Madhya Pradesh Government, under School Education Department

Madhya Pradesh

Madhyamik Shikshak (Subject)

Selection Exam 2025

English

Compiled & Edited by
Neetu Arora

ARIHANT PUBLICATIONS (INDIA) LIMITED

卐 **Administrative & Production Offices**

Regd. Office

'Ramchhaya' 4577/15, Agarwal Road, Darya Ganj, New Delhi -110002
Tele: 011- 47630600, 43518550

卐 **Head Office**

Kalindi, TP Nagar, Meerut (UP) - 250002
Tel: 0121-7156203, 7156204

卐 **Sales & Support Offices**

Agra, Ahmedabad, Bengaluru, Bareilly, Chennai, Delhi, Guwahati, Hyderabad, Jaipur, Jhansi, Kolkata, Lucknow, Nagpur & Pune.

卐 **PRICE** ₹425.00

卐 **PO No :** TXT-59-T063191-02-25

Published by Arihant Publications (India) Ltd.

For further information about the books published by Arihant, log on to www.arihantbooks.com or e-mail at info@arihantbooks.com

CONTENTS

Syllabus

Unit-1 : Reading: Unseen Passage- Prose (Factual, descriptive or literary) to assess comprehension, interpretation, inference and vocabulary

Unit-2 : Reading: Unseen Passage- Poetry (to assess comprehension, interpretation, inference and vocabulary)

Unit-3 : Noun, Pronoun, Prepositions, Conjunctions, Verb, Adverbs, Adjectives ,Determiners (Articles, Degree),

Unit-4 : Tense, Subject-verb Agreement, Transformation of Sentences, Active to Passive, Direct to Indirect Narration, Negative, Interrogative, Punctuation

Unit-5 : Compound Sentences, Complex Sentences – Clause (Noun Clause, Adjective /Relative Clause, Adverb Clause)

Unit-6 : Vocabulary-Synonyms, Antonyms, One-word Substitution, Idioms and Phrases, Homophone, Homonyms, Homographs, Prefix, Suffix

Unit-7 : Figures of speech-Simile, Metaphor, Personification, Paradox, Irony, Alliteration, Hyperbole, Assonance

Unit-8 : Forms of poetry- Sonnet, Ode, Elegy, Satire, Blank Verse. Forms of stanza, Syllable division, Rhyme scheme

Unit-9 : The Fun They Had, The Sound of Music, The Little Girl, A Truly Beautiful Mind, The Snake and Mirror, My Childhood, Reach for the Top, If I Were You (Class IX SCERT MP)

Unit-10 : A Letter to God, Nelson Mandela: Long Walk to Freedom, From the Diary of Anne Frank, Mijbil the Otter, Madam Rides the Bus, The Proposal, Glimpses of India (Baker from Goa, Coorg, Tea from Assam) (Class X SCERT MP)

Unit-11 : The Lost Child, The Happy Prince, The Last Leaf, Iswaran the Storyteller, The Accidental Tourist (Class IX SCERT MP)

Unit-12 : A Triumph of Surgery, The Thief's Story, The Necklace, The Midnight Visitor, Bholi (Class IX & X SCERT MP)

Unit-13 : Rain on the Roof, The Lake Isle of Innisfree, Wind, On A Slumber Did My Spirit Seal, A Legend of The Northland, (Class IX SCERT MP)

Unit-14 : Dust of Snow, A Tiger in the Zoo, The Ball Poem, Amanda, On killing a Tree (Class X SCERT MP)

From unit 9 to 14 (author's purpose, analysis and evaluation of themes and characters, vocabulary in context will be assessed)

Unit-15 : Poetry

- John Keats- Ode to Autumn,
- Toru Dutt- Our Casuarina Tree
- W. B. Yeats- A Prayer for My Daughter
- Sarojini Naidu- Indian Weavers
- Guru Nanak Dev- The Sky is Your Platter

Unit-16 : Prose

- William Hazlitt-On Going a Journey
- A.G. Gardiner-On Umbrella Morals
- Francis Bacon- Of Studies

Unit-17 : Fiction

- Charles Dickens- David Copperfield
- Virginia Woolf-Mrs. Dalloway

Unit-18 : Drama

- William Shakespeare-The Merchant of Venice
- John Galsworthy-The Silver Box

Unit-19 : Short stories

- R. K. Narayan- The English Teacher
- Ruskin Bond- The Room on the Roof
- Rabindranath Tagore - Kabuliwala

Unit-20 : History of Indian Writing in English (renowned authors/poets and their works)

Unit-01

01 Reading : Unseen Passage Prose

Reading Comprehension is defined as the understanding of a passage or a text. Basically, it tests the reader's ability to understand the content as well as style and theme of the passage. In examination, questions on the passage generally appear in a chronological order.

Types of Passages

In the examination, two unseen passages are asked from the following categories

1. The passage could be of any one of the following types
   (i) **Factual** A factual passage includes some facts about the physical aspects of a subject. It includes instructions, descriptions and reports. It helps the student to get a detailed view of the subject and develop a complete mental picture of a specific person, place, object or being.
   (ii) **Discursive** A discursive passage includes argumentative, interpretative and persuasive text. Such passages may include opinions or feedback. It allows students to arrive at a conclusion through reasoning and understanding rather than intuition. It presents a balanced and objective approach towards the subject being discussed.
   (iii) **Literary** A literary passage may include an extract from fiction, drama, biography, autobiography, travelogue, poetry, etc.
2. **Case Based Factual Passages** A case based factual passage is based on graphical data or charts.

Types of Questions

In the examination, the students are tested on a variety of questions that assess comprehension, interpretation inference and vocabulary. In examination, Questions including MCQs and objective are asked from factual, discursive and literary passages and Questions including MCQs and objective are asked from case based factual passages.

Steps to Attempt Reading Comprehension

The following steps have to be attempted while reading comprehension

- Read each and every line in the passage carefully.
- Reading the passage twice is always favourable as it helps in better understanding and makes it easier for a student to find answers. If the title of the passage is given, read it first as it gives the central insight of the passage.
- Underline all the difficult words while reading the passage, as you might be tested on these words in the vocabulary questions.
- Always give emphasis on the beginning and end of the passages. These paragraphs often hold the most important information of the passage.
- While answering, be sure that you've clearly understood the question. Answer must be relevant to the question.
- Ensure that you answer the question according to the marks it carries. Subjective questions should be answered in complete sentences.
- Try to use your own language and modify the answer according to the question.
- Answers should be based on information given/inference derived from the information in the passage.
- Make sure that you use the same tense in which the question has been asked.
- In MCQs analyse the questions and options carefully before selecting the correct option because some of the four options are often closely related.
- Write the correct question number on each answer sheet to avoid mistakes.

Unseen Passage

(Factual, Discursive & Literary Passages)

Read the following passages carefully and answer the questions that follow.

Passage 1

The outer solar system is the name of the planets beyond the asteroid belt. These planets are called gas giants because they are made up of gas and ice.

The first stop of our tour is the fifth planet, Jupiter. Jupiter is bigger than three hundred Earths! It is made up of hydrogen and helium and a few other gases. There are violent wind storms that circle around Jupiter. The most famous storm is called the Great Red Spot. It has been churning for more than four hundred years already. At last count, Jupiter has sixty-three known moons and a faint ring around it too.

Next in our space neighbourhood comes Saturn. It is well-known for the series of beautiful rings that circle it. They are made up of tiny bits of frozen dirt and ice. Like Jupiter, Saturn is made up of mostly hydrogen and helium. It is smaller though, at only ninety-five times the size of Earth. Saturn has sixty-two moons.

The seventh planet, Uranus and its twenty-seven moons orbit very far from the sun. In addition to helium and hydrogen, Uranus atmosphere also contains ammonia ice and methane ice. It is a very cold planet, with no internal heat source. One of the strangest things about Uranus is that it is tipped over and orbits the sun on its side at a ninety-degree angle. The twenty-seven moons it has orbits from top to bottom, instead of left to right like our moon.

The eighth planet is Neptune. Like Uranus, it is made up of hydrogen, helium, ammonia ice and methane ice. But unlike Uranus, Neptune does have an inner heat source, just like Earth. It radiates twice as much heat as it receives from the sun. Neptune's most distinctive quality is its blue colour. Most of the information we know about it came from the Voyager 2 spacecraft passing close by it in 1989.

Pluto is the last and was considered a planet after its discovery in 1930. In 2006, Pluto was demoted and reclassified as a dwarf planet. Pluto exists in the Kuiper belt. That's just a fancy name for the band of rocks, dust and ice that lies beyond the gas giants. Scientists have found objects bigger than Pluto in this belt. Thus, the outer solar system has many secrets to explore.

Questions

On the basis of your reading of the passage, answer the following questions.

(i) What do you understand by " Pluto was demoted and reclassified"?

(a) Pluto is no longer called planet.
(b) Pluto was categorised as a different kind of planet.
(c) Pluto was renamed.
(d) Pluto was removed from our planetary system.

(ii) Complete the sentence by choosing the correct option.
The Kuiper belt is an area of rocks, dust and ice that ....

(a) is between Jupiter and Saturn
(b) is beyond Pluto
(c) includes Pluto
(d) surrounds Saturn's rings

(iii) Which of the following options lists the planets without any internal heat source?

(a) Jupiter and Uranus
(b) Earth and Neptune
(c) Saturn and Pluto
(d) Jupiter and Saturn

(iv) Which one of the following is a synonym of 'faint' as used in paragraph?

(a) Indistinct (b) Slight
(c) Muffled (d) Unconscious

(v) Pick the option showing the correct use of 'churning' as used in the passage.

(a) Programme-makers seem irresponsibly about churning out violence.
(b) The churning, pressing crowds made her feel claustrophobic.
(c) I had my driving test that morning and my stomach was churning.
(d) Guided by the churning within the planet, the crust of the Earth has been in a constant state of flux.

(vi) Select the option that conveys the opposite of 'gentle' from the passage.

(a) Violent (b) Discovery
(c) Reclassified (d) Bigger

Passage 2

Today's wars have little in common with the battles of the 19th century. The fighting has gradually moved from clearly defined battlefields to populated areas. Traditional war between armies of opposing states is an exception, while non-international conflicts have become the norm. Nowadays, civilians bear the brunt of armed conflicts.

International humanitarian law has adapted to this change. Appalled by the destruction and suffering caused by the Second World War, states agreed in the four Geneva Conventions of 1949 on comprehensive protection for those who are not or are no longer participating in hostilities — wounded and sick soldiers, prisoners of war and civilians. This cornerstone of international humanitarian law was supplemented in 1977 and 2005 by three additional protocols. The use of certain weapons, such as biological or chemical weapons, cluster munitions and anti-personnel mines is now widely outlawed. The law has placed barriers to protect the most vulnerable from the brutality of war. Its implementation has also seen a certain amount of progress, such as in the training of soldiers or in the prosecution of the worst war crimes, thanks in particular to the founding of the International Criminal Court (ICC).

Nevertheless, regular serious breaches of international humanitarian law are a cause of suffering. Underlying it all is our collective failure. The contracting states undertook in Article 1—common to the four Geneva Conventions of 1949—"to respect and to ensure respect" for these conventions "in all circumstances."

International humanitarian law has, since its conception, lacked mechanisms for encouraging effective compliance. This impotence has often meant death and destruction for those affected by war.

Since the adoption of the first Geneva Convention 150 years ago, international humanitarian law has become a central pillar of the international legal order. Ultimately its provisions serve to protect our key characteristic as human beings: our humanity.

This is an irrevocable right. It is based on the belief, forged over centuries and in all our cultures, according to which it is essential to lay down rules if we want to prevent wars from degenerating into barbarism.

It is up to our generation to consolidate these achievements and to create an institutional framework to ensure these rules are respected. If it is to be fully effective, the law needs suitable instruments. Never in the history of humankind have we been closer to a solution than we are today.

Questions

On the basis of your reading of the passage, answer the following questions.

(i) How did the International humanitarian law change between 1977 and 2005?
(a) It abolished use of biological and chemical weapons
(b) It abolished use of cluster munitions
(c) It abolished use of anti-personnel mines
(d) All of the above

(ii) When and why were the Geneva Conventions adopted?
(a) 1949; to prevent wars from taking place
(b) 1977-2005; to preserve humanity during wars
(c) 1949; to preserve humanity during wars
(d) 100 years ago; to prevent wars from taking place

(iii) The significant change that the Geneva Conventions of 1949 brought about was that the countries agreed to protect the people who were no longer fighting the war. Which of the following categories of people did it include?
(a) Prisoners of war and civilians
(b) Wounded and sick soldiers
(c) Both (a) and (b)
(d) None of the above

(iv) Complete the sentence by choosing an appropriate option. The International Humanitarian Law believes that ....
(a) humanity is the central pillar of existence
(b) it is essential for all countries to follow it in all circumstances
(c) it is essential to lay down rules to prevent wars from degenerating
(d) the law needs sustainable instruments to be effective

(v) Pick the option showing the correct use of 'cornerstone' as used in the passage.
(a) This study is the cornerstone of the whole research programme.
(b) The cornerstone of that ideology is the doctrine of judicial independence, to which we now turn.
(c) The prohibition of discrimination on grounds of nationality remains a cornerstone of unification.
(d) All of the above

(vi) Select the option that conveys the meaning of 'forged'.
(a) Adoption
(b) Provisions
(c) Established
(d) Effective

Passage 3

Had Dr. Johnson written his own life, in conformity with the opinion which he has given, that every man's life may be best written by himself; had he employed in the preservation of his own history, that clearness of narration and elegance of language in which he has embalmed so many eminent persons, the world would probably have had the most perfect example of biography that was ever exhibited.

Wherever narrative is necessary to explain, connect, and supply, I furnish it to the best of my abilities; but in the chronological series of Johnson's life, which I trace as distinctly as I can, year by year, I produce, wherever it is in my power, his own minutes, letters or conversation, being convinced that this mode is more lively and will make my readers better acquainted with him, than even most of those were who actually knew him, but could know him only partially; whereas there is here an accumulation of intelligence from various points, by which his character is more fully understood and illustrated.

Indeed I cannot conceive a more perfect mode of writing any man's life, than not only relating all the most important events of it in their order, but interweaving what he privately wrote and said and thought.

Had his other friends been as diligent and ardent as I was, he might have been almost entirely preserved.

As it is, I will venture to say that he will be seen in this work more completely than any man who has ever yet lived.

And he will be seen as he really was, for I profess to write, not his panegyric, which must be all praise, but his life; which, great and good as he was, must not be supposed to be entirely perfect.

To be as he was, is indeed subject of panegyric enough to any man in this state of being; but in every picture there should be shade as well as light and when I delineate him without reserve, I do what he himself recommended, both by his precept and his example, as quoted below.

"If the biographer writes from personal knowledge, and makes haste to gratify the public curiosity, there is danger lest his interest, his fear, his gratitude, or his tenderness, overpower his fidelity and tempt him to conceal, if not to invent."

Questions

On the basis of your reading of the passage, answer the following questions.

(i) Complete the sentence by choosing an appropriate option.
It can be inferred from the passage that Dr Johnson ....

(a) wrote many biographies
(b) wrote his own autobiography
(c) was against writing his autobiography
(d) did not want the author to write about him

(ii) Dr. Johnson would probably have agreed with none of the given statements, EXCEPT:

(a) A biography tends to over-praise.
(b) An autobiography is always misleading.
(c) An autobiographer is the greatest authority on his own life.
(d) All of the above

(iii) According to the passage, the author goes through the various letters, conversations and minutes for which of the following reasons?

(a) To give a correct chronology of Johnson
(b) To illustrate Johnson's characteristics with utmost precision
(c) To write a perfect biography
(d) To present his thought in his works

(iv) The author does not want to write a panegyric because

(a) he feels that it would not be a perfect biography.
(b) he feels that it would harm dr. johnson's reputation.
(c) he believes that dr. johnson was not perfect.
(d) he believes that only dr. johnson's friends would do so.

(v) Select the option that conveys the meaning of 'panegyric' used in Paragraph 4.

(a) Eulogy (b) Myth (c) Portrait (d) Fame

(vi) Select the most appropriate title for the above passage.

(a) Dr. Johnson: A Biography
(b) Dr. Johnson: An Autobiographer
(c) Dr. Johnson: An Autobiography
(d) Dr. Johnson: A Biographer

Passage 4

The kingdom of books is as vast as the universe, for there is no corner of it which they have left unexplored. There is no dearth of books on any topic, be it as simple as the composition of sodium nitrate or as intricate as the mechanism of a spacecraft. Books report the fruits of our research in various fields of knowledge, and spread our progressive view on matters which are of vital concern to our fellow beings.

In fact, no single product of human labour has been as helpful to the advancement of civilisation as books, which are written in all languages of the world and are decoratively placed in bookshelves in our homes and tastefully displayed in bookstall and libraries. If to Keats, works of ancient poets like Homer were realms of gold from which he derived much joy as well as inspiration, to the modern lover of books, the labours of all geniuses, including those of Keats, are mines of inestimable intellectual wealth which he goes on exploring for the sake of his mental and spiritual advancement.

There was a time some five centuries back, when books as we know them today did not exist, and when there were few people who could read things written on stuff which certainly was not paper. At that time our ancestors used rocks, pillars and parchment with a view to recording and perpetuating their most important thoughts and achievements in the language they then understood.

Nowadays, the book-producing machinery gives to the works of every great scientific thinker, poet or philosopher the character of permanence, reproduces in attractive forms old and rare manuscripts and caters to the differing tastes of millions of people for whom book-reading is an extremely pleasant, intellectual exercise. Moreover, the high percentage of literacy, the growth of libraries in towns and villages and the tendency of intellectuals to have their own private collection of useful books, have given birth to a number of big publishing houses with branches in many parts of the world and publications numbering thousands.

In recent years, paperbacks have begun to reveal their attraction for the reading public, and although they have not completely thrown into neglect the hard cover markets, they have appealed to people who would not have thought of buying books not so very long ago. These paperbacks are generally reprints of popular fiction or of established classics or translations from foreign works which are in constant demand at all bookstalls.

Questions

On the basis of your reading of the passage, answer the following questions.

(i) Complete the sentence by choosing an appropriate option.
For the majority of people, book-reading is ....

(a) an enjoyable intellectual exercise
(b) a boring job
(c) not interesting
(d) waste of time

(ii) Books are helpful for which of the following?

(a) Reporting research results
(b) Spread progressive view on vital matters
(c) Advancement of civilisation
(d) All of the above

(iii) Which of the following has contributed to the growth of publishing houses?

(a) High literacy
(b) Growth of libraries
(c) People's desire to have their own collection
(d) All of the above

(iv) Which has been one of the most helpful product of human labour to the advancement of civilisation?

(a) Books
(b) Publishing houses
(c) Paper
(d) Spacecraft

(v) Select the option that conveys the opposite of 'displeased' in the passage.

(a) Appealed
(b) Pleased
(c) Enjoyed
(d) Delighted

(vi) Pick the option showing the correct use of the word 'appealed' as used in the passage.

(a) The bowler appealed to the umpire for the LBW.
(b) I am appealed today.
(c) A career in forensic science appealed Shweta.
(d) Sumit was appealed to see the poverty in the slums.

Passage 5

There's no concept of good or bad food in nutrition science. What matters is the amount of food you consume, something that can be measured in terms of portion or size of serving. Portions and sizes vary from country to country and community to community. Large portions are commonly consumed in the advanced economies while smaller size portions are found mostly in developing economies of Africa and Asia.

Incidentally, portion sizes have undergone a considerable change over the years and continue to do so even today. The trend, in general, has been towards consuming larger and larger food portions (expanding waistlines are proof of this). The human mind seems to count the number of portions rather than the portion size. For example, when people say they have only one chapatti for lunch or dinner, they rarely discuss its size.

Short-term studies have also shown that people eat more when confronted with larger portion sizes. A study at a restaurant setting showed that when pasta was served in different portion sizes on different days, people ate larger amounts on being served larger portions, regardless of the taste. Also, studies show that people do not adjust or eat less in subsequent meals if they have already had larger portions.

Technically a portion means the amount of food you choose to eat at one time – at a restaurant, from a package, or at home. A 'serving' size indicates the calories and nutrients in a certain serving listed under a product's 'nutrition facts' or a single unit or commonly regarded unit of food. The serving size is not the recommended amount to be eaten.

Sometimes, the portion size and serving size match; sometimes they don't. For example, one slice of bread equals one serving of bread. But the number of slices you eat would be the number of portions you have eaten, so if you have eaten two slices, you have consumed two portions.

So how do we recognise what's the right amount of food to eat on a regular basis? Learn to recognise standard serving sizes as they help you judge how much you are eating. It may also help to compare serving sizes to common objects.

Questions

On the basis of your reading of the passage, answer the following questions.

(i) Complete the sentence by choosing an appropriate option.
Portions and sizes vary ....

(a) from country to country
(b) from community to community
(c) from developed economies to developing economies
(d) All of the above

(ii) According to the passage, which of the following statements is TRUE?

(a) Portion sizes are increasing.
(b) Developed economies have larger portions of food.
(c) Portion varies from community to community only.
(d) People do not adjust the size of meals regularly.

(iii) The write would agree with the given information based on the passage EXCEPT :

(a) Africa and Asia have smaller portions of food.
(b) Larger food portions means larger consumptions.
(c) After larger food portions are consumed people opt for smaller portions.
(d) Portion sizes always match.

(iv) Pick the option showing the CORRECT use of 'serving' as used in the passage.

(a) The number of prisoners serving life sentences has fallen.
(b) He is eating one serving of pasta.
(c) He is serving on a warship in the Pacific.
(d) There was only one girl serving customers.

(v) Which of the following words cannot replace 'regardless' as used in the passage?

(a) Despite (b) Notwithstanding
(c) Whatever (d) Ignoring

(vi) According to the passage, what is central to the concept of nutritional science?

(a) Portions and sizes
(b) Excercise and sleep
(c) Hotels and restaurants
(d) Junk food

Passage 6

Last week was spent glued to T.V, watching India getting thrashed by a rejuvenated England at Lord's. Like most Indians, I too was dispirited by India's inability to live up to its reputation as the number one team. But at least there was the immense satisfaction of watching the match live and even listening to BBC's good-humoured Test Match Special on Internet radio.

It was such a change from my schooldays when you had to tune in to a crackling short wave broadcast for intermittent radio commentary. Alternatively, we could go to the cinema, some three weeks after the match, to see a two-minute capsule in the Indian News Review that preceded the feature film.

It is not that there was no technology available to make life a little more rewarding. Yet, in 1971, when B.S Chandrasekhar mesmerised the opposition and gave India its first Test victory at the Oval, there was no T.V, except in Delhi.

Those were the bad old days of the shortage economy when everything, from cinema tickets to two-wheelers, had a black market premium. Telephones were a particular source of exasperation. By the 1970s, the telephone system in cities had collapsed. You may have possessed one of those heavy, black bakelite instruments but there was no guarantee of a dial tone when you picked up the receiver. The ubiquitous 'cable fault' would render a telephone useless for months on end.

What was particularly frustrating was that there was precious little you could do about whimsical public services. In the early 1980s, when opposition MPs complained about dysfunctional telephones, the then Communications Minister C.M. Stephen retorted that phones were a luxury and not a right. If people were dissatisfied, he pronounced haughtily, they could return their phones.

Inefficiency was, in fact, elevated into an ideal. When capital-intensive public sector units began running into the red, the regime's economists deemed that their performance shouldn't be judged by a narrow capitalist yardstick. The public sector, they pronounced, had to exercise 'social' choices. 'India', wrote Jagdish Bhagwati (one of the few genuine dissidents of that era), "suffered the tyranny of anticipated consequences from the wrong premises."

Questions

On the basis of your reading of the passage, answer the following questions.

(i) The narrator felt dispirited as his team ....
(a) was the number one team of the world
(b) could not perform as per people's expectations
(c) could not play even 100 overs
(d) performed like professionals

(ii) How does the passage describe the telephone?
1. Fashionable 2. Unpredictable
3. Faulty 4. Luxury
5. Whimsical
(a) 1, 2, 3 (b) 2, 3, 4 (c) 3, 4, 5 (d) 2 and 3

(iii) Which of the following statements is CORRECT as per the passage?
(a) The public services needed a revolution in the author's childhood.
(b) There was a great transparency in public services.
(c) The author of the passage as a grown up did not have access to technology.
(d) The telephone lines were great during the author's childhood.

(iv) Pick the option showing the CORRECT use of 'whimsical' as used in the passage.
(a) Despite his kind and whimsical air, he was a shrewd observer of people.
(b) The whimsical imagery of Martinez's work plays on colour and shape.
(c) Love is whimsical and temperamental.
(d) All of the above

(v) In Paragraph 6, the word .... is the antonym of 'lowered'.
(a) promoted (b) denigrated
(c) elevated (d) deemed

(vi) The tone of the author of the given passage is
(a) nostalgic (b) critical
(c) bitter (d) doubtful

Passage 7

A dance which is created or choreographed and performed according to the tenets of the Natya Shastra is called a classical dance. The two broad aspects of classical dancing are the tandava and the lasya. Power and force are typical of the tandava; grace and delicacy, of the lasya. Tandava is associated with Shiva, and lasya with Parvati. Dance which is pure movement is called nritta, and dance which is interpretative in nature is called nritya. The four main schools of classical dancing in India are Bharatanatyam, Kathakali, Manipuri and Kathak.

Bharatanatyam is the oldest and most popular dance form of India. Earlier, it was known by various names. Some called it Bharatam, some Natyam, some Desi Attam and some Sadir. The districts of Tanjore and Kanchipuram in Tamil Nadu were the focal points in the development of Bharatanatyam.

It was performed as a solo performance by devadasis (temple dancers) on all auspicious occasions. Later, kings and rich people lent their patronage to it and it started shedding its purely sacred character. The dancer is directed by the natuvanar, who is a musician and, invariably, a teacher. Another musician plays the cymbals. The music for Bharatanatyam is from the Carnatic School of music. The mridangam (a drum), played on both sides with the hands, provides the rhythm.

The home of Kathakali is Kerala. Kathakali literally means 'story-play'. It combines music, dance, poetry, drama and mime. Its present form has evolved out of older forms such as Ramanattam and Krishnanattam.

Kathakali dance-dramas last from dusk to dawn. The artistes use elaborate costumes; mask-like make-up and towering head-dresses. The dancers are all males. Female roles are usually played by boys. There is no stage - a few mats are spread on the ground for the audience to sit on. The only 'stage-lighting' is a brass lamp fed with coconut oil.

Two singers provide the vocal music. The chenda, a large drum, which is beaten on one side with two slender curved sticks, is an integral part of the Kathakali performance. A metal gong, a pair of cymbals and another drum complete the orchestra. Besides providing the beat, they are also the means by which all the sound-effects are created.

Questions

On the basis of your reading of the passage, answer the following questions.

(i) What is the Natya Shastra?
(a) A scientific study of classical dance
(b) The science of dances
(c) Shiva's sacred thread
(d) None of the above

(ii) When did Bharatanatyam start shedding its purely sacred character?
(a) When the devadasis stopped dancing
(b) When it was danced as a solo performance
(c) When kings and the rich patronised it
(d) When they used Carnatic music

(iii) Which of the following lists the elements not present in Kathakali?

1. Drama	2. Costume
3. Mime	4. Stage
5. Dance	6. Tabla

(a) 4 and 6 (b) 1, 2, 3
(c) 3, 4, 5 (d) 1 and 3

(iv) The phrase 'focal point' indicates
(a) origin
(b) popularity
(c) teaching center
(d) home to popular dancers

(v) The word 'invariably' in the passage denotes
(a) the temporary nature
(b) the unchanging nature
(c) the domination
(d) the usual

(vi) Pick the option showing the CORRECT use of 'slender' as used in the passage.
(a) She's got a beautiful slender figure.
(b) A slender hope still flickered within him.
(c) These claims are based on slender evidence.
(d) The builders have perched a light concrete dome on eight slender columns.

(vii) Which of the following statements is true for Kathakali?
(a) Kathakali is performed on drums.
(b) Kathakali performance starts at dusk and ends at dawn.
(c) Kathakali is performed as street plays.
(d) Kathakali is generally based on universal social issues.

(viii) The 'Natuvanar' in a dance performance is a
(a) background dancer (b) musician
(c) teacher (d) Both (b) and (c)

Passage 8

The power of our body to fight against various disease producing agents is known as defence mechanism. This defence mechanism depends upon various factors which can be categorised mainly into two types-common factors and special factors.

Amongst the common factors, the most important is the health of human beings. For keeping good health, one should take a nutritious balanced diet. A balanced diet is that which contains carbohydrates, fat, proteins, vitamins in proportionate amount.

The skin saves us against many micro-organisms producing diseases, provided that it is intact. In case there are cuts or abrasions on it, the micro-organisms penetrate the body through those cuts and abrasions and can cause diseases. Therefore, a cut or an abrasion should never be left open. In case there is no bandage available, it may be covered by a clean cloth.

Some bacteria reside on and inside the human body. They do not cause any disease and by their presence they do not allow disease-causing organisms to settle on those places. The human body secretes a variety of fluids, which are killers for disease causing micro-organisms. For instance, gastric juice (acidic in nature) secreted by our intestinal tract kills all organisms which enter our body through food.

There are a few automatic activities of our body known as 'reflex phenomenon or action', which protects the body against many infections. This reflex phenomenon includes sneezing, coughing and vomiting.

Fever is one of the most important constituents of the defence mechanism of our body. The organ which regulates the temperature of our body is known as Hypothalamus and is situated in the brain. When micro-organisms after entering the body release toxic products and these reach the brain through blood, the hypothalamus starts increasing the temperature of the body and the person gets fever. This fever is very useful for the human body because due to the increase of temperature, the micro-organisms which are the root cause of the problem get killed. We are living in an environment which is full of bacteria. Many of these bacteria can produce serious diseases, but all of us do not suffer from such diseases. It is due to a special power present in our body to fight these diseases, known as Innate Immunity.

In a nutshell, we can say that since nature has provided us with defence mechanism to fight against so many diseases, let us maintain it or rather increase it by way of immunisation.

Questions

On the basis of your reading of the passage, answer the following questions.

(i) Why should one have a nutritious balanced diet?

1. Keep healthy

2. Ensure that recommendations of a dietician are followed

3. Have essential items

4. Enjoy all tastes

(a) Only 1 (b) Only 2
(c) Both 2 and 3 (d) Only 4

(ii) The defence mechanism of the human body ………… .

(a) checks body deterioration
(b) ensures wear and tear of the body
(c) saves us from depression
(d) protects us from diseases

(iii) The power of our body to fight against various diseases producing agents is called ……… .

(a) Defence mechanism (b) Health
(c) Immunisation (d) Fever

(iv) Why should a cut or abrasion never be left open?

1. It causes pain. 2. It causes itching.

3. Micro-organisms penetrate the body and can cause disease.

4. It grows deeper.

(a) Only 1 (b) Both 1 and 2
(c) Only 3 (d) Only 4

(v) Reflex phenomenon includes ……… .

(a) sneezing (b) coughing
(c) vomiting (d) All of these

(vi) Which of the following statements is/are NOT TRUE as per the passage.

1. Hypothalamus is situated in the liver.

2. The power to fight the diseases is called Innate Immunity.

3. Fever is one of the most important constituents of our defence mechanism.

4. We should never increase our defence mechanism by immunisation.

(a) Both 1 and 4
(b) Both 2 and 3
(c) Only 2
(d) Only 3

(vii) Pick the option showing the CORRECT use of the word 'abrasion'.

(a) The abrasion is slow and steady.
(b) Nutan had a small abrasion on her knee.
(c) Abrasions are for one and all.
(d) I like abrasion very much.

(viii) The word 'innate' means ………… .

(a) instinctive (b) intuitive
(c) inborn (d) acquired

PASSAGE 9

These days, it is not unusual to see people listening to music or using their electronic gadgets while crossing busy roads or travelling on public transport, regardless of the risks involved. I have often wondered why they take such risks: is it because they want to exude a sense of independence or is it that they want to tell the world to stop bothering them? Or is it that they just want to show how cool they are?

Whether it is a workman or an executive, earphones have become an inseparable part of our lives, sometimes even leading to tragicomic situations. The other day, an electrician had come to our house to fix something. We told him in detail what needed to be done. But after he left, I found that the man had done almost nothing. It later turned out that he could not hear our directions clearly because he had his earphones on.

Hundreds of such earphones addicts commute by the Delhi Metro every day. While one should not begrudge anyone their moments of privacy or their love for music, the fact is 'iPod oblivion' can sometimes be very dangerous. Recently, I was travelling with my wife on the Delhi Metro. Since the train was approaching the terminus, there weren't too many passengers. In our compartment, other than us, there were only two women sitting on the other side of the aisle. And then suddenly, I spotted a duffel bag. The bomb scare lasted for several minutes.

Then suddenly, a youth emerged from nowhere and picked up the bag. When we tried to stop him, he looked at us, surprised. Then he took off his earpieces, lifted the bag, and told us that the bag belonged to him and that he was going to get off at the next station.

We were stunned but recovered in time to ask him where he was all this while? His answer: he was in the compartment, leaning against the door, totally immersed in the music. He had no clue about what was going on around him. When he got off, earplugs in his hand, we could hear strains of the song.

Questions

On the basis of your reading of the passage, answer the following questions.

(i) The reason for people listening to music or using their electronic gadgets while crossing busy roads or travelling on public transport is that they ....

(a) do not want to be disturbed
(b) want to show how fashionable they are
(c) want to show their independence
(d) All of the above

(ii) Why had the electrician done nothing?

(a) Because he hadn't heard them.
(b) Because he was listening to music.
(c) Because he was not interested in the job.
(d) Because he couldn't understand what needed to be fixed.

(iii) The electrician episode is explained by the narrator as

(a) exasperating (b) infuriating
(c) tragicomedy (d) disgusting

(iv) Which of the following correctly lists the tone with which the author had written the passage?

1. Humorous 2. Sarcastic
3. Serious 4. Informative
5. Resentful

(a) 1 and 5 (b) 2 and 4
(c) 3 and 5 (d) 1 and 4

(v) The author says that we should not resent people ....

(a) indulging in their love for music
(b) wanting privacy
(c) Both (a) and (b)
(d) Neither (a) nor (b)

(vi) The passengers were stunned because ....

(a) the youth was careless
(b) the bag contained a bomb
(c) the youth had not been visible anywhere near the bag earlier
(d) None of the above

(vii) Pick the option showing the CORRECT use of 'stunned' as used in the passage.

(a) The animals are stunned before slaughter.
(b) The robber stunned the guard by banging him on the head.
(c) Many cinema-goers were stunned by the film's violent and tragic end.
(d) The impact of the ball had stunned her.

(viii) The word .... in the passage is an antonym of absorb.

(a) exude (b) bothering (c) commute (d) stunned

Passage 10

I was lucky, I found what I loved to do early in life. Woz and I started Apple in my parent's garage when I was 20. We worked hard and in 10 years Apple had grown into a $ 2 billion company with over 4000 employees. We had just released our finest creation - the Macintosh - a year earlier and I had just turned 30. And then I got fired. How can you get fired from a company you started? Well, as Apple grew, we hired someone, who I thought was very talented, to run the company and for the first year or so things went well.

But then eventually we had a falling out. When we did, our Board of Directors sided with him. So at 30 I was out. What had been the focus of my entire adult life was gone and it was devastating.

I really didn't know what to do for a few months. I felt that I had let the previous generation of entrepreneurs down - that I had dropped the baton as it was being passed to me. But something slowly began to dawn on me: I still loved what I did. The turn of events at Apple had not changed that one bit. I had been rejected, but I was still in love. And so I decided to start over.

I didn't see it then, but it turned out that getting fired from Apple was the best thing that could have ever happened to me. It freed me to enter one of the most creative periods of my life.

During the next 5 years, I started a company named NeXT and another company named Pixar. Pixar went on to create the world's first computer Animated Feature Film, Toy Story and is now the most successful animation studio in the world. In a remarkable turn of events, Apple bought NeXT, I returned to Apple and the technology we developed at NeXT is at the heart of Apple's current renaissance.

I'm pretty sure none of this would have happened if I hadn't been fired from Apple. It was awful tasting medicine, but I guess the patient needed it. Sometimes life hits you in the head with a brick. Don't lose faith. I'm convinced that the only thing that kept me going was that I loved what I did. You've got to find what you love.

Questions

On the basis of your reading of the passage, answer the following questions.

(i) What can be inferred from the line "But something slowly began to dawn on me"?
(a) He realised he still loved what he did.
(b) He realised he was a public failure.
(c) He realised that he had let down the other entrepreneurs.
(d) He realised he wanted to return to Apple.

(ii) Complete the sentence by choosing an appropriate option.
Getting fired from Apple was ....
(a) the worst thing that ever happened to the author
(b) a planned decision
(c) helpful to make him successful again
(d) the best part of his life

(iii) Pixar is credited for
(a) being the first animation studio
(b) creating the world's first computer animated movie
(c) being a bigger company than Apple
(d) buying NeXT

(iv) Select the option that conveys the opposite of 'ordinary' from words used in the passage.
(a) Extraordinary (b) Remarkable
(c) Finest (d) Lucky

(v) What is the meaning of the phrase 'dropped the baton'?
(a) Dropped the rod
(b) Feeling of depression
(c) Not sure of future
(d) Not living upto expectations

(vi) Pick the option showing the CORRECT use of 'falling out' as used in the passage.
(a) The passengers came falling out when the bus went down the hill.
(b) After falling out with her husband, she started living downstairs.
(c) Many rocks and lava were falling out from the volcano.
(d) Did you see people falling out from the pedestal?

Passage 11

Recently, a particular brand of noodles was found to contain inadmissible levels of harmful substances in it. But there is something else as important as the controversy about harmful substances. It is that instant noodles are not healthy for anybody, with or without lead and MSG. So, we should have a simplified classification system and scale for junk versus healthy food.

Eating refined starch that is processed, dried and kept for months with the help of chemical preservatives is unlikely to be good for us. Its advertisements may be emotionally moving, the brand ambassador highly credible and the soupy noodles may taste good. But it is still not good for you.

Of course, the noodles won't kill you. Our diet today has plenty of other unhealthy things as well. For instance, almost all Indian sweets are unhealthy, as are many of our gravy 'delicacies'. We have given up health benefits of food in favour of cost, convenience or taste. Such compromises are acceptable only up to an extent. However, if done in excess, they can lead to major health problems such as obesity, heart disease and diabetes.

How does one limit unhealthy food then? The problem comes when 'junk' is marketed as 'healthy'. Our advertising standards for food are extraordinarily lax. Junk food manufacturers not only hide the nature of their food, but also position their products as 'healthy' alternatives. Armed with advertisements of smiling mothers feeding bright-looking kids, we find junk being marketed as emotional nectar. Food, be it for nourishment or pleasure, has positive associations for us.

Any food is good and the kind of food doesn't seem to matter. Perhaps, this has developed from a time when India was poor and food was scarce. When we worked twelve hours a day in the fields, we could eat and burn as many calories as we wanted.

However, times have changed. Physical labour is reducing and we don't burn calories as easily. Hence, we need to monitor our food intake carefully. If a big part of our diet has to come from packaged food, we need to understand and label it accordingly.

This will increase awareness about what we are eating and over sometime, incentivise us as well as manufacturers to move towards healthier foods. A healthy society will lead to lower healthcare costs, improved productivity at work and a better quality of life for citizens.

Questions

On the basis of your reading of the passage, answer the following questions.

(i) The writer of the above passage would agree with the statement.

(a) Instant noodles are not tasty.
(b) All types of instant noodles are bad for health.
(c) Noodles are good for health.
(d) Instant noodles will slowly kill us.

(ii) What is the problem with advertisements of junk food?

(a) They market junk food as healthy
(b) They are only half correct
(c) They show smiling mothers
(d) They have misleading taglines

(iii) Complete the sentence by choosing an appropriate option.

Our attitude towards food has its roots in the time when India ....

(a) was a golden bird
(b) was poor and food was scarce
(c) when agriculture was predominant
(d) was a British colony

(iv) Which of the following statement is incorrect?

(a) All junk food are unhealthy.
(b) All instant noodles are unhealthy.
(c) Only the junk food in our diet is unhealthy.
(d) We compromise with food for its taste or convenience.

(v) Select the option that conveys the opposite of 'coarse'.

(a) Processed (b) Credible
(c) Refined (d) Unlikely

(vi) Select the most suitable title for the passage.

(a) The Harm in Jank Food
(b) Junk Food not Healthy
(c) Ancient Food Habits of India
(d) All of the above

Passage 12

If you're addicted to coffee and doctors warn you to quit the habit, don't worry and keep relishing the beverage, because it's not that bad after all! In fact, according to a new study, the steaming cup of java even beats fruits and vegetables as the primary source of antioxidants. A study by the University of Scranton states that coffee is the number one source of antioxidants in the American diet and both caffeinated and decaf versions appear to provide similar antioxidant levels.

"Americans get more of their antioxidants from coffee than any other dietary source. Nothing else comes close to it.", said the study's lead researcher, Dr Joe Vinson, adding that high antioxidant levels in food and beverages don't necessarily translate into levels found in the body. Antioxidants in general have been linked to a number of potential health benefits, including protection against heart disease and cancer, but Vinson said that the benefits ultimately depend on how they are absorbed and utilised in the body.

The researchers analysed the antioxidant content of more than 100 different food items, including vegetables, fruits, nuts, spices, oils and common beverages. The data was compared to an existing US Department of Agriculture database on the contribution of each type of food item to the average estimated US per capita consumption.

The results were surprising. Coffee came out on the top, on the combined basis of both antioxidants per serving size and frequency of consumption. It outranked popular antioxidant sources like tea, milk, chocolate and cranberries.

Of all the food and beverages studies, dates actually have the most antioxidants of all based solely on serving size, but since dates are not consumed at anywhere near the level of coffee, the drink comes as the top source of antioxidants, Vinson said.

Besides keeping you alert and awake, coffee has been linked to an increasing number of potential health benefits, including protection against liver and colon cancer, type 2 diabetes and Parkinson's disease, according to some recently published studies.

The researchers, however, advised that one should consume coffee in moderation, because it can make you jittery and cause stomach pains.

Questions

On the basis of your reading of the passage, answer the following questions.

(i) On what basis does coffee rank as the top source of antioxidants?

(a) Due to its consumption
(b) A study by the University of Scranton
(c) Because it is a primary source
(d) Due to its potential health benefits

(ii) Potential health benefits of antioxidants include ....

(a) protection against heart disease
(b) protection against cancer
(c) Both (a) and (b)
(d) Neither (a) nor (b)

(iii) Other popular sources of antioxidants include ....

(a) tea (b) milk
(c) chocolate (d) All of these

(iv) Potential Health benefits of coffee include protection against ....

(a) liver and colon cancer (b) type 2 diabetes
(c) Parkinson's disease (d) All of these

(v) Which of the following words in the first paragraph means the same as 'enjoying'?

(a) Delighting (b) Steaming
(c) Relishing (d) Tasting

(vi) The benefits of consuming coffee are dependent on

(a) consumption
(b) portion size
(c) utilisation
(d) Both (a) and (c)

Passage 13

It is said that everyone lives by selling something. What you can understand by this statement is that teachers live by selling knowledge, philosophers live by selling wisdom and priests earn their living by selling spiritual comfort. Though it may be possible to measure the value of material goods in terms of money, it is extremely difficult to estimate the true value of the services which people perform for us.

There are times when we would willingly give everything we possess to save our lives, yet we might grudge paying a surgeon a high fee for offering us precisely the same service. The conditions of society are such that skills have to be paid for in the same way that goods are paid for at a shop. Everyone has something to sell.

Tramps seem to be the only exception to this general rule. Beggars almost sell themselves as human beings to arouse the pity of passers-by. But real tramps are not beggars. They have nothing to sell and require nothing from others. In seeking independence, they do not sacrifice their human dignity. A tramp may ask you for money but he will never ask you to feel sorry for him. He has deliberately chosen to lead the life he leads and is fully aware of the consequences. He may never be sure where his next meal is coming from, but he is free from the thousands of anxieties which afflict other people. His few material possessions make it possible for him to move from place to place with ease. By having to sleep in the open, he gets far closer to the world of nature than most of us ever do.

He may hunt, beg or steal occasionally to keep himself alive; he may even, in times of real need, do a little work; but he will never sacrifice his freedom.

We often speak with contempt for tramps and put them in the same class as beggars. But how many of us can honestly say that we have not felt a little envious of their simple way of life and their freedom from any care in the world?

Questions

On the basis of your reading of the passage, answer the following questions.

(i) Which of the following is difficult to judge?

(a) The actual value of services given by people
(b) The actual value of material goods
(c) Both (a) and (b)
(d) Neither (a) nor (b)

(ii) A .... does not sell services.

(a) surgeon (b) teacher
(c) priest (d) None of these

(iii) According to the passage, which of the following correctly lists the qualities of a tramp?

1. Anxious 2. Tranquil
3. Independent 4. Traveler 5. Beggarly

(a) 1 and 5 (b) 2 and 3
(c) 1,3,4 (d) 2,3,4

(iv) A beggar is different from a tramp because

(a) a beggar sells but tramps don't
(b) beggars do not travel but tramps are always on the move
(c) beggars don't know when they will eat their next meal but tramps find a means to earn their meals
(d) All of the above

(v) Which of the following words is the synonym of 'estimate' in Paragraph 1?

(a) Calculate (b) Evaluation
(c) Appraisal (d) Determine

(vi) Pick the option showing the CORRECT use of 'afflict' as used in the passage.

(a) There are two main problems which afflict people with hearing impairments.
(b) They return to afflict the living, so they have to be sent packing.
(c) You shall not afflict any widow or fatherless child.
(d) I wish you wouldn't afflict me with your constant complains.

(vii) .... Paragraph 3 is the antonym of 'unconsciously'.

(a) Purposefully (b) Occasionally
(c) Deliberately (d) Specifically

(viii) .... means the same as 'feel aggrieved about'.

(a) Anxieties (b) Grude
(c) Spiritual (d) Envious

Passage 14

Travel is a bug that was in me when I was born, probably inherited from my father. In 24 years of travelling widely through India, I have been most fascinated by those little islands that dot the Bay of Bengal off the East Coast of India. Yes, I am talking about the Andaman Islands. Andamans somehow seemed almost sinister, with images of being haunted, bleak and scary, until my parents actually returned from a trip to Port Blair and told us about these serene islands. We immediately awaited the first opportunity to take a break and check them out. Finally, the D-Day came and we were all ready. We boarded the aircraft and, to our surprise, found that there were several empty seats. On enquiry, we learnt that all supplies to the Andamans including newspapers and meat go from the mainland, and so there is always more cargo and less people.

Port Blair airport is a small, old airport that was constructed in 1947. On my way to the hotel, I noticed that there are none of the usual auto-rickshaws that noisily wend their way through most Indian towns. There was only one traffic signal in the entire town and the roads were more up and down than level. This was all surprising for a person like me who has lived in the coastal towns of Chennai and Mumbai.

The colour of the sea was an unpolluted blue, a colour that I had not seen in any of the beaches in India. It was calm and beautiful. I was thrilled with the fact that we were going to spend 10 entire days there. All we had to do was sit in the open restaurant, look at the sea, enjoy the cool breeze and feel good.

The Andaman Islands are a group of several islands, so most of our sightseeing was by boats. There are a total of more than 356 islands there. Even the oldest boatman, Rathnam, had seen only 200 of them. I figured that 10 days was surely not enough to get a full picture of this place, so I started to store every sight, every sound and every smell. The sound and light show at the jail sent a shiver down my spine. (This trip was before the movie 'Kalapani' was released). The realisation that those who fought for our independence had lived, struggled, suffered and even died here, left an impact.

Questions

On the basis of your reading of the passage, answer the following questions.

(i) Complete the sentence by choosing the correct option.

One thing that left a major impact on the author was ....

(a) the serenity of the place
(b) the wholesome experience
(c) vastness of the islands
(d) the realisation that freedom fighters had lived, struggled and died there.

(ii) The writer agree with the given statements EXCEPT:

(a) The narrator liked travelling.
(b) There were no empty seats in the aircraft.
(c) The Port Blair Airport is small.
(d) The Andaman Islands are a group of Islands.

(iii) **What was the author's initial impression about the Andaman Islands?**
(a) They were beautiful and serene.
(b) They were uninhabitable.
(c) They were sinister, haunted and scary.
(d) They were difficult to explore.

(iv) **Where are Andaman Islands located?**
(a) In the Arabian Sea
(b) In the Bay of Bengal
(c) In the Indian Ocean
(d) In the Atlantic Ocean

(v) **Pick the option showing the CORRECT use of the word 'boarded' as used in the passage.**
(a) I was the last to board the tourist bus.
(b) I felt board when I went to Denmark.
(c) Einstein was boared in his school classes.
(d) Did you took my board today?

(vi) **Select the option that conveys the meaning of 'sinister' as used in Paragraph 1.**
(a) Inconclusive (b) Threatening
(c) Fascinating (d) Obscure

Passage 15

A poor farmer lived with his wife and son in a small village. One day, exhausted by the heat, he lay down under the shadow of a tree to take a nap. All of a sudden he saw a giant cobra crawling out of an ant hill. The farmer thought to himself, "Surely this snake must be a deity guarding my field. So far I have not noticed it and that is why all my farming is in vain. Let me pay my respects to it now and worship it thereafter."

He then made up his mind, brought some milk in a bowl and placed it before the ant hill. He said aloud, "O lord guardian of my field! I did not know you dwell here. Please forgive me for not paying respects to you."

He left the milk bowl there and went back to his house. The next morning, he was surprised to see a gold coin in the bowl. Since then the farmer placed a bowl of milk every day and got back a gold coin the next morning. Soon the farmer became rich and happy.

One day the farmer had to go to a nearby city for a few days and so he directed his son to place the milk bowl near the ant hill every day. The son kept the milk bowl and left, only to find a gold coin the next day. He then thought to himself, "This ant hill must be full of gold coins: I'll kill the serpent and take all of them."

The next day, while placing the bowl of milk, the farmer's son struck the snake with a club. But the serpent escaped and bit him with its sharp fangs instead. He was dead at once. When the farmer returned, he learnt about his son's fate and grieved. The next morning, he took the bowl of milk and went to the ant hill. The snake came out and said, "Your greed made you overlook even the loss of your son. Your son struck me in ignorance and I had bitten him to death.

I cannot forget the blow on my head and you cannot forget the loss of your son. Hereafter, the friendship between us is not possible." The snake gave a costly coin and disappeared. The farmer returned home cursing the foolishness of his son.

Questions

On the basis of your reading of the passage, answer the following questions.

(i) **Based on your understanding of the passage, choose the option that lists the CORRECT sequence of the occurrence of incidents in the passage.**

1. The farmer brought some milk in a bowl.
2. A giant cobra was seen by the farmer.
3. The farmer's son placed a bowl of milk near the ant hill.
4. The snake was struck with a club.

(a) 2, 4, 1, 3 (b) 2, 1, 3, 4
(c) 1, 2, 3, 4 (d) 4, 3, 2, 1

(ii) **Pick the option showing the CORRECT use of the word 'directed' as used in the passage.**
(a) The administrator has direct access to all the files on every computer.
(b) One's educational level has a direct effect on one's income.
(c) Which is the most direct route to Chandni Chowk?
(d) The Principal directed the teachers to make online videos for their students.

(iii) **What did the son do to get all the gold?**
(a) He requested the cobra to give him all the gold.
(b) He stole all the gold from the ant hill.
(c) He tried to kill the cobra.
(d) None of these

(iv) **The word 'deity' in Paragraph 1 means ....**
(a) guard (b) sentry (c) divine being (d) idol

(v) **The word 'exhausted' in Paragraph 1 is an antonym of ....**
(a) started (b) finished
(c) fresh (d) invigorated

(vi) Pick the option that CORRECTLY lists the final feelings of the farmer.

1. Annoyance
2. Contentment
3. Repentance
4. Joy
5. Empathy

(a) 2 and 4 (b) 1 and 4
(c) 1 and 5 (d) 1 and 3

Passage 16

"Did you see that?" Joe said to his friend Bill. "You're a great shooter!"

Bill caught the basketball and bounced it before throwing it again. The ball flew into the net.

"Bill, you never miss!" Joe said admiringly.

"Unless I'm in a real game," Bill complained.

"Then I miss all the time."

Joe knew that Bill was right. Bill performed much better when he was having fun with Joe in the school yard than he did when he was playing for the school team in front of a large crowd.

"Maybe you just need to practice more," Joe suggested.

"But I practice all the time with you!" Bill objected.

He shook his head. "I just can't play well when people are watching me."

"You play well when I'm watching," Joe pointed out.

"That's because I've known you since we were five years old," Bill said with a smile.

Joe nodded and understood, but he also had an idea. The next day Joe and Bill met in the school yard again to practice. After a few minutes, Joe excused himself. "Practice without me," Joe said to his friend. "I'll be back in a minute."

Joe hastened through the school building, gathering together whomever he could find—two students, a math teacher, two secretaries, and a janitor. When Joe explained why he needed them, everyone was happy to help. Joe reminded the group to stay quiet as they all went toward the school's basketball court.

As Joe had hoped, Bill was still practicing basketball. He made five baskets in a row without noticing the people standing behind him.

"Hey, Bill!" Joe called out finally. Bill turned. A look of surprise came over his face.

"I just wanted to show you that you could play well with people watching you," Joe said. "Now you'll have nothing to worry about for the next game!"

Questions

On the basis of your reading of the passage, answer the following questions.

(i) What would be the best title for the above literary passage?

(a) Bill Joins the Team
(b) Practice Makes Perfect
(c) Bill Wins the Big Game
(d) Bill's Basketball Problem

(ii) Which of the following characteristics can you associate with Joe?

1. Kind
2. Confused
3. Encouraging
4. Friendly
5. Intelligent
6. Knowledgeable

(a) 1 and 3 (b) 2 and 6
(c) 4 and 5 (d) Both (a) and (c)

(iii) Which of the following words can replace the word 'complained' as used in the passage?

(a) Resented (b) Cribbed
(c) Lamented (d) Protested

(iv) Pick the option showing the CORRECT use of 'objected' as used in the passage.

(a) He stood up and objected in strong language.
(b) The director objected to the cuts ordered by the censor.
(c) She objected to this invasion of her personal space.
(d) All of the above

(v) Which word in the passage can be replaced by 'hurried'?

(a) Hastened (b) Excused
(c) Bounced (d) Pointed

(vi) Which of the following can be attributed to the people who Joe had gathered?

(a) Motivating (b) Courageous
(c) Self conscious (d) Critical

Passage 17

Archimedes with his lever desired a place to stand that he might move the world of matter. [William Lloyd] Garrison with his paper, having found a place for his feet, demonstrated speedily his ability to push from its solid base the world of mind. His plan was very simple, viz., to reveal slavery as it then existed in its naked enormity, to the conscience of the North, to be "as harsh as truth and as uncompromising as justice." And so, week after week, he packed in the columns of the Liberator facts, the most damning facts, against slaveholders, their cruelty and tyranny. He painted the woes of the slaves as if he, too, had been a slave. For the first time the masters found a man who rebuked them as not before had they been rebuked. Others may have equivocated, but this man called things by their proper names, a spade, a spade and sin, sin.

Others may have contented themselves with denunciations of the sins and with excuses for the sinner, as a creature of circumstances, the victim of ancestral transgressions, but this man offered no excuses for the slave-holding sinner. Him and his sin he denounced in language, which the Eternal puts only into the mouths of his prophets.

It was, as he had said, "On this subject I do not wish to think, or speak, or write, with moderation." The strength and resources of his mother-tongue seemed to him wholly inadequate for his needs, to express the transcendent wickedness of slave-holding. All the harsh, the stern, the terrible and tremendous energies of the English speech he drew upon and launched at slaveholders. Amid all of this excess of the enthusiast there was the method of a calculating mind. He aimed to kindle a conflagration because he had icebergs to melt. "The public shall not be imposed upon," he replied to one of his critics, "and men and things shall be called by their right names. I retract nothing, I blot out nothing. My language is exactly such as suits me; it will displease many, I know; to displease them is my intention."

He was philosopher enough to see that he could reach the national conscience only by exciting the national anger. It was not popular rage, which he feared but popular apathy. If he could goad the people to anger on the subject of slavery he would soon be rid of their apathy. And so week after week he piled every sort of combustible material, which he was able to collect on board the Liberator and lighting it all, sent the fiery messenger blazing among the icebergs of the Union. Slaveholders were robbers, murderers, oppressors; they were guilty of all the sins.

At the same moment that the reformer denied their right of property in the slave, he attacked their character also, held them up in their relation of masters to the reprobation of the nation and of mankind as monsters of injustice and inhumanity.

The tone which he held toward them, steadily, without shadow of change, was the tone of a righteous man toward the workers of iniquity. The indifference, the apathy, the pro-slavery sympathy and prejudice of the free States rendered the people of the North hardly less culpable.

Questions

On the basis of your reading of the passage, answer the following questions.

(i) What made William Lloyd Garrison different from other abolitionists?

(a) He went onto Southern plantations and freed slaves.

(b) He worked in Congress to pass abolitionist legislation.

(c) He didn't make any excuses in his writings and exposed the truth.

(d) He operated an underground railroad to help slaves escape to the North.

(ii) Complete the sentence by choosing an appropriate option.
According to the passage, Garrison's language was so strong because ....

(a) He had been a slave himself and wrote from experience.

(b) He saw himself as a sort of Prophet and his language was given to him by God.

(c) He feared having the people being angry with him.

(d) He felt like he was the only person talking about this topic.

(iii) All of the following statements are true about Garrison's intentions EXCEPT

(a) He hoped that people would ignore his writings and keep owning slaves.

(b) He wanted to provoke the national anger.

(c) He attacked the character of the slave-owners, showing them to be monsters.

(d) He wanted people to react so that they wouldn't be apathetic any more.

(iv) Based on the context clues in the passage, what was the Liberator?

(a) A novel (b) A movie

(c) A train (d) A pamphlet

(v) Select the option that conveys the meaning of 'conflagration'.

(a) Fire (b) Shipwreck (c) Mess (d) Waterfall

(vi) Pick the option showing the CORRECT use of 'goad' as used in the passage.

(a) "I want somebody very goad, very safe , to plant that gun," he told Clemenza.

(b) The thought of exams next week is a great goad to the students to work hard.

(c) His opposition acted as a goad to her determination to succeed.

(d) All of the above

Passage 18

Among the vast number of men who have thought fit to write down the history of their own lives, three or four have achieved masterpieces which stand out pre-eminently: Saint Augustine in his Confessions, Samuel Pepys in his Diary, Rousseau in his Confessions. It is among these extraordinary documents and unsurpassed by any of them, that the autobiography of Benvenuto Cellini takes its place.

The life of himself which Cellini wrote was due to other motives than those which produced its chief competitors for first place in its class. St. Augustines aim was religious and didactic, Pepys noted down in his diary the daily events of his life for his sole satisfaction and with no intention that any one should read the cipher in which they were recorded. But Cellini wrote that the world might know, after he was dead, what a fellow he had been; what great things he had attempted and against what odds he had carried them through. All men, he held, whatever be their condition, who have done anything of merit, or which verily has a semblance of merit, if so be they are men of truth and good repute, should write the tale of their life with their own hand. That he had done many things of merit, he had no manner of doubt. His repute was great in his day and perhaps good in the sense in which he meant goodness; as to whether he was a man of truth, there is still dispute among scholars.

Of some misrepresentations, some suppressions of damaging facts, there seems to be evidence only too good-a man with Cellini's passion for proving himself in the right could hardly have avoided being guilty of such; but of the general trustworthiness of his record, of the kind of man he was and the kind of life he led, there is no reasonable doubt.

The period covered by the autobiography is from Cellini's birth in 1500 to 1562; the scene is mainly in Italy and France. Of the great events of the time, the time of the Reformation and the Counter-Reformation, of the strife of Pope and Emperor and King, we get only glimpses. The leaders in these events appear in the foreground of the picture only when they come into personal relations with the hero; and then not mainly as statesmen or warriors, but as connoisseurs and patrons of art. Such an event as the Sack of Rome is described because Benvenuto himself fought in it.

Much more complete is the view he gives of the artistic life of the time. It was the age of Michelangelo, and in the throng of great artists which then filled the Italian cities, Cellini was no inconsiderable figure. Michelangelo himself he knew and adored. Nowhere, can we gain a better idea than in this book of the passionate enthusiasm for the creation of beauty which has bestowed upon the Italy of the Renaissance its greatest glory.

Very vivid, too, is the impression we receive of the social life of the sixteenth century; of its violence, of its zeal for fine craftsmanship, of its abounding vitality, its versatility and its idealism. For Cellini himself is an epitome of that century. This man who tells here the story of his life was a murderer - insolent, sensual, inordinately proud and passionate; but he was also a worker in gold and silver, rejoicing in delicate and subtle modelling of precious surfaces; a sculptor and a musician; and as all who read his book must testify, a great master of narrative.

Keen as was Benvenutos interest in himself and much as he loved to dwell on the splendor of his exploits and achievements, he had little idea that centuries after his death he would live again, less by his statue of Perseus and his goldsmiths work than by the book which he dictated casually to a lad of fourteen, while he went about his work.

The autobiography was composed between 1558 and 1566, but it brings the record down only to 1562. The remainder of Cellini's life seems to have been somewhat more peaceful. He died at Florence, 13th May, 1571 and was buried in The Church of the Annunziata in that city.

Questions

On the basis of your reading of the passage, answer the following questions.

(i) In the given passage, the author talks about

(a) Cellini's life
(b) Cellini's competitors
(c) Cellini's autobiography
(d) Cellini's literary works

(ii) What CANNOT be inferred from this passage?

(a) Most of Cellini's life was peaceful.
(b) Cellini's autobiography is not entirely truthful in all respects.
(c) Cellini was well-known during his day.
(d) Cellini's autobiography is full of self-love.

(iii) Which of the following lists the characteristics that can be associated with Cellini?

1. Narcissist
2. Courageous
3. Criminal
4. Artistic
5. Exploitative

(a) 1 and 2 (b) 3 and 4
(c) 4 and 5 (d) All of these

(iv) **As described by the author, what is NOT true about Cellini's autobiography?**
(a) It focuses on the political events of the time.
(b) It is one of the perfect example of a biography.
(c) It gives the reader insight into the artistic and social life of the 16th century.
(d) It tells us about Cellini's exploits and achievements.

(v) **What do the words 'these extraordinary documents' refer to?**
(a) Historical books
(b) The autobiographies of St. Augustine, Pepys and Rousseau
(c) Cellini's autobiographies
(d) All biographies

(vi) **What is the meaning of the words 'unsurpassed by' as used in the passage?**
(a) Better than
(b) Cannot be compared to
(c) Equal to
(d) Unable to cross

(vii) **Pick the option showing the CORRECT use of 'repute' as used in the passage.**
(a) His Wessex - wide repute was among them alone.
(b) This repute seemed to give the new managers the confidence to approach their bosses as resources.
(c) A mountaineer of repute, whether local or not, is conspicuous by his or her absence.
(d) Are you acquainted if only by repute with a Mr. Landor who is a poet?

(viii) **Which word in the passage is synonym of 'slight'?**
(a) Inconsiderable (b) Versatility
(c) Vivid (d) Suppressions

Passage 19

The forces that generate conditions conducive to crime and riots are stronger in urban communities than in rural areas. Urban living is more anonymous living. It often releases the individual from community restraints more common in tradition-oriented societies. But more freedom from constraints and controls also provides greater freedom to deviate. And living in the more impersonalised, formally controlled urban society means that regulatory orders of conduct are often directed by distant bureaucrats. The police are strangers executing these prescriptions on an anonymous set of subjects. Minor offences in small town or village are often handled without resort to official police action. As disputable as such action may seem to be, it results in fewer recorded violations of the law compared to the big cities. Although, perhaps causing some decision-difficulties for the police in small town, formal and objective law enforcement is not always acceptable to villagers.

Urban areas with mass population, greater wealth, more commercial establishments and more products of our technology also provide more frequent opportunities for theft. Victims are impersonalised, property is insured, consumer goods in more abundance are vividly displayed and are more portable. The crime-rate increases despite formal moral education given in schools.

(i) **According to the passage, which of the following contribute to higher crime-rates in urban areas except**
(a) higher standard of living
(b) urban impersonalised living
(c) increasing population
(d) inadequate police force

(ii) **Which of the following is a characteristic of an urban setting?**
(a) Unreported minor crimes
(b) Deviation from freedom
(c) Less forceful social control
(d) Minimal opportunities of crime due to better law enforcement

(iii) **The author's view of 'Traditional Societies' is best expressed by which of the following?**
(a) They provide less freedom for the individual in many circumstances
(b) They have lower crime-rates because of the moral teachings in schools
(c) They provide inadequate freedom for personal movements and travel
(d) They are ruled and controlled by distant bureaucrats

(iv) **People live under more social control in**
(a) formally controlled urban societies
(b) an anonymous form of living
(c) non-traditional societies
(d) None of the above

(v) **It can be inferred from the passage that urban crime can be controlled by**
(a) enforcement of law by distant bureaucrats
(b) vivid display of expensive consumer goods

(c) making the expensive consumer goods less portable

(d) None of the above

(vi) Which of the following statements is true in the context of the passage?

(a) The display of consumer goods is the main cause of crime

(b) Lack of personal contacts increases crimes in urban areas

(c) Small communities have more minor crimes than in urban centres

(d) Police in urban areas settle minor disputes without official action

Passage 20

A close look at the facts relating to political interference in administration shows that it is not a one-way process. There is often a nexus between power-hungry and corrupt politicians and civil servants with convenient principles. Many civil servants are only too anxious to oblige the politicians, and then cash the obligation when they need some special favour. So, the attitude of self-righteousness adopted by the civil service is sometimes only a way of covering their own flaws by blaming others.

Every now and then some retired civil servants come out with his memoirs, painting a glorious picture of the heights of administrative efficiency reached during his reign. There is often the suggestion that had there not been so much political interference, things would have been even more fantastic. It is not unusual for the self-styled hero to blame not only interfering politicians but also fellow civil servants who were idiots or crooks, for his failures.

This attitude of smug self-satisfaction is, unfortunately, developed during the years of service. Self-preservation rather than service is encouraged by our whole system of rules and procedures. The remedy has to be drastic and quickly effective. The over-protection now granted of civil servants must end. Today to remove an erring civil servant is just not possible. And the only thing that the highest authority in the Government, both in the State and at the Centre, can do is to transfer an official from one job to another.

The rules for taking disciplinary action are so complicated that, in the end, the defaulting civil servant gets away, and gets his full emoluments even for the period of the disciplinary proceedings, thus making it a paid holiday for him. The result is that the administration has become rule-oriented and not result oriented. Action is possible against the official who takes some interest in his work, but no action is ever taken against a person who does not deliver the goods. If the country is to adopt a result-oriented approach, it is necessary to link job performance with job retention.

(i) The facts relating to the problem of political interference indicate that

(a) honest bureaucrats are always being troubled by politician

(b) politicians are often misled and trapped by civil servants

(c) politicians and civil servants co-operate to gain mutual advantages

(d) politicians and civil servants use interference as an excuse for victimising the common man

(ii) The attitude of self-righteousness adopted by the civil service, according to the writer

(a) is not welcomed and supported by politicians

(b) is dishonest and conceals the facts

(c) is very difficult to maintain because of opposition

(d) does not really help the public get fair treatment

(iii) Civil servants who write their memoirs after retiring

(a) claim that they would have achieved outstanding success if interference had not come in the way

(b) prove that constant political interference made it impossible for them to do anything properly

(c) complain that the credit for their achievements goes to dishonest politicians

(d) prove that people of inferior quality in the civil service bring about interference

(iv) The existing system of administration seems to encourage civil servants

(a) to become self-styled heroes and boss over others

(b) to present a glorious picture of the administration

(c) to become self-centred and concerned mainly about their own gain

(d) to become self-righteous and fight back against corrupt politicians

(v) The problem with the present set-up needing urgent action is
(a) a lack of accountability on the part of civil servants
(b) a lack of control over the power of politicians
(c) a neglect of the ideals of self-righteousness
(d) complicated rules and procedures that greatly reduce efficiency

(vi) The main principle of the remedy proposed by the writer is, that
(a) the politicians should be made accountable for all their decisions
(b) the high level of protection enjoyed by civil servants should be reduced
(c) the common man's right to efficient and fair administration must be protected
(d) rules should be simplified so that there is less scope for misuse

Passage 21

True, it is the function of the army to maintain law and order in abnormal times. But in normal times there is another force that compels citizens to obey the laws and to act with due regard to the rights of others. The force also protects the lives and the properties of law abiding men. Laws are made to secure the personal safety of its subjects and to prevent murder and crimes of violence.

They are made to secure the property of the citizens against theft and damage to protect the rights of communities and castes to carry out their customs and ceremonies, so long as they do not conflict with the rights of others.

Now the good citizen, of his own free will obey these laws and he takes care that everything he does is done with due regard to the rights and well-being of others.

But the bad citizen is only restrained from breaking these laws by fear of the consequence of his actions. And the necessary steps to compel the bad citizen to act as a good citizen are taken by this force. The supreme control of law and order in a State is in the hands of a Minister who is responsible to the State Assembly and acts through the Inspector General of Police.

(i) The expression 'customs and ceremonies' means
(a) fairs and festivals
(b) habits and traditions
(c) usual practices and religious rites
(d) superstitions and formalities

(ii) A suitable title for the passage would be
(a) The Function of the Army
(b) Laws and the People's Rights
(c) The Fear of the Law and Citizen's Security
(d) The Functions of The Police

(iii) Which of the following is not implied in the passage?
(a) Law protects those who respect it
(b) Law ensures people's religious and social rights absolutely and unconditionally
(c) A criminal is deterred from committing crimes only for fear of the law
(d) The forces of law help to transform irresponsible citizens into responsible ones

(iv) According to the writer, which one of the following is not the responsibility of the police?
(a) To protect the privileges of all citizens
(b) To check violent activities of citizens
(c) To ensure peace among citizens by safeguarding individual rights
(d) To maintain peace during extra-ordinary circumstances

(v) Which of the following reflects the main thrust of the passage?
(a) It deals with the importance of the army in maintaining law and order
(b) It highlights role of the police as superior to that of the army
(c) It discusses the roles of the army and the police in different circumstances
(d) It points to the responsibility of the Minister and the Inspector General of Police

(vi) "They are made to secure the property of citizens against theft and damage", means that the law
(a) helps in recovering the stolen property of the citizens
(b) assist the citizens whose property has been stolen or destroyed
(c) initiate process against offenders of law
(d) safeguard people's possessions against being stolen or lost

Passage 22

On attending a conference which focused on the role of the services sector in Indian economy, I was amazed. The conference gave a very interesting **perspective** on the role of the service sector in the growth of Indian economy in relation to growth rates in agriculture and industry.

The current situation in India is that the growth rate of services has overtaken both agriculture and industry and is now contributing to more than 50% of GDP. The service sector has the highest growth rate and is the least **volatile** sector, Growth is particularly marked in public services, IT and financial services. In some areas, the growth rate of the service sector is 40-50% due to increased use of mobile technologies. India, therefore has, a service-oriented economy. It hasn't followed traditional growth models as in China. However, in the process of doing so it has skipped the manufacturing stage and has jumped straight from the agriculture stage to service stage, which is also the main reason for the expansion of the service sector.

In fact, the situation now is such that the growth in the service sector can and will support in the agriculture and industrial sectors.

However, the only setback for Indian economy is the lack of growth in the manufacturing sector which causes dependence on other countries, which is not so desirable in terms of job creation and increased prosperity.

Population is also a major concern of the Indian economy. As the population of India grows so also does the number of dependents in the population in both the lower and higher age groups. In such a scenario of increasing population, especially in an economy which still recovering from crisis, growth becomes difficult. For such an economy to grow it has to invest. Currently, the public sector invests more than it saves. The household sector saves in surplus, but it is not increasing so it cannot continue to support private and public sectors. There is a **massive** need to spend on agriculture and infrastructure development of the country, Apart from that health and education should also be the priority of the government particularly the education of women in order to reduce the birth rate.

(i) Choose the word which is most opposite in meaning to word given in bold as used in the passage.

Volatile

(a) Erratic (b) Impatient
(c) Stable (d) Solid

(ii) According to the passage, which of the following is/are true about the impact of increasing population on Indian economy?

A. If India attempts to absorb all the labour force, it will impact the growth of service sector negatively and in turn hamper the economic growth of the country.

B. As the population of the country increases, the number of dependants in the country also increase which in turn increases the pressure on the economy.

C. An increasing population can never lead the economy of the country towards prosperity; in fact it can only put strain on the economy of a country.

Codes

(a) Only B (b) Only C (c) B and C (d) A and C

(iii) According to the passage, which of the following can be said about the agriculture and industry sectors in India?

A. Looking at the growth of the services sector in India it can be safely said that the service sector will soon be in a position to support both agriculture and industry sector.

B. The agriculture and the industrial sector of the country have reached their threshold and there would be no use of further investment in these sectors.

C. Currently, the agriculture and industry sectors contribute lesser as compared to service sector to the GDP of the country.

Codes

(a) Only A (b) Only C
(c) A and C (d) B and C

(iv) What does the author mean by the statement, ... a 'growth window' for India will open?

(a) In the coming years, the Indian economy will grow as the service sector of the country would be booming due to the focus of the government in that sector

(b) In the next two decades, Indian economy will have an opportunity to grow as the working population of India will be high as compared to the dependant population

(c) There would be only a small period of time in which the economy of India has to grow and if it fails to do so it will never be able to recover from the economic downfall

(d) Only upto the next two decades would Indian people interested in finding jobs in the country beyond which they would search for jobs abroad thus, hampering the growth of Indian economy

(v) **Choose the word which is most similar in meaning to the word given in bold as used in the passage.**
Massive
(a) Huge (b) Bulky (c) Solid (d) Grand

(vi) **Choose the word which is most similar in meaning to the word given in bold as used in the passage.**
Perspective
(a) Viewpoint (b) Prospect
(c) Attitude (d) Agreement

Passage 23

The great recession hasn't been great for free trade. As unemployment has risen throughout the world, governments have become more focused on protecting their own industries than on promoting international commerce. The US, though typically an enthusiastic supporter of open markets, included failing 'buy American' clauses in its stimulus package and propped up its falling auto industry with handouts. But according to the Asian Development Bank (ADB), in the part of the world that was hit hardest by the trade crash -Asia the number of Free-Trade Agreements (FTAs) signed by Asian countries has grown from just three in 2000 to 56 by the end of August 2009. Nineteen of those FTAs are among 16 Asian economies, a trend that could help the region become a powerful trading bloc.

The drive to lower trade barriers has taken on fresh urgency amid the recession. As Asian manufacturing networks become more intertwined - and as Asian consumers become wealthier - regional commerce is becoming critical to future economic expansion. Intra-regional trade last year made up 57% of total Asian trade, up from 37% in 1930. In the past Asia produced for America and Europe, now Asia is producing for Asia. Of course, Asia is still dependent on sales to the West. But FTAs could reduce the region's exposure to the United States by giving Asian companies preferential treatment in selling to Asian companies and consumers. However, these benefits could come with downsides. According to experts, FTAs create a 'non-level playing field with advantages for Asian countries.'

If the most dynamically growing part of the global economy gives the US restricted access, it will impact global balance.

Companies in countries like the United States left out of the trade pacts could face disadvantages when trying to tap fast-growing Asian markets. This, in turn, could have a negative impact of efforts to rebalance excessive debt in the US and excessive savings in Asia. Still, the benefits of greater regional integration could prove powerful enough to overcome the roadblocks. In Asia, the only thing everyone agrees upon is business. If it does, the world economy may never be the same.

(i) **What do the Asian Development Bank (ADB) statistics indicate?**
(a) Asian economies are financially more sound than those of the developed world
(b) The financial crisis impacted the West far more than it did Asia
(c) Asian countries have aligned themselves on lines similar to the European Union
(d) Asian countries have been actively opening their markets to one another

(ii) **What has given rise to the large number of trade agreements between Asian countries?**
(a) The need to insulate Asian economies from over exposure to the American economy
(b) Angry reaction among Asian countries owing to America's protectionist policy
(c) The aim of empowering the poorer Asian economies and being them on par with Western economies
(d) The desire to achieve conditions conducive to global consensus on trade regulations and tariffs

(iii) **Which of the following is/ are not true in the context of the passage?**
I. **Political and economic rivalries between Asian countries are non-existent today.**
II. **Asian countries hold America responsible for the recession and have imposed economic sanctions against the US.**
III. **America has adopted a protectionist strategy after the recession.**

Codes
(a) Only I (b) II and III (c) I and II (d) Only III

(iv) **Which of the following describes expert predictions about trade pacts between Asian countries?**
(a) These will be beneficial and are likely to give rise to a common Asian currency
(b) Tariffs will be lowered and bureaucratic regulations will become transparent
(c) Widening of differences between participant and non-participant countries will hamper global stability
(d) Regional conflicts will increase as competition and inequities between Asian nations will intensify

(v) Which of the following has/have not been (an) impact(s) of the recession?

I. Various trade agreements signed between developed and Asian countries have not been honoured.

II. The US Government has restructured the automobile industry.

III. Regional conflicts in Asia have substantially reduced.

Codes

(a) Only IIII (b) Only I
(c) I and II (d) All of these

(vi) According to the author, what danger does creating an Asian trading bloc pose?

(a) Political instability in Asia will rise as some countries are wealthier than others
(b) American consumers have ceased their demands for Asian goods
(c) Unemployment in Asian countries will rise as many plants will be forced to close down
(d) None of the above

Passage 24

The small village of Somnathpur contains an extraordinary temple, built around AD 1268 by the Hoyasalas of Karnataka- one of the most prolific temple builders. Belur and Helebid are among their better known works. While these suffered during the invasion of the 14th century, the Somnathpur temple stands more or less intact in near-original condition.

This small temple captivates the beauty and vitality of its detailed sculpture, covering almost every inch of the walls, pillars and even ceilings. It has three shikharas and stands on a star shaped platform with 24 edges. The outer walls have a profusion of detailed carvings: the entire surface runs over by a carved plaque of stone.

There were vertical panels covered by exquisite figures of Gods and Goddesses. Vishnu seemed the most popular, with many of his incarnations being depicted. Shiv, Brahma and Indra weren't left out and there were plenty of female deities too like Durga and Saraswati. There were shapely nymphs too, some carrying an ear of maize.

The elaborate ornamentation, very characteristic of Hoyasalas sculptures, was a remarkable feature.

On closer look and it is worth it- the series of friezes on the outer walls revealed intricately carved caparisoned elephants, charging horsemen, stylised flowers, warriors, musicians, crocodiles and swans.

The temple was actually commissioned by Soma Dandanayaka or (Somnath), he named the temple after him, the minister of the Hoyasalas king, Narsimha the Third. The temple was built to house three versions of Krishna. The inner center of the temple was Kalyana Mandapa.

Leading from here were three corridors, each ending in a shrine, one for each kind of Krishna-Venugopala, Janardana and Prasanna Keshava, though only two remain in their original form. In the darkness of the sanctum, I tried to discern the different images. The temple's sculptural perfection is amazing and it includes the doors of the temple and the three elegantly carved towers.

(i) After whom was the temple named?

(a) Kalyana Mandapa
(b) Lord Shiva
(c) Minister of the Hoyasalas King
(d) Lord Krishna

(ii) What would the word 'maize' mean here?

(a) Grain (b) Deer
(c) Symbol of prosperity (d) Symbol of weakness

(iii) The most remarkable feature of Hoyasalas sculptures was

(a) elaborate ornamentation
(b) beautiful clothing
(c) sharply cut sculptures
(d) real expression

(iv) What stands on the 24 edges star shaped raised platform?

(a) Shrines (b) Temple (c) Shikharas (d) Pillars

(v) What will be the most suitable antonym of 'reveal'?

(a) Impart (b) Disclose
(c) Conceal (d) Refuse

(vi) The word 'intricately' can also mean

(a) easy (b) complicated
(c) tangled (d) simple

Passage 25

There was a time when the aged were revered in India as symbols of tradition, respect, wisdom and experience. They controlled and guided the destinies of all the members of joint families. Urbanisation and industrialisation has led to the breaking up of the joint family system. The disintegration of joint families has had an adverse impact on the elderly people. Many elderly people get neglected because of the nuclear set up of families. The aged are now viewed as a useless and non-productive entity. Modernisation has led to the degradation of their status and authority. Their existence as integral part of the family is now uprooted. With the decline in their functional position as the head of the family, they have lost their authority, respect and prestige they used to command earlier.

The changing values and the dependence of the aged on their sons and daughters-in-law has complicated the problems. The aged are marginalised, alienated and left out of mainstream. Neglect, lack of respect, verbal taunts, inter-actional stress and increasing gap in communication make the aged feel unwanted and unpleasant entities. The only peaceful place for these weak, sad and depressed people in the evening of their life are the homes of the aged. Under the existing circumstances, the need for old age homes has certainly increased and they have become a must for the elderly to lead a peaceful and happy life among those who share and care for them.

(i) Urbanisation and industrialisation has led to
(a) neglect and stress
(b) degradation of the families
(c) breakup of joint family set up
(d) non-productive entity

(ii) The elderly people are getting neglected because of
(a) the joint family system
(b) nuclear set up
(c) their age
(d) their ailing health

(iii) We should behave more responsibly and revise our
(a) past
(b) moral values
(c) behaviour and conduct
(d) strengths and weakness

(iv) The only peaceful place left for the aged is
(a) their native place (b) their parents home
(c) old age home (d) orphanage

(v) Who were seen as symbols of tradition, respect and experience?
(a) The palatial buildings (b) The aged
(c) The new generation (d) Joint families

(vi) Neglect, lack of respect, verbal taunts, communication gap make the aged feel
(a) unwanted and unpleasant
(b) cared and concerned
(c) stressed and strained
(d) unavailable and outdated

Passage 26

In spite of all the honours that we heaped upon him, Pasteur, as has been said, remained simple at heart. Perhaps the imagery of his boyhood days, when he drew the familiar scenes of his birthplace and the longing to be a great artist, never wholly left him. In truth he did become a great artist, though after his sixteenth year he abandoned the brush forever.

Like every artist of worth, he put his whole soul and energy into his work and it was this very energy that in the end wore him out. For to him, each sufferer was more than just a case that was to be cured.

He looked upon the fight against hydrophobia as a battle and he was absorbed in his determination to win.

The sight of injured children, particularly, moved him to an indescribable extent. He suffered with his patients and yet he would not deny himself a share in that suffering. His greatest grief was when sheer physical exhaustion made him give up his active work.

He retired to the estate of Villeneuve Etang, where he had his Kennels for the study of rabies and there he passed his last summer, as his great biographer, Vallery Robot, has said, 'practicing the gospel virtues'.

The attitude of this man to the science, he had done so much to perfect, can be best summed up in a sentence that he is reputed once to have uttered, concerning the materialism of many of his contemporaries in similar branches of learning to his own: "the more I contemplate the mysteries of nature, the more my faith becomes like that of a peasant."

But even then, in retirement he loved to see his former pupils, and it was then he would reiterate his life's principles: 'Work,' he would say, 'never cease to work'.

He passed as simply as a child, the greatest man France had ever produced, derived from a plebiscite among the French people. Napoleon, the idol of France was placed fifth.

No greater tribute could have been given to Louis Pasteur, the tanner's son, the scientist, the man of peace and the patient worker for humanity.

(i) What advice Pasteur always gave to his pupils?
(a) Never to stop working
(b) To work according to one's health
(c) Work and rest at the same time
(d) Work to earn money

(ii) How did Pasteur engage himself in the estate?
(a) He took enough rest as he was very exhausted
(b) Conducted study on rabies
(c) Practiced the Gospel Virtues
(d) Both (b) and (c)

(iii) How did Pasteur view those who suffered from diseases?
(a) He gave them best treatment
(b) As subjects of pity
(c) The sufferer was more than just a case for him
(d) He dealt carefully not to give pain in wounded areas

(iv) Give one word for the phrase- Vote by the people of the country to decide a matter of national importance.
(a) Election (b) Plebiscite
(c) Hydrophobia (d) Contemporaries

(v) Who was ranked fifth after the achievements of Louis Pasteur?
(a) Napoleon (b) Hitler
(c) Nelson Mandela (d) Thomas Addison

(vi) Even accolades and honours did not change the simple man that Pasteur was
(a) because he did not like false praises
(b) he was very simple and child like at heart
(c) he wanted more than what he had achieved
(d) he was very egoistic

(vii) Opposite word for 'humanity' is
(a) callousness (b) early man
(c) homogeneous (d) people

Passage 27

The modern youth are more intelligent and hardworking than the previous generations. They have more facilities for education and they do utilise them. But they lack proper direction. In the absence of proper guidance, young boys and girls go on increasing their academic qualifications. Some of them secure high percentage of marks whereas most of them get average or below average marks. Since the number of aspirants for a job is much higher than the number of vacancies, most of the young boys and girls do not get any employment. This causes the problem of the educated unemployment and depression among the youth.

The problem of the educated unemployed can be solved partly through proper guidance and counselling and partly through grooming. Young students often disregard the advice of their parents and go on imitating their peers. This sets in the chain of the blind leading the blind. Uneducated or semi-educated parents think of academic qualification as achievement. Young students must seek the advice of the school counsellors and select a course of studies that suit their aptitude. Instead of pursuit of academic excellence, they must go in for proficiency in technical field of information technology, computers, biotechnology, biochemistry and consumer services. In this way, their youthful energy will get directed in the proper channel and they may get fruitful employment or become competent enough to launch their own project and give employment to others.

(i) What is the positive aspect of today's generation?
(a) They are more intelligent and hardworking
(b) They are more into fashion and time pass
(c) They have the power to work less and get more
(d) The youth now knows what he has to do

(ii) Academic qualification is seen as an achievement, which adds to the problem due to
(a) uneducated or semi-educated parents
(b) increase in the urge of getting higher remunerations
(c) lack of focus and attention
(d) disillusionment and depression

(iii) Frustration, irritation, anger, indiscipline, arrogance, disillusionment and depression are all the result of
(a) growing modernisation
(b) educated unemployment
(c) aspirations not meeting goals
(d) lack of grooming and counselling

(iv) Suggest a suitable title for this extract.
(a) Educated Unemployed
(b) Education-A Revolution
(c) Fight for Power
(d) Professionalism

(v) The synonym for 'cautioned' is
(a) ignorance (b) negligence
(c) prudence (d) discretion

(vi) Identify the correct statement.
(a) Young students must seek the advice of the school counsellors to select a course.
(b) Young students must take a course which their friends are opting for.

(c) Young students must take a course as suggested by their parents.

(d) Young students get the employment easily.

(vii) Opposite word for 'proficiency' is

(a) incompetence (b) expertise

(c) skill (d) formula

Passage 28

'Why did you keep away yesterday? Asked the head master, looking up. Swaminathan's first impulse was to protest that he had never been absent. But the attendance register was there. 'No-No-I was stoned. I tried to come, but they took away my cap and burnt it. Many strong men held me down when I tried to come ... When a great man is sent to gaol ... I am surprised to see you a slave of the Englishmen ... Didn't they cut off - Dacca Muslin - Slaves of Slaves ....'

These were some of the disjoined explanations which streamed into his head and which, even at that moment, he was discreet enough not to express. He wanted to mention a headache, but he found to his distress that others beside him had one. The headmaster shouted, 'won't you open your mouth?' He brought the cane sharply down on Swaminathan's right shoulder. Swaminathan kept staring at the headmaster with tearful eyes, massaging with his left hand the spot, where the cane was laid. 'I will kill you if you keep on staring without answering my question,' cried the headmaster.

'I-I- couldn't come', stammered Swaminathan.

"Is that so? Asked the headmaster and turning to a boy said, bring the peon".

Swaminathan thought What ! is he going to ask the peon to thrash me? If he does any such thing, 'I will bite everybody dead'. The peon came. The headmaster said to him, 'now say what you know about this rascal on the desk.'

The peon eyed Swaminathan with a sinister look, grunted and demanded, 'Didn't I see you break the panes?'

Of the ventilators in my room? added the headmaster with zest.

Here, there was no chance of escape. Swaminathan kept staring foolishly till he received another whack on the back. The headmaster demanded what the young brigand had to say about it. The brigand had nothing to say. It was a fact that he had broken the panes.

They had seen it. There was nothing more to it. He had unconsciously become defiant and did not care to deny the charge. When another whack came on his back, he ejaculated, 'don't beat me, Sir. It pains.' This was an invitation to the head master to bring down the cane four times again. He said, "keep standing here, on this desk , staring like an idiot, till I announce your dismissal".

(i) The headmaster's reaction to Swami's pleading is

(a) to beat Swami more (b) to forgive Swami

(c) to allow him to go (d) not to allow him to go

(ii) The title of the passage can be

(a) The Peon's Evidence (b) Swami's Punishment

(c) Swami's Excuses (d) Swami at School

(iii) In the end, Swami is

(a) defiant (b) submissive

(c) calm (d) indifferent

(iv) According to the peon, Swami had

(a) broken the panes (b) bitten someone

(c) been rude (d) been absent from school

(v) If Swami is not 'discreet', he would be

(a) careless (b) intelligent

(c) wise (d) smart

(vi) The headmaster's attitude towards Swami is one of

(a) kindness for Swami

(b) pleasure in punishing him

(c) pleasure in asking questions

(d) hatred for Swami

Passage 29

Your attitudes are the perspectives from which you view life. Some people seem to have a good attitude towards most things. Some people seem to have a bad attitude towards everything. But when you look closer, you will find that most of us have a combination of attitudes, some good, some not so good. Whatever attitude we have towards anything will affect how we feel about it, which in turn determines whether or not we will do well. So our right attitudes play a very important part in helping us become successful.

In fact, as we can see, a good attitude is essential for achievement of any kind! We so often hear of someone who is said to have a 'bad attitude'. The term is often applied to young people, especially to teenagers who frequently get into trouble, but we often hear it about adults, too .The implication is always that the individual in question is not going to make it if he doesn't change his attitude.

I would agree, without a good attitude it is not possible to see the opportunities ahead and set one's sights to reach them. But even more important is the fact that in order to possess the kind of feelings which work for us we've got to have the right attitude to start with. But where do we get our attitudes from? Are we born with them or do they just appear out of nowhere? Our attitudes are no accident: They don't just happen. Our attitudes are created and influenced entirely by our beliefs.

(i) Which one of the following statements is correct?
(a) Our attitudes are influenced by our parents only
(b) Our attitudes are created and controlled by our beliefs
(c) Our attitudes are the results of own personal experience
(d) We are born with our attitudes

(ii) The word 'determine' most nearly means
(a) influence (b) overcome
(c) engage (d) govern

(iii) Which part of speech is the underlined word in the sentence given below?
'Some people seem to have a good attitude towards most things.'
(a) Preposition (b) Adjective
(c) Conjunction (d) Adverb

(iv) A/An .... attitude is absolutely necessary for attainment of any kind.
(a) cheerful (b) optimistic
(c) good (d) virtuous

(v) The term 'bad attitude' is used for young people because they
(a) behave irresponsibly
(b) often get into difficulty
(c) are unpredictable
(d) defy all kinds of authority

Passage 30

Your body is made up of sixty per cent water and you lose the essential fluid every minute of every day as you breathe, digest and hopefully work up a sweat. It is important that you put back every drop. Starting now, drink eight 230 ml glasses of water every single day—that's the minimum, your body needs daily. That is the non-negotiable sugar savvy hydration mantra. Many times when you think you're hungry, sleepy, depressed and/or irritated, you're actually just dehydrated. Drinking enough water actually helps you combat water retention. Sounds counterintuitive, but think about it. If you are running around in a semi-dehydrated state all the time, your body is going to hang on to every single drop, giving you that puffy, unhealthy appearance.

When you are properly hydrated, your body gets the message that all systems are operating smoothly and it continues its work of flushing out your system and ridding itself of the excess fluids.

If your goal is to lose weight, water is a must. When you're dehydrated, your body sends out signals that you need assistance. Many people mistake those thirsty SOS signals for hunger and take in hundreds of extra calories. They also don't solve the real problem—thirst! Drinking water can be a powerful appetite suppressant and allows you to cue into your real hunger.

Your body also needs plenty of water for proper digestion, so you can get the most from the foods you eat. You are less susceptible to food cravings when your stomach is full and you're getting all the nutrients you need. Drink two glasses of water before every meal— you'll eat less ! Your body uses water for fat.

(i) .... helps fight water retention.
(a) Having a balanced diet
(b) Drinking enough water
(c) Exercising regularly
(d) A regular morning walk

(ii) Our systems operate satisfactorily
(a) if excess fat is reduced
(b) when we enjoy a sound sleep
(c) when we are properly hydrated
(d) if we consume lots of fruits and vegetables

(iii) The best way to lose weight is to
(a) eat less starchy food
(b) take weight-reducing pills
(c) exercise at least twice a day
(d) drink plenty of water

(iv) When we are dehydrated, we think we
(a) are about to collapse (b) want to vomit
(c) are tired (d) need food

(v) The word 'irritated' most nearly means
(a) annoyed (b) troubled
(c) uneasy (d) frustrated

(vi) The word which is opposite in meaning to 'assistance' is
(a) fragrance (b) hinderance
(c) persistence (d) existence

Passage 31

Raja Ram Mohan Roy is considered the pioneer of modern Indian Renaissance for the remarkable reforms he brought about in the 18th century India. Among his efforts, the abolition of the *Sati-pratha*—a practice in which the widow was compelled to sacrifice herself on the funeral pyre of her husband—was prominent. His efforts were also instrumental in eradicating the *Purdah* System and child marriage. In 1828, Ram Mohan Roy formed the Brahmo Samaj, a group of people, who had no faith in idol-worship and were against the caste restrictions.

Raja Ram Mohan Roy's father was a wealthy Brahmin and strictly performed the duties set by the religion. Ram Mohan himself was also devoted to Lord Vishnu and in his 14th year, he wanted to become a monk but his mother, Tarini Devi objected to his desire.

Ram Mohan viewed education as a medium to implement the social reforms. So, in 1815, Ram Mohan came to Calcutta and the very next year, started an English College by putting in his own savings. He was well aware that the students should learn the English language and scientific subjects and that's why he criticised the government's policy of opening only Sanskrit schools. According to him, Indians would lag behind if they do not get to study modern subjects like Mathematics, Geography and Latin. The government accepted this idea of Ram Mohan and also implemented it but not before his death. Ram Mohan was also the first to give importance to the development of mother tongue. His Gaudiya Byakaran in Bengali is the best of his prose works.

Rabindranath Tagore and Bankimchandra also followed in the footsteps of Ram Mohan Roy. Ram Mohan Roy was a staunch supporter of free speech and expression and fought for the rights of Vernacular Press. He also brought out a newspaper in Persian called Miratul-Akhbar (the Mirror of News) and a Bengali weekly called Sambad Kaumudi (the Moon of Intelligence). In those days, items of news and articles had to be approved by the government before being published. Ram Mohan protested against this control by arguing that newspapers should be free and that the truth should not be suppressed simply because the government did not like it.

(i) Raja Ram Mohan Roy is known for his
(a) economic reforms (b) literary reforms
(c) political reforms (d) social reforms

(ii) When he was a teenager, Raja Ram Mohan Roy expressed his desire to become a
(a) journalist (b) monk
(c) teacher (d) businessman

(iii) Raja Ram Mohan Roy believed that Indians would lag behind if they
(a) forgot their cultural roots
(b) did not learn traditional skills
(c) gave up study of Sanskrit
(d) did not study modern subjects

(iv) Raja Ram Mohan Roy strongly supported
(a) rituals and observances
(b) physical education
(c) freedom of speech and expression
(d) moral education

(v) The word 'eliminating' most nearly means
(a) banishing (b) eradicating
(c) banning (d) dismissing

(vi) The word which is opposite in meaning to 'encouraged' is
(a) crushed (b) misled
(c) disheartened (d) suppressed

(vii) Which 'part of speech' is the underlined word in the sentence given below?
"He was a staunch supporter of free <u>speech</u> and expression."
(a) Adjective (b) Conjunction
(c) Noun (d) Adverb

(viii) 'Raja Ram Mohan Roy viewed education ... .' The 'voice' in the above sentence has been correctly changed in
(a) education was viewed
(b) education is viewed
(c) education has been viewed
(d) education had been viewed

Passage 32

A remarkable feature of Edison's inventions was their basic simplicity. There were innumerable scientists possessing deep knowledge of electricity, chemistry etc. but it was this unschooled genius who succeeded where they failed. What were his unique qualities? *Firstly,* he had an uncanny ability to judge the practical use of any scientific fact.

Secondly, he was blessed with patience and perseverance. He would try out countless ideas till he found the right one. *Third* was his business acumen, which enabled him to earn the large sums of money necessary to conduct experimental work. Edison's enthusiasm for work and optimistic attitude ensured a long and productive life. Only after crossing the age of seventy-five did he start slowing down. During his final illness, his curiosity about his condition, medicines and treatment, made the doctors think that possibly he was taking this too as one of his scientific investigations! He passed away on 18th October, 1931, at the ripe old age of eight-four. During his lifetime itself Edison became one of the most famous men in the world. Honours were showered on him. Among them was the Congressional Gold Medal in 1928 for his contributions to human welfare. In 1960, he was posthumously elected to the Hall of Fame for Great Americans at New York University. But the tribute that was most eloquent was quite unintended. The authorities contemplated switching off the power supply in New York, the scene of his triumph in 1882, for two minutes as a mark of respect on his death. But 1931 was not 1882. Since normal life would have come to a standstill by the two minutes power cutoff, the idea was given up. There could be no greater tribute to the man than this negative tribute!

(i) The most remarkable feature of Edison's inventions was their

(a) low cost (b) aesthetic aspect
(c) fundamental simplicity (d) multiple usefulness

(ii) According to the author, Edison became prosperous because he

(a) had great business sense
(b) had luck on his side
(c) worked very hard
(d) made the best use of his time

(iii) To conduct experimental work, Edison needed

(a) calm and quiet atmosphere
(b) sophisticated gadgets
(c) support of generous patrons
(d) huge amounts of money

(iv) Edison's long and productive life can be attributed to

(a) his positive attitude
(b) his immensely good health
(c) a large circle of friends
(d) his involvement in charitable work

(v) The word 'uncanny' as used in the passage means

(a) astonishing (b) weird (c) great (d) terrific

(vi) The opposite of 'famous' is

(a) negligible (b) unnoticeable
(c) unpopular (d) unknown

(vii) Which 'part of speech' is the underlined word?

"He had an uncanny ability to judge the practical use of any scientific fact."

(a) Adverb (b) Preposition
(c) Noun (d) Adjective

Passage 33

The art of Madhubani painting is the traditional style developed in the Mithila region, in the villages around Madhubani, Bihar. Madhubani literally means a forest of honey. This style of painting has been traditionally used by the women of the region, though today men are also involved to meet the demand. The work is done on freshly plastered mud walls. For commercial purposes, it is now being done on paper, cloth etc.

The paintings are basically of religious nature. They are done in the special rooms of their homes (in the Pooja room, ritual area, bridal room), on the main village walls, etc. for ceremonial or ritualistic purposes. The women offer prayers to the deity before starting the work. Figures from nature and mythology are adapted to suit their style. The themes and designs widely painted are the worship of Hindu deities such as Krishna, Rama, Shiva, Durga, Lakshmi, Saraswati, Sun and Moon, Tulsi plant, court scenes, wedding scenes and other social events taking place around them.

Floral, animal and bird motifs, geometrical designs are used to fill up all the gaps. There is hardly any empty space in this style. Cotton wrapped around a bamboo stick forms the brush. The colours applied are prepared by the artists. The skill is handed down the generations, and hence the traditional design and patterns are widely maintained. It is believed that genesis of Madhubani paintings came about when King Janaka asked for paintings to be developed for his daughter Sita's wedding.

(i) Madhubani paintings are no longer done exclusively by women on walls

(a) as paper is cheaper
(b) because cloth is more durable
(c) to meet their widespread demand
(d) as men are better painters

(ii) Madhubani paintings are essentially of religious nature when they are done

(a) using figures from nature
(b) in the Pooja room
(c) in the bridal room
(d) on the village walls

(iii) These paintings become secular when they depict

(a) wedding scenes (b) court scenes
(c) worship of Saraswati (d) Tulsi plant

(iv) A Madhubani painting shows only

(a) geometrical designs
(b) a balanced portrayal of all of them
(c) Hindu deities
(d) flowers and plants

(v) The art of Madhubani painting is learnt in the
(a) homes of renowned artists
(b) Ashrams of Madhubani
(c) schools of art
(d) families at home

(vi) 'Floral' is an adjective derived from the noun, 'flower'. 'Aural' is derived from the noun
(a) eye (b) mouth (c) morning (d) ear

(vii) The word 'genesis' means the same as
(a) spirit (b) growth (c) birth (d) original

Passage 34

World Animal Day has been observed on 4th October since 1931, as a way of highlighting the plight of endangered species. Since then, it has become a day for remembering and paying tribute to all animals and the people who love and respect them. It's celebrated in different ways in every country, with no regard to nationality, religion, faith or political ideology.

Since the official World Animal Day website was launched by Naturewatch Foundation, the number of events taking place throughout the world has increased and the trend continues. And, that is the aim of the World Animal Day initiative to encourage everybody to use this special day to highlight their importance in the world; celebrate animal life in all its forms; celebrate humankind's relationship with the animal kingdom; acknowledge the diverse roles that animals play in our lives- from being our companions, supporting and helping us, to bringing a sense of wonder into our lives; and acknowledge and be thankful for the way in which animals enrich our lives.

Increased awareness will lead the way to improved standards of animal welfare throughout the world. Building the initiative is a way to unite the animal welfare movement with something that everyone can join in, whether they are part of an organisation, group or as an individual. Through education, we can help to create a new culture of respect and sensitivity, to make this world a fairer place for all living creatures. On the website, people will find everything they need to make World Animal Day a reality in their area. If we care about animals, we should not miss this special day to help make animal welfare issues front page news around the globe-a vital catalyst for change.

(i) In reading this passage, we learn that the World Animal Day is an/a .... celebration.
(a) monthly on the 4th
(b) year long
(c) annual
(d) commemoration held in 1931

(ii) The writer points out that animals are important because they
(a) can replace people by being more resourceful
(b) will outlive human beings in the years to come
(c) be put to work in many ways
(d) make us appreciate the diversity of life

(iii) The launch of the website is to
(a) promote social networking by animal lovers
(b) provide guidelines to celebrate Animal Day
(c) information about endangered animals species
(d) serve as a source of reference about animals

(iv) The writer implies that animals are
(a) treated cruelly by human beings
(b) given due protection
(c) ignored altogether
(d) subject to mistreatment

(v) Identify the correct statement.
(a) often pose a danger to people
(b) People tend to forget to celebrate Animal Day
(c) Animal Day reminds us to care for other species
(d) The new website was started by the writer

(vi) The expression : 'a sense of wonder' means
(a) a critical reaction (b) a sympathetic attitude
(c) an emotional response (d) a deep understanding

(vii) A closest synonym for the word 'sensitivity' as used here is
(a) passivity (b) affection
(c) awareness (d) tolerance

(viii) The antonym of the word 'initiative' is
(a) enterprise (b) idleness
(c) ambition (d) advance

Passage 35

Meditating can have an almost instant effect on reducing stress, researchers have found. They say three consecutive days of 25-minute sessions can have a dramatic effect. Researchers studied 'mindful meditation'- the guiding principle is to live more 'in the moment,' spending less time going over past stresses and worrying about future problems. Techniques include moving the focus of attention around the body and observing sensations that arise- the so-called 'body scan'. A secular practice, it is said to help people recognise and overcome negative thoughts. For the study, the research team had 66 healthy individuals aged 18-30 years old participate in a three-day experiment. Some participants went through a brief mindfulness meditation training programme for 25 minutes for three consecutive days, the individuals were given breathing exercises to help them monitor their breath and pay attention to their present moment experiences. A second group of participants completed a matched three day cognitive training programme in which they were asked to critically analyse poetry in an effort to enhance problem-solving skills. Following the fined training activity, all participants were asked to complete stressful speech and mathematical tasks in front of stern-faced evaluators. Each individual reported their stress levels in response to **stressful** speech and mathematical performance stress tasks and provided saliva samples for measurement of cortisol, commonly referred to as the stress hormone. The participants who received the brief mindfulness meditation training reported reduced stress **perceptions** to the speech and mathematical tasks, indicating that the mindfulness meditation fostered psychological stress resilience.

(i) **The text is a .... piece of writing.**
(a) factual (b) descriptive
(c) biographical (d) reflective

(ii) **The writer's attitude to mediation is**
(a) indifferent (b) different
(c) suspicious sometimes (d) supportive

(iii) **The writer, by referring to the experiment, suggests that, it is**
(a) stress that cannot be controlled
(b) possible for us to control stress
(c) mathematics that is a stressful subject
(d) poetry analysis is easier than solving Mathematical problems

(iv) **The 'body scan' is a reference to**
(a) an experiment in a lab
(b) a form of meditation
(c) a research experiment
(d) a problem solving activity

(v) **An antonym for the word 'stressful' would be**
(a) annoying (b) calming
(c) challenging (d) erasing

(vi) **The word that can replace 'perception' in the text is**
(a) belief (b) attention
(c) conceptualisation (d) trust

Passage 36

As District Employment Officer, my father was given a jeep by the government. There was no garage in the office, so the jeep was parked in our house. My father refused to use it to commute to the office. He told us that the jeep is an expensive resource given by the government-he reiterated to us that it was not 'his jeep' but the government's jeep. Insisting that he would use it only to tour the interiors, he would walk to his office on normal days. He also made sure that we never sat in the government jeep-we could sit in it only when it was stationary. That was our early childhood lesson in governance-a lesson that corporate managers learn the hard way, some never do.

The driver of the jeep was treated with respect due to any other member of my father's office. As small children, we were taught not to call him by his name. We had to use the suffix 'dada' whenever we were to refer to him in public or private. When I grew up to own a car and a driver by the name of Raju was appointed, I repeated the lesson to my two small daughters. They have, as a result, grown up calling him 'Raju Uncle'—very different from many of their friends who refer to their family drivers as 'my driver.' When I hear that term from a school or college going person, I cringe, to me the lesson was significant—you treat small people with more respect than you treat big people. It is more important to respect your subordinates than your superiors.

(i) **The author's father would not allow his family to use the jeep because**
(a) it was not their private vehicle
(b) the roads were full of potholes
(c) he was afraid of accidents
(d) the jeep was in a bad condition

(ii) **The author taught his children to**
(a) be firm with servants
(b) treat small people with respect
(c) maintain a discreet distance from servants
(d) be kind to small people

(iii) **The author was critical of his children's friends because their attitude to servants smacked of**
(a) weakness (b) coarseness
(c) arrogance (d) loftiness

(iv) **The author's attitude towards servants can be described as**
(a) respectful (b) indifferent
(c) rational (d) affectionate

(v) **The opposite of the word 'refused' is**
(a) accepted (b) received
(c) justified (d) admired

(vi) **The word that can replace 'reiterated' is**
(a) revised (b) repeated
(c) recalled (d) reconsidered

Answers

Passage 1
(i) (b) (ii) (c) (iii) (d) (iv) (a) (v) (d) (vi) (a)

Passage 2
(i) (d) (ii) (c) (iii) (c) (iv) (c) (v) (d) (vi) (c)

Passage 3
(i) (a) (ii) (c) (iii) (b) (iv) (c) (v) (a) (vi) (a)

Passage 4
(i) (a) (ii) (d) (iii) (d) (iv) (a) (v) (b) (vi) (c)

Passage 5
(i) (d) (ii) (b) (iii) (d) (iv) (b) (v) (c) (vi) (a)

Passage 6
(i) (b) (ii) (d) (iii) (a) (iv) (d) (v) (c) (vi) (c)

Passage 7
(i) (a) (ii) (c) (iii) (a) (iv) (b) (v) (b) (vi) (d)
(vii) (b) (viii) (d)

Passage 8
(i) (a) (ii) (d) (iii) (a) (v) (d) (vii) (b) (viii) (c)

Passage 9
(i) (d) (ii) (a) (iii) (c) (iv) (b) (v) (c) (vi) (c)
(vii) (c) (viii) (a)

Passage 10
(i) (a) (ii) (c) (iii) (b) (iv) (b) (v) (d) (vi) (b)

Passage 11
(i) (b) (ii) (a) (iii) (b) (iv) (c) (v) (c) (vi) (a)

Passage 12
(i) (b) (ii) (c) (iii) (d) (iv) (d) (v) (c) (vi) (d)

Passage 13
(i) (a) (ii) (d) (iii) (d) (iv) (a) (v) (d) (vi) (a)
(vii) (c) (viii) (b)

Passage 14
(i) (d) (ii) (b) (iii) (c) (iv) (b) (v) (vi) (a)
(vii) (b)

Passage 15
(i) (b) (ii) (d) (iii) (c) (iv) (c) (v) (d) (vi) (d)

Passage 16
(i) (d) (ii) (d) (iii) (c) (iv) (d) (v) (a) (vi) (a)

Passage 17
(i) (c) (ii) (b) (iii) (a) (iv) (d) (v) (a) (vi) (c)

Passage 18
(i) (c) (ii) (a) (iii) (d) (iv) (b) (v) (b) (vi) (a)
(vii) (c) (viii) (a)

Passage 19
(i) (c) (ii) (c) (iii) (a) (iv) (d) (v) (d) (vi) (b)

Passage 20
(i) (c) (ii) (b) (iii) (a) (iv) (c) (v) (c) (vi) (b)

Passage 21
(i) (c) (ii) (d) (iii) (b) (iv) (d) (v) (c) (vi) (d)

Passage 22
(i) (c) (ii) (a) (iii) (c) (iv) (b) (v) (a) (vi) (a)

Passage 23
(i) (d) (ii) (a) (iii) (c) (iv) (c) (v) (d) (vi) (d)

Passage 24
(i) (c) (ii) (c) (iii) (a) (iv) (b) (v) (c) (vi) (b)

Passage 25
(i) (c) (ii) (b) (iii) (b) (iv) (c) (v) (b) (vi) (a)

Passage 26
(i) (a) (ii) (d) (iii) (c) (iv) (b) (v) (a) (vi) (b)
7. (a)

Passage 27
(i) (a) (ii) (a) (iii) (b) (iv) (a) (v) (c) (vi) (a)
7. (a)

Passage 28
(i) (a) (ii) (d) (iii) (b) (iv) (a) (v) (a) (vi) (b)

Passage 29
(i) (b) (ii) (a) (iii) (b) (iv) (b) (v) (b)

Passage 30
(i) (b) (ii) (c) (iii) (d) (iv) (d) (v) (a) (vi) (b)

Passage 31
(i) (d) (ii) (b) (iii) (d) (iv) (c) (v) (b) (vi) (c)
7. (c) 8. (a)

Passage 32
(i) (c) (ii) (a) (iii) (d) (iv) (a) (v) (b) (vi) (d)
7. (c)

Passage 33
(i) (c) (ii) (b) (iii) (b) (iv) (b) (v) (d) (vi) (d)
7. (c)

Passage 34
(i) (c) (ii) (d) (iii) (b) (iv) (d) (v) (c) (vi) (c)
7. (c) 8. (b)

Passage 35
(i) (b) (ii) (d) (iii) (b) (iv) (c) (v) (b) (vi) (c)

Passage 36
(i) (a) (ii) (b) (iii) (c) (iv) (a) (v) (a) (vi) (b)

Case Based

Read the following passages carefully and answer the questions that follow.

Passage 1

Present-day India owes an immeasurable debt of gratitude to the vision, tact, diplomacy and pragmatic approach of Sardar Vallabhbhai Patel, the indomitable man who integrated 562 princely states with the Union of India and prevented the Balkanisation of the newly-independent country.

Back in 1947, India had finally gained a hard-fought independence but it had come with besetting problems - partition, communal riots and a refugee crisis. Add to that crippling resource constraint, fledgling institutions and an ill-equipped colonial machinery and it's not difficult to understand why India's new government found the integration of more than 500 princely states a tough nut to crack.

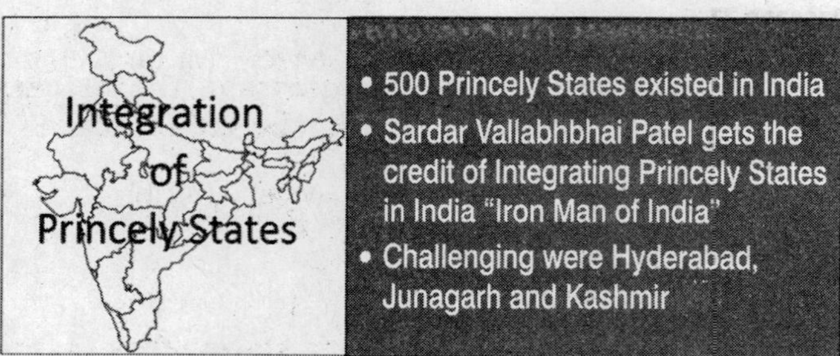

The Indian Independence Act of 1947, (based on the Mountbatten Plan) provided for the lapse of paramountcy of the British Crown over the Indian states. It also gave each of these rulers the option to accede to the newly born dominions India or Pakistan or continue as an independent sovereign state.

By 15th August, 1947, the process of integration of Princely States was almost complete except for a few, who held out. Some simply delayed signing the Instrument of Accession-like Piploda, a small state in central India that did not accede to India until March 1948.

The biggest problems, however, arose with Jodhpur, which tried to negotiate better deals with Pakistan, with Junagarh, which actually did accede to Pakistan and with Hyderabad and Kashmir, both of which declared that they intended to remain independent.

Realising the need to get these 500-odd chiefdoms to accede to India before the day of independence, Patel and VP Menon began using all the tricks in the bag - including the use of both force and friendly advice - to achieve their integration with the Indian dominion.

Questions

On the basis of your reading of the passage, answer the following questions.

(i) What was the biggest contribution of Sardar Patel?

(a) He fought for the independence of India.
(b) He was the first Home Minister of India.
(c) He merged 562 Princely States with India.
(d) He prevented partition of India.

(ii) Complete the given sentence by selecting the most appropriate option.

Central Provinces was a part of ....

(a) British India (b) Princely States
(c) West Pakistan (d) East Pakistan

(iii) Complete the given sentence by selecting the most appropriate option.

The method used by Sardar Patel for the unification of India was ....

(a) Force
(b) Friendly advice
(c) Both (a) and (b)
(d) Neither (a) nor (b)

(iv) The word 'accede to' as used in the second last paragraph means

(a) to disagree to a demand, proposal, etc. especially after first agreeing to it
(b) to fail
(c) to agree to a demand, request, etc. especially after first disagreeing to it
(d) to recognise something as good

(v) The common thing between Mysore, Hyderabad and Benaras is that ....

Passage 2

The 2004 Olympic Games returned home to Greece, birthplace of the ancient Games and site of the inaugural modern Olympics. The excitement surrounding the homecoming was tempered by security concerns related to Athens's proximity to the politically volatile Middle East. Moreover, serious construction delays and worries that Athens's hot, humid weather and high levels of air pollution would be detrimental to the athletes prompted the International Olympic Committee (IOC) to briefly consider moving the Games to another city. The media seized on these matters and predicted dismal failure. None of the expected calamities occurred. By opening day the city had been splendidly rebuilt. All venues and facilities were ready; exceptionally modern transportation systems functioned well; and security was the best ever.

The world press raved about the success of the Games as it apologised to Greece for its dire but groundless predictions. IOC president Jacques Rogge declared the Athens Olympics 'unforgettable, dream Games.' Nearly 11,100 athletes competed in 37 disciplines in 28 sports; women participated in freestyle wrestling and sabre fencing for the first time.

American swimming phenomenon Michael Phelps topped the medals table with a record-tying eight (six gold and two bronze). On the track, Kelly Holmes of Great Britain and Ethiopia's Hicham El Guerrouj were double gold medalists, and hurdler Liu Xiang won China's first gold medal in men's athletics (track and field). The concluding event, the men's marathon, was won by Stefano Baldini of Italy. Lima, who recovered to take the bronze, was awarded the Pierre de Coubertin medal for 'his exceptional demonstration of fair play and Olympic values.'

Rank ◆	Nation ◆	Gold ◆	Silver ◆	Bronze ◆	Total ◆
1	United States (USA)	36	39	26	101
2	China (CHN)	32	17	14	63
3	Russia (RUS)	28	26	36	90
4	Australia (AUS)	17	16	17	50
5	Japan (JPN)	16	9	12	37
6	Germany (GER)	13	16	20	49
7	France (FRA)	11	9	13	33
8	Italy (ITA)	10	11	11	32
9	South Korea (KOR)	9	12	9	30
10	Great Britain (GBR)	9	9	12	30
11–74	*Remaining*	120	136	156	412
Totals (74 nations)		**301**	**300**	**326**	**927**

Questions

On the basis of your reading of the passage, answer of the following questions.

(i) Complete the following sentence by choosing the most appropriate option.

The significant thing about 2004 Summer Olympics was that ....

(a) it was organised amidst heavy security
(b) it was being hosted by the city where it originated
(c) it was being organised against many political disturbances
(d) more female athletes participated in comparison to male athletes

(ii) Select the option that displays the reason the IOC considered moving the Olympics to another city.

(a) Construction delays
(b) The hot and humid weather
(c) High levels of air pollution
(d) All of these

(iii) According to the given passage, the success of the 2004 Olympics can be seen through

(a) the cool climate
(b) the modern transportation and facilities
(c) the opening day
(d) security system

(iv) Which of the following statements is not substantiated by information given in the passage?

(a) As per the media, the Olympic games were going to be a failure.
(b) Women participated in freestyle wrestling and sabre fencing for the first time in the 2004 Olympics.
(c) Greece is the birth place of the ancient games.
(d) Kelly Holmes of Great Britain was a triple gold medalist at the 2004 Olympics.

(v) Which of the following words is similar in meaning to the word 'unforgettable'?

(a) Raved
(b) Memorable
(c) Declared
(d) Dismal

Passage 3

India is likely to continue for several decades as a country with the largest share of rural population in the world. Rural labour and the sources of their employment are not only predominantly informal but also not very productive in nature and often spread across several activities. Though estimates of visible unemployment are very low, under-employment is widely prevalent. Rural employment, which was for a long time considered as equal to employment in agriculture, is no longer true.

During the last two decades there have been rapid changes in the structure of rural employment, and rural non-farm employment has been growing at a faster pace and there are significant changes within the structure of non-farm employment.

Notwithstanding these changes there is persistence of certain characteristics of unorganised informal rural labour, such as dependence on multiple activities for work, segmentation by gender and social groups, seasonal nature of work and work which is temporary and vulnerable to low levels of earnings and high levels of persisting poverty.

Distribution of Occupation of 200 Males of a Village in Uttar Pradesh

OCCUPATION	NUMBER
Farmers	02
Government service, clerks	44
Lawyers	03
Newspapers and presses	05
No occupation	25
Not recorded	08
Students	68
Teachers	11
Trade and commerce	23
Other	08

Questions

On the basis of your reading of the passage, answer the following questions.

(i) Pick the option that lists statements that are NOT TRUE according to the passage.

1. Sources of rural employments in India are productive
2. Segmentation by gender occurs in India
3. Currently, India does not have the largest share of rural population
4. The work in the rural sector is temporary

(a) 1 and 3 (b) 2 and 4
(c) 3 and 4 (d) 1 and 2

(ii) The least number of men in the village are involved in which field?

(a) Education (b) Agriculture
(c) Government service (d) Publishing

(iii) India predominantly consists of ....

(a) urban population (b) rural population
(c) literate population (d) illiterate population

(iv) Which statement is true?

1.The number of lawyers is more than teachers.
2.The number of teachers is more than clerks.
3.The number of people involved in trade and commerce is less than those without any employment.
4.The students are less than teachers.

(a) 1 and 2 (b) 2 and 3
(c) Only 3 (d) Only 4

(v) Which statement is incorrect?

(a) Sources of employment of rural labour are not very productive.
(b) Rural employment means employment in agriculture only.
(c) Underemployment in rural labour is widely prevalent.
(d) Rural non-farm employment has been growing at a faster pace.

Passage 4

A tornado is a violent rotating column of air extending from a thunderstorm to the ground. The most violent tornadoes are capable of tremendous destruction with wind speeds of up to 300 mph. They can destroy large buildings, uproot trees and hurl vehicles hundreds of yards. They can also drive straw into trees. Damage paths can be in excess of one mile wide to 50 miles long. Most tornadoes form from thunderstorms. A change in wind direction and an increase in wind speed with increasing height creates an invisible, horizontal spinning effect in the lower atmosphere. Rising air within the updraft tilts the rotating air from horizontal to vertical. An area of rotation, 2-6 miles wide, now extends through much of the storm. Most strong and violent tornadoes form within this area of strong rotation.

Several conditions are required for the development of tornadoes and the thunderstorm clouds with which most tornadoes are associated. Abundant low level moisture is necessary to contribute to the development of a thunderstorm and a 'trigger' (perhaps a cold front or other low level zone of converging winds) is needed to lift the moist air aloft. Once the air begins to rise and becomes saturated, it will continue rising to great heights to produce a thunderstorm cloud, if the atmosphere is unstable. An unstable atmosphere is one where the temperature decreases rapidly with height. Atmospheric instability can also occur when dry air overlays moist air near the Earth's surface. Finally, tornadoes usually form in areas where winds at all levels of the atmosphere are not only strong, but also turn with height in a clockwise or veering direction.

Tornadoes can appear as a traditional funnel shape or in a slender rope-like form. Some have a churning, smoky look to them, and other contain 'multiple vortices', which are small, individual tornadoes rotating around a common centre. Even others may be nearly invisible, with only swirling dust or debris at ground levels as the only indication of the tornado's presence.

Classification	Wind Speed	Damage
F0	40–72 mph	Mild
F1	73–112 mph	Moderate
F2	113–157 mph	Significant
F3	158–206 mph	Severe
F4	207–260 mph	Devastating
F5	261–318 mph	Incredible
F6	319–379 mph	Inconceivable

The Fujita-Pearson Tornado Intensity Scale

Questions

On the basis of your reading of the passage, answer of the following questions.

(i) Complete the following sentence by selecting the most appropriate option.

The names of the categories in the third column, labelled 'Damage,' could best be described as ....

(a) scientific
(b) descriptive
(c) objective
(d) whimsical

(ii) Complete the following sentence by selecting the most appropriate option.

The range of damage path of tornadoes can be ....

(a) 2-3 miles (b) 1-50 miles
(c) 3-7 miles (d) 10-15 miles

(iii) Complete the following sentence by selecting the most appropriate option.

The major cause for the development of thunderstorms is ....

(a) abundant low level moisture
(b) difference in temperature
(c) high humidity
(d) high pressure

(iv) Pick the option showing the correct use of the word 'debris'.

(a) Debris are lying here and there.
(b) Debris from the train explosion was scattered here and there.
(c) I cannot believe the debris he said.
(d) He is a good debris.

Tornadoes usually form in areas where winds are ....

(v) Which of the following words is the antonym of the word 'invisible' given in Paragraph 3?

(a) Veering
(b) Swirling
(c) Saturated
(d) Apparent

Passage 5

Prime Minister Narendra Modi launched Swachh Bharat Mission on 2nd October, 2014, by wielding a broom on the streets of Delhi. The program, which has Mahatma Gandhi's iconic spectacles as its logo, is one of the most hyped schemes of the Modi Government. Its primary goal is to make India open defecation-free by 2019.

As of 1st February, 2019, the Modi Government claimed that 5.5 lakh villages and 28 of India's 36 states and Union Territories had become open defecation free. But independent surveys show a mixed picture.

The Research Institute for Compassionate Economics surveyed 3,235 households in four states in North India in 2014 and 2018. It found open defecation had reduced by 26% in the four years since Swachh Bharat was launched. But access to toilets does not mean open defecation has ended. The RICE survey found 23% of people who own a toilet continue to defecate in the open, including people in Rajasthan and Madhya Pradesh, which have been declared open defecation-free states.

To achieve its goals under the Swachh Bharat Mission, the government outlined a three-pronged strategy: using social messaging, education and communication to trigger behaviour change, providing subsidies to vulnerable social groups to help them construct latrines at home and verifying and monitoring the continued use of these latrines through surveys and social audits.

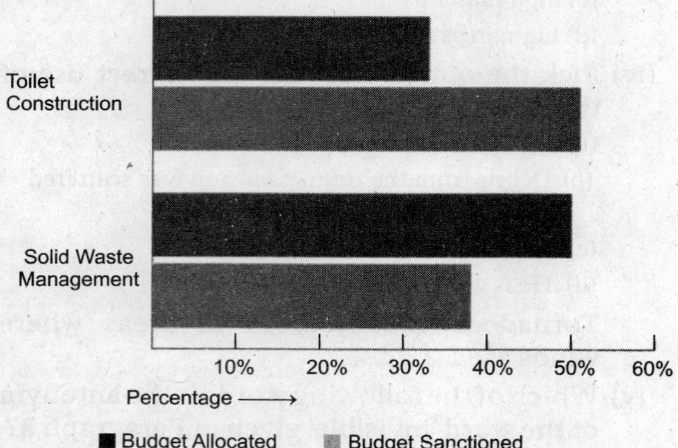

The Mission's objectives also include creating sustainable solid and liquid waste management systems, promoting social inclusion by improving sanitation for women and marginalised communities and eradicating manual scavenging. In the four years since it was rolled out, the Mission has focussed almost entirely on toilet construction and ownership.

In the urban component of Swachh Bharat, toilet construction was meant to take up 33% of the budgetary allocation, while 50% was allocated towards improving solid waste management. However, in the past four years, the Centre has sanctioned 51% of its share of the urban budget towards toilet construction and only 38% towards solid waste management.

India generates over 1,50,000 tons of municipal solid waste per day. Only 83% of waste is collected and less than 30% is treated. As noted above, the government has chosen to priortise toilet construction at the cost of waste management services.

Even though the budget for waste management has increased over the years, at least 23 States/Union Territories were yet to receive that year's funds for it.

Questions

On the basis of your reading of the passage, answer the following questions.

(i) What is the goal of the mission?

1. To make India open-defecation free
2. To clean the Indian rivers
3. To make completely clean
4. To pay respect to sweepers and cleaners

(a) Only 1 (b) 1 and 2
(c) 3 and 4 (d) Only 4

(ii) Pick the option that lists statements that are NOT TRUE according to the passage.

1. India is free from open defecation.
2. Now India needs to focus on solid-waste management.
3. The success rate of the mission is 97%.
4. 28 out of 36 Indian states and UTs are open defecation free.

(a) 1 and 2
(b) 2 and 3
(c) 1 and 3
(d) Only 4

(iii) Which two states have been used as an example to show the contradictory picture of Swachh Bharat Abhiyaan?

(a) Odisha and Maharashtra
(b) Rajasthan and Madhya Pradesh
(c) Gujarat and Kerala
(d) Assam and Andhra Pradesh

(iv) Which strategy is the government using to make the mission successful?

(a) Using social messaging, education and communication to trigger behaviour change.
(b) Providing subsidies to vulnerable social groups to help them construct toilets.
(c) Verifying and monitoring the continued use of toilets.
(d) All of the above

(v) Which of the following is an objective of the mission?

(a) Creating sustainable waste management systems
(b) Eradicating manual scavenging
(c) Toilet construction
(d) Both (a) and (b)

(vi) The budget allocated for the mission for urban areas is stated by which option?

(a) Toilet construction had 33% of the budgetary allocation, while 50% was allocated towards improving solid waste management.
(b) 51% of its share of the budget towards toilet construction, and only 38% towards solid waste management.

(c) Toilet construction got 38% of the budgetary allocation, while 51% was allocated towards improving solid waste management.

(d) Toilet construction got 50% of the budgetary allocation, while 33% was allocated towards improving solid waste management.

(vii) What does the data show?

(a) Solid waste management budget needs to be increased.

(b) Budget should focus on eradicating manual scavenging.

(c) The government priortise toilet construction.

(d) All of the above

(viii) Which of the following figures shows the CORRECT percentage of treatment of solid waste in India?

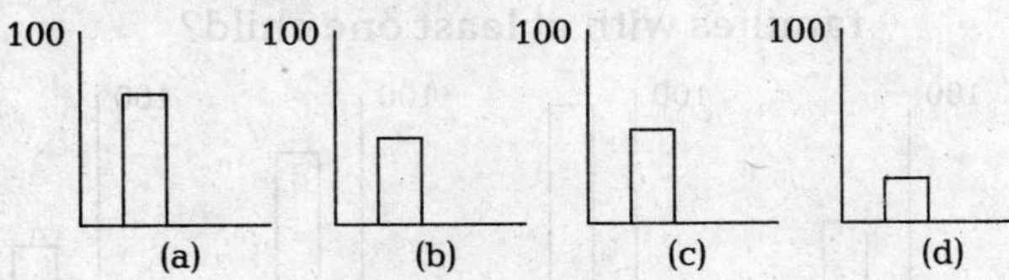

Passage 6

Over the last four decades, the number and proportion of couples in which both parents work, especially full-time, have increased considerably. Recent studies show that approximately 69% of couple families with at least one child were dual-earner families, up from 36% in last 19th century.

In this context of evolving professional and family roles, concerns about work-life balance have also grown. This is especially true for women. Despite men's increased involvement in raising children and doing household chores, women continue to devote an average more time to both. They are also more likely to be caregivers, which can have an impact on their time use and possibly on their ability to balance work and family life. This data examines the satisfaction with work-life balance of mothers and fathers of children aged 17 and under who work full-time (i.e. 30 hours or more per week).

Overall, most parents who work full-time are satisfied with their work-life balance. In the study, 3 out of 4 parents said they were satisfied or very satisfied with this balance (75%). The others were 'neither satisfied nor dissatisfied' (15%), 'dissatisfied' (8%) or 'very dissatisfied' (1%).

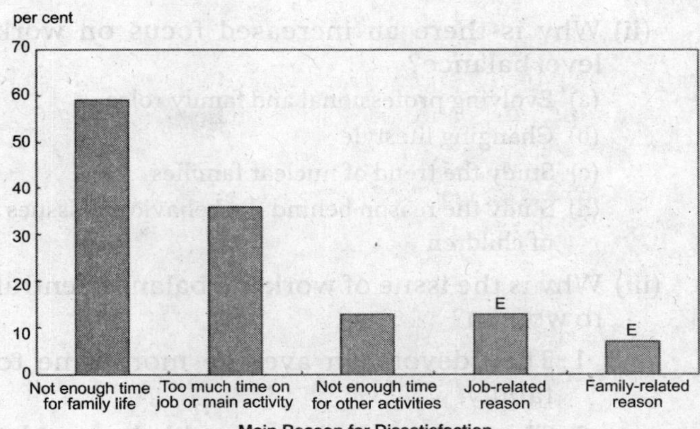

Of the parents who said that they were not satisfied, the most frequently mentioned reason for the dissatisfaction was not having enough time for family life. This was followed by spending too much time on their job or main activity, and not having enough time for other activities. Of the respondents, it was found that lone parents who work full-time obviously assume more responsibilities; they must prepare meals, transport children, help with homework, etc. This pressure may be even greater when the children are very young and the parents have little or no social support.

Only 67% of lone parents reported that they were satisfied or very satisfied with their work-life balance, compared with 76% of couple parents. Among individuals in couples, women were less satisfied than men, perhaps in part because they assume more family responsibilities than men. Furthermore, parents with at least one child aged 0 to 4 years were less likely to report being satisfied with the balance between their job and home life (72%) than those whose children were all between 5 and 17 years of age (77%). Among parents with at least one young child, 75% of fathers reported that they were nonetheless satisfied with their work-life balance, compared with 68% of women.

Questions

On the basis of your reading of the passage, answer the following questions.

(i) What is the data about?

1. Unemployed people with children

2. Work-life balance of working parents

3. Satisfaction level of working parents

4. How do working parents divide their time

(a) Only 1 (b) Both 2 and 3

(c) Only 3 (d) Only 4

(ii) Why is there an increased focus on work level balance?
(a) Evolving professional and family roles
(b) Changing lifestyle
(c) Study the trend of nuclear families
(d) Study the reason behind the behavioural issues of children

(iii) Why is the issue of work life balance central to women?
1. They devote on average more time to family.
2. They are also more likely to be caregivers.
3. They are the primary person responsible for children.
4. They are the secondary person responsible for children.
(a) Both 1 and 2 (b) Only 1
(c) Both 2 and 3 (d) Only 4

(iv) Parents who were surveyed
(a) had children under the age of 17.
(b) worked for 17 hours a day.
(c) had infant and toddler.
(d) were on top level position.

(v) Pick the statement that is TRUE as per the data given in the passage.
(a) Maximum number of parents were dissatisfied.
(b) Fathers were not very satisfied with the balance.
(c) Lone parents were equally satisfied as couple parents.
(d) Most parents believed that they did not give much time to family.

(vi) Approximately 40% of the parents believe that
(a) they spend quality time with children but it is not enough.
(b) they are dissatisfied was not having enough time for family life.
(c) they spend too much time on their job or main activity.
(d) they do not have enough time for other activities.

(vii) Which of the following figures shows the CORRECT latest percentage of dual-earner families with at least one child?

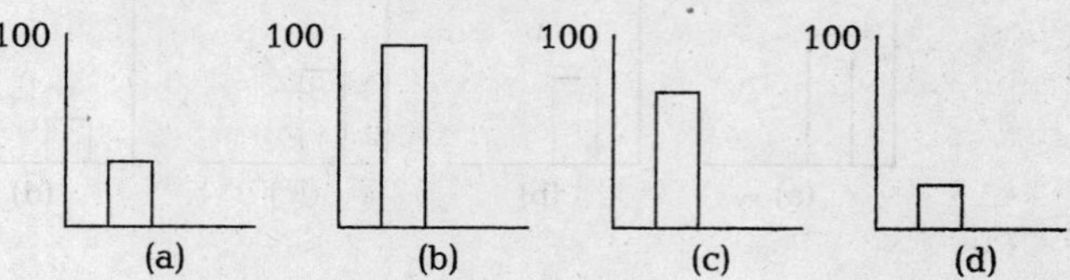

(viii) Why is there a pressure on lone parents?
(a) They alone take the responsibility.
(b) The children are very young.
(c) They have little or no social support.
(d) All of the above

Answers

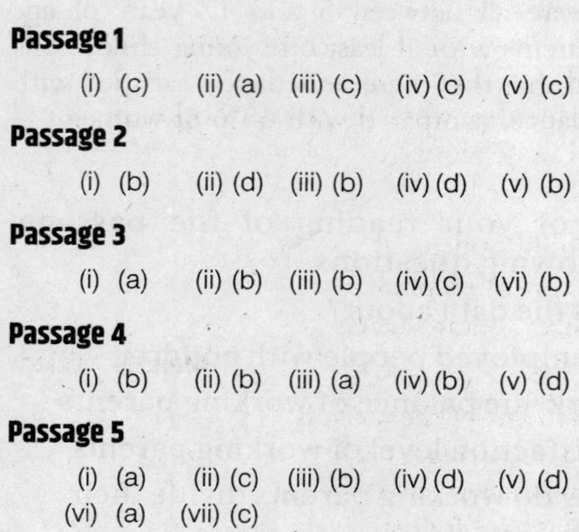

Passage 1

(i) (c) (ii) (a) (iii) (c) (iv) (c) (v) (c)

Passage 2

(i) (b) (ii) (d) (iii) (b) (iv) (d) (v) (b)

Passage 3

(i) (a) (ii) (b) (iii) (b) (iv) (c) (vi) (b)

Passage 4

(i) (b) (ii) (b) (iii) (a) (iv) (b) (v) (d)

Passage 5

(i) (a) (ii) (c) (iii) (b) (iv) (d) (v) (d)
(vi) (a) (vii) (c)

(viii) (b)

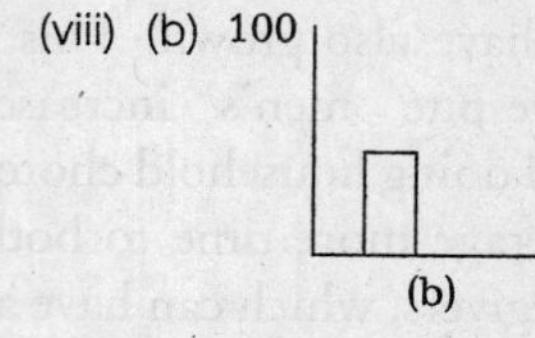

Passage 6

(i) (c) (ii) (a) (iii) (a) (iv) (a) (v) (d) (vi) (c)
(vii) (c)

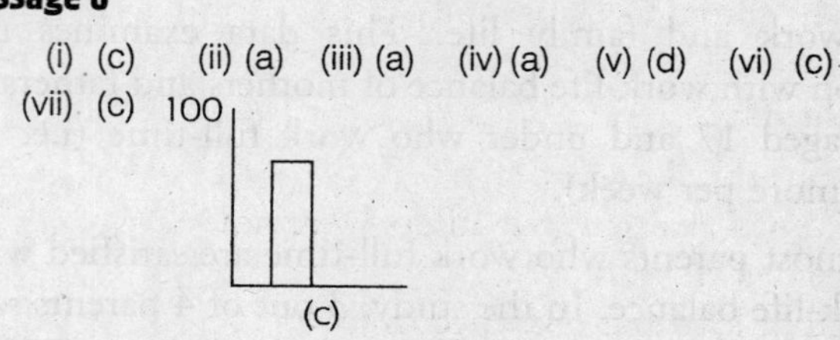

(viii) (d)

Unit-02

01 Unseen Passage-Poetry

English Language I consists of 1 Poem from which 6 questions are asked. The candidate has to go through the poem and answer the questions by selecting the most appropriate option from the given options.

Types of Questions Asked

Questions asked are either on title, theme, or central idea of the poem. Some questions are asked on certain words or phrases or lines of the poem. The students must be well versed in knowledge of figures of speech and rhyming schemes of the poem as one or two questions are asked on these also.

Tips to Solve Poetry Reading Comprehension

- Read the poem thoroughly to understand what the poet is trying to convey through the poem.
- Reread the poem to find out the theme or central idea of the poem.
- Pay attention to the key words also that may help to understand the tone or mood of the poem.
- One must try to attempt vocabulary questions very carefully as apart from knowing the literal meaning of a phrase or a line, these questions focus on 'understanding' the meaning in context of the poem.
- Questions on figures of speech and rhyming scheme can be attempted only if one is aware of these, so candidates must try to learn the different figures of speech while preparing for the exam.
- To know the rhyming scheme one must pay attention to pronunciation than spelling of words.

Unseen Poem

DIRECTIONS (Poem Nos. 1 and 2) **Read the following poems and answer the questions that follow.**

Poem 1

When did my childhood go?
Was it the day I ceased to be eleven.
Was it the time I realised that Hell and Heaven,
Could not be found in Geography,
And therefore could not be,
Was that the day!

When did my childhood go?
Was it the time I realised that adults were not
All they seemed to be,
They talked of love and preached of love,
But did not act so lovingly,
Was that the day!

When did my childhood go?
Was it when I found my mind was really mine,
To use whichever way I choose,
Producing thoughts that were not those of other people
But my own and mine alone
Was that the day!

Where did my childhood go?
It went to some forgotten place,
That is hidden in an infant's face,
That's all I know.

-Marcus Natten

1. The central theme of the poem is
(a) childhood never comes back
(b) identifying the lost childhood
(c) childhood is a swift dream
(d) a childhood memory of the poet

2. Identify the figure of speech in the line–'Was it the time I realised that Hell and Heaven'.
(a) Personification (b) Hyperbole
(c) Oxymoron (d) Alliteration

3. The poet .... when he lost his childhood.
(a) dumfounded (b) wonders
(c) shocked (d) realised

4. The poet realised that he could form his own .... as he grew up.
(a) unique decision (b) prejudiced opinions
(c) thoughts and experience (d) reality of some other infant

5. What would be a suitable title for the poem?
(a) The Lost Childhood (b) Child : A Dream
(c) Childhood (d) None of these

6. What made the poet question his faith more rationally?
(a) Geography (b) Education
(c) Childhood (d) Sense of realisation

Poem 2

Two roads diverged in a yellow wood,
And sorry I could not travel both
And be one traveller, long I stood
And looked down one as far as I could

To where it bent in the undergrowth;
Then, took the other, as just as fair,
And having perhaps the better claim
Because it was grassy and wanted wear,
Though as for that the passing there
Had worn them really about the same,
And both that morning equally lay
In leaves no step had trodden black.

Oh, I kept the first for another day!
Yet knowing how way leads on to way
I doubted if I should ever come back.
I shall be telling this with a sigh
Somewhere ages and ages hence:
Two roads diverged in a wood, and I,
I took the one less travelled by,
And that has made all the difference. **-Robert Frost**

1. The poet writes 'Two roads diverged in a yellow wood'. The word 'diverged' means
(a) appeared (b) curved
(c) branched off (d) continued on

2. In the poem, a traveller comes to a fork in the road and needs to decide which way to go, to continue his journey. Figuratively, the choice of the road denotes
(a) the tough choices people make in the road of life
(b) the time wasted on deciding what to do
(c) life is like a forest
(d) one must travel a lot to realise his dreams

3. The tone of the speaker in the first stanza is that of
(a) excitement
(b) anger
(c) hesitation and thoughtfulness
(d) sorrow

4. Rhyme scheme of the poem is
(a) aabba (b) abababc (c) abaab (d) abcb

5. The poet chooses
(a) the road which was less travelled by the people
(b) two roads which diverged in a yellow wood
(c) the unknown road
(d) to sit alone near the road side

6. An example of 'Alliteration' is
(a) to where it bent
(b) I shall be telling this
(c) because it was grassy
(d) though as for that the passing there

Poem 3

The Laburnum Top is silent, quite still
in the afternoon yellow September sunlight,
A few leaves yellowing, all its seeds fallen

Till the goldfinch comes, with a twitching chirrup
A suddeness, a startlement, at a branch end
Then, sleek as a lizard, and alert and abrupt,
She enters the thickness, and a machine starts up
Of chitterings, and of tremor of wings, and trillings

The whole tree trembles and thrills
It is the engine of her family.
She stokes it full, then flirts out to a branch-end
Showing her barred face identity mask

Then with eerie delicate whistle chirrup whisperings.
She launches away, towards the infinite
And the laburnum subsides to empty **-Ted Hughes**

1. Laburnum is a kind of
(a) sweetmeat which is served after meal
(b) the golden chain tree. A commonly found tree with golden flowers that hang in bunches
(c) a strange bird which is short fly itself
(d) rays of sunlight

2. The poet 'Ted Hughes' got the inspiration from .... to compose the poem.
(a) the top of laburnum
(b) the relationship between goldfinch and the poet
(c) the romantic pro-nature poets William Blake
(d) None of the above

3. What do you notice about the beginning of the poem?
(a) Some laburnum were getting yellowish gradually
(b) Sunlight has added beauty to laburnum
(c) The laburnum top is silent and still
(d) Activity of some goldfinches

4. The line 'A suddeness, a startlement at a branch end' contains which figure of speech
(a) Alliteration (b) Simile
(c) Personification (d) Hyperbole

5. The poet evoked the image of engine,
(a) it produces a variety of sounds
(b) it moves faster than other
(c) it has been compared with the tree
(d) it makes the machine work

6. What does the phrase 'her barred face identity mask' mean
(a) the beauty of laburnum top
(b) the rays of sunlight
(c) the striped face of the goldfinch
(d) the image of the engine of her family

Poem 4

I do not understand this child
Though we have lived together now
In the same house for years. I know
Nothing of him, so try to build
Up a relationship from how
He was when small. Yet have I killed
The seed I spent or sown it where
The land is his and none of mine?

We speak like strangers, there's no sign
Of understanding in the air.
This child is built to my design
Yet what he loves I cannot share,

Silence surrounds us. I would have
Him prodigal, returning to
His father's house, the home he knew,
Rather than see him make and move
His world. I would forgive him too,
Shaping from sorrow a new love.
Father and son, we both must live
On the same globe and the same land.

He speaks: I cannot understand
Myself, why anger grows from grief.
We each put out an empty hand,
Longing for something to forgive.

-Elizabeth Jennings

1. What is the title of the poem from which these lines have been extracted?
(a) Son to Father (b) Son to Mother
(c) Father to Son (d) Son and Father

2. This poem seems to be a
(a) personal (b) non-subjective
(c) subjective (d) memory of childhood

3. This poem deals with
(a) general issue of generation gap
(b) extravagance of son
(c) caring for elderly
(d) comfortable relationship

4. The father's helplessness is brought out very
(a) differently (b) poignantly (c) seriously (d) commonly

5. The rhyme scheme is
(a) a, b, b, a, b, a (b) abcdef, faebdc
(c) aaba (d) a, b, a, b, ab, c, c

6. Identify the phrase or line from the poem that indicates distance between father and son.
(a) In the same house for years
(b) Silence surrounds us
(c) On the same globe and the same land
(d) Shaping from sorrow a new love

Poem 5

A chieftain, to the Highlands bound, Cries,
"Boatman, do not tarry!
And I'll give thee a silver pound
To row us o'er the ferry!"--

"Now, who be ye, would cross Lochgyle,
This dark and stormy weather?"
"O, I'm the chief of Ulva's isle,
And this, Lord Ullin's daughter".

"And fast before her father's men
Three days we've fled together,
For should he find us in the glen,
My blood would stain the heather.

"His horsemen hard behind us ride
Should they our steps discover,
Then, who will cheer my bonny bride
When they have slain her lover?"--

"And by my word! the bonny bird
In danger shall not tarry;
So, though the waves are raging white,
I'll row you o'er the ferry."-

By this the storm grew loud space,
The water-wraith was shrieking;
And in the scowl of heaven each face
Grew dark as they were speaking.
But still as wilder blew the wind,
And as the night grew drearer,
Adown the glen rode armed men,
Their trampling sounded nearer.

-Thomas Campbell

1. Lord Ullin's daughter and her lover are trying to
(a) escape the wrath of her father
(b) settle in a distant land
(c) challenge the storm in the lake
(d) trying to prove their love for each other

2. The boatman agrees to ferry them across because
(a) he has fallen in love with Lord Ullin's daughter
(b) he wants to avenge Lord Ullin
(c) he has lost his love
(d) he is sorry for the childlike innocence of the lady

3. The poem is an example of a
(a) folk tale (b) Ballad
(c) Narrative Poem (d) Lyric

4. The phrase 'raging white' is an example of
(a) personification (b) alliteration
(c) imagery (d) onomatopoeia

5. The title of the poem is
(a) The Love Has no Bound (b) Wishful
(c) Lord Ullin's Daughter (d) The Last First Again

6. Who is the lover of Lord Ullin's daughter?
(a) A chieftain (b) The boatman
(c) Lord Ullin (d) Daughter of Lord Ullin

Poem 6

All the world's a stage,
And all the men and women merely players;
They have their exits and their entrances,
And one man in his time plays many parts.

His acts being seven ages. At first the infant,
Mewling and puking in the nurse's arms;
And then the whining schoolboy, with his satchel
And shining morning face, creeping like snail.

Unwillingly to school. And then the lover,
Sighing like furnace, with a woeful ballad,
Made to his mistress' eyebrow. Then, a soldier,
Full of strange oaths, and bearded like the pard,

Jealous in honour, sudden and quick in quarrel,
Seeking the bubble reputation
Even in the cannon's mouth. And then the justice,
In fair round belly with good capon lined,

With eyes severe and beard of formal cut,
Full of wise saws and modern instances;
And so he plays his part. The sixth age shifts
Into the lean and slippered pantaloon,

With spectacles on nose and pouch on side;
His youthful hose, well saved, a world too wide
For his shrunk shank: and his big manly voice,
Turning again toward childish treble, pipes

And whistles in his sound. Last scene of all,
That ends this strange eventful history,
Is second childishness and mere oblivion,
Sans teeth, sans eyes, sans taste, sans everything.

-William Shakespeare

1. All the world's a stage is an extended metaphor for
(a) the life shown in well known plays
(b) seeing the well known plays
(c) life of well known actors
(d) life of man that comes to an end

2. All 'have their exits and their entrances'. 'Exits and entrances' refer to
(a) death and birth
(b) beginning and end of play
(c) coming and going of actors
(d) the end of the Shakespearean era

3. The seven roles that a man plays correspond to his
(a) chronological age in life (b) desires
(c) mental age in life (d) idea of a perfect life

4. These lines have been taken from
(a) The famous play "As You Like It"
(b) Responsibilities
(c) The Stages of life
(d) Turning Again Toward Childish

5. The line 'Creeping like snail unwilling to go to school' contains the poetic device of
(a) Metaphor (b) Simile
(c) Personification (d) Hyperbole

6. In the first stage 'Infancy', what are the characteristic feature?
(a) Complaining, properly dressed
(b) Wise, protective
(c) Weak, dependent
(d) Teethless, poor eyesight

Poem 7

Oh, I wish I'd looked after me teeth,
And spotted the perils beneath
All the toffees I chewed,
And the sweet sticky food.

Oh, I wish I'd looked after me teeth.
I wish I'd been that much more willin'
When I had more tooth there than fillin'
To give up gobstoppers.

From respect to me choppers,
And to buy something else with me shillin'.
When I think of the lollies I licked
And the liquorice all sorts I picked,
Sherbet dabs, big and little,
All that hard peanut brittle,
My conscience gets horribly pricked.
My mother, she told me no end,
'If you got a tooth, you got a friend'.
I was young then, and careless,
My toothbrush was hairless,
I never had much time to spend.

-Pam Ayres

1. The poetess went to the .... for the treatment.
(a) doctor (b) surgeon
(c) dental college (d) dentist

2. The title 'Oh, I wish I'd Looked After Me Teeth', expresses
(a) regret and longing (b) humour
(c) excitement (d) pleasure

3. The conscience of the speaker pricks her as she has
(a) been careless (b) been ignorant
(c) been fun loving (d) been rude

4. The speaker says that she has paved the way for cavities and decay by
(a) eating the wrong food and not brushing
(b) not listening to his mother
(c) laughing at his mother's false teeth
(d) not listening to the dentist

5. The words that can replace 'gobstoppers' is ....
(a) dark chocolate (b) bunch of flowers
(c) a hard round candy (d) boiled sweets

6. The line 'I never had much time to spend' means that the poetess
(a) was very busy
(b) was too lazy
(c) did not take out time for brushing her teeth
(d) was very tired to brush her teeth

Poem 8

I am dotted silver threads dropped from heaven
By the gods. Nature then takes me, to adorn
Her fields and valleys.
I am beautiful pearls, plucked from the
Crown of Ishtar by the daughter of Dawn
To embellish the gardens.
When I cry the hills laugh;
When I humble myself the flowers rejoice;
When I bow, all things are elated.
The field and the cloud are lovers
And between them I am a messenger of mercy.
I quench the thirst of one;
I cure the ailment of the other.
The voice of thunder declares my arrival;
The rainbow announces my departure.
I am like earthly life, which begins at
The feet of the mad elements and ends
Under the upraised wings of death.
I emerge from the heart of the sea
Soar with the breeze. When I see a field in
Need, I descend and embrace the flowers and
The trees in a million little ways.

-Khalil Gibran

1. What is 'I' in the poem?
(a) The poet (b) The rain
(c) The nature (d) The heaven

2. The rain calls itself the 'dotted silver threads' as
(a) the shimmering drops fall one after the other
(b) it ties heaven and Earth
(c) it dots the Earth with shimmering water
(d) it decorates the fields

3. The tone and mood of the rain in the poem reflect its
(a) love for the Earth
(b) desire to take revenge
(c) merriment as it destroys
(d) desire to look beautiful

4. 'When I cry, the hills laugh' here cry refers to
(a) heavy rain (b) drizzling
(c) rain like cats and dogs (d) flood

5. The poet wants to convey the idea that
(a) rain is blissful
(b) everybody hears the sound of rain
(c) it gives freshness and sorrow
(d) it provides us prosperity

6. The poetic device used in the line 'Rain embraces the trees' is
(a) Metaphor (b) Simile
(c) Alliteration (d) Personification

Poem 9

Where is the peace, the wishful thinking of us all?
Where is the law and order, the basic desire of each and all?
We look for a thing, which we have seldom wished for from our genuine heart.

How to get rid of this rotten society where everyone is sick, but calls himself healthy?

Life is short but the wish to live is too long.
The more and more we are heading towards death,

The more and more the allurements of the world do seize us,
The germs of discord and dissension prey on us,
And life is reduced to a mere dream;
What a strange world this is indeed, which keeps us all restless and dissatisfied;

Perhaps this is all the leela the play of Maya, entrapping us all.
O God! You have made us all slaves to Maya, seizing us from all sides and keeping us disturbed;
I don't know what is good and what is evil,
I fail to distinguish between Maya and reality, the foul and the fair,

As if being born in this world was a punishment;
Are we condemned to live in this hell once and for all?
Where we have to come again and again to suffer,
God! Make us get rid of all that glitters but is not gold.

-Anonymous

1. According to the poet, what is a punishment for us?
(a) To be born in this world (b) To live in discord
(c) The play of Maya (d) Death

2. The poet is not being able to distinguish between
(a) life and death (b) foul and fair
(c) rich and poor (d) strong and weak

3. What does the line 'Where we have to come again and again to suffer' signify?
(a) Cycle of birth and death (b) Place to visit
(c) Our homes (d) This world

4. In the above poem 'allurement' refers to
(a) being unsatisfied (b) getting carried away
(c) worldly pleasures (d) emotions

5. What, according to the poet, is our wishful thinking?
(a) Law and order (b) Outer peace
(c) Inner peace (d) Genuine heart

6. Our life has been condemned to like
(a) living in hell (b) living in luxury
(c) Maya (d) Leela

Poem 10

She lives in a garret
Up a haunted stair,
And even when she's frightened
There's nobody to care.

She cooks so small a dinner
She dines on the smell,
And even if she's hungry
There's nobody to tell.

She sweeps her musty lodging
As the dawn steals near,
And even when she's crying
There's nobody to hear.

I haven't seen my neighbour
Since a long time ago,
And even if she's dead
There's nobody to know.

-Frances Park

1. The line 'She dines on the smell' means
(a) her food is stale
(b) she eats very little
(c) she dislikes the smell of her food
(d) she dislikes the food

2. Who is 'she' in the poem?
(a) A miserly woman
(b) A hungry woman
(c) A woman who lives next door
(d) A woman who lives in an old age home

3. The woman cooks a small dinner because
(a) she has no food to cook (b) she is alone
(c) she is stingy (d) she dislikes food

4. The attitude of the speaker is
(a) indifferent (b) uncaring
(c) sympathetic (c) pitiable

5. The purpose of the poem is to tell us that
(a) no one cares for lonely people
(b) the speaker's neighbour is dead
(c) the speaker's neighbour is hungry
(d) the woman was treated badly

6. The woman described in the poem is
(a) brave
(b) helpless
(c) sad and lonely
(d) disappointed

Poem 11

These few precepts in thy memory
See thou character. Give thy thoughts no tongue,
Nor any unproportioned thought this act:
Be thou familiar, but by no means vulgar

Those friends thou hast, and their adoption tried
Grapple them to thy soul with hoops of steel,
But do not dull thy palm with entertainment
One each new hatched, unfledged comrade. Beware

Of entrance to a quarrel, but being in,
Bear that the opposed may beware of thee.
Give every man thy ear, but few thy voice,
Take each man's censure, but reserve thy judgement.
Costly thy habit as thy purse can buy,

But not expressed in fancy; rich not gaudy;
For the apparel often proclaims the man.
Neither a borrower nor a lender be;
For loan oft loses both itself and friend,
And borrowing dulls the edge of husbandry.

-William Shakespeare

1. It is always suggested to beware of
(a) dogs
(b) backbiting
(c) quarrels
(d) artificial policies

2. Here, the poet proposes that habit should be in ratio
(a) to one's pocket (b) to what suits him
(c) with the ability
(d) what are his engagements

3. What is seen through percepts in memory?
(a) Face (b) Character
(c) Appearance (d) Clause

4. It is always said to speak less
(a) still you can see everything
(b) but you can hear everyone
(c) and eat properly
(d) and be more productive

5. What is the side effect of taking a loan?
(a) You will have to pay interest
(b) It loses friend and itself
(c) It earns bad name
(d) You can die in debt

6. What is the opposite of 'rich' here in line 14?
(a) Poor (b) Borrower
(c) Poverty (d) Gaudy

Poem 12

A nightingale, that all day long
Had cheered the village with his song
Not yet at eve his note suspended,
Nor yet when eventide was ended,
Began to feel, as well he might,
The keen demands of appetite;
When, looking eagerly around,
He spied far off, upon the ground
A something shining in the dark,
And knew the glow-worm by his spark;
So, stooping down from hawthorn top,
He thought to put him in his crop

The worm, aware of his intent,
Harangued him thus, right eloquent-
'Did you admire my lamp,' quoth he,
'As much as I your minstrelsy',

You would abhor to do me wrong,
As much as I to spoil your song;
For't was the self-same power divine,
Taught you to sing, and me to shine;

That you with music, I with light,
Might beautify and cheer the night;
The songster heard his short oration
And warbling out his approbation,

Released him as my story tells,
And found a supper somewhere else.

-William Cowper

1. Whom did the nightingale wish to make his crop?
(a) Hawthorn top (b) Glow worm
(c) Mils insects (d) Something else

2. Who taught the nightingale to sing and worm to shine?
(a) Their parents (b) God
(c) Right from birth (d) Each other

3. Explain- 'The keen demands of appetite'.
(a) Good appetite is important for singing
(b) The nightingale was now very hungry
(c) He had a very large appetite
(d) He thought he could not fulfill his appetite

4. What is the rhyming scheme of the poem?
(a) Abba (b) Abab
(c) Baba (d) Aabb

5. What did the nightingale finally decide?
(a) To make the glowworm his supper
(b) To find his supper somewhere else
(c) To sit and wait for something else
(d) To keep singing for the whole night

6. Suggest a suitable topic for the poem.
(a) Song Versus Light
(b) Power of Divine
(c) The Nightingale and the Glowworm
(d) The Nightingale's Tragedy

Poem 13

Snug in mother's bosom
The newly born
Rests in warm embrace,
Listening to mother's heart beat

Love takes another form
In the friendship of mates,
Eating, playing and fighting,
Childhood moves on to youth,
The irresistible attraction
Of the opposite sexes,
Brings a fiery love
Through tempestuous adulthood.

This melts into paternal love
Losing sleep when a child is sick
Untold pleasure in his achievements,
And anxiety in his misfortunes.

Old age brings another love,
And lust for life
Seeking pleasures when pleasure recedes,
And love gets colder by the day.

Inexorably moving towards the end
The ultimate love lies ahead.
But through changing seasons,
It has been all the way.

-Anonymous

1. What is the significant aspect of childhood?
(a) Friendship of mates (b) Eating
(c) Playing and fighting (d) All of these

2. Who is snug in the mother's bosom?
(a) The new born baby (b) A child
(c) A boy (d) A girl

3. What is the person attracted to most in adulthood?
(a) Studies
(b) Opposite sex
(c) Games
(d) Roaming here and there

4. We receive untold pleasures
(a) when we grow up
(b) when we become a parent
(c) in a child's achievements
(d) in misfortunes

5. Which line indicates the closeness of the baby to mother?
(a) Melts into paternal love
(b) Ultimate love lies ahead
(c) Listening to mother's heartbeat
(d) Fiery love

6. What does 'tempestuous mean'?
(a) Stormy (b) Testing patience
(c) Violent (d) High in temper

Poem 14

Our constant march towards infinity,
Seems to have jeopardised the real identity.
What are we sent for?
Is it to experience the exuberance of Nature?

Or to plunge into an eternal race of rivalry,
Where a man devours his divine self,
And strives to show his supremacy.
Really a blind race, full of strife,
That has soaked the sap of human life.
O, Misguided soul,
Listen patiently the songs of divinity,
That'll subdue the passion of brutality,
And lead you to the Great White Throne,
Which all of us must vie to own. **-Anonymous**

1. Man is just running to get the most of worldly pleasures. Amidst these, he forgets
(a) his divine self (b) his family
(c) his other priorities (d) the society

2. What does the line – 'March towards Infinity' mean?
(a) Getting misdirected
(b) Lack of guidance
(c) Forwarding oneself to means, that have no ends
(d) Proceeding towards God

3. The poet wants the man to listen to what kind of songs?
(a) Traditional songs (b) Songs of divinity
(c) Eternal songs (d) Patriotic songs

4. Life is like a fight, full of struggle. Find the line in the poem that relates to this line.
(a) Has soaked the sap of human life
(b) And strives to show his supremacy
(c) Subdue the passion of brutality
(d) Really a blind race, full of strife

5. What is 'The Great White Throne'?
(a) Place where God lives
(b) The ultimate place of being
(c) Door of salvation
(d) A very peaceful place

6. Instead of facing the eternal race of rivalry, a man should?
(a) Jeopardise the real identity
(b) Experience the exuberance of nature
(c) Patiently listen the songs of divinity
(d) Should not march towards infinity

Poem 15

The Last Conqueror

Victorious men of Earth, no more
Proclaim how wide your empires are;
Though you bind-in every shore
And your triumphs reach as far
As night or day,
Yet you, proud monarchs, must obey
And mingle with forgotten ashes, when
Death calls ye to the crowd of common men.

Devouring Famine, Plague and War,
Each able to undo mankind,
Death's servile emissaries are;
Nor to these alone confined,
He hath at will
More quaint and subtle ways to kill;
A smile or kiss, as he will use the art,
Shall have to cunning skill to break a heart.

1. '........... servile emissaries' means
(a) Risky behaviour (b) Humble messengers
(c) Those who protect (d) Messengers of peace

2. The line – 'More quaint and subtle ways to kill;
A smile or kiss, as he will use the art,'
-tell the reader that the speaker
(a) believes in human goodness
(b) is afraid of his enemies
(c) hates wars
(d) distrusts human nature

3. '....... the cunning skill' refers to
(a) A weapon of war
(b) Skillful soldier
(c) A manipulative king
(d) Hidden threat

4. '........ mingle with forgotten ashes' means
(a) dead persons
(b) fires on the battlefield
(c) threats to life
(d) hidden dangers

5. In the above poem, 'subtle' means
(a) stupid (b) hidden
(c) suggestive (d) sullen

6. 'And your triumphs reach as far
As night or day'
The poetic device found in these words is a
(a) pathetic fallacy (b) metaphor
(c) simile (d) formula

Poem 16

Human Nature

Is it human nature
to desire forbidden fruit,
to hunger for a blossom
so obsessed with passion

that we forget the pain,
which inevitably arises
once we tease ourselves
with the thought of it

or taste a tiny part of it,
and it becomes the predator
eating at us like a carnivore
that saves the head for last

savouring the brain to feed its own
and we, still craving illicit nectar
enjoying the fact that it is devouring us? -C.J Grant

1. Another word in the poem that suggests 'forbidden' is
(a) obsess (b) crave
(c) savour (d) illicit

2. 'It becomes the predator' means
(a) strong emotions influence one negatively
(b) pursuit of happiness
(c) being cautious against outside influences
(d) being strong and positive against any threat

3. An example of personification in the poem is
(a) saves the head
(b) tease ourselves
(c) illicit nectar
(d) like a carnivore

4. 'Eating at us like a carnivore' refers to
(a) being attacked by a wild beast
(b) being attacked by a human enemy
(c) being eaten up by an unknown entity
(d) exerting a strong influence

5. 'We, still craving illicit nectar' can be explained by focusing on the word
(a) we (b) craving
(c) illicit (d) nectar

6. A synonym for the word 'savouring' is
(a) Smelling
(b) Flavouring
(c) Experiencing
(d) Avoiding

Poem 17

I cannot rest from travel : I will drink
Life to the lees : All times I have enjoy'd
Greatly, have suffer'd greatly both with those
That loved me, and alone, on shore and when
Thro' scudding drifts the rainy Hyades

Vext the dim sea : I am become a name;
For always roaming with a hungry heart
Much have I seen and known; cities of men
And manners, climates, councils, governments,
Myself not least, but honour'd of them all;

1. The speaker can be described as
(a) an adventurer
(b) a frolicsome person
(c) a vagabond
(d) a seeker after the truth

2. The expression, 'drink life to the lees' means
(a) to live a life of adventure
(b) to live life to the fullest
(c) to live a life of pleasure
(d) to face challenges bravely

3. Which of the following statements is true?
(a) He has suffered and enjoyed greatly.
(b) He has lost interest in life.
(c) The speaker is an aimless wanderer.
(d) His adventures have not changed his outlook.

4. The line – 'Myself not least, but honour'd of them all' reveals that the speaker is
(a) conscious of his merits
(b) arrogant
(c) prone to bragging
(d) a garrulous person

5. The figure of speech used in 'drink life to the lees' is
(a) personification
(b) assonance
(c) simile
(d) metaphor

6. Which literary device has been used in 'hungry heart'?
(a) Alliteration (b) Irony
(c) Assonance (d) Simile

Poem 18

On a Tired Housewife

Here lies a poor woman who was always tired.
She lived in a house where help wasn't hired
Her last words on Earth were : 'Dear friends, I am going

To where there's no cooking, or washing, or sewing,
For everything there is exact to my wishes,
For where they don't eat there's no washing of dishes.
I'll be where loud anthems will always be ringing,
But having no voice I'll be quit of the singing.
Don't mourn for me now, don't mourn for me never,
I am going to do nothing for ever and ever.' -Anonymous

1. The woman described in the poem
(a) lived in her own house
(b) worked in the house of a rich man
(c) was very busy doing chores
(d) was no more

2. The woman was always tired because
(a) she did all the household work without any help
(b) she had hardly anything to eat
(c) she was physically very weak
(d) she was suffering from a serious ailment

3. The woman wanted to go to a place where
(a) people would take good care of her
(b) people would sincerely mourn for her
(c) people didn't sing or dance
(d) people didn't cook, wash or sew

4. The woman's account in the poem shows
(a) how a woman can escape from work
(b) how we should help each other
(c) how overworked a housewife is
(d) that there is no work in heaven

5. 'For everything there is exact to my wishes'.
In this line, the word 'exact' can be interpreted to mean
(a) according (b) leading
(c) contrary (d) contributing

6. The rhyme pattern in the poem is
(a) aa, bb, cc, dd, ee (b) aa, ab, bc, cd, de
(c) ab, ab, ab, ab, ab (d) aa, ab, cd, cd, ee

Poem 19

Night
The Sun descending in the West,
The evening star does shine;
The birds are silent in their nest,
And I must seek for mine.

The Moon, like a flower,
In heaven's high bower,
With silent delight
Sits and smiles on the night.

Farewell, green fields and happy groves,
Where flocks have took delight.
Where lambs have nibbled, silent moves
The feet of angels bright;

Unseen they pour blessing,
And joy without ceasing,
On each bud and blossom,
And each sleeping bosom.

They look in every thoughtless nest,
Where birds are covered warm;
They visit caves of every beast,
To keep them all from harm.

If they see any weeping
That should have been sleeping,
They pour sleep on their head,
And sit down by their bed.

1. The evening star rises when
(a) the Sun descends in the West
(b) the birds leave their nests
(c) it is midnight
(d) it is dawn

2. Here, 'bower' represents
(a) a flower vase
(b) a potted plant
(c) a framework that supports climbing plants
(d) a bouquet of flowers

3. The poet compares the moon to
(a) an angel (b) a flower
(c) a bird in the nest (d) an evening star

4. The angels come down on Earth to
(a) take blessing and joy
(b) spread moonlight
(c) give blessing and joy
(d) make people dance and have fun

5. Birds nest is described as 'thoughtless' because
(a) the occupants are asleep without any care
(b) the angels are blessing the birds to be happy
(c) the birds are covered in the warmth of their nest
(d) it is made without any thought

6. The figure of speech used in the line 'In heaven's high bower' is
(a) simile (b) metaphor
(c) personification (d) alliteration

Poem 20

Between the Miles
Because existence can become
severe in one day,
just sense me and I'll be there
In the mind's eye,

I'm not so far away.
If you hold out your hand,
in the whispers,
I'll become the zephyr...

and besiege you.
If your eye's upon the stars,
in the crystalline darkness,
I'll become the Moon.

And the light shall guide you.
If you rest upon the ground,
in the warmth,
I'll become the grass

And embrace you.
If you turn outside,
in the wetness,
I'll become the rain.

An upon your forhead, kiss you
If you free the air,
in the light of day,
I'll become the Sun.

And smile for you.
Between the miles
if you need me
If you need a friend
Let me be the friend, I want to be.

-Heather Stoop

1. The theme of the poem is about
(a) nature (b) separation
(c) relationship (d) travel

2. The 'crystalline darkness' suggests that surrounding is
(a) pitch dark and quiet
(b) black and sombre
(c) in the moonlight
(d) lit up by the stars only

3. In the poem, the poet suggests that friendship is unaffected by
(a) differences in attitude (b) individual independence
(c) changing feelings (d) time and distance

4. 'The zephyr' is a
(a) gentle, mild breeze (b) fine quality of cloth
(c) scent or odour (d) strong stream of air

5. An example of a metaphor is
(a) 'If you rest upon the ground'
(b) 'I'll become the grass'
(c) 'Between the miles'
(d) 'I want to be'

6. A synonym of the word 'besiege' is
(a) Trap (b) Surround
(c) Attack (d) Befriend

Poem 21

Sprinkle, squish between my toes,
The smell of ocean to my nose.
I can feel each grain of sand,
It falls from air into my hand.

The shells I find along the shore,
Picked up by birds
that fly and soar.
They sparkle like the ocean's waves,
And carry sand from all the lakes.
I walk
That's where my feet leave prints to be.
I walk all the way to the end of the land,
The land that holds this beautiful sand. **-Morgan Swain**

1. The poem's central theme is
(a) a factual description of nature
(b) sharing experiences with nature
(c) a recollection of a visit
(d) an introspection by the writer

2. Here, 'to the end of the land' refers to the
(a) sealine (b) land
(c) sky (d) horizon

3. Here, 'That's where my feet leave prints to be' means that the writer
(a) knows that everything is temporary
(b) relives past visits
(c) expects to forget the experience
(d) hopes to remember his visit

4. The phrase in the poem that conveys the same meaning as 'along the tip of the sea' is
(a) each grain of sand
(b) end of the land
(c) air into my hand
(d) like the ocean's waves

5. The poetic device used in the line 'They sparkle like the ocean's waves' is a/an
(a) hyperbole (b) exaggeration
(c) simile (d) allegory

6. A word that can replace 'squish' is
(a) crush (b) hold
(c) scrunch (d) trample

Poem 22

Invictus

Out of the night that covers me,
Black as the pit from pole to pole,
I thank whatever gods may be
For my unconquerable soul.
In the fell clutch of circumstance
I have not winced nor cried aloud.
Under the bludgeonings of chance
My head is bloody, but unbowed.
Beyond this place of wrath and tears
Looms but the Horror of the shade,
And yet the menace of the years
Finds and shall find, me unafraid. **-William Ernest Henley**

1. The phrase 'unconquerable soul' means a person who is
(a) invincible (b) compassionate
(c) noble (d) sensitive

2. Lines 5 and 6 show that the speaker
(a) refuses to surrender
(b) remains undaunted even under the worst circumstances
(c) is overwhelmed by adverse circumstances
(d) accepts life's challenges

3. 'Wrath and tears' means
(a) unbearable suffering
(b) anger causing havoc
(c) anger and sorrow
(d) unfavourable circumstances

4. The phrase 'menace of the years' suggests
(a) threats of the times (b) danger to life
(c) cruel fate (d) evils of life

5. The word 'winced' in the above poem means
(a) recoiled (b) ruffled
(c) frightened (d) worried

6. The poetic device used in 'Black as the pit from pole to pole' is
(a) metaphor (b) irony
(c) simile (d) parallelism

Poem 23

So he spoke, mildly; Sohrab heard his voice
The mighty voice of Rustum and he saw
His giant figure planted on the sand,
Sole, like some single tower, which a chief

Hath builded on the waste in former years
Against the robbers; and he saw that head,
Streak'd with its first grey hairs; hope filled his soul,
And he ran forward and embraced his knees,
And clasp'd his hand within his own, ...

1. The way Sohrab reacted when he saw Rustum shows that
(a) he felt great love and admiration for him
(b) he was utterly confused
(c) he was overcome with grief
(d) he was enraged, when he saw Rustum

2. The poet describes Rustum's voice as
(a) booming (b) shrill
(c) loud (d) powerful

3. The figure of speech used in lines 3 and 4 is
(a) personification (b) metonymy
(c) simile (d) metaphor

4. Identify the literary device used in
'......... he saw that head
Streak'd with its first grey hairs'
(a) Imagery (b) Alliteration
(c) Simile (d) Contrast

5. The encounter between Rustum and Sohrab took place
(a) on the sea-shore
(b) in a desert
(c) in a valley
(d) in a forest

6. The description of Rustum's physical appearance shows that he was
(a) middle-aged (b) a teenager
(c) young (d) old

Poem 24

How soon hath Time, the subtle thief of youth,
Stol'n on his wing my three-and-twentieth year!
My hasting days fly on with full career,
But my late spring no bud or blossom shew'th.

Perhaps my semblance might deceive the truth
That I to manhood am arriv'd so near;
And inward ripeness doth much less appear,
That some more timely-happy
spirits endu'th.
Yet be it less or more, or soon or slow,
It shall be still in strictest measure ev'n
To that same lot, however mean or high,
Toward which Time leads me, and the will of Heav'n.

1. The poet presents 'Time' as a/an
(a) enemy (b) spirit (c) friend (d) thief

2. The poet regrets that
(a) he has not attained inner maturity
(b) his teachers are not happy with his progress
(c) his academic progress has been very slow
(d) he is not popular with his peers

3. The poet envies his friends because they
(a) have achieved name and fame
(b) are popular with their friends
(c) are blessed with robust health
(d) have attained inward ripeness

4. The inner maturity the poet longs for will come
(a) with the help of peers
(b) with the help of teachers
(c) only by the will of God
(d) through hard work

5. The poet is .... about his future.
(a) pessimistic (b) unconcerned
(c) cynical (d) optimistic

6. The 'figure of speech' used in lines (a) and (b) is
(a) personification (b) a hyperbole
(c) an irony (d) a simile

Poem 25

My mother bore me in the Southern wild,
And I am black, but O ! my soul is white;
White as an angel is the English child:
But I am black as if bereav'd of light.
My mother taught me underneath a tree
And sitting down before the heat of day,
She took me on her lap and kissed me,
And pointing to the East began to say.
Look on the rising Sun : there God does live
And gives his light, and gives his heat away.
And flowers and trees and beasts and men receive
Comfort in morning joy in the noonday.
And we are put on Earth a little space,
That, we may learn to bear the beams of love,
And these black bodies and this Sun-burnt face
Is but a cloud, and like a shady grove.

1. 'The Little Black Boy' was born in
(a) the East coast (b) the desert wastes
(c) the servants' house (d) the Southern wild

2. 'The Little Black Boy' wished that he could be
(a) white (b) educated (c) older (d) free

3. The mother of 'the Little Black Boy' says God put people on Earth
(a) to learn how to treat one another as equals
(b) to learn to endure his love
(c) to work off their sins
(d) to prepare them for future trials

4. The mother of 'The Little Black Boy' says his dark skin and face are
(a) a cloud (b) a blessing
(c) a veil (d) a curse

5. The phrase 'like a shady grove' is
(a) a personification
(b) a metaphor
(c) a simile
(d) an example of alliteration

6. Through the phrase 'as if bereav'd of light', the poet hints at the
(a) colour of the boy
(b) low self-esteem of the child
(c) lack of hope for the future
(d) All of the above

Poem 26

All creation drinks with pleasure
Drinks at Mother Nature's breast;
All the just and all the evil,
Follow down her rosy path.
Kisses she bestowed, and grape wine,
Friendship true, proved e'en in death;
Every worm knows nature's pleasure,
Every cherub meets his God.
Gladly, like the planets flying
True to heaven's mighty plan,
Brothers, run your course now,
Happy as a knight in victory.

1. What does the expression, 'Brothers, run your course now' mean?
(a) Cultivate a positive attitude to life
(b) Keep on moving towards your goal
(c) Don't let failures upset you
(d) Seek God's help when you are in difficulty

2. How can we say that God's creatures are most fortunate and happy?
(a) They have benevolent Mother Nature to look after them
(b) The world they live in lacks romance and beauty
(c) They have no friends to share their joys and sorrows
(d) They do not have enough pleasures at their disposal

3. Which of the following does not support the idea that Mother Nature's love embraces all?
(a) She also blesses us with true friendship
(b) All creation drinks at Mother Nature's heart
(c) She bestows kisses on all her children
(d) She loves all the just but not all the evil

4. What is the hallmark of a true friend?
(a) He can take on all the evils for you
(b) He saves you from troubles
(c) He helps you to enjoy the fruits of nature
(d) He proves true even in death

5. Rosy path is followed by
(a) neither the just nor the evil
(b) the honest
(c) the evil
(d) Both (b) and (c)

6. Identify the figure of speech used in 'All creation drinks at Mother Nature's breast.'
(a) Alliteration (b) Metonymy
(c) Simile (d) Personification

Poem 27

Light Brigade
By Alfred Tennyson
Half a league, half a league,
Half a league onward,
All in the valley of Death
Rode the six hundred.
"Forward the Light Brigade!
Charge for the guns !" he said.
Into the valley of Death
Rode the six hundred.
Forward, the Light Brigade!"
Was there a man dismay'd ?
Not tho' the soldier knew
Some one had blunder'd.
Theirs not to make reply,
Theirs not to reason why,
Theirs but to do and die.
Into the valley of Death
Rode the six hundred.

1. The expression' the valley of death' refers to
(a) the place where the dead soldiers are lying buried
(b) the impending death of soldiers
(c) the house of death
(d) a nightmarish place

2. Which of the following statement is not true? The military discipline teaches the soldiers
(a) to do and die
(b) to obey their commander's order
(c) to act tactfully in the battlefield
(d) not to ask any question

3. Which of the following adjectives does not apply to the soldiers?
(a) courageous (b) disciplined
(c) patriotic (d) impractical

4. Identify the figure of speech used in 'the Valley of Death'.
(a) Metaphor (b) Simile (c) Synecdoche (d) Metonymy

5. Which literary device is used in the expression, 'to do and die'?
(a) Assonance
(b) Alliteration
(c) Simile
(d) Personification

6. In the first stanza of the extract, the soldiers are
(a) talking to each other about their personal problems
(b) waiting for their commander's order
(c) thinking about the result of the war
(d) seen riding fast to the enemy territory

Poem 28

I come from haunts of coot and hern.
I make a sudden sally
And sparkle out among the fern,
To bicker down a valley,
By thirty hills I hurry down,
Or slip between the ridges,
By twenty thorpes, a little town,
And half a hundred bridges,
Till last by Philip's farm I flow
To join the brimming river,
For men may come and men may go,
But I go on forever,
I chatter over stony ways,
In little sharps and trebles,
I bubble into eddying bays,
I babble on the pebbles,
With many a curve my banks I fret
By many a field and fallow,
And many a fairy foreland set
With willow-weed and mallow,

1. Identify the figure of speech used in the line, 'I come from haunts of coot and herm'.
(a) Metaphor (b) Synecdoche
(c) Personification (d) Hyperbole

2. The brook chatters over stony ways
(a) noiselessly
(b) in little sharps and trebles
(c) in a meandering fashion
(d) gleefully

3. Which of the following is not true according to the poem?
(a) The brook chatters over stony ways.
(b) Man is moral and Nature is eternal.
(c) The brook will finally join the brimming river.
(d) Man may go and come anywhere and everywhere.

4. The line 'I make a sudden sally' means:
(a) I flow evenly
(b) I flow by fits and starts
(c) I leap enthusiastically
(d) I move in a zig zag manner

5. Where is the brook headed for?
(a) Philip's farm
(b) a valley
(c) the brimming river
(d) fields and bays

6. Identify the figure of speech used in 'with willow-weed' in stanza 5?
(a) Hyperbole (b) Alliteration
(c) Metaphor (d) Metonymy

Poem 29

When you're up against a trouble,
Meet it squarely, face to face;
Lift your chin and set your shoulders.
Plant your feet and take a brace.

When it's vain to try to dodge it,
Do the best you can do;
You may fail, but you may conquer,
See it through!

Black may be the clouds about you
And your future may seen grim,
But don't let your nerve desert you;
Keep yourself in fighting trim.

If the worst is bound to happen,
Spite of all that you can do,
Running from it will no save you,
See it through!

1. What does the poet want to 'brace' for?
(a) planting one's feet firmly (b) setting up shoulders
(c) facing difficulties (d) dodging someone

2. In 'dodge it' line 5, 'it' stands for
(a) nerves (b) the problems
(c) black clouds (d) vanity

3. By 'lift your chin' (line 3) the poet wants us to be
(a) alert (b) punctual
(c) smart (d) bold

4. The poet wants us to avoid
(a) black clouds (b) grim future
(c) meanness (d) failing nerves

5. What is the rhyme scheme in lines no 9-12?
(a) abab (b) abcd
(c) abac (d) abbb

6. 'Your future may see grim'
The underlined word means the same as:
(a) soft (b) bright
(c) depressing (d) sure

Poem 30

'Will you walk into my parlour?' said the spider to the fly;
"It is the prettiest little parlour that you may ever spy
The way into my parlour is up a winding stair,
And I have many curious things to show when you are there."
"O no, no," said the little fly; "to ask me is in vain,
For who goes up your winding stair can n'ver come down again."

1. The spider is very eager to invite the fly to his home because he wants to
(a) show her the architectural beauty of his home.
(b) trap her into the web and gobble her up
(c) show her many pretty things in his possession.
(d) make her envious of his beautiful home

2. The spider can be compared to a
(a) clever business man (b) greedy dog
(c) crafty person (d) heartless hunter

3. What prompts the fly to say an emphatic 'no' to the spider's proposal?
(a) Her innate wisdom.
(b) The instinctive fear of spiders.
(c) Her friend's warning against the spiders.
(d) Her personal experience.

4. The central idea of the extract is
(a) Spiders are ugly, scary creatures
(b) Beware of honey-tongued people
(c) One should not miss opportunities to see beautiful things
(d) We should not be cynical about everything

5. The word, 'parlour' in the line – "Will you walk into my parlour?" is an example of
(a) a metaphor (b) euphemism
(c) a hyperbole (d) a simile

6. Which literary device has been used in the words, "O no, no"?
(a) Assonance (b) Pun
(c) Simile (d) Repetition

Poem 31

Behold her, single in the field,
Yon solitary Highland Lass!
Reaping and singing by herself;
Stop here, or gently pass!
Alone she cuts and binds the grain,
And sings a melancholy strain;
O listen! For the Vale profound
Is overflowing with the sound.

No Nightingale did ever chaunt
More welcome notes to weary bands
Of travellers in some shady haunt,
Among Arabian sands:
A voice so thrilling ne'er was heard
In spring-time from the Cuckoo-bird,
Breaking the silence of the seas
Among the farthest Hebrides.

Will no one tell me what she sings?
Perhaps the plaintive numbers flow
For old, unhappy, far-off things,
And battles long ago:
Or is it some more humble lay,
Familiar matter of to-day?
Some natural sorrow, loss or pain,
That has been, and may be again?

1. The poem suggests that
(a) The song the girl is singing is meant for others.
(b) The poet is greatly moved by the song.
(c) The song that the girl is singing is one of ecstasy.
(d) The theme of the song concerns familiar matters of today.

2. The song is addressed to
(a) the travellers who pass by her
(b) herself
(c) the vale around her
(d) the poet

3. The phrase 'a melancholy strain' means
(a) a playful song (b) a lilting song
(c) a sad song (d) a mysterious song

4. The tone of the poem is
(a) cheerful (b) passionate
(c) loud (d) sad

5. Which figure of speech is used in 'Among Arabian sands'?
(a) Metaphor (b) Metonymy
(c) Personification (d) Alliteration

6. Which figure of speech has been used in the following lines?
"Breaking the silence of the seas
Among the farthest Hebrides"
(a) Metaphor (b) Simile
(c) Personification (d) Assonance

Poem 32

In friction land there is a family
With some confusions as you will see.
There is Raghu aged fifteen and others all grown.
'Please will someone let me ever be on my own!'

Rejection, refusal, Raghu saw red.
'Am I the Prefect at school? or the baby at home?'
Crazy! What adventures! Bah teenagers! Papa saw the threat
They Think they can manage everything on their own

'Look at your clothes, looks like you haven't bathed in years.
Cut your hair, you look like a scream! Raghu was in tears
'Why can't I live like I wanna be':
I won't change! My friends love it and the girls-look at me.'

Days passed by, things looked better, sometimes worse.
'Papa, there is a band, that wants me to sing a verse'.
"Join a band! yelled flabbergasted papa 'you've surely gone mad'.

Think of a career, for things gonna be sad.

1. 'Friction land' here stands for
(a) a mysterious island (b) a confused family
(c) a desert (d) wonderland

2. 'Saw red in line 5 means'
(a) was angry (b) was in danger
(c) was excited (d) was nervous

3. Which of the following is not a point of clash between Raghu and his father?
(a) different lifestyle (b) different interests
(c) different food habits (d) age difference

4. Which line shows the dilemma faced by Raghu?
(a) Line 2 (b) Line 4
(c) Line 6 (d) Line 8

5. What is the rhyme in 1st stanza?
(a) abab (b) abcd
(c) acbd (d) abcc

6. In 'flabbergasted papa', flabbergasted is used as a/an
(a) verb
(b) adverb
(c) adjective
(d) noun

Answers

Poem 1.	1. (b)	2. (d)	3. (b)	4. (a)	5. (c)	6. (b)
Poem 2.	1. (c)	2. (a)	3. (c)	4. (c)	5. (a)	6. (d)
Poem 3.	1. (b)	2. (c)	3. (c)	4. (a)	5. (c)	6. (c)
Poem 4.	1. (c)	2. (c)	3. (a)	4. (b)	5. (a)	6. (b)
Poem 5.	1. (a)	2. (d)	3. (b)	4. (c)	5. (c)	6. (a)
Poem 6.	1. (d)	2. (a)	3. (a)	4. (a)	5. (b)	6. (c)
Poem 7.	1. (d)	2. (a)	3. (a)	4. (a)	5. (c)	6. (c)
Poem 8.	1. (b)	2. (a)	3. (a)	4. (a)	5. (a)	6. (d)
Poem 9.	1. (a)	2. (b)	3. (a)	4. (c)	5. (c)	6. (a)
Poem 10.	1. (b)	2. (c)	3. (b)	4. (c)	5. (a)	6. (c)
Poem 11.	1. (c)	2. (a)	3. (b)	4. (d)	5. (b)	6. (a)
Poem 12.	1. (b)	2. (b)	3. (b)	4. (d)	5. (b)	6. (c)
Poem 13.	1. (d)	2. (a)	3. (b)	4. (c)	5. (c)	6. (c)
Poem 14.	1. (a)	2. (c)	3. (b)	4. (d)	5. (c)	6. (b)
Poem 15.	1. (b)	2. (d)	3. (d)	4. (a)	5. (b)	6. (c)
Poem 16.	1. (d)	2. (a)	3. (a)	4. (d)	5. (b)	6. (b)
Poem 17.	1. (a)	2. (b)	3. (a)	4. (c)	5. (d)	6. (a)
Poem 18.	1. (d)	2. (a)	3. (d)	4. (c)	5. (a)	6. (a)
Poem 19.	1. (a)	2. (c)	3. (b)	4. (c)	5. (a)	6. (d)
Poem 20.	1. (c)	2. (d)	3. (d)	4. (a)	5. (b)	6. (b)
Poem 21.	1. (b)	2. (a)	3. (d)	4. (b)	5. (c)	6. (a)
Poem 22.	1. (a)	2. (b)	3. (c)	4. (a)	5. (a)	6. (c)
Poem 23.	1. (a)	2. (d)	3. (c)	4. (a)	5. (b)	6. (a)
Poem 24.	1. (d)	2. (a)	3. (d)	4. (c)	5. (d)	6. (a)
Poem 25.	1. (d)	2. (a)	3. (b)	4. (a)	5. (c)	6. (d)
Poem 26.	1. (b)	2. (a)	3. (d)	4. (d)	5. (d)	6. (d)
Poem 27.	1. (a)	2. (c)	3. (d)	4. (a)	5. (b)	6. (d)
Poem 28.	1. (c)	2. (d)	3. (d)	4. (c)	5. (a)	6. (b)
Poem 29.	1. (c)	2. (b)	3. (d)	4. (d)	5. (a)	6. (c)
Poem 30.	1. (b)	2. (c)	3. (a)	4. (b)	5. (b)	6. (d)
Poem 31.	1. (b)	2. (b)	3. (c)	4. (d)	5. (d)	6. (c)
Poem 32.	1. (d)	2. (a)	3. (c)	4. (c)	5. (d)	6. (c)

Unit-03

01 Noun

किसी व्यक्ति (Person), वस्तु (Thing), स्थान (Place), गुण (Quality), कार्य (Action), या अवस्था (State) के नाम को Noun (संज्ञा) कहते हैं।

e.g., Rahul (Person), Pen (Thing), Delhi (Place), Punctual (Quality), Anxiety (State) and Discussion (Action).

Kinds of Noun There are five kinds of Noun

1. **Proper Noun** किसी particular person, place या thing के नाम को Proper Noun कहते हैं।
   e.g., Amit, Taj Mahal, Parker Pen etc.
   - I live in Alwar.
   - He is Shalabh.
2. **Common Noun** किसी person, place या things को particular ना बताकर बल्कि उसकी पूरी class को denote करने वाले words को Common Noun कहते हैं।
   e.g., woman, cow, village, roads, computers etc.
   - The nearest town is 80 km away from here.
   - All the gardens were invaded by beetles this summer.
3. **Collective Noun** एक ही प्रकार के persons, things or animals के group (समूह) को denote करने वाले words को Collective Noun कहते हैं।
   e.g., Bunch (group of flowers), Family (a group of persons living together), Class (a group of students)
   - The jury were different in their opinions.
   - A flock of sheep is grazing in the field.

   Following is the list of some Collective Nouns
   - A Barren of Mules (खच्चरों की बजंर)
   - An Army of Ants (चींटीयों का झुण्ड)
   - A Herd of Swine (सुअरों का झुण्ड)
   - A Stock of Wood (लकड़ियों का ढेर)
   - A Flock of Geese (कलहंस का झुण्ड)
   - A Shoal of fish (मछलियों का समूह)
   - A Heap of Rubbish (कूड़े-कचरे का ढेर)
   - A Team of Players (खिलाड़ियों का दल)
   - A Gang of Robbers (डाकुओं का समूह)
   - A Herd of Cattles (पशुओं का झुण्ड)
   - A Cloud of Locusts (टिड्डियों का दल)
   - A Cluster of Galaxy (आकाशगंगा का समूह)
   - A Cluster/Galaxy of Stars (तारों का झुण्ड)
   - A Cluster of Grapes (अंगूर का गुच्छा)
   - A Flock of Sheep/Goats (भेड़/बकरों का झुण्ड)
   - A Crew of Sailors (नाविकों का दल)
   - A Detachment of Soldiers (सैनिकों की टुकड़ी)
   - A Crowd of People (लोगों की भीड़)
   - A Group of Students (छात्रों का समूह)
   - An Assembly of Listeners (श्रोताओं की मण्डली)
   - A Swarm of Ants (चीटियों का समूह)
   - A Sheaf of Grains (अनाज का गट्ठर)
   - A Heap of Sand (बालू रेत का ढेर)
   - A Museum of Art (कला संग्राहलय)
   - A Clique of People (लोगों का समूह)
   - A Drove of Cattle (पशुओं का समुदाय)
   - A Clump of Trees (वृक्षों का समूह)
   - An Assembly of Worshippers (श्रद्धालुओं की मण्डली)
   - A Flight of Locusts (उड़ते हुए टिड्डियों का झुण्ड)
   - A Tissue of Lies/Crimes (झूठ/अपराधों का पुलिंदाआ)
   - A Course of Lectures (व्याख्यान/भाषण का क्रम)
   - A Peal of Bells (घण्टों की जोरदार आवाज का समूह)
   - A Fleet of Ships (जहाजों का बेड़ा)
   - A Covery of Patridges (तीतरों का झुण्ड)
   - A Brace of Pigeons (कबूतरों का जोड़ा)
   - A Council of Advisors (सलाहकारों की परिषद)
   - A Series of Events (घटनाओं का क्रम)
   - A Delegation of Students (छात्रों का शिष्टमण्डल)
   - A Choir of Singers (गायकों की मण्डली)
   - A Bouquet of Flowers (फूलों का गुच्छा)
   - A Bundle of Clothes (कपड़ों की लाट)
   - A Flock of Birds (चिड़ियों का झुण्ड)
   - A Troupe of Dancers (नृतकों की मण्डली)
   - A Library of Books (पुस्तकों का संग्राहलय)
   - A Tuft of Grass (घास का गुच्छा)
   - An Association of Labourers (मजदूरों का संघ)
   - A Packet of Cigarettes (सिगरेट का डिब्बा)
   - A Regiment of Soldiers (सैन्यदलों का समूह)
   - A Band of Nomads (घुमक्कड़ों का जत्था)
   - A Tribe of Natives (स्वदेशियों का वर्ग/जाति)

- A String of Onions (प्याज की पक्तियाँ)
- A Pack of Wolves/hounds (भेड़ियों या शिकारी कुत्तों का झुण्ड)
- A Chain of Mountains (पर्वतों की श्रेणी)
- A Volley of Arrows (बाणों की वर्षा)
- A Board of Directors (निदेशकों की मण्डली)

4. **Material Noun** ऐसे materials या substance जिनके द्वारा अन्य वस्तुएँ बनाई जा सके, उन्हें Material Noun कहते हैं।
e.g., wood, leather, gold, plastic, steel, sugar etc.
   - The necklace is made of gold.
   - He got his furniture made of teak wood.

5. **Abstract Noun** जो Noun quality, state या action को denote करते हैं, उन्हें Abstract Noun कहते हैं।
e.g., love, expectation, hatred, childhood, honesty etc.
   - We have to get at the truth of the matter.
   - Death is the last scene of a man on the stage of Earth.

Conversion of Common Noun to Abstract Noun

Common Noun	Abstract Noun	Common Noun	Abstract Noun
Brother	Brotherhood	Neighbour	Neighbourhood
Child	Childhood	Scholar	Scholarship
Friend	Friendship	Act	Action
King	Kingship	Bond	Bondage
Leader	Leadership	Patriot	Patriotism
Man	Manhood	Robber	Robbery
Member	Membership	Slave	Slavery
Mother	Motherhood	Regular	Regularity

Other Kinds of Nouns

There are also two other kinds of Noun

- **Countable Noun** जिन Nouns की counting की जा सकती है, उन्हें Countable Nouns कहते हैं। Countable nouns को singular form से plural form में बदला जा सकता है।
e.g., Book, Boy, Chair, Pen, Rupee etc.
- **Uncountable Noun** जिन Nouns की counting नहीं की जा सकती, उन्हें Uncountable Nouns कहते हैं। Uncountable Nouns को singular form से plural form में नहीं बदला जा सकता है।
e.g., Grass, Air, Water, Health, Patience etc.

Noun : Numbers

Grammar में Noun के दो Number होते हैं

- Singular Number
- Plural Number

(i) **Singular Number** जो Noun किसी एक person, place or thing को denote करते हैं, वो Singular Nouns होते हैं।
e.g., Boy, Girl, Table, City etc.

(ii) **Plural Number** जो Noun दो या दो से अधिक person, place or thing को denote करते हैं, वो Plural Nouns होते हैं।
e.g., Boys, Girls, Tables, Cities etc.

Following is the list of some singulars with their plurals

Singular	Plural	Singular	Plural
Bus	Buses	Class	Classes
Fox	Foxes	Church	Churches
Watch	Watches	Quiz	Quizzes
Switch	Switches	Tax	Taxes
Ass	Asses	Dish	Dishes
Canvas	Canvases	Box	Boxes
Fix	Fixes	Coach	Coaches
Kiss	Kisses	Glass	Glasses
Bush	Bushes	Match	Matches
Gas	Gases	Brush	Brushes
Bench	Benches	Branch	Branches
Hero	Heroes	Mango	Mangoes
Potato	Potatoes	Cargo	Cargoes
Mosquito	Mosquitoes	Echo	Echoes
Canto	Cantos	Piano	Pianos
Dynamo	Dynamos	Solo	Solos
Memento	Mementos	Photo	Photos
Ratio	Ratios	Quarto	Quartos
Motto	Mottoes	Volcano	Volcanoes
Torpedo	Torpedoes	Calico	Calicoes
Momento	Momentoes	Eskimo	Eskimoes
Commando	Commandos	Proviso	Provisos
Embryo	Embryos	Maestro	Maestros
Bee	Bees	Radio	Radios
Tree	Trees	Woe	Woes
Zoo	Zoos	Portfolio	Portfolios
Bamboo	Bamboos	Cuckoo	Cuckoos
Cameo	Cameos	Curio	Curios
Ratio	Ratios	Sterio	Sterios
Video	Videos	Scenario	Scenarios
Cry	Cries	City	Cities
Doll	Dolls	Bomb	Bombs
Country	Countries	Dictionary	Dictionaries
Family	Families	Lorry	Lorries
Pony	Ponies	Reply	Replies
Valley	Valleys	Pay	Pays
Journey	Journeys	Chimney	Chimneys

Singular	Plural	Singular	Plural
Day	Days	Storey	Storeys
Calf	Calves	Life	Lives
Half	Halves	Leaf	Leaves
Wife	Wives	Elf	Elves
Thief	Thieves	Knife	Knives
Wolf	Wolves	Shelf	Shelves
Belief	Beliefs	Proof	Proofs
Chief	Chiefs	Roof	Roofs
Cliff	Cliffs	Safe	Safes
Dwarf	Dwarfs	Scarf	Scarfs
Grief	Griefs	Strife	Strifes
Gulf	Gulfs	Turf	Turfs
Mischief	Mischiefs	Puff	Puffs
Reef	Reefs	Staff	Staffs
Brother-in-law	Brothers-in-law	Bed-room	Bed-rooms
Commander-in-chief	Commanders-in-chief	Step-daughter	Step-daughters
Maid-servant	Maid-servants	Pea-hen	Pea-hens
Peacock	Peacocks	Mother-in-law	Mothers-in-law
Sister-in-law	Sisters-in-law	Member of Parliament	Members of Parliament
**Man servant	Men servants	**Woman conductor	Women conductors
**Man nurse	Men nurses	**Woman engineer	Women engineers
*Man hater	Man haters	*Woman lover	Woman lovers
*Man lover	Man lovers		
Man	Men	Mouse	Mice
Woman	Women	Louse	Lice
Foot	Feet	Goose	Geese
Tooth	Teeth	Dormouse	Dormice
Child	Children	Cow	Kine
Ox	Oxen	Brother	Brothers
Looker on	Lookers-on	Hanger-on	Hangers-on
Knight-Errant	Knights-Errants	Spend-thrift	Spend-thrifts
Lord-Justice	Lords-Justices	Knight-Templar	Knights-Templars
Lord-Lieutenant	Lords-Lieutenants	Go-between	Go-betweens

Noun : Gender

There are four kinds of Gender in Noun,

(i) **Masculine Gender** ये nouns 'Male' representing होते हैं।
e.g., Man, Boy, Tiger, Husband, Father etc.

(ii) **Feminine Gender** ये nouns 'Female' representing होते हैं।
e.g., Woman, Girl, Tigress, Wife, Mother etc.

(iii) **Common Gender** ये nouns 'Male and Female' दोनों को represent करते हैं।
e.g., Child, Servant, Teacher, Cousin, Driver etc.

(iv) **Neuter Gender** ये nouns Non-living things or objects को represent करते हैं।
e.g., Bag, Pen, Car, Computer, Paper etc.

Following is the list of some words of masculine with their feminine

Masculine	Feminine
Author (लेखक)	Authoress (लेखिका)
Count (सामंत)	Countess (सामंत की पत्नी)
Host (मेजबान)	Hostess (महिला मेजबान)
Jew (यहूदी)	Jewess (यहूदिन)
Mayor (महापौर)	Mayoress (महिला महापौर)
Peer (सामंत)	Peeress (सामंत की पत्नी)
Poet (कवि)	Poetess (कवयित्री)
Prophet (पैगम्बर)	Prophetess (पैगम्बरी)
Tutor (अध्यापिका)	Tutoress (अध्यापिका)
Shepherd (गड़ेरिया)	Shepherdess (गड़ेरिन)
Baron (सामंत)	Baroness (सामंत की पत्नी)
Giant (राक्षस)	Giantess (राक्षसनी)
Heir (उत्तराधिकारी)	Heiress (उत्तराधिकारिणी)
Lion (शेर)	Lioness (शेरनी)
Manager (प्रबन्धक)	Manageress (प्रबन्धिका)
Patron (संरक्षक)	Patroness (संरक्षिका)
Priest (पुजारी)	Priestess (पुजारिन)
Tailor (दर्जी)	Tailoress (दर्जानि)
Steward (भण्डारी)	Stewardess (भण्डारिन)
Postmaster (डाकपाल)	Postmistress (महिला डाकपाल)
Abbot (मठाधिकारी)	Abbess (मठाधिकारीणी)
Emperor (सम्राट)	Empress (साम्राज्ञी)
Governor (राज्यपाल)	Governess (महिला राज्यपाल)
Duke (सामन्त)	Duchess (सामन्तनी)
God (देवता)	Goddess (देवी)
Master (स्वामी)	Mistress (स्वामिनी)
Sorcerer (जादूगर)	Sorceress (जादूगरनी)
Man-servant (नौकर)	Maid-servant (नौकरानी/दाई)
Washer-man (धोबी)	Washer-woman (धोबिन)
Bull-calf (बछड़ा)	Cow-calf (बछड़ी)
Cock-sparrow (नर गौरैया-चिड़िया)	Hen-sparrow (मादा गौरैया)
Jack-ass (गधा)	Jenny-ass (गधी)
Drone (नर मधुमक्खी)	Bee (मादा मधुमक्खी)
Ox (बैल)	Cow (गाय)
Brother-in-law (साला/बहनोई)	Sister-in-law (साली/जेठसर)
Son-in-law (दामाद)	Daughter-in-law (पुत्रवधू)

Masculine	Feminine
Step-son (सौतेला बेटा)	Step-daughter (सौतेली बेटी)
Step-father (सौतेला पिता)	Step-mother (सौतेली माँ)
Step-brother (सौतेला भाई)	Step-sister (सौतेली बहन)
Maternal-uncle (मामा)	Maternal-aunt (मामी)
Maternal-grand father (नाना)	Maternal-Grand mother (नानी)
Adopted-son (दत्तक पुत्र)	Adopted-daughter (दत्तक पुत्री)
Bullock (बाछा)	Heifer (बाछी)
Buck (नर हिरन/साम्भर/खरगोश)	Doe (मादा हिरन/साम्भर/खरगोश)
Hart (हिरन)	Roe (हिरनी)
Friar (महन्त, संयासी)	Nun (महन्तनी, संयासिन)
Swain (युवा पुरुष, गड़ेरिया, देहाती)	Nymph (युवती, गड़ेरिन देहातिन)
Ambassador (राजदूत)	Ambassadress (राजदूतिन, राजदूत की पत्नी)
Boar (सूअर)	Sow (सूअरी)
Dog (कुत्ता)	Bitch (कुतिया)
Monk (महंथ)	Nun (महंथनी)
Bridegroom (दुल्हा)	Bride (दुल्हन)
Widower (विधुर)	Widow (विधवा)
Lad (लड़का)	Lass (लड़की)
Lover (प्रेमी)	Beloved (प्रेमिका)
Wizard (जादूंगर)	Witch (जादूगरनी)
Mr (श्रीमान/महाशय)	Mrs (श्रीमती/महाशया)
School master (पाठशाला का अध्यापक)	School mistress (पाठशाला की अध्यापिका)
Beggar-man (भिखारी)	Beggar-woman (भिखारिन)
Great uncle (असामान्य चाचा)	Great-aunt (असामान्य चाची)
Mer man (दरियाई मर्द)	Mer maid (दरियाई औरत)
Prosecutor (मुद्दई/अभियोक्ता)	Prosecutrix (अभियोग चलानेवाली)
Viceroy (राज्यप्रतिनिधि (पुरुष)	Vicereine (राज्यप्रतिनिधि महिला)
He-buffalo (भैंसा)	She-buffalo (भैंस)
Dairy-man (दूध बेचनेवाला)	Dairy-maid (दूध बेचनेवाली)
Director (संचालक/निर्देशक)	Directress (संचालिका/निर्देशिका)
Votary (भक्त/उपासक)	Votaress (भक्तिन/उपासिका)
Boy friend (लड़का दोस्त)	Girl friend (लड़की दोस्त)
Stag (हिरन)	Hind (हिरनी)
Gander (नरहंस)	Goose (मादा हंस)
Earl (सामंत)	Countess (सामंत की पत्नी)
Drake (नर-बत्तख)	Duck (मादा-बत्तख)
Colt (घोड़े का बछड़ा)	Filly (घोड़े की बाछी)
Buck (नर-खरगोश)	Doe (मादा-खरगोश)
Viscount	Viscountess
Tiger (बाघ)	Tigress (बाघिन)

Masculine	Feminine
Emperor (सम्राट्)	Empress (साम्राज्ञी)
Benefactor (पुरुष दानदाता)	Benefactoress (महिला दानदाता)
Conductor (पथ-प्रदर्शक, बस या ट्राम का परिचालक)	Conductress (परिचालिका/संवाहिका)
Enchanter (जादूगर)	Enchantress (जादूगरनी)
Founder (संस्थापक)	Foundress (संस्थापिका)
Hunter (शिकारी)	Huntress (शिकारी की पत्नी)
Instructor (प्रशिक्षक)	Instructress (प्रशिक्षिका)
Negro (हब्शी)	Negress (हब्शिन)
Preceptor (उपदेशक)	Preceptress (उपदेशिका)
Songster (गायक)	Songstress (गायिका)
Seamster (दर्जी)	Seamstress (दर्जिन)
Nephew (भतीजा)	Niece (भतीजी)
Sir (महाशय)	Madam (महाशया)
Bachelor (कुँआरा लड़का)	Maid/Spinster (कुँआरी लड़की)
Bull (बैल)	Cow (गाय)
Cock (मुर्गा)	Hen (मुर्गी)
Traitor (देशद्रोही, धोखेबाज)	Traitoress (धोखेबाज औरत)
Waiter (होटल का सेवक)	Waitress (सेविका)
Marquis (सामन्त)	Marchioness (सामन्तनी)
Murderer (हत्यारा)	Murderess (हत्यारिन)
Hero (अभिनेता)	Heroine (अभिनेत्री)
Sultan (सुल्तान)	Sultana (सुल्ताना)
Administrator (प्रशासक)	Administratrix (प्रशासिका)
Executor (सम्पादनकर्त्ता)	Executrix (सम्पादन करने वाली)
Testator (बसीयत करनेवाला)	Testatrix (बसीयत करने वाली)
Czar (रूस का सम्राट)	Czarina (रूस की सम्राज्ञी)
Signor (महाशय-इटालियन भाषा में)	Signora (महाशया)
Milkman (ग्वाला)	Milk-maid (ग्वालिन)
Grand-father (दादा)	Grand-mother (दादी)
Land-lord (जमीदार)	Land-lady (जमीदारिन)
Pea-cock (मोर)	Pea-hen (मोरनी)
He-goat (बकरा)	She-goat (बकरी)
He-cat (बिलाव)	She-cat (बिल्ली)
He-bear (रीछ)	She-bear (रिंछनी)

Important Rules of Noun

Rule 1 कुछ Nouns का प्रयोग सिर्फ plural form में ही किया जाता है। इन Nouns के अन्त में लगे 's' को हटाकर, इन्हें singular नहीं बनाया जा सकता है। इनके साथ हमेशा plural verb ही use होती है। ऐसे Nouns निम्न हैं

Amends, ashes, athletics, species, scissors, trousers, pants, clippers, eyeglasses, goggles, belongings, breeches, braces, binoculars, customs, congratulations, earnings, fireworks, lodgings, odds, etc.

e.g., (i) Where are my trousers?

(ii) The proceeds were deposited in the court.

Rule 2 कुछ nouns जैसे news, politics, summons, physics, ethics, economics, ethics, mechanics, mathematics, mumps, rickets, billiards, draughts etc. दिखने में plural लगते हैं, लेकिन इनका प्रयोग हमेशा singular में ही किया जाता है।

e.g., (i) Economics is a good subject.

(ii) Ethics demands honesty in working.

Rule 3 कुछ nouns दिखने में singular लगते हैं, लेकिन इनका प्रयोग हमेशा plural from में किया जाता है। इनके साथ भी 's' नहीं लगाया जाता, क्योंकि ये noun स्वयं में ही plural हैं। ऐसे nouns निम्न हैं

Public, police, people, gentry, vermin, folk, poultry, peasantry, cattle, infantry, children, electorate, nobility, data, criteria, bacteria etc.

e.g., (i) Our infantry have marched forward.

(ii) Cattle are fastened with a rope.

Rule 4 कुछ Nouns का प्रयोग, केवल singular form में ही किया जाता है। इनके साथ helping verb भी singular होती है। ये Uncountable nouns होते हैं और इनके साथ article 'a/an' का प्रयोग भी नहीं किया जाता है। ऐसे Nouns निम्न हैं

e.g., Homage, luggage, baggage, lineage, percentage, postage, stationery, bakery, crockery, jewellery, information, anger, money, honesty, magic, fuel, gratitude, music, travel, hair, work etc.

e.g., (i) Your luggage is too heavy to lift up.

(ii) I have no information about her residere.

Note ऊपर दिए गए Nouns के साथ कुछ अन्य words जोड़कर इनका प्रयोग plural form में भी किया जाता है।

e.g., (i) He gave me a piece of Information.

(ii) Items of this stationery are of bad quality.

Rule 5 कुछ nouns का प्रयोग singular एवं plural दोनों forms में एक समान किया जाता है। ऐसे nouns निम्न हैं

Innings, jury, carp, deer, sheep, swine, issues, offspring, corps, means, series, team, counsel, species, crops etc.

e.g., (i) Our team is the best.

Our team are wearing their new uniform.

(ii) There are four innings in the match.

The first innings of this match has been finished.

Rule 6 कुछ Nouns ऐसे होते हैं यदि इनके पहले किसी definite numeral adjective (one, two, three, etc.) का प्रयोग किया जाता है, तो इन Nouns को pluralise नहीं किया जाता है। ऐसे Nouns निम्न हैं

Score, gross, pair, hundred, thousand, dozen, million, billion etc.

e.g., (i) I have four pair of shoes.

(ii) They bought five dozen bananas.

Rule 7 यदि किसी noun के बाद preposition आता है एवं फिर वही noun आता है, तो वह noun singular रहता है।

e.g., (i) Town after town was devastated.

(ii) He enquired from door to door.

Rule 8 Common gender nouns (Teacher, Student, Child, Clerk, Advocate, Worker, Writer, Author, Leader Musician etc.) का प्रयोग जब singular में किया जाता है, तो third person, singular pronoun का एवं masculine gender (he/his/him) का use सामान्य रूप से किया जाता है।

e.g., (i) Every candidate should write his/her name.

(ii) Every person should perform his duty.

Rule 9 Apostrophe का use possessive case के लिए निम्न स्थिति में करना ही उचित है। जैसे

(i) Living things

(a) Mohan's book (b) a cow's horn

(ii) Thing personified as

(a) week's holiday (b) earth's surface

(iii) Space time or weight as

(a) a day's leave (b) well's water

(iv) Certain dignified objects as

(a) the court's orders

(b) at duty's call

(c) a razor's edge

(d) a needle's point

(v) Familiar phrases as

(a) at his wit's end

(b) at a stone's throw

अन्य cases में apostrophe को avoid करना उचित होगा।

Rule 10 यदि किसी plural word का last alphabet 's' है, तो apostrophe का use करते समय 's' नहीं लगाते हैं, केवल (') apostrophe का ही प्रयोग करते हैं। जैसे

(i) Horses' tail.

(ii) Boys' college.

(iii) Girls' school.

(iv) Working girls' hostel.

Words with hissing sound of s में भी 's' नहीं लगता है।

for peace' sake, for conscience' sake, for goodness' sake, for Jesus' sake

Rule 11 कुछ words his, hers, yours, mine, ours, its, theirs के साथ apostrophe नहीं लगाते हैं, जैसे–Yours faithfully, Yours truly, Ours garden , his pen, hers purse, theirs room.

Rule 12 निम्न titles के साथ apostrophe अन्तिम शब्द के साथ ही लगाते हैं। जैसे

(i) Governor-general's instructions.
(ii) Commander-in-chief's orders.
(iii) My son-in-law's sister.
(iv) Ram and Sons's shop.

Rule 13 Do not use 'Double apostrophe': We should try to avoid double apostrophe in a sentence:

(i) My wife's secretary's mother has expired. *(Incorrect)*
The mother of my wife's secretary has expired. *(Correct)*
(ii) Mrs. Kuwrani's now chairperson of society's proposal was rejected. *(Incorrect)*
The proposal of Mrs. Kuwrani, now chairperson of society was rejected. *(Correct)*

Rule 14 Anybody/Nobody/Everybody/ Somebody/ Anyone/Someone/No one/Everyone के साथ apostrophe 's' का प्रयोग किया जाता है। जैसे

(i) Everyone's concern is no one's concern.
(ii) Everybody's business is nobody's business.

Exercise 1

Directions (Q. Nos. 1-10) Identify the Proper Noun among the following.

1. (a) Cleopatra (b) Anger (c) Year (d) Class

2. (a) San Francisco (b) People (c) Violence (d) Herd

3. (a) Jury (b) Wilson (c) Way (d) Culture

4. (a) Calm (b) Council (c)) Israel (d) Day

5. (a) Paris (b) Woman (c) Generosity (d) Crowd

6. (a) Life (b) London (c) Loyalty (d) Gang

7. (a) Child (b) Patience (c) Mob (d) New York

8. (a) England (b) Work (c) Warmth (d) Crew

9. (a) Mars (b) School (c) Wisdom (d) Pile

10. (a) Wit (b) Child (c) Micrsoft (d) Bunch

Directions (Q. Nos. 11-20) In each question, four nouns are given. Identify the Common Noun among them.

11. (a) Water (b) Air (c) Mug (d) All of these

12. (a) Shylock (b) Farmer (c) Banker (d) Both (b) and (c)

13. (a) Antonio (b) Honesty (c) Anger (d) Nomad

14. (a) France (b) Africa (c) Lawyer (d) Both (a) and (c)

15. (a) Tourist (b) Monastery (c) Kennel (d) All of these

16. (a) Architect (b) Sword (c) Christian (d) Both (a) and (b)

17. (a) Wisdom (b) New York (c) River (d) Both (a) and (c)

18. (a) Jew (b) Car (c) Market (d) Both (b) and (c)

19. (a) Heart (b) Fruits (c) Story (d) All of these

20. (a) Mary (b) Leopard (c) Worry (d) All of these

Directions (Q. Nos. 21-30) Choose the correct Abstract Noun from the following options.

21. (a) Determination (b) Distracted (c) Mysterious (d) Reliably

22. (a) Beneficial (b) Significantly (c) Magnificent (d) Disbelief

23. (a) Differentiate (b) Justifiable (c) Fascination (d) Aimless

24. (a) Zealous (b) Sophistication (c) Strengthen (d) Obnoxious

25. (a) Brilliance (b) Thoughtless (c) Materialistic (d) Embarrassed

26. (a) Luxury (b) Duchess (c) Stone (d) Heifer

27. (a) Charity (b) Hosepipe (c) Shiver (d) Fireman

28. (a) Liberty (b) Cathedral (c) Island (d) Continent

29. (a) Youth (b) Oak (c) Vase (d) Hourglass

30. (a) Thrill (b) Packet (c) Garden (d) Angel

Directions (Q. Nos. 31-33) Identify the Countable Noun among the following.

31. (a) News (b) Rice (c) Homework (d) Essay

32. (a) Progress (b) Help (c) Job (d) Advice

33. (a) Peace (b) Luggage (c) Suitcase (d) Research

Directions (Q. Nos. 34-36) Identify the Uncountable Noun among the following.

34. (a) Language (b) Building (c) Festival (d) Presence

35. (a) Thirst (b) Question (c) Monument (d) Flower

36. (a) Toy (b) Story (c) Day (d) Grief

Directions (Q. Nos. 37-51) Choose the correct Collective Noun for the given blanks.

37. A/An .... of alligators
(a) congregation (b) herd (c) army (d) bike

38. A .... of antelope
(a) flock (b) troupe (c) roll (d) tribe

39. A ...... of doves
(a) herd (b) group (c) team (d) dole

40. A ...... of chickens
(a) cast (b) brood
(c) flight (d) pride

41. A ...... of monkeys
(a) troop (b) nest
(c) litter (d) cluster

42. A .... of locusts.
(a) litter (b) herd
(c) swarm (d) colony

43. A ...... of hornets
(a) nest (b) horde
(c) cloud (d) swarm

44. A/An ...... of stars
(a) galaxy (b) system
(c) album (d) fleet

45. A .... of judges.
(a) mob (b) band
(c) pack (d) bench

46. A ...... of sparrows
(a) haul (b) host
(c) shoal (d) murder

47. A ...... of puppies
(a) team (b) litter
(c) burrow (d) pack

48. A ...... of natives
(a) board (b) panel
(c) tribe (d) crowd

49. A .... of musicians
(a) bunch (b) gang
(c) band (d) mafia

50. A .... of dancers
(a) crowd (b) pack
(c) troupe (d) panel

51. A .... of ships
(a) crew (b) fleet (c) tribe (d) shoal

Directions (Q. Nos. 52-61) Choose the correct Abstract Noun for the given words.

52. Agent : ....
(a) agency (b) agenda
(c) agents (d) agentment

53. Act : ....
(a) acting (b) actor
(c) actress (d) action

54. Child : ....
(a) parent (b) childhood
(c) playfulness (d) kids

55. Friend : ....
(a) friends (b) group
(c) friendship (d) school

56. Able : ....
(a) disable (b) ability
(c) unable (d) enable

57. Safe : ....
(a) danger (b) secure
(c) unsafe (d) safety

58. Strong : ....
(a) weakness (b) strength
(c) powerful (d) brave

59. Poor : ....
(a) beggar (b) rich
(c) poverty (d) hunger

60. Obey : ....
(a) obedience (b) disobey
(c) obeying (d) obeyed

61. Fly : ....
(a) flying (b) flight
(c) flown (d) flew

Directions (Q. Nos. 62-71) In each of the following questions, four words are given. Identify the words which are not Nouns.

62. (a) Slate (b) Won
(c) Boy (d) Toys

63. (a) Wept (b) Whip
(c) News (d) Mr. Smith

64. (a) Coach (b) Blackboard
(c) Fond (d) Sky

65. (a) Mangoes (b) Grate
(c) Temple (d) Son

66. (a) Serena (b) Till
(c) Fleet (d) Both (b) and (c)

67. (a) Went (b) Earth
(c) Rosy (d) All of these

68. (a) University (b) James
(c) Gems (d) Refer

69. (a) Pole (b) Kit
(c) Yolk (d) Nibble

70. (a) Moon (b) Give
(c) Light (d) Sky

71. (a) Quran (b) Horse
(c) Envious (d) Hudson

Directions (Q. Nos. 72-81) Identify the type of Noun in each of the following questions.

72. Crowd
(a) Common noun
(b) Proper noun
(c) Collective noun
(d) Abstract noun

73. Goodness
(a) Collective noun
(b) Abstract noun
(c) Proper noun
(d) Common noun

74. Slavery
(a) Collective noun
(b) Proper noun
(c) Abstract noun
(d) Common noun

75. Honesty
(a) Abstract noun
(b) Collective noun
(c) Countable noun
(d) Uncountable noun

76. Sister
(a) Proper noun
(b) Collective noun
(c) Countable noun
(d) Uncountable noun

77. Mug
(a) Common noun
(b) Proper noun
(c) Collective noun
(d) Abstract noun

78. Germany
(a) Common noun
(b) Proper noun
(c) Collective noun
(d) Abstract noun

79. Dentist
(a) Common noun
(b) Proper noun
(c) Collective noun
(d) Abstract noun

80. Loyalty
(a) Common noun
(b) Proper noun
(c) Collective noun
(d) Abstract noun

81. Envy
(a) Common noun (b) Proper noun
(c) Collective noun (d) Abstract noun

Directions (Q. Nos. 82-96) Identify the type of underlined noun in the following sentences. Choose the correct option.

82. Always speak the <u>truth</u>.
(a) Proper (b) Common
(c) Collective (d) Abstract

83. Solomon was the wisest of all kings.
(a) Proper (b) Common
(c) Collective (d) Abstract

84. Cleanliness is next to godliness.
(a) Proper (b) Common
(c) Collective (d) Abstract

85. The Nile is the longest of all rivers.
(a) Proper (b) Common
(c) Collective (d) Abstract

86. Jawaharlal Nehru was the first Prime Minister of India.
(a) Proper (b) Common
(c) Collective (d) Abstract

87. Birds of a feather flock together.
(a) Proper (b) Common
(c) Collective (d) Abstract

88. Silver and gold are precious metals.
(a) Proper (b) Common
(c) Collective (d) Abstract

89. Man pollutes the environment.
(a) Proper (b) Common
(c) Collective (d) Abstract

90. The audience began clapping and cheering.
(a) Proper (b) Common
(c) Collective (d) Abstract

91. Edison invented the phonograph.
(a) Proper (b) Common
(c) Collective (d) Abstract

92. The society is not affiliated with any political party.
(a) Abstract (b) Common
(c) Proper (d) Collective

93. The friends promised to stay together in sickness and death.
(a) Both Common
(b) Both Collective
(c) Both Abstract
(d) Both Proper

94. Dresses are made of cotton, wool and silk.
(a) All Collective
(b) All Common
(c) All Abstract
(d) All Material

95. The school committee has selected him as the secretary by unanimous vote.
(a) Proper (b) Common
(c) Abstract (d) Collective

96. Work is worship.
(a) Common (b) Abstract
(c) Collective (d) Material

Directions (Q. Nos. 97-111) Identify the noun in the given sentence with the help of given alternatives.

97. Many of these people have been ignored.
(a) Many (b) These
(c) People (d) Ignored

98. Most of the calls to this company are placed on lengthy holds.
(a) Most (b) Placed
(c) Lengthy (d) Holds

99. Rosemary, come and meet our new dog!
(a) Come (b) Meet (c) Our (d) Dog

100. Keeping warm in the winter is both more difficult and more important for elderly persons.
(a) Keeping (b) Difficult
(c) Persons (d) Elderly

101. Tom and Dave were in the same platoon during the Gulf War.
(a) War (b) And
(c) Were (d) During

102. It will take all of your energy but you will be able to walk again.
(a) Take (b) All
(c) Your (d) Energy

103. The works of many great poets have been placed on reserve.
(a) Many (b) Great
(c) Placed (d) Reserve

104. The Brooklyn Bridge was opened in 1883.
(a) Bridge (b) Was
(c) Opened (d) In

105. Sparta and Athens were enemies during the Peloponnesian War.
(a) And (b) Were
(c) During (d) War

106. Sharks and lampreys are not true fish because their skeletons are made of cartilage rather than bone.
(a) True (b) Because
(c) Their (d) Bone

107. John, have you met your new boss?
(a) Have (b) Met
(c) Your (d) Boss

108. Her parents tried living in North India, but they could not adapt to the cold.
(a) Cold (b) But
(c) Not (d) Adapt

109. Mastering basic mathematics is an important goal for younger students.
(a) Mastering (b) Important
(c) Younger (d) Students

110. To seize a foreign embassy and its inhabitants is flagrant disregard for diplomatic neutrality.
(a) Seize (b) Its
(c) Flagrant (d) Neutrality

111. The Trojans' rash decision to accept the wooden horse led to their destruction.
(a) Their (b) Led
(c) Accept (d) Destruction

Directions (Q. Nos. 112-140) In the following questions, fill the given blanks with appropriate noun.

112. There were five .... at the office.
(a) man (b) men
(c) boy (d) servant

113. A .... of robbers surrounded us.
(a) army (b) band
(c) gang (d) mob

114. The chair was made of ....
(a) water (b) wood
(c) milk (d) oil

115. While coming back home, I saw a crowd of ....
(a) soldiers (b) merchants
(c) singers (d) people

116. The children were tired after climbing up a .... of stairs.
(a) galaxy (b) fleet
(c) flight (d) library

117. Marina dropped the .... of rice before it reached the table.
(a) stack (b) piece
(c) basket (d) bowl

118. The children were happy to look after the .... of puppies they found in the park.
(a) litter (b) hive
(c) flock (d) catch

119. The thieves hid the loot in a .... of hay.
(a) bunch (b) stack
(c) bowl (d) group

120. A .... of ships sailed towards the harbor.
(a) string (b) flight
(c) fleet (d) herd

121. The chain of my .... became loose, due to which I had to stop pedaling and put it back again.
(a) bicycle (b) shirt
(c) book (d) home

122. We need .... to help us when we run into problems.
(a) birds (b) animals
(c) friends (d) cars

123. Jamshed left his .... to find work in the nearby town.
(a) chimney (b) village
(c) certificate (d) toys

124. I added new books to my ....
(a) room (b) home
(c) school (d) library

125. Our .... fought with great courage during the Kargil War.
(a) men
(b) soldiers
(c) politicians
(d) students

126. Farmers keep a .... of buffaloes.
(a) bees (b) band
(c) herd (d) bevy

127. A large .... is expected.
(a) crowd (b) crowds
(c) holiday (d) children

128. Forest shows you a clump of ....
(a) fruits
(b) vegetables
(c) animals
(d) trees

129. I have just filled forty .... of petrol in the car.
(a) kilos (b) litres
(c) boxes (d) metres

130. The .... was attended by guests from both the bride's and the groom's families.
(a) school (b) wedding
(c) picnic (d) village

131. I would like to have a .... of coffee, please.
(a) cup (b) plate
(c) piece (d) sip

132. A .... of oxen helped the farmers till the field.
(a) drove (b) horde
(c) brood (d) army

133. We enjoyed seeing the .... of ducks flying.
(a) herd (b) flock
(c) string (d) charm

134. The crop was attacked by a/an .... of caterpillars.
(a) army (b) horde
(c) litter (d) herd

135. The leaping .... of dolphins was fun to watch.
(a) army (b) school
(c) colony (d) nest

136. The carrots in the field were all eaten up by a .... of mice.
(a) army (b) horde
(c) parliament (d) mischief

137. I do not travel with much ....
(a) furniture (b) food
(c) luggage (d) work

138. .... is on the banks of river Hooghly .
(a) Bihar
(b) Kolkata
(c) Delhi
(d) None of the above

139. The .... has still not taken our order.
(a) porter (b) manager
(c) shopkeeper (d) waiter

140. Life of a/an .... is luxurious.
(a) farmer
(b) shopkeeper
(c) engineer
(d) king

Exercise 2

Directions (Q. Nos. 1-30) Choose the correct alternative for the following questions.

1. We met at McDonalds at noon. The word 'McDonalds' is a .... noun.
(a) Common (b) Collective
(c) Abstract (d) Proper

2. Identify the proper noun in the given sentence.
He could not remember who signed the Declaration of Independence.
(a) Remember
(b) Signed
(c) Declaration of Independence
(d) He

3. I study in Springdales School. Here, 'Springdales School' is a ....
(a) Proper noun
(b) Material noun
(c) Common noun
(d) Collective noun

4. Fill in the blank with the correct collective noun.
The .... were on the march for several days.
(a) officers (b) armies
(c) soldiers (d) cadets

5. The plural form of 'focus' is
(a) focus (b) focuss
(c) foci (d) focusies

6. My family lives in different parts of India.
Here, 'family' is ....
(a) Collective noun
(b) Abstract noun
(c) Common noun
(d) Proper noun

7. Identify all the common nouns in the given sentence.
Rohan took his bike to the hills for a ride.
(a) Rohan, bike, his
(b) His, bike, hills
(c) Bike, hills, ride
(d) Rohan, hills, ride

8. Masons build houses.
Here, 'masons' is a ....
(a) Collective noun
(b) Abstract noun
(c) Common noun
(d) Proper noun

9. Identify the material noun in the given sentence.
Lomani Paris is my favourite perfume.
(a) Lomani Paris (b) favourite
(c) my (d) perfume

10. Fill in the blank with the correct material noun.
.... dresses are very cheap and comfortable.
(a) Cotton (b) Silk
(c) Paper (d) Rubber

11. What is the plural of 'Father-in-law'?
(a) Father-in-laws
(b) Fathers-in-law
(c) Fathers-ins-laws
(d) Father-ins-law

12. Select the noun which remains unchanged in its plural form.
(a) Bottle (b) Deer
(c) Tiger (d) Shirt

13. Select the abstract noun in the given sentence.
It's a pleasure to meet you after five years.
(a) you (b) meet
(c) five years (d) pleasure

14. What is the feminine gender of 'gander'?
(a) goose (b) horse
(c) bull (d) sheep

15. Childhood is the best part of life.
Here, 'childhood' is ....
(a) Collective noun
(b) Common noun
(c) Proper noun
(d) Abstract noun

16. A crew of ....
(a) soldiers (b) keys
(c) sailors (d) flowers

17. A herd of ......
(a) stars (b) cattle
(c) people (d) sticks

18. A ...... of sheep
(a) gang (b) army
(c) bench (d) flock

19. A ...... of sticks
(a) crew (b) bundle
(c) bunch (d) team

20. A board of ....
(a) people (b) directors
(c) judges (d) stars

21. 'Thieves' is for 'Thief', 'Mice' is for ....
(a) Moose (b) Mouse
(c) Mise (d) Mices

22. 'Queen' is for ...., 'king' is for 'Gentleman'.
(a) Woman (b) Girl
(c) Princess (d) Lady

23. 'Boxes' is for 'Box', ... is for 'Ox'.
(a) Oxen (b) Oxes
(c) Cows (d) Horse

24. 'Army' is for 'Soldiers', 'Gang' is for ....
(a) People
(b) Leaders
(c) Robbers
(d) Merchants

25. 'Mistress' is for 'Master', 'Nun' is for ....
(a) Man (b) Poet
(c) Lad (d) Monk

26. The plural of 'sheep' is
(a) sheeps (b) sheepes
(c) sheep (d) shap

27. The plural of 'step daughter' is ....
(a) steps daughter
(b) step daughters
(c) steps daughters
(d) step daughter

28. The plural form of 'curriculum' is
(a) curriculums
(b) curriculi
(c) curricula
(d) Both (a) and (c)

29. The feminine gender of 'milkman' is ....
(a) milkwoman (b) milklady
(c) milkgirl (d) milkmaid

30. The feminine gender of 'headmaster' is ....
(a) head man (b) head maid
(c) head mistress (d) head lady

Directions (Q. Nos. 31-105) Identify the part of the sentence that has an error.

31. There was (a)/a bunch of parrots (b)/ roosting on the Mango tree. (c)/ No error (d)

32. The jewelleries (a)/ displayed in the showroom (b)/ was stunning. (c)/ No error (d)

33. No news (a)/ is (b)/ good news. (c)/ No error (d)

34. My spectacle (a)/ are lying (b)/on the table. (c)/No error (d)

35. Inspite of the doctor's stern warning, (a)/Latika continued taking (b)/sugars in her milk. (c)/ No error (d)

36. Professor Amartya Sen (a)/ is an alumunus of (b)/ Presidency College, Kolkata. (c)/ No error (d)

37. My two daughter-in-laws (a)/ work at (b)/ the government hospital in the city. (c)/ No error (d)

38. It is very difficult (a)/to chase a huge (b)/score in the second inning. (c)/ No error (d)

39. Wordsworth wrote (a)/ poetries on (b)/ romantic themes. (c)/ No error (d)

40. Israel has made (a)/ a large investment in research (b)/ which has resulted in much progresses on the technical front. (c)/ No error (d)

41. They bought (a)/ a pen, an inkpot, a pencil (b)/and a soap from a store. (c)/ No error (d)

42. The table's wood (a)/is infested with milk (b)/and I am likely to dispose it off. (c)/ No error (d)

43. He says that he (a)/has given you (b)/twenty-rupees note. (c)/ No error (d)

44. All the boys students are (a)/advised to attend (b)/the meeting positively. (c)/ No error (d)

45. You shall get (a)/all the informations (b)/if you read this book carefully. (c)/ No error (d)

46. The same board is (a) / used for chess as (b) / well as for draughts. (c) / No error (d)

47. The company (a)/ has ordered (b)/ some new equipments. (c)/ No error (d)

48. I feel (a)/ that the circumstances (b)/ here is quite bad. (c)/ No error (d)

49. He acted not as (a)/ per my advice (b)/ but somebody else. (c)/ No error (d)

50. The shopkeeper said that the (a)/ fault was the (b)/ manufactures responsibility. (c)/ No error (d)

51. Unfortunately, (a)/ hunters kill many (b)/ deers every year. (c)/ No error (d)

52. Two summons have been issued by the court (a)/ but Sohan has not (b)/ yet appeared before the count. (c)/ No error (d)

53. Sneha has (a)/ read pages after pages (b)/ of Gita. (c)/ No error (d).

54. All the evidences were (a)/against him and he was (b)/held guilty. (c)/ No error (d)

55. The shepherd had (a)/ a flock of sheeps, (b)/ whom he used for wool. (c)/ No error (d)

56. He likes (a)/ the sceneries (b)/ of the hills. (c)/ No error (d)

57. All the girls students are (a)/ advised to attend (b)/ the meeting positively. (c)/ No error (d)

58. You know it well that your success (a)/ in life depends not on my (b)/ advice but on him. (c) / No error (d)

59. I went to the house and (a)/ found that the (b)/ car's wheel was broken. (c)/ No error (d)

60. She wanted me to (a)/ bring two breads and (b)/ some butter for breakfast. (c)/ No error (d)

61. The English teacher gave (a)/ him a home work to complete (b)/ by that night positively. (c)/ No error (d)

62. I just saw the group of (a)/ mouse on the upper floor of the (b)/ university and ran away in fear. (c)/ No error (d)

63. Pakistan's problems (a)/are also as (b)/serious as (c)/ India. (d)

64. The mother-in-laws (a)/ gathered together (b)/ to discuss certain family issues. (c)/ No error (d)

65. Many of the question (a)/ in this question paper (b)/are too difficult (c)/to solve. (d)

66. I visited (a)/Ram's and Sita's house (b)/and found the couple missing. (c)/ No error (d)

67. My friends bat (a)/was broken during (b)/ last week's cricket game. (c)/ No error (d)

68. She gave me (a)/two important informations (b)/I had been waiting for (c)/the last two months. (d)

69. Beautiful lies in (a)/ eyes of (b)/ the beholder. (c)/ No error (d)

70. She could not complete (a)/even the two-third (b)/of the book (c)/owing to her busy schedule. (d)

71. All the woman teachers (a)/are annoyed (b)/ with the haughty attitude (c)/of the Principal. (d)

72. He informed that (a)/he had lost a packet (b)/of the hundred (c)/rupees notes. (d)

73. He has ordered (a)/bricks for the proposed (b)/shopping complex. (c)/No error (d)

74. She has ordered (a)/two dozens of copies (b)/of English Book by Mr. Gupta. (c)/No eeror (d)

75. She uses a good (a)/quality of shampoo (b)/so her hairs are (c)/black. (d)

76. I know nothing (a)/about her (b)/ whereabout. (c)/No error (d)

77. Order has been issued (a)/ for his transfer to another district (b)/ but he has not received them so far. (c)/ No error (d)

78. Although she has studied (a)/ English for almost a year (b)/ she is yet to learn the alphabets. (c)/ No error (d)

79. There are two scores of books (a)/ which are lying (b)/ unused in the library. (c)/ No error (d)

80. Children are prone (a)/ to making mischiefs (b)/ if they have nothing to do. (c)/ No error (d)

81. Sheeps are economically useful (a)/ and so they are reared (b)/ in the hills. (c)/ No error (d)

82. I have not gone through (a)/ the letter and so I am not aware (b)/ of its content. (c)/ No error (d)

83. I shall not attend the meeting (a)/ since I have many works to complete (b)/ within allotted time. (c)/ No error (d)

84. You should always be (a)/ true to your words (b)/ if you are to succeed in life. (c)/ No error (d)

85. It is a pity (a)/ that even five years old boys (b)/ are engaged in hazardous factories. (c)/ No error (d)

86. I gave him (a)/ two hundred rupees notes (b)/ for depositing. (c)/ No error (d)

87. It is not my business (a)/ to give an advice to those (b)/who are not sensible enough to deal with their own problems. (c)/ No error (d)

88. Women athletes have (a)/ performed far better (b)/ than man athletes. (c)/ No error (d)

89. She misplaced her spectacle (a)/ and is now feeling (b)/ great difficulty in studying. (c)/ No error (d)

90. Arabian Nights are (a)/ a collection of (b)/ very interesting episodes of adventure. (c)/ No error (d)

91. I hope to visit (a)/ my uncle only next year (b)/ during summer vacations. (c)/ No error (d)

92. Ration has run out (a)/ and the District Magistrate (b)/ has been informed. (c)/ No error (d)

93. The table's wood (a)/ is infested with mite (b)/ and I am likely to dispose it off. (c)/ No error (d)

94. I can't come to you now (a)/ because a lot of works (b)/ remains to be done. (c)/ No error (d)

95. A farmer was leading oxes (a)/ to his field for ploughing (b)/ early in the morning. (c)/ No error (d)

96. My sister-in-laws (a)/who live in Mumbai (b)/ have come to stay with us. (c)/ No error (d)

97. This article (a)/ is not available (b)/ in any of the shop in the market. (c)/No error (d)

98. The morale of the army (a)/ was high because the news (b)/ coming from the front are very encouraging. (c)/ No error (d)

99. A flock of lions (a)/ roamed about (b)/ fearlessly in the jungle. (c)/ No error (d)

100. I have done my best; (a)/ the whole thing is now (b)/ in the laps of God. (c)/ No error (d)

101. A trained gang of sailors (a)/ was employed (b)/ on the ship. (c)/ No error (d)

102. Interviews for (a)/ the posts of lecturers (b)/ will begin from Monday. (c)/ No error (d)

103. What (a)/ is the criteria (b)/ of selection in the examination? (c)/ No error (d)

104. The company (a)/ has ordered (b)/ some new equipments. (c)/ No error (d)

105. One of the most (a)/ widespread bad habit (b)/ is the use of tobacco. (c)/ No error (d)

ANSWERS

Exercise 1

1	(a)	2	(a)	3	(b)	4	(c)	5	(a)	6	(b)	7	(d)	8	(a)	9	(a)	10	(c)
11	(d)	12	(d)	13	(d)	14	(c)	15	(d)	16	(d)	17	(c)	18	(d)	19	(d)	20	(b)
21	(a)	22	(d)	23	(c)	24	(b)	25	(a)	26	(a)	27	(a)	28	(a)	29	(a)	30	(a)
31	(d)	32	(c)	33	(c)	34	(d)	35	(a)	36	(d)	37	(a)	38	(d)	39	(d)	40	(b)
41	(a)	42	(c)	43	(a)	44	(a)	45	(d)	46	(b)	47	(b)	48	(c)	49	(c)	50	(c)
51	(b)	52	(a)	53	(d)	54	(b)	55	(c)	56	(b)	57	(d)	58	(b)	59	(c)	60	(a)
61	(b)	62	(b)	63	(a)	64	(c)	65	(b)	66	(b)	67	(a)	68	(d)	69	(d)	70	(b)
71	(c)	72	(c)	73	(b)	74	(c)	75	(a)	76	(c)	77	(a)	78	(b)	79	(a)	80	(d)
81	(d)	82	(d)	83	(a)	84	(d)	85	(b)	86	(a)	87	(b)	88	(b)	89	(b)	90	(c)
91	(a)	92	(d)	93	(c)	94	(d)	95	(d)	96	(a)	97	(c)	98	(d)	99	(d)	100	(c)
101	(a)	102	(d)	103	(d)	104	(a)	105	(d)	106	(d)	107	(d)	108	(a)	109	(d)	110	(d)
111	(d)	112	(b)	113	(c)	114	(b)	115	(d)	116	(c)	117	(d)	118	(a)	119	(b)	120	(c)
121	(a)	122	(c)	123	(b)	124	(d)	125	(b)	126	(c)	127	(a)	128	(d)	129	(b)	130	(b)
131	(a)	132	(a)	133	(c)	134	(a)	135	(b)	136	(d)	137	(c)	138	(b)	139	(d)	140	(d)

Exercise 2

1 (d)	2 (c)	3 (a)	4 (b)	5 (c)	6 (a)	7 (c)	8 (c)	9 (d)	10 (a)
11 (b)	12 (b)	13 (d)	14 (a)	15 (d)	16 (c)	17 (b)	18 (d)	19 (b)	20 (b)
21 (b)	22 (d)	23 (a)	24 (c)	25 (d)	26 (c)	27 (b)	28 (c)	29 (d)	30 (c)
31 (b)	32 (a)	33 (d)	34 (a)	35 (c)	36 (d)	37 (a)	38 (c)	39 (b)	40 (c)
41 (c)	42 (a)	43 (c)	44 (a)	45 (b)	46 (d)	47 (c)	48 (c)	49 (c)	50 (c)
51 (c)	52 (a)	53 (b)	54 (a)	55 (b)	56 (b)	57 (a)	58 (c)	59 (c)	60 (b)
61 (d)	62 (b)	63 (d)	64 (a)	65 (a)	66 (b)	67 (a)	68 (b)	69 (a)	70 (b)
71 (a)	72 (d)	73 (b)	74 (b)	75 (c)	76 (c)	77 (a)	78 (c)	79 (a)	80 (b)
81 (a)	82 (c)	83 (b)	84 (b)	85 (b)	86 (b)	87 (b)	88 (c)	89 (a)	90 (a)
91 (c)	92 (a)	93 (a)	94 (b)	95 (a)	96 (a)	97 (c)	98 (c)	99 (a)	100 (c)
101 (a)	102 (b)	103 (b)	104 (c)	105 (b)					

Explanations

Exercise 2

31. *(b)* 'Bunch' is not the correct collective noun for parrots. It should be replaced by 'pandemonium'.

32. *(a)* There is no plural form of 'jewellery'. Hence, 'jewellery' should be used.

33. *(d)* The given sentence has 'no error'.

34. *(a)* 'Spectacle' should be replaced by 'spectacles' as 'spectacles' is used in its plural form always.

35. *(c)* Use 'sugar' in place of 'sugars' as 'sugar' is uncountable noun. It does not have a plural form.

36. *(d)* The given sentence has 'no error'.

37. *(a)* The correct plural form is 'daughters-in-law'.

38. *(c)* Use 'innings' in place of 'inning' as the word is used as both singular and plural form.

39. *(b)* 'Poetry' should be used in place of 'poetries' as the plural of word 'poetry' is also same.

40. *(c)* 'Progress' does not have a plural form. It is used as 'progress'.

41. *(c)* Remove 'a' before soap because 'soap' is used as uncountable noun in the sentence. It should be 'a piece of soap'.

42. *(a)* Replace 'table's wood' with 'wood of the table' to make the sentence error free.

43. *(c)* Use 'twenty rupee note' in place of 'twenty rupees note' because 'note' indicates a singular unit.

44. *(a)* Replace 'boys' with 'boy' because in the sentence 'boy' is used as an adjective.

45. *(b)* Use 'information' in place of 'informations' as information is an uncountable noun and thus, does not have a plural form.

46. *(d)* The given sentence has no error.

47. *(c)* दिए गए sentence में 'equipments' के स्थान पर 'equipment' का use होगा, because यह एक uncountable noun है और इसकी कोई plural form नहीं होती है।

48. *(c)* 'Is quite' के स्थान पर 'are quite' का प्रयोग होगा, क्योंकि वाक्य में helping verb का प्रयोग circumstances (noun) के अनुसार किया गया है।

49. *(c)* 'Somebody else' के स्थान पर 'somebody else's' का प्रयोग किया जाना चाहिए, क्योंकि apostrophe + s ('s) का प्रयोग अधिकार (possession) दर्शाने के लिए किया जाता है।

50. *(c)* 'Manufactures responsibility' के स्थान पर 'manufacture's responsibility' का प्रयोग होगा।

52. *(a)* यहाँ 'Summons' के स्थान पर 'Summonses' का use किया जाएगा। 'Summons' is a noun and the plural of Summons is 'Summonses'.

53. *(b)* यहाँ part (b) में 'page after page' का use किया जाएगा।

54. *(a)* दिए गए sentence के part (a) में 'evidence' का use किया जाएगा। 'Evidence' is an uncountable noun. So, 's' or 'es' is not added with it and takes singular verb.

56. *(b)* 'Sceneries' के स्थान पर 'scenery' का प्रयोग होगा।

57. *(a)* Girls students की जगह girl students का use किया जाएगा, क्योंकि एक compound noun में मुख्य शब्द को ही plural किया जाता है।

58. *(c)* Replace 'him' with 'his' to make the sentence error free.

59. *(c)* 'Car's wheel' के स्थान पर 'wheel of car' का प्रयोग होगा।

60. *(b)* 'Two breads' के स्थान पर 'two pieces of bread' का प्रयोग होगा, क्योंकि 'bread' एक uncountable noun है, इसलिए इसको plural form में नहीं प्रयोग कर सकते हैं।

62. *(b)* Replace 'mouse' with 'mice' as plural form should be used.

63. *(d)* India की जगह India's होगा। यहाँ Pakistan की problems की तुलना India की problem से की जा रही है न कि India से।

64. *(a)* There is an error in part (a). Here, 'mothers-in-law' should be used in place of 'mother-in-laws'.

65. *(a)* question की जगह questions आएगा। After phrases : 'of the' like 'one of the', 'many of the', plural noun is used.

66. *(b)* Ram's and Sita's की जगह Ram and Sita's होना चाहिए। जब दो noun एक ही वस्तु के possession को बता रहे हों तो एक ही apostrophe का प्रयोग होगा।

67. *(a)* Replace 'friends' with 'friend's' to correct the sentence.

68. *(b)* two important informations की जगह two important pieces of information होगा। Information एक uncountable noun है। अत: इसके साथ a, two, three etc नहीं लगता है।

69. *(a)* 'Beauty' is the correct abstract noun to be used in the sentence. Hence, replace 'beautiful' with 'beauty'.

70. *(b)* two-third की जगह two-thirds होगा। यहाँ Book के एक part के बारे में बात हो रही है। अत: thirds लिखा जाएगा।

71. *(a)* Woman teachers की जगह women teachers होगा। man, woman के साथ plural noun आता है, तो men, women हो जाता है। जैसे:

Man supervisor —Men supervisors

Woman cleaner— Women cleaners

72. *(d)* rupees की जगह rupee लिखें। साधारणतया हम one hundred rupees कहते हैं। यहाँ one hundred rupees केवल adjective की तरह कार्य कर रहा है, अत: rupee singular ही रहेगा।

73. *(b)* Bricks की जगह pieces of brick होगा क्योंकि brick, stone, iron chalk, uncountable, material noun हैं।

74. *(b)* two dozen copies होगा। Q. No. 72 का Explanation देखें।

75. *(c)* hairs are की जगह 'hair is' होगा।

76. *(c)* Whereabout की जगह Whereabouts (पता) होगा।

77. *(a)* दिए गए sentence में part (a) के अन्तर्गत 'order has been issued' के स्थान पर 'orders has been issued' का use किया जाएगा।

When a person is assigned to a new station, he receives his 'orders' not 'order' to be used here.

78. *(c)* यहाँ दिए गए sentence में part (c) के अन्तर्गत 'alphabets' के स्थान पर 'alphabet' का use किया जाएगा। 'Alphabet' is the set of letters in a language. English alphabet has 26 letters from A to Z.

79. *(a)* यदि 'score' word से पहले quantity like 2, 5, 3 etc. दी गई हो, तब 'score' को plural form में use नहीं किया जाएगा। अत: दिए गए sentence के part (a) के अन्तर्गत 'scores' के स्थान पर 'score' का use किया जाएगा।

80. *(b)* 'Mischief' की कोई plural form नहीं होती है। इसलिए part (b) के अन्तर्गत 'mischiefs' के स्थान पर 'mischief' का use उपयुक्त होगा। The word 'mischief' does not have a plural form.

81. *(a)* 'Sheep' की plural form 'sheep' ही होती है। इसलिए यहाँ part (a) के अन्तर्गत 'sheeps' के स्थान पर 'sheep' का ही use होगा।

82. *(c)* 'Content' के स्थान पर 'contents' का use किया जाएगा। The word 'content' is used in its plural form 'contents' when it is used to mean 'something contained'.

83. *(b)* 'work' एक uncountable noun है। इसकी plural form भी work ही होती है इसलिए यहाँ part (b) के अन्तर्गत 'many works' के स्थान पर 'much work' का use किया जाएगा।

84. *(b)* 'True to your word' का अर्थ होता है 'Promise'। अत: यहाँ part (b) के अन्तर्गत 'your words' के स्थान पर 'your word' का use किया जाएगा।

85. *(b)* यहाँ part (b) के अन्तर्गत 'five years old' के स्थान पर 'five year old' का use किया जाएगा as we know that in a compound noun, a compound word is not used in plural if a noun does not work of an adjective.

86. *(b)* यहाँ part (b) के अन्तर्गत 'two hundred rupees' के स्थान पर 'two hundred rupee' का use किया जाएगा because in the given sentence 'two hundred rupees' is used as an adjective of the noun 'notes'.

87. *(b)* 'Advice' एक uncountable noun है इसलिए इससे पहले article 'an' का use नहीं किया जाएगा। अत: 'an advice' के स्थान पर सिर्फ 'advice' का use किया जाएगा।

88. *(c)* यहाँ sentence में comparison किया गया है, इसलिए दोनों noun same form में होने चाहिए। अत: 'man athletes' के स्थान पर 'men athletes' का use किया जाएगा क्योंकि comparison women athletes से किया गया है।

89. *(a)* यहाँ 'spectacle' के स्थान पर 'spectacles' का use किया जाएगा।

90. *(a)* Book 'Arabian Nights' एक singular noun है, इसलिए 'are' के स्थान पर 'is' का use किया जाएगा।

91. *(c)* 'vacations' के स्थान पर 'vacation' का use किया जाएगा।

92. *(a)* 'Ration has run out' के स्थान पर 'Rations have run out' का use किया जाएगा।

93. *(a)* दिए गए sentence में 'The table's wood' के स्थान पर 'The wood of the table' का use किया जाएगा, to make the sentence grammatically correct.

94. *(b)* 'lot of works' के स्थान पर 'lot of work' का use किया जाएगा क्योंकि 'work' एक uncountable noun है।

95. *(a)* 'Ox' का plural 'oxen' होता है, इसलिए यहाँ 'oxes' के स्थान पर 'oxen' का use किया जाएगा।

96. *(a)* 'sister-in-law' का plural 'sisters-in-law' होता है। अत: 'sister-in-laws' के स्थान पर 'sisters-in-law' का use उचित होगा।

97. *(c)* यहाँ 'shop' के स्थान पर 'shops' का use होगा because 'Any' refers to a number of things (here shops).

98. *(c)* 'News' एक singular noun है इसलिए 'are very' के स्थान पर 'is very' का use होगा।

99. *(a)* यहाँ 'flock of lions' की जगह 'pride of lions' का use होगा because 'pride' is the right word to refer to a group of lions.

100. *(c)* यहाँ 'laps' का use incorrect है, इसलिए यहाँ 'lap' का use किया जाएगा।

101. *(a)* यहाँ 'gang of sailors' की जगह 'crew of sailors' का use किया जाएगा because a group of sailors is called a crew.

102. *(b)* 'Posts' के स्थान पर 'post' का use किया जाएगा।

103. *(b)* यहाँ part (b) के अन्तर्गत 'criteria' के स्थान पर 'criterion' का use उचित होगा, to make the sentence grammatically correct.

104. *(c)* यहाँ 'equipments' के स्थान पर 'equipment' का use होगा क्योंकि equipment एक uncountable noun है और इसकी कोई plural form नहीं होती है।

105. *(b)* 'One of' के साथ हमेशा plural noun का use किया जाता है इसलिए 'habit' के स्थान पर 'habits' का use किया जाएगा।

02 Pronoun

जो words किसी Noun के लिए या Noun के स्थान पर use किए जाते हैं, उन्हें Pronouns कहते हैं। They are used to avoid repetitions of nouns. e.g.,

I saw Pooja. Pooja is a good girl. Pooja has a scooty. (✗)

I saw Pooja. She is a good girl. She has a scooty. (✓)

He, She, It, They, Either, This, Those, One another, Everyone etc all are called Pronouns.

Kinds of Pronoun There are total ten kinds of pronoun which are as follows

1. Personal Pronoun

Personal pronouns, sentence में persons को denote करते हैं। I, We-First person pronoun, You-Second person pronoun, तथा He, She, It, They-Third Person Pronoun कहलाते हैं। Personal pronouns की निम्नलिखित forms होती है

Person	Subjective Case		Objective Case		Possessive Case	
	Singular	Plural	Singular	Plural	Singular	Plural
First	I	We	Me	Us	My, Mine	Our, Ours
Second	You	You	You	You	Your	Yours
Third	He, She, It	They	Him, Her, it	Them	His, Her, Its	Their, Theirs

Use and Rules of Personal Pronoun

Rule 1 यदि कोई noun किसी verb का subject हो, तो वह nominative/subjective case में होता है और यदि कोई noun किसी verb का object हो, तो वह objective case में होता है।

e.g., (i) She went to Delhi by train.
(ii) He abused them.

Rule 2 'Let' के बाद objective case pronoun का use किया जाता है क्योंकि 'let' transitive verb है।

e.g., (i) Let him sit. (Not 'he sit')
(ii) Let you and me eat. (Not 'you and I')

Rule 3 As/than के बाद nominative case के pronoun का use होगा।

e.g., Reena is as tall as I. (×)
Reena is as tall as me. (✓)

Rule 4 यदि वाक्य में एक से अधिक singular pronouns (I, he, she, you) का प्रयोग हुआ हो, तो उनको लिखने का सही क्रम निम्न प्रकार है

Second person → Third person → First person
(you) (He/She) (I)

e.g., You, He and I are good friends.

परन्तु यदि वाक्य में एक से अधिक plural pronouns (we, you, they) का प्रयोग हुआ हों, तो उनको लिखने का सही क्रम निम्न प्रकार है

First person → Second person → Third person
(We) (You) (They)

e.g., We, you and they are leaving for Mumbai.

Rule 5 यदि किसी वाक्य में एक से अधिक pronouns का प्रयोग हुआ हो तथा उस वाक्य में गलती, अपराध या भूल का जिक्र हों या वाक्य negative हो, तो उनका क्रम है

First person → Second person → Third person
(I/We) (You) (He/She/They)

e.g., I, you and she killed a bird.

Rule 6 यदि किसी वाक्य में दो subjects को with, along with, together with, but, besides, rather than, no less than, nothing but, as well as, and not etc. से जोड़ा जाता है, तब वाक्य में pronoun और possessive adjective का प्रयोग पहले subject के अनुसार किया जाता है।

e.g., Meena as well as her parents has packed their clothes. (×)
Meena as well as her parents has packed her clothes. (✓)

Pronoun 'It' का use निम्न के लिए होता है

1. For thing without life (निर्जीव वस्तुओं के लिए)
   (a) Here is your pen. Please take it.
2. For Animals (पशुओं के लिए)
   - He has a cat. It is very beautiful.
   - I have a dog. It is very faithful.
3. For young child (यदि उनमें male-female का अन्तर न करना हो)
   - When he saw the child, it was playing.
   - The baby has spoiled its dress.

4. किसी Noun या Pronoun को महत्त्व देने हेतु 'It' का प्रयोग निम्न प्रकार किया जाता है
- It is you, who can solve this problem.
- It was I, who called you.

5. एक अनिश्चित कर्त्ता (Indefinite Nominative) के रूप में 'It' का प्रयोग निम्न प्रकार होता है
- It rains
- It thunders

6. समय, मौसम के सन्दर्भ में 'It' का प्रयोग निम्न प्रकार होता है
- It is 7 O'clock.
- It is winter.

7. Exclamatory वाक्य में It का प्रयोग निम्न प्रकार किया जाता है
- What a beautiful bird it is!
- What a large building it is!.

8. It का प्रयोग निम्न प्रकार के वाक्यों में भी किया जाता है
- It is easy to find faults with others.
- It is confirm that he is wrong.
- It is doubtful whether she will join here.

2. Possessive Pronoun

ये pronouns, sentence में प्रयुक्त Noun/Pronoun के प्रति अधिकार (Possession) दर्शाते हैं। His, Hers, Ours, Yours, Mine, Theirs etc, possessive pronoun होते हैं।

e.g., (i) My phone is dead. Pass me yours.
(ii) The house on the corner is theirs.

Use and Rules of Possessive Pronoun

Rule 1 Possessive pronoun का use sentence के subject के रूप में भी हो सकता है।

e.g., (i) Yours bike is an old bike. (✗)
(ii) Yours is an old bike. (✓)

Rule 2 यदि sentence में noun का use पहले ही हो गया हो, तो repetition से बचने के लिए possessive pronoun का use किया जाता है।

e.g., (i) This house is yours house. (✗)
(ii) This house is yours. (✓)

3. Distributive Pronoun

ये pronouns किसी group में से एक person or thing (one at a time) को denote करते हैं। अत: ये singular होते हैं एवं इनके साथ हमेशा singular verb का use किया जाता है। Each, Either, Neither, Everyone distributive pronouns होते हैं।

e.g., (i) Each of the students gets a prize.
(ii) Either of the two will win the race.

Use and Rules of Distributive Pronoun

Rule 1 Each का use 'प्रत्येक' के अर्थ में दो या दो से अधिक persons/things के लिए किया जाता है।

e.g., (i) Each got his turn.
(ii) Each of the two girls is beautiful.

Rule 2 दो persons या दो things में से कोई एक के लिए 'either' का use किया जाता है, जबकि दो से अधिक के लिए 'any/one' का use किया जाता है।

e.g., (i) Either of these two pens is blue.
(ii) Any of these three books is useful for our exam.

Rule 3 दो persons या दो things में से कोई भी नहीं के लिए 'neither' का use किया जाता है जबकि दो से अधिक में से कोई भी नहीं के लिए 'none' का use किया जाता है।

e.g., (i) None of these three writers writes well.
(ii) Neither of his two movies is superhit.

Rule 4 Each of/Either of/Neither of के बाद 'the + plural noun' या सिर्फ plural pronoun का ही use किया जाता है।

e.g.,
(i) Each of the students has completed this project.
↓
Plural Noun
(ii) Either of you did this crime.
↓
Plural Pronoun

4. Reciprocal Pronouns

ये दो pronouns से मिलकर बनते हैं तथा एक-दूसरे से सम्बन्धित होते हैं। Each other and one another, reciprocal pronouns होते हैं।

e.g., (i) The two friends quarrelled with each other.
(ii) They all wish Diwali to one another.

Use and Rules of Reciprocal Pronouns

Rule 1 Reciprocal pronoun 'each other' का use दो persons/things के लिए किया जाता है, जबकि 'one another' का use दो से अधिक 'persons/things' के बीच परस्पर सम्बन्ध बताने के लिए किया जाता है।

e.g., (i) Babita and Amita never liked each other.
(ii) All the students are talking to one another.

Rule 2 Reciprocal pronouns का use कभी भी sentence के subject के रूप में नहीं किया जाता है।

e.g., Each other are trying to solve this question. (✗)
They are trying to solve this question. (✓)

Rule 3 अधिकार (Possession) दर्शाने के लिए 'Each other' तथा 'One another' के साथ apostrophe + s ('s) का भी use किया जा सकता है।

e.g., Saurav and Gaurav had broken each other toys. (✗)
Saurav and Gaurav had broken each other's toys. (✓)

5. Reflexive/Intensive Pronoun

ये pronouns, sentence में 'अपने आपको या स्वयं' के अर्थ में use किए जाते हैं। My, Your, Him, Her, It में 'self' जोड़ने पर एवं our, your, them में 'selves' जोड़ने पर Reflexive pronoun बनाए जाते हैं। Myself, yourself, themselves, ourselves, itself etc. reflexive pronoun होते हैं।

e.g., (i) He hurt himself.
(ii) They ruined themselves.

Use and Rules of Reflexive Pronoun

Rule 1 कुछ verbs ऐसी होती हैं, जिनके बाद reflexive pronoun का use जरूरी होता है।

Exert (परिश्रम करना)	Reconcile (मेल-मिलाप करना)	Apply (ध्यान करना)
Avail (लाभ उठाना)	Absent (अनुपस्थित रहना)	Revenge (बदला लेना)
Acquit (अच्छा व्यवहार करना)	Amuse (मन बहलाना)	Adapt (रुपान्तरित करना)
Pride (स्वाभिमान)	Avenge (प्रतिशोध लेना)	Enjoy (आनन्द उठाना)
Adjust (व्यवस्थित करना)	Resign (पदत्याग करना)	

उपरोक्त verbs के बाद यदि object नहीं लिखा हो, तो इनके बाद Reflexive pronoun का प्रयोग किया जाता है। e.g.,

(i) The bear adapted to the surroundings of the jungle. (✗)
The bear adapted itself to the surroundings of the jungle. (✓)
(ii) He could solve this problem if he applied. (✗)
He could solve this problem if he applied himself. (✓)

Rule 2 अगर 'Enjoy' के बाद कोई object नहीं दिया गया हो, तो इसके बाद reflexive pronoun का use किया जाता है, लेकिन अगर 'Enjoy' के बाद कोई object दिया गया हो, तो इसके बाद reflexive pronoun का use नहीं किया जाता है। e.g.,

(i) Let the children enjoy themselves this movie. (✗)
Let the children enjoy this movie. (✓)
(ii) Time passed so quickly when we were enjoying. (✗)
Time passed so quickly when we were enjoying ourselves. (✓)

उपरोक्त पहले example में object 'this movie' का use हुआ है, इसलिए यहाँ 'reflexive pronoun' का use नहीं होगा, जबकि दूसरे example में कोई object नहीं दिया गया है, इसलिए यहाँ reflexive pronoun का use होगा।

Rule 3 किसी sentence में अगर absent का use object की तरह हो, तो इसके बाद reflexive pronoun का use नहीं किया जाता है, लेकिन इसका verb की तरह use होने पर, इसके साथ reflexive pronoun का use होगा। e.g.,

(i) He is absent himself today. (✗)
(absent → Object; himself → Reflexive pronoun)
He is absent today. (✓)
(absent → Object)
(ii) The manager absented from the meeting. (✗)
(absented → Verb)
The manager absented himself from the meeting. (✓)
(absented → Verb; himself → Reflexive pronoun)

Rule 4 निम्नलिखित verbs के बाद reflexive pronoun का प्रयोग नहीं किया जाता है।
Wash, dress, bathe, shave, keep, turn, move, rest, stop, hide, qualify, start, think, etc.

e.g., One must bathe every morning.
(Not 'bathe oneself ')

6. Demonstrative Pronouns

इन pronouns का use पास या दूर स्थित persons or things को point out करने के लिए किया जाता है।

This, That, These, Those, the same, such etc. demonstrative pronouns होते हैं।

e.g., (i) This is a gift from my uncle.
(ii) These boys are my friends.

Use and Rules of Demonstrative Pronouns

Rule 1 'This' का use निकट के व्यक्ति/वस्तु के लिए किया जाता है, जबकि 'that' का use दूर के लिए किया जाता है। This/That के साथ singular noun का use किया जाता है।

e.g., (i) This is a book.
(ii) That is a student.

Rule 2 'These' का use निकट के एक से अधिक व्यक्तियों/वस्तुओं के लिए किया जाता है, जबकि 'those' का use दूर के एक से अधिक व्यक्तियों/वस्तुओं के लिए किया जाता है। These/Those के साथ plural noun का use किया जाता है।

e.g., (i) Those were terrorists.
(ii) These are intelligent boys.

Rule 3 This/That के बाद 'kind of/sort of ' का use किया जाता हैं जबकि These तथा Those के बाद 'kinds of/sorts of ' का use किया जाता है।

e.g., (i) This kind of food is harmful for you.
(ii) Those sorts of men are industrious.

7. Indefinite Pronouns

ये pronouns, sentence में किसी definite person या definite things को denote नहीं करते हैं। Everyone, someone, none, anyone, everybody, somebody, nobody, everything, something, nothing, any, all, same etc indefinite pronouns हो हैं।

e.g., (i) Some have joined the party.
(ii) Can anyone answer this question?

Use and Rules of Indefinite Pronouns

Rule 1 अगर Everybody, somebody, nobody, anyone, someone, anybody, everyone etc. का प्रयोग subject के रूप में हुआ हो, तो इनके लिए singular pronoun (he, she, him, her, herself) का प्रयोग किया जाता है, plural pronoun/adjective (they, them, their, theirs) का नहीं।

e.g.,
(i) Everyone can solve this puzzle, if they try again and again. (✗)
(ii) Everyone can solve this puzzle, if he tries again and again. (✓)

Rule 2 Everything, nothing, anything, something का use subject की तरह किए जाने पर इनके लिए singular pronoun (it, itself) का use किया जाता है।

e.g., Everything has its limit.

Rule 3 यदि किसी sentence में 'one' का use, subject की तरह किया गया हैं, तो इसके लिए 'one's' तथा 'oneself' का use किया जाता है।

e.g., (i) One should do one's duty.
(ii) One should try oneself.

Rule 4 'All' के साथ 'who' का use 'person' के लिए किया जाता है तथा 'all' के साथ 'that' का use 'things' के लिए किया जाता हैं।

e.g., (i) All who have the essential qualification can fill this form.
(ii) All that can be seen may not be true.

8. Relative Pronoun

ये pronouns, sentence में प्रयुक्त (used) दूसरे Noun/Pronoun से relation (सम्बन्ध) को denote करते हैं। Who, Which, That, Whose, Whom etc सभी relative pronouns होते हैं।

e.g., (i) Reena saw the boy who was jumping.
(ii) I have found the bag which I lost yesterday.

Use and Rules of Relative Pronoun

Rule 1 Relative pronouns who/whom का use person के लिए किया जाता है। People एवं Those के साथ 'who' का ही use किया जाता है।

e.g., (i) I know all those who were involved in the case.
(ii) This is the girl whom all admire.

Rule 2 'Whose' का possessive case में use, generally persons and animals के लिए किया जाता है।

e.g., (i) This is the boy whose parents have died.
(ii) The dog whose color is white, has become mad.

कई स्थितियों में whose का use non-living nouns के लिए भी किया जाता है।

e.g., A girl whose hair is curly looks beautiful.

Rule 3 'Which' का use Non-living things एवं animals के लिए किया जाता हैं।

e.g., (i) The book which I purchased yesterday is useless.
(ii) The dog which was caught by the municipality has died.

Rule 4 'That' का use living एवं Non-living nouns के लिए singular एवं plural दोनों Nouns के साथ होता है।

e.g., (i) I have lost the book that you gave me.
(ii) This is the lady that looks so pretty.

Rule 5 That से पहले कोई preposition नहीं लगाया जाता हैं। यदि preposition लगाने की आवश्यकता हो तो वह sentence के end में use किया जाता है।

e.g., (i) We know the hotel that she lives in.
(ii) This is the house that I told you about.

Much, little, the little, the same, no, none, nobody, nothing, any, all, the only, everything, everyone के बाद relative pronoun 'that' का प्रयोग किया जाता है।

e.g., (i) This is the same boy that I saw yesterday.
(ii) These was none that didn't support the cause.

9. Interrogative Pronoun

इन pronouns का use sentence में questions पूछने के लिए किया जाता है। Who, Whom, What, Which, Whose etc interrogative pronouns होते हैं।

e.g., (i) Whose pen is this?
(ii) What is your father's occupation?

Use and Rules of Interrogative Pronoun

Rule 1 Who (कौन) का use किसी वाक्य में subject के लिए Interrogative sentence में किया जाता है।

e.g., The students were studying.
↓
'Subject
Who were studying?
↓
Subject के लिए

Rule 2 Whom (किसे) का use वाक्य में object के लिए Interrogative sentence में किया जाता है। इसका use भी सिर्फ व्यक्ति (person) के लिए होता है।

e.g., The teacher punished the students.
↓
Object

Whom did the teacher punish?
↓
Object के लिए

Rule 3 Whose (किसका) का use स्वामित्व या अधिकार (possession) दर्शाने के लिए Interrogative sentence में किया जाता है। इसका use व्यक्ति (person) और वस्तु (thing) दोनों के लिए होता है।

e.g., This mobile is yours.
Whose mobile is this?
↓
'Possession के लिए'

Rule 4 Which (कौन सा/सी) का use वाक्य में subject और object दोनों के लिए होता है। इसका use वस्तुओं के बीच विकल्प (choice) या चुनाव (selection) के लिए होता है।

e.g., The red car is yours.
↓
Subject

Which is your car?
↓
Subject के लिए

Rule 5 किसी वाक्य में 'preposition + whom' का प्रयोग किया जा सकता है, लेकिन 'preposition + who' का नहीं।

e.g., (i) With who are you going? (×)
(ii) With whom are you going? (✓)

10. Exclamatory Pronoun

जब Interrogative words का use surprise (आश्चर्य) व्यक्त करने के लिए किया जताा है, तो उसे Exclamatory pronoun कहते हैं। What, Such, How, etc exclamatory pronouns होते हैं।

e.g., (i) What! You lost the gold chain.
(ii) How bright they have grown in the sunlight!

Exercise 1

Directions (Q. Nos. 1-20) Identify the kind of pronoun for the underlined words in the following sentences.

1. She often reads books.
(a) Reflexive pronoun
(b) Personal pronoun
(c) Possessive pronoun
(d) Interrogative pronoun

2. They are on the wall.
(a) Demonstrative pronoun
(b) Possessive pronoun
(c) Reflexive pronoun
(d) Personal pronoun

3. Which colour do you prefer?
(a) Interrogative pronoun
(b) Emphatic pronoun
(c) Reflexive pronoun
(d) Demonstrative pronoun

4. Whose car is that?
(a) Reflexive pronoun
(b) Personal pronoun
(c) Possessive pronoun
(d) Interrogative pronoun

5. I fed myself with the grapes.
(a) Reflexive pronoun
(b) Personal pronoun
(c) Possessive pronoun
(d) Emphatic pronoun

6. Sophie herself told me that she was going abroad.
(a) Demonstrative pronoun
(b) Personal pronoun
(c) Possessive pronoun
(d) Emphatic pronoun

7. This cat is mine.
(a) Reflexive pronoun
(b) Emphatic pronoun
(c) Possessive pronoun
(d) Personal pronoun

8. What do you want for dinner?
(a) Interrogative pronoun
(b) Personal pronoun
(c) Possessive pronoun
(d) Reflexive pronoun

9. He has climbed to the top of that tree.
(a) Reflexive pronoun
(b) Personal pronoun
(c) Possessive pronoun
(d) Emphatic pronoun

10. Rita enjoyed herself.
(a) Reflexive pronoun
(b) Personal pronoun
(c) Possessive pronoun
(d) Interrogative pronoun

11. Yours is a new bag.
(a) Personal (b) Possessive
(c) Reflexive (d) Relative

12. The new house on the street is theirs.
(a) Personal (b) Possessive
(c) Reflexive (d) Relative

13. I had to remind myself to speak clearly and loudly.
(a) Personal (b) Possessive
(c) Reflexive (d) Relative

14. This is the model which Vaani made.
(a) Personal (b) Possessive
(c) Reflexive (d) Relative

15. Linda is my sister. She does not like sports.
(a) Personal (b) Possessive
(c) Reflexive (d) Relative

16. John blamed himself for the poor performance.
(a) Personal (b) Possessive
(c) Reflexive (d) Relative

17. She received many toys: two of which she gave to her sister.
(a) Personal (b) Possessive
(c) Reflexive (d) Relative

18. My mother's name is Anita. She is from India.
(a) Personal (b) Possessive
(c) Reflexive (d) Relative

19. This is our pet, not theirs.
(a) Personal (b) Possessive
(c) Reflexive (d) Relative

20. They thanked themselves for their luck.
(a) Personal (b) Possessive
(c) Reflexive (d) Relative

Directions (Q. Nos. 21-30) Do as directed by choosing the correct option.

21. Identify the personal pronoun among the following.
(a) It
(b) This
(c) Myself
(d) Both (a) and (c)

22. Which among the following is NOT a possessive pronoun?
(a) His (b) Our
(c) Mine (d) Yours

23. Which among the following is a reflexive pronoun?
(a) Herself
(b) Ours
(c) Their
(d) Both (a) and (c)

24. Which among the following is NOT a demonstrative pronoun?
(a) This (b) These
(c) That (d) Them

25. Which among the following is NOT an interrogative pronoun?
(a) What
(b) Yours
(c) Who
(d) Both (b) and (c)

26. Identify the emphatic pronoun among the following.
(a) Herself (b) Whose
(c) Yours (d) Both (b) and (c)

27. Identify the personal pronoun among the following.
(a) I (b) We
(c) You (d) All of these

28. Which among the following is NOT an interrogative pronoun?
(a) What (b) Which
(c) Whom (d) None of these

29. Which among the following is a reflexive pronoun?
(a) Themselves
(b) Yours
(c) Hers
(d) Both (b) and (c)

30. Which among the following is NOT a possessive pronoun?
(a) Each
(b) Ours
(c) His
(d) Both (a) and (b)

Directions (Q. Nos. 31-82) Fill the given blanks by choosing the most appropriate option.

31. We knew that .... was free.
(a) him (b) her
(c) he (d) they

32. I will give this book to ....
(a) he (b) they
(c) she (d) you

33. The duck can swim because .... has webbed feet.
(a) their (b) we
(c) it (d) she

34. When I met Anu, I invited .... to my house.
(a) them (b) her
(c) they (d) us

35. They looked at ....
(a) their (b) it
(c) we (d) my

36. To .... did you tell this?
(a) who (b) whom
(c) which (d) whose

37. .... book is this?
(a) Who (b) Whom
(c) When (d) Whose

38. .... is beautiful ?
(a) When (b) How
(c) Why (d) Which

39. .... went there?
(a) Who (b) Whom
(c) Whose (d) When

40. .... is this person?
(a) Who (b) Which
(c) Whose (d) Whom

41. I congratulated the girls .... won prizes.
(a) which (b) who
(c) whose (d) they

42. I plucked the mangoes .... hung low.
(a) who (b) those
(c) these (d) which

43. I liked the boy .... accepted his mistake.
(a) he (b) whom
(c) who (d) they

44. Talk to the girl .... brother is the school leader.
(a) whose (b) which
(c) who (d) whom

45. Show me the place .... you bought this phone.
(a) whose (b) who
(c) where (d) when

46. .... is the time when you can play, as you have now completed your work.
(a) This (b) That
(c) These (d) Those

47. Look at .... , see how it is racing away.
(a) this (b) that
(c) these (d) those

48. .... flowers in my hand are wilting.
(a) This (b) That
(c) These (d) Those

49. Arrange .... books that are scattered in the next room.
(a) this (b) that
(c) these (d) those

50. .... is the car that has recently been launched.
(a) This (b) That
(c) These (d) Those

51. Stella and Maria haven't met .... for a long time.
(a) each other (b) each
(c) other (d) others

52. My friends enjoyed .... very much at the concert.
(a) himself (b) themselves
(c) herself (d) yourself

53. Sam repaired his car ....
(a) myself (b) himself
(c) yourself (d) itself

54. We helped .... with our report.
(a) himself (b) ourself
(c) each other (d) yourself

55. The old woman lived alone, with .... to look after ....
(a) no one, her
(b) someone, her
(c) anyone, her
(d) everyone, her

56. I .... wash .... clothes.
(a) my, mine
(b) myself, mine
(c) mine, my
(d) myself, my

57. He gave .... a book.
(a) my (b) me
(c) I (d) myself

58. We decided to do all the cooking ....
(a) itself
(b) of our own
(c) by ourselves
(d) each other

59. He .... answered the phone.
(a) himself (b) his
(c) itself (d) either

60. .... of her poems have been published.
(a) Every (b) None
(c) Any (d) Whichever

61. The butterfly tried .... best.
(a) her (b) hers
(c) its (d) his

62. Have .... prepared well for the exam?
(a) he (b) she
(c) you (d) them

63. There are a lot of pets in our colony, but .... is the most disciplined.
(a) our
(b) ours
(c) your
(d) their

64. Radhika's sincerity as a student made the teacher believe that .... would never cheat.
(a) his (b) her
(c) she (d) him

65. At home, my mother gives .... cooking lessons.
(a) I (b) her
(c) me (d) mine

66. The women in blue saree is .... mother.
(a) my (b) mine
(c) ours (d) theirs

67. He wanted to play the prank but .... was afraid that he would be caught.
(a) him (b) his
(c) he (d) he's

68. Pedro and I like to play tennis. .... play at the club.
(a) We (b) I
(c) He (d) Us

69. Please put our name on the gift so that .... know that it's from ....
(a) us/they
(b) they/us
(c) them/they
(d) he/us

70. Our English teacher taught ...... Shakespeare this year.
(a) our (b) ours
(c) us (d) me

71. My parents will not allow .... to spend the night outside.
(a) me (b) mine
(c) I (d) her

72. The man ...... I met yesterday was Ajay.
(a) which (b) whose
(c) who (d) when

73. The story began to puzzle .... when it did not make any sense.
(a) they (b) he
(c) me (d) she

74. My best friend wants me to stay with .... tonight.
(a) she (b) hers
(c) her (d) she's

75. .... house is located on a hill.
(a) Ours (b) Our
(c) Theirs (d) Who's

76. The baby started recognizing .... in the mirror.
(a) she (b) her
(c) herself (d) it

77. We had to remind .... that it's just a game.
(a) us (b) our
(c) ours (d) ourselves

78. Mom asked .... to be careful and not to spill the sauce.
(a) I (b) mine
(c) me (d) she

79. I intend to be at home immediately after the movie is over but .... may be a little bit late.
(a) me (b) I
(c) mine (d) myself

80. He is not a good friend but he is an acquaintance of ....
(a) mine (b) me
(c) myself (d) I

81. The gangster flashed .... gun at us.
(a) him (b) his
(c) himself (d) his's

82. I took a picture of .... with my new hat.
(a) my (b) me (c) mine (d) myself

Exercise 2

Directions (Q. Nos. 1-15) Fill in the blanks with suitable pronoun.

1. Abha is more beautiful and more intelligent than ....
(a) I (b) me
(c) myself (d) mine

2. Have you any objection to .... going to your house?
(a) mine (b) I
(c) myself (d) me

3. This is only thing .... I want.
(a) as (b) that
(c) which (d) whose

4. I do not like .... of these two magazines.
(a) any (b) one
(c) either (d) some

5. My views are quite different from ....
(a) you (b) your
(c) yourself (d) yours

6. Come and have supper with us if you are not doing .... thing tonight.
(a) some (b) any
(c) one (d) all

7. I was unable to say whether .... was a boy or not.
(a) it (b) he
(c) she (d) that

8. Rakhi is the girl .... has failed.
(a) whom (b) who
(c) which (d) whose

9. There was none .... did not enjoy the show.
(a) who (b) which
(c) that (d) whom

10. My ambition is far different than ....
(a) mine (b) your
(c) our (d) yours

11. Hello Harish, Kavita and Praveen. Help.....to buy some food and I'II be with you in a moment.
(a) you (b) yours
(c) yourself (d) yourselves

12. The ball that my dog took was ....
(a) him (b) he
(c) his (d) my

13. When Sunanda won the lottery, she pinched .... to make sure she wasn't dreaming.
(a) hers (b) herself
(c) her (d) himself

14. Almost no friend of.... came to the funeral.
(a) her (b) myself
(c) theirs (d) them

15. It's partly finished. There is .... left.
(a) nothing (b) everything
(c) anything (d) something

Directions (Q. Nos. 16-25) Do as directed by choosing the correct option.

16. Fill in the blank with the correct pronoun.
Jason and James took their bike with ....
(a) they (b) them (c) their (d) us

17. Find the personal pronoun in the given sentence.
Jerry's mother asked him to clean the garden.
(a) Jerry (b) mother
(c) him (d) garden

18. Fill in the blank with the correct pronoun.
Don't blame yourself for the mistake. .... is perfect.
(a) Nobody (b) Anybody
(c) Everybody (d) Somebody

19. Someone caught twelve fish.
Here 'someone' is ....
(a) Personal pronoun
(b) Possessive pronoun
(c) Reflexive pronoun
(d) Indefinite pronoun

20. Fill in the blank with the correct pronoun.
Someone must do .... about the human rights in this country or it will be too late.
(a) anything (b) everything
(c) something (d) nothing

21. Fill in the blank with the correct interrogative pronoun.
.... sister works as a doctor in the hospital?
(a) whose (b) whom
(c) what (d) how

22. Select the distributive pronouns from the following options.
(a) Himself, Herself, Ourselves
(b) Every, Each, Both
(c) Anybody, Somebody, Nobody
(d) What, Which, Whom

23. None of the books are hers. They belong to Mary's sons.
Here, 'none' is ....
(a) Distributive pronoun
(b) Personal pronoun
(c) Possessive pronoun
(d) Reflexive pronoun

24. Select the distributive pronoun in the given sentence.
I enjoyed every minute of my stay in Africa.
(a) I (b) my stay
(c) Africa (d) every

25. Fill in the blank with the correct possessive pronoun.
His view eventually prevailed over ....
(a) our (b) their
(c) theirs (d) its

Directions (Q. Nos. 26-55) In the following questions, select the option which is the correct form of the given sentence. If none of the option is correct, mark the answer a option (d).

26. I, he and you are class fellows.
(a) I, you and he are class fellows.
(b) You, he and I are class fellows.
(c) He, you and I are class fellows.
(d) None of the above

27. Both didn't go.
(a) Both of you don't go.
(b) Neither of you didn't go.
(c) Neither went.
(d) None of the above

28. They and you can go outside.
(a) You and they can go outside.
(b) They and you can goes outside.
(c) You and they can goes outside.
(d) None of the above

29. John, Peter and Micky help each other.
(a) Peter, John and Micky help each other.
(b) John, Peter and Micky help one another.
(c) John, Peter and Micky helps one another.
(d) None of the above

30. Distribute these apples between four friends.
(a) Distribute these apples between four friend.
(b) Distribute these apples among four friends.
(c) Distribute these apples among four friend.
(d) None of the above

31. Every boy was in their best mood.
(a) Every boys were in their best mood.
(b) Every boy was in his best mood.
(c) Every boy was in his best moods.
(d) None of the above

32. The two friends like one another.
(a) The two friends like each other.
(b) The two friend likes each other.
(c) The two friends likes each other.
(d) None of the above

33. Who do you like the best?
(a) Who does you like the best?
(b) Whom do you like the best?
(c) Whom does you like the best?
(d) None of the above

34. Either Satish or Rakesh has been ordered to bring their books.
(a) Either Satish or Rakesh has been ordered to bring his books.
(b) Either Satish or Rakesh have been ordered to bring his books.
(c) Either Satish or Rakesh have been ordered to bring their books.
(d) None of the above

35. One must do his duty
(a) One must do their duty
(b) One must do your duty
(c) One must do one's duty
(d) None of the above

36. Distribute these sweets among two brother.
(a) Distribute these sweets between two brothers.
(b) Distribute these sweet among two brothers.
(c) Distribute these sweets between two brother.
(d) None of the above

37. It is one of the best novels that has been written by Leo Tolstoy.
(a) ... the best novel that have been written ...
(b) ... the best novels that have been written ...
(c) ... the best novel that has been written ...
(d) None of the above

38. These books are for he and I.
(a) These books are for him and me.
(b) There books are for I and he.
(c) These books are for his as well as mine.
(d) None of the anove

39. Any of these two books will serve my purpose.
(a) Any of these two book ....
(b) Each of these two book ....
(c) Either of these two books ....
(d) None of the above

40. He availed of that chance.
(a) He availed himself of that chance.
(b) He availed him of that chance.
(c) He availed his of that chance.
(d) None of the above

41. We went in the garden and enjoyed.
(a) We went in the garden and enjoyed there.
(b) We went in the garden and enjoyed ourselves.
(c) We went in the garden and enjoyed themselves.
(d) None of the above

42. Neither of your five brothers have helped you.
(a) None of your five brothers have helped you.
(b) None of your five brothers has helped you.
(c) Neither of your five brothers has helped you.
(d) None of the above

43. This is the book whose pages have been torn.
(a) This is the book whose pages has been torn.
(b) This is the book whom pages have been torn.
(c) This is the book the pages of which have been torn.
(d) None of the above

44. He kept himself away from the dog.
(a) He kept away from the dog.
(b) He kept the dog away from himself.
(c) He kept himself from the dog.
(d) None of the above

45. It was her, who stole your purse.
(a) It was she, who stole your purse.
(b) It was hers who stole your purse.
(c) It was herself who stole your purse.
(d) None of the above

46. Neither Sohan nor his friends attend his class.
(a) ...his friends attend him class.
(b) ...him friends attend his class.
(c) ...his friends attend their class.
(d) None of the above

47. None of the four boys were there.
(a) Neither of the four boys was there.
(b) None of the four boys was there.
(c) None of the four boy were there.
(d) None of the above

48. He was happy at his brother arrival.
(a) He was happy at his brother's arrival.
(b) He was happy at him brother's arrival.
(c) He was happy at himself brother's arrival.
(d) None of the above

49. If I was him, I would not abuse him.
(a) If I were he, I would not abuse him.
(b) If I were him, I would not abuse him.
(c) If I was he, I would not abuse him.
(d) None of the above

50. Whom do you think will win the match?
(a) Whose do you think will win the match?
(b) Whom does you think will win the match?
(c) Who do you think will win the match?
(d) None of the above

51. He abstained himself from the meat.
(a) He abstained from meat.
(b) He abstained his from the meat.
(c) He abstained he from the meat.
(d) None of the above

52. The rabbit hid itself behind a bush.
(a) The rabbit hid himself behind a bush.
(b) The rabbit hid behind a bush.
(c) The rabit hid herself behind a bush.
(d) None of the above

53. He absented from the meeting.
(a) He absented itself from the meeting.
(b) He absented himself from the meeting.
(c) He absented him from the meeting.
(d) None of the above

54. Whom do you think he is?
(a) Who do you think he is?
(b) Why do you think he is?
(c) Whom does you think he is?
(d) None of the above

55. Everyone of us should do our duty.
(a) Everyone of us should do her duty.
(b) Everyone of us should do their duty.
(c) Everyone of us should do his duty.
(d) None of the above

Directions (Q. Nos. 56-135) Read the following sentences carefully and identify the part of the sentence which has an error.

56. The board of directors (a)/want the facilities (b)/of car and accommodation (c)/for itself. (d)

57. Every teacher (a)/and every student (b)/of this school is determined to do their best for the benefit of all. (c)/ No error (d)

58. The officer, Jatin, as (a)/ well as the clerks (b)/ absented themselves (c)/ from the office. (d)

59. There were (a)/five active workers (b)/and three lazy one (c)/in the factory. (d)

60. There is none (a)/who can support you (b)/in this crucial period. (c)

61. Any of the (a)/two photos which reflect (b)/the natural beauty of Kashmir (c)/is worthseeing. (d)

62. The guests (a)/whom we were talking (b)/about have arrived. (c)/ No error. (d)

63. He introduced (a)/to the chairman as (b)/the President of the (c)/workers association. (d)

64. As a student (a)/of arts (b)/you are much better (c)/than him. (d)

65. He hates everybody (a)/and everything who (b)/reminds him (c)/of his blunder. (d)

66. Whomever (a)/does not come in time (b)/will not be allowed (c)/to mark his presence. (d)

67. The six partners (a)/are at daggers drawn (b)/so they do not talk (c)/ to each other. (d)

68. If some one has (a)/completed the work (b)/they may leave (c)/No error. (d)

69. She lent me (a)/some money with the condition (b)/that I should return (c)/the same within the month. (d)

70. The teacher instructed (a)/ the peon to let (b)/ the students and I (c)/ go into the office of Principal. (d)

71. The candidate (a)/ being a commerce graduate (b)/she is eligible (c)/for the post of accountant. (d)

72. In all circumstances (a)/I have helped him (b)/and he knows. (c)

73. I asked he (a)/ to complete the (b)/ presentation by the (c)/ end of that day. (d)

74. You and myself (a)/ will enjo the function (b)/being arranged in honour of (c)/ the new Principal. (d)

75. He asked for (a)/ permission to go to the cinema (b)/ but his mother(c)/did not give. (d

76. Either of the two (a)/ hockey players were (b)/ also an athlete. (c)/ No error (d)

77. (a) You and he/ (b) tried his best/ (c) to pass the examination but failed/(d) No error.

78. (a) Each/ (b) of these/ (c) boy play./ (d) No error.

79. (a) Whoever/ (b) does the best/ (c) he will get a prize./ (d) No error.

80. (a) One/ (b) should not/ (c) waste his time/ (d) No error.

81. (a) I and she/ (b) are/ (c) sisters./ (d) No error.

82. (a) He/ (b) is wiser/ (c) than me./ (d) No error.

83. (a) Between/ (b) you and I,/ (c) Anil is not to be trusted./ (d) No error.

84. (a) Nobody/ (b) was there/(c) but I./ (d) No error.

85. You accidentally (a)/ cut you last (b)/ Thursday while making (c)/ dinner for everyone. (d)

86. (a) Only/ (b) he and me / (c) can use this card./ (d) No error.

87. (a) Let/ (b) him and I / (c) go now./ (d) No error.

88. (a) Everyone/ (b) got/ (c) one's pay./ (d) No error

89. (a) Everyone is/ (b) frightened when/ (c) they see a tiger./ (d) No error

90. (a) These two friends/ (b) are fond of/ (c) one another./ (d) No error

91. (a) I did not like/ (b) him coming/ (c) at that hour./(d) No error

92. (a) Who/ (b) do you think/ (c) I met?/ (d) No error

93. (a) You should/ (b) avail this/ (c) opportunity./ (d) No error

94. (a) When you have/ (b) read the books, / (c) please return the same to me./(d) No error

95. (a) They that are/ (b) humble need/ (c) fear no fall./ (d) No error

96. One should (a)/ do your duty (b)/ honestly and sincerely. (c) No error (d)

97. The movie who (a)/ was really good (b)/ came out last week . (c)/ No error (d)

98. You, he and I (a)/ have broken (b)/ the glass of the window (c)/No error (d)

99. Only (a)/ you and him (b)/ can do this work fast. (c)/ No error (d)

100. The coach and mentor, Amit, (a)/ of the team (b)/ blamed themselves for the defeat. (c)/ No error (d)

101. When I am (a)/ sick, it is (b)/ her who cures me. (c)/ No error (d)

102. Neither of the boys (a) has (b) / submitted their records. (c)/ No error (d)

103. The city it (a)/ does not receive too (b)/ much rainfall during winters. (c)/ No error (d).

104. India and Pakistan (a)/ should cooperate with (b)/ one another in this matter. (c)/ No error (d)

105. Anyone of these two students (a)/ can be sent to participate (b)/ in the drawing competition. (c)/No error (d)

106. The master did not know (a)/ who of the servants (b)/ broke the glass. (c)/ No error (d)

107. The ruling party stood (a)/ for the implementation of the bill (b)/ and was ready to stake their political existence. (c)/ No error (d)

108. Wherever they go (a)/ the Indians easily adapt to (b)/ local circumstances. (c)/ No error (d)

109. It is not easy for anyone to command (a)/ respect from one's friends as well as critics (b)/ as Dr. Neil did for his integrity and honesty. (c)/ No error (d)

110. Mahatma Gandhi taught us (a)/ that one should respect (b)/ the religions of others as much as his own. (c)/ No error (d)

111. He, You and I (a)/ shall manage (b)/ this problem together. (c)/ No error (d) .

112. Was it him (a)/ who got injured (b)/ in an accident this morning? (c)/ No error (d)

113. As soon as he (a)/ saw his mother (b)/ he ran to her and embraced. (c)/ No error (d)

114. Due to me being a newcomer (a)/ I was unable to get a house (b)/ suitable for my wife and me. (c)/ No error (d)

115. The audience (a)/ is requested (b)/ to be in its seats. (c)/ No error (d)

116. A scientist must follow (a)/ his hunches and his data (b)/ wherever it may lead. (c)/ No error (d)

117. The number of vehicles (a)/ on this road (b)/ is more than on the main road. (c)/ No error (d)

118. Being a destitute (a)/ I admitted him (b)/ to an old people's home. (c)/ No error (d)

119. One should make (a)/ his best efforts if one wishes to achieve (b)/ success in this organisation. (c)/ No error (d)

120. May I (a)/ know who you want (b)/ to see please? (c)/ No error (d)

121. Our is the only country (a)/ in the world that can boast of (b)/ unity in diversity. (c)/ No error (d)

122. Last summer he went (a)/ to his uncle's village (b)/ and enjoyed very much. (c)/ No error (d)

123. If I were him (a)/ I would have taught (b)/ those cheats a lesson. (c)/ No error (d)

124. Those sort of people (a)/ usually do not (b)/ earn fame in society. (c)/ No error (d)

125. Had I come (a)/ to know about his difficulties (b)/ I would have certainly helped. (c)/ No error (d)

126. One of the boys (a)/ forgot to take their bag (b)/ from the school. (c)/ No error (d)

127. Civil servants should (a)/ acquit efficiently (b)/ in the service of a common man. (c)/ No error (d)

128. Avail every chance that comes your way (a)/ lest you should (b)/ repent in the long run. (c)/ No error (d)

Answers

Exercise 1

1 (b)	2 (d)	3 (a)	4 (d)	5 (a)	6 (d)	7 (c)	8 (a)	9 (b)	10 (a)
11 (b)	12 (b)	13 (c)	14 (d)	15 (a)	16 (c)	17 (d)	18 (a)	19 (b)	20 (c)
21 (a)	22 (b)	23 (a)	24 (d)	25 (b)	26 (a)	27 (d)	28 (d)	29 (a)	30 (a)
31 (c)	32 (d)	33 (c)	34 (b)	35 (b)	36 (b)	37 (d)	38 (d)	39 (a)	40 (a)
41 (b)	42 (d)	43 (c)	44 (a)	45 (c)	46 (a)	47 (b)	48 (c)	49 (d)	50 (a)
51 (a)	52 (b)	53 (b)	54 (c)	55 (a)	56 (d)	57 (b)	58 (c)	59 (a)	60 (b)
61 (c)	62 (c)	63 (b)	64 (c)	65 (c)	66 (a)	67 (c)	68 (a)	69 (b)	70 (c)
71 (a)	72 (c)	73 (c)	74 (c)	75 (b)	76 (c)	77 (d)	78 (c)	79 (b)	80 (a)
81 (b)	82 (d)								

Exercise 2

1 (b)	2 (d)	3 (b)	4 (c)	5 (d)	6 (b)	7 (a)	8 (b)	9 (a)	10 (d)
11 (d)	12 (c)	13 (b)	14 (c)	15 (d)	16 (b)	17 (c)	18 (a)	19 (d)	20 (c)
21 (a)	22 (b)	23 (a)	24 *(d)*	25 (c)	26 (b)	27 (c)	28 (a)	29 (b)	30 (b)
31 (b)	32 (a)	33 (b)	34 (a)	35 (c)	36 (a)	37 (b)	38 (a)	39 (c)	40 (a)
41 (b)	42 (b)	43 (c)	44 (a)	45 (a)	46 (c)	47 (b)	48 (a)	49 (a)	50 (c)
51 (a)	52 (b)	53 (b)	54 (a)	55 (c)	56 (d)	57 (d)	58 (c)	59 (c)	60 (b)
61 (a)	62 (b)	63 (a)	64 (d)	65 (b)	66 (a)	67 (d)	68 (d)	69 (d)	70 (c)
71 (c)	72 (c)	73 (a)	74 (a)	75 (d)	76 (b)	77 (b)	78 (c)	79 (c)	80 (c)
81 (a)	82 (d)	83 (b)	84 (c)	85 (b)	86 (b)	87 (b)	88 (c)	89 (d)	90 (c)
91 (b)	92 (a)	93 (b)	94 (c)	95 (a)	96 (b)	97 (a)	98 (a)	99 (b)	100 (c)
101 (c)	102 (c)	103 (a)	104 (c)	105 (a)	106 (b)	107 (c)	108 (b)	109 (b)	110 (c)
111 (a)	112 (a)	113 (c)	114 (d)	115 (c)	116 (c)	117 (c)	118 (a)	119 (b)	120 (b)
121 (a)	122 (c)	123 (a)	124 (a)	125 (c)	126 (b)	127 (b)	128 (a)		

Explanations

Exercise 2

26. *(b)* यहाँ 231 pattern follow किया जाएगा i.e., IInd Person; IIIrd Person and 1st Person.

27. *(c)* दो व्यक्तियों के लिए negative sense के लिए neither का प्रयोग करें।

28. *(a)* (Note केवल किसी unpleasant या बुरे काम या मामले के सम्बन्ध में, 'I, he and you' (या इनका plural forms) का प्रयोग होता है। यहाँ ऐसी कोई बात नहीं है।)

29. *(b)* दो से अधिक व्यक्तियों या वस्तुओं के लिए one another का प्रयोग करें।

30. *(b)* 'Among' दो से अधिक व्यक्तियों के लिए प्रयोग में लाया जाता है। दो व्यक्तियों के लिए between शब्द प्रयोग में लाया जाता है।

31. *(b)* 'Everybody' शब्द singular माना जाता है अत: इसके लिए singular verb तथा singular pronoun का प्रयोग किया जाता है।

32. *(a)* 'Each other' परस्पर दो व्यक्तियों के लिए प्रयोग में लाया जाता है।

33. *(b)* 'Who' subject को denote करता है किन्तु 'whom' object को denote करता है।

34. *(a)* 'Either ... or' सदैव 'last' subject के आधार पर verb और pronoun लेता है। यहाँ पर Rakesh शब्द singular है। अत: verb तथा pronoun भी singular ही चाहिए।

35. *(c)* Pronoun 'one' का possessive pronoun 'one's' होता है।

36. *(a)* 'Between' शब्द दो व्यक्तियों के लिए प्रयोग में लाया जाता है। Among दो से अधिक व्यक्तियों के case में प्रयोग में लाया जाता है।

37. *(b)* इस case में 'the best novels' का अर्थ है 'the best among many'. अत: इस केस में Plural verb 'have' लगाना चाहिए, सबसे बढ़कर बात यह है कि Relative Pronoun सदैव antecedent से gender number तथा person के लिए agree करना चाहिए।

38. *(a)* जब कोई pronoun verb के object के तौर पर प्रयोग में लाया जाता है तो यह सदैव objective case होना चाहिए।

39. *(c)* दो व्यक्तियों तथा वस्तुओं में एक समान choice के लिए 'Either' शब्द का प्रयोग करें।

40. *(a)* 'Avail' शब्द के साथ reflexive pronoun का प्रयोग करें।

41. *(b)* 'Enjoy' शब्द के साथ reflexive pronoun का प्रयोग करें।

42. *(b)* दो से अधिक व्यक्तियों के लिए 'none' का प्रयोग करें। None के साथ singular verb का प्रयोग होता है।

43. *(c)* 'Non-living thing' के लिए 'which' Pronoun का प्रयोग किया जाता है। 'whose' शब्द 'living beings' की possession दर्शाता है।

44. *(a)* 'Keep' शब्द के साथ प्राय: reflexive pronoun का प्रयोग नहीं किया जाता।

45. *(a)* Complement क्रिया का object जब किसी pronoun के रूप में दिखाया जाता है, तो यह nominative case में होना चाहिए।

46. *(c)* 'Neither ...nor' के case में verb तथा pronoun सदैव 'last subject' के आधार पर प्रयोग में लाए जाते हैं।

47. *(b)* 'None' शब्द दो से अधिक व्यक्तियों के सन्दर्भ में प्रयोग में लाया जाता है तथा यह singular होता है।

48. *(a)* यह एक possessive case है।

49. *(a)* Imaginary situations में I were + nominative case का प्रयोग करें।

50. *(c)* 'Who' शब्द Subject को denote करता है। 'Whose' शब्द possession बताता है। 'Whom' शब्द object को denote करता है।

51. *(a)* 'Abstain' शब्द के साथ reflexive pronoun प्रयोग में नहीं लाया जाता।

52. *(b)* 'Hide' शब्द के साथ reflexive Pronoun प्रयोग न करें।

53. *(b)* 'Absent' जब Verb हो तो इसके साथ reflexive pronoun लगाएँ।

54. *(a)* वाक्य सही है।

55. *(c)* 'Our' के स्थान पर 'his' आएगा।

56. *(d)* 'Itself' की जगह 'themselves' आएगा। यहाँ Board of Directors का प्रयोग as collective noun की तरह नहीं हुआ है।

57. *(d)* The given sentence is error free.

58. *(c)* In a sentence, when two nouns are connected with 'as well as', the verb and the pronoun should be in coordination with the first noun. Hence, replace 'themselves' with 'himself' to make the sentence grammatically correct.

59. *(c)* 'Lazy one' की जगह 'lazy ones' होना चाहिए। One का प्रयोग singular के लिए एवं ones का प्रयोग plural हेतु किया जाता है।

60. *(b)* 'Who' की जगह 'that' का प्रयोग करें। याद रखें, All/none/same/only/ के साथ सामान्यतया relative pronoun 'that' का प्रयोग होता है। जैसे:
All that glitter is not gold.
He is the same man that supported me.
Same के साथ relative pronoun 'as' का प्रयोग किया जाएगा, यदि इसके बाद verb का प्रयोग नहीं हुआ है। This is the same house as mine.

61. *(a)* 'Any' की जगह 'Either' का प्रयोग होगा। Either का प्रयोग दो के लिए होता है।

62. *(b)* 'Whom' की जगह 'who' का प्रयोग किया जाएगा। **Whom**—objective case है, **Who**—Subject case है।

63. *(a)* introduced के बाद reflexive pronoun himself भी लगाना होगा।

64. *(d)* 'Him' की जगह 'he' ही आएगा। 'than' के बाद यदि दो subjects के मध्य तुलना की जाए तो nominative case का प्रयोग होगा न कि object case का। 'he'nominative case एवं 'him'object case है। देखें : She was more surprised than me to see the circus girl coming towards us.

यहाँ भी 'me' की जगह I का प्रयोग होगा क्योंकि तुलना दो subjects,'she' एवं I में है।

65. *(b)* 'Who' की जगह 'Which' या 'That' का प्रयोग करना होगा।

जब किसी pronoun के पहले आए दो noun, and से संयुक्त होते हैं तो pronoun अपने पास आए noun से govern होता है।

यहाँ पास वाला noun, everything है अत: यहाँ 'Which' या 'That' का प्रयोग होगा।

66. *(a)* 'Whomever' की जगह 'Whoever' होगा। Whomever, objective case है जबकि, whoever nominative case है जो अपने साथ verb, does not come ले रहा है।

67. *(d)* 'Each other' की जगह 'one another' होगा। each other का सामान्यतया प्रयोग दो के लिए किया जाता है।

68. *(d)* वाक्य सही है।

69. *(d)* 'The same' की जगह 'it' आयेगा। 'the same' का प्रयोग हमेशा एक adjective की तरह होता है। 'the same' का प्रयोग pronoun की तरह करना गलत है। जैसे :

(1) This is the same pen as mine.

(2) It is the same chair as yours.

70. *(c)* 'I' की जगह 'me' होगा। Let के साथ pronoun हमेशा objective case में आता है। जैसे :

(1) Let you and me go there.

(2) Let you and him prepare a proposal.

71. *(c)* She को delete करें क्योंकि यहाँ She लगाने की आवश्यकता नहीं है। This is the pen, which I lost it yesterday. यहाँ भी it का प्रयोग अनावश्यक है।

72. *(c)* Knows के बाद it लगाना आवश्यक है।

73. *(a)* Replace 'he' with 'him' to make the sentence grammatically correct.

74. *(a)*'Myself' के बदले 'I' होगा। ध्यान दें, reflexive pronoun, कभी भी वाक्य में subject की तरह प्रयुक्त नहीं हो सकता है। साधारण बोलचाल में हम myself को subject की तरह प्रयोग करते हैं। जैसे:

Myself is Suresh. *Incorrect*
I am Suresh. *Correct*
Yourself is responsible. *Incorrect*
You are responsible. *Correct*

75. *(d)* give के बाद 'it' लगेगा। Give एक transitive verb है, इसके साथ object लगाना आवश्यक है।

76. *(b)* When 'either' is used in a sentence, singular form of verb is used. Hence, replace 'were' with 'was' to make the sentence grammatically correct.

77. *(b)* 'his best' के स्थान पर 'your best' आएगा।

78. *(c)* 'boys play' के स्थान पर 'boys plays' आएगा।

79. *(c)* वाक्य में 'he' की आवश्यकता नहीं है।

80. *(c)* Replace 'his' with 'one's'.

81. *(a)* 'I and she' के स्थान पर 'She and I' आएगा।

82. *(d)* The given sentence is error free.

83. *(b)* 'And I' के स्थान पर 'and me' आएगा।

84. *(c)* 'I' के स्थान पर 'me' आएगा।

85. *(b)* Replace 'you' with 'yourself' to make the sentence grammatically correct.

86. *(b)* 'Me' के स्थान पर 'I' आएगा।

87. *(b)* 'I' के स्थान पर 'me' आएगा।

88. *(d)* 'One's pay' के स्थान पर 'their pay' आएगा।

89. *(c)* The given sentence is error free.

90. *(c)* 'One another' के स्थान पर 'each other' आएगा।

91. *(b)* 'Him coming' के स्थान पर 'his coming' आएगा।

92. *(a)* 'Who' के स्थान पर 'whom' आएगा।

93. *(b)* 'avail' के साथ 'yourself' प्रयुक्त होगा।

94. *(c)* 'the same' के स्थान पर 'them' आएगा।

95. *(a)* 'They' के स्थान पर 'Those' आएगा।

96. *(b)* 'you duty' के स्थान पर 'one's duty' का use किया जाएगा because if 'one' is used as a subject in a sentence then 'one's' or 'oneself' is used.

97. *(a)* यहाँ part (a) के अन्तर्गत 'who' के स्थान पर 'which' का use किया जाएगा क्योंकि lifeless object or things के लिए 'which' का use किया जाता है और persons के लिए who का।

98. *(a)* 'You, he and I' के स्थान पर 'I, you and he' का use किया जाएगा as they admitted their fault.

99. *(b)* यहाँ 'you and him' के स्थान पर 'you and he' का use suitable होगा as subjective case of a pronoun will be used here.

100. *(c)* यहाँ 'themselves' के स्थान पर 'himself' का use किया जाएगा क्योंकि दोनों nouns (coach and mentor) एक ही person के लिए use किए गए हैं।

101. *(c)* यहाँ part (c) के अन्तर्गत 'her' के स्थान पर 'she' का use किया जाएगा because the subjective case of pronoun is used when it is to be placed after 'to be'.

102. *(c)* Pronoun 'Neither' singular noun के लिए use किया जाता है इसलिए यहाँ part (c) के अन्तर्गत 'their' के स्थान पर 'his' का use किया जाएगा।

103. *(a)* Replace 'it' with 'itself' to make the sentence grammatically correct.

104. *(c)* यहाँ part (c) के अन्तर्गत 'one another' के स्थान पर 'each other' का use किया जाएगा as reciprocal noun 'each other' is used for two nouns while 'one another' is used for more than two nouns.

105. *(a)* यहाँ 'anyone' के स्थान पर 'either' का use किया जाएगा। For two persons or things, 'either' is used and for more than two, 'anyone' is used.

106. *(b)* यहाँ part (b) के अन्तर्गत 'who' के स्थान पर 'which' का use किया जाएगा। As the sentence refers to a choice among more than two persons (servants), 'which' will be used in place of 'who'.

107. *(c)* यहाँ part (c) के अन्तर्गत 'their' के स्थान पर 'its' का use किया जाएगा। When a pronoun stands for a collective noun (ruling party), it must be in the neuter gender.

108. *(b)* दिए गए sentence में 'adapt' के बाद reflexive pronoun 'themselves' का use किया जाएगा। As the sentence refers to a particular set of people (Indians), it will contain a reflexive pronoun.

109. *(b)* दिए गए sentence में 'critics' से पहले pronoun 'one's' का use किया जाएगा, to make the sentence grammatically correct.

110. *(c)* Sentence में 'one' का use किया गया है इसलिए part (c) के अन्तर्गत 'his own' के स्थान पर 'one's own' का use किया जाएगा।

111. *(a)* यदि sentence में एक से अधिक singular pronouns का use हुआ हो, तो उनको लिखने का सही क्रम You—He/She—I होता है। अत: यहाँ part (a) के अन्तर्गत 'He, You and I' के स्थान पर 'You, He and I' का use किया जाएगा।

112. *(a)* यहाँ 'was it him' के स्थान पर 'was it he' का use किया जाएगा।

As per the rule, the component of the verb 'to be' (was) when expressed by a pronoun should be in the nominative case.

113. *(c)* दिया गया sentence incomplete है इसलिए यहाँ part (c) में 'embraced' के बाद 'her' का use किया जाएगा, to make the sentence error free.

114. *(d)* No error.

115. *(c)* यहाँ part (c) में 'its' के स्थान पर 'their' का use किया जाएगा क्योंकि living beings (audience) के लिए 'their' का use किया जाता है।

116. *(c)* यहाँ part (c) के अन्तर्गत 'it' के स्थान पर 'they' का use किया जाएगा। as the sentence refers to 'his hunches' and 'his data'.

117. *(c)* यहाँ 'than' के साथ 'that' का use होना जरुरी है, to make the sentence meaningful and correct.

118. *(a)* दिया गया sentence 'he' से शुरू होगा इसलिए यहाँ part (a) के अन्तर्गत 'being' से पहले 'he' का use किया जाएगा।

The sentence does not convey the intended meaning as it has 'he' missing in the beginning.

119. *(b)* यहाँ 'his' के स्थान पर 'one's' का use किया जाएगा क्योकि sentence, indefinite pronoun 'one' से start हुआ है।

120. *(b)* यहाँ part (b) के अन्तर्गत 'who' के स्थान पर 'whom' का use किया जाएगा to make the sentence grammatically correct.

121. *(a)* यहाँ 'our' के स्थान पर 'ours' का use किया जाएगा to make the sentence grammatically correct.

122. *(c)* यहाँ 'enjoyed' के बाद reflexive pronoun 'himself' का use किया जाएगा to make the sentence grammatically correct.

123. *(a)* यहाँ 'him' के स्थान पर 'he' का use किया जाएगा because the verb 'were' when expressed by a pronoun, it should be in the nominative case.

124. *(a)* यहाँ 'sort of' का use incorrect है। It should be replaced by 'sorts of' to make the sentence grammatically correct.

125. *(c)* दिया गया sentence incomplete है इसलिए यहाँ part (c) में 'helped' के बाद 'him' का use किया जाएगा। The sentence is incomplete as it does not answer the question 'helped whom'.

126. *(b)* यहाँ 'their' के स्थान पर 'his' का use किया जाएगा to make the sentence grammatically correct.

127. *(b)* यहाँ part (b) के अन्तर्गत 'acquit' के बाद reflexive pronoun 'themselves' का use किया जाएगा to make the sentence grammatically correct.

128. *(a)* यहाँ part (a) के अन्तर्गत 'avail' के बाद 'yourself of' का use किया जाएगा to make the sentence error free.

03 Prepositions

वे शब्द जो किसी noun या pronoun से पहले प्रयुक्त होकर उसका सम्बन्ध, sentence के किसी अन्य noun या pronoun के साथ बताते हैं, उन्हें prepositions कहते हैं। जैसे—on, at, in, by, to, of, from etc.

e.g., (i) He is sitting on the chair.
(ii) They are in the room.

Kinds of Prepositions

Prepositions मुख्यत: निम्न प्रकार की होती हैं—

- **Simple Prepositions** At, on, in, for, to, of, up, over etc.
- **Compound Prepositions** Inside, outside, beneath, beside, beyond etc.
- **Phrasal Prepositions** Along with, because of, by means of, with regard to etc.

Correct Use of Some Prepositions

1. **At** (पर) का use

(a) छोटे स्थानों, गाँवों, कस्बों या बड़े स्थान के एक भाग के लिए
e.g., (i) I live at Balbir Nagar.
(ii) He has arrived at Chandni Chowk.

(b) किसी निश्चित समय के लिए
e.g., (i) The train departs at 5 am.
(ii) Come at 6 o'clock.

(c) किसी स्थान के विशेष बिन्दु की ओर इशारा करने के लिए
e.g., (i) Do not look at the door.
(ii) He is at the platform.

(d) कीमत/दर/चाल की दर को अभिव्यक्त करने के लिए
e.g., (i) Milk sells at ₹ 16/ litre.
(ii) He got that book at ₹ 50.

(e) उम्र (age) तथा चरण (stage) को अभिव्यक्त करने के लिए
e.g., (i) My grandfather died at the age of sixty.
(ii) I left college at twenty five.

(f) Particular time (dawn, midnight, noon, two o'clock etc.), meal/calendar, festival seasons (New year, Christmas etc), start/end of/week/month के लिए
e.g., (i) She will come at Christmas.
(ii) Richa went home at lunch time.

2. **In** (में) का use

(a) देश, प्रदेश या बड़े नगरों के लिए
e.g., (i) Mukti lives in Canada.
(ii) I work in Delhi.

(b) समय के किसी भाग की समाप्ति के लिए या भविष्य की अवधि बताने के लिए अर्थात् कार्य कुछ समय में होगा, यह बताने के लिए
e.g., (i) Complete the task in two days.
(ii) The Taj Mahal was built in 21 years.

(c) सन्, वर्ष या महीने के नाम से पूर्व
e.g., (i) I was born in July.
(ii) We got freedom in 1947.

(d) स्थिरता तथा विश्राम (Rest) की दशा में
e.g., (i) The tea is in the cup.
(ii) My mother is cooking food in the kitchen.

(e) In + the + room, places, weather, kitchen, bedroom, Sun, rain, show etc.
e.g., (i) She was working in the Sun.
(ii) He was sleeping in the bedroom.

3. **On** (पर) का use

(a) किसी वस्तु की स्थिरता को प्रकट करने के लिए तथा जब एक वस्तु दूसरी के ऊपर हो और उसे छू रही हो।
e.g., (i) Do not sit on the bench.
(ii) We live on the Earth.

(b) दिनों के नामों से पूर्व या तिथियों से पूर्व
e.g., (i) They got married on 10th March.
(ii) He came here on Sunday.

(c) On + name of day/name of day with part of day/particular date etc.
e.g., (i) Her birthday is on 26th April.
(ii) He will meet you on Tuesday morning.

'At night' और 'In the night' में difference = 'At night' का अर्थ होता है किसी भी रात के दौरान लेकिन 'In the night' का अर्थ किसी particular रात के दौरान होता है।

- Time [In time : समय से पहले (Scheduled time), On time : समय पर (Exact on time)]
  e.g. We reached the examination centre in time and the exam started on time.
- Hour → Month → Year → Day → Date
  at in in on on
- The use of the preposition of time 'in' and 'on' in these common expressions :

In	on
in the morning	on Tuesday morning
in the mornings	on Saturday morning
in the afternoon(s)	on Sunday afternoons
in the evening(s)	on Monday evening

- At/In/On
  'At' is used for a precise time.
  'In' is used for Months, Years, Centuries and long periods.
  'On' is used for days and dates.

AT Precise Time	IN Months, Years, Centuries and Long Periods	ON Days and Dates
at 3 o'clock	in May	on Sunday
at 10:30 am	in summer	on Tuesday
at noon	in the summer	on 6th March
at dinner time	in 1990	on 25th January, 2007
at bed time	in the 1990s	on Christmas Day
at sunrise	in the next century	on Independence Day
at sunset	in the Ice Age	on my birthday
at the moment	in the past/future	on New Yeas's Eve

4. **Upon** (पर) का use

किसी वस्तु की गति का भाव (in motion) बताने के लिए तथा स्थान परिवर्तन के रूप में upon का use किया जाता है।

e.g., (i) A dog jumped upon me.
(ii) The lion sprang upon the prey.

5. **With** (से या साथ) का प्रयोग

(a) किसी यन्त्र (instrument) के लिए
e.g., (i) Do not play with guns.
(ii) The mother cut the apple with a knife.

(b) दो व्यक्तियों के मिलन या संयोग की दशा में
e.g., (i) Come with your father.
(ii) He bought this house with her help.

6. **By** (के द्वारा) का प्रयोग

(a) कार्य करने वाले के लिए कर्त्ता (agent) से पूर्व passive voice में
e.g. (i) You are helped by a monk.
(ii) He is beaten by you.

(b) किसी निश्चित समय के लिए
e.g., Try to come by 5 am.

(c) साधन से पूर्व
e.g., (i) Satish is hit by a car.
(ii) Madan goes everywhere by cycle.

(d) नाप या तोल की इकाई से पूर्व
e.g., (i) Sugar is sold by gram.
(ii) Banana is sold by dozen.

'With' का use instrument हेतु और 'By' का use agent (कर्ता) हेतु किया जा सकता है।
e.g., The snake was killed by him with a stick.

7. **Within** (में) का use

समय की अवधि की समाप्ति से पूर्व के लिए
e.g., (i) Finish the chapter within an hour.
(ii) I will be transferred within a week.

8. **After** (बाद में) का use

समय की अवधि की समाप्ति के लिए
e.g. (i) He had come after she died.
(ii) She will join you after the lunch.

9. **Behind** (के पीछे) का use

स्थान के लिए और विश्राम की अवस्था को बताने के लिए
e.g. (i) The temple is behind the house.
(ii) There are two men behind my car.

10. **Between** (के बीच) तथा Among (के बीच) का use

Between का प्रयोग 'दो के लिए' जबकि among का प्रयोग 'दो से अधिक' के लिए
e.g., (i) There is a conflict between Sapna and Vinay.
(ii) Prasad Should be distributed among the devotees.

- 'दो से अधिक' के लिए भी between का प्रयोग कर सकते हैं, बशर्ते स्थिति व्यवस्थित हो।
  e.g. Delhi is between UP, Rajasthan, Punjab and Haryana.
- यदि स्थिति अव्यवस्थित हो, तो among का प्रयोग करते हैं।
  e.g. His seat is among the employees.

11. **Beside** (के पास) तथा Besides (के अतिरिक्त) का use

Beside का use के बगल में (at the side of) जबकि besides का use 'अतिरिक्त, के अलावा' के अर्थ में किया जाता है।
e.g. (i) My office is beside the Meerut Mall.
(ii) Besides the shirts he sold his jeans.

12. **Since** (के बाद से), For (के लिए) तथा From (से) का use

Since तथा for का use समय बताने के लिए perfect continuous tense में होता है। Since निश्चित समय तथा for अनुमानित समय के लिए प्रयुक्त होता है। From का use किसी भी tense में हो सकता है। यह समय बिन्दु (point of time) को दर्शाता है।

e.g., (i) He has been reading a book since 5 o'clook.
(ii) They have been cooking the food for two hours.
(iii) I will use this bag from 10th March, 2016.

For + a/an + minute/hour/day/week, etc.
For + a long period/time
For + numerical adjective (जैसे-two, three) + minutes/hours/day/weeks/months, etc.
For + the last/past + numerical adjective + minute (s)/hour(s)/day(s)/decade etc.
e.g., (i) She has been absent from the office for a week.
(ii) They have not seen her for the last past five months.

- Last/past (month/week, etc) के पहले यदि the का use हो, तो इनसे period of time का बोध होता है, न कि point of time का इसलिए ऐसे case में for का use किया जाता है, न कि since का।

e.g., (i) She has been here since last week. (Point of time) (✗)
(ii) She has been here for the last week. (Period of time) (✓)

Since + fixed time/date/day/month/years.
Since + definite event/occasion (Holi, Diwali, Eid etc.)
Since + part of the day (Morning, Evening etc.)
Since + stage of life (Childhood, Adolescence etc.)
Since का use सिर्फ present/past time दर्शाने वाले शब्दों के साथ किया जाता है, जबकि future समय के case में from का use since की जगह किया जाता है।
e.g., (i) They will come here from next Monday.
(ii)They have been visiting us since childhood.

13. **Till** (जब तक) का use

अनिश्चित समय के लिए

e.g., (i) Do not turn the page till I order.
(ii) Karishma will wait till 6 o'clock.

14. **Onto** (पर) का use

जब कोई वस्तु गतिशील हो तथा किसी सतह (surface) पर आ रही हो

e.g., (i) The helicopter is falling onto the runway.
(ii) The cat jumped and sat onto the table.

15. **Of** (का) का use

(a) सम्बन्ध को प्रकट करने के लिए

e.g., (i) I am the writer of this book.
(ii) He is the owner of this house.

(b) विशेषता या कारण बताने के लिए

e.g., (i) Madan died of cancer. (कारण)
(ii) You should be the man of principal. (विशेषता)

16. **Off** (से दूर) का use

(a) विभाजन (separation) के लिए

e.g., (i) Come off the car.
(ii) The cap of the pen came off while opening.

(b) कार्य जो ऊपर से नीचे के लिए प्रकट हो

e.g. He fell off the building.

17. **To** (को) का use

किसी स्थान या व्यक्ति से जुड़ने के लिए

e.g., Shobhit has gone to Nepal.

18. **Beyond** (के परे) का use

(a) नियन्त्रण या आपे से बाहर होने के लिए

e.g. This situation is beyond your limit.

(b) दूसरी ओर (Place) के लिए

e.g. Do not go beyond the fence.

19. **Under** (के नीचे) का use

(a) नीचे (place) के लिए

e.g. We sat under the table.

(b) कम के लिए

e.g. It is illegal to marry if you are under 18 years.

20. **Towards** (की ओर), Across (के ओर पार), Along (के साथ), Through (के माध्यम से) का use

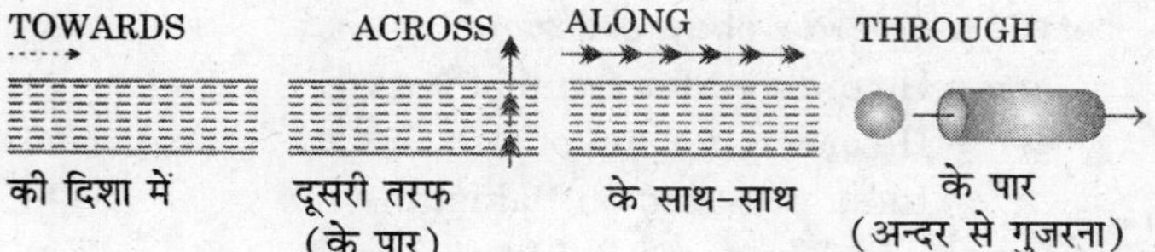

- Towards का use **'दिशा'** (In the direction of) के लिए किया जाता है।
- Across का use 'के पार' (The opposite side), 'एक ओर से दूसरी ओर' (From one side to another one) तथा दोनों ओर' (Both sides) के लिए किया जाता है।
- Along का use 'के साथ-साथ चलने' या समानांतर (Parallel) को दर्शाने के लिए किया जाता है। Along के साथ noun का use किया जाता है, जब यह preposition के रूप में use किया जाता है।
- Through का use 'के पार और के माध्यम से' (By means of/From one side to another one) तथा 'शुरूआत से अन्त तक' को दर्शाने के लिए किया जाता है।
- Throughout का use 'प्रत्येक जगह' (in every part of a place or object) के अर्थ में किया जाता है।

e.g., (i) Students are going towards the school.
(ii) I saw Rohit, walking along the river.
(iii) The rest house is across the river.
(iv) Students knew their result through a newspaper.

21. **Beneath** (नीचे) का use

Beneath का use (नीचे) under के लिए किया जाता है।

e.g., (i) The deer was sitting beneath the tree.
(ii) Alex was pale beneath the golden skin.

Some Important Rules of Prepositions

Rule 1 जब object-interrogative pronoun (What, Who, When, Which, Where etc) होता है, तो preposition को sentence के end में लगाया जाता है।

e.g., (i) What are you thinking of ?
(ii) What is he crying for ?

Rule 2 जब object-relative pronoun, 'that' होता है, तब भी preposition को sentence के end में लगाया जाता है।

e.g., (i) This is the girl that I told you of.
(ii) Here is the magazine that you asked for.

Rule 3 कुछ sentences में preposition का use शुरु में ही किया जाता है। सामान्यतया ऐसे sentences interrogative होते हैं।

e.g., (i) By which train did you come?
(ii) For whom was instructions given?

Rule 4 सामान्यतया transitive verbs के साथ preposition का use नहीं किया जाता है। इस तरह की verbs हैं-Reach, resist, resemble, afford, accompany, attack, assist, pick, pervade, precede, obey, order etc.

e.g., He ordered for a cup of tea. (✗)
He ordered a cup of tea. (✓)
India attacked on Pakistan. (✗)
India attacked Pakistan. (✓)

Rule 5 स्थान एवं समय व्यक्त करने वाले words (e.g. last week, last month, abroad, minute, inside, outside etc) के साथ भी generally preposition नहीं लगता है।

e.g., (i) He came here last month.
(ii) Please come inside.

Significant Expressions of Prepositions

1. I agree to you. (Incorrect)
I agree with you or to your proposal. (Correct)
2. deal for (Incorrect)
deal in (business) (Correct)
3. deal to (Incorrect)
deal with (behave) (Correct)
4. write with black ink (Incorrect)
write in black ink (Correct)
5. accompany with somebody (Incorrect)
accompany somebody (Correct)
6. accused with murder (Incorrect)
accused of murder (Correct)
7. accustom with some habit (Incorrect)
accustom to some habit (Correct)
8. acquit for murder (Incorrect)
acquit of murder (Correct)
9. anxious for something (Incorrect)
anxious about something (Correct)
10. apply to a job (Incorrect)
apply for a job (Correct)
11. apply for a person (Incorrect)
apply to a person (Correct)
12. appose with something (Incorrect)
appose to something (Correct)
13. ashamed at or for (Incorrect)
ashamed of (Correct)
14. ask on (Incorrect)
ask after (Correct)
15. be assessed on, for (Incorrect)
be assessed at (Correct)
16. be assimilated in, at (Incorrect)
be assimilated into (Correct)
17. assign for (Incorrect)
assign to (Correct)
18. tired with someone (Incorrect)
tired of someone or some job (Correct)
19. complain for somebody (Incorrect)
complain against somebody (Correct)
20. complain with somebody against somebody (Incorrect)
complain to somebody against somebody (Correct)
21. catch from or for arm, etc. (Incorrect)
catch by arm or collar (Correct)
22. contribute for some firm (Incorrect)
contribute to some firm (Correct)
23. angry at somebody (Incorrect)
angry with somebody (Correct)
24. angry with somebody's behaviour (Incorrect)
angry at somebody's behaviour (Correct)
25. died from some disease (Incorrect)
died of some disease (Correct)
26. died of overwork (Incorrect)
died from overwork (Correct)

27. guard at something bad (Incorrect)
guard against something bad (Correct)
28. burst in tears (Incorrect)
burst into tears (Correct)
29. fond for something (Incorrect)
fond of something (Correct)
30. taste with something (Incorrect)
taste for something (Correct)
31. quarrel on trifles (Incorrect)
quarrel over trifles (Correct)
32. jealous with somebody (Incorrect)
jealous of somebody (Correct)
33. convicted for the charge of theft (Incorrect)
convicted of the charge of theft (Correct)
34. suffering with fever (Incorrect)
suffering from fever (Correct)
35. slow on studies (Incorrect)
slow at studies (Correct)
36. slow at hearing (Incorrect)
slow of hearing (Correct)
37. get rid from something or somebody (Incorrect)
get rid of something or somebody (Correct)
38. invite at, of etc. (Incorrect)
invite to (Correct)
39. unfit with somebody (Incorrect)
unfit for somebody (Correct)
40. add with something (Incorrect)
add up something (Correct)
41. add up on (Incorrect)
add up to give out a total
e.g., add up to ₹9000 (Correct)
42. order for something (Incorrect)
order something (Correct)
43. resemble with somebody (Incorrect)
resemble somebody (Correct)
44. knock for (Incorrect)
knock on or at (Correct)

Note
(i) 'knock on' का अर्थ है उसी स्थान पर जिसका वर्णन किया गया है, जैसे 'door'.
(ii) 'knoch at' का अर्थ है उस स्थान के पास जैसे door के पास window पर

45. abound with something (Incorrect)
abound in something (Correct)
46. afraid from something (Incorrect)
afraid of something (Correct)
47. apologize from a person (Incorrect)
apologize to a person (Correct)
48. apologize with the rude behaviour (Incorrect)
apologize for the rude behaviour (Correct)
49. confident for success (Incorrect)
confident of success (Correct)
50. eager about praise (Incorrect)
eager for praise (Correct)
51. eligible with a post (Incorrect)
eligible for a post (Correct)
52. engage with studies (Incorrect)
engage in studies (Correct)
53. absorb with studies (Incorrect)
absorb in studies (Correct)
54. differ to you (Incorrect)
differ from or with you (Correct)
55. desirous for doing something (Incorrect)
desirous of doing something (Correct)
56. confidence on you (Incorrect)
confidence in somebody (Correct)
57. devoid from something (Incorrect)
devoid of something (Correct)
58. envious from (Incorrect)
envious of (Correct)
59. escape on (Incorrect)
escape from (Correct)
60. born in poor parents (Incorrect)
born of poor parents (Correct)
61. born from him or her (Incorrect)
born to him or her (Correct)
62. blind with one eye (Incorrect)
blind in or of one eye (Correct)
63. famous from something (Incorrect)
famous for something (Correct)
64. famous in some people (Incorrect)
famous with some people (Correct)
65. attend for someone's lesson (Incorrect)
attend to someone's lesson (Correct)
66. beware from (Incorrect)
beware of (Correct)
67. bend for (Incorrect)
bend on (Correct)
68. introduce for someone (Incorrect)
introduce to someone (Correct)
69. inferior from (Incorrect)
inferior to (Correct)

70. superior from (Incorrect)
superior to (Correct)

71. junior from (Incorrect)
junior to (Correct)

72. senior from (Incorrect)
senior to (Correct)

73. neglectful with one's duty (Incorrect)
neglectful to one's duty (Correct)

74. kind with someone (Incorrect)
kind to someone (Correct)

75. married with (Incorrect)
married to (Correct)

76. loyal for one's country (Incorrect)
loyal to one's country (Correct)

77. laugh on someone (Incorrect)
laugh at someone (Correct)

78. infested from rats (Incorrect)
infested with rats (Correct)

79. necessary with you (Incorrect)
necessary for you (Correct)

80. greed for something (Incorrect)
greed of something (Correct)

81. hope to success (Incorrect)
hope for or of success (Correct)

82. ignorant from (Incorrect)
ignorant of (Correct)

83. innocent from (Incorrect)
innocent of (Correct)

84. false from one's promise (Incorrect)
false to one's promise (Correct)

85. familiar in some place (Incorrect)
familiar with some place (Correct)

86. familiar for somebody (Incorrect)
familiar to somebody (Correct)

87. free of germs (Incorrect)
free from germs (Correct)

88. furnished on (Incorrect)
furnished with (Correct)

89. notorious from (Incorrect)
notorious for (Correct)

90. popular to (Incorrect)
popular with (Correct)

91. prevent to (Incorrect)
prevent from (Correct)

92. proud for (Incorrect)
proud of (Correct)

93. reduced from a skeleton (Incorrect)
reduced to a skeleton (Correct)

94. pray for God (Incorrect)
pray to God (Correct)

95. pray from somebody (Incorrect)
pray for somebody (Correct)

96. relate for (Incorrect)
relate to (Correct)

97. respect in (Incorrect)
respect for (Correct)

98. regard with (Incorrect)
regard for (Correct)

99. worthy from (Incorrect)
worthy of (Correct)

100. useful with (Incorrect)
useful for (Correct)

101. zeal on something (Incorrect)
zeal for some mission (Correct)

102. thankful with (Incorrect)
thankful to (Correct)

103. search to something (Incorrect)
search for something (Correct)

104. belong for (Incorrect)
belong to (Correct)

105. boast for something (Incorrect)
boast of something (Correct)

106. close for (Incorrect)
close to (Correct)

107. dear for someone (Incorrect)
dear to someone (Correct)

108. lost from (Incorrect)
lost to (Correct)

109. honest to (Incorrect)
honest in (Correct)

110. sick with (Incorrect)
sick of (Correct)

111. sorry at (Incorrect)
sorry for (Correct)

112. reply at somebody (Incorrect)
reply to somebody (Correct)

113. wait to somebody (Incorrect)
wait for somebody (Correct)

114. respectful with (Incorrect)
respectful to (Correct)

115. interest with a subject (Incorrect)
interest in a subject (Correct)

116. interest in a person (Incorrect)
interest with a person (Correct)

117. studded in (Incorrect)
studded with (Correct)

118. stare to (Incorrect)
stare at (Correct)

119. passion to (Incorrect)
passion for (Correct)

120. full in something (Incorrect)
full of something (Correct)

121. exempt for (Incorrect)
exempt from (Correct)

122. mad to laughter (Incorrect)
mad with laughter (Correct)

123. opposite with (Incorrect)
opposite to (Correct)

124. made with (Incorrect)
made of (Correct)

125. involved to (Incorrect)
involved in (Correct)

126. injurious for health (Incorrect)
injurious to health (Correct)

127. delighted for (Incorrect)
delighted with (Correct)

128. loaded in (Incorrect)
loaded with (Correct)

129. objection for (Incorrect)
objection to (Correct)

130. obnoxious on (Incorrect)
obnoxious to (Correct)

131. identical to (Incorrect)
identical with (Correct)

132. rob in money (Incorrect)
rob of money (Correct)

133. wonder on (Incorrect)
wonder at (Correct)

134. astonish on (Incorrect)
astonish at (Correct)

135. overwhelmed of (Incorrect)
overwhelmed with (Correct)

136. vexed on (Incorrect)
vexed at (Correct)

137. accurate with (Incorrect)
accurate in (Correct)

138. attentive on (Incorrect)
attentive to (Correct)

139. repent for (Incorrect)
repent of (Correct)

140. abide with (Incorrect)
abide by (Correct)

Exercise 1

Directions (Q. Nos. 1-50) Fill in the blanks with appropriate prepositions.

1. The dog snapped .... the thief and caught his leg.
(a) of (b) at (c) on (d) over

2. I shall proceed .... him.
(a) against (b) to
(c) for (d) on

3. When I heard of my grandmother's death, I burst .... tears.
(a) at (b) upon (c) into (d) in

4. She was removed .... the office of the director.
(a) to (b) of
(c) from (d) through

5. President Saddam Hussain has been familiar .... a gun all his life.
(a) with (b) for
(c) by (d) on

6. I am confident .... winning.
(a) to (b) of
(c) at (d) in

7. He hindered me .... doing this.
(a) from (b) of
(c) over (d) at

8. Munni is good .... music.
(a) by (b) to
(c) with (d) at

9. I must be faithful .... you.
(a) to (b) on (c) in (d) by

10. He is coming .... plane.
(a) on (b) by (c) with (d) in

11. This is different .... the other.
(a) from (b) to
(c) with (d) in

12. This is no cause .... anxiety.
(a) of (b) for
(c) to (d) on

13. I sold my car for .... its half cost.
(a) below (b) under
(c) in (d) upon

14. He entered .... the bus.
(a) in
(b) into
(c) with
(d) None of the above

15. He is not ashamed .... his conduct.
(a) of (b) on
(c) in (d) with

16. A policeman rescued the child .... danger.
(a) from (b) of
(c) against (d) for

17. That rule is not applicable .... your case.
(a) on (b) to
(c) at (d) for

18. He is addicted .... gambling.
(a) to (b) of
(c) on (d) with

19. He lives .... 48 Banjara Hills .... Hyderabad.
(a) at, in (b) in, at
(c) on, in (d) in, on

20. He started .... six .... the morning.
(a) at, on (b) at, in
(c) in, at (d) at, of

21. He was killed .... the robber .... a knife.
(a) with, by (b) by, with
(c) from, with (d) by, to

22. I was angry .... him .... lying to me.
(a) with, for (b) to, for
(c) with, on (d) to, with

23. Nobody is .... the reach of the law?
(a) beyond (b) above
(c) over (d) beside

24. Our factory turns .... two thousand new cars a month.
(a) out (b) up
(c) at (d) with

25. Shivaji fought .... every kind of aggression.
(a) against (b) to
(c) with (d) at

26. This week the rupee dropped .... its lowest level.
(a) on (b) to
(c) at (d) for

27. He dispensed .... the services of his dishonest clerk.
(a) with (b) to
(c) at (d) for

28. The godown is infested .... rats.
(a) with (b) to
(c) by (d) for

29. I am obliged .... you .... your kindness.
(a) with, for (b) to, for
(c) at, on (d) at, for

30. Alcohol is injurious .... health.
(a) with (b) to
(c) at (d) for

31. I am not satisfied .... your explanation.
(a) with (b) to
(c) at (d) for

32. Her activities are harmful .... my own interests.
(a) upon (b) with
(c) to (d) at

33. Has the train arrived .... the station?
(a) in (b) to
(c) at (d) for

34. The man jumped .... the river.
(a) in (b) into
(c) on (d) for

35. I go .... school every day.
(a) on (b) to
(c) with (d) by

36. They went home .... foot.
(a) at (b) with
(c) by (d) on

37. The streets are lit .... electricity.
(a) up with (b) by
(c) on (d) up to

38. My best friend lives .... Boxtz road.
(a) in (b) on
(c) at (d) for

39. I prefer tea .... coffee.
(a) to (b) of
(c) with (d) on

40. The frog fell .... the well.
(a) into (b) under
(c) over (d) in

41. He lives .... Bombay .... India.
(a) at, of (b) in, of
(c) at, in (d) in,at

42. She sat .... a chair.
(a) to (b) in
(c) at (d) on

43. What is the time .... your watch?
(a) by (b) in
(c) into (d) on

44. He is angry .... me.
(a) to (b) with
(c) on (d) by

45. We are shocked .... the news .... your failure.
(a) at, of (b) at, to
(c) on, to (d) to with

46. Be polite .... all and trust .... God.
(a) with, over (b) at, in
(c) to, in (d) by, in

47. Let us move ....
(a) on (b) in
(c) to (d) of

48. Nothing lasts .... ever.
(a) from (b) for
(c) over (d) on

49. None .... the brave deserves the fair.
(a) to (b) from
(c) for (d) but

50. What are you looking ...... ?
(a) to (b) for
(c) with (d) by

Directions (Q.Nos. 51-75) Select the option which is the correct form of the sentence.

51. I agreed to you.
(a) I agreed with you.
(b) I agreed for you.
(c) I agreed on you.
(d) None of the above

52. Tony reached at the station in time.
(a) Tony reached on the station in time.
(b) Tony reached the station in time.
(c) Tony reached to the station in time.
(d) None of the above

53. A gang of robbers attacked on the bank manager.
(a) A gang of robbers attacked the bank manager.
(b) A gang of robbers attacked at the bank manager.
(c) A gang of robbers attacked to the bank manager.
(d) None of the above

54. He accompanied with us to Mumbai.
(a) He accompanied us to Mumbai.
(b) He accompanied to us to Mumbai.
(c) He accompanied on us to Mumbai.
(d) None of the above

55. He was accused with murder.
(a) He was accused for murder.
(b) He was accused to murder.
(c) He was accused of murder.
(d) None of the above

56. He was accustomed on going for a walking in the morning.
(a) He was accustomed to going for a walk...
(b) He was accustomed for going for a walk.
(c) He was accustomed at going for a walk...
(d) None of the above

57. He achieved on a great success in life.
(a) He achieved a great success in life.
(b) He achieved to a great success in life.
(c) He achieved for a great success in life.
(d) None of the above

58. The jury acquitted Tony for murder.
(a) The jury acquitted Tony to murder.
(b) The jury acquitted Tony of murder.
(c) The jury acquitted Tony on murder.
(d) None of the above

59. Ajit was anxious on his mother's health.
(a) Ajit was anxious for his mother's health.
(b) Ajit was anxious about his mother's health.
(c) Ajit was anxious at his mother's health.
(d) None of the above

60. Rupesh applied for a Principal.
(a) Rupesh applied to the post of a Principal.
(b) Rupesh applied for the post of a Principal.
(c) Rupesh applied on the post of a Principal.
(d) None of the above

61. The pen was apposed on the ink-pot.
(a) The pen was apposed to the inkpot.
(b) The pen was apposed for the inkpot.
(c) The pen was apposed with the inkpot.
(d) None of the above

62. Your father deals with sugar.
(a) Your father deals on sugar.
(b) Your father deals to sugar.
(c) Your father deals in sugar.
(d) None of the above

63. He was ashamed to himself.
(a) He was ashamed of himself.
(b) He was ashamed with himself.
(c) He was ashamed for himself.
(d) None of the above

64. He was asking on you.
(a) He was asking to you.
(b) He was asking after you.
(c) He was asking with you.
(d) None of the above

65. I never aspired on such grand success in life.
(a) I never aspired to such grand...
(b) I never aspired with such...
(c) I never aspired for such grand...
(d) None of the above

66. A big crowd assembled to the outside.
(a) A big crowd assembled on the outside.
(b) A big crowd assembled at the outside.
(c) A big crowd assembled outside.
(d) None of the above

67. The damage due to floods was assessed for £ 8 million.
(a) The damage due to floods was assessed at £ 8 million.
(b) The damage due to floods was assessed on £ 8 million.
(c) The damage due to floods was assessed with £ 8 million.
(d) None of the above

68. The gambling trends are assimilated in the modern society with lightning speed.
(a) The gambling trends are assimilated into...
(b) The gambling trends are assimilated to...
(c) The gambling trends are assimilated with...
(d) None of the above

69. He has been appointed on the job of a manager.
(a) He has been appointed to the job of...
(b) He has been appointed for the job of...
(c) He has been appointed at the job of...
(d) None of the above

70. I have ordered for a cup of coffee.
(a) I have ordered to a cup...
(b) I have ordered a cup....
(c) I have ordered in a cup....
(d) None of the above

71. Tom resembles with his father.
(a) Tom resembles to his father.
(b) Tom resembles in his father.
(c) Tom resembles his father.
(d) None of the above

72. I am tired from you.
(a) I am tired of you.
(b) I am tired on you.
(c) I am tired with you.
(d) None of the above

73. He has no faith for God.
(a) He has no faith with God.
(b) He has no faith in God.
(c) He has no faith to God.
(d) None of the above

74. I lodged a complaint about the arrogant clerk.
(a) I lodged a complaint for the arrogant.
(b) I lodged a complaint against the arrogant...
(c) I lodged a complaint on the arrogant...
(d) None of the above

75. Mukesh caught Rakesh from the arm.
(a) Mukesh caught Rakesh on the arm.
(b) Mukesh caught Rakesh to the arm.
(c) Mukesh caught Rakesh by the arm.
(d) None of the above

Exercise 2

Directions (Q. Nos. 1-45) Fill in the blanks with suitable preposition.

1. In the month of December, the temperature falls .... 4°C.
(a) from (b) below
(c) at (d) into

2. A jeep hit him while he was going .... the main road.
(a) on
(b) across
(c) behind
(d) through

3. She is .... a noble family of Rajputs.
(a) from (b) of
(c) among (d) at

4. The case was put .... the judge and the judge decided it within an year.
(a) at (b) from
(c) before (d) of

5. The bridge .... this river was built in the year 1995.
(a) at (b) over
(c) above (d) on

6. She is suffering .... fever.
(a) with (b) of
(c) through (d) from

7. We saw wounded tiger while passing .... the forest.
(a) from (b) through
(c) along (d) among

8. Chairs are made .... wood.
(a) of (b) from
(c) on (d) through

9. There are tall beautiful coconut trees .... the river.
(a) along (b) at
(c) into (d) over

10. We are proud .... our children.
(a) on (b) at
(c) after (d) of

11. Mt Abu is about five thousand feet .... the sea-level.
(a) above (b) along
(c) after (d) behind

12. I shall always be indebted ... you for this timely help.
(a) from (b) of (c) to (d) with

13. He broke the jug ... hundred pieces.
(a) an (b) into
(c) at (d) of

14. Do not cry ...... spilt milk.
(a) above (b) under
(c) over (d) on

15. He looked ...... his watch all around the house.
(a) of (b) for
(c) to (d) from

16. I am fond ...... watching movies.
(a) from (b) for
(c) of (d) about

17. Don't loiter ...... the street.
(a) onto (b) about
(c) on (d) into

18. They will go to Bengaluru ...... plane.
(a) on (b) in
(c) by (d) from

19. He drained what was left ...... his drink.
(a) from (b) in
(c) of (d) off

20. It became clear that the strangers were heading ...... a serious disaster.
(a) along (b) towards
(c) for (d) into

21. He is so proud of his wealth that he looks down ...... the poor.
(a) for (b) at
(c) with (d) upon

22. The government aims ...... rehabilitating the affected victims in the calamity.
(a) to (b) for
(c) at (d) over

23. He complained ...... me to the police.
(a) about (b) against
(c) for (d) with

24. The climate is not conducive ...... good health.
(a) with (b) from
(c) in (d) to

25. The city was plunged ...... darkness due to a sudden power failure.
(a) at (b) to
(c) under (d) into

26. The students did not pay attention ...... what the teachers said.
(a) to (b) over
(c) on (d) at

27. I saw him felling a big tree ...... an axe.
(a) with (b) from
(c) to (d) of

28. The mother was anxious ...... the safety of her son.
(a) at (b) about
(c) for (d) upon

29. The four brothers are always quarreling ...... themselves.
(a) between (b) among
(c) for (d) with in

30. She lost her ring ...... the beach.
(a) upon (b) at
(c) from (d) to

31. We have lots of things in common ...... music.
(a) beside (b) below
(c) among (d) besides

32. Pakistan has ever been hostile ...... India, since it came ...... being.
(a) to, in (b) to, into
(c) of, in (d) from, out

33. How can a highly successful person like him be devoid ...... common sense.
(a) from (b) of
(c) to (d) in

34. The Hindus believe in many rituals to ward ...... evils.
(a) of (b) from
(c) off (d) with

35. His mother was overwhelmed ...... love for her son.
(a) to (b) with
(c) in (d) for

36. After all hard work has come to tell ...... your health.
(a) on (b) at
(c) upon (d) into

37. One should be true ...... one's promises ...... order ...... earn name and fame ...... life.
(a) to, in, to, in
(b) in, from, to, in
(c) to, into, from, in
(d) at, in, to, on

38. I have requested the police commissioner ...... look ...... the matter ...... increasing crime ...... our locality.
(a) into, from, of, in
(b) to, in, from, in
(c) of, into, to, in
(d) to, into, of, in

39. High rate ...... employment depends ...... growth ...... economy.
(a) on, in, of
(b) of, on, of
(c) of, in, of
(d) from, on, of

40. Indian Airlines had no positive response ...... the incident occurred ...... the failure ...... an aeroplane engine.
(a) to, in, of (b) of, in, to
(c) in, to, of (d) to, into from

41. The captain called ...... at one or two ports and sent ...... his long-boat ...... food and fresh water.
(a) at, in, for (b) in, at, for
(c) in, in, for (d) for, in, at

42. I was very fond ...... the old soldier ...... our little town. He used ...... tell me ...... his adventures.
(a) off, at, for, about
(b) of, in, to, about
(c) of, to, to, for
(d) in, at, of, before

43. Koala bear has been made ...... stuffed toys all ...... the world. But it is rare ...... see this creature alive and moving.
(a) into, over, to
(b) to, around, at
(c) into, about, to
(d) in, over, to

44. King Vikramaditya's verdicts were always just and people ...... all over vast kingdom came ...... him ...... crder ...... settle their disputes.
(a) of, at, for, into
(b) for, at, to, in
(c) from, in, to, on
(d) from, to, in, to

45. Laws are made ...... secure the personal safety ...... its subjects and ...... prevent murder and crimes ...... violence.
(a) off, to, to, of
(b) to, of, to, of
(c) for, to, of, in
(d) to, in, at, with

Directions (Q. Nos. 46-75) Read each sentence to find out whether there is an error in any part.

46. He was sleeping (a)/in his room when a thief (b)/entered into his house (c)/and took away a lot of things. (d)

47. In her concluding speech (a)/she said almost nothing (b)/worth listening to. (c)

48. It was apparent for (a)/everyone present (b)/that if the patient did not receive (c)/immediate medical aid (d)/he would die. (e)

49. He proposed me (a)/that we should go to the Disco (b)/and then have (c)/dinner at a restra. (d)

50. There appears (a)/to be a little liaison (b)/among the (c)/two groups of the society. (d)

51. The team (a)/complained to the manager (b)/against the captain (c)/and the poor facilities provided in the hotel. (d)

52. Yesterday I met (a)/a man (b)/who was blind with the right eye. (c)/ No error (d)

53. The principal distributed (a)/the sweet among our friends (b)/who bade him forewell. (c)/ No error (d)

54. As per the invitation care (a)/Rahim marries with Sayra (b)/on 13th December Monday. (c)/ No error (d)

55. The debacle of the Congress party (a)/admit no other explanation (b)/than its (c)/poor performance during the last five years. (d)

56. The society does not (a)/hold itself responsible (b)/for the loss or damage to (c)/ any item. (d)

57. In spite of being (a)/very busy at project work (b)/he saves time (c)/to the relatives. (d)

58. Some persons (a)/get promotions (b)/even if they are not (c)/worthy for them. (d)

59. While he was returning (a)/from the office (b)/a man attacked on (c)/him with a dagger. (d)

60. The decline of her moral (a)/was caused by a lot of (b)/factors that were once (c)/fascinating to her. (d)

61. He took me to a restra (a)/and ordered for two cups (b)/of cold coffee (c)/which the waiter brought in an hour. (d)

62. There are some animals (a)/that can live both in water and land (b)/without any difficulty. (c)/ No error (d)

63. During his tour (a)/to the South (b)/he visited not only to Chennai (c)/but also Karnataka. (d)

64. The President Mr Kalam (a)/is much sought after (b)/by school students and (c)/is invited for many functions. (d)

65. His mother is not well (a)/but he (b)/ does not look for her (c)/properly. (d)

66. We may have to await for (a)/a new political revival (b)/to eradicate the (c)/corruption from our economy. (d)

67. When she was (a)/in jail (b)/she was debarred to send (c)/a letter even to her son. (d)

68. Despite of the best efforts (a)/put by the doctors (b)/the condition of the patient (c)/is detereorating from bad to worse. (d)

69. The militant yielded for (a)/the temptation and fell (b)/into the trap (c)/of police. (d)

70. Many people in India (a)/ are dying from hunger (b)/ but government seems (c)/ to be ignorant of such crude fact. (d)

71. In difficult times (a)/she prefers keeping her counsel (b)/rather than wandering (c)/here and there for relief. (d)

72. The persons who are (a)/suffering from diabetes are (b)/advised to substitute (c)/saccharine by sugar. (d)

73. He is guilty (a)/for killing (b)/an innocent bird. (c)/No error (d)

74. Hardly had we settled down (a)/for the rest (b)/when we were started by the (c)/strange sound of trumpets. (d)

75. He was able to (a)/free himself with (b)/the debts by (c)/working day and night. (d)

Answers

Exercise 1

1 (b)	2 (a)	3 (c)	4 (c)	5 (a)	6 (b)	7 (a)	8 (d)	9 (a)	10 (b)
11 (a)	12 (b)	13 (a)	14 (d)	15 (a)	16 (a)	17 (b)	18 (a)	19 (a)	20 (b)
21 (b)	22 (a)	23 (a)	24 (a)	25 (a)	26 (b)	27 (a)	28 (a)	29 (b)	30 (b)
31 (a)	32 (c)	33 (c)	34 (b)	35 (b)	36 (d)	37 (a)	38 (c)	39 (a)	40 (a)
41 (c)	42 (d)	43 (a)	44 (b)	45 (a)	46 (c)	47 (a)	48 (b)	49 (d)	50 (b)
51 (a)	52 (b)	53 (a)	54 (a)	55 (c)	56 (a)	57 (a)	58 (b)	59 (b)	60 (b)
61 (a)	62 (c)	63 (a)	64 (b)	65 (a)	66 (c)	67 (a)	68 (a)	69 (a)	70 (b)
71 (c)	72 (a)	73 (b)	74 (b)	75 (c)					

Exercise 2

1 (b)	2 (b)	3 (a)	4 (c)	5 (b)	6 (d)	7 (b)	8 (a)	9 (a)	10 (d)
11 (a)	12 (c)	13 (b)	14 (c)	15 (b)	16 (c)	17 (c)	18 (c)	19 (c)	20 (b)
21 (d)	22 (c)	23 (b)	24 (d)	25 (d)	26 (a)	27 (a)	28 (b)	29 (b)	30 (b)
31 (d)	32 (b)	33 (b)	34 (c)	35 (c)	36 (c)	37 (a)	38 (d)	39 (b)	40 (a)
41 (c)	42 (b)	43 (a)	44 (d)	45 (b)	46 (c)	47 (c)	48 (a)	49 (a)	50 (c)
51 (d)	52 (c)	53 (b)	54 (b)	55 (b)	56 (c)	57 (d)	58 (d)	59 (c)	60 (a)
61 (b)	62 (b)	63 (c)	64 (d)	65 (c)	66 (a)	67 (c)	68 (a)	69 (a)	70 (b)
71 (c)	72 (d)	73 (b)	74 (c)	75 (b)					

Explanations

46. *(c)* 'Entered into' की जगह 'entered his' आयेगा। Go into, jump into हो सकता है।

47. *(c)* 'Listening to' की जगह केवल 'listening' ही होगा। यदि listen के बाद कोई object न हो, तो 'to' का प्रयोग नहीं होता है।

48. *(a)* 'Apparent for' की जगह 'Apparent to' होगा।

49. *(a)* 'Proposed' की जगह 'Proposed to' का use होगा। 'Proposed के साथ preposition 'to' का प्रयोग किया जाता है।

50. *(c)* 'Among' की जगह 'between' आयेगा। सामान्यत: 'between' का प्रयोग दो के लिए तथा 'among' का प्रयोग 'more than two' के लिए किया जाता है।

51. *(d)* 'And the poor' की जगह 'And about the poor ......' होगा।

52. *(c)* यहाँ 'blind with' के स्थान पर 'Blind in' का use होगा।

blind in left or right eye या blind of an eye या blind with both eyes आदि होता है।

53. *(b)* 'Among' की जगह 'amongst' होगा।

54. *(b)* यहाँ 'marries' के साथ 'with' का प्रयोग नहीं होगा। जब marry का प्रयोग मुख्य verb के रूप में होता है, तो इसके साथ कोई preposition नहीं लगता है।

55. *(b)* यहाँ 'admit' की जगह 'admits of' का use होगा। 'of' का प्रयोग 'admits' के बाद होगा।

56. *(c)* यहाँ 'loss or' की जगह 'loss of or' का use किया जाएगा।

यदि दो words, or या and संयुक्त हों एवं अलग-अलग prepositions लेते हों तो अलग - अलग prepositions लगाने आवश्यक हैं।

57. *(d)* 'To the relatives' की जगह 'for the relatives' का प्रयोग होगा। Save के साथ preposition निम्न प्रकार से लगते हैं : Save for something, save somebody from something.

(i) He has saved some money for medicines.

(ii) She saved me from drowning.

58. *(d)* 'Worthy for' की जगह 'worthy of का use होगा क्योंकि 'worthy' के बाद 'of', preposition लगता है।

59. *(c)* 'On' का प्रयोग अनुचित है। 'attacked on' की जगह 'attacked' का use suitable होगा। यदि attack का प्रयोग verb के रूप में किया जाये, तो इसके बाद object आता है। लेकिन यदि make के साथ attack का प्रयोग होता है, तो preposition 'on' लगता है। China made an attack on India.

60. *(a)* 'Decline of' की जगह 'Decline in' का use होगा। Decline in moral/ Decline in prices में decline के साथ 'in' आता है।

61. *(b)* 'Order' के बाद 'for' का प्रयोग नहीं होगा, क्योंकि 'order' एक transitive verb है, जिसके तुरन्त बाद object आता है।

(i) He ordered a glass of wine.

(ii) He ordered him to go to market.

62. *(b)* यहाँ 'and land' की जगह 'and on land' आयेगा।

यदि दो words 'and' या 'or' से संयुक्त हों एवं दोनों के साथ अलग-अलग preposition लगता हो, तो अलग-अलग prepositions लगने चाहिए।

63. *(c)* 'To' का प्रयोग गलत है। अत: यहाँ 'not only to Chennai' की जगह 'not only Chennai' आएगा। Visited का प्रयोग जब एक verb के रूप में किया जाता है, तो इसके बाद object आता है लेकिन make के साथ जब visit का प्रयोग किया जाता है, तो 'to' का प्रयोग होता है।

He made a visit to Agra last year.

64. *(d)* Invited के साथ to का प्रयोग होगा for की जगह to लगायें।

65. *(c)* 'Look for' की जगह 'Look after' का use होगा। 'Look after' का अर्थ है देखभाल करना।

66. *(a)* 'Await' के साथ for नहीं लगेगा। wait for होता है await for गलत है।

67. *(c)* 'Debarred to send की जगह 'Debarred from sending' का use होगा।

Debar/abstain/refrain के साथ preposition 'from' का प्रयोग + verb + ing का प्रयोग होता है।

He abstained from drinking wine.

68. *(a)* 'Despite' के साथ 'of' नहीं लगता है। 'Despite' का अर्थ होता है In spite of.

69. *(a)* 'Yielded for' की जगह 'Yielded to' का use होगा। Yield to का अर्थ होता है 'समर्पण' 'yielded for' की जगह (yield to somebody, yield to something) करना।

70. *(b)* 'Dying from hunger' की जगह 'Dying of hunger' का use होगा। 'Die of hunger/die of a disease' होता है। 'Die from over working/die from over drinking/die from food poisoning' आदि होता है।

71. *(c)* 'Rather than' की जगह 'rather' का use होगा। Prefer, senior, junior, prior इत्यादि के साथ preposition 'to' लगता है।

72. *(d)* 'By sugar' की जगह 'for sugar' का use होगा। substitute something for something होता है।

73. *(b)* 'Guilty' के साथ preposition 'of' का use किया जाता है, इसलिए यहाँ part (b) के अन्तगर्त 'for killing' की जगह 'of killing' का प्रयोग किया जएगा।

74. *(c)* 'Startled by' की जगह 'Startled at' होगा। Surprised / startled/ amazed/ astonished के साथ preposition 'at' लगता है।

75. *(b)* 'Free himself with' की जगह 'Free himself from' का use होगा। Free somebody from something या free from something होता है।

04 Conjunctions

A conjunction is a word which joins two or more than two words, phrases, clauses or sentences अर्थात् conjunction वह शब्द है जो दो या दो से अधिक शब्दो, शब्द समूहों, वाक्याशों या वाक्यों को जोड़ता है।

e.g., (i) He was in the class but he did not listen to the teacher.

(ii) He was misbehaving with the teacher therefore he was expelled.

Main Conjunctions

Conjunctions	Hindi Meaning	Conjunctions	Hindi Meaning
As (conj.)	तब उस समय	As to	विषय में
So as to	ताकि	As far as	जहाँ तक
As	क्योंकि	Because	क्योंकि
As...as	उतना...जितना	Consequently	परिणामत:
Either...or	या तो ... या	Neither...nor	न तो ... न
So ... that	इतना ... कि	Too...to	इतना ... कि
And	और	As well as	और भी, तथा/साथ-साथ
So...as	इतना ... जितना कि	As ... as	इतना ... जितना कि
Whether...or	चाहे ... या	Therefore	अत: इसलिए, फलत:
So	अत: इसलिए, फलत:	Hence	अत: इसलिए, फलत:
Scarcely ... when	मुश्किल/कठिनता से ... कि	Not only ... but also	मुश्किल/कठिनता से ... कि
As ... so	जैसा ... वैसा ही	As soon as	ज्योंही ... त्योंही
But...	पर, परन्तु, लेकिन, मगर, किन्तु	Or...	या, अथवा, नहीं तो
No sooner... than	ज्योंही ... त्योंही	Both... and	दोनों, और ... भी
Otherwise	नहीं तो, अन्यथा	Or else	नहीं तो, वरना
Hardly ... when	मुश्किल/कठिनता से ... कि	Where	जहाँ
Wherever	जहाँ कहीं भी	Whence	जहाँ से/कहाँ से

Conjunctions	Hindi Meaning	Conjunctions	Hindi Meaning
When	जब	Whenever	चाहे कभी, जब चाहे, किसी भी अवसर पर
Till or until	तब तक ... जब तक	While	जब तक ... तब, तक/जबकि
Though	यद्यपि ...	Although	यद्यपि
However	चाहे कितनी ही	No less than	अपेक्षाकृत कम नहीं
Whereas	विरोधी भावना में, जबकि	Nevertheless	तथापि, तो भी
Since	चूँकि	That	ताकि, कि
Lest	ताकि ... न, ऐसा न हो ... कि	Such.... that	इतना ... कि
If	यदि	Unless	जब तक ... तब तक, यदि ... नहीं
Provided	बशर्ते ... कि	As if	माना ... कि
As though	माना	As (adv.)	उसी प्रकार से, उतना
How (adv.)	कैसे, किस प्रकार	However (conj.)	तथापि
However (adv.)	कुछ भी हो, यद्यपि, कितना भी	As yet	इस समय तक
Yet (adv.)	अब तक, तब तक, अभी तक, अब तक भी	Not yet	अभी नहीं
		Yet (conj.)	फिर भी

Kinds of Conjunctions

Conjunctions मुख्यत: चार प्रकार के होते हैं

1. Co-ordinating Conjunctions
2. Sub-ordinating Conjunctions
3. Correlative Conjunctions
4. Compound Conjunctions

I. Co-ordinating Conjunctions

Co-ordinating conjunctions भी चार प्रकार के होते हैं

(i) Cumulative (ii) Adversative

(iii) Alternative (iv) Illative

Cumulative Conjunctions

इन conjunctions का use दो statements को जोड़ने के लिए किया जाता है। इसके अन्तर्गत and, also, both... and, as well as, now, too, no less than etc. का use किया जाता है।

e.g., (i) Neeru as well as Sushma is proud.
(ii) Vinita is a singer and a dancer too.

Adversative Conjunctions

इन conjunctions का use दो statements के बीच contrast (अंतर/विरोध) बताने के लिए किया जाता है। इसके अन्तर्गत but, yet, still, only, while, whereas, nevertheless etc. conjunctions का use किया जाता है।

Alternative Conjunctions

इन conjunctions का use ऐसे वाक्यों को जोड़ने के लिए किया जाता है, जिनमें कोई विकल्प (Alternate) व्यक्त किया जाता है, या जिनसे दो विकल्पों में से एक को चुनने का बोध होता है। इनमें मुख्यत: otherwise, else, neither... nor, either ... or, etc. conjunctions का use किया जाता है।

e.g., (i) You must run fast else you will miss the train.
(ii) Either work hard or repent forever.

Illative Conjunctions

इन conjunctions का use ऐसे sentences को जोड़ने के लिए किया जाता है, जिनमे एक sentence, दूसरे sentence का नतीजा या परिणाम हैं। इनमे मुख्यत: so, for, therefore, so then, then etc conjunctions का use किया जाता है।

e.g., (i) Something has broken, for I have heard a splash.
(ii) He came late so the teacher scolded him.

II. Subordinating Conjunctions

Subordinating conjunctions को इनके द्वारा व्यक्त कार्य। अर्थ के अनुसार निम्न भागों में वर्गीकृत किया गया है—

1. **Time** When, whenever, till, until, before, after, since, while, as soon as, as long as, just as.
   e.g., (i) When I called on her, she was sleeping.
   (ii) I have been searching her since I met her.
2. **Cause or Reason** Since, because, as, that etc.
   e.g., (i) As my father has fever, he cannot see you now.
   (ii) She is crying because someone has stolen her purse.
3. **Condition** As if, if, unless, provided, provided that, supposing etc.
   e.g., (i) He will help you if you ask him.
   (ii) I shall help her provided that she comes to me.
4. **Purpose** That, so that, in order that, lest, etc.
   e.g., (i) She applied for a loan so that she might pay the fee of her course.
   (ii) She walked carefully lest she should slip.
5. **Result or Effect** So... that, such... that, that etc.
   e.g., (i) He spoke in such a low voice that few could hear him.
   (ii) The coffee is so hot that I can't drink it.
6. **Manner or Extent** as far as, as though, as, as if, so for etc.
   e.g., (i) He acted upon as he was instructed.
   (ii) Meena Kumari was a good actress as far as we know.
7. **Concession or contrast** though, although, yet, however, notwithstanding etc.
   e.g., (i) Although he is a billionaire, he does not show off.
8. **Comparison** as, than, as...as, so...as etc.
   e.g., (i) He is as strong as your brother.
   (ii) Kamal is taller than Priya.

III. Correlative Conjunction

इन conjunctions का use हमेशा pairs (जोड़ें) में किया जाता है। जैसे though...yet, whether ... or, neither ... nor, either...or, both...and, not only ... but also etc.

e.g., (i) He is neither useful nor social.
(ii) I do not care whether you attend the class or not.

IV. Compound Conjunction

वे conjunctions जो दो या दो से अधिक शब्दों का समूह हो, compound conjunctions कहलाते हैं। जैसे–as though, although, as if, in order that, provided that etc.

e.g., (i) She worked as if the earth belonged to her.
(ii) Anand finished the work even though he was ill.

Some Important Rules of Conjunction

Rule 1 Either...or/ Neither...nor/ Not only... but also का use एक ही प्रकार के words या phrases को जोड़ने के लिए किया जाता है।

e.g., (i) Either Monika is careless or ignorant. (✗)
Monika is either careless or ignorant. (✓)
(ii) Anurag both likes coke and pepsi. (✗)
Anurag likes both coke and pepsi. (✓)

Rule 2 Although या though के बाद yet या comma(,) का use होता है, न कि 'but' का

e.g. (i) Although he is poor he is happy. (✗)
(ii) Although he is poor yet he is happy. (✓)

Rule 3 Between...and तथा from...to का use करते समय ध्यान रखना चाहिए कि 'between' के साथ 'to' एवं 'from' के साथ 'and' नही आता है।

e.g., (i) The shop will remain closed from 2pm and 4pm. (✗)
(ii) The shop will remain closed from 2pm to 4pm. (✓)

Rule 4 The reason एवं the reason why के बाद because, because of, on account of तथा due to का use ना होकर 'that' का use होता है।

e.g., (i) This is the reason that Nilesh is not behaving sensible.

Rule 5 Such .... that का use कारण/परिणाम बताने के लिए किया जता है।

Such .... as का use तुलना करने के लिए किया जाता है।

e.g., (i) It was such a bad weather that we had to cancel the tour.

(ii) Annu is such a studious girl as we thought of.

Rule 6 As...as का अर्थ 'इतना...जितना' होता है। इनका use affirmative तथा negative sentence में होता हैं, जबकि so...as का use सिर्फ negative sentences में होता है।

e.g., (i) Delhi is not as big as Mumbai.

(ii) Mohan is not so killed as we need for this job.

Rule 7 Positive sentences में doubtful/doubt के साथ if/whether तथा negative/interrogative sentences में doubtful/doubt के साथ 'that' का use किया जाता है।

e.g., (i) Meena doubts if/whether she may qualify the physical fitness test.

(ii) I do not have any doubt that he is a graduate.

Rule 8 Since/because/as के साथ therefore/so का use नही किया जा सकता।

e.g., (i) Since it is sunday therefore all the shops are closed.

(therefore की जगह comma (,) आएगा)

(ii) As he finished his meals, so he asked for a towel.

(so की जगह comma (,) आएगा)

Exercise 1

Directions (Q.Nos 1-35) Choose the appropriate conjunction from the options to fill in the given blanks.

1. Either you .... your sister has done it.
(a) or (b) but
(c) nor (d) and

2. I waited for him .... the clock struck seven.
(a) until (b) unless
(c) upto (d) as

3. Both Veena .... Meena are beautiful.
(a) also (b) and
(c) as well as (d) but

4. Make hay .... the sun shines
(a) but (b) or
(c) while (d) when

5. Although she works hard .... she fails.
(a) but (b) and
(c) yet (d) than

6. He is no other .... my brother.
(a) but (b) except
(c) since (d) than

7. Rita .... Gita is very intelligent.
(a) as well as (b) but
(c) or (d) and

8. Believe in your mother .... do your duty.
(a) though (b) unless
(c) and (d) because

9. Make haste .... you will be late.
(a) but (b) lest
(c) else (d) as

10. He finished first .... he began late.
(a) but (b) though
(c) since (d) yet

11. He behaved .... a brave man should do.
(a) that (b) lest
(c) else (d) as

12. She writes slowly .... neatly.
(a) but (b) and
(c) else (d) since

13. I wanted to go on the beach, ... Mary refused.
(a) but (b) or
(c) so (d) for

14. He will starve .... he steals.
(a) but (b) lest
(c) else (d) before

15. .... I am poor, I am not dishonest.
(a) But (b) Lest
(c) Though (d) As

16. We all know .... sin and sorrow go together.
(a) that (b) lest
(c) else (d) as

17. Veena will succeed .... she is working hard.
(a) but (b) till
(c) since (d) unless

18. I need an umbrella .... it is raining.
(a) but (b) because
(c) though (d) if

19. Although my father is sick ... he goes to the office
(a) if (b) unless
(c) yet (d) for

20. .... the story is true or it is a widespread rumour.
(a) Neither (b) Either
(c) Or (d) But

21. I shall wait .... my father comes.
(a) but (b) by
(c) till (d) unless

22. The sky is .... cloudy nor bright.
(a) neither (b) unless
(c) either (d) though

23. She is noble .... kind too.
(a) therefore (b) so that
(c) and (d) or

24. We eat .... we remain healthy.
(a) as soon as (b) so that
(c) still (d) otherwise

25. Raja is poor .... he is honest.
(a) but (b) therefore
(c) so that (d) or

26. The Sun rose .... the fog disappeared
(a) still (b) and
(c) as soon as (d) so

27. .... she saw the tiger, she shouted.
(a) So that (b) Still
(c) As soon as (d) As well as

28. Work hard, ... you will fail.
(a) unless (b) since
(c) so that (d) otherwise

29. Thomas worked very hard, ... he did not stand first.
(a) therefore (b) and
(c) still (d) so that

30. She must cry .... she will die. He .... his brother has committed the crime.
(a) or, or
(b) so, as well as
(c) otherwise, and
(d) as soon as, and

31. The box was heavy; .... he could not lift it.
(a) still (b) so
(c) so that (d) therefore

32. He has been ill .... he reached Mumbai.
(a) since (b) and
(c) therefore (d) as soon as

33. .... being very rich, he never shows off.
(a) Other than (b) Despite
(c) Instead (d) Otherwise

34. I am not feeling well; ...., I will come to the party.
(a) because
(b) however
(c) since
(d) unless

35. .... I have had my lunch, my hunger has not gone.
(a) Although
(b) Moreover
(c) Finally
(d) Already

Directions (Q.Nos 36-55) In each of the following questions a sentence is given which may or may not be correct. Select the option which is the correct form of the sentence.

36. Although he is poor but he is honest.
(a) Although he is a poor but he is a honest.
(b) Although he is poor yet he is honest.
(c) Although he is the poor yet he is the honest.
(d) None of the above

37. No sooner I step out of the house when it started raining.
(a) No sooner did I step out of the house than it started raining.
(b) No sooner did I step out of the house when it started raining.
(c) No sooner did I stepped out of the house than it started raining.
(d) None of the above

38. Hardly had I step out of the house there it started raining.
(a) Hardly had I stepped out of the house when it started raining.
(b) Hardly had I stepped out of the house then it started raining.
(c) Hardly had I step out of the house when it started raining.
(d) None of the above

39. I had scarcely opened the door then a cool breeze rushed in.
(a) I had scarcely open the door when a cool breeze rushed in.
(b) Scarcely had I opened the door when a cool breeze rushed in.
(c) Scarcely had I open the door then a coll breeze rushed in.
(d) None of the above

40. Tony is not only wise but honest.
(a) Tony is not only a wise boy but an honest boy.
(b) Tony is not only a wise boy but honest boy.
(c) Tony is not only wise but honest also.
(d) None of the above

41. I and you am to blame.
(a) I as well as you am to blame.
(b) I as well as you are to blame.
(c) I as well as you is to blame.
(d) None of the above

42. Mohan is rich. Mohan help the poor.
(a) Mohan is rich yet he helps the poor.
(b) Mohan is rich and he helps the poor.
(c) Mohan is rich because he helps the poor.
(d) None of the above

43. Unless you do not disclose the secret, I shall not let you go.
(a) Unless you do not disclose the secret, yet I shall not let you go.
(b) Unless you disclose the secret, I shall not let you go.
(c) Unless you disclose the secret yet I shall not let you go.
(d) None of the above

44. She is as happy like you.
(a) She is as happy as you are
(b) She is as happy like you are.
(c) She is as happy so like you.
(d) None of the above

45. This horse runs as fast like the tiger.
(a) This horse runs as fast as the tiger.
(b) This horse runs as fast as like the tiger.
(c) This horse runs as fast like as the tiger.
(d) None of the above

46. Tony met no other but his fast friend Lucky.
(a) Tony met no other but than his fast friend Lucky.
(b) Tony met no other than his fast friend Lucky.
(c) Tony met no other than his fast friend but Lucky.
(d) None of the above

47. My father likes such boys who are honest.
(a) My father likes such boys as are honest.
(b) My father likes such boys who as are honest.
(c) My father likes such boys those are honest.
(d) None of the above

48. Work hard lest you may not fail.
(a) Work hard lest you might not fail.
(b) Work hard lest you are not fail.
(c) Work hard lest you should fail.
(d) None of the above

49. Wait until I do not return.
(a) Wait until I return.
(b) Wait until I am not return.
(c) Wait until I not return.
(d) None of the above

50. Both Raju as well as Ravi are intelligent boys.
(a) Both Raju and Ravi are intelligent boys.
(b) Both Raju or Ravi are intelligent boys.
(c) Both Raju as well as Ravi are intelligent.
(d) None of the above

51. Neither did Rakhi attend the meeting nor Mohan attend.
(a) Neither did Rakhi attend the meeting nor did Mohan attend it.
(b) Neither did Rakhi attend the meeting nor Mohan did attend.
(c) Neither did Rakhi attend the meeting nor do Mohan.
(d) None of the above

52. Neither did Sohan open the window nor his sister opened.
(a) Neither did Sohan open the window nor did his sister open it.
(b) Neither did Sohan open the window not his sister did open.
(c) Neither did Sohan open the window not his sister open it.
(d) None of the above

53. My shirt is as good if not better than yours.
(a) My shirt is as good as if not better than yours.
(b) My shirt is as good as not better than yours.
(c) My shirt is as good if as not better than yours.
(d) None of the above

54. Both of them not go there.
(a) Both of them was not go there.
(b) Neither of them or of the two went there.
(c) Neither of them did not go there.
(d) None of the above

55. Immediately the car started I came back.
(a) At once the car started I came back.
(b) As soon as the car started I came back.
(c) Instantaneously the car started I came back.
(d) None of the above

Exercise 2

Directions (Q. Nos. 1-35) Choose the appropriate conjunction from the options to fill in the given blanks.

1. We shall fail .... we are industrious.
(a) even (b) unless
(c) whether (d) until

2. I went to the shop .... bought some pens.
(a) and (b) to
(c) as (d) for

3. Don't talk .... she is singing.
(a) as (b) since
(c) while (d) so

4. They were ordered to wait .... the signal was given.
(a) unless (b) till
(c) up to (d) when

5. Write it down .... you should forget about it.
(a) lest
(b) because
(c) for
(d) or

6. They spoke in a low voice .... the child wouldn't wake up.
(a) for (b) because
(c) that (d) so that

7. I will not pay .... he sends me the bill again.
(a) if (b) until
(c) unless (d) whether

8. He sells oranges .... mangoes.
(a) as well (b) also
(c) as well as (d) but

9. He is rich .... he is not happy.
(a) and (b) but
(c) though (d) as well as

10. He is neither a cheat .... a fool.
(a) or (b) either
(c) nor (d) not

11. You must be quiet .... you must leave the room.
(a) or (b) while
(c) but (d) and

12. I asked him .... he would help me.
(a) that (b) if
(c) unless (d) or

13. The passengers got off the plane .... it landed.
(a) while (b) as soon as
(c) if (d) as well as

14. He lost .... his ticket, but also his bag.
(a) not only (b) not
(c) neither (d) either

15. The teacher says .... the Earth moves around the Sun.
(a) when (b) why
(c) that (d) what

16. .... she is pretty, I don't like her.
(a) As (b) Unless
(c) Though (d) While

17. Do .... you have been directed.
(a) so (b) that
(c) which (d) as

18. He went to the US .... he finished his studies.
(a) and (b) when
(c) till (d) but

19. Put it .... you can find it later.
(a) if (b) where
(c) because (d) as

20. He is weak .... he does a lot of work.
(a) because (b) so
(c) and (d) yet

21. I was ill .... I didn't go to work.
(a) so (b) because
(c) as (d) when

22. A student will fail .... he does not work hard.
(a) because (b) if
(c) until (d) though

23. He was late .... it was raining heavily.
(a) so (b) that
(c) when (d) because

24. .... you have any doubt, please ask me.
(a) In case (b) Because
(c) Unless (d) Until

25. She is more intelligent .... her sister.
(a) as (b) than
(c) before (d) because

26. She has changed a lot .... I saw her last.
(a) before (b) while
(c) as (d) since

27. He could not get the prize, ... he tried hard for it.
(a) yet (b) though
(c) but (d) when

28. We must leave now .... it is getting dark.
(a) as long as
(b) as soon as
(c) when
(d) since

29. I was taking a bath .... somebody rang the bell.
(a) as
(b) while
(c) when
(d) as soon as

30. He failed in the examination; ...., he didn't lose heart.
(a) moreover (b) than
(c) while (d) nevertheless

31. This is the place .... we stayed last time we visited.
(a) where (b) when
(c) since (d) than

32. We lost the key. We had .... break the lock to open.
(a) still (b) for
(c) therefore (d) when

33. A mechanic was sent for .... our car broke down.
(a) since (b) as soon as
(c) until (d) because

34. Both my father .... my wife are ill.
(a) and (b) or
(c) but (d) if

35. He is not only strong .... also brave.
(a) though (b) but
(c) or (d) however

Directions (Q.Nos. 36-65) Find out which part of the sentence has an error.

36. The reason Navita (a)/felt exhausted was (b)/ if she worked non-stop for 12 hours. (c)/ No error (d)

37. There is no other way (a)/ of beating stress (b)/than to accept yourself as you are. (c)/ No error (d)

38. This picture is so (a)/ beautiful as (b)/ that one. (c)/ No error (d)

39. I not only did (a)/ my homework (b)/ but even revised my lesson. (c)/ No error (d)

40. Although we worked (a)/ the whole day (b)/ but we were not paid well. (c)/ No error (d)

41. We will remind you (a)/ in order to you arrive on time (b)/ for the appointment (c)/ No error (d)

42. You must keep (a)/ the main door locked (b)/ until I do not return. (c)/ No error (d)

43. Both the dresses (a)/ look good (b)/ on you. (c)/ No error (d)

44. Rashmi will go to Nainital (a)/ whether she stands (b)/ first in her class. (c)/ No error (d)

45. I have travelled (a)/ not only Nepal (b)/ and Bhutan. (c)/ No error (d)

46. No sooner did I enter (a)/ the house I saw my uncle (b)/ going out for a walk. (c)/ No error (d)

47. Seldom or ever have I tried (a)/ my best to defend my friends (b)/ who are after all guilty to some extent. (c)/ No error (d)

48. The robber had hardly (a)/ put the ornaments in his bag (b)/ than the housewife woke up. (c)/ No error (d)

49. The teacher said to the students, (a)/ "Go through the notes as many times (b)/ as possible lest you would fail." (c)/ No error (d)

50. This is perhaps the same dog (a)/ which bite her while she (b)/ was returning from market. (c)/ No error (d)

51. You will not (a)/ get well until (b)/ you take medicine regularly. (c)/ No error (d)

52. Her name is so glorious (a)/ in our history (b)/ as any other leader. (c)/ No error (d)

53. Either he nor his brother (a)/ was informed about the venue (b)/ of the meeting of our society. (c)/ No error (d)

54. He not only believes (a)/ in hard work but also (b)/ in honesty of the highest order. (c)/ No error (d)

Answers

Exercise 1

1 (a)	2 (a)	3 (b)	4 (c)	5 (c)	6 (d)	7 (a)	8 (c)	9 (c)	10 (b)
11 (d)	12 (a)	13 (a)	14 (d)	15 (c)	16 (a)	17 (c)	18 (b)	19 (c)	20 (b)
21 (c)	22 (a)	23 (c)	24 (b)	25 (a)	26 (b)	27 (c)	28 (d)	29 (c)	30 (a)
31 (d)	32 (a)	33 (b)	34 (b)	35 (a)	36 (b)	37 (a)	38 (a)	39 (b)	40 (c)
41 (b)	42 (b)	43 (b)	44 (a)	45 (a)	46 (b)	47 (a)	48 (c)	49 (a)	50 (a)
51 (a)	52 (a)	53 (a)	54 (b)	55 (b)					

Exercise 2

1 (b)	2 (a)	3 (c)	4 (b)	5 (a)	6 (d)	7 (c)	8 (c)	9 (b)	10 (c)
11 (a)	12 (b)	13 (b)	14 (a)	15 (c)	16 (c)	17 (d)	18 (b)	19 (b)	20 (d)
21 (a)	22 (b)	23 (d)	24 (a)	25 (b)	26 (d)	27 (b)	28 (d)	29 (c)	30 (d)
31 (a)	32 (c)	33 (d)	34 (a)	35 (b)	36 (c)	37 (d)	38 (a)	39 (c)	40 (c)
41 (b)	42 (c)	43 (d)	44 (b)	45 (c)	46 (a)	47 (a)	48 (c)	49 (c)	50 (b)
51 (b)	52 (a)	53 (a)	54 (a)						

Explanations

Exercise 2

36. *(c)* 'if' के स्थान पर 'because' का use होगा क्योंकि because clause with reasons को जोड़ता है।

37. *(d)* No error

38. *(a)* दिया गया sentence positive हैं इसलिए 'so' के स्थान पर 'as' का use किया जाएगा।

39. *(c)* 'not only' के साथ 'but also' का use किया जाता है। इसलिए 'even' के स्थान पर 'also' का use suitable होगा। Not only... but also co-relative conjunction होते हैं।

40. *(c)* यहाँ 'but' के स्थान पर 'yet' का use किया जाएगा क्योंकि 'although/though' के आगे 'yet' का use किया जाता हैं।

41. *(b)* दिए गए sentence के according, 'in order to' incorrect है, यहाँ 'in order that' use होगा।

42. *(c)* Sentence में 'do not' का use नही किया जाएगा क्योंकि already 'until' का use किया गया है। दो negatives एक ही sentence में use नहीं किये जाते हैं।

43. *(d)* No error

44. *(b)* दिए गए sentence के according, 'whether' के स्थान पर 'if ' का use किया जाएगा।

45. *(c)* दिए गए sentence के part (c) में error हैं। यहाँ 'and' के स्थान पर 'but also' का use किया जाएगा।

46. *(a)* 'I' के पहले 'than' का प्रयोग होगा क्योंकि 'no sooner' के बाद 'than' का प्रयोग अवश्यक होता है।

47. *(a)* 'or' के स्थान पर 'if ' का प्रयाग होगा क्योंकि 'seldom if ever' तथा 'seldom of never' का प्रयोग होता है।

48. *(c)* 'than' के स्थान पर 'when' का प्रयोग होगा क्योंकि 'hardly/scarcely' के बाद 'when/ before' का प्रयाग होता है न कि 'than' का।

49. *(c)* 'would' के स्थान पर 'should' का use होगा क्योंकि 'lest' के बाद हमेशा 'should' का use होता है।

50. *(b)* 'which' के स्थान पर 'that' का प्रयोग होगा क्योंकि 'the same' के बाद 'that' का प्रयोग होता है यदि verb स्पष्ट हो और 'as' का प्रयोग होता है यदि verb अस्पष्ट हो।

51. *(b)* 'until' के स्थान पर 'unless' का use होगा क्योंकि 'until' का प्रयोग समय (जब तक नहीं) तथा 'unless' का प्रयाग शर्त (यदि नहीं) के लिए होता है।

52. *(a)* 'so' के स्थान पर 'as' का प्रयोग होगा क्योंकि 'so...as' का प्रयोग negative वाक्य में होता है जबकि 'as...as' का प्रयोग negative तथा affirmative दोनों में होता है।

53. *(a)* 'nor' के स्थान पर 'or' का प्रयोग होगा क्योंकि 'either' के बाद 'or' का प्रयोग होता है और 'neither' के बाद 'nor' का।

54. *(a)* 'not only' का प्रयोग 'believes' के बाद होगा क्योंकि यहाँ not only...but also से prepositional phrases 'in hard work' तथा 'in honesty' को जोड़ा गया है।

05 Verb

वह शब्द जो किसी action (कार्य) के करने या होने को दर्शाता है, उसे 'verb' कहा जाता है। कोई भी sentence बिना verb के incomplete होता है।

Verb के द्वारा हमें निम्न बातों का पता चलता है

(i) किसी person या thing का होना (the state of being of persons or things)
e.g., (i) My father is a professor.
(ii) Jaipur is a nice city.

(ii) किसी person या thing का अधिकार (the possession on persons or things)
e.g., (i) A spider has natural venom.
(ii) My school has hundred teachers.

(iii) किसी person या thing ने क्या किया (What does a person or thing do)
e.g., (i) Ashok writes a letter.
(ii) The plane flew over the mountains.

(iv) किसी person या thing की state (अवस्था) (The physical or mental state of persons or things)
e.g., (i) He looks happy.
(ii) A moat surrounds the castle.

Kinds of Verb

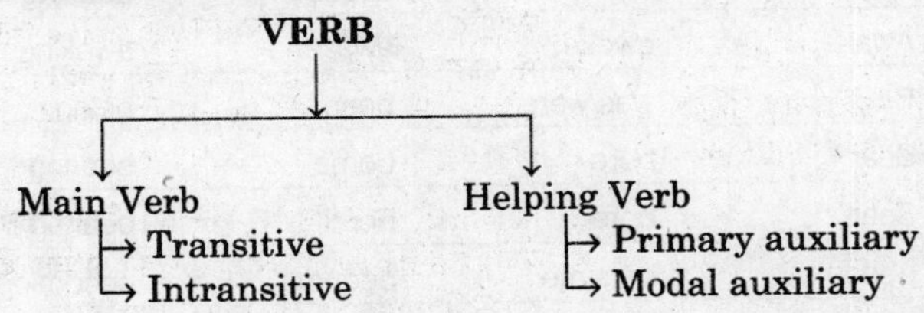

1. Main Verb Main verb वह होती है, जो subject के द्वारा किए गए actions (कार्य) को बताती है, जैसे- Play, Write, Read, Laugh etc.
e.g., (i) He sang a song.
(ii) They are reading.

Main verb के दो प्रकार होते हैं

(i) **Transitive Verbs** Transitive का अर्थ है passing over अर्थात् जिन verbs में action, subject (कर्त्ता) तक ही सीमित ना रहकर object (किसी अन्य वस्तु) पर pass over होता है। Transitive verbs, वो verb होती है, जिनके बाद हमेशा एक object का use किया जाता है।

e.g., (i) Ramesh → Subject; hits → Transitive verb; a ball → Object
(ii) I → Subject; admire → Transitive verb; your honesty → Object

Transitive verbs-Bring, give, raise, borrow, have, admire, offer, hits, face, pay, write, promise etc.

(ii) **Intransitive Verbs** Intransitive verbs में actions, subject तक ही सीमित रहता है, object पर pass over नहीं होता है। ये वो verbs होती है, जिनके बाद object की आवश्यकता नहीं होती है।

e.g., (i) We talked for hours. (talked → Intransitive)
(ii) Shyam speaks loudly. (speaks → Intransitive)

Some Intransitive verbs are - work, cry, talk, laugh, sit, speak, increase, originate, fluctuate etc.

2. Helping Verb वह verb जो main verb के साथ मिलकर काम करती है, Helping verb कहलाती है। यह verbs, subject की state (अवस्था) के बारे में बताती है। इन्हें हम auxiliaries भी कहते हैं। इनकी संख्या 24 होती है- do, does did, is, am, are, was, were, has, have, had, can, will, shall, may, might, could, would, should, must, ought to, need, dare, used to.

Helping verb के भी दो प्रकार होते हैं

- **Primary Auxiliary** Primary auxiliary verbs को तीन भागों में वर्गीकृत किया गया है
  - (i) Verbs 'to be' : Is, am, are, was, were
  - (ii) Verbs 'to have' : Have, has, had
  - (iii) Verbs 'to do' : Do, does, did

  e.g., (i) She is taking her lunch.
  (ii) I do drive the bike.
- **Modal Auxiliary** ये ऐसी Helping verbs होती है, जो कि speaker के mood को दर्शाती है, जैसे कि permission, prohibition, obligation, suggestion etc.

  e.g., (i) You can leave early. (Permission)
  (ii) The sky is cloudy, it may rain today. (Possibility).

Grammar में, इनके अतिरिक्त तीन प्रकार की verbs और भी होती है

- Linking verb
- Causative verb
- Inchoative verb

Linking Verbs

जब helping verb, किसी sentence में main verb को support नहीं करती है बल्कि main verb की तरह प्रयुक्त होती है, तो उस स्थिति में इन्हें Linking verbs या Notional verbs कहा जाता है। ये verbs केवल अपने subjects से ही linked या connected होती है या केवल subjects को ही प्रभावित करती है। इस तरह की verbs निम्नलिखित है

- **Is** He is my elder brother.
- **Am** I am a teacher.
- **Are** They are players.
- **Was** She was sad.
- **Were** They were happy.
- **Appear** She appear upset about the announcement.
- **Become** She became a doctor.
- **Fell** She fell ill.
- **Grow** Some couples are lucky enough to grow old together.
- **Look** You look exhausted, after studying all night.
- **Seem** All the children seem satisfied with the bouncy-castle.
- **Smell** The eggs smell rotten.
- **Remain** The spectators remained silent after the injury.
- **Taste** The cinnamon rolls taste heavenly.

Causative Verbs

जब कोई कार्य, subject स्वयं न करके, किसी other person से करँवाए, तब causative verbs का use किया जाता है। इस तरह की verbs हैं

- **Let** Our boss doesn't let us smoke at office premises.
- **Make** The teacher made students work hard.
- **Get** I can never get my husband to wash the clothes.
- **Have** The CEO have his secretary note all the important meetings.
- **Help** I can help you search for a new job.

Inchoative Verbs

जो verbs किसी action की beginning, development or final stage या change of condition को denote करती है, उन्हें Inchoative verbs कहते हैं। इस तरह की मुख्य verbs निम्नलिखित है

- **Get** My father is getting weaker.
- **Become** The leaves become red in autumn.
- **Grow** It is growing dark.
- **Come** My dreams have come true.
- **Go** He is going bald.
- **Turn** The weather has turned much colder.
- **Run** Supplies are running short.

Forms of Verb

Basically, verb की four forms होती है

- Base form (Present Tense) v_1
- Past Form v_2
- Past Participle form (v_3-ed form)
- Present Participle v_4 (v_1+ ing)

Following is the list of verbs with their forms

V_1 Present	V_2 Past	V_3 Past Participle	V_4 Present Participle
Arise	arose	arisen	arising
Arrive	arrived	arrived	arriving
Abide	abode	abode	abiding
Abuse	abused	abused	abusing
Awake	awoke	awaken	awaking
Be	was/were	been	being
Bear	bore	borne	bearing
Bear	bore	born	bearing
Become	became	become	becoming
Blow	blew	blown	blowing
Borrow	borrowed	borrowed	borrowing
Break	broke	broken	breaking
Bring	brought	brought	bringing
Behold	beheld	beheld	beholding
Buy	bought	bought	buying
Catch	caught	caught	catching
Climb	climbed	climbed	climbing
Come	came	come	coming
Choose	chose	chosen	choosing

V_1 Present	V_2 Past	V_3 Past Participle	V_4 Present Participle
Dig	dug	dug	digging
Do	did	done	doing
Draw	drew	drawn	drawing
Drink	drank	drunk	drinking
Deal	dealt	dealt	dealing
Dream	dreamt	dreamt	dreaming
Dwell	dwelt	dwelt	dwelling
Eat	ate	eaten	eating
Earn	earned	earned	earning
Elect	elected	elected	electing
Electrify	electrified	electrified	electrifying
Enjoy	enjoyed	enjoyed	enjoying
Enrol	enrolled	enrolled	enrolling
Enter	entered	entered	entering
Err	erred	erred	erring
Excite	excited	excited	exciting
Excuse	excused	excused	excusing
Feed	fed	fed	feeding
Fall	fell	fallen	falling
Fight	fought	fought	fighting
Find	found	found	finding
Flow	flowed	flowed	flowing
Fly	flew	flown	flying
Forget	forgot	forgotten	forgetting
Forbid	forbade	forbidden	forbidding
Freeze	froze	frozen	freezing
Forsake	forsook	forsaken	forsaking
Get	got	got	getting
Give	gave	given	giving
Grow	grew	grown	growing
Gain	gained	gained	gaining
Gamble	gambled	gambled	gambling
Govern	governed	governed	governing
Graze	grazed	grazed	grazing
Greet	greeted	greeted	greeting
Guide	guided	guided	guiding
Hide	hid	hidden	hiding
Hang	hung	hung	hanging
Hold	held	held	holding
Have	had	had	having
Hurt	hurt	hurt	hurting

V_1 Present	V_2 Past	V_3 Past Participle	V_4 Present Participle
Ignore	ignored	ignored	ignoring
Imagine	imagined	imagined	imagining
Injure	injured	injured	injuring
Insult	insulted	insulted	insulting
Intend	intended	intended	intending
Invade	invaded	invaded	invading
Invent	invented	invented	inventing
Join	joined	joined	joining
Joke	joked	joked	joking
Judge	judged	judged	judging
Jump	jumped	jumped	jumping
Kneel	knelt	knelt	kneeling
Kill	killed	killed	killing
Kick	kicked	kicked	kicking
Lie	lay	lain	lying
Lend	lent	lent	lending
Light	lighted	lighted	lighting
Lose	lost	lost	losing
Let	let	let	letting
Leak	leaked	leaked	leaking
Lead	led	led	leading
Lick	licked	licked	licking
Like	liked	liked	liking
Listen	listened	listened	listening
Look	looked	looked	looking
Love	loved	loved	loving
Make	made	made	making
Mean	meant	meant	meaning
Mar	marred	marred	marring
March	marched	marched	marching
Marry	married	married	marrying
Mind	minded	minded	minding
Miss	missed	missed	missing
Mix	mixed	mixed	mixing
Mortgage	mortgaged	mortgaged	mortgaging
Nap	napped	napped	napping
Neglect	neglected	neglected	neglecting
Nurse	nursed	nursed	nursing
Obey	obeyed	obeyed	obeying
Object	objected	objected	objecting
Offend	offended	offended	offending

V_1 Present	V_2 Past	V_3 Past Participle	V_4 Present Participle
Open	opened	opened	opening
Oppose	opposed	opposed	opposing
Oppress	oppressed	oppressed	oppressing
Order	ordered	ordered	ordering
Prove	proved	proved	proving
Purchase	purchased	purchased	purchasing
Pay	paid	paid	paying
Pardon	pardoned	pardoned	pardoning
Persist	persisted	persisted	persisting
Polish	polished	polished	polishing
Ponder	pondered	pondered	pondering
Post	posted	posted	posting
Practise	practised	practised	practising
Pray	prayed	prayed	praying
Prepare	prepared	prepared	preparing
Press	pressed	pressed	pressing
Pretend	pretended	pretended	pretending
Progress	progressed	progressed	progressing
Quit	quit	quit	quitting
Quarrel	quarrelled	quarrelled	quarrelling
Question	questioned	questioned	questioning
Quench	quenched	quenched	quenching
Ride	rode	ridden	riding
Read	read	read	reading
Ring	rang	rung	ringing
Sell	sold	sold	selling
Send	sent	sent	sending
Sow	sowed	sown	sowing
Spend	spent	spent	spending
Sit	sat	sat	sitting
Speak	spoke	spoken	speaking
Spell	spelt	spelt	spelling
Sweep	swept	swept	sweeping
See	saw	seen	seeing
Shake	shook	shaken	shaking
Shine	shone	shone	shining
Sink	sank	sunk	sinking
Swear	swore	sworn	swearing
Swim	swam	swum	swimming
Shoot	shot	shot	shooting

V_1 Present	V_2 Past	V_3 Past Participle	V_4 Present Participle
Sling	slung	slung	slinging
Saw	sawed	sawn	sawing
Shear	sheared	sheared	shearing
Spoil	spoiled	spoilt	spoiling
Strive	strove	striven	striving
Swell	swelled	swelled	swelling
Set	set	set	setting
Shut	shut	shut	shutting
Take	took	taken	taking
Teach	taught	taught	teaching
Think	thought	thought	thinking
Thrust	thrust	thrust	thrusting
Tread	trod	trodden	treading
Undergo	underwent	undergone	undergoing
Undo	undid	undone	undoing
Unify	unified	unified	unifying
Vacate	vacated	vacated	vacating
Value	valued	valued	valuing
Vanish	vanished	vanished	vanishing
Violate	violated	violated	violating
Vomit	vomited	vomited	vomiting
Win	won	won	winning
Weep	wept	wept	weeping
Wake	woke	waked	waking
Wear	wore	worn	wearing
Weave	wove	woven	weaving
Wash	washed	washed	washing
Wed	wedded	wedded	wedding
Wound	wounded	wounded	wounding
Water	watered	watered	watering
Want	wanted	wanted	wanting
Waste	wasted	wasted	wasting
Wave	waved	waved	waving
Weaken	weakened	weakened	wakening
Weigh	weighed	weighed	weighing
Wink	winked	winked	winking
Wipe	wiped	wiped	wiping
Wire	wired	wired	wiring
Yawn	yawned	yawned	yawning
Yield	yielded	yielded	yielding

Some Important Rules of Verb

Rule 1 कुछ verbs, transitive और intransitive दोनों का कार्य कर सकती है। जैसे- sing, leave, start, stop, do, set, close, open, run, live, wash, write, continue, change, move, return, grow, etc.

e.g., (i) Mitali sang classic blues.
↓
Transitive verb

(ii) Divyansh always sings during the bath.
↓
Intransitive verb

(iii) My friend returned the books.
↓
Transitive verb

(iv) The child returned to its home.
↓
Intransitive verb

Rule 2 यदि किसी sentence में 'क्या (what)' या 'किसे (Whom)' का जवाब मिलता है, तब उस sentence में use की हुई verb transitive होती है।

e.g. (i) Baby is sleeping. (Intransitive)
(ii) Priyanka is eating fruit. (Transitive)

Rule 3 Is/Am/Are का use present tense में तथा was/were का use past tense में किया जाता है। 'Am' का use केवल 'I' के साथ होता है तथा 'was' का use past tense में singular subject के साथ होता है।

e.g., (i) I am a man.
(ii) It was me.

Rule 4 Have/Has/Had का use किसी वस्तु पर Possession (मालिकाना हक), Ownership (स्वामित्व) को denote करने के लिए किया जाता है।

e.g., (i) I have a car.
(ii) He had a beautiful house.

Rule 5 Have/Has/Had का causative verb की तरह भी use किया जाता है।

e.g., (i) I have a house built by her.
(ii) I had him punished for his negligence.

Rule 6 Verbs-Expect, hope, wish, want etc के साथ had का use past perfect में ऐसी past इच्छाओं को व्यक्त करता है जो पूर्ण नहीं हुई।

e.g., (i) I had expected to pass IAS.
(ii) I had hoped to meet her in the party.

Rule 7 Auxiliary verb 'to do' (does/do/did) का use negative एवं interrogative sentences में किया जाता है। सामान्यतया इनका use Present एवं Past tense में किया जाता है।

e.g., (i) Does he love her?
(ii) They do not want to teach you.

निम्नलिखित Structures को याद रखे

1. Verb 'to be' + V_4 (V + ing) परन्तु Passive voice में verb 'to be' + V_3
2. Verb 'to have' + V_3
3. Verb 'to do' + V_1
4. Modal verbs + V_1 OR Modal verbs + have + V_3

Exercise 1

Directions (Q. Nos. 1-35) In the following questions, fill the blanks with suitable verbs.

1. Kanak ……… sick the day before because she got caught in the rain.
(a) be (b) did
(c) was (d) had

2. They ……… best friends until they quarrelled a month ago.
(a) be (b) did
(c) had (d) were

3. I ……… so hungry that I can eat three bowls of rice.
(a) am (b) is
(c) does (s) has

4. ……… you like to read' books in your free time?
(a) Do (b) Be
(c) Have (d) Are

5. Richa ……… the most wonderful birthday party last year.
(a) was (b) be
(c) had (d) did

6. Milan ……… not want to go swimming today because the sky is dark.
(a) is (b) has
(c) be (d) does

7. Farhan ……… an enjoyable time at the theme park.
(a) had (b) is
(c) does (d) be

8. You ……… very tall for according to your age.
(a) be (b) has
(c) are (d) does

9. ……… you go to the movies yesterday ?
(a) Was
(b) Had
(c) Did
(d) Doing

10. My grandparents ……… nine children altogether.
(a) be (b) do
(c) have (d) are

11. ……… she going to be late for the concert ?
(a) Is (b) Has
(c) Be (d) Does

12. I .... the only child in my family.
(a) do (b) am
(c) has (d) be

13. Mehar was scolded because she .... not bring her homework.
(a) was (b) be
(c) did (d) had

14. They .... going to the park for a picnic later.
(a) do (b) be
(c) have (d) are

15. What are you .... with all these flowers?
(a) be (b) being
(c) having (d) doing

16. Manya .... the best time of her life in Australia last year.
(a) did (b) be
(c) had (d) was

17. He .... not have any interest in computer games now.
(a) do (b) did
(c) does (d) doing

18. I .... a glass of milk and a sandwich for breakfast every morning.
(a) has (b) had
(c) have (d) having

19. .... the ladies now need more materials for the embroidery lesson?
(a) Do (b) Did
(c) Does (d) Doing

20. The puppies .... running in the park an hour ago.
(a) am (b) are
(c) was (d) were

21. They .... visiting their grandmother next month.
(a) are (b) is
(c) am (d) was

22. I .... looking for a way out of the maze.
(a) are (b) is
(c) am (d) was

23. Last evening, I .... looking for my lost dog in the park.
(a) are (b) is
(c) am (d) was

24. The last time we met, you .... shopping in the mall.
(a) were (b) is
(c) am (d) was

25. We .... painting the house this weekend.
(a) are (b) is
(c) am (d) was

26. My brothers, Niki and Riki, ... playing soccer this weekend.
(a) are (b) is (c) am (d) was

27. Who .... going to get the grocery this week?
(a) are (b) is
(c) am (d) were

28. It's hard to predict who will win but they .... putting in their best effort.
(a) are (b) is
(c) am (d) was

29. I did not eat breakfast this morning, so I .... getting a little hungry now.
(a) are (b) is
(c) am (d) was

30. Compared to my older brother, I .... much shorter.
(a) are (b) is
(c) am (d) was

31. Rick was the only one without a project, as he .... not listening in class yesterday.
(a) are (b) is
(c) am (d) was

32. The smell of garbage .... awful.
(a) are (b) were
(c) am (d) was

33. I .... doubtful about the outcome, so I am waiting eagerly.
(a) are (b) is
(c) am (d) was

34. Animals can become fierce if they .... trapped.
(a) are (b) is
(c) am (d) was

35. What .... you doing last year?
(a) are (b) is
(c) am (d) were

Directions (Q. Nos. 36-53) Fill in the blanks with the correct form of action verb.

36. My sister .... her homework late.
(a) submitted (b) submit
(c) submits (d) submitting

37. My younger brother .... earlier in the night, even before his test.
(a) sleep (b) slept
(c) sleeping (d) sleeps

38. The teachers .... us in all the remaining problems.
(a) guide (b) guides
(c) guided (d) guiding

39. The Moon .... brightly at night.
(a) shining (b) shiny
(c) shine (d) shines

40. Manners .... a man.
(a) makes (b) make
(c) made (d) making

41. My sister got me a ...... doll.
(a) danced (b) dances
(c) dance (d) dancing

42. .... football is not only his hobby, but also his profession.
(a) Played (b) Play
(c) Playing (d) Player

43. We .... home from the picnic with the setting the Sun behind us.
(a) returned (b) returning
(c) return (d) returns

44. In order to .... early in the morning, you must go to bed early at night.
(a) wakes (b) wake
(c) waking (d) awaken

45. We are encouraged .... our teeth after every meal.
(a) to brush (b) brush
(c) brushing (d) brushed

46. I had a hard time staying .... during the boring speech.
(a) awoke (b) awake
(c) awaken (d) awakened

47. I .... to the park today.
(a) to walk (b) walking
(c) walk (d) walked

48. Peter .... in China in 1965.
(a) lived (b) lives
(c) living (d) life

49. She goes .... every morning.
(a) run (b) running
(c) ran (d) runs

50. My father .... a newspaper every day.
(a) buy (b) bought
(c) buys (d) buying

51. The lion is .... the deer.
(a) Choosing (b) Cheering
(c) Clanging (d) Chasing

52. The universe is .... and has been so since its beginning.
(a) Exposing (b) Expanding
(c) Passing (d) Questioning

53. My dog .... last night in pain last night.
(a) Bloomed (b) Zipped
(c) Whined (d) Rattled

Directions (Q. Nos. 54-63) Choose the third form of the verbs given in capital letters below.

54. ARISE
(a) Arose (b) Arosed
(c) Arisen (d) Arised

55. WIN
(a) Win (b) Won
(c) Winner (d) Wins

56. WEAR
(a) Wears (b) Wearn
(c) Wore (d) Worn

57. DRINK
(a) Drunk (b) Drank
(c) Drink (d) Drinks

58. BE
(a) Was (b) Were
(c) Been (d) Be

59. BEAT
(a) Beat (b) Beated
(c) Beating (d) Beaten

60. BITE
(a) Bitten (b) Bit
(c) Bite (d) Bited

61. KEEP
(a) Kept (b) Keeping
(c) Kepted (d) Keep

62. SEND
(a) Sented (b) Sending
(c) Sent (d) Sended

63. RISE
(a) Rise (b) Rose
(c) Rosen (d) Risen

Exercise 2

Directions (Q. Nos. 1-30) Identify the underlined part of speech. Choose the correct answer.

1. The burglar <u>disappeared</u> with the cash
(a) transitive verb
(b) intransitive verb
(c) linking verb
(d) auxiliary verb

2. The director <u>told</u> the actors, 'Do your best, and we'll be a hit.'
(a) transitive verb
(b) intransitive verb
(c) linking verb
(d) auxiliary verb

3. He <u>would</u> tell me if he thought we were in danger
(a) transitive verb
(b) intransitive verb
(c) linking verb
(d) auxiliary verb

4. His ability to concentrate <u>is</u> legendary.
(a) transitive verb
(b) intransitive verb
(c) linking verb
(d) auxiliary verb

5. The campers <u>hid</u> inside the cabin when they saw the bear.
(a) transitive verb
(b) intransitive verb
(c) linking verb
(d) auxiliary verb

6. Alexis <u>is</u> swimming in the state championship contest next week.
(a) transitive verb
(b) intransitive verb
(c) linking verb
(d) auxiliary verb

7. Frustrated with the official's call, Ethan <u>kicked</u> the bench.
(a) transitive verb
(b) intransitive verb
(c) linking verb
(d) auxiliary verb

8. The student <u>procrastinated</u> too long and failed to finish the project.
(a) transitive verb
(b) intransitive verb
(c) linking verb
(d) auxiliary verb

9. The vegetarian burger <u>tasted</u> like salted cardboard.
(a) transitive verb
(b) intransitive verb
(c) linking verb
(d) auxiliary verb

10. Ellen <u>nodded</u> to the audience and sang her song.
(a) transitive verb
(b) intransitive verb
(c) linking verb
(d) auxiliary verb

11. Her brother <u>likes</u> bananas, but she likes peaches.
(a) transitive verb
(b) intransitive verb
(c) linking verb
(d) auxiliary verb

12. Adjunct faculty <u>are teaching</u> in several of the lower division courses.
(a) transitive verb
(b) intransitive verb
(c) linking verb
(d) auxiliary verb

13. The ladies <u>curried</u> the fruits to the markets.
(a) transitive verb
(b) intransitive verb

(c) linking verb
(d) auxiliary verb

14. Regis Philbin, the host of 'Who Wants to be a Millionaire,' **smiled** at her answer.
(a) transitive verb
(b) intransitive verb
(c) linking verb
(d) auxiliary verb

15. When the contestant **completed** the first test, she received another clue.
(a) transitive verb
(b) intransitive verb
(c) linking verb
(d) auxiliary verb

16. Dennis **became** impatient when Thomas took too long to choose a movie.
(a) transitive verb
(b) intransitive verb
(c) linking verb
(d) auxiliary verb

17. President Clinton **pushed** into the crowd and shook her hand.
(a) transitive verb
(b) intransitive verb
(c) linking verb
(d) auxiliary verb

18. The hiker **turned** quickly toward the noise behind him.
(a) transitive verb
(b) intransitive verb
(c) linking verb
(d) auxiliary verb

19. Our teacher **gave** each of us another chance to take the exam.
(a) transitive verb
(b) intransitive verb
(c) linking verb
(d) auxiliary verb

20. After the chef **completed** the demonstration, she left the students to clean the kitchen.
(a) transitive verb
(b) intransitive verb
(c) linking verb
(d) auxiliary verb

Directions (Q. Nos. 21-30) In the given sentences, an error has been underlined. Choose the correct word from the given options to replace the underlined word.

21. She buys a new dress last week.
(a) was buying (b) is buying
(c) bought (d) buy

22. Varun prefer milk to tea.
(a) prefers
(b) has preferred
(c) preferring
(d) No improvement

23. My mother is fond of travel.
(a) travelled (b) travelling
(c) has travel (d) travels

24. The Earth revolved around the Sun.
(a) was revolving (b) is revolving
(c) had revolved (d) revolves

25. Four miles are not a long distance for a person like you.
(a) had
(b) is
(c) were
(d) No improvement

26. The traders suddenly rise the prices of crude oil last year.
(a) rose (b) raised (c) raise (d) risen

27. In old age neither of his two sons are prepared to come to help him.
(a) is prepared
(b) were prepared
(c) is preparing
(d) No improvement

28. In the morning, I found it was raining the whole night.
(a) is raining
(b) has been raining
(c) had been raining
(d) No improvement

29. Manav has broken a cup last evening.
(a) break (b) broke
(c) broken (d) No improvement

30. One is bounded in duty to help the ageing parents.
(a) bound (b) binding
(c) bind (d) No improvement

Directions (Q. Nos. 31-65) In each of the following questions, one part of the sentence has an error. Identify the part that has an error, and choose that part as your answer. If a sentence is free from error, then choose option (d) as your answer.

31. He flowed into a rage (a)/ at the very (b)/ sight of that man. (c)/ No error (d)

32. Now that I am back at work, (a)/I have beginning (b)/to feel much better. (c)/No error (d)

33. Have someone (a)/ to break (b)/ this lock. (c)/ No error (d)

34. His initials is engraved (a)/ on the back of (b)/ the watch. (c)/ No error (d)

35. People are wanting (a)/ to see the home team (b)/ win the game. (c)/ No error (d)

36. As they climb (a)/ higher, the air (b) /became cooler. (c)/ No error (d)

37. We have done everything (a)/ that could be done (b)/ to avert the storm which is now coming on. (c)/ No error (d)

38. Riches are uncertain things and the fame (a)/ that power give or is won by foul means (b)/ is as shortlived as a dewdrop. (c)/No error (d)

39. There be a long queue (a)/ for entry into (b)/ the exhibition ground. (c)/ No error (d)

40. I meant to repair the radio (a)/ but hadn't time (b)/ to do it today. (c)/No error (d)

41. The students were nervous (a)/ as the exam did not begun (b)/ on time (c)/ No error (d)

42. Various species of birds (a)/ can be saw during (b)/ the monsoon season in northern part of India. (c)/ No error (d)

43. I was got defeated (a)/ by my best friend (b)/ in the online typing speed test. (c)/ No error (d)

44. Three people were arrested (a)/ by the police but (b)/ one released. (c)/ No error (d)

45. The coach (a)/ alongwith the players (b)/ is watching a movie. (c)/ No error (d)

46. One hundred and eight thousand (a)/ miles are (b)/ the speed of light. (c)/ No error (d)

47. Every participant (a)/ in the meeting (b)/ are required to make this script. (c)/ No error (d)

48. Neither of the teams (a)/ are sensible enough (b)/ to do this task (c)/ No error (d)

49. All the boys (a)/ has been (b)/ selected. (c)/ No error (d)

50. Yesterday I founded (a)/ that my friend stole (b)/ the money from my purse. (c)/ No error (d)

51. If vehicle drivers do not observe (a)/ the rules of traffic, they (b) / will be prosecuted and have to pay fine. (c) / No error (d)

52. While the old man was entering (a)/ the shrine, he slipped and fall headlong (b) / on the floor. (c) / No error (d)

53. Some of the students were standing (a)/ in the college ground and watched the NCC parade (b)/ while a few others were sitting in the college canteen. (c) / No error (d)

54. The food that is being (a) / cooked in the neighbour's house (b) / is smelling delicious. (c)/ No error (d)

55. Gayatri has finished checking (a)/ the books last night and will dispatch (b) / them to the University on Monday. (c) / No error (d)

56. This practice does not confirm (a)/ to the rules (b)/ laid down by the committee. (c)/ No error (d)

57. Their opinion of (a)/the President would not effect (b)/her/his popularity in the country. (c)/No error (d)

58. The reporter (a)/ was unable (b)/ to illicit information from the police. (c)/ No error (d)

59. Lay your books aside and (a)/lay down to rest (b)/for a while. (c)/No error (d)

60. Sudeep must attended the class (a)/ regularly else he will not to be (b)/ allowed to sit in the final examinations. (c)/ No error (d).

61. Shyam is telling (a)/ that I have (b)/ stolen his pen. (c)/No error (d)

62. The timid creature was driven (a)/ into a narrow lane(b)/ where it was slewed by the kidnapper. (c)/ No error (d)

63. The river is in spate (a)/ and it has overflow (b)/ its banks. (c)/No error (d)

64. A rise in rents and wages (a)/ have been found (b)/ to go together. (c)/No error (d)

65. I have met him yesterday (a)/ while he was on his (b)/ way to college. (c)/No error (d)

Answers

Exercise 1

1 (c)	2 (d)	3 (a)	4 (a)	5 (c)	6 (d)	7 (a)	8 (c)	9 (c)	10 (c)
11 (a)	12 (b)	13 (c)	14 (d)	15 (d)	16 (c)	17 (c)	18 (c)	19 (a)	20 (d)
21 (a)	22 (c)	23 (d)	24 (a)	25 (a)	26 (a)	27 (b)	28 (a)	29 (c)	30 (c)
31 (d)	32 (d)	33 (c)	34 (a)	35 (d)	36 (a)	37 (b)	38 (a)	39 (d)	40 (b)
41 (d)	42 (c)	43 (a)	44 (b)	45 (a)	46 (b)	47 (d)	48 (a)	49 (b)	50 (c)
51 (d)	52 (b)	53 (c)	54 (c)	55 (b)	56 (d)	57 (a)	58 (c)	59 (d)	60 (a)
61 (a)	62 (c)	63 (d)							

Exercise 2

1 (b)	2 (a)	3 (d)	4 (c)	5 (b)	6 (d)	7 (a)	8 (b)	9 (c)	10 (b)
11 (a)	12 (b)	13 (a)	14 (b)	15 (a)	16 (c)	17 (b)	18 (b)	19 (a)	20 (a)
21 (c)	22 (a)	23 (b)	24 (d)	25 (b)	26 (b)	27 (a)	28 (c)	29 (b)	30 (a)
31 (a)	32 (b)	33 (b)	34 (a)	35 (a)	36 (a)	37 (d)	38 (b)	39 (a)	40 (b)
41 (b)	42 (b)	43 (a)	44 (c)	45 (d)	46 (b)	47 (c)	48 (b)	49 (b)	50 (a)
51 (c)	52 (b)	53 (b)	54 (c)	55 (a)	56 (d)	57 (b)	58 (c)	59 (b)	60 (a)
61 (a)	62 (c)	63 (b)	64 (b)	65 (a)					

Explanations

Exercise 2

31. *(a)* 'Flowed' की जगह 'flew' का प्रयोग करें 'Fly into a rage' एक phrasal verb है और 'flew', 'fly' की IInd form है।

32. *(b)* 'Have' की जगह 'am' का प्रयोग करें, क्योंकि progressive action को present में दर्शाने के लिए (I) am का प्रयोग उचित रहेगा।

33. *(b)* यहाँ 'to' का प्रयोग नहीं किया जाना चाहिए, क्योंकि causative verbs (let, make, have, get and help) के साथ bare infinitive (बिना 'to' के verb का प्रयोग) का प्रयोग किया जाता है।

34. *(a)* यहाँ 'is' के स्थान पर 'are' का प्रयोग किया जाना चाहिए, क्योंकि वाक्य का subject 'initials' एक plural noun है।

35. *(a)* 'Are wanting' के स्थान पर 'want' का प्रयोग किया जाना चाहिए, क्योंकि अधिकतर 'verb of sensation' को 'ing' form में प्रयोग नहीं किया जाता है।

36. *(a)* इस वाक्य में 'climb' के स्थान पर 'climbed' का प्रयोग किया जाना चाहिए, क्योंकि वाक्य का दूसरा भाग भी past में है।

37. *(d)* No error

38. *(b)* इस वाक्य में 'give' के स्थान पर 'gives' का प्रयोग किया जाना चाहिए, क्योंकि 'power' एक singular noun है, जिसके बाद singular verb (gives) का प्रयोग होगा।

39. *(a)* 'Be' के स्थान पर was/is का प्रयोग किया जाना चाहिए।

40. *(b)* यहाँ पर 'hadn't had' or 'did not have' का प्रयोग किया जाना चाहिए, क्योंकि Sentence के सही structure के लिए helping verb की आवश्यकता होती है।

41. *(b)* यदि sentence में didnot का use किया गया है, तब verb की base form का use किया जाता है। अत: यहाँ part (b) के अन्तर्गत 'begun' के स्थान पर 'begin' का use किया जाएगा।

42. *(b)* दिया गया sentence passive form में है, इसलिए यहाँ IIIrd form of verb का use किया जाएगा। अत: 'saw' की जगह 'seen' का use किया जाएगा।

43. *(a)* Sentence में part (a) के अन्तर्गत 'get' का use किया जाएगा।
Two verbs in simple past tense can not be used consecutively in a sentence. Hence, remove 'got' to correct the sentence.

44. *(c)* यहाँ part (c) के अन्तर्गत 'one released' के स्थान पर 'one was released' का use किया जाएगा to make the sentence grammatically correct.

45. *(d)* No error.

46. *(b)* यहाँ part (b) के अन्तर्गत 'are' के स्थान पर 'is' का use किया जाएगा।
Distance, money, time etc. when used as a unit takes singular verb.

47. *(c)* Part (c) के अन्तर्गत helping verb 'are' की जगह 'is' का use किया जाएगा as 'every' takes singular noun and singular verb.

48. *(b)* यहाँ part (b) के अन्तर्गत 'are' की जगह 'is' का use किया जाएगा। Singular verb should be used with neither of, either of, none of, one of etc.

49. *(b)* यहाँ part (b) के अन्तर्गत 'has' के स्थान पर 'have' का use किया जाएगा।
'All' and 'some' are followed by plural verb and plural noun.

50. *(a)* यहाँ part (a) के अन्तर्गत 'founded' के स्थान पर 'found' का use किया जाएगा as here the sentence requires the verb 'found'.

51. *(c)* 'And have to pay' के स्थान पर 'and will have to pay' का प्रयोग होगा, क्योंकि 'and' से जुड़ने वाले verb/helping verb दोनों एक ही form में होने चाहिए।

52. *(b)* 'Fall' के स्थान पर 'fell' का प्रयोग होगा।
Fall—Fell—Fallen = गिरना
Fell—Felled—Felled = गिराना

53. *(b)* 'Watched' के स्थान पर 'watching' का प्रयोग होगा, क्योंकि 'watched' को 'were standing' के अनुसार present participle में ही बदलना होगा।

54. *(c)* 'Is smelling' के स्थान पर 'smells' का प्रयोग होगा। 'Smell' यहाँ पर एक verb of perception है, इसलिए इसको 'ing' form में प्रयोग नहीं किया जा सकता।

55. *(a)* 'Has finished' के स्थान पर 'finished' का प्रयोग होगा, क्योंकि वाक्य में 'last night' का प्रयोग है।

56. *(d)* No error

57. *(b)* 'Effect' के स्थान पर 'affect' का प्रयोग करें, क्योंकि जब 'effect' को एक verb की तरह प्रयोग किया जाता है, तो इसका अर्थ 'अमल में लाना' (to cause something to happen) होता है, जबकि verb 'affect' का अर्थ 'प्रभावित करना' होता है।

58. *(c)* 'Illicit' के स्थान पर 'elicit' का प्रयोग किया जाना चाहिए, क्योंकि 'elicit' का अर्थ है 'कुछ पाना या उत्पन्न करना' खासतौर पर 'information' या 'reaction' जबकि 'illicit' का अर्थ 'गैर कानूनी' होता है।

59. *(b)* 'Lay down' के स्थान पर 'lie down' का प्रयोग किया जाना चाहिए, क्योंकि 'lay' के बाद एक direct object की आवश्यकता होती है परन्तु 'Lay'-Put down and set in position for use. (रखना)
Lie - A resting position on a supporting surface (of a person or animal). (लेटना)
(A) You lie down on the sofa. (No direct object)
(b) You lay the book down on the table. (Book is direct object).

60. *(a)* यहाँ part (a) के अन्तर्गत 'attended' की जगह 'attend' का use किया जाएगा because all modal verbs are followed by first form of verb.

61. *(a)* 'Is telling' के स्थान पर 'is telling me' या 'is saying' का प्रयोग किया जाना चाहिए। 'Tell' एक transitive verb है, जिसके बाद एक object का प्रयोग होता है। Verb 'say' का प्रयोग भी किया जा सकता है, जिसके बाद object की आवश्यकता नहीं होती है।

62. *(c)* 'Slewed' के स्थान पर 'slain' का प्रयोग किया जाना चाहिए। 'Slain' की present form 'slay' है, जिसका अर्थ है 'to kill in a violent way' (जान से मारना).

63. *(b)* 'Overflow' के स्थान पर 'Overflowed' का प्रयोग किया जाना चाहिए, क्योंकि present perfect tense में verb की third form का प्रयोग होगा।

V_1	V_2	V_1
Fly	Flew	Flown (उड़ना)
overflow	overflowed	overflowed (बहना)

64. *(b)* 'Have' के स्थान पर 'has' का प्रयोग किया जाना चाहिए, क्योंकि वाक्य का subject 'A rise' singular है, जिसके साथ singular verb का ही प्रयोग किया जाएगा।

65. *(a)* 'Have met' के स्थान पर 'met' का प्रयोग होगा, क्योंकि वाक्य में 'yesterday' का प्रयोग किया गया है, जो past को दर्शाता है।

06 Adverbs

Adverb वह शब्द होता हैं, जो किसी sentence में verb, adjective तथा किसी अन्य adverb की विशेषता बताता हैं या उसको define करता हैं। जैसे-Gently, really, very, simply, etc.

e.g. (i) He was horribly busy.
Adv. Adj.

(ii) He speaks English quite fluently.
Verb Adv. Adv.

(iii) Anand is really much dejected.
Adv. Adv. Adj.

Kinds of Adverbs

Adverbs को सामान्यतया तीन भागों में वर्गीकृत किया गया है

- Simple Adverbs
- Interrogative Adverbs
- Relative Adverbs

Simple Adverbs

Simple Adverbs ऐसे adverbs होते हैं, जो Time (समय), Place (जगह), Manner (ढ़ंग/तरीके), Frequency /Number (संख्या), Cause/Reason (कारण) तथा Affirmation/Negation को व्यक्त करते हैं।

1. **Adverb of Time** Daily, since, yesterday, soon, tomorrow, etc.
2. **Adverb of Place** Here, there, everywhere, in, away, up, etc.
3. **Adverb of Frequency or Number** Frequently, again, often, seldom, once, twice, etc.
4. **Adverb of Manner** Fast, swiftly, quickly, easily, slowly, loudly, so, bravely, etc.
5. **Adverb of Degree or Quantity** Fully, very, rather, perfectly, pretty, almost, etc.
6. **Adverb of Affirmation and Negation** Certainly, surely, seldom, never, always, definitely, etc.
7. **Adverb of Reasons** Therefore, hence, on account of, etc.
8. **Adverb of Contrast** However, though, etc.
9. **Adverb of Condition** Had, if, etc.
10. **Adverb of Extent** So far, till now, etc.

Interrogative Adverbs

ये adverbs, प्रश्न पूछने के लिए use किये जाते हैं। जैसे-why, when, who, how, which, where, wherefore (for what reason), whence (from where), whither (at what place) etc.

e.g. (i) When will you do the work ?

(ii) Wherefore do you cry ?

Yes or No Adverbs जो adverbs, Yes or No के रूप में पूरे sentence को ही स्पष्ट करते हैं, Yes or No adverbs कहलाते हैं।

e.g., (i) Do you know me ? Yes.

(ii) Have you played ? No.

Relative Adverbs

जो words, दो sentences को जोड़कर conjunction का काम करते हैं, relative adverbs के अन्तर्गत आते हैं। जैसे— what, when, where, how, etc.

e.g., (i) I know the time when he comes.

(ii) This is the reason why he failed.

Correct use of Adverbs

Very	Much
Very का use positive degree के लिए adjective से पहले किया जाता है। (er/est) (✗) जैसे–very good, very honest, very smart, etc. e.g., He is a very honest person.	Much का use comparative degree से पहले किया जाता हैं। (er-est) (✓) जैसे–Much better, much more honest, much smarter, etc. e.g., She works much faster than her sister.
Very का use present participle (ing) के साथ किया जाता है। जैसे–Very interesting, very admiring, very amusing, etc. e.g. It is a very interesting picture.	Much का use past participle (ed) के लिए किया जाता है। जैसे–Much interested, much admired, much amused, etc. e.g. I was much exhausted in the evening.

Too (–ve)	Very (+ve)
Too का use unpleasant adjective के साथ किया जाता हैं। जैसे–Too bad, too sad, too cold, etc.	Very का use pleasant adjective के लिए किया जाता है। जैसे– Very happy, very good, very intelligent, etc.
Too का अर्थ आवश्यकता से अधिक के लिए किया जाता है, जो एक Negative sense दिखाता हैं। e.g. Reena is too poor to afford anything.	Very का अर्थ सिर्फ अधिक के लिए किया जाता है, जो एक Positive sense दिखाता हैं। e.g. Rahul is very good at maths.

Position and Rules of Adverbs

Rule 1 Adverb of time का use सामान्यत: sentence के अन्त में होता है।

e.g., (i) I met him yesterday.
(ii) He celebrated his birthday with his friends last month.

Rule 2 Adverb of place का use सामान्यत: वाक्य के अन्त में होता है।

e.g., (i) Ravi did not come here.
(ii) Shekhar lives in a small village.

Rule 3 Adverb of manner का use सामान्यत: verb या sentence के अन्त में होता है।

e.g., (i) He ran quickly.
(ii) Heena delivered the speech fluently.

Rule 4 यदि Verb + Preposition + Object का use हो, तो Adverb of manner का प्रयोग preposition के पहले या object के बाद किया जा सकता है।

e.g., (i) He spoke angrily with his friend.
(ii) He spoke with his friend angrily.

Rule 5 यदि किसी sentence के last में Adverb of place, Adverb of manner and Adverb of time का use किया गया है तो इनका क्रम

Verb/Object + Manner + Place + Time होता है।

e.g., Shikha spoke fluently (Manner) in the class (Place) yesterday (Time).

यदि किसी sentence में Adverb of place, frequency और time का use हो तो इनका क्रम verb/object + place + frequency + time होता हैं।

e.g., Gaurav goes there (Place) three times (Frequency) in a day (Time).

Rule 6 निम्नलिखित Verbs के साथ Adverb 'as' का use superflous होता है जैसे—Make, elect, select, choose, appoint, consider, think, nominate, name, call, etc.

e.g., (i) Rahul has called his brother fool.
(Not 'as fool')
(ii) Mr. Sharma is selected company representative by them.
(Not 'as company representative')

परन्तु निम्नलिखित Verbs के साथ Adverbs 'as' का use correct होता है, जैसे—Mention, describe, regard, define, treat, view, know, etc.

e.g., (i) Everyone regards Mr. Rajeev as true mentor.
(ii) They treated me as one of the most important guests in the party.

Rule 7 Adverb of degree के रूप में so के बाद that का use होना चाहिए, प्राय: 'so' का use अकेले नही किया जाता है, यदि 'so' अकेला use हो तो उसकी जगह very का use किया जाता है।

e.g., (i) She is so brave. (✗)
She is very brave. (✓)
(ii) She is so brave that she can face any danger. (✓)

Exercise 1

Directions (Q. Nos. 1-6) Choose the correct answer from the given options based on the adverb given in the brackets.

1. I'm late (never).
(a) I am never late.
(b) Never I am late.
(c) I'm late never.
(d) I never am late.

2. They go out in the week (seldom).
(a) They go out seldom in the week.
(b) They seldom go out in the week.
(c) They go out in the week very seldom.
(d) They go out in the seldom week.

3. We don't see her (often)
(a) We don't often see her.
(b) We often don't see her.
(c) We don't see her often
(d) Often we don't see her.

4. I take too long in the shower (always).
(a) I take always too long in the shower.
(b) I always take too long in the shower.
(c) I take too long always in the shower.
(d) I take too long in the shower always.

5. Sam arrives on time (usually).
(a) Sam arrives usually on time.
(b) Sam usually arrives on time.
(c) Sam arrives on time usually.
(d) Usually sam arrives on time.

6. Do you go to the cinemas on Fridays (always)?
(a) Do you always go to the cinemas on Fridays ?
(b) Do you go to cinemas always on Fridays ?
(c) Do you go always to cinema on Fridays ?
(d) Always do you go to the cinemas on Fridays ?

Directions (Q. No. 7-35) Fill in the blanks with the correct adverb.

7. I...........want to know what happened.
(a) exactly (b) purely
(c) simply (d) highly

8. Don't worry. It's ....safe. You won't fall.
(a) finely (b) deeply
(c) fully (d) completely

9. The future will be ....shaped by technology.
(a) merely (b) specially
(c) largely (d) purely

10. Everything will be .... cheaper in the sales .
(a) widely (b) greatly
(c) considerably (d) particularly

11. There's nothing ....similar to this product.
(a) closely (b) remotely
(c) nearly (d) wildly

12. They succeeded in ....exploiting their opportunities.
(a) hardly (b) entirely
(c) fully (d) deeply

13. Nobody answering the phone doesn't ....mean there is no one there.
(a) necessarily (b) surely
(c) wholly (d) strictly

14. It's ....true that education is becoming global.
(a) exactly (b) reliably
(c) certainly (d) fully

15. We were ....considering selling the house.
(a) heavily (b) seriously
(c) brightly (d) fully

16. It was a long time ago, but I .... do remember when we first arrived in our new home.
(a) specially (b) surely
(c) seriously (d) strictly

17. I ....go to bed at 10 o'clock.
(a) usually (b) occasionally
(c) once (d) often

18. I have ....been to the USA.
(a) mostly (b) never
(c) sometimes (d) rarely

19. I have been to Australia just ....
(a) always (b) occasionally
(c) once (d) rarely

20. I ....take a bath before I go to bed.
(a) never (b) rarely
(c) sometimes (d) always

21. My grandparents live in Calcutta. I visit them......
(a) once (b) never
(c) always (d) often

22. My friends are .... non-smokers.
(a) often (b) rarely
(c) mostly (d) occasionally

23. I was ....impressed with her performance.
(a) mostly (b) very
(c) always (d) once

24. They .... go for a walk in the park.
(a) sometimes (b) once
(c) twice (d) really

25. I ....watch English films.
(a) twice (b) always
(c) again (d) once

26. They ....go out in the evening because of the cold.
(a) sometimes (b) mostly
(c) rarely (d) once

27. Our holiday was too short. The time passed very ....
(a) continuously (b) fluently
(c) perfectly (d) quickly

28. Tom doesn't take risks when he is driving. He is always ....
(a) happy (b) nervous
(c) perfect (d) careful

29. Shelly works .... She never stops in between.
(a) continuously (b) completely
(c) happily (d) quickly

30. Aditya and Sanjana are very ....married.
(a) happily (b) completely
(c) perfectly (d) quickly

31. I cooked this meal ....for you, so I hope you like it.
(a) happily (b) quickly
(c) especially (d) completely

32. Everything was very quiet. There was ....silence.
(a) special (b) complete
(c) perfectly (d) careful

33. I tried the shoes and they fitted me ......
(a) quickly (b) completely
(c) perfectly (d) specially

34. Do you usually feel ....before an interview ?
(a) nervous (b) special
(c) fluent (d) careful

35. I'd like to buy a car but it is ....impossible for me at the moment.
(a) completely (b) perfecty
(c) specially (d) financially

Exercise 2

Directions (Q.No. 1-20) Fill in the blanks with suitable adverbs.

1. ....I met my childhood friend Meeta.
(a) Yesterday (b) Today
(c) Tomorrow (d) This sunday

2. You need to run ....to win this race.
(a) slow (b) steadily
(c) fast (d) lazily

3. I won't say it ....
(a) progressively (b) repeatedly
(c) necessarily (d) correctly

4. Speak ...., I cannot hear you.
(a) loudly (b) slowly
(c) hardly (d) quickly

5. You should ....smoke as it is dangerous for your health.
(a) always (b) usually
(c) never (d) hardly

6. We searched ......but we were unable to find her lost jewellery.
(a) nowhere (b) anywhere
(c) everywhere (d) all where

7. I hope to see you ....!
(a) soon (b) never
(c) randomly (d) occasionally

8. Deepak never dressed .... for work.
(a) formally (b) coolly
(c) dirtily (d) casually

9. The manager looked at me with an ....expression when I reached late.
(a) sad (b) regret
(c) angry (d) polite

10. Ranjit speaks ....good French, he can be of great help to you.
(a) he (b) great
(c) quite (d) English

11. He .... goes to office in the weekends as his office remains shut.
(a) always (b) never
(c) often (d) sometime

12. I belive in punctuality, so I go to work on time and .... come home by 8.
(a) always (b) sometimes
(c) never (d) often

13. He has not ....applied for the job we told him about.
(a) still (b) yet
(c) now (d) since

14. Tom is ....clever, but Peter is rather stupid.
(a) fairly (b) rather
(c) almost (d) just

15. Her case is so heavy that she can ....lift it.
(a) hardly (b) have
(c) nearly (d) fairly

16. The ballerina moved .... as she danced.
(a) softly (b) politely
(c) gracefully (d) None of these

17. He and his friends work ....
(a) hardly (b) hard
(c) only (d) diligent

18. Sanjay is .... better today.
(a) fairly (b) rather
(c) very (d) too

19. We waited .... for the bus to arrive.
(a) patiently (b) promptly
(c) punctually (d) gently

20. If you do something you don't really want to do, you do it ....
(a) eagerly (b) reluctantly
(c) accidently (d) exactly

Directions (Q. Nos. 21-40) In each of the following questions, a sentence is given which may or may not be correct. Select the option which is the correct form of the sentence.

21. My brother smokes seldom.
(a) My brother smokes little.
(b) My brother seldom smokes.
(c) My brother smokes less.
(d) None of the above

22. Tom is enough rich to help the poor.
(a) Tom is rich enough to help the poor.
(b) Tom is enough rich than to help the poor.
(c) Tom is rich enough than to help the poor.
(d) None of the above

23. It is nothing else than pride.
(a) It is nothing else but pride.
(b) It is nothing else than a pride.
(c) It is nothing else but a pride.
(d) None of the above

24. It is too cold today.
(a) It is very cold today.
(b) It is too cold today.
(c) It is very a cold today.
(d) None of the above

25. I shall come back just now.
(a) I shall come back just after.
(b) I shall come back presently.
(c) I shall come back just then.
(d) None of the above

26. She works quick than you.
(a) She works quickly than you.
(b) She works more quickly than you.
(c) She works much more quick than you.
(d) None of the above

27. You are so nice.
(a) You are so a nice.
(b) You are very nice
(c) You are a very nice.
(d) None of the above

28. My brother met me presently.
(a) My brother met me just now.
(b) My brother met me now.
(c) My brother met me just
(d) None of the above

29. The almirah is too much heavy for me.
(a) The almirah is too heavy for me.
(b) The almirah is too very heavy for me.
(c) The almirah is much heavy for me.
(d) None of the above

30. She only spent ten rupees.
(a) She spent only ten rupees.
(b) She only spent a ten rupee notes.

(c) She only spent a ten rupee note.
(d) None of the above

31. He speaks much fluently
(a) He speaks very fluently.
(b) He speaks more fluently
(c) He speaks most fluently
(d) None of the above

32. Mohan compelled Sonu to at once leave the place.
(a) Mohan compelled Sonu at once to leave the place.
(b) Mohan compelled Sonu to leave the place at once.
(c) Mohan compelled Sonu leave the place to at once.
(d) None of the above

33. I shall tomorrow go there.
(a) I shall tomorrow went there
(b) I shall tomorrow there go.
(c) I shall go there tomorrow
(d) None of the above

34. I visit the castle often.
(a) I visit often the castle.
(b) I often visit the castle.
(c) I visit the often castle.
(d) None of the above

35. He tried to hurriedly reach the hotel.
(a) He tried to reach the hotel hurriedly.
(b) He hurriedly tried to reach the hotel.
(c) He tried to hurriedly the hotel reach.
(d) None of the above

36. He ran very fastly
(a) He ran much fastly.
(b) He ran most fastly.
(c) He ran very fast.
(d) None of the above

37. Ravi is wiser than Yogesh.
(a) Ravi is many wiser than Yogesh.
(b) Ravi is much wiser than Yogesh.
(c) Ravi is too wiser than Yogesh.
(d) None of the above

38. You should speak the truth always.
(a) You should always speak the truth.
(b) You should speak always the truth.
(c) You always should speak the truth.
(d) None of the above

39. She is wonderful beautiful.
(a) She is wonderfully beautiful.
(b) She is wonderfully beautify.
(c) She is wonderful beautify.
(d) None of the above

40. It is very cold to go out.
(a) It is very too cold to go out.
(b) It is much too cold to go out.
(c) It is too cold to go out.
(d) None of the above

Directions (Q. Nos. 41-60) Read the following sentences and find out the error part in the given sentences. If there is no error, in any part, the answer is option (d) i.e., No error.

41. Somebody informed the contractor (a)/ that his brother (b)/ had only died five days before. (c)/No error (d)

42. The teacher (a)/scolded him always (b)/because he rarely reached school on time. (c)/No error (d)

43. Who can believe that (a)/she was not hardly hit (b)/by the death of her son. (c)/No error (d)

44. It is a common misconception (a)/that every policeman badly behaves (b)/with the citizens. (c)/ No error (d)

45. Only by discussing with the officer (a)/ concerned they found out (b)/ the person behind the fraud. (c)/No error (d)

46. The house is very good (a)/ but too much small (b)/to accommodate the full family. (c)/No error (d)

47. He does not know (a)/ to make friends (b)/ so he is leading a lonely life. (c)/No error (d)

48. Every member of the family (a)/ is addicted to drinking (b)/ and so Asha is. (c)/No error (d)

49. As I had been very bad (a)/ with calculations, she asked me (b)/ to carefully solve the questions (c)/ No error (d)

50. Shakshi was exorbitantly paid (a) for how skilful she (b)/ welcomed the visitors. (c)/No error (d)

51. "Please listen to the announcement with carefully", (a)/ said the manager (b)/ to his employees. (c)/ No error (d)

52. The student requested (a)/the principal to be enough kind (b)/to grant him seven days leave. (c)/No error (d)

53. He has been trying (a)/to persuade her for several months (b)/but he has not still succeeded. (c)/No error (d)

54. Meera had hardly (a)/ reached the airport (b)/ when the flight took off. (c)/ No error (d)

55. The amount which the company paid (a)/ to the dependents of the deceased (b)/ was fairly unjustified. (c)/No error (d).

56. Although he only earns (a)/sixteen hundred rupees per month (b)/yet he manages his family well. (c)/No error (d)

57. I liked that opportune moment (a)/where the workers proved themselves (b)/and came out victorious. (c)/No error (d)

58. One should face (a)/ the challenges posed by (b)/ life manly. (c)/No error (d)

59. I hardly ever see him (a)/ because in my opinion (b)/he is not a reliable man. (c)/No error (d)

60. I meet Shivangi often (a)/ near the (b)/ cafe shop. (c)/ No error (d)

Answers

Exercise 1

1 (a)	2 (b)	3 (c)	4 (b)	5 (b)	6 (a)	7 (c)	8 (d)	9 (c)	10 (c)
11 (b)	12 (c)	13 (a)	14 (c)	15 (b)	16 (b)	17 (a)	18 (b)	19 (c)	20 (d)
21 (d)	22 (c)	23 (b)	24 *(a)*	25 (b)	26 (c)	27 (d)	28 (d)	29 (a)	30 (a)
31 (c)	32 (b)	33 (c)	34 (a)	35 (d)					

Exercise 2

1 (a)	2 (c)	3 (b)	4 (a)	5 (c)	6 (c)	7 (a)	8 (a)	9 (c)	10 (c)
11 (b)	12 (a)	13 (b)	14 (a)	15 (a)	16 (c)	17 (b)	18 (b)	19 (a)	20 (b)
21 (b)	22 (a)	23 (a)	24 (a)	25 (b)	26 (b)	27 (b)	28 (a)	29 (a)	30 (a)
31 (a)	32 (b)	33 (c)	34 (b)	35 (a)	36 (c)	37 (b)	38 (a)	39 (a)	40 (c)
41 (c)	42 (b)	43 (b)	44 (b)	45 (a)	46 (b)	47 (b)	48 (c)	49 (c)	50 (b)
51 (a)	52 (b)	53 (c)	54 (d)	55 (c)	56 (a)	57 (b)	58 (c)	59 (d)	60 (a)

Explanations

Exercise 2

41. *(c)* 'Only' का प्रयोग 'died' के बाद होगा। brother had died only five days before. He only died का अर्थ है केवल वह मरा' He died only three days ago. का अर्थ है 'वह केवल तीन दिन पहले मरा'।

42. *(b)* यहाँ part (b) के अनतर्गत 'scolded him always' के स्थान पर 'always scolded him' का use किया जाएगा। Adverbs like always, seldom, never etc. are used before the main verb.

43. *(b)* 'Hardly hit' की जगह 'hit hard' का use होगा। Hardly का अर्थ 'न के बराबर' (negative) होता है, जबकि hard का अर्थ 'कठिन'/'कड़ा' होता है।

44. *(b)* यहाँ 'badly behaves' की जगह 'behaves badly' का use किया जाएगा, as the adverbs of manner are used after the main verb.

45. *(a)* Only को 'with' से पहले लिखें। By discussing only with. Only का प्रयोग सामान्यतया उस word से पहले किया जाता है जिसे महत्त्व दिया जा रहा है।

46. *(b)* 'Too much' की जगह 'much too small' होना चाहिए। सामान्यतया 'too much' का प्रयोग noun से पूर्व होता है, 'much too' का प्रयोग adjective से पूर्व होता है।

47. *(b)* यहाँ 'to make' की जगह 'how to make' का use होगा।

48. *(c)* 'So Asha is' की जगह 'so is Asha' होगा। इस तरह के वाक्यों में सहायक क्रिया Subject से पहले आती है।

49. *(c)* यहाँ part (c) के अन्तर्गत 'carefully' का use 'questions' के बाद किया जाएगा। It is incorrect to use adverbs in between participles. Hence, 'to solve the questions carefully' is correct.

50. *(b)* यहाँ part (b) के अन्तर्गत 'skilful' के स्थान पर 'skilfully' का use किया जाएगा। 'Skilful' एक adjective है जबकि यहाँ skilfully (Adverb), verb received को qualify कर रहा है।

51. *(a)* यहाँ part (a) के अन्तर्गत 'with' का use नहीं किया जाएगा। Prepositions are never used with adverbs.

52. *(b)* यहाँ part (b) के अन्तर्गत 'to be enough kind' की जगह 'to be kind enough' होगा। 'Enough' (as adverb) का use उस शब्द के बाद होता है जिसे वह qualify कर रहा है।

53. *(c)* 'Still' की जगह 'yet' आएगा। Still का प्रयोग affirmative वाक्यों में होता है, जबकि yet का प्रयोग सामान्तया negative वाक्यों में किया जाता है।

54. *(d)* No error

55. *(c)* 'Fairly' की जगह 'rather' या 'quite' का प्रयोग होगा। Fairly का use सामान्यतया good sense में होता है।

56. *(a)* 'He earns only' होगा only, almost, even etc. का प्रयोग हमेशा उस Phrase या शब्द से पहले किया जाता है जिसे वह qualify करता है।

57. *(b)* 'Where' की जगह 'When' का प्रयोग होगा। 'Where'– adverb of place है तथा Time के लिए Adverb of time, 'when' का प्रयोग किया जाता है।

58. *(c)* यहाँ 'Manly' की जगह 'manfully' का use किया जाएगा। 'manly' एक adjective है और 'manfully' एक adverb.

59. *(d)* No error

60. *(a)* यहाँ 'I meet Shivangi often' की जगह 'I often meet Shivangi' का use किया जाएगा। Adverbs of time are used before the verbs that they modify.

07 Adjective

जो words sentence में किसी Noun या Pronoun की विशेषता (जैसे-रंग-रूप, गुण-दोष, आकार-प्रकार आदि) denote करते हैं, Adjectives कहलाते हैं, जैसे-tall boy, thin girl, white hat etc.

e.g., (i) Sakshi is a good girl.

↓ ↓
Adj. Noun

(ii) He is smart and handsome.

↓ ↓ ↓
Pronoun Adj. Adj.

Kind of Adjective

1. **Proper Adjective** ⇒ Proper noun से बनने वाले adjectives, proper adjectives कहलाते हैं; जैसे- India से Indian, Africa से African, China से Chinese etc.

   e.g., This is a Chinese belt.

   ↓
   Proper Adj.

   Kabaddi is an Indian game.

   ↓
   Proper Adj.

2. **Demonstrative Adjective** ⇒ ऐसे adjectives जिनका use sentence में निकट या दूर के Noun/Pronoun को denote करने के लिए किया जाता हैं, उन्हें demonstrative adjective कहते हैं; जैसे- This, That, These, Those, Such etc.

   e.g., These novels are interesting.
   This shirt is dirty.

> **Note** This/That के बाद **singular noun** तथा **These/Those** के बाद **plural noun** का **use** किया जाता है। जैसे- **This dog, These dogs, That boy, Those boys.**
>
> यदि किसी sentence में **This/That/These/Those** के तुरन्त बाद किसी **Noun** के स्थान पर **verb** का **use** किया गया हो, तो फिर ये **Demonstrative Adjective** नहीं, बल्कि **Demostrative Pronoun** की तरह प्रयुक्त होंगे।
>
> **Demonstrative Pronoun** This is an intelligent boy.
> Those were my friends.
>
> **Demonstrative Adjective** This shirt is dirty.
> Those men are Indian.

3. **Adjective of Quantity** ⇒ ऐसे adjectives जिनका use sentence में किसी noun की quantity (मात्रा) बताने के लिए किया जाए, उन्हें adjective of quantity कहते हैं; जैसे– Whole, some, enough, sufficient, no, full, little etc.

   e.g., I need some food.
   There is enough water in the jug.

4. **Adjective of number** ये adjectives व्यक्तियों या वस्तुओं की संख्या का बोध कराते हैं। इन्हें दो भागों में विभाजित किया गया है।

   Definite Number Adjectives ये adjectives exact number or order (निश्चित संख्या या क्रम) का बोध कराते हैं; जैसे- One, two, three ......, first, second, third ...

   e.g. I have three pencils.

   Indefinite Number Adjectives ये adjectives exact number or order (निश्चित संख्या या क्रम) का बोध नहीं कराते हैं, जैसे- All, few, some, several, many, certain etc.

   e.g., Many boys have come here.

> **Note** Indefinite number adjectives are used for persons only.

5. **Adjective of Quality** ऐसे adjectives, जो किसी noun (persons, things, animals) के गुण, दोष, रंग आकार-प्रकार, स्वभाव, दशा आदि को denote करता है, उन्हें adjectives of quality कहते हैं; जैसे- Intelligent, beautiful, long, tall, red, round, square etc.

   e.g., I have a black skirt.
   She is an old lady.

6. **Distributive Adjectives** ⇒ ऐसे adjectives, जिनका sentence में प्रयुक्त व्यक्तियों/वस्तुओं के group में से किसी एक, प्रत्येक, या एक भी नहीं के सन्दर्भ में use किया जाता है; जैसे- Each, every, either, neither etc.

   e.g., Neither of these boys went there.
   Each boy is responsible for littering classroom.

7. **Interrogative Adjectives** ⇒ ऐसे adjectives, जिनका use sentence में प्रश्न पूछने के लिए किया जाता है, उन्हें interrogative adjectivies कहते हैं; जैसे- What, which, whose etc.

   e.g., Whose shirt is this?
   What is your name?

8. **Emphasizing Adjectives** ⇒ ऐसे adjectives, जिनका use sentence में किसी noun पर stress (विशेष दबाव), importance (प्रमुखता) या emphasize (जोर) देने के लिए किया जाए, उन्हें emphasizing adjectives कहते हैं; जैसे– Own, very, quite.

   e.g., This is her own dress.
   This is the very costly gift I wanted.

Position of Adjectives

1. Generally, adjective का use उस Noun के पहले किया जाता है, जिसकी वह विशेषता बताता है।

   e.g., • He is a good boy.
   Adj. Noun

   • She is a beautiful girl.
   Adj. Noun

2. जब एक से ज्यादा adjectives, एक ही noun के साथ प्रयुक्त होते हैं, तो इन adjectives को noun के बाद लगाया जाता है।

   e.g., The soldier, fearless and determined attacked the enemy.
   Noun Adj.

   A girl intelligent and beautiful won the race.
   ↓ ↓
   Noun Adj.

3. यदि sentence में indefinite pronoun का use हो तो, adjective का use इसके बाद करते हैं।

   e.g., • It is something important.
   ↓ ↓
   Pronoun Adj.

   • I have nothing new to say.
   ↓ ↓
   Pronoun Adj.

4. कुछ निम्न phrases में adjective, noun के बाद आता है। जैसे Notary public, Time immemorial, Body politic, God Almighty, Heir Apparent, Sum total, God Incarnate, Governor-General etc.

   कुछ adjectives जैसे—Asleep, alone, ashamed, alike का use वाक्य में predicatively होता है।

   e.g., • The child is asleep.

   • The baby is awake.

5. जब adjective के साथ कोई phrase या words उसे स्पष्ट करने हेतु प्रयुक्त होते हैं तो adjective को noun के बाद लगाते हैं।

   e.g., • A man, wiser than his fellows solved the question within a minute.

   • She is a girl, benevolent in nature.

Some Important Rules of Adjectives

Rule 1 यदि किसी sentence में ordinal तथा numerical (or cardinals) दोनो का use किया गया हो, तो पहले हमेशा ordinal adjectives का तथा बाद में cardinal adjective का use किया जाएगा।

e.g., You must study the first three topics of the syllabus.
↓ ↓
Ordinal Cardinal

The last two or three chapters of the book are important.
↓ ↓
ordinal Cardinals

Rule 2 जब किसी sentence में noun से पहले एक से अधिक adjectives का use किया गया हो, तो इन adjectives का क्रम निम्न प्रकार होना चाहिए

Quantity or Number (मात्रा या संख्या)	Two, three, many, etc.
Opinion (राय/विचार)	Lovely, Dirty, Beautiful, etc.
Size (आकार)	Tall, Big, Tiny, etc.
Age (आयु/उम्र)	Young, old, new, 10-year-old, etc.
Shape (आकृति/रूप)	Circular, Round, Rectangular, etc.
Colour (रंग)	Green, white, black, etc.
Origin (उत्पत्ति/उद्भव)	Indian, Chinese, Dutch, etc.
Material (पदार्थ)	Plastic, Silver, Metal, etc.
Purpose (उद्देश्य)	Wedding or any occasion.

e.g., Number → Size → Shape → Material.
↑ ↑ ↑ ↑
I have two, long, narrow, plastic brushes. (Correct)

Nitin wants to buy a comfortable black sleeping bed. (Correct)
↓
(qualifier)

Rule 3 कुछ adjectives ऐसे होते हैं; जिनका प्रयोग किसी वाक्य में केवल attributive position में ही किया जा सकता है, यानि इन adjectives के बाद एक noun का होना जरूरी है। ऐसे adjectives है- Elder, eldest, live, little, mere, sheer, chief, main, principal etc.

e.g., His elder brother is a politician.
Adj. Noun

This suggestion is sheer nonsense.
Adj. Noun

इस adjectives का प्रयोग verb के बाद बिना noun के नहीं किया जा सकता है। इनके स्थान पर हम दूसरे शब्दों का प्रयोग कर सकते हैं।

(✗) (✔)
e.g. This snake is still live/alive.

Ajeet's house is little/small.
(✗) (✔)

Rule 4 कुछ adjectives ऐसे होते हैं, जिनका प्रयोग केवल predicative position में ही किया जा सकता है, यानि इनका प्रयोग verb के बाद किया जाता है तथा इनके तुरन्त बाद किसी noun का प्रयोग नहीं किया जाता है। ऐसे adjectives हैं afloat, afraid, aglow, alive, alone, asleep, etc.

e.g., You were afraid.
Verb Adj.

The animal is alive.
Verb Adj.

Rule 5 किसी sentence में result को दर्शाने के लिए transitive verb तथा object के बाद, adjective का use किया जाता है, adverb का नहीं।

Subject + Transitive verb + Object + Adjective

e.g., I thought the plan unwise.
verb obj Adj.

He made him fool.
verb obj. Adj.

Rule 6 जब दो या दो से अधिक adjectives को एक ही noun/pronoun को qualify करने के लिए hyphen (-) से जोड़ा जाता है, तो उसे compound adjective कहते है। ये adjectives हमेशा singular form में ही use किए जाते हैं।

e.g., (i) Meera adopted a two-years-old dog. (✗)
Meera adopted a two-year-old dog. (✔)
(ii) She took a six-weeks course. (✗)
She took a six-week course. (✔)

इसी तरह जब एक noun को adjective की तरह use किया जाता है, तो वह adjective सिर्फ singular form में होना चाहिए।

e.g., He bought a ticket to see boats race. (✗)
He bought a ticket to see boat race. (✓)

इस sentence में noun 'boat', का use adjective की तरह हुआ है, इसलिए यह singular form में ही होना चाहिए, plural form में नहीं।

Degrees of Comparison of Adjectives

Degrees of comparison का use एक, दो या दो से अधिक person/places/things के बीच तुलना (comparison) करने के लिए किया जाता है। Adjectives के अन्तर्गत निम्नलिखित तीन प्रकार की degrees होती हैं

1. Positive Degree
2. Comparative Degree
3. Superlative Degree

Positive Degree

जब किसी adjective को उसके वास्तविक रूप में use किया जाता है, तब वह positive degree को दर्शाता है।

e.g., (i) Ria is a beautiful girl.
(ii) Abhishek is a tall boy.

Positive degree के adjectives को as ... as तथा so ... as के बीच में भी रखा जाता है।

e.g., (i) She is as beautiful as Veenu.
(ii) He is not so good as I.

Note ⇒ so ... as का use mostly negative sentences में किया जाता है।

Comparative Degree

जब किसी adjective का use दो व्यक्तियों या वस्तुओं के गुण, मात्रा आदि की तुलना करने के लिए किया जाता है, वह comparative degree को denote करता है। Comparative degree में adjective के बाद 'than' का use किया जाता है।

e.g., (i) He is taller than I.
(ii) She is more beautiful than Reena.

The + comparative + of the two + plural noun का प्रयोग selection (चुनाव) के भाव के लिए होता है। जैसे–

She is the better of the two girls.
He was the more intelligent of the two boys.

Note Subject के बाद transitive verb का प्रयोग हो, तो than के बाद objective case के pronoun का प्रयोग होता है।
जैसे– You love him more than me.

Superlative Degree

जब comparison (तुलना) दो से अधिक व्यक्तियों, वस्तुओं तथा समूहों के बीच हो, तब superlative degree का use किया जाता है। Superlative degree से पहले article 'the' का use किया जाता है।

e.g., He is the tallest boy in my class.
He is the cleverest of all the six brothers.

Following is the list of some adjectives with their Comparatives and Superlatives

Positive	Comparative	Superlative
Sweet	Sweeter	Sweetest
Young	Younger	Youngest
High	Higher	Highest
Old	Older	Oldest
Tall	Taller	Tallest
Poor	Poorer	Poorest
Rich	Richer	Richest
Slow	Slower	Slowest
Bright	Brighter	Brightest
Thick	Thicker	Thickest
Clever	Cleverer	Cleverest
Deep	Deeper	Deepest
Long	Longer	Longest
Small	Smaller	Smallest
Cheap	Cheaper	Cheapest
Clear	Clearer	Clearest
Great	Greater	Greatest
White	Whiter	Whitest
Noble	Nobler	Noblest
Wise	Wiser	Wisest
Large	Larger	Largest
Safe	Safer	Safest
Fine	Finer	Finest
Brave	Braver	Bravest
Wide	Wider	Wisest

Positive	Comparative	Superlative
Able	Abler	Ablest
True	Truer	Truest
Wet	Wetter	Wettest
Big	Bigger	Biggest
Hot	Hotter	Hottest
Fat	Fatter	Fattest
Sad	Sadder	Saddest
Thin	Thinner	Thinnest
Fit	Fitter	Fittest
Dim	Dimmer	Dimmest
Slim	Slimmer	Slimmest
Easy	Easier	Easiest
Lovely	Lovelier	Loveliest
Happy	Happier	Happiest
Heavy	Heavier	Heaviest
Healthy	Healthier	Healthiest
Pretty	Prettier	Prettiest
Merry	Merrier	Merriest
Lazy	Lazier	Laziest
Wealthy	Wealthier	Wealthiest
Dry	Drier	Driest
Merry	Meerier	Merriest
Holy	Holier	Holiest
Gay	Gayer	Gayest
Grey	Greyer	Greyest
Bad	Worse	Worst
Much	More	Most
Fore	Former	Foremost, First
Late	Later	Latest
Good, Well	Better	Best
Ill/Evil	Worse	Worst
Far	Farther	Farthest
Late	Later/Latter	Latest/Last
Little	Less/Lesser	Least
Much/Many	More	Most
Nigh	Nigher	Nighest, Next
In	Inner	Innermost, Inmost
Difficult	More Difficult	Most Difficult
Important	More Important	Most Important
Careless	More Careless	Most Careless
Beautiful	More Beautiful	Most Beautiful
Courageous	More Courageous	Most Courageous
Useful	More Useful	Most Useful

Positive	Comparative	Superlative
Laborious	More Laborious	Most Laborious
Intelligent	More Intelligent	Most Intelligent
Handsome	More Handsome	Most Handsome
Interesting	More Interesting	Most Interesting
Expensive	More Expensive	Most Expensive
Magnificent	More Magnificent	Most Magnificent
Splendid	More Splendid	Most Splendid
Useful	More Useful	Most Useful
Honest	More Honest	Most Honest
Famous	More Famous	Most Famous

Some Important Rules Regarding Degree of Adjectives

Rule 1 यदि किसी sentence में दो adjectives को किसी भी conjunction (and, or, but etc) से जोड़ा जाता है, तो दोनों ही adjectives, same degree में होने चाहिए; या तो सब comparative में हो या superlative में।

Subject + H.V. + Adjective + or/but/and + Adjective +Object
+ ER/more .... + ER/More
+ ER/most .... + ER/most
How much/many .... How much/many

e.g., Anita is cleverer and braver than her sister.
Ram is wiser and stronger than Shyam.

Rule 2 As + positive degree + as का use किसी sentence में दो persons या things की qualitites में समानता दर्शाने के लिए किया जाता है।

e.g., (i) Sunita is as intelligent as Ankit.
(ii) She is as beautiful as Karishma.

(As ...... as के बीच केवल positive degree का ही use किया जाता है, comparative या superlative का नहीं)

Rule 3 ऐसा जरूरी नहीं की हमेशा ही comparative degree के साथ than का use किया जाएगा। अगर comparison का दूसरा part पहले से ही स्पष्ट हो तो comparative का use बिना 'than' के भी किया जा सकता है।

e.g., He does not want to walk much farther than this.
(Comparison का दूसरा part 'than this' पहले से ही स्पष्ट है।)

Rule 6 Noun/pronoun के स्वभाव या स्थिति (condition) में निरन्तर होने वाले बदलाव को दर्शाने के लिए 'comparative degree + and + comparative degree' का use किया जाता है। इस स्थिति में adjective की comparative degree का प्रयोग predicative position में ही किया जा सकता है।

इस प्रकार के construction में ज्यादातर get, grow, become, इत्यादि verbs का use किया जाता है।

e.g., (i) The noise is becoming louder and louder.

(ii) The condition of this city is getting better and better.

Rule 7 कुछ adjectives जिनके अन्त में 'ior' होता है, उनके बाद 'than' का नहीं 'to' का use किया जाता है।

ऐसे adjectives हैं -Superior, anterior, senior, junior, prior, posterior, inferior.

e.g., (i) Manvi is superior to Anshu. (✓)

(ii) Yogesh is junior to me. (✓)

Rule 8 कुछ adjectives ऐसें होते हैं जिनसे पहले more या most लगाकर उनको comparative या superlative degree में नहीं बदला जा सकता है। ऐसे adjectives हैं- Unique, chief, entire, universal, milky, spherical, dead, blind, extreme, golden, ideal, unmatched, monthly, lunar, solar, singular, external, invincible, right, incorrigible, wrong, round, square, triangular, rectangular, whole, excellent, eternal, major, minor, interior, ulterior, exterior, etc.

e.g., (i) This is the most unique opportunity. (×)

This is a unique opportunity. (✓)

(ii) The food was more excellent. (×)

The food was excellent. (✓)

Rule 9 Adjective 'preferable' के साथ 'to' का प्रयोग किया जाता है न कि 'than' का और इसके साथ 'more' का भी प्रयोग नहीं किया जाता है। Preferable का प्रयोग सिर्फ comparative degree में ही किया जाता है।

e.g., (i) A diplomatic solution is preferable than war. (×)

A diplomatic solution is preferable to war. (✓)

(ii) Online shopping is more preferable to offline shopping. (×)

Online shopping is preferable to offline shopping. (✓)

Rule 10 वाक्य में दो comparative या दो superlative degree का प्रयोग एक साथ नहीं किया जाता है।

e.g., (i) Radha is taller than her. (Not 'more taller')

(ii) This is the safest place in this town. (Not 'most safest')

Rule 11 'Fairly' तथा 'Comparatively' का use comparative degree से पहले नहीं किया जाता है।

e.g., The bag is fairly heavy. (Not 'fairly heavier')

She was comparatively well yesterday. (Not 'Comparatively better')

Rule 12 दो व्यक्तियों (persons) या वस्तुओं (things) के बीच अन्तर (comparison) दर्शाने के लिए 'the + comparative degree + of का use किया जाता है, लेकिन अगर अन्तर दो से अधिक के बीच हो तो 'the + superlative degree + of का use किया जाता है।

e.g., (i) He is the noblest of the two friends. (×)

He is the nobler of the two friends. (✓)

(ii) He is the wiser of all the boys. (×)

He is the wisest of all the boys. (✓)

उपरोक्त पहले वाक्य में comparison सिर्फ दो के बीच किया गया है, इसलिए यहाँ पर 'the nobler of' का use होगा, जबकि दूसरे वाक्य में comparison सभी के साथ किया गया है, इसलिए यहाँ पर 'the wisest of' का use होगा।

Rule 13 जब किसी एक ही person/thing की दो qualities के बीच comparison किया गया हो तो comparative degree के स्थान पर 'more + positive degree' का use किया जाता है।

e.g., John is funnier than serious. (×)

John is more funny than serious. (✓)

Ram is more strong than intelligent. (✓)

I quality II quality

Rule 14 जब किसी person/things का comparison उसी के समूह से किया जाता है, जिस समूह (group) का वह व्यक्ति या वस्तु स्वयं एक हिस्सा (part) है, तो उस व्यक्ति/वस्तु को उस समूह से अलग दर्शाने के लिए 'any other' का use किया जाता है।

e.g., (i) Wular is larger than any lake in India. (×)

Wular is larger than any other lake in India. (✓)

(ii) Caspean Sea is larger than any other lake in India. (×)

Caspean Sea is larger than any lake in India. (✓)

उपरोक्त पहले वाक्य में 'any other' का प्रयोग होगा, क्योंकि 'wular' भारतीय झीलों (Indian lakes) का ही एक हिस्सा है। जबकि दूसरे वाक्य में 'any other' का प्रयोग नहीं होगा, क्योंकि Caspean Sea भारतीय झील (Indian lake) नहीं है, इसलिए यह इसका एक हिस्सा नहीं है।

> **Note** Adjective की superlative degree के साथ 'other' का प्रयोग नहीं होता है।

Rule 15 जब किसी व्यक्ति/स्थान की किसी खास चीज का comparison किसी दूसरे व्यक्ति/स्थान की उसी चीज से हो, तो उस दूसरे व्यक्ति/वस्तु से पहले that of, those of या उसके साथ apostrophe 's'('s) का use किया जाता है। Singular के लिए 'that of' तथा plural के लिए 'those of' का use किया जाता है।

e.g., (i) The climate of Patna is better than that of Gaya. (✓)

(ii) The climate of Patna is better than Gaya. (×)

(iii) The people of Jajuar are wiser than those of Bishnupur. (✓)

(iv) The people of Jajuar are wiser than Bishnupur. (×)

(v) The people of Jajuar are wiser than that of Bishnupur. (×)

Example no. (ii) तथा (iv) से यह स्पष्ट है कि दो असमान वस्तुओं के बीच तुलना नहीं होती है। Example no. (ii) में The climate of Patna की तुलना Gaya शहर से की गई है, जो गलत है। The climate of Patna की तुलना The climate of Gaya से होनी चाहिए थी। The climate-singular noun का प्रयोग of Patna के पहले हुआ है। अत: than के बाद that of का प्रयोग होना चाहिए था।

Example no. (iii) में The people of Jajuar की तुलना Bishnupur गाँव से की गई है, जो गलत है। The people of Jajuar की तुलना The people of Bishnupur से होनी चाहिए थी। The people-plural noun का प्रयोग of Jajuar से पहले हुआ है, अत: than के बाद those of का प्रयोग होना चाहिए था।

Rule 16 साथ साथ होने वाले increment (वृद्धि) या decrement (कमी) को denote करने के लिए इस structure का use किया जाता है-

The + Comparative degree + sub + verb, the + comparative degree + sub + verb

e.g., (i) The more you study, the much you know. (×)
Comparative D   Positive D
The more you study, the more you know. (✓)
Comparative D   Comparative D

(ii) The slim you are, the quicker you run. (×)
Positive D   Comparative D
The slimmer you are, the quicker you run. (✓)
Comparative D   Comparative D

Rule 17 Adverb 'enough' से पहले सिर्फ positive degree का use किया जाता है।

e.g., The water of this bucket is hot enough to bath.

Rule 18 Comparison के लिए 'so ... as' का use केवल negative sentence में किया जाता है, जबकि 'as ... as' का use negative तथा positive दोनों sentences में होता है। So ... as के साथ भी positive degree का ही use किया जाता है।

e.g., This structure is so bigger as the previous structure. (×)
This structure is as big as the previous structure. (✓)

Rule 19 किसी व्यक्ति/वस्तु के बीच comparison को measrue (माप) या weight (वजन) में denote करने के लिए 'as ... as' से पहले numerical adjective (three, four, five) + times का use किया जाता है।

e.g., This tree is four times as long as that one.

Rule 20 यदि कोई भी दो adjectives किसी conjunction से जुड़े हो और दोनों ही adjectives same degree में हो, तब दोनों adjectives के साथ उचित preposition (in, at, on, to, etc) का use किया जाना चाहिए।

e.g., (i) She is senior and more intelligent than her friend. (×)
She is senior to and more intelligent than her friend. (✓)

(ii) He was angry and disagree with this irrelevant proposal. (×)
He was angry at and disagree with this irrelevant proposal. (✓)

Rule 21 कुछ adjectives ऐसे होते है जो preposition के साथ use किए जाने पर noun बन जाते हैं। ऐसे adjectives है- in general, in short, for good, at best, before long, in black and white, through thick and thin.

e.g., (i) I have left Delhi for good.
(ii) Give me your application in black and white.

Exercise 1

Directions (Q. Nos. 1-11) Fill in the blanks with suitable adjective.

1. Make sure you wear a scarf because the weather outside is quite ....
(a) windy (b) humid
(c) hot (d) rainy

2. My new bed not only looks good but also very ....
(a) heavy (b) ugly
(c) comfortable (d) stiff

3. The little .... kitten climbed up the curtains and spilled her milk.
(a) naughty (b) lazy
(c) old (d) fat

4. We sat and watched as the setting sun created a .... sky.
(a) dull (b) clear
(c) gorgeous (d) dark

5. I will be performing in front of a large audience tomorrow, so I am feeling ....
(a) angry (b) anxious
(c) jealous (d) sleepy

6. The younger sister felt .... as the, elder one was being showered with presents on her birthday.
(a) foolish (b) wise
(c) jealous (d) poor

7. Helping my mother with the chores seemed fun at first, but soon it became ....
(a) relaxed (b) tedious
(c) exciting (d) happening

8. She is too .... to learn the error of her ways.
(a) arrogant (b) hardworking
(c) disciplined (d) wise

9. She was .... to receive the bad news.
(a) happy (b) excited
(c) shocked (d) elated

10. It was so .... of you to offer them help.
(a) rude (b) horrible
(c) kind (d) terrible

11. Ramesh has joined a .... cause.
(a) three-year (b) three-year
(c) one-year (d) None of these

Directions (Q. Nos. 12-47) Fill in the blanks with correct form of adjective.

12. Of his three sisters, Susan is the ....
(a) old (b) elder
(c) eldest (d) None of these

13. Black is the .... colour.
(a) dark (b) darker
(c) darkest (d) None of these

14. Maya is the .... girl in the class.
(a) pretty (b) prettier
(c) prettiest (d) None of these

15. Tina is .... than Priti.
(a) intelligent
(b) more intelligent
(c) most intelligent
(d) None of the above

16. The weather today is .... than the weather yesterday, but not as .... as it was four days ago.
(a) worse/bad (b) bad/bad
(c) worse/worse (d) bad/worst

17. The road was .... than we expected.
(a) long (b) longer
(c) longest (d) None of these

18. Planes are the .... means of travelling today.
(a) convenient
(b) more convenient
(c) most convenient
(d) None of the above

19. These jeans are the ...., in fact they are .... than the trousers.
(a) dirty/dirtier
(b) dirtiest/dirtier
(c) dirty/dirty
(d) None of the above

20. A candle gives .... light than a lamp.
(a) little (b) less
(c) least (d) None of these

21. That boy is the .... runner of all.
(a) fast (b) faster
(c) fastest (d) None of these

22. His badminton skills are .... among the players in the team.
(a) good (b) better
(c) best (d) None of these

23. The cake is just as .... as the ice-cream.
(a) sweet (b) sweeter
(c) sweetest (d) None of these

24. Shakespeare is .... than any other English poet.
(a) great (b) greater
(c) greatest (d) None of these

25. Shakespeare is the .... of all English poets.
(a) great (b) greater
(c) greatest (d) None of these

26. The pen is .... than the sword.
(a) mighty (b) mightier
(c) mightiest (d) None of these

27. Mount Everest is the .... peak in the world.
(a) high (b) higher
(c) highest (d) None of these

28. Mango is .... than lime.
(a) sweet (b) sweeter
(c) sweetest (d) None of these

29. I have .... books than you.
(a) many (b) more
(c) most (d) None of these

30. Very few nations are as .... as the USA.
(a) powerful
(b) more powerful
(c) most powerful
(d) None of the above

31. This is the .... painting he ever made.
(a) more beautiful
(b) beautiful
(c) beautier
(d) most beautiful

32. My luggage is .... than yours.
(a) heavy (b) heaviest
(c) heavier (d) heavily

33. The rides at the fair were .... than I thought.
(a) expensive
(b) more expensive
(c) most expensive
(d) not expensive

34. The weather today is .... than it was yesterday.
(a) more good (b) best
(c) better (d) worst

35. Ravi is more .... than expected.
(a) lately (b) late
(c) later (d) latter

36. I saw a rainbow in the sky. It was a .... sight than I had ever seen.
(a) splendid
(b) splendier
(c) most splendid
(d) more splendid

37. They claim that the new computers are ....
(a) most sturdy (b) sturdiest
(c) sturdier (d) very sturdy

38. Chimpanzees are .... than most people think.
(a) clever (b) more clever
(c) cleverer (d) cleverest

39. The classroom is .... and full of freshness after the cleaning.
(a) brighter
(b) bright
(c) most bright
(d) more brighter

40. Our childhood years always seem .... to us.
(a) happy (b) happiest
(c) more happy
(d) most happy

41. The latter proposal was .... than the former.
(a) the better (b) the best
(c) better (d) best

42. This room is .... preferable to that of your sister.
(a) more (b) most
(c) very (d) No word

43. Her birthday is the .... day for her.
(a) most happiest
(b) more happier
(c) happier
(d) happiest

44. This is comparatively a .... pen.
(a) cheaper (b) cheap
(c) cheapest (d) better

45. Santosh is .... than prudent.
(a) braver (b) more braver
(c) more brave (d) braver enough

46. This sum is .... difficult than that.
(a) very (b) more
(c) most (d) the most

47. Among the politicians, who could be called ....
(a) the more honest
(b) more honest
(c) the most honest
(d) most honest

Directions (Q. Nos. 48-62) Choose the adjective in the given sentences.

48. The unique design of the building was praised much.
(a) The unique (b) design of
(c) building (d) praised

49. Lord Mountbatten was the last Governor-General of India.
(a) Lord Mountbatten
(b) last
(c) Governor-General
(d) India

50. The first book of author is about poverty.
(a) first (b) book
(c) author (d) poverty

51. They are wise enough to not fight with others.
(a) They (b) wise
(c) enough (d) fight

52. His command over English is excellent.
(a) command (b) His
(c) English (d) excellent

53. It is relatively colder today.
(a) It (b) colder
(c) today (d) None of these

54. The baby has drunk much milk.
(a) The baby (b) drunk
(c) much (d) milk

55. Mumbai is the busiest city in India.
(a) Mumbai (b) busiest
(c) city (d) India

56. The beauty of Kashmir is unmatched.
(a) beauty
(b) Kashmir
(c) unmatched
(d) None of the above

57. The interior decoration of the temple was excellent.
(a) interior
(b) decoration
(c) excellent
(d) Both (a) and (c)

58. The shy boy hid behind his mother's skirt.
(a) boy (b) behind
(c) shy (d) skirt

59. I opened the door to find a tattered envelope on the step.
(a) door (b) opened
(c) envelope (d) tattered

60. Please open the door to let that poor dog inside.
(a) poor (b) Please
(c) let (d) inside

61. The baby was making sleepy noises and rubbing her eyes.
(a) noises (b) sleepy
(c) rubbing (d) making

62. How many times have you been to the new restaurant?
(a) times (b) have
(c) restaurant (d) new

Exercise 2

Directions (Q. Nos. 1-15) Do as directed.

1. Choose the superlative form of 'Fast'.
(a) Fast (b) Faster
(c) Fastest (d) Fastly

2. If the superlative is least than the positive is
(a) Least (b) Less
(c) Little (d) Lesser

3. My sister is a beautiful girl. Here, 'beautiful' is a/an ....
(a) adjective of quality
(b) adjective of quantity
(c) demonstrative adjective
(d) possessive adjective

4. Find out the adjectives of quality from the following options.
(a) Most, few, little
(b) Tall, small, sweet
(c) One, five, ten
(d) My, your, his

5. Select the distributive adjective in the following sentence.
Each cheerleader is given props along with dress.
(a) Each (b) along
(c) given (d) props

6. Neither my son nor my husband could lock the door. Here, 'neither' is a/an ....
(a) possessive adjective
(b) demonstrative adjective
(c) interrogative adjective
(d) distributive adjective

7. Comparative degree of 'well' is
(a) best (b) well
(c) very well (d) better

8. Find out the indefinite adjective in the given sentence.
A man can fail many times, but he isn't a failure until he begins to blame somebody else.
(a) many (b) somebody
(c) failure (d) times

9. Identify the type of word that is underlined in the given sentence.
<u>All</u> the people cheered.
(a) Noun (b) Pronoun
(c) Adjective (d) Verb

10. Identify the type of word that is underlined in the given sentence.
It's <u>Sheer</u> rubbish.
(a) Noun (b) Pronoun
(c) Adjective (d) Verb

11. Find out the adjective from the given options.
(a) Walking (b) Punished
(c) Punishment (d) Punishable

12. Find out the correct word (Adjective) of the word 'Accent.'
(a) Accentuate
(b) Accentual
(c) Accentuated
(d) Accentuation

13. Choose the correct adjective of the following noun 'Advice.'
(a) Advisable (b) Advise
(c) Advisedly (d) Adviser

14. Which of the following has the three degrees of the adjectives in their correct form?
(a) Early earlier, earliest
(b) Hot,more hot, hottest
(c) Easy, more easy, most easy
(d) Special, specialer, specialist

15. Fill in the blank with the correct degree of comparison of the word given in the bracket.
My cold is definitely .... (bad) this morning.
(a) worst (b) worse
(c) bad (d) more bad

Directions (Q. Nos. 16-40) In the following questions, select the option which is the correct form of the sentence. If you think none of the options is correct, your answer is 'd'.

16. Harish is senior than you.
(a) Harish is more senior than you.
(b) Harish is more senior to you.
(c) Harish is senior to you.
(d) None of the above

17. My shirt is more superior than yours.
(a) My shirt is superior than yours.
(b) My shirt is more superior to yours.
(c) My shirt is superior to yours.
(d) None of the above

18. Sangeeta is more wiser than Sunita.
(a) Sangeeta is wise than Sunita.
(b) Sangeeta is more much wiser than Sunita.
(c) Sangeeta is wiser than Sunita.
(d) None of the above

19. It is the most impossible to stay in the flames of fire for a long time.
(a) It is the more impossible to stay in the flames of fire for a long time.
(b) It is impossible to stay in the flames of fire for a long time.
(c) It is more impossible in the flames of fire for a long time.
(d) None of the above

20. Tony is the most happiest boy in the world.
(a) Tony is most happiest boy...
(b) Tony is the happiest boy...
(c) Tony is the most happy boy...
(d) None of the above

21. Sonu is more cleverer than industrious.
(a) Sonu is more cleverer to industrious.
(b) Sonu is more clever to industrious.
(c) Sonu is more clever than industrious.
(d) None of the above

22. Surjeet is better than any player in the team.
(a) Surjeet is better than any other player in the team.
(b) Surjeet is more better than any other player in the team.
(c) Surjeet is better than any players in the team.
(d) None of the above

23. Rohit is my oldest son.
(a) Rohit is my most oldest son.
(b) Rohit is my eldest son.
(c) Rohit is my most eldest son.
(d) None of the above

24. These sort of people are not liked by me.
(a) This sort of people are not liked by me.
(b) These sorts of people are not liked by me.
(c) This sort of peoples are not liked by me.
(d) None of the above

25. I sat nearest to her.
(a) I sat nearer to her.
(b) I sat more nearer to her.
(c) I sat next to her.
(d) None of the above

26. You are becoming clever day-by-day.
(a) You are becoming more cleverer day-by-day.
(b) You are becoming much cleverer day-by-day
(c) You are becoming cleverer day-by-day.
(d) None of the above

27. The best team won the final match.
(a) The better team won the final match.
(b) Best team won the final match.
(c) More best team won the final match.
(d) None of the above

28. Open your books at nine page.
(a) Open your books in nine page.
(b) Open your books at page nine.
(c) Open your books in page nine.
(d) None of the above

29. My brother bought much apples.
(a) My brother bought many apples.
(b) My brother bought much more apples.
(c) My brother bought many more apples.
(d) None of the above

30. His statement is truthful.
(a) His statement is truth.
(b) His statement is true.
(c) His statement is more true.
(d) None of the above

31. Whole town is under water.
(a) Whole of town is under water.
(b) The whole town is under water.
(c) Whole the town is under water.
(d) None of the above

32. Sachin is more famous than any player of cricket.
(a) Sachin is more famous than any other player of cricket.
(b) Sachin is famouser than any other player of cricket.
(c) Sachin is the most famous than any other player of cricket.
(d) None of the above

33. Less dresses are needed for the circus men.
(a) Lesser dresses are needed for the circus men.
(b) Fewer dresses are needed for the circus men.
(c) Least dresses are needed for the circus men.
(d) None of the above

34. What is the last news?
(a) What is the lest news?
(b) What is the latest news?
(c) What is the end news?
(d) None of the above

35. There are only fewer bananas left in the basket.
(a) There are only a few bananas left in the basket.
(b) There are only the few bananas left in the basket.
(c) There are only more few bananas left in the basket.
(d) None of the above

36. Mukesh got cent per cent marks in Mathematics.
(a) Mukesh got absolute marks in Mathematics.
(b) Mukesh got full marks or hundred per cent marks in Mathematics.
(c) Mukesh got up to date marks in Mathematics.
(d) None of the above

37. Tony is a miser boy.
(a) Tony is miser boy.
(b) Tony is miser.
(c) Tony is a miser.
(d) None of the above

38. John has spent little money he had.
(a) John has spent the little money he had.
(b) John has spend a little money he had.
(c) John has spent more little money he had.
(d) None of the above

39. Sandeep is five years smaller than I or me.
(a) Sandeep is five years more smaller than I.
(b) Sandeep is five years smaller to I.
(c) Sandeep is five years younger than I or me.
(d) None of the above

40. My pants are more inferior than you.
(a) My pants are more inferior than yours.
(b) My pants are inferior to yours.
(c) My pants are inferior than yours.
(d) None of the above

Directions (Q. Nos. 41-100) Find out which part of the sentence has an error.

41. Kolkata is further (a)/from Alwar (b)/than Jaipur (c)/the capital of Rajasthan. (d)

42. Ramesh is smarter (a)/enough to get (b)/selected for this (c)/post, without any recommendations. (d)

43. He said, "Priyanka (a)/is the most unique (b) /singer of (c)/our college. (d)"

44. This shirt is (a)/comparatively better (b)/than that (c)/we saw in corner shop yesterday. (d)

45. Everyone was surprised to note (a)/that Rahim married a girl (b)/who was more beautiful and more tall (c)/than he. (d)

46. Shivangi is a beautiful (a)/if not (b)/more than Meera. (c)/ No error (d)

47. I told her (a)/that it would be all (b)/the more better (c)/if she herself talked to the groom. (d)

48. She does not have (a)/some money to buy (b)/a new refrigerator (c)/so she is worried. (d)

49. Now-a-days (a)/the weather (b)/is getting more cold (c)/and colder. (d)

50. The books (a)/were indeed interesting (b)/but that one was (c)/the more interesting. (d)

51. There were only two (a)/warriors but each and every (b)/warrior was equal (c)/to six persons. (d)

52. A dark spacious (a)/cell has been found (b)/in a recent discovery. (c)/ No error (d)

53. Can we rely (a)/on this agency (b)/for the last news (c)/of the day. (d)

54. Ram is junior than (a)/Shyam and (b)/Ram is older (c)/than Ganesh. (d)

55. The militants (a)/entered the palace (b)/from the utmost gate (c)/with guns hidden in their clothes. (d)

56. "She can't sing (a)/much than (b)/four songs at (c)/a stretch", he informed. (d)

57. It is well know (a)/that Mrs. Indira Gandhi (b)/was the first statesman (c)/of her time. (d)

58. It is a (a)/ desert (b)/ place. (c)/ No error (d)

59. It is believed that (a)/ hundreds of people (b)/ have lost lives. (c)/ No error (d)

60. That was (a)/ the most unique- opportunity (b)/ he got in his life. (c)/ No error (d)

61. Shelley is (a)/ superior than Byron (b)/ in his vision of democracy. (c)/ No error (d)

62. To the ordinary man, in fact, the pealing of bells (a)/ is a monotonous jangle and a nuisance (b)/ tolerably only when mitigated by remote distance and sentimental association. (c)/ No error (d)

63. If you have a way with words, (a)/ a good sense of design and administration ability (b)/ you may enjoy working in the high pressure world of advertising. (c)/ No error (d)

64. Of the two great cities (a)/ the former is (b)/ biggest. (c)/ No error (d)

65. I feel certain problems (a) / in the execution (b) / of this plan. (c) / No error (d).

66. Everybody knows (a)/that Bhutan is the most peaceful (b)/of all other countries of the world. (c)/ No error(d)

67. The pollution level in (a)/ Delhi is higher (b)/ than that of last year. (c)/ No error (d)

68. I prefer (a)/ to have tea (b)/ than coffee. (c)/ No error (d)

69. India Gate is (a)/ a historical (b)/ monument located in New Delhi. (c)/ No error (d)

70. The half first (a)/ of the movie (b)/ was very interesting. (c)/ No error (d)

71. Samar is (a)/ the oldest (b)/ of his siblings. (c)/ No error (d)

72. Rupali is (a)/ wise of (b)/ the two students. (c)/ No error (d)

73. Manmohan Singh is (a) our former than (b)/ Prime Minister. (c)/ No error (d)

74. Sachin is (a)/ the best cricketer (b)/ of the two. (c)/ No error (d)

75. Toto is shorter (a)/ than (b)/ fat. (c)/ No error (d)

76. Chilika is the (a)/largest brackish water (b)/lagoon in Asia. (c)/ No error (d)

77. On Sundays (a)/I prefer reading (b)/than going out visiting my friends. (c)/ No error (d)

78. The student asked me (a)/if I knew that Kalidas was the greater (b)/than any other poet. (c)/ No error (d)

79. Each child (a)/was given (b)/red beautiful balloon. (c)/ No error (d)

80. Rahul is older than his brother (a)/Sanjay by (b)/eight years. (c)/ No error (d)

81. It is an. infirmity of the political leaders (a)/ that they feel highly grateful when they are praised (b) / in eloquent terms on the stage before a vast gathering. (c) / No error. (d)

82. Rohan will be suspended because he (a)/ opened an account without: obtaining none (b)/ of the necessary documents. (c)/I No error (d)

83. Rahul is older than his brother (a)/ Sanjay by (b)/ eight years. (c)/ No error (d)

84. No American President (a)/ has been so famous as (b)/ Abraham Lincoln. (c)/ No error (d)

85. According to a survey more of the forty percent (a)/ of Indians do not (b)/ have access to banks. (c)/ No error (d)

86. The ten captains had (a)/ an achievement (b)/ of his own. (c)/ No error (d)

87. When your in doubt (a)/ about your best friend's loyalty (b)/ you can't help being disappointed. (c)/ No error (d)

88. I recall you telling me (a)/ the story of the seven witches (b)/ but I cannot remember where or when. (c)/ No error (d)

89. Ramesh is smarter enough (a)/ to get selected for this post, (b)/ without any recommendations. (c)/ No. error (d)

90. No method of making other (a)/ people agree to (b)/ your view point is as effective as this method. (c)/ No error (d)

91. The house (a)/ is built in an (b)/ attractive manner. (c)/ No error (d)

92. We received (a)/ much help (b)/ from the neighbours. (c)/ No error (d)

93. Henry is (a)/ a capable boy (b)/ of doing anything. (c)/ No error (d)

94. This is the girl (a)/ whose brother (b)/ is a doctor. (c)/ No error (d)

95. Mobile phones are so importance these days (a)/ that they are no longer (b)/ luxury items but have become a necessity. (c)/No. error (d)

96. Education is the only affective tool (a)/ to help eradicate (b)/ the problem of violence against & women. (c)/ No. error (d)

97. Jewellery retailers across India decided (a)/ to suspend sold (b)/ of gold coins and bars for six months. (c)/ No. error (d)

98. The more contented we are (a)/ with what we already have (b)/ the happy we will be. (c)/ No error (d)

99. The uniform (a)/ of St. Martin's school (d)/ is blue colour. (c)/ No error(c)

100. One should respect (a)/ the religions of others (b)/ as much as his own. (c)/ No error (d)

Answers

Exercise 1

1	(a)	2	(c)	3	(a)	4	(c)	5	(b)	6	(c)	7	(b)	8	(a)	9	(c)	10	(c)
11	(a)	12	(c)	13	(a)	14	(c)	15	(b)	16	(a)	17	(b)	18	(c)	19	(b)	20	(b)
21	(c)	22	(c)	23	(a)	24	(b)	25	(c)	26	(b)	27	(c)	28	(b)	29	(b)	30	(a)
31	(d)	32	(c)	33	(b)	34	(c)	35	(b)	36	(d)	37	(d)	38	(c)	39	(a)	40	(a)
41	(c)	42	(a)	43	(d)	44	(b)	45	(c)	46	(b)	47	(c)	48	(a)	49	(b)	50	(a)
51	(b)	52	(d)	53	(b)	54	(c)	55	(b)	56	(c)	57	(d)	58	(c)	59	(d)	60	(a)
61	(b)	62	(d)																

Exercise 2

1	(c)	2	(c)	3	(a)	4	(b)	5	(d)	6	(a)	7	(c)	8	(a)	9	(c)	10	(c)
11	(d)	12	(b)	13	(a)	14	(a)	15	(b)	16	(c)	17	(c)	18	(c)	19	(b)	20	(b)
21	(c)	22	(a)	23	(b)	24	(a)	25	(c)	26	(c)	27	(a)	28	(b)	29	(a)	30	(b)
31	(b)	32	(a)	33	(b)	34	(b)	35	(a)	36	(b)	37	(c)	38	(a)	39	(c)	40	(b)
41	(a)	42	(a)	43	(b)	44	(b)	45	(c)	46	(a)	47	(c)	48	(b)	49	(c)	50	(d)
51	(b)	52	(a)	53	(c)	54	(a)	55	(c)	56	(b)	57	(c)	58	(b)	59	(c)	60	(b)
61	(b)	62	(c)	63	(b)	64	(c)	65	(d)	66	(c)	67	(d)	68	(c)	69	(b)	70	(a)
71	(b)	72	(b)	73	(b)	74	(b)	75	(a)	76	(d)	77	(c)	78	(b)	79	(c)	80	(a)
81	(b)	82	(b)	83	(a)	84	(a)	85	(a)	86	(c)	87	(a)	88	(a)	89	(a)	90	(a)
91	(d)	92	(d)	93	(b)	94	(d)	95	(a)	96	(a)	97	(b)	98	(c)	99	(c)	100	(c)

Explanations

Exercise 2

41. *(a)* यहाँ 'further' के स्थान पर 'farther' का use किया जाएगा क्योंकि Farther का अर्थ अधिक दूर तथा further का अर्थ आगे होता है। Farther 'far' की comparative degree है।

42. *(a)* 'Smarter' की जगह 'smart' लिखा जायेगा। ध्यान रखें: enough के पूर्व, positive degree का प्रयोग होता है।

43. *(b)* Unique के पूर्व, the most को delete करें। कुछ adjectives unique, full, whole, square universal etc. अपने अर्थ के कारण superlative degree की तरह प्रयुक्त होते हैं। इनको compare नहीं किया जा सकता है। More unique, more complete या more square लिखना एवं most unique, most complete या most square लिखना गलत है।

44. *(b)* Comparatively के साथ positive degree के adjective का प्रयोग होता है। अत: या तो comparatively good लिखा जायेगा या केवल better लिखा जायेगा।

45. *(c)* 'More tall' की जगह 'taller' होगा। सामान्यतया one syllable adjective का comparative उसमें 'er' या 'r' जोड़कर बनाया जाता है।

46. *(a)* यहाँ part (a) के अन्तर्गत beautiful के बाद 'as' का use किया जाएगा to make the sentence error free.

47. *(c)* 'More better' लिखना गलत है। avoid double comparative. 'more' को delete करें।

48. *(b)* 'Some money' की जगह 'any money' लिखा जायेगा। इस तरह के negative वाक्यों में 'some' की जगह 'any' का प्रयोग होता है।

49. *(c)* 'More cold' की जगह 'colder' लिखा जायेगा। इस तरह के वाक्यों में comparative degree of adjective का प्रयोग निम्न प्रकार से होता है। जैसे: He is becoming stronger and stronger.

50. *(d)* 'More' की जगह 'most' का प्रयोग किया जायेगा। जब दो से अधिक वस्तुओं के साथ तुलना हो तो superlative degree of adjective का प्रयोग किया जाता है। दो वस्तुओं हेतु comparative degree का प्रयोग होता है।

51. *(b)* Change 'each and every' to 'each'. ध्यान रखें : each का प्रयोग दो हेतु, किन्तु 'each and every' या 'every' का प्रयोग हमेशा दो से अधिक के लिए होता है।

52. *(a)* यहाँ 'dark spacious' की जगह 'spacious dark' का use suitable होगा according to sequence of adjectives.

53. *(c)* 'Last' की अपेक्षा 'latest' लिखा जायेगा। समय के सन्दर्भ late की comparative एवं superlative degree later, latest है।

54. *(a)* 'Than' की जगह 'to' का प्रयोग होगा। Junior, senior, prior etc. के साथ to का प्रयोग किया जाता है।

55. *(c)* 'Utmost' की जगह 'outermost' लिखा जायेगा। Out का comparative, outer एवं superlative; outermost होता है। Utmost का अर्थ complete (पूर्णतया) होता है। यहाँ utmost का गलत प्रयोग हुआ है।

56. *(b)* Much' की जगह 'more' का प्रयोग होगा। much-positive degree का adjective है जिसका comparative more है।

57. *(c)* यहाँ 'first' की जगह 'foremost' का प्रयोग किया जायेगा first का अर्थ प्रथम होता है जबकि foremost का अर्थ most notable (सर्वाधिक चर्चित) होता है। वाक्य के सन्दर्भ के अनुसार foremost का प्रयोग ही उचित है।

58. *(b)* यहाँ 'desert' के स्थान पर 'deserted' का प्रयोग किया जाना चाहिए, क्योंकि 'deserted' एक adjective है, जिसका अर्थ 'वीरान या निर्जन' होता है, जबकि 'desert' एक noun है, जिसका अर्थ 'रेगिस्तान' होता है।

59. *(c)* 'Lives' से पहले 'their' का प्रयोग किया जाना चाहिए। 'Hundreds of people' plural है, इसलिए इसके बाद एक possessive adjective 'their' का प्रयोग किया जाएगा।

60. *(b)* 'The most' के स्थान पर 'a' का प्रयोग किया जाना चाहिए। कुछ words जैसे unique, perfect, full, absolute, etc. के साथ adjective 'more' या 'most' का प्रयोग नहीं किया जाता है।

61. *(b)* 'Than' के स्थान पर 'to' का प्रयोग किया जाना चाहिए। कुछ words जैसे- superior, junior, prefer, senior, etc. के बाद preposition 'to' का प्रयोग किया जाता है।

62. *(c)* Adverb 'tolerably' के स्थान पर adjective 'tolerable' का प्रयोग किया जाना चाहिए, क्योंकि यहाँ 'the pealing of bells' को qualify करने के लिए एक adjective की आवश्यकता है।

63. *(b)* Noun 'administration' के स्थान पर adjective 'administrative' का प्रयोग किया जाना चाहिए, क्योंकि यहाँ noun 'ability' को qualify करने के लिए एक adjective की आवश्यकता है, न कि noun की।

64. *(c)* यहाँ दो cities के बीच comparative degree 'bigger' का प्रयोग किया जाना चाहिए, न कि 'biggest' का।

65. *(d)* No error.

66. *(c)* Remove 'other' because 'other' is not used with superlative degree, it is used in comparative degree.`

67. *(d)* No error

68. *(c)* यहाँ part (c) के अन्तर्गत 'Than' के स्थान पर 'to' का use किया जाएगा क्योंकि 'prefer' के साथ 'to' का use किया जाता है।

69. *(b)* Part (b) में 'historical' के स्थान पर 'historic' का use किया जाएगा।

70. *(a)* Part (a) के अन्तर्गत 'Half first' का use incorrect है। इसकी जगह 'first half' का use किया जाएगा as ordinal numbers are followed by cardinal numbers.

71. *(b)* यहाँ 'oldest' का use inappropriate है। 'Oldest' के स्थान पर यहाँ 'eldest' का use किया जाएगा as eldest is used for member of same family.

72. *(b)* यहाँ 'wise' के स्थान पर comparative degree 'wiser' का use किया जाएगा क्योंकि comparison दो nouns के बीच में किया गया है।

73. *(b)* यहाँ part (b) में 'than' का use नहीं किया जाएगा। Use of 'than' is superfluous here.

74. *(b)* यहाँ 'best' के स्थान पर 'better' का use किया जाएगा as the sentence compares two peoples.

75. *(a)* यहाँ part (a) के अन्तर्गत 'shorter' के स्थान पर 'more short' का use किया जाएगा as two qualities of the same person are compared.

76. *(d)* No error

77. *(c)* यहाँ 'than' के स्थान पर 'to' का use किया जाएगा because 'prefer' is followed by 'to'.

78. *(b)* यहाँ part (b) के अन्तर्गत article 'the' का use नहीं किया जाएगा क्योंकि 'the' का use superlative degree के साथ किया जाता है और दिया गया sentcence comparative degree से belong करता है।

79. *(c)* यहाँ 'red beautiful ballon' की जगह 'beautiful red ballon' का use किया जाएगा because adjective of opinion (beautiful) is used before adjective of colour.

80. *(a)* यहाँ part (a) के अन्तर्गत 'older than' के स्थान पर 'elder to' का use किया जाएगा as we know that 'elder' is used only for sibling or for blood relations.

81. *(b)* 'Grateful' के स्थान पर 'gratified' का प्रयोग होगा। यह दोनों शब्द adjective हैं लेकिन sentece के according यहाँ 'gratified' का use appropriate होगा।

Grafteful = One is thankful to somebody for something. (आभारी)

Gratified = One is satisfied or pleased. (सन्तुष्ट/प्रसन्न)

82. *(b)* 'None' के स्थान पर 'any' का प्रयोग होगा, क्योंकि Negative/Interrogative वाक्यों में हमेशा any का ही प्रयोग किया जाता है।

83. *(a)* 'Older than' के स्थान पर 'elder to' का प्रयोग होगा, क्योंकि elder का प्रयोग सिर्फ siblings के लिए किया जाता है।

84. *(a)* 'No American' के स्थान पर 'no other American' का प्रयोग होगा, क्योंकि यहाँ President 'Abraham Lincoln' की तुलना अपने ही देश के अन्य Presidents के साथ की गई है।

85. *(a)* 'More of the forty percent' के स्थान पर 'most of the forty percent' का प्रयोग होगा, यहाँ 'most' का अर्थ है, 'अधिकांश/ज्यादातर'।

86. *(c)* 'His' के स्थान पर 'their' का प्रयोग होगा, क्योंकि plural noun (ten captains) के लिए plural possessive adjective (their) का प्रयोग किया जाता है।

87. *(a)* 'Your' के स्थान पर 'your are' का प्रयोग किया जाना चाहिए, क्योंकि 'your' एक possessive adjective है, जिसका प्रयोग possession दिखाने के लिए noun से पहले किया जाता है।

88. *(a)* 'You' के स्थान पर 'your' का प्रयोग किया जाना चाहिए, क्योंकि gerund (telling) से पहले possessive adjective (my, your, our, their, his, her) का प्रयोग किया जाता है।

89. *(a)* 'Smarter' के स्थान पर 'smart' का प्रयोग किया जाना चाहिए, क्योंकि 'enough' से पहले हमेशा adjective की positive degree का प्रयोग किया जाता है।

90. *(a)* 'No method' के स्थान पर 'no other method' का प्रयोग किया जाना चाहिए, क्योंकि वाक्य में आगे comparison को दर्शाया गया है।

91. *(d)* No error

92. *(d)* No error

93. *(b)* यहाँ 'capable boy' के स्थान पर 'boy capable' का use होगा। इस वाक्य की सही संरचना है 'Henry is a boy capable of doing anything'.

94. *(d)* No error

95. *(a)* इस वाक्य में noun 'importance' के स्थान पर adjective 'important' का प्रयोग किया जाना चाहिए, क्योंकि यहाँ एक adjective की आवश्यकता है।

96. *(a)* यहाँ 'affective' के स्थान पर 'effective' का प्रयोग किया जाना चाहिए, क्योंकि 'effective' का अर्थ होता है 'प्रभावी', जबकि 'affective' का अर्थ होता है 'भावात्मक'।

97. *(b)* यहाँ adjective 'sold' के स्थान पर noun 'sale' का प्रयोग किया जाना चाहिए, क्योंकि यहाँ एक noun की आवश्यकता है, adjective की नहीं।

98. *(c)* 'Happy' के स्थान पर 'happier' का प्रयोग करें, क्योंकि वाक्य के पहले भाग में comparative degree 'more' का प्रयोग किया गया है।

99. *(c)* 'Blue colour' के स्थान पर 'blue' का प्रयोग करें, क्योंकि blue में ही colour की sense होती है। अत: यहाँ colour का use superfluous है।

100. *(c)* 'His' के स्थान पर 'one's' का प्रयोग करें क्योंकि 'one' एक subject है, जिसके अनुसार possessive case 'one's' का प्रयोग किया जाएगा।

08 Determiners

Determiners वह शब्द होते हैं, जो noun की व्याख्या करते हैं या जो noun को quantify करते हैं। Determiners का use हमेशा noun से पहले किया जाता है।

The most common determiners are as follows

1. **Demonstratives** ⇒ This, That, These, Those
2. **Possessives** ⇒ His, Her, Its, My, Our, Their, Own etc.
3. **Numerals** ⇒ One, two, three, First, Second, Third etc.
4. **Quantifiers** ⇒ All, Few, Many, Several, Some etc.
5. **Articles** ⇒ A, An, The

⇒ Determiners की form में कोई परिवर्तन नहीं होता है; जैसे A, An, The, Some, All, Much, Both, Few, Whole etc. इनमें कोई suffix या prefix जोड़कर कोई परिवर्तन नहीं किया जा सकता है।

⇒ Sentence में determiners का use होने पर यह निश्चित हो जाता है कि इसके बाद noun अवश्य आएगा।

⇒ Sentence में यदि determiner एवं adjective दोनों का use किया गया हो, तो पहले determiner, फिर adjective उसके बाद noun आता है। Adjective का use determiner के पहले नहीं किया जा सकता है।

e.g., (a) He is a boy. (b) He is a good boy. (c) I have some pencils. (d) I have some coloured pencils.

उपरोक्त sentences में a, some; determiners हैं तथा good एवं coloured adjectives हैं। Sentence (a) एवं (c) में determiners का use noun से पहले हुआ है। (b) एवं (d) में determiner + adjective + noun का use हुआ है।

I. Demonstrative determiners ये determiners noun से पहले use किए जाते हैं परन्तु वे noun के तौर पर use नहीं किए जा सकते हैं।

e.g., (i) This pen is mine. (ii) This is my pen.

Sentence (i) में 'This', noun-'pen' से पहले use हो रहा है तथा उसे modify भी कर रहा हैं, इसलिए वह एक determiner है। Sentence (ii) में 'This' का use pronoun के तौर पर हुआ है और वह 'noun-pen' के एकदम पहले नहीं लगा इसलिए वह determiner नहीं है।

II. Possessive determiners ये determiners, noun का possession (अधिकार) व्यक्त करते हैं तथा noun से पहले use किए जाते हैं।

Possessive determiner + Noun

e.g., Anjali gave me your book.

Possessive Noun

III. Numerals and Quantifiers ये determiners, noun से तुरन्त पहले use किए जाते हैं व noun की मात्रा (quantity) के बारे में बताते हैं। ये काफी हद तक quantitative determiners से मिलते जुलते हैं। Numerical determiners गिने जा सकते हैं लेकिन quantitative determiners गिने नहीं जा सकते अपितु measure किए जा सकते हैं।

e.g., (i) There is a lot of milk in the glass.
(Quantitative determiner)

(ii) Give me one more piece of bread.
(Numerical determiner)

Uses of Some Important Determiners

1. Little, A Little, The Little

- इनका प्रयोग uncountable noun के साथ मात्रा (quantity) बताने के लिए किया जाता है।
- Little का use negative sense में किया जाता है तथा इसका अर्थ होता है 'कुछ नहीं, या ना के बराबर'।
- 'A Little' का use positive sense में किया जाता है तथा इसका अर्थ होता है 'कुछ, थोड़ा सा'।
- 'The Little' का use specific sense में किया जाता है तथा इसका अर्थ होता है- 'जो सब कुछ थोड़ा सा'।

e.g., (i) A little money that you are earning should not be wasted. (×)
The little money that you are earning should not be wasted. (✓)
(ii) Little common sense can bring success to you. (×)
A little common sense can bring success to you. (✓)
(iii) Ravi knows the little French therefore, he wanted to join special classes. (×)
Ravi knows little French therefore, he wanted to join special classes. (✓)

- उपरोक्त पहले sentence में 'A little' के स्थान पर 'The little' का use होगा क्योंकि यहाँ 'that you are earning' से पता चलता है कि वह money जितनी भी है, specific है।
- दूसरे sentence में 'Little' के स्थान पर 'A little' का use होगा, क्योंकि 'little' का अर्थ होता है ना के बराबर जबकि 'a little' का अर्थ होता है मात्रा में कम लेकिन है। इसलिए यहाँ sentence के according 'A little' का ही use होना चाहिए।
- तीसरे sentence में 'the little' के स्थान पर 'little' का use होना चाहिए क्योंकि 'the little' का use सिर्फ specific sense में ही किया जाता है जबकि 'little' negative sense दर्शाता है और यहाँ इस वाक्य का sense negative ही है।

2. Few, A few, The few

- इनका use countable noun से पहले संख्या (Number) बताने के लिए किया जाता है।
- 'Few' का use negative sense में किया जाता है। Few का अर्थ होता है-संख्या में ना के बराबर होना।
- 'A Few' का use positive sense में किया जाता है। A Few का अर्थ होता है-कुछ है लेकिन संख्या में कम।
- 'The Few' का use specific sense में किया जाता हैं। 'The Few' का अर्थ होता है संख्या में इतना नहीं लेकिन जितना भी है वह सब कुछ।

e.g., (i) The few persons are free from worries. (✗)
Few persons are free from worries. (✓)
(ii) I requested him to bring me few books. (✗)
I requested him to bring me a few books. (✓)
(iii) A few days that I passed in her company were exciting. (✗)
The few days that I passed in her company were exciting. (✓)

- उपरोक्त पहले sentence में 'The few' के स्थान पर 'Few' का use होगा, क्योंकि 'the few' का use सिर्फ specific sense में किया जाता है और यहाँ पर 'persons' specific नहीं है। यहाँ पर 'few person' का अर्थ है' ना के बराबर लोग।
- दूसरे sentence में 'few books' का अर्थ है ना के बराबर किताबे यानि 'few' के use से sentence का अर्थ गलत हो गया है, इसलिए यहाँ पर 'a few books' का use होना चाहिए, जिसका अर्थ है 'कुछ किताबें'।
- तीसरे sentence में 'A few' के स्थान पर 'the few' का use होना चाहिए, क्योंकि यहाँ 'that I passed' से पता चलता है कि यहाँ उन दिनों (days) की बात हो रही है, जो कि बीत चुके है, इसलिए वे specific हैं।

3. Later, Latest, Latter, Last

- 'Later' का अर्थ है-'बाद में' तथा इसका use दो से अधिक के सन्दर्भ में (बाद वाले को बताने के लिए) किया जाता है। 'Latest' का अर्थ होता हैं- Last upto now only हाल-फिलहाल का। इन दोनों का use समय (time) के सन्दर्भ में किया जाता है।

e.g., (i) I will come later.
(ii) This is the latest technology.

- 'Latter' का अर्थ है 'बाद वाला' तथा 'Last' का अर्थ है 'अन्तिम'। ये दोनों ही position (क्रम) के सन्दर्भ में use किए जाते हैं। जब दो के लिए स्थिति/क्रम के सन्दर्भ में use किया जाना हो तो latter का, एवं दो से अधिक के सन्दर्भ में last का use किया जाता है।

e.g., (i) Between Ram and Shyam, the latter is more intelligent.
(ii) Lord Mountbatten was the last Governor General of India.

4. Farther, Further, Farthest

'Farther' का अर्थ होता है- 'अधिक दूर' एवं 'Farthest' का अर्थ 'सबसे अधिक दूर'। Farther एवं farthest का use सिर्फ दूरी (distance) के लिए किया जाता हैं। 'Further' का अर्थ होता है-अतिरिक्त (additional) और इसका use समय (time) के लिए भी किया जाता है।

e.g., (i) Mumbai is farther from Alwar than from Jaipur.
(ii) It is the farthest place from the railway station.
(iii) Further investigation is needed.

5. Elder, Eldest, Older, Oldest

- Elder एवं eldest का use एक ही परिवार के सदस्यों के लिए seniority दर्शाने के लिए किया जाता है। इनका use केवल persons के लिए किया जाता है।
- Older, oldest का use किसी अन्य व्यक्तियों एवं वस्तुओं की age दर्शाने के लिए किया जाता है। Elder के साथ हमेशा 'to' जबकि older के साथ हमेशा 'than' का use किया जाता है।

e.g., (i) Shivam is my elder brother.
(ii) My mother is the eldest member of our family.
(iii) This machine is older than that.
(iv) This is the oldest college in our city.

6. Fewer, Less, Lesser

- 'Fewer' का use countables के साथ संख्या (number) बताने के लिए किया जाता है। इसका अर्थ होता है 'कम'।
- 'Less' का use uncountables के साथ मात्रा (quantity) बताने के लिए किया जाता है। इसका भी अर्थ कर्म होता है।
- 'Lesser' का अर्थ होता है 'कम महत्त्वपूर्ण'।

e.g., (i) I found <u>fewer</u> books in the library than that.
(ii) He has <u>less</u> source to expand his business.
(iii) Many <u>lesser</u> speakers also came to speak.

7. Some; Any

- 'Some' का use generally affirmative sentence में countables एवं uncountables दोनों के साथ किया जा सकता है। Interrogative sentences में some का use request या command के रूप में किया जाता हैं। Some के साथ request का अर्थ सामान्य रूप से मान ली जाने वाली request के लिए होता है।

e.g., (i) I shall buy some books. (Countables)
(ii) They have purchased some fruit. (Uncountables)
(iii) Will you give me some milk? (Request)
(iv) Can you lend me some rupees? (Request)

- 'Any' का use generally negative एवं interrogative sentences में countables एवं uncountables दोनों के लिए किया जा सकता है।

e.g., (i) I don't have any pen.
(ii) He hasn't give any advice.
(iii) Have you any novel?

8. Each and Every

- Each एवं Every दोनों का अर्थ समान है यानि 'प्रत्येक'। 'Each' का use दो या दो से अधिक व्यक्तियों/वस्तुओं के लिए होता है जबकि 'Every' का use दो से अधिक के लिए ही किया जाता है। Each का use निश्चित संख्या (Definite number) हेतु तथा every का use अनिश्चित संख्या (Indefinite number) हेतु किया जाता है।

Each → Two or more than two

Every → More than two

e.g., (i) <u>Each</u> of the ten students gets a prize.
(ii) <u>Every</u> candidate was given a certificate.

- Each का use किसी समूह (group) को सम्मिलित रूप से न दर्शाकर, उस समूह के प्रत्येक व्यक्ति या वस्तु को अलग-अलग दर्शाता है जबकि every का use पूरे group को सम्मिलित रूप से दर्शाता हैं।

e.g., (i) <u>Each</u> student went to meet the chairman in line.
(ii) <u>Every</u> student has a book.

> 'Each' and 'Every' के साथ हमेशा singular noun + singular verb का ही use होता है परन्तु यदि every के बाद कोई plural adjective of number (two, three, four etc.) का use हो, तो उसके बाद आने वाला noun, plural होगा।
>
> e.g., She takes medicine every three hours.

9. Either, Neither

'Either' का use 'दो में से एक' तथा 'Neither' का use 'दो में से एक भी नहीं' के लिए किया जाता है।

e.g., (i) <u>Either</u> book will be useful for the project.
(ii) <u>Neither</u> bike gives good mileage.

10. Much, Many

'Much' का use हम singular uncountable noun से पहले मात्रा (quantity) को denote करने के लिए तथा 'Many' का use plural countable noun से पहले संख्या (number) दर्शाने के लिए किया जाता है।

e.g., (i) This job requires <u>much</u> patience.
(ii) Sakshi made <u>many</u> friends in the college.

11. Whole, All

- Whole का प्रयोग जब एक adjective की तरह किया जाता है, तो इससे पहले 'the' का use करना चाहिए।

e.g., (i) He wasted the whole day.
(ii) I worked the whole day.

- Whole का use जब proper noun के पहले किया जाता है, तो इससे पहले 'the' तथा बाद में 'of ' का use किया जाता है।

e.g., (i) The whole of India mourned the death of Rajeev Gandhi.
(ii) The whole of Rajas than was in the grip of drought.

- All का use जब plural noun के साथ किया जाता है, तो all के बाद 'the' का use करना होता है। Possessive noun या pronoun के साथ all हमेशा उससे पहले लगता है।

e.g., (i) All the students were happy.
(ii) All my friends went to party.

12. Another, Other, Any other

Another का use singular noun के साथ तथा other का use plural noun के साथ किया जाता है। Any other का use generally negative sentences में singular-plural दोनों nouns के साथ हो सकता है।

e.g., (i) He has purchased <u>another</u> book.
(ii) They haven't visited <u>any</u> other places.

Articles

A, An, The articles कहलाते हैं। Articles, noun को specify करते हैं तथा articles को generally noun से पहले लगाया जाता है।

Articles के दो प्रकार होते है

1. Indefinite article - A, An 2. Definite article - The

Indefinite Articles - A, An

Generally A/An का use singular countable noun से पहले किया जाता है; अत: इसका अर्थ 'एक' निकलता है। निम्नलिखित के माध्यम से a/an के use को समझा जा सकता है

1. जब किसी word का first letter consonant हो और उस word की initial sound भी consonant हो, तब ऐसे words से पहले article 'a' का use किया जाता है।

e.g., (i) Pooja has a cat.
(ii) He is a doctor.

2. जब किसी word का first letter vowel (a, e, i, o, u) होता है और उस word की initial sound of pronunciation भी vowel हो, तब ऐसे words से पहले article 'an' का use किया जाता है।
e.g., (i) She has an umbrella.
(ii) This is an inkpot.

3. यदि किसी word का first letter consonant हो लेकिन first letter की ध्वनि (Initial sound of pronunciation) vowel हो, तब ऐसे words से पहले article 'an' का use किया जाता है।
e.g., (i) He is an MLA. (एम एल ए)
(ii) He is an heir (ऐअर) to the throne.

Correct use of A/An

1. A house	2. A heinous crime
3. A unity	4. A one eyed man
5. A unique decision	6. A USA ally
7. An hour	8. An honorary post
9. An honorarium	10. An SP/SDO
11. A historical fair	12. A young man
13. A union	14. A uniform
15. A united front	16. A forest officer
17. An hourly meeting	18. An honourable person
19. An F.O.	20. An M.A/M.Sc/M. Com
21. A humble person	22. A ewe
23. A eulogy	24. A useful book
25. A unified plan	
26. A Member of Parliament	
27. An hour's daybreak	28. An honest man
29. An MP/MLC	30. An RTS/RTC/RO
31. A husband	32. A university
33. A one rupee note	34. A useful feature
35. A year	36. A UK ship/European
37. An honour	38. An heir
39. An IAS/IPS/ILO	40. An RC worker

4. यदि किसी sentence में adjective, किसी noun को qualify कर रहा हो, तो article का use उस adjective से पहले किया जाता है।
e.g., (i) Anita is an honest employee.
Adj.
(ii) Sita is a beautiful girl.
Adj.

5. Generally proper noun से पहले a/an का use नहीं होता है, लेकिन निम्न स्थिति में proper noun से पूर्व a/an का use किया जा सकता है।
e.g., (i) This novel is written by a Maneesh.
(ii) This book is written by a Suresh.

Note जब proper noun का use common noun की तरह किया जाए, तब proper noun से पहले a/an का use किया जा सकता है।
e.g., He is a Ram.
↓
Proper noun used as a common noun
She looks like a Cinderella.
↓
Proper noun used a common noun

6. जब किसी verb का use common noun की तरह किया जाता है, तब उस noun से पहले a/an का use किया जाता है।
e.g., (i) I want a drink.
↓
verb as noun
(ii) He has gone for a ride.
↓
verb as a noun

7. Many/Rather/Quite/Such के बाद यदि singular noun आता है, तो उससे पहले a/an का use किया जाता है।
e.g., (i) It was quite an impossible task.
(ii) Many a boy comes late to the class.

8. Exclamatory sentence में How/What के बाद singular countable noun से पहले a/an का use किया जाता है।
e.g., (i) What a beautiful girl!
(ii) What an exceptional child!

9. किसी जाति विशेष (as a common noun) को व्यक्त करने के लिए singular countable noun से पूर्व a/an का use किया जाता है।
e.g., (i) A dog is an animal.
(ii) A peacock is a bird.

10. प्रति/की दर से (per) के लिए a/an का use किया जाता है।
e.g., (i) Sugar is sold at fifty a kilo.
(ii) Bullet train can run at 220 kilometers an hour.

11. कुछ गिनती बताने वाले शब्द जैसे –A hundred, A Thousand, A Million, A Dozen, A couple से पूर्व article 'A' का use किया जाता है; जैसे: $3\frac{1}{2}$ Kilo → Three and a half Kilo, $2\frac{1}{4}$ Metre → Two and a half quarter metre etc.
e.g., (i) I have a hundred pens.
(ii) I have to walk two and a half miles everyday.

12. Profession (व्यवसाय) से पूर्व a/an का use किया जाता है।
e.g., (i) He is an MP.
(ii) She is a nurse.

13. कुछ विशेष Phrases जिनमें a/an का use किया जाता है

Take a fancy to	To have a drink	Have a good education
Tell a lie	A short while ago	Make a noise
Make a fool	Keep a secret	Go for a walk

As a rule	In a nutshell	At a discount
Take a bath	In a hurry	Take an interest in
Half a kilo	A matter of chance	At a stone's throw
In a fix	At a loss	Have an interest in
Take a risk	Keep a promise	Make an excuse
Catch a cold	Have an opportunity	In a range
At a premium	A short time ago	In a dilemma

Have a headache/toothache/stomach ache

e.g., (i) It is a pity to trust a dishonest person.

(ii) I bought this shirt at a discount.

14. Article 'A' का use मात्रा (quantity) और संख्या (number) के बारे में बताने वाले expression में भी होता हैं।

जैसे- a lot of, a number of, a great many of, a great deal of, a great number of, a good deal of, a large number of , a quarter of etc.

e.g., A number of employees were absent yesterday.

Omission of Articles-A/An

1. A/An का use proper noun से पहले नहीं किया जाता है।

e.g., (i) We live in a Bihar. (Use 'in Bihar')

(ii) A Nilu is a naughty girl. (Use only 'Nilu')

2. Uncountable noun से पहले a/an का use नहीं किया जाता है; जैसे- a coal, an accommodation, an advice, a luck, a coffee, a petrol, a rice, a dust, a knowledge, a news, a wine etc.

e.g., (i) She has gone to purchase bread. (Not 'a bread')

(ii) The wall is made of stone and brick. (Not 'a stone')

लेकिन uncountables से पहले कुछ words का use करके इन्हें countable बनाया जा सकता है; जैसे- A glass of water, a piece of bread, a piece of furniture, a stick of chalk, a kilo of rice, a piece of paper, a bottle of whisky etc.

e.g., (i) I have a piece of bread.

(ii) I have a good news for you. ('one good news')

3. Plural nouns के पहले भी a/an का use नहीं किया जाता है; जैसे-

A children (×)	Children (✓)
A boys (×)	Boys (✓)
An oxen (×)	Oxen (✓)

4. Kind of, Sort of, Type of, Variety of के बाद प्रयुक्त nouns के पहले a/an का use नहीं किया जाता है। जैसे :

Kind of a suit (×)	Kind of suit (✓)
Type of a notebook (×)	Type of notebook (✓)
Sort of a radio (×)	Sort of radio (✓) etc.

परन्तु interrogative sentences में इन words के साथ a/an का use किया जा सकता है; जैसे- What kind of a animal is he?

5. यदि sentence में सिर्फ adjective का use किया गया है, Adjective + Noun का नहीं, तब उस adjective से पहले a/an का use नहीं किया जाएगा।

e.g., He is an honest. (×)

He is honest. (✓)

Ghosh babu is a popular in his village. (×)

Ghosh babu is popular in his village. (✓)

6. Demonstrative adjective (This, that, these, those etc) तथा distributive adjectives (Each, every, either, neither) के बाद प्रयुक्त nouns के पहले भी a/an का use नहीं होता है।

e.g.,	
This a car (×)	This car (✓)
That a pencil (×)	That pencil (✓)
Every a girl (×)	Every girl (✓)
Either a room (×)	Either room (✓)

Definite Article-The

- 'The' का use उस countable या uncountable से पहले किया जाता है, जो definite (निश्चित) है, विशेष (particular) है या जिसके बारे में sentence में पहले बताया जा चुका है, इसलिए article 'The' को definite article भी कहा जाता है।

e.g., (i) I found a bag. The bag contained a coin. The coin was made of gold.

(ii) She brought a silk saree. The saree is very costly.

- Sentence (i) में bag से पूर्व सर्वप्रथम 'a' का प्रयोग किया गया है, बाद में 'The' का प्रयोग किया गया है, क्योंकि यह bag पूर्व निर्धारित, निश्चित हो गया है। इसी तरह coin से पहले 'a' का प्रयोग किया गया है, बाद में 'The' का, क्योंकि अब coin पूर्व निर्धारित, निश्चित हो चुका है। इसी तरह वाक्य (ii) में पहले saree से पूर्व 'a' तथा बाद में 'The' का प्रयोग किया गया है। अन्य उदाहरण देखें

(a) This is the hotel where she lives.

(b) The man in blue dress is my brother.

Uses of Definite article - 'The'

1. धार्मिक समुदायों के नाम, साम्राज्यों के नाम, इतिहास की घटनाओं, वंशजों के नाम, राजनीतिक दलों के नाम, ट्रेन, जहाज, अखबार के नाम, महत्त्वपूर्ण भवनों के नाम, नदियों के नाम, नहरों के नाम समुद्र के नाम आदि के पूर्व 'The' का use किया जाता है। जैसे:

e.g., **Rivers** (नदियाँ) ⇒ The Gange (The Ganges), The Kaveri, The Nile, The Danube, The Thames etc.

Sea (सागर) ⇒ The Red Sea, The Mediterranean Sea, The Arabian sea etc.

Ocean (महासागर) ⇒ The Atlantic Ocean, The Pacific Ocean, The Great Indian Ocean etc.

Bay (मुहाना) ⇒ The Bay of Bengal, The Bay of Biscay etc.

Group of Islands (द्वीपों के समूह) ⇒ The Philippines, The Bahamas etc.

Canal (नहर) ⇒ The KP Canal, The Suez Canal, The Albert Canal, The Erie canal etc.

Political Parties (राजनीतिक दलों के नाम से पहले) ⇒ The BJP, The Congress, The communist party

Train, Ships, Newspaper (के नाम से पहले) ⇒ The Hindu, The India Express, The Rajdhani Express etc.

> **Note** Hudson Bay से पहले 'The' का use नहीं होता है।
> जब किसी river के नाम के साथ उसके शहर का नाम जुड़ा हो, तब ऐसी स्थिति में river के नाम से पहले 'The' का use नहीं किया जाता है।
> e.g., Pryagraj on Ganges, Kingston on Thames, Stratford on Avon etc.

2. धार्मिक ग्रन्थो तथा महाकाव्यों (epics) के नाम से पहले 'the' का use किया जाता है। जैसे- The Ramayana, The Quran, The Geeta, The Bible etc.

   e.g., <u>The Ramayana</u> is a sacred book.
   <u>The Quran is also a sacred book.</u>

   लेकिन Valmiki's Ramayan, Banabhatta's Kadambari जैसी स्थिति में इनके पूर्व 'The' नहीं लगता है।

3. 'The' का use country के नाम से पूर्व नहीं होता है लेकिन यदि country के नाम के साथ Republic, Kingdom, States जुड़े हुए हों तो 'The' का use इनसे पूर्व किया जाता है। जैसे; The Republic of Ireland, The Dominican Republic, The United States, The United Kingdom etc.

   (a) He visited India and The United States.
   (b) They went to Canara and The United Kingdom.

4. 'The' का use Plural names of Countries/Islands /Mountains/Person के साथ होता है। जैसे- The Netherlands, The Lakshadweep islands, The Philippines, The Andes, The Alps, The Himalayas, The Ambanis, The Raymonds etc.

5. East, West, North, South के साथ 'The' का use होता है लेकिन यदि इनके साथ किसी Place का नाम जोड़ा गया हो तो 'The' का use नहीं होगा। इसी तरह Northern, Southern , Eastern, Western से पूर्व 'The' का use नहीं होगा।

   (a) The sun rises in the east.
   (b) He is going to North America.

6. जो things अपने-आप में unique हैं, उससे पूर्व भी 'The' का use किया जाएगा; जैसे- The Sun, The Earth, The Venus, The World etc लेकिन Heaven, Hell, God, Parliament से पहले 'The' का use नहीं होता है।

   e.g., (i) The Sun sets in the West.
   (ii) Go to hell.

7. पहाड़ो की श्रृंखला (Ranges of Mountains) के नाम से पहले 'The' का use किया जाता है; जैसे- The Andes, The Alps, The Vindhyas, The Himalayas, The Eastern Ghats etc.

   लेकिन श्रृंखला के किसी एक पहाड़ या द्वीप (individual hill or island) और mountain peak के नाम से पहले 'the' का use नहीं किया जाता है;

   जैसे–The Mt. Everest (✗), The Kanchanjunga (✗), The Kamat (✗), The K_2 (✗), The Mt. Abu (✗), The Nanda Devi (✗), The Java (✗), The Sumatra (✗) etc.

8. किसी person के पद (post) के नाम से पहले 'The' का use किया जाता है; जैसे- The Chief Minister, The Governor, The Chairman, The Editor etc.

   e.g., (i) The meeting was presided over <u>the Executive Director.</u>
   (ii) The decision is taken by <u>the Prime Minister.</u>

   लेकिन जब title के बाद उस पद पर आसीन व्यक्ति का नाम आता हैं, तब 'The' का use नहीं किया जाता है।

   e.g., Prime Minister Narendra Modi, Prince Charles etc.

9. बहुत सी महत्त्वपूर्ण buildings एवं institutions के नाम शब्दों से मिलकर बने होते हैं, जिनमें से एक शब्द किसी व्यक्ति या स्थान का नाम होता है, ऐसे नाम के साथ 'The' का प्रयोग नहीं किया जाता है। जैसे : Delhi Airport, Victoria Station, London Zoo, Jaisingh Palace, Indira Gandhi Airport, Edinburgh Castle, Jaipur Place etc., लेकिन अन्य नामों जैसे-The Royal Palace, The Char Minar, The White House, The Red Square, The Taj Mahal इनके साथ 'The का प्रयोग होता है।

10. यदि किसी Proper Noun के बाद कोई Adjective उसी noun को qualify करते हुए लगाया जाता है, तब उस adjective के साथ article 'the' का use किया जाता है।

    e.g., Ambani-The Capitalist, Napoleon-The Warrior, Ashoka-The Great.

11. दिन तथा महीनों के नामों से पहले article का use नहीं किया जाता है, परन्तु दिनों तथा महीनों को definite/indefinite बताने के लिए article का use किया जा सकता है।

    e.g., In a december (किसी december में) in the november of 1993 (1993 के नवम्बर में)

12. Job एवं profession से पूर्व the का प्रयोग होता है।

    e.g. (i) He likes the banking profession.
    (ii) Do you like the teaching job?

13. Ordinals से पूर्व 'The' का प्रयोग किया जाता है। First, second, third .....(ordinals) तथा one, two, three... (cardinals) कहलाते हैं।

    e.g., (i) The second lesson of this book is very difficult.
    (ii) He is the first to arrive in the meeting.

14. Musical instrument, किसी आविष्कार (Invention) के नाम के पूर्व, 'The' का प्रयोग किया जाता है।
    e.g., (i) She can play the Tabla / Violin / Trumpet.
    (ii) Who invented the Telephone / Telescope?
15. Cinema एवं theatre से पूर्व 'The' लगता है।
    e.g., (i) He went to the cinema yesterday.
    (ii) She is going to the theatre.
16. Committee, club, foundation तथा trust के नाम के पूर्व 'The' लगता है। जैसे- The Lions Club, The Rotary Club, The United Nation, The WHO, The Ford Foundation, The Rajiv Gandhi Trust etc.
17. कुछ phrases में 'The' का प्रयोग स्वत: ही होता है।
    e.g., (i) What is the matter?
    (ii) Come to the point.
    (iii) She came to the rescue.
    (iv) Keep to the left.
18. Plural nouns से पहले 'The' का प्रयोग किया जाता है, यदि वाक्य के reference के अनुसार plural noun, particular/definite हो गया हो।
    e.g., (i) The boys of this college are very intelligent.
    (ii) The girls of this hostel are very beautiful.
19. Nationality denote करने वाले शब्दों से पूर्व 'The' का use किया जाता है; जैसे- The English, The French, The Russians etc.
    e.g., (i) The English defeated The French.
    (ii) The Indian Cricket team has won the match.
20. जब adjective का प्रयोग noun की तरहं किया जाता है, तो उससे पहले 'The' लगाने पर वह पूरे समुदाय को दर्शाता है। जैसे: The young, The old, The rich, The youth, The disabled etc.
    e.g., (i) The young and the old, the poor and the rich, the male and the female all supported Gandhi ji.
    (ii) Three per cent posts are reserved for the disabled.
21. जब कोई वस्तु understood होती है, तो उससे पूर्व 'The' का प्रयोग किया जाता है।
    e.g., (i) Kindly return the book. (That I gave you)
    (ii) Can you turn off the light?
    (The light in the room.)
    (iii) He has gone to the railway station.
    (The railway station of the town)
22. Part of the body के नामों से पहले article 'the' का use किया जाता है।
    e.g., (i) He was wounded in the arm.
    (ii) Ram hit him in the head.
23. Superlative degree से पहले 'The' का use किया जाता है।
    e.g., (i) He is the tallest boy in the class.
    (ii) She is the most beautiful girl in this school.

    लेकिन यदि superlative degree से पहले possessive case (yours, his, her, mine, its, their) का use किया जाए, तो 'The' का use नहीं किया जाता है।
    e.g., (i) I am your best friend.
    (ii) Mr. Verma is my wisest colleague.

    ⇒ Most भी much का superlative है, लेकिन यदि most का use very के अर्थ में किया जाए, तो इससे पहले 'The' का use न करके 'A' का use किया जाता है।
    e.g., (i) He is a most interesting man.
    (ii) Tanya was a most famous dancer.
24. जब कोई noun किसी दूसरे noun के गुण या भाव को denote करे, तो उससे पूर्व भी 'The' का use किया जाता है।
    e.g., (i) The mother in Sujata made her soothe the crying child.
    (यहाँ Sujata किसी की माँ नहीं हैं अपितु उसमें माँ का भाव व्यक्त किया गया है।)
    (ii) The moralist in Gandhiji revolted against the tyranny of the British.
25. यदि sentence में comparative degree + of the two का use किया गया हो, तब comparative degree से पहले 'the' का use किया जाता है।
    e.g., (i) He is the better of the two boys.
    (ii) She is the stronger of the two.
26. Comparative degree से पहले 'the' का use तब किया जाता हैं, जब इसका use adverb की तरह किया जाए।
    e.g., (i) The more she gets, the more she demand.
    (ii) The sooner he completes, the better it is.
27. Sky, Moon, World, Sea, Country, Environment से पूर्व 'The' का use किया जाता है।
    e.g., (i) The sky is dark and the Moon is shinning.
    (ii) The sea seems calm today.
    (iii) Do you live in a town or in the country?
    (iv) We must do something to protect the environment.

    Space से पूर्व 'The' नहीं लगता है, जब space का अर्थ 'अन्तरिक्ष' से होता है, लेकिन यदि space, 'जगह' के अर्थ में use हुआ हो तो 'The' का use होता है।
    e.g., (i) There are lacs of stars in space.
    (ii) He tried to park his car there, but the space was too small.

    'Sea' के साथ 'The' का use नहीं होगा।
    e.g., (i) We go to sea as sailors.
    (ii) He is at sea now-a-days (on a voyage).

28. Same से पूर्व 'The' का use comparison हेतु होता है।
    e.g., (i) These books are the same as we saw in that shop.
    (ii) Your pen is the same as mine.
29. यदि दो या अधिक noun एक ही व्यक्ति या वस्तु के लिए प्रयुक्त हुए हों तो 'The' का use पहले noun के पूर्व किया जाता है।
    e.g., (i) The secretary and treasurer was present there.
    (ii) The counsellor and faculty was working in the office.

यहाँ secretary and treasurer तथा counsellor and faculty एक ही व्यक्ति है।

Omission of Article-'the'

निम्नलिखित जगहों पर article-'the' का use नहीं किया जाता हैं-

1. School, College, University, Bed, Church, Court, Hospital, Prison, Market से पूर्व article 'The' का प्रयोग उस स्थिति में नहीं किया जाता जब वहाँ जाने का उद्देश्य, वही हो, जिस हेतु इनका निर्माण किया गया है।
    e.g., (i) I go to college at 10 am. (For the purpose of study)
    (ii) He went to church on Sunday. (For making prayer)
    (iii) He went to market to purchase a TV. (To purchase)

    लेकिन यदि इन स्थानों पर जाने का उद्देश्य अलग हो तो इनसे पहले 'The' लगता है।
    e.g., (i) The school is near to Ram's house.
    (ii) I will meet you near the court.
    (iii) I found her near the church.
    (iv) We went to the Prison to meet the superintendent.
2. Appoint, made, nominate, elect, declare के बाद यदि कोई noun आता है तो उससे पहले भी article 'the' का use नहीं होता है।
    e.g., (i) He was elected MLA.
    (ii) He was appointed supervisor.
    (iii) He was nominated secretary.
    (iv) We made him monitor.
3. खाने के नाम (Lunch, dinner, supper, breakfast) से पहले articles का use सामान्य स्थिति में नहीं किया जाता है।
    e.g., (i) I couldn't have breakfast this morning.
    (ii) He was invited to dinner.

    लेकिन यदि खाने के नाम के साथ कोई adjective लगा हो या खाना particular हो गया हो तो articles का use किया जाता है।
    e.g., (a) He arranged a nice dinner.
    (b) The dinner hosted by the queen was superb.
4. बीमारियों (Disease) के नाम से पहले कोई article नहीं लगता है।
    e.g., (i) She is suffering from fever.
    (ii) He died of Cholera.

    लेकिन यदि diseases का नाम Plural में हो जैसे: Mumps, Measles तो इनके पूर्व The का use किया जाता है।
    e.g., The measles is a contagious disease.
5. भाषा के नाम, रंगों के नाम से पहले article का use नहीं होता है।
    e.g., (i) I can speak Hindi, but I can't speak English.
    (ii) He likes blue and white colour.

    लेकिन यदि colour का नाम एक adjective की तरह किसी countable noun के साथ प्रयुक्त हुआ है तो article का use किया जाता है।
    e.g., (i) She has a blue saree.
    (ii) I have a red pen.
6. यदि दो अलग-अलग adjective एक ही countable noun के लिए प्रयुक्त हों तो article का प्रयोग पहले वाले adjective के साथ ही होगा।
    e.g., (i) This is a Hindi and English learning book.
    (ii) This is an English and Hindi dictionary.
7. Plural noun से पूर्व article को use तब नहीं किया जाता, जब plural noun किसी वर्ग जैसे doctors, lawyers, teachers etc. को व्यक्त करता है।
    e.g., (i) Lawyers are generally witty.
    (ii) Bankers are generally honest.
    (iii) Doctor are paid more than teachers.
    (iv) Teachers are generally hard workers.
8. 'The' का use noun + number के साथ नहीं होता है।
    e.g., (i) Our train arrives at platform 6.
    (ii) I need shoes in size 18.
9. कई Shops, Restaurants, Hotels, Banks के साथ उन व्यक्तियों के नाम जुड़े रहते हैं जिन्होंने इन्हें शुरू किया है। इनके साथ 'The' का use नहीं किया जाता है।
    e.g., Lloyds Bank, Mcdonalds, Jack's Guest House, Harrods (shop), Raymonds (shop).
10. Church के नाम के साथ Saints के नाम जुड़े रहते हैं, इसके साथ भी 'The' का use नहीं किया जाता है।
    e.g., St John's Church, St Paul's Cathedral.
11. Companies के नाम, Airlines के नाम के साथ भी 'The' का use नहीं होता है।
    e.g., Fiat (not the fiat), Sony, Kodak, British, Airways, IBM, Reliance etc.
12. Subjects के नाम के पूर्व सामान्यतया Articles का use नहीं किया जाता है।
    e.g., (i) I am student of Political Science.
    (ii) He is learning French.
    (iii) I secured 88% marks in English.
    (iv) He is good at Physics.

13. Kind of, sort of, type of के बाद 'The' का use नहीं किया जाता है।
 e.g., (i) What kind of bird it was!
 (ii) What kind of girl she is!

14. कुछ ऐसे phrases जिनमें preposition के बाद object आता है इनमें articles का use नहीं होता है। जैसे:
at hand, by name, by bus, by train, by plane, in jail, at dinner, underground, in jest, by water, on horseback, at sunset, in debt, in hand, all day, all night, at noon, at night, by post etc.
 e.g., (i) Ramesh is at school.
 (ii) Askak works by day.

15. कुछ ऐसे phrases जिनमें transitive verb के बाद object आता है इनमें articles का use नहीं होता है।
 e.g., to catch fire, to leave school / college, to give ear, to bring word, to lay size, to lose heart, to set sail, to send word, to cast anchor etc.

16. जब किसी abstract noun द्वारा feelings या emotions को साधारण भाव में व्यक्त किया जाए तो articles का use नहीं किया जाता है।
 e.g., (i) Honesty is the best policy. (Not 'The Honesty')
 (ii) Virtue has its own reward. (Not The Virtue)

लेकिन यदि abstract noun द्वारा किसी व्यक्ति/जीव या वस्तु की qualities बताई जाए तो उसके पूर्व article 'the' लगता है।
 e.g., (i) He possesses the swiftness of a tiger.
 (ii) He has the cunningness of crow.

17. जब common noun का use विस्तृत अर्थ में किया जाता है तो उससे पूर्व articles नहीं लगता है।
 e.g., (i) Man is an intelligent animal. (Not 'The Man')
 (ii) Birds fly. (Not 'The Birds')

18. Generally proper noun से पहले articles का use नहीं किया जाता है, लेकिन यदि proper noun का use एक common noun की तरह होता है तो उससे पहले article 'the' का use किया जाता है।
 e.g., (i) Akbar was a great king.
 (ii) Agra is a beautiful city.

यहाँ Akbar, Agra, proper noun है
 (i) Jaipur is the Paris of India.
 (ii) Mumbai is the Manchester of India.

यहाँ Paris एवं Manchester का प्रयोग common noun की तरह हुआ है।

19. बहुत सी महत्त्वपूर्ण buildings एवं institutions के नाम दो शब्दों से मिलकर बने होते हैं। जिनमें से एक शब्द किसी व्यक्ति या स्थान का नाम होता है, ऐसे नाम के साथ 'The' का use नहीं किया जाता है।
 e.g., Delhi Airport, Victoria Station, London Zoo, Jaisingh Palace, Indira Gandhi Airport, Edinburgh Castle, Jaipur Place इत्यादि इनके साथ 'The' का use नहीं किया जाता है

20. 'The' का use country के नाम के पूर्व नहीं होता है लेकिन यदि country के नाम के साथ Republic, Kingdom, States जुड़े हुए हों तो 'The' का use इनसे पूर्व किया जाता है। जैसे The Republic of Ireland, The Dominican Republic, The United States, The United Kingdom etc.
 e.g., (i) He visited Mexico and The United States.
 (ii) They went to Canara and then The United Kingdom.

21. Work के साथ सामान्यतया 'The' का use नहीं किया जाता है।
 e.g., (i) She is at work.
 (ii) They haven't back from work yet.

22. 'Nature' का use जब प्रकृति के अर्थ में हो तो इसके पूर्व 'The' का use नहीं होगा।
 e.g., If you interfere with nature you will suffer for it.

23. 'Games' के नाम के पूर्व 'The' का use नहीं होता।
 e.g., (i) I play golf.
 (ii) He plays cricket.

24. 'Seasons' के नाम से पहले 'The' का use नहीं होता है।
 e.g., (i) In Spring, we like to clean the house.
 (ii) She is planning to visit her parents in winter.

25. 'Time of day' के नामों से पहले 'The' का use नहीं होता है।
 e.g., (i) We travelled mostly by night.
 (ii) We'll be there around midnight.

Exercise 1

Directions (Q. Nos. 1-70) Fill in the blanks with suitable determiners.

1. You will have to wait for .... hour.
(a) an (b) a
(c) the (d) No article

2. We should have filed ...... FIR against the wrong doers.
(a) a (b) an
(c) the (d) No article

3. He is wearing .... new uniform.
(a) a (b) an
(c) the (d) No article

4. What .... car it is!
(a) an (b) the
(c) a (d) No article

5. .... water of this river is very pure.
(a) The (b) An
(c) A (d) No article

6. Ramesh earns ₹ 10000 .... month.
(a) a (b) the
(c) an (d) No article

7. Yesterday .... old man came my home.
(a) a (b) an
(c) the (d) No article

8. .... experience is the best teacher.
(a) A (b) An
(c) The (d) No article

9. This year I will see .... Redfort.
(a) a (b) the
(c) an (d) No article

10. His mother reads .... Ramayana daily.
(a) the (b) a
(c) an (d) No article

11. The furniture is made of .... wood.
(a) the (b) an
(c) a (d) No article

12. I have an uncle who is .... engineer.
(a) the (b) an
(c) a (d) No article

13. Last year we would go for .... walk daily.
(a) a
(b) an
(c) the
(d) No article

14. .... boy standing behind the tree, is my cousin.
(a) The (b) A
(c) An (d) No article

15. We should help .... poor.
(a) a (b) an
(c) the (d) No article

16. .... first five chapters will come in the exam.
(a) A (b) The
(c) An (d) No article

17. She has got .... headache.
(a) A (b) An
(c) The (d) No article

18. Mohan was .... strongest player in our team.
(a) a (b) an
(c) the (d) No article

19. They took admission in this college in .... April.
(a) a (b) an
(c) the (d) No article

20. He has ...... great knowledge.
(a) an (b) a
(c) the (d) No article

21. Sheela will not buy .... book.
(a) these (b) those
(c) some (d) this

22. Her brother had .... work.
(a) a lot of (b) a number of
(c) the few (d) few

23. There was .... milk in the glass.
(a) many a (b) a little
(c) each (d) a few

24. .... the soldiers hide behind the rock.
(a) Few (b) Many (c) All (d) Each

25. It was his .... day at the office.
(a) each (b) few
(c) every (d) first

26. He could not prepare the .... two lessons.
(a) last (b) latter
(c) later (d) latest

27. The .... money he had, was spent on his education.
(a) more (b) much
(c) little (d) few

28. ...... employees were dismissed from their job.
(a) Each (b) Some
(c) Every (d) First

29. He will have to count .... note.
(a) these (b) those
(c) each (d) many

30. I was .... intelligent than my elder brother.
(a) much (b) very
(c) too (d) more

31. Do you have ...... post card?
(a) one (b) any
(c) none (d) some

32. She showed .... concern for her step- daughter.
(a) a little (b) little
(c) few (d) some

33. Did ...... write with my pen when I was away?
(a) some (b) someone
(c) anyone (d) None of these

34. All the boys went to beach but only .... could swim.
(a) few (b) a few
(c) little (d) the little

35. There are .... countries in the world where population is not growing fast.
(a) any (b) many
(c) most (d) much

36. Dr. Radha Krishnan was .... more famous philosopher than a politician.
(a) the (b) an
(c) a (d) None of these

37. The eggs are sold by .... dozen.
(a) a (b) an
(c) the (d) None of these

38. Last month we went to see .... National book fair with our teacher.
(a) some (b) the
(c) a (d) an

39. We bought .... books.
(a) much (b) more
(c) any (d) many

40. .... of them were story books, while the others were of General Knowledge.
(a) Much (b) Any
(c) Some (d) The little

41. I need a pencil. Please give me ....
(a) any (b) one
(c) same (d) a pencil

42. Though they were sent last week .... of the parcels have arrived yet.
(a) none (b) some
(c) all (d) most

43. I have .... glass of milk every morning.
(a) the (b) a
(c) any (d) some

44. My neighbour is .... honest person.
(a) a (b) an
(c) the (d) any

45. .... student in the class is capable of passing the examination.
(a) All (b) Every
(c) Many (d) Some

46. There aren't .... people here.
(a) much (b) many
(c) a lot (d) some

47. .... first item in today's programme is a song.
(a) The (b) A
(c) Any (d) Some

48. ...... dog is a faithful animal.
(a) A (b) The
(c) One (d) An

49. .... villages were washed away by floods.
(a) One (b) None
(c) Any (d) Many

50. I need a pen. Could you give me .... ?
(a) any (b) one
(c) same (d) a pen

51. We were watching .... news on BBC last evening.
(a) a (b) the
(c) an (d) None of these

52. Between Manu and Tanu, the .... is more intelligent.
(a) last (b) later
(c) latest (d) latter

53. It is a work of .... month.
(a) few
(b) a few
(c) the few
(d) None of the above

54. I have .... influence in the political field now.
(a) little (b) a little
(c) some (d) the little

55. How .... students are there in the hostel?
(a) much
(b) any
(c) many
(d) None of the above

56. I have read all .... novels, I had.
(a) the few (b) few
(c) a few (d) None of these

57. At .... the President gave thanks to the audience.
(a) latter (b) latest
(c) later (d) last

58. Ram is .... than me.
(a) elder (b) older
(c) eldest (d) oldest

59. My brother is .... to me.
(a) elder (b) eldest
(c) older (d) oldest

60. She had donated .... she had.
(a) little (b) a little
(c) the little (d) None of these

61. .... people can speak English correctly.
(a) A few
(b) Few
(c) Elder
(d) The few

62. This is the .... building in our village.
(a) many (b) some
(c) older (d) oldest

63. ...... Sun rises in ...... East.
(a) A, the (b) The, the
(c) The, a (d) An, a

64. Ritu is .... most active girl in .... family.
(a) the, a (b) the, the
(c) a, the (d) a, a

65. There was .... accident near .... market this morning.
(a) the, a (b) an, the
(c) a, the (d) the, the

66. One of the students of the class writes .... date on .... black board every day.
(a) a, the (b) the, a
(c) the, the (d) the, an

67. .... higher you go .... colder it is.
(a) A, the (b) The, the
(c) A, an (d) An, the

68. .... doctor says it is .... hopeless case.
(a) The, a (b) A, the
(c) The, the (d) A, a

69. .... man who is wearing .... white cap is my neighbour.
(a) A, the (b) The, the
(c) The, a (d) A, a

70. .... Taj Mahal is .... monument symbolising love.
(a) The, a
(b) A, an
(c) The, an
(d) A, the

Directions (Q. Nos. 71-95) In each of the following questions a sentence is given which may or may not be correct. Select the option which is the correct form of the sentence. If you think none of the options is correct your answer is option 'd'.

71. Ganga is a holy river.
(a) Ganga is the holy river.
(b) The Ganga is a holy river.
(c) The Ganga is the holy river.
(d) None of the above

72. Hindustan Times is published from Delhi.
(a) Hindustan Times is published from the Delhi.
(b) The Hindustan Times is published from the Delhi.
(c) The Hindustan Times is published from Delhi.
(d) None of the above

73. Bible is a holy book.
(a) Bible is the holy book.
(b) The Bible is the holy book.
(c) The Bible is a holy book.
(d) None of the above

74. Earth revolves round sun.
(a) The Earth revolves round sun.
(b) Earth revolves round the sun.
(c) The Earth revolves round the sun.
(d) None of the above

75. Higher you go, cooler it is.
(a) The higher you go, cooler it is.
(b) Higher you go, the cooler it is.
(c) The higher you go, the cooler it is.
(d) None of the above

76. The gold is a precious metal.
(a) The gold is the precious metal.
(b) Gold is a precious metal.
(c) The gold is one of the precious metals.
(d) None of the above

77. The honey is sweet when tasted.
(a) Honey is sweet when tasted.
(b) The honey is sweet when it is tasted.
(c) The honey is the sweet when tasted.
(d) None of the above

78. Taj Mahal is a wonderful building.
(a) The Taj Mahal is a wonderful building.
(b) The Taj Mahal is the wonderful building.
(c) The Taj Mahal is the wonderfully building.
(d) None of the above

79. Rich should help poor.
(a) Rich should help the poor.
(b) The rich should help poor.
(c) The rich should help the poor.
(d) None of the above

80. The Delhi is the capital of the India.
(a) The Delhi is the capital of India.
(b) Delhi is the capital of India.
(c) Delhi is the capital of the India.
(d) None of the above

81. My elder brother is a M.A.
(a) My elder brother is an M.A.
(b) My elder brother is M.A.
(c) My elder brother is M.A.'s
(d) None of the above

82. He is an European.
(a) He is European.
(b) He is a European.
(c) He is a European's.
(d) None of the above

83. The water is a good solvent.
(a) Water is a good solvent.
(b) Water is good solvent.
(c) The water is good solvent.
(d) None of the above

84. My brother is an university professor.
(a) My brother is university professor.
(b) My brother is a university professor.
(c) My brother is an university professors.
(d) None of the above

85. Tony is Dhoni of our team.
(a) Tony is the Dhoni of our team.
(b) Tony is an Dhoni of our team.
(c) Tony is Dhoni's of our team.
(d) None of the above

86. Punjab is richest state of India.
(a) Punjab is the richest state of India.
(b) The Punjab is the richest state of India.
(c) The Punjab is richest state of India.
(d) None of the above

87. I requested the clerk to make a F.D.R.
(a) I requested the clerk to make an F.D.R.
(b) I requested the clerk to make F.D.R.
(c) I requested a clerk to make a F.D.R.
(d) None of the above

88. The death is a great leveller.
(a) A death is a great leveller.
(b) An death is a great leveller.
(c) Death is a great leveller.
(d) None of the above

89. Himalayas is in the north of India.
(a) The Himalayas is in the north of India.
(b) Himalayas are in the north of India.
(c) The Himalayas are in the north of India.
(d) None of the above

90. A religious person worships the God and the Nature.
(a) A religious person worships the God and Nature.
(b) A religious person worships God and the Nature.
(c) A religious person worships God and Nature.
(d) None of the above

91. Sonu is a honest boy.
(a) Sonu is an honest boy.
(b) Sonu is the honest boy.
(c) Sonu is honest's boy.
(d) None of the above

92. Shatabdi Express is fastest train in India.
(a) The Shatabdi Express is fastest train in India.
(b) The Shatabdi Express is the fastest train in India.
(c) A Shatabdi Express is the fastest train in India.
(d) None of the above

93. An man is mortal.
(a) A man is mortal.
(b) The man is mortal.
(c) Man is mortal.
(d) None of the above

94. The man needs the waters and the air to live.
(a) The man needs the water and air to live.
(b) A man needs water and the air to live.
(c) Man needs water and air to live.
(d) None of the above

95. Arjun walked two miles and half at stretch.
(a) Arjun walked two miles and a half at stretch.
(b) Arjun walked two miles and half at a stretch.
(c) Arjun walked two miles and a half at a stretch.
(d) None of the above

Exercise 2

Directions (Q. Nos. 1-75) Fill in the blanks with suitable determiners.

1. This car hardly uses ....
(a) petrol (b) any petrol
(c) some petrol (d) no petrol

2. Could you lend me ...... for a few days?
(a) money (b) any money
(c) some money (d) a little money

3. There's ...... ice cream in the fridge, if you'd like some.
(a) little
(b) a little
(c) few
(d) a few

4. She walked out without ...... explanation.
(a) any (b) no
(c) some (d) least

5. Those people have ...... money.
(a) much (b) a lot
(c) a lot of (d) lots of

6. I bought the ...... expensive bike.
(a) less (b) least
(c) another (d) other

7. I can write with ...... hand.
(a) every (b) two
(c) either (d) both

8. Today ...... people who enjoy winter sports is bigger than that twenty years ago.
(a) a number of
(b) many
(c) the number of
(d) several

9. Switch on .... light.
(a) the (b) a
(c) an (d) None of these

10. He is .... unlucky man.
(a) the (b) an
(c) a (d) No article

11. We have .... apples in the fridge. They are not enough for me.
(a) a few (b) few
(c) the (d) little

12. I have not received my salary. I don't have .... money today.
(a) any (b) some
(c) little (d) the few

13. Do you remember, ... is the place where we met for the first time?
(a) this (b) which
(c) where (d) those

14. .... is the house where my brother lived for many years.
(a) These
(b) Those
(c) This
(d) Both (b) and (c)

15. I don't have .... money to spend on wasteful things.
(a) a little (b) a few
(c) some (d) much

16. Please bring me .... purse that was kept on the table.
(a) a (b) my
(c) any (d) few

17. It is very difficult to talk to him. He knows .... English.
(a) a little (b) the little
(c) few (d) little

18. .... were the days when we enjoyed our college life.
(a) Those (b) These
(c) This (d) That

19. Please get me .... vegetables from the market.
(a) few (b) any
(c) some (d) the

20. The dogs were .... given a bone.
(a) any (b) many
(c) every (d) each

21. She got her license without .... problems.
(a) some (b) little
(c) every (d) any

22. I always keep .... money in my wallet for emergencies.
(a) little (b) any
(c) every (d) some

23. Very .... people fly just because of terrorist activities.
(a) little (b) much
(c) many (d) few

24. The lion is .... king of beasts.
(a) the (b) an
(c) a (d) No article

25. I eat an egg .... day.
(a) the
(b) an
(c) a
(d) No article

26. Johny is a keen player but unfortunately he has .... skills.
(a) few (b) none
(c) some (d) little

27. If we don't move faster, we will miss our transfer to Munich. There isn't .... time to waste.
(a) little (b) any
(c) many (d) few

28. I want to be .... M. P.
(a) the (b) an
(c) a (d) No article

29. Give me .... umbrella which you bought yesterday.
(a) the (b) an
(c) a (d) No article

30. Unfortunately, I haven't got .... time for watching T.V.
(a) few (b) no
(c) much (d) little

31. You can buy these maps at .... station. They all have them.
(a) a lot of (b) several
(c) some (d) any

32. If you have .... question, I'm ready to answer.
(a) little (b) any
(c) much (d) plenty

33. I didn't have .... trouble getting the passports. I only had a problem with my photo.
(a) much (b) any
(c) no (d) several

34. He died without .... heir.
(a) the (b) an
(c) a (d) No article

35. The thief was sent to .... prison.
(a) a (b) an
(c) No article (d) the

36. You should always carry .... umbrella with you.
(a) a (b) an
(c) any (d) a few

37. .... meat you cooked tasted good.
(a) A (b) An
(c) The (d) No article

38. There is .... water left, so drink only if you must.
(a) some (b) little
(c) few (d) much

39. There isn't .... point at all in getting upset about it.
(a) few (b) several
(c) many (d) any

40. .... coat is suitable. It doesn't need to be a raincoat.
(a) Little (b) No
(c) Any (d) Few

41. Our city will have .... university soon.
(a) a
(b) an
(c) the
(d) No article

42. .... elephant is vegetarian.
(a) An (b) A
(c) No article (d) The

43. With hardwork and ...... luck nothing can stop you in your way to success.
(a) little (b) a little
(c) plenty (d) few

44. As .... each of the individuals in a society is supposed to be responsible for their own deeds.
(a) either (b) the whole
(c) each (d) none

45. .... of the students use their students IDs to enter the building.
(a) All (b) The whole
(c) Every (d) Each

46. This is .... car I bought yesterday.
(a) No article (b) a
(c) an (d) the

47. .... unit means a measurement.
(a) A (b) An
(c) No article (d) The

48. I know .... of the book is not worth reading but most of the readers like the end of the book.
(a) much (b) many
(c) a few (d) several

49. Taj Mahal is built of .... marble.
(a) a (b) an
(c) the (d) No article

50. Let us play .... chess.
(a) a (b) an
(c) No article (d) the

51. Though it is a densely populated city, there are surprisingly .... people seen on the streets.
(a) few (b) a few
(c) a little (d) little

52. I'd like to have helped my friend but I had very .... time, so I had to refuse her.
(a) few (b) plenty
(c) a little (d) little

53. .... of the animals that live in the desert are nocturnal.
(a) Much (b) Some
(c) Each (d) Every

54. There were .... people on the beach, so we weren't completely alone.
(a) a few (b) fewer
(c) little (d) only a little

55. The new job isn't .... different from the old one.
(a) much (b) many
(c) most (d) more

56. We have .... advantage over them.
(a) all (b) none
(c) every (d) much

57. .... my friends like black metal.
(a) A few of (b) few of
(c) A little of (d) None of

58. In .... countries, you have to pay for the medical treatment.
(a) any (b) many
(c) a few (d) little

59. Their car is running at 150 miles .... hour.
(a) a (b) an
(c) the (d) No article

60. Rahul's father works as .... electrician.
(a) a (b) an
(c) the (d) No article

61. You must learn .... English every day to improve your language.
(a) little (b) a little
(c) any (d) a few

62. They cancelled the concert because .... tickets had been sold.
(a) few (b) a few
(c) little (d) a little

63. With this, you have lost .... chance that you had.
(a) a little (b) little
(c) the little (d) slight

64. .... man that we saw turned out to be a thief.
(a) A (b) The
(c) That (d) This

65. During ...... meal he talks about ..... garden.
(a) a, a (b) the, the
(c) a, the (d) the, a

66. ...... youngest boy has just started going to .....school.
(a) A, the (b) The, the
(c) The, a (d) A, a

67. According to the studies, dolphins, whales and ...... other sea creatures use highly sophisticated navigation systems.
(a) any (b) a little
(c) many (d) much

68. The dietary habits of a child often have ...... to do with that child's eating habits as an adult.
(a) little (b) whole
(c) every (d) most

69. In the United States of America, there are adult literacy classes for workers, ... of whom never graduated from high school.
(a) a little (b) much
(c) any (d) many

70. In the first ...... months of life, an infant learns how to lift its head, how to smile and how to recognise its parents.
(a) many (b) a lot of
(c) any (d) few

71. After ...... terms in Congress, Shirley Chisholm became an important United States politician.
(a) several (b) a lot
(c) much (d) whole

72. Although the language learning abilities of apes have surprised ...... scientists, they generally agree that apes do not progress beyond the linguistic abilities of a two-year-old child.
(a) few (b) a little
(c) many (d) much

73. The storm continued for ...... of the days when we were in New Orleans, but fortunately there wasn't ...... damage in the city.
(a) a few, many
(b) several, a lot
(c) all, a little
(d) most, much

74. Heavy fines and jail sentence have made ...... difference in preventing elephant poaching for their tusks.
(a) a few
(b) little
(c) many
(d) None of the above

75. Although ...... species of fox are reddish in colour, the Arctic fox is often pure white.
(a) any (b) plenty
(c) all (d) most

Directions (Q. Nos. 76-110) Find out which part of the sentence has an error. If there is no error, mark option (d) as your answer.

76. There were (a)/ no fewer than fifty persons (b)/ present in the room. (c)/ No error (d)

77. Few remarks (a)/ that he made were (b)/ offensive to my friend. (c)/ No error (d)

78. There is (a)/ few information (b)/that I can give you. (c)/ no error (d)

79. I think it is quite all right (a)/ if you stay their (b)/ for one more week. (c)/ No error (d)

80. He had to cut a sorry figure (a)/ when he realised that he had (b)/ no any money in his purse. (c)/No error (d)

81. There is (a)/ so many fifths (b)/ all around the place. (c) No error (d)

82. I requested him (a)/ to lend me few books (b)/ that might help me in my studies. (c)/ No error (d)

83. What kind of a friend are you (a)/ who is not ready (b)/ to help your friend in need? (c)/ No error (d)

84. I was happy to see that (a)/there were few students in the calss (b)/ ready to volunteer for the event. (c)/ No error (d)

85. Little care on your part (a)/ would have made you (b)/ more successful than your friend. (c)/ No error (d)

86. She will not (a)/ be having some garments (b)/ for the party. (c)/ No error (d)

87. The latest chapter of this novel (a)/ is the most comprehensive of all (b)/ the chapters in the book. (c)/ No error (d)

88. She was not punished (a)/ though she came (b)/ latter than I. (c)/ No error (d)

89. Headmaster (a)/ has instructed (b)/ the teachers to follow the rules of the school. (c)/ No error (d)

90. I told the teacher (a)/ that the homework set for the day (b)/ was much too heavy for us to complete. (c)/ No error (d)

91. I saw portion (a)/ of the manuscript (b) on birds. (c)/ No error (d)

92. The road (a)/ to famous monument (b)/ passes through a forest. (c)/ No error (d)

93. Our Housing Society comprises of (a)/ six blocks and (b)/ thirty three flats in an area of about thousand sq. metres. (c)/ No error (d)

94. Now that she is living in her own flat, (a)/ she cleans the windows (b)/ twice a week in the summer and once a week in the winter. (c)/ No error (d)

95. With little imagination and enterprise, (a)/ the tournament could have been transformed (b)/ into a major attraction. (c)/ No error (d)

96. These display (a)/ the (b)/ remarkable variety. (c)/ No error (d)

97. If you have faith in Almighty (a)/ everything will turn out (b)/ to be all right. (c)/ No error (d)

98. According to the Bible (a)/ it is meek and humble (b)/ who shall inherit the Earth. (c)/ No error (d)

99. On my request (a)/ Lalit introduced me to his friend (b)/ who is singer and a scientist. (c)/ No error (d)

100. This town isn't very well known (a)/ and there isn't much to see (b)/ so a few tourists come here. (c)/ No error (d)

101. He took to (a)/ reading Times (b)/ for better knowledge of the facts. (c)/ No error (d)

102. The accelerating pace of life in our metropolitan city (a)/ has had the tremendous effect (b)/ on the culture and life-style of the people. (c)/ No error (d)

103. Both the civilians (a)/ and armymen (b)/ joined the First World War. (c)/ No error (d)

104. The school is (a)/ within hundred yards (b)/ from my house. (c)/ No error (d)

105. Fortunately, less people (a)/ last their lives (b)/ in the recent bus accident. (c)/ No error (d)

106. The person I met (a)/ in the theatre (b)/ was the playwright himself. (c)/ No error (d)

107. After toiling very hard (a)/ over a long period, he found (b)/ he had hardly made no profit. (c)/ No error (d)

108. He got to the hill top (a)/ and was many disappointed (b)/ when someone else had reached it earlier. (c)/ No error (d)

109. he sold a little gold (a)/ he got from his mother (b)/ for his marriage. (c)/ No error (d)

110. My father (a)/was (b)/ an honest and God fearing man. (c)/ No error (d)

Answers

Exercise 1

1	(a)	2	(b)	3	(a)	4	(c)	5	(a)	6	(a)	7	(b)	8	(d)	9	(b)	10	(a)
11	(d)	12	(b)	13	(a)	14	(a)	15	(c)	16	(b)	17	(a)	18	(c)	19	(d)	20	(b)
21	(d)	22	(a)	23	(b)	24	(c)	25	(d)	26	(a)	27	(c)	28	(b)	29	(c)	30	(d)
31	(b)	32	(b)	33	(b)	34	(b)	35	(b)	36	(c)	37	(c)	38	(b)	39	(d)	40	(c)
41	(b)	42	(a)	43	(b)	44	(b)	45	(b)	46	(b)	47	(a)	48	(b)	49	(d)	50	(a)
51	(b)	52	(d)	53	(b)	54	(a)	55	(c)	56	(a)	57	(d)	58	(b)	59	(a)	60	(c)
61	(a)	62	(d)	63	(b)	64	(b)	65	(b)	66	(c)	67	(b)	68	(a)	69	(c)	70	(a)
71	(b)	72	(c)	73	(c)	74	(c)	75	(c)	76	(b)	77	(a)	78	(a)	79	(c)	80	(b)
81	(a)	82	(b)	83	(a)	84	(b)	85	(a)	86	(b)	87	(a)	88	(c)	89	(c)	90	(c)
91	(a)	92	(b)	93	(c)	94	(c)	95	(c)										

Exercise 2

1	(b)	2	(c)	3	(b)	4	(a)	5	(c)	6	(b)	7	(c)	8	(c)	9	(a)	10	(b)
11	(b)	12	(a)	13	(a)	14	(c)	15	(d)	16	(b)	17	(d)	18	(a)	19	(c)	20	(d)
21	(d)	22	(d)	23	(d)	24	(a)	25	(c)	26	(a)	27	(b)	28	(b)	29	(a)	30	(c)
31	(d)	32	(b)	33	(a)	34	(b)	35	(c)	36	(b)	37	(c)	38	(b)	39	(d)	40	(c)
41	(a)	42	(d)	43	(b)	44	(c)	45	(a)	46	(d)	47	(c)	48	(a)	49	(d)	50	(c)
51	(a)	52	(d)	53	(b)	54	(a)	55	(a)	56	(c)	57	(c)	58	(b)	59	(b)	60	(b)
61	(b)	62	(a)	63	(c)	64	(b)	65	(b)	66	(b)	67	(c)	68	(a)	69	(d)	70	(d)
71	(a)	72	(c)	73	(d)	74	(b)	75	(d)	76	(b)	77	(a)	78	(b)	79	(b)	80	(c)
81	(b)	82	(b)	83	(a)	84	(b)	85	(a)	86	(b)	87	(a)	88	(c)	89	(a)	90	(c)
91	(a)	92	(b)	93	(c)	94	(c)	95	(a)	96	(b)	97	(a)	98	(b)	99	(c)	100	(c)
101	(b)	102	(b)	103	(b)	104	(b)	105	(a)	106	(d)	107	(c)	108	(b)	109	(a)	110	(d)

Explanations

Exercise 2

76. *(b)* यहाँ 'no fewer than' के स्थान पर 'no less than' का use किया जाएगा, to make the sentence grammatically correct.

77. *(a)* यहाँ 'few' के स्थान पर 'a few' का use suitable होगा।

78. *(b)* यहाँ 'few information' के स्थान पर 'little information' का use किया जाएगा। 'Few' cannot be used with uncountable nouns.

79. *(b)* किसी जगह के बारे में बताने के लिए determiner का use किया जाता है। अत: यहाँ 'their' के स्थान पर 'there' का use किया जाएगा।

80. *(c)* यहाँ 'any' का use superfluous है इसलिए sentence में 'any' का use नहीं किया जाएगा, to make the sentence grammatically correct.

81. *(b)* 'Filth' एक uncountable noun है, thus, it cannot be in the plural form. इसके साथ determiner 'much' का use किया जाएगा। अत: 'so many filths' के स्थान पर 'much filth' का use suitable होगा to make the sentence grammatically correct.

82. *(b)* यहाँ 'few' के स्थान पर 'a few' का use किया जाएगा। 'Few' means nothing. So, we will use 'a few' in the given sentence to make the sentence grammatically correct.

83. *(a)* 'Type of, sort of, kind of' के साथ articles का use नहीं किया जाता है इसलिए 'kind of a friend' के स्थान पर 'kind of friend' का use होगा, to make the sentence grammatically correct.

84. *(b)* यहाँ part (b) के अन्तर्गत 'few' के स्थान पर 'a few' का use किया जाएगा। 'A few' means some or quite a number. On the other hand, 'few' means very less or almost no one. Since the person was happy, it cannot be that almost no one volunteered for the event. So, 'few' is wrong here.

85. *(a)* यहाँ part (a) के अन्तर्गत 'little' के स्थान पर 'a little' का use किया जाएगा, to make the sentence grammatically correct.

86. *(b)* यहाँ 'some garments' की जगह, 'any garments' का use किया जाएगा। to make the sentence error free. In a negative/interrogative sentences the quantity of something is expressed using the word 'any'.

87. *(a)* दिए गए sentence में 'latest' के स्थान पर 'last' का use किया जाएगा।

88. *(c)* दिए गए sentence के according, 'latter' के स्थान पर 'later' का use किया जाएगा, to make the sentence grammatically correct.

89. *(a)* 'Headmaster' की जगह 'The Headmaster' का use किया जाएगा। For a person specified, we should use article 'the'.

90. *(c)* 'was much too heavy' के स्थान पर 'was too heavy' का use suitable होगा as 'much' is superfluous here.

91. *(a)* यहाँ portion से पहले article 'a' का use किया जाएगा because 'portion' is a countable noun and article 'a' is used with a countable noun.

92. *(b)* यहाँ 'famous' से पहले article 'the' का use किया जएगा, as the sentence refers to a particular thing.

93. *(c)* यहाँ 'about thousand sq. metres' से पहले 'a' का use किया जाएगा। Article 'a' is used before a common noun to suggest the sense of one.

94. *(c)* Seasons (summer, winter, spring etc.) के नामों से पहले articles का use नहीं किया जाता है। अत: 'summer' and 'winter' से पहले article 'the' का use नहीं किया जाएगा।

95. *(a)* यहाँ 'little' के स्थान पर 'a little' का use किया जाएगा, to make the sentence grammatically correct.

96. *(b)* यहाँ part (b) के अन्तर्गत article 'the' के स्थान पर article 'a' का use किया जाएगा, to make the sentence grammatically correct.

97. *(a)* 'Almighty' से पहले article 'the' का use किया जाएगा, because 'almighty' in the given sentence refers to 'God'.

98. *(b)* यहाँ 'meek' और 'humble' दोनों से पहले article 'the' का use किया जाएगा। The given sentence implies to represent a class of people i.e. 'the meek' and 'the humble'.

99. *(c)* यहाँ part (c) के अन्तर्गत 'singer' से पहले article 'a' का use किया जाएगा।

100. *(c)* यहाँ 'a few' के स्थान पर 'few' का use किया जाएगा। 'A few' means some and 'few' means 'hardly any'. As per the sentence, 'few' should be used instead of 'a few'.

101. *(b)* 'Times' एक newspaper का नाम है इसलिए इससे पहले article 'the' का use किया जाएगा। It should be written as 'the times'.

102. *(b)* यहाँ 'tremendous' से पहले article 'the' की जगह article 'a' का use किया जाएगा। The sentence is incorrect as 'the' is used before the adjective 'tremendous'.

103. *(b)* यहाँ 'armymen' के पहले article 'the' का use किया जाएगा। As per the rule, 'the' should come before an adjective which represents a class of people.

104. *(b)* यहाँ hundred yards से पहले article 'a' का use किया जाएगा, to convey the meaning that the school is within one hundred yards from the house.

105. *(a)* यहाँ part (a) के अन्तर्गत 'less' के स्थान पर 'few' का use किया जाएगा। 'Less' denotes quantity, 'few' denotes number.

106. *(d)* No error

107. *(c)* यहाँ 'no profit' के स्थान पर 'any profit' का use suitable होगा, as two negative words in the same sentence change the meaning. 'Hardly' is a negative word and thus 'no' should be replaced with 'any' to have a proper meaning.

108. *(b)* Part (b) के अन्तर्गत 'many' के स्थान पर 'much' का use किया जाएगा। Here, disappointment is an uncountable noun. So, 'much' should be used instead of 'many'.

109. *(a)* यहाँ 'a little' के स्थान पर 'the little' का use किया जाएगा। 'A little' means some though not much and 'the little' means not much but all that is.

110. *(d)* No error.

01 Tense

Tense शब्द की उत्पत्ति Latin word 'Tempus' से हुई है, जिसका सीधा सम्बन्ध 'समय' से है। Tense किसी कार्य के समय तथा उसकी अवस्था को दर्शाता है।

Tense is that form of verb which shows not only the time of an actions, but also the state of an action or event.

Kinds of Tense

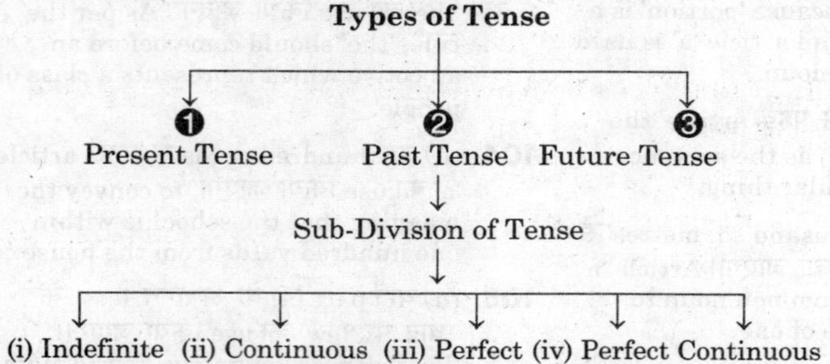

1. Present Tense

कार्य सम्पन्न होने की स्थिति; State of an action के according, present tense को चार भागों में विभाजित किया गया है—

- Present Indefinite
- Present Continuous
- Present Perfect
- Present Perfect Continuous

I. Present Indefinite Tense

Present indefinite tense में present में होने वाले actions के बारे में बताया जाता है अर्थात् जिन sentences में वर्तमान समय में किसी काम का करना या होना पाया जाता है, वह present indefinite tense कहलाता है।

e.g., (i) She watches emotional movies.
(ii) She loves her brother.

Affirmative = Subject + V_1 + es/s + Object
Negative = Subject + do/does + not + V_1 + Object
Interrogative = Do/Does + Sub + V_1 + Object
Do = I, We, You, They (Plural Noun) (Plural Subject)
Does = He, She, It (Singular Noun) (Singular Subject)

Important facts of Present Indefinite Tense

1. प्रतिदिन सामान्य रूप से या बार-बार किए जाने वाले कार्य (Regular or Repeated actions)
   e.g., (i) I go for a walk every morning.
   (ii) My father gets up early in the morning.
2. सार्वभौमिक सत्य (Universal Truth)
   e.g., (i) The sun rises in the East.
   (ii) The earth revolves around the Sun.
3. अनियमित कार्य (Irregular work)
   e.g., Earthquake comes in Nepal oftenly.
4. T.V. एवं Radio पर commentaries में भी simple present tense का use होता है।
   e.g. (i) Tendulkar strikes the ball.
   (ii) The Cabinet Minister signs the deal.
5. तथ्यों (facts) के लिए भी simple present tense का use किया जाता है।
   e.g., (i) A cow has four legs.
   (ii) My brother lives in England.
6. निर्धारित कार्य (scheduled action) जो नियमित रूप (daily) से होते हैं।
   e.g., (i) The shop opens at 10 A.M.
   (ii) The assembly bell rings at 7:30.
7. Here तथा There से शुरू होने वाले exclamatory sentences में भी simple present tense का ही use किया जाता है।
   e.g., (i) Here comes the bus!
   (ii) There goes she!
8. Future planned action के लिए भी present indefinite tense का use किया जाता है।
   e.g., (i) The Prime Minister leaves for America next week.
   (ii) Mr. Sharma retires on 31st March.
9. यदि किसी sentence में always, never, usually, daily, every year, every week, twice a year आदि दिये गये हों, तो भी present indefinite tense का use किया जाता है।

e.g., (i) He usually goes to movie.
(ii) Reena often comes late.

II. Present Continuous Tense

Present continuous tense, वर्तमान में चल रहे किसी कार्य या वर्तमान में हो रही किसी बात या घटना को दर्शाता है। सामान्यतया, इस तरह के वाक्यों के अन्त में रहा, रहे, रही हैं जैसे शब्द आते हैं।

e.g., (i) The students are learning poem.
(ii) We are going to attend the seminar.

Affirmative = Subject + is/am/are + V_1 + ing + Object
Negative = Subject + is/am/are + not + V_1 + ing + Object
Interrogative = Is/Am/Are + Subject + V_1 + ing + Object + ?
I + am, You + are, They + are, He/She/It + is

Important facts of Present Continuous Tense

1. यदि किसी sentence में now/these days/at present/at this moment etc शब्दों का use किया गया हो, तब present continuous tense का use होता हैं।
   e.g., (i) He is sleeping now.
   (ii) Gita is learning english these days.
2. Near future (निकट भविष्य) में खत्म होने वाले planned कार्य को बताने के लिए भी present continuous tense का use किया जाता है।
   e.g., (i) He is coming tomorrow.
   (ii) We are meeting today in the evening.
3. कुछ verbs का use continuous tense में नहीं किया जाता, जो निम्न हैं

   Remember, mind, mean, think, know, suppose, please, see, taste, smell prefer, hear, recognise, notice, have, belong, comprise, contain, own, possess, believe, dislike, adore, wish, hate, like, love, want, desire, agree, imagine, look, appear, resemble, require, hope, seem, affect, cost, become, refuse.

   e.g., (i) We see with our eyes. (Not 'are seeing')
   (ii) Do you smell something burning? (Not 'Are you smelling')

   उपरोक्त verbs में से कुछ verbs का प्रयोग continuous tense में किया जा सकता है, जब इनका अर्थ अलग हो।

   (i) जब 'see' का अर्थ meet (मिलना) हो तथा feel का अर्थ touch (छूना) या examine (जाँचना) हो, तो इनका प्रयोग 'ing' form में किया जा सकता है।

   e.g., (i) I am seeing my lawyer today.
   (ii) The doctor is feeling the pulse of the patient.

III. Present Perfect Tense

इस tense से यह पता चलता है कि कोई काम वर्तमान काल में अभी-अभी समाप्त हुआ है।

e.g., (i) He has gone.
(ii) I have taken bath.

Affirmative = Subject + has/have + V_3 + Object
Negative = Subject + has/have + not + V_3 + Object
Interrogative = Has/Have + Subject + V_3 + Object + ?
Has = He, She, It, Singular noun
Have = I, We, You, They, Plural noun

Important facts of Present Perfect Tense

1. यदि sentence में yet, already, upto, lately, recently, so far, ever etc जैसे words का use हो, तो present perfect tense का use किया जाता है।
   e.g., (i) Haven't you finished the work yet?
   (ii) I have already seen the match.
2. यदि कोई कार्य past का बोध करवाता है, तो उसमें present perfect का use ना करके past indefinite का use होता है।
   e.g., (i) I have visited Mumbai two years ago. (✗)
   I visited Mumbai two years ago. (✓)
   (ii) Harshit Saumitra has ascended at Kala Pathar in 2015. (✗)
   Harshit Saumitra ascended at Kala Pathar in 2015. (✓)
3. इन sentences में भी present perfect tense का use किया जा सकता है,

This is the first time It is the first time This is the worst This is the easiest	(,/that) + subject + has/have + V_3

   e.g., (i) This is the best whisky, I have ever drunk.
   (ii) This is the first time that I have heard her song.

IV. Present Perfect Continuous Tense

ये कुछ ऐसे कार्यों के लिए प्रयोग किया जाता है, जो past में किसी समय में शुरू हुए हो तथा अभी तक चल रहे हो।

e.g., (i) He has been studying for two hours.
(ii) It has been raining for a long time.

Affirmative = Subject + has/have + been + V_1 + ing + object + since/for + time
Negative = Subject + has/have + not + been + V_2 + ing + object + since/for + time
Interrogative = Has/have + subject + been + V_1 + ing + object + since/for + time + ?
Since is used point of time
For is used period of time

Important fact of Present Perfect Continuous Tense

सामान्यत: Present perfect continuous tense का use तब भी हो सकता है, जब sentence से यह पता चल जाए कि कार्य शुरू होने के समय से आज तक चल रहा है।

e.g., He has been taking classes for one year.

2. Past Tense

कार्य की अवस्था के अनुसार past tense को चार भागों में वर्गीकृत किया गया है

- Past Indefinite
- Past Continuous
- Past Perfect
- Past Perfect Continuous

I. Past Indefinite Tense

Simple past या past indefinite tense किसी ऐसे action को दर्शाता है, जो past में शुरू हुआ और past में ही किसी specific time पर finish हो गया हो।

e.g., (i) They played football.
(ii) Anand purchased a new car.

⇒ Past में एक के बाद एक होने वाले completed action की series दर्शाने वाले sentence, simple past में बनाए जाते हैं—

e.g., She came home, took off her jacket and sat down.

Affirmative = Subject + V_2 + Object
Negative = Subject + did + not + V_1 + Object
Interrogative = Did + Subject + V_1 + Object + ?

Important facts of Past Indefinite Tense

1. यदि किसी sentence में yesterday, previous day, ago, last day, last week, last year, last month etc का use हो तो हमेश simple past का ही use होगा।
2. यदि किसी sentence की शुरूआत It is time/It is about time/It is high time etc से हो, तो हमेश past indefinite का ही use होगा।
   e.g., (i) It is about time they took their children to school.
   (ii) It is time we renovated our house.
3. Past के habitual actions को व्यक्त करने हेतु भी simple past का use किया जाता है।
   e.g., (i) He always carried this bag.
   (ii) She always asked for a cup of tea.
4. जब दो actions, sequence में एक के बाद दूसरा तुरन्त समाप्त हो जाता है तो past indefinite का use किया जाता है। ऐसे sentences में सामान्यतया 'before' का use होता है।
   e.g., (i) He changed his dress before he went to bed.
   (ii) The train started just before I reached the station.

II. Past Continuous Tense

ऐसे कार्य (action) हेतु जो past में continue थे, वह past continuous का बोध करवाते हैं।

e.g., (i) He was going to market.
(ii) She was sleeping.

Affirmative = Subject + was/were + V_1 + ing + Object.
Negative = Subject + was/were + not + V_1 + ing + Object
Interrogative = Was/Were + Subject + not + V_1 + ing + Object + ?
Was = I/He/She/It/(Singular noun)
Were = We/You/They/(Plural noun)

Important facts of Past Continuous Tense

1. यदि sentence में 'Those days' दिया गया हो, तो past continuous tense का use किया जाता है।
   e.g., Anand and Anubhav were going to gym those days. (Not 'Went to gym')
2. ऐसी स्थिति में भी past continuous का use किया जाता है, जब काई दूसरी घटना घटित हुई हो, एवं अन्य कोई कार्य भी जारी रहा हो।
   e.g., (i) When he arrived, his wife was washing her clothes.
   (ii) The Sun was just setting as they reached the hill.
3. निरंतर होने वाली वृद्धि या कमी (gradual increase/ decrease) को दर्शाने के लिए भी get, grow तथा become के साथ past continuous tense का use किया जाता है।
   e.g., (i) It was getting colder and colder day by day.
   (ii) That tree was growing larger and larger.

III. Past Perfect Tense

Past perfect tense का use ऐसे actions के लिए किया जाता है, जो past में खत्म हो चुके हो।

e.g. (i) I had eaten the food.
(ii) You had warned him.

Affirmative = Subject + had + V_3 + Object
Negative = Subject + had + not + V_3 + Object
Interrogative = Had + Subject + V_3 = Object + ?

Important facts of Past Perfect Tense

1. यदि कोई भी दो कार्य sequence में दिए गए हो, तो उसमे जो काम पहले खत्म हो, वह हमेशा past perfect में तथा दूसरा sentence past indefinite में बनता है।
   e.g., Before we reached (Past Indef.) the station, the train had left (Past Perfect).
2. Before तथा after का use, sentences में इस प्रकार किया जा सकता है—
   Before + Subject + $_2$, Subject + had + $_3$ + Object
   After + Subject + had + $_3$, Subject + $_2$ + Object
   e.g., We had got (had +V_3) everything ready, before they arrived (V_2).
3. Conditional sentences या sentences of imaginary condition में भी past perfect tense का use किया जाता है।
   e.g., If I had completed that work, I would have informed you.

IV. Past Perfect Continuous Tense

यदि कोई action past में शुरु होकर past में ही खत्म हुआ हो, तब past perfect continuous tense का use किया जाता है, जिसमें समय का भी बोध होता है।

e.g., (i) It had been raining since morning.
(ii) He had been watching TV for two hours.

Affirmative = Sub + had + been + V_1 + ing + Object + since/for + time
Negative = Sub + had + not + been + V_1 + ing + Object + since/for + time
Interrogative = Had + Subject + been + V_1 + ing + Object + since/for + time + ?

Important facts of Past Perfect Continuous Tense

1. Past perfect के repeated action को भी past perfect continuous में व्यक्त किया जा सकता है।
   e.g., (i) He had tried five times to contact her. (Past Perfect)
   (ii) He had been trying to contact her. (Past Perfect Continuous)

3. Future Tense

कार्य की अवस्था के अनुसार Future tense को चार भागों में वर्गीकृत किया गया है

- Future Indefinite
- Future Continuous
- Future Perfect Continuous

I. Future Indefinite Tense

ऐसे कोई भी कार्य, जो future में किए जाएगे, वे future indefinite में आते हैं।

e.g., (i) He will go to Jaipur.
(ii) We shall clean the house.

Affirmative = Subject + will/shall + V_1 + Object.
Negative = Subject + will/shall + not + V_1 + Object.
Interrogative = Will/shall + subject + V_1 + Object + ?
Shall = I, we, Will = He, She, It, They, We

Important facts of Future Indefinite Tense

1. यदि किसी sentence में future denoting words (e.g., tomorrow, next year, next month, next week etc) का use हो, तो future indefinite tense का use किया जाता है।
   e.g., (i) I shall take my examination next year.
   (ii) I shall be thirty on my next birthday.
2. जैसा कि present indefinite में बताया गया है कि planned future कार्य को future में न बताकर presnet indefinite में बताया जाता है।
   e.g., (i) Mr. Gupta retires on 31st October.
   (ii) The PM visits Maharashtra tomorrow.
3. जब sentence में promise, (वादा), threat (धमकी) या determination (दृढ़ संकल्प) का बोध हो, तब He, She, You, They तथा It के साथ कुछ conditions में shall का तथा I, we के साथ will का use किया जाता है।
   e.g., (i) I will inform your father about your failure. (Threat)
   (ii) He shall help me. (Promise)
4. Verb की 'going to' form का use सामान्यतया ऐसी स्थिति में किया जाता है, जब वक्ता की intention भविष्य में होने वाले किसी कार्य के शीघ्र सम्पन्न होने के संदर्भ में जाहिर करना होता है।
   e.g., (i) I am going to buy a laptop.
   (ii) We are going to do this work.
5. Future actions हेतु 'about to' का use निम्न प्रकार से किया जा सकता है
   e.g., (i) The train is about to start.
   (ट्रेन जाने वाली है।)
   (ii) The shop is about to close.
   (दुकान बन्द होने वाली है।)

II. Future Continuous Tense

ऐसे actions जो future में जारी रहते हैं, वे future continuous tense के अन्तर्गत आते हैं।

e.g., (i) I shall be writing the thesis in the evening.
(ii) He will be coming today in the evening.

Affirmative = Subject + Will/Shall + be + V_1 + ing + Object
Negative = Subject + Will/shall + not + be + V_1 + ing + Object
Interrogative = Will/shall + Subject + be + V_1 + ing + Object + ?

Important facts of Future Continuous Tense

1. Future के किसी निश्चित कार्यक्रम या योजना (fixed programme or plan) को दर्शाने के लिए भी future continuous tense का use किया जाता है।
   e.g., (i) Nitin will be going to Jaipur next month.
   (ii) We shall be working on this project till the end of this month.

Difference between Present Continuous and Future Continuous

(a) I am seeing the Principal tomorrow.
(Present Continuous)

(b) I'll be seeing the Principal tomorrow.
(Future Continuous)

Sentence (a) एक planned action या arrangement (पहले से तय) को बताता है जबकि sentence (b) normal course में action होने को बताता है।

III. Future Perfect Tense

Future perfect tense से ऐसे कार्य का पता चलता है, जो कि future में किसी निश्चित समय तक खत्म हो चुके होगें।

e.g., (i) He will have completed this project by next year.
(ii) I shall have reached school before the bell rings.

Affirmative = Subject + will/shall + have + V_3 + Object
Negative = Subject + will/shall + not + have + V_3 + Object
Interrogative = Will/Shall + Subject + have + V_3 + Object

Important fact of Future Perfect Tense

जब कोई एक कार्य दूसरे कार्य के पूर्ण होने के बाद पूर्ण हो तो इस तरह के sentences में पहले पूर्ण होने वाले कार्य के लिए future perfect एवं जो कार्य बाद में पूर्ण होगा, उसके लिए present indefinite का use किया जाता है।

e.g., (i) He will have (Future Perfect) left before you reach (Present Indef.) there.

(ii) The mechanic will have repaired the TV before it strikes eight.

IV. Future Perfect Continuous Tense

इस tense का use हमेशा भविष्य की उस घटना के लिए होता है, जो भविष्य में किसी निश्चित समय तक जारी रहेगे।

e.g. (i) They will have been playing for two hours by 7'o clock.

(ii) We shall have been flying kites since morning on next monday.

> Affirmative = Subject + shall/will + have been + V_1 + ing + from/for + time
> Negative = Subject + shall/will + not + have been + V_1 + ing + from/for + time
> Interrogative = Shall/Will + sub + have been + V_1 + ing + from/for + time + ?

Important facts of Future Perfect Continuous Tense

1. Future perfect continuous tense में since का use न करके, from का use किया जाता है। Since का use हम past time के sense को व्यक्त करने के लिए करते हैं परन्तु 'from' का use इस tense में भविष्य के समय के लिए किया जाता है।

   e.g., I shall have been teaching the students from 12 January, 2020.

2. 'From' का use past/present/future में time बताने के लिए भी किया जाता है।

   e.g., You will attend the class from next Tuesday.

Since और For का प्रयोग निम्न tenses में किया जाता है

- Present Perfect Continuous
- Past Perfect Continuous
- Future Perfect Continuous

1. Since का प्रयोग हमेश निश्चित समय (point of time), जैसे since 7:00 o'clock/last night/Monday आदि के साथ होता है।
2. For का प्रयोग 'अनिश्चित समय अवधि' को दर्शाता है, जैसे—For two hours, for four days, for a long time, for centuries etc.

FOR	SINCE
One hour	
2 days	Years = 1929, 2015, 2000, etc.
3 weeks	Month = June, August, October, etc.
4 months	Days = Sunday, Monday, Tuesday, etc.
5 Years	Dates = 7th August, 2nd of September, etc.
Centuries	Time = 09:00 o' clock, 07:00 o' clock, 08:00 o' clock
Decades	Occasions = Holi, Diwali, Eid, etc.
A long time	Part of the day = Morning/ Evening/ Noon, etc.
Last 3 days	Stage of life = Childhood /Old age / Adolescence, etc.
Last 4 years	Time immemorial, Last Monday, Last year, Last week, etc.
Last 5 months	
Last 1 hour	

Exercise 1

Directions (Q. Nos. 1-25) Fill in the blanks with correct Present Tense forms of the verbs given in brackets. Select your answer from the given options.

1. They .... (live) in Shri Nagar for five years.
(a) are living (b) were living
(c) has been living
(d) have been living

2. At the moment the child .... (play) in the garden.
(a) playing
(c) plays
(b) is playing
(d) has been playing

3. I .... (tell) you already about it.
(a) told (b) have told
(c) tells (d) am telling

4. If you .... (study) hard, you will secure a first division.
(a) studied (b) study
(c) have studies (d) are study

5. She .... (pass) the post office on her way to school every day.
(a) is passing
(b) has been passing
(c) passes
(d) passed

6. He ...... (read) since morning.
(a) have been reading
(b) has been reading
(c) is reading
(d) had been reading

7. This pen .... (cost) me ten rupees.
(a) costs (b) costing
(c) has cost (d) costed

8. He .... (wait) for me since morning.
(a) has been waiting
(b) have been waiting
(c) had been waiting
(d) is waiting

9. The Sun .... (shine) by day.
(a) shining
(b) has been shining
(c) shines
(d) is shining

10. The bell .... (ring) just now.
(a) rings (b) ringing
(c) rung (d) has rung

11. She .... (attend) college since 4th July.
(a) has been attending
(b) attends
(c) is attending
(d) attended

12. Why ....(you come) late every day?
(a) do you come (b) did you come
(c) have you come (d) did you came

13. When he .... (meet) you, he will love you.
(a) will meet (b) is meeting
(c) meets (d) has met

14. It .... (not rain) now.
(a) does not rain
(b) did not rain
(c) has not rained
(d) is not raining

15. I .... (not yet give) up hope.
(a) have not yet given
(b) do not yet given
(c) did not yet give
(d) am not giving

16. If you .... (be) hungry, you can eat.
(a) being (b) are
(c) have been (d) will be

17. The Earth .... (move) round the Sun.
(a) is moving
(b) has been moving
(c) moves
(d) moving

18. The Sun .... (rise) in the East and .... (set) in the West.
(a) rising, is setting
(b) rises, sets
(c) rising, setting
(d) has been rising, has been setting

19. He .... (suffer) from Malaria since day before yesterday.
(a) has been suffering
(b) have been suffering
(c) suffers
(d) is suffering

20. It .... (rain) all the year round here.
(a) has rained
(b) is raining
(c) rains
(d) has been raining

21. He .... (write) to me every month.
(a) is writing
(b) writes
(c) has been writing
(d) had been writing

22. Where .... he .... (go) to play in the evening?
(a) did, go (b) has, gone
(c) does, go (d) does, going

23. This servant .... (work) with us for ten years.
(a) works
(b) has been working
(c) is working
(d) does work

24. What time .... you .... (reach) home in the evening?
(a) do, reach
(b) does, reach
(c) did, reached
(d) have, reached

25. How .... you .... (get) on with your studies?
(a) is, get (b) do, get
(c) is, getting (d) have, got

Directions (Q Nos. 26-45) Fill in the blanks with correct Past Tense forms of the verbs given in brackets. Select your answer from the given options.

26. He .... (buy) a car one month ago.
(a) bought
(b) has bought
(c) has been buying
(d) had been buying

27. She .... (leave) for Jammu yesterday.
(a) leaves
(b) is leaving
(c) has been leaving
(d) left

28. He ....(teach) in this college for five years.
(a) teaches
(b) is teaching
(c) taught
(d) has been teaching

29. I .... (write) to her last week.
(a) wrote
(b) have been writing
(c) had been writing
(d) written

30. He .... (be) weak in English in the beginning.
(a) being (b) been
(c) was (d) had been

31. People .... (vote) them out in the recent elections.
(a) were voting
(b) have been voting
(c) voted
(d) have voted

32. I .... (have) my breakfast at 8.30 a.m. yesterday.
(a) am having
(b) was having
(c) will be having
(d) have been doing

33. I .... (write) a letter when she knocked at the door.
(a) wrote (b) had writing
(c) have written (d) was writing

34. We .... (bathe) in the river when it was raining.
(a) were bathing
(b) have been bathing
(c) are bathing
(d) did bath

35. He .... (watch) television when I came in.
(a) watched
(b) was watching
(c) had watched
(d) has been watching

36. He .... (tell) me that he had never met you.
(a) is telling (b) did tell
(c) told (d) has told

37. He .... (arrive) before I came.
(a) was arriving
(b) is arriving
(c) had arrived
(d) has been arriving

38. He .... (arrive) here only last night.
(a) has arrived
(b) arrived
(c) had arrived
(d) was arriving

39. If you .... (work hard), you would have passed.
(a) have worked hard
(b) had worked hard
(c) have been working hard
(d) worked hard

40. She .... (come) to see me yesterday.
(a) came
(b) has came
(c) had came
(d) had been coming

41. When I reached his home, he .... (sleep).
(a) has slept (b) had sleep
(c) was sleeping (d) slept

42. When he left this morning, the Sun .... (shine).
(a) shines (b) has shone
(c) had shone (d) was shining

43. Madhu .... (not attend) the office yesterday.
(a) was not attending
(b) did not attend
(c) was not attend
(d) had not attend

44. Last year, it .... (not rain) heavily.
(a) did not rain (b) had not rain
(c) has not rain (d) was not rain

45. I .... (write) to him yesterday.
(a) has written
(b) and written
(c) wrote
(d) have been writing

Directions (Q. Nos. 46-50) Fill in the blanks with correct Future Tense forms of the verbs given in brackets. Select your answer from the given options.

46. I don't think we .... (meet) agian.
(a) are meeting
(b) will be meeting
(c) will meet
(d) can meet

47. He .... (be) here early next month.
(a) was (b) has been
(c) had been (d) will be

48. If I go to school late, the teacher .... (punish) me.
(a) is punishing (b) punishing
(c) will punish (d) shall punish

49. If you study hard, you .... (get) a first class.
(a) are getting
(b) will get
(c) will be getting
(d) shall get

50. He .... (leave) for Sri Nagar next week.
(a) will leave
(b) shall leave
(c) going to leave
(d) will be leaving

Directions (Q. Nos. 51-62) From the options given below, complete the sentences in the Future Continuous or Future Perfect, Simple and Continuous Tenses. Do not change the meaning of the sentences.

51. I will be on the 10:25 train to Manali.
At 10:25 .... to Manali.
(a) I'II travel
(b) I will have been travelling
(c) I am going to travel
(d) I'II be travelling

52. The tickets will be available on Tuesday.
The tickets .... by Tuesday.
(a) are going to be printed
(b) will print
(c) will be printed
(d) will have been printed

53. I am busy now but .... the lock after lunch.
(a) I am going to repair
(b) I will repair
(c) I will be repairing
(d) I will have been repairing

54. Bruce is not willing to give us a hand on Saturday morning.
Bruce .... on Saturday morning.
(a) will not be helping us
(b) will not help us
(c) is not going to help us
(d) will not have been helping us

55. There's film watching in our programme tonight.
We .... a film tonight.
(a) are going to watch
(b) will watch
(c) will be watching
(d) will have been watching

56. I like this pen. Will you need it today?
I like this pen. .... ?
(a) Are you going to use it today?
(b) Will you be using it today?
(c) Will you use it today?
(d) Will you have been using it today?

57. In ten year's time most teenagers will have their own cars.
In ten year's time more and more teenagers .... their own cars.
(a) will drive
(b) will be driving
(c) are going to drive
(d) will have been driving

58. We will have new motorway this year.
They .... a new motorway by the end of this year.
(a) will have built
(b) will be building
(c) will build
(d) will have been built

59. They started to build this motorway two years ago.
By the end of this year they .... this motorway for three years.
(a) will build
(b) will be building
(c) will have built
(d) will have been building

60. I have a lot of texts to translate for tomorrow.
.... a lot of texts tomorrow.
(a) I will be translating
(b) I am going to translate
(c) I will translate
(d) I will have translated

61. By the year 2020 there will be no water in the lake.
By the year 2020 all the water .... from this lake.
(a) will disappear
(b) is going to disappear
(c) will have disappeared
(d) will have been disappeared

62. This is my fifth day at bed. Tonight .... at my bed for five days.
(a) I'll be lying
(b) I'll have been lying
(c) I'll have laid
(d) I'll lay

Directions (Q. Nos. 63-70) Replace the underlined forms with the Future Simple or Future Continuous Tense, from the options given below.

63. Don't call me at 10 o'clock. My mobile phone will be switched off. I am going to fly to Spain.
(a) will fly
(b) will have flown
(c) will have been flying
(d) will be flying

64. I suppose we are going to stay at a hotel next summer.
(a) we will have been staying
(b) we will be staying
(c) we will stay
(d) we will have stayed

65. If you come to see me in the afternoon. I work in the garden.
(a) will be working
(b) will work
(c) will have been working
(d) am going to work

66. Do you think it is snowing at the weekend?
(a) will be snowing
(b) will snow
(c) is going to snow
(d) will have been snowing

67. Is the coat OK? Yes, I am taking it.
(a) will be taking it
(b) will have taken it
(c) will take it
(d) am going to take it

68. This time on Sunday we are going to ski in France.
(a) will ski
(b) will have been skiing
(c) will have ski
(d) will have been moving

69. I don't know if I will stay here, Perhaps I move to a big city one day.
(a) will move
(b) will be moving
(c) am going to move
(d) will have been moving

70. Every student is using a computer in the future.
(a) is going to use
(b) will be using
(c) will have use
(d) will have been using

Directions (Q. Nos. 71-90) Each of the following sentences has underlined word/phrase. Identify the best replacement from the options given below. If none of the substitutes improve the sentence, indicate option (d) as your answer.

71. If he had time he will call you.
(a) would have
(b) would have had
(c) has
(d) no improvement

72. If he has his book he would bring.
(a) would have (b) would have had
(c) had (d) no improvement

73. I have still to meet a person who is perfectly satisfied with his job.
(a) am still to meet
(b) am yet to meet
(c) might still meet
(d) no improvement

74. Had you helped me in time, I shall not have failed so badly.
(a) would not be
(b) would not have
(c) should not be
(d) No improvement

75. If I were a millionaire, I would have helped the poor.
(a) can help
(b) could have helped
(c) would help
(d) No improvement

76. If the room had been brighter, I would have been able to read for a while before bed time.

(a) If the room was brighter
(b) If the room are brighter
(c) Had the room been brighter
(d) No improvement

77. I <u>would wish to know</u> more about my country.
(a) would have wished to know
(b) wish I knew
(c) shall wish to know
(d) No improvement

78. It depends on your early <u>brought up</u> in the family.
(a) bringing up
(b) bringing on
(c) upbringing
(d) No improvement

79. The small child does whatever his father <u>was done</u>.
(a) has done
(b) did
(c) does
(d) No improvement

80. Why did you <u>not threw</u> the bag away?
(a) not throw
(b) had not threw
(c) not thrown
(d) No improvement

81. He dislikes the word dislike, <u>isn't he</u>?
(a) didn't he
(b) doesn't he
(c) hasn't he
(d) No improvement

82. You will be late if you <u>do not leave</u> now.
(a) did not leave
(b) left
(c) will not leave
(d) No improvement

83. If I were a millionaire, I <u>would have helped</u> the poor.
(a) would help
(b) can help
(c) could have helped
(d) No improvement

84. Children like to eat sweets, <u>isn't it</u>?
(a) do they?
(b) is it?
(c) don't they?
(d) No improvement

85. I <u>did not saw</u> my cousin in Madras.
(a) not seen
(b) did not see
(c) did not seen
(d) No improvement

86. He was weary of failure, <u>Didn't he</u>?
(a) Isn't he?
(b) Wasn't he?
(c) Doesn't he?
(d) No improvement

87. Keats <u>says</u> the idea very well in his poems.
(a) speaks
(b) describes
(c) expresses
(d) No improvement

88. We can buy anything in this shop, <u>Can we</u>?
(a) Isn't it?
(b) Can't we?
(c) Don't we?
(d) No improvement

89. If I had followed your advice, I <u>would not regret</u> today.
(a) will not regret
(b) had not regretted
(c) would not have regretted
(d) No improvement

90. It is time we <u>leave</u>.
(a) left
(b) have to leave
(c) would leave
(d) No improvement

Exercise 2

1. Only one of the boys .... not done the home-work given yesterday.
(a) have (b) has
(c) can (d) could

2. It is time we .... with determination.
(a) act
(b) acted
(c) have acted
(d) will act

3. When the thief entered the house, the inmates .... in the hall.
(a) were slept
(b) were sleeping
(c) slept
(d) had been sleeping

4. The thief explained how he .... from the jail.
(a) escapes (b) had escaped
(c) escaped (d) has escaped

5. They did not know where they .... from.
(a) had come (b) have come
(c) has come (d) come

6. Madhu has not been able to recall where ....
(a) Does she live (b) She lived
(c) Did she live (d) Lived the girl

7. When he died, Ramanujan .... behind three notebooks.
(a) was leaving (b) had left
(c) left (d) leaves

8. All the applicants .... and the results will be announced next week.
(a) rank
(b) are to rank
(c) are to be ranked
(d) are ranking

9. Tourists always enjoyed .... the setting Sun in the Darjeeling hills.
(a) to watch (b) watching
(c) in seeing (d) seeing

10. Ramappa .... as the mayor of the town and he will assume charge this Friday.
(a) elects (b) elected
(c) is elected (d) is electing

11. Just as in a family it is the willing cooperation of its members that .... happiness and contentment, so is it in the larger family of the nation.
(a) brought (b) will bring
(c) brings (d) bought

12. The old man could not remember where he .... his money.
(a) deposits (b) is depositing
(c) had deposited (d) will deposit

13. Hamid .... in Mumbai for three years when his parents came to visit.
(a) has lived
(b) had lived
(c) was living
(d) had been living.

14. Two years have passed since he .... here.
(a) has come (b) come
(c) came (d) had come

15. Will those of you who have objections to this proposal .... put up your hands, please?
(a) discussed
(b) being discussed
(c) having discussed
(d) discussing

16. She had frequent toothaches. So she decided to ....
(a) remove her teeth
(b) removing her teeth
(c) have her teeth removed
(d) having her teeth removed

17. The mechanic .... the vehicle since this morning.
(a) repaired
(b) repairing
(c) has been repairing
(d) will be repairing

18. If I had worked here, I .... very high marks in the examination.
(a) scored
(b) would score
(c) could score
(d) would have scored

19. I got used .... on the right when I was in the U.S. for two years.
(a) driving (b) to drive
(c) to driving (d) by driving

20. Had you told me earlier I .... the meeting.
(a) had attended
(b) have attended
(c) attended
(d) would have attended

21. There will be a rush for seats when the train ....
(a) will arrive (b) arrived
(c) is arriving (d) arrives

22. By the time I reach America, it .... morning.
(a) is (b) would be
(c) must be (d) was

23. She feared that she ....
(a) will fail
(b) may fail
(c) might have fail
(d) would fail

24. I was washing my face as the insect .... quietly into the bedroom.
(a) crept (b) creeps
(c) was creeping (d) has crept

25. During the recent floods two thirds of our city .... in ruins.
(a) are (b) were
(c) is (d) was

26. I have .... Lakshmi for the past twelve years.
(a) know (b) knew
(c) known (d) knows

27. The engineers .... this bridge since last year.
(a) have repaired
(b) had repaired
(c) have been repairing
(d) are repairing

28. If I had helped him, he ....
(a) will not be drowned
(b) would not be drowned
(c) will not have drowned
(d) would not have drowned

29. The housewife .... cakes burning, and ran to switch off the oven.
(a) smell (b) smells
(c) smelt (d) smelling

30. If you had followed the rules, you .... disqualified.
(a) will not be
(b) would not be
(c) will not have been
(d) would not have been

31. The farmers .... their farms, if they had known that a thunderstorm was approaching.
(a) will leave
(b) would leave
(c) will have left
(d) would have left.

32. .... you hear the President's speech?
(a) Have (b) Has
(c) Had (d) Did

33. I .... to the movies with some friends last night.
(a) have gone (b) went
(c) am gone (d) am going

34. If I .... a doctor, I would serve the poor,
(a) am (b) had been
(c) were (d) was

35. The plane will take off when the thunderstorm ....
(a) stops (b) stopped
(c) would stop (d) will stop

36. When the doctor .... the patient was already ....
(a) arrived; died
(b) arrived; dead
(c) arrive; dead
(d) arriving; dying

37. If you litter, you .... to pay a fine.
(a) will have (b) would have
(c) will had (d) would had

38. The life-guard would not let the children .... at the deep end of the pool.
(a) swims (b) swim
(c) swam (d) to swim

39. The audience watched the clowns ....
(a) performs (b) perform
(c) performed (d) are performing

40. We shall go for a picnic if the weather .... good.
(a) is (b) was
(c) has been (d) had been

41. I .... hard to establish the validity of the theory from morning.
(a) have been trying
(b) had tried
(c) tried
(d) am trying.

42. I wish I .... her to clean the room.
(a) have asking (b) have asked
(c) asked (d) had asked

43. Simon .... very polite at the moment, because he wants to make a good impression.
(a) was being (b) has been
(c) is behaving (d) is being.

44. Had I saved money, I .... a new car.
(a) will purchase
(b) would purchase
(c) would have purchased
(d) purchased

45. He told me that he .... the movie.
(a) is watched (b) was watched
(c) had watched (d) not watched

46. The railway coaches .... by the Integral Coach Factory, Chennai.
(a) is manufactured
(b) are manufactured
(c) are manufacture
(d) is being manufactured

47. The car broke down and we .... get a taxi.
(a) were to (b) are to
(c) had to (d) have to

48. He said I .... use his car when ever I wanted.
(a) could (b) can
(c) will (d) would

49. While he was working at the site, a block of wood suddenly .... his right shoulder.
(a) was hitted (b) was hit
(c) had hitted (d) hit

50. In the tragic incident, none of the passengers ....
(a) could survived
(b) survive
(c) survived
(d) is surviving

Directions (Q.Nos. 51-95) Read the following sentences to find out whether there is any error in any part.

51. The students sitting on the dais (a)/ studied here (b)/ for three years but (c)/ they have never created any problem. (d)

52. A philogynist is a person (a)/ who loves woman (b)/ but a misogynist is a person (c)/ who is hating woman. (d)

53. It is appearing to me (a)/ that you are (b)/ trying to destabilise (c)/ the present committee. (d)

54. I have been knowing her (a)/ for many years (b)/ but I don't know (c)/ where she works. (d)

55. If he would have done this (a)/ he would have done wrong (b)/ and would have deceived (c)/ many of his relatives. (d)

56. The victim tried to tell us (a)/ what has happened (b)/ but his words (c)/ were not audible. (d)

57. I want you to (a)/ pick up the box of eggs gently (b)/ and kept it in (c)/ the corner carefully. (d)

58. She came to (a)/ the party much (b)/ later than (c)/ I expect. (d)

59. I lived here (a)/for five years (b)/ so I know about the (c)/ problems of this colony. (d)

60. The chairman had not taken (a)/ any decision until (b)/ he had studied (c) the case thoroughly. (d)

61. They got everything (a)/ ready for the visitors (b)/ long before (c)/ they reached there. (d)

62. He switched on the light (a)/ before he entered (b)/ the room. (c)/No error (d)

63. I have been admiring (a)/ her for the (b)/ voice with which (c)/ she is gifted. (d)

64. He was with me (a)/ till now (b)/ so don't (c)/ punish him for the delay. (d)

65. Several survey reports (a)/ indicate that (b)/ the number of (c) drug addicts is grown gradually. (d)

66. "Here is coming up Bachchan!", (a)/ said he (b)/ when he was (c)/ waiting for him. (d)

67. I could not recall (a)/ when she has told me (b)/ about her (c)/ affair with Gopal. (d)

68. Four and four (a)/ always made eight (b)/ cannot (c)/ be questioned by anyone. (d)

69. She hopes to (a)/ become an engineer (b)/ after she will complete (c)/ her education. (d)

70. When you will find (a)/ a solution to this problem (b)/ you will be able (c)/ to get this project. (d)

71. The teacher told us (a)/ that we should remain (b)/ in the hostel (c)/ if it rains. (d)

72. I could not recall (a)/ what she has advised me (b)/ in this matter. (c)/ No error (d)

73. By this time tomorrow (a)/ she has had reached (b)/ there positively. (c)

74. I will inform (a)/ you as soon as (b)/ I will get any news (c)/ about his health. (d)/ No error

75. A recent survey (a)/ indicates (b)/ that the number of drug addicts (c)/ grew day by day. (d)

76. Before the alarm (a)/ had stopped ringing (b)/ Reena had pulled up the shade. (c)/ No error (d)

77. If I was you (a)/ I would have told (b)/ the principal (c)/ to keep his mouth shut. (d)

78. The police brought the cover (a)/ to the villages (b)/ so that they can identify then. (c)/ No error (d)

79. The victim tried (a)/ to tell us what has happened (b)/ but his words (c)/ were not audible. (d)

80. The Mumbai police have found (a)/the body of a man (b)/ who they believe to be (c)/ the prime suspect in a murder case (d)

81. I am taking case (a)/ of the garden (b) since my father's death. (c)/ No error (d)

82. The secret of his (a)/ good health lies (b)/ in the fact (c)/ that he is getting up before sunrise. (d)

83. John has eaten (a)/ the cookies last night (b)/ while watching the match. (c)/ No error (d)

84. I came to know (a)/ that your father (b)/ has died (c)/ last month. (d)

85. If we had Ramesh (a)/ in our team, we (b)/ would have won the match. (c)

86. My friend said to me, (a)/"When have (b)/ you come here?" (c)

87. I have been knowing (a)/ him for the last five years (b)/ but now I don't know (c)/ where he lives. (d)

88. He lived here (a)/ since 1998, (b)/ so he knows everything (c)/ about this town. (d)

89. I have been working (a)/ in this firm (b)/ for the last twenty years. (c)/No error (d)

90. (a) Whenever he is coming (a)/ here, he brings (b)/ many (c)/ gifts for me. (d)

Answers

Exercise 1

1 (d)	2 (b)	3 (b)	4 (b)	5 (c)	6 (b)	7 (c)	8 (a)	9 (c)	10 (d)
11 (a)	12 (a)	13 (c)	14 (d)	15 (a)	16 (b)	17 (c)	18 (b)	19 (a)	20 (a)
21 (b)	22 (c)	23 (b)	24 (a)	25 (b)	26 (a)	27 (d)	28 (c)	29 (a)	30 (c)
31 (c)	32 (b)	33 (d)	34 (a)	35 (b)	36 (c)	37 (c)	38 (b)	39 (b)	40 (a)
41 (c)	42 (d)	43 (b)	44 (a)	45 (c)	46 (c)	47 (d)	48 (c)	49 (b)	50 (a)
51 (d)	52 (d)	53 (c)	54 (a)	55 (c)	56 (b)	57 (b)	58 (a)	59 (d)	60 (a)
61 (c)	62 (b)	63 (d)	64 (c)	65 (a)	66 (b)	67 (c)	68 (a)	69 (a)	70 (b)
71 (c)	72 (c)	73 (a)	74 (b)	75 (c)	76 (d)	77 (b)	78 (a)	79 (a)	80 (a)
81 (b)	82 (d)	83 (a)	84 (c)	85 (b)	86 (b)	87 (c)	88 (b)	89 (c)	90 (a)

Exercise 2

1 (a)	2 (d)	3 (a)	4 (a)	5 (b)	6 (c)	7 (a)	8 (d)	9 (b)	10 (d)
11 (d)	12 (a)	13 (b)	14 (c)	15 (c)	16 (a)	17 (b)	18 (c)	19 (b)	20 (d)
21 (b)	22 (a)	23 (c)	24 (a)	25 (b)	26 (a)	27 (b)	28 (b)	29 (a)	30 (a)
31 (c)	32 (c)	33 (c)	34 (d)	35 (c)	36 (d)	37 (b)	38 (c)	39 (a)	40 (c)
41 (c)	42 (b)	43 (a)	44 (c)	45 (b)	46 (d)	47 (b)	48 (a)	49 (c)	50 (d)
51 (b)	52 (d)	53 (a)	54 (a)	55 (a)	56 (b)	57 (c)	58 (d)	59 (a)	60 (a)
61 (a)	62 (d)	63 (a)	64 (a)	65 (d)	66 (a)	67 (b)	68 (b)	69 (c)	70 (a)
71 (d)	72 (b)	73 (b)	74 (c)	75 (d)	76 (b)	77 (a)	78 (c)	79 (b)	80 (c)
81 (a)	82 (d)	83 (a)	84 (c)	85 (a)	86 (b)	87 (a)	88 (a)	89 (d)	90 (a)

Explanations

51. *(b)* Studied की जगह have studied होगा। sitting on the dais एवं have never created का use यह show करता है कि वाक्य को present tense में माना गया है।

52. *(d)* Who is hating की जगह who hates लिखा जाएगा। Universal truth/eternal truth के लिए present indefinite का प्रयोग होता है।

53. *(a)* It is appearing की जगह it appears लिखा जाएगा। यहाँ appear का प्रयोग seem के अर्थ में हुआ है अत: present continuous का प्रयोग नहीं किया जाएगा। Present indefinite का प्रयोग किया जाएगा। Appear का प्रयोग यदि 'जनता' के सामने आने या प्रकाशित होने के mevoYe& ceW nes lees continuous में इसका प्रयोग किया जा सकता है; जैसे:

His next novel is appearing this month.

54. *(a)* I have been knowing की जगह I have known का use लिखा जाएगा। Verb know का प्रयोग continuous में नहीं किया जाता है।

55. *(a)* यहाँ 'If he would have done this' की जगह 'If he had done this' का use लिखा जाएगा। इस तरह के conditional sentences वाक्यों का structure निम्न होगा :
It + subject + had + V_3 ....would have + V_3

56. *(b)* Has happened की जगह had happened लिखा जाएगा। जब वाक्य में सब जगह past tense है, तो present perfect का प्रयोग गलत है।

57. *(c)* Kept it की जगह keep it होगा। वाक्य में past tense का प्रयोग अनावश्यक किया गया है।

58. *(d)* I expect की जगह I had expected आएगा। कार्य past में हुआ है, अत: expect के साथ had expected (past to past) का प्रयोग होगा।

59. *(a)* यहाँ I lived की जगह I have lived होगा क्योंकि sentence present tense में है।

60. *(a)* यहाँ 'had not taken' की जगह did not take लिखा जाना चाहिए। जब वाक्य में एक clause had+ V_3 का प्रयोग होता है तो दूसरे clause में past indefinite का प्रयोग होता है।

61. *(a)* They got की जगह they had got लिखा जाएगा जब वाक्य में दो कार्य एक के बाद दूसरा पूर्ण होता है तो पहले पूर्ण होने वाले कार्य के लिए past perfect का प्रयोग किया जाता है।

63. *(a)* I have been admiring की जगह I admire लिखा जाना चाहिए, क्योंकि know, admire, adore, trust, believe, rely, hope etc. का प्रयोग सामान्यतया Continuous में नहीं किया जाता है।

64. *(a)* He was की जगह He has been लिखा जाएगा, क्योंकि till now, के साथ past का प्रयोग नहीं होता है।

65. *(d)* Is grown की जगह is growing आएगा।

66. *(a)* Here is coming की जगह Here comes लिखा जाएगा। Exclamatory वाक्यों में Present Indefinite का निम्न प्रकार से प्रयोग होता है :
Here comes the train!
There works Sita!

67. *(b)* She has told की जगह she had told लिखा जाना चाहिए। जब वाक्य में Past Tense का प्रयोग हो तो Present Perfect का प्रयोग नहीं होगा।

68. *(b)* made की जगह makes लिखें। Universal truth/mathematical calculations/historical facts हेतु Present Indefinite का प्रयोग किया जाता है।

69. *(c)* She will complete की जगह she has completed लिखा जाना चाहिए। She hopes का प्रयोग future अर्थ के लिए किया गया है चूँकि engineer बनने से पूर्व education पूर्ण करनी है अत: present perfect का प्रयोग होगा।

70. *(a)* 'Will' को delete करें। When के बाद वाक्य में will का प्रयोग नहीं करते हैं। When, it, before, after, until के बाद will का प्रयोग नहीं किया जाता है।

71. *(d)* If it rains की जगह if it rained होना चाहिए। जब reporting verb, past tense में है, तो reported speech भी past tense में होगा।

72. *(b)* She has की जगह she had होना चाहिए। principal clause में past की घटना है, तो subordinate clause में भी past tense ही आएगा।

73. *(b)* Has had reached की जगह will have reached होगा। यह future perfect का वाक्य है।

74. *(c)* 'Will' को delete करें। Conditional clauses में as soon as, when, after, before if, के बाद future tense का प्रयोग नहीं होता है।

75. *(d)* Grew की जगह is growing होगा। The sentence is in present tense.

76. *(b)* Had stopped की जगह केवल stopped होगा।
Conditional sentences में जो कार्य बाद में होता है, उसमें past indefinite tense का प्रयोग होता है।

77. *(a)* If I was का जगह if I were होगा इस तरह के conditional वाक्यों में 'were' का प्रयोग किया जाता है।

78. *(c)* दिया गया sentence past tense को belong करता हैं इसलिए यहाँ part (c) के अन्तर्गत 'can' की जगह 'could' का use किया जाएगा।

79. *(b)* What has happened की जगह what had happened का use होगा। जब वाक्य past में है तो यहाँ present perfect का use करना गलत है।

80. *(c)* यहाँ part (c) के अन्तर्गत 'believe' के स्थान पर believed का use किया जाएगा। The action of 'believing' preceded the action of 'finding the body'. Thus, the verb should be used in past tense.

81. *(a)* यहाँ 'I am taking care' के स्थान पर 'I have been taking care' का use किया जाएगा। The subject of the sentence denotes the activity, in the past and continuous to do so. Thus, present perfect continuous tense is suitable here.

82. *(d)* He is getting up की जगह he gets up होगा। Present habit को बताने हेतु present indefinite का use किया जाता है।

83. *(a)* यहाँ part (a) के अन्तर्गत 'John has eaten' की जगह 'John ate' आएगा। The correct verb would be 'ate' as it should be in the simple past tense as the action had already taken place in the past.

84. *(c)* has died की जगह died आएगा। past time के adverbs (यहाँ last month, ago, last year) के साथ, present perfect का use नहीं होता है।

85. *(a)* We had की जगह we had had होना चाहिए।

86. *(b)* When have की जगह when did use किया जाएगा। Past में किसी question हेतु when did का use होता है।

87. *(a)* I have been knowing की जगह I have known होगा। Know, see, appear, believe आदि verbs का प्रयोग continuous tense में करना अनुचित है।

88. *(a)* Lived की जगह has been living होगा। Sentence से अभी भी उसका रहना जाहिर होता है।

90. *(a)* यहाँ 'he is coming' की जगज 'he comes here' use होगा। यह आदतन किया जाने वाला act है, जिसके लिए present indefinite का use suitable होगा।

02 Subject-Verb Agreement

Subject-verb concord का अर्थ होता है, sentence में verb और subject के बीच का agreement. किसी भी sentence में verb का use उसके subject के according करना subject-verb concord या subject-verb agreement कहलाता है। यदि sentence में subject singular है, तो verb भी singular होगी और यदि subject plural हैं, तो verb भी plural होगी।

e.g. (i) Rohan is dancing.
(ii) We are swimming.

उपरोक्त examples में singular subject Rohan के साथ singular verb 'is' का use किया गया है तथा plural subject 'we' के साथ plural verb 'are' का use किया गया है।

Some Singular/Plural subjects with their Singular/ Plural verbs are given as follows

Subject	Helping verb		
I	Am	Was	Have/had
He/she/it	Is	Was	Has/had
We/you/they	Are	Were	Have/had

Following are the some important rules of subject-verb concord

Rule 1 कुछ sentences ऐसे होते हैं, जिनमें singular subject होते हुए भी plural verb का use किया जाता है।

(A) जब sentence में imagination (कल्पना) का भाव होता है या असम्भव शर्त का भाव प्रदर्शित होता है।

e.g., (i) I wish, I were the Prime Minister.
(ii) She ordered, if she were my mother.

उपरोक्त examples में 'were' का use singular subject के साथ किया गया है।

(B) यदि sentences में verbs; bless, save, help, live का use desire, wish या blessing का भाव प्रकट करता है, तब singular subject के साथ भी इन verb का use plural form (blesses, saves, helps, lives) में नहीं किया जा सकता।

e.g., (i) God save the queen. (Not 'saves')
(ii) God bless you with a son. (Not 'Blesses')

Rule 2 किसी sentence में यदि दो subjects 'and' से जुड़े हो तथा सिर्फ first subject से पहले article (A, An, The) का use किया गया हो, तो वह subject एक ही person का बोध करवाता है तथा singular verb का use किया जाता है।

The poet and painter has died.
(ii) The director and producer of the film has arrived.

Rule 3 यदि कोई भी दो subjects 'and' से जुड़े हो तथा दोनों से पहले article का use किया गया हो, तो वे अलग-अलग persons का बोध करवाते है तथा plural verb का use किया जाता है।

e.g., (i) The musician and the singer have died in a car accident.
(ii) The editor and the writer have been awarded by the President.

Rule 4 दो noun जो same नहीं हैं, लेकिन एक phrase की तरह प्रयुक्त होते हैं, तो भी verb singular लगती है।

e.g., (i) Bread and Butter is a good breakfast.
(ii) Cost and Creed is a major problem.

Exception : जब दो uncountable nouns को 'and' से जोड़ा जाता है तथा वे दो अलग-अलग subjects का बोध करँवाए, तो plural verb का use किया जाता है।
e.g., Love and Happiness are necessary for a peaceful life.

Rule 5 नीचे दिए गए words का use किसी sentence में किया जाए तो इनके बाद use होने वाले Noun, Adjective, Verb तथा Pronoun, Singular form में होते हैं।

Words	Noun/ Pronoun	Helping Verb/ Main verb	Adjective
Each, Someone, No one, Every, Anyone, one, Nobody, Everyone, Anybody, Many a, Somebody, More than one	Singular	Singular	Singular

e.g. Each book and pen is brown.
Many a man has sacrificed for his country.

Key Point

Each का प्रयोग दो व्यक्तियों/वस्तुओं के लिए किया जाता है, जबकि 'every', 'each and every' का प्रयोग दो से अधिक व्यक्तियों/वस्तुओं के लिए किया जाता है।

e.g. (i) There were only two soldiers, **each and every** soldiers was equal to five policeman. (×)
(ii) They were only two soldiers, **each** solider **was** (singular verb) equal to five policeman. (✓)

Rule 6 यदि sentence में each of, every of, one of , any of, everyone of, either of/neither of का use किया गया हो, तो इनके बाद आने वाला Noun/Pronoun हमेशा plural होता है, लेकिन verb singular use होती है।

e.g. (i) One of the boys in our class has won a prize. *(Not 'have')*

(ii) One of the most widely spread bad habit is use of cigarette. *(Not 'habit are')*

Key Point

Neither तथा **Either** का प्रयोग सिर्फ दो के लिए किया जाता है।

None, one तथा **any** का प्रयोग दो से अधिक के लिए किया जाता है।

e.g., (i) **Neither** of the Pandvas was to be blamed for the battle. (✗)
None of the Pandvas was to be blamed for the battle. (✓)

(ii) **Any** of the two roads leads to the park. (✗)
Either of the two roads leads to the park. (✓)

Rule 7 यदि किसी sentence में subjects को इन शब्दों से जोड़ा जाए, तो उस sentence में verb हमेशा पहले वाले subject के according ही use की जाती हैं। ऐसे words निम्न है—with/alongwith/together with/ as well as/ like/ unlike/ but/ except/ rather than/ besides/ in addition to / accompanied by/ headed by/ guided by/ governed by/ controlled by/ led by/ dominated by/ run by, etc.

e.g. (i) She together with her sisters has gone to the market.

(ii) The father with his son was missing from his home.

Rule 8 यदि दो subjects को neither ... nor, either ... or, not only ... but also, none ... but, nor, or, etc से जोड़ा जाए, तो verb हमेशा (नजदीक वाले) दूसरे subject के according use की जाती है।

e.g. (i) Neither he nor his brother is guilty.

(ii) Not only the doctor but also the nurses are very kind to the patients.

Rule 9 नीचे दिए गए words का use, sentence में निम्न प्रकार से किया जाता है।

Words	Noun	Helping Verb/ Main Verb
A number of A large number of A great number of	Plural countable noun	Plural
The number of The large number of The great number of	Plural countable noun	Singular
The quantity of The amount of A large amount of A great deal of	Uncountable noun	Singular

e.g. (i) The number of candidates is absent today.

(ii) A large number of books are printed on this topic.

Note Number of के साथ यदि **article 'A'** का प्रयोग हो, तो हमेशा **H.V/M.V plural form** में होगा लेकिन यदि **'the'** का प्रयोग हो, तो **H.V. singular** होगा। ध्यान रखें, **subjects** दोनों के **plural countable noun** होंगे, परन्तु **uncountable noun** के लिए **quantity** या **amount** शब्द का प्रयोग किया जाता है।

Rule 10 Optative sentences (वह sentence जो किसी इच्छा को denote करे) में singular subject तथा plural verb का use किया जाता है।

e.g. (i) God bless you!

(ii) May you live long!

Rule 11 यदि sentence में little/ the little/ much/ not much के साथ 'of' का use किया गया हैं, तो singular noun के साथ singular helping verb का use किया जाएगा।

e.g. (i) Not much of her work was appreciated by the team.

(ii) A little of the milks is used for a cup of tea.

Rule 12 यदि sentence में the percent/the percentage के साथ 'of' का use किया गया हो, तो singular uncountable या plural countable noun के साथ singular helping verb का use किया जाएगा।

e.g. (i) The percentage of the students is (singular) increasing day by day.

(ii) The percent of her devotion has increased by the time.

Rule 13 किसी sentence में countable noun के साथ यदि 'all' एवं 'some' का use हो, तो उसमें plural verb का use किया जाता है, लेकिन 'all' के साथ यदि uncountable noun आता है, तो singular verb का use किया जाता है।

e.g. (i) Some animals are trustworthy.

(ii) All the furniture was sent to the market.

Rule 14 यदि sentence में relative pronoun (Who, Which, That etc) का use किया गया हो, तब verb का use, relative pronoun के पहले आने वाले noun/pronoun के according use की जाएगी (Singular के साथ Singular, तथा Plural के साथ Plural)

e.g. (i) It is I who have telephoned you.

(ii) The books that are here are mine.

Rule 15 यदि किसी sentence में indefinite pronoun 'one' का use subject की तरह किया जाए, तो उस sentence में singular verb का use किया जाता हैं।

e.g., One has to take care of one's health.

Rule 16 यदि sentence में प्रत्येक noun से पहले 'each' and 'every' का use किया जाए तो Singular verb का use किया जाता है।

e.g. (i) Each man and every woman is guilty.
(ii) Each boy and each girl was given gift by the principal.

Rule 17 जब sentence में इन phrases : a good deal of, remainder of, most of, a number of, many of, a quarter of, proportion of, none of, a great deal of, two-third of, lots of, plenty of, some of, majority of, much of, part of, percent of, heaps of, आदि का use होता है, तो verb आने वाले noun के according use की जाती है। यदि of के बाद आने वाला noun plural countable है, तो verb भी plural, use की जाएगी, और यदि noun uncountable है तो singular verb use की जाएगी।

e.g. (i) Some of the workers are on strike.
(ii) Some of the sugar is littered on the floor.

Rule 18 यदि sentence में 'None' का use किया जाता हैं तो निम्न structure use किया जाता है

None + of + uncountable noun + singular verb
None + of + plural countable noun + plural verb

e.g. (i) **None** of the counterfeit money (Uncountable) **has** (Singular H.V.) been found.
(ii) **None** of my children (Countable Noun) **are** (Plural verb) able to communicate in English.

Rule 19 The French, The English, The Japanese, The Chinese, The poor, The young, The old etc. इनके साथ definite article 'The' का use किया जाता हैं तथा ये पूरी class (जाति) को denote करते है, इसलिए इनके साथ plural verb का use किया जाता है।

e.g. (i) The Japanese are intelligent.
(ii) The English have great sense of humour.

Rule 20 जो दो singular nouns को किसी preposition के द्वारा जोड़ा जाता है, तो singular helping verb का use किया जाता हैं।

Noun + Preposition + Noun + Singular Verb

e.g. (i) Village after village was destroyed.
(ii) Ship after ship is heading toward the shore.

Rule 21 यदि एक plural noun एक निश्चित quantity या amount को एक unit की तरह व्यक्त करता हैं, तो verb singular लगती है।

e.g. (i) Five kilograms is not a heavy weight.
(ii) Hundred rupees is a big amount for him.

लेकिन यदि इनसे plurality का बोध होता है तो verb plural लगेगी।

e.g. (i) Five years have passed.
(ii) Two thousand rupees were charged by him.

Rule 22 जब किसी sentence में other या another के बाद कोई noun आए तो ध्यान रखे other के बाद plural noun and plural verb का use होगा और another के बाद singular noun and singular verb का use किया जाएगा।

e.g. (i) There are so many other hotels better than this.
(ii) There is another hotel near the railway station.

Rule 23 जब collective noun (Committee, Army, Parliament, Fleet, Mob, Assembly, Jury, Majority etc.) एक unit (इकाई) की तरह use की जाती है तो verb singular लगती है।

e.g. (i) The Parliament has passed the bill.
(ii) Army was deployed at the border.

लेकिन यदि collective noun, sentence में divided प्रतीत होती है या विभिन्न सदस्यो में एकमत नहीं होती, तो plural verb use की जाती हैं।

e.g. (i) The committee are divided over the proposal.
(ii) The audience were getting bored.

Exercise 1

Directions (Q. Nos. 1-45) Complete the following sentences with a verb form that agrees with the subject.

1. Ram and Shyam .... brothers.
(a) is (b) are
(c) have (d) had

2. Slow and Steady .... the race.
(a) wins (b) winning
(c) win (d) is winning

3. Eggs and butter .... sold here.
(a) has (b) is
(c) are (d) None of these

4. I and Ramesh .... going to do this work now.
(a) am (b) is
(c) are (d) has

5. The rise and fall .... caused by the storm.
(a) are (b) am
(c) has (d) is

6. Mr. Bose or Mr. Ghosh .... to give the class.
(a) were (b) was
(c) are (d) had

7. A few men ...... good natured.
(a) were (b) are
(c) is (d) has

8. Neither of the bags ...... black.
(a) was (b) were
(c) are (d) had

9. Ram as well as his brothers .... come today.
(a) are (b) were
(c) is (d) have been

10. Economics .... no attraction for me
(a) have (b) had
(c) were (d) has

11. 'Northern Lights' .... one of Suzanne's favourite books.
(a) are (b) is
(c) was (d) have

12. .... effort is required for financial planning,
(a) A lots of (b) A lot of
(c) A number of (d) Something

13. A number of apartment blocks here .... their own swimming pool.
(a) are (b) has (c) have (d) had

14. Dr. Jone's whereabouts .... kept a closely guarded secret by his friend.
(a) are (b) were
(c) is (d) has been

15. .... somebody taken my note book? I can't find it anywhere.
(a) has (b) have
(c) is (d) was

16. The truth about those two rival companies .... going to be exposed.
(a) was (b) is
(c) has (d) are

17. All precautions .... taken to prevent the river from bursting its bank.
(a) has been (b) have been
(c) had been (d) were

18. Second-hand furniture .... here at reasonable prices.
(a) are sold (b) were selling
(c) has sold (d) is sold

19. Something .... wrong with my car. It just refuses to start.
(a) are (b) is
(c) was (d) were

20. Sita told them that they .... wrong.
(a) are (b) will be
(c) were (d) can

21. Each of them boys .... intelligent.
(a) is (b) wer
(c) has (d) are

22. The person together with three other saints .... to make a number of startling predictions.
(a) plans (b) plan
(c) is planning (d) has planned

23. These predictions .... not to be believed.
(a) was (b) were
(c) is (d) are

24. My sister, along with her husband and my parents .... driving to a wedding this weekend.
(a) is (b) are
(c) was (d) were

25. Manoj is one of the few students who .... passed the exam.
(a) have (b) has
(c) had been (d) would have

26. One of my brothers .... in Atlanta last weekend.
(a) was (b) are
(c) were (d) is

27. The teacher as well as her students .... that practise makes a man perfect.
(a) are believing (b) believes
(c) believe (d) believed

28. Neither of the two politicians .... to lose the race.
(a) expect
(b) expected
(c) expects
(d) have expected

29. Each of the twins .... some unusual habits.
(a) has (b) have
(c) had (d) is having

30. She is one of the students who always .... correctly.
(a) answer
(b) answering
(c) answers
(d) have answered

31. Either the physicians in this hospital or Cheif administrator .... going to have to make a decision.
(a) is (b) are
(c) was (d) were

32. The other boys or Henry .... to blame.
(a) is (b) are
(c) were (d) will

33. Some of the votes .... to have been miscounted.
(a) seems (b) seem
(c) seemed (d) has seemed

34. Each of the Girl Scouts .... a community project.
(a) does (b) do
(c) participates (d) participate

35. Everyone selected to serve on this jury .... to be willing to give up a lot of time.
(a) have (b) had
(c) has (d) are

36. Shivani Wangu together with her teammates, ... a formidable opponent on the cricket ground.
(a) present (b) presents
(c) presented (d) have presented

37. He seems to forget that there .... things to be done before he can graduate.
(a) is (b) are
(c) were (d) was

38. Some people .... still left in the town after yesterday's earthquake.
(a) is (b) were
(c) are (d) was

39. Some of the grain .... to be contaminated.
(a) appears (b) appeared
(c) have appeared
(d) appear

40. Three quarters of the students .... against the tuition hike.
(a) were (b) is
(c) are (d) was

41. A high percentage of the population .... voting for the new school.
(a) was (b) were
(c) is (d) are

42. Neither of the two boys .... done it.
(a) have (b) has
(c) had (d) are

43. Two hundred rupees .... a large amount fifty years ago.
(a) were (b) are
(c) is (d) was

44. More than one students .... absent.
(a) was (b) were
(c) are (d) is

45. The mother and not her children .... been arrested for committing the theft.
(a) have
(b) has
(c) are
(d) had

Exercise 2

Directions (Q. Nos. 1-40) Choose the most appropriate alternative to make a proper sentence.

1. The owner of these books ....
(a) have gone (b) were gone
(c) has gone (d) is gone

2. Ten books of this library ....
(a) is missing
(b) are missing
(c) has been missing
(d) has missed

3. Either he or you ....
(a) has to go (b) have to go
(c) is to go (d) was going

4. The father with his sons ....
(a) was sleeping (b) have slept
(c) are sleeping (d) sleep

5. He and I .... like them.
(a) does not (b) has not
(c) do not (d) cannot

6. The news .... by him.
(a) were brought (b) have brought
(c) has brought (d) was brought

7. Neither he nor I ....
(a) is going (b) am going
(c) were going (d) has gone

8. The frogs at the cottage .... very loudly.
(a) croaks (b) croak
(c) croaked (d) croaking

9. Many a girl ....
(a) has seen this movie
(b) have seen this movie
(c) see this movie
(d) are going to see this movie

10. There .... a cow and a horse in the field.
(a) was (b) is
(c) were (d) will

11. Your friend .... too much.
(a) talk (b) talks
(c) talking (d) None of these

12. The man with the roses .... like your brother.
(a) look (b) looks
(c) looking (d) None of these

13. The women in the pool .... well.
(a) swimming (b) swims
(c) swim (d) had swimming

14. Basant .... a cab.
(a) drives (b) drive
(c) driving (d) were driving

15. The football players .... five kilometres every day.
(a) run (b) running
(c) was running (d) were run

16. That red-haired lady in the fur hat ...... across the street.
(a) live
(b) lives
(c) living
(d) were lived

17. Each of the girls .... good on stage.
(a) look (b) looks
(c) looking (d) are looking

18. Everybody .... asked to remain quiet.
(a) are (b) is
(c) were (d) was

19. Neither of the men .... here yet.
(a) is (b) were
(c) are (d) was

20. Some members of the faculty .... present.
(a) is (b) are
(c) was (d) has

21. Nobody in the class .... the answer.
(a) have (b) has
(c) has been (d) have been

22. .... each of the girls ready to leave?
(a) Are (b) Was
(c) Is (d) Were

23. Each of the girls .... all the regulations.
(a) observe (b) observes
(c) observing (d) None of these

24. Each of these options .... its own benefit.
(a) has (b) have
(c) have been (d) has been

25. The level of drunkenness .... for person to person for the same amount of wine.
(a) vary (b) varies
(c) varying (d) None of these

26. Mr. Sanyal's family members .... going to USA next week.
(a) are (b) is
(c) was (d) has

27. Many of my friends .... working in the private sector.
(a) is (b) are
(c) was (d) had

28. A large number of people .... in the earthquake in London.
(a) dies (b) die
(c) died (d) dying

29. The decoration of Mayank's home .... it look impressive.
(a) make (b) makes
(c) making (d) are making

30. Nobody .... come for the party yet we're still waiting.
(a) has (b) have
(c) was (d) is

31. The members of the committee _______ to the proposal.
(a) have consented
(b) was consented
(c) had been consented
(d) has consented

32. Where .... the earrings that I left by the bathroom sink?
(a) was (b) were
(c) is (d) are

33. Neither of those sharks circling your boogie board .... hungry enough to bite.
(a) looks (b) look
(c) looked (d) had looked

34. Neither food nor water .... to be found there.
(a) are (b) have
(c) be (d) was

35. Someone - perhaps Ekant or Pushp .... the right wine to serve with mushroom lasagna.
(a) knew (b) will know
(c) knows (d) know

36. These scissors .... so dull that I'm not sure you could slice butter with them!
(a) is (b) are
(c) has been (d) had been

37. Physics .... proven to be Samridhi's easiest subject this semester.
(a) has (b) have
(c) had (d) will have

38. .... road is safe.
(a) Not a (b) Neither
(c) Nor (d) Either

39. Every cereal bowl and casserole dish .... slipped out of Sheila's soapy hands.
(a) has (b) have
(c) will have (d) had

40. Not only fat caterpillars, but also my neighbour's rabbits, ... chewed my poor tomato plants.
(a) has (b) have
(c) will have (d) had

Directions (Q. Nos. 41-65) In each of the following questions, a sentence is given which may or may not be correct. Select the option which is the correct form of the sentence. If you think none of the options is correct, your answer is 'D'.

41. Slow and steady win the race.
(a) Slowly and steady wins the race.
(b) Slow and steadily wins the race.
(c) Slow and steady wins the race.
(d) None of the above

42. These news were broadcasted on Radio BBC.
(a) These news were broadcast on Radio BBC.
(b) This news was,broadcast on Radio BBC.
(c) This news was broadcasted on Radio BBC.
(d) None of the above

43. Every boy and girl were given a prize
(a) Every boy and girl were given prizes.
(b) Every boy and girl was given prizes.
(c) Every boy and girl was given a prize.
(d) None of the above

44. Everyone of them were clapping at the performance of the clown.
(a) Everyone of them were clapping at the performance of the clowns.
(b) Everyone of them was clapping at the performance of the clowns.
(c) Everyone of them was clapping at the performances about the clowns.
(d) None of the above

45. Law and order are to be maintained at all costs.
(a) Law and orders are to be maintained at all costs.
(b) Law and order is to be maintained at all costs.
(c) Laws and orders are to be maintained at all costs.
(d) None of the above

46. Five hundred rupees are a long sum.
(a) Five hundred rupee is a long sum.
(b) Five hundred rupee is a big sum.
(c) Five hundred rupees is a big sum.
(d) None of the above

47. Mohit not his friends are to blame.
(a) Mohit, not his friends, is to blame.
(b) Mohit, not his friend are to blame.
(c) Mohit, not his friends is on to blame.
(d) None of the above

48. I as well as you are to blame.
(a) I as well as you, is to blame.
(b) I as well as you are to blame.
(c) I as well as you, am to blame.
(d) None of the above

49. You did not do so, nor he did.
(a) You did not do so, he nor did.
(b) You did not do so, nor did he.
(c) You did not do so, he did nor.
(d) None of the above

50. Hardly I had opened the window when a stream of cool breeze started rushing in.
(a) Hardly I had opened the window then ....
(b) Hardly had I opened the window when ....
(c) Hardly had I opened the window then ....
(d) None of the above

51. He is one of the greatest player who has participated in one day cricket matches.
(a) He is one of the greatest players who has ......
(b) He is one of the greatest players who have ......
(c) He is one of the greatest player who have ......
(d) None of the above

52. Neither she laughed nor I did.
(a) Neither she laughed nor did I.
(b) Neither she laughed did nor I.
(c) Neither she laughed I did nor.
(d) None of the above

53. Deepak alongwith his aunts were present in the party.
(a) Deepak alongwith his aunts were present in the parties.
(b) Deepak alongwith his aunts was present in the party.
(c) Deepak alongwith his aunt were present in the party.
(d) No error.

54. The white and the black dog is dead.
(a) The white and black dog are dead.
(b) The white and the black dog are dead.
(c) The white and blacks dog are dead.
(d) None of the above

55. The painter and poet are dead.
(a) The painter and the poet is dead.
(b) The painter and poets are dead.
(c) The painter and poet is dead.
(d) None of the above

56. The committee has announced their decision.
(a) The committees has announced their decision.
(b) The committee has announced its decision.
(c) The committee have announced its decision.
(d) None of the above

57. I wish I am a millionaire.
(a) I wish I was a millionaire.
(b) I wish I are a millionaire.
(c) I wish I were a millionaire.
(d) None of the above

58. A large number of students is absent.
(a) A large numbers of students is absent.
(b) A large number of students are absent.
(c) A large number of student is absent.
(d) None of the above

59. Walking on the road, I met one of my old friends.
(a) When I was walking on the road, I met one of my old friend.
(b) When I was walking on the road, I met one of my old friends.
(c) Walking on the road, I met one of my friend.
(d) None of the above

60. Our only guide were the stars.
(a) Our only guide were the star.
(b) Our only guides was the star.
(c) Our only guide was the stars.
(d) None of the above

61. Many a girls have gone to see the movie.
(a) Many a girl have gone to see the movie.
(b) Many a girls has went to see the movies.
(c) Many a girl has gone to see the movie.
(d) None of the above

62. Either he or she has done his work.
(a) Either he or she has done their work.
(b) Either he or she has done her work.
(c) Either he or she has done their work.
(d) None of the above

63. A hundred miles are a high distance.
(a) A hundred miles are a big distance.
(b) A hundred miles are a long distance.
(c) A hundred mile is a long distance.
(d) None of the above

64. 'A Tale of Two Cities' were written by Charles Dickens.
(a) 'A Tale of Two Cities' was written by Charles Dickens.
(b) 'A Tale of Two Cities' is wrote by Charles Dickens.
(c) 'A Tale of Two Cities' are wrote by Charles Dickens.
(d) None of the above

65. Many a boys were playing in the garden.
(a) Many a boy were playing in the garden.
(b) Many a boys was playing in the garden.
(c) Many a boy was playing in the garden.
(d) None of the above

Directions (Q. Nos. 66-100) In the following questions, find out which part of the sentence has an error.

66. He ordered (a)/ as if he (b)/ was my master. (c)/ No error (d)

67. God (a)/ saves (b)/ the queen Victoria. (c)/ No error (d)

68. If it was so (a)/ poetry (b)/ would cease to matter. (c)/ No error (d)

69. The merit (a)/ of these books (b)/ are known to everyone. (c)/ No error (d)

70. The condition of (a)/ people living in (b)/ rural area (c)/ are very bad. (d)

71. The smell (a)/of these rose (b)/ flowers are (c)/ very sweet. (d)

72. The condolence messages (a)/ received on the (b)/ death of Mrs. Gandhi (c)/ speaks highly of her greatness. (d)

73. Economic cooperation (a)/ between the two countries (b)/ have increased substantially. (c)

74. A band of musicians (a)/ have been engaged (b)/ for the inaugural function. (c)

75. The number (a)/ of persons interested (b)/in psychology are (c)/generally small. (d)

76. The manager's comments (a)/on the preparation of the test matches (b)/ for this tour (c)/ has been generally praised. (d)

77. The details (a)/of the incident (b)/was not known (c)/to me. (d)

78. The majority of (a)/writers never (b)/passes this stage. (c)/ No error (d)

79. A large part of (a)/the distinctive features (b)/of the mind is due to its being (c)/ an instrument of communication. (d)

80. A part of (a)/the mango (b)/are rotten. (c)No error (d)

81. A part of (a)/the mangoes (b)/are rather. (c)/ No error (d)

82. The governing body at (a)/its first meeting (b)/ have decided (c)/to conduct the test again. (d)

83. Neither of them (a) are going to attend (b) the party on 10th October (c) / No error (d)

84. Five quintals of wooden coal (a)/are (b)/his annual requirement (c)/for the unit. (d)

85. Dickens have criticised (a)/the philosophy (b)/in'Hard Times'. (c)/ No error (d)

86. All his money (a)/is spent (b) /and all his (c)/hopes ruined.(d)

87. Every woman in the world (a)/ fervently hope that her child (b)/ will be normal and healthy baby. (c)/ No error (d)

88. Neither of them (a)/ sent his papers (b)/ in time for the last seminar (c)/ No error (d)

89. Many a students (a)/ participated (b)/ in the competition. (c)/ No error (d)

90. Every (a)/Tom, Dick and Harry (b)/drink wine these days. (c)

91. He and I (a)/is partners in (b)/this firm. (c)

92. Shivangi never (a)/ has and never will allow (b)/ her brother to join army. (c)/ No error (d)

93. The magistrate and collector (a)/were (b)/present there (c)/on the spot. (d)

94. Horse and Carriage (a)/are (b)/ waiting there (c)/for the couple. (d)

95. Rice and fish (a)/are (b)/my favourite dish. (c)

Answers

Exercise 1

1 (b)	2 (a)	3 (c)	4 (a)	5 (d)	6 (b)	7 (b)	8 (a)	9 (c)	10 (d)
11 (b)	12 (b)	13 (c)	14 (b)	15 (a)	16 (a)	17 (b)	18 (d)	19 (b)	20 (c)
21 (a)	22 (a)	23 (d)	24 (a)	25 (a)	26 (a)	27 (c)	28 (c)	29 (a)	30 (c)
31 (a)	32 (a)	33 (b)	34 (a)	35 (c)	36 (b)	37 (b)	38 (c)	39 (a)	40 (c)
41 (b)	42 (b)	43 (c)	44 (b)	45 (a)					

Exercise 2

1 (c)	2 (b)	3 (b)	4 (a)	5 (c)	6 (d)	7 (b)	8 (b)	9 (a)	10 (c)
11 (b)	12 (b)	13 (c)	14 (a)	15 (a)	16 (b)	17 (b)	18 (d)	19 (a)	20 (b)
21 (b)	22 (c)	23 (b)	24 (a)	25 (b)	26 (a)	27 (b)	28 (c)	29 (b)	30 (a)
31 (a)	32 (d)	33 (a)	34 (d)	35 (c)	36 (b)	37 (a)	38 (b)	39 (a)	40 (b)
41 (c)	42 (b)	43 (c)	44 (b)	45 (b)	46 (c)	47 (a)	48 (c)	49 (b)	50 (b)
51 (b)	52 (a)	53 (b)	54 (b)	55 (c)	56 (b)	57 (c)	58 (b)	59 (b)	60 (c)
61 (c)	62 (b)	63 (c)	64 (a)	65 (c)	66 (c)	67 (b)	68 (a)	69 (c)	70 (d)
71 (c)	72 (d)	73 (c)	74 (b)	75 (c)	76 (d)	77 (c)	78 (c)	79 (c)	80 (c)
81 (d)	82 (c)	83 (b)	84 (b)	85 (a)	86 (d)	87 (b)	88 (d)	89 (a)	90 (c)
91 (b)	92 (b)	93 (b)	94 (b)	95 (b)					

Explanations

Exercise-2

66. *(c)* was की जगह 'were' आएगा। जब sentence में कल्पना (Imaginations) का भाव हो, तो singular subject के साथ 'were' का प्रयोग होता है।

67. *(b)* saves की जगह save आएगा। ऐसे वाक्य जिनमें कोई इच्छा (desire), अभिलाषा (wish) या आशीर्वाद (blessing) का भाव हो तो verbs; bless, live, save एवं help हमेशा plural में आती है अर्थात् इनके साथ s नहीं लगता है।

68. *(a)* यहाँ was की जगह 'were' आएगा। 'If it was so' reflects imaginations.

69. *(c)* 'are' की जगह 'is' आएगा। यहाँ subject 'merit' है, जो singular है अत: verb singular होगी।

70. *(d)* 'are' की जगह 'is' आएगा। यहाँ subject of the verb, condition है जो singular है। अत: verb भी singular होगी।

71. *(c)* 'are' की जगह 'is' लिखें। यहाँ subject of the verb is 'The smell' which is singular अत: verb (is) भी singular ही लगेगी।

72. *(d)* speaks की जगह speak आएगा verb (speak) का subject, 'condolence messages' plural है अत: verb, plural use होगी।

73. *(c)* 'have' की जगह 'has' आएगा subject economic cooperation singular है। अत: verb भी singular होगा।

74. *(b)* have been की जगह has been आएगा। 'A band of musicians' collective noun है जिसके साथ singular verb का प्रयोग होगा।

75. *(c)* 'are' की जगह 'is' आएगा। 'The number' एक निश्चित संख्या को बताता है, अत: इसके साथ हमेशा singular verb का प्रयोग किया जाता है।

76. *(d)* 'has been' की जगह 'have been' आएगा। Sentence का subject, 'manager's comments plural है अत: verb भी plural use होगी।

77. *(c)* 'was' की जगह were आएगा। Subject of the sentence—'The details, plural है। अत: verb भी plural (were) use होगी।

78. *(c)* passes की जगह pass आएगा। यहाँ 'of' के बाद जो noun आया है, वह plural (writers) है, अत: verb भी plural ही रहेगी।

79. *(c)* यहाँ 'mind is due' की जगह mind are due आएगा।

80. *(c)* 'are' की जगह 'is' लिखें। Sentence का subject (A part of the mango) singular है, अत: verb भी singular लगेगी।

81. *(d)* No error.

82. *(c)* have की जगह has लिखें क्योंकि governing body, collective noun है अत: collective nouns के साथ verb singular use होती है।

83. *(b)* यहाँ 'are' के स्थान पर 'is' का use किया जाएगा। 'Neither of' के बाद आने वाला Noun/Pronoun plural होता है लेकिन verb singular use की जाती है।

84. *(b)* 'are' की जगह 'is' लिखें 'five quintals एक निश्चित weight को व्यक्त करता है जो collective noun की तरह singular noun का बोध कराता है, अत: verb singular (is) ही लगेगी।

85. *(a)* have की जगह has लगेगा। Dickens एक व्यक्ति का नाम है, जो की singular subject को belong करता है।

86. *(d)* hopes के बाद 'are' insert करें। जब वाक्य में पहले आने वाली verb (यहाँ 'is') दूसरे noun के number एवं person से मेल नहीं खाती है, तो दूसरे noun के अनुसार अलग से verb का प्रयोग होता है। Hopes, plural है अत: यहाँ plural verb 'are' का use किया जाएगा।

87. *(b)* यहाँ part (b) के अनतर्गत 'hope' के स्थान पर 'hopes' का use किया जाएगा। 'Every woman' takes singular verb so, verb also used in plural form.

88. *(d)* No error.

89. *(a)* 'Many a' के साथ singular subject का use किया जाता है इसलिए यहाँ 'students' के स्थान पर 'student' का use किया जाता है।

90. *(c)* drink की जगह drinks आएगा। Every, Each के साथ इस तरह के वाक्यों में singular verb लगती है।

91. *(b)* 'is' की जगह 'are' आएगा। जब दो nouns को and से जोड़ा जाता है तो verb, plural आती है।

92. *(b)* यहाँ part (b) के अन्तर्गत 'has' के बाद 'allowed' का use किया जाएगा। In a compound sentence both auxiliary verbs and principal verbs should be mentioned separately if they differ in number, form or voice. In such cases, one verb can't act for both the clauses.

93. *(b)* were की जगह 'was' लिखें। यहाँ magistrate एवं collector एक ही व्यक्ति को refer करते हैं। इसलिए singular verb का use किया जाएगा।

94. *(b)* 'are' की जगह 'is' लिखें। Horse and carriage जोड़े की तरह एक ही वस्तु का ज्ञान कराते हैं। अत: verb singular लगेगी।

95. *(b)* are की जगह 'is' लिखें Rice and fish एक pair की तरह, एक चीज का ही संकेत करते हैं। अत: verb, singular लगेगी।

03 Transformation of Sentences

A. Direct-Indirect

किसी व्यक्ति द्वारा कही गई बात को हम दो प्रकार से व्यक्त कर सकते हैं

1. बोलने वाले के शब्दों को बिल्कुल वैसे ही प्रस्तुत करके जैसे उसके द्वारा कहा गया है।
2. बोलने वाले के शब्दों को उस तरह न बोलकर अर्थात् उस बात को अपने शब्दों में प्रस्तुत करके।

Direct Speech प्रत्यक्ष कथन

जब किसी व्यक्ति द्वारा कही गई बात को अन्य व्यक्ति द्वारा बिल्कुल वैसे ही प्रस्तुत किया जाता है जैसे उसके द्वारा कही गई है, तो इस प्रकार कहने के ढंग को direct speech कहा जाता है। Direct speech में व्यक्ति द्वारा कही गई बात को inverted commas (" ") के अन्दर तथा पहला अक्षर Capital letter से लिखा जाता है।

e.g., (i) Krishna said, "I am a teacher."
(ii) Raman says, "Tushar plays cricket very well."

Direct speech के निम्नलिखित दो भाग होते हैं

(i) **Reporting Clause** वाक्य में inverted commas (" ") से पहले का भाग reporting clause कहलाता है, जिसमें subject, verb तथा object होते हैं। वाक्य में प्रयुक्त subject को speaker or reporter (बोलने वाला), verb को reporting verb तथा object को listener (सुनने वाला) कहा जाता है।

(ii) **Reported Clause** वाक्य में inverted commas (" ") के अन्दर का भाग reported clause कहलाता है, जिसमें speaker द्वारा कहा गया कथन (Statement) होता है।

e.g. Rohan said to his father, "I want to purchase a car."
उपरोक्त वाक्य में 'Rohan' — speaker or reporter, 'said' –reporting verb, 'his father'–listener तथा "I want to purchase a car." –reported clause है।

Indirect Speech अप्रत्यक्ष कथन

जब किसी व्यक्ति द्वारा कही गई बात को कोई अन्य व्यक्ति उस तरह न बोलकर अपने शब्दों में प्रस्तुत करता है, तो इस प्रकार कहने के ढंग को indirect speech कहा जाता है। Indirect speech में inverted commas का प्रयोग नहीं किया जाता परन्तु reported clause से पहले that का प्रयोग किया जाता है।

e.g. Rohan said to his father, "I want to purchase a car." (Direct)
Rohan told his father that he wanted to purchase a car. (Indirect)

Direct Speech से Indirect Speech में परिवर्तन के नियम

Direct speech से Indirect speech बनाते समय निम्नलिखित परिवर्तन किए जाते हैं

Reporting Verb में होने वाले परिवर्तन

Rule 1

यदि reporting verb केवल says, say, said, will say अथवा shall say है, तब indirect speech में परिवर्तित करते समय reporting verb में कोई परिवर्तन नहीं होता।

e.g. (i) He says, "I am a singer." (Direct)
He says that he is a singer. (Indirect)
(ii) She said, "My father is an engineer." (Direct)
She said that her father was an engineer. (Indirect)

Rule 2

यदि reporting verb, says to, say to, said to, will say to अथवा shall say to है, तब indirect speech बनाते समय reporting verb को क्रमश: tells, tell, told, will tell एवं shall tell में परिवर्तित कर दिया जाता है।

e.g. (i) Hari said to me, "You are a good boy." (Direct)
Hari told me that I was a good boy. (Indirect)
(ii) My father says to me, "You are a good player." (Direct)
My father tells me that I am a good player. (Indirect)

Reported Clause के Verb (Tense) में होने वाले परिवर्तन

Rule 1

यदि reporting verb, Present tense में या Future tense में हो, तो reported clause के verb में कोई परिवर्तन नहीं होता।

e.g. (i) She says to me, "You are a handsome boy." (Direct)
She tells me that I am a handsome boy. (Indirect)
(ii) I shall say to her, " He has an umbrella." (Direct)
I shall tell her that he has an umbrella. (Indirect)

Rule 2

यदि reporting verb, Past tense में हो, तो reported clause के verb (tense) में निम्नलिखित परिवर्तन होते हैं

(a) Present Indefinite —changes into→ Past Indefinite
(s/es) (IInd form of verb)

e.g. (i) I said, "He eats mangoes." (Direct)
I said that he ate mangoes. (Indirect)

(ii) My mother said, "They work very hard." (Direct)
My mother said that they worked very hard. (Indirect)

(b) Present Continuous —changes into→ Past Continuous
(is/am/are + verb + ing) (was/were + verb + ing)

e.g. (i) Rahul said, "I am dancing." (Direct)
Rahul said that he was dancing. (Indirect)

(ii) He said, "They are playing." (Direct)
He said that they were playing. (Indirect)

(c) Present Perfect —changes into→ Past Perfect
(has/have + IIIrd form of verb) (had + IIIrd form of verb)

e.g. (i) She said, "I have sung a song." (Direct)
She said that she had sung a song. (Indirect)

(ii) Bharti said to me, "You have danced very well." (Direct)
Bharti told me that I had danced very well. (Indirect)

(d) Present Perfect Continuous —changes into→ Past Perfect Continuous
(has/have been + verb + ing) (had been + verb + ing)

e.g. (i) Amar said to her, "We have been working hard since morning." (Direct)
Amar told her that they had been working hard since morning. (Indirect)

(ii) My mother said to me, "You have been playing for two hours." (Direct)
My mother told me that I had been playing for two hours. (Indirect)

(e) Past Indefinite —changes into→ Past Perfect
(IInd form of verb) (had + IIIrd form of verb)

e.g. (i) He said, "I played guitar." (Direct)
He said that he had played guitar. (Indirect)

(ii) She said to me, "I bought a black dress." (Direct)
She told me that she had bought a black dress. (Indirect)

(f) Past Continuous —changes into→ Past Perfect Continuous
(was/were + verb + ing) (had been + verb + ing)

e.g. (i) I said, "He was writing a letter." (Direct)
I said that he had been writing a letter. (Indirect)

(ii) My father said, "They were going to market." (Direct)
My father said that they had been going to market. (Indirect)

(g) Past Perfect —no change→ Past Perfect
(had + IIIrd form of verb) (had + IIIrd form of verb)

e.g. (i) I said, "He had played football." (Direct)
I said that he had played football. (Indirect)

(ii) He said to me, "I had seen the Taj Mahal". (Direct)
He told me that he had seen the Taj Mahal. (Indirect)

(h) Past Perfect Continuous —no change→ Past Perfect Continuous
(had been + verb + ing) (had been + verb + ing)

e.g.(i) My sister said, "I had been watching TV for two hours." (Direct)
My sister said that she had been watching TV for two hours. (Indirect)

(ii) She said to me, "I had been dancing for five years." (Direct)
She told me that she had been dancing for five years. (Indirect)

(i) Future Tense —changes into→ Future का ही Past equivalent
(चारों रूप)

(will + Ist form of verb/shall + Ist form of verb/will be + verb ceW ing/will have + IIIrd form of verb/will have been + verb ceW ing) (would + Ist form of verb/should + Ist form of verb/would be + verb ceW ing/would have + IIIrd form of verb/would have been + verb ceW ing)

e.g. (i) He said to me, "You will teach her." (Direct)
He told me that I would teach her. (Indirect)

(ii) My brother said to me, "She will be playing in the ground." (Direct)
My brother told me that she would be playing in the ground. (Indirect)

(j) अन्य परिवर्तन

Do/Does ⟶ Did

Can ⟶ Could

May ⟶ Might

Did not + Ist form of verb ⟶ had not + IIIrd form of verb

was/were + IIIrd form of verb ⟶ had been + IIIrd form of verb

Should ⟶ Should

Must ⟶ Must

To go ⟶ To go

e.g. (i) The teacher said to the principal, "They do not study." (Direct)
The teacher told the principal that they did not study. (Indirect)
(ii) The doctor said to me, "You can walk." (Direct)
The doctor told me that I could walk. (Indirect)
(iii) My mother said, "You may go outside." (Direct)
My mother said that you might go outside. (Indirect)
(iv) She said to me, "You must work hard. (Direct)
She told me that I must work hard. (Indirect)

Rule 3

यदि reported clause में कोई सदैव सत्य रहने वाली बात (Universal truth), स्वभाव (आदत) से सम्बन्धित तथ्य या past में हुआ कोई ऐतिहासिक तथ्य (Historical fact) बताया गया हो, तो indirect speech बनाते समय उसके tense में कोई परिवर्तन नहीं होता।

e.g. (i) The teacher said to the students, "The Moon moves round the Earth." (Direct)
The teacher told the students that the Moon moves round the Earth. (Indirect)
(ii) He said, "Jawaharlal Nehru was the first Prime Minister of India." (Direct)
He said that Jawaharlal Nehru was the first Prime Minister of India. (Indirect)

Rule 4

यदि past में किसी एक ही समय पर एक साथ दो कार्य हो रहे हों, तो indirect speech बनाते समय उनके tense में कोई परिवर्तन नहीं होता।

e.g. (i) She said to me, "When we went out, it started raining." (Direct)
She told me that when they went out, it started raining. (Indirect)
(ii) He said, "When she reached the party, the light had gone." (Direct)
He said that when she reached the party, the light had gone.(Indirect)

Pronoun में होने वाले परिवर्तन

Pronoun में निम्नलिखित प्रकार से परिवर्तन किए जाते हैं

Person	Subjective Case	Objective Case	Possessive Case
First	I	Me	My, Mine
	We	Us	Our, Ours
Second	You	You	Your, Yours
Third	He	Him	His
	She	Her	Her, Hers
	It	It	Its
	They	Them	Their, Theirs

Reported clause के pronoun (subjective case/objective case) में परिवर्तन reporting clause के speaker (subject) एवं listener (object) के अनुसार होते हैं।

Rule 1

Reported clause के First person के pronouns सदैव speaker (subject) के person, gender और number के अनुसार बदलते हैं।

e.g. (i) Mohan said, "I write a letter. (Direct)
Mohan said that he wrote a letter. (Indirect)
(ii) Kiran said to me, "I am going to market with my mother." (Direct)
Kiran told me that she was going to market with her mother. (Indirect)

उपरोक्त वाक्य (i) में reported clause के I को Mohan (subject) के अनुसार he में बदला गया है तथा वाक्य (ii) में reported clause और I के my को Kiran (subject) के अनुसार she व her में बदला गया है।

Rule 2

Reported clause के Second person के pronouns सदैव listener (object) के person, gender और number के अनुसार बदलते हैं।

e.g. (i) He said to me, "You are a good boy." (Direct)
He told me that I was a good boy. (Indirect)
(ii) Rohan said to Prince, "You are a good singer." (Direct)
Rohan told Prince that he was a good singer. (Indirect)

उपरोक्त वाक्य (i) में reported clause के you को me (object) के अनुसार I में बदला गया है तथा वाक्य (ii) में reported clause के you को Prince (object) के अनुसार he में बदला गया है।

Rule 3

Reported clause के Third person के pronouns में कोई change नहीं होता।

e.g. (i) I said to him, "She was playing Tennis." (Direct)
I told him that she had been playing Tennis. (Indirect)
(ii) He said to her, "They are going to Lucknow." (Direct)
He told her that they were going to Lucknow. (Indirect)

Note

Reporting clause में object (listener) न होने पर third person के pronoun को ही object मान लिया जाता है reported clause में उसी के अनुसार परिवर्तन किए जाते हैं।

e.g. The teacher said, "You will be punished." (Direct)
The teacher said that he/she/they would be punished. (Indirect)

Time or Place में होने वाले परिवर्तन

Reporting verb के Past tense में होने पर reported clause में दिए गए time or place को दर्शाने वाले शब्दों में *निम्नलिखित प्रकार से परिवर्तन किए जाते हैं*

Direct Speech	Indirect Speech	Direct Speech	Indirect Speech
This	That	These	Those
Here	There	Now	Then
Ago	Before, Earlier	Thus	So, In that way
Come	Go	Hence	Thence
Hither	Thither	Today	That day
Tomorrow	The next day	Yesterday	The previous day
Tonight	That night	Last night	The previous night
Last week	The previous week	Last month	The previous month
Next week	The following week	Next month	The following month

Rule 1

जब Come के बाद कोई समीपता दिखाने वाला शब्द प्रयुक्त हुआ हो, तब come को go में बदल दिया जाता है।

e.g. (i) He said to me, "He is coming here." (Direct)
He told me that he was going there. (Indirect)

(ii) She asked me, "Come here". (Direct)
She asked me to go there. (Indirect)

Rule 2

जब this तथा here किसी ऐसी वस्तु, समय तथा स्थान की ओर संकेत करते हैं, जो बात करते समय speaker के सामने हो, तो indirect speech बनाते समय इनमें कोई परिवर्तन नहीं होता।

e.g. (i) She said, "This is my home." (Direct)
She said that this was her home. (Indirect)

(ii) Rohan said to me, "I have no time to talk to you here". (Direct)
Rohan told me that he had no time to talk to me here. (Indirect)

Interrogative Sentences में होने वाले परिवर्तन

Rule 1

यदि reported clause, auxiliary verbs (is, am, are, was, were, do, does, did, will, can, could, may, might, आदि) से प्रारम्भ हो, तो निम्नलिखित नियमों का पालन किया जाता है

(a) Say/said to को ask/asked में बदल देते हैं तथा कभी-कभी ask/asked के स्थान पर enquire/enquired या interrogate/ interrogated का भी प्रयोग किया जाता है।

(b) Conjunction 'that' का प्रयोग नहीं किया जाता बल्कि if/whether का प्रयोग किया जाता है।

(c) Reported clause को interrogative sentence से उसके assertive sentence में बदल देते हैं।

(d) वाक्य के अन्त में question mark (?) के स्थान पर full stop (.) का प्रयोग किया जाता है।

e.g. (i) Neelam said, "Are you mad?" (Direct)
Neelam asked if he/she was mad. (Indirect)

(ii) Kapil said to his mother, "Can I go to market with my friends?" (Direct)
Kapil asked his mother if he could go to market with his friends. (Indirect)

Rule 2

यदि reported clause, question words (what, why, where, who, when, which) आदि से प्रारम्भ हो, तो निम्नलिखित नियमों का पालन किया जाता है

(a) Say/said to को ask/asked में बदल देते हैं तथा कभी-कभी ask/asked के स्थान पर enquire/enquired या interrogate/ interrogated का भी प्रयोग किया जाता है।

(b) Conjunction 'that' के स्थान पर if/whether का प्रयोग नहीं किया जाता बल्कि direct speech में प्रयुक्त question word का ही प्रयोग किया जाता है तथा उसके बाद subject को लिखा जाता है।

(c) Reported clause को interrogative sentence से उसके assertive sentence में बदल देते हैं।

(d) वाक्य के अन्त में question mark (?) के स्थान पर full stop (.) का प्रयोग किया जाता है।

e.g. (i) I said to my father, "What did you do?" (Direct)
I asked my father what he had done. (Indirect)

(ii) I said to my brother, "Where were you going yesterday?" (Direct)
I asked my brother where he had been going the previous day. (Indirect)

Imperative Sentences में होने वाले परिवर्तन

Rule 1

(a) Said to के स्थान पर commanded, ordered, requested, suggested, advised, आदि शब्दों का भाव के अनुसार प्रयोग किया जाता है।

(b) Conjunction 'that' का प्रयोग नहीं किया जाता बल्कि to का प्रयोग किया जाता है।

(c) प्रार्थनासूचक वाक्यों में requested का प्रयोग करके Please, Kindly, Sir, Madam, आदि शब्दों को हटा दिया जाता है।

e.g. (i) I said to him, "Please, help me." (Direct)
I requested him to help me. (Indirect)

(ii) The teacher said to the boy, "Leave the class". (Direct)
The teacher ordered the boy to leave the class. (Indirect)

Rule 2

Negative sentence बनाते समय Do not के स्थान पर not to का प्रयोग किया जाता है अथवा said to को forbade में बदलकर not का प्रयोग नहीं किया जाता, केवल to का प्रयोग किया जाता है।

e.g. (i) The monitor said to us, "Do not make a noise." (Direct)
The monitor ordered us not to make a noise. (Indirect)
Or The monitor forbade us to make a noise. (Indirect)

(ii) He said to me, "Don't be lazy for your targets". (Direct)

He advised me not to be lazy for my targets. (Indirect)

Or He forbade me to be lazy for my targets. (Indirect)

'Let' से प्रारम्भ होने वाले Sentences में परिवर्तन

Rule 1

(a) Said to के स्थान पर proposed, advised, commanded, suggested, ordered, declared, आदि शब्दों का वाक्य के भाव के अनुसार प्रयोग किया जाता है।

(b) Conjunction 'that' का प्रयोग किया जाता है तथा reported clause में should का प्रयोग करते हैं।

e.g. (i) He said, "Let us sing". (Direct)

He proposed/suggested that we/they should sing. (Indirect)

(ii) She said to me, "Let us visit the India Gate." (Direct)

She proposed me that we/they should visit the India Gate. (Indirect)

Rule 2

Order या request की दशा में said to के स्थान पर ordered या requested का प्रयोग होता है परन्तु inverted commas (" ") को हटाकर to let का प्रयोग करते हैं।

e.g. (i) The officer said to his guards, "Let the crowd move away." (Direct)

The officer ordered his guards to let the crowd move away. (Indirect)

(ii) The principal said to the manager, "Let him go early." (Direct)

The principal requested the manager to let him go early. (Indirect)

Exclamatory Sentences में होने वाले परिवर्तन

Rule 1

(a) Said to के स्थान पर exclaimed, prayed, applauded, wished, cried out शब्दों तथा इनके साथ with joy, with surprise, with sorrow, with regret, आदि शब्दों का वाक्य के भाव के अनुसार प्रयोग किया जाता है।

(b) Conjunction 'that' का प्रयोग किया जाता है।

(c) What एवं how को हटाकर very या great का प्रयोग किया जाता है।

(d) वाक्य के अन्त में exclamation mark (!) को हटाकर full stop (.) का प्रयोग किया जाता है।

e.g. (i) He said, "Hurrah! We have won". (Direct)

He exclaimed with joy that they had won. (Indirect)

(ii) He said, "Alas! We can't be successful". (Direct)

He exclaimed with sorrow that they couldn't be successful. (Indirect)

(iii) They said, "How nonsense you are!" (Direct)

They exclaimed with surprise that I was very nonsense. (Indirect)

(iv) He said to me, "May you be successful in your life!". (Direct)

He wished that I might be successful in my life. (Indirect)

Note

यदि reported clause में Good morning, Good bye, Good night, आदि हो, तो indirect speech बनाते समय said to के स्थान पर 'bade' का प्रयोग करते हैं तथा Conjunction 'that' का प्रयोग नहीं किया जाता।

e.g. (i) She said to me, "Good bye". (Direct)

She bade me good bye. (Indirect)

(ii) Prabhas said to her wife, "Good night dear!" (Direct)

Prabhas bade her wife good night. (Indirect)

Exercise

Directions (1-100) Change the following sentences into direct/indirect narration.

1. Ramesh informed his friend that he could make use of his car while he was away.
(a) Ramesh said to his friend, "You will make use of my car while I was away".
(b) Ramesh said to his friend, "Use my car while I go away".
(c) Ramesh said to his friend, "You can make use of my car while I am away".
(d) Ramesh asked his friend, "Will you make use of my car while I am away?".

2. Kala said to Radha, "Who were you speaking to over the phone?"
(a) Kala asked Radha who she had been speaking to over the phone.
(b) Kala asked Radha who she has been speaking to over the phone.
(c) Kala asked Radha that who she was speaking to over the phone.
(d) Kala asked Radha that who she had been speaking to over the phone.

3. She said, "I'm going shopping. Can I get you something?"
(a) She said she was going shopping and said to me if I wanted something.
(b) She said she was going shopping and asked if I wanted something.
(c) She said she was going shopping and asked if she could get me something.
(d) She said she is going shopping and asked if she could get me something.

4. The girl wondered where the sparrows had gone.
(a) The girl said, "Oh !Where the sparrows have gone?"
(b) The girl said "Oh !Where are the sparrows?"
(c) The girl said, "Oh ! Where had the sparrows gone?"
(d) The girl said, "Oh ! Where have the sparrows gone?"

5. She said, "I am sorry, I am not able to submit those papers."
(a) She said she was sorry, she is not able to submit those papers.
(b) She said that she was sorry and she will not be able to submit those papers.
(c) She apologised for not being able to submit those papers.
(d) She exclaimed with sorrow that she was sorry and she will not be able to submit those papers.

6. The boys respectfully wished their teacher good morning.
(a) "Good morning," said the boys to their teacher.
(b) "Good morning," said the boys to the teacher.
(c) "Good morning Madam" said the boys to the teacher.
(d) "Good morning, Madam", said the boys to his teacher.

7. Mr Robinson asked his son what he wanted to be when he grew up.
(a) "My son," said Mr Robinson, "What will you be when you grow up?"
(b) "My son," said Mr Robinson, "What do you want to be when you grow up?"
(c) "Mr Robinson said," "My son, what did you want to be when you grew up?"
(d) Mr Robinson said, "My son, what would you be when you grow up?

8. My uncle said, "I will be here again tomorrow."
(a) My uncle said that he would be here again tomorrow.
(b) My uncle said that he would be there again the next day.
(c) My uncle said that he would be here again the next day.
(d) My uncle said that I will be here again tomorrow.

9. She asked me, "How is your father?"
(a) She asked me how was my father?
(b) She asked him how my father is?
(c) She asked how father was?
(d) She asked me how my father was?

10. Rakesh said to his boss, "Please allow me to do the presentation."
(a) Rakesh requested his boss to allow him to do the presentation.
(b) Rakesh requested his boss to please allow him to do the presentation.
(c) Rakesh requested his boss to let him to do the presentation.
(d) Rakesh said to his boss to please allow him to do the presentation.

11. The boss said to his secretary, "Did you discuss this matter with the manager?"
(a) The boss asked his secretary whether he discussed that matter with the manager.
(b) The boss asked his secretary If you have discussed that matter with the manager.
(c) The boss asked his secretary if he had discussed that matter with the manager.
(d) The boss asked his secretary whether he has discussed that matter with the manager.

12. Kannan said to Subha, "I'll return the book after I have read it."
(a) Kannan told Subha that he will return the book after he has read it.
(b) Kannan told Subha that he would return the book after he has read it.
(c) Kannan told Subha that he will return the book after he read it.
(d) Kannan told Subha that he would return the book after he had read it.

13. Mohan's father asked him, "Have you passed the examination?"
(a) Mohan's father asked him whether he had passed the examination.
(b) Mohan was asked by his father about passing the examination.
(c) His father asked Mohan had he passed the examination.
(d) Mohan's father asked did he pass the examination.

14. Nita said to the teacher, "Could you please repeat the question?"
(a) Nita requested the teacher whether she could please repeat the question.
(b) Nita asked the teacher whether, if she could repeat the question.
(c) Nita requested the teacher to repeat the question.
(d) Nita asked the teacher, if please she could repeat the question.

15. He said to me, "Is there any possibility of my getting promotion this year?"
(a) He asked me if there was any possibility of my getting promotion this year?
(b) He asked me if there was any possibility of his getting promotion this year?
(c) He asked me if there was any possibility of his getting promotion that year?"
(d) He asked me if there is any possibility of his getting It promotion this year?

16. He said, "I do not wish to see any of you, go away."
(a) He said that he had not wished to see any of them and ordered them to go away.
(b) He said that he did not wish to see any of them and ordered them to go away.
(c) He told that he did not wish to see any of them and ordered them to go away.
(d) He said that he does not wish to see any of us and ordered us to go away.

17. "When will I be able to vote?", I asked my mother.
(a) I asked my mother when would he be able to vote.
(b) I asked to my mother when I will be able to vote.
(c) I asked my mother when I would be able to vote.
(d) I asked my mother when would I be able to vote.

18. The dealer said, "Either make your purchases or walk out of my shop."
(a) The dealer told the customer that he would either make his purchases or walk out of his shop.
(b) The dealer ordered the customer to make his purchases and walk out of his shop.
(c) The dealer told the customer that he should either make his purchases or walk out of his shop.
(d) The dealer requested the customer to make his purchases or walk out of his shop.

19. He said to us, "Why are you all sitting about there doing nothing?"
(a) He asked us why are we all sitting about there doing nothing.
(b) He asked us why we are all sitting about there doing nothing.
(c) He asked us why we were all sitting about there doing nothing.
(d) He asked us why were we all sitting about there doing nothing.

20. I said, "Father, when will you buy me a motor cycle?"
(a) I asked my father when will he buy me a motor cycle.
(b) I asked my father when he will buy me a motor cycle.
(c) I asked my father when would he buy me a motor cycle.
(d) I asked my father when he would buy me a motor cycle.

21. He said to me, "You are getting lazy day by day."
(a) He informed me that I am getting lazy day by day".
(b) He told me that I have been getting lazy day by day.
(c) He told me that I was getting lazy day by day.
(d) He told me that you were getting lazy day by day.

22. The lady said to the servant, "If you don't wash the clothes properly, I will dismiss you."
(a) The lady warned the servant that she would dismiss her if she didn't wash the clothes properly.
(b) The lady told the servant that she would dismiss her on the event of bad work.
(c) The lady cautioned the servant that she must wash the clothes properly.
(d) The lady advised the se[illegible]t to wash the clothes properly.

23. The teacher said to the student, "Why do you disturb the class?"
(a) The teacher said to the student why he disturbed the class.
(b) The teacher told the student why he had disturbed the class.
(c) The teacher asked the student why he disturbed the class.
(d) The teacher asked the student why he had disturbed the class.

24. Rita said to me, "Will you lend me this classic? Rita asked me
(a) if I would lend her that classic.
(b) if she would lend me that classic.
(c) if I will lend her that classic.
(d) would I lend her that classic.

25. The teacher said, "Gandhiji was born in India"
(a) The teacher said that Gandhiji had been born in India.
(b) The teacher says that Gandhiji was born in India.
(c) The teacher said that Gandhiji was born in India.
(d) The teacher will say that Gandhiji was born in India.

26. Would you open the door please?
(a) She asked me to please open the door.
(b) She requested me to open the door.
(c) She requested me to please open the door.
(d) She asked me open the door.

27. "There are ceremonies going on", he said to me.
(a) He told me that there were ceremonies going on.
(b) He told that there had been ceremonies going on.
(c) He told that there had been ceremonies going on.
(d) He told that there are ceremonies going on.

28. I said to my sister, "I brought you a doll yesterday."
(a) I told my sister that I brought you a doll the previous day.

(b) I told my sister that I had brought her a doll the previous day.
(c) I told my sister that I had brought her a doll yesterday.
(d) I told my sister that I brought her a doll yesterday.

29. The captain said to the army, "March forward, now."
(a) The captain said to the army that march forward now.
(b) The captain ordered the army to march forward then.
(c) To captain ordered the army to march on that day.
(d) The captain ordered the army to attack the enemy.

30. They said, "We've lived here for a long time."
(a) They said they have lived there for a long time.
(b) They said they lived here for a long time
(c) They said they had lived there for a long time.
(d) They said they have lived for a long time.

31. He asked me if I would like to have lunch with him that day.
(a) He said to me, "Can you have lunch with me today?"
(b) He said to me, "Would you like to have lunch with me today?"
(c) He said to me, "You can if you like to have lunch with me today."
(d) He said to me, "Do you like to have lunch with me today?"

32. The officer said, "Cowards! you shall soon be put to death."
(a) The officer said that they were cowards and should be put to death soon.
(b) The officer called them cowards and said that they would soon be put to death.
(c) The officer said that they would soon be put to death.
(d) The officer called them cowards and said that they must be put to death soon.

33. The commander said, "Let the gates be left open."
(a) The commander wanted that the gates be left open.
(b) The commander ordered that the gates will be left open.
(c) The commander ordered for the gates to be left open.
(d) The commander ordered that let the gates be left open.

34. "There is no need for you to be so angry" said Mrs Sen to her husband.
(a) Mrs Sen told to her husband that there was no need for his anger.
(b) Mrs Sen told her husband that no need was there to be so in anger.
(c) Mrs Sen told her husband that there was no need for him to be so angry.
(d) Mrs Sen told her husband to not be so angry.

35. He said to me, "Where are you going?"
(a) He said to me that where I was going.
(b) He asked that where I was going.
(c) He said me to where I was going.
(d) He asked me where I was going.

36. "Sam, will you help me carry my bags?" asked the old woman.
(a) The old woman asked Sam whether he would help her carry her bags.
(b) The old woman told Sam to helped her carry her bags.
(c) The old woman said to Sam to help her carried her bags.
(d) The old Woman asked to Sam to help her carry her bags.

37. My father said to me, "Will you sit and study at least now?"
(a) My father asked me whether I can sit and study at least then.
(b) My father asked me if I will sit and study at least then.
(c) My father asked me if I would sit and study at least then.
(d) My father required me if I would sit and study at least then.

38. Rahul said, "Yes I am mistaken."
(a) Rahul said that he was on mistake.
(b) Rahul admitted that I was mistaken.
(c) Rahul admitted that he was mistaken.
(d) Rahul said that he is mistaken.

39. Rajiv said to me, "He plays with right hand."
(a) Rajiv told me that he plays with right hand.
(b) Rajiv said that he played with right hand.
(c) Rajiv asked if he could play with right hand.
(d) Rajiv told me that he could play with right hand.

40. They are late, "she has already told us".
(a) She told us that they are late already.
(b) She has already been telling us that they are late.
(c) She told us that they are already late.
(d) She has already told us (that) they are late.

41. I said to my friend, "Can I borrow your dictionary for one day only?"
(a) I requested my friend if I can borrow his dictionary for one day only.
(b) I asked my friend if I might borrow his dictionary for one day only.
(c) I told my friend I could borrow his dictionary for one day only.
(d) I asked my friend if I could borrow his dictionary for one day only.

42. The teacher said to me, "I hope you will bring credit to my school."
(a) The teacher hoped that I would bring credit to his school.
(b) The teacher wished that I would bring credit to my school.
(c) The teacher said that I will bring credit to his school.
(d) The teacher desired that I bring credit to his school.

43. I said to my mother, "Please warm this milk. Don't boil it."
(a) I asked my mother that she may warm that milk but not boil it.
(b) I requested my mother that she warm that milk and not to boil it.
(c) I requested my mother to warm that milk and asked not to boil it.
(d) I told my mother respectfully that she will warm that milk and not to boil it.

44. "What an excellent piece of art!" she said.
(a) She exclaimed with appreciation that it was an excellent piece of art.

(b) She exclaimed what an excellent piece of art was it.
(c) She had exclaimed that it was an excellent piece of art.
(d) She exclaimed with surprise was it an excellent piece of art.

45. He said to his father, "Shall I go to market now?"
(a) He asked his father if he will go to market then.
(b) He asked his father if he shall go to market now.
(c) He asked his father if he would go to market then.
(d) He asked his father if he should go to market then.

46. The guide said to the swimmer, "Don't swim out too far."
(a) The guide asked the swimmer not swim out too far.
(b) The guide suggested the swimmer that don't swim out too far.
(c) The guide told the swimmer to not swim out too far.
(d) The guide forbade the swimmer to swim out too far.

47. The teacher said to his student, "Do you have any excuse for coming late to the school, today?"
(a) The teacher asked his student whether he has any excuse for coming late to the school that day.
(b) The teacher asked his student whether did he have any excuse for coming late to the school that day.
(c) The teacher asked his student whether he had any excuse for coming late to the school that day.
(d) The teacher asked his student whether he did have any excuse for coming late to the school that day.

48. The teacher said to him, "Do not go out."
(a) The teacher commanded him that he should not go out.
(b) The teacher advised him not to go out.
(c) The teacher told him do not go out.
(d) The teacher ordered him not to go out.

49. I'll say to my friends, "I have started learning computer."
(a) I'll tell my friends that I had started learning computer.
(b) I'll tell my friends that I am learning computer.
(c) I'll tell my friends that I have started learning computer.
(d) I'll tell my friends that I learn computer.

50. Dr Ratan said to the patient, "Take light food and to not go out in the Sun".
(a) Dr Ratan advised the patient to take light food and not to go out in the Sun.
(b) Dr Ratan advised the patient to take light food and to do not go out in the Sun.
(c) Dr Ratan advised the patient to take light food and do not go out in the sun.
(d) Dr Ratan advised the patient to take light food and not go out in the Sun.

51. He wished me respectfully and told that he had come to join the office.
(a) He said, "Good Morning Sir! I want to join the office".
(b) He said to me, "Good morning, Sir! I'm here to join the office".
(c) He said to me, "Good morning Sir! I'll join the office today".
(d) He said to me, "Good morning Sir! I have come to join the office".

52. I said, "Good-bye, my beloved friends."
(a) I wished my beloved friends good-bye.
(b) I bided good-bye to my beloved friends.
(c) I said good-bye to my beloved friends.
(d) I bade my beloved friends good-bye.

53. The teacher said, "Don't come to school on Monday because it is a holiday".
(a) The teacher asked if we were coming to school on Monday because it is a holiday.
(b) The teacher told us don't come to school on Monday because it is a holiday.
(c) The teacher told us not to come to school on Monday because it was a holiday.
(d) The teacher asked us don't come to school on Monday because it is a holiday.

54. Oh! how foolish I have been in money matters!"?
(a) He expressed with regret that he could be so foolish in money matters.
(b) He confessed regretfully that he had been very foolish in money matters.
(c) He confessed to himself that he is being very foolish in money matters.
(d) He exclaimed regretfully that he was very foolish in money matters.

55. The boy thanked the Principal for granting him a fee concession.
(a) The boy told the Principal, "You are kind enough to grant me a fee-concession".
(b) The boy said to the Principal, "Thank you, madam for granting me a fee-concession."
(c) The boy said to the principal, "I am thankful to you for a fee-concession."
(d) The boy said to the Principal, "I express my thanks that you have granted me a fee-concession."

56. He said, "Ravi, why are you sounding so depressed today?"
(a) He asked Ravi why did he sound so depressed that day.
(b) He asked Ravi why he was sounding so depressed that day.
(c) He told Ravi why he sounded so depressed today.
(d) He asked Ravi that why was he sounding so depressed that day.

57. He asked me, "What time will the sun set tomorrow?"
(a) He asked me what time does the sun set the next day.
(b) He asked me what time the sun would set tomorrow.
(c) He asked me what time the sun would set the next day.
(d) He asked me what time would the sun set the next day.

58. "Tinu, where have you been all these days?" asked the Principal.
(a) The Principal asked Tinu where he had been all those days.
(b) The Principal asked Tinu where he has been all those days.
(c) The Principal asked Tinu where had he been all those days.
(d) The Principal asked to Tinu where was he all those days.

59. "Have you finished your assignment, Minu?" said her brother.
(a) Minu' brother asked Minu if you have finished your assignemnt.
(b) Minu's brother said to Minu if she had finished her assignment.
(c) Minu's brother asked her if she had finished her assignment.
(d) Minu's brother asked Minu if she has finished her assignment.

60. The king said to his men, "Do not be afraid of the enemy face them bravely".
(a) The king ordered his men to not be afraid of the enemy and that they had to be faced bravely.
(b) The king asked his men to not be afraid of the enemy but they should be faced bravely.
(c) The king advised his men not to be afraid of the enemy but to face them bravely.
(d) The king told his men not to be afraid of the enemy and they had faced them bravely.

61. He says, "I go for a walk every morning."
(a) He says that he goes for a walk every morning.
(b) He said that he used to go for a walk every morning.
(c) He said that he goes for a walk every morning.
(d) He says he went for a walk every morning.

62. The Principal said, "Why didn't you attend the flag hoisting ceremony, Anuj?"
(a) The Principal asked Anuj why hadn't he attended the flag hoisting ceremony.
(b) The Principal asked to Anuj why he hadn't attended the flag hoisting ceremony.
(c) The Principal asked Anuj why didn't he attend the flag hoisting ceremony.
(d) The Principal asked Anuj why he didn't attend the flag hoisting ceremony.

63. I said to him, "Will you go to Delhi?"
(a) I asked him will he go to Delhi.
(b) I said to him would he go to Delhi.
(c) I asked him if he would go to Delhi.
(d) I said to him would you go to Delhi.

64. He said, "I have read this novel".
(a) He said that he has read this novel.
(b) He said that he had read that novel.
(c) He said that he read that novel.
(d) He said that he had read this novel.

65. I said to him, "Where have you lost the pen I brought for you yesterday?"
(a) I asked him where he had lost the pen I had brought him yesterday.
(b) I asked him where he had lost the pen I have brought for him the previous day.
(c) I asked him where he had lost the pen I had brought for him the previous day.
(d) I asked him where had he lost the pen I had brought him the previous day.

66. Sita said, "I may go there."
(a) Sita says that she may go there.
(b) Sita says that she is going there.
(c) Sita said that she will go there.
(d) Sita said that she might go there.

67. My friend requested me to bring him a sandwich.
(a) He said, "My friend, please bring me a sandwich."
(b) My friend said, "Will you bring me a sandwich".
(c) "Please bring me a sandwich", said my friend.
(d) "Please bring my friend a sandwich", said he.

68. He said, "If I had the tools I could mend the car."
(a) He said that if he had the tools he could mend the car.
(b) He tells that he had the tools he could mend the car.
(c) He said I could mend the car if I have the tools.
(d) He told he could mend the car.

69. She said to the children, "You mustn't play with fire."
(a) She told the children they were not to play with fire.
(b) She told the children that they mustn't play with fire.
(c) She told the children not to play with fire.
(d) She told the children they are not to play with fire.

70. Everybody says, "How well she sings!"
(a) Everybody comments that she sings well.
(b) Everybody says how well she sings.
(c) Everybody tells that she sang very well.
(d) Everybody says that she sang well.

71. He says that he is very sorry.
(a) He said, "He was very sorry".
(b) He says, "I am very sorry".
(c) He said, "He is very sorry".
(d) He told me, "I felt sorry".

72. Daman says, "Priya is working in Ahmedabad".
(a) Daman say that Priya was worring in Ahmedabad.
(b) Daman said that Priya was working in Ahmedabad.
(c) Daman said that Priya works in Ahmedabad.
(d) Daman says that Priya is working in Ahmedabad.

73. Anne said, "It is time to leave for the meeting."
(a) Anne said that it was time to leave for the meeting.
(b) Anne told that it is time to leave for the meeting.
(c) Anne said its time to leave for the meeting.
(d) Anne said that it was time for the meeting.

74. The old man said that he would soon be leaving the world.
(a) The old man said, "I shall soon be leaving the world."
(b) The old man said, "I am soon leaving the world."
(c) The old man said, "I would soon leave the world."
(d) The old man said, "I am going to leave the world soon."

75. "Come home early" said Mr Matthew to his clerk.
(a) Mr Matthew told his clerk to come home as early as possible.
(b) Mr Matthew asked his clerk to be home early.
(c) Mr Matthew ordered his clerk to come home early.
(d) Mr Matthew requested his clerk to come home a little early.

76. I said, "Water is essential for life."
(a) Water is essential for life was said by me.

(b) I told that water was essential for life.
(c) I exclaimed that water was essential for life.
(d) I said that water is essential for life.

77. She asked me if I was going to college.
(a) She said, "Am I going to college?"
(b) She said to me, "Are you going to college?"
(c) She asked me, "Will you go to college?"
(d) She asked to me, "Was I going to college?"

78. Iba said that she might go home the next day with her sister.
(a) Iba said, "I could go home tomorrow with my sister."
(b) Iba said, "I may go home tomorrow with my sister."
(c) Iba said, "I can go home tomorrow with my sister."
(d) Iba said, "I will go home tomorrow with my sister."

79. He said, "I was doing it."
(a) He said that he had been doing it.
(b) He said that he had done it.
(c) He said that he has done it.
(d) He said that he did it.

80. The lady asked me how my uncle was.
(a) The lady said to me, "How is your uncle ?"
(b) The lady asked me, "How has your uncle been ?"
(c) The lady said to me, "How was your uncle ?"
(d) The lady asked me, "How is your uncle doing?"

81. He said, "Honesty is the best policy."
(a) He said that honesty is the best policy.
(b) He said that honesty was the best policy.
(c) He said that honesty had been the best policy.
(d) He said that honesty has been the best policy.

82. He said that, he intended to leave for Surat that night.
(a) "I intend to leave for Surat, that night", he said.
(b) "I intend to left for Surat that night", he said.
(c) "I intended to leave for Surat tonight", he said.
(d) "I intend to leave for Surat tonight", he said.

83. The teacher said to him, "Is poverty not a curse ?"
(a) The teacher asked him is poverty not a curse.
(b) The teacher asked him if poverty was not a curse.
(c) The teacher asked him was poverty not a curse.
(d) The teacher asked him whether poverty is not a curse.

84. The prisoner enquired if a lawyer had been arranged for him.
(a) The prisoner enquired, "Is there a lawyer for me ?"
(b) The prisoner asked, "Has a lawyer been arranged for me?"
(c) The prisoner enquired, "Had a lawyer been arranged for me?"
(d) The prisoner said, "Have you arranged a lawyer for me?"

85. Phila ordered her brother to turn down the television and let her work in peace.
(a) Phila said to her brother, "Turn down the television, that let let me do my work in peace?
(b) Phila said to her brother, "Turn down the television and let me work in peace."
(c) Phila said to her brother, "Turn down the television, let me do my work in peace.
(d) Phila said to her brother, "Turned down the television and let me do my work in Peace.".

86. You will say, "I am ill."
(a) You will say that you are ill.
(b) You would say that you were ill.
(c) You would say that you are ill.
(d) You will say that you were ill.

87. He said, "Garima wants to take up a job while her husband wants her to look after the family."
(a) He said that Garima wanted to take up a job while her husband wanted her to look after the family.
(b) He said that Garima wants to take up a job while her husband wanted her to look after the family.
(c) He told that Garima wanted to take up a job while her husband wants her to look after the family.
(d) He said to Garima that though she wanted to take up a job while her husband wanted her to look after the family.

88. He exclaimed with joy that their team had won the tournament.
(a) He said, "Our team has won the tournament."
(b) He said, "Wow! Our team won the tournament."
(c) He exclaimed, "Hurrah ! Our team has won the tournament."
(d) He said, "Our team won the tournament,"

89. His father said that it was time he visited his uncle.
(a) "It was time you visited your uncle", said his father.
(b) It is time you visited my uncle", said his father.
(c) "It is time you visit your uncle", said his father.
(d) "It is time you visited your uncle", said his father.

90. The Project Manager asked Vivek, "How much time will you take to finish this project?"
(a) The Project Manager asked Vivek how much time would he take to finish that project.
(b) The Project Manager enquired of Vivek how much time he would take to finish that project.
(c) The Project Manager enquired of Vivek how much time he will be taking to finish that project.
(d) The Project Manager asked Vivek how much time he would take to finish this project.

91. The ox asked the dog not to sit there.
(a) The ox said to the dog, "Not to sit here."
(b) The ox said to the dog, "Do not sit here."
(c) The ox said to the dog, "Does not sit here."
(d) The ox said to the dog, "Did not sit here."

92. He said, "I am writing a poem."
(a) He said that I am writing a poem.
(b) He said that he is writing a poem.

(c) He said that the poem is being written.
(d) He said that he was writing a poem.

93. He said, "Asha washed the clothes."
(a) He said that Asha washed the clothes.
(b) He said that clothes were washed by Asha.
(c) He said that Asha had washed the clothes.
(d) He said that Asha has washed the clothes.

94. Martha said, "I am going to Mexico next year."
(a) Martha said that she had been going to Mexico next year.
(b) Martha said that she was going to Mexico next year.
(c) Martha said that she had gone to Mexico next year.
(d) Martha said that she will be going to Mexico next year.

95. My mother said to me, "Wish you a happy and prosperous life!"
(a) My mother wished me a happy and prosperous life.
(b) My mother told me that I should lead a happy and prosperous life.
(c) My mother wished that I enjoy a happy and prosperous life.
(d) My mother wished that I should be living a happy and prosperous life.

96. You said to me, "Why are you talking so much?"
(a) You asked me why he was talking so much.
(b) You asked me why I was talking so much.
(c) You asked me why was I talking so much.
(d) You asked me why I had been talking so much.

97. Sandy said, "I have already written a letter to my family."
(a) Sandy said that she had already written a letter to her family.
(b) Sandy said that she wrote a letter to her family.
(c) Sandy said that she was writing a letter to her family.
(d) Sandy said that she will write a letter to her family.

98. You said, "They were busy the whole day."
(a) You said that they had busy the whole day.
(b) You said that they were busy the whole day.
(c) You said that they had been busy the whole day.
(d) You said that they have been busy the whole day.

99. I said to her, "I will have written letters."
(a) I told her that she will have written letters.
(b) I told her that she would have written letters.
(c) I told her that I will have written letters.
(d) I told her that I would have written letters .

100. I asked him, "Will you go to Agra tomorrow?"
(a) I asked him whether I would go to Agra the next day.
(b) I asked him whether he would go to Agra the next day.
(c) I asked him whether you would go to Agra the next day.
(d) I asked him whether he will go to Agra the next day.

Answers

1. (c)	**2.** (a)	**3.** (c)	**4.** (a)	**5.** (c)	**6.** (d)	**7.** (b)	**8.** (b)	**9.** (d)	**10.** (a)
11. (c)	**12.** (d)	**13.** (a)	**14.** (c)	**15.** (c)	**16.** (b)	**17.** (c)	**18.** (c)	**19.** (c)	**20.** (d)
21. (c)	**22.** (a)	**23.** (c)	**24.** (a)	**25.** (c)	**26.** (b)	**27.** (a)	**28.** (b)	**29.** (b)	**30.** (c)
31. (b)	**32.** (b)	**33.** (c)	**34.** (c)	**35.** (d)	**36.** (a)	**37.** (c)	**38.** (c)	**39.** (a)	**40.** (d)
41. (d)	**42.** (a)	**43.** (c)	**44.** (a)	**45.** (c)	**46.** (d)	**47.** (c)	**48.** (d)	**49.** (c)	**50.** (a)
51. (d)	**52.** (d)	**53.** (c)	**54.** (b)	**55.** (b)	**56.** (b)	**57.** (c)	**58.** (a)	**59.** (c)	**60.** (c)
61. (a)	**62.** (d)	**63.** (c)	**64.** (b)	**65.** (c)	**66.** (d)	**67.** (c)	**68.** (a)	**69.** (b)	**70.** (a)
71. (b)	**72.** (d)	**73.** (a)	**74.** (a)	**75.** (c)	**76.** (d)	**77.** (b)	**78.** (b)	**79.** (a)	**80.** (a)
81. (a)	**82.** (d)	**83.** (b)	**84.** (b)	**85.** (b)	**86.** (a)	**87.** (a)	**88.** (c)	**89.** (d)	**90.** (d)
91. (b)	**92.** (d)	**93.** (c)	**94.** (b)	**95.** (a)	**96.** (b)	**97.** (a)	**98.** (c)	**99.** (d)	**100.** (b)

B. Active-Passive

Voice is that property of the verb which points out whether the subject performs an action or the action is experienced by the doer.

Kinds of Voice

Voice निम्नलिखित दो प्रकार की होती हैं

1. **Active Voice** जब किसी वाक्य में प्रयुक्त क्रिया (Verb) से ऐसा प्रकट हो कि कर्ता (Subject) स्वयं कार्य कर रहा है, तो वह वाक्य active voice में होता है। अत: वह voice जिसमें verb द्वारा subject को प्रधानता दी जाती है, active voice कहलाती है। इसमें subject के अनुसार verb की form बदली जाती है।
2. **Passive Voice** जब किसी वाक्य में प्रयुक्त क्रिया (Verb) से ऐसा प्रकट हो कि कर्ता स्वयं कार्य नहीं कर रहा है बल्कि किसी के द्वारा उसके लिए कार्य किया जा रहा है, तो वाक्य passive voice में होता है। अत: वह voice जिसमें verb द्वारा object को प्रधानता दी जाती है, passive voice कहलाती है। इसमें object के अनुसार verb की form बदली जाती है।

e.g. (i) They cook the food. (Active voice)
The food is cooked by them. (Passive voice)
(ii) He writes a book. (Active voice)
A book is written by him. (Passive voice)

उपरोक्त वाक्यों से स्पष्ट है कि Active voice में subject प्रमुख होता है तथा subject स्वयं कार्य करता है परन्तु Passive voice में verb के द्वारा object को प्रमुख बनाया जाता है तथा किसी के द्वारा subject के लिए कार्य किया जाता है।

Active Voice से Passive Voice बनाने के नियम

1. Active voice के object को passive voice में subject के रूप में प्रयोग किया जाता है।
2. Active voice के subject को passive voice में object के रूप में प्रयोग किया जाता है।
3. Passive voice के object से पहले by लगाया जाता है।
4. Passive voice में main verb की IIIrd form का प्रयोग किया जाता है।
5. Pronoun/Noun (Subjective case तथा Objective case) में परिवर्तन निम्नलिखित प्रकार से किए जाते हैं

Subjective Case के लिए

Subject (Active voice)		Object (Passive voice)
I	⟶	by me
We	⟶	by us
You	⟶	by you
He	⟶	by him
She	⟶	by her
They	⟶	by them
Someone/Somebody/ Everyone/Everybody/Any one/Anybody	⟶	No object (Object को हटा दिया जाता है)
Any Noun	⟶	by Noun (as it is)

Objective Case के लिए

Object (Active voice)		Subject (Passive voice)
me	⟶	I
us	⟶	We
you	⟶	You
him	⟶	He
her	⟶	She
them	⟶	They
Any Noun	⟶	Noun (as it is)

Active voice में 12 tenses होते हैं परन्तु passive voice केवल 8 tenses की ही बनाई जा सकती है। निम्नलिखित 4 tenses की passive voice नहीं बनती है

(i) Present Perfect Continuous
(ii) Past Perfect Continuous
(iii) Future Continuous
(iv) Future Perfect Continuous

Present Indefinite Tense का Active Voice से Passive Voice में परिवर्तन

Present Indefinite tense का भिन्न-भिन्न वाक्यों में active voice से passive voice में परिवर्तन निम्न प्रकार से होता है

Affirmative Sentence के लिए

Verb की Ist form के साथ s/es $\xrightarrow{\text{change into}}$ is/am/are (subject kesâ Devegmeej) + verb keâer IIIrd form

e.g. (i) He teaches English. (Active)
English is taught by him. (Passive)
(ii) Rahul eats a mango. (Active)
A mango is eaten by Rahul. (Passive)

Negative Sentence के लिए

Do/does + not + verb की Ist form $\xrightarrow{\text{change into}}$ is/am/are (subject के अनुसार) + not + verb की IIIrd form

e.g. (i) He does not teach English. (Active)
English is not taught by him. (Passive)
(ii) Rahul does not eat a mango. (Active)
A mango is not eaten by Rahul. (Passive)

Interrogative Sentence के लिए

Do/Does + subject + verb की Ist form $\xrightarrow{\text{change into}}$ Is/Am/Are (subject के अनुसार) + subject + verb की IIIrd form

e.g. (i) Does he teach English? (Active)
Is English taught by him? (Passive)
(ii) Does Rahul eat a mango? (Active)
Is a mango eaten by Rahul? (Passive)

Interrogative-Negative Sentence के लिए

Do/Does + subject + not + verb की Ist form $\xrightarrow{\text{change into}}$ Is/Am/Are (subject के अनुसार) + subject + not + verb की IIIrd form

e.g. (i) Does he not teach English? (Active)
Is English not taught by him? (Passive)
(ii) Does Rahul not eat a mango? (Active)
Is a mango not eaten by Rahul? (Passive)

Present Continuous Tense का Active Voice से Passive Voice में परिवर्तन

Present Continuous tense का भिन्न-भिन्न वाक्यों में active voice से passive voice में परिवर्तन निम्न प्रकार से होता है

Affirmative Sentence के लिए

Is/am/are + verb की ing form $\xrightarrow{\text{change into}}$ is/am/are (subject के अनुसार) + being + verb की IIIrd form

e.g. (i) Rohan is cooking the food. (Active)
The food is being cooked by Rohan. (Passive)
(ii) She is reading a newspaper. (Active)
A newspaper is being read by her. (Passive)

Negative Sentence के लिए

Is/am/are + not + verb की ing form $\xrightarrow{\text{change into}}$ is/am/are (subject के अनुसार) + not + being + verb की IIIrd form

e.g. (i) Rohan is not cooking the food. (Active)
The food is not being cooked by Rohan. (Passive)
(ii) She is not reading a newspaper. (Active)
A newspaper is not being read by her. (Passive)

Interrogative Sentence के लिए

Is/Am/Are + subject + verb की ing form $\xrightarrow{\text{change into}}$ Is/Am/Are (subject के अनुसार) + subject + being + verb की IIIrd form

e.g. (i) Is Rohan cooking the food? (Active)
Is the food being cooked by Rohan? (Passive)
(ii) Is she reading a newspaper? (Active)
Is a newspaper being read by her? (Passive)

Interrogative-Negative Sentence के लिए

Is/Am/Are + subject + not +verb की ing form $\xrightarrow{\text{change into}}$ Is/Am/Are (subject के अनुसार) subject + not + being + verb की IIIrd form

e.g. (i) Is Rohan not cooking the food? (Active)
Is the food not being cooked by Rohan? (Passive)
(ii) Is she not reading a newspaper? (Active)
Is a newspaper not being read by her? (Passive)

Present Perfect Tense का Active Voice से Passive Voice में परिवर्तन

Present Perfect Tense का भिन्न-भिन्न वाक्यों में active voice से passive voice में परिवर्तन निम्न प्रकार से होता है

Affirmative Sentence के लिए

has/have + verb की IIIrd form $\xrightarrow{\text{change into}}$ has/have (subject के अनुसार) + been + verb की IIIrd form

e.g. (i) Someone has broken the glass. (Active)
The glass has been broken. (Passive)
(ii) You have stolen the books. (Active)
The books have been stolen by you. (Passive)

Negative Sentence के लिए

Has/have + not + verb की IIIrd form $\xrightarrow{\text{change into}}$ has/have (subject के अनुसार) + not + been + verb की IIIrd form

e.g. (i) Someone has not broken the glass. (Active)
The glass has not been broken. (Passive)
(ii) You have not stolen the books. (Active)
The books have not been stolen by you. (Passive)

Interrogative Sentence के लिए

Has/Have + subject + verb की IIIrd form $\xrightarrow{\text{change into}}$ Has/Have (subject के अनुसार) + subject + been + verb की IIIrd form

e.g. (i) Has someone broken the glass? (Active)
Has the glass been broken? (Passive)
(ii) Have you stolen the books? (Active)
Have the books been stolen by you? (Passive)

Interrogative-Negative Sentence के लिए

Has/Have + subject + not + verb की IIIrd form $\xrightarrow{\text{change into}}$ Has/Have (subject के अनुसार) + subject + not + been + verb की IIIrd form

e.g. (i) Has someone not broken the glass? (Active)
Has the glass not been broken? (Passive)
(ii) Have you not stolen the books? (Active)
Have the books not been stolen by you? (Passive)

Past Indefinite Tense का Active Voice से Passive Voice में परिवर्तन

Past Indefinite tense का भिन्न-भिन्न वाक्यों में active voice से passive voice में परिवर्तन निम्न प्रकार से होता है

Affirmative Sentence के लिए

verb की IInd form $\xrightarrow{\text{change into}}$ was/were (subject के अनुसार) + verb की IIIrd form

e.g. (i) Dinesh killed a snake. (Active)
A snake was killed by Dinesh. (Passive)
(ii) My father bought sweets. (Active)
Sweets were bought by my father. (Passive)

Negative Sentence के लिए

did + not + verb की Ist form $\xrightarrow{\text{change into}}$ was/were (subject के अनुसार) + not + verb की IIIrd form

e.g. (i) Dinesh did not kill a snake. (Active)
A snake was not killed by Dinesh. (Passive)
(ii) My father did not buy sweets. (Active)
Sweets were not bought by my father. (Passive)

Interrogative Sentence के लिए

Did + subject + verb की Ist form $\xrightarrow{\text{change into}}$ Was/Were (subject के अनुसार) + subject + verb की IIIrd form

e.g. (i) Did Dinesh kill a snake? (Active)
Was a snake killed by Dinesh? (Passive)
(ii) Did my father buy sweets? (Active)
Were sweets bought by my father? (Passive)

Interrogative-Negative Sentence के लिए

Did + subject + not + verb की Ist form $\xrightarrow{\text{change into}}$ Was/ Were (subject के अनुसार) + subject + not + verb की IIIrd form

e.g. (i) Did Dinesh not kill a snake? (Active)
Was a snake not killed by Dinesh? (Passive)
(ii) Did my father not buy sweets? (Active)
Were sweets not bought by my father? (Passive)

Past Continuous Tense का Active Voice से Passive Voice में परिवर्तन

Past Continuous Tense का भिन्न-भिन्न वाक्यों में active voice से passive voice में परिवर्तन निम्न प्रकार से होता है

Affirmative Sentence के लिए

Was/were + verb की ing form $\xrightarrow{\text{change into}}$ was/were (subject के अनुसार) + being + verb की IIIrd form

e.g. (i) She was drinking milk. (Active)
Milk was being drunk by her. (Passive)
(ii) We were buying crackers. (Active)
Crackers were being bought by us. (Passive)

Negative Sentence के लिए

Was/were + not + verb की ing form $\xrightarrow{\text{change into}}$ was/were (subject के अनुसार) + not + being + verb की IIIrd form

e.g. (i) She was not drinking milk. (Active)
Milk was not being drunk by her. (Passive)
(ii) We were not buying crackers. (Active)
Crackers were not being bought by us. (Passive)

Interrogative Sentence के लिए

Was/Were + subject + verb की ing form $\xrightarrow{\text{change into}}$ Was/Were (subject के अनुसार) + subject + being + verb की IIIrd form

e.g. (i) Was she drinking milk? (Active)
Was milk being drunk by her? (Passive)
(ii) Were we buying crackers? (Active)
Were crackers being bought by us? (Passive)

Interrogative-Negative Sentence के लिए

Was/Were + subject + not + verb की ing form $\xrightarrow{\text{change into}}$ Was/Were (subject के अनुसार) + subject + not + being + verb की IIIrd form

e.g. (i) Was she not drinking milk? (Active)
Was milk not being drunk by her? (Passive)
(ii) Were we not buying crackers? (Active)
Were crackers not being bought by us? (Passive)

Past Perfect Tense का Active Voice से Passive Voice में परिवर्तन

Past Perfect tense का भिन्न-भिन्न वाक्यों में active voice से passive voice में परिवर्तन निम्न प्रकार से होता है

Affirmative Sentence के लिए

Had + verb की IIIrd form $\xrightarrow{\text{change into}}$ had + been + verb की IIIrd form

e.g. (i) You had informed him. (Active)
He had been informed by you. (Passive)
(ii) We had completed the work. (Active)
The work had been completed by us. (Passive)

Negative Sentence के लिए

had + not + verb की IIIrd form $\xrightarrow{\text{change into}}$ had + not + been + verb की IIIrd form

e.g. (i) You had not informed him. (Active)
He had not been informed by you. (Passive)
(ii) We had not completed the work. (Active)
The work had not been completed by us. (Passive)

Interrogative Sentence के लिए

Had + subject + verb की IIIrd form $\xrightarrow{\text{change into}}$ Had + subject + been + verb की IIIrd form

e.g. (i) Had you informed him? (Active)
Had he been informed by you? (Passive)

(ii) Had we completed the work? (Active)
Had the work been completed by us? (Passive)

Interrogative-Negative Sentence के लिए

Had + subject + not + verb की IIIrd form —change into→ Had + subject + not + been + verb की IIIrd form

e.g. (i) Had you not informed him? (Active)
Had he not been informed by you? (Passive)

(ii) Had we not completed the work? (Active)
Had the work not been completed by us? (Passive)

Future Indefinite Tense का Active Voice से Passive Voice में परिवर्तन

Future Indefinite tense का भिन्न-भिन्न वाक्यों में active voice से passive voice में परिवर्तन निम्न प्रकार से होता है

Affirmative Sentence के लिए

Shall/will + verb की Ist form —change into→ Shall/will + be + verb की IIIrd form

e.g. (i) I shall teach you. (Active)
You will be taught by me. (Passive)

(ii) I shall buy a car. (Active)
A car will be bought by me. (Passive)

Negative Sentence के लिए

Shall/will + not + verb की Ist form —change into→ Shall/will + not + be + verb की IIIrd form

e.g. (i) I shall not teach you. (Active)
You will not be taught by me. (Passive)

(ii) I shall not buy a car. (Active)
A car will not be bought by me. (Passive)

Interrogative Sentence के लिए

Shall/Will + subject + verb की Ist form —change into→ Shall/Will + subject + be + verb की IIIrd form

e.g. (i) Shall I teach you? (Active)
Will you be taught by me? (Passive)

(ii) Shall I buy a car? (Active)
Will a car be bought by me? (Passive)

(iii) Will she call the servants? (Active)
Will the servants be called by her? (Passive)

Interrogative-Negative Sentence के लिए

Shall/Will + subject + not + verb की Ist form —change into→ Shall/Will + subject + not + be + verb की IIIrd form

e.g. (i) Shall I not teach you? (Active)
Will you not be taught by me? (Passive)

(ii) Shall I not buy a car? (Active)
Will a car not be bought by me? (Passive)

Future Perfect Tense का Active Voice से Passive Voice में परिवर्तन

Future Perfect tense का भिन्न-भिन्न वाक्यों में active voice से passive voice में परिवर्तन निम्न प्रकार से होता है

Affirmative Sentence के लिए

Shall/will + have + verb की IIIrd form —change into→ shall/will + have + been + verb की IIIrd form

e.g. (i) She will have helped the poor. (Active)
The poor will have been helped by her. (Passive)

(ii) They will have distributed fruits. (Active)
Fruits will have been distributed by them. (Passive)

Negative Sentence के लिए

Shall/will + not + have + verb की IIIrd form —change into→ Shall/will + not + have + been + verb की IIIrd form

e.g. (i) She will not have helped the poor. (Active)
The poor will not have been helped by her. (Passive)

(ii) They will not have distributed fruits. (Active)
Fruits will not have been distributed by them. (Passive)

Interrogative Sentence के लिए

Shall/Will + subject + have + verb की IIIrd form —change into→ Shall/Will + subject + have + been + verb की IIIrd form

e.g. (i) Will she have helped the poor? (Active)
Will the poor have been helped by her? (Passive)

(ii) Will they have distributed fruits? (Active)
Will fruits have been distributed by them? (Passive)

Interrogative-Negative Sentence के लिए

Shall/Will + subject + not + have + verb की IIIrd form —change into→ Shall/Will + subject + not + have + been + verb की IIIrd form

e.g. (i) Will she not have helped the poor? (Active)
Will the poor not have been helped by her? (Passive)

(ii) Shall they not have distributed fruits? (Active)
Shall fruits not have been distributed by them? (Passive)

Exercise

Directions (1-100) Choose any one of the given alternatives which best represents change of voice.

1. It is time to take tea.
(a) It was time that tea was taken.
(b) It is time for tea to be taken.
(c) It is time that tea should be taken.
(d) It is time that tea had been taken.

2. The members should adhere to all the decisions.
(a) All the decisions should adhere to the members
(b) All the decisions adhered to the members
(c) All the decisions should be adhered to by the members
(d) All should adhere to the decisions of the members

3. His subordinates accused him of various offences.
(a) They accused him of various offences.
(b) It was accused by his subordinates that he had done various offences.
(c) His subordinates accused that he had done various offences.
(d) He was accused of various offences by his subordinates.

4. Has someone made all the necessary arrangements?
(a) Has all the necessary arrangements been made by someone?
(b) Have the necessary arrangements been all made by someone?
(c) Have all the necessary arrangements been made by someone?
(d) Have all the necessary arrangements have been made by one?

5. We will know the outcome of these experiments after six months.
(a) The outcome of these experiments will be known after six months.
(b) The outcomes will be known of these experiments after six months.
(c) After six months, we will know the outcome of these experiments.
(d) These experiments will have a known outcome after six months.

6. Don't speak until someone speaks to you.
(a) Don't speak until you are spoken to
(b) Don't speak until someone is spoken to
(c) Don't speak until you have been spoken to
(d) Don't speak until someone has been spoken to

7. Did the noise frighten you?
(a) Did you frighten the noise?
(b) Was the frightened by the noise?
(c) Were you frightened by the noise?
(d) Were you frighten by the noise?

8. We are reaching the end of this exercise.
(a) This exercise is ended by us.
(b) The end of this exercise is being reached by us.
(c) This is our end to the exercise.
(d) The exercise has reached its end by us.

9. I expect you to complete this work before sunset.
(a) I except you to be completed this work before sunset.
(b) I am expected you to complete this work before sunset.
(c) You are expected to complete this work before sunset.
(d) You are expected to be completed this work before sunset.

10. The storm did much damage.
(a) Much damage was done by the storm.
(b) The storm damaged much.
(c) Much damage did the storm.
(d) The storm was damaged.

11. The boy has rung the bell.
(a) The bell has been rung by the boy.
(b) The bell was being rung by the boy.
(c) The bell was rung by the boy.
(d) The bell has been being rung by the boy.

12. He likes people to call him Sir.
(a) He likes to be called Sir by people.
(b) He likes to be call Sir by people.
(c) He likes people who call him Sir.
(d) To call him Sir is liked by people.

13. We added up the money and found that it was correct.
(a) The money was added up and found to be correct.
(b) Correct it was found and the money was added up.
(c) The money added up by us and it was correctly found.
(d) The money added up by us found it was correct.

14. The telegraph wires have been cut.
(a) Someone has been cut the telegraph wires.
(b) No one has cut the telegraph wires.
(c) The telegraph wires have cut someone.
(d) Someone has cut the telegraph wires.

15. Will she tell us the truth?
(a) Is the truth told to us by her?
(b) The truth will be told to us by her.
(c) Will the truth be told to us by her?
(d) Will the truth be told us by her?

16. Mr. Sen asked him a question.
(a) He was asked a question Mr Sen.
(b) He was asked a question to Mr Sen.
(c) He was asked a question by Mr Sen.
(d) A question was being asked by Mr Sen.

17. People speak English all over the world.
(a) English is spoken all over the world.
(b) English was spoken all over the world.
(c) English was spoken by people.
(d) English is spoken by people.

18. The teacher punished the boys who had not done their homework.
(a) The boys who had not done their homework had been punished by their teacher.

(b) The boys were punished by their teacher who had not done their homework.
(c) The boys who had not done their homework were punished by the teacher.
(d) The boys who had not done their homework were being punished by the teacher.

19. The Principal has granted him a scholarship.
(a) A scholarship has granted to him by the Principal.
(b) He has been granted a scholarship by the Principal.
(c) He has granted a scholarship by the Principal.
(d) A scholarship was granted to him by the Principal.

20. Somebody told me that there had been an explosion in the Town Hall.
(a) I was told by somebody about the explosion in the Town Hall.
(b) I was told about the explosion in the Town Hall.
(c) I was informed that there was an explosion in the Town Hall.
(d) I was told by somebody that there had been an explosion in the Town Hall.

21. Why haven't they allowed you to go?
(a) Why you haven't been allowed to go?
(b) Why haven't you been allowed to go?
(c) Why were you not allowed to go?
(d) Why you were not allowed to go?

22. I expected him to give us financial aid.
(a) It was expected of him to give us financial aid.
(b) Let it be expected that he would give us financial aid.
(c) It was expected by me that he will give us financial aid.
(d) He may be expected to give us financial aid.

23. Tobacco manufacturers are making considerable efforts to gain new clients.
(a) Considerable efforts are being made by tobacco manufacturers to gain new clients.
(b) Considerable efforts being made by tobacco manufacturers to gain new clients.
(c) Considerable efforts are made by tobacco manufacturers to gain new clients.
(d) To gain new clients by tobacco manufacturers considerable efforts are being made.

24. Has anybody done all the work?
(a) Have all the work been done by somebody?
(b) Somebody has done all the work.
(c) The work has been done by somebody.
(d) Has all the work been done by somebody?

25. Cigarette smoking causes two million deaths annually in the industrial states.
(a) Cigarette smoking has been causing two million deaths annually in the industrial states.
(b) Two million deaths are caused annually by cigarette smoking in the industrial states.
(c) Two million deaths are being caused by cigarette smoking annually in the industrial states.
(d) Two million deaths have been caused annually by cigarette smoking in the industrial states.

26. Circumstances will oblige me to go.
(a) I will oblige the circumstances and go.
(b) I shall be obliged to go by the circumstances.
(c) Under the circumstances, I should go.
(d) I would be obliged by the circumstances to go.

27. We waste much time on trifles.
(a) Much time was wasted on trifles.
(b) Much time will be wasted on trifles.
(c) Much time is wasted by us on trifles.
(d) Much time is wasted on trifles.

28. Mohan gave the beggar an old shirt.
(a) An old shirt was given to Mohan by the beggar.
(b) An old shirt was given to the beggar by Mohan.
(c) The beggar was gave an old shirt by Mohan.
(d) An old shirt was gave to the beggar by Mohan.

29. They have made him a king.
(a) A kind has been made by him.
(b) He was made a king by them.
(c) They have been made kings by him.
(d) He has been made a king by them.

30. Who taught you English?
(a) By whom English was taught to you?
(b) By whom you were taught English?
(c) By whom was English taught to you?
(d) By whom are you taught English?

31. You surprise me.
(a) I am to be surprised.
(b) You are surprised.
(c) I am surprised.
(d) Me is surprised.

32. The boys killed the snake with a stick.
(a) The snake was killed by the boys with a stick.
(b) A stick was killed by the boys with the snake.
(c) A snake with a stick was killed by the boys.
(d) A snake is killed by the boys with a stick.

33. Let me do this.
(a) Let us do this.
(b) This be done by me.
(c) Let this be done by me.
(d) Let do this.

34. The tiger caught a fox.
(a) A fox has been caught by the tiger
(b) A fox was caught by the tiger
(c) A fox is caught by the tiger
(d) A fox has been caught by the tiger.

35. Someone has lit the fire.
(a) The fire was lit by someone.
(b) You are requested to light the fire by someone
(c) The fire has been lit by someone.
(d) The fire had been lit by someone.

36. Has the price rise affected all the people?
(a) Have all the people been affected by the price rise?
(b) Are all the people being affected by the price rise?

(c) Had all the people being affected by the price rise?
(d) Are all the people affected by the price rise?

37. They pick the flowers, fresh, every morning.
(a) The fresh flowers are picked every morning by them.
(b) The flowers are fresh and picked every morning by them.
(c) The flowers are picked fresh every morning by them.
(d) The picked flowers are fresh every morning by them.

38. Everyone looked up to him.
(a) He was looked up to by everyone.
(b) He was looked up by everyone.
(c) He is looked up by everyone.
(d) He looks up by everyone.

39. Tell him to get out of our house.
(a) He is told to get out of our house.
(b) Let him be told to get out of our house.
(c) He might be told to get out of our house.
(d) He should be told that he may get out of our house.

40. Those who worked hard seldom obtained good marks.
(a) Good marks were seldom being obtained by those who worked hard.
(b) Good marks are seldom obtained by those who worked hard.
(c) Seldom had good marks been obtained by those who worked hard.
(d) Good marks were seldom obtained by those who worked hard.

41. The accountant took the money from the customer.
(a) The money is taken from the customer by the accountant.
(b) The money was taken from the customer by the accountant.
(c) The customer was taken the money by the accountant.
(d) The money had been taken from the customer by the accountant.

42. The peon refused him admittance.
(a) He was refused admittance by the peon.
(b) Admittance is refused to him by the peon.
(c) Admittance was refused by the peon to him.
(d) Admittance is refused him by the peon.

43. The reporter was interviewing the political leaders.
(a) The political leaders were being interviewed by the reporter.
(b) The political leaders was being interviewed by the reporter.
(c) The political leaders are being interviewed by the reporter.
(d) The political leader is being interviewed by the reporter.

44. The beavers have built a perfect dam across the stream.
(a) A perfect dam had been built by the beavers across the stream.
(b) A perfect dam had been built by the beavers across the stream.
(c) A perfect dam have been built by the beavers across the stream.
(d) A perfect dam was being built by the beavers across the stream.

45. You should follow all the instructions carefully.
(a) All the instructions are carefully followed by you.
(b) All the instructions were carefully followed by you.
(c) All the instructions should be carefully followed by you
(d) All the instruction can be carefully followed by you.

46. The school was damaged by the earthquake which caused havoc to other buildings as well.
(a) The earthquake damaged the school and other buildings.
(b) The earthquake damaged other buildings.
(c) The earthquake caused havoc to other
(d) The earthquake damaged the school besides causing havoc to other buildings.

47. You don't need to wind this watch.
(a) This watch need not be wound.
(b) This watch does not wind.
(c) This watch need not be wounded.
(d) This watch need not be winded up.

48. Has somebody broken the window?
(a) Have the window been broken?
(b) Had the window been broken by somebody?
(c) Has the window been broken by somebody?
(d) Has been the window broken?

49. The children are making a noise.
(a) A noise is made by the children.
(b) A noise is being made by the children.
(c) The children should be making a noise.
(d) A noise has been made by the silence.

50. The child's shrill wail broke the silence.
(a) The silence was being broken by the child's shrill wall.
(b) The child's shrill wail was broken by the silence.
(c) The silence was broken by the child's shrill wail.
(d) The silence was being broken by the child's shrill wail.

51. The cat is running after the rat.
(a) The rat was being run after by the cat.
(b) The rat is being run after by the cat.
(c) The rat is run after by the cat.
(d) The cat is being run after by the rat.

52. English is spoken all over the world.
(a) All over the world English speaks.
(b) English speaks all over the world.
(c) The whole world speaks English.
(d) People speak English all over the world.

53. The boys elected Mohan captain.
(a) The boys were elected captain by Mohan.
(b) Mohan is elected captain by the boys.
(c) Mohan was elected captain by the boys.
(d) Mohan and the boys elected the captain.

54. They threw away the rubbish.
(a) The rubbish will be thrown away.
(b) The rubbish was being thrown away.
(c) The rubbish was thrown away.
(d) The rubbish thrown away.

55. Let him see the picture.
(a) Let the picture be seen by him.
(b) The picture is seen by him.
(c) Let him the picture be seen.
(d) The picture is seen by him.

56. We have already done the exercise.
(a) Already, the exercise has been done by us.
(b) The exercise has already been done by us.
(c) The exercise had been already done by us.
(d) The exercise is already done by us.

57. The main skills we seek to develop include analysing, interpreting and evaluating ideas.
(a) The main skills sought by us to develop include analysing, interpreting and evaluating ideas.
(b) The main skills sought to be developed by us include analysing, interpreting and evaluating ideas.
(c) The main skills that we are seeking to be developed include analysing, interpreting and evaluating ideas.
(d) The main skills include analysing, interpreting and evaluating ideas which are sought by us to develop.

58. Who can question Gandhi's integrity?
(a) By whom Gandhi's integrity can be questioned ?
(b) By whom can Gandhi's integrity be questioned ?
(c) Gandhi's integrity can be questioned by whom
(d) Who could have questioned Gandhi's integrity ?

59. He presented me a bouquet on my birthday.
(a) A bouquet is presented to me on my birthday by him.
(b) I was presented on my birth day bouquet by him.
(c) I was presented a bouquet on my birthday by him.
(d) I will be presented a bouquet on my birthday by him.

60. Drinking has ruined many people.
(a) Many people has been ruined by drinking.
(b) Many people have been ruined by drinking
(c) Many people are ruined by drinking.
(d) Many people has ruined drinking.

61. The king mocked at the servant.
(a) The servant was mocked at by the king
(b) The servant was being mocked at by the king.
(c) The servant was to be mocked at by the king .
(d) The servant was mocked by the king.

62. The labourers were digging a canal.
(a) A canal is being digged by the labourers.
(b) A canal was dug by the labouresrs.
(c) A canal was being dug by the labourers.
(d) A canal had been dug by the labourers.

63. The watchman switched on the lights before it began to grow dark.
(a) The lights were only switched on the lights before it began to grow dark.
(b) The lights were only switched on before it began to grow dark.
(c) The lights were being switched on by the watchman before it began to grow dark.
(d) The lights were switched on by the watchman before it began to grow dark.

64. Where do you keep the current magazines?
(a) Where were the current magazines kept?
(b) Where have the current magazines been kept ?
(c) Where are the current magazines being kept?
(d) Where are the current magazines kept by you?

65. She will be rewarded for her kind deed.
(a) Her kind deed will reward her.
(b) Her kind deed will have rewarded her.
(c) Her kind deed will be her reward.
(d) Her kind deed will have been her reward.

66. God gives up happiness.
(a) Happiness is given by God.
(b) happiness is being given to us by God.
(c) Happiness has been given by God.
(d) Happiness will be given by God.

67. The situation could hardly have been altered by the interference of the police force.
(a) The interference of the police force can hardly alter the situation.
(b) The interference of the police force could hardly have altered the situation.
(c) The interference of the police force could alter the situation with hardness.
(d) The interference of the police force had altered the situation.

68. We prohibit smoking.
(a) Smoking is prohibited.
(b) Smoking will be prohibited.
(c) Smoking has been prohibited.
(d) Smoking is being prohibited.

69. Rajesh could not complete his paper because he had a headache.
(a) The paper could not be completed by Rajesh because he had a headache.
(b) Rajesh's paper could not be completed because he had a headache.
(c) Rajesh's paper would not be completed because he had a headache.
(d) The paper of Rajesh could not be completed by him because he had a headache.

70. I didn't speak even a single word in the meeting.
(a) Even a single word had not been spoken by me in the meeting.
(b) Even a single word was not spoken by me in the meeting.
(c) Even a single word has not been spoken by me in the meeting.
(d) Even a single word have not been spoken by me in the meeting.

71. The Swiss regarded him as an impostor and called him a Villain.
(a) He is regarded as an impostor and called a Villain by the Swiss.
(b) He has been regarded as an impostor and called a Villain by the Swiss.
(c) He was regarded as an impostor and is called a Villain by the Swiss.
(d) He was regarded as an impostor and was called a Villain by the Swiss.

72. These days most of the students do their assignments with the help of the internet.
(a) These days most of the assignments are done with the help of the internet by the students.
(b) These days most of the students are doing their assignments with the help of the internet.
(c) These days the assignments are done with the help of the internet by most of the students.
(d) These days the assignments are being done with the help of the internet by most of the students.

73. That too many cooks spoil the broth is known to all.
(a) All knew that too many cooks spoilt the broth.
(b) All know that the broth is spoilt by too many cooks.
(c) All knows that the broth is spoilt by too many cooks.
(d) All know that too many cooks spoil the broth.

74. Shut the door.
(a) Let door be shut. (b) Let door be shut by you.
(c) Let the door be shutted. (d) Let the door be shut.

75. We shall write a novel.
(a) A novel would be written by us.
(b) A novel will have been written by us.
(c) A novel is written by us.
(d) A novel will be written by us.

76. Who tore the curtains yesterday?
(a) By whom were the curtains torn yesterday ?
(b) BY whom are the curtains torn yesterday?
(c) By whom were the curtains teared yesterday?
(d) By whom were the curtains teared yesterday?

77. He knew that his own life was unjust.
(a) It was known to him that his own life had been unjust.
(b) It was known by him that his own life was unjust.
(c) It was known to him that his own life was unjust.
(d) it was known by him that life was unjust.

78. The student has learnt the answer by heart.
(a) The answer was learnt by the student by heart.
(b) The answer is learnt by heart by the student.
(c) The answer by the student was learnt by heart.
(d) The answer has been learnt by heart by the student.

79. The old lady touched and patted the cow.
(a) The cow patted and touched the old lady.
(b) The cow was touched by the old lady patted her.
(c) The cow was touched and patted by the old lady.
(d) The patted cow touched the old lady.

80. This watch was given to me by my grandfather.
(a) My grandfather gave me this watch.
(b) My grandfather gives me this watch.
(c) My grandfather had given this watch to me.
(d) My grandfather has given this watch to me.

81. By whom is the child being fed?
(a) Who is feeding the child?
(b) Who has fed the child ?
(c) Who was feeding the child ?
(d) Who has been feeding the child ?

82. Alexander expected to conquer the world.
(a) It was expected by Alexander that he should conquer the world.
(b) It was expected by Alexander that he would conquer the world.
(c) It was expected by Alexander that he will conquer the world.
(d) It had been expected by Alexander that he would conquer the world.

83. She begins her day with a cup of coffee.
(a) Her day is being begun with a cup of coffee.
(b) Her day is begun with a cup of coffee.
(c) A cup of coffee is beginning her day.
(d) A cup of coffee has begun her day.

84. I shall be obliged to go.
(a) Circumstances would oblige me to go.
(b) Circumstances could oblige me to go.
(c) Circumstances will oblige me to go.
(d) Circumstances may oblige me to go.

85. It is time to water the plants.
(a) It is time when plants are watered.
(b) it is time the plants be watered.
(c) It is time for the plants to be watered.
(d) The plants should be watered.

86. Sita learns her lessons daily.
(a) Her lessons were learnt daily by Sita.
(b) Her lessons was learnt daily by Sita.
(c) Her lessons is learnt daily by Sita.
(d) Her lessons are learnt daily by Sita.

87. Ratan is performing an experiment.
(a) An experiment is performed by Ratan.
(b) An experiment was performed by Ratan.
(c) An experiment is being performed by Ratan.
(d) Experiments were performed by Ratan.

88. Who had laughed at you?
(a) Who had you been laughed at?
(b) By whom had you been laughed at?
(c) By whom were you been laughed at?
(d) By whom you had been laughed at?

89. Kindly offer your remarks.
(a) You have been requested to offer your remarks.
(b) You were requested to offer your remarks.
(c) You are requested to offer your remarks.
(d) You are being requested to offer your remarks.

90. By this time he will have received my letter.
(a) By this time my letter will have been received by him.
(b) By this time the letter has reached him.
(c) The letter, by this time, has been delivered to him.
(d) By this time the letter has been received by him.

91. You have to do this immediately.
(a) This has been done by you immediately.
(b) This is being done by you immediately.
(c) This was being done by you immediately.
(d) This has to be done by you immediately.

92. Let us help him.
(a) Let him help us.
(b) Let he is helped.
(c) Let he be helped.
(d) Let him be helped by us.

93. Cacao is bitter when it is tasted.
(a) Cacao is bitter.
(b) Cacao tastes bitter.
(c) Cacao's taste is bitter.
(d) Cacao tasted bitter.

94. A great man acknowledges me as a flatterer to him.
(a) I was acknowledged by a great man to be a flatterer.
(b) I was acknowledged by a great man to have been a flatterer.
(c) I am acknowledged as a flatterer by a great man.
(d) I was acknowledged by as a flatterer to a great man.

95. Has she worked out all the sums?
(a) Have all the sums worked out by her?
(b) Has all the sums been worked out by her?
(c) Have all the sums been worked by her?
(d) Have all the sums been worked out by her?

96. Can those happy moments be ever forgotten by me?
(a) Shall I ever forget those happy moments?
(b) Can I ever forget those happy moments?
(c) Will I ever forget those happy moments?
(d) Could I ever forget those happy moments?

97. Did he plan an excursion to mountains
(a) Was an excursion to mountains planned by him?
(b) Is an excursion to mountains planned by him?
(c) Had an excursion to mountains planned by him?
(d) Has an excursion to mountains planned by him?

98. Our vehicle had been stolen from our garage by the same burglary team.
(a) The same burglary team has stolen our vehicle from our garage.
(b) The same burglary team had stolen our vehicle from our garage.
(c) The same burglary team is stealing our vehicle from our garage.
(d) The same burglary team will have stolen our vehicle from our garage.

99. The judge ordered the murderer to be hanged.
(a) The murderer was to be hanged according to the order of the judge.
(b) The murderer was ordered by the judge to be hanged.
(c) It was ordered by the judge to hang the murderer.
(d) The order was given by the judge to hang the murderer.

100. Who gave you the money?
(a) Who was given the money by you ?
(b) By whom were you given the money?
(c) Who gave the money to you?
(d) By whom was you given the money?

Answers

1. (b)	2. (c)	3. (d)	4. (c)	5. (a)	6. (a)	7. (c)	8. (b)	9. (c)	10. (a)
11. (a)	12. (a)	13. (a)	14. (d)	15. (c)	16. (c)	17. (a)	18. (c)	19. (b)	20. (d)
21. (b)	22. (a)	23. (a)	24. (d)	25. (b)	26. (b)	27. (c)	28. (b)	29. (d)	30. (c)
31. (c)	32. (a)	33. (c)	34. (b)	35. (c)	36. (a)	37. (c)	38. (a)	39. (b)	40. (d)
41. (b)	42. (a)	43. (a)	44. (b)	45. (c)	46. (d)	47. (a)	48. (c)	49. (b)	50. (c)
51. (b)	52. (d)	53. (c)	54. (c)	55. (a)	56. (b)	57. (b)	58. (b)	59. (c)	60. (b)
61. (a)	62. (c)	63. (d)	64. (d)	65. (a)	66. (a)	67. (b)	68. (a)	69. (a)	70. (b)
71. (d)	72. (c)	73. (d)	74. (d)	75. (d)	76. (a)	77. (c)	78. (d)	79. (c)	80. (a)
81. (a)	82. (b)	83. (b)	84. (c)	85. (c)	86. (d)	87. (c)	88. (b)	89. (c)	90. (a)
91. (d)	92. (d)	93. (b)	94. (c)	95. (d)	96. (b)	97. (a)	98. (b)	99. (b)	100. (b)

C. Negative-Interrogative

एक प्रकार के वाक्य को दूसरे प्रकार के वाक्य में बदलने की प्रक्रिया, conversion of sentences कहलाती है। वाक्यों के conversion में निम्नलिखित नियमों का पालन किया जाता है।

Affirmative से Negative में Conversion

Rule 1

जब affirmative वाक्यों में verb 'be' के रूप (is, am, are, was, were) तथा verb 'have' के रूप (have, has, had) का प्रयोग main verb की तरह किया गया हो, तो इन verbs के बाद not का प्रयोग करके negative sentence बनाते हैं।

e.g. (i) Sonam was a musician. (Affirmative)
Sonam was not a musician. (Negative)

(ii) He has a new book. (Affirmative)
He has not a new book. (Negative)
or He does not have a new book.

Rule 2

जब primary auxiliaries (be and have) तथा modal auxiliaries (can, should, could, may, might, etc) का प्रयोग सहायक क्रिया (Helping verb) की तरह किया गया हो, तो helping verb और main verb के बीच not का प्रयोग करके negative sentence बनाया जाता है।

e.g. (i) I am purchasing a shirt. (Affirmative)
I am not purchasing a shirt. (Negative)

(ii) You should go there. (Affirmative)
You should not go there. (Negative)

Rule 3

जब primary auxiliary (be, do, have) तथा modal auxiliary (might, can, may, could, should, etc) का प्रयोग एक साथ किया गया हो, तो इनके बीच में not का प्रयोग करके negative sentence बनाया जाता है।

e.g. (i) She might be a winner. (Affirmative)
She might not be a winner. (Negative)

(ii) I can be a good player. (Affirmative)
I cannot be a good player. (Negative)

Rule 4

Present Indefinite Tense में singular के साथ does not का प्रयोग करके verb के अन्त में लगा s या es हटा देते हैं तथा does not, verb के पहले लिखा जाता है। इसी प्रकार, plural के साथ do not का प्रयोग करके negative sentence बनाया जाता है।

e.g. (i) He plays football. (Affirmative)
He does not play football. (Negative)

(ii) They work hard. (Affirmative)
They do not work hard. (Negative)

Rule 5

Past Indefinite Tense में verb से पहले did not का प्रयोग करके negative sentence बनाया जाता है तथा verb की second form को first form में बदल देते हैं।

e.g. (i) I played cricket yesterday. (Affirmative)
I did not play cricket yesterday. (Negative)

(ii) He purchased a car. (Affirmative)
He did not purchase a car. (Negative)

Rule 6

कुछ वाक्यों में शब्द बदलकर negative sentence बनाया जाता है। ऐसे वाक्यों में nothing, no one, nobody, no where, आदि शब्दों का प्रयोग किया जाता है।

e.g. (i) Something is wrong here. (Affirmative)
Nothing is wrong here. (Negative)

(ii) He saw someone in the room. (Affirmative)
He saw no one in the room. (Negative)

Rule 7

कुछ वाक्यों में noun से पहले no का प्रयोग करके negative sentence बनाया जाता है।

e.g. (i) He has respect in the society. (Affirmative)
He has no respect in the society. (Negative)

(ii) They have chance of playing. (Affirmative)
They have no chance of playing. (Negative)

Rule 8

जहाँ किसी कार्य को कभी न करने की बात कही गई हो, वहाँ verb से पहले never का प्रयोग करके negative sentence बनाया जाता है।

e.g. (i) I have always read English books. (Affirmative)
I have never read English books. (Negative)

(ii) He has always gone to temple. (Affirmative)
He has never gone to temple. (Negative)

Rule 9

जिन वाक्यों में either...or का प्रयोग किया गया हो, उनमें either के स्थान पर neither तथा or के स्थान पर nor का प्रयोग करके negative sentence बनाया जाता है।

e.g. (i) Either his mother or his father is a teacher. (Affirmative)
Neither his mother nor his father is a teacher. (Negative)

(ii) Either Sohan or Rohan did this. (Affirmative)
Neither Sohan nor Rohan did this. (Negative)

Note No body व no one का प्रयोग व्यक्ति के लिए, nothing का प्रयोग वस्तु के लिए, no where का प्रयोग स्थान के लिए तथा none का प्रयोग सजीव एवं निर्जीव दोनों के लिए किया जाता है।

Affirmative से Interrogative में Conversion

Rule 1

जब affirmative वाक्यों में verb 'be' के रूप (is, am, are, was ,were) का प्रयोग main verb की तरह किया गया हो, तो इन्हें subject से पहले प्रयोग करके interrogative sentence बनाया जाता है।

e.g. (i) He is a boy. (Affirmative)
Is he a boy? (Interrogative)

(ii) Reema was a painter. (Affirmative)
Was Reema a painter? (Interrogative)

Rule 2

जब affirmative वाक्यों में verb 'have' के रूप (have, has व had) का प्रयोग main verb की तरह किया गया हो, तो इन्हें subject से पहले प्रयोग करके अथवा subject से पहले verb 'do' के रूप (do, does, did) का प्रयोग करके interrogative sentence बनाया जाता है।

e.g. (i) You have a car. (Affirmative)
Have you a car?
or Do you have a car? (Interrogative)
(ii) Hema has a bicycle. (Affirmative)
Has Hema a bicycle?
or Does Hema have a bicycle? (Interrogative)
(iii) They had a sound sleep. (Affirmative)
Had they a sound sleep?
or Did they have a sound sleep? (Interrogative)

Rule 3

जब affirmative वाक्यों में primary auxiliaries (be and have) तथा modal auxiliaries (can, could, should, would, etc) का प्रयोग helping verb की तरह किया गया हो, तो helping verb को subject से पहले तथा main verb को subject के बाद प्रयोग करके interrogative sentence बनाया जाता है।

e.g. (i) He has eaten a mango. (Affirmative)
Has he eaten a mango? (Interrogative)
(ii) Mohan will draw a picture. (Affirmative)
Will Mohan draw a picture? (Interrogative)

Rule 4

जब affirmative वाक्यों में primary auxiliary तथा modal auxiliary का प्रयोग एक साथ किया गया हो, तो subject को इन दोनों के बीच में प्रयोग करके interrogative sentence बनाया जाता है।

e.g. (i) He may be a good dancer. (Affirmative)
May he be a good dancer? (Interrogative)
(ii) You can do this work. (Affirmative)
Can you do this work? (Interrogative)

Rule 5

Present Indefinite Tense में singular subject से पहले does का प्रयोग करके व plural subject से पहले do का प्रयोग करके interrogative sentence बनाया जाता है तथा verb के अन्त में लगा s व es हटा देते हैं।

e.g. (i) He loves me a lot. (Affirmative)
Does he love me a lot? (Interrogative)
(ii) They go to temple every Thursday. (Affirmative)
Do they go to temple every Thursday? (Interrogative)

Rule 6

Past Indefinite Tense में subject से पहले did का प्रयोग करके interrogative sentence बनाया जाता है तथा verb की second form को first form में बदल देते हैं।

e.g. (i) She danced very well. (Affirmative)
Did she dance very well? (Interrogative)
(ii) They went to watch a movie. (Affirmative)
Did they go to watch a movie? (Interrogative)

Interrogative से Interrogative-Negative में Conversion

प्रत्येक प्रकार के interrogative sentences में सदैव subject के बाद not का प्रयोग करके negative sentence बनाया जाता है।

e.g. (i) Does he go to school daily? (Interrogative)
Does he not go to school daily? (Negative)
(ii) Is she a good dancer? (Interrogative)
Is she not a good dancer? (Negative)

Imperative से Negative में Conversion

Imperative sentences में वाक्य के शुरु में do not का प्रयोग करके negative sentence बनाया जाता है।

e.g. (i) Pluck the flower. (Imperative)
Do not pluck the flower. (Negative)
(ii) Sit here. (Imperative)
Do not sit here. (Negative)

Affirmative से Exclamatory में Conversion

Affirmative वाक्यों के आरम्भ में exclamatory words; जैसे What!, How!, Wow!, आदि को वाक्य के भाव के अनुसार प्रयोग करके इसे exclamatory sentence में बदला जा सकता है तथा subject + verb को वाक्य के अन्त में लिखा जाता है।

e.g. (i) This is a good shot.
Wow! What a good shot this is.
(ii) The journey was pleasant.
What a pleasant journey that was!
(iii) This is a beautiful scenery.
What a beautiful scenery this is!
(iv) It is very wonderful weather.
How wonderful the weather is!

Exercise

Directions (1-30) Answer the following questions by choosing the most appropriate option.

1. Transform the given sentence into assertive.
How gorgeous is the sunset!
(a) How is the sunset so gorgeous?
(b) The sunset is gorgeous, isn't it?
(c) The sunset is very gorgeous.
(d) How gorgeous the sunset is!

2. Transform the given sentence into superlative.
No other metal is as expensive as gold.
(a) No other metal except gold is expensive.
(b) Gold is expensive of all the metals.
(c) Isn't gold the most expensive of all metals.
(d) Gold is the most expensive of all metals.

3. Transform the given sentence into simple.
She said that she was coming.
(a) She will come today.
(b) She is coming.
(c) She told of her coming.
(d) She told that she was coming.

4. Transform the given sentence into adjective.
She treated me respectfully.
(a) She treated me with respect.
(b) She respectfully treats me.
(c) She was respectful to me.
(d) She treats me respect.

5. Transform the given sentence into negative.
Human is mortal.
(a) Human is immortal.
(b) Human is not immortal.
(c) Not all humans are mortal.
(d) Not all humans are immortal.

6. Transform the given sentence into complex.
My ambition is to serve the country.
(a) My ambition is that I should serve my country.
(b) My ambition is that I shall serve my country.
(c) To serve my country is my ambition.
(d) I serve my country is my great ambition.

7. Transform the given sentence into negative.
Many people want to travel the world.
(a) Many people want to travel the world, isn't it?
(b) Many people don't want to travel the world.
(c) Don't many people want to travel the world?
(d) Not many people want to travel the world.

8. Transform the given sentence into comparative.
That chocolate is not as sweet as this one.
(a) The chocolates vary in their sweetness.
(b) This chocolate is sweeter than that chocolate.
(c) This chocolate is not sweeter than that chocolate.
(d) This chocolate is sweeter than that one.

9. Transform the given assertive sentence into interrogative.
Everybody has heard of Amitabh Bachchan.
(a) Has everybody heard of Amitabh Bachchan?
(b) Isn't that everybody has heard of Amitabh Bachchan?
(c) Everybody has heard of Amitabh Bachchan, isn't it?
(d) Amitabh Bachchan is known to all, isn't it?

10. Transform the given sentence into complex.
Her looks proclaim her innocence.
(a) Her looks proclaim that she is innocent.
(b) She is innocent, her looks proclaim.
(c) Her innocence is seen on her looks.
(d) She is innocent, proclaims her looks.

11. Transform the given sentence and change into noun. Parul sympathises with the needy and poor.
(a) Parul is sympathetic towards needy and poor.
(b) Parul treats needy and poor with sympathy.
(c) Parul has sympathy for the needy and poor.
(d) Needy and poor are sympathised by Parul.

12. Transform the given sentence by changing into verb.
The examination result gave her pleasure.
(a) The examination result pleased her.
(b) Her examination result gave her pleasure.
(c) She was pleased by her examination result.
(d) She was pleased to see her examination result.

13. Transform the given sentence into interrogative.
Great deal of research has been done on the science project.
(a) Has much research been done on the Science project?
(b) Has the Science project undergone research?
(c) The Science project is thoroughly researched, isn't it?
(d) Much research has been done on the Science project, isn't it?

14. Transform the given sentence into complex sentence.
We have informed her of her success.
(a) We have informed her of her being successful.
(b) She has been informed by us of her success.
(c) We have informed her that she has succeeded.
(d) She has been informed that she has succeeded.

15. Transform the given sentence into compound sentence.
Everyone knows that the earth is round.
(a) The earth is round and everyone knows it.
(b) Everyone knows that earth is circular in shape.
(c) The Earth is round is a known fact.
(d) The Earth is round is known to everyone.

16. Which of the transformations of the sentence 'Rajdhani Express is the fastest train' is correctly changed into positive sentence?
(a) There is no other train as fast as Rajdhani Express.
(b) No other train is as fast as Rajdhani Express.
(c) Both (a) and (b)
(d) None of the above.

17. Transform the given sentence by removing too.
This tea is too hot for me.
(a) This tea is so hot that I cannot take it.
(b) This tea is very hot for me.
(c) This tea is hot for me.
(d) This tea is hot that I cannot take it.

18. Transform the given sentence into compound.
Coming to me, Anita delivered the letter.
(a) Anita came to me and delivered the letter.
(b) Anita delivered the letter while she was coming to me.
(c) Anita came to deliver the letter.
(d) Anita came to me to deliver the letter.

19. Transform the given sentence into complex.
Buy one shirt and get one free.
(a) If you buy one shirt, you get another shirt free.
(b) If you buy one shirt, you get one free.
(c) A shirt free on purchase of a shirt.
(d) Buy one shirt to get one free.

20. Transform the given sentence into complex.
Listen and I will tell you all.
(a) If you listen, I will tell you all.
(b) Listen and know all.
(c) Listen carefully to know all.
(d) If you listen to me, I will tell you everything.

21. Transform the given sentence by removing too.
The oranges are too cheap to be good.
(a) The oranges are cheap and good.
(b) The oranges are cheap as well as good.
(c) The oranges are very cheap good.
(d) The oranges are so cheap that they cannot be good.

22. Transform the given complex sentence into compound sentence.
If you cannot obey me you have to leave.
(a) If you don't obey me, you will have to leave.
(b) Obey or leave.
(c) Either obey me or leave.
(d) Obey me or leave.

23. Transform the given sentence into interrogative.
Stop it.
(a) Will you stop it?
(b) Please stop it.
(c) Can you stop it?
(d) Please stop.

24. Transform the given compound sentence into complex sentence.
Cancer is curable and everybody knows this.
(a) Cancer is curable is known to all.
(b) Cancer is curable is a known fact.
(c) Everybody knows that cancer is curable.
(d) Everybody knows that cancer can be cured.

25. Transform the given complex sentence into compound sentence.
As soon as we heard the shout, we rushed to the spot.
(a) We heard the shout and rushed to the spot.
(b) Hearing the shout, we rushed to the spot.
(c) We heard the shout and rushed.
(d) We rushed to the spot as soon as we heard the shout.

26. Transform the given compound sentence into complex sentence.
You have to be 18 years old or you can't drive.
(a) You can't drive because you are under 18.
(b) To drive, you have to be 18 years old.
(c) If you are under 18, you can't drive.
(d) If you are 18 year old, you can't drive.

27. Transform the given exclamatory sentence into assertive sentence.
How kind of you to help her like that.
(a) How kind of you that you helped her like that.
(b) It is very kind of you to help her.
(c) You are very kind to help her like that.
(d) It is very kind of you to help her like that.

28. Transform the given complex sentence into compound sentence.
Although he is rich, he is not happy.
(a) He isn't happy but he is rich.
(b) He is rich and still not happy.
(c) He is rich but he is not happy.
(d) He is rich but not happy.

29. Transform the given sentence into negative.
Ajay loved his parents.
(a) Ajay hates his parents.
(b) Ajay did not love his parents.
(c) Ajay does not love his parents.
(d) Ajay did not hate his parents.

30. Transform the given sentence into positive.
Samay writes more neatly than any other boy in the class.
(a) No other boy of Samay's class writes as neatly as he.
(b) Samay writes neatly than all his classmates.
(c) Samay's writing is very neat.
(d) Samay's writing is neater than all the boys in his class.

Directions (31-40) Combine each of the following pairs of sentences using infinitives.

31. They wanted to win. They worked hard for that reason.
(a) They worked hard to win.
(b) They worked hard for that reason to win.
(c) To win they worked hard.
(d) They wanted to win and worked hard

32. She was sensible. She did the right thing.
(a) She was sensible to do the right thing.

(b) She did the right thing to be sensible.
(c) She was sensible enough to do the right thing.
(d) To be sensible she did right thing.

33. The students were not able to solve the problem. It was too difficult for them.
(a) It was too difficult to solve the problem.
(b) To the students it was too difficult to solve the problem.
(c) The problem for the students was too difficult to solve.
(d) The problem was too difficult for the students to solve.

34. It is too late. We can't start a new lesson now.
(a) It is too late for us to start a new lesson.
(b) It is too late that can't start a new lesson now.
(c) It is getting late to start a new lesson.
(d) We are too late starting a new lesson.

35. The manager appointed John. He will do the accounts.
(a) He will do the accounts the manager appointed John.
(b) The manager appointed John to do the accounts.
(c) The manager appointed to John he will do the accounts.
(d) Being appointed by manager John will do the accounts.

36. We went to the theater. We saw a movie there.
(a) We went to the theater seeing a movie.
(b) We saw a movie there went to the theater.
(c) To seeing a movie we went to the theatre.
(d) We went to the theater to see a movie.

37. I have no interest in politics. I must tell it frankly.
(a) I have no interest in politics to tell it frankly.
(b) I must tell it frankly to no interest in politics.
(c) To be frank, I have no interest in politics.
(d) I must tell it frankly to having no interest in politics.

38. The man took out a knife. He intended to frighten all of us.
(a) The man took out a knife to frighten all of us.
(b) He intended to frighten all of us took out a knife.
(c) To frighten all of us he took out knife.
(d) The man took out a knife to intend to frighten all of us.

39. Mary collects old stamps. It is her hobby.
(a) It is her hobby to collect stamps.
(b) It is Mary's hobby to collect old stamps.
(c) Mary collects old stamps it is her hobby.
(d) Mary's old hobby is collecting stamps.

40. The men held a meeting. They wanted to elect a manager for the company.
(a) They wanted to elect a manager for the company, the men held a meeting.
(b) They wanted a manager to held a meeting.
(c) The men held a meeting to elect a manager for the company.
(d) A meeting was held to elect a manager.

Directions (41-50) Identify the following sentences or clauses from the given options.

41. We can wait here until Sourav calls us.
(a) Compound
(b) Simple
(c) Complex
(d) None of the above

42. Either the engine starts, or we will remain here all night.
(a) Compound (b) Simple
(c) Complex (d) None of these

43. A group of my classmates studied the problem and solved it in a few minutes.
(a) Compound
(b) Simple
(c) Complex
(d) None of these

44. The old car was in fairly good operating condition, but the condition of the body was poor.
(a) Compound (b) Simple
(c) Complex (d) None of these

45. The small streams <u>that run through the area</u> are loaded with fish.
(a) Adverb clause
(b) Adjective clause
(c) Noun clause
(d) None of the above

46. <u>When the leaves begin to fall,</u> we will harvest the last of our crops.
(a) Adverb clause
(b) Adjective clause
(c) Noun clause
(d) None of the above

47. Your sister said <u>you haven't slept in two or three nights.</u>
(a) Adverb clause
(b) Adjective clause
(c) Noun clause
(d) None of the above

48. People <u>who have poor diets</u> are likely to catch colds.
(a) Adverb clause
(b) Adjective clause
(c) Noun clause
(d) None of the above

49. The crew checked the ship and prepared it for sea.
(a) Compound (b) Simple
(c) Complex (d) None of these

50. We must prepare the dam, or the water will rush through.
(a) Compound (b) Simple
(c) Complex (d) None of these

Directions (51-54) Transform the simple sentence into a compound sentence.

51. He must work hard to make up for the lost time.
(a) He should make up the lost of time working hard.
(b) He must worked hard and make up for the lost time.
(c) Working hard he can make up the lost time
(d) He has to make up the lost time working hard.

52. To his eternal disgrace, he betrayed his country.
(a) He betrayed his country is an eternal disgrace.
(b) For him betraying his country was an eternal disgrace.
(c) He betrayed his country and this was to his eternal disgrace.
(d) Eternal disgrace was his betraying the country.

53. Besides robbing the poor child, he also murdered the child.

(a) He not only robbed the poor child but also murdered the child.

(b) He robbed the child and murdered the child.

(c) The poor child was robbed and murdered by him.

(d) After robbing the poor child he murdered him.

54. The teacher punished the children for disobedience.

(a) For disobedience the teacher punished the children.

(b) The teacher punished the children for their disobedience.

(c) The children were disobedient so the teacher punished them.

(d) Being disobedient the teacher punished the students.

Directions (55-60) Change one part of a sentence for another part without changing the meaning.

55. This kind of joke never amuses me.

(a) This kind of jokes are always amusing.

(b) I am not amused by this kind of jokes.

(c) This kind of joke never gives me any amusement.

(d) Always amusing this kind of jokes.

56. It costs twelve dollars.

(a) Its cost is twelve dollars.

(b) The cost is twelve dollars.

(c) Twelve dollar is the cost of it.

(d) The cost stands at twelve dollars.

57. Direction: Transform the following without changing the meaning.

He gave a curt reply.

(a) His reply was curtly.

(b) He always gives replies in a curtly manner.

(c) Curtly replies are his habit.

(d) He replied curtly.

58. I see him every day.

(a) I see him always.

(b) I see him daily.

(c) I see him all the time.

(d) I see him every time.

59. This scene is surpassingly beautiful.

(a) Surpassingly beautiful is the scene.

(b) The beauty of this scene is surpassing.

(c) How surpassingly the beautiful scene.

(d) Surpassing beautiful the scene is.

60. He is admittedly the greatest general of this country.

(a) This is admitted he is the greatest general of this country

(b) This country's greatest general he is.

(c) It has been admitted that he is the greatest general of this country.

(d) Admittedly the greatest general of this country he is.

Answers

1. (c)	2. (d)	3. (c)	4. (c)	5. (b)	6. (a)	7. (d)	8. (d)	9. (a)	10. (a)
11. (c)	12. (a)	13. (a)	14. (c)	15. (a)	16. (c)	17. (a)	18. (a)	19. (b)	20. (a)
21. (d)	22. (d)	23. (a)	24. (c)	25. (a)	26. (c)	27. (d)	28. (c)	29. (d)	30. (a)
31. (a)	32. (c)	33. (d)	34. (a)	35. (b)	36. (d)	37. (c)	38. (a)	39. (b)	40. (c)
41. (c)	42. (a)	43. (a)	44. (a)	45. (b)	46. (a)	47. (c)	48. (b)	49. (a)	50. (a)
51. (b)	52. (c)	53. (a)	54. (c)	55. (c)	56. (a)	57. (d)	58. (b)	59. (b)	60. (c)

D. Punctuation

The right use of putting in marks or stops in writing is called Punctuation अर्थात् लिखते समय mark, stops या points का सही रूप में use करना Punctuation कहलाता है।

Kinds of Punctuation Marks

English language के अन्तर्गत निम्न punctuation marks use किये जाते हैं

S.N.	Name of the Punctuation mark	Sign
1.	Full stop (also called 'Period')	(.)
2.	Comma	(,)
3.	Note (or sign) of Interrogation (also called 'the question mark')	(?)
4.	Note (or sign) of exclamation	(!)
5.	Apostrophe	(')
6.	Quotation marks (or inverted commas)	
	(i) Double	("…")
	(ii) Single	('…')
7.	Capital Letters	A, B, C etc.
8.	Colon	(:)
9.	Semi colon	(;)
10.	Dash	(—)
11.	Hyphen	(-)
12.	Parentheses (or Brackets)	( )
13.	Oblique	(/)

Usage of Punctuation Marks

1. Full Stop [पूर्ण विराम (.)]

(a) Interrogative एवं exclamatory sentences के अतिरिक्त सभी प्रकार के sentences के अन्त में full stop लगता है। चाहे वह sentence सामान्य statement हो अथवा command हो या sentence के मध्य में कोई प्रश्न हो।

e.g., He is a good boy. (Statement)
Do not open the gate. (Command)

(b) Abbreviation के प्रत्येक अक्षर या भाग को पृथक करने के लिए

e.g., Single letter : M.A., B.A., L.L.B. etc.
Double letter : Ph.D., B.Ed., Dr., Er. etc.
A number of letters : Dist., Abbr., Adv. etc.

(c) प्रत्येक closed couplet के अन्त में

e.g., "For forms of government, let fools contest,
Whate'er is best administered is best".
— Alexander Pope.

(d) कविता की उन पंक्तियों के अन्त में जहाँ चल रहा विचार समाप्त होता है

e.g., Our sincerest laughter, with some pain is fraught;
Our sweetest songs are those that tell of saddest thought. — P.B. Shelley

(e) Letter लिखते समय date के अन्त मे

e.g., 21st May, 2014.
or May 21, 2014.

2. Comma (अल्प या अद्ध विराम) (,)

Comma सबसे महत्त्वपूर्ण तथा सबसे अधिक प्रयोग होने वाला punctuation mark है। इसका प्रयोग निम्नलिखित स्थानों पर किया जाता है।

(a) एक ही parts of speech के एक जैसे वर्ग के शब्दों को अलग करने के लिए

e.g., (i) Sachin, Saurabh, Gautam and Deepak are my classmates.
(ii) He is very innocent, honest and hard-working.

(b) तिथि को वर्ष से अलग करने के लिए

e.g. (i) She was born on May 12, 1987.
(ii) I got the job on July 15, 2010.

(c) Nominative of address के बाद

e.g., (i) Apeksha, come to me.
(ii) Ankit, do your work.

(d) यदि nominative of address वाक्य के अन्त में प्रयुक्त हो, तो इससे पहले

e.g., (i) Come to me, Kiran.
(ii) Listen to me, Tushar.

(e) Nominative absolute phrase के बाद

e.g., (i) My work having been finished, I went home.
(ii) The weather being bad, we did not go to market.

(f) यदि case in apposition वाक्य के बीच में आए, तो उसके पहले और बाद दोनों स्थानों पर

e.g., (i) My friend, Richa, is an engineer.
(ii) Milton, the great poet of English literature, was blind.

(g) Reported speech को वाक्य से अलग करने पर

e.g., (i) Priya said, "I am feeling well now".
(ii) She said to me, "I have a gift for you".

(h) And से जुड़े हुए जोड़ों को एक-दूसरे से अलग करने के लिए

e.g., (i) Chavi and Priyanka, Seema and Nitika, Kiran and Kavita will play together.

(ii) King and beggar, wise and foolish, rich and poor are alike in the court of God.

(i) Continuative sense में प्रयोग होने वाले relative adverbs या relative pronouns से पहले

e.g., (i) I went to Jaipur, where we stayed for two days.

(ii) This movie, which I watched last sunday, is very boring.

(j) वाक्य में क्रिया को बार-बार न लिखने के लिए

e.g., (i) My sister ate dosa and my brother, noodles.

(ii) Komal bought a suit and Ankita, a saree.

(k) Yes या no के बाद

e.g., (i) Yes, I shall go there.

(ii) No, I will not do this work.

(*l*) पत्र (letter) में salutation (अभिवादन) तथा complementary close (सम्मानसूचक) के बाद

e.g., (i) Dear Sir,

(ii) Yours Sincerely,

(m) Clauses को अलग करने के लिए

e.g., (i) If you come, I shall help you.

(ii) The girls came, sat down and went after two hours.

(n) Adverbial phrase और adverbial clause को अलग करने के लिए जब वह वाक्य के आरम्भ में प्रयुक्त हो

e.g., (i) In case of need, please come to me.

(ii) In spite of so many instructions, she did the same thing.

(o) कुछ coordinate conjunctions से पहले

e.g., (i) He is tired, still he is working.

(ii) She did not come, still he is waiting for her.

(p) कुछ शब्दों या phrases के पहले और बाद में, जो वाक्य के अन्दर किसी बात पर जोर डालने के लिए प्रयुक्त हों, ऐसे शब्द however, therefore, doubtless, too, hence, in short, moreover, nevertheless, at least, of course, finally, may, after all, आदि हैं।

e.g. (i) I, therefore, cannot go there.

(ii) I, after all, selected you to go with me.

3. Note (or Mark) of Interrogation [प्रश्नवाचक चिन्ह (?)]

(a) Interrogative sentence के अन्त में तथा एक sentence में question पूछने वाले word, clause या phrase के बाद

e.g., (i) Who invited you to dinner?

(ii) "Is everything ok?", Ram asked.

(b) जब sentence में किसी प्रकार की अनिश्चितता या शंकात्मक प्रश्न जैसा भाव हो तो question mark लगाया जाता है।

e.g., (i) Gandhiji died in 1948?

(ii) The Sun is the hottest star in the sky?

(c) Question tag के बाद

e.g., (i) You are happy, aren't you?

(ii) He is there, isn't he?

4. Note of Exclamation [विस्मयादिबोधक चिन्ह (!)]

(a) प्रत्येक exclamatory अथवा optative sentences के अन्त में

e.g., (i) How beautiful the Taj is!

(ii) May you live long!

(b) Interjections के बाद

e.g., (i) Bravo! well done

(ii) Alas! He's ruined.

5. Apostrophe [सम्बोधन चिन्ह (')]

(a) सम्बन्ध प्रकट करने के लिए (singular के साथ s से पहले व plural के साथ s के बाद)

e.g., (i) This is Ashwani's watch.

(ii) This is girls's hostel.

(b) शब्दों को संक्षिप्त बनाने के लिए

e.g., don't (do not), can't (can not), it's (it is), I've (I have), I'II (I will), आदि।

(c) Abbreviations को plural बनाने के लिए

e.g., M.L.A's, B.A.'s etc.

(d) जब किसी singular को possessive case में show करना हो, तो singular noun के बाद 's' लगेगा, परन्तु यदि plural को possessive case में show करना हो, तो plural (अर्थात् word + s) के बाद (') का use होगा।

e.g., (i) Is there a boys' hostel in your college?

(ii) How many girls' colleges are there in your city?

6. Quotation marks or Inverted commas ("...")

(a) Direct reported speech दर्शाने के लिए

e.g., (i) He said to you, "I am glad to see you".

(ii) She says to her mother, "Where is Shyam?"

(b) किसी लेखक आदि को quote करने के लिए

e.g., (i) According to Shakespeare, "Sweet are the uses of adversity".

(ii) According to Milton, "Better to reign in hell than to serve in heaven".

(c) किसी word पर जोर देने के लिए

e.g., (i) Take care of your "spellings".

(ii) We should lay stress on "national integration".

7. Capital Letters (ABC ...)

(a) वाक्य आरम्भ करने के लिए
e.g., (i) Komal is a teacher.
(ii) She is very innocent.

(b) Personal pronoun 'I' एवं interjection 'O' के लिए
e.g., (i) What can I say to him?
(ii) O man! what is wrong with you?

(c) Abbreviations के लिए प्रयुक्त प्रत्येक अक्षर के लिए
e.g., (i) N.A.T.O. (North Atlantic Treaty Organisation)
(ii) P.M. (Prime Minister)

(d) Proper noun और proper adjective के लिए
e.g., (i) Ram lives in Delhi.
(ii) Sakshi belongs to Maharashtra.

(e) महीनों के नाम, दिनों के नाम तथा holidays के लिए
e.g., (i) January is the first month of the year.
(ii) Sunday is a holiday.
(iii) We celebrate Children's Day on 14th November.

(f) देश के नाम, भाषा, राष्ट्रीयता (Nationality), धर्म (Religion) तथा विषय (Subject) के लिए
e.g., (i) I want to visit China.
(ii) Indian people are very intelligent.
(iii) Hindi is our national language.
(iv) Holi is the festival of colours.
(v) My mother teaches me English.

(g) ऐतिहासिक जगह एवं घटनाओं के लिए
e.g., (i) The Taj Majal is in Agra.
(ii) Green Revolution in India was a period during which agriculture in India increased its yields.

(h) Title के लिए
e.g., (i) 'War and Peace' is one of the best novels.
(ii) 'Complete Course' is the best series of Arihant Publications.

(i) समाचार पत्रों, जहाजों, रेलों, आदि के नाम के लिए
e.g., (i) The Times of India is the best newspaper.
(ii) The Titanic was the biggest ship in the world.
(iii) Metro train runs in Delhi.

(j) भगवान के नामों के लिए
e.g. (i) I pray to God daily.
(ii) I believe in Lord Vishnu.

(k) Reported speech के लिए
e.g., (i) Rishabh says, "My father is a doctor."
(ii) Kalpana said, "I am a best teacher for my daughter."

(l) राजनैतिक दलों के नाम के लिए
e.g., Bhartiya Janta Party, Congress, Samajwadi Party, आदि।

8. Colon (:)

(a) Colon का use किसी उदाहरण या सूची को शुरू करने हेतु किया जाता है।
e.g., (i) The three committes are as follows : Finance, Administration and Sports.
(ii) He nominated five members : Rahul, Sarla, Rajni, Girish and Janardhan.

(b) Expression जैसे What I suggest is this के बाद
e.g., What I suggest is this :
(i) Fill the form
(ii) Submit it to the counter
(iii) Wait for the reply

(c) Expression जैसे What really happened was this के बाद
e.g., What really happened was this:
(i) The manager came there
(ii) He listened to the problems
(iii) He assured everyone

(d) Expression जैसे as follows, the following, for example, namely, आदि के बाद अर्थात् किसी list को लिखने से पहले
e.g. (i) Everyone wants the following things :
- Car
- Flat
- Job

(ii) Please send me all your proof namely:
- Age certificate
- Passport
- Family income

(d) Complete sentence के बाद किसी quotation को लिखने के लिए
e.g., (i) Follow the words of Chanakya : "A man is great by deeds, not by birth."
(ii) Remember the words of the great Yogi Berra: "It ain't over until it's over."

(f) Hours, minutes तथा seconds के बीच
e.g., (i) It is 11: 30: 45 by my watch.
(ii) I will reach at 9: 30 am.

(g) अनुपात (Ratio) के लिए
e.g., (i) The ratio of students and teachers is 10 : 1.
(ii) The ratio of blue and red balls is 3 : 1.

9. Semi-Colon (;)

(a) Independent clauses को जोड़ने के लिए comma या conjunction के स्थान पर semicolon का use किया जाता है।
e.g., (i) I am upset; he insulted my father.
(ii) I am very happy; my brother has been selected for this post.

(b) जब विभिन्न प्रकार के नाम व पदनाम एक series में, एक ही sentence में एक-दूसरे के साथ आएँ तो इन्हें अलग एवं स्पष्ट रूप से व्यक्त/प्रदर्शित करने के लिए semi-colon का use किया जाता है।

e.g., The nominated members are S. Krishna, Chairman; K. Krishnan, Vice chairman; L. Krishnan, Secretary; and M. Krishnan, Joint Secretary.

(c) कभी-कभी poetry की lines में भी use किया जाता है।

e.g., "Heart,
Why not the heart?
A fittest flower to God;
Does flower please God; ...."
— Anonymous.

10. Dash (–)

(a) Colon के साथ जहाँ इसे "Colon Dash" कहते हैं

e.g., Please try to learn the following points :

(b) कई बार अकेले Dash ही "Colon Dash" का काम करते है

e.g ., Please pay full attention to the point mentioned below –

(c) अचानक किसी विचार को व्यक्त करने के लिए भी यह प्रयोग में लाई जाती है,

e.g., Now, nobody will have to go to the town for small items of daily use–and that's novelty behind this idea of starting a multi-trading complex in the rural areas.

(d) कविता में विभिन्न प्रकार के भाव प्रकट करने के लिए

e.g., "Wordsworth has gone from us – and ye, Ah, may ye feel his voice as we!"
— Matthew Arnold (in Memorial Verses, April, 1850)

11. Hyppen (-)

(a) Compound words बनाने के लिए भी hyphen का प्रयोग होता है, e.g.,

(a) Commander-in-chief

(b) Man-of-war

(c) Man-sized

(b) इसका प्रयोग pin Code लिखने के लिए भी होता है, e.g.,

(a) Delhi-110001

(b) Ludhina-141425

(c) इसका प्रयोग telecom के codes लिखने के लिए भी होता है,

e.g., (a) 91-011-2249543

(b) 92-161-454112

(d) E-mail शब्द के दो भागों के बीच में सदा hyphen का प्रयोग होता है।

(e) कई बार पाठकों का ध्यान आकर्षित करने के लिए भी इसका प्रयोग होता है,

e.g., Through-us-you-can-visit
USA-UK-Germany-France

12. Parenthesis or Brackets [( )]

(a) जब कोई term या expression के साथ उसकी abbreviation देनी हो,

e.g., (i) He is the Managing Director (M.D.) of this firm.

(ii) He is Bachelor of Arts (B.A.)

(b) जब किसी abbreviation के पूरे शब्द देने हों,

e.g., (i) This matter pertains to W.H.O. (World Health Orgaisation).

(ii) India has manufactured the M.B.T. (Main Battle Tank).

13. Oblique (/)

(a) दो में से एक सम्भावना व्यक्त करने के लिए,

e.g., (i) Please express your view/s on this matter.

(ii) You can get a prize/prizes if you work hard.

(b) To express certain terms in abbreviated forms

e.g., (i) c/f (carried forward)

(ii) b/d (brougt down)

(iii) r/o (resident of)

Exercise 1

Directions (Q. Nos. 1-50) In the questions given below, which one alternative out of four has been applied with correct punctuation marks?

1. Hurry up the train leaves at six o'clock
(a) Hurry up; the train leaves at six o'clock.
(b) Hurry up, the train leaves at six o'clock.
(c) Hurry up! the train leaves at six o'clock.
(d) Hurry up, the train leaves at six o'clock.

2. It is a sin to waste food said the father
(a) It is a sin to waste food said the father.
(b) 'It is a sin to waste food' said the father.
(c) "It is a sin to waste food" said the father.
(d) "It is a sin to waste food," said the father.

3. This is his fathers car
(a) This is his Fathers Car
(b) This is his father car
(c) This is his father's car.
(d) This is his fathers' car.

4. The man asked the taxi driver will you take me to the airport
(a) The man asked the taxi driver, will you take me to the airport?
(b) The man asked the taxi driver, "Will you take me to the airport?"
(c) The man asked the taxi driver, "Will you take me to the airport."
(d) The man asked the taxi driver, "will you take me to the airport!"

5. Bring me a glass of water said the teacher I am feeling very thirsty
(a) "Bring me a glass of water," said the teacher, "I am feeling very thirsty."
(b) "Bring me a glass of water" said the teacher, I am feeling very thirsty.
(c) "Bring me a glass of water" said the teacher 'I am feeling very thirsty.'
(d) "Bring me a glass of water, said the teacher "i am feeling very thirsty."

6. Ram said I am in a hurry I cannot spare time
(a) Ram said, "I am in a hurry" "I cannot spare time."
(b) Ram said "I am in a hurry I cannot spare time."
(c) Ram said, "I am in a hurry, I cannot spare time."
(d) Ram said, 'I am in a hurry I cannot spare time.'

7. How have you found so much wealth asked Anil's wife
(a) "How have you found so much wealth!" asked Anil's wife.
(b) "How have you found so much wealth?" asked Anil's wife.
(c) "How have you found so much wealth." asked Anil's wife.
(d) "How have you found so much wealth?", asked Anil's wife.

8. What is the matter why are you crying he asked the child
(a) "What is the matter, why are you crying?" he asked the child.
(b) "What is the matter? why are you crying?" he asked the child
(c) "What is the matter" "why are you crying?" he asked the child.
(d) "What is the matter? Why are you crying?" he asked the child.

9. I am going to marry and I want a house to live in said the young man
(a) "I am going to marry and I want a house to live in", said the young man.
(b) "I am going to marry" and "I want a house to live in" said the young man.
(c) "I am going to marry and I want a house to live in" said the young man.
(d) "I am going to marry and I want a house to live in." said the young man.

10. What harm is there if we admit the error the lawyer said
(a) "What harm is there, if we admit the error?" the lawyer said.
(b) "What harm is there if, we admit the error?" The lawyer said.
(c) "What harm is there if we admit the error?" the lawyer said.
(d) "What harm is there? if we admit the error". the lawyer said.

11. The more we hate one another the worse it will be for everybody
(a) The more we hate one another the worse, it will be for everybody.
(b) The more we hate one another, the worse it will be for everybody.
(c) The more we hate one another; The worse it will be for everybody.
(d) The more we hate one another - The worse it will be for everybody.

12. Anita's father Mr. Anil Kumar is a teacher
(a) Anita's father Mr anil Kumar is a teacher.
(b) Anita's father, mr. Anil Kumar is a teacher.
(c) Anita's father : Mr. Anil Kumar, is a teacher.
(d) Anita's father, Mr. Anil Kumar, is a teacher.

13. Considering all aspects of the matter they decided to give up the plan
(a) Considering all aspects of the matter, they decided to give up the plan.
(b) considering, all aspects of the matter, they decided to give up the plan.
(c) Considering all aspects, of the matter, they decided to give up the plan.
(d) Considering, All aspects of the matter they decided to give up the plan.

14. The Narmada the Ganga and the Yamuna are three of the largest Indian rivers

(a) The narmada, the ganga and the yamuna are three of the largest Indian rivers.
(b) The Narmada, the Ganga, and the Yamuna are three of the largest Indian rivers
(c) The Narmada, the Ganga and the Yamuna are three of the largest Indian rivers.
(d) The Narmada, the Ganga and, the Yamuna are three of the largest Indian rivers.

15. What a remarkable victory
(a) What, a remarkable victory.
(b) What a remarkable victory.
(c) What a remarkable victory?
(d) What a remarkable victory!

16. The election many people said would spring a big surprise and they were proved right
(a) The election, many people said, "would spring a big surprise and they were proved right."
(b) "The election," many people said, "would spring a big surprise and they were proved right."
(c) "The election" many people said, 'Would spring a big surprise and they were proved right'.
(d) "The election" many people said "would spring a big surprise and they were proved right.

17. Are you going he asked we are not I replied
(a) "Are you going?" he asked, 'we are not.' I replied.
(b) "Are you going?" he asked, "we are not" I replied.
(c) "Are you going?" he asked. "We are not," I replied.
(d) "Are you going?" he asked, "we are not" I replied.

18. Here I am master I am ready to go wherever you want me to go he said
(a) "Here I am, Master, I am ready to go," wherever you want me to go he said.
(b) "Here I am master, I am ready to go wherever you want me to go" he said.
(c) "Here I am master i am ready to go wherever you want me to go", He said.
(d) "Here I am, master, I am ready to go wherever you want me to go", he said.

19. What is your reason for refusing to marry this girl asked his mother
(a) "What is your reason for refusing to marry this girl?" asked his mother.
(b) "What is your reason, for refusing to marry this girl?" asked his mother.
(c) What is your reason for refusing to marry this girl? asked his mother
(d) "What is your reason for refusing to marry this girl," asked his mother.

20. He said my brother had an accident on Sunday the 28th April, 2013 and is still confined to bed
(a) He said "my brother had an accident on Sunday the 28th April, 2013 and is still confined to bed."
(b) He said "My brother had an accident on Sunday the 28th April, 2013 and is still confined to bed."
(c) He said", My brother had an accident on Sunday, the 28th April, 2013, and is still confined to bed."
(d) He said," My brother had an accident on Sunday, the 28th April, 2013 and is still confined to bed."

21. How many r's are there in referred I asked
(a) How many r's are there in referred? I asked.
(b) "How many r's are there, in referred" I asked.
(c) "How many r's are there in referred?" I asked.
(d) "How many rs' are there in referred?" I asked.

22. Friends colleagues relatives none stood by him
(a) Friends, colleagues, relatives none stood by him.
(b) Friends, colleagues, relatives, none stood by him.
(c) Friends, colleagues, relatives, none, stood by him
(d) Friends, colleagues, relatives none, stood by him.

23. He said, I am sorry I could not reach in time
(a) He said, "I am sorry I could not reach in time."
(b) He said "I am sorry. I could not reach in time."
(c) He said : "I am sorry I could not reach in time."
(d) He said "I am sorry I could not reach in time."

24. Never listen to his stories dont believe what he says and always distrust him
(a) Never listen to his stories, don't believe what he says? and always distrust him.
(b) Never listen to his stories, don't believe, what he says? and always distrust him.
(c) Never listen to his stories, do'nt believe what he says and always distrust him.
(d) Never listen to his stories, don't believe what he says and always distrust him.

25. Man proposes God disposes
(a) Man proposes God disposes.
(b) Man proposes, God disposes.
(b) Man proposes, God disposes!
(d) Man proposes God disposes!

26. He asked me what I wanted
(a) He asked me, what I wanted?
(b) He asked me "what I wanted"?
(c) He asked me what I wanted.
(d) He asked me "what I wanted!"

27. He said to me lets wait for him
(a) He said to me, "Let's wait for him."
(b) He said to me "Lets wait for him.'
(c) He said to me, "let's wait for him."
(d) He said to me, "Let's wait for him."

28. In India the ganga and the yamuna are regarded as sacred rivers
(a) In India, the Ganga and the Yamuna are regarded as sacred rivers.
(b) In India, the ganga and the Yamuna are regarded as sacred rivers.
(c) In India, the ganga and the yamuna are regarded as sacred rivers.
(d) In India–the Ganga and the yamuna are regarded as sacred rivers.

29. To err is human to forgive divine
(a) To err is human to forgive divine.

(b) To err is human, to forgive divine.
(c) To err, is human to forgive, divine.
(d) To err is human; to forgive, divine.

30. He was born on August 16, 1944 in Howrah West Bengal
(a) He was born on August 16, 1944 in howrah west bengal.
(b) He was born on August 16, 1944, in Howrah West Bengal.
(c) He was born on, August 16 1944 in Howrah west bengal.
(d) He was born on August, 16 1944, in Howrah West Bengal.

31. He is to tell you the truth is a fool
(a) He is, to tell you the truth, is a fool.
(b) He is to tell you, the truth is a fool.
(c) He is to tell you the truth; is a fool.
(d) He is; to tell you the truth is a fool.

32. This in brief is what he said
(a) This in brief is what he said.
(b) This in brief, is what he said.
(c) This, in brief, is what he said.
(d) This, in brief is what, he said.

33. If you need my help write to me
(a) If you need my help write to me.
(b) If, you need my help, write to me.
(c) If you need, my help, write to me.
(d) If you need my help, write to me.

34. They started running for they were getting late
(a) They started running, for they were getting late.
(b) They started running for they were getting late.
(c) They started running for, they were getting late.
(d) They started, running for, they were getting late.

35. The sun having set it became pleasant
(a) The Sun having set it became pleasant.
(b) The sun, having set, it became pleasant.
(c) The Sun having set, it became pleasant.
(d) The sun, having set it, became pleasant.

36. Mr. Sushil please listen to me
(a) Mr. Sushil please listen to me.
(b) Mr. Sushil, please listen to me.
(c) Mr. Sushil Please, listen to me.
(d) Mr. Sushil, please; listen to me.

37. Wherever you go you face the same difficulties
(a) Wherever you go you face the same difficulties.
(b) Wherever, you go, you face the same difficulties.
(c) Wherever you go; you face, the same difficulties.
(d) Wherever you go, you face the same difficulties.

38. Tell me what I can do for you
(a) Tell me what I can do for you.
(b) Tell me what I can do for you!
(c) Tell me what I can do for you?
(d) Tell me, what I can do for you?

39. May you live long
(a) May you live long.
(b) May you live long?
(c) May you live long!
(d) May, you live long!

40. May God the Greatest bless you
(a) May God the Greatest bless you.
(b) May God, the Greatest bless you!
(c) May God, the Greatest, bless you.
(d) May God, the Greatest, bless you!

41. The sun having risen the fog disappeared
(a) The Sun having; risen the fog disappeared.
(b) The Sun having risen, the fog disappeared.
(c) The Sun having risen; the fog disappeared.
(d) The Sun, having risen, the fog disappeared!

42. Having done his homework he went to bed
(a) Having done his homework he went to bed.
(b) Having done, his homework he went to bed.
(c) Having done, his homework, he went to bed.
(d) Having done his homework, he went to bed.

43. He is indeed a foolish boy
(a) He is indeed, a foolish boy.
(b) He is indeed a foolish boy.
(c) He is, indeed, a foolish boy.
(d) He, is indeed, a foolish boy.

44. Naresh my younger brother has gone to Patna
(a) Naresh, my younger brother, has gone to Patna.
(b) Naresh, my younger brother has gone to Patna.
(c) Naresh my younger brother, has gone to Patna.
(d) Naresh! my younger brother has gone to Patna.

45. Well I shall look into the matter
(a) Well I shall look into the matter.
(b) Well, I shall look into the matter.
(c) Well I shall, look into the matter.
(d) Well I shall, look into, the matter.

46. All right you can go
(a) All, right you can go.
(b) All right-you, can go.
(c) All right, you can go.
(d) All right! you can go.

47. Carry on your work I am watching you
(a) Carry on your work I am watching you.
(b) Carry on, your work, I am watching you.
(c) Carry on, your work, I am watching you.
(d) Carry on your work, I am watching you.

48. He was a kind bold man and we all praised him.
(a) He was a kind bold man and We all praised him.
(b) He was a kind, bold man and we all praised him.
(c) He was a kind bold, man and we all praised him.
(d) He was, a kind bold man, and we all praised him.

49. He said Honesty is the best policy
(a) He said 'Honesty is the best policy'.
(b) He said, Honesty is the best policy.
(c) He said "Honesty is the best policy."
(d) He said, "Honesty is the best policy."

50. What a beautiful flower it is
(a) What, A beautiful flower it is.
(b) What a beautiful flower it is?
(c) What a beautiful flower it is!
(d) What! a beautiful flower it is

Exercise 2

Directions (Q. Nos. 1-20) Select the correctly punctuated sentence from the options given below.

1. (a) Spain is a beautiful country; the beache's are warm sandy and spotlessly clean.
(b) Spain is a beautiful country: the beaches are warm, sandy and spotlessly clean.
(c) Spain is a beautiful country, the beaches are warm, sandy and spotlessly clean.
(d) Spain is a beautiful country; the beaches are warm, sandy and spotlessly clean.

2. (a) I can't see Tim's car, there must have been an accident.
(b) I cant see Tim's car; there must have been an accident.
(c) I can't see Tim's car there must have been an accident.
(d) I can't see Tim's car; there must havebeenanaccident.

3. (a) After stealing Tims car, the thief lost his way and ended up at the Chief Constable's garage.
(b) After stealing Tim's car the thief lost his way and ended up at the Chief Constable's garage.
(c) After stealing Tim's car, the thief lost his way and ended up at the Chief Constable's garage.
(d) After stealing Tim's car, the thief lost his' way and ended up at the Chief Constable's garage.

4. (a) That tall man, Paul's grandad, is this month's winner.
(b) That tall man Paul's grandad is this month's winner.
(c) That tall man, Paul's grandad, is this months winner.
(d) That tall man, Pauls grandad, is this month's winner.

5. (a) Please move your bicycle, said Dad.
(b) "Please move your bicycle", said Dad.
(c) "Please move your bicycle" said Dad.
(d) "Please move your bicycle"; said Dad.

6. (a) Dron concluded "it's to our advantage to accept their offer".
(b) Dron concluded, "Its to our advantage to accept their offer".
(c) Dron concluded "Its to our advantage to accept their offer".
(d) Dron concluded, "It's to our advantage to accept their offer."

7. (a) This tree is very recognisable: its long slender branches droop almost to the ground.
(b) This tree is very recognisable; its long slender branches droop almost to the ground.
(c) This tree is very recognisable. It's long slender branches droop almost to the ground.
(d) This tree is very recognisable, Its long slender branches droop almost to the ground.

8. (a) The age of the gigantic high rise apartment block is far from over.
(b) The age of the gigantic high-rise apartment block is far from over.
(c) The age of the gigantic high-rise apartment block, is far from over.
(d) The age of the gigantic high-rise apartment-block, is far from over.

9. (a) Grasp your opportunities while you may; you never know what the future holds.
(b) Grasp your opportunities while you may, you never know what the future holds.
(c) Grasp your opportunities, while you may, you never know what the future holds.
(d) Grasp your opportunities while you may, you never know what the future holds!

10. (a) In last week's Brunch, one of my favourite magazines, I enjoyed reading Ananya's article-How Not to Go camping.
(b) In last week's Brunch; one of my favourite magazines, I enjoyed reading Ananya's article: How Not to Go Camping.
(c) In last week's Brunch, one of my favourite magazines, I enjoyed reading Ananya's article 'How Not to Go Camping.'
(d) In last week's Brunch, one of my favourite magazines; I enjoyed reading Ananya's article 'How Not to Go Camping.

11. (a) Montaigne wrote the following : "A wise man never loses anything, if he has himself."
(b) Montaigne, wrote the following- "A wise man never loses anything, if he has himself."
(c) Montaigne, write the following- A wise man never loses anything, if he has himself.
(d) Montaigne wrote the following: A wise man never loses anything, if he has himself.

12. (a) There was a very interesting article entitled - The New Rage for Folk Singing in last Sunday's The Times of India newspaper.
(b) There was a very interesting article entitled, The New Rage for Folk Singing in last Sunday's The Times of India newspaper.
(c) There was a very interesting article entitled 'The New Rage for Folk Singing' in last Sunday's The Times of India newspaper.
(d) There was a very interesting article entitled 'The New Rage for Folk Singing in last Sunday's The Times of India newspaper.

13. (a) Ms. Anuradha has offered to coach the team this year, however, the competition for the job is intense.
(b) Ms. Anuradha has offered to coach the team this year; however, the competition for the job is intense.
(c) Ms. Anuradha has offered, to coach the team, this year. However, the competition for the job is intense.
(d) Ms. Anuradha, has offered to each the team this year. However, the competition for the job is intense.

14. (a) My favourite teacher, who just happens to be my uncle, retired from the University last summer.
(b) My favourite teacher who just happens to be my uncle, retired from the University last summer.

(c) My favourite teacher, who just happens to be my uncle; retired from the University last summer.
(d) My favourite teacher who just happens to be my uncle retired from the University last summer.

15. (a) Given the hard choices our coach has had to make this year it's no wonder she's decided to retire.
(b) Given the hard choices our coach has had to make this year, it's no wonder she's decided to retire.
(c) Given the hard choices, our coach has had, to make this year. It's no wonder she's decided to retire.
(d) Given the hard choices, our coach has had to make this year; it's no wonder she's decided to retire.

16. (a) Rajiv has been too busy to keep up with his courses because he took on too many extracurricular activities.
(b) Rajiv has been too busy to keep up with his courses, because he took on too many extracurricular activities.
(c) Rajiv has been too busy to keep up with his courses because, he took on too many extracurricular activities.
(d) Rajiv has been too busy to keep up with his courses; because he took on too many extracurricular activities.

17. (a) Mrs. Shivani has offered to donate a large part of her money to coach the best team this year however the competition for donations is quite intense.
(b) Mrs. Shivani has offered to donate a large part of her money to coach the best team this year; however, the competition for the donations is quite intense.
(c) Mrs. Shivani, has offered to donate, a large part of her money to coach the best team this year, however, the competition for the donation is quiet intense.
(d) Mrs. Shivani has offered to donate — a large part of her money to coach the best team this year, however, the competition for the donation is quiet intense.

18. (a) Brazil which is nearly as large as the whole of europe is covered with a vegetation of incredible profusion.
(b) Brazil, which is nearly as large, as the whole of Europe, is covered with a vegetation of incredible profusion.
(c) Brazil, which is nearly as large as the whole of Europe, is covered with a vegetation of incredible profusion.
(d) Brazil which is nearly as large as the whole of Europe: is covered with, a vegetation of incredible profusion.

19. (a) Ramesh ran and ran but there was no way he could keep pace with his brother Abhinav.
(b) Ramesh ran and ran, but there was no way he could keep pace with his brother, Abhinav.
(c) ramesh ran and ran, but, there was no way, he could keep pace with his Brother abhinav.
(d) Ramesh ran and ran! but there was no way – he could keep pace with his brother–Abhinav.

20. (a) At midnight however I was aroused by the tramp of horses hoofs in the yard.
(b) at midnight however I was aroused by the tramp of horses' hoofs in the yard.
(c) At midnight, however, I was aroused by the tramp of horses' hoofs in the yard.
(d) at the midnight–however– I was aroused by the tramp of horse's hoofs in the yard.

Directions (Q. Nos. 21-24) Choose the answer that shows that best punctuation for the underlined part of the sentence. If the sentence is correct, the answer is 'No error'.

21. Most residents of the building have air conditioners however I've always found that a ceiling fan is sufficient.
(a) air conditioners however : I've
(b) air conditioners, however, I've
(c) air conditioners; however, I've
(d) No error

22. Most owners of the restaurant maintain that only organic ingredients are used in their kitchen.
(a) maintain, that only
(b) maintain that, only
(c) maintain: that only
(d) No error

23. Before the student could be hired by the company the students adviser had to provide a letter of recommendation.
(a) company the students
(b) company, the student's
(c) company, the students'
(d) No error

24. The sky is blue, but I hear thunder in the distance.
(a) sky, is blue (b) sky is blue;
(c) sky is; blue (d) No error

Answers

Exercise 1

1 (d)	2 (d)	3 (c)	4 (b)	5 (a)	6 (c)	7 (b)	8 (d)	9 (a)	10 (c)
11 (b)	12 (d)	13 (a)	14 (c)	15 (d)	16 (b)	17 (c)	18 (d)	19 (a)	20 (d)
21 (c)	22 (b)	23 (a)	24 (d)	25 (b)	26 (c)	27 (a)	28 (a)	29 (d)	30 (b)
31 (a)	32 (c)	33 (d)	34 (a)	35 (c)	36 (b)	37 (d)	38 (a)	39 (c)	40 (d)
41 (b)	42 (d)	43 (c)	44 (a)	45 (b)	46 (c)	47 (d)	48 (b)	49 (d)	50 (c)

Exercise 2

1 (d)	2 (d)	3 (c)	4 (a)	5 (b)	6 (d)	7 (a)	8 (b)	9 (a)	10 (c)
11 (a)	12 (c)	13 (b)	14 (a)	15 (b)	16 (a)	17 (b)	18 (c)	19 (b)	20 (c)
21 (c)	22 (d)	23 (b)	24 (d)						

Unit-05

01 Compound Sentence and Complex Sentence Clause

Synthesis of sentences या Synthesis का अर्थ है—दो या दो से अधिक वाक्यों को जोड़कर एक वाक्य बनाना। यह वाक्य simple, compound या complex हो सकता है। Sentence के मुख्यत: तीन प्रकार हैं, जो synthesis के अन्तर्गत प्रयोग में आते हैं।

- **Simple Sentence** इन वाक्यों में एक Finite verb होता है।
  e.g. The boy is going to school.
- **Complex Sentence** इन वाक्यों में एक Principal clause पर दूसरा अन्य Subordinate clause (आश्रित वाक्य) बनाना होता है।
  e.g. Ram was very sad because his father was not feeling well.
- **Compound Sentence** इन वाक्यों में दो या दो से अधिक Principal clause (प्रमुख वाक्य-खण्ड) होते है तथा वे एक-दूसरे पर पूर्ण रूप से आश्रित न होकर स्वतन्त्र रूप से भी अपना अर्थ देते हैं।
  e.g. God gave the land and man built house on land.

Synthesis of sentences का प्रयोग मुख्यत: निम्नलिखित तीन स्थितियों में किया जाता है

(i) दो या दो से अधिक Simple sentences से एक Simple sentence बनाना।

(ii) दो या दो से अधिक Simple sentences से एक Complex sentence बनाना।

(iii) दो या दो से अधिक Simple sentences से एक Compound sentence बनाना।

Simple Sentence

Simple sentence ऐसा sentence है, जिसमें एक ही Finite verb होती है। अत: दो या अधिक Simple Sentences को संयुक्त कर जो Simple Sentence बनेगा, उसमें एक ही Finite verb होनी चाहिए। यह निम्न प्रकार से किया जा सकता है :

(A) Using Participle

(a) Simple Sentences को जोड़ने हेतु Participle का प्रयोग सामान्यतया तब किया जाता है जब वाक्यों में एक ही कर्त्ता (subject) हो या एक वाक्य में It का प्रयोग हो।

(b) वाक्य इस तरह के हों, जिनसे यह ज्ञात हो कि एक कार्य दूसरे कार्य के बाद सम्पन्न हुआ है।

Rule 1

यदि एक वाक्य में is/am/are/was/were जैसी verb का प्रयोग हुआ है, तो इनकी जगह being का प्रयोग करके नया simple वाक्य बनाया जाता है। जैसे:

(1) (a) He is very weak. (b) He cannot go alone.
Being very weak he cannot go alone.

(2) (a) He is intelligent
(b) He can solve this question.
Being intelligent he can solve this question.

(3) (a) It was Sunday. (b) The market was closed.
Being Sunday the market was closed.

Rule 2

यदि दूसरे वाक्य में Action में fastness व्यक्त हो तो पहले वाक्य की verb को participle की तरह प्रयुक्त करते हैं जो कार्य पहले हुआ है, उस वाक्य की verb को participle के तरह प्रयोग करके नया वाक्य बनाना चाहिए। जैसे:

(1) (a) He saw a lion. (b) He fled away.
Seeing a lion he fled away.

(2) (a) She heard a noise. (b) She ran out.
Hearing a noise she ran out.

(3) (a) He was late. (b) He ran to the station.
It being late he ran to the station.

Rule 3

यदि वाक्य में Action में fastness व्यक्त न हो तो having + V-III को प्रयोग किया जाता है। जैसे :

(1) (a) I took my lunch. (b) I went to office.
Having taken my lunch I went to office.

(2) (a) He wrote a letter. (b) He posted it.
Having written a letter he posted it.

(3) (a) He played a match. (b) He went to college.
Having played a match he went to college.

Rule 4

Past participle का adjective की तरह प्रयोग करके भी simple sentence बनाया जा सकता है जैसे :

(1) (a) He met a child. (b) The child was weeping.
He met a weeping child.

(2) (a) She found a dog. (b) The dog was black.
She found a black dog.

(3) (a) I saw a lion. (b) The lion was wounded.
I saw a wounded lion.

(B) By Using Conjunction 'And'

'And' conjunction द्वारा इस तरह के वाक्यों को जोड़ा जा सकता है,जिनमें predicate समान हो, subject अलग हों। ऐसे वाक्यों को and से जोड़कर नया Simple sentence बनाया जा सकता है। जैसे :

(1) (a) Harish played cricket.
(b) Ramesh played cricket.
Harish and Ramesh played cricket.

(2) (a) Ram knows driving. (b) Shyam knows driving.
Ram and Shyam know driving.

(3) (a) Ram went to hospital.
(b) Sita went to hospital.
Ram and Sita went to hospital.

जब predicate अलग हो एवं subject समान हो, तो वाक्यों को निम्न प्रकार जोड़ा जाता है :

(1) (a) Ram can write. (b) Ram can read.
Ram can write and read.

(2) (a) Sita can dance. (b) Sita can swim.
Sita can dance and swim.

(3) (a) He will play. (b) He will support us.
He will play and support us.

(C) By Using Nominative Absolute

जब वाक्यों में Subject अलग-अलग हो एवं वाक्यों में व्यक्त कार्यों के बीच कारण परिणाम का सम्बन्ध हो, अर्थात् एक कार्य के होने के बाद दूसरा कार्य उसका परिणाम हो, तो ऐसे वाक्यों को जोड़ने हेतु Nominative absolute का प्रयोग किया जाता है।

Nominative absolute उस कर्त्ता (nominative) को कहा जाता है जो वाक्य की क्रिया पर प्रभाव नहीं डालता है। जैसे :

(i) (a) The police arrived.
(b) The thieves fled away.

यहाँ Police (Nominative absolute) है।

वाक्य The police arrived में police द्वारा कोई कार्य नहीं किया गया है। Verb arrived, police के द्वारा किया कोई कार्य नहीं है (The police arrested him. यहाँ arrested, police द्वारा किया कार्य है) इसका Norminative thieves है।

ऐसे वाक्यों को निम्न प्रकार एक Simple sentence में बदला जाता है।
The police having arrived the thieves fled away.

Rule

यदि वाक्य Active voice में है, तो having + V-III का प्रयोग किया जाता है एवं Passive voice में having been + V-III का प्रयोग किया जाता है।
See the following examples :

(1) (a) The sun rose.
(b) The fog disappeared.
The sun having risen the fog disappeared.

(2) (a) The building caught fire.
(b) All household articles were burnt to ashes.
The building having caught fire, all the household articles were burnt to ashes.

(3) (a) The job was completed.
(b) He went on leave.
The job having been completed he went on leave.

(4) (a) The lion was caught in the net.
(b) He struggled to get free.
Having been caught in the net the lion struggled to get free.

(D) By Using Noun or Phrase in Apposition

Apposition का अर्थ होता है,'side by side', जब वाक्य इस तरह के होते हैं कि पहले वाक्य में आए किसी noun के बारे में ही दूसरे वाक्य में कुछ details दी जाती है, तो ऐसे वाक्यों में noun के साथ ही उस detail को देखा (apposition) जाता है। जैसे :

(1) (a) I went to London.
(b) London is the capital of Britain.
I went to London, the capital of Britain.

(2) (a) I like Sakshi.
(b) Sakshi is the most beautiful girl in this town.
I like Sakshi, the most beautiful girl in this town.

(3) (a) Gandhiji was a moralist.
(b) He had once been a lawyer.
(c) He struggled hard to attain freedom.
Gandhiji, a moralist, once a lawyer, struggled hard to attain freedom.

(E) By Using Preposition with Noun or Gerund

ऐसे Simple sentences को जोड़ने हेतु Preposition का प्रयोग किया जाता है, जिनमें आपस में कोई कारण या अन्य प्रकार का सम्बन्ध होता है। जैसे :

(1) (a) He was rusticated.
(b) He had broken the school window.
He was rusticated for breaking the school window.

(2) (a) He completed his work.
(b) It struck seven.
He completed his work upto seven O'clock.

(3) (a) His wife died. (b) He heard the news.
(c) He lost consciousness.
On hearing the news of his wife's death, he lost consciousness.

(F) By Using Infinitive

Infinitive का प्रयोग ऐसे वाक्यों को जोड़ने हेतु किया जाता है, जिन वाक्यों में आपस में Inter dependence दृष्टिगोचर होती है। ऐसे वाक्यों में भी Infinitive का प्रयोग किया जाता है, जिनमें आपस में कारण-परिणाम का सम्बन्ध दिखाई देता है। (ध्यान रखें ऐसे वाक्यों को Nominative absolute द्वारा इसलिए नहीं जोड़ा जा सकता क्योंकि Nominative absolute के मामले में कर्त्ता भिन्न होते हैं तथा एक कार्य के बाद दूसरा कार्य होता है)।

Infinitive द्वारा जोड़े गए वाक्यों में कार्य आगे-पीछे नहीं होता है बल्कि साथ-साथ होने का आपस मे सम्बन्ध-सा होता है। जैसे :

(1) (a) I will go there. (b) I will settle the matter.
I will go there to settle the matter.

(2) (a) He came here.
(b) He signed the agreement.
He came here to sign the agreement.

(3) (a) I have no money. (b) I cannot pay you now.
I have no money to pay you now.

(G) By Using Adjective or Adverb

जब दो वाक्य इस तरह के होते हैं कि एक में कार्य होने का कारण, दूसरा वाक्य होता है, तो ऐसे वाक्यों में enough का प्रयोग करके एक Simple sentence बनाया जाता है। जैसे :

(1) (a) He is intelligent.
(b) He can solve this puzzle.
He is intelligent enough to solve this puzzle.

(2) (a) I have time. (b) I can go to hospital.
I have time enough to go to hospital.

(3) (a) He is rich. (b) He can buy this hotel.
He is rich enough to buy this hotel.

(H) By Using 'Too -to'

जब दो Simple sentences में किसी कार्य के न होने का कारण, पहले वाक्य में दिया गया हो, तो 'Too-to' का प्रयोग करके एक Simple sentence बनाया जाता है। जैसे :

(1) (a) He is very weak. (b) He cannot walk.
He is too weak to walk.

(2) (a) He is very poor. (b) He cannot pay his fees.
He is too poor to pay his fees.

(3) (a) The tea is very hot. (b) I cannot drink it.
The tea is too hot to drink.

Compound Sentence

Compound sentence में दो Principal clause होती हैं। उनमें कोई Subordinate clause नहीं होती है। Compound sentence को बनाने के लिए दो Simple sentences को एक Coordinating conjunction द्वारा जोड़ा जाता है, जो निम्नलिखित हैं :

And, both....and, also, too, as well as, not only....but also, either....or, neither....nor, for, otherwise, or, but, yet, however, so, therefore etc.

मुख्य बात यह है कि Compound sentence बनाते समय Subordinating conjunction का प्रयोग कदापि न करें। कौन-सा Coordinating conjunction प्रयोग किया जाएगा, यह वाक्यों के अर्थ से पता चलेगा। यदि वाक्यों में कोई choice है तो either....or यदि कोई विरोधाभास है, तो but, however, yet इत्यादि का प्रयोग किया जाता है।

(A) By using Cumulative Conjunction

दो Simple sentences को Cumulative conjunnction द्वारा जोड़कर, एक Compound sentence बनाया जाता है। मुख्य Cumulative conjunctions निम्नलिखित हैं:

And, both ...... and, as well as, not only ...... but also, not less than etc.

(a) Using 'And' :

(1) (a) I watched T.V. (b) He played football.
I watched T.V and he played football.

(2) (a) The police came. (b) The thief ran away.
The police came and the thief ran away.

(3) (a) She came. (b) She watched T.V.
She came and watched T.V.

(b) Using 'Both ...... and' :

(1) (a) He ate a biscuit. (b) He ate an orange.
He ate both a biscuit and an orange.

(2) (a) He is a student. (b) He is a painter.
He is both a student and a painter.

(3) (a) She purchased a pen.
(b) She purchased a pencil.
She purchased both a pen and a pencil.

(c) Using 'As well as' :

(1) (a) Suresh is going to Jaipur.
(b) Kukku is going to Jaipur.
Suresh as well as Kukku is going to Jaipur.

(2) (a) Saurav is playing cricket.
(b) Sachin is playing cricket.
Saurav as well as Sachin is playing cricket.

(3) (a) He is intelligent. (b) He is smart.
He is intelligent as well as smart.

(d) Using 'Not only ...... but also' :

(1) (a) He is a painter.
(b) He is a student.
He is not only a painter but also a student.

(2) (a) Ram will go to Jaipur.
(b) Sita will go to Jaipur.
Not only Ram but also Sita will go to Jaipur.

(3) (a) Sita is intelligent.
(b) Sita is beautiful.
Sita is not only intelligent but also beautiful.

(B) By Using Adversative Conjunction

But, still, yet, however, where, whereas, only, while इत्यादि Adversative conjunctions कहलाते हैं। इनका प्रयोग दो विरोधाभासी वाक्यों को जोड़ने हेतु किया जाता है। जैसे :

(a) Using 'But' :

(1) (a) He is smart.
(b) He is not intelligent.
He is smart but he is not intelligent.

(2) (a) He worked hard. (b) He could not pass.
He worked hard but he could not pass.

(3) (a) He is rich. (b) He is miser.
He is rich but he is miser.

(b) Using 'Still or yet' :

(1) (a) I don't support her. (b) She respects me.
I do not support her still she respects me.

(2) (a) He is poor. (b) He is honest.
He is poor yet he is honest.

(3) (a) He worked hard. (b) He failed.
He worked hard yet he failed.

(c) Using 'However' :

(1) (a) She did not prepare well.
(b) She succeeded.
She did not prepare well however she succeeded.

(2) (a) Your leaves are not due.
(b) You may go.
Your leaves are not due however you may go.

(3) (a) I do not like this pen.
(b) I may buy it for you.
I do not like this pen however I may buy it for you.

(d) Using 'Nevertheless' :

(1) (a) He is a miser.
(b) He spent one lac in the marriage.
He is a miser nevertheless he spent one lac in the marriage.

(2) (a) He is a rich man.
(b) He is not contented.
He is a rich man nevertheless he is not contented.

(3) (a) He is poor. (b) He is trustworthy.
He is poor nevertheless he is trustworthy.

(e) Using 'Or' :

(1) (a) Go away. (b) Come in.
Go away or come in.

(2) (a) Run fast. (b) You will miss the train.
Run fast or you will miss the train.

(3) (a) Work hard. (b) You will be failed.
Work hard or you will be failed.

(f) Using 'Only' :

(1) (a) He could solve it.
(b) He became hopeless.
He could solve it only he became hopeless.

(2) (a) Go anywhere you like.
(b) You inform me.
Go anywhere you like only inform me.

(3) (a) You can do whatever you like.
(b) You don't make unnecessary telephones.
You can do whatever you like only you don't make unnecessary telephones.

(g) Using 'While/Whereas' :

(1) (a) He was playing.
(b) She was watching TV.
He was playing while she was watching TV.

(2) (a) I was reading.
(b) He was flying kites.
While I was reading, he was flying kites.

(3) (a) Ram won the game.
(b) Shyam lost this chance.
Ram won the game whereas Shyam lost this chance.

(C) By Using Causative Conjunction

जब वाक्यों में कारण परिणाम का सम्बन्ध होता है, तो Causative conjunction का प्रयोग करके Compound sentence बनाया जाता है। मुख्य Causative conjunction हैं; therefore, so, for, hence etc.

(a) Using 'Therefore' :

(1) (a) He broke the glass.
(b) He was punished.
He broke the glass therefore he was punished.

(2) (a) He is honest.
(b) He was rewarded.
He is honest therefore he was rewarded.

(b) Using 'So' :

(1) (a) You are late.
(b) You are fined.
You are late so you are fined.

(2) (a) We are late.
(b) We should move fast.
We are late so we should move fast.

(c) Using 'For'

(1) (a) Everyone has to die one day.
(b) Man is mortal.
Everyone has to die one day for man is mortal.

(2) (a) He forgave her.
(b) She apologized publicly.
He forgave her for she apologized publicly.

(d) Using 'Hence' :

(1) (a) It is very cold.
(b) We purchased some winter wears.
It is very cold hence we purchased some winter wears.

(2) (a) He is a sincere worker.
(b) He was promoted.
He is a sincere worker hence he was promoted.

(D) By Using Who, When, Where, Which, In Continuative Sense

Who, which, where, when का प्रयोग Continuative sense में किया जाता है, तो ये Subordinating conjunction की तरह प्रयुक्त नहीं होते हैं एवं शुरू होने वाली clause भी Principal clause होती है। जैसे :

(1) (a) I went to London. (b) I got a job.
I went to London, where I got a job.

(2) (a) I worked there for three days.
(b) I received a telegram.
I worked there for three days, where I received a telegram.

(3) (a) There is a girl.
(b) She is very intelligent.
There is a girl, who is very intelligent.

(4) (a) I killed a rat.
(b) It was a cruel act.
I killed a rat, which was a cruel act.

Complex Sentence

Complex sentence में एक Principal clause होती है तथा एक या अधिक Subordinate clause होती है जो Subordinating conjunction द्वारा Principal clause से जुड़ी रहती है। अत: जब दो या अधिक Simple sentences को जोड़कर एक Complex sentence बनाना हो, तो एक sentence को Principal clause बनाएँ तथा अन्य को Subordinate clause बनाएँ।

Subordinate clause जैसा आपने analysis के अध्याय में पढ़ा है तीन प्रकार की होती हैं

(a) Noun clause (b) Adjective clause
(c) Adverb clause

Subordinate clause को Principal clause के साथ Subordinating conjunction; जैसे : that, who, which, what because, since, so that, in order that, as, as if, as if, as soon as, though, before, after if, when, till untill etc., द्वारा जोड़ा जाता है।

कौन-सा Subordinating conjunction, प्रयुक्त होगा, यह वाक्यों के आशय या अर्थ पर निर्भर करता है।

(A) By Using Noun Clause

I. Use of conjunction

(who/which/whom/whose/what/when/where/why/how/if/whether) : जब दो Simple sentences में एक तो Assertive/Imperative/Interrogative वाक्य होता है एवं दूसरा वाक्य Interrogative होता है, तो Complex वाक्य बनाते समय दूसरे Interrogative वाक्य को Assertive बनाते हुए पहले वाक्य से जोड़ा जाता है। यहाँ इन words से जो clause शुरू होती है वह Noun clause है। जैसे :

(1) (a) I do not know.
(b) Who is he?
(Assertive + Interrogative)
I do not know who he is.

(2) (a) I cannot say.
(b) Has he come?
(Assertive + Interrogative)
I cannot say whether he has come.

(3) (a) Tell me.
(b) Where does she live ?
(Imperative + Interrogative)
Tell me where she lives.

(4) (a) Inform him.
(b) When will she go ?
(Imperative + Interrogative)
Inform him when she will go.

(5) (a) Do you know?
(b) What does he do ?
(Interrogative + Interrogative)
Do you know what he does ?

(6) (a) Can you inform me?
(b) Where has she gone ?
(Interrogative + Interrogative)
Can you inform me where she has gone?

निम्न प्रकार के वाक्यों को भी Wh-word का प्रयोग करके (वाक्यों के आशय के अनुसार) Complex sentence बनाया जा सकता है। Wh-words से शुरू होने वाली clause, Noun, clause है। जैसे :

(1) (a) Someone telephoned me.
(b) I do not know who.
I do not know who telephoned me.

(2) (a) She will not come.
(b) I do not know why.
I do not know why she will not come.

(3) (a) How had he performed !
(b) None could expect this.
None could expect how had he performed.

(4) (a) What a beautiful bird it is !
(b) I cannot imagine.
I cannot imagine what a beautiful bird it is.

II. Use of 'That' :

यदि दो simple sentence इस तरह के हैं कि कथनों के स्वीकार या अस्वीकार का सम्बन्ध आपस में स्थापित किया जा सकता है, तो ऐसे वाक्यों का Complex sentence बनाने के लिए 'that' का प्रयोग निम्न प्रकार किया जाता है जैसे :

(1) (a) He is innocent.
(b) I am confident of it.
I am confident that he is innocent.

(2) (a) He has committed a mistake.
(b) I believe so.
I believe that he has committed a mistake.

(3) (a) She is an intelligent girl.
(b) I do not doubt it.
I do not doubt that she is an intelligent girl.

III.

इस तरह के वाक्यों को जोड़कर भी Complex sentence बनाया जा सकता है, जिनमें कोई इच्छा व्यक्त की गई हो। जैसे :

(1) (a) I wish to be a queen.
(b) I am not a queen.
I wish I were a queen.

(2) (a) I wished to marry her.
(b) I did not marry her.
I wished I had married her.

(B) By Using Adjective Clause

Adjective clause का प्रयोग उस स्थिति में करना उपयुक्त होता है जब एक वाक्य में किसी व्यक्ति/वस्तु के बारे में बताया गया है एवं अन्य वाक्यों में उसी noun के सम्बन्ध में कुछ कहा गया है, तो where/which/when/who/that etc. का प्रयोग करके एक या अधिक वाक्यों को Subordinate adjective clause बनाया जाता है एवं एक वाक्य को Principal clause बनाकर जोड़ा जाता है। जैसे :

(1) (a) This is the magazine.
(b) I want to purchase.
This is the magazine that I want to purchase.

(2) (a) This is the hotel.
(b) I lived here for three months.
This is the hotel where I lived for three months.

(3) (a) This is the girl.
(b) She secured first position.
This is the girl who secured first position.

(C) By Using Adverb Clause

Adverb clause का प्रयोग तब किया जाता है, जब दो वाक्यों में किए गए कथनों में आपस में, विरोधाभास, तुलनात्मक, समय, स्थान, कारण या शर्त का सम्बन्ध व्यक्त हो। ध्यान रखें Adverb के functions के अनुसार जब दो वाक्यों में परस्पर सम्बन्ध हो, तो Adverb clause का प्रयोग करके, वाक्यों को जोड़कर Complex sentence बनाया जाता है। जैसे :

(1) (a) I wrote a letter.
(b) I posted it.
I posted the letter after I had written it.

(2) (a) I watched T.V.
(b) I went to market.
I went to market after I had watched T.V.

(3) (a) He is so poor.
(b) He cannot buy his books.
He is so poor that he cannot buy his books.

(4) (a) He is intelligent.
(b) His sister is equally intelligent .
He is as intelligent as his sister.

(5) (a) He finished his work.
(b) Then he watched a movie.
He didn't watch a movie until he finished his work.

(6) (a) He is an intelligent student.
(b) No other student in the class is more intelligent.
No other student in the class is more intelligent than he.

Synthesis of a Mixed Sentence

Mixed sentence ऐसा वाक्य होता है जिसमें कम-से-कम दो Principal clauses होती हैं एवं कम-से-कम एक Subordinate clause होती है अर्थात् Mixed sentence एक Compound sentence में Subordinate clause जोड़कर बनाया जा सकता है या एक Simple sentence, जिसे Principal clause माना जाए, के साथ एक Complex sentence को संयुक्त कर एक Mixed sentence बनाया जा सकता है। इस हेतु Coordinating एवं Subordinating Conjunctions का प्रयोग किया जाता है, जिनके बारे में विस्तृत रूप से Synthesis of Simple/Compound/Complex sentences में बताया जा चुका है।

Exercise

Directions (1-9) Combine the following simple sentences into one simple sentence.

1. Mahatma Gandhi was a great visionary. He realised the danger of communal conflicts. He sacrificed his life to bring about unity.

(a) A great visionary, Mahatma Gandhi realised the danger of communal conflicts and sacrificed his life to bring about unity.
(b) Mahatma Gandhi, a great visionary, He sacrificed his life to bring about unity on realising the danger of communal conflicts.
(c) Mahatma Gandhi sacrificed his life to bring about unity when he realised the danger of communal conflicts.
(d) Having realised the danger of communal conflicts Mahatma Gandhi, a great visionary, sacrificed his life to bring about unity.

2. She stood on tip-toe. She reached for the mangoes on tree.

(a) She reached for the mangoes on tree by standing tip-toed.
(b) She reached for the mangoes on tree when she stood on tip-toe.
(c) Standing on tip-toe she reached for the mangoes on tree.
(d) She reached the mangoes on tree standing on tip-toe.

3. India will win the World cup. That is certain.

(a) It is certain that India will win the World Cup.
(b) India will certainly win the World Cup.
(c) Certainly, India will win the World Cup.
(d) India will win the World Cup certainly.

4. The US Trade Centre caught fire. The building was burnt to ashes.

(a) The US Trade Centre having caught fire, the building was burnt to ashes.
(b) The building of US Trade Centre caught fire and burnt to ashes.
(c) The building of US Trade Centre was burnt to ashes when it caught fire.
(d) The US Trade Centre caught fire and the building was burnt to ashes.

5. The servant mopped the room; she found a wallet lying in the corner.

(a) The servant found a wallet while mopping the corner of the room.
(b) The servant founded a wallet lying in the corner while mopping the room.
(c) The servant mopped the room and found a wallet lying in the corner.
(d) While mopping the room, the servant found a wallet lying in a corner.

6. Ashoka was a great conqueror. But he failed to unite the various conquered territories into a well-knit empire.

(a) Ashoka was a great conqueror, but he failed to unite the various conquered territories into a well-knit empire.
(b) Though Ashoka was a great conqueror, but he failed to unite the various conquered territories into a well-knit empire.
(c) Despite being a great conqueror, Ashoka failed to unite the various conquered territories into a well-knit empire.
(d) Ashoka failed to unite the various conquered territories into a well-knit empire, in spite of being a great conqueror.

7. I must finish this novel. There are still few chapters.

(a) I have still few chapters in this novel to finish.
(b) I still have few chapters in the novel before I finish it.
(c) Few chapters are still left for me to finish the novel.
(d) There are still few chapters for me to finish this novel.

8. They decided to start a travel group. All agreed to this.

(a) They all agreed to start a travel group.
(b) They jointly decided to start a travel group.
(c) They agreed to jointly start a travel group.
(d) They unanimously decided to start a travel group.

9. Rabindranath Tagore was a great poet. He was a good painter.

(a) Rabindranath Tagore was not only a great poet, but also a good painter.
(b) Besides being a great poet, Rabindranath Tagore was a good painter.
(c) Rabindranath Tagore was a great poet as well as a good painter.
(d) Rabindranath Tagore was a great poet and painter.

Direction (10-15) Combine the following simple sentences into a compound sentence.

10. There was little hope of success. She tried hard.

(a) There was little hope of success, still she tried hard.
(b) There was little hope of success, but she tried hard.
(c) She tried hard but there was little hope of success.
(d) There was little hope of success, nevertheless she tried hard.

11. Sheena will not spend her money. She will not invest it.

(a) Sheena will neither spend her money nor invest it.
(b) Sheena will not spend her money and will not invest it.
(c) Sheena will either spend her money or invest it.
(d) Sheena will not spend her money or will not invest it either.

12. Ani speaks English. She also speaks French.

(a) Ani speaks English as well as French.
(b) Ani speaks English apart from French.
(c) Ani speaks both English and French.
(d) Ani speaks English and French.

13. Get inside. You may catch cold.
(a) Get inside else you may catch cold.
(b) You may catch cold, get inside.
(c) Get inside, otherwise you may catch cold.
(d) Get inside or you may catch cold.

14. He went to the market. He saw the latest gadget. He could not, however purchase it.
(a) He went to the market and could not purchase the latest gadget that he saw.
(b) He went to the market and saw the latest gadget but he could not purchase it.
(c) He saw the latest gadget in the market and could not purchase it.
(d) He could not purchase the latest gadget he saw in the market.

15. Mohan is industrious. He is very particular in his work.
(a) Mohan is very particular in his work as he is industrious.
(b) Mohan is not only industrious but also very particular in his work.
(c) Mohan is industrious and particular in his work.
(d) Mohan is industrious as well as particular in his work.

Directions (16-19) Combine the following simple sentences into a complex sentence.

16. India will have a good monsoon season this year. The meteorologists expect this.
(a) The meteorologists expect a good monsoon season this year in India.
(b) The meteorologists expect that India will have a good monsoon season this year.
(c) As expected by the meteorologists, India will have a good monsoon season this year.
(d) The meteorologists expect India to have a good monsoon season this year.

17. We visited the Golden Temple. Gurunanak Devji preached his first sermon here.
(a) We visited the Golden Temple wherein Gurunanak Devji preached his first sermon.
(b) We visited the Golden Temple because Gurunanak Devji preached his first sermon.
(c) We visited the Golden Temple where Gurunanak Devji preached his first sermon.
(d) Gurunanak Devji preached his first sermon at the Golden Temple.

18. She was honest. This was his statement. It was right.
(a) He rightly said in his statement that she was honest.
(b) She was rightly said as honest in his statement.
(c) His statement was right in which he said that she was honest.
(d) His statement that she was honest was right.

19. Her younger brother is in Canada. He is a lecturer at a prestigious University.
(a) Her younger brother is a lecturer at a prestigious University in Canada.
(b) Her younger brother, who is in Canada, is a lecturer at a prestigious University.
(c) Her younger brother is a lecturer at a prestigious Canadian University.
(d) Her Canada based younger brother is a lecturer at a prestigious University.

20. Which of the following statements about synthesis of sentence is incorrect?
(a) Synthesis means combining two or more simple sentences in one sentence.
(b) Synthesis is opposite of transformation of sentences.
(c) Synthesis leads to the formation of either a simple, complex or compound sentence.
(d) All are correct.

21. Which of the following statements is incorrect?
(a) When we combine two simple sentences by using an adverb or an adverbial phrase, we change the adverb of the sentence into adjective.
(b) Two simple sentences are joined using a participle when they have a common subject.
(c) The conjunction for noun clause in synthesis of complex sentences is that.
(d) Compound sentences are joined using coordinating conjunctions.

Directions (22-26) Study the given simple sentences that have been combined to form a simple sentence. Decipher how they have been combined.

22. Separate: She wanted to educate her son. She sent him to London.
Combined: She sent her son to London to educate him.
(a) By using an adverb or an Adverbial Phrase
(b) By using a participle
(c) By using an infinitive
(d) By using, Nominative Absolute Construction

23. Separate: Anita was scolded. Her uncle scolded badly.
Combined: Anita was badly scolded by her uncle
(a) By using a preposition with noun or gerund
(b) By using, Nominative Absolute Construction
(c) By using a noun or a phrase in apposition
(d) By using an adverb or an Adverbial Phrase

24. Separate: She has failed many times. She still hopes to get success at last.
Combined: In spite of many failures she still hopes to get success at last.
(a) By using a preposition with noun or gerund
(b) By using a Participle
(c) By using a noun or a phrase in apposition
(d) By using an infinitive

25. Separate: I love Sanchit very much. He is my brother.
Combined: I love my brother Sanchit very much.
(a) By using a noun or a phrase in apposition
(b) By using a preposition with noun or gerund
(c) By using an adverb or an Adverbial Phrase
(d) By using an infinitive Synthesis of Sentences l 61

26. **Separate :** The monkey sat on a branch. He gibbered.
Combined : Sitting on a branch the monkey gibbered.
(a) By using an infinitive
(b) By using a noun or a phrase in apposition
(c) By using a participle
(d) By using a preposition with noun or gerund

27. Given are two simple sentences, decipher which of the following is a correctly combined complex sentence by using a noun clause?
She has failed. The reason is her illness.
(a) The reason of her failure is that she is ill.
(b) She was ill and thus failed.
(c) She failed because of her illness.
(d) The reason behind her failure is her illness.

28. Given are two simple sentences, decipher which of the following is a correctly combined complex sentence by using an adjective clause?
I met your friend. His wallet was stolen in the market.
(a) I met your friend and his wallet was stolen in the market.
(b) As soon as I met your friend, his wallet was stolen in the market.
(c) I met your friend whose wallet was stolen in the market.
(d) I met your friend because his wallet was stolen in the market.

29. Given are two simple sentences, decipher which of the following is a correctly combined complex sentence by using an adverb clause?
The burglar saw the police. He took his heels.
(a) Seeing the police, the burglar took his heels.
(b) On seeing the police, the burglar took his heels.
(c) As soon as the burglar saw the police, he took his heels.
(d) As the burglar saw the police, he took his heels.

30. Given are two simple sentences, decipher which of the following is a correctly combined complex sentence by using an adjective clause?
I saw a car. It was black in colour.
(a) I saw a car in black colour.
(b) I saw a black coloured car.
(c) I saw a black car.
(d) I saw a car which was black in colour.

Directions (31-40) Combine the following sentences using an appropriate conjunction from the given options.

31. He is snobbish. I like him.
(a) Though he is snobbish, I like him.
(b) He is snobbish and I like him
(c) He is snobbish but I like him
(d) I like him because he is snobbish

32. My mother attended the wedding. My father attended the wedding.
(a) My mother and father attended the wedding.
(b) My mother attended the wedding also my father.
(c) Both my mother and father attended the wedding.
(d) My father, mother attended the wedding.

33. He has walked five miles. It is possible that he is tired.
(a) He has walked five miles; it is possible that he is tired.
(b) He has walked five miles, so he must be tired.
(c) He has walked five miles therefore it is possible that he is tired.
(d) He has walked five miles and possible that he is tired.

34. I went to the shop. I bought a watch.
(a) I went to the shop bought a watch.
(b) I went to the shop to buy a watch.
(c) I went to the shop and bought a watch.
(d) To buy a watch I went to the shop.

35. You must be quiet. You must leave the room.
(a) You must be quiet. You must leave the room.
(b) You must leave the room and quiet.
(c) Must you leave and quiet the room
(d) You must be quiet or you must leave the room.

36. The prisoner fell down on his knees. He begged for mercy.
(a) The prisoner fell down on his knees, he begged for mercy
(b) The prisoner fell down on his knees and begged for mercy.
(c) The prisoner begged for mercy felling down on his knees.
(d) He begged mercy the prisoner felling down on his knees.

37. I left home early. I could not get to work on time.
(a) Because I left home early I could not get to work on time.
(b) But I left home early could not get to work on time,
(c) Though / although I left home early, I could not get to work on time.
(d) I could not get to work on time as I left home early.

38. Azim works hard. Kabir works harder.
(a) Azim works hard but Kabir works harder.
(b) Both Azim and Kabir work harder.
(c) Kabir and Azim work harder.
(d) Kabir, Azim work harder.

39. You must start at once. You will be late.
(a) You will be late must start at once.
(b) You must start at once or you will be late.
(c) You must start at once because you will be late.
(d) You must start at once for you will be late.

40. You are not interested in this offer. I know it.
(a) I know it you are not interested in this offer.
(b) You are not interested in this offer this I know it.
(c) I know that you are not interested in this offer.
(d) I know as you are not interested in this offer.

Directions (41-62) Choose the right combined sentence from the following options.

41. I say it. He is a good man.
(a) I say he is a good man.
(b) He is good man I say
(c) I say that he is a good man.
(d) I say he is good man it.

42. I cannot say. Will he come tomorrow?
(a) I cannot say he will come tomorrow.
(b) I cannot say if/whether he will come tomorrow.
(c) He will come tomorrow I cannot say.
(d) Will he come tomorrow I cannot say.

43. I don't know. What is he doing?
(a) I don't know he is doing what?
(b) What is he doing I don't know?
(c) He is doing what I don't know.
(d) I don't know what he is doing.

44. Everybody was pleased to know. She was absent.
(a) Everybody was pleased to know that she was absent.
(b) She was absent everybody was pleased.
(c) Everybody was pleased to know she was absent.
(d) Everybody was pleased she was absent to know.

45. She kept on asking. When will her mother return?
(a) She kept on asking when her mother would return.
(b) When will her mother return kept on asking she.
(c) She kept on asking when her mother return would.
(d) Would her mother return she kept on asking.

46. I don't believe. She said something.
(a) I don't believe what she said.
(b) What she said I don't believe.
(c) I don't believe in what she said.
(d) She said something don't believe I.

47. Please listen. Your teacher is telling something.
(a) Please listen what your teacher is telling you.
(b) Please listen to what your teacher is telling.
(c) Your teacher is telling something to listen.
(d) Please listen your teacher to telling something.

48. The hope is. She will return tomorrow.
(a) The hope is that she will return tomorrow.
(b) The hope is that she would return tomorrow.
(c) She will return tomorrow is the hope.
(d) That she will return is the hope.

49. The fact is. Nisha has not qualified the test.
(a) Nisha has not qualified the test is the fact.
(b) The fact, Nisha has not qualified the test.
(c) The fact is that Nisha has not qualified the test.
(d) Nisha is the fact not qualified the test.

50. She never believed in his statement. His father is a doctor.
(a) She never believed in his statement that his father was a doctor.
(b) His father is a doctor she never believed statement.
(c) In his statement she never believed his father is a doctor.
(d) His father is a doctor she never believed in his statement.

51. It is true. My brother has left for America.
(a) It is true my brother has left for America
(b) My brother has left for America, it is true.
(c) It is true that my brother has left for America.
(d) It is my brother left for America is true.

52. It was not known. What is she doing in Indore.
(a) It was not known what she was doing in Indore.
(b) It was known she is doing what in Indore.
(c) What she was doing in Indore is not known.
(d) Not known she was doing what in Indore.

53. I know the man. He is a doctor.
(a) Who is a doctor I know the man.
(b) He is a doctor I know the man.
(c) I know the man who is a doctor.
(d) He is the man I know the doctor.

54. I don't know any of the men. They live here.
(a) They live here I don't know any of them.
(b) I don't know any of the men that live here.
(c) I don't know they live here any of the men.
(d) Any of the men I don't know live here.

55. The monster was proud of his power. He was defeated by Hercules.
(a) The monster who was proud of his power was defeated by Hercules.
(b) The monster was defeated by Hercules was proud of his power.
(c) He was defeated by Hercules was proud of his power.
(d) The monster proud of his power was defeated by Hercules.

56. It was midnight. The trains collided then.
(a) The trains collided then it was midnight.
(b) In the midnight collided then the trains.
(c) It was midnight when the trains collided.
(d) Midnight trains collided then.

57. He settled in Nagpur. He was born there.
(a) He was born there settled in Nagpur.
(b) He settled in Nagpur was born there.
(c) Settled in Nagpur was born there he.
(d) He settled in Nagpur where he was born.

58. I will get money for you. Don't go till then.
(a) Don't go till then I will get money for you.
(b) I will get money for you, don't go.
(c) Don't go I will get money for you.
(d) Don't go until I get money for you.

59. He was going to school. He was caught in the train.
(a) Going to school he was in the train was caught.
(b) He was caught in the train going to school.

(c) Caught in the train he was going to school.
(d) While he was going to school, he was caught in train.

60. His father retired last year. He has been idle from that time.
(a) He has been idle from that time his father retired.
(b) Since his father retired last year he has been idle.
(c) His father retired last year, he has been idle from that time.
(d) Idle from that time his father retired last year.

61. He will win the first prize. That is certain.
(a) He will certainly win the first prize.
(b) He will win the first prize that is certain.
(c) That is certain the first prize he will win.
(d) The first prize that is certain he will win.

62. She had many shortcomings. But she was a nice woman.
(a) She had many shortcomings but she was a nice woman.
(b) In spite of having many shortcomings, she was a nice woman.
(c) She was a nice woman had many shortcomings.
(d) She was a nice woman have many shortcomings.

Directions (63-70) Combine the following pairs of sentences with suitable conjunctions.

63. He didn't get admission. His grades were not very good.
(a) He didn't get admission; his grades were not very good.
(b) He didn't get admission because his grades were not very good.
(c) His grades were not very good and he didn't get admission.
(d) As his grades were not very good he didn't get admission.

64. The teacher enters the classroom. You should get up.
(a) When the teacher enters the classroom, you should get up.
(b) You should get up as the teacher enters the classroom.
(c) With the teacher enters the classroom you should get up.
(d) As soon as the teacher enters you should get up.

65. You will find it. You look for it.
(a) If you look for it will find it.
(b) When you look for it you will find it.
(c) You look for it if you will find it.
(d) You will find it if you look for it.

66. I told you not to do it. You have done it again.
(a) You have done it again when I told you not to do it.
(b) I told you not to do it but you have done it again.
(c) I told you not to do it, you have done it again.
(d) Despite I told you not to do it you have done it again.

67. She was really upset with him. She said nothing.
(a) She was really upset with him she said nothing.
(b) Being she was really upset with him she said nothing
(c) As she was really upset with him, she said nothing.
(d) She said nothing was really upset with him.

68. You heat ice. It melts.
(a) If/when you heat ice, it melts.
(b) You heat ice it melts.
(c) It melts heating ice.
(d) Heating ice it melts.

69. It will start working. You give it a kick.
(a) It will start working you give it a kick.
(b) It will start working by giving it a kick.
(c) It will start working when/if you give it a kick.
(d) You give it a kick it will start working.

70. He paid the subscription fee. His membership was renewed.
(a) He paid the subscription fee his membership was renewed.
(b) His membership was renewed as he paid the subscription fee.
(c) He paid the subscription fee so his membership was renewed.
(d) His membership was renewed by paying subscription fee.

Answers

1. (d)	2. (c)	3. (b)	4. (a)	5. (d)	6. (c)	7. (a)	8. (d)	9. (b)	10. (d)
11. (a)	12. (a)	13. (d)	14. (b)	15. (b)	16. (b)	17. (c)	18. (d)	19. (b)	20. (b)
21. (a)	22. (c)	23. (d)	24. (a)	25. (a)	26. (c)	27. (a)	28. (c)	29. (a)	30. (d)
31. (a)	32. (c)	33. (b)	34. (c)	35. (d)	36. (b)	37. (c)	38. (a)	39. (b)	40. (c)
41. (c)	42. (b)	43. (d)	44. (a)	45. (a)	46. (c)	47. (b)	48. (a)	49. (c)	50. (a)
51. (c)	52. (a)	53. (c)	54. (b)	55. (a)	56. (c)	57. (d)	58. (d)	59. (d)	60. (b)
61. (a)	62. (b)	63. (b)	64. (a)	65. (d)	66. (b)	67. (c)	68. (a)	69. (c)	70. (c)

Unit-06

01 Synonyms

Synonyms वे शब्द हैं, जो परस्पर एकसमान अर्थ प्रकट करते हैं। अर्थात् जिन शब्दों का meaning बिल्कुल एक-सा हो ऐसे ही शब्दों को synonym कहा जाता है। इस प्रकार के प्रश्नों का मुख्य उद्देश्य अभ्यर्थी की vocabulary एवं शब्दों के उचित उपयोग की क्षमता का आकलन करना होता है।

List of Words and their Synonyms

Word	Synonym
Awkward (भद्दा/कठिन/व्यग्र)	Clumsy, Rough
Allure (प्रलोभन/आकर्षण)	Entice, Fascinate
Abortive (निष्फल)	Vain, Unproductive
Allay (पीड़ा/भय कम करना)	Pacify, Soothe
Axiom (स्वयं सिद्ध कथन)	Maxim, Truth
Abjure (छोड़ देना/त्यागना)	Forsake, Renounce
Abject (निन्दनीय)	Despicable, Servile
Authentic (प्रामाणिक/सच्चा)	Genuine, Reliable
Audacity (साहस/ढिठाई)	Boldness, Arrogance
Abate (कम करना/शान्त करना)	Moderate, Decrease
Arraign (दोषारोपण)	Charge, Blame
Apathy (उदासीनता)	Unconcern, Indifference
Alien (विजातीय/विदेशी)	Foreigner, Outsider
Affront (सार्वजनिक अपमान)	Provoke, Irreverence
Adversity (दुर्भाग्य/विपत्ति)	Misfortune, Calamity
Antipathy (घृणा/अनिच्छा)	Hostility, Aversion
Amplify (विस्तार करना)	Nlarge, Extend
Alleviate (पीड़ा कम करना)	Abate, Relieve
Admonish (चेतावनी/भर्त्सना/सलाह देना)	Counsel, Reprove
Adherent (समर्थक/अनुयायी)	Follower, Disciple
Absolve (क्षमादान/पापमोचन)	Pardon, Forgive
Acrimony (झुंझलाहट)	Harshness, Bitterness
Accord (सहमति/स्वेच्छा)	Agreement, Harmony
Adamant (कठोर/वज्र)	Stubborn, Inflexible
Adjunct (मिला हुआ/जुड़ा हुआ)	Complement, Addition
Abandon (त्याग करना)	Leave
Attain (प्राप्त करना)	Gain, Acquire
Ascent (उठना)	Rise, Lift

Word	Synonym
Anguish (दुःख)	Distress, Sorrow
Arrogant (अहंकार)	Disdainful, Imperious
Avoid (टोकना)	Ignore, Shun
Ability (योग्यता)	Capacity, Skill
Acknowledge (स्वीकार करना)	Admit, Confess
Aid (सहायता)	Help, Relief
Apology (क्षमा माँगना)	Pardon, Excuse
Anger (नाराज होना)	Fury, Rage
Adept (अनुभवी होना)	Proficient, Expert
Answer (उत्तर देना)	Reply, Response
Bustle (आकुलता/शीघ्रता)	Haste, Flurry
Brittle (कुरकुरा/टूटने योग्य)	Delicate, Fragile
Bleak (रूखा/आनन्दरहित)	Dismal, Gloomy
Benevolence (दया/परोपकारिता)	Humanity, Generosity
Barbarous (असभ्य/निर्दयी)	Uncivilized, Savage
Baffle (घबराना)	Frustrate, Perplex
Bewitching (मोहिनी/लुभाने वाली)	Magical, Fascinating
Brilliant (चतुर)	Clever, Intelligent
Bliss (हर्ष)	Happiness, Joy
Brave (बहादुर)	Valiant, Bold
Build (निर्माण करना)	Construct, Make
Barbarous (जंगली)	Uncivilized
Bane (अभिशाप)	Curse, Harm
Benefit (लाभ)	Advantage, Gain
Banish (वनवास)	Exile, Expel
Beautiful (सुन्दर)	Lovely, Pretty
Bold (निडर)	Fearless
Bear (सहन)	Tolerate, Endure
Busy (व्यस्त)	Engaged
Careful (सावधान)	Cautious, Part, Portion
Cease (रोकना)	Desist, Stop
Competent (योग्य)	Able, Capable
Chaste (पवित्र)	Pure, Simple
Confess (स्वीकार करना)	Admit

Word	Synonym
Consolation (आश्वासन)	Solace
Convict (अपराधी)	Criminal, Prisoner
Candid (स्पष्ट)	Frank, Outspoken
Contrary (विरुद्ध/प्रतिकूल)	Dissimilar, Conflicting
Contradict (विरोध करना)	Deny, Oppose
Contempt (अपमान/उपेक्षा)	Scorn, Disregard
Conspicuous (प्रत्यक्ष/उत्कृष्ट)	Prominent, Obvious
Consolidate (ठोस/पुष्ट)	Compact, Strong
Consequence (परिणाम/प्रभाव)	Effect, Outcome
Consent (सहमत होना)	Agree, Permit
Concede (स्वीकार करना)	Yield, Assent
Comprise (सम्मिलित करना)	Include, Contain
Compassion (कृपा/दया)	Kindness, Sympathy
Concur (सहमत होना)	Approve, Agree
Chastise (दण्ड देना)	Punish, Admonish
Caricature (हँसी उड़ाना)	Exaggeration, Imitation
Captivity (कारावास/अधीनता)	Imprisonment, Confinement
Captivate (मोहित करना/लुभाना)	Charm, Fascinate
Calumny (आक्षेप/झूठा अभियोग)	Defamation, Aspersion
Callous (कठोर)	Obdurate, Unfeeling
Calamity (दु:ख/संकट)	Adversity, Misfortune
Cavity (छेद/खोह)	Depth, Hole
Despicable (नीच/घृणित)	Worthless, Shameless
Disdain (अवहेलना/तिरस्कार)	Detest, Despise
Deride (उपहास करना)	Mock, Taunt
Deprive (वंचित करना)	Despoil, Divest
Demolish (नष्ट करना)	Ruin, Devastate
Delicious (सुस्वादु/मधुर)	Palatable, Tasteful
Deliberate (विचारपूर्वक/ निश्चित)	Ponder, Intentional
Defray (देना/अदा करना)	Spend, Pay
Defile (दूषित करना/अपवित्र करना)	Contaminate, Pollute
Defer (विलम्ब करना)	Prolong, Suspend
Dedicate (अर्पित करना)	Devote, Consecrate
Decipher (अर्थ निकालना)	Interpret, Reveal
Deceit (कपट/छल)	Deception, Artifice
Decay (क्षय होना/नाश होना)	Collapse, Decomposition
Dainty (मृदु/सुन्दर)	Elegant, Exquisite
Evident (स्पष्ट/प्रत्यक्ष)	Obvious, Apparent
Eternal (नित्य/अनन्त)	Perpetual, Endless
Esteem (सम्मान एवं श्रद्धा)	Respect, Reverence
Eradicate (समाप्त करना/नष्ट करना)	Destroy, Exterminate
Equivocal (अस्पष्ट/अनिश्चित)	Uncertain, Ambiguous
Epitome (संक्षेप संग्रह)	Precise, Example
Endowment (धर्मदान/ वृत्तिदान)	Grant, Benefit

Word	Synonym
Endeavour (प्रयत्न करना)	Undertake, Aspire
Encumbrance (बाधा/भार)	Hindrance, Obstacle
Eloquence (वाक्पटुता)	Expression, Fluency
Eliminate (हटा देना)	Expel, Oust
Elevate (ऊपर उठाना/उन्नत करना)	Dignify, Heighten
Efface (मिटा देना)	Destroy, Obliterate
Ecstasy (परम हर्ष)	Delight, Exultation
Eccentric (विचित्र/सनकी)	Strange, Abnormal
Fabricate (बनाना/निर्माण करना)	Construct, Produce
Frugality (किफायत)	Economy, Providence
Frivolous (अमहत्त्वपूर्ण/ओछा)	Petty, Worthless
Frantic (उत्तेजित/व्यग्र)	Violent, Agitated
Fragile (भंगुर/नाजुक)	Weak, Infirm
Forsake (त्याग देना/छोड़ देना)	Desert, Renounce
Fluctuate (अनियमित/उतार-चढ़ाव)	Deflect, Vacillate
Flimsy (पतली/हल्की सामग्री)	Trifling, Transparent
Fleeting (क्षणिक)	Transient, Temporary
Feud (दुश्मनी/बैर)	Strife, Quarrel
Ferocious (क्रूर/खूँखार)	Untamed, Barbarous
Feeble (क्षीण/कमजोर)	Weak, Frail
Fantastic (विलक्षण)	Fanciful, Uncommon
Fanatical (कट्टर/दुराग्रही)	Narrow-minded, Biased
Falter (लड़खड़ाना)	Fluctuate, Demur
Fallacy (भ्रामकता/भ्रांति)	Delusion, Mistake
Guile (छल-कपट)	Cunning, Deceit
Grudge (अनिच्छा/दुर्भावना)	Hatred, Aversion
Grisly (विकट/क्रूर)	Disgusting, Atrocious
Gracious (उदार)	Courteous, Beneficent
Gorgeous (शानदार)	Magnificent, Dazzling
Glut (अतितृप्ति/भरमार)	Stuff, Satiate
Gloom (उदासी/गहरी छाया)	Obscurity, Darkness
Hypocrisy (पाखण्ड/ढोंग)	Deception, Affectation
Hideous (घृणित)	Frightful, Shocking
Heretic (विधर्मी)	Non-conformist, Secularist
Hazard (संकट)	Presumption, Danger
Haughty (अहंकारी)	Arrogant, Pompous
Harass (सताना/तंग करना)	Irritable, Molest
Hardship (कष्ट झेलना)	Misfortune, Difficulty
Holy (पवित्र)	Godly, Pious
Homage (उपासना)	Tribute, Respect
Humane (दयालु)	Kind, Sympathetic
Humble (विनम्र)	Modest, Meek
Haven (ठहरने का स्थान)	Refuge, Shelter
Hygiene (स्वच्छ, साफ)	Cleanliness, Sanitation

Word	Synonym
Irrepressible (जो दबाया न जा सके)	Irresistible, Unconfined
Invincible (अजेय)	Unconquerable, Impregnable
Intricate (जटिल/पेचीदा)	Tangled, Complicated
Intrigue (षड्यन्त्र)	Scheme, Conspiracy
Intrinsic (आन्तरिक गुण)	Genuine, Fundamental
Invective (आक्षेप/निन्दा)	Accusation, Censure
Instil (धीर-धीरे प्रवेश करना)	Inculcate, Inject
Insolvent (निर्धन/दिवालिया)	Indigent, Destitute
Insipid (बेस्वाद/अरोचक)	Tasteless, Vapid
Insinuate (अप्रिय संकेत देना)	Communicate, Allude
Ingenuous (निष्कपट/सच्चा)	Undisguised, Naive
Infringe (हनन/अतिक्रमण)	Violate, Encroach
Inevitable (अवश्य होने वाला/अपरिहार्य)	Unavoidable, Ascertained
Incongruous (अनुपयुक्त/असंगत)	Inappropriate, Absurd
Incompetent (असमर्थ/अयोग्य)	Inefficient, Unskilled
Inclination (झुकाव/अभिरुचि)	Disposition, Affection
Impute (आरोप लगाना)	Attribute, Ascribe
Impious (नास्तिक/अधर्मी)	Irreligious, Unholy
Impediment (बाधा/अड़चन)	Hurdle, Obstruction
Impartial (निष्पक्ष)	Just, Unbiased
Impair (हानि पहुँचाना)	Diminish, Deteriorate
Immunity (प्रतिरक्षा)	Prerogative, Privilege
Imminent (निकट भविष्य/समीपता)	Impending, Brewing
Immerse (मग्न/डूबना)	Submerge, Involve
Immense (विशाल)	Huge, Enormous
Immaculate (बेदाग/शुद्ध)	Unsullied, Spotless
Juvenile (तरुण/किशोर)	Young, Tender
Justify (स्पष्टीकरण/औचित्य सिद्ध करना)	Defend, Exculpate
Just (न्यायसंगत/उचित)	Honest, Impartial
Judicious (विवेकपूर्ण)	Thoughtful, Prudent
Jubilant (उल्लासपूर्ण)	Rejoicing, triumphant
Jovial (प्रसन्नचित्त)	Frolicsome, Cheerful
Jaded (थका हुआ)	Tired, Exhausted
Jejune (नीरसता से)	Dull, Boring
Kindred (सम्बन्ध/सजातीय)	Relation, Species
Keen (तीव्र/उत्सुक)	Sharp, Poignant
Knave (धूर्त/दुष्ट)	Dishonest, Scoundrel
Knell (मृत्युघण्टा/अशुभ सूचक)	Death knell, Last blow
Knotty (कठिन/पेंचदार)	Complicated, Difficult
Luxuriant (प्रचुर)	Profuse, Abundant
Luscious (स्वादिष्ट/सुमधुर)	Palatable, Delicious
Lure (प्रलोभन)	Attract, Entice
Lunacy (पागलपन/उन्माद)	Delusion, Insanity

Word	Synonym
Lucid (सुबोध/साफ-साफ)	Sound, Rational
Listless (निरुत्साह)	Lazy, Inattentive
Linger (धीरे-धीरे/देर तक)	Loiter, Prolong
Liberal (उदार/सहृदय)	Magnanimous, Generous
Liable (प्रवृत्ति/सम्भावना)	Accountable, Bound
Lenient (उदार)	Compassionate, Merciful
Lax (असावधान/लापरवाह)	Slack, Careless
Lavish (मुक्तहस्त/फिजूलखर्च)	Abundant, Excessive
Mutual (पारस्परिक/सहभावना)	Joint, Identical
Mutinous (विद्रोही)	Recalcitrant, Insurgent
Murky (अन्धकारमय)	Dusky, Dreary
Munificent (दानी/उदार)	Liberal, Hospitable
Monotonous (एकसुरा/नीरस)	Irksome, Tedious
Momentous (अति महत्त्वपूर्ण)	Notable, Eventful
Mollify (शान्त करना/मुलायम करना)	Appease, Assuage
Molest (छेड़खानी)	Paster, Harass
Modest (विनम्र/सुशील)	Humble, Courteous
Mitigate (कम करना)	Alleviate, Relieve
Miraculous (चमत्कार/असाधारण)	Marvellous, Extraordinary
Minute (सूक्ष्म)	Diminutive, Miniature
Numerous (बहुसंख्यक)	Profuse, Various
Nullify (रद्द करना)	Cancel, Annul
Noxious (हानिकारक/अहितकारी)	Baneful, Injurious
Novice (नौसिखिया)	Tyro, Beginner
Nonchalant (उदासीन/शान्त)	Indifferent, Negligent
Nimble (फुर्तीला/दक्ष)	Prompt, Brisk
Niggardly (लालची/कंजूसी से)	Miserly, Covetous
Negligent (लापरवाह)	Inattentive, Careless
Overwhelm (कुचलना)	Triumph, Subjugate
Outrage (अत्याचार/उपद्रव)	Offence, Maltreatment
Outbreak (विस्फोट/उद्वेग)	Eruption, Insurrection
Ornamental (शोभाकार/विभूषक)	Decorative, Adorned
Ordain (निर्दिष्ट करना/प्रबन्ध करना)	Order, Impose
Oracular (आकाशवाणी/अनिश्चित)	Cryptic, Vague
Opaque (अपारदर्शी)	Obscure, Shady
Offspring (सन्तान/सन्तति)	Descendants, Siblings
Offensive (क्षतिकर/घृणित)	Abhorrent, Arrogant
Odious (उदासीन)	Malevolent, Obnoxious
Occult (गुप्त/रहस्यमय)	Latent, Ambiguous
Obvious (स्पष्ट/प्रत्यक्ष)	Evident, Apparent
Obstruct (अवरोध/विघ्न)	Impede, Prevent
Prudent (चतुर/विवेकी)	Cautious, Discreet
Queer (अजीब)	Strange, Odd
Quit (त्यागना)	Leave, Abandon

Word	Synonym	Word	Synonym
Regard (सम्मान)	Respect, Esteem	Target (लक्ष्य)	Goal, Object
Rival (प्रतिद्वन्द्वी)	Competitor, Opponent	Tedious (थका देने वाली)	Boring, Dull
Raise (उठना/उत्थान)	Increase, Lift	Timid (कायर/डरपोक)	Cowardly, Shy
Recover (प्राप्त करना)	Regain, Obtain	Trust (विश्वास)	Faith, Confidence
Release (मुक्त करना)	Free, Liberate	Uproar (शोरगुल)	Tumult
Reliable (विश्वास करना)	Trustworthy, Dependable	Unique (एकमात्र)	Unequalled, Matchless
Ruin (नष्ट करना)	Destruction, Downfall	Urge (गिड़गिड़ाना, निवेदन करना)	Solicit, Plead
Realize (महसूस करना)	Accomplish, Fulfil	Understanding (समझ)	Insight, Perception
Significant (महत्त्वपूर्ण)	Distinctive, Important	Variety (विभिन्न प्रकार के)	Assortment, Diversify
Settle (समझौता करना)	Adjust, Compromise	Vanish (गायब होना)	Disappear
Separate (पृथक् होना)	Part, Divide	Vice (अवगुण, दोष)	Wickedness
Simple (साधारण)	Plain, Natural	Vigour (ऊर्जा)	Energy, Force
Summary (सारांश)	Synopsis, Substance	Victory (विजय)	Conguest, Success
Sacred (पवित्र)	Holy, Consecrated	Vigilant (जागरण)	Cautious, Alert
Savage (जंगली)	Wild, Uncivilized	Venture (खतरा मोल लेना)	Dare, Risk
Scorn (घृणा)	Contempt, Disdain	Wicked (क्रूर)	Immoral, Sinful
Splendid (अतिशानदार)	Glorious, Magnificient	Withhold (छिपाए रखना)	Retrain, Detain
Strife (राड़/झगड़ा)	Dispute, Discord	Wisdom (बुद्धिमानी)	Intelligence, Foresight
Struggle (संघर्ष करना)	Fight, Battle	Wreck (विध्वंस करना/बर्बाद करना)	Destruction, Ruin
Summit (चोटी/ऊँचाई पर/शिखर)	Top, Peak	Wilt (मुरझाना)	Wither, Perish
Seize (जब्त करना)	Capture, Arrest	Yoke (जुड़ा हुआ/सन्नद्ध)	Connect, Harness
Temper (मिजाज)	Mood, Nature	Yield (आत्मसमर्पण/उपज)	Surrender, Abdicate
Tough (कठिन)	Aggressive, Unyielding	Yearn (ललक/उत्कण्ठा)	Languish, Crave
Tremendous (शानदार)	Huge, Colossal	Zest (रुचि/दिलचस्पी)	Delight, Enthusiasm
Thin (पतला)	Slim, Slender	Zenith (पराकाष्ठा/चरम बिन्दु)	Summit, Apex
Thick (मोटा)	Dense, Compact	Zeal (उत्साह/जोश)	Eagerness, Fervour
Teach (पढ़ाना/शिक्षा देना)	Instruct, Educate		

Exercise 1

Directions (Q. Nos. 1-50) In each of the following questions, choose the alternative which is most nearly the same in meaning of the given word.

1. INDICT
(a) Condemn (b) Reprimand
(c) Accuse (d) Allege

2. SCINTILLATING
(a) Smouldering (b) Glittering
(c) Touching (d) Warming

3. REFECTORY
(a) Restaurant (b) Parlour
(c) Living Room (d) Dining Room

4. DISTINCTION
(a) Diffusion (b) Disagreement
(c) Different (d) Degree

5. IMPROVEMENT
(a) Advancement (b) Betterment
(c) Promotion (d) Preference

6. ADVERSITY
(a) Failure (b) Helplessness
(c) Misfortune (d) Crisis

7. TURN UP
(a) Land up (b) Show up
(c) Crop up (d) Come up

8. DEIFY
(a) Flatter (b) Challenge
(c) Worship (d) Face

9. ERROR
(a) Misadventure
(b) Misgiving
(c) Ambiguity
(d) Blunder

10. SHALLOW
(a) Artificial (b) Superficial
(c) Foolish (d) Worthless

11. MASSACRE
(a) Murder (b) Stab
(c) Assassinate (d) Slaughter

12. COMBAT
(a) Conflict (b) Quarrel
(c) Feud (d) Fight

13. VORACIOUS
(a) Wild (b) Hungry
(c) Angry (d) Quick

14. IMPROMPTU
(a) Offhand (b) Unimportant
(c) Unreal (d) Effective

15. RABBLE
(a) Mob (b) Noise
(c) Roar (d) Rubbish

16. TEPID
(a) Hot (b) Warm
(c) Cold (d) Boiling

17. MAYHEM
(a) Jubilation (b) Havoc
(c) Excitement (d) Defeat

18. TIMID
(a) Fast (b) Slow
(c) Medium (d) Shy

19. CANTANKEROUS
(a) Quarrelsome (b) Rash
(c) Disrespectful (d) Noisy

20. PRECARIOUS
(a) Cautious (b) Critical
(c) Perilous (d) Brittle

21. TACITURNITY
(a) Dumbness
(b) Changeableness
(c) Hesitation
(d) Reserve

22. INEBRIATE
(a) Dreamy (b) Stupefied
(c) Unsteady (d) Drunken

23. HARBINGER
(a) Massenger (b) Steward
(c) Forerunner (d) Pilot

24. INTIMIDATE
(a) To hint (b) Frighten
(c) Bluff (d) Harass

25. IRONIC
(a) Inflexible
(b) Bitter
(c) Good-natured
(d) Disguisedly sarcastic

26. STRINGENT
(a) Tense
(b) Stringy
(c) Strict
(d) Causing to shrink

27. ECSTATIC
(a) Animated (b) Bewildered
(c) Enraptured (d) Illful

28. COMMENSURATE
(a) Measurable
(b) Proportionate
(c) Beginning
(d) Appropriate

29. DESTITUTION
(a) Humility (b) Moderation
(c) Poverty (d) Beggary

30. ASCEND
(a) Leap (b) Grow
(c) Deviate (d) Mount

31. UNCOUTH
(a) Ungraceful (b) Rough
(c) Slovenly (d) Dirty

32. LYNCH
(a) Hang (b) Madden
(c) Killed (d) Shoot

33. LAUD
(a) Lord (b) Eulogy
(c) Praise (d) Extolled

34. CORRESPONDENCE
(a) Agreements (b) Contracts
(c) Documents (d) Letters

35. VENUE
(a) Place (b) Agenda
(c) Time (d) Duration

36. STERILE
(a) Barren (b) Arid
(c) Childless (d) Dry

37. SYNOPSIS
(a) Index (b) Mixture
(c) Summary (d) Puzzle

38. GERMANE
(a) Responsible (b) Logical
(c) Possible (d) Relevant

39. PONDER
(a) Think (b) Evaluate
(c) Anticipate (d) Increase

40. CANNY
(a) Obstinate (b) Handsome
(c) Clever (d) Stout

41. ABUNDANT
(a) Ripe (b) Cheap
(c) Plenty (d) Absent

42. CONSEQUENCES
(a) Results (b) Conclusions
(c) Difficulties (d) Applications

43. SHIVER
(a) Shake (b) Rock
(c) Tremble (d) Move

44. DILIGENT
(a) Progressive (b) Brilliant
(c) Inventive (d) Hard-working

45. DISTANT
(a) Far (b) Removed
(c) Reserved (d) Separate

46. FORAY
(a) Excursion (b) Contest
(c) Ranger (d) Intuition

47. FRUGALITY
(a) Foolishness (b) Extremity
(c) Enthusiasm (d) Economy

48. GARNISH
(a) Paint (b) Garner
(c) Adorn (d) Abuse

49. VIGOUR
(a) Strength (b) Boldness
(c) Warmth (d) Enthusiasm

50. CANDID
(a) Apparent (b) Explicit
(c) Frank (d) Bright

Directions (Q. Nos. 51-80) Pick out the word which is the same in meaning to the italicised word in the given sentence.

51. Plants that grow and exist in deserts have highly specialised means of adapting themselves to the **arid** environment.
(a) unproductive
(b) useless
(c) withering
(d) dry

52. *Eventually* vision is affected and the patient is only able to see if light is present.
(a) primarily (b) initially
(c) gradually (d) ultimately

53. Reading of poetry is not **congenial** to his taste.
(a) preferable (b) helpful
(c) beneficial (d) suited

54. He had a *penchant* for fine phrases.
(a) bias (b) liking
(c) training (d) desire

55. There is no **gainsaying** that the country is in difficulties.
(a) forgetting (b) denying
(c) ignoring (d) hiding

56. He **alleged** that the victim had been with the accused on the night of the murder.
(a) said (without giving proof)
(b) boasted (without hesitation)
(c) proved
(d) gossiped

57. Our art treasures must be kept for **posterity**.
(a) prosperity
(b) future generations
(c) the wealthy
(d) art connoisseurs

58. He was trying to put **across** his ideas to his audience.
(a) to convey
(b) to cross
(c) to convince
(d) to influence

59. The growing **disparity** between the rich and the poor has been a cause for concern for those who are committed to the establishment of a just and egalitarian social order.
(a) unity (b) diversity
(c) togetherness (d) inequality

60. The man **vehemently** denied all the charges of corruption that were levelled against him.
(a) devoutly (b) serenely
(c) hysterically (d) forcefully

61. The rebels returned home under an **amnesty**.
(a) Police security
(b) Judicial trial
(c) General pardon
(d) Financial assistance

62. A **posthumous** award was given to the poet.
(a) Postal (b) After death
(c) Literary (d) Creditable

63. He is so **meticulous** that he can never do anything in a hurry.
(a) slow (b) secretive
(c) lazy (d) very careful

64. The children suffer from having a **domineering** mother.
(a) sick and unhealthy
(b) tending to order people about
(c) nagging
(d) incapable of affection

65. This was his **maiden** performance on the stage and he did very well.
(a) opening (b) girlish
(c) first (d) primary

66. Please suggest an **appropriate** title for this passage.
(a) precise (b) alternate
(c) concise (d) suitable

67. The first **indication** of a storm is the long, slow swell at sea.
(a) danger (b) appearance
(c) sign (d) forecast

68. He obtained all the information available from public records and this helped him to compile the **biography** of the famous politician.
(a) life-history
(b) political activities
(c) report
(d) study

69. When the teacher saw John looking idly at the walls, he **admonished** him to study.
(a) warned (b) guided
(c) punished (d) implored

70. I doubt the **veracity** of your statements.
(a) wisdom
(b) reliability
(c) truthfulness
(d) tenacity

71. He is quite **parsimonious** by nature.
(a) cruel (b) spendthrift
(c) haughty (d) miserly

72. He is notorious for his **voracious** appetite.
(a) strong (b) gluttonous
(c) acute (d) explosive

73. She **called out** for help as soon as she sensed something was wrong
(a) pushed (b) shouted
(c) walked (d) advised

74. Despite his **lavish** preparation, he was not appreciated by his guest.
(a) sufficient (b) inadequate
(c) excessive (d) wonderful

75. If he gives his **assent** we shall be ready for tomorrow's journey.
(a) word (b) consent
(c) judgement (d) blessing

76. The manager deeply **regretted** his decision to dispense with the services of his assistant.
(a) discredited
(b) considered
(c) lamented
(d) blamed

77. The government can only afford to provide the poor with a meagre **subsistence**.
(a) allowance (b) food
(c) assistance (d) salary

78. I am certain that the audience will be alarmed when he expresses his **frank** views on the matter.
(a) comic (b) serious
(c) candid (d) intelligent

79. His mother **rebuked** him for not drinking the milk.
(a) praised (b) awarded
(c) teased (d) scolded

80. The *envoy* was not able to reach their place on time.
(a) spy (b) mail
(c) greetings (d) messanger

Exercise 2

Directions (Q. Nos. 1-25) Choose the correct synonym for the following words.

1. Acquaint
(a) Withhold (b) Conceal
(c) Familiarise (d) Risky

2. Authorise
(a) Disallow (b) Question
(c) Permit (d) Verify

3. Defamation
(a) Insult (b) Debt
(c) Infection (d) Deterioration

4. Invoice
(a) Language (b) Immoral
(c) Statement (d) Weariness

5. Assimilate
(a) Absorb (b) Arrange
(c) Receive (d) Assemble

6. Cherish
(a) Accuse (b) Flatter
(c) Demolish (d) Appreciate

7. Abandon
(a) Leave (b) Admit
(c) Refrain (d) Abstain

8. Clumsy
(a) Adroit (b) Dexterous
(c) Rough (d) Ungraceful

9. Comprehend
(a) Agree (b) Understand
(c) Reprieve (d) Settle

10. Coalition
(a) Alone (b) Disintegration
(c) Alliance (d) Perfection

11. Buoyant
(a) Joyful (b) Sad
(c) Angry (d) Clever

12. Calibre
(a) Straightness (b) Ability
(c) Shortcut (d) Streamline

13. Melancholy
(a) Animated (b) Carefree
(c) Depression (d) Forgivable

14. Illegible
(a) Fit (b) Illegal
(c) Not readable (d) Elective

15. Illicit
(a) Illegal (b) Draw
(c) Differ (d) Postpone

16. Ridiculous
(a) Anticipate (b) Absurd
(c) Satisfaction (d) Moderate

17. Delighted
(a) Despair (b) Overjoyed
(c) Careless (d) Depression

18. Conservation
(a) Environment (b) Preservation
(c) Agriculture (d) Technology

19. Omen
(a) Prophecy (b) Superstition
(c) Imagery (d) Imagination

20. Prolific
(a) Barren (b) Scanty
(c) Fertile (d) Graceful

21. Remote
(a) Distant (b) Barren
(c) Regular (d) Rude

22. Summit
(a) Base (b) Slope
(c) Declivity (d) Peak

23. Proceed
(a) Begin (b) End
(c) Engage (d) Continue

24. Persuade
(a) Assure (b) Discourage
(c) Convince (d) Cheat

25. Liberty
(a) Law (b) Moral
(c) Freedom (d) Rights

Directions (Q. Nos. 26-50) In the following sentences, select the word which is the same in meaning to the given underlined word.

26. Ritika didn't want to wait for dinner because she was starving.
(a) full (b) busy
(c) hungry (d) angry

27. Teena could not remember what happened that day.
(a) forget (b) recall
(c) discuss (d) explain

28. We're told that there is safety in numbers.
(a) danger (b) risk
(c) hazard (d) security

29. You look so gloomy today.
(a) delighted (b) rested
(c) unhappy (d) tired

30. She looked as serene as she always did.
(a) solemn (b) meek
(c) delicate (d) calm

31. Rohit made himself indispensable to his institution.
(a) redundant (b) essential
(c) negligible (d) superfluous

32. Because firemen are often in dangerous situations, they must be courageous.
(a) rugged (b) brave
(c) cowardly (d) volunteer

33. The newspaper hired an accomplished reporter to cover the story.
(a) unsinkable (b) unskilled
(c) skilled (d) suspected

34. The train arrived at the depot ahead of schedule.
(a) station (b) wreckage
(c) shanty (d) blizzard

35. Last night for homework we finished reading a story about the Pilgrim's voyage to India.
(a) monument (b) homeland
(c) refuge (d) journey

36. Although the situation is bad there is no cause for concern.
(a) caution (b) desire
(c) attention (d) anxiety

37. He has a genuine desire to help the poor people.
(a) maximum (b) selfish
(c) right (d) real

38. The function was attended by some eminent persons.
(a) important (b) rich
(c) cultured (d) related

39. It is very rare for him to arrive late in office.
(a) different (b) regular
(c) unusual (d) possible

40. He could not remember the incident due to the long lapse of time.
(a) period (b) memory
(c) delay (d) error

41. The beauty of the furniture does not concern me as much as its utility.
(a) cheapness (b) usefulness
(c) durability (d) weakness

42. During his stay at the office, he dealt with essential matters.
(a) few (b) vital
(c) insignificant (d) factual

43. Special areas in the town have been allocated for commercial activities.
(a) social (b) official
(c) business (d) clerical

44. Soon after the slaves were emancipated the industry collapsed.
(a) imprisoned (b) freed
(c) punished (d) enslaved

45. We gave him assurance regarding the safety of his things.
(a) decision (b) payment
(c) permission (d) promise

46. He is considered by every one as a man of virtues.
(a) power
(b) dishonesty
(c) goodness
(d) responsibility

47. The garage is at the rear part of his house.
(a) home (b) unusual
(c) invisible (d) back

48. Aparna is so intelligent that she stands first always.
(a) completes (b) ranks
(c) scores (d) establishes

49. We all tried to prevent her from leaving this town.
(a) control
(b) persuade
(c) stop
(d) resist

50. There appears to be some confusion in the planning.
(a) looks (b) thinks
(c) suppose (d) seems

Answers

Exercise 1

1 (c)	2 (b)	3 (d)	4 (c)	5 (b)	6 (c)	7 (b)	8 (c)	9 (d)	10 (b)
11 (d)	12 (d)	13 (b)	14 (a)	15 (a)	16 (b)	17 (b)	18 (d)	19 (a)	20 (b)
21 (d)	22 (d)	23 (c)	24 (b)	25 (d)	26 (c)	27 (c)	28 (b)	29 (c)	30 (d)
31 (a)	32 (c)	33 (c)	34 (d)	35 (a)	36 (a)	37 (c)	38 (d)	39 (a)	40 (c)
41 (c)	42 (a)	43 (c)	44 (d)	45 (a)	46 (a)	47 (d)	48 (c)	49 (a)	50 (c)
51 (d)	52 (d)	53 (d)	54 (b)	55 (b)	56 (a)	57 (b)	58 (a)	59 (d)	60 (d)
61 (c)	62 (b)	63 (d)	64 (b)	65 (c)	66 (d)	67 (c)	68 (a)	69 (a)	70 (c)
71 (d)	72 (b)	73 (b)	74 (d)	75 (b)	76 (a)	77 (a)	78 (c)	79 (d)	80 (d)

Exercise 2

1 (c)	2 (c)	3 (a)	4 (c)	5 (a)	6 (d)	7 (a)	8 (d)	9 (b)	10 (c)
11 (a)	12 (b)	13 (c)	14 (c)	15 (a)	16 (b)	17 (b)	18 (b)	19 (a)	20 (c)
21 (a)	22 (d)	23 (d)	24 (c)	25 (c)	26 (c)	27 (b)	28 (d)	29 (c)	30 (d)
31 (b)	32 (b)	33 (c)	34 (a)	35 (d)	36 (d)	37 (d)	38 (a)	39 (c)	40 (a)
41 (b)	42 (b)	43 (c)	44 (b)	45 (d)	46 (c)	47 (d)	48 (b)	49 (c)	50 (d)

02 Antonyms

Opposites/Antonyms वे शब्द हैं, जो अपने मूल अर्थ से विपरीत शब्द होते हैं। अर्थात् opposite अर्थ रखने वाले शब्दों को antonyms कहा जाता है। Opposites/Antonyms का मुख्य उद्देश्य अभ्यर्थी की vocabulary एवं शब्दों के उचित उपयोग करने की क्षमता का आकलन करने से होता है ताकि candidates अपनी अंग्रेजी को और दृढ़ बना पाए और अपने को बेहतर साबित करें।

List of Words and the Opposites

Word	Opposite
Above (ऊपर)	Below
Attack (आक्रमण)	Defend
Ability (योग्यता)	Inability
Advance (आगे)	Retreat
Adversity (विपत्ति)	Prosperity
Arrival (पहुँच)	Departure
Arrest (बन्दी बनाना)	Release, Free
Ascent (चढ़ाव)	Descent
Acceptance (स्वीकार)	Rejection
Armament (युद्ध करने की सामग्री)	Disarmament
Absurd (भद्दा)	Reasonable
Agree (सहमति)	Disagree
Angel (दूत)	Devil
Ancient (प्राचीन)	Modern
Alive (जीवित)	Dead
Bottom (नीचे)	Top
Broad (चौड़ा)	Narrow
Buy (खरीदना)	Sell
Blunt (खुदरा)	Sharp
Busy (व्यस्त)	Idle
Beautiful (सुन्दर)	Ugly
Blessing (आशीर्वाद)	Curse
Bravery (बहादुरी)	Cowardice
Belief (विश्वास)	Disbelief
Beneficial (लाभ)	Harmful
Barren (बंजर)	Fertile
Boon (वरदान)	Bane, Curse
Better (बेहतर)	Worse
Bold (निडर)	Meek

Word	Opposite
Bitter (कड़वा)	Sweet
Cheerful (खुशी)	Gloomy
Complicated (जटिल)	Simple
Confess (स्वीकार करना)	Deny
Compare (तुलना)	Contrast
Courageous (साहस)	Timid
Care (परवाह करना)	Neglect
Creation (निर्माण)	Destruction
Civilized (सभ्य)	Uncivilized, Wild
Cause (कारण)	Effect
Certain (निश्चित)	Uncertain
Contrary (विरुद्ध/प्रतिकूल)	Similar, Alike
Contradict (विरोध करना)	Approve, Confirm
Contempt (अपमान/उपेक्षा)	Regard, Praise
Conspicuous (प्रत्यक्ष/उत्कृष्ट)	Concealed, Hidden
Consolidate (ठोस/पुष्ट)	Separate, Weak
Consequence (परिणाम/प्रभाव)	Origin, Start
Consent (सहमत होना)	Object, Disagree
Concede (स्वीकार करना)	Deny, Reject
Comprise (सम्मिलित करना)	Reject, Lack
Compassion (कृपा/दया)	Cruelty, Barbarity
Concur (सहमत होना)	Differ, Disagree
Chastise (दण्ड देना)	Cheer, Encourage
Chaste (पवित्र/आडम्बर रहित)	Sullied, Lustful
Caricature (हँसी उड़ाना)	Exactness, Precision
Captivity (कारावास/अधीनता)	Freedom, Liberty
Captivate (मोहित करना/लुभाना)	Disillusion, Offend
Calumny (आक्षेप/झूठा अभियोग)	Commendation, Praise
Callous (कठोर)	Compassionate, Tender
Calamity (दुःख/संकट)	Happiness, Fortune
Cavity (छेद/खोह)	Elevation, Projection
Cease (रुकना/समाप्त होना)	Continue, Originate
Despicable (नीच/घृणित)	Worthy, Decent
Disdain (अवहेलना/तिरस्कार)	Approve, Praise

Word	Opposite
Deride (उपहास करना)	Inspire, Encourage
Deprive (वंचित करना)	Restore, Renew
Demolish (नष्ट करना)	Repair, Construct
Delicious (सुस्वादु /मधुर)	Distasteful, Unsavoury
Deliberate (विचारपूर्वक/निश्चित)	Rash, Sudden
Defray (देना/अदा करना)	Disclaim, Repudiate
Defile (दूषित करना/अपवित्र करना)	Purify, Sanctity
Defer (विलम्ब करना)	Accelerate, Expedite
Dedicate (अर्पित करना)	Refuse, Negate
Decipher (अर्थ निकालना)	Misinterpret, Distort
Deceit (कपट/छल)	Veracity, Sincerity
Decay (क्षय होना/नाश होना)	Flourish, Progress
Dainty (मृदु/सुन्दर)	Clumsy, Insipid
Evident (स्पष्ट/प्रत्यक्ष)	Obscure, Concealed
Esteem (सम्मान एवं श्रद्धा)	Ridicule, Spurn
Eradicate (समाप्त करना/नष्ट करना)	Secure, Plant
Equivocal (अस्पष्ट/अनिश्चित)	Obvious, Lucid
Epitome (संक्षेप संग्रह)	Increment, Expansion
Endowment (धर्मदान/वृत्तिदान)	Drawback, Damage
Endeavour (प्रयत्न करना)	Cease, Quit
Encumbrance (बाधा/भार)	Incentive, Stimulant
Eloquence (वाक्पटुता)	Halting, Stammering
Eliminate (हटा देना)	Restore, Accept
Elevate (ऊपर उठाना/उन्नत करना)	Deprecate, Denounce
Efface (मिटा देना)	Retain, Maintain
Ecstasy (परम हर्ष)	Despair, Calamity
Eccentric (विचित्र/सनकी)	Natural, Conventional
Fabricate (बनाना/निर्माण करना)	Destroy, Dismantle
Frugality (किफायत)	Lavishness, Extravagance
Frivolous (अमहत्त्वपूर्ण/ओछा)	Solemn, Significant
Frantic (उत्तेजित/व्यग्र)	Subdued, Gentle
Fragile (भंगुर/नाजुक)	Enduring, Tough
Forsake (त्याग देना/छोड़ देना)	Hold, Maintain
Fluctuate (अनियमित/उतार-चढ़ाव)	Stable, Resolute
Flimsy (पतली/हल्की सामग्री)	Firm, Tenacious
Fleeting (क्षणिक)	Enduring, Eternal
Feud (दुश्मनी/बैर)	Fraternity, Harmony
Ferocious (क्रूर/खूँखार)	Gentle, Innocent
Feeble (क्षीण/कमजोर)	Strong, Robust
Fantastic (विलक्षण)	Ordinary, Normal
Fanatical (कट्टर/दुराग्रही)	Liberal, Tolerant
Falter (लड़खड़ाना)	Persist, Endure

Word	Opposite
Fallacy (भ्रामकता/भ्रान्ति)	Veracity, Truth
Guile (छलकपट)	Honesty, Frankness
Grudge (अनिच्छा/दुर्भावना)	Benevolence, Affection
Grisly (विकट/क्रूर)	Pleasing, Attractive
Gracious (उदार)	Rude, Unforgiving
Gorgeous (शानदार)	Dull, Unpretentious
Glut (अतितृप्ति/भरमार)	Reduce, Abstain
Gloom (उदासी/गहरी छाया)	Delight, Mirth
Hypocrisy (पाखण्ड/ढोंग)	Sincerity, Honesty
Hideous (घृणित)	Attractive, Alluring
Heretic (विधर्मी)	Conformable, Religious
Hazard (संकट)	Conviction, Security
Haughty (अहंकारी)	Humble, Submissive
Harass (सताना/तंग करना)	Assist, Comfort
Import (आयात)	Export
Include (सम्मिलित करना)	Exclude
Increase (बढ़ाना)	Decrease
Innocent (निर्दोष)	Guilty
Initial (आरम्भिक)	Final
Inhale (अन्दर की ओर साँस लेना)	Exhale
Junior (कनिष्ठ)	Senior
Justice (न्याय देना)	Injustice
Joy (खुशी)	Sorrow
Known (ज्ञात होना)	Unknown
King (राजा)	Subject
Knowledge (ज्ञान)	Ignorance
Kind (दयालु)	Cruel
Like (पसन्द करना)	Dislike
Literate (शिक्षित)	Illiterate
Logical (तर्क-वितर्क करना)	Illogical
Lack (कमी)	Abundance
Legitimate (कानूनी)	Illegitimate
Laugh (हँसना)	Cry
Lend (उधार देना)	Borrow
Material (सांसारिक)	Spiritual
Maximum (अधिकतम)	Minimum
Mortal (नश्वर)	Immortal
Miser (कंजूस)	Spendthrift
Merit (योग्य)	Demerit
Mourn (विलाप करना)	Rejoice
Mature (परिपक्व)	Immature
Mad (पागल)	Sane

Word	Opposite
Noble (आदर्श)	Ignoble
Natural (प्राकृतिक)	Unnatural, Artificial
Night (रात)	Day
Noise (शोर-शराबा)	Quiet
Oral (मौखिक)	Written
Odd (विचित्र/विषम)	Even
Offer (प्रदान करना/देना)	Refuse
Order (आदेश देना)	Disorder
Optimistic (आशावादी)	Pessimistic
Provoke (उकसाना/उत्तेजित करना)	Pacify, Comfort
Protract (विलम्ब)	Abbreviate, Curtail
Proscribe (बहिष्कार/त्यागना)	Solicit, Include
Profuse (अतिव्ययी/विपुल)	Scarce, Meagre
Profligate (भ्रष्टचरित्र/व्यसनी)	Virtuous, Upright
Prodigy (अद्भुत/विलक्षण)	Normal, Average
Prodigious (बहुत बड़ा/विलक्षणता)	Unimpressive, Diminutive
Premature (असामयिक/समय से पूर्व)	Belated, Opportune
Predicament (दशा/स्थिति)	Resolution, Confidence
Precarious (संदिग्ध/अनिश्चित)	Assured, Undeniable
Pompous (गर्वित)	Unpretentious, Humble
Perverse (हठी/दुष्ट)	Complacent, Docile
Pertness (ढिठाई)	Modesty, Diffidence
Peevish (झगड़ालू/चिड़चिड़ा)	Suave, Amiable
Quaint (विचित्र)	Familiar, Usual
Quack (ठग विद्या करने वाला/कुवैद्य)	Upright, Unfeigned
Quibble (वाकछल करना)	Unfeign, Plain
Ruthless (निर्दयी/क्रूर)	Compassionate, Lenient
Rustic (असभ्य/गँवार)	Cultured, Refined
Rout (उपद्रव/बलवा)	Succumb, Withdraw
Retract (पीछे हटना)	Confirm, Assert
Remote (दूरस्थ/दूरवर्ती)	Adjoining, Adjacent
Remorse (पश्चाताप)	Ruthless, Obduracy
Resentment (द्वेष/ईर्ष्या)	Content, Cheer
Rescind (खण्डन/लोप करना)	Delegate, Permit
Remonstrate (प्रतिवाद)	Agree, Laud
Remnant (अवशेष/बचा हुआ)	Entire, Whole
Sycophant (चापलूस/नीच)	Devoted, Loyal

Word	Opposite
Superficial (ऊपरी/छिछला)	Profound, Discerning
Subvert (ढहाना/नाश करना)	Generate, Organise
Substantial (वास्तविक/ठोस)	Tenuous, Abstract
Subsequent (उत्तरगामी/आगामी)	Preceding, Previous
Stain (धब्बा/कलंक)	Honour, Purify
Sporadic (छितराया हुआ)	Incessant, Frequent
Solicit (सविनय माँगना/आग्रह करना)	Protest, Oppose
Sneer (उपहास/तिरस्कार)	Flatter, Praise
Trenchant (तीक्ष्ण/तीव्र)	Feeble, Vacillating
Transient (नश्वर/अस्थिर)	Lasting, Enduring
Tranquil (शान्त/निश्चल)	Violent, Furious
Timid (भीरु/कायर)	Bold, Intrepid
Temperate (संयमी/उत्तेजनारहित)	Boisterous, Violent
Tedious (थकाने वाला)	Exhilarating, Lively
Taciturn (अल्पभाषी)	Talkative, Extrovert
Utterly (सम्पूर्णत:)	Deficient, Incomplete
Usurp (अधिकार छीनना/शक्तिहनन)	Restore, Compensate
Uncouth (गँवार/असभ्य)	Elegant, Graceful
Umbrage (कटु अनुभव/बुरा मानना)	Sympathy, Goodwill
Vulgar (अशिष्ट/अभद्र)	Elegant, Civil
Vouch (जिम्मा लेना/आश्वासन देना)	Repudiate, Prohibit
Volatile (चंचल/वाष्पशील)	Heavy, Ponderous
Vicious (भ्रष्ट/दूषित)	Noble, Virtuous
Venerable (पूजनीय/श्रद्धेय)	Unworthy, Immature
Vanity (दम्भ)	Modesty, Humility
Valour (पराक्रम)	Fear, Cowardice
Waive (दावा छोड़ना/त्यागना)	Impose, Clamp
Wary (सतर्क/सावधान)	Heedless, Negligent
Wane (क्षीण होना/निर्बल होना)	Ameliorate, Rise
Welt (मुरझाना)	Revive, Bloom
Yoke (जुड़ा हुआ/सन्नद्ध)	Liberate, Release
Yield (आत्मसमर्पण/उपज)	Resist, Protest
Yearn (ललक/उत्कण्ठा)	Content, Satisfied
Zest (रुचि/दिलचस्पी)	Disgust, Passive
Zenith (पराकाष्ठा/चरम बिन्दु)	Nadir, Base
Zeal (उत्साह/जोश)	Apathy, Lethargy

Exercise 1

Directions (Q. Nos. 1-50) In the following questions, choose the word which is the exact opposite of the given word.

1. DEAR
(a) Priceless (b) Free
(c) Worthless (d) Cheap

2. FLAGITIOUS
(a) Innocent (b) Vapid
(c) Ignorant (d) Frivolous

3. LIABILITY
(a) Property (b) Assets
(c) Debt (d) Teasure

4. VIRTUOUS
(a) Wicked (b) Corrupt
(c) Vicious (d) Scandalous

5. ENCOURAGE
(a) Dampen (b) Disapprove
(c) Discourage (d) Warn

6. MORTAL
(a) Divine (b) Immortal
(c) Spiritual (d) Eternal

7. LEND
(a) Borrow (b) Cheat
(c) Pawn (d) Hire

8. COMIC
(a) Emotional (b) Tragic
(c) Fearful (d) Painful

9. ADDITION
(a) Division (b) Enumeration
(c) Subtraction (d) Multiplication

10. MINOR
(a) Big (b) Major
(c) Tall (d) Heavy

11. REPEL
(a) Attend (b) Concentrate
(c) Continue (d) Attract

12. ARTIFICIAL
(a) Red (b) Natural
(c) Truthful (d) Solid

13. CAPACIOUS
(a) Limited (b) Caring
(c) Foolish (d) Changeable

14. PROVOCATION
(a) Vocation (b) Pacification
(c) Peace (d) Destruction

15. METICULOUS
(a) Mutual (b) Shaggy
(c) Meretricious (d) Slovenly

16. ABLE
(a) Disable (b) Inable
(c) Unable (d) Misable

17. COMFORT
(a) Uncomfort
(b) Miscomfort
(c) Discomfort
(d) None of the above

18. GAIN
(a) Loose (b) Fall
(c) Lost (d) Loss

19. SYNTHETIC
(a) Affable (b) Natural
(c) Plastic (d) Cosmetic

20. ACQUITTED
(a) Freed (b) Burdened
(c) Convicted (d) Entrusted

21. STRINGENT
(a) General (b) Vehement
(c) Lenient (d) Magnanimous

22. FLIMSY
(a) Frail (b) Filthy
(c) Firm (d) Flippant

23. BUSY
(a) Occupied (b) Engrossed
(c) Relaxed (d) Engaged

24. ADAPTABLE
(a) Adoptable (b) Flexible
(c) Yielding (d) Rigid

25. LOVE
(a) Villainy (b) Hatred
(c) Compulsion (d) Force

26. BALANCE
(a) Disbalance (b) Misbalance
(c) Debalance (d) Imbalance

27. RELINQUISH
(a) Abdicate (b) Renounce
(c) Possess (d) Deny

28. MOUNTAIN
(a) Plain (b) Plateau
(c) Precipice (d) Valley

29. FICKLE
(a) Courageous (b) Sincere
(c) Steadfast (d) Humble

30. PERENNIAL
(a) Frequent (b) Regular
(c) Lasting (d) Rare

31. RARELY
(a) Hardly (b) Definitely
(c) Frequently (d) Periodically

32. STARTLED
(a) Amused (b) Relaxed
(c) Endless (d) Astonished

33. ADHERENT
(a) Detractor (b) Enemy
(c) Alien (d) Rival

34. QUIESCENT
(a) Indifferent (b) Troublesome
(c) Weak (d) Unconcerned

35. CONDENSE
(a) Expand (b) Distribute
(c) Interpret (d) Lengthen

36. BENIGN
(a) Malevolent (b) Soft
(c) Friendly (d) Unwise

37. OBSCURE
(a) Implicit (b) Obnoxious
(c) Explicit (d) Pedantic

38. HYPOCRITICAL
(a) Gentle (b) Sincere
(c) Amiable (d) Dependable

39. EVASIVE
(a) Free (b) Honest
(c) Liberal (d) Frank

40. INDUSTRIOUS
(a) Indifferent (b) Indolent
(c) Casual (d) Passive

41. EXTRICATE
(a) Manifest (b) Palpable
(c) Release (d) Entangle

42. LUCID
(a) Glory (b) Noisy
(c) Obscure (d) Distinct

43. INSIPID
(a) Tasty (b) Stupid
(c) Discreet (d) Feast

44. OBEYING
(a) Ordering
(b) Following
(c) Refusing
(d) Contradicting

45. VICTORIOUS
(a) Defeated (b) Annexed
(c) Destroyed (d) Vanquished

46. COMMISSIONED
(a) Started (b) Closed
(c) Finished (d) Terminated

47. VANITY
(a) Pride (b) Humility
(c) Conceit (d) Ostentious

48. ZENITH
(a) Acme (b) Top
(c) Nadir (d) Pinnacle

49. TANGIBLE
(a) Ethereal (b) Concrete
(c) Actual (d) Solid

50. REPRESS
(a) Inhibit (b) Liberate
(c) Curb (d) Quell

Directions (Q. Nos. 51-80) In the following sentences, a word or phrase is written in italicised letter. For each italicised part, four words are listed below each sentence. Choose the word which is opposite in meaning of the italicised word.

51. He was dejected when he heard the news.
(a) elated (b) impressed
(c) hilariours (d) gleeful

52. After meeting the holy man, his nagging mood of diffidence suddenly changed.
(a) confusion (b) self assurance
(c) contentment (d) consternation

53. The deliberate suavity of Dev's behaviour made the emotions of the audience volatile.
(a) politeness (b) impetuosity
(c) stupidity (d) pleasant

54. Sanjay's point of view was correct but his behaviour with his father was quite impertinent.
(a) impressive (b) smooth
(c) healthy (d) respectful

55. Atleast some students are in the habit of doing their exercises in a *slovenly* manner.
(a) near (b) proper
(c) decent (d) correct

56. The last show of the concert at the Ritz theatre was a fiasco.
(a) triumph (b) victory
(c) fruitful (d) success

57. He proved utterly capricious in his dealings with his friends.
(a) helpful
(b) steadfast
(c) understanding
(d) obstinate

58. It is surprising to find her condoning such an act.
(a) disparaging (b) condemning
(c) disliking (d) forbidding

59. They had an *insipid* conversation.
(a) curious
(b) loud
(c) argumentative
(d) lively

60. His partners felt that it was a viable business proposition.
(a) impracticable (b) inviolable
(c) unavailable (d) enviable

61. Overeating can often be detrimental to health.
(a) beneficial (b) injurious
(c) useful (d) destructive

62. Miscellaneous items were discussed at the meeting.
(a) Minor (b) Unrelated
(c) Mixed (d) Classified

63. The author has perspicuity in his style.
(a) frankness (b) bluntness
(c) obstruseness (d) vivacity

64. The officer exaggerated the damage caused by the rowdies.
(a) underwrote
(b) condemned
(c) ignored
(d) underestimated

65. The speaker was unable to pacify the crowd.
(a) excite (b) antagonize
(c) threaten (d) challenge

66. His officer was a very strict person.
(a) pleasant
(b) open hearted
(c) lenient
(d) indifferent

67. Servitude is not helpful for mental growth.
(a) Disservice
(b) Retirement
(c) Freedom
(d) Termination

68. His attitude to poor people is deplorable.
(a) commendable
(b) miserable
(c) equitable
(d) desirable

69. The guest made derogatory remarks about the food he was served.
(a) interesting
(b) complimentary
(c) unnecessary
(d) cheerful

70. He has an aversion to milk.
(a) dear (b) loving
(c) liking (d) pet

71. The paucity of good teachers is the chief reason for the present condition of these schools.
(a) presence (b) appointment
(c) surplus (d) retention

72. Don't you think his account of things was monotonous?
(a) agreeable (b) acceptable
(c) varied (d) indecent

73. Spurious drugs can prove to be fatal.
(a) Virtuous (b) Inferior
(c) Genuine (d) Contemptuous

74. Because of the failure of the monsoon, there was paucity of foodgrains.
(a) overflow (b) inflow
(c) plenty (d) glut

75. The evidence against the accused is conclusive.
(a) powerful (b) indecisive
(c) exclusive (d) partial

76. Their careers followed a parallel path.
(a) divergent (b) difficult
(c) similar (d) dissimilar

77. The old man manifested his greed at the sight of a huge amount of money.
(a) displayed (b) concealed
(c) suppressed (d) marked

78. The fallen trees blocked our passage to freedom from the word.
(a) facilitated (b) started
(c) checked (d) promoted

79. The outcome of his mission was more rewarding than he had expected.
(a) lucrative (b) disappointing
(c) thrilling (d) nail-biting

80. He wanted to inaugrate the project right on schedule.
(a) terminate (b) inculcate
(c) facilitate (d) ameliorate

Exercise 2

Directions (Q. Nos. 1-25) *Choose the correct antonym of the following words.*

1. Dearth
(a) Abundance (b) Scarcity
(c) Replenish (d) Expensive

2. Wrath
(a) Agitated (b) Gentleness
(c) Anger (d) Worship

3. Brisk
(a) Agile (b) Nimble
(c) Sluggish (d) Quick

4. Dormant
(a) Domestic (b) Inactive
(c) Dorsal (d) Active

5. Terminate
(a) Begin (b) Stop
(c) End (d) Halt

6. Enormous
(a) Soft (b) Average
(c) Tiny (d) Weak

7. Dreadful
(a) Beastly (b) Pleasant
(c) Atrocious (d) Awful

8. Diverge
(a) Converge (b) Condense
(c) Separate (d) Part

9. Reckless
(a) Cautious (b) Careless
(c) Hasty (d) Irresponsible

10. Obeying
(a) Refusing (b) Following
(c) Complying (d) Contradicting

11. Busy
(a) Occupied (b) Engrossed
(c) Idle (d) Engaged

12. Fresh
(a) Faulty (b) Sluggish
(c) Disgraceful (d) Stale

13. Aware
(a) Uncertain (b) Ignorant
(c) Sure (d) Doubtful

14. Benevolent
(a) Caring (b) Humane
(c) Gracious (d) Selfish

15. Blustered
(a) Angry (b) Gentle
(c) Neglect (d) Impede

16. Arrogant
(a) Humble
(b) Cowardly
(c) Egoistic
(d) Gentlemanly

17. Victorious
(a) Annexed (b) Destroyed
(c) Bravery (d) Defeated

18. Graceful
(a) Rough (b) Expert
(c) Awkward (d) Miserable

19. Treacherous
(a) Doubtful (b) Faithful
(c) Immoral (d) Fraud

20. Adaptable
(a) Rigid (b) Flexible
(c) Yielding (d) Adoptable

21. Suppress
(a) Allow (b) Praise
(c) Permit (d) Encourage

22. Haphazard
(a) Fortuitous (b) Indifferent
(c) Deliberate (d) Accidental

23. Hollow
(a) Filled (b) Solid
(c) Strong (d) Substantial

24. Valuable
(a) Worthless (b) Invaluable
(c) Inferior (d) Lowly

25. Autonomy
(a) Slavery (b) Subordination
(c) Dependence (d) Submissive

Directions (Q. Nos. 26-50) *Select the correct antonym of the word underlined in the given sentences.*

26. Jia felt a lot of pride.
(a) happiness (b) shame
(c) joy (d) enjoyment

27. Zayed is modest.
(a) boastful (b) unaware
(c) clumsy (d) shabby

28. The medicine tasted awful.
(a) terrible (b) bitter
(c) great (d) sour

29. Tanya gathered some wood for the campfire.
(a) burned (b) soaked
(c) collected (d) scattered

30. You can't admit what you've done!
(a) deny (b) hide
(c) change (d) conceal

31. The detective will try to expose new facts to solve the case.
(a) show (b) reveal
(c) uncover (d) conceal

32. With the light bulb burnt out, the room was very dim.
(a) dark (b) badly lit
(c) bright (d) shadowy

33. We'll be lucky if the weather is mild on the day of the big game.
(a) calm (b) gentle
(c) severe (d) moderate

34. Sushant was filled with glee when he saw he'd made the horror roll.
(a) joy (b) cheer
(c) sadness (d) happiness

35. Carpenters always start with wood that's as straight as possible.
(a) solid (b) curved
(c) direct (d) simple

36. Self reliance has been adopted as an important objective of economic planning in modern India.
(a) refused
(b) forsaken
(c) denied
(d) discarded

37. His appointment was confirmed last month.
(a) disappointment
(b) suspension
(c) dismissal
(d) discharge

38. She has a passion for indigenous goods.
(a) native (b) foreign
(c) silly (d) cheap

39. He made an exhaustive list of the items his secretary should attend to.
(a) short (b) incomplete
(c) interesting (d) meticulous

40. I like his friendly attitude.
(a) jealous (b) envious
(c) hostile (d) vicious

41. He appears to be a phony person.
(a) beautiful (b) unread
(c) genuine (d) ugly

42. He was in a dejected mood.
(a) jubilant (b) rejected
(c) irritable (d) romantic

43. Philosophers say that the world is an <u>illusion</u>.
(a) a fact (b) a reality
(c) an actuality (d) a truth

44. He was a marked <u>deterioration</u> in his condition.
(a) improvement (b) revision
(c) reformation (d) amendment

45. This offer has come as a great <u>boon</u> to me.
(a) curse (b) blemish
(c) trouble (d) misfortune

46. I liked the poem for its <u>literal</u> meaning.
(a) deep (b) complex
(c) fictitious (d) figurative

47. His book has a short but useful <u>introduction</u>.
(a) end (b) conclusion
(c) termination (d) deduction

48. The Principal hardly managed to give the papers a <u>cursory</u> glance.
(a) curious (b) thorough
(c) through (d) superficial

49. The attack on the freedom of the press is a <u>retrograde</u> step.
(a) progressive
(b) stubborn
(c) punitive
(d) aggressive

50. We received a <u>cordial</u> welcome from our host.
(a) indifferent
(b) distrustful
(c) cold
(d) official

Answers

Exercise 1

1 (d)	2 (a)	3 (b)	4 (c)	5 (c)	6 (b)	7 (a)	8 (b)	9 (c)	10 (b)
11 (d)	12 (b)	13 (a)	14 (b)	15 (d)	16 (c)	17 (c)	18 (d)	19 (b)	20 (c)
21 (c)	22 (c)	23 (c)	24 (d)	25 (b)	26 (d)	27 (c)	28 (d)	29 (c)	30 (d)
31 (d)	32 (b)	33 (b)	34 (a)	35 (c)	36 (a)	37 (c)	38 (b)	39 (b)	40 (b)
41 (d)	42 (c)	43 (a)	44 (a)	45 (a)	46 (d)	47 (b)	48 (c)	49 (a)	50 (b)
51 (a)	52 (b)	53 (b)	54 (d)	55 (a)	56 (a)	57 (b)	58 (b)	59 (d)	60 (a)
61 (a)	62 (d)	63 (c)	64 (d)	65 (a)	66 (c)	67 (c)	68 (a)	69 (b)	70 (c)
71 (c)	72 (c)	73 (c)	74 (d)	75 (b)	76 (a)	77 (c)	78 (a)	79 (b)	80 (a)

Exercise 2

1 (a)	2 (b)	3 (c)	4 (d)	5 (a)	6 (c)	7 (b)	8 (a)	9 (a)	10 (a)
11 (c)	12 (d)	13 (b)	14 (d)	15 (b)	16 (a)	17 (d)	18 (c)	19 (b)	20 (a)
21 (d)	22 (c)	23 (b)	24 (a)	25 (c)	26 (b)	27 (a)	28 (c)	29 (d)	30 (a)
31 (d)	32 (c)	33 (c)	34 (c)	35 (b)	36 (d)	37 (c)	38 (b)	39 (b)	40 (c)
41 (c)	42 (a)	43 (b)	44 (a)	45 (a)	46 (d)	47 (b)	48 (b)	49 (a)	50 (a)

03 Words Often Confused (Homonyms, Homographs)

Word similar in sound or pronunciation, but different in meaning, are called Homonyms.

English में ऐसे बहुत से शब्द हैं जिनका pronunciation लगभग एक जैसा होता है, लेकिन उनके meaning में अन्तर होता है, ऐसे शब्दों को Homonyms or Homophones कहा जाता है। जैसे : Access, Excess, Affect, Effect इन शब्दों का उचित ज्ञान न होने पर एक की जगह पर दूसरे शब्द को लिखने से सब कुछ गलत हो जाता है अत: छात्रों को ऐसे शब्दों का बहुत ध्यानपूर्वक अध्ययन करना आवश्यक है। नीचे इस तरह के बहुत से शब्दों के बारे में बताया गया है।

1. **Affect** (to act upon, to pretend प्रभाव डालना) She affects too much innocence.

   Effect (Result–प्रभाव) Internet produces a bad effect on the young generation.

2. **Adapt** (accomodate-व्यवहार) One should adapt oneself to the new circumstances.

   Adept (expert-निपुण) He is an adept in Folk dance.

   Adopt (take up-गृहण करना) One should not adopt unfair means to secure good marks.

3. **Accede** (Agree–स्वीकार करना) He will not accede to your request.

   Exceed (to be greater–बढ़ना, बढ़ाना) Write an essay not exceeding three hundred words.

4. **Access** (approach, reach–पहुँच) Now-a-days, every person has an easy access to the temples irrespective to his caste.

   Excess (more than enough–अधिकता) Excess of everything is bad.

5. **Accept** (to take–स्वीकार करना) He cannot accept this gift.

   Except (leaving out–बजाय) Except Nisha everyone was present in the party.

6. **Antic** (odd, strange–अपरिचित) His behaviour on yesterday was antic.

   Antique (ancient–प्राचीन) I am fond of collecting antique items.

7. **All ready** (all are ready–सभी तैयार) They were all ready to welcome the groom.

   Already (earlier–पूर्व में) I have already informed him.

8. **Apposite** (proper–योग्य) His arguments were not apposite to the subject.

   Opposite (contrary–विपरीत, in front of) His house is opposite to the college.

9. **Assent** (agreement–स्वीकारोक्ति)He gave his assent to the new proposal.

   Ascent (going up–ऊपर चढ़ना) He pushed the button and the elevator began its slow ascent.

10. **Aloud** (high volume–ऊँचा स्वर) I can't hear you well, please speak aloud.

    Allowed (permitted–इजाजत दी) He was allowed to enter.

11. **Advice** (noun–सलाह) I need your expert advice in this matter.

    Advise (verb–सलाह देना) Please advise me in this matter.

12. **Amiable** (lovable–प्यार योग्य) She is not only a beautiful but also an amiable girl.

    Amicable (friendly–मित्रवत्) Finally they came to an amicable settlement.

13. **All together** (in a body–साथ-साथ) Let us move there all together.

    Altogether (completely–पूर्णतया) It seems altogether impossible to cross the river in the night.

14. **Aid** (to assist–सहायता करना) He has given aid of ₹ 5000/- to the poor family.

    Aide (an assistant) He is a close aide to the Prime Minister.

15. **All** (everything–सब) He has donated all his property.

    Awl (a small pointed tool for pricking or piercing holes, esp. such a tool used by shoemakers– औजार)

16. **Auger** [(a drill (tool–औजार)] I need an auger to make a hole.

Augur (foretell–भविष्य कहना) The recent communal riots do not augur well for the smooth running of government.

17. Aural (of hearing–सुनने सम्बन्धित) He became famous as an inventor of astonishing visual and aural effects)

Oral (of the mouth–मौखिक) He presented his ideas in a nice way orally.

18. Awed (in a state of wonder–चकित) Awedly she was unable to recall his name.

Odd (not usual) Find the odd word from the following passage.

19. Bale (package–गाँठ) I received thirty bales of cotton last month.

Bail (security–जमानत) The magistrate didn't grant him bail in theft case.

20. Berth (sleeping place in train–ट्रेन में बर्थ) I have booked two berths in Shatabadi Express.

Birth (coming to life–जन्म)This is not the birth place of Buddha.

21. Bare (*uncovered*–नंगा, बिना ढका) He came here bare footed.

Bear (to tolerate–सहन करना) I cannot bear your insulting remarks.

(an animal–रीछ) There are three bears in that circus.

Beer (a kind of wine–बीयर) I prefer to take beer.

22. Blow (to whistle–बजाना) A cool wind is blowing. Don't blow the whistle.

Below (underneath–नीचे) Hitting below the belt is not allowed.

23. Born (to take birth–जन्म) My wife was born in 1960.

Borne (supported–सहन किया) He is suffering from water borne disease.

24. Bad (not good–बुरा) He is a bad man.

Bed (sleeping place–बिस्तर) I go to bed at 11 P.M.

25. By (assistance–द्वारा) A snake was killed by Ram with a stick.

Buy (purchase–खरीदना) I want to buy a car.

26. Beet (a vegetable–चुकन्दर) I prefer mango to beet.

Beat (to thrash–पीटना) It is wrong to beat the students with a stick.

27. Borrow (to take loan–उधार लेना) I have borrowed some money from Bank.

Burrow (a hole in earth–छेद) A mouse lives in this burrow.

28. Cell (a small cottage–छोटी कोठरी) There are more than twenty cells in that prison.

Sell (to dispose off–बेचना) He sells fruits and vegetables.

Sale (noun-act of selling–बिक्री) I have purchased this dress from that shop.

29. Beach (shore–किनारा) Many people like to walk along the sea beach.

Beech (a kind of tree–पेड़) There are many beech trees near the railway station.

30. Brake (make a moving vehicle slow down or stop by using a brake–पहियों की रोक) I am going to get the brake wire changed.

Break (to make a part–तोड़ना) Can you break this stick with your hands?

31. Baron (a landlord–जमींदार) There was a time when all powers rested in the hands of rich barons.

Barren (not fertile–अनुपजाऊ) In barren land you can't cultivate any thing.

32. Blue (a colour–नीला) I like blue colour.

Blew (whistled–बजाई) The refree blew the whistle again and again.

33. Bald (hairless–गंजा) She is bald headed.

Balled (carnal knowledge) He picked up the sheets of paper and balled them tightly in his fists.

Bawled (cried aloud–जोर से पुकारना) Someone in the audience bawled out 'Once More'.

34. Bard (a poet–कवि) People sometimes refer to William Shakespeare as the Bard.

Barred (enclosed by poles–घेरना) The windows were closed and shuttered and the door was barred.

35. Base (the bottom support *for anything*–आधार) The base of the bottle is very narrow.

Bass (the lowest musical pitch or range–धीमी आवाज) A bass is also a man with deep singing voice.

36. Better (superior–अच्छा) It is always better to drive carefully.

Bettor (one who bets–जुंआरी) The person who bets is called a bettor.

37. Bight (the loop of a rope–रस्सा) is called bight.

Bite (a mouthful–गुस्सा) You can have a bite of chocolates.

Byte (eight bits–बइट) Byte is a unit of storage in computers.

38. Bloc (an alliance–मित्रगण) A bloc is a group of countries which have similar aims and interest and that generally act together over some issue.

Block (a block in a town is an area of land with streets on all its sides–घरों की पंक्ति) She walked four blocks down High Street.

39. Boar (wild pig–जंगली सुअर) We can find wild boars in the valleys .

Boer (a South African of Dutch descent) He is a boer.

Boor (tasteless buffoon–स्वादरहित) If we refer someone as a boor, we think his behaviour and attitude rough and rude.

Bore (not interesting–अरुचिकर) He bored me all through the meal with stories of the army life.

40. Bole (trunk–पेड़ का धड़) He was standing behind the bole of a tree.

Bowl (dish–बर्तन) Put all the soup in a large bowl.

41. Braid (A narrow piece of twisted thread or cloth used to decorate clothes)

He was wearing a coloured uniform with lots of gold braid.

Brayed (a donkey cried–गधे की आवाज) The donkey brayed and tried to bolt.

42. Bread (a loaf–रोटी) Bread is necessary for the living.

Bred (past tense of breed–नस्ल का भूतकाल) He is an ill bred fellow.

43. Bruise (an injury–चोट) How did you get that bruise on your cheek?

Brews (making beer–बीयर बनाना) I brew my own beer.

44. Brows (multiple foreheads–भौंहें) Your brows on your forehead.

Browse (grazing–चरना) Three red deer were browsing near my lodge.

45. Burger (meat sandwich–बर्गर) I do not like eating burger.

Burgher (merchant–व्यवसायी) The burghers of a town are the people who live there especially the richer or more respectable people.

46. But (excepting–लेकिन) He is but a good man.

Butt (the thick end–मोटा सिरा) A number of cigarette butts are lying there.

47. Buyer (one who purchases–खरीदार) Only a prospective buyer can purchase this house.

Byre (a cow barn–गौशाला) A byre is a cowshed.

48. Check (to verify, to stop–जाँचना) He checked my passport. He checked me from leaving the function.

Cheque (bank document–चेक) I issued a cheque favouring P.N.B.

49. Calendar (chart showing dates etc–कलैण्डर) I have only one calendar in my office.

Calender (to press paper, cloth etc.–प्रेस करना) Please calender my dress.

50. Cannon (big gun–तोप) A cannon of ancient time is placed near the railway station.

Canon (rule–सिद्धान्त) He believes in canons of justice.

51. Casual (accidental, occasional–आकस्मिक) I was granted only one day casual leave.

Causal (showing cause–कारण बनाने वाला) There is a causal link between balanced diet and sound mind.

52. Corpse (dead body–लाश) The corpse was covered with a white bedsheet.

Corps (a body of troops–सेना की टुकडी) I want to join National Cadet Corps.

53. Coma (state of senselessness–बेहोशी) The patient has been in coma since Monday.

Comma (mark of punctuation–कोमा) One should be careful about proper use of comma.

54. Censer (a pot in which incense is burnt–यज्ञ की वेदी) Place some incense into the censer.

Censor (an official examination–सेंसर) The Censor Board has awarded 'U' certificate to this film.

Censure (criticise adversely–निन्दा) His conduct was censured by the Parliament.

55. Cease (discontinue–छोड़ना) He resigned and thus, ceased to be the Chairman of our society.

Seize (to catch–पकड़ना) Heroin worth 2 lacks rupees was seized from his office.

Siege (surrounded–घेरना) Akbar's army sieged the castle of Chittorgarh.

56. Career (profession–व्यवसाय) For better career opportunities, join computer courses.

Carrier (one who carries–ले जाने वाला) Mosquitoes are carriers of virus.

57. Coarse (rough–खुरदरा) Do not use a coarse cloth to clean the glasses.

Course (line of action–कार्य की दिशा) A disciplined course of action is required to achieve success.

58. Collision (clashing–टकराना) In a collision between train and bus, three persons died on the spot.

Collusion (secret agreement for an evil plan–षड्यन्त्र) He planned to execute a robbery in collusion with the clerk.

59. Cloth (unstitched cloth–बिना सिले कपड़े) I want to purchase cloth for a shirt and a trousers.

Clothe (stitched cloth–सिले हुए कपड़े) I have given my clothes to washerman for drycleaning.

60. Capital (centre of administration–राजधानी) Delhi is the capital of India.

Capitol (roman temple of Jupiter, US Congress House–एक बिल्डिंग का नाम)

A meeting of US Congress be held in capitol tomorrow.

61. **Defy** (challenge–चुनौती) One should not defy the orders of one's superiors.
Deify (worship a God–ईश्वर की तरह पूजना) Mr. M.K. Gandhi is defied by all Indians.

62. **Complement** (which completes–पूरक) Husband and wife are complementary to each other.
Compliment (regards–अभिनन्दन) Please convey my best compliments to your parents.

63. **Council** (assembly–सदन) He was nominated to the Council of State .
Counsel (advice–सलाह) He counsels in a right way.

64. **Cymbal** (a musical instrument–मंजीरा) I like the melodious sound of the Cymbal.
Symbol (sign–चिन्ह) What is the symbol of 2004 Olympic Games?

65. **Current** (present–वर्तमान, ताजा) What is the current news?
Currant (dried grapes–किशमिश) I am fond of currants.

66. **Cite** (speak–कहना) He cited the example of bravery of Maharana Pratap.
Site (location–स्थान) In my opinion this site for the departmental store is commercially viable.
Sight (view–दृश्य) (vision–दृष्टि) It was a pitiable sight. Get your eyesight checked at the earliest.

67. **Caste** (Community–जाति) He belongs to schedule caste.
Cast (to give–देना) Please cast your votes in favour of me.

68. **Cattle** (animal–पशु) Cattle were grazing in the field.
Kettle (vessel–पतीली) Put the kettle on the gas burner.

69. **Corporal** (pertaining to body–शारीरिक) Corporal punishment are banned now-a-days in all schools and colleges.
Corporeal (bodily–शरीर सम्बन्धित) God has no corporeal existence.

70. **Carat** (unit of weight for precious stones, equal to 200 milligrams)
Caret (proofreader's insertion mark–छुटा हुआ शब्द दिखाने का चिन्ह)
Carrot (edible orange root–गाजर) Carrot contains aburdent iron.
Karat (one-24th part of otherwise pure gold–24वाँ भाग या पूर्ण सोना)

71. **Cause** (generative force–कारण) Smoking is the biggest preventive cause of death.
Caws (sounds of crows–कौओं की आवाज) When a crow caws it makes a loud sound.

72. **Cent** (one hundredth of a dollar–डॉलर का सौवाँ हिस्सा)
Scent (an aroma–सुगन्ध) I like the aroma of freshly baked bread .
Sent (dispatched–भेजा) I have sent you a packet of wool.

73. **Cents** (hundredths of a dollar–डॉलर का सौवाँ हिस्सा) A dollar has hundred cents.
Scents (many things to smell–सुगन्ध) Flowers are chosen for their scent as well as their look.
Sense (physical abilities of sight, smell, hearing, touch and taste–चेतना)
She has a good sense of humour.

74. **Chews** (masticating–चबाना) Chew your food well and eat slowly.
Choose (to select–चुनना) They will be able to choose their own leader through election.

75. **Claus** (fat, jolly guy with presents–सांताक्लॉज) Santa Claus comes to town on every Christmas.
Clause (clause is a group of words–शब्द समूह) Containing a verb, contractual unit.
Claws (big fingernails–पंजा) The cat tried to cling to the edge by its claws.

76. **Click** (ticking noise–क्लिक करना) You can check your e-mail with a click of your mouse.
Clique (exclusive group–अलग समूह) Clique is a group of people that spend a lot of time together and seem unfriendly towards people who are not in the group.

77. **Climb** (ascending–चढ़ना) He climbed up the stairs.
Clime (climate–वातावरण) She left Britain for the sunnier climes of Southern France.

78. **Coal** (black mineral–कोयला) A number of families even today use the coal for cooking.
Cold (opposite to warm–ठण्डा) I like tea neither too hot nor too cold.

79. **Coax** (persuade–बहलाना) The government coaxed them to give up their strike by promising them some temporary benefits.
Cokes (more than one soft drink–रूपये पदार्थ) Several kinds of cokes were available in the party.
Cocks (more than one male bird–मुर्गे) I have two beautiful cocks.
Cox (नाव में अधिकारी) In a rowing boat, the cox is the person, who gives instructions to the rowers.

80. **Desert** (a waste track of land –रेगिस्तान noun, to forsked; verb त्यागना) Churu is a desert area in Rajasthan. He has deserted his wife.
Dessert (fruit served after dinner–भोजन के बाद फल आहार) The dessert course after dinner was liked by all.

81. **Dye** (a verb-to colour–रँगना) Dye my shirt in sky blue.
Die (expire–मरना) He died from cholera.

82. **Dose** (quantity of medicine–दवा की खुराक) I have already taken four doses of this medicine by now.
Doze (sleep–ऊँघना) You were dozing in the class yesterday.

83. **Draught** (a quantity of liquid–तरल की मात्रा) The patient was given a draught of medicine.
Drought (want of rain–सूखा) Due to scanty rain whole of the district is in the grip of drought.

84. **Dam** (surrounding area to stop flow of water–बाँध) A dam is being built up here to storage the rainy water.
Damn (condemn–निन्दा) His behaviour is damned by all the members of the society.

85. **Dear** (loving–प्रिय) He is my very dear friend.
Deer (an animal–हिरण) I saw many deer in that forest.

86. **Deduce** (draw conclusion–नतीजा निकालना) You can't deduce such a conclusion of the discussion.
Deduct (to take something–कम करना) Deduct cash discount 3% and make the payment by tomorrow.

87. **Deference** (respect–आदर) I treat my elders with due deference.
Difference (dissimilarity–अन्तर) There was a difference of opinion on this point.

88. **Decent** (good–बढ़िया) Because of his decent behaviour he was promoted to the post of General Manager.
Descent (coming down–नीचे उतरना) That hill has a steep descent to the south.
Dissent (to differ–मतभेद) He recorded his dissent on this proposal.

89. **Device** (noun-plan–योजना) He used all devices to popularise the game.
Devise (verb—to plan–योजना बनाना) You are to devise a plan to increase the turn over.

90. **Duel** (a fight between two–दो के बीच युद्ध) There was a duel between Dara Singh and Kingkong.
Dual (double–दोहरा) Dual system of governance is a bad governance.

91. **Disease** (illness–रोग) Malaria is a curable disease.
Decease (death–मृत्यु) The sudden decease of his father forced him to abandon his studies.

92. **Dam** (holds back water–बाँध) Government is building a dam on this river.
Damn (a curse–शाप देना) Don't be flippant , damn it! This is serious.

93. **Dire** (desperate–भयानक) He was in dire need of hospital treatment.
Dyer (one who dyes–रँगने वाला) Ram is working in the firm of drycleaners as dyer.

94. **Do** (an auxiliary in grammar–करना) They do not know me. Do come tomorrow again.
Doe (a female deer–मादा हिरण) There are several does in the forest.
Dough (uncooked bread–साना हुआ) Roll out the dough into one large circle.

95. **Done** (completed–पूर्ण करना) I have done my job.
Dun (something that is dun is a dull grey-brown colour.)

96. **Eminent** (distinguish–विशिष्ट) Indira Gandhi was an eminent politician.
Imminent (impending–तुरन्त) Indian army is ready to face any imminent attack of Pakistan.

97. **Eligible** (fit to be chosen–योग्य) He is eligible for the post.
Illegible (that which cannot be read–अपठनीय) His writing is illegible.

98. **Facility** (ease, opportunity–सुविधा) Facility of STD is also available in this hotel.
Felicity (happiness–प्रसन्नता) True felicity can't be enjoyed by a dishonest man.

99. **Foul** (unfair–अनुचित) One can't achieve true success through foul means.
Fowl (a bird–पक्षी) He is fond of fowl's meat.

100. **Floor** (surface–फर्श) Clean the floor with dettol and water.
Flour (wheat meal–आटा) He has a flour mill.

101. **Forth** (onward–आगे आना) He alone came forth to assist that poor lady.
Fourth (third-fourth–चौथा) April is the fourth month of the year.

102. **Farther** (more distant–दूर) Delhi is farther from Alwar in comparison to Jaipur.
Further (next-आगे) Please settle the case without any further delay.

103. **Fair** (pure, a show–पवित्र, मेला) I believe in using fair means to achieve the target.
Let us go to the fair.
Fare (passage money–किराया) A strike was called by the truckers demanding hike in minimum fare.

104. Feat (an exploit–साहसिक कार्य) A racing car is an extraordinary feat of engineering.

Feet (plural of foot–पाँव) Do not put your feet on the table.

105. Fairy (imaginary magic person–जादूगर) Fairies are often represented as small people with wings.

Ferry (river-crossing boat–छोटी नाव) They crossed the river by ferry.

106. Few (not many–थोड़ा) I gave a dinner party for a few close friends.

Phew (expression of relief) Phew, what a relief, I am feeling now!

107. Finish (to complete–समाप्त) I will finish my work by tomorrow.

Finnish (from Finland–फिनलैण्ड के निवासी) Finnish is the language spoken in Finland.

108. Flair (verve, talent–प्रवृत्ति) If you have a flair for a particular thing , you have a natural ability to do it well.

Flare (to spread–बढ़ाना) Camp fire flares like beacons in the dark.

109. Flew (past tense of fly–उड़ायी) He flew many kites yesterday.

Flu (short for influenza–बुखार) I got flu day before yesterday.

Flue (chimney pipe–चिमनी पाइप) The flue of the chimney required to be changed.

110. Gage (security–जमानत) I do not lend without sufficient gage.

Gaze (to look attentively–एकटक देखना) She stood gazing at herself in the mirror.

111. Gait (manner of walk–चाल) That model girl has a graceful and sexy gait.

Gate (large door–दरवाजा) You should not enter through the main gate.

112. Goal (aim–उद्देश्य) To achieve this goal you are to work hard.

Gaol (jail–जेल) He has been to gaol earlier also.

113. Galley (ship's kitchen–जहाज की रसोई) The galley of this ship is well maintained and full of eatables.

Gally (to frighten or terrify–डराना) He tried to gally the child with a mask of demon.

114. Gilt (gold-plated–धातु की परत चढ़ा हुआ) This is a gilt ornament.

Guilt (culpable–दोषी) You aren't convinced of Mr. Charles guilt.

115. Grate (a lattice–जाली) A grate is a framework of metal bars in a fireplace, which holds the coal or wood. A wood fire burned in the grate.

Great (extremely good–बड़ा, महान) Gandhi was a great man.

116. Groan (a long low sound uttered in pain –कराहना) He opened his eyes and he began to groan with pain.

Grown (has gotten larger–बड़ा, बढ़ना) Dad, I am a grown woman. I know what I am doing.

117. Guise (appearance–दिखना) She presented her dance in the guise of a rabbit.

Guys (man–व्यक्ति) Hi, guys! How are you doing?

118. Hail (frozen rain–ओले) It is hailing. It hailed yesterday.

Hale (healthy–स्वस्थ) May God keep you hale and healthy!

119. Horde (a gang–समूह) A horde of mischievous students attacked the shopkeepers.

Hoard (to store–एकत्र करना) Hoarding of sugar beyond the prescribed limit is an offence.

120. Hair (बाल) She has black hair.

Heir (successor–उत्तराधिकारी) He is an heir apparent to the throne.

121. Hurt (injury–चोट) Your comments can hurt her feelings.

Hart (a male deer–हिरण) I have a beautiful pair of harts.

Heart (an organ in the body–दिल) He is suffering from heart disease.

122. Humane (kind–दयालु) UNO has advised the member countries to meet out humane treatment to Prisoners of war.

Human (pertaining to mankind–मनुष्य से सम्बन्धित) You will find almost the same human nature everywhere.

123. Heel (part of shoe–जूते की एड़ी) The heels of my shoe are pinching.

Heal (to cure–अच्छा होना) This medicine will help you in quick healing.

124. Hole (a burrow–छेद) A serpent lives in this hole.

Whole (complete–सम्पूर्ण) He ate whole of the breakfast.

125. Hall (a large room–बड़ा कमरा) He has hired a hall for the concert.

Haul (a–उठाना) If you haul something which is heavy or difficult to move, you move it using a lot of effort.

A crane had to be used to haul the car out of the stream...(b) If someone is hauled before a court or someone in authority, they are made to appear before them because they are accused of having done something wrong.

He was hauled before the managing director and fired.

126. **Hangar** (garage for airplanes–हवाई जहाज रखने का स्थान) Some repairing is going on in the hangar of the airport.

Hanger (from which things hang–लटकाने वाला) I want to purchase a coat hanger.

127. **Ho** (an expression of admiration or surprise–हो-हो) Ho ! you are here.

Hoe (a garden tool–औजार) Today he is hoeing in the vineyard.

128. **Hear** (to listen) I hear his voice.

Here (at this location–यहाँ) Come here.

129. **Heard** (listened to–सुनना) I heard a strange sound yesterday in the night.

Herd (a group of animals–भीड़) They are individuals. They will not follow the herd.

130. **Hi** (greetings–हाय) "Hi Luis", she said.

High (way up–ऊँचा) I looked down from the high window.

131. **Heroin** (narcotic–अफीम) Heroin is a powder drug.

Heroine (female hero–एक्ट्रेस) My favourite heroine is Ash.

132. **Hew** (to chop–काटना) He fell, peeled and hewed his own timber.

Hue (a colour–रंग) The same hue will look different in different light.

133. **Higher** (farther up–अपेक्षाकृत ऊँचा) He has gone to USA for higher studies.

Hire (to employ–किराए पर लेना) Cars are available for hire.

134. **Hoard** (store–एकत्र करना) They have begun to hoard food and sugar .

Horde (a great many people–भीड़-भाड़) This attracted hordes of tourists to Las Vegas.

135. **Hoarse** (rough voice–कर्कश ध्वनि) His voice is hoarse.

Horse (equine–घोड़ा) He has a black horse.

136. **Hold** (to grip–पकड़ना) Hold the bucket please.

Holed (full of holes–छिद्रदार) The wall seems to be holed by a drill.

137. **Holy** (with religious significance–पवित्र) Ayodhya is a holy place for the Hindus.

Wholly (completely–पूर्णतया) This approach for the urban area is wholly inadequate.

138. **Hostel** (inexpensive lodging for travelers–छात्रावास) He is living in the college hostel.

Hostile (unfriendly–दुश्मनी) Pakistan has not yet changed its hostile attitude towards India.

139. **Idle** (indolent–निकम्मा) An idle man can't make any progress.

Ideal (visionary–आदर्श) My teacher, Mr. Shrivastava, is an ideal for me.

Idol (an image of a deity–मूर्ति) A section of the Hindus believe in idol worship.

140. **Incite** (to provoke–उत्तेजित करना) His arrogant behaviour incited me a lot.

Insight (a clear vision–स्पष्ट देखना) Do you know the insight story of this murder?

141. **In** (expressing inclusion–में) He is in the room.

Inn (hotel–होटल) This is a well maintained inn.

142. **Jealous** (envious–ईर्ष्या) He is not liked by anybody because of his jealous nature.

Zealous (enthusiastic–उत्साही) She is very zealous about her new book.

143. **Jewel** (precious stone–जवाहरात) This watch contains many jewels.

Joule (unit of energy measure–ऊर्जा की इकाई) In Physics joule is a unit of energy or work.

144. **Naughty** (mischievous–शैतान) She is a naughty girl.

Knotty (difficult–कठिन) This was indeed a knotty problem.

145. **Knead** (working bread dough–गुंदना) He kneaded the mixture on a floured surface.

She felt him knead the aching muscles.

Need (must have–आवश्यकता) He needs your help.

146. **Knight** (chivalrous man–बहादुर) He was knighted on the queen's birthday.

Night (darkness–रात) Night comes after day.

147. **Knit** (interlocking loops of yarn–बुनना) She has already started knitting baby sweators.

Nit (louse egg–जूं के अण्डे)

(a) Nits are the eggs of insects called lice which live in people's hair.

(b) If you refer to someone as a nit, you think they are stupid or silly. You'd rather leave the business than work with such a nit.

148. **Knock** (to rap–ठोकना) Someone had knocked him unconscious. I heard a knock at the front door.

Nock (a notch in an arrow–तीर का सिरा जैसा) A V shape cut or indentation in an edge or across a surface.

149. Knot (fastening in cord–गाँठ) He tied a knot at the end of the lace.

Naught (or nought is zero–शून्य) Sales rose by naught point four percent last month.

Not (negation–नहीं) He was not present in the party.

150. Know (to possess knowledge–जानना) I know him.

No (negation–नहीं) I have no pen.

151. Knows (only the shadow knows–जानना) Everyone knows about Mahatma Gandhi.

Nose (plain as the nose on your face–नाक) Clean your nose daily.

152. Lightening (make lighter–हल्का करना) We had appealed to the court for lightening the punishment, but of no avail.

Lightning (electric discharge in clouds–बिजली चमकना) There was occasional lightning in the sky last night.

153. Loath (unwilling–इच्छा के विरुद्ध) Nothing loath he did, as he was saying.

Loathe (to dislike greatly–घृणा करना) I loathe her dressing pattern and arrogant way of talking.

154. Latter (antonym of former–बाद में आने वाला) Between Ram and Shyam, the latter (Shyam) is a diligent student.

Later (comparative of late–देरी से आने वाला) He came later than his friend.

155. Lose (to part with–खोना) Where did you lose your briefcase?

Loose (to slack–ढीला करना) He was wearing a loose cotton shirt.

156. Lesson (chapter–पाठ) Learn your lesson well.

Lessen (to make less–कम करना) Even this medicine has not lessen my pain.

157. Last (antonym to first–अन्तिम) Bahadur Shah was the last emperor of India.

Latest (superlative of late–ताजा) She always prefers latest design clothes.

158. Lain (past tense of lay or lie–लेटना) He has lain there for sometime.

Lane (narrow road–गली)
Shyam lives at the end of the lane.

159. Lam (headlong flight–भागना) If someone is on the lam or if they go on the lam, they are trying to escape or hide from someone such as the police or an enemy. He was on the lam for seven years.

Lamb (baby sheep–भेड़ का बच्चा) A lamb is a young sheep.

160. Lay (to recline–समर्पण) Lay a sheet of paper on the floor.

Lei (a flower necklace–फूलों का हार) A garland made of flowers, feathers, shells etc, often given as a symbol of affection.

161. Lea (a meadow–सूत की लम्बाई) They live in a hut constructed in the lea.

Lee (a sheltered position–सुरक्षित स्थिति) The lee of a place is the shelter that it gives from the wind or bad weather.

Lease (rented-किराए पर) She leased out her bungalow at a good rent.

162. Leak (accidental escape of liquid-रिसना) The roof is leaking.

Leek (variety of onion–प्याज) I like leek vegetables.

163. Liar (tells falsehoods–झूठा) He is a liar and a cheat.

Lyre (stringed instrument–यन्त्र) A lyre is a stringed instrument that looks like a harp.

164. Lie (an untruth–झूठ) He is telling a lie.

Lieu (instead–बजाय) He gave his T.V. to the landlord in lieu of rent.

165. Load (cargo–सामान) I have just loaded my truck up.

Lowed (a cow mooed–रम्भाना) The cow lowed in agony.

166. Loan (allow to borrow–ऋण) She has taken loan from a bank.

Lone (by itself–अकेला) He was shot by a lone gunmen.

167. Meat (flesh–मांस) I don't like eating meat.

Meet (to assemble–मिलना) She came here only to meet me.

168. Metal (iron, brass etc.–धातु) Silver is a white metal.

Mettle (spirit, courage–साहस) Our leaders have no mettle to fight against corruption.

169. Metre (poetic rhythm–छन्द) Can you tell me in what metre Shelley's 'Skylark' is written?

Meter (a measuring instrument =100 cm., –मीटर) One meter is equal to hundred centimetres.

170. Minor (underage–छोटा) Minors are not allowed to open current account in Banks.

Miner (one who works in mine–खान पर काम करने वाला) He is a miner, works in a coal mine.

171. **Moat** (a ditch surrounding a castle–खाई) There is a bridge over the moat near main gate.
Mote (a particle of dust–धूल का कण) You cannot see small mote by naked eyes.

172. **Monetary** (pertaining to money–मुद्रा सम्बन्धित) Have you any book on monetary theory?
Monitory (giving advice–सलाह देना) He acted against the monitory advise of his friends and so failed.

173. **Male** (opposite to female–पुरुष) A male candidate can't be posted against the post reserved for a woman.
Mail (post–डाक) Have you received my mail ?

174. **Mite** (small thing–अल्प मात्रा) He contributed his mite for the service of mankind.
Might (strength–शक्ति Your might will be tested in battle against the foreign power.
Might (past of may–सकना) He told me that he might come to attend the function.

175. **Marry** (to get married–विवाह करना) I want to marry your sister.
Merry (joyous–आनन्द करना) Don't lose heart and be merry.

176. **Main** (chief–मुख्य) Ramesh is the main culprit in the bank robbery case.
Mane (long hair of an animal's neck–गर्दन के बाल) His horse had a fine mane.

177. **Marshal** (a military officer–मार्शल) He is a marshal of the court.
Martial (war like–युद्ध जैसा) He has martial spirit and courage to fight in odd circumstances.

178. **Maize** (corn–मक्का) I like to eat maize cake.
Maze (labyrinth–घुमाव) This castle has many hidden mazes.

179. **Made** (accomplished–बनाया) The table is made of wood.
Maid (young woman–नौकरानी) She is our maid-servant.

180. **Manner** (method–तरीका) I am a professional and I have to conduct myself in a professional manner. She smiled in a friendly manner.
Manor (lord's house or a large private house–बड़ा व्यैक्तिक घराना) The thieves broke into the manor at night.

181. **Marc** (coarse brandy–ब्रांडी) I don't like the taste of marc.
Mark (a sign–निशान) He made some peculiar marks with a pen.

182. **Marshal** (to organise–संयोजक) He was marshalling the teachers and other officials, showing them where to go.
Martial (warlike–पुत्र समान स्थिति) The newspapers were banned during martial regime.

183. **Mind** (thinking unit–मस्तिष्क) Mind your business, please.
Mined (looked for ore–खनिज कार्य) The pit was shut down because it hadn't enough that could be mined economically.

184. **Missal** (hymn book– किताब) A book containing the service of the Mass for the whole year; loosely a Roman Catholic book of prayers.
Missile (projectile–मिसाइल) The football supporters began throwing missiles one of which it the captain of the rival team.

185. **Mist** (fog–कोहरा) The mist made the flying impossible.
Missed (not hit–चूकना) He scored four of the goals but missed a penalty.

186. **Moose** (a large elk–बड़ा हिरण) Moose are large type of deer have big flat horns.
Mousse (dessert of whipped cream and eggs) Mousse is a sweet light food made from eggs and cream.

187. **Morning** (A.M.–प्रात:) I get up early in the morning.
Mourning (remembering the dead–मृतक हेतु मातम) On the death of Rajeev Gandhi, the whole of India was in the mourning.

188. **Muscle** (fibrous, contracting tissue–मांसपेशी) He is doing a lot of exercises to keep his muscles strong.
Mussel (mussels are a kind of shellfish that you can eat from their shells–एक प्रकार की मछली)

189. **Mustard** (spicy yellow sauce–सरसों) This is fried in mustard oil.
Mustered (assembled for roll call–एकत्र होना) He travelled through out India to muster support for his movement.

190. **Nice** (good–अच्छा) She is a nice and beautiful girl.
Niece (daughter of brother–भतीजी) I am going to attend the marriage of my niece positively.

191. **Our** (plural of 'my'–हमारा) This is our house.
Hour (a period of time–घण्टा) I have been waiting for you for half an hour.

192. **Oar** (used for rowing a boat–नाव का डण्डा Life without aim is like a boat without an oar.
Ore (mineral from which metal can be extracted–खनिज) Iron is extracted from its ore by melting.

193. Ordinance (A rule–अध्यादेश) The President has promulgated an ordinance for administering the minority community.

Ordnance (Gun–युद्ध सामग्री) There is an ordnance factory in Jamshedpur Bihar.

194. Overdo (carried to excess–अधिक) It is important never to overdo new exercises.

Overdue (past time for payment or some action–देर) The meeting is long overdue.

195. Pray (entreat–प्रार्थना) I pray to God everyday.

Prey (hunt–शिकार) Do not prey upon the innocent animals.

196. Principal (head of school or college–प्राचार्य) Sh. R.C. Jha is the new Principal of our college.

Principle (rule–सिद्धान्त) Do you understand anything about the principles of justice?

197. Proffer (offer–प्रस्ताव) Many lucrative proposals were proffered to him for acceptance.

Prefer (like–पसन्द) I prefer coffee to tea.

198. Practice (noun–अभ्यास) Practice makes a man perfect.

Practise (verb—to practise) Don't preach but practise.

199. Plain (easy, simple–साधारण) One should try to write his thoughts in plain language.

Plane (to smoothen, level–चमकदार करना) I use cream to plane my hair.

200Peel (to remove the skin–छीलना) You cannot eat a banana without peeling it.

Peal (sound of thunder or Bells–घंटियों की ध्वनि) I am hearing peals of trumpets.

201. Pare (to trim–टुकड़े करना) Pare your nails and then polish them.

Pair (two–जोड़ी) I have only three pair of shoes.

202. Peace (tranquility–शान्ति) Peace of mind is more precious than the materialistic richness.

Piece (fragment–टुकड़ा) The dog found a piece of meat.

203. Price (value–कीमत) What is the price of this shirt?

Prize (reward–ईनाम) She could not win any prize this time.

204. Persecute (to harass–परेशान करना) Pakistani soldiers persecuted the Hindus in a cruel manner.

Prosecute (to bring before a court–अभियोग चलाना) He was prosecuted for murdering his wife.

205. Physic (medicine–दवा) No physic can cure him of cancer.

Physique (bodily fitness–शारीरिक बनावट) He possesses an attractive physique.

206. Prescribe (to direct–निर्देश देना) The doctor has prescribed three doses of medicine after four hours daily.

Proscribe (to banish–देश निकाला देना) The minister was proscribed by the king.

207. Patrol (going round–गश्त लगाना) A chowkidar was patrolling at the main gate.

Petrol (oil–पकठ-पेट्रोल) Petrol is required to run vehicles.

208. Popular (Familiar–लोकप्रिय) Rajeev Gandhi was a very popular leader.

Populous (Thickly inhabited–आबादी वाला) Delhi is a highly populous city.

Pail (Bucket–बाल्टी) I have two pails full of water.

Pale (Yellowish appearance–पीला) On seeing a lion, his face turned pale.

209. Pain (It hurts–दर्द) I felt a sharp pain in my lower back.

Pane (A single panel of glass–पैनल) The left pane of this window required change.

210. Pair (A set of two–जोड़ा) I need a new pair of socks.

Pare (Cutting down–काटना) Local authorities were instructed to pare their budget.

Pear (Bottom-heavy fruit–नाशपाती) I am fond of red pears.

211. Pea (round, green legume–मटर) I like peas vegetable.

Pee (piss–पेशाब करना) The driver was probably having a pee. He needed to pee.

212. Peak (mountain top–पहाड़ की चोटी) He climbed up to the peak of the mountain.

Peek (secret look–चोरी से देखना) On one occasion she had peeked at him through a hole in the door.

213. Pearl (round, luminescent gem from an oyster–मोती) She wore a string of pearls at her throat.

Purl (धातु का तारा) Thread or cord of twisted gold or silver wire, used esp. for edging; edging etc made from this.

214. Pedal (foot control–पैडल) I am too tired to pedal again.

Peddle (to sell–बेचना) He attempted to peddle his paintings around the city.

215. Pistil (डोडी) Seed-bearing organ of a flower.

Pistol (hand gun–पिस्तौल) He was caught with a pistol.

216. **Place** (a location–स्थान) This is a good place to live at.
Plaice (एक प्रकार की मछली) Plaice are a type of flat sea fish.

217. **Plait** (braid–तह बनाना) She parted her hair and then began to plait it into two thick braids.
Plate (a dish–थाली) She pushed her plate away. She had eaten nothing.

218. **Pole** (a person from Poland–पोलैण्ड के निवासी) He is a Pole.
Pole (big stick–बड़ी लकड़ी) I need a pole to climb up that house.
Poll (a voting–चुनाव कार्य) More than 60 percent of those polled said that they approved of his record as Chairman.

219. **Poor** (no money–निर्धन) A poor man can't afford a car.
Pore (careful study; microscopic hole–ध्यान में लीन, छोटा छिद्र) We spent hours poring over the visa rules.
Pour (to flow freely–बहना)
He poured himself another drink.

220. **Presence** (the state of being present–उपस्थिति) The meeting took place in the presence of the Judge.
Presents (gifts–उपहार) He gave a nice present to his friend on his wedding anniversary.

221. **Pride** (ego–गर्व) We take pride in offering you the best services.
Pried (opened–खोला) I pried the top off a can of chilli.

222. **Profit** (money earned–लाभ) The company has earned good profit in this quarter.
Prophet (seer–महान् व्यक्ति) He did it as per the instructions of the prophet.

223. **Pros** (benefits–फायदा) Motherhood has both its pros and cons.
Prose (ordinary language–गद्य) Shute's prose is stark and chillingly unsentimental.

224. **Quite** (altogether–पूरी तरह से) I am quite well now.
Quiet (silent–शान्त) Please keep quiet.

225. **Rein** (bridle–लगाम) Keep the rein tight, otherwise you may be thrown out by the horse.
Reign (rule–शासन करना) The reign of Akbar is known for communal harmony.

226. **Rite** (ceremony–रस्म) Only a few rites were performed in his wedding.
Write (compose–लिखना) I am to write a letter immediately.
Right (antonym of left–दायाँ) This is my right leg.
Right (antonym to wrong–सही) You have taken a right decision.
Wright (a worker–बनाने वाला) He is a wonderful play wright.

227. **Raise** (to life–ऊँचा उठाना) I will raise this issue in Parliament.
Raze (to destroy–नष्ट करना) The storm razed many buildings to the ground.

228. **Route** (course–रास्ता) By which route you came here.
Rout (flight–भगाना) The Pakistan armies were put to rout.

229. **Rap** (a sharp blow–थप्पड़) He rapped her on the cheek.
Rape (to ravish–बलात्कार) He raped a college girl.
Wrap (to enclose–बन्द करना) The book was wrapped in a piece of white paper.

230. **Recover** (regain–ठीक होना) He has now recovered a lot from the weakness.
Re-cover (to cover again–पुन: ढकना) Re-cover the sweets with some clean cloth.

231. **Road** (way–रास्ता) The road has recently been repaired.
Rode (past of ride–सवारी की) He rode on the horse yesterday.

232. **Ring** (an ornament for fingers–अँगूठी) This ring is made of gold.
Wring (to twist, to squeeze–ऐठना निचोड़ना) Wring the clothes well and put them on the ground.

233. **Rest** (respite–आराम) I want some rest before starting the next assignment.
Wrest (snatch by force–छीनना) Ram wrested a bag from Shyam.

234. **Roll** (to run overly – नामावली, लोटपोट होना) He rolled over the log to the right side of river.
Role (part–भाग लेना) I am playing the role of Ravana in this serial.

235. **Raise** (elevate–उठाना) He raised is hand in support of the resolution.
Rays (thin beams of light–किरण) The sun rays can penetrate water up to ten feet.
Raze (to tear down completely–नष्ट करना) Many of villages have been razed.

236. **Read** (having knowledge from reading–पढ़ना) I have read this novel.
Red (a primary colour–लाल रंग) I like red colour shirt.

237. **Real** (authentic–वास्तविक) Yes it is a real story.
Reel (wavering move–चक्कर) He lost is balance and reeled back.

238. Recede (to move backward–पीछे जाना) As he receded she waved goodbye.

Reseed (to plant again–पुन: बीजारोपण) He is trying to reseed the rose plant.

239. Reek (smells bad–गंदी बदबू) Your breah reeks of stale cigar smoke.

Wreak (to inflict–बदला लेना) She threatened to wreak vengeance on the men who toppled him some years ago.

240. Retch (heave–वमन करना) If you retch, your stomach moves as if you are vomiting. The smell made me retch.

Wretch (wicked–नीच व्यक्ति) Oh, what have you done, you wretch!

241. Review (a general survey or assessment–विचार करना) The P.M. reviewed the situation with his cabinet.

Revue (a series of theatrical sketches or songs) A revue is a theatrical performance consisting of songs, dances, and jokes about recent events.

242. Rise (to stand up–उठना) The sun rises in the east.

Ryes (varieties of grain–राई) I am fond of cheese on rye.

243. Rood (a cross–क्रॉस चिन्ह) A cross as an instrument of execution; The Cross on which Jesus suffered; the cross as the symbol of the Christian faith. We wears a graden rood.

Rude (coarse–असभ्य) He is rude to her friends and obsessively jealous.

244. Rough (coarse–कठोर) His hands are rough.

Ruff (pleated collar–कॉलर) A ruff is a stiff strip of cloth or other material with many small folds in it, which some people wore round their neck in former times.

245. Sooth (truth सच) Sooth to speak, he is not a good boy.

Soothe (to calm–शान्त करना) You can't soothe his anger with lame excuses.

246. Spacious (enough space–खुला) His office is quite spacious and well decorated.

Specious (attractive–आकर्षक) With your specious look, you can't be foot her.

247. Stationary (Fixed–स्थिर) Earth is not stationary, it moves round the sun.

Stationery (Writing material–स्टेशनरी) I am going to market to purchase several stationery items for the office.

248. Straight (opposed to curved–सीधा) I believe in straight talks.

Strait (narrow–तंग) The lane is too strait to pass through for an elephant.

249. Sore (painful–दर्दकारक) I can't sing as my throat is sore.

Soar (to fly high–ऊँचा उड़ना) Birds soar in sky.

Sour (not sweet–खट्टा) The grapes were sour.

250. Suit (an action in court–दावा) Bank has filed a civil suit against you for recovery.

Suite (a set of room–कमरों का सेट) I have reserved a suite for you in Ashoka Hotel.

251. Story (a tale–कहानी) My grandmother told me a story of an oldman.

Storey (floor of a building–मंजिल) I have taken a room at first storey.

252. Serge (a kind of cloth–एक प्रकार का कपड़ा) This suit is made of serge.

Surge (move like waves –तरंगों की तरह) The waves of ocean surge violently in night.

253. Shear (to clip the wool–ऊन कतरना) The sheep are being shorn.

Sheer (downright–एकमात्र) He achieved success by the sheer force of his hard labour.

254. Sun (सूर्य) The sun is a far.

Son (a person's male child–पुत्र) He is my son.

255. Sole (lower surface of shoe–जूते का तला एकमात्र) The sole of the right shoe requires repairing. The sole aim of my life is to earn reputation in the society.

Soul (immaterial part–आत्मा) You can't see soul. Soul is immortal.

256. Stair (step–सीढ़ी) Let us go up stairs.

Stare (gaze–घूरना) It is wrong to stare at girls.

257. Sing (melodious sound–गाना) She will sing a sweet song.

Swing (to oscillate–झूलना) She has gone to enjoy swing ride.

258. Saver (one who saves–बचाने वाला) Low interest rates are bad news for savers.

Savor (to relish a taste–स्वादिष्ट) People come here to savor the exquisite food provided by the owner.

259. Seal (to close–बन्द करना) He sealed the envelope and put on a stamp.

Seel (to close someone's eyes–आँखे बन्द करना) Close the eyes of (a hawk etc.) by stitching up the eyelids·

260. Seamen (sailors–नाविक) He emigrated to work as seamen.

Semen (male discharge–वीर्य) He is being treated for some semen problem.

261. Sewer (मल मार्ग) A sewer is a large underground channel that carries waste matter and rain water away, usually to a place where it is treated and made harmless.

Sower (one who sows–बोने वाला)

Suer (one who sues –दावा करने वाला)

262. Side (lateral–बगल) There is a park on the left side of the road.

Sighed (breathed sorrowfully–आह भरना) He sighed wearily.

263. Sign (displayed board bearing information–निशान) Equations are generally written with a two bar equals sign.

Sine (reciprocal of the cosecant) Find the sine value of this angle.

264. Sloe (blackthorn berries–जंगली बेर) A sloe is a small, sour fruit that has a dark purple skin. It is often used to flavour gin.

Slow (not fast–धीमा) The traffic is heavy and slow.

265. Some (a few–कुछ) Please give me some money.

Sum (result of addition–फेड़) The sum of all the angles of a triangle is 180 degree.

266. Suit (clothes–पहनने का सूट) I have a blue suit.

Suite (a set of rooms–कमरों का समूह) We enjoyed our time during the week in a suite at London.

267. Spade (shovel–फावड़ा) He used a spade for digging this pit.

Spayed (to sterilise a female animal–बधिया करना) When a female animal is spayed, it has its ovaries removed so that it cannot become pregnant.

268. Sundae (आईसक्रीम) A sundae is a tall glass of ice cream with whipped cream and nuts or fruit on top.

Sunday (the first day of the week–रविवार) Today is Sunday.

269. Team (a group of players–टीम) Our college team has won the trophy.

Teem (to be full of–बहुतायात) Rajasthan is a state teeming with natural resources.

270. Toe (a part of foot–पैर का अँगूठा) She hurt her left toe in an accident.

Tow (to draw by a rope–बाँधना) The boat was towed with a tree near the shore.

271. Tail (part of body–पूँछ) Cow has a long tail.

Tale (story–कहानी) My grandmother told me an interesting tale.

272. Their (belong to they–उनका) They have learnt their lessons.

There (at that place–वहाँ) I am to go there now.

273. Throne (royal seat–सिंहासन) All the brothers are fighting for the throne.

Thrown (third form of throw–फेंक दिया) She has thrown her certificates into the river.

Thorn (impediment–काँटा) You need a needle to get the thorn out.

274. Tare (the seed of a vetch used in refence *to its small size*–एक प्रकार की घास) When the harvest is gleaned the evil tares will be separated from the good wheat.

Tear (salty drops from eyes–आँसू) Her eyes are filled with tears.

Tier (a horizontal row–पंक्ति) I have booked your seats in two tier compartment.

275. Taught (past tense of teach–पढ़ाया) Who taught you English?

Taut (stretched tight–तना हुआ) The clothes line is pulled taut and secured.

276. Tea (herbal infusion–चाय) I am fond of tea.

Tee (golfball prop–गोल्फ से सम्बन्धित) The tee was broken accidentally.

277. Tenner (english slang for a ten pound *note*–दस का) I have only a tenner in my pocket.

Tenor (tendency–तात्पर्य) The whole tenor of discussion has changed.

278. Tern (a shorebird–एक चिड़िया) A tern is a small black and white seabird with long wings and a forked tail.

Terne (alloy of lead and tin–मिश्रित धातु) This plate is made of terne.

Turn (rotate–घुमाव) He turned left and went away.

279. The (denoting persons already mentioned–आर्टिकल) The is the definite article.

Thee (objective case of thou–तुझे) I missed thee , beloved mother.

280. Through (from end to end–बीच से) Go straight through that door under the 'exit' word.

Throw (to discharge through the air–फेंकना) The crowd began throwing stones.

281. Timber (wood for building–लकड़ी) In Japan timber is used for construction of house.

Timbre (musical quality–ध्वनि) The timbre of someone's voice or of a musical instrument is the particular quality of sound that it has. (FORMAL)

282. Toad (frog–मेढक) A toad is a creature similar to frog.

Toed (to conform a policy–अनुसरण) He tried to persuade the rivals to toe the line of his party.

Towed (pulled ahead–ले जाना) The policeman threatened to tow away my car.

283. Told (what was spoken–बोला) He told me how to do it.

Tolled (a bell was rung–घण्टी बजाना) The pilgrims tolled the bell.

284. Track (narrow path or road–संकरा रास्ता) We set of once more , over a rough mountain track.

Tract (a plot of land–भूमि) A vast tract of land is available for stadium.

285. Tray (a platter–ट्रे) I need a tray for six cups of tea.

Trey (three–तीन) The side of a die marked with three pips or spots; a throw which turns up this side.

286. Troop (a company of soldiers–सिपाहियों का समूह) Twenty thousands troops were deployed on the border.

Troup (a company of actors–एक्टर्स का समूह) She belongs to an acrobatic performing troup.

287. Umpire (a referee–अम्पायर) You must not disobey the umpire.

Empire (dominion–राज्य) The king was unable to manage his empire properly.

288. Vein (a blood vessel–शिरा) Veins take the blood to all parts of body.

Vane (weather cock–मुर्गा) There is a vane at the top of the temple.

289. Wave (unevenness–लहर) The waves of ocean are rising higher and higher.

Wave (movement–हिलाना) She waved her hand as the bus started.

Waive (relinquish–छोड़ना, I request the officer to waive the punishment.

290. Waste (useless–व्यर्थ करना) Don't waste your precious time.

Waist (part of body–कमर) The boy had a chain round his waist.

291. Weather (atmosphere–मौसम) It is cold weather today.

Whether (which of two–यदि) I asked her whether she would come

292. Vain (useless–व्यर्थ) I made several request to our Principal but all in vain .

Wane (to decrease–कम होना) I see the moon waning these nights.

293. Vice (bad habit–गलत आदत) She described that those responsible for offences are connected with vice, like drugs or gaming.

Vise (bench-mounted clamp–क्लैंप) I need a good vise while I repair the furniture.

294. Weigh (to ascertain the weight–तौलना) I am to purchase one weighing machine.

Way (passage–रास्ता) This way leads to hospital.

295. Weight (weight–वजन) He gained ten kg. of weight within a month.

Wait (to attend–इन्तजार) Don't wait for me, I will go myself.

296. Week (period of seven days–सप्ताह) Monday is the first day of a week.

Weak (feeble–कमजोर) Ram is too weak to walk.

297. Ware (article–समान) He has sold all his cook wares.

Wear (to put on–पहनना) I like to wear silk sarees.

Wear (to diminish–घिसना) My shirt has worn out.

298. Wine (drink–शराब) Drinking wine is harmful for lever.

Vine (creeper–बेल) The hut is covered with grapevines.

299. Wade (talk in shallow water–पानी में हलचल) Rescuers had to wade across a river to reach them.

Weighed (weight was measured–वजन मापना) He weighed approximately 270 kilos.

300. Wain (a wagon–छकड़ा गाड़ी) He has hired a wain for transporting his household goods.

Wane (decrease, fad-कम होना) His interest in sports began to wane, a passion for golf developed.

301. War (large scale armed conflict-युद्ध) A war like situation is prevailed between India and Pakistan.

Wore (past tense of wear-पहना) She wore a silken saree last night.

Ware (merchandise–सामान) The box seems to contain glass wares.

302. Wary (cautious-सावधानी) People do not teach their wards to be wary of strangers.

Wherry (छोटी नाव) A light rowing boat used chiefly on rivers and in harbours for carrying passengers.

303. Weld (to join metal by melting its edges–वेल्डिंग) Where did you learn to weld?

Welled (pouring forth–अधिक होना) Her love for him welled stronger than ever.

304. Which (selection-किसका) Which dress do you like most ?

Witch (जादूगरनी) In fairy stories, a witch is a woman, usually an old woman, who has evil magic powers. Witches often wear a pointed black, hat and have a pet black cat.

305. **While** (during–जबकि) He was reading while she was cooking.

Wile (a crafty, cunning or deceitful trick; *a stratagem, a ruse*–चालाक धोखेबाज)
She used all her wiles to earn his favour.

306. **Whine** (annoying cry–दर्द भरी आवाज) I can hear my dog whining in the courtyard.

Wine (fermented grape juice–दारू) This is a nice wine.

307. **Whit** (insignificant amount–बहुत थोड़ी राशि) He cared not a whit for the social, political or religious aspects of literature.

Wit (cleverness; sense of humour–चतुराई) He was at his wit's end.

308. **Whither** (to which place, point, condition, etc? –कौनसा स्थान) They knew not whither they went.

Wither (shrivel up–मुरझाना) The flowers withered away within three hours.

309. **Yearn** (to long–इच्छा करना) I am anxiously yearning to meet my wife.

Yarn (thread–धागा) I have purchased three bundles of yarn.

310. **Yoke** (slavery–दास बनाना) He is under the yoke of his master.

Yolk (yellow portion of an egg–अण्डे की पीली जर्दी) Some people eat only the yolk of an egg.

Homographs

Homographs are words that are spelled the same but have different meanings.

Homographs can be pronounced differently (like bass the fish and bass the instrument) or the same (like fair meaning "equitable" or "a carnival")

Homographs that are pronounced differently

- **minute** (the noun meaning "60 seconds"; the adjective meaning "very small")
- **bass** (the fish; the instrument)
- **Polish** (from Poland) and polish (to make something shiny)
- **bow** (the noun referring to a ribbon tied in a decorative way; the verb meaning to bend reverently)
- **close** (the adjective meaning "nearby"; the verb meaning "to shut")
- **lead** (the metal; the verb meaning "to act as a leader")

Homographs that are pronounced the same

- **bear** (the animal; the verb meaning "to carry")
- **ring** (a circle; a type of jewelry; what a phone does)
- **fan** (the appliance that makes wind; an admirer/appreciator)
- **band** (music group; a ring or strap)
- **bat** (the animal; a baseball bat)
- **kind** (the adjective meaning "nice"; the noun meaning "type")
- **part** (a component of something; a line in one's hair; the verb meaning "to separate")

Exercise 1

Directions (Q. Nos. 1-28) Fill in the blanks with the correct alternative.

1. I love the .... of the fresh flowers.
(a) scent (b) sent
(c) cent (d) None of these

2. The dog likes to .... his bone in the sand.
(a) bury (b) berry
(c) barry (d) None of these

3. The contractor plans to .... a skyscraper.
(a) bill (b) billed
(c) build (d) Either a or c

4. The weather outside is very ....
(a) chilly (b) chile
(c) chili (d) None of these

5. The cat has a .... around his neck.
(a) caller (b) collar
(c) caul (d) None of these

6. I ordered a loaf of .... from the bakery.
(a) breed
(b) bread
(c) bred
(d) None of the above

7. Is it .... late to sign up for the golf tournament?
(a) to
(b) too
(c) two
(d) None of the above

8. The government has the right to .... the stolen property.
(a) sees (b) seas
(c) seize (d) size

9. Though he was already tired, the farmer had to .... the seeds.
(a) so (b) sew
(c) sow (d) chew

10. You .... of onions! What did you eat?
(a) wreak (b) reek
(c) wreck (d) reeked

11. Could you tell me .... I might find a camp stove?
(a) wear (b) ware
(c) where (d) None of these

12. The metal pipe in chimney through which the smoke and heat passes is called a ....
(a) flew (b) flue
(c) few (d) None of these

13. Watch the hen .... an egg!
(a) lay (b) lei (c) lea (d) laid

14. The fisherman .... to shore as soon as the storm clouds appeared on the horizon.
(a) road (b) rode
(c) rowed (d) None of these

15. You must......... in a wild horse.
(a) rein (b) reign
(c) rain (d) None of these

16. She vanished into thin ....
(a) air (b) heir
(c) ere (d) err

17. Prasanna had a good .... for stage.
(a) trup (b) troop
(c) trupe (d) troupe

18. In the forest, you might see a grizzly ....
(a) bear (b) bare
(c) barer (d) bariest

19. Don't get too close to the bear, it might ....you!
(a) byte (b) bite
(c) bytes (d) beats

20. The king died......... .
(a) hareless (b) heirless
(c) hairless (d) airless

21. He is bent upon taking ....
(a) avenge (b) arc
(c) ark (d) revenge

22. Draw an .... touching this square.
(a) arc (b) ark
(c) revenge (d) essay

23. The .... to this hill is very difficult.
(a) avenge
(b) revenge
(c) assent
(d) ascent

24. I .... him to join the armed services.
(a) access (b) excess
(c) advise (d) advice

25. .... Ram, all his friends were present there.
(a) Accept
(b) Except
(c) Adapt
(d) Adopt

26. .... is a sale on parrots at the pet store.
(a) They're (b) Their
(c) There (d) They

27. Which is an example of homophones?
(a) bear and bare
(b) cat and dog
(c) read and read
(d) pretty and beautiful

28. The words friar and fryer are ....
(a) Synonyms (b) Antonyms
(c) Homonyms (d) None of these

29. Which word is a homophone of 'four'?
(a) fir (b) hair
(c) for (d) foreign

30. Which of these is the homophone for the word 'new'?
(a) nwew (b) knew
(c) know (d) nue

Exercise 2

Directions (Q. Nos.1-30) Fill in the blanks with the correct alternatives.

1. The .... of a snow clad mountain is exciting.
(a) site (b) cite
(c) sight (d) None of these

2. I .... him very well.
(a) now (b) no
(c) know (d) None of these

3. His legal .... is Sheela.
(a) heir (b) hare
(c) hair (d) here

4. Raman was .... by the English king.
(a) nighted (b) nighed
(c) knighted (d) None of these

5. The king died ....
(a) hareless (b) heirless
(c) hairless (d) airless

6. Avoid eating .... for healthy living.
(a) meet (b) meat
(c) mute (d) mate

7. The .... of the cats are sharp.
(a) paws (b) pauses
(c) pause (d) None of these

8. .... lands have no market.
(a) Baren (b) Barren
(c) Baron (d) None of these

9. .... is a heavy metal.
(a) Led (b) Lid
(c) Lead (d) None of these

10. Pramod had a good .... for stage plays.
(a) trip (b) troop
(c) troupe (d) None of these

11. The .... rises in the East.
(a) Sun (b) son
(c) sin (d) soon

12. The child is .... young to go to school alone.
(a) to (b) too
(c) two (d) None of these

13. It is not healthy to .... hair.
(a) dice (b) dye (c) die (d) dyes

14. The cattle are ....on the meadow.
(a) gracing
(b) grace
(c) grazing
(d) None of these

15. .... of you must do the work.
(a) Sum (b) Some
(c) Same (d) None of these

16. In the forest, you might see a grizzly ....
(a) bear (b) bare
(c) beer (d) None of these

17. Don't get too close to the bear, it might .... you!
(a) byte (b) bite
(c) bytes (d) None of these

18. I can see my house from ....
(a) hear (b) here
(c) heir (d) None of these

19. I feel ....
(a) week (b) weak
(c) wick (d) None of these

20. I hope the .... is fine.
(a) weather
(b) whether
(c) wither
(d) None of the above

21. My sister cooks ....
(a) raise (b) rise
(c) rice (d) None of these

22. Balls were .... into the sack.
(a) throne (b) thrown
(c) thrawn (d) None of these

23. You have got bigger piece of cake than me. That's not ....
(a) fair (b) fare
(c) fire (d) None of these

24. I have got a hole in the .... of my shoe.
(a) sole (b) soul
(c) shawl (d) None of these

25. She writes everyday in her ....
(a) dairy (b) diary
(c) deary (d) None of these

26. .... refers to the second-mentioned thing of two things.
(a) Later (b) Latter
(c) Letter (d) None of these

27. The .... is the most important city of any country.
(a) Capitol (b) Septal
(c) Capital (d) None of these

28. The servant .... up the mat.
(a) role
(b) scroll
(c) rolls
(d) None of the above

29. It is good to eat orange .... also.
(a) peal (b) peels
(c) pull (d) None of these

30. The .... of cotton is very heavy.
(a) belle (b) bail
(c) bale (d) None of these

Directions (Q. Nos. 31-40) Which of the following is not a homonym pair?

31. (a) Coarse-Course
(b) Caste-Cast
(c) Pate-pat
(d) Bale-Bail

32. (a) Berth-Birth (b) Bole-Bowl
(c) Braise-Brays (d) But-Burst

33. (a) Defy-Deify (b) Chord-Cord
(c) Cattle-Kettle (d) Cent-Saint

34. (a) Floor- Flour (b) Few-Phew
(c) Gilt-Guilt (d) Cent-Saint

35. (a) Patrol-Petrol (b) Pare-Pair
(c) Pain-Pane (d) Fear-Fare

36. (a) Rest-Wrest (b) Pole-Poll
(c) Quite-Quit (d) Suit-Suite

37. (a) Bite-Byte
(b) Cell-Sell
(c) Aloud-Allowed
(d) Noisy-Nose

38. (a) Sell-Sale
(b) Boar-Bore
(c) All together-Altogether
(d) Complement-Compliment

39. (a) Dire-Dyre
(b) Less-Lasy
(c) Gild-Guild
(d) Career-Carrier

40. (a) Heard-Herd
(b) Peel-Peal
(c) Right- Write
(d) Wring-Wrong

Directions (Q. Nos 41-45) Which of the following is a homonym pair.

41. (a) Counsil-Counsel
(b) Course-Curse
(c) Buyer-Bare
(d) Corpse-Crops

42. (a) Symbol-Simple
(b) Check-Cheque
(c) Cite-Sit
(d) Chase-Case

43. (a) Cloth-Sloth
(b) Aloud-Allowed
(c) Carrier-Barrier
(d) Stair-Star

44. (a) Chess-Chaise
(b) Review-Revenue
(c) Sun-Son
(d) Sick-Six

45. (a) Staid-Stay
(b) Heir–Ware
(c) Throne-Thorn
(d) Idle-Idol

Answers

Exercise 1

1 (a)	2 (a)	3 (c)	4 (a)	5 (b)	6 (b)	7 (b)	8 (c)	9 (c)	10 (b)
11 (c)	12 (b)	13 (a)	14 (c)	15 (a)	16 (a)	17 (c)	18 (a)	19 (b)	20 (b)
21 (d)	22 (a)	23 (d)	24 (c)	25 (b)	26 (c)	27 (a)	28 (c)	29 (c)	30 (b)

Exercise 2

1 (c)	2 (c)	3 (a)	4 (c)	5 (b)	6 (b)	7 (a)	8 (b)	9 (c)	10 (c)
11 (a)	12 (b)	13 (b)	14 (c)	15 (b)	16 (a)	17 (b)	18 (b)	19 (b)	20 (a)
21 (c)	22 (b)	23 (a)	24 (a)	25 (b)	26 (b)	27 (c)	28 (c)	29 (b)	30 (c)
31 (c)	32 (d)	33 (d)	34 (d)	35 (d)	36 (c)	37 (d)	38 (a)	39 (b)	40 (d)
41 (a)	42 (b)	43 (b)	44 (c)	45 (d)					

04 One Word Substitution

One word substitution में हम शब्दों के समूह को किसी एक word से ही विस्थापित कर देते हैं। शब्द-समूह तथा विस्थापित करने वाले शब्द समान अर्थ रखते हैं।

उदाहरण के लिए, "Without the name of the writer" यानि "बिना लेखक के नाम का" के स्थान पर यदि हम एक शब्द का प्रयोग करना चाहें, तो हम anonymous (गुमनाम) का प्रयोग करेंगे।

Following are the substitutes for the given group of expressions

1. Set free by. **Acquit** (दोषमुक्त करना)
2. A person who is out to destroy all government law and order. **Anarchist** (अराजकतावादी)
3. Yearly return of the date of an event. **Anniversary** (वार्षिकी)
4. The letter which does not bear the name of the writer. **Anonymous** (गुमनाम)
5. A traveller in space. **Astronaut** (अन्तरिक्ष यात्री)
6. One who does not believe in the existence of God. **Atheist** (नास्तिक)
7. Capable of being heard. **Audible** (श्रव्य)
8. Story of a person written by himself. **Autobiography** (आत्मकथा)
9. A person who is fond of fishing. **Angler** (मछेरा)
10. A statement or proposition on which an abstractly accepted or self-evident true. **Axiom** (स्वयंसिद्ध)
11. A person who can easily be approached. **Accessible** (सुलभ)
12. Government by one person only. **Autocracy** (निरंकुश शासन)
13. Animals which live in water. **Aquatic** (जल में रहने वाले जन्तु)
14. A medicine which counteracts poison. **Antidote** (विषनाशक)
15. One who has infinite power. **Almight** (सर्वशक्तिमान)
16. A man who remains unmarried.
Or The state of being unmarried. **Bachelor** (कुँवारा)
17. A person who is unable to pay debts. **Bankrupt** (दिवालिया)
18. One who loves books. **Bibliophile** (पुस्तक-प्रेमी)
19. The life history of a man written by someone else. **Biography** (जीवनकथा)
20. Speaking two languages. **Bilingual** (द्विभाषिक)
21. The scientific study of plants and their structure. **Botany** (वनस्पति विज्ञान)
22. A person who studies plants. **Botanist** (वनस्पति विज्ञानी)
23. That which happens once in two years. **Biennial** (द्विवार्षिक)
24. Speaking disrespectfully about sacred things. **Blasphemy** (ईश्वर निन्दा)
25. A list of books. **Catalogue** (सूची-पत्र)
26. An animal living on flesh of other animals. **Carnivorous** (माँसाहारी)
27. A disease which spreads over a wide area. **Communicable** (संक्रामक रोग)
28. Persons living at the same time. **Contemporary** (तत्कालीन)
29. A person who has done something wrong. **Convict** (अपराधी)
30. That which can be believed. **Credible** (विश्वसनीय)
31. A person who is very simple and easily believes whatever is told. **Credulous** (त्वरित विश्वासी)
32. A person who is opposed to changes. **Conservative** (रूढ़िवादी)
33. A list of books. **Catalogue** (सूचीपत्र)
34. A period of hundred years. **Century** (शताब्दी)
35. The goods carried by a ship, plane or vehicle. **Cargo** (जहाज का भार)
36. A government of the people, by the people and for the people. **Democracy** (प्रजातन्त्र)
37. Want of rain. **Drought** (सूखा)
38. The art practised by statesmen and politicians. **Diplomacy** (कूटनीति)
39. Words written on the tombstone after one's death. **Epitaph** (अभिलेख)
40. A person who talks too much about himself. Egotist (स्वप्रशंसी)
41. A speech delivered without preparation. **Extempore** (तात्कालिक)
42. That which is fit to be eaten. **Edible** (खाद्य)
43. Liable to error. **Err** (चूक)
44. A person who studies insects. **Enomologist** (कृमि शास्त्री)
45. A person who leaves his own country to live in another country. **Emigrant** (परदेश में बसने वाला)
46. Which is fit to eat or consume. **Edible** (खाने योग्य)

47. The state of being or living. **Existence** (अस्तित्व)
48. Which ends in death. **Fatal** (घातक)
49. That which can be easily broken into many pieces. **Fragile** (भंगुर)
50. One who believes in fate. **Fatalist** (भाग्यवादी)
51. The murder of one's brother. **Fratricide** (भ्रातृहंता)
52. A man who is devoted to the welfare of the women. **Feminist** (नारीवादी)
53. A medicine that kills germs. **Germicides** (जीवाणु-नाशी)
54. Excessive eater. **Glutton** (पेटू)
Or One who eats too much.
55. A person who is fond of company. **Gregarious** (झुण्ड में रहने वाला व्यक्ति)
56. For which no salary is paid. **Honorary** (अवैतनिक)
Or A post for which no salary is paid.
57. Animals which live on herbs. **Herbivorous** (शाकाहारी)
58. Belief in pleasure as humankind's proper aim. **Hedonism** (सुखवाद)
59. A person who is very careful about his health. **Hygienist** (आरोग्यशास्त्री)
60. Anything which is contrary to law. **Illegal** (गैर-कानूनी)
61. Not liable to error or mistake. **Infallible** (अचूक)
62. Which cannot be corrected. **Incorrigible** (असुधार्य)
63. Which is difficult to believe. **Incredible** (अविश्वसनीय)
64. A person who can neither read, nor write. **Illiterate** (अनपढ़)
65. Which cannot be read. Illegible (अपठनीय)
66. A piece of land surrounded by water. **Island** (द्वीप)
67. Which can't be conquered. **Invincible** (अविजित)
68. Which can't be divided. **Indivisible** (अखण्डनीय)
69. Which can't be seen. **Invisible** (अदृश्य)
70. Murder of an infant. **Infanticide** (बालवध)
71. Difficult to hear. **Inaudible** (अश्रव्य)
72. Which cannot be repaired or remedied. **Irreparable** (जो सुधारा न जा सके)
73. Which must happen on day. **Inevitable** (अवश्यम्भावी)
74. Incapable of being reached**Inaccessible** (पहुँच के बाहर)
75. A person who is unable to pay his debts. **Insolvent** (दिवालिया)
76. Easily made angry. **Irritable** (जल्दी नाराज होने वाला)
77. A disease which spreads by contact. **Infectious** (संक्रामक)
78. Articles received by one country form the other. **Import** (आयात)
79. Not qualified for the post. **Ineligible** (अयोग्य)
80. To carry away or stealing a person by force. **Kidnap** (अपहरण)
81. One who knows many languages. **Linguist** (भाषाविद्)
Or A person who is proficient in many languages.
82. Eclipse of moon. **Lunar** eclipse (चन्द्र ग्रहण)
83. A place where experiments are carried out. **Laboratory** (प्रयोगशाला)
84. A speech made for the first time.
Or The first speech delivered by a person. **Maiden speech** (प्रथम भाषण)
85. A document written by hand. **Manuscript** (पाण्डुलिपि)
86. Leaving one's country. **Migrate** (प्रवर्जन)
87. A person who is hater of womankind. **Misogynist** (स्त्री जाति से घृणा करने वाला)
88. A person who hates mankind. **Misanthropist** (मानव से घृणा करने वाला)
89. A person who hates the institution of marriage. **Misogamist** (विवाह से घृणा करने वाला)
90. A person who undergoes of death or suffering for any great cause. **Martyr** (शहीद)
91. Government by a monarch. **Monarchy** (राजतन्त्र, साम्राज्यवाद)
92. Residence for monks and priests. **Monasteries** (मठ, आश्रम)
93. Animals which give milk. **Mammals** (स्तनधारी)
94. Practice of marrying one at a time. **Monogamy** (एक बार विवाह करने की प्रथा)
95. A man who eats meat. **Non-vegetarian** (माँसाहारी)
96. A person widely known for evil deeds. **Notorious** (कुख्यात)
97. A medicine that induces sleep. **Narcotic** (निद्राकारी)
98. That which cannot be seen through. **Opaque** (अपारदर्शी)
99. A garden where fruit are found/grown. **Orchard** (फलों का बगीचा)
100. One who looks at the bright side of things. **Optimist** (आशावादी)
101. All powerful. **Omnipotent** (सर्वशक्तिमान)
102. One who is present everywhere at the same time. **Omnipresent** (सर्वव्यापी)
103. One who knows everything. **Omniscient** (सर्वज्ञ)
104. A child whose parents are dead. **Orphan** (अनाथ)
105. No longer in use. **Obsolete** (अप्रचलित)
106. Government by few. **Oligarchy** (अल्पजन का शासन)
107. One who goes on foot. **Pedestrian** (पदयात्री)
108. One who looks at the dark side of things.
Or A person who looks the dark side of things. **Pessimist** (निराशावादी)
109. One who is a lover of mankind. **Philanthropist** (जन-हितैषी)
110. Remedy for all diseases. **Panacea** (रामबाण)
Or Sometimg that will solve all the problems of a particular situation.
Or A remedy of all kinds of diseases.
111. Born after the death of its father. **Posthumous** (मरणोपरान्त)

112. A person who loves his own country. **Patriot** (देशभक्त)
113. A man who amuses himself by love making. **Philanderer** (प्रेमालापी)
114. Belief in many Gods. **Polytheism** (अनेक देवताओं में विश्वास)
115. A person who depends on others. **Parasite** (परजीवी)
116. A short sentence often quoted. **Proverb** (कहावत)
117. Medical examination of the dead body. **Postmortem** (मृत्यु के बाद की डॉक्टरी परीक्षा)
118. Extreme poverty. **Penury** (दरिद्रता)
119. Substance used to destroy insects, etc. that cause danger to the crop. **Pesticide** (प्रदूषण)
120. The murder of a king. **Regicide** (राजहत्या)
121. A person who takes arms against the government of his own country. **Rebel** (विद्रोही)
122. Fit to be chosen. **Suitable** (योग्य)
123. Murder of oneself. **Suicide** (आत्महत्या)
124. An aged unmarried woman. **Spinster** (कुँआरी)
125. Eclipse of the Sun. **Solar** eclipse (सूर्य ग्रहण)
126. A person who exports or imports goods without paying custom duty and other taxes. **Smuggler** (तस्कर)
127. Walking in sleep. **Somnambulate** (नींद में चलना)
128. Talking in sleep. **Somniloquity** (नींद में बोलना)
129. A person who hesitates in meeting with people. **Shy** (शर्मीला)
130. Which takes place at the same time. **Simultaneous** (साथ-साथ)
131. One who totally abstains from liquor. **Teetotaller** (मद्य-निषेधी)
132. A person who believes in God. **Theist** (आस्तिक)
Or One who believes in the existence of God.
133. That which can be seen through. **Transparent** (पारदर्शी)
134. A student who runs away from his class without permission. **Truant** (गैर-हाजिर रहने वाला)
135. A person who saves money. **Thrifty** (मितव्ययी)
136. Two childern born of the same mother at one and the same time. **Twins** (जुड़वाँ बच्चे)
137. Government by the Gods. **Thearchy** (देवताओं का शासन)
138. Lasting for a short time. **Transient** (क्षणभंगुर)
139. A person who lends money at a high rate of interst. **Usurer** (अधिक सूदखोर)
140. Incapable of being understood. **Unintelligible** (समझ के बाहर)
141. The right to refuse, especially the right to stop a law from being passed or a decision from being taken. **Veto** (निषेधाधिकार)
142. A person with long experience. **Veteran** (अनुभवी)
143. One who does not eat meat. **Vegetarian** (शाकाहारी)
144. A fault that may be forgiven. **Venial** (क्षम्य)
145. Evening prayer in the church. **Vespers** (गिरजाघर की सायंकालीन प्रार्थना)
146. A man whose wife is dead. **Widower** (विधुर)
147. That which cannot be tamed. **Wild** (जंगली)
148. A place where clothes are placed. **Wardrobe** (कपड़े रखने की अलमारी)
149. A person who studies animals. **Zoologist** (जन्तु विज्ञान का शास्त्री)
150. A place for keeping various animals. **Zoo** (चिड़ियाघर)

Exercise 1

Directions (Q. Nos. 1-75) In the following questions, out of the four alternatives, select the alternative which is the best substitute of the words/sentence.

1. To examine one's own thoughts and feelings
(a) Meditation (b) Retrospection
(c) Reflection (d) Introspection

2. Custom of having many wives
(a) Monogamy (b) Bigamy
(c) Polygamy (d) Matrimony

3. To cause troops to spread out in readiness for battle
(a) Align (b) Collocate
(c) Deploy (d) Disperse

4. Anything written in a letter after it is signed
(a) Posterity (b) Postdiction
(c) Postscript (d) Corrigendum

5. The policy of extending a country's empire and influence
(a) Imperialism
(b) Capitalism
(c) Internationalism
(d) Communism

6. The custom of having more than one husband at the same time
(a) Polygamy (b) Polyandry
(c) Debauchery (d) Bigamy

7. List of headings of the business to be transacted at a meeting
(a) Schedule (b) Agenda
(c) Proceedings (d) Excerpts

8. To send an unwanted person out of the country
(a) Exclude (b) Ostracise
(c) Deport (d) Expatriate

9. A government run by a dictator
(a) Democracy (b) Autocracy
(c) Oligarchy (d) Theocracy

10. One who is determined to exact full vengeance for wrongs done to him
(a) Vindicator (b) Usurer
(c) Vindictive (d) Virulent

11. An office or post with no work but high pay
(a) Honorary (b) Sinecure
(c) Gratis (d) Ex-officio

12. Murder of a brother
(a) Patricide (b) Regicide
(c) Homicide (d) Fratricide

13. A person living permanently in a certain place
(a) Native (b) Resident
(c) Domicile (d) Subject

14. A place where money is coined
(a) Bank (b) Mint
(c) Treasury (d) Press

15. Regard for others as a principle of action or selflessly
(a) Cynicism (b) Nepotism
(c) Philanthropy (d) Altruism

16. Person who believes that God is everything and everything is God
(a) Agnostic (b) Theist
(c) Pantheist (d) Pantechnicon

17. Simplest and smallest form of plant life, present in air, water and soil; essential to life but may cause disease
(a) Virus (b) Amoeba
(c) Bacteria (d) Toxin

18. Relationship by blood or birth
(a) Parentage
(b) Affiliation
(c) Consanguinity
(d) Nepotism

19. Opposed to great or sudden change
(a) Static (b) Revolutionary
(c) Conservative (d) Evolutionary

20. Walking in sleep
(a) Somniloquism
(b) Somnambulism
(c) Obsession
(d) Hallucination

21. Belief or opinion contrary to what is generally accepted
(a) Unbelief
(b) Superstition
(c) Non-conformity
(d) Heresy

22. A person who kills somebody especially for political reason
(a) Criminal
(b) Murderer
(c) Assassin
(d) Hangman

23. A person who rules without consulting the opinion of others
(a) Democrat (b) Bureaucrat
(c) Autocrat (d) Fanatic

24. Study of mankind
(a) Pathology (b) Physiology
(c) Philology (d) Anthropology

25. Through which light cannot pass
(a) Dull (b) Dark
(c) Obscure (d) Opaque

26. Stealing from the writings of others
(a) Copying (b) Reframing
(c) Reproducing (d) Plagiarism

27. A short stay at a place
(a) Halt (b) Interlude
(c) Intermission (d) Sojourn

28. Constant effort to achieve something
(a) Perseverance (b) Attempt
(c) Enthusiasm (d) Vigour

29. A person not sure of the existence of God
(a) Theist (b) Atheist
(c) Agnostic (d) Cynic

30. Design made by putting together coloured pieces of glass or stones
(a) Oleograph (b) Mosaic
(c) Tracery (d) Relief

31. One who deserts his religion
(a) Deserter (b) Turn-coat
(c) Fanatic (d) Apostate

32. One who uses fear as a weapon of power
(a) Terrorist (b) Militant
(c) Extremist (d) Anarchist

33. The original inhabitants of a country
(a) Aborigines (b) Citizens
(c) Natives (d) Primitive

34. Place where birds are kept
(a) Zoo (b) Apiary
(c) Armoury (d) Aviary

35. One who does not care for literature or art or is hostile or undifferent to it
(a) Barbarian (b) Philistine
(c) Illiterate (d) Primitive

36. A man of odd habits
(a) Eccentric (b) Cynical
(c) Introvert (d) Moody

37. Deriving pleasure from inflicting pain on others
(a) Sadism (b) Malevolence
(c) Bigotry (d) Masochism

38. The power of reading the thoughts of others
(a) Psychopathy
(b) Telecommunication
(c) Psychology
(d) Telepathy

39. Animals living on land and in water
(a) Ambiguous (b) Amphibian
(c) Amorphous (d) Ambivalent

40. A light sailing boat built especially for racing
(a) Dinghy (b) Canoe
(c) Yacht (d) Frigate

41. Be the embodiment or perfect example of
(a) Signify (b) Characterise
(c) Personify (d) Masquerade

42. An opinion or conclusion formed on the basis of incomplete information
(a) Proof (b) Conjecture
(c) Clincher (d) Averment

43. An event or a group of events occurring as part of a sequence
(a) Stanza (b) Episode
(c) Series (d) Lesson

44. The study of human history and prehistory through the excavation of sites
(a) Archeology (b) Psephology
(c) Anthropology (d) Geology

45. Average in amount, intensity, quality, or degree
(a) Moderate (b) Supernatant
(c) Hobble (d) Hum

46. One who eats too much
(a) Overweight (b) Glutton
(c) Corpulent (d) Obese

47. The action of repeating something aloud from memory
(a) Paraphrase
(b) Rendition
(c) Erudition
(d) Recitation

48. A remedy for all diseases
(a) Panacea (b) Antidote
(c) Antibiotic (d) Patent

49. Something that cannot be avoided
(a) Indelible (b) Infallible
(c) Inevitable (d) Invincible

50. A person who sells and arranges cut flowers
(a) Nutritionist (b) Agriculturist
(c) Florist (d) Botanist

51. Place for collection of dried plant specimens
(a) Green house (b) Nursery
(c) Warehouse (d) Herbarium

52. Match of surpass a person by imitation
(a) Parallel (b) Emulate
(c) Ditto (d) Impression

53. Living in air
(a) Heavenly (b) Feathery
(c) Aerial (d) Visual

54. Guide the course of a ship especially by using instruments or maps
(a) Amchor (b) Sail
(c) Travel (d) Navigate

55. A person who can speak only two languages
(a) Monolingual (b) Multilingual
(c) Linguist (d) Bilingual

56. A person who is skilled at writing beautifully
(a) Painter (b) Artist
(c) Calligrapher (d) Cartoonist

57. One who is in charge of a museum or art gallery
(a) Monitor (b) Curator
(c) Instructor (d) Collector

58. Willing to be guided or controlled
(a) Adorable (b) Adamant
(c) Amenable (d) Abominable

59. A game in which no one wins
(a) Conquest (b) Draw
(c) Triumph (d) Feat

60. A word formed from the initial letters of other words and pronounced as a word
(a) Ellipsis (b) Precise
(c) Epitome (d) Acronym

61. Concerned with beauty or the appreciation of beauty
(a) Foul (b) Aesthetic
(c) Hideous (d) Gross

62. The statistical study of the population
(a) Demography (b) Sociology
(c) Psychology (d) Anthropology

63. The art of cleaning and preserving animal skins
(a) Etymology (b) Taxonomy
(c) Dermatology (d) Taxidermy

64. The original inhabitants of a country
(a) Slaves (b) Immigrants
(c) Aborigines (d) Residents

65. A strong and fast moving stream of water
(a) Rivulet (b) Creek
(c) Torrent (d) Trickle

66. One who makes and sells sweets and pastries
(a) Grocer (b) Confectioner
(c) Cobbler (d) Barber

67. A large impressive house
(a) Mansion (b) Cabin
(c) Shack (d) Fort

68. A gesture expressing respect, such as a bow
(a) Consensual (b) Obeisance
(c) Perk (d) Germinate

69. Impossible or extremely difficult to understand
(a) Inaudible
(b) Incomprehensible
(c) Incompatible
(d) Inevitable

70. Something widely feared as a possible dangerous occurrence
(a) Spectre (b) Beguile
(c) Monolith (d) Canny

71. Showing poor taste and quality
(a) Savour (b) Pike
(c) Tacky (d) Exquisite

72. Regard something as being due to a cause
(a) Adventitious (b) Superfluous
(c) Incidental (d) Ascribe

73. Something that catches fire easily
(a) Inflammable (b) Inflatable
(c) Incredible (d) Infallible

74. One who is difficult to please
(a) Feminist (b) Fastidious
(c) Fatalist (d) Fanatic

75. A person belonging to a foreign country
(a) Native (b) Resident
(c) Alien (d) Inhabitant

Exercise 2

Directions (Q. Nos. 1-50) In the following questions, out of the four alternatives, select the alternative which is the best substitute of the given phrase.

1. One who draws or produces maps
(a) Cartographer (b) Photographer
(c) Designer (d) Draftsman

2. Having a limited or narrow outlook or scope
(a) Indulgent (b) Parochial
(c) Egotistical (d) Liberal

3. Well chosen or suited to the circumstances
(a) Bias (b) Disparity
(c) Asperity (d) Felicitous

4. Preserve a right, tradition or idea in a form that ensures it will be protected and respected
(a) Profane (b) Sacrilege
(c) Enshrine (d) Blaspheme

5. Ask or beg for something earnestly or humbly
(a) Bequeath (b) Bestow
(c) Accord (d) Supplicate

6. Praise highly in speech or writing
(a) Chide (b) Eulogise
(c) Chastise (d) Reprimand

7. Become liquid, typically during decomposition
(a) Deliquesce (b) Petrify
(c) Cohere (d) Anneal

8. Extremely happy, peaceful or picturesque
(a) Idyllic (b) Abominable
(c) Iota (d) Amiss

9. Showing a lack of courage or confidence
(a) Tenacious (b) Indomitable
(c) Timid (d) Gutsy

10. To rummage about in a place or container in search of something
(a) To rake (b) To excavate
(c) To ferret (d) To poke

11. Things that have been discarded as worthless
(a) Remains (b) Flotsam
(c) Shambles (d) Havoc

12. One who does not tire easily
(a) Infallible (b) Indefatigable
(c) Inevitable (d) Indelible

13. Open to more than one interpretation; not having one obvious meaning
(a) Trite (b) Opposite
(c) Exceptional (d) Ambiguous

14. That which is no longer useful
(a) Redundant (b) Abundant
(c) Reluctant (d) Dominant

15. Able to adapt to many different functions or activities
(a) Expert (b) Versatile
(c) Surrogate (d) Deputy

16. One who treats skin diseases
(a) Dermatologist (b) Radiologist
(c) Geologist (d) Cardiologist

17. People living at the same time
(a) Comrades
(b) Friends
(c) Contemporaries
(d) Cosmopolitans

18. One who can use both hands efficiently
(a) Genius (b) Skillful
(c) Ambivalent (d) Ambidextrous

19. People who enjoy social company
(a) Gregarious (b) Unanimous
(c) Gorgeous (d) Herbivorous

20. The state of remaining unmarried
(a) Feminism (b) Polygamy
(c) Celibacy (d) Monogamy

21. That which cannot be heard
(a) Inaudible (b) Invisible
(c) Incorrigible (d) Incredible

22. Rapid increase in the number of amount of something
(a) Proliferation
(b) Promotion
(c) Propensity
(d) Paucity

23. One who criticises popular beliefs which he thinks are mistaken or unwise
(a) Philistine (b) Imposter
(c) Cannibal (d) Iconoclast

24. A short statement of a general truth or rule of conduct
(a) Instance (b) Illustration
(c) Maxim (d) Parable

25. A group of singers in a church
(a) choir (b) band
(c) host (d) troop

26. One who walks on foot
(a) Pauper (b) Pediatrician
(c) Pedestrian (d) Protagonist

27. An official pardon
(a) Regicide (b) Redemption
(c) Amnesty (d) Amnesia

28. A type of dome-shaped shelter built from blocks of solid snow
(a) Chalet (b) Wigwam
(c) Hut (d) Igloo

29. Protection or exemption from something, especially an obligation or penalty
(a) Castigation (b) Immunity
(c) Penance (d) Ostracism

30. Rub a part of the body to restore warmth or sensation.
(a) Fuzz (b) Chafe
(c) Scum (d) Oblique

31. A group of people leading the way in new developments or ideas
(a) Sycophant (b) Stooge
(c) Zealot (d) Vanguard

32. An upright bar, post or frame forming a support or barrier
(a) Repose (b) Stanchion
(c) Recumbent (d) Supine

33. A routine task, especially a household one
(a) Chore (b) Servitude
(c) Moil (d) Travail

34. A military or political group that rules a country after taking power by force
(a) Junta
(b) Suffrage
(c) Emancipation
(d) Egalitarianism

35. A person who lives outside his native country
(a) Indigenous (b) Natal
(c) Expatriate (d) Intrinsic

36. A warning of impending danger
(a) Naive (b) Monition
(c) Obtuse (d) Daft

37. Beyond or above the range of normal or physical human experience
(a) Mundane (b) Transcendent
(c) Ribald (d) Coarse

38. Capable of being imagined or grasped mentally
(a) Dazzling (b) Conceivable
(c) Stunning (d) Spectacular

39. One whose hobby is stamp collection
(a) Phonologist (b) Philanthropist
(c) Philatelist (d) Panegyrist

40. To lift or haul something heavy with great effort
(a) Heave (b) Shrimp
(c) Wimp (d) Runt

41. A factory, where workers are employed at very low wages for long hours and under poor conditions
(a) Impalpable (b) Outset
(c) Bloomy (d) Sweatshop

42. Eager or quick to argue or fight; aggressively defiant
(a) Docile (b) Truculent
(c) Pliable (d) Pliant

43. A political leader who seeks support by appealing to popular desires and prejudices rather than by using rational argument
(a) Rebel (b) Radical
(c) Demagogue (d) Anarchistic

44. Very rude or coarse; vulgar
(a) Gross (b) Adipose
(c) Porcine (d) Corpulent

45. To divide by cutting or slicing, especially suddenly and forcibly
(a) To detach
(b) To bisect
(c) To sever
(d) To dissect

46. The punishment of being kept in school after hours
(a) Pretension (b) Isolate
(c) Detention (d) Blender

47. A hot spring in which water intermittently boils, pushing a tall column of water and steam into the air
(a) Geyser (b) Smite
(c) Brew (d) Pitted

48. Represent something as being less important than it really is
(a) Discriminant
(b) Stride
(c) Underplay
(d) Imperious

49. Lack of skill, ability or competence
(a) Ineptitude
(b) Dexterity
(c) Proficiency
(d) Prowess

50. Extreme old age when a man behaves like a fool
(a) Imbecility
(b) Senility
(c) Dotage
(d) Incorrigible

Answers

Exercise 1

1 (d)	2 (c)	3 (c)	4 (c)	5 (a)	6 (b)	7 (b)	8 (c)	9 (b)	10 (c)
11 (b)	12 (d)	13 (c)	14 (b)	15 (d)	16 (c)	17 (c)	18 (c)	19 (c)	20 (b)
21 (d)	22 (c)	23 (c)	24 (d)	25 (d)	26 (d)	27 (d)	28 (a)	29 (c)	30 (b)
31 (d)	32 (a)	33 (a)	34 (d)	35 (b)	36 (a)	37 (a)	38 (d)	39 (b)	40 (c)
41 (c)	42 (b)	43 (b)	44 (a)	45 (a)	46 (b)	47 (d)	48 (a)	49 (c)	50 (c)
51 (d)	52 (b)	53 (c)	54 (d)	55 (d)	56 (c)	57 (b)	58 (c)	59 (b)	60 (d)
61 (b)	62 (a)	63 (d)	64 (c)	65 (c)	66 (b)	67 (a)	68 (b)	69 (b)	70 (a)
71 (c)	72 (d)	73 (a)	74 (b)	75 (c)					

Exercise 2

1 (a)	2 (b)	3 (d)	4 (c)	5 (d)	6 (b)	7 (a)	8 (a)	9 (c)	10 (c)
11 (b)	12 (b)	13 (d)	14 (a)	15 (b)	16 (a)	17 (c)	18 (d)	19 (a)	20 (c)
21 (a)	22 (a)	23 (d)	24 (c)	25 (a)	26 (c)	27 (c)	28 (d)	29 (b)	30 (b)
31 (d)	32 (b)	33 (a)	34 (a)	35 (c)	36 (b)	37 (b)	38 (b)	39 (c)	40 (a)
41 (d)	42 (b)	43 (c)	44 (a)	45 (c)	46 (c)	47 (a)	48 (c)	49 (a)	50 (c)

05 Idioms and Phrases

- An idiom is a commonly used expression, whose meaning does not relate to the literal meaning of its words.
  e.g.,
  (i) **An early bird** means someone who wake up early in the morning.
  (ii) **Snake in the grass** means a hidden energy.
- A 'proverb' is a brief, simple and popular saying or phrase that gives advice and effectively embodies a common truth, based on practical experience or common sense.
  e.g.,
  (i) **All that glitters is not gold** means not everything that looks precious or true turns out to be so.
  (ii) **An apple a day keeps the doctor away** means if one eats healthy foods, will always remain in good health and will not need to see the doctor after.

Important Idioms and Proverbs

- **Heart and soul** (the central core of something) Now, we are getting to the heart and soul of the matter.
- **Helter skelter** (disorderly) On arrival of the police the strikers ran helter skelter.
- **First and foremost** (first of all) to be sincere and devoted is the first and formost requirement for this job.
- **Might and main** (with as much effort or strength as one can muster) She attacked the punching bag with might and main.
- **Milk and water** (weak) The foreign policy of India is nothing more than a milk and water policy.
- **Live-wire** (a very lively or energetic person) Gurvind is such a live-wire that its tough to keep up with his stories.
- **Ins and outs** (the intricate details of situation) Before starting any new business you must know all ins and outs of it.
- **Intents and purposes** (almost completely) My wife is the incharge of the house for all intents and purposes.
- **To be weak or vacant in the upper storey** (lack in willpower) I can't assign such work to him, as he is vacant in the upper storey.
- **To be under one's thumb** (under the control of someone) She is no more under the thumb of her mother-in-law.
- **To be at daggers drawn** (to be angry with each other) Both the brothers are at daggers drawn.
- **To pull a long face** (look sad) My son pulled a long face when he was scolded by his mother.
- **To play truant** (absent from school without leave) It is a very bad habit of the students to play truant from class.
- **To flog a dead horse** (to waste time to do something) He keeps trying to get his essay published, but I think he is flogging a dead horse.
- **To fall flat** (to fail miserably) The Principal's speech fell flat on the students.
- **To get into hot water** (in trouble) The manager got into hot water while participating in the union meeting.
- **Fair field and no favour** (with honesty and sincerity) The staff wants a fair field and no favour in the matter of transfer.
- **Far and wide** (having great extent) Many tourists come to see the Taj from far and wide.
- **To move heaven and earth** (to do everything possible) He can move heaven and earth to get it done on time.
- **To make light of** (to treat something as not very serious)
  I wish you wouldn't make light of his problems.
- **To make both ends meet** (to earn the minimum amount of money necessary for living) Sudden increase in prices has made it difficult for the employees to make both ends meet.
- **Right and left** (on all sides or everywhere) The robbers looted the village right and left and fled away.
- **Safe and sound** (unharmed) She reached there safe & sound.

- **To go on a fool's errand** (a fruitless mission) The key was in his pocket and he sent me on a fool's errand to search the same at the shopping complex.
- **To gain ground** (become more popular or accepted) The belief in the abolition of Sati rites has gained ground.
- **The last nail in the coffin** (to shorten life) The reservation policy of VP Singh was the last nail in the coffin of the Janta Party.
- **Thick and thin** (good and bad times) I shall support you through thick and thin.
- **To make sure** (to ensure) I went to the college to make sure if our exams would commence from the next week.
- **To make neither head nor tail** (to fail to understand) The leader spoke so rapidly that the audience could make neither head nor tail of his lecture.
- **To nip in the bud** (to stop something from developing further) Many serious illnesses can be nipped in the bud if they are detected early enough.
- **Tooth and nail** (with every available resources) Students of general caste opposed the reservation policy tooth and nail but to no avail.
- **To knit the brow** (to frown) My father always knits his brow at everything I do.
- **To kick the bucket** (to die) She had kicked the bucket after suffering from cancer for several years.
- **To keep someone at arm's length** (to avoid) She is not a good girl and must be kept at arm's length.
- **Confusion worse confounded** (a still worse state of disorder or confusion) Recess was already going on when the fire alarm rang, leading to confusion worse confounded.
- **To gild the pill** (To make something unpleasant seem appealing) I knew that my daughter won't go to the doctor, so I gilded the pill by reminding her about the toys that are at the clinic.
- **To stem the tide of** (to resist) As a true social worker, first of all you stem the tide of poverty and unemployment.
- **To speak volumes for** (to express something clearly and completely) The sacrifice made by freedom fighters speak volumes for their true love for the country.
- **Rhyme or reason** (without meaning) He resigned from the service without any rhyme or reason.
- **Cut and dried** (fixed) There is no cut and dried method of English speaking.
- **To keep abreast of** (to have recent information) It is very important for the youth to keep abreast of all current events.
- **To keep one's fingers crossed** (to wish or hope for good luck) We should keep our fingers crossed till the last ball is bowled.
- **Nook and corner** (at every corner) I searched her in every nook and corner.
- **Now and then** (sometimes) I visit church now and then.
- **Stuff and nonsense** (foolishness) The judge found all his arguments stuff and nonsense.
- **Sum and substance** (a summary) The sum and substance of the paragraph must be reflected in a good precis.
- **To put all eggs in one basket** (To invest all of one's energy or resources into a single goal) Mrs Tan's financial advisor urged her to be careful and not put all her eggs in one basket.
- **To pour oil on troubled water** (to calm someone down) Both of them were fighting for the property but the justified decision of their mother poured oil on troubled water.
- **With tail between the legs** (to feel ashamed or defeated) The Minister was talking a lot about the values of honesty etc. but when Ramesh reminded him about the money paid to him for the work, he went away with his tail between the legs.
- **To get off scot free** (free from harm or penalty) He got off scot free for lack of evidence.
- **To be worth its weight in gold** (very useful) For a hungry man a piece of bread is often worth its weight in gold.
- **To be lost in clouds** (lost in thoughts) Philosophers are often lost in clouds.
- **Pins and needless** (in a state of tense anticipation nervousness) He was on pins and needles while waiting for the test results.
- **Pin money** (A small amount of money to buy things that you want but don't need) She teaches a little french now and then, just for pin money.
- **Out of gear** (in worse condition) The strike of employees always put the Government machinery out of gear.
- **Out and out** (abosolute or definitely) Mahatma Gandhi was a great leader out and out.
- **Hornet's nest** (unusal difficulty) The speaker of Lok Sabha stirred up hornet's nest by referring to impending changes in several rules.
- **Hole and corner policy** (secretive) The officer adopted a hole and corner policy to get his personal assistant transferred.
- **To live in a fool's paradise** (foolish ideas) It is wrong to live in a fool's paradise and not put hard efforts to achieve success.

- **To lie in the bed one has made** (suffer for one's misdeed) He has made his fortune so he must lie in the bed he has made.
- **To give one a long rope** (to allow a person full scope to commit mistakes) He never gives his employees a long rope.
- **To give currency** (to make something credible by providing additional details) You are famous in this field if you comment on this guy's stupid ideas, you will just give currency to them.
- **To grease the palm** (to give money as bribe) You cannot get this contract unless you grease the palm of the officials.
- **To have gift of the gab** (the ability to talk readily) Ram may seem different but he has the gift of the gab.
- **To have an iron will** (strong will) A person with iron will can achieve anything.
- **Once and again** (a few times) I have told you once and again that I have no money to purchase the car at the moment.
- **Achilles heel** (the most weak point) Her involvement in corruption scandal has been her Achilles heel.
- **To turn the corner** (to advance beyond a difficult stage) He turned the corner by passing the examinations with good marks.
- **To take to one's heels** (to flee away) On seeing the police, the thief took to his heels.
- **Over and above** (in addition to) I paid him rupees ten thousand over and above what he demanded.
- **Over head and ears** (completely/hopelessly) He is over head and ears in debt.
- **To make much ado about nothing** (make a fuss) He is a quarrelsome man, he makes much ado about nothing.
- **To make hay while the sun shines** (make the best of a good situation) As the Congress party came into power, he became chairman of UTI. He rightly says to make hay while the sun shines.
- **To make the most of** (to use or enjoy something as much as possible) Students should make the most of their time if they want to secure good marks.
- **To be at a loss** (to not know what do or say) In the interview he found himself at a loss and could not answer even very simple questions.
- **To be at one's wit's end** (not knowing what to do next) Seeing the income tax officer at his shop, he was at his wit's end.
- **To come to a standstill** (to stop completely) As the car came to standstill for want of petrol, the thief ran away on foot.
- **Open and aboveboard** (completely and openly honest) He believes in open and aboveboard discussion on every point before arriving at a conclusion.
- **Seamy side of life** (the most unpleasant) The present day cinema depicts the seamy side of life.
- **Spick and span** (neat and clean) Mr. Jawaharlal Nehru was always spick and span in his dressing style.
- **Null and void** (having no legal effect) The law passed by legislature was declared null and void by the Supreme Court.
- **To steal a march** (to gain advantage secretly) Shalini stole a march on her friend in marketing her products slowly and steadily.
- **To steer clear of** (to stay away) You should try to steer clear of such nasty people.
- **To give the devil his dues** (to give your enemy a proper credit) No doubt he is a naughty man, but to give the devil his dues he is dedicated and hard working.
- **To give chapter and verse for a thing** (to give a detailed account of something without missing anything) He can give chapter and verse for all the allegations, he made against the minister.
- **To add a new feather in one's cap** (great achievement) His success in his ICFAI exams has added a new feather in his cap.
- **To be at sea** (confused) My wife is quite at sea in maths.
- **To be in fix** (to be in dilemma) The police department was in a fix about the threatning calls sent by the militants.
- **To lead up the garden path** (to deceive someone) The tricky traders try to lead the customers up the garden path by assuring them of warranty and good discount.
- **To hang fire** (to hold back as if in suspense) The problem of poverty has been hanging fire for the last fifty five years.
- **To have feet of clay** (a weakness or failure) The inquiry has revealed that most of the politicians have feet of clay.
- **To have thing at one's finger tips** (complete knowledge) He has all the statistics of employment at his finger tips.
- **To have an axe to grind** (self interest) I am sure, he has an axe to grind in this proposal.
- **Watch and ward** (a continuous watch) At least three guards are required to have perfect watch and ward of the building.
- **Whip and spur** (in utmost haste) He completed the project in a whip and spur.
- **Willy nilly** (whether one agrees or not) After her boss fell sick, she willy nilly found herself directing the project.

- **Take bull by horns** (handle difficult situation directly) One should have courage to take bull by horns if one wants to succeed in life.
- **The die is cast** (a decision has been made) There is no point of discussing the matter now as the die is cast.
- **Flesh and blood** (physical existence) I am only flesh and blood as anybody else.
- **Gall and wormwood** (bitter resentment) Ever since I lost the election for school president, I only feel gall and wormwood when I think of my unworthy opponent.
- **To rub one the wrong way** (to irritate) If you rub him the wrong way, he will oppose the proposal.
- **To rule the roost** (to be the boss or manager) Today the scheduled caste minister rules the roost in the Government.
- **Yellow press** (sensational journalism) These days newspapers with yellow press are earning like anything.
- **To add fuel to the flame or fire** (make a problem worse) With the arrest of the leader of agitators, the Government only added fuel to the flame.
- **To assume airs** (to be proud of) He is in the habit of assuming airs in the presence of his inlaws.
- **Pick and choose** (to select with a great care) The management adopted pick and choose policy in the promotions from clerical to assistant cadre.
- **Through fire and water** (endure danger) He can go through fire and water to achieve his goal.
- **Time and tide** (time and opportunity) Time and tide waits for none.
- **To and fro** (back and forth) What are the to and fro taxi charges for travelling from Alwar to Delhi?
- **To be not worth one's salt** (not deserving) You should not help Ramesh, he is not worth his salt.
- **To be in tune** (agreeing) The Principal asked the students if they were in tune for organising the annual function.
- **To be out of sorts** (to feel slightly ill) She had been out of sorts for several days and so could not do her office work.
- **Herculean task** (a difficult task) Getting selected in IAS is a herculean task for everybody.
- **Hit below the belt** (to give someone an unfair blow) By making his private secrets public he hit him below the belt.
- **Hither and thither** (here and there) He is in the habit of putting his goods hither and thither.
- **To take people by storm** (impress greatly) The refusal by Soniya to accept the Prime Ministership took the nation by storm.
- **To the backbone** (thoroughly) We need leaders who are honest to the backbone.
- **Toil and moil** (hard work) It requires too much of toil and moil to secure first position.
- **Tom, Dick and Harry** (everyone) Every Tom, Dick and Harry knows that MS Dhoni is a wonderful cricketer.
- **Ups and downs** (the mixture of good and bad) There are ups and downs in every business.
- **Uphill task** (a difficult and challenging task) Passing CAT examination is an uphill task.
- **Warp and woof** (a base or a foundation) Blood and bones are warp and woof of human body.
- **To put a spoke in one's wheel** (hinder someone) Every competitor in the market is trying to put a spoke in the wheel of others.
- **To rip up old sores** (reopen the quarrel) Ramesh and his wife can't live in peace, they are always ripping up old soros.
- **Fire and brimstone** (to punish) The USA has threatened Iraq with fire and brimstone if it refuses follow the resolutions of UNO.
- **Fire and fury** (full of haughty temper) The speech of the leader was full of fire and fury.
- **To be in the good books** (to have approval) A good student is always in the good books of his teachers.
- **To be under a cloud** (under suspicious) His connections with the militants have brought him under a cloud.
- **To be at large** (to be free) The man who tried to kill her is still at large.
- **To get oneself into a mess** (get into muddle) He seems to have got himself into a mess because of the involvement of his wife in a criminal case.
- **To go to the dogs** (to go to ruin) He went to the dogs because of his son's involvement in the murder of a girl.
- **To keep body and soul together** (to manage to keep existing) Because of the inflation it has become difficult for many to keep body and soul together.
- **To keep the wolf from the door** (to prevent starvation) In our country the poor have to struggle hard to keep the wolf from the door.
- **To break the news** (to tell someone some important news) He broke the news of her husband's death very cautiously in order to lessen the shock.
- **To burn the midnight oil** (to work very hard) I have to burn the midnight oil for several days in order to complete the work in time.
- **To be born with a silver spoon in one's mouth** (to be born in wealthy family) Indira Gandhi was born with a silver spoon in her mouth.

- **To lose ground** (fail to hold one's position) He has lost ground and so his opponent has won the election.
- **To leave no stone unturned** (to make every possible effort) The Prime Minister has assured the country that he shall leave no stone unturned to uplift the condition of the countrymen.
- **To get down to brass tacks** (to begin to discuss the important details) Instead of wasting time in discussion please get down to brass tacks.
- **To give a wide berth** (to keep far away) I try my best to give a wide berth to such a selfish person.
- **To see a thing through coloured glasses** (to see only one aspect of things) A prejudiced man will see the thing through coloured glasses. He can't judge the things properly.
- **To show the white feather** (to betray or cowardise) He will show the white feather when the real time or action comes.
- **Ivory tower** (a place away from practical affairs) Those who talk of non-violence as a useful tool in tackling the militants live in ivory tower.
- **Kith and kin** (one's relatives) All kith and kin were invited in the marriage of his son.
- **To hold a candle to** (compare to) She is the daughter of a famous dancer, but she does not hold a candle to her mother.
- **To have brush with** (to have a brief contact with something) Our neighbours had a brush with one another over the matter of throwing the garbage.
- **To pay one back in the same coin** (to seek revenge on someone by treating them in the same negative manner as they had done) I believe in the policy of paying back in the same coin.
- **To put the cart before the horse** (to do things in improper order) He made a contract with the publisher, without getting the book ready. He put the cart before the horse as such.
- **Hue and cry** (commotion) A lot of hue and cry was raised in Parliament against this bill.
- **Hush money** (a bribe paid to keep something secret) He managed to escape punishment by paying hush money.
- **Goods and chattels** (all kinds of personal possessions) They have been turned out of their house on short notice and don't know where to store their goods and chattels.
- **To play fast and loose** (to ignore social conventions to suit one's purpose) There is a willingness to play fast and loose with the facts.
- **To pay off old scores** (to get revenge) By suspending the clerk on frivolous grounds the officer paid off old scores.
- **Egg on** (urge on) The captain egged the players on to continue the struggle.
- **Fair and square** (just and honest) He is fair and square in his dealings.
- **Fabian policy** (a policy of delays and cautions) Mr. Narsimha Rao always followed a Fabian policy in all political issues.
- **Few and far between** His visits to his parents are few and far between because of his busy schedule.
- **Pros and cons** (*considering all the fact*) Before signing this agreement you must understand all pros and cons well.
- **Queer fish** (*odd person*) He is such a queer fish that we can't expect anything positive from him.
- **Rank and ruin** (*complete destruction*) The present drought has put the farmers at the verge of rank and ruin.
- **Oily tongue** (*too smooth of speech*) One should be aware of the persons with oily tongue.
- **Part and parcel** (*an essential element*) Each employee should feel himself part and parcel of the business enterprises.
- **Foot the bill** (to pay the bill) Although she hosted the feast, her father had to foot the bill.
- **Free and easy** (casual, calm and relaxed) If you're free and easy with your savings, you'll be broke again in no time.
- **To take heart** (to be confident or courageous) You must take heart and face the failures boldly.
- **To take up arms** (commence hostilities) We must not shy for taking up arms against the misdeeds of the public departments.
- **To have no backbone** (lacking strength) The movement against the reservation based on caste, had no backbone and collapsed too soon.
- **To harp on the same string** (to dwell upon one subject) The speakers had nothing new to say, everyone harped on the same string of his predecessor.
- **Loaves and fish** (benefits or rewards) Now-a-days Government servants are concerned with the loaves and fish of the office than to solve the problems of common public.
- **Lock and key** (full security) He keeps jewellery under lock and key.
- **Length and breadth** (throughout the place) Anti English agitation spread through the length and breadth of country.
- **Life and Soul** (very lively and entertaining, good with mixing with people) Soniya Gandhi is the life and soul of Congress (I).
- **Like a fish out of water** (in a very awakward manner) Ram was given an unremunerative post. He is feeling like a fish out of water.

- **To sail under false colours** (disguise your true nature) We should not believe the politicians because they sail under false colours.
- **To set Thames on fire** (do something remarkable work) Qualifying civil services examination for you is like setting Thames on fire.
- **To say ditto to** (a copy) You are bound to say ditto to what your boss says.
- **Neck and crop** (altogether) The Pak army ruined the border village neck and crop.
- **Need of the hour** (most essential need or requirement) Providing full security for the residents of border area is the need of the hour.
- **To cry for the moon** (ask for impossible thing) Your hope for marrying with Aishwarya is like a cry for the moon.
- **To curry favour** (gain favour by flattery) By giving present and visiting again and again, you are trying to curry his favour.
- **To draw the long bow** (to exaggerate or overstate) In calling her the best racer of the world, her admirers draw the long bow.
- **Fishy** (suspicious) There seems to be something fishy going on.
- **Call a spade a spade** (to speak clearly) He believes in calling a spade a spade.
- **Cats and dogs** (contrary to belief unusually) It has been raining cats and dogs for the last three hours.
- **Cock and bull story** (concocted story) All his excuses seem a cock and bull story.
- **To play ducks and drakes** (to waste foolishly) He is playing ducks and drakes with parental money.
- **Hard and fast** (fixed) There are no hard and fast rules to sanction the loan in the banks.
- **Haughty and naughty** (rude and old) The haughty and naughty attitude of the President is not liked by any member of the society.
- **Dig the grave** (do something foolish) By taking a side of the thief, he dug the grave of his honest image.
- **To end in smoke/fiasco** (to not get a positive result) He spoke a lot about his new book but it all ended in fiasco, when the book was in the market.
- **To feather one's own nest** (to grow wealthy by taking advantage of one position) Our leaders are busy feathering their own nests and have no concern for the general mass.
- **To pass the buck** (pass the blame) Political parties pass the buck on to one another on all small or big matters.
- **To play the gallery** (try to win approval) Every action of the political leaders is aimed to play the gallery.
- **To send about one's business** (to dismiss or fire) His employer sent him about his business when he was caught involved in forgery.
- **To stand ones ground** (to maintain one's position) He did not yield to pressure and stood his ground till he won the game.
- **Gird up the loin** (to get ready) We should gird up the loin to fight the poverty and menace of dowery.

Exercise 1

Directions (Q.Nos 1-75) Some proverbs and idioms are given below with their meanings. Choose the correct meaning of the proverb/idiom.

1. To beg the question
(a) To refer to
(b) To take for granted
(c) To raise objections
(d) To be discussed

2. To drive home
(a) To find one's roots
(b) To return to place of rest
(c) Back to original position
(d) To emphasise

3. To hit the right nail on the head
(a) To do the right thing
(b) To destroy one's reputation
(c) To announce one's fixed views
(d) To teach someone a lesson

4. To pick holes
(a) To find some reason to quarrel
(b) To destory something
(c) To criticise someone
(d) To cut some part of an item

5. To smell a rat
(a) To see signs of plague epidemic
(b) To get bad smell of a dead rat
(c) To suspect foul dealings
(d) To be in a bad mood

6. A black sheep
(a) An unlucky person
(b) A negro
(c) An ugly person
(d) None of the above

7. To catch a tarter
(a) To trap wanted criminal with great difficulty
(b) To catch a dangerous person
(c) To meet with disaster
(d) To deal with a person who is more than one's watch

8. To be above board
(a) To have a good height
(b) To be honest in any business deal
(c) To have no debts
(d) To try to be beautiful

9. To keep one's temper
(a) To become angry
(b) To be in good mood
(c) To preserve one's energy
(d) To be a loof from

10. To have an axe to grind
(a) A private end to serve
(b) To fail to arouse interest
(c) To have no result
(d) To work for both sides

11. To cry wolf
(a) To listen eagerly
(b) To give false alarm
(c) To turn pale
(d) To keep off starvation

12. A man of straw
(a) A man of no substance
(b) A very active person
(c) A worthy fellow
(d) An unreasonable person

13. To make clean breast of
(a) To gain prominence
(b) To praise oneself
(c) To confess without reserve
(d) To destroy before it blooms

14. To end in smoke
(a) To make completely understand
(b) To ruin oneself
(c) To excite great applause
(d) None of the above

15. To leave someone in the lurch
(a) To come to compromise with someone
(b) Constant source of annoyance to someone
(c) To put someone at ease
(d) To desert someone in his difficulties

16. To play second fiddle
(a) To be happy, cheerful and healthy
(b) To reduce importance of one's senior
(c) To support the role and view of another person
(d) To do back seat driving

17. To set one's face against
(a) To oppose with determination
(b) To judge by appearance
(c) To get out of difficulty
(d) To look at one steadily

18. To put one's hand to the plough
(a) To take up agricultural farming
(b) To take a difficult task
(c) To get entangled into unnecessary things
(d) Take interest in technical work

19. To join issue with
(a) To cooperate with others for a cause
(b) To join any voluntary organisation for good purpose
(c) To resolve dispute and restore peace
(d) To enter into argument over any issue

20. To do oneself justice
(a) To dispense justice on our own
(b) To treat others with due respect
(c) To defend one's point of view
(d) None of the above

21. Once in a blue moon
(a) Once in a while
(b) Often
(c) At a short interval
(d) At a particular time

22. Crocodile tears
(a) Big tears
(b) Cry in a huge voice
(c) To feel sorry
(d) Hypocritical tears

23. To beat about the bush
(a) To do something wrong
(b) To beat somebody badly
(c) To open some secret
(d) To talk meaninglessly or in a roundabout way

24. To be at sixes and sevens
(a) To be in a proper order
(b) To be in an improper order
(c) To be in a good mood
(d) Something in abundance

25. A big mouth
(a) A man having a large mouth
(b) A strong man
(c) A boastful person
(d) A heavy cannon

26. French leave
(a) A leave without permission
(b) A leave for a long time
(c) A leave for a short period of time
(d) A leave forever

27. To cool one's heals
(a) To run away
(b) To stand in comfort
(c) To keep (to be kept) waiting for someone
(d) To stand firmly

28. Chips of the same block
(a) Persons of the same caste
(b) Persons of the same taste
(c) Persons from the same family
(d) Foolish persons

29. To kick the bucket
(a) To fall unconsciously
(b) To hate someone
(c) To beat Someone
(d) To die

30. To make out
(a) To prepare something
(b) To understand
(c) To guess
(d) To complete something

31. To call a spade a spade
(a) To speak the truth
(b) To tell a lie
(c) To open the secret
(d) To say something on somebody's face

32. To bank upon
(a) To go to bank
(b) To depend upon
(c) To sit on the bank of a lake
(d) To say something in a quick manner

33. To spread like wild fire
(a) To spread in a large area
(b) To spread rapidly
(c) To spread at a great height
(d) To be very colourful or shining

34. Burn the candles at both ends
(a) A wealthy person
(b) A lazy person
(c) Treat as important
(d) Use up too much energy

35. To be cut out
(a) To be fit for
(b) To fight
(c) To get a deep wound
(d) To be a great enemy of

36. Dark horse
(a) Unexpected winner
(b) To be indifferent
(c) Natives of Africa
(d) Decide for good reasons

37. Yeoman service
(a) To do something in a mysterious way
(b) Good commendable service
(c) Service to the peasants
(d) A religious service

38. Through thick and thin
(a) To pass through a narrow passage
(b) In all circumstances
(c) To be in a great trouble
(d) To become weak

39. Of the first water
(a) Of high order
(b) Of a foreigner
(c) Of a strong person
(d) Of an elder one

40. To go to the wall
(a) A cold welcome
(b) To be pushed to the worst position
(c) To be in a cheerful mood
(d) To move towards the wall

41. To look into the matter
(a) To be serious
(b) To investigate
(c) To look in a surprised manner
(d) To understand

42. To pass away
(a) To go abroad
(b) To go out for hunting
(c) To die
(d) To move away rapidly

43. To show the cat out of the bag
(a) To boast
(b) To keep weapons (illegally)
(c) To keep weapons (legally)
(d) To open the secret

44. Ups and downs
(a) Uneven path
(b) Hills and plains
(c) Successes and failures
(d) To ride a sea-saw

45. A chicken-hearted fellow
(a) An honest person
(b) A cowardly person
(c) A weak person
(d) A cunning person

46. A cold reception
(a) A reception in winter session
(b) A reception in an AC room
(c) A reception wanting in love and enthusiasm
(d) A heartiest reception

47. A man of mark
(a) A bully
(b) A man with a scar on his face
(c) A crack-shot
(d) A man of distinction

48. An open question
(a) A question not yet decided
(b) A different question
(c) A common talk
(d) An important talk

49. To build castles in the air
(a) To be a great artist
(b) To frame imaginary schemes
(c) To be rich
(d) To have full knowledge of modern science and technology

50. To have blue blood (in one's veins)
(a) To be a cruel person
(b) To be an infectious person
(c) To belong to a noble or rich family
(d) To be a foolish person

51. Never-never land
(a) An imaginary utopian place or situation.
(b) A place that is worse than hell.
(c) A place that you know that you will never be able to visit.
(d) A popular place about which you have heard such stories that you would not like to go there.

52. Through thick and thin
(a) To be scared of small dangers
(b) Passing through a thick forest
(c) Support under all circumstances
(d) To be hard hearted in times of loss

53. New kid on the block
(a) New rules which are bound to fail
(b) A junior
(c) A new social trend
(d) A newcomer

54. Kitty-corner
(a) Favourite place of cats
(b) A place where ladies meet to party
(c) A very small place
(d) Things located diagonally opposite each other

55. In a nutshell
(a) Add nuts into something
(b) Put everything in a shell
(c) Packed very tightly
(d) Express very briefly

56. To go for broke
(a) To risk everything in an all-out effort

(b) Failure in relationship or partnership
(c) Losing all money in an effort to revive a failing business
(d) To start again after failing in a business

57. Put your best foot forward
(a) Take care to dress well
(b) Walk very cautiously
(c) Try as hard as one can
(d) Check every step

58. Fixed in one's ways
(a) Not wanting to change how one does things
(b) One will succeed if one does not change their path
(c) Trapped in a particular unpleasant situation
(d) A dilemma of two different paths

59. Be in two minds
(a) Behave smart at sometime and stupid at other.
(b) Unable to decide
(c) Having a split personality disorder.
(d) Trying to do two things at the same time.

60. Dance to someone's tune
(a) Argue with others on petty matters
(b) Delay in making a decision
(c) Do what others want you to do
(d) Be engaged in an energetic activity

61. At large
(a) A very big opportunity
(b) A criminal escaped or not yet captured.
(c) To have a big heart
(d) A big appetite

62. Leave no stone unturned
(a) Leave the path halfway
(b) Not make enough efforts
(c) Turn everything upside down
(d) Try everything possible

63. Variety is the spice of life
(a) New experiences make life more interesting
(b) Experimentation may be risky
(c) Life is very beautiful
(d) There is no life without excitement

64. Rule the roost
(a) To make all the decisions
(b) To be prosperous but generous
(c) To frequently pick a quarrel
(d) To blindly follow others

65. At somebody's expense
(a) Paid for by someone
(b) To blame a crime on someone else
(c) The unlucky persons who lose a race
(d) If one person benefits it is always at the loss of another

66. Actions speak louder than words
(a) Achievers are better than those who talk big
(b) No action can compensate for saying bad words
(c) A pen is mightier than a sword
(d) What someone does mean more than what they say they will do

67. Acid test
(a) A malicious way of taking revenge
(b) A test that shows how to harm someone
(c) Proof that an attack has been made
(d) Definitive proof of truth or falsehood

68. Bolt from the blue
(a) Winning after losing a game many times
(b) Something sudden that happens unexpectedly
(c) Someone who runs fast and wins a race
(d) Locking the doors to keep the rain out

69. Be on the air
(a) Broadcast over the radio or on TV
(b) Float like a bird
(c) To pass bodily gases
(d) Be very arrogant

70. At snail's pace
(a) Do something very carefully
(b) Be very persistent
(c) Do something very slowly
(d) Keep your moves secret

71. Hanging by a thread
(a) In a sorry or humble estate
(b) Be extremely weak
(c) Unable to act as desired
(d) Be in a dangerous situation

72. Zero tolerance
(a) Accuracy is paramount
(b) Non-acceptance of antisocial behaviour
(c) No return without risk
(d) No problem at all

73. Turn a deaf ear
(a) To pay attention
(b) To listen carefully
(c) To make someone deaf
(d) To pay no need

74. Green thumb
(a) To have talent in gardening
(b) To be envious
(c) To be angry
(d) To have talent in painting

75. A blessing in disguise
(a) A misfortune that eventually has good results
(b) A person who has changed so much that he is now unrecognisable
(c) A prayer asking for God's favour
(d) A bad person hiding his face behind a mask

Exercise 2

Directions (Q. Nos. 1-60) In the following questions, out of the four alternatives, select the alternative, which best expresses the meaning of the idion-phrase.

1. Silver bullet
(a) A very expensive solution used only as the last measure
(b) A simple and seemingly magical solution to a complicated problem
(c) A solution which is worse than the problem
(d) A thing of beauty but which is actually deadly

2. Take to task
(a) To assign work
(b) To rebuke
(c) To praise
(d) To give an award

3. At arm's length
(a) Checking the length of fabric
(b) As close as one can touch
(c) Avoiding too much closeness
(d) Using one's arm to measure length

4. Against the clock
(a) To do a job fast to finish it before a deadline
(b) Time is money
(c) Man is a victim of time
(d) It is useless to fight destiny

5. Four corners of the earth
(a) From the very beginning
(b) From morning till night
(c) From all parts of the world
(d) From beginning to end

6. Gift of the gab
(a) Receive a precious gift
(b) Achieve sudden greatness
(c) Have the ability to adapt
(d) Have the talent to speak well

7. Red letter day
(a) A very special day
(b) A very hot day
(c) A frightful day
(d) A very cold day

8. As the crow flies
(a) To be uncertain
(b) A long winding path
(c) The shortest route
(d) To be directionless

9. A hot potato
(a) A war like situation which could have been easily avoided
(b) A common eatery but favoured by celebrities
(c) A controversial situation which is awkward to deal with
(d) A celebrity who keeps getting into some or the other controversy

10. Pull the plug
(a) Make a firm refusal
(b) Save a situation by acting in the nick of time
(c) To waste away somebody's effort
(d) Prevent something from continuing

11. Ethnic cleansing
(a) A social revolution where negative aspects of a culture are removed
(b) To perform mass religious conversions
(c) The mass killing of members of one ethnic group
(d) Removal of all signs of culture from a society

12. Pull the wool over someone's eyes
(a) To protect someone
(b) To keep oneself warm
(c) Deceive someone by telling lies
(d) To pretend to be blind to the other person's bad behaviour

13. Head in the clouds
(a) To daydream
(b) To be very tall
(c) To be very lazy
(d) To feel giddy

14. To shake off
(a) To denounce (b) To get rid of
(c) To recollect (d) To pass off

15. Mind your language
(a) To speak first and think later
(b) To put a lot of efforts to understand what the other person is trying to say
(c) Tell someone to speak politely
(d) To speak grammatically incorrect language

16. Face the music
(a) Face the enemy
(b) Enjoy the harmony
(c) Get appreciation
(d) Face the criticism

17. Hand in glove
(a) Working together in the same office
(b) Wearing gloves while working
(c) In partnership for something dishonest
(d) Doing work in the garden

18. To grease the palm
(a) To give support
(b) To bribe someone
(c) To cheat someone
(d) To give a massage

19. Add fuel to the fire
(a) Go from one bad situation to another
(b) A cause becomes stronger when more people join
(c) The flame will extinguish if it runs out of oil
(d) Cause a situation to become worse

20. Pass the hat
(a) To sell something
(b) To collect money
(c) To play a game
(d) To avoid work

21. Make no headway
(a) Check if the head can pass through
(b) Unable to progress ahead
(c) Unable to overtake anyone
(d) Forced to fix a new goal

22. Flesh and blood
(a) A very gory murder scene
(b) A lot of hard work
(c) Loss of lives in battle
(d) A person's physical body and their needs and frailties

23. Flea market
(a) A market for semi-precious stones and jewellery
(b) A market where stolen goods are sold
(c) A street market selling second hand goods
(d) A small but crowded and noisy place

24. In a pickle
(a) In great pain (b) In jubiliation
(c) In trouble (d) In deep sorrow

25. A walk of life
(a) An easy comfortable life not necessarily prosperous
(b) The most important day of your life
(c) A person's occupation or position within society
(d) Walking is the best form of exercise

26. Up in arms
(a) Throw up arms in joy
(b) Divide into armed groups
(c) Give up fighting and surrender
(d) Angry about

27. Stir up a hornet's nest
(a) Call for dialogue
(b) Lead a revolt
(c) Provoke trouble
(d) Destroy a nest

28. Draw a blank
(a) Be unsuccessful
(b) Be happy about something
(c) Be unable to sketch
(d) Be lucky in a game

29. Dark hourse
(a) someone who is fond of horse racing
(b) someone who has a wheatish complexion
(c) someone who breeds race horses
(d) someone who unexpectedly succeeds

30. Have one's hands full
(a) To be very rich
(b) To be very clumsy
(c) To be very busy
(d) To be very generous

31. Left handed compliment
(a) Praise that is given directly
(b) Insulting someone in front of others
(c) Insulting remark appearing as praise
(d) Making fun of someone to tease them

32. The crux of the matter
(a) The unknown point
(b) The lesser issue
(c) The critical point
(d) The interesting thing

33. To bark up the wrong tree
(a) To be wrong about the reason for something
(b) To bury money under a tree and forget the place
(c) To be mistaken about the name of a tree
(d) To eat an unpalatable fruit by mistake

34. Be an old hat
(a) Be superstitious (b) Be outdated
(c) Be crazy (d) Be foolish

35. Feather your own nest
(a) Make money unfairly
(b) Win a competition
(c) Be in a comfortable position
(d) Disturb others in their work

36. To take the bull by the horns
(a) To face danger boldly
(b) To escape unhurt
(c) To act foolishly
(d) To enjoy risky sports

37. Chew something over
(a) Discuss or consider something at length
(b) Grab what belongs to someone else
(c) Take a large bite, more than you can eat
(d) Talk while eating

38. By courtesy of
(a) Be very polite
(b) Do a philanthropic act forcefully
(c) Be brave and face risks for the team
(d) Given or allowed by

39. Be in force
(a) To enjoy a short period of fame or power
(b) In great strength or numbers
(c) A hateful act done in a haste
(d) Be the current winner

40. A thorn in the flesh
(a) A minor discomfort which is easily ignored
(b) To fight despite being injured
(c) A source of continual annoyance or trouble
(d) A person within close family whom you secretly hate

41. A wet blanket
(a) A safety net of precaution from fires
(b) A person who discourages enjoyment or enthusiasm
(c) An extremely uncomfortable place to sleep
(d) A trick to shoo away unwelcome guests

42. Drive someone up the wall
(a) To help someone achieve success
(b) To overcome an obstacle by going over it
(c) To close someone's path of escape
(d) Make someone very irritated or angry

43. I can't think straight
(a) Accept that the puzzle is too difficult for you.
(b) Faced with a dilemma.
(c) Cannot think rationally due to being overwhelmed with emotion.
(d) Ask for advice on a difficult problem.

44. Every dog has his day
(a) The weakest will become the strongest, that is the cycle of life
(b) Everyone will have good luck at some point in their lives
(c) Loyalty will not go unrewarded
(d) Every person has a talent, and one will discover it one day

45. On a wing and a prayer
(a) A prayer can move mountains
(b) A prayer has the strength to make you achieve great heights just like wings do
(c) The more one gets into prayer the closer one feels to God
(d) With only the slightest chance of success

46. In the same boat
(a) When the option that you have is equally bad as the situation you are in
(b) Life like the river throws the same challenges for all boats
(c) Be in the same difficult circumstances as others
(d) Big and small boats suffer the same fate in a storm

47. A ray of hope
(a) Even in a very bad situation one should try to see a good thing
(b) Good days are sure to follow difficult ones
(c) Be very happy even if the reason is very small
(d) Something that provides a small amount of optimism in a difficult situation

48. At short notice
(a) With little warning or time for preparation
(b) To ignore something important at your own peril
(c) To notice a small leak which can sink a ship
(d) Inform somebody that they are fired from a job

49. Alphabet soup
(a) A beautiful poem
(b) A text which nourishes your soul
(c) A book that is close to your heart
(d) A confusing or confused mixture of things.

50. A dime a dozen
(a) Strength is in numbers
(b) People who say bad things have no value
(c) Very common and of no particular value
(d) You save more if you buy in large numbers

51. Practice makes a man perfect
(a) Perfection demands patience
(b) Any problem can be solved if you are willing to try many times
(c) Regular activity is the way to become proficient in it
(d) It takes a long time to form a good habit

52. A slap on the wrist
(a) A mild punishment
(b) Punishing the wrong person
(c) To hit someone where it hurts the most
(d) To threaten someone

53. Wag the dog
(a) To divert attention from something of greater importance to something of lesser importance
(b) To be nice to someone if you want that person's loyalty
(c) To praise someone to get that person's love
(d) A small favour to a person who loves you matters a lot to that person

54. Scapegoat
(a) Animal sacrifice as an offering to God
(b) The most useful animal or person
(c) A lucky person who is forgiven for his crimes
(d) A person who is blamed for the mistakes of others

55. Water under the bridge
(a) To create solutions to overcome any problem
(b) Past events are no longer important
(c) Young days can never be brought back again
(d) Time keeps flowing endlessly

56. To go the extra mile
(a) To get an unexpected bonus
(b) To make a special effort to achieve something
(c) To lose one's way and walk aimlessly
(d) A vehicle which is very fuel efficient

57. A drop in the bucket
(a) So much silence that even a drop can be heard
(b) A very small amount compared with what is needed
(c) The final act before the task is done
(d) A small favour is worth a lot to a person in trouble

58. When it rains, it pours
(a) One getting much less than what one expected
(b) Calamity always occurs in bad times
(c) You always fall into trouble when you are least prepared
(d) When something bad occurs, it usually occurs more than once

59. Wear your heart on your sleeve
(a) A very bold person
(b) A noble pure person
(c) Make one's feelings apparent
(d) Being overtly polite at all times

60. To drink like a fish
(a) A person who spends a lot
(b) A person who keeps cheating for a very long time without getting noticed
(c) A person who needs to relive himself very frequently
(d) To drink excessive amounts of alcohol

Answers

Exercise 1

1 (b)	2 (d)	3 (a)	4 (c)	5 (c)	6 (d)	7 (b)	8 (b)	9 (b)	10 (a)
11 (b)	12 (a)	13 (c)	14 (d)	15 (d)	16 (c)	17 (a)	18 (b)	19 (b)	20 (d)
21 (a)	22 (d)	23 (d)	24 (b)	25 (c)	26 (a)	27 (c)	28 (b)	29 (d)	30 (b)
31 (a)	32 (b)	33 (b)	34 (d)	35 (a)	36 (a)	37 (b)	38 (b)	39 (a)	40 (b)
41 (b)	42 (c)	43 (d)	44 (c)	45 (b)	46 (c)	47 (d)	48 (a)	49 (b)	50 (c)
51 (a)	52 (c)	53 (d)	54 (d)	55 (d)	56 (a)	57 (c)	58 (a)	59 (b)	60 (c)
61 (b)	62 (d)	63 (a)	64 (a)	65 (a)	66 (d)	67 (d)	68 (b)	69 (a)	70 (c)
71 (d)	72 (b)	73 (d)	74 (a)	75 (a)					

Exercise 2

1 (b)	2 (b)	3 (c)	4 (a)	5 (c)	6 (d)	7 (a)	8 (c)	9 (c)	10 (d)
11 (c)	12 (c)	13 (a)	14 (b)	15 (c)	16 (d)	17 (c)	18 (b)	19 (d)	20 (b)
21 (b)	22 (d)	23 (c)	24 (c)	25 (c)	26 (d)	27 (c)	28 (a)	29 (d)	30 (c)
31 (c)	32 (c)	33 (a)	34 (b)	35 (a)	36 (a)	37 (a)	38 (d)	39 (b)	40 (c)
41 (b)	42 (d)	43 (c)	44 (b)	45 (d)	46 (c)	47 (d)	48 (a)	49 (d)	50 (c)
51 (c)	52 (a)	53 (a)	54 (d)	55 (b)	56 (b)	57 (b)	58 (d)	59 (c)	60 (d)

06 Prefix, Suffix

Prefix It is kind of syllable placed before the root of a word. For example Unhappy conists of prefix 'Un' which means not and root word is happy.

Suffix A suffix is a group of letters placed after the end of a word to form a new word.

For example Improvement Here the root word is improve and we have added suffix ment. To the addition of a suffix often changes a word from one part of speech to another.

Suffixes Used to Form Nouns

ee — Payee, examiness, employee
sion — submission, recession, discussion
al — survival, revival
ion — action, selection, attraction
ance — brilliance, acceptance, appearance
ment — improvement, payment
ar, er, or — beggar, actor, preacher, spectator
ery, ary, ory — victory, misery, missionary
ence — excellence, inncence, difference
ure — pleasure, treasure
mony — patrimony, harmony, testimony
dom — freedom
ship — friendship, studentship, hardship
ness — bitterness, sweetness
th — death, dearth, worth, growth
hood — manhood, womanhood, childhood
ty — cruelty, enemity, entity
ism — rationalism, communism
ing — riding, waiting, sleeping, gardening

Suffixes Used to Form Verbs

se — cleanse
ise/ize — memorise, fertilize, advertise
er — weaker, harder, quicker, broader, faster
fy — simplify, falsify, purify
ate — rotate, captivate, activate

Suffixes Used to Form Adjectives

ful — beautiful, hopeful, playful
some — winsome, wholesome, quarrelsome
less — fearless, cashless, jouless, cheerless
al — multinational, bilateral, loyal
ine — bovine, canine, feline
ate — fortunate, temperate, sedate
ary — necessary, customary
ly — cowardly, manly, glutlemanly, likely
en — woollen, golden, rotten
y — sundry, needy, sandy, ready
like — childlike, womanlike, slatelike
ish — womanish, childish, prudish
ic — phonetic, organic, cyclic, heroic
que — picturesque, grotesque, unique

Suffix 'ly' is Used with Adjective to make adverb

beautiful — beautifully
innocent — innocently
pleasant — pleasantly
hard — hardly
violent — violently

Prefixes Used to Form Verbs

em — empower, embody, embolden
be — bemoan, befriend, besiege,
en — enable, enlarge, entail, enslave, endanger
de — decode, defame, devalue, degrade
hyper — hyper active, hyper sensitive
ex — export, excessive, exonerate
Re — Return, Refund, Refuse, Reconsider, Rewrite
mis — misuse, misrepresent, mistook
dis — disappear, disappointment, dislike, dis disembark, disagree

Prefixes Used to Form Adjectives

Anti — Anticlockwise, anticlimax, antidote
Il — Illegal, Illegible, Illiterate, Ill-informed
Im — Impossible, Impatient, immobile, Impolite
In — Independent, incoherence, Incompatibility

Prefixes Used to Form Nouns

Auto — autobiography, automobile, autocorrect
Anti — Anti government, antiracist, antiwar
dis — discomfort, dislike
Inter — Interaction, Interference
Mal — Matreatment, matrutition
Mis — Misconduct, misdeed, Mismanagement
Mono — Monosyllable, monograph, Monogamy

Exercise

1. The Suffix in the word comfortable is
(a) for (b) table (c) able (d) ible
2. The Prefix in the word Irreligious is
(a) ar (b) Irr (c) Ir (d) Irre
3. What is the prefix in the word dissociate?
(a) Ate (b) Dis (c) Sociale (d) As
4. Which word below contains a suffix?
(a) Beauty (b) Empower
(c) Attraction (d) Export
5. Which word below contains a prefix?
(a) Uncle (b) Unhappy
(c) Under (d) Understand
6. Which suffix will form a word from 'dent' which means a person who fixes teeth.
(a) ic (b) ist (c) tion (d) atiou
7. What is the suffix in the word Reformation?
(a) on (b) mation
(c) ation (d) ion
8. Add the correct suffix to form a word from 'journal which means the writing and publishing of newspaper and magazine'.
(a) ist (b) ism (c) ly (d) ic
9. What suffix you will add in the noun Memory to make it a verb?
(a) able (b) ation (c) ize (d) ion
10. What prefix you will use to make the opposite of word 'credible?
(a) Un (b) em (c) In (d) Ir
11. What suffix you will use in the noun 'miser' to make it an adjective?
(a) able (b) y (c) ary (d) ent
12. What is the suffix which will be used to make noun 'captive' into a verb?
(a) se (b) ate (c) en (d) ize
13. What prefix you will add to the word 'active' to mean extremely energetic and active?
(a) de (b) un (c) hyper (d) re
14. The word missionary has a suffix. Find it out.
(a) nary (b) ary (c) ry (d) onary
15. The adjective 'beautiful' contain which suffix?
(a) iful (b) ul (c) tiful (d) ful

Directions (Q. Nos.16-20) complete the sentences by using a prefix or suffix.

16. In many countries it is .... legal to keep a gun in your house.
(a) un (b) il
(c) in (d) is
17. She is thinking of going back to university and taking a ....graduate course.
(a) post (b) under
(c) pro (d) for
18. You should not eat any food which is .... cooked.
(a) anti (b) under
(c) mis (d) up
19. She works in a/an .... national company which is headquartered in US
(a) in (b) inter
(c) multi (d) bi
20. Everyone was watching me and I felt very .... conscious.
(a) un (b) over
(c) self (d) pi

Answers

1. (c)	2. (c)	3. (b)	4. (c)	5. (b)	6. (b)	7. (c)	8. (b)	9. (c)	10. (c)
11. (a)	12. (b)	13. (c)	14. (b)	15. (d)	16. (b)	17. (a)	18. (b)	19. (b)	20. (c)

Unit-07

01 Figures of Speech

Introduction

Figures of speech are everywhere, from classical works like Shakespeare or the Bible, to everyday speech, pop music and television commercials. It makes the reader or listener use their imagination and understand much more than the plain words. It is the opposite of literal language. Literal language means exactly what it says. Figure of speech means something different to (and usually more than) what it says on the surface.

Figures of speech basically deal with the vehicles which primarily make the expression of language more beautiful and effective. In a traditional way, these devices have been described as poetic ornaments in a traditional way of analyzing the poem. The author in poetry, using these devices; metaphors, images, symbols, personification, etc. can deliver the message indirectly to the readers. As a result language becomes connotative and or referential. As we look at these figures of speech from linguistics point of view, we find them full of language features. A figure of speech is a way of saying something other than the literal way. It adds extra dimensions to language and reveals one thing by relating it to something else.

1. Simile

The word Simile comes from a Latin word 'similis' which means 'like' and 'likeness'. A simile, therefore, is an expression of likeness between different objects or events. It consists in placing two different thing side by side and comparing them with regard to some quality common to them. There are two essential elements in a simile. First, the two objects or events compared **must be different in kind.** Secondly, the **point of resemblance** between the different objects or events compared must be clearly brought out. The words as……as, so, like, such etc must be used.

For example:

(i) My brother is as brave as a lion.
(ii) She is delicate like a flower.
(iii) The younger brother is as good as gold.

2. Metaphor

The word Metaphor comes from the Greek word 'Meta' (means 'over') and 'Pherp' (means 'carry'). Thus, it literally means 'to carry over'. By this figure of speech the quality is transferred or carried over from the object to which it belongs or to the object which it refers to. A metaphor is a figure of speech that directly refers to one thing by mentioning another for rhetorical effect. It may provide clarity or identify hidden similarities between two ideas.

For example:

(i) My brother was **boiling mad**. (This implies he was too angry)
(ii) The assignment was a **breeze**. (This implies that the assignment was not difficult)
(iii) He was a **lion** on the battle field.

3. Alliteration

Alliteration is derived from Latin's 'Latira'. It means 'letters of alphabet'. It is a stylistic device in which a number of words, having the same first consonant sound, occur close together in a series. It is a device used to enhance the musical quality of the poetry.

Consider the following examples:

(i) **B**ut a **b**etter **b**utter makes a **b**utter **b**etter.
(ii) A **b**ig bully **b**eats a **b**aby **b**oy.

Both sentences are alliterative because the same first letter of words (B) occurs close together and produces alliteration in the sentence. An important point to remember here is that alliteration does not depend on letters but on sounds.

From Samuel Taylor Coleridge's 'The Rime of the Ancient Mariner'

'The fair breeze blew, the white foam flew,
The furrow followed free;
We were the first that ever burst
Into that silent sea.'

In the above lines we see alliteration ('b', 'f' and 's') in the phrases 'breeze blew', 'foam flew', 'furrow followed free', and 'silent sea'.

4. Assonance

The word is derived from the Latin phrase 'assonare', meaning to answer with the same sound. Assonance takes place when two or more words, close to one another repeat the same vowel sound, but start with different consonant sounds. Assonance can be used in all types of literature, but is commonly found in poetry. It also enhances the musical quality of the poetry. It also mirrors or changes the mood of a poem in order to match the subject matter. Beyond literature, assonance is also found in pop culture, especially in music.

For example:

(i) The early bird catches the worm.

(ii) Honesty is the best policy.

(iii) Let the cat out of the bag.

5. Personification

Personification is a type of metaphor and a common literary tool. It is when you assign the qualities of a person to something that isn't human or that isn't even alive, like nature or emotions. There are many reasons for using personification. It can be used as a method of describing something so that others can more easily understand it. It can be used to emphasize a point. It can be used to help paint a picture in your mind. You may in fact use personification without even knowing it.

For example:

(i) **Opportunity** knocks at the door but once.

(ii) **Death** lays his icy hands on kings.

(iii) **Nature** bemoaned the death of the bride.

6. Paradox

The term paradox is from the Greek word 'paradoxon', which means 'contrary to expectations, existing belief, or perceived opinion'. A statement that seems to say two opposite things which at first seem to be impossible but that may be true.

For example:

(i) I must be cruel to be kind. (How can an individual treat others kindly even when he is cruel?)

(ii) The child is father of the man. (How can a child be father of the man?)

(iii) Truth is honey, which is bitter. (How can honey be bitter?)

A paradox is often used in everyday speech as well to criticise an idea in order to show its faults or to provoke a new thought. In poetry, the use of paradox is not confined to mere wit and pleasure; rather, it becomes an integral part of poetic diction. Paradoxes are also a fun concept that can add a witty element to a situation or writing. They are interesting or amusing statements that contradict common beliefs and are sure to add intrigue to whatever situation they are used in.

Note Antithesis needs **two clauses/ sentences** to show opposition; oxymoron shows opposition in a **single phrase** and paradox shows opposition in a **single sentence**.

7. Hyperbole

'Hyper' means 'beyond' and 'ballo' means 'throw', thus it literally means 'a throwing beyond' or 'exaggeration'. It consists in represnting things as much greater or smaller than they really are with the intention of producing a more striking effect than a plain statement can.

For example:

(i) Why, man, if the rivers were dry, I am able to fill it with tears.

(ii) I had to wait in the station for ten days – an eternity.

(iii) His classmates laughed at him, saying he had a pea-sized brain.

By using hyperbole, a writer or a poet makes common human feelings remarkable and intense to such an extent that they do not remain ordinary. In literature, usage of hyperbole develops contrasts. When one thing is described with an over-statement, and the other thing is presented normally, a striking contrast is developed. This technique is employed to catch the reader's attention.

8. Irony

In Greek, 'eiron' meant 'a dissembler — someone who hides their true intentions'. Irony is a figure of speech in which words are used in such a way that their intended meaning is different from the actual meaning of the words. It may also be a situation that ends up in quite a different way than what is generally anticipated. In simple words, it is a difference between appearance and reality.

For example:

(i) 'Go ask his name: if he be married.
My grave is like to be my wedding bed.'
(Here 'grave' is ironical)

(ii) 'Here under leave of Brutus and the rest
(for Brutus is an honourable man
So are they, all honourable man)
Come I to speak in Caeser's funeral....'
(Use of 'honourable' here is ironical)

Exercise

Directions (1-29) Choose the best answers from the given option.

1. What kind of figure of speech is a direct comparison of two unlike things without using like and as?
(a) Paradox (b) Oxymoron
(c) Metaphor (d) Simile

2. A rich man is no richer than a poor man is an example of?
(a) Metonymy (b) Onomatopoeia
(c) Irony (d) Antithesis

3. The camel is the ship of the desert.
(a) Metaphor (b) Simile
(c) Oxymoron (d) Epigram

4. Death lays its icy hands on Kings.
(a) Epigram (b) Antithesis
(c) Metaphor (d) Personification

5. Life is as tedious as a twice-told tale.
(a) Simile (b) Metaphor
(c) Hyperbole (d) Apostrophe

6. Variety is the spice of life.
(a) Metaphor (b) Simile
(c) Hyperbole (d) Antithesis

7. Pride goeth forth on horseback, grand and gay
(a) Personification
(b) Hyperbole
(c) Apostrophe
(d) Metaphor

8. Here is the smell of blood still; all the perfumes of Arabia will not sweeten this little hand.
(a) Hyperbole (b) Antithesis
(c) Personification (d) Metaphor

9. What is the term for repetition of consonant sounds?
(a) Allegory (b) Alliteration
(c) Anapest (d) Aside

10. My love is like a red, red rose.
(a) Personification
(b) Metaphor
(c) Simile
(d) Paradox

11. She hangs like a star in the dew of our song.
(a) Metaphor (b) Simile
(c) Irony (d) Personification

12. Look like the innocent flower.
(a) Personification
(b) Metaphor
(c) Simile (d) Paradox

13. Life is a tale told by an idiot.
(a) Personification
(b) Metaphor
(c) Simile (d) Paradox

14. Life is but a walking shadow.
(a) Metaphor (b) Simile
(c) Irony (d) Personification

15. Hope is the poor man's bread.
(a) Simile (b) Metaphor
(c) Irony (d) Personification

16. Opportunity knocks at the door but once.
(a) Irony (b) Simile
(c) Metaphor (d) Personification

17. This sea that bares her bosom to the moon.
(a) Personification
(b) Simile
(c) Irony (d) Metaphor

18. Truth sits upon the lips of dying men.
(a) Metaphor (b) Simile
(c) Irony (d) Personification

19. Live like a hermit.
(a) Paradox (b) Metaphor
(c) Simile (d) Personification

20. She skims like a bird on the foam of a stream.
(a) Personification
(b) Metaphor
(c) Simile
(d) Paradox

21. The city's voice itself is soft like solitude's.
(a) Personification
(b) Simile
(c) Metaphor
(d) Paradox

22. Life is as tedious as a twice-told tale.
(a) Metaphor (b) Simile
(c) Personification (d) Paradox

23. She is the pillar of the state.
(a) Personification
(b) Metaphor
(c) Paradox
(d) Simile

24. If you wish to preserve your secret, wrap it up in frankness."
(a) Paradox (b) Metaphor
(c) Simile (d) Personification

25. "I have found the paradox, that if you love until it hurts, there can be no more hurt, only more love."
(a) Personification
(b) Metaphor
(c) Simile
(d) Paradox

26. "War is peace."
"Freedom is slavery."
"Ignorance is strength."
(a) Personification
(b) Metaphor
(c) Paradox (d) Simile

27. I posted a video on YouTube about how boring and useless YouTube is.
(a) Personification
(b) Metaphor
(c) Irony
(d) Paradox

28. The name of Britain's biggest dog was 'Tiny'.
(a) Personification
(b) Irony
(c) Simile
(d) Paradox

29. You laugh at a person who slipped stepping on a banana peel, and the next thing you know, you've slipped too.
(a) Personification
(b) Metaphor
(c) Simile
(d) Irony

Answers

1. (d)	2. (c)	3. (a)	4. (d)	5. (a)	6. (a)	7. (a)	8. (a)	9. (b)	10. (c)
11. (b)	12. (c)	13. (b)	14. (a)	15. (b)	16. (d)	17. (a)	18. (d)	19. (c)	20. (c)
21. (b)	22. (b)	23. (b)	24. (a)	25. (d)	26. (c)	27. (c)	28. (d)	29. (d)	

01 Forms of Poetry

The Sonnet

- Sonnet is a short poem of fourteen lines expressing one single thought, feeling, sound or strain. It is of lyrical nature to be sung with a musical instrument.
- Sonnet is originally associated with the name of great Italian poet. Petrarch, the father of Sonnet-Italian or Petrarchan sonnet. Petrarchan Sonnet is composed of two parts–Octave (8 lines) and Sestet (6 lines).
- In England, sonnet writing began during the reign of Queen Elizabeth. Wyatt Surrey and Spenser were the earlier ones. Then came Shakespeare, he gave new structure, beauty and flexibility to the Sonnet.
- Shakespeare wrote 154 sonnets. This new form of Sonnet introduced by him is known as the Shakespearean or English Sonnet. It concludes with a couplet. (Second kind of Sonnet).
- After Shakespeare, there came up a third kind of Sonnet. It is a combination of two kinds of Sonnet - Petrarchan and English Sonnet. It is called Irregular Sonnet.
- Poets generally wrote 'sonnet sequences' all of which had the theme of 'Love'. Some poets, especially Milton, changed this practice of writing in sequences. Wordsworth took further liberties with the Italian Sonnet and broke up the rhyme scheme of the octave to be 'abba acca' in place of 'abba abba'.
- The sonnet was introduced to England by Wyatt and developed by Surrey and was there after, widely used, notably in the sonnet sequences of Shakespeare, Sidney, Spenser and other poets of the Golden period.

The Elegy

- The Elegy is a poem of mourning or sorrow. It is often written on the death of a person.
- It is full of pathetic feelings. Sometimes the poet discusses some philosophical thought in place of giving expression to his personal grief.
- The Elegy is a mourning song in which the poet mourns the death of some friend or relative. It is as spontaneous as a lyric and like the ode.
- The Elegy is often serious and philosophical in tone. It is a poem of serious, pensive or reflective mood in memory of something loved and lost.
- In the current literary language, an elegy is a short lyric of the poet's lament or expression of sorrow over the death of someone dear. Its theme must be reflective and melancholic.
- 'Elegy on the Death of a Mad Dog' and 'In Memoriam' are the best examples of elegy.
- The Elegy can be divided into two parts :
  (i) Personal Elegy
  (ii) Impersonal Elegy

The Ode

- The ode may be defined as "a rhymed lyric often in the form of an address, generally dignified or exalted in subject and style."
- Its theme may be an important public event like a National Jubilee, the death of a distinguished personage, the commemoration of the founding of a great university etc.
- Like its parent form, the lyric, an ode is of Greek origin. It is dignified and exalted in tone.
- There are four kinds of ode – Pindaric Ode, Horatian ode, Regular or Irregular ode.
- An ode is longer than lyric, but it is the result of hard labour, not spontaneous. It is always serious and elevated in tone.

The Lyric

- Lyric was most popular form of poetry during the 16th century.
- A lyric is a short poem. The word 'Lyric' is derived from the Greek work 'lyre' a musical instrument.
- It is personal in mood and emotions.
- The first great poet who introudced lyric in English literature in England was Sir Thomas Wyatt.
- In the beginning lyrics were composed by ancient Greeks. The greatest writers of lyrics were Pindar, Aeschylus and Sopocles.

- Ben Jonson has written a number of lyrics that are ideal and superb. The subject matter of a lyric is emotion and feeling, it appeals more to the heart than to the intellect.
- It is a subjective poem. It has a simple and single emotion. In English lyric there is powereful personal emotion.

The Satire

- The word satire is derived from the Greek word 'Satyrs', a type of Greek comedy.
- Satire is a technique or literacy device which is used by the writer to criticise or expose something.
- Satire has been also called the oldest form of Social Commentary.
- The writer uses fictional characters in a satire but they stand for real characters or people to expose and condemn the ills prevailing in the society.
- Satirist uses irony and humour to emphasise the flaws prevalent in a sociely.
- People may pick up a satirical book or watch a satirical movie hoping to be entertained but end up thinking about issues and perspectives they never thought of before.
- The writer's intention of using satire is improving society by criticising their follies and foibles. The writer sees a problem and wants it corrected. Alexander Pope's 'Rape of Lock' and George orwell's 'Animal Farm' are perfect example of satires in literature.

Blanks Verse

- "Blank verse" is a literary term that refers to poetry written in unrhymed but metered lines, almost always iambic pentameter.
- "Iambic pentameter" refers to the meter of the poetic line: a line of poetry written this way is composed of five "iambs," groups of two syllables that fall into an "unstres sed-stressed" pattern: famously, like a heartbeat: buh -BUM, buh-BUM.
- Traditionally – say, in a Shakespeare sonnet – lines of iambic pentameter are then combined with end-rhymes to create various rhyming patterns.
- You can hear this very clearly in the famous opening quatrain -- the first four lines -- of Shakespeare's Sonnet 18:"Shall I compare thee to a summer's day?Thou are more lovely and more temperate.Rough winds do shake the darling buds of May;And summer's lease hath all too short a date"
- Blank verse is not a recent invention: Christopher Marlowe and Shakespeare, among others, popularized the use of blank verse in their plays. But the most famous early example of a poem composed in blank verse is without a doubt John Milton's epic masterpiece, Paradise Lost, which appeared in its twelve-book form in 1674.
- In a prefatory note to the poem, Milton explains that he has chosen to write Paradise Lost in what he calls "English heroic verse without rhyme" – that is, in unrhymed iambic pentameter.
- And Milton says that he's done so because Homer and Virgil wrote their epics in unrhymed Greek and Latin, respectively.
- So Milton is very much setting himself up as their successor. Rhyme, he goes on, was "the invention of a barbarous age, to set off wretched matter and lame meter." Some of Milton's co ntemporaries use it pretty well, he admits, but he still finds that they do so because they are "carried away by custom, but much to their own vexation, hindrance and constraint to express many things otherwise, and for the most part worse than else they w ould have expressed them."

Form of Stanza

In poetry, a stanza is a division of four or more lines having a fixed length, meter or rhyming scheme. Stanza divides a poem in such a way that does not harm its balance but rather it adds beauty to the symmetry of a poem. Moreover, it allows poets to shift their moods and present different subject matters in their poems. Stanzas are a series of lines grouped together and separated by an empty line from other stanzas. They are the equivalent of a paragraph in an essay. One way to identify a stanza is to count the number of lines.

Traditional English language poems have the following kinds of stanzas

(i) **Couplet** It consists of two rhyming lines having the same meter.

(ii) **Tercet** A tercet comprises three lines following a same rhyming scheme a a a or have a rhyming pattern a b a. Sir Thomas Wyatt introduced tercet in 16th century.

(iii) **Quatrain** It is a form of stanza having four lines popularised by a Persian poet, Omar Khayyam, who called it a Rubai. It has common rhyming schemes a a a a, a a b b, a b a b.

(iv) **Quintain** It also referred to as cinquain is a stanza of five lines which may be rhymed or unrhymed and has a typical stress pattern. Its invention is attributed to Crapsey.

(v) **Sestet** It is a kind of stanza that consists of six lines. It is the second division of Italian or sonnets of Petrarch following an octave or the first division comprising eight lines.

Rhyme

A rhyme is a repetition of similar sounding words occurring at the end of lines in poems or songs. A rhyme is a tool utilising repeating patterns that brings rhythm or musicality in poems which differentiate them from prose which is plain. A rhyme is employed for the specific purpose of rendering a pleasing effect to a poem which makes its recital an enjoyable experience. For example

Had we but world enough, and time,
"This coyness, lady, were no crime.
We would sit down and think which way,
To walk and pars our long love's day."

Syllable Division

Syllable division is the process of breaking words into smaller units called syllables, where each unit contains at least one vowel sound. Understanding how to divide syllables helps with pronunciation, reading, and spelling.

Basic Rules of Syllable Division

(i) Every syllable must have at least one vowel sound (a, e, i, o, u, and sometimes y). For example: apple ? ap/ple

(ii) Divide between two consonants when they come between two vowels (VC/CV rule). For example: basket ? bas/ket

(iii) A single consonant between vowels usually joins the second vowel (if the first vowel is long, V/CV rule; if short, VC/V rule). Fro example: tiger ? ti/ger, lemon ? lem/on

(iv) Do not split consonant blends or digraphs (e.g., sh, ch, th, bl, cl). For example: thunder ? thun/der

(v) Prefixes and suffixes form separate syllables. For example: unhappy ? un/hap/py

(vi) Words ending in -le form a separate syllable with the preceding consonant. For example: candle ? can/dle

Examples of Syllable Division

(i) Basket ? bas/ket (VC/CV rule)

(ii) Tiger ? ti/ger (V/CV rule)

(iii) Wonderful ? won/der/ful (r-controlled syllable)

(iv) Unhappy ? un/hap/py (prefix + root)

(v) Candle ? can/dle (-Cle syllable rule) .

Importance of Syllable Division

(i) Improves pronunciation by helping with word breakdown.

(ii) Enhances reading fluency by making words easier to recognize.

(iii) Aids spelling by identifying patterns in words.

(iv) Develops phonemic awareness, strengthening language skills.

(v) Syllable division is a fundamental skill for reading and writing, helping learners break down and understand words more effectively.

Exercise

The Sonnet

1. What is Sonnet?
(a) A prose of special nature
(b) A sacred poem of a reputed poet
(c) A poem of fourteen lines
(d) A criticism of a poet

2. How many lines does a sonnet have?
(a) 10 (b) 14 (c) 12 (d) 15

3. The sonnet is known to have originated in
(a) Spain (b) Greece
(c) England (d) Italy

4. The word 'sonnet' comes from .... origin.
(a) Greek (b) Spanish
(c) Latin (d) Italian

5. There are .... types of sonnets.
(a) three (b) two (c) four (d) five

6. Who was the first one to use sonnet in England?
(a) Shakespeare
(b) Petrarch
(c) Milton
(d) Sir Thomas Wyatt

7. .... was the first to use this form of lyric to express his love for his beloved Lauka.
(a) Petrarch (b) Shakespeare
(c) Milton (d) Earl of Surrey

8. Petrarchan sonnet has two parts
(a) Octave and sestet
(b) Quatrains and couplet
(c) Octave and couplet
(d) Quatrains and sestet

9. There are............... lines in octave of Petrarchan sonnet.
(a) ten (b) eight (c) six (d) four

10. The octave of Petrarchan sonnet presents a ....
(a) question/problem
(b) describes something
(c) confesses mistake
(d) addresses someone

11. The rhyming scheme of sestet is ....
(a) cde cde (b) cd cd ef
(c) cd ef ef (d) cd cd cd

12. Petrarchan sonnet is also called ....
(a) the Shakespearean Sonnet
(b) the Miltonic Sonnet
(c) the Jacobian Sonnet
(d) None of these

13. In which year were Shakespeare's sonnets first published?
(a) 1600 (b) 1609 (c) 1619 (d) 1630

14. How many sonnets does Shakespeare's collection contain?
(a) 154 (b) 160
(c) 164 (d) 170

15. What are the last two lines of a Shakespearean sonnet called?
(a) Quatrain (b) Triple
(c) Couplet (d) Sestet

16. How is the rhyme's scheme of the couplet represented?
(a) gg (b) ab (c) cc (d) ee

17. Shakespeare's sonnets are addressed to
(a) Queen Elizabeth
(b) A Dark lady
(c) Mr W.H.
(d) Both (b) and (c)

18. This type of sonnet is made up of three quatrains and one couplet.
(a) Petrarchan sonnet
(b) Free verse
(c) Shakespearean sonnet
(d) Poetry

19. The main characteristic of sonnet are
(a) highly personal
(b) in form of love song
(c) musical and addressed to someone
(d) All of the above

20. Spenserian sonnet is an important varient of
(a) Petrarchan Sonnet
(b) Shakespearean Sonnet
(c) Classical Sonnet
(d) None of the above

21. Faerie Queene is written in the form of
(a) Petrarchan Sonnet
(b) Spenserian Sonnet
(c) Shakespearean Sonnet
(d) Miltonic Sonnet

22. Spenser's motto in writing his Faerie Queene was
(a) to please and humour Queen Elizabeth
(b) to justify holiness as the greatest virtue
(c) to save the honour of womanhood
(d) to fashion a gentleman in virtuous and gentle discipline

23. The last six lines of a Miltonic Sonnet are divided into two groups of three lines each what is the group of three lines called
(a) Tercet (b) Tricet
(c) Triplet (d) Trilet

24. The rhyming scheme 'abab bcbc, cd cd, ee' belongs to
(a) Miltonic Sonnet
(b) Petrarchan Sonnet
(c) Spenserian Sonnet
(d) Shakespearean Sonnet

The Elegy

25. An Elegy is a type of lyric and focusses on expressing emotions and thoughts using
(a) heroic couplet
(b) an octave and a sestet
(c) formal language and structure
(d) alliteration

26. An Elegy is a
(a) historical poem
(b) figurative story
(c) song of lamentation
(d) short story

27. Which is a special kind of lyrics?
(a) Sonnet (b) Ode
(c) Elegy (d) Epic

28. The best elegies are characterised by
(a) personal sorrow to general sorrow of mankind
(b) a gentle melancholy
(c) dignified and solemn in tone
(d) All of the above

29. The first elegy was written by
(a) Thomas Gray (b) Spenser
(c) Milton (d) John Donne

30. The elegy 'Astrophel' is about
(a) the death of Sir Philip Sidney
(b) the death of villagers
(c) the death of Sir Richard
(d) None of these

31. Tennyson's 'In Memoriam' is a good example of
(a) Impersonal elegy
(b) Personal elegy
(c) Pastoral elegy
(d) None of the above

32. 'Elegy written in a Country Churchyard' was written by
(a) Tennyson (b) Thomas Gray
(c) Milton (d) P.B. Shelley

33. A pastoral elegy is a lament of a
(a) poet (b) villager
(c) king (d) shepherd

34. An elegy written with a particular convention and rural background, is called
(a) Pastoral elegy
(b) Personal elegy
(c) Impersonal elegy
(d) None of these

35. In England, pastoral elegies have been written down from
(a) the restoration age
(b) the renaissance age
(c) the victorian age
(d) the romantic age

36. Milton's Lycidas is
(a) a lyric
(b) a sonnet
(c) a pastoral elegy
(d) a personal elegy

37. Elegy is said to be originated from
(a) Greek (b) England
(c) Italy (d) France

38. An elegy is a brief lyric of
(a) ceremony (b) religious event
(c) mourning (d) None of these

39. What is Sidney's Arcadia?
(a) A pastoral verse tale
(b) A pastoral romance
(c) A pastoral elegy
(d) A pastoral lyric

40. Shelley wrote a Pastoral Elegy on the death of Keats, what is its title?
(a) Lycidas
(b) Endymion
(c) Adonais
(d) Thyrsis

The Ode

41. An ode is generally defined as a serious long poem in which the poet pours out his
(a) aspirations (b) anger
(c) horror (d) terror

42. Ode is a type of
(a) lyrical verse
(b) short poem
(c) narrative poem
(d) non-narrative poem

43. Classical ode or Pindaric ode is structured in three major parts
(a) Strophe, Antistrophe, Epode
(b) Strophe, Epode, Antistrophe
(c) Epode, Strophe, Antistrophe
(d) Antistrophe, Epode, Strophe

44. Strophe forms the .... part of ode.
(a) first
(b) second
(c) third
(d) fourth

45. Pindaric ode's another name is
(a) The Dorian Ode
(b) Horatian Ode
(c) Irregular Ode
(d) Regular Ode

46. Pindaric Odes were written for
(a) the honour of victory
(b) the mourning
(c) singing in simple and sober style
(d) None of the above

47. .... is the example of Pindaric ode.
(a) The progress of Poesy
(b) The Bard
(c) Both (a) and (b)
(d) None of the above

48. The most common rhyme scheme of English ode is
(a) ababcdecde
(b) aa bb cc dd
(c) abbai, abba
(d) Both (a) and (b)

49. Ode is a poem that written for an
(a) occasion
(b) religion
(c) Both (a) and (b)
(d) None of the above

50. The forms of odes are
(a) Pindaric, Horatian and irregular
(b) Irregular, Horatian
(c) Pindaric and Horatian
(d) Both (a) and (c)

51. The earliest odes in the English literature were
(a) Epithalamion, Prothalamion by Spenser
(b) Ode to evening by Collins
(c) Ode to Nightingale by Keats
(d) None of the above

52. Horatian ode is also known as
(a) The Dorian ode
(b) The Irregular ode
(c) Lesbian ode
(d) The English ode

53. Dryden's 'ode on solitude' is an example of
(a) Pindaric ode (b) Horatian ode
(c) Irregular ode (d) None of these

54. Romantic ode expresses
(a) personal emotions
(b) emotional and romantic responses
(c) patriotism and national adoration
(d) None of the above

55. The greatest writer of victorian ode is
(a) Wordsworth (b) Watson
(c) Collins (d) Tennyson

56. 'Ode to West Wind' is written by
(a) Shelley (b) Keats
(c) Wordsworth (d) Tennyson

57. 'Couch' is an ode singing of
(a) the old glories of the past
(b) death of the duke of Wellington
(c) celebrations
(d) victory

58. Which one is known as the irregular ode?
(a) Strophe (b) Anti-strophe
(c) Epode (d) Cowleyan ode

59. Cowleyan ode was established by
(a) Horace (b) Abraham Cowley
(c) Pindar (d) Collins

60. John Keats 'Ode to Autumn' is a .... ode.
(a) Pindaric (b) Horatian
(c) Cowleyan (d) None of these

61. Which one is known as the Regular ode?
(a) Strophe (b) Anti strophe
(c) Epode (d) None of these

62. Which odes were generally written for public occasions?
(a) Pindaric odes
(b) Horatian odes
(c) Cowleyan odes
(d) None of the above

63. What is the most distinctive feature of an ode?
(a) It is longer than a lyric
(b) It is in the form of an address
(c) It is written on a sublime subject
(d) It is written on a historical theme

64. Who is the most important poet who has written Pindaric Odes in English?
(a) Thomas Gray (b) John Keats
(c) PB Shelley (d) Walter Scott

65. Who is the poet of an 'ode to himself'?
(a) Abraham Cowley
(b) John Donne
(c) Ben Jonson
(d) Robert Herrick

66. This is a form of a classical ode
(a) Gray's odes
(b) Pindaric ode
(c) Shelley's Adonais
(d) None of the above

67. Odes had originated in religious celebrations and were performed at
(a) festivals and other important occasions
(b) stage
(c) classrooms
(d) parties hall

68. Odes normally included the following
(a) Prayers or praise to the Gods
(b) Stories or myth from the heroic past
(c) Moral maxims and personal references
(d) All of the above

The Satire

69. The word satire is derived from
(a) French word (b) Greek word
(c) English word (d) Sanskrit word

70. A satire uses what type of characters in satire?
(a) Real character
(b) Religious characters
(c) Fictional characters
(d) None of these

71. The purpose of satire is.......
(a) to make people laugh
(b) to provide philosophical thoughts
(c) just a causal reading
(d) to expose the problem prevailing in society

72. The writer users satire in his writing with the intertion of
(a) criticism only
(b) entertaining people
(c) bringing improvement
(d) make people think

73. Which are two main components of satire?
(a) Ornamental language and poetry
(b) Irony and humour
(c) Preaching and logical explanation
(d) Use of Lyrics and dramatisation

74. Which best describes the relationship between Impersonation and satire?
(a) Impersonation and satire are synonyms
(b) Impersonation is a tool of satire
(c) Impersonation is opposite of satire
(d) Satire is a tool of impersonation.

75. Which is not a type of satire?
(a) Hovation (b) Juvenalism
(c) Calm (d) Menippean

76. Alexander Pope's 'Rape of the Lock' is an example of ......
(a) parody
(b) Romantic literature
(c) satire
(d) ironic

77. Who wrote 'Animal Farm'– (a satire)?
(a) Tennyson
(b) Jonathan Swift
(c) George Or Well
(d) Bernard Shaw

Blanks Verse

78. Blank verse is iambic pentameter
(a) without rhyme
(b) with rhyme
(c) with alternate rhyme
(d) without alternate rhyme

79. How many syllables are usually in a line of blank verse?
(a) 5 (b) 8 (c) 10 (d) 12

80. Blank verse is made up of .... iams, a specific kind of metric foot.
(a) 1 (b) 2 (c) 4 (d) 5

81. Which of the following characteristics defines blank verse?
(a) It is written in unrhymed lines of iambic pentameter.

(b) It is written in rhymed couplets.
(c) It uses a specific number of syllables per line, usually ten, but follows no specific meter.
(d) It is written in free verse with no particular meter or rhyme scheme.

82. Which of the following is the main characteristics of blank verse?
(a) It has a rhyme scheme.
(b) It consists of unrhymed lines in iambic pentameter.
(c) It follows a strict pattern of stressed and unstressed syllables, but rhymes.
(d) It is written in free verse with no specific structure.

83. From the given options,.Blank verse is most commonly associated with which type of literature?
(a) Prose poetry
(b) Classical tragedies and Shakespearean drama
(c) Limericks
(d) Haiku

84. What does "iambic pentameter" refer to in blank verse?
(a) A meter with ten stressed syllables per line.
(b) A meter with five stressed syllables per line.
(c) A meter with five pairs of unstressed and stressed syllables.
(d) A line of poetry that contains exactly 10 syllables with no stress pattern.

85. Which of the following is an example of blank verse?
(a) "Shall I compare thee to a summer's day?"
(b) "To be or not to be, that is the question."
(c) "The cat sat on the mat."
(d) "Once upon a midnight dreary, while I pondered, weak and weary."

86. Which of the following authors is most famous for using blank verse in his plays?
(a) Charles Dickens
(b) William Shakespeare
(c) Edgar Allan Poe
(d) Emily Dickinson

87. Blank verse is most commonly used in which of the following genres?
(a) Epic poetry
(b) Drama, especially tragedies
(c) Narrative fiction
(d) Sonnet

88. Which of the following is true about blank verse?
(a) It consists of rhymed couplets.
(b) It is written in iambic pentameter without rhyme.
(c) It has no specific rhythm or meter.
(d) It is always written in four-line stanzas.

89. Blank verse is most commonly used in which type of work?
(a) Epic poetry (b) Comic verse
(c) Dramatic plays (d) Haikus

90. What distinguishes blank verse from heroic couplets?
(a) Blank verse is written in iambic pentameter, but heroic couplets are written in pairs of rhyming lines.
(b) Blank verse is always written with 14 lines, but heroic couplets are written with 10 lines.
(c) Blank verse is used only in drama, while heroic couplets are used in poetry.
(d) Blank verse is written in quatrains, while heroic couplets are written in stanzas.

Stanza

91. A stanza is a group of lines in a poem, similar to a ____ in prose.
(a) Sentence (b) Paragraph
(c) Word (d) Letter

92. A two-line stanza called?
(a) Quatrain (b) Couplet
(c) Tercet (d) Sestet

93. A three-line stanza is known as a ....
(a) Tercet (b) Quatrain
(c) Cinquain (d) Sestet

94. From the given options,. Which stanza form consists of four lines?
(a) Octave (b) Tercet
(c) Quatrain (d) Couplet

95. A five-line stanza is called a ....
(a) Cinquain (b) Quatrain
(c) Septet (d) Sestet

96. A stanza with six lines is known as a ....
(a) Sestet (b) Quintain
(c) Octave (d) Couplet

97. Which stanza type consists of eight lines?
(a) Octave (b) Tercet
(c) Quatrain (d) Couplet

98. What is a seven-line stanza called?
(a) Heptastich
(b) Quintain
(c) Sonnet
(d) Limerick

99. A stanza with only one line is called a ....
(a) Monostich
(b) Singleton
(c) Lineverse
(d) Verselet

100. The rhyme scheme of a Shakespearean sonnet?
(a) ABABCDCDEFEFGG
(b) ABBAABBA CDECDE
(c) AABBAA
(d) AABBCC

101. A stanza with alternating lines of iambic tetrameter and iambic trimeter is called a ____.
(a) Villanelle (b) Ballad stanza
(c) Haiku (d) Ottava Rima

102. Which stanza form is commonly used in limericks?
(a) Quatrain (b) Couplet
(c) Quintain (d) Sestet

103. The Spenserian stanza consists of how many lines?
(a) 7 (b) 8
(c) 9 (d) 10

104. Which stanza form follows the rhyme scheme ABABBCC?
(a) Ottava Rima (b) Terza Rima
(c) Rhyme Royal (d) Limerick

105. A Villanelle consists of how many stanzas?
(a) 3 (b) 5
(c) 6 (d) 7

106. Ottava Rima has which rhyme scheme?
(a) ABABABCC (b) ABCABC
(c) AABBCC (d) ABBAABBA

107. What is the common rhyme scheme of a quatrain?
(a) ABAB (b) AABB
(c) ABCB (d) All of these

108. A Haiku follows which syllable pattern?
(a) 5-7-5 (b) 7-5-7
(c) 5-5-7 (d) 7-7-7

109. What is the final stanza of a Villanelle called?
(a) Couplet (b) Quatrain
(c) Sestet (d) Tercet

110. The Petrarchan sonnet consists of how many lines?
(a) 10 (b) 12 (c) 14 (d) 16

111. The rhyme scheme of a Limerick is ....
(a) ABAB (b) ABCB
(c) AABBA (d) AABBCC

112. What is a stanza called in free verse poetry?
(a) Verse paragraph
(b) Couplet
(c) Quatrain
(d) Tercet

113. Which poet popularized the Rhyme Royal stanza?
(a) Geoffrey Chaucer
(b) William Blake
(c) John Keats
(d) William Wordsworth

114. The heroic couplet is written in which meter?
(a) Trochaic tetrameter
(b) Iambic pentameter
(c) Dactylic hexameter
(d) Anapestic trimeter

115. Which stanza form is used in Dante's "Divine Comedy"?
(a) Villanelle
(b) Terza Rima
(c) Spenserian Stanza
(d) Rhyme Royal

116. A poem that consists of 14 lines is called a:
(a) Haiku (b) Sonnet
(c) Limerick (d) Ballad

117. A stanza that repeats at intervals in a poem, similar to a chorus, is called a:
(a) Verse (b) Refrain
(c) Line break (d) Tercet

118. The first eight lines of a Petrarchan sonnet are called:
(a) Couplet (b) Sestet
(c) Octave (d) Tercet

119. A stanza that contains a question-answer pattern is often found in:
(a) Haiku (b) Ballad
(c) Elegy (d) Limerick

120. The common rhyme scheme of a Shakespearean sonnet's final two lines is:
(a) AA (b) AB
(c) CC (d) BB

121. A stanza form that follows an AABBA rhyme scheme is most commonly found in:
(a) Haiku (b) Villanelle
(c) Limerick (d) Sonnet

122. What is the name of a poem that is composed entirely of quatrains?
(a) Ballad (b) Haiku
(c) Free Verse (d) Sonnet

123. Which poetic form consists of five tercets and a quatrain?
(a) Haiku
(b) Villanelle
(c) Rhyme Royal
(d) Ottava Rima

124. What type of poem often consists of quatrains with an ABCB rhyme scheme?
(a) Limerick (b) Haiku
(c) Ballad (d) Sonnet

125. What is the primary characteristic of blank verse?
(a) Rhyming quatrains
(b) Unrhymed iambic pentameter
(c) Free verse
(d) Fixed syllabic pattern

126. Which stanza form follows the rhyme scheme ABABBCBCC?
(a) Rhyme Royal
(b) Ottava Rima
(c) Spenserian Stanza
(d) Terza Rima

127. A Petrarchan sonnet is divided into how many stanzas?
(a) One (b) Two
(c) Three (d) Four

128. Which poetic form uses repeated refrains in a fixed pattern?
(a) Sestina (b) Villanelle
(c) Limerick (d) Haiku

129. The term "alexandrine" refers to a line of poetry that has:
(a) 8 syllables
(b) 10 syllables
(c) 12 syllables
(d) 14 syllables

130. In Rhyme Royal, the stanza consists of how many lines?
(a) 4 (b) 6
(c) 7 (d) 8

131. Which form of poetry follows a strict pattern of six stanzas of six lines each, with a final three-line stanza?
(a) Villanelle (b) Sestina
(c) Terza Rima (d) Rondeau

132. The term "terza rima" refers to a stanzaic pattern using which rhyme scheme?
(a) ABAB
(b) AABB
(c) ABA BCB CDC
(d) AABBCC

133. Which of the following poetic forms traditionally has unrhymed tercets?
(a) Haiku (b) Sonnet
(c) Ballad (d) Limerick

134. Which stanza form was frequently used by Lord Byron in "Don Juan"?
(a) Spenserian Stanza
(b) Ottava Rima
(c) Terza Rima
(d) Quatrain

135. What is the standard syllabic pattern of a Shakespearean sonnet?
(a) 8 syllables per line
(b) 10 syllables per line
(c) 12 syllables per line
(d) 14 syllables per line

136. Which poetic form consists of three quatrains followed by a couplet?
(a) Spenserian Sonnet
(b) Shakespearean Sonnet
(c) Petrarchan Sonnet
(d) Rondeau

137. The heroic couplet is commonly associated with which poet?
(a) John Milton
(b) Alexander Pope
(c) William Wordsworth
(d) Emily Dickinson

138. What is the rhyme scheme of a ballad stanza?
(a) AABB (b) ABAB
(c) ABCB (d) AAAB

139. In poetry, what does an "enjambment" mean?
(a) A break in the stanza
(b) A pause at the end of a line
(c) A line that continues without a pause to the next line
(d) A repeated refrain

140. What is the difference between blank verse and free verse?
(a) Blank verse has a fixed meter but no rhyme, while free verse has neither
(b) Blank verse is always rhymed, while free verse is not
(c) Free verse is more structured than blank verse
(d) Blank verse does not follow any rhythm

Rhyme

141. What is a rhyme scheme?
(a) The number of lines in a poem
(b) The pattern of rhymes at the end of lines
(c) The use of alliteration
(d) The way a poem is divided into stanzas

142. How is a rhyme scheme represented?
(a) Using numbers
(b) Using symbols
(c) Using letters
(d) Using words

143. What is the rhyme scheme of a Shakespearean sonnet?
(a) ABABBCBCDEE
(b) ABABCDCDEFEFGG
(c) AABBCCDD
(d) ABBAABBA

144. In the rhyme scheme ABAB, which lines rhyme?
(a) The first and second
(b) The first and third, second and fourth
(c) The second and third
(d) All four lines

145. What is the rhyme scheme of a limerick?
(a) AABB (b) AABBA
(c) ABAB (d) ABCB

146. Which of the following rhyme schemes is a couplet?
(a) ABAB (b) AABB
(c) ABCB (d) ABBA

147. What is a monorhyme?
(a) A poem where every line rhymes the same
(b) A poem with no rhyme
(c) A poem with alternating rhyme
(d) A poem with a repeating refrain

148. What is the rhyme scheme of the following stanza?
The moon is bright
It lights the night
The sky is high
With stars in sight
(a) AABB (b) AAAA
(c) ABAB (d) ABBA

149. What does an enclosed rhyme look like?
(a) AABB (b) ABAB
(c) ABBA (d) AAAA

150. Which poetic form uses ABA BCB CDC?
(a) Sonnet (b) Terza Rima
(c) Limerick (d) Free verse

151. What is the rhyme scheme of a Petrarchan sonnet?
(a) ABABCDCDEFEFGG
(b) ABBAABBACDCDCD
(c) AABBAA
(d) ABCABC

152. The last two lines of a Shakespearean sonnet are always a...
(a) Quatrain (b) Couplet
(c) Octave (d) Free verse

153. Which of these is NOT a common rhyme scheme?
(a) ABCD (b) ABAB
(c) AABB (d) ABBA

154. How many lines are in a limerick?
(a) 3 (b) 5 (c) 7 (d) 9

155. What is the rhyme scheme of this stanza?
The waves do rise upon the shore (A)
They crash and break with mighty roar (A)
The sky above is clear and bright (B)
A peaceful scene, a lovely sight (B)
(a) ABAB (b) AABB
(c) AAAA (d) ABCB

156. What is the rhyme scheme of a villanelle?
(a) ABA ABA ABA ABA ABA ABAA
(b) AABB CCDD
(c) ABBA ABBA CDECDE
(d) ABCABC

157. From the given options,What is a tercet?
(a) A four-line stanza
(b) A three-line stanza
(c) A two-line stanza
(d) A stanza with no rhyme

158. Which famous poet used terza rima?
(a) Shakespeare
(b) Dante Alighieri
(c) Emily Dickinson
(d) Robert Frost

159. What is the rhyme scheme of a haiku?
(a) AAA (b) AABB
(c) No set rhyme (d) ABAB

160. Which of these poetic forms usually has no rhyme scheme?
(a) Free verse (b) Limerick
(c) Sonnet (d) Villanelle

161. What is an eye rhyme?
(a) Words that look like they should rhyme but don't
(b) Words that rhyme perfectly
(c) Words that sound similar
(d) Words with opposite meanings

162. What is slant rhyme?
(a) A perfect rhyme
(b) A forced rhyme
(c) A near rhyme
(d) A rhyme that follows no pattern

163. Which type of rhyme scheme is common in nursery rhymes?
(a) ABAB (b) AABB
(c) ABCD (d) ABBA

164. Which is NOT a rhyme scheme used in sonnets?
(a) ABABCDCDEFEFGG
(b) AABBCCDD
(c) ABBAABBACDCDCD
(d) ABBAABBACDECDE

165. What is a ballad's rhyme scheme?
(a) ABAB or ABCB (b) AAAA
(c) ABBA (d) AABB

166. The rhyme scheme ABAB BCBC CDCD EE is found in what form?
(a) Lmerick
(b) Rondeau
(c) Spenserian sonnet
(d) Free verse

167. From the given options,What is internal rhyme?
(a) Rhymes inside a line
(b) Rhymes at the end of lines
(c) A repeated refrain
(d) Unrhymed poetry

168. Which poet is famous for using unconventional rhyme schemes?
(a) Shakespeare
(b) Emily Dickinson
(c) Edgar Allan Poe
(d) Robert Frost

169. A pantoum follows which pattern?
(a) ABAB BCBC CDCD DA
(b) AABB
(c) ABBAABBA
(d) AAAA

170. In a rondeau, which line is repeated?
(a) First line
(b) Last line
(c) Third line
(d) Every other line

Syllable Division

171. From the given options,How many syllables are in the word "elephant"?
(a) 1 (b) 2
(c) 3 (d) 4

172. What is a syllable?
(a) A group of letters
(b) A unit of pronunciation with at least one vowel sound
(c) A word with only consonants
(d) A complete sentence

173. How many syllables are in the word "banana"?
(a) 1 (b) 2
(c) 3 (d) 4

174. Which word has only one syllable?
(a) Water (b) Cat
(c) Banana (d) Elephant

175. Which word is divided correctly into syllables?
(a) Ap/ple (b) Appl/e
(c) A/pple (d) Ap/p/le

176. Which of these words is a compound word?
(a) Butterfly (b) Tiger
(c) Apple (d) Window

177. How many syllables are in the word "computer"?
(a) 1 (b) 2
(c) 3 (d) 4

178. Which word has two syllables?
(a) Dog (b) Table
(c) Butterfly (d) Elephant

179. Which of these is a closed syllable?
(a) Be (b) Hi
(c) Cat (d) Go

180. Which of the following words has an open syllable?
(a) Go (b) Hat
(c) Cup (d) Dog

181. Where do you divide the word "basket"?
(a) Ba/sket (b) Bask/et
(c) Bas/ket (d) B/asket

182. How do you divide "tiger" correctly?
(a) Tig/er (b) Ti/ger
(c) Tig/e/r (d) Ti/g/er

183. Which of these is a consonant-le syllable?
(a) Table (b) Happy
(c) Tiger (d) Window

184. Where should "rabbit" be divided?
(a) Rab/bit (b) Ra/bbit
(c) Rabb/it (d) R/abbit

185. What type of syllable is "hope" in "hopeful"?
(a) Closed
(b) Open
(c) Vowel-consonant-e
(d) R-controlled

186. How do you divide "music" correctly?
(a) Mu/sic (b) Mus/ic
(c) Mu/s/ic (d) M/u/sic

187. Which word follows the V/CV division pattern?
(a) Lemon (b) Robot
(c) Napkin (d) Basket

188. Where should "wonderful" be divided?
(a) Won/der/ful (b) Wo/nder/ful
(c) Wond/erful (d) Wonder/ful

189. What type of syllable is "star" in "starfish"?
(a) Open (b) Closed
(c) R-controlled (d) Vowel team

190. How do you divide "little"?
(a) Lit/tle (b) Li/ttle
(c) Litt/le (d) L/ittle

191. How do you divide "dining"?
(a) Din/ing (b) Di/ning
(c) Din/i/ng (d) D/ining

192. What is the correct syllable division for "family"?
(a) Fam/i/ly (b) Fa/mi/ly
(c) Fam/ily (d) Fam/i/l/y

193. Which word follows the VC/V rule?
(a) Paper (b) Lemon
(c) Table (d) Robot

Answers

1. (c)	2. (b)	3. (d)	4. (d)	5. (b)	6. (d)	7. (a)	8. (a)	9. (b)	10. (a)
11. (a)	12. (b)	13. (a)	14. (a)	15. (c)	16. (a)	17. (d)	18. (c)	19. (d)	20. (b)
21. (b)	22. (a)	23. (c)	24. (c)	25. (c)	26. (c)	27. (c)	28. (d)	29. (b)	30. (a)
31. (b)	32. (b)	33. (d)	34. (a)	35. (b)	36. (c)	37. (a)	38. (c)	39. (c)	40. (c)
41. (a)	42. (a)	43. (a)	44. (a)	45. (a)	46. (a)	47. (a)	48. (c)	49. (a)	50. (a)
51. (a)	52. (c)	53. (b)	54. (b)	55. (d)	56. (a)	57. (a)	58. (d)	59. (b)	60. (b)
61. (c)	62. (a)	63. (b)	64. (b)	65. (c)	66. (b)	67. (a)	68. (d)	69. (b)	70. (c)
71. (d)	72. (c)	73. (b)	74. (b)	75. (c)	76. (c)	77. (c)	78. (a)	79. (c)	80. (d)
81. (a)	82. (b)	83. (b)	84. (c)	85. (b)	86. (b)	87. (b)	88. (b)	89. (c)	90. (a)
91. (b)	92. (b)	93. (a)	94. (c)	95. (a)	96. (a)	97. (a)	98. (a)	99. (a)	100. (a)
101. (b)	102. (c)	103. (c)	104. (c)	105. (c)	106. (a)	107. (d)	108. (a)	109. (b)	110 (c)
111. (c)	112. (a)	113. (a)	114. (b)	115. (b)	116. (b)	117. (b)	118. (c)	119. (b)	120. (a)
121. (c)	122. (a)	123. (b)	124. (c)	125. (b)	126. (c)	127. (b)	128. (b)	129. (c)	130. (c)
131. (b)	132. (c)	133. (a)	134. (b)	135. (b)	136. (b)	137. (b)	138. (b)	139. (c)	140. (a)
141. (b)	142. (c)	143. (b)	144. (b)	145. (b)	146. (b)	147. (a)	148. (b)	149. (c)	150. (b)
151. (b)	152. (b)	153. (a)	154. (b)	155. (b)	156. (a)	157. (b)	158. (b)	159. (c)	160. (a)
161. (a)	162. (c)	163. (b)	164. (b)	165. (a)	166. (c)	167. (a)	168. (b)	169. (a)	170. (a)
171. (c)	172. (b)	173. (c)	174. (b)	175. (a)	176. (a)	177. (c)	178. (b)	179. (c)	180. (a)
181. (c)	182. (b)	183. (a)	184. (a)	185. (c)	186. (a)	187. (b)	188. (a)	189. (c)	190. (a)
191. (a)	192. (a)	193. (b)							

Unit-09

01 The Fun They Had

The story is a fictional account of how the schools and books will be in the future. It compares the educational system of today with that of the future. It is based on a young girl, Margie's diary entry dated 17th May, 2157.

In future, students will be taught alone at their homes in a room called the 'Schoolroom'. The human teachers of today's era will be replaced by mechanical teachers which can be adjusted as per the level of a student.

Important Characters

Margie मार्गी	A small 11 year old girl who is one of the main characters in the story. She is not happy with her schooling system and longs for a change in it. ग्यारह साल की एक छोटी लड़की जो कहानी में मुख्य पात्रों में से एक है। वह अपनी स्कूली शिक्षा प्रणाली से खुश नही है और उसमें बदलाव की इच्छा रखती है।
Tommy टॉमी	He is Margie's friend and thirteen years old. He found a real book from the old times. वह मार्गी का दोस्त है और उसकी उम्र तेरह वर्ष है। उसे पुराने समय की एक वास्तविक पुस्तक मिली।
Mrs. Jones मिसेज जोन्स	Mrs. Jones is Margie's mother who is strict about Margie's studies. मिसेज जोन्स, मार्गी की माँ है जो मार्गी की पढ़ाई के प्रति सख्त है।
Mechanical Teacher मैकेनिकल टीचर	The electronic teacher of Margie who has taught her everything. मार्गी का इलेक्ट्रॉनिक टीचर जिसने उसे सब कुछ सिखाया है।
County Inspector काउण्टी इन्स्पेक्टर	The computer engineer/expert who had adjusted Margie's mechanical teacher to her level. कम्प्यूटर इंजीनियर/विशेषज्ञ जिसने मार्गी के मैकेनिकल टीचर को उसके स्तर के अनुसार कर दिया था।

The characters of the story learn about the education system of the past and want to be a part of that. They do not like the mechanical teachers of their era which lack human interaction and fun. They rejoice at the feeling of being taught by a human teacher and wish to go to a school together with fellow students.

Summary of the Lesson पाठ का सार

Diary Entry by Margie and the Real Book

Margie, a 11 years little girl wrote a diary entry dated 17th May, 2157, titled "Today Tommy found a real book!". It was a very old book. Once Margie's grandfather had told her about the time when all stories were printed on paper.

Tommy found the book in the attic of his house. Margie and Tommy turned the pages of the book, which were yellow and crinkly (wrinkled). Margie found it funny to read the book as the words in it were not moving like they moved on her telebook.

Opinion about the Book

Tommy, a 13 year old boy, called the book a waste because after one time reading, it could be thrown away. Margie also felt the same way. They compared the book with their television screen which could have a million books on it and still had space for more. Moreover, it had not to be thrown away after reading.

मार्गी द्वारा डायरी प्रविष्टि (एंट्री) और वास्तविक पुस्तक

11 वर्ष की एक छोटी लड़की मार्गी ने 17 मई, 2157 दिनांक अंकित कर एक डायरी प्रविष्टि (एंट्री) लिखी जिसका शीर्षक था "आज टॉमी को एक वास्तविक पुस्तक मिली।" यह एक बहुत पुरानी पुस्तक थी। एक बार मार्गी के दादाजी ने उसे ऐसे समय के विषय में बताया था जब सभी कहानियाँ कागज पर छापी जाती थीं।

टॉमी को यह पुस्तक उसके घर की अटारी पर मिली थी। मार्गी और टॉमी ने पुस्तक के पन्ने पलटे, जो पीले और सलवटों भरे थे। मार्गी को यह पुस्तक पढ़ना हास्यास्पद लगा, क्योंकि इसमें शब्द चल नहीं रहे थे, जैसे वे उसकी टेलीबुक में चलते थे।

पुस्तक के बारे में विचार

13 वर्ष का लड़का, टॉमी, इस पुस्तक को व्यर्थ बताता है, क्योंकि इसे एक बार पढ़ने के बाद फेंका जा सकता था। मार्गी ने भी ऐसा ही महसूस किया। उन्होंने पुस्तक की तुलना अपनी टेलीविजन स्क्रीन के साथ की जिस पर दस लाख पुस्तकें हो सकती थीं और अभी भी ओर अधिक पुस्तकों के लिए जगह थी। इसके अलावा, इसे पढ़ने के बाद फेंकने की आवश्यकता भी नहीं थी।

Margie's Hatred about her School

Tommy told Margie that the book he found was about the school, but Margie showed no interest as Margie hated her school and her mechanical teacher.

Her mechanical teacher was large, black and ugly and had a big screen. All the lessons were shown on the screen and the questions were asked.

Margie hated the slot where she had to put her homework and test papers daily. She had to write them in a punch code which she had learned when she was 6 years old.

Margie's Poor Performance in the Tests

The mechanical teacher gave Margie test continuously in geography. She had not been doing well in the tests. Margie's mother, Mrs Jones, was worried about the poor performance of Margie in the tests. So, she called the County Inspector to find out the cause of Margie's poor performance.

The Arrival of the County Inspector

The County Inspector was a round little man, with red face. He carried a whole box of tools with dials and wires. Margie hoped that the County Inspector would not be able to fix the mechanical teacher and would take it with him. She was hoping this as Tommy's teacher was once taken away by the County Inspector for one month when there was a problem with history sector.

The Geography Sector Set Right

The County Inspector took the mechanical teacher out. He told Margie's mother that there was no fault of Margie. In fact, the geography sector was little too quick for Margie to read and understand.

He had fixed the geography sector by slowing down the speed according to the level of a 10 year-old child. He also told that the overall performance of Margie had been quite satisfactory.

Discussion about Old Schools

Tommy had a discussion with Margie after reading the book which described the schools of the past. The schools in the past were located in special buildings away from the students' houses.

The students were taught by human teachers. All the kids of the same age learnt the same thing. The teacher taught them lessons, asked questions and gave them homework. Margie wanted to know more about those funny schools, but it was the time for both Tommy and Margie to go to their school. So they decided to read the book later.

Margie's Schoolroom

Margie's schoolroom was located next to her bedroom. Her mechanical teacher was always on at the same time everyday except on Saturday and Sunday because her mother believed that little girls learned better if they learned at regular hours. On that day, the mechanical teacher was going to teach her a lesson on arithmetic about the addition of proper fractions but she was not interested in studying.

अपने स्कूल के प्रति मार्गी की घृणा

टॉमी ने मार्गी को बताया कि उसे जो पुस्तक मिली वह स्कूल के बारे में थी, लेकिन मार्गी ने कोई दिलचस्पी नहीं दिखाई, क्योंकि मार्गी अपने स्कूल और अपने मैकेनिकल टीचर से घृणा करती थी।

उसका मैकेनिकल टीचर बड़ा, काला और भद्दा था जिसकी एक बड़ी स्क्रीन थी। सभी पाठ स्क्रीन पर प्रदर्शित किए जाते थे और प्रश्न पूछे जाते थे।

मार्गी को उस दरार से नफरत थी जहाँ उसे रोजाना अपना गृहकार्य और टेस्ट पेपर डालने होते थे। उसे (मार्गी को), उन्हें एक पंच कोड में लिखना होता था जो उसने तब सीखा था जब वह 6 वर्ष की थी।

टेस्ट में मार्गी का खराब प्रदर्शन

मैकेनिकल टीचर ने मार्गी को लगातार भूगोल के टेस्ट दिए। वह टेस्ट में अच्छा नहीं कर रही थी। मार्गी की माँ, श्रीमती जोन्स, टेस्ट में मार्गी के खराब प्रदर्शन के विषय में चिंतित थी। इसलिए, मार्गी के खराब प्रदर्शन का कारण जानने के लिए उन्होंने काउण्टी इंस्पेक्टर को बुलावा भेजा।

काउण्टी इंस्पेक्टर का आगमन

काउण्टी इंस्पेक्टर एक लाल चेहरे वाला छोटे कद का गोल-मटोल सा व्यक्ति था। वह औजारों के साथ डायलों और तारों से भरा एक बक्सा लिए हुए था। मार्गी को उम्मीद थी, कि काउण्टी इंस्पेक्टर मैकेनिकल टीचर को ठीक नहीं कर पाएगा और उसे अपने साथ ले जाएगा। वह यह उम्मीद इसलिए कर रही थी, क्योंकि एक बार जब टॉमी के टीचर के इतिहास वाले भाग में कुछ समस्या थी, तब काउण्टी इंस्पेक्टर द्वारा उसे एक महीने के लिए ले जाया गया था।

भूगोल वाला भाग ठीक होना

काउण्टी इंस्पेक्टर मैकेनिकल टीचर को बाहर ले गया। उसने मार्गी की माँ को बताया, कि इसमें मार्गी की गलती नहीं थी। वास्तव में भूगोल वाला भाग मार्गी के पढ़ने और समझने के लिए कुछ ज्यादा तेज था।

उसने (काउण्टी इंस्पेक्टर ने) गति को एक 10 वर्षीय बच्चे के स्तर के अनुसार धीमा करके भूगोल वाले भाग को ठीक कर दिया है। उसने यह भी बताया कि मार्गी का सम्पूर्ण प्रदर्शन काफी सन्तोषजनक था।

पुराने स्कूलों के विषय में चर्चा

टॉमी ने पुस्तक जिसमें अतीत के स्कूलों का वर्णन किया गया था, पढ़ने के बाद मार्गी से चर्चा की। अतीत के स्कूल छात्रों के घरों से दूर विशेष इमारतों में स्थित थे।

छात्रों को मानव शिक्षकों द्वारा पढ़ाया जाता था। समान उम्र के सभी बच्चे एक समान सीखते थे। शिक्षक उन्हें पाठ पढ़ाते, प्रश्न पूछते और उन्हें गृहकार्य देते थे। मार्गी उन हास्यास्पद स्कूलों के विषय में और अधिक जानना चाहती थी, लेकिन टॉमी और मार्गी दोनों के लिए यह उनके स्कूल जाने का समय था। इसलिए उन्होंने बाद में पुस्तक को पढ़ने का निर्णय किया।

मार्गी का स्कूल रूम

मार्गी का स्कूल रूम उसके शयनकक्ष के समीप स्थित था। स्कूल का समय शुरू होने पर उसका (मार्गी) मैकेनिकल टीचर शनिवार और रविवार को छोड़कर प्रत्येक दिन एक निश्चित समय पर ऑन होता था, क्योंकि मार्गी की माँ मानती थी कि छोटी लड़कियाँ अगर नियमित समय पर सीखें तो वे अच्छा सीखती हैं। उस दिन मैकेनिकल टीचर उसे उचित भिन्नों के जोड़ के विषय में अंकगणित का एक पाठ पढ़ाने जा रहा था, लेकिन उसे (मार्गी को) पढ़ने में कोई दिलचस्पी नहीं थी।

Margie Thinks of Old Schools

Margie put her home work in a slot as commanded by the mechanical teacher. She was thinking about the old schools where all the kids came laughing and shouting in the schoolyard and sat together in the schoolroom. They were taught by human teachers, learnt the same things and helped each other in their homework. The mechanical teacher was flashing a question of fractions on the screen but Margie was thinking of the fun kids had at the school in the past.

मार्गी का पुराने स्कूलों के विषय में सोचना

मार्गी ने अपने गृहकार्य को एक स्थान में रखा, जैसा कि मैकेनिकल टीचर ने निर्देश दिया था। वह अतीत के स्कूलों के विषय में सोच रही थी जहाँ सभी बच्चे स्कूल के मैदान में हँसते और चिल्लाते हुए आते थे और स्कूल रूम में साथ बैठते थे। उन्हें मानव शिक्षकों द्वारा पढ़ाया जाता था, वे समान चीजें सीखते थे और अपने गृहकार्य में एक-दूसरे की सहायता करते थे। मैकेनिकल टीचर स्क्रीन पर भिन्नों पर आधारित प्रश्न प्रकाशित कर रहा था, लेकिन मार्गी उस आनन्द के विषय में सोच रही थी जो बच्चों को अतीत के स्कूल में होता था।

Objective Questions

Extract Based Questions

Read the following extracts carefully and answer the questions that follow.

1 It was a very old book. Margie's grandfather once said that when he was a little boy his grandfather told him that there was a time when stories were printed on paper.

They turned the pages, which were yellow and crinkly and it was awfully funny to read words that stood still instead of moving the way they were supposed to on a screen, you know.

(i) Who found the old book?
(a) Margie (b) Margie's mother
(c) Tommy (d) Tommy's father

(ii) Where was the book found?
(a) In the attic of Margie's house.
(b) In the drawing room of Tommy's house.
(c) In the basement of Tommy's house.
(d) In the attic of Tommy's house.

(iii) They are surprised to turn the pages because they now study
(a) on machines (b) on computers
(c) on mobiles (d) on tablets

(iv) The pages were crinkly and yellow because they were
(a) crepe papers (b) very old
(c) printed yellow (d) designed that way

(v) What does 'crinkly' in the extract mean?
(a) With no folds or lines (b) Fresh
(c) With many folds or lines (d) Old

2 Margie was scornful. "School? What's there to write about school? I hate school." Margie always hated school, but now she hated it more than ever. Margie always hated school, but now she hated it more than ever. The mechanical teacher had been giving her test after test in geography and she had been doing worse and worse until her mother had shaken her head sorrowfully and sent for the County Inspector.

He was a round little man with a red face and a whole box of tools with dials and wires. He smiled at Margie and gave her an apple, then took the teacher apart.

(i) Who is 'he' in the given extract?
(a) A teacher (b) A mechanic
(c) An engineer (d) The County Inspector

(ii) When the writer says, "he wouldn't know how to put it together again," he means
(a) modify it (b) correct it
(c) replace it (d) repair it

(iii) What is being talked about in the given extract?
(a) Margie's laptop (b) Margie's T.V
(c) Margie's mechanical teacher (d) Margie's cell phone

(iv) Margie was scornful because
(a) she was worse in geography.
(b) she had been doing good in subjects other than geography.
(c) the geography teacher was a machine.
(d) a and c both

(v) Find a word in the passage which is the opposite of 'never'.
(a) forever (b) always (c) about (d) there

3 Margie was disappointed. She had been hoping they would take the teacher away altogether. They had once taken Tommy's teacher away for nearly a month because the history sector had blanked out completely.

So, she said to Tommy, "Why would anyone write about school?"

Tommy looked at her with very superior eyes. "Because it's not our kind of school, stupid. This is the old kind of school that they had hundreds and hundreds of years ago." He added loftily, pronouncing the word carefully, "Centuries ago".

(i) Why was Margie disappointed?
(a) Because she had to attend the school.
(b) Because her mechanical school teacher was corrected.
(c) Because she had hoped that her mechanical teacher would be taken away for some time.
(d) All of the above

(ii) Tommy in the extract is
(a) Margie's brother (b) Margie's neighbour
(c) Margie's friend (d) Margie's cousin

(iii) Which of the following is the opposite of 'disappointed' as used in the extract?
(a) hopeless (b) sad (c) ignorant (d) pleased

(iv) 'Old kind of school' in the extract refers to
(a) the mechanical school
(b) the online school
(c) the coaching institute
(d) a school with a building and teachers.

(v) 'Loftily' in the extract means
(a) carefully (b) in an inferior way
(c) in a superior way (d) in a formal way

4 They weren't even half finished when Margie's mother called, "Margie! School!"

Margie looked up. "Not yet, Mamma."

"Now!" said Mrs. Jones. "And it's probably time for Tommy, too."

Margie said to Tommy, "Can I read the book some more with you after school?"

"May be," he said nonchalantly. He walked away whistling, the dusty old book tucked beneath his arm.

(i) How did Margie feel when she was called for school?
(a) Angry (b) Irritated (c) Excited (d) Gloomy

(ii) Choose the option that is not true according to the given extract.
(a) The printed book interested Margie and Tommy.
(b) Tommy and Margie had mechanical school teachers.
(c) The book that they were reading belonged to Margie's grandfather.
(d) The book was about schools.

(iii) Why was the book dusty and old?
(a) Because it was lying in the attic
(b) Because it was one of its kind
(c) Because it was a rare piece
(d) Because it was a very old book

(iv) Tommy and Margie were .... when Margie's mother called Margie.
(a) playing
(b) reading an old book about schools
(c) reading an article about schools
(d) sleeping

(v) The word 'nonchalantly' in the extract means
(a) carefully (b) slowly (c) loudly (d) carelessly

Multiple Choice Questions

1. When did Margie write in her diary?
(a) In the morning (b) In the evening
(c) In the afternoon (d) At night

2. Margie wrote in her diary that Tommy found a .... book.
(a) odd (b) real (c) old (d) yellow

3. What were the colour of the pages in the book?
(a) Dull white (b) Grey
(c) Yellow (d) Orange

4. .... considered the book as a waste.
(a) Tommy (b) Margie
(c) Tommy's father (d) Mrs. Jones

5. How old are Margie and Tommy?
(a) Margie is eleven and Tommy is twelve.
(b) Margie is twelve and Tommy is thirteen.
(c) Margie is thirteen and Tommy is fourteen.
(d) Margie is eleven and Tommy is thirteen.

6. The test that the mechanical teacher gave repeatedly was from which subject?
(a) English (b) History
(c) Mathematics (d) Geography

7. Which part about the mechanical teacher did Margie hate the most?
(a) The large, black and ugly screen
(b) The slot where she had to put the homework
(c) The dials and the wires
(d) The part that gave the test

8. What kind of teacher taught in the schools mentioned in Tommy's book?
(a) A female teacher (b) A male teacher
(c) A mechanical teacher (d) Human teacher

9. Who said the following line?
"Why would anyone write about school?"
(a) Tommy (b) Margie
(c) Mrs. Jones (d) County Inspector

10. Why did Mrs. Jones call Margie when she was reading the book with Tommy?
(a) To go to school (b) To eat her lunch
(c) To go to sleep (d) To do her homework

11. Where was Margie's school?
(a) In a special building (b) In Tommy's house
(c) Right next to her bedroom (d) Outside her house

12. On which days, Margie did not have school?
(a) Sunday (b) Saturday
(c) Monday (d) Both (a) and (b)

13. What subjects did Margie learn?
(a) Geography (b) Arithmetic
(c) History (d) All of these

Answer

Extract Based Questions

1. (i) (c), (ii) (d), (iii) (a), (iv) (b), (v) (c) 2. (i) (d), (ii) (b), (iii) (c), (iv) (d), (v) (b) 3. (i) (d), (ii) (c), (iii) (d), (iv) (d), (v) (c)
4. (i) (b), (ii) (c), (iii) (d), (iv) (b), (v) (d)

Multiple Choice Questions

1. (d) 2. (b) 3. (c) 4. (a) 5. (d) 6. (d) 7. (b) 8. (d) 9. (b) 10. (a) 11. (c) 12. (d) 13. (d)

02 The Sound of Music

The chapter is divided into two parts. Both deal with aspects of music and the legendary musicians who achieved excellence in their respective fields.

Part I

Evelyn Glennie Listens to Sound without Hearing it
by Deborah Cowley

Part-I This part is about the famous multi-percussionist, Evelyn Glennie. Evelyn became deaf at a young age. However, she worked hard to learn music and became one of the world's most famous multi-percussionist. She has won many awards. She is a role model for the handicapped people. She was honoured with the Royal Philharmonic Society's prestigious Soloist of the year Award.

Important Characters

Evelyn Glennie एवलिन ग्लेनी	A renowned multi-percussionist who was deaf but managed to overcome her disability with the help of her strong will power. एक प्रसिद्ध बहुतालवादक जो बधिर थी, लेकिन अपनी दृढ़ इच्छाशक्ति से अपनी विकलांगता पर विजय पाने में सफल हुई।
Ron Forbes रॉन फॉर्बस	A percussionist who spotted the potential of Evelyn and supported her in achieving her goal. एक महान तालवादक थे, जिन्होंने एवलिन की क्षमता को पहचाना तथा उसे अपने लक्ष्य तक पहुँचने में मदद की।
Isabel Glennie इसाबेल ग्लेनी	Mother of Evelyn Glennie एवलिन ग्लेनी की माँ

Summary of the Lesson पाठ का सार

Evelyn Lost her Hearing at a Young Age

Evelyn lost her sense of hearing gradually at a young age. It was first noticed by her mother, Isabel Glennie, when Evelyn was eight years old. However, Evelyn managed to hide her growing deafness from her friends and teachers for a long time. But by the time she was eleven years old her performance in school became worse. Her headmistress advised her parents to take her to a specialist. The specialist conformed her deafness due to a gradual nerve damage and asked her parents to get her fitted with hearing aids. He also told them to send her to the school for the deaf.

एवलिन का युवा उम्र में अपनी सुनने की क्षमता को खो देना

एवलिन ने युवा उम्र में धीरे-धीरे अपनी सुनने की क्षमता को खो दिया। इसका पता पहली बार उसकी माँ, इसाबेल ग्लेनी को तब चला, जब एवलिन आठ वर्ष की थी। हालाँकि, एवलिन लम्बे समय तक अपने दोस्तों और शिक्षकों से अपने बढ़ते हुए बहरेपन को छिपाने में कामयाब रही। लेकिन जब वह 11 वर्ष की हुई तो विद्यालय में उसका प्रदर्शन खराब होने लगा। उसकी (एवलिन की) प्रधानाध्यापिका ने उसके माता-पिता को उसे एक विशेषज्ञ के पास ले जाने की सलाह दी। विशेषज्ञ ने स्नायु के धीरे-धीरे क्षति होने के कारण उसके बहरेपन की पुष्टि की और उसके माता-पिता को उसे श्रवण यन्त्र लगाने के लिए कहा। उसने उन्हें उसे (एवलिन को) बधिरों के विद्यालय भेजने के लिए भी कहा।

Evelyn didn't Give up Hope and Never Looked Back

Despite her deafness, Evelyn was determined to lead a normal life and pursue her interest in music. One day, she noticed a girl playing a xylophone and decided to learn to play it. Most of the teachers discouraged Evelyn but the percussionist Ron Forbes recognised her potential. He supported Evelyn in achieving her goal. He began by tuning two large drums to different notes. He advised Evelyn not to hear music through her ears but try to sense in different way.

Evelyn tried to feel the notes of drums in different way. Suddenly, Evelyn realised that she could feel the higher drum from the waist up and the lower one from the waist down. Later, she discovered that she could sense the vibrations in different parts of her body. She had learnt to open her mind and body to the sounds and vibrations.

Achievements of Evelyn

Evelyn joined a youth orchestra and toured the United Kingdom with them. When she was sixteen, she decided to make music her life. She auditioned for the Royal Academy of Music and scored one of the highest marks in the history of the academy. She gradually left the orchestral work and started giving solo performances. At the end of her three year course, she had received most of the top awards. She became the world's most famous multi-percussionist with a mastery over some thousand instruments. She speaks Scottish flawlessly and also learnt French and Japanese.

In 1991, she was honoured with the Royal Philharmonic Society's prestigious Soloist of the year Award.

Evelyn Senses Music

Evelyn told that music flows through every part of her body. It tingles in her skin, her cheekbones and even in her hair. When she plays the xylophone, she can sense the sound passing up the stick into her fingertips.

By leaning against the drums, she can feel the resonances (sounds) flowing into her body. On a wooden platform, she removes her shoes so that the vibrations pass through her bare feet and up her legs.

Evelyn : An Inspiration for the Handicapped

Evelyn admitted that she was a workaholic and works harder than other classical musicians. Apart from the regular concerts, she gives free concerts in prisons and hospitals and also gives priority to classes for young musicians. She delights her audiences and has given great pleasure to millions.

She has promoted percussion to the front of the orchestra. She has given an inspiration to the handicapped people.

एवलिन ने उम्मीद नहीं छोड़ी और कभी पीछे मुड़कर नहीं देखा

अपने बहरेपन के बावजूद एवलिन ने एक सामान्य जीवन जीने और संगीत में अपनी रुचि को जारी रखने का दृढ़-संकल्प लिया। एक दिन उसने एक लड़की को जाइलोफोन बजाते हुए देखा और उसे बजाना सीखने का निश्चय किया। अधिकांश शिक्षकों ने एवलिन को हतोत्साहित किया, लेकिन तबलावादक रॉन फोर्ब्स ने उसकी क्षमता को पहचाना। उसने उसका (एवलिन का) लक्ष्य हासिल करने में एवलिन का साथ दिया। उसने दो बड़े ड्रमों को भिन्न ध्वनियों में बजाकर शुरूआत की। उसने एवलिन को संगीत को अपने कानों के माध्यम से न सुनकर, बल्कि अलग तरीके से महसूस करने का प्रयास करने की सलाह दी।

एवलिन ने ड्रम की ध्वनियों को अलग तरीके से महसूस करने का प्रयास किया। अचानक, एवलिन को एहसास हुआ कि वह ऊपर बँधे हुए ड्रम की ध्वनि को कमर के ऊपर और नीचे बँधे हुए ड्रम की ध्वनि को कमर के नीचे के हिस्से में महसूस कर सकती थी। बाद में उसने (एवलिन ने) पाया कि वह अपने शरीर के विभिन्न हिस्से में ध्वनि की कंपन को महसूस कर सकती थी। उसने ध्वनि और कंपन के प्रति अपने मस्तिष्क और शरीर के द्वारा प्रतिक्रिया देना सीख लिया था।

एवलिन की उपलब्धियाँ

एवलिन एक युवा ऑर्केस्ट्रा में शामिल हो गई और उनके साथ यूनाइटेड किंगडम का दौरा किया। जब वह सोलह वर्ष की थी, तब उसने संगीत को अपना जीवन बनाने का फैसला किया। उसने रॉयल एकेडमी ऑफ म्यूजिक के लिए ऑडिशन दिया और एकेडमी के इतिहास में सर्वाधिक अंक प्राप्त किए। उसने धीरे-धीरे समूह प्रदर्शन का कार्य छोड़ दिया और एकल प्रदर्शन करना शुरू कर दिया। अपने तीन साल के पाठ्यक्रम के अन्त में उसने शीर्ष पुरस्कारों में से अधिकांश प्राप्त कर लिए थे। वह कुछ हजार वाद्ययन्त्रों में निपुणता के साथ दुनिया की सबसे प्रसिद्ध बहु-तालवादक बन गई। वह बिना रुके स्कॉटिश भाषा में बोलती और उसने फ्रेंच और जापानी भाषा भी सीखी।

वर्ष 1991 में उसे रॉयल फिलहारमोनिक सोसायटी के प्रतिष्ठित सोलोइस्ट ऑफ द ईयर के पुरस्कार से सम्मानित किया गया।

एवलिन का संगीत महसूस करना

एवलिन ने बताया कि संगीत उसके शरीर के प्रत्येक हिस्से में बहता है। यह उसकी त्वचा उसके गालों की हड्डियों तक यहाँ तक कि उसके बालों में भी सनसनाहट उत्पन्न करता है। जब वह जायलोफोन बजाती है, तो वह उसकी ध्वनि को छड़ियों में से होकर अपनी अँगुलियों के पोरों में महसूस कर सकती है।

ड्रम की तरफ झुककर, वह उसकी गूँज के प्रवाह को अपने शरीर में महसूस कर सकती है। लकड़ी से बने मंच पर, वह अपने जूते उतार देती है जिससे वाद्ययन्त्र का कंपन उसके नंगे पैरों से होता हुआ पैरों के ऊपर की तरफ जा सके।

एवलिन : विकलांगों के लिए एक प्रेरणा

एवलिन ने स्वीकार किया कि वह बहुत मेहनती थी और अन्य शास्त्रीय संगीतकारों से अधिक मेहनत करती है। नियमित संगीत कार्यक्रमों के अतिरिक्त, वह जेलों और अस्पतालों में निःशुल्क संगीत कार्यक्रम देती है और युवा संगीतकारों के लिए संगीत की कक्षाओं को भी महत्त्व देती है। वह अपने दर्शकों को प्रसन्न करती है और लाखों लोगों को बहुत खुशी प्रदान करती है।

उसने तबलावादन को ऑर्केस्ट्रा में आगे का स्थान दिलवाया। उसने विकलांग लोगों को एक प्रेरणा दी है।

Objective Questions

Extract Based Questions

Part I

Read the following extracts and answer the questions given below them.

1 Rush hour crowds jostle for position on the underground train platform. A slight girl, looking younger than her seventeen years, was nervous yet excited as she felt the vibrations of the approaching train. It was her first day at the prestigious Royal Academy of Music in London and daunting enough for any teenager fresh from a Scottish farm.

(i) The girl referred to here is
(a) Evelyn Glennie (b) Isabel Glennie
(c) James Blades (d) Ann Richlin

(ii) Where was she going?
(a) She was going to give her audition at Royal Academy of Music.
(b) She was going to attend her first day at Royal Academy of Music.
(c) She was going to meet Ron Forbes at Royal Academy of Music.
(d) She was going to the concert being played at Royal Academy of Music.

(iii) The bigger challenge was
(a) she was dumb (b) she was blind
(c) she was profoundly deaf (d) she was lame

(iv) The first line gives us the impression that it was
(a) an isolated place
(b) a crowded place
(c) a busy underground platform
(d) Both (b) and (c)

(v) The word 'daunting' means
(a) pleasing (b) frightening
(c) taxing (d) challenging

2 But Evelyn was not going to give up. She was determined to lead a normal life and pursue her interest in music. One day she noticed a girl playing a xylophone and decided that she wanted to play it too. Most of the teachers discouraged her but percussionist Ron Forbes spotted her potential. He began by tuning two large drums to different notes.

"Don't listen through your ears", he would say, "try to sense it some other way." Says Evelyn, "Suddenly I realised I could feel the higher drum from the waist up and the lower one from the waist down." Forbes repeated the exercise and soon Evelyn discovered that she could sense certain notes in different parts of her body.

(i) What was Evelyn not going to give up?
(a) Leading a normal life
(b) Pursue her Interest in music
(c) Her dream of joining Royal Academy of Music
(d) Both (a) and (b)

(ii) In the given extract, Ron Forbes comes out as a
(a) Motivator (b) Mentor
(c) Role model (d) All of these

(iii) Why does the extract pose that Evelyn was not going to give up?
(a) Because she was deaf (b) Because she was poor
(c) Because she was blind (d) Because she was ill

(iv) Which of the following is opposite in meaning to 'discouraged'?
(a) disheartened (b) pleased
(c) encouraged (d) confused

(v) Which word in the options means 'someone's ability to develop, achieve or succeed'?
(a) Tuning (b) Determined
(c) Pursue (d) Potential

3 And for all this, Evelyn won't accept any hint of heroic achievement. "If you work hard and know where you are going, you'll get there." And she got right to the top, the world's most sought-after multi percussionist with a mastery of some thousand instruments and hectic international schedule.

It is intriguing to watch Evelyn function so effortlessly without hearing. In our two-hour discussion she never missed a word. "Men with bushy beards give me trouble," she laughed. "It is not just watching the lips, it's the whole face, especially the eyes."

(i) 'All this' in the given extract refers to
(a) her career as a percussionist
(b) her journey in the Royal Academy of Music
(c) receiving the highest marks in the history of Royal Academy of Music
(d) Both (b) and (c)

(ii) Which of the following statements is not true according to the given extract?
(a) Evelyn did not participate in international concerts.
(b) Evelyn was very determined.
(c) Evelyn became a very iminent percussionist.
(d) Evelyn studied at the Royal Academy of Music.

(iii) According to Evelyn, the secret of her success is
(a) hard work (b) patience
(c) gossip (d) idleness

(iv) The phrase 'most sought after' indicates
(a) popularity (b) stardom
(c) fan following (d) Both (a) and (c)

(v) The word 'hectic' means
(a) busy (b) leisurely
(c) vibrant (d) flush

Multiple Choice Questions

1. How old was Evelyn when she went to the Royal Academy of Music?
   (a) Eight years old (b) Eleven years old
   (c) Seventeen years old (d) Twenty-three years old
2. Evelyn was.........when she wanted to leam music.
   (a) fat girl (b) slight girl
   (c) small girl (d) tall girl
3. Which nationality did Evelyn Glennie belong to ?
   (a) British (b) American
   (c) Scottish (d) Russian
4. Which disability was Evelyn Glennie suffering from?
   (a) Hearing disability (b) Blindness
   (c) Learning disability (d) Walking disability
5. Who was the first to notice that something was wrong with Evelyn?
   (a) Evelyn's friend (b) Evelyn's teacher
   (c) Evelyn's father (d) Evelyn's mother
6. Evelyn's deafness was first noticed when
   (a) she was eight (b) she was five
   (c) she was six (d) she was nine
7. ....told Evelyn to try to sense music some other way.
   (a) Jack Forbes (b) Evelyn's headmistress
   (c) James Blades (d) Ron Forbes
8. Evelyn's headmistress urged her parents to take her to
   (a) a special school (b) a teacher
   (c) a specialist (d) a music school
9. Evelyn senses the words of other persons by watching
   (a) their lips
   (b) especially the eyes
   (c) the whole face
   (d) All of these
10. Evelyn gives high priority to classes for
    (a) young musicians (b) aged musicians
    (c) young dancers (d) girl musicians
11. What is the name of Evelyn's mother?
    (a) Laura Glennie (b) Isabel Glennie
    (c) Robin Glennie (d) Kelly Glennie
12. How many instruments had Evelyn mastered?
    (a) Two: piano and xylophone (b) Only one: drums
    (c) Around thousand (d) Less than a hundred
13. Which of the following statments is true?
    (a) Evelyn hid her deafness from her friends and teachers.
    (b) Evelyn hid her friends from her parents.
    (c) Evelyn used her deafness as an excuse.
    (d) Evelyn did not hide her deafness.
14. Why does Evelyn say that her speech is clear?
    (a) Because she wasn't mute.
    (b) Because she loved to sing and would practice a lot.
    (c) Because she could read other people's lips very nicely.
    (d) Because she could hear till she was eleven years old.
15. Which foreign languages did Evelyn learn?
    (a) French and Japanese
    (b) German and Japanese
    (c) German
    (d) Chinese

Answers

Extract Based Questions

1. (i) (a), (ii) (b), (iii) (c), (iv) (d), (v) (b) 2. (i) (d), (ii) (d), (iii) (a), (iv) (c), (v) (d) 3. (i) (d), (ii) (a), (iii) (a), (iv) (d), (v) (a)

Multiple Choice Questions

1. (c) 2. (b) 3. (a) 4. (a) 5. (d) 6. (a) 7. (d) 8. (c) 9. (d) 10. (a) 11. (b) 12. (c) 13. (a) 14. (d) 15. (a)

Part II
The Shehnai of Bismillah Khan

This part is about the renowned shehnai player, Bismillah Khan. He belonged to a well-known family of musicians from Bihar. He practised hard on the banks of the Ganga in Benaras and invented ragas that were considered to be beyond the range of the shehnai. He played the shehnai on the auspicious occasion of national freedom on 15th August, 1947. He was honoured with the highest civilian award the Bharat Ratna in 2001.

Important Characters

Bismillah Khan	A great shehnai player, devout, patriot and liberal human being.
बिस्मिल्लाह खान	वे महान शहनाई वादक, धार्मिक, देशभक्त एवं उदार व्यक्ति थे।
Ali Bux	Maternal uncle of Ustad Bismillah Khan, a shehnai player who didn't discriminate with anyone on the basis of religion.
अली बक्स	उस्ताद बिस्मिल्लाह खान के मामा थे। वे शहनाई वादक भी थे तथा धर्म के आधार पर कोई भेदभाव नहीं करते थे।

Ban on Pungi and Origin of Shehnai

Emperor Aurangzeb banned the playing of the pungi (a musical instrument) in the royal palace as it had a loud and unpleasant sound.

A barber who belonged to a family of professional musicians decided to improve the tonal quality of the pungi. He took a pipe with a natural hollow stem. It was longer and broader than the pungi. He made seven holes on its body. When it was played by closing and opening some of these holes, soft and melodious sounds were produced. Everyone was impressed when barber played the instrument in the palace.

Naming of Shehnai and its Importance

As the instrument was first played in the Shah's (King's) Chambers and was played by a nai (a barber), it was named as the 'shehnai'. The sound of the shehnai gradually became popular and it started to be considered auspicious with time. It is still played in temples and at weddings in North India. In the past, the shehnai was part of the naubat or the traditional group of nine instruments found at royal courts.

Bismillah Khan's Birth and Family

Bismillah Khan was born on 21st March, 1916 in a well-known family of musicians in Dumraon, Bihar. His grandfather, Rasool Bux Khan, was the shehnai-nawaz of the Bhojpur king's Court. His father, Paigambar Bux and other ancestors were great shehnai players.

Bismillah Got Interested in Music

Bismillah got interested in music at a small age. His mother took him to his maternal uncle's house in Banaras (now Varanasi) when he was three years old. He was fascinated by watching his uncle, Ali Bux playing the shehnai. Soon, he started accompanying his uncle to the Vishnu temple of Banaras where he was employed to play shehnai. Gradually, he started getting lessons on playing the shehnai.

He practised playing it in the temples of Balaji and Mangala Maiya and at the banks of the river Ganga. The flowing waters of the Ganga inspired him to invent new raagas. He accompanied his uncle to the Allahabad Music Conference at the age of fourteen. Ustad Faiyaz Khan was impressed by his performance and encouraged him to work hard to achieve his goal.

पुंगी पर प्रतिबन्ध और शहनाई की उत्पत्ति

सम्राट औरंगजेब ने शाही महल में पुंगी (एक वाद्ययन्त्र) के बजाने पर प्रतिबन्ध लगा दिया, क्योंकि इसकी आवाज बहुत ऊँची और अप्रिय थी।

पेशेवर संगीतकारों के परिवारों से सम्बन्ध रखने वाले एक नाई ने पुंगी की सुर-सम्बन्धी गुणवत्ता को सुधारने का निर्णय किया। उसने एक प्राकृतिक खोखले तने वाला पाइप लिया। यह पुंगी की तुलना में अधिक लम्बा और चौड़ा था। उसने इस पाइप पर सात छिद्र बनाए। जब इनमें से कुछ छिद्रों को बन्द व खोलते हुए इसे बजाया, तो कोमल और मधुर ध्वनि उत्पन्न हुई। जब नाई ने वाद्ययन्त्र को महल में बजाया, तो सभी उससे प्रभावित हुए।

शहनाई का नामकरण और उसका महत्त्व

चूँकि यन्त्र सबसे पहले शाह की (राजा की) सभा में बजाया गया था और एक नाई के द्वारा बजाया गया था, इसे 'शहनाई' नाम दिया गया। शहनाई की आवाज धीरे-धीरे लोकप्रिय हो गई और इसे समय के साथ शुभ माना जाने लगा। यह अभी भी उत्तर भारत में मन्दिरों और शादियों में बजाई जाती है। अतीत में शहनाई नौबत या शाही दरबारों में पाए जाने वाले नौ वाद्ययन्त्रों के पारम्परिक समूह का हिस्सा थी।

बिस्मिल्लाह खान का जन्म और परिवार

बिस्मिल्लाह खान का जन्म 21 मार्च, 1916 को बिहार के डुमरॉव में संगीतकारों के एक प्रसिद्ध परिवार में हुआ था। इनके दादा, रसलू बख्श खान भोजपुर राजा के दरबार के शहनाई-नवाज थे। उनके पिता, पैगम्बर बख्श और अन्य पूर्वज महान शहनाई वादक थे।

बिस्मिल्लाह को संगीत में रुचि होना

बिस्मिल्लाह को छोटी उम्र में ही संगीत में रुचि हो गई थी। जब वे तीन साल के थे तब उनकी माँ उन्हें बनारस (अब वाराणसी) में उनके मामा के घर ले गई। वे अपने मामा अली बख्श को शहनाई बजाते देखकर शहनाई की ओर आकर्षित हो गए। शीघ्र ही, वे अपने मामा के साथ बनारस के विष्णु मन्दिर में जाने लगे, जहाँ उनके मामा शहनाई बजाने के लिए नियुक्त थे। धीरे-धीरे उन्होंने शहनाई बजाने की शिक्षा लेना शुरू कर दिया।

उन्होंने बालाजी और मंगला मैया के मन्दिरों में और गंगा नदी के किनारों पर इसे बजाने का अभ्यास किया। गंगा के बहते पानी ने उन्हें नए रागों की रचना करने के लिए प्रेरित किया। वे चौदह वर्ष की उम्र में अपने मामा के साथ इलाहाबाद संगीत सभा में गए। उस्ताद फैयाज खान उनके प्रदर्शन से प्रभावित हुए और उन्हें अपने लक्ष्य को हासिल करने के लिए कड़ी मेहनत करने के लिए प्रोत्साहित किया।

Bismillah's Rise to Fame

Bismillah Khan got the first big break with the opening of the All India Radio in Lucknow in 1938. Soon he became a popular shehnai player on the radio. Bismillah became the first Indian to greet the nation with his shehnai on 15th August, 1947 when India gained independence. He played Shehnai from the Red Fort in front of an audience including Pandit Jawaharlal Nehru. He gave many memorable performances in India and abroad. His first trip to abroad was to Afghanistan where King Zahir Khan became impressed by his performance and gifted him his priceless Persian carpets and other things.

Bismillah's Contribution in the Film World

Film director Vijay Bhatt named a film *'Goonj* Uthi *Shehnai'* after he was fascinated on hearing Bismillah playing the shehnai at a festival. One of Bismillah Khan's compositions in the film 'Dil Ka Khilona Hai Toot Gaya' became a national chartbuster. Bismillah only gave music in two films–Goonj Uthi Shehnai and a Kannada film Sanadhi Apanna. This was because he did not like the artificiality and glamour of the film world.

A Renowned Musician

Ustad Bismillah Khan was the first Indian to be invited to perform at the prestigious Lincoln Centre Hall in the USA. He also took part in The World Exposition in Montreal, Cannes Art Festival and the Osaka Trade Fair. He became so popular internationally that an auditorium in Tehran was named after him.

Bismillah's Awards

Bismillah received the National awards like the Padma Shri, the Padma Bhushan and the Padma Vibhushan. In 2001, he was awarded the India's highest civilian award, the Bharat Ratna. He recommended Indians to teach the music to their children as it is Hindustan's richest tradition.

Bismillah's Love for his Roots

Bismillah Khan travelled to many countries, but he was fond of Banaras and Dumraon. These remained the most wonderful towns of the world for him. He also refused one of his student's offer to head a Shehnai school in the USA by saying that he could not find the Ganga there. His life is a perfect example of the rich, cultural heritage and seniority of India.

प्रसिद्धि की ओर बिस्मिल्लाह

वर्ष 1938 में लखनऊ में ऑल इण्डिया रेडियो की शुरूआत के साथ बिस्मिल्लाह खान को पहला बड़ा अवसर मिला। शीघ्र ही वे रेडियो पर एक लोकप्रिय शहनाई वादक बन गए। 15 अगस्त, 1947 को जब भारत ने स्वतन्त्रता प्राप्त की, तो बिस्मिल्लाह अपनी शहनाई के साथ राष्ट्र का अभिवादन करने वाले पहले भारतीय बने। उन्होंने लाल किले से पण्डित जवाहर लाल नेहरू समेत सभी दर्शकों के सामने शहनाई बजाई। उन्होंने भारत और विदेशों में कई यादगार प्रस्तुतियाँ दीं। उनकी प्रथम विदेश यात्रा अफगानिस्तान की थी, वहाँ के राजा जहीर खान उनके प्रदर्शन से प्रभावित हुए और उन्हें अपनी बेशकीमती फारसी कालीन और अन्य चीजें भेंट की।

फिल्मी जगत में बिस्मिल्लाह का योगदान

फिल्म निर्देशक विजय भट्ट ने बिस्मिल्लाह को एक समारोह में शहनाई वादन से प्रभावित होकर अपनी एक फिल्म का नाम 'गूँज उठी शहनाई' रखा। फिल्म में बिस्मिल्लाह खान द्वारा रचित गाना 'दिल का खिलौना है टूट गया' देश में बहुत प्रसिद्ध हुआ। बिस्मिल्लाह ने केवल दो फिल्मों में संगीत दिया—'गूँज उठी शहनाई' और एक कन्नड़ फिल्म 'सनधी अपन्ना'। ऐसा इसलिए था, क्योंकि उन्हें फिल्मी दुनिया का बनावटीपन और तड़क-भड़क पसन्द नहीं था।

एक प्रसिद्ध संगीतकार

उस्ताद बिस्मिल्लाह खान पहले भारतीय थे, जिन्हें संयुक्त राज्य अमेरिका के प्रतिष्ठित लिंकन सेण्टर हॉल में प्रदर्शन के लिए आमन्त्रित किया गया था। उन्होंने मॉन्ट्रियल में वैश्विक प्रदर्शनी, कला महोत्सव और ओसाका व्यापार मेले में भी हिस्सा लिया। वे अन्तर्राष्ट्रीय स्तर पर इतना लोकप्रिय हुए कि तेहरान में एक ऑडिटोरियम का नाम उनके नाम पर रखा गया।

बिस्मिल्लाह के पुरस्कार

बिस्मिल्ला ने पद्म श्री, पद्म भूषण और पद्म विभूषण जैसे राष्ट्रीय पुरस्कार प्राप्त किए। 2001 में उन्हें भारत के सर्वोच्च नागरिक पुरस्कार, भारत रत्न से सम्मानित किया गया। उन्होंने भारतीयों को अपने बच्चों को संगीत सिखाने की सलाह दी, क्योंकि यह हिन्दुस्तान की सबसे समृद्ध परम्परा है।

अपने देश के लिए बिस्मिल्लाह का प्यार

बिस्मिल्लाह खान ने कई देशों की यात्रा की, लेकिन वे बनारस और डुमराँव के आदी थे। ये उनके लिए दुनिया के सबसे अद्भुत नगर बने रहे। उन्होंने अपने एक छात्र का संयुक्त राज्य अमेरिका के एक शहनाई स्कूल का प्रमुख बनने का प्रस्ताव को भी यह कहते हुए ठुकरा दिया कि वे वहाँ गंगा नहीं खोज सकते थे। उनका जीवन भारत की समृद्ध सांस्कृतिक विरासत और वरिष्ठता का आदर्श उदाहरण है।

Objective Questions

Extract Based Questions

Part II

Read the following extracts and answer the questions given below them.

1 He chose a pipe with a natural hollow stem that was longer and broader than the pungi and made seven holes on the body of the pipe. When he played on it, closing and opening some of these holes, soft and melodious sounds were produced.

He played the instrument before royalty and everyone was impressed. The instrument so different from the pungi had to be given a new name. As the story goes, since it was first played in the Shah's chambers and was played by a nai (barber), the instrument was named the 'shehnai'.

(i) Who does 'he' refer to?
(a) Aurangzeb (b) A Barber
(c) Bismillah Khan (d) Rasool Bux Khan

(ii) What is the name of the new instrument?
(a) Shehnai (b) Pungi (c) Sitar (d) Guitar

(iii) Why was pungi banned from the court of Aurangzeb?
(a) It was inauspicious.
(b) It could be used as a weapon.
(c) It had a very unpleasant sound.
(d) It caused deafness.

(iv) Where was the new instrument played traditionally?
(a) In temples (b) In wedding ceremonies
(c) In auspicious ceremonies (d) All of these

(v) From where did the new instrument get its name?
(a) By combining the words of 'King' and 'Barber'.
(b) It was named by a barber.
(c) A king gave its name.
(d) It was named by a writer.

2 Awards and recognition came thick and fast. Bismillah Khan became the first Indian to be invited to perform at the prestigious Lincoln Centre Hall in the United States of America. He also took part in the World Exposition in Montreal, in the Cannes Art Festival and in the Osaka Trade Fair.

So, well known did he become internationally that an auditorium in Teheran was named after him — Tahar Mosiquee Ustaad Bismillah Khan.

(i) What did Bismillah perform at the Lincoln Centre Hall?
(a) He played the shehnai (b) He played the sarod
(c) He sang the National Anthem (d) He sang a song

(ii) The phrase 'thick and fast' indicates
(a) from all over the world
(b) rapidly and in large numbers
(c) suddenly and in large numbers
(d) suddenly and deservingly

(iii) Which of the following words can replace 'prestigious' in the given extract?
(a) honourable (b) deserving
(c) reputable (d) estimable

(iv) The statement that is true according to the extract is
(a) Bismillah Khan played the shehnai at various prestigious locations worldwide.
(b) Bismillah Khan was enjoying his new found stardom.
(c) Bismillah Khan wanted to open a music school in London.
(d) Bismillah Khan won all prestigious awards related to music.

(v) Bismillah Khan was fondly called
(a) Bismil (b) Khansaab
(c) Khanji (d) Masterji

3 In spite of having travelled all over the world – Khansaab as he is fondly called – is exceedingly fond of Benaras and Dumraon and they remain for him the most wonderful towns of the world. A student of his once wanted him to head a Shehnai school in the U.S.A., and the student promised to recreate the atmosphere of Banaras by replicating the temples there. But Khansaab asked him if he would be able to transport river Ganga as well.

(i) 'Khansaab' in the extract refers to
(a) the student (b) King of Bhojpur
(c) Rasool Bux (d) Bismillah Khan

(ii) The given extract shows that Bismillah Khan was
(a) too fond of his culture and land
(b) disliked foreigners
(c) wanted to open a school but in India
(d) loved to drink milk

(iii) The statement that is true according to the given extract is
(a) Bismillah Khan's popularity had spread worldwide.
(b) Bismillah Khan grew up in Banaras.
(c) Bismillah Khan always had the river Ganga in his memory.
(d) All of the above

(iv) What is the nickname of Bismillah Khan?
(a) Ustad (b) Khan
(c) Khansaab (d) None of these

(v) His favourite place was
(a) Prayagraj and Banaras (b) Banaras and Lucknow
(c) Banaras and Dumraon (d) Dumraon and Agra

Multiple Choice Questions

1. Why was 'pungi' banned in the royal residence?
(a) It had a strange shape.
(b) It had a shrill unpleasant sound.
(c) The emperor did not like any musical instrument.
(d) It distracted everyone from important work.

2. The shehnai is the refined version of ....
(a) the guitar (b) harmonium
(c) sitar (d) pungi

3. What was the 'shehnai' part of?
(a) The Naubat
(b) The royal wedding
(c) The weapons to fight the enemy
(d) The kitchen utensils

4. Ustad Bismillah Khan belonged to the state of ....
(a) Bihar (b) Uttar Pradesh
(c) Madhya Pradesh (d) Rajasthan

5. Where was the 'shehnai' played before it was brought onto the classical stage?
(a) Temples (b) Weddings
(c) Theatres (d) Both (a) and (b)

6. Which award did the little boy earn?
(a) The Gem of Aurangzeb's Court
(b) India's highest civilian award – the Bharat Ratna
(c) Best Musician in Benaras
(d) Best Musician in the World

7. Rasool Bux Khan's .... was the *shehnai nawaz* of the Bhojpur king's court.
(a) father (b) uncle
(c) grandfather (d) brother

8. At the age of three, where would Bismillah Khan accompany his uncle to?
(a) Vishnu temple of Banaras
(b) Banks of the River Ganga
(c) Bhojpur king's court
(d) Ancient estate of Dumraon

9. Who did Bismillah Khan meet at the Allahabad Music Conference?
(a) Ustad Faiyaz Khan
(b) Pandit Jawaharlal Nehru
(c) King Zahir Shah
(d) Vijay Bhatt

10. In which country is the Lincoln Centre Hall situated?
(a) India (b) Afghanistan
(c) The United States of America (d) Canada

11. Bismillah Khan took part in which of the following events?
(a) World Exposition in Montreal
(b) Cannes Art Festival
(c) Osaka Trade Fair
(d) All of the above

12. Shehnai is still played at the temples and North Indian weddings because its sound
(a) promises to bring good news
(b) promises to bring money
(c) promises to bring good fortune
(d) promises to bring fight

13. Bismillah Khan played the shehnai at the Red Fort, Delhi on
(a) 15th August, 1947
(b) 14th August, 1948
(c) 14th August, 1947
(d) 13th August, 1948

14. Bismillah Khan's first trip abroad was to
(a) Afghanistan (b) Pakistan
(c) Nepal (d) Burma

15. The most important members of the audience of the shehnai recital at the Red Fort was
(a) Mahatma Gandhi
(b) Pandit Jawaharlal Nehru
(c) Both (a) and (b)
(d) None of the above

Answers

Extract Based Questions

1. (i) (b), (ii) (a), (iii) (c), (iv) (d), (v) (a) 2. (i) (a), (ii) (b), (iii) (c), (iv) (a), (v) (b) 3. (i) (d), (ii) (a), (iii) (d), (iv) (c), (v) (c)

Multiple Choice Questions

1. (b) 2. (d) 3. (a) 4. (a) 5. (d) 6. (b) 7. (c) 8. (a) 9. (a) 10. (c) 11. (d) 12. (c)
13. (a) 14. (a) 15. (b)

03 The Little Girl

The story describes the relationship between a strict father and his sensitive daughter (Kezia). The father is shown as a very busy person in the story. He wants his daughter to be a good girl and does not tolerate any kind of mischief. He beats her when she does something wrong. Kezia is very afraid of her father and avoids him. She gets a sense of relief when he is not around. However, in the end of the story Kezia's perception about her father changes. This happens when her mother gets hospitalised and she is left alone at home. At this time, her father takes care of Kezia with love and sympathy. She finds that her father loves her and hence she develops affection for him.

Important Characters

Kezia	A little girl who was afraid of her father. Her perception towards her father changes at the end due to care taken by her father in her mother's absence.
केज़िया	एक छोटी लडकी जो अपने पिता से डरती थी। अन्त में उसकी माँ की अनुपस्थिति में उसके पिता द्वारा उसकी देखभाल करने के कारण वह अपने पिता के प्रति अपना नजरिया बदल लेती है।
Kezia's Father	A hard working man and a strict disciplinarian whose tender side is revealed at the end of the story.
केज़िया के पिता	एक मेहनती और सख्त अनुशासनवादी व्यक्ति जिसका कोमल रूप कहानी के अन्त में सामने आता है।
Kezia's Grandmother	A woman who told Kezia about her father's birthday.
केज़िया की दादी	एक महिला जिसने केज़िया को उसके (केज़िया के) पिता के जन्मदिन के बारे में बताया।
Alice	The cook at Kezia's house who was assigned the duty to look after Kezia in the absense of Kezia's mother and grandmother
ऐलिस	केज़िया के घर पर रसोइया जिसे केज़िया की माँ और दादी की अनुपस्थिति में केज़िया की देखभाल की जिम्मेदारी सौंपी गई थी।

Summary of the Lesson पाठ का सार

Kezia is Afraid of her Father

The little girl, Kezia was afraid of her father. She always avoided meeting him. Every morning before going to the office, her father went to Kezia's room and gave her a casual kiss. Kezia felt a sense of relief when her father went out to work. In the evening, when Kezia's father came home, her mother would call Kezia to take off father's shoes. Kezia used to stammer in front of her father whereas with others she used to talk normally. Kezia considered her father as a giant. According to Kezia, he had big hands and neck, his mouth appeared very big to her when he yawns.

Incident on Sunday Afternoon

On Sunday afternoons, Kezia's grandmother sent her to the drawing room to have a talk with her parents. When Kezia went there she always found her mother reading and her father sleeping on the sofa with a handkerchief on his face and his feet on the cushion. He snore while he slept. Kezia kept waiting for her father to wake up. After waking up, Kezia's father asked her not to stare at him as she looked like a little brown owl while staring.

केज़िया का अपने पिता से डरना

छोटी लड़की केज़िया अपने पिता से डरती थी। वह हमेशा उनसे मिलने से बचती थी। प्रत्येक सुबह ऑफिस जाने से पहले, केज़िया के पिता उसके कमरे में जाते और उसे स्नेह करते। जब केज़िया के पिता काम पर चले जाते थे, तब वह राहत महसूस करती थी। शाम को, जब केज़िया के पिता घर लौटते, तब केज़िया की माँ उसको पिता के जूते उतारने के लिए आवाज लगाती। केज़िया अपने पिता के सामने हकलाती थी, जबकि अन्य लोगों के साथ वह सामान्य रूप से बात कर पाती थी। केज़िया अपने पिता को एक दैत्य (राक्षस) की तरह समझती थी। केज़िया के अनुसार उसके पिता के हाथ और गर्दन बड़े थे और जम्हाई लेने पर केज़िया को उसके पिता का मुँह बहुत बड़ा लगता था।

रविवार की दोपहर की घटना

रविवार की दोपहर को केज़िया की दादी उसे अपने माता-पिता के साथ बात करने के लिए ड्राइंग-रूम में भेजा करती थी। जब केज़िया वहाँ जाती तो वह हमेशा अपनी माँ को कुछ पढ़ते हुए और अपने पिता को सोफे पर सोते हुए पाती थी जिनके चेहरे पर रूमाल ढका होता और पैर तकिये पर होते थे। उसके पिता सोते समय खर्राटे भरते थें। केज़िया अपने पिता के जागने का इंतजार करती। जागने के बाद केज़िया के पिता ने उसे अपनी ओर घूरने के लिए मना किया, क्योंकि घूरते समय वह एक छोटे भूरे उल्लू की तरह दिखाई देती थी।

Kezia Makes a Birthday Gift for her Father

One day Kezia had a cold and did not go to school. Her grandmother told her that her father's birthday was coming next week. She suggested Kezia to make a pin-cushion of yellow silk as a gift for her father. So, Kezia made a pin-cushion by stitching its three sides. She needed something to fill in the pin-cushion.

She went into her mother's bedroom and found some papers on the table. She tore these papers and stuffed them into the pin-cushion. The paper contained an important speech that her father would deliver for the Port Authority next day.

Kezia gets Punished

Kezia's father was very angry when he could not find his papers of speech. Everyone in the house was questioned about the papers. When Kezia was asked about the papers, she told that she had torn up the papers and stuffed them into the pin-cushion. For this, Kezia's father punished her by hitting her palms with a ruler. He wanted to teach Kezia not to touch anything that did not belong to her. Kezia cried a lot.

After a few hours, her grandmother wrapped Kezia in a shawl. Kezia was very disturbed about the incident of getting punished by her father. She cried and asked her grandmother, "What did God make fathers for?"

Kezia's Neighbours : The Macdonalds

The Macdonalds had five children and they lived in the house next to Kezia. Mr. Macdonald always played with his children when he was free. They laughed and enjoyed each others company. Seeing all this, Kezia realised that there were different kinds of fathers.

Kezia's Nightmare

One day Kezia's mother fell ill and had to be hospitalised. Her grandmother went to the hospital with her mother. Kezia was alone in the house with the cook, Alice and her father was sleeping in his room. Kezia was not comfortable sleeping alone at night as she used to have nightmares.

At that night also, Kezia had a frightful nightmare. In the nightmare, she saw a butcher with a knife and a rope, smiling and coming nearer to her. She was unable to move and was crying and calling her grandmother.

Kezia Changes her Opinion about her Father

Kezia's father came to her room after hearing her scream. Her father took Kezia in his arms to his bedroom and lay down beside her to give her comfort. He also asked Kezia to rub her feet against his legs to get warmth.

He fell asleep after sometime. Kezia found that her father's body was harder than her grandmother. Kezia also realised that her father had to work very hard all day and would get tired to play with her like Mr. Macdonald. She felt sorry for tearing his papers. She told her father that he had a very big heart.

केज़िया द्वारा अपने पिता के लिए जन्मदिन का उपहार बनाना

एक दिन केज़िया को ठण्ड लग गई और वह स्कूल नहीं गई। उसकी दादी ने उसे बताया, कि अगले सप्ताह उसके पिता का जन्मदिन आने वाला है। उसने केज़िया को अपने पिता के लिए उपहार के रूप में पीले रेशमी कपड़े से एक पिन-कुशन बनाने का भी सुझाव दिया। अत: केज़िया ने तीन तरफ से सिलाई करके पिन-कुशन बनाया। उसे पिंन-कुशन में भरने के लिए कुछ चाहिए था।

वह अपनी माँ के बैडरूम में गई और उसे वहाँ टेबल पर कुछ कागज रखे मिले। उसने इन कागजों को फाड़कर उन्हें पिन-कुशन में भर दिया। कागजों पर बन्दरगाह प्राधिकरण के लिए तैयार किया गया भाषण था जो उसके पिता को अगले दिन देना था।

केज़िया को सजा मिलना

केज़िया के पिता अपने भाषण के कागज न मिलने पर बहुत गुस्सा थे। घर में सभी से कागजों के विषय में पूछताछ की गई। जब केज़िया से कागजों के विषय में पूछा गया, तो उसने बताया कि उसने कागजों को फाड़कर पिन-कुशन में भर दिया था। इसके लिए केज़िया के पिता ने एक छड़ी से उसकी हथेलियों पर मारकर उसे दण्डित किया। वह केज़िया को सिखाना चाहते थे कि वह ऐसी किसी भी चीज को न छुए जो उसकी नहीं है। केज़िया बहुत रोई।

कुछ घण्टों के बाद, उसकी दादी ने केज़िया को एक शॉल में लपेट दिया। केज़िया अपने पिता से सजा पाने की घटना को लेकर बहुत परेशान थी। उसने रोते हुए अपनी दादी से पूछा, "ईश्वर ने पिता किसलिए बनाए?"

केज़िया के पड़ोसी : मैकडोनाल्ड परिवार

मैकडोनाल्ड्स परिवार में पाँच बच्चे थे और वे केज़िया के समीप वाले घर में रहते थे। मि. मैकडोनाल्ड हमेशा खाली समय में अपने बच्चों के साथ खेलते थे। वे हँसते और एक-दूसरे के साथ का आनन्द लेते थे। यह सब देखकर, केज़िया को एहसास हुआ कि पिता विभिन्न प्रकार के थे।

केज़िया का बुरा सपना

एक दिन केज़िया की माँ बीमार पड़ गई और उन्हें अस्पताल में भर्ती कराना पड़ा। उसकी दादी उसकी माँ के साथ अस्पताल चली गई। केज़िया घर में ऐलिस नामक रसोइया के साथ अकेली थी और उसके पिता अपने कमरे में सो रहे थे। केज़िया रात को अकेले सोने में सहज नहीं थी, क्योंकि उसे बुरे सपने आते थे।

उस रात भी केज़िया को एक डरावना सपना आया। सपने में, उसने एक कसाई को एक चाकू और एक रस्सी के साथ, मुसकुराते हुए और उसके (केज़िया के) पास आते हुए देखा। वह हिल नहीं पा रही थी और रोते हुए अपनी दादी को बुला रही थी।

केज़िया का अपने पिता के विषय में अपने विचारों में बदलाव

केज़िया के पिता उसकी चीख सुनकर उसके कमरे में आए। केज़िया के पिता केज़िया को अपनी बाँहों में लेकर अपने बैडरूम में ले गए और उसे सुरक्षित महसूस कराने के लिए उसके बगल में लेट गए। उन्होंने केज़िया को अपने पैरों को गर्म करने के लिए उनकी (पिता की) टाँगों से रगड़ने के लिए भी कहा।

वह कुछ समय बाद सो गए। केज़िया ने अपने पिता के शरीर को अपनी दादी से कठोर पाया। केज़िया को यह भी एहसास हुआ कि उसके पिता को पूरे दिन बहुत मेहनत करनी पड़ती थी वे बहुत थक जाते होंगे और मैकडोनाल्ड की तरह खेल नहीं सकते। उसे (केज़िया को) अपने पिता के कागज फाड़ने के लिए अफसोस हुआ। उसने अपने पिता को बताया कि उनका दिल बहुत बड़ा था।

Objective Questions

Extract Based Questions

Read the following extracts and answer the questions given below them.

1 To the little girl he was a figure to be feared and avoided. Every morning before going to work he came into her room and gave her a casual kiss, to which she responded with 'Goodbye, Father'. And Oh, there was a glad sense of relief when she heard the noise of the carriage growing fainter and fainter.

down the long road! In the evening when he came home she stood near the staircase and heard his loud voice in the hall. "Bring my tea into the drawing-room... Hasn't the paper come yet? Mother, go and see if my paper's out there — and bring me my slippers."

(i) 'He' in the extract refers to
- (a) Mr. Macdonald
- (b) The butcher
- (c) Kezia's grandfather
- (d) Kezia's father

(ii) Kezia used to
- (a) avoid her father
- (b) fear her father
- (c) like her father
- (d) Both (a) and (b)

(iii) 'a figure to be feared' means
- (a) a thing to be feared
- (b) a person to be feared
- (c) a situation to be feared
- (d) All of these

(iv) Why was he a figure to be feared?
- (a) Because he never spoke to her with love.
- (b) Because he terrorised her.
- (c) Because he used to beat her.
- (d) Because he was her step father.

(v) Why was there a glad sense of relief when she heard the noise of the carriage growing fainter?
- (a) Because she felt comfortable when he was not around.
- (b) Because she was afraid of her father.
- (c) Because he tortured her.
- (d) Both (a) and (b)

2 He was so big his hands and his neck, especially his mouth when he yawned. Thinking about him alone was like thinking about a giant. On Sunday afternoons grandmother sent her down to the drawing room to have a "nice talk with father and mother". But he little girl always found mother reading and father stretched out on the sofa, his handkerchief on his face.

(i) 'He' here refers to
- (a) Kezia's cook
- (b) Kezia's neighbour
- (c) Kezia's father
- (d) Kezia's friend

(ii) The statement that is true regarding the person referred in the above extract as per Kezia is
- (a) Kezia wasn't attached to that person.
- (b) He gave her appropriate attention.
- (c) He didn't pamper Kezia like her grandmother does.
- (d) Both (a) and (c)

(iii) The little girl always found
- (a) father relaxing
- (b) mother reading
- (c) mother knitting
- (d) Both (a) and (b)

(iv) The physical appearance of the person mentioned above is compared to a
- (a) dwarf
- (b) giant
- (c) miniature
- (d) god

(v) The grandmother sent her down to them to make her
- (a) feel scared
- (b) feel miserable
- (c) feel comfortable with her parents
- (d) feel sad

3 Laboriously, with a double cotton, the little girl stitched three sides. But what to fill it with? That was the question. The grandmother was out in the garden and she wandered into mother's bedroom to look for scraps. On the bed-table she discovered a great many sheets of fine paper, gathered them up, tore them into tiny pieces and stuffed her case, then sewed up the fourth side.

(i) Who is 'the little girl'?
- (a) Margie
- (b) Kezia
- (c) Mao
- (d) Evelyn

(ii) Why was she searching for scraps?
- (a) For arts and crafts
- (b) To complete her homework
- (c) To fill the pin-cushion
- (d) To make a present for her father

(iii) The fine sheets of paper contained
- (a) her father's contract
- (b) her father's business deal
- (c) her father's speech
- (d) her father's documents

(iv) Why was the little girl making it?
- (a) To pass her time
- (b) To gift it to her father on his birthday
- (c) To gift it to her father on his anniversary
- (d) To do something creative

(v) How did Kezia's father react on finding his torn speech?
- (a) He reacted angrily
- (b) He reacted happily
- (c) He reacted sadly
- (d) He did not react in any way

4 And she was dragged down to where father was pacing to and fro, hands behind his back. 'Well'? He said sharply. Mother explained. He stopped and stared at the child. "Did you do that?" 'N-No,' she whispered? "Mother, go up to her room and fetch down the damned thing — see that the child's put to bed this instant." Crying too much to explain, she lay in the shadowed room watching the evening light make a sad little pattern on the floor. Then Father came into the room with a ruler in his hands.

(i) Who was dragged down?
(a) Kezia's grandmother (b) Kezia
(c) Kezia's mother (d) Evelyn

(ii) Why was 'she' dragged?
(a) Because she had stolen some money.
(b) Because she had torn the important papers.
(c) Because she had made the pin-cushion without permission.
(d) Because of her mischief.

(iii) What was the mother trying to explain the father?
(a) That Kezia tore the papers to fill in the pin-cushion.
(b) That Kezia didn't tear the papers.
(c) That Kezia is a responsible girl.
(d) That Kezia will not do this again in the future.

(iv) The statement that is true about the incident discussed in the above extract is
(a) Kezia didn't tear the papers.
(b) Grandmother encouraged her to tear the papers.
(c) Father wanted to enquire if Kezia had torn the papers.
(d) Kezia was never afraid of her father.

(v) Which of the following gives the correct meaning of 'whispered'?
(a) To speak loudly (b) To speak very softly
(c) to speak the truth (d) To speak carefully

Multiple Choice Questions

1. Kezia's father went to work in a ....
(a) bus (b) carriage (c) train (d) rickshaw

2. What was Kezia asked to do by her mother in the evening?
(a) To carry the teacup back to the table carefully
(b) To take off her father's boots
(c) To bring the tea to the drawing room
(d) To bring the slippers to the drawing room

3. Kezia stammered only in front of her ....
(a) father (b) mother
(c) grand mother (d) teacher

4. What was thinking about her father like for Kezia?
(a) It was scary like having the nightmare.
(b) It was fun to think about her father.
(c) It was like thinking about a giant.
(d) It made her very angry to think about her father.

5. Kezia's father told her that she looked like a
(a) little brown duck (b) big brown owl
(c) big brown duck (d) little brown owl

6. What did Kezia's mother do on Sunday afternoons?
(a) She would rest all day long.
(b) She would make lunch on Sunday afternoons.
(c) She would sleep on the sofa.
(d) She would read on Sunday afternoons.

7. Kezia's grandmother sent her down to the drawing room to have a nice talk with
(a) father (b) grandfather
(c) mother (d) Both (a) and (c)

8. Why was Kezia making a pin-cushion?
(a) Because it was a gift for her mother's birthday.
(b) Because it was a gift for her grandmother's birthday.
(c) Because it was a gift for her father's birthday.
(d) Because it was a gift for herself.

9. What did Kezia fill the pin-cushion with before sewing the fourth side?
(a) Many little cotton balls
(b) Many sheets of fine paper
(c) Many lengths of yellow silk
(d) Scraps she gathered from the garbage can

10. What was her father's speech for?
(a) The Port Authority
(b) The Award Function he had to go to
(c) The Birthday Party
(d) The Office Meeting

11. Who was Alice?
(a) Kezia's friend (b) Kezia's aunt
(c) The cook (d) The neighbour's wife

12. Kezia's father commented that she looked like a
(a) little brown cat (b) little brown owl
(c) little brown rat (d) little brown mole

13. How did Kezia's father look when she thought about him alone?
(a) Ghost (b) Giant (c) Monster (d) Huge

14. The Macdonalds were Kezia's
(a) friends (b) classmates
(c) next-door neighbours (d) acquaintances

15. Mr. Macdonald was a .... father.
(a) rude (b) tyrant
(c) loving (d) caring

Answers

Extract Based Questions

1. (i) (d), (ii) (d), (iii) (b), (iv) (a), (v) (d) 2. (i) (c), (ii) (d), (iii) (d), (iv) (b), (v) (c) 3. (i) (b), (ii) (c), (iii) (c), (iv) (b), (v) (a)
4. (i) (b), (ii) (b), (iii) (a), (iv) (c), (v) (b)

Multiple Choice Questions

1. (b) 2. (b) 3. (a) 4. (c) 5. (d) 6. (d) 7. (d) 8. (c) 9. (b) 10. (a) 11. (c) 12. (b)
13. (b) 14. (c) 15. (c)

04 A Truly Beautiful Mind

The chapter recounts the life of Albert Einstein, the greatest scientist of the 20th century. Einstein was considered unusual by his mother. He was highly skilled in mathematics and physics. After graduating in 1900, he worked as a technical expert in 1902 where he assessed other people's inventions and secretly developed his own ideas. He became world famous after he published his General Theory of Relativity in 1915. He was awarded the Nobel Prize for Physics in 1921. He worked for world peace and democracy in the later years of his life.

Important Characters

Albert Einstein	A world famous scientist and a humanitarian who was considered as a world citzen.
एल्बर्ट आईन्स्टाइन	एक विश्व प्रसिद्ध वैज्ञानिक और मानवतावादी जिन्हें विश्व नागरिक के रूप में माना गया।
Einstein's Mother	A conservative woman who could not accept Mileva as she was three years older to Albert.
आईन्स्टाइन की माँ	एक रूढ़िवादी महिला जो मिलेवा को स्वीकार नहीं कर सकती थी, क्योंकि वह एल्बर्ट से तीन वर्ष बड़ी थी।
Mileva Maric	Einstein's fellow student and his first wife. Her initial intellectual ambition later converted into unhappiness as a house wife.
मिलेवा मेरिक	आईन्स्टाइन की सहपाठी छात्रा और उनकी पहली पत्नी। उसकी प्रारम्भिक बौद्धिक महत्त्वाकांक्षा, बाद में एक गृहिणी के रूप में अप्रसन्नता में बदल गई।

Summary of the Lesson पाठ का सार

Early Life of Einstein

Albert Einstein was born on 14th March 1879 in the city named Ulm in Germany. His mother thought that he was a freak (abnormal) because unlike other children, he had a large head. He was unable to speak even at the age of two and a helf years. When he started speaking, he spoke everything twice.

Einstein did not like the company of friends. His friends called him 'Brother Boring'. He played by himself with mechanical toys. Einstein learnt to play the violin at the age of six and later became an amateur violinist.

Einstein's Education and Clash with Teachers

Einstein went to high school in Munich where his family had moved. He was a good student and scored good marks in every subject. Einstein did not like the strict discipline of the school and often had arguments with his teachers. He left the school at the age of 15 years. His parents shifted to Milan but Einstein continued his schooling in Switzerland.

Einstein at University

Einstein was extraordinary in mathematics and had an interest in physics. After finishing school, he decided to study at a university in Munich. Einstein graduated at the age of 21 in the year 1900. At the university in Munich, Einstein fell in love with a Serbian girl named Mileva Maric.

आईन्स्टाइन का प्रारम्भिक जीवन

एल्बर्ट आईन्स्टाइन का जन्म 14 मार्च, 1879 को जर्मनी के उल्म नामक शहर में हुआ था। उनकी माँ ने सोचा कि वे सनकी (असाधारण) थे, क्योंकि अन्य बच्चों की तुलना में, उनका सिर बड़ा था। वे ढाई वर्ष की आयु में भी बोलने में असमर्थ थे। जब उन्होंने बोलना प्रारम्भ किया तो हर बात को दो बार बोलते थे।

आईन्स्टाइन को दोस्तों की संगति पसन्द नहीं थी। उनके दोस्त उन्हें 'ब्रदर बोरिंग' कहते थे। वे अकेले ही यांत्रिक खिलौनों के साथ खेलते थे। आईन्स्टाइन ने 6 वर्ष की आयु में वायलिन बजाना सीखा और बाद में एक शौकिया वायलिन वादक बन गए।

आईन्स्टाइन की शिक्षा और शिक्षकों के साथ टकराव

आईन्स्टाइन म्यूनिख के हाई स्कूल में पढ़ने गए, जहाँ उनका परिवार चला गया था। वे एक अच्छे छात्र थे और प्रत्येक विषय में अच्छे अंक हासिल करते थे। आईन्स्टाइन को स्कूल का सख्त अनुशासन पसन्द नहीं था और अकसर अपने शिक्षकों के साथ उनकी बहस होती थी। उन्होंने 15 वर्ष की आयु में स्कूल छोड़ दिया। उनके माता-पिता मिलान में स्थानान्तरित हो गए, लेकिन आईन्स्टाइन ने स्विट्जरलैंड में अपनी स्कूली शिक्षा जारी रखी।

विश्वविद्यालय में आईन्स्टाइन

आइन्स्टाइन गणित में असाधारण थे, और भौतिकी में उनकी रुचि थी। स्कूल की पढ़ाई पूरी करने के बाद, उन्होंने म्यूनिख के एक विश्वविद्यालय में अध्ययन करने का निर्णय लिया। आईन्स्टाइन ने वर्ष 1900 में 21 वर्ष की आयु में स्नातक की उपाधि प्राप्त की। म्यूनिख के विश्वविद्यालय में, आईन्स्टाइन को मिलेवा मेरिक नाम की सर्बियाई लड़की से प्यार हो गया।

Einstein's Special Theory of Relativity

After graduation, he worked as a teaching assistant and also gave private lessons. He got a job as a technical expert in the patent office in Bern in 1902. At the same time, he developed his own ideas secretly. He published his Special Theory of Relativity in 1905, according to which time and distance are not absolute. From this theory, he derived the world's most famous formula which described the relationship between mass and energy, $E = mc^2$. (where E is energy, m is mass and c is the speed of the light in a vacuum)

Einstein's Marriage

Mileva Maric was an intelligent girl. Einstein wanted to marry her but his mother was against it. She thought that Mileva was too old for Einstein. However, Einstein married her in 1903. They had two sons but their marriage failed and they finally got divorced in 1919. Einstein married his cousin Elsa in the same year.

Einstein's Published His General Theory of Relativity and Nobel Prize

In 1915, Einstein published his General Theory of Relativity. It gave a new interpretation of gravity. An eclipse of the sun in 1919 proved his theory correct. He became famous as his work was considered as a scientific revolution. He received the Nobel Prize for Physics in 1921.

Einstein Emigrates to US

Einstein emigrated (moved) to the United States when the Nazis came to power in 1933. The process of nuclear fission was discovered in Berlin in 1938. The American physicists feared that the Nazis could build an atomic bomb. On 2nd August, 1939 Einstein wrote a letter to the American President, Franklin D. Roosevelt about the massive destruction that can be caused by a single atomic bomb.

The Americans developed the atomic bomb secretly and dropped it on the Japanese cities of Hiroshima and Nagasaki in August 1945 during the World War II.

Einstein Works for Peace and Democracy

Einstein was very upset about the huge destruction caused by the atomic bomb. So, he wrote a long official letter to the United Nations in which he proposed the formation of a world government. But, this did not have any effect.

He continued to work for world peace and democracy and involved himself more in politics in the coming years. He campaigned to end the arms build up. He died in 1955 at the age. of 76. He was admired as a visionary, a world citizen and a scientific genius.

आईन्स्टाइन का सापेक्षता का विशेष सिद्धान्त

स्नातक स्तर की शिक्षा के बाद, उन्होंने एक सहायक अध्यापक के रूप में काम किया और निजी शिक्षण भी दिया। उन्हें 1902 में बर्न के पेटेंट कार्यालय में एक तकनीकी विशेषज्ञ के रूप में नौकरी मिली। उसी समय, उन्होंने गुप्त रूप से अपने विचारों को विकसित किया। उन्होंने 1905 में अपना सापेक्षता का विशेष सिद्धान्त प्रकाशित किया, जिसके अनुसार समय व दूरी निरपेक्ष नहीं है। इस सिद्धान्त से, उन्होंने विश्व का सबसे प्रसिद्ध सूत्र निकाला, जिसने द्रव्यमान और ऊर्जा के बीच के सम्बन्ध का वर्णन किया, $E=mc^2$. (जहाँ E ऊर्जा है, m द्रव्यमान है और c निर्वात में प्रकाश की गति)

आईन्स्टाइन का विवाह

मिलेवा मेरिक एक बुद्धिमान लड़की थी। आईन्स्टाइन उससे शादी करना चाहते थे लेकिन उनकी माँ इसके खिलाफ थी। उन्होंने (आइन्स्टाइन की माँ ने) सोचा कि मिलेवा आईन्स्टाइन के लिए आयु में बहुत बड़ी थी। हालाँकि, आईन्स्टाइन ने 1903 में मिलेवा से विवाह किया। उनके दो पुत्र थे लेकिन उनकी शादी विफल रही और 1919 में उन्होंने मिलेवा से तलाक ले लिया। आईन्स्टाइन ने उसी वर्ष अपनी मौसी की बेटी एल्सा से विवाह कर लिया।

आईन्स्टाइन का सापेक्षता के सामान्य सिद्धान्त को प्रकाशित करना और नोबेल पुरस्कार

वर्ष 1915 में, आईन्स्टाइन ने अपना सापेक्षता का सामान्य सिद्धान्त प्रकाशित किया। इसने गुरुत्वाकर्षण की एक नई व्याख्या प्रदान की। 1919 में सूर्य के ग्रहण ने उनके सिद्धान्त को सही साबित किया। वे प्रसिद्ध हुए, क्योंकि उनके काम को 'वैज्ञानिक क्रान्ति' के रूप में माना गया। उन्होंने 1921 में भौतिकी का नोबेल पुरस्कार प्राप्त किया।

आईन्स्टाइन का यू.एस. चले जाना

वर्ष 1933 में नाजियों के सत्ता में आने पर आईन्स्टाइन यू.एस. जाकर बस गए। 1938 में बर्लिन में नाभिकीय विखण्डन की प्रक्रिया की खोज की गई। अमेरिकी भौतिकविदो को डर था कि नाजी परमाणु बम बना सकते थे। 2 अगस्त, 1939 को आईन्स्टाइन ने परमाणु बम से बड़े पैमाने पर होने वाले विनाश के बारे में अमेरिकी राष्ट्रपति फ्रैंकलिन डी. रूजवेल्ट को एक पत्र लिखा।

अमेरिकियों ने गुप्त रूप से परमाणु बम विकसित किया और द्वितीय विश्वयुद्ध के दौरान अगस्त, 1945 में जापानी नगरों हिरोशिमा और नागासाकी पर गिरा दिया।

आईन्स्टाइन का शान्ति और लोकतन्त्र के लिए कार्य करना

आईन्स्टाइन परमाणु बम से हुए विनाश से बहुत परेशान थे। इसलिए, उन्होंने संयुक्त राष्ट्र को एक आधिकारिक पत्र लिखा जिसमें उन्होंने एक विश्व सरकार के गठन का प्रस्ताव रखा। लेकिन इसका कोई प्रभाव नहीं हुआ।

उन्होंने विश्व शान्ति और लोकतन्त्र के लिए काम करना जारी रखा और आने वाले वर्षों में स्वयं को राजनीति में अधिक शामिल किया। उन्होंने शस्त्रों के निर्माण की होड़ को समाप्त करने के लिए अभियान चलाया। 1955 में 76 वर्ष की आयु में उनका निधन हो गया। उन्हें एक दूरदर्शी एक विश्व नागरिक और एक प्रतिभाशाली वैज्ञानिक के रूप में सराहा गया।

Objective Questions

Extract Based Questions

Read the following extracts and answer the questions given below them.

1 To her, his head seemed too large? At the age of two-and-a-half, Einstein still wasn't talking. When he finally did learn to speak, he uttered everything twice. Einstein did not know what to do with other children, and his playmates called him 'Brother Boring'.

So the youngster played by himself much of the time. He especially loved mechanical toys. Looking at his newborn sister, Maja, he is said to have said: "Fine, but where are her wheels?"

(i) To whom does 'her' refer to?
(a) Einstein's cousin (b) Einstein's teacher
(c) Einstein's mother (d) Einstein's grandmother

(ii) What does she think about him?
(a) He was dumb. (b) He was too intelligent.
(c) He will be very wealthy. (d) He was a freak.

(iii) What abnormality did Einstein suffer from in his childhood?
(a) Learning disability (b) Speaking disability
(c) Walking disability (d) Social disability

(iv) Einstein uttered everything twice
(a) he started speaking late
(b) was very friendly with other children
(c) Both (a) and (b)
(d) None of the above

(v) Who called him boring?
(a) Playmates (b) Teacher
(c) Headmaster (d) Mother

2 A headmaster once told his father that what Einstein chose as a profession wouldn't matter, because "he'll never make a success at anything." Einstein began learning to play the violin at the age of six, because his mother wanted him to; he later became a gifted amateur violinist, maintaining this skill throughout his life.

But Albert Einstein was not a bad pupil. He went to high school in Munich, where Einstein's family had moved when he was 15 months old, and scored good marks in almost every subject.

(i) What was headmaster's opinion about Einstein?
(a) He will be a failure.
(b) He will not succeed in any profession.
(c) He will be able to perform much later.
(d) His hard work will not pay him.

(ii) Why did Einstein begin learning to play the violin?
(a) He loved playing the violin since childhood.
(b) His father wanted him to learn the violin.
(c) His mother wanted him to learn the violin.
(d) His friends supported him to learn the violin.

(iii) Which word from the extract means the same as 'not a professional'?
(a) Gifted (b) Amateur
(c) Skilled (d) Professional

(iv) How can we say that the headmaster was not correct in his opinion of Einstein?
(a) Headmaster could not recognise Einstein's talent.
(b) Einstein was an average person.
(c) Einstein was a gifted child.
(d) Einstein was skilled enough to handle everything.

(v) The statement that is true regarding Einstein is
(a) He was a slow child during his childhood.
(b) He was overfriendly.
(c) He was intelligent but his headmaster didn't realise this fact.
(d) Both (a) and (c)

3 But Albert Einstein was not a bad pupil. He went to high school in Munich, where Einstein's family had moved when he was 15 months old and scored good marks in every subject. Einstein hated the school's regimentation and often clashed with his teachers. At the age of 15, Einstein felt so stifled there that he left the school for good. The previous year, Albert's parents had moved to Milan and left their son with relatives. After prolonged discussion, Einstein got his wish to continue his education in German-speaking Switzerland, in a city which was more liberal than Munich.

(i) 'Bad pupil' in the extract means
(a) bad son (b) bad husband
(c) bad student (d) bad teacher

(ii) When did Einstein leave school?
(a) When he was 12 years old.
(b) When he was 15 years old.
(c) When he was 16 years old.
(d) When he was 17 years old.

(iii) Where did Albert's parents move from Munich?
(a) Zurich (b) Paris (c) Milan (d) Brussels

(iv) 'Clashed' in the extract means
(a) to argue (b) to agree (c) to meet (d) to obey

(v) How did Einstein feel at school?
(a) Happy (b) Suffocated (c) Lively (d) Bored

4 While Einstein was solving the most difficult problems in physics, his private life was unravelling. Albert had wanted to marry Mileva right after finishing his studies, but his mother was against it. She thought Mileva,who was three years older than her son, was too old for him. She was also bothered by Mileva's intelligence. "She is a book like you", his mother said. Einstein put the wedding off.

(i) Why did Einstein's mother oppose his marriage to Mileva?
(a) Because Mileva was three years older than Einstein.
(b) Because Mileva was very dumb.
(c) Because Mileva was very intelligent.
(d) Both (a) and (c)

(ii) Mileva belonged to
(a) Germany (b) Russia
(c) France (d) Serbia

(iii) Einstein put the wedding off because
(a) he was busy with his research work.
(b) he did not have money.
(c) his mother was against his marriage with Mileva.
(d) his father was against his marriage with Mileva.

(iv) Which word in the extract is the opposite of 'stupidity'?
(a) Unravelling (b) Intelligence
(c) Difficult (d) Book

(v) The word 'unravelling in the extract means
(a) starting to fail (b) starting to happen
(c) starting to succeed (d) starting to show

Multiple Choice Questions

1. Where was Albert Einstein born?
(a) Ulm, Germany (b) Munich, Germany
(c) Switzerland (d) Milan

2. What did Einstein's playmates call him?
(a) Albert (b) Albie
(c) Brother boring (d) Freak

3. What was the name of Einstein's little sister?
(a) Mileva (b) Maja
(c) Elsa (d) Zurich

4. Einstein's loved to play with
(a) soft toys (b) mechanical toys
(c) dolls (d) All of these

5. At what age did Einstein begin learning to play the violin?
(a) At two and half years (b) At fifteen years
(c) At six years (d) At twenty-one years

6. Which of the following statements about Einstein is true?
(a) His points knew that he was destined for greatness.
(b) Einstein's could talk when he was years old.
(c) His mother discouraged him from playing the violin.
(d) He scored good marks in almost every subject.

7. Why did Einstein leave the school at the age of fifteen?
(a) He often clashed with the teachers.
(b) He hated the school's regimentation.
(c) He didn't want to study anymore.
(d) Both (a) and (b)

8. In which of the following subjects was Einstein highly gifted and interested?
(a) Mathematics (b) History
(c) Physics (d) Both (a) and (c)

9. What kind of a moustache did Einstein have?
(a) A bushy moustache
(b) A walrus moustache
(c) A slim moustache
(d) He didn't have any moustache.

10. Whom did Einstein show a special interest in?
(a) Mileva (b) Elsa (c) Maja (d) Himself

11. Who is referred to as 'philistines' in the story?
(a) People in his family and at university with whom he was constantly at odds.
(b) His teachers from the university who disliked him.
(c) His friends from college who thought he was a freak.
(d) His colleagues at work who found him to be unusual.

12. When Einstein was a little child his mother thought him a
(a) bully (b) freak (c) weak (d) innovative

13. When Albert's parents moved to Milan, they left their son with
(a) cousins (b) neighbours
(c) relatives (d) friends

14. Albert Einstein became a university graduate in
(a) 1899 (b) 1901 (c) 1902 (d) 1900

15. The world's most famous formula was the relationship between
(a) mass and velocity (b) energy and velocity
(c) mass and distance (d) mass and energy

Answers

Extract Based Questions

1. (i) (c), (ii) (d), (iii) (b), (iv) (a), (v) (a) 2. (i) (b), (ii) (c), (iii) (b), (iv) (c), (v) (d) 3. (i) (c), (ii) (b), (iii) (c), (iv) (a), (v) (b)
4. (i) (d), (ii) (d), (iii) (c), (iv) (b), (v) (a)

Multiple Choice Questions

1. (a) 2. (c) 3. (b) 4. (b) 5. (c) 6. (d) 7. (d) 8. (d) 9. (b) 10. (a)
11. (a) 12. (b) 13. (c) 14. (d) 15. (d)

05 The Snake and the Mirror

In this story, the narrator is a homeopathic doctor. He narrates his encounter with a snake in a frightening and humourous way. One night, the doctor was sitting in his room and admiring himself in the mirror. Suddenly, a snake falls on his shoulder and coils itself around his left arm. Luckily, the snake turns its head and looks into the mirror. Then, it uncoils itself from the doctor's arm and moves closer to the mirror. The doctor, thus, gets an opportunity to escape.

Important Characters

The Doctor एक डॉक्टर	He is a young bachelor homeopathic doctor who is conscious of how to look smart. He is also the narrator of the story who shares his experience of encounter with a snake in a humorous way. वह एक जवान, कुँवारा होम्योपैथिक डॉक्टर है, जो इस बात को लेकर सजग है कि सुन्दर कैसे दिखे। वह कहानी का कथाकार भी है, जो एक साँप के साथ अपनी आकस्मिक भेंट के अपने अनुभव को हास्यपूर्ण ढंग से साझा करता है।

Summary of the Lesson पाठ का सार

The Narrator Starts Narrating His Experience

The narrator was a homeopathic doctor. He lived in a small rented room which did not have an electricity connection. He had just started his medical practice and his earning was small. The narrator describes his experience with a snake to his friends.

It was a hot summer night. The doctor had returned to his room at about ten O'clock after having meal at the restaurant. When he opened the door, he heard a noise from above. As his room had a lot of rats in it, he ignored the noise.

He lighted the kerosene lamp and took off his clothes. He then opened the two windows and lay down on his bed but was unable to sleep as it was very hot. He got up and went to the veranda to get some fresh air.

The Doctor Admires Himself Seeing in the Mirror

After coming back into his room, the doctor sat on a chair. He took out a medical book and opened it on the table. A lamp and a large mirror were kept on the table. A small comb also lay beside the mirror. The doctor was a bachelor and believed in making himself look handsome.

The doctor again heard the same sound but ignored it. He looked closely at his face in the mirror and made two important decisions. First, he would shave daily and grow a thin moustache and second, he would always keep an attractive smile on his face. Suddenly, he heard the same noise again from above. The doctor also thought that he would marry a woman doctor who had a lot of money and a good medical practice. She had to be fat because if he made some silly mistake and needed to run away, she would not be able to catch him.

कथावाचक का अपने अनुभव बताना शुरू करना

कथावाचक एक होम्योपैथिक डॉक्टर था। वह एक छोटे से किराए के कमरे में रहता था, जिसमें बिजली का कनेक्शन नहीं था। उसने अभी-अभी अपनी मेडिकल प्रैक्टिस शुरू की थी और उसकी आमदनी कम थी। कथावाचक अपने दोस्तों को एक साँप के साथ अपने अनुभव का वर्णन करता है।

ग्रीष्म ऋतु की गर्म रात्रि थी। डॉक्टर रेस्तराँ में भोजन करने के बाद लगभग दस बजे अपने कमरे में लौट आया था। जब उसने दरवाजा खोला तो उसे ऊपर से कुछ आवाज सुनाई दी। चूँकि उसके कमरे में बहुत सारे चूहे थे, उसने आवाज को अनदेखा कर दिया।

उसने केरोसीन का लैम्प जलाया और अपने कपड़े उतार दिए। फिर उसने दोनों खिड़कियाँ खोलीं और अपने बिस्तर पर लेट गया, लेकिन अधिक गर्मी के कारण वो सो नहीं सका। वह उठा और कुछ ताजी हवा लेने के लिए बरामदे में चला गया।

डॉक्टर का दर्पण में देखकर स्वयं की प्रशंसा करना

अपने कमरे में वापस आने के बाद, डॉक्टर एक कुर्सी पर बैठ गया। उसने एक चिकित्सा सम्बन्धी पुस्तक निकाली और उसे मेज पर खोलकर रख दिया। मेज पर एक लैम्प और एक बड़ा दर्पण रखा हुआ था। दर्पण के पास में एक छोटा-सा कंघा भी पड़ा हुआ था। डॉक्टर कुँवारा था और स्वयं को सुन्दर दिखाने में विश्वास रखता था।

डॉक्टर ने फिर से वही आवाज सुनी लेकिन उसे अनदेखा कर दिया। उसने अपने चेहरे को दर्पण में बहुत करीब से देखा और दो महत्त्वपूर्ण निर्णय लिए। पहला, वह प्रतिदिन दाढ़ी बनाएगा और एक पतली सी मूँछ उगाएगा और दूसरा, वह हमेशा अपने चेहरे पर एक आकर्षक मुस्कान बनाए रखेगा। अचानक, उसने ऊपर से फिर वही आवाज सुनी। डॉक्टर ने यह भी विचार किया कि वह एक महिला डॉक्टर से शादी करेगा, जिसके पास बहुत सारा धन हो और जिसकी मेडिकल प्रैक्टिस अच्छी हो। वह मोटी होनी चाहिए, क्योंकि यदि वह (डॉक्टर) कुछ मूर्खतापूर्ण गलती कर दे और उसे भागने की आवश्यकता पड़े, तो वह उसे (डॉक्टर को) पकड़ ना सके।

A Snake Falls on the Doctor

For sometime, the doctor did not hear any sound from above. Suddenly, there was a dull thud as if a rubber tube had fallen to the ground. As he turned around, a fat snake landed on his shoulder. The snake coiled around the doctor's left arm above the elbow. Its head was only 3-4 inches away from the doctor's face. The doctor did not move as if he had turned into stone. He felt pain in his left arm.

Doctor's Escape From the Snake

The doctor prayed to God for help and then realised that he was a foolish and stupid doctor as he did not have any medicine for snakebite with him. He forgot his danger and smiled at himself.

The snake turned his head. It looked into the mirror and saw its reflection. Then it uncoiled itself from the doctor's arm and slowly moved towards his lap. From there, the snake crawled over to the table and moved towards the mirror as if it liked to see its reflection more closely.

The doctor, thus, got an opportunity to escape from the house. He got up from the chair and quietly went out through the door into the veranda. Then he ran as fast as he could into the yard.

Doctor decides to Shift to a Different Place

The doctor ran till he reached his friend's house. He took a bath and changed his clothes there. He decided to shift to a different place. So, the next morning at about eight thirty the doctor went to his room with his friend to shift his belongings. However, after reaching, the doctor and his friend found that some thief had taken most of his things. From that day, the doctor never saw that snake again.

एक साँप का डॉक्टर पर गिरना

कुछ समय तक, डॉक्टर ने ऊपर से कोई आवाज नहीं सुनी। अचानक वहाँ धीमी-सी धम्म की आवाज आई जैसे कोई रबर की ट्यूब जमीन पर गिर गई हो। जैसे ही वह पीछे मुड़ा एक मोटा साँप उसके कंधे पर आकर बैठ गया। साँप डॉक्टर के बाएँ हाथ की कोहनी के ऊपर चारों ओर लिपट गया। उसका फन डॉक्टर के चेहरे से केवल 3-4 इंच की दूरी पर था। डॉक्टर हिला नही, जैसे वह पत्थर में बदल गया हो। उसने अपनी बाईं भुजा में दर्द महसूस किया।

डॉक्टर का साँप से बचना

डॉक्टर ने मदद के लिए भगवान् से प्रार्थना की और फिर उसे एहसास हुआ कि वह एक मूर्ख और बेवकूफ डॉक्टर था, क्योंकि उसके पास साँप के काटने की कोई दवा नहीं थी। वह अपने खतरे को भूल गया और स्वयं पर मुस्कुराया।

साँप ने अपना सिर घुमाया। उसने दर्पण में देखा और उसे उसका प्रतिबिम्ब दिखाई दिया। फिर उसने स्वयं को डॉक्टर की भुजा से हटा दिया और धीरे से उसकी (डॉक्टर की) गोद की ओर बढ़ गया। वहाँ से, साँप रेंगता हुआ मेज की ओर चला गया और दर्पण की ओर बढ़ गया, जैसे कि वह अपने प्रतिबिम्ब को और करीब से देखना चाहता था।

इस प्रकार, डॉक्टर को घर से बच निकलने का अवसर मिला। वह कुर्सी से उठा और धीरे से दरवाजे से बरामदे में चला गया। फिर वह जितना तेज मैदान में भाग सकता था, उतना तेज भागा।

डॉक्टर का रहने के स्थान को बदलने का निर्णय

डॉक्टर तब तक भागा जब तक वह अपने मित्र के घर नहीं पहुँच गया। उसने वहाँ स्नान किया और अपने कपड़े बदले। उसने रहने का स्थान बदलने का निर्णय किया। इसलिए, अगली सुबह करीब साढ़े आठ बजे डॉक्टर अपने दोस्त के साथ अपना सामान लेने के लिए अपने कमरे पर गया। हालाँकि, वहाँ पहुँचकर, डॉक्टर और उसके दोस्त ने पाया कि कोई चोर उसका अधिकतर सामान ले जा चुका था।

Objective Questions

Extract Based Questions

Read the following extracts and answer the questions given below them.

1 Has a snake ever coiled itself round any part of your body? A full-blooded cobra? All of us fell silent. The question came from the homeopath. The topic came up when we were discussing snakes. We listened attentively as the doctor continued with his tale. It was a hot summer night; about ten o'clock.

(i) Who is asking the question in the extract?
(a) The doctor's father (b) A homeopath doctor
(c) A heart specialist (d) A dentist

(ii) 'We' in the extract refers to
(a) the author and his doctor friends
(b) the author and his cousins
(c) the author and his engineer friends
(d) the author and his siblings

(iii) Why did all of them fell silent?
(a) Because they were afraid of animals.
(b) Because they were afraid of the narrator.
(c) Because they were afraid of snakes.
(d) Because they were afraid of the dark.

(iv) The opposite of 'silent' is
(a) quite (b) noisy
(c) indifferent (d) calm

(v) The extract has been taken from
(a) The Snake and the Mirror
(b) A Truly Beautiful Mind
(c) The Lost Child
(d) The Little Girl

2 It was a hot summer night; about ten O'clock I had my meal at a restaurant and returned to my room. I heard a noise from above as I opened the door. The sound was a familiar one. The house was not electrified; it was a small rented room. I had just set up medical practice and my earnings were meagre. I had about sixty rupees in my suitcase. Along with some shirts and dhotis, I also possessed one solitary black coat which I was then wearing.

(i) Who is 'I' in these lines?
(a) The patient (b) Doctor-narrator
(c) The landlord (d) The neighbour

(ii) It was a night of
(a) winter (b) summer (c) spring (d) autumn

(iii) I heard a noise from above as 'I' opened the
(a) window (b) door (c) almirah (d) cupboard

(iv) The word 'meagre' in the passage means
(a) huge (b) very little (c) small (d) big

(v) 'I' had about sixty rupees in his
(a) bag (b) box
(c) suitcase (d) cupboard

3 I didn't jump. I didn't tremble. I didn't cry out. There was no time to do any such thing. The snake slithered along my shoulder and coiled around my left arm above the elbow. The hood was spread out and its head was hardly three or four inches from my face!

It would not be correct to say merely that I sat there holding my breath. I was turned to stone. But my mind was very active. The door opened into darkness. The room was surrounded by darkness. In the light of the lamp I sat there like a stone image in the flesh.

(i) The given lines show that the narrator is
(a) terrified
(b) awed
(c) surprised
(d) nervous

(ii) Which of the following statements is not true?
(a) The incident took place in the narrator's clinic.
(b) The narrator is recounting this experience.
(c) The snake is an admirer of beauty.
(d) The narrator is a doctor.

(iii) The snake mentioned in the extract was
(a) thin (b) fat
(c) injured (d) restless

(iv) The phrase 'slithered along' in the extract means
(a) to surround
(b) to crawl
(c) to slide
(d) to push

(v) When the snake fell on the narrator, he was
(a) sleeping
(b) standing
(c) writing
(d) seated on a chair

4 I forgot my danger and smiled feebly at myself. It seemed as if God appreciated that. The snake turned its head. It looked into the mirror and saw its reflection. I do not claim that it was the first snake that had ever looked into a mirror. But it was certain that the snake was looking into the mirror.

(i) The tone of the narrator in the given extract is
(a) alarmed (b) relieved
(c) surprised (d) happy

(ii) From the given extract it seems that the snake is
(a) trying to copy the narrator
(b) a narcissist
(c) attracted to the mirror
(d) not hungry

(iii) The danger referred to here is
(a) the snake (b) the broken house
(c) the glass (d) the book

(iv) The snake turned its
(a) tail (b) body (c) eyes (d) head

(v) The snake was
(a) lying still (b) trying to move outside
(c) looking into the mirror (d) doing nothing

Multiple Choice Questions

1. Who asked the first question in the story?
(a) The narrator's friend
(b) A thief
(c) The homeopath
(d) The hospital receptionist

2. What kind of night was it when the narrator returned to his room?
(a) Hot winter night
(b) Cold summer night
(c) Cold winter night
(d) Hot summer night

3. The narrator shared his room with ....
(a) snakes (b) his friends
(c) rats (d) All of these

4. What does the doctor say about the room where he lived?
(a) It was not electrified.
(b) It was a small rented room.
(c) There were too many rats in it.
(d) All of the above

5. How many rupees did the narrator have in his suitcase?
(a) Eighty rupees
(b) Sixty rupees
(c) Twenty rupees
(d) Forty rupees

6. These were .... windows in the narrator's room.
(a) three (b) four
(c) many (d) two

7. Which of the following items of clothing did the narrator have?
(a) Some shirts
(b) Dhotis
(c) Single black coat
(d) All of the above

8. Why was it a valid reason for the woman he marries to be fat?
(a) If he runs away after making a mistake, she won't be able to catch him.
(b) She would be round and soft.
(c) She wouldn't be able to beat him.
(d) None of the above

9. Which of the following statements about the narrator is true?
(a) The narrator was a medical student.
(b) The narrator shared the room with his friend.
(c) The narrator wanted to marry a rich doctor.
(d) The narrator wanted to marry a poor doctor.

10. Where did the narrator have his meal?
(a) At his uncle's house
(b) At home
(c) At his friend's house
(d) At a restaurant

11. What did he do after coming into the room?
(a) He lighted a candle.
(b) He lighted a kerosene lamp.
(c) He switched on the light.
(d) He sat down in the dark.

12. Why did the doctor live in a small rented room?
(a) He was unmarried.
(b) There was no other room available.
(c) His earnings were small.
(d) It was very close to his clinic.

13. What did the snake do after landing on the doctor's shoulder?
(a) Coiled around his head
(b) Coiled around his neck
(c) Coiled around his left arm above the elbow
(d) Coiled around his right arm above the elbow

14. The doctor's life was saved
(a) because of rats (b) because of mirror
(c) because of his dirty vest (d) None of these

15. Why did the doctor decide to smile?
(a) To attract people
(b) To attract customers
(c) To look more handsome
(d) None of the above

Answers

Extract Based Questions

1. (i) (b), (ii) (a), (iii) (c), (iv) (b), (v) (a) 2. (i) (b), (ii) (b), (iii) (b), (iv) (b), (v) (c) 3. (i) (a), (ii) (a), (iii) (b), (iv) (c), (v) (d)
4. (i) (b), (ii) (b), (iii) (a), (iv) (d), (v) (c)

Multiple Choice Questions

1. (c) 2. (d) 3. (c) 4. (d) 5. (b) 6. (d) 7. (d) 8. (a) 9. (c) 10. (d)
11. (b) 12. (c) 13. (c) 14. (b) 15. (c)

06 My Childhood

This chapter is an extract taken from the autobiography of APJ Abdul Kalam, 'Wings of Fire'. This chapter is about his childhood. He became India's eleventh President in 2002. His hard work, sincerity and dedication made him a world class scientist. In this chapter, he describes his house, family, friends and teachers. It also mentions how he earned his first wages. During his childhood, he faced religious discrimination but was able to overcome it with the support of some progressive people. The motivation was given to him by his father and science teacher to pursue his goals made him a great scientist in the future.

Important Characters

Abdul Kalam अब्दुल कलाम	He was a former President of India and a great scientist. He was also known as 'Missile Man'. ये भारत के पूर्व राष्ट्रपति थे तथा महान वैज्ञानिक थे। ये 'मिसाइल मैन' के नाम से भी जाने जाते थे।
Jainulabdeen जैनुलाब्दीन	He was Abdul Kalam's father. He possessed great innate wisdom and true generosity of spirit. वे अब्दुल कलाम के पिता थे। उनके पास जन्म से ही बुद्धिमत्ता और सच्ची आध्यात्मिक उदारता थी।
Ashiamma आशिम्मा	She was the mother of Abdul Kalam and a woman with simple thoughts. वे अब्दुल कलाम की माता थी और एक सरल विचारों वाली महिला थी।
Samsuddin समसुददीन	He was cousin of Abdul Kalam who helped Kalam in earning his first wages. वह अब्दुल कलाम का चचेरा भाई था, जिसने कलाम की पहली कमाई कमाने में मदद की थी।
Ramanadha Sastry रामनधा शास्त्री	Abdul Kalam's friend who was the son of Pakshi Lakshmana Sastry, the high priest of Rameswaram temple. अब्दुल कलाम के दोस्त थे, जो पाक्षी लक्ष्मण शास्त्री (रामेश्वरम मन्दिर के बड़े पुजारी) के पुत्र थे।
Pakshi Lakshmana Sastry पक्षी लक्ष्मण शास्त्री	He was the high priest of Rameshwaram temple. वे रामेश्वर मन्दिर के बड़े पुजारी थे।
Aravindan अरविन्द	He was childhood friend of Abdul Kalam. वह अब्दुल कलाम का बचपन का दोस्त था।
Sivaprakasan शिवप्रकाशन	He was childhood friend of Abdul Kalam. वह अब्दुल कलाम का बचपन का दोस्त था।
Sivasubramania Iyer शिवसुब्रमणिया अय्यर	He was science teacher of Abdul Kalam and he was an orthodox Brahmin. वे अब्दुल कलाम के विज्ञान के शिक्षक थे और रूढ़िवादी ब्राह्मण थे।

Summary of the Lesson पाठ का सार

Kalam's Birth and Family

Abdul Kalam was born in 1931 into a middle-class Tamil family in the island town of Rameswaram in Madras. His father's name was Jainulabdeen and his mother's name was Ashiamma. He had three brothers and one sister.

Kalam's father was not much educated but he had great wisdom and generosity. He was not rich but he provided Kalam a very secure childhood. His mother fed many poor people and outsiders everyday.

The family lived in its ancestral house. It was a large pucca house, made of limestone and brick on the Mosque Street in Rameswaram. Kalam inherited honesty and self-discipline from his father and faith in goodness and deep kindness from his mother.

कलाम का जन्म और परिवार

अब्दुल कलाम का जन्म 1931 में मद्रास के एक द्वीपीय कस्बे रामेश्वरम के मध्यम-वर्गीय तमिल परिवार में हुआ था। उनके पिता का नाम जैनुलाब्दीन और उनकी माता का नाम अशियम्मा था। उनके तीन भाई और एक बहन थी।

कलाम के पिता अधिक पढ़े-लिखे नहीं थे लेकिन वे अत्यधिक बुद्धिमान एवं उदार व्यक्ति थे। वे अमीर नहीं थे, लेकिन उन्होंने कलाम को बहुत सुरक्षित बचपन प्रदान किया। उनकी माता प्रतिदिन कई गरीब लोगों और बाहरी व्यक्तियों को खाना खिलाती थी।

परिवार उनके पैतृक घर में रहता था। यह रामेश्वरम की मस्जिद वाली गली में चूना पत्थर और ईंटों से बना हुआ, एक बड़ा पक्का घर था। कलाम को विरासत में अपने पिता से ईमानदारी और आत्म-अनुशासन और अपनी माता से अच्छाई में विश्वास और गहरी दया भावना प्राप्त हुई थी।

Kalam's First Earning

Kalam was eight years old when the Second World War started in 1939. There was a great demand for tamarind seeds at that time. Kalam used to collect these seeds and got a sufficient amount by selling them at a provision store.

Kalam's brother-in-law, Jallaluddin told him stories about the war which Kalam later read in the newspaper, Dinamani. Kalam earned his first wages by working as a helper to his cousin, Samsuddin, who distributed newspapers in Rameswaram.

Kalam's Childhood Friends

Kalam had three close friends in his childhood. They were Ramanadha Sastry, Aravindan and Sivaprakasan. All of them belonged to orthodox Hindu Brahmin Families. Ramanadha was the son of the high priest of the Rameswaram temple. He later took over the priesthood of the Rameswaram temple from his father.

Aravindan joined the business of arranging transport for visiting pilgrims. Sivaprakasan became a catering contractor for the Southern Railways.

Discriminatory Attitude of New Teacher in Kalam's School

Kalam sat in the front row in the class when he was studying in fifth standard at the Rameswaram Elementary School. His friend, Ramanadha Sastry, sat next to him.

One day a new teacher came to the class. The teacher could not tolerate a Muslim boy (Kalam) sitting with a Hindu priest's son (Ramanadha). So, he asked Kalam to go and sit on the back bench. Both Kalam and Ramanadha felt very sad about this. When Kalam went to the last row Ramanadha started crying. It had a deep and lasting impression on Kalam's mind.

Later, Ramanadha's father called the teacher and warned him against spreading social separation among the children. The teacher felt sorry for his behaviour.

Kalam's Science Teacher

Kalam's science teacher, Sivasubramania Iyer, was a high-caste Brahmin. His wife was very conservative. On the other hand, he was very liberal and did his best to break social barriers.

One day, he invited Kalam to his house for dinner. His wife refused to serve a Muslim boy (Kalam) in her kitchen. So, the teacher himself served Kalam with his own hands and sat next to him to eat.

He again invited Kalam for dinner next weekend. When Kalam went to his house the next time, Sivasubramania's wife took him inside her kitchen and served him food with her own hands.

Kalam Seeks Permission to leave Rameswaram

After the Second World War was over, India's freedom was certain. Gandhiji urged Indians to build their own country. Kalam took his father's permission to leave Rameswaram as he wanted to continue his studies at the district headquarters in Ramanathapuram. His father allowed him but his mother did not like it. So, his father comforted his wife by quoting Khalil Gibran.

कलाम की प्रथम आमदनी (कमाई)

कलाम आठ वर्ष के थे जब 1939 में द्वितीय विश्वयुद्ध प्रारम्भ हुआ। उस समय इमली के बीजों की अत्यधिक माँग थी। कलाम इन बीजों को इकट्ठा करते थे और इन्हें किराना की दुकान पर बेचकर पर्याप्त धनराशि प्राप्त कर लेते थे।

कलाम के जीजाजी, जलालुद्दीन उसे युद्ध की कहानियाँ सुनाते थे, जिन्हें बाद में कलाम ने दीनामणी अखबार में पढ़ा था। कलाम को अपना पहला वेतन अपने चचेरे भाई, समसुद्दीन के सहायक के रूप में कार्य करने पर मिला, जो रामेश्वरम में अखबार बाँटता था।

कलाम के बचपन के दोस्त

बचपन में कलाम के तीन घनिष्ठ मित्र थे। वे रामनधा शास्त्री, अरविन्दन और शिवप्रकाशन थे। वे सभी रूढ़िवादी ब्राह्मण परिवारों से थे। रामनधा रामेश्वरम मन्दिर के उच्च पुजारी का बेटा था। बाद में उन्होंने अपने पिता के रामेश्वरम मन्दिर के पुरोहित का पदभार संभाला।

अरविन्दन तीर्थ स्थलों के भ्रमण के लिए यातायात साधनों की व्यवस्था करने के व्यवसाय से जुड़ गया। शिवप्रकाशन दक्षिण रेलवे के लिए कैटरिंग कांट्रैक्टर बन गया।

कलाम के विद्यालय के नये अध्यापक का भेदभावपूर्ण व्यवहार

कलाम जब रामेश्वरम प्राथमिक विद्यालय की पाँचवीं कक्षा में पढ़ते थे। तब वे प्रथम पंक्ति में बैठते थे। उनके मित्र, रामनधा शास्त्री, उनके साथ बैठते थे।

एक दिन, एक नया अध्यापक कक्षा में आया। अध्यापक को एक मुस्लिम लड़के (कलाम) का हिन्दू पुजारी के बेटे (रामनधा) के साथ बैठना सहन नहीं हुआ। इसलिए, उन्होंने कलाम को पीछे वाली बेंच पर जाकर बैठने के लिए कहा। कलाम और रामनधा दोनों को इस बात से बहुत दु:ख हुआ। जब कलाम आखिरी पंक्ति में चले गए, तो रामनधा रोने लगा। इसका कलाम के मस्तिष्क पर गहरा और स्थायी प्रभाव पड़ा।

बाद में, रामनधा के पिताजी ने अध्यापक को बुलाया और उसे बच्चों के बीच में सामाजिक अलगाव (भेदभाव) फैलाने के खिलाफ चेतावनी दी। अध्यापक को अपने व्यवहार पर शर्मिंदगी हुई।

कलाम के विज्ञान के अध्यापक

कलाम के विज्ञान के अध्यापक, शिवसुब्रमणिया अय्यर, उच्च-जाति के ब्राह्मण थे। उनकी पत्नी बहुत रूढ़िवादी थी। दूसरी तरफ, वे बहुत उदार थे और सामाजिक प्रतिबन्धों को तोड़ने का पूरा प्रयत्न करते थे।

एक दिन, उन्होंने कलाम को अपने घर रात्रिभोज के लिए आमन्त्रित किया। उनकी पत्नी ने एक मुस्लिम लड़के (कलाम) को अपनी रसोई में भोजन परोसने से इन्कार कर दिया। इसलिए, अध्यापक ने स्वयं अपने हाथों से कलाम को भोजन परोसा और भोजन करने के लिए उसके साथ बैठ गए।

उन्होंने अगले सप्ताहान्त पर फिर से कलाम को रात्रि-भोज के लिए आमन्त्रित किया। जब अगली बार कलाम उनके घर गए, शिवसुब्रमणिया की पत्नी उन्हें अपनी रसोई में लेकर गई और स्वयं अपने हाथों से उन्हें खाना परोसा।

कलाम का रामेश्वरम् छोड़ने की अनुमति माँगना

द्वितीय विश्वयुद्ध की समाप्ति के बाद, भारत की स्वतन्त्रता निश्चित थी। गांधीजी ने भारतीयों से अपना देश स्वयं बनाने का आग्रह किया। कलाम ने अपने पिता से रामेश्वरम छोड़ने की अनुमति माँगी, क्योंकि वह रामानाथापुरम के जिला मुख्यालय से अपनी शिक्षा जारी रखना चाहते थे। उनके पिता ने उन्हें अनुमति दे दी लेकिन उनकी माता को यह पसन्द नहीं था। इसलिए, उनके पिता ने खलील जिब्रान की पंक्तियाँ सुनाकर अपनी पत्नी को सांत्वना दी।

He told her that her children are not hers but are sons and daughters of life's longing for itself. They came through her and not from her. She could only give her love to them and should not impose her will on them.

कलाम के पिता ने अपनी पत्नी से कहा कि हमें अपने बच्चों को उनके जीवन की आकांक्षाओं के अनुसार जीने की आजादी देनी चाहिए और उस पर अपनी इच्छाएँ नहीं थोपनी चाहिए। वह जब तक हमारे साथ है हमें उन्हें अपना स्नेह देना चाहिए।

Objective Questions

Extract Based Questions

Read the following extracts and answer the questions given below them.

1 I was born into a middle-class Tamil family in the island town of Rameswaram in the erstwhile Madras state. My father, Jainulabdeen, had neither much formal education nor much wealth; despite these disadvantages, he possessed great innate wisdom and a true generosity of spirit.

(i) In which family was Abdul Kalam born?
(a) A rich family
(b) A middle-class Tamil family
(c) A middle-class Kannad family
(d) A rich Maratha family

(ii) What is true about Abdul Kalam's father?
(a) He did not have much formal education
(b) He was highly emotional
(c) He did not have much wealth
(d) Both (a) and (c)

(iii) Who was Jainulabdeen's ideal helpmate?
(a) Abdul Kalam (b) Samsuddin
(c) Ashiamma (d) Aravindan

(iv) 'erstwhile' in the extract means
(a) former (b) later (c) great (d) small

(v) Which word in the extract means 'inborn'?
(a) island (b) innate (c) spirit (d) possessed

2 For reasons I have never been able to understand, a sudden demand for tamarind seeds erupted in the market. I used to collect the seeds and sell them to a provision shop on Mosque street. A day's collection would fetch me the princely sum of one anna. My brother-in-law Jallaluddin would tell me stories about the war which I would later attempt to trace in the headlines in *Dinamani*.

(i) Here, which war is referred in the above extract?
(a) First World War (b) Second World War
(c) India-China War (d) India-Pakistan War

(ii) Why were tamarind seeds collected by Kalam?
(a) So that he can earn some money.
(b) So that he can help his friends.
(c) It was an essential service to do so at that time.
(d) It would benefit his family.

(iii) The statement that is true which reflects the characteristics of Kalam from the above extract is
(a) he was hard working.
(b) he had a faith in dignity of labour.
(c) he was impatient.
(d) Both (a) and (b)

(iv) 'Dinamani' is the name of a
(a) magazine (b) newspaper
(c) book (d) dictionary

(v) The phrase 'attempt to trace' here means
(a) try to find
(b) try to draw
(c) try to make
(d) try to concoct

3 That forced my cousin Samsuddin, who distributed newspapers in Rameswaram, to look for a helping hand to catch the bundles and, as if naturally, I filled the slot. Samsuddin helped me earn my first wages. Half a century later, I can still feel the surge of pride in earning my own money for the first time.

(i) 'I' in the extract later on become a
(a) scientist (b) statesman
(c) photographer (d) Both (a) and (b)

(ii) What did Samsuddin do?
(a) He distributed newspapers in Rameswaram.
(b) He sold seeds.
(c) He printed newspapers.
(d) He drove the train.

(iii) What made Samsuddin look for a helping hand?
(a) Lack of conveyance
(b) No train stopping at their station
(c) Second World War
(d) His injury

(iv) What would the helping hand do?
(a) Distribute the newspapers
(b) Get on the moving train to get the newspapers
(c) Sell the newspapers
(d) Catch the newspapers

(v) From which chapter has this extract been taken?
(a) My Childhood
(b) The Little Girl
(c) Reach For The Top
(d) The Snake and the Mirror

4 One day, he invited me to his home for a meal. His wife was horrified at the idea of a Muslim boy being invited to dine in her ritually pure kitchen. She refused to serve me in her kitchen. Sivasubramania Iyer was not perturbed, nor did he get angry with his wife, but instead, served me with his own hands and sat down beside me to eat his meal.

His wife watched us from behind the kitchen door. I wondered whether she had observed any difference in the way I ate rice, drank water or cleaned the floor after the meal. When I was leaving his house, Sivasubramania Iyer invited me to join him for dinner again the next weekend.

(i) Why did the teacher's wife watched them from behind the kitchen door?
(a) She believed in segregation of different people.
(b) She didn't want Kalam to enter the kitchen area.
(c) She was observing the behaviour of Kalam.
(d) Both (a) and (b)

(ii) Why was Kalam hesitant to eat food with the Hindu family?
(a) He didn't want to eat with the Hindu family.
(b) He felt ashamed of his religion.
(c) He felt that he was not welcomed in the family.
(d) He wasn't accepted in the Hindu family due to his beliefs.

(iii) Why did the teacher invite him home?
(a) For music (b) For meal
(c) For exercise (d) For discussion

(iv) Which of the following is not true as per the extract?
(a) Abdul's teacher believed in the caste system.
(b) Abdul went to his teacher's house thrice for dinner.
(c) The teacher wanted Kalam to develop.
(d) Both (a) and (b)

(v) What did Iyer's wife refuse to do?
(a) To serve food (b) To give book
(c) To give cloth (d) None of these

Multiple Choice Questions

1. Where was Abdul's ancestral house situated?
(a) Kanyakumari (b) Kochi
(c) Rishikund (d) Rameswaram

2. What qualities did the narrator's father have?
(a) Wisdom (b) Generosity of spirit
(c) Formal education (d) Both (a) and (b)

3. Abdul was ...... while his parents were ....
(a) tall, short (b) short, tall (c) fat, thin (d) thin, fat

4. Kalam's father was
(a) wealthy (b) simple
(c) strict (d) Both (b) and (c)

5. What was Kalam's age during the Second World War?
(a) 10 years (b) 9 years (c) 11 years (d) 8 years

6. Which of the following statements is true?
(a) Jallaluddin was Abdul's brother–in–law.
(b) Samsuddin told Kalam stoics about World War I.
(c) The Second World War stroked in 1940.
(d) Abdul sold tamarind to a chemist shop.

7. Where were the bundled newspaper thrown on?
(a) The Rameswaram Road
(b) The Dhanuskodi Road
(c) The Ramanathapuram Road
(d) In the front of the narrator's house

8. 'My Childhood' chapter is taken from the famous book
(a) Discovery of India (b) Wings of Fire
(c) Tempest (d) India Wins Freedom

9. What was the name of Abdul Kalam's father?
(a) Samsuddin (b) Ashraf Kalam
(c) Shahbaaz Kalam (d) Jainulabdeen Kalam

10. "Indians will build their own India." Who said this?
(a) APJ Abdul Kalam
(b) Sivasubramania Iyer
(c) Netaji Subhas Chandra Bose
(d) Mahatma Gandhi

11. Abdul Kalam became the 11th .... of India.
(a) Prime Minister (b) President
(c) Army Chief (d) Chief Justice

12. Dinamani is the name of
(a) book (b) a newspaper
(c) a woman (d) a friend

13. What is the theme of the story 'My Childhood'?
(a) Children are precious.
(b) Society must be in harmony.
(c) Society, environment and childhood experiences shape one's life.
(d) None of the above

14. Why did Kalam collect tamarind seeds?
(a) To eat them (b) To earn money
(c) To grow plant (d) None of these

15. Who was Kalam's close friend?
(a) Ramanadha Sastry (b) Samsuddin
(c) His father (d) All of these

Answers

Extract Based Questions

1. (i) (b), (ii) (d), (iii) (c), (iv) (a), (v) (b) 2. (i) (b), (ii) (a), (iii) (d), (iv) (b), (v) (a) 3. (i) (d), (ii) (a), (iii) (b), (iv) (d), (v) (a)
4. (i) (d), (ii) (c), (iii) (b), (iv) (d), (v) (a)

Multiple Choice Questions

1. (d) 2. (d) 3. (b) 4. (d) 5. (d) 6. (a) 7. (a) 8. (b) 9. (d) 10. (d)
11. (b) 12. (b) 13. (c) 14. (b) 15. (a)

07 Reach for the Top

This chapter presents the journey of two successful women, Santosh Yadav and Maria Sharapova. Both the women show that with determination and hard work, one can overcome all obstacles and achieve success.

Important Characters (Part I)

Santosh Yadav सन्तोष यादव	She is the first woman mountaineer to climb Mount Everest twice. In recognition of her achievements, she was honoured with one of the top honours, the Padmashri. वह पहली पर्वतारोही हैं, जिन्होंने दो बार माउण्ट ऐवरेस्ट की चढाई की। उनकी उपलब्धियों के लिए उन्हें सबसे बड़े सम्मान, पद्म श्री से सम्मानित किया गया।

Summary of the Lesson पाठ का सार

Part I : Santosh Yadav

It is about Santosh Yadav, a record holding mountaineer. Santosh was born in a very conservative society in Haryana where daughters had no freedom. But Santosh, with her will and dedication, took control of her life. As a result, she became the first woman to climb Mt Everest twice.

Santosh's Birth and Family Background

Santosh Yadav is the first woman in the world who has climbed Mt Everest twice. She was born in a society where the birth of a son was considered as a blessing and a daughter was not welcomed. Once, a holy man visited the family to bless Santosh's mother with a son but Santosh's grandmother told him that they wanted a daughter. Santosh, a sister five elder brothers, was born in a small village of Joniyawas of Rewari district in Haryana.

Santosh's Rebellion

Santosh's name means 'contentment' but she was never satisfied with the traditional life of her society. So, she started to live her life according to her own terms. The other girls of the society wore traditional dresses while Santosh wore shorts. Santosh believed that if she followed the right path, the other people around her would have to change.

Education of Santosh

Santosh's parents were rich landowners. They had the capacity to send Santosh to the best schools of Delhi. But due to the prevailing custom in the family, she was sent to the local village school. Santosh decided to fight this system.

Santosh's parents wanted to marry her at the age of 16 because in her village, most of the girls got married at this age. Santosh refused to marry and threatened her parents that she would not get married until she gets proper education.

सन्तोष का जन्म और पारिवारिक पृष्ठभूमि

सन्तोष यादव दुनिया की पहली महिला हैं, जिन्होंने दो बार माउण्ट ऐवरेस्ट की चढ़ाई की। उनका जन्म एक ऐसे समाज में हुआ जहाँ, एक बेटे के जन्म को आशीर्वाद समझा जाता था और एक बेटी के जन्म का स्वागत नहीं किया जाता था। एक बार, एक साधु सन्तोष की माता को बेटे के जन्म का आशीर्वाद देने के लिए आया, लेकिन सन्तोष की दादी ने उससे कहा कि वे एक बेटी चाहते थे। सन्तोष, पाँच बड़े भाइयों की एक बहन, का जन्म हरियाणा के रेवाड़ी जिले के एक छोटे से गाँव जोनियावास में हुआ था।

सन्तोष का विद्रोह

'सन्तोष' नाम का अर्थ 'सन्तुष्टि' होता है, लेकिन वह अपने समाज के परम्परागत जीवन से कभी भी सन्तुष्ट नहीं थी। इसलिए, उसने अपना जीवन अपनी शर्त पर जीना प्रारम्भ किया। समाज की अन्य लड़कियाँ पारम्परिक वस्त्र पहनती थीं, जबकि सन्तोष ने शॉर्ट्स पहने। सन्तोष मानती थी कि यदि वह सही रास्ते पर है, तो उसके आस-पास के लोगों को बदलना ही होगा।

सन्तोष की शिक्षा

सन्तोष के माता-पिता अमीर जमींदार थे। वे सन्तोष को दिल्ली के सबसे अच्छे स्कूल में भेजने मे समर्थ थे, लेकिन परिवार में प्रचलित प्रथा के अनुरूप सन्तोष को गाँव के स्कूल में भेजा गया। सन्तोष ने इस व्यवस्था से लड़ने का निश्चय किया।

सन्तोष के माता-पिता उसकी शादी 16 वर्ष की आयु में करवा देना चाहते थे क्योंकि उसके गाँव में ज्यादातर लड़कियों की शादी इस उम्र तक हो जाती थी। सन्तोष ने शादी से इनकार कर दिया और अपने माता-पिता को धमकी दी कि वह तब तक शादी नहीं करेंगी जब तक वह उच्च शिक्षा प्राप्त न कर ले।

Santosh left her home and got admission in a school in Delhi. Her parents initially refused to pay the school fees, but when she told them about her plans of working part time to pay the fees, they agreed to pay for her education.

सन्तोष ने अपना घर छोड़ दिया और दिल्ली के एक विद्यालय में दाखिला ले लिया। प्रारम्भ में उसके माता-पिता ने उसकी स्कूल फीस देने से इनकार कर दिया, लेकिन जब उसने उन्हें अपनी स्कूल फीस के भुगतान के लिए अंशकालिक काम करने की अपनी योजना के विषय में बताया, तो वे उसकी शिक्षा का खर्च देने के लिए सहमत हो गए।

Santosh's Interest in Climbing

Santosh passed her high school and got admission in Maharani college in Jaipur. She got a room in Kasturba Hostel which faced the Aravalli Hills. She used to see some villagers going up the hills and then disappearing after some time. One day, Santosh decided to check it out herself. She found nobody except a few mountaineers. They motivated Santosh to take interest in climbing.

सन्तोष की चढ़ाई में रुचि

सन्तोष ने अपनी हाई स्कूल की परीक्षा उत्तीर्ण की और जयपुर के महारानी कॉलेज में दाखिला ले लिया। उसे कस्तूरबा हॉस्टल में एक कमरा मिल गया, जिसके बिल्कुल सामने अरावंली की पहाड़ियाँ थीं। वह कुछ ग्रामीणों को पहाड़ी के ऊपर जाते हुए और कुछ समय पश्चात् गायब होते हुए देखती थी। एक दिन, सन्तोष ने स्वयं इसे जाँचने का फैसला किया। उसे कुछ पर्वतारोहियों के अतिरिक्त कोई नहीं मिला। उन्होंने सन्तोष को चढ़ाई में रुचि लेने के लिए प्रेरित किया।

Admission in a Mountaineering Institute

Santosh was a determined girl. She took admission in Nehru Institute of Mountaineering located in Uttarkashi. After completing her course in Jaipur, she directly left for Uttarkashi. Santosh wrote a letter to her father and apologised for taking admission at Uttarkashi without his permission.

पर्वतारोहण संस्थान में दाखिला

सन्तोष दृढ़-निश्चय वाली लड़की थी। उसने उत्तरकाशी के नेहरू पर्वतारोहण संस्थान में दाखिला ले लिया। जयपुर में अपनी पढ़ाई पूरी करने के बाद, वह सीधे उत्तरकाशी चली गई। सन्तोष ने अपने पिता को पत्र लिखकर उनकी अनुमति के बिना उत्तरकाशी में दाखिला लेने के लिए माँफी माँगी।

Santosh as a Mountaineer

In Uttarkashi, Santosh went on an expedition every year. Alongwith her climbing skills she developed an amazing immunity to cold and high altitude. As a mountaineer, she had an iron will, physical endurace (capacity to tolerate) and mental toughness.

पर्वतारोही के रूप में सन्तोष

उत्तरकाशी में, सन्तोष हर साल एक चढ़ाई अभियान पर जाती थी। पर्वतारोहण कौशल के साथ-साथ उसने सर्दी और ऊँचाई के लिए अद्भुत प्रतिरोधक क्षमता विकसित की। एक पर्वतारोही के रूप में उसमें इच्छाशक्ति, शारीरिक सहनशक्ति (सहन करने की ताकत) और मानसिक दृढ़ता थी।

Climbing Mt. Everest

Santosh's hard work and determination led her to climb Mt Everest, the highest peak in the world in 1992. She had climbed Mt. Everest at just 20 years of age. She became the youngest female to climb Mt Everest.

माउण्ट एवरेस्ट की चढ़ाई

सन्तोष की कड़ी मेहनत और दृढ़-निश्चय ने 1992 में उसे विश्व की सबसे ऊँची पर्वत चोटी, माउण्ट एवरेस्ट तक पहुँचा दिया। उसने मात्र 20 वर्ष की आयु में माउण्ट एवरेस्ट की चढ़ाई की। वह माउण्ट एवरेस्ट पर चढ़ने वाली सबसे कम उम्र की महिला बन गई।

Santosh's Humanity

Apart from her mountaineering skills, Santosh also impressed her seniors with her humanity. Her concern for others and her desire to work together as a team made her a special person. During Everest mission in 1992, she provided special care to her teammate in South Col. Unfortunately, she could not save him. However, she saved another climber, Mohan Singh by sharing her oxygen with him.

सन्तोष की मानवता

अपने पर्वतारोहण कौशल के अतिरिक्त, सन्तोष ने अपनी मानवता से अपने वरिष्ठों को प्रभावित किया। दूसरों के लिए उसकी चिन्ता और एक संगठन के रूप में काम करने की इच्छा उसे विशेष व्यक्ति बनाती थी। 1992 के एवरेस्ट मिशन में, उसने अपने एक साथी की दक्षिण कोल में विशेष देखभाल की थी। दुर्भाग्य से, वह उसे बचा नहीं सकी। हालाँकि, उसने एक अन्य पर्वतारोही, मोहन सिंह के साथ अपनी ऑक्सीजन साझा करके, उसे बचा लिया।

The Second Climb to Mt. Everest

After a year of her first success, Santosh, joined an Indo-Nepalese Women's Expedition and again climbed Mt Everest. She became the first women to climb Mt Everest twice. Her achievements brought glory to her and also gave India a unique place in mountaineering.

माउण्ट एवरेस्ट की दूसरी चढ़ाई

अपनी सफलता के एक साल बाद सन्तोष एक भारतीय-नेपाली महिला चढ़ाई अभियान से जुड़ गई और दोबारा माउण्ट ऐवरेस्ट की चढ़ाई की। वह माउण्ट एवरेस्ट पर दो बार चढ़ने वाली प्रथम महिला बनी। उसकी उपलब्धियों ने उसे प्रतिष्ठा प्रदान की और भारत को पर्वतारोहण में विशिष्ट स्थान प्रदान किया।

The Happiest Moment of Santosh's Life

The Indian government recognised Santosh's achievements and awarded her with the Padma Shri. Santosh felt the happiest moment of her life when she climbed Mt. Everest. She describes the feeling as unreal. She felt proud when she unfurled the Indian flag. Santosh Yadav is not only a mountaineer but she is also an environmentalist. She collected and brought down 500 kgs of garbage from the Himalayas.

सन्तोष के जीवन का सबसे अधिक खुशी का पल

भारत सरकार ने सन्तोष की उपलब्धियों को मान्यता दी और उन्हें पद्म श्री से सम्मानित किया। सन्तोष ने अपने जीवन का सबसे अधिक खुशी का पल तब महसूस किया जब उसने माउण्ट एवरेस्ट की चढ़ाई पूरी की। वह उस अनुभूति को कल्पना के रूप में बताती है। उसने राष्ट्रीय ध्वज को फहराकर गर्व महसूस किया। सन्तोष यादव केवल एक पर्वतारोही ही नहीं है बल्कि वह एक पर्यावरण रक्षक भी है। वह हिमालय से 500 किलो कचरा इकट्ठा करके नीचे लेकर आई।

Objective Questions

Extract Based Questions

Part I

Read the following extracts and answer the questions given below them.

1 A marriage as early as that was the last thing on her mind. She threatened her parents that she would never marry if she did not get a proper education. She left home and got herself enrolled in a school in Delhi. When her parents refused to pay for her education, she politely informed them of her plans to earn money by working part time to pay her school fees. Her parents then agreed to pay for her education.

(i) 'She' in the given extract is
(a) Maria Sharapova (b) Santosh Yadav
(c) Sania Mirza (d) Arunima Sinha

(ii) The given extract shows that she is
(a) courageous (b) rebellious
(c) resilient (d) All of these

(iii) The given extract shows that the society in which she lives is
(a) orthodox and rural (b) rural and modern
(c) urban and orthodox (d) can't say

(iv) The phrase 'last thing on her mind' means
(a) in the to do list
(b) not thought about or considered
(c) very well thought and rejected
(d) very well thought and accepted with a condition

(v) Which word is opposite in meaning to 'early' as used in the extract?
(a) late (b) later
(c) quick (d) timely

2 "I used to watch villagers from my room, going up the hill and suddenly vanishing after a while. One day I decided to check it out myself. I found nobody except a few mountaineers. I asked if I could join them. To my pleasant surprise, they answered in the affirmative and motivated me to take to climbing."

(i) The 'hill' in the extract refers to
(a) Aravalli Hills
(b) Mount Everest
(c) Shivalik Hills
(d) Sahyadri Hills

(ii) The incident in the extract took place in
(a) Delhi (b) Jaipur
(c) Uttarkashi (d) South col

(iii) When the writer says, 'vanishing after a while', he means to say
(a) entering a building
(b) becoming invisible
(c) climbing the hill and not being visible
(d) doing something mysterious

(iv) The phrase 'take to climbing' means
(a) learn climbing (b) practice climbing
(c) teach climbing (d) Both (a) and (b)

(v) The people the speaker met .... the speaker.
(a) entertained (b) encouraged
(c) discouraged (d) ignored

3 Within twelve months, Santosh found herself a member of an Indo-Nepalese Women's Expedition that invited her to join them. She then scaled the Everest a second time, thus setting a record as the only woman to have scaled the Everest twice and securing for herself and India a unique place in the annals of mountaineering.

(i) When did Santosh conquer Mount Everest the second time?
(a) In 1992 (b) In 1993
(c) In 1994 (d) In 1995

(ii) What made Santosh scale Mt. Everest the second time?
(a) She was invited by a French team.
(b) She was invited by an Indo-Canadian team.
(c) She was invited by an Indo-Nepalese Women's Expedition.
(d) She was invited by an Indo-Japanese Women's Expedition.

(iii) How many times did she scale Mount Everest?
(a) Thrice (b) Once
(c) Twice (d) None of these

(iv) Which award was bestowed upon her?
(a) The Padma Shri (b) The Padma Bhushan
(c) Civil Award (d) None of these

(v) The word 'scaled' in the extract means
(a) went (b) climbed
(c) hunted (d) conquered

Multiple Choice Questions

1. Which peak did Santosh Yadav scale twice?
(a) Aravalli Hills (b) The Himalayas
(c) Mt. Everest (d) The Joniyawas

2. Which of the following statements about Santosh is true?
(a) Santosh was always content with her life.
(b) She was born in Revari, Rajasthan.
(c) Santosh's parents did not pressurise her to get married.
(d) She went to Jaipur after pursuing high school examination.

3. What did Santosh's grandmother say that surprised the 'holy man'?
   (a) They wanted a son.
   (b) They did not want a son.
   (c) They didn't care if it was a son or a daughter.
   (d) They didn't want any children.
4. Santosh was the .... child of her parents.
   (a) fifth (b) sixth
   (c) fourth (d) ninth
5. Parents of Santosh were
   (a) rich landowners (b) poor
   (c) highly educated (d) cruel
6. What is the meaning of the name 'Santosh'?
   (a) Satisfaction (b) Sacred
   (c) Pure (d) Laughter
7. What did Santosh prefer to wear?
   (a) Suits (b) Shorts
   (c) Shirt (d) Long Kurta
8. What was the prevailing custom in the family?
   (a) Children will never go away from home.
   (b) Children would not involve themselves in adventure activities like mountaineering.
   (c) Girls would not go away from home to work.
   (d) Girls would not go away from home to study.
9. What was Santosh equipped with when she started climbing the mountains?
   (a) Iron will (b) Physical tolerance
   (c) Mental toughness (d) All of these
10. Why was Santosh sent to a local school?
   (a) Because her parents were poor.
   (b) Because her parents were rich.
   (c) Because of the prevailing trend.
   (d) Because they did not love her.
11. Why did Santosh leave home for Delhi?
   (a) To meet a friend
   (b) To get proper education and avoid marriage
   (c) To roam about
   (d) All of the above
12. How was Santosh attracted to mountain climbing?
   (a) Seeing her friends
   (b) Neighbours prompted her
   (c) Classmates prompted her
   (d) Watching some people going up the Aravalli hills from her hostel room
13. How was Santosh different from other girls?
   (a) She was slim (b) She did things of her choice
   (c) She was prettier (d) She was very rich
14. What kind of girl was Santosh?
   (a) A hardworking girl with a strong mind
   (b) A brat
   (c) Arrogant (d) Very shy
15. Why did senior climbers praise Santosh?
   (a) Physical fitness and mental strength
   (b) Climbing skills
   (c) For being helpful to teammates
   (d) All of the above

Answers

Extract Based Questions

1. (i) (b), (ii) (d), (iii) (a), (iv) (b), (v) (a) **2.** (i) (a), (ii) (b), (iii) (c), (iv) (d), (v) (b) **3.** (i) (b), (ii) (b), (iii) (c), (iv) (a), (v) (b)

Multiple Choice Questions

1. (c) 2. (d) 3. (b) 4. (b) 5. (a) 6. (a) 7. (b) 8. (d) 9. (d) 10. (c)
11. (b) 12. (d) 13. (b) 14. (a) 15. (d)

Important Characters (Part II)

Maria Sharapova मारिया शारापोवा	She has been the brightest tennis star. She is a Russian citizen. She secured the world number one position in women's tennis in 2005. वह टेनिस की सबसे सिद्ध खिलाड़ी है। वह रूसी नागरिक है। उसने 2005 में दुनिया के महिला टेनिस खिलाड़ियों में प्रथम स्थान प्राप्त किया था।
Yuri यूरी	He is Maria's father. He encouraged Maria and worked as much as he could to keep Maria's tennis training going. वह मारिया के पिता हैं। उन्होंने मारिया को हौसला दिया और उसकी टेनिस-ट्रेनिंग को जारी रखने के लिए अत्यधिक मेहनत की।
Yelana येलिना	She is Maria's mother. She could not go with Maria because of visa restriction. वह मारिया की माँ है। वह वीजा प्रतिबन्ध के कारण मारिया के साथ नहीं जा सकी थी।

Summary of the Lesson पाठ का सार

Part II Maria Sharapova

This part is about Maria Sharapova, a teenager, who achieved number one position in World's Women Tennis. In her journey, Maria had made many sacrifices and also had suffered through insults. However, all these only made her more determined and tough. Her hard work and her mental toughness finally led her to achieve her goal.

Number One Position in World Tennis

On 22nd August, 2005, Maria Sharapova gained number one position in world's women tennis. Maria was born in Siberia, Russia. She is a calm and confident girl who took only four years as a professional to reach the pinnacle.

Maria's Journey and her Sacrifice

Maria's journey towards becoming the biggest woman tennis player started when she was nine years old. She went to America to get training. In her journey to Florida, US only her father, Yuri, went with her. Maria's mother, Yelena could not go with Maria due to her visa restrictions. Maria lived without her mother for two years. During that time Maria realised that she had to sacrifice a lot to gain excellence in Tennis.

Maria's Training in the US

In US, Maria stayed alone and missed her mother very badly. Maria could not even spend much time with her father as he was working hard to earn money for Maria's training. Maria was the youngest child at her training center so she used to sleep at 8 pm. But the other senior players used to wake her up by 11 pm. Then, they ordered her to clean the room.

Maria's Determination and Toughness

Maria's experience of her training period made her more determined and tough. She struggled hard and learned to take care of herself. She was determined to reach her goal so she never thought about quitting. Due to her determination and toughness, Maria won the women's singles crown at Wimbledon in 2004. She became number one woman tennis player in the world in 2005.

Maria's Success Mantra

Maria's journey inspired many youngsters. She believes that all the sacrifices that she had made were worth it. Maria's way of answering clearly indicated her confidence. She says that she is very competitive. She always works hard at what she does. For her, hardwork is her mantra for success.

Maria Proud of her Russian Roots

Maria speaks with an American accent but, she is very proud of her Russian nationality. She says that US is a big part of her life but her blood is Russian. She also has Russian citizenship and wishes to play in Olympics for Russia.

टेनिस की दुनिया में प्रथम स्थान

22 अगस्त, 2005 को मारिया शारापोवा ने दुनिया के महिला टेनिस में प्रथम स्थान प्राप्त किया। मारिया का जन्म रूस के साइबेरिया में हुआ। वह एक शान्त और आत्म-विश्वास से परिपूर्ण लड़की है, जो एक पेशेवर खिलाड़ी के रूप में केवल चार वर्षों में सफलता के शिखर तक पहुँची।

मारिया की यात्रा और उसका बलिदान

मारिया की सबसे महान महिला टेनिस खिलाड़ी बनने की यात्रा तब प्रारम्भ हुई जब वह नौ वर्ष की थी। वह ट्रेनिंग के लिए अमेरिका गई। उसकी संयुक्त राष्ट्र के फ्लोरिडा की यात्रा में केवल उसके पिता यूरी, उसके साथ थे। मारिया की माता, येलेना वीजा प्रतिबन्धों के कारण उसके साथ नहीं जा सकी। मारिया दो साल तक अपनी माँ के बिना रही। उस समय मारिया ने अनुभव किया कि टेनिस में उत्कृष्टता प्राप्त करने के लिए उसे बहुत से बलिदान देने होंगे।

संयुक्त राष्ट्र में मारिया की ट्रेनिंग

संयुक्त राष्ट्र में मारिया अकेली रहती थी और अपनी माँ को बहुत अधिक याद करती थी। मारिया अपने पिता के साथ भी अधिक समय व्यतीत नहीं कर पाती थी, क्योंकि वे मारिया की ट्रेनिंग के लिए धन कमाने के लिए कड़ी-मेहनत कर रहे थे। मारिया अपने ट्रेनिंग केन्द्र में सबसे छोटी आयु की लड़की थी, इसलिए वह 8 बजे सो जाया करती थी। लेकिन दूसरे सीनियर खिलाड़ी उसे 11 बजे जगा दिया करते थे। तब वे उसे (मारिया को) कमरा साफ करने का आदेश दिया करते थे।

मारिया का दृढ़-संकल्प और मजबूती

मारिया के ट्रेनिंग के अनुभव ने उसे अधिक दृढ़-संकल्प और मजबूत बनाया। उसने कठोर संघर्ष किया और स्वयं की देखभाल करना सीखा। वह अपने लक्ष्य की प्राप्ति के लिए दृढ़-संकल्प थी इसलिए उसने कभी छोड़कर भागने के विषय में नहीं सोचा। अपने दृढ़-संकल्प और मजबूती के कारण 2004 में मारिया ने विम्बलडन में महिलाओं का एकल खिताब जीता। 2005 में वह दुनिया की सर्वश्रेष्ठ महिला टेनिस खिलाड़ी बन गई।

मारिया की सफलता का मंत्र

मारिया की जीवन-यात्रा ने कई युवाओं को प्रेरित किया। वह मानती है कि उसके द्वारा किए गए सभी बलिदान महत्त्वपूर्ण थे। मारिया का प्रश्नों के उत्तर देने का तरीका उसके आत्म-विश्वास को दर्शाता है। वह कहती है कि वह बहुत अधिक प्रतिस्पर्धात्मक है। वह जो भी कार्य करती है उसे हमेशा ही मेहनत के साथ करती है। उसके लिए कड़ी मेहनत ही सफलता का मंत्र है।

मारिया का अपने रूसी होने पर गर्व करना

मारिया अमेरिकन लहजे में बात करती है, लेकिन उसे अपनी रूसी नागरिकता पर बहुत गर्व है। वह कहती है कि संयुक्त राष्ट्र उसके जीवन का महत्त्वपूर्ण भाग है, लेकिन उसका खून रूसी है। उसकी नागरिकता रूसी है और वह ओलम्पिक में रूस के लिए खेलना चाहती है।

Maria's Hobbies and Her View on Tennis

Maria's hobbies include fashion, singing and dancing. She loves reading the Novels of Arthur Conan Doyle and is very fond of evening gowns. She also loves to eat pancakes with chocolate spread and drink fizzy orange drinks.

Maria's talent, determination and readiness to sacrifice led her to the path of success and fame. For Maria, apart from money, the dream of becoming number one in the world is her main motivation.

मारिया की अभिरुचियाँ और टेनिस के विषय में उसके विचार

मारिया की अभिरुचियों में फैशन, गाना और नाचना है। वह आर्थर कोनन डोयल के उपन्यास पढ़ना पसन्द करती है और उसे इवनिंग गाउन पहनना बहुत पसन्द है। उसे चॉकलेट से भरे पैनकेक खाना और फिजी ऑरेंज ड्रिंक पीना भी पसन्द है।

मारिया की प्रतिभा, दृढ़-निश्चय और बलिदान के लिए तत्परता, उसे सफलता और प्रसिद्धि के पथ पर ले गई। धन के अतिरिक्त मारिया के लिए मुख्य प्रेरणा दुनिया में प्रथम स्थान प्राप्त करना है।

Objective Questions

Extract Based Questions

Read the following extracts and answer the questions given below them.

1 There is something disarming about Maria Sharapova, something at odds with her ready smile and glamorous attire. And that something in her lifted her on Monday, 22nd August, 2005 to the world number one position in women's tennis. All this happened in almost no time. Poised beyond her years, the Siberian born teenager took just four years as a professional to reach the pinnacle. However, the rapid ascent in a fiercely competitive world began nine years before with a level of sacrifice few children would be prepared to endure.

(i) The Siberian born teenager is
(a) Serena Williams (b) Maria Sharapova
(c) Sania Mirza (d) Simona Halep

(ii) What according to you is 'that something', as mentioned in the extract?
(a) Dedication (b) Courage
(c) Sincerity (d) All of these

(iii) The sentence 'All this happened in almost no time' indicates
(a) laziness (b) suddenness
(c) inevitability (d) gradual process

(iv) How much time did Maria takes to reach the top position?
(a) 2 years (b) 4 years (c) 3 years (d) 5 years

(v) Where was Maria Sharapova born?
(a) America (b) Siberia (c) Paris (d) Poland

2 "I used to be so lonely," Maria Sharapova recalls. "I missed my mother terribly. My father was working as much as he could to keep my tennis-training going." so, he couldn't see me either.

However, the rapid ascent in a fiercely competitive world began nine years before with a level of sacrifice few children would be prepared to endure. Little Maria had not yet celebrated her tenth birthday when she was packed off to train in the United States. That trip to Florida with her father Yuri launched her on the path to success and stardom.

(i) Which of the following is not true as per the given extract?
(a) Maria was born in the USA.
(b) Maria had to sacrifice her childhood to achieve success.
(c) Maria was bullied by her batchmates.
(d) Maria's trip to Florida launched her on the path to success.

(ii) How did staying in the USA changed her life?
(a) It provided her with the path to success and stardom.
(b) It provided her with the confidence.
(c) It motivated her to achieve her goals.
(d) It gave her the strength to face problems.

(iii) "I used to be so lonely." Who said this?
(a) Mother (b) Father
(c) Maria (d) Another player

(iv) Find a word which means 'awfully'.
(a) terribly (b) lonely
(c) recall (d) willingly

(v) Choose the option that gives the correct meaning of 'endure'.
(a) suffer (b) realise (c) release (d) transfer

3 The straight looks and the answers she gives when asked about her ambition make it amply clear that she considers the sacrifices were worth it. "I am very, very competitive. I work hard at what I do. It's my job." This is her mantra for success.

Though Maria Sharapova speaks with a pronounced American accent, she proudly parades her Russian nationality.

(i) The sacrifices referred to in the extract refer to
(a) staying away from parents
(b) going through bullying
(c) staying all alone
(d) All of the above

(ii) Choose the correct option that lists the sport that Maria Sharapova plays.
(a) Table Tennis (b) Hockey
(c) Badminton (d) Tennis

(iii) Which of the following statements is not true about Maria Sharapova?
(a) Maria is very ambitious.
(b) Maria would like to play for Russia as well.
(c) Maria speaks in an American accent.
(d) Maria does not have a Russian citizenship.

(iv) The phrase 'proudly parades' means
(a) to show off
(b) to display publicly
(c) to be proud of
(d) Both (b) and (c)

(v) The straight look is a
(a) happy look (b) blank face
(c) serious look (d) laughing face

Multiple Choice Questions

1. Which of the following is not associated with Maria Sharapova?
(a) Ready smile
(b) Hard stare
(c) Glamorous attire
(d) Both (a) and (c)

2. Maria stayed away from her mother for .... years when she went to train in the US.
(a) two (b) three
(c) four (d) five

3. What was the date when she gained number one position in the world's women tennis?
(a) 22nd August, 2005
(b) 22nd August, 2004
(c) 21st August, 2005
(d) 21st August, 2004

4. Maria Sharapova belongs to
(a) Germany (b) England
(c) India (d) Russia

5. In how many years as a professional did Maria reach the most successful point?
(a) Two years (b) Three years
(c) Four years (d) Five years

6. How old was Maria when she was sent to the United States?
(a) More than 10 years
(b) Less than 10 years
(c) Less than 5 years
(d) More than 15 years

7. Maria Sharapova wishes to play the .... for Russia, if allowed.
(a) National League (b) Australian Open
(c) French Open (d) Olympics

8. Which of the following qualities was the key to her winning the Women's Singles in 2004?
(a) Her sentiments (b) Her toughness
(c) Her glamorous beauty (d) Her rise to success

9. What was Maria's mantra for success?
(a) Work hard at your job.
(b) Work lazily at your job.
(c) Work or don't work – it's up to you.
(d) Don't ever be competitive.

10. Which accent does Maria Sharapova speak in?
(a) Siberian (b) Russian
(c) American (d) Australian

11. Which game is Maria attached to?
(a) Volleyball (b) Tennis
(c) Hockey (d) Cricket

12. Which title did Maria Sharapova win in 2004?
(a) Wimbledon (b) Australian Open
(c) American Open (d) All of these

13. Maria Sharapova reached the summit of women's tennis when she was barely
(a) 17 (b) 19
(c) 18 (d) 20

14. Where was Maria sent to learn Tennis?
(a) England (b) The United States
(c) India (d) Germany

15. What was the name of Maria's father?
(a) Michael (b) Yelena
(c) Jimmy (d) Yuri

Answers

Extract Based Questions

1. (i) (b), (ii) (d), (iii) (b), (iv) (c), (v) (b) 2. (i) (a), (ii) (a), (iii) (c), (iv) (a), (v) (a) 3. (i) (d), (ii) (d), (iii) (d), (iv) (d), (v) (b)

Multiple Choice Questions

1. (b) 2. (a) 3. (a) 4. (d) 5. (c) 6. (b) 7. (d) 8. (b) 9. (a) 10. (c)
11. (b) 12. (a) 13. (c) 14. (b) 15. (d)

08 If I Were You

This chapter 'If I Were You' is a dialogue drama written by Douglas James. In this play, Gerrard is the main character. He uses his presence of mind and outplays the intruder. During the conversation he learns the intention of the intruder.
Gerrard smartly cooks a fake story to outwit the intruder. The use of intelligence and sense of humour often helps us at the time of crises as shown in the play. Gerrard outsmarts the intruder by trapping him in his own net.

Important Characters

Gerrard जैरार्ड	A playwright by profession, who has a great presence of mind. He was successful in trapping the Intruder. पेशे से एक नाटककार है, जिसके पास उच्च बुद्धि तत्परता है। घुसपैठिए को फँसाने में वह सफल रहा।
Intruder घुसपैठिया	The intruder is a criminal who specialises in stealing jewellery. He intrudes into the cottage of Gerrard to kill Gerrard and to take on his identity. घुसपैठिया एक अपराधी है, जो आभूषण (गहने) चुराने में विशिष्ट है। वह जैरार्ड को मारने और उसकी पहचान लेने के लिए जैरार्ड की कुटिया में घुस गया।

Summary of the Lesson पाठ का सार

Gerrard, the Protagonist

The play opens with Gerrard talking on the phone. He was a man of medium height and lived in a lonely cottage in the forests (wilds) of Essex. He was wearing his glasses, a lounge suit and a long coat. After he put down the phone, he started packing a travelling bag, it appeared that he was going somewhere.

The Intruder Entered the House

While Gerrard was busy packing, a man with a revolver in his hand quietly entered the house. He looked similar to Gerrard. He was wearing a long coat and a soft hat. The intruder ordered Gerrard to put his hands up and also asked him to answer some of his questions. Gerrard remains calm and talks to the intruder politely.

Gerrard told the intruder that he was feeling uncomfortable while standing with his hands lifted up. So, the intruder allows Gerrard to sit on the chair and he himself sat on the diwan. He then started to ask questions. The intruder wanted to know the basic information (like full name, habits, talking style, etc.) about Gerrard.

The Intruder's Motive

The intruder told Gerrard that he was a jewel robber. He had killed a policeman and he was running away from the police.

He further informed Gerrard that he had planned to kill him and take his identity. He wanted to live a peaceful life as Vincent Charles Gerrard.

जैरार्ड मुख्य पात्र

नाटक की शुरुआत में जैरार्ड फोन पर बात कर रहा होता है। वह एक मध्यम कद का व्यक्ति था और एसेक्स के जंगलों (जंगली) में एक एकान्त कुटिया में रहता था। उसने चश्मा, लाउन्ज सूट और एक लम्बा कोट पहन रखा था। फोन रखने के बाद, वह एक यात्रा पर ले जाने वाला बैग पैक करने लगा, ऐसा प्रतीत होता है, कि वह कहीं जा रहा है।

घुसपैठिए का घर में प्रवेश करना

जब जैरार्ड सामान समेटने में व्यस्त था, एक व्यक्ति घर में चुपचाप घुसता है, जिसके हाथ में रिवाल्वर है। वह जैरार्ड के समान दिखता था। उसने एक लम्बा कोट और एक मुलायम टोपी पहन रखी थी। घुसपैठिए ने जैरार्ड को हाथ ऊपर करने का आदेश दिया और उससे अपने कुछ प्रश्नों के उत्तर देने को भी कहा। जैरार्ड शान्त रहता है और घुसपैठिए से नम्रतापूर्वक बात करता है।

जैरार्ड ने घुसपैठिए को बताया कि वह अपने हाथों को ऊपर उठाकर खड़े करने से असहज महसूस कर रहा है। इसलिए, घुसपैठिया जैरार्ड को कुर्सी पर बैठने की अनुमति देता है और वह स्वयं दीवान पर बैठ जाता है। फिर वह प्रश्न पूछना प्रारम्भ करता है। घुसपैठिया जैरार्ड के बारे में मूलभूत जानकारी (जैसे—पूरा नाम, आदतें, बात करने का तरीका आदि) जानना चाहता था।

घुसपैठिए का उद्देश्य

घुसपैठिए ने जैरार्ड को बताया कि वह एक आभूषण चोर था। उसने एक पुलिसकर्मी को मार डाला और वह पुलिस से भाग रहा था।

उसने जैरार्ड को आगे बताया कि उसने उसे मारने और उसकी पहचान लेने की योजना बनाई थी। वह विन्सेंट चार्ल्स जैरार्ड के रूप में एक शान्तिपूर्ण जीवन जीना चाहता था।

Gerrard's False Story

After listening to the intruder, Gerrard cleverly made up a false story and informed the intruder that he himself was a criminal. Gerrard had murdered someone and had run away. However, one of his men had been caught.

He (Gerrard) was also running away from the police and had already packed his bag to run. He convinced the intruder by showing his disguise outfits including false moustache, etc.

Intruder's Reaction

Gerrard's story almost convinced the intruder. The intruder began to think after this. This was an opportunity for Gerrard to work on his plan. Gerrard asked the intruder to hurry and run with him in his car as police was about to reach there soon.

Gerrard opened the door to exit the house, which was actually the door of a cupboard. The intruder looked inside to make sure that it was actually a door.

The Intruder is Trapped

While the intruder looked inside, Gerrard gave him a push and locked him in the cupboard. The gun fell down from the intruder's hand. Gerrard picked the gun and called up the Sergeant to arrest the intruder. The true identity of Gerrard, who was actually a playwright got revealed when he said that he got something for his next play from this experience.

जैरार्ड की झूठी कहानी

घुसपैठिए की बात सुनने के बाद, जैरार्ड ने चतुराई से एक झूठी कहानी बनाई और घुसपैठिए को बताया कि वह स्वयं एक अपराधी था। जैरार्ड ने किसी की हत्या कर दी थी और भाग गया था। हालाँकि, उसका एक आदमी पकड़ा गया था।

वह (जैरार्ड) भी पुलिस से भाग रहा था और भागने के लिए अपना बैग पैक कर चुका था। उसने नकली मूंछे आदि सहित अपनी वेश भूषा दिखाकर घुसपैठिए को विश्वास दिला दिया।

घुसपैठिए की प्रतिक्रिया

जैरार्ड की कहानी ने घुसपैठिए को लगभग आश्वस्त कर दिया था। घुसपैठिए ने इसके बाद सोचना शुरू कर दिया था। यह जैरार्ड के लिए अपनी योजना पर काम करने का एक अवसर था। जैरार्ड ने घुसपैठिए को जल्दी से अपनी कार में उसके साथ भागने को कहा, क्योंकि पुलिस जल्द ही वहाँ पहुँचने वाली है।

जैरार्ड ने घर से बाहर निकालने के लिए दरवाजा खोला, जो वास्तव में एक अलमारी का दरवाजा था। घुसपैठिए ने यह सुनिश्चित करने के लिए अन्दर देखा कि यह वास्तव में एक दरवाजा है।

घुसपैठिए फँस गया

जब घुसपैठिए ने अन्दर देखा, जैरार्ड ने उसे धक्का दिया और उसे अलमारी में बन्द कर दिया। घुसपैठिए के हाथ से बन्दूक नीचे गिर गई। जैरार्ड ने बन्दूक उठाई और घुसपैठिए को गिरफ्तार करने के लिए पुलिस वाले को बुलाया। जैरार्ड, जो वास्तव में एक नाटककार था, उसकी असली पहचान तब सामने आई, जब उसने कहा कि इस अनुभव से उसे अपने अगले नाटक के लिए कुछ प्राप्त हुआ है।

Objective Questions

Extract Based Questions

I. Read the following extract and answer the questions that given below them.

1

Gerrard : (pleasantly) Why, this is a surprise, Mr— er —

Intruder : I'm glad you're pleased to see me. I don't think you'll be pleased for long. Put those paws up!

Gerrard : This is all very melodramatic, not very original, perhaps, but...

Intruder : Trying to be calm and — er—

Gerrard : 'Nonchalant' is your word, I think.

Intruder : Thanks a lot. You'll soon stop being smart. I'll make you crawl. I want to know a few things, see.

Gerrard : Anything you like. I know all the answers. But before we begin I should like to change my position; you may be comfortable, but I am not.

Intruder : Sit down there, and no funny business. (Motions to a chair, and seats himself on the divan by the bag.) Now then, we'll have a nice little talk about yourself!

(i) Why does Gerrard struggle with the other person's name?
(a) He has forgotten him.
(b) He is meeting him after a long time.
(c) He doesn't know him.
(d) He dislikes him.

(ii) When will Gerrard stop being smart according to the intruder?
(a) When he will leave.
(b) When the intruder shows his smartness.
(c) When he will be dead.
(d) When the intruder's partners arrive.

(iii) Why did Gerrard want to change his position?
(a) He was uncomfortable.
(b) It was his strategy.
(c) He wanted to call the police.
(d) All of the above

(iv) Why did the intruder want to talk about Gerrard?
(a) To know more about him (b) To take on his identity
(c) To betray him to the police (d) Both (a) and (b)

(v) Which of the following words is similar in meaning to 'nonchalant'?
(a) anxious (b) concerned
(c) composed (d) apprehensive

2

Intruder : Never mind my name. I like yours better, Mr Gerrard. What are your Christian names?
Gerrard : Vincent Charles.
Intruder : Do you run a car?
Gerrard : No.
Intruder : That's a lie. You're not dealing with a fool. I'm as smart as you and smarter, and I know you run a car. Better be careful, wise guy!
Gerrard : Are you American, or is that merely a clever imitation?
Intruder : Listen, this gun's no toy. I can hurt you without killing you, and still get my answers.
Gerrard : Of course, if you put it like that, I'll be glad to assist you. I do possess a car, and it's in the garage round the corner.
Intruder : That's better. Do people often come out here?
Gerrard : Very rarely. Surprisingly few people take the trouble to visit me. There's the baker and the greengrocer, of course; and then there's the milkman — quite charming, but no one so interesting as yourself.
Intruder : I happen to know that you never see tradespeople.

(i) What is the intruder's name?
(a) Vincent Charles
(b) Gerrard
(c) Not mentioned in the extract
(d) Both (a) and (b)

(ii) Which vehicle does the intruder ask if Gerrard can drive?
(a) Bike
(b) Truck
(c) Scooter
(d) Car

(iii) Who comes to visit Gerrard?
(a) Baker (b) Greengrocer
(c) Milkman (d) All of these

(iv) Who is Gerrard's most interesting visitor?
(a) Baker
(b) The intruder
(c) Greengrocer
(d) Milkman

(v) What is Gerrard's full name?
(a) Mr. Gerrard
(b) Vincent Charles
(c) Vincent Charles Gerrard
(d) Vincent Gerrard

3

Gerrard : And where precisely have you got? It didn't require a great brain to break into my little cottage.
Intruder : When you know why I've broken into your little cottage, you'll be surprised, and it won't be a pleasant surprise.
Gerrard : With you figuring so largely in it, that is understandable. By the way, what particular line of crime do you embrace, or aren't you a specialist?
Intruder : My speciality's jewel robbery. Your car will do me a treat. It's certainly a dandy bus.
Gerrard : I'm afraid jewels are few and far between in the wilds of Essex.
Intruder : So are the cops. I can retire here nicely for a little while.
Gerrard : You mean to live with me? A trifle sudden isn't it; you've not been invited.
Intruder : You won't be here long; so I didn't trouble to ask.
Gerrard : What do you mean?
Intruder : This is your big surprise. I'm going to kill you.

(i) Why does the intruder choose Gerrard's house?
(a) Because he was safe there.
(b) Because he could hide from the police.
(c) Because he could be peaceful.
(d) All of the above

(ii) What is happening in the given lines?
(a) Gerrard is wasting his time.
(b) Gerrard is getting to know the intruder.
(c) Gerrard is taking his time to come up with a plan.
(d) The intruder is informing Gerrard about his purpose.

(iii) What is the intruder's speciality?
(a) Stealing cars (b) Jewel robbery
(c) Bank robbery (d) All of these

(iv) What is the intruder's big surprise?
(a) He is going to kidnap Gerrard.
(b) He is going to betray Gerrard.
(c) He is going to kill Gerrard.
(d) All of the above

(v) The phrase 'few and far between' means
(a) rare (b) in abundance
(c) more in intensity (d) less populated

Multiple Choice Questions

1. The scene for the play has been set in ....
(a) a small cottage (b) a huge mansion
(c) a bungalow (d) a theatre

2. What is on the table at the beginning of the play?
(a) A book (b) A play
(c) A mobile phone (d) A telephone

3. How was Gerrard dressed?
(a) He was wearing horn-rimmed glasses.
(b) He was dressed in a lounge suit and a great coat.
(c) He was smoking a pipe.
(d) Both (a) and (b)

4. From which side did the intruder enter?
(a) Back (b) Front (c) Left (d) Right

5. Where did the intruder sit when Gerrard said he was uncomfortable?
(a) On the table (b) On the divan
(c) On the chair (d) On the floor

6. What was the Christian name of Gerrard?
(a) Vincent (b) Charles
(c) Vincent Charles (d) Charles Vincent

7. Where is Gerrard's car?
(a) Someone stole it
(b) His friend has it
(c) The intruder took it
(d) In the garage

8. What was the tone of Gerrard when he said, 'You have been so modest'?
(a) Sarcastic (b) Angry
(c) Calm (d) Serious

9. When the intruder said, 'you won't be here long', he meant that
(a) Gerrard was going somewhere.
(b) He would kidnap Gerrard.
(c) He was going to kill Gerrard.
(d) None of the above

10. To which animal does the intruder compare himself?
(a) Rat (b) Cat (c) Dog (d) Raccoon

11. Where did the intruder see Gerrard?
(a) Drury (b) London
(c) America (d) Aylesbury

12. What does the intruder mean by saying, "Hearing about you was one of my luckiest breaks"?
(a) It was the luckiest thing for the intruder.
(b) It was a lucky tea break to listen about Gerrard.
(c) It was a lucky lunch break.
(d) None of the above

13. All the while Gerrard was talking to the intruder he ....
(a) was saying the truth
(b) wanted to arrest the intruder
(c) was befooling the intruder
(d) wanted to kill the intruder

14. Why did Gerrard say that the intruder would be hanged for sure?
(a) Gerrard told him that he himself was a murderer too.
(b) Gerrard told him police was after him.
(c) Both (a) and (b)
(d) None of the above

15. What did Gerrard say about his outfit?
(a) It was his evening dress.
(b) It was a disguised outfit to elude police.
(c) He was going for a party.
(d) He was going to attend a wedding.

Answers

Extract Based Questions

1. (i) (c), (ii) (c), (iii) (a), (iv) (d), (v) (c) 2. (i) (c), (ii) (d), (iii) (d), (iv) (b), (v) (c) 3. (i) (d), (ii) (c), (iii) (b), (iv) (c), (v) (a)

Multiple Choice Questions

1. (a) 2. (d) 3. (d) 4. (d) 5. (b) 6. (c) 7. (d) 8. (a) 9. (c) 10. (a)
11. (d) 12. (a) 13. (c) 14. (c) 15. (b)

01 A Letter to God

Summary of the Lesson पाठ का सार

This chapter is about a farmer, Lencho and his firm faith in God. Lencho lived on the crest of a low hill with his family. He was eagerly waiting for a good rain to have a good harvest, so he could earn money for his family. As Lencho had expected, it started raining at the time of supper (dinner). He felt happy. But suddenly, the rain turned into a hailstorm, destroying all of Lencho's corn. Lencho knew that his family would suffer because they wouldn't have enough food.

Despite their tough situation, Lencho and his family kept on believing in God for help. With his firm faith, Lencho wrote a letter to God. He asked for a hundred pesos to plant crops and feed his family. He took the letter to the post office, addressing it to 'God.' After reading Lencho's letter addressing God, the postmaster laughed. But the postmaster was a kind person and he was touched by Lencho's strong faith.

To keep Lencho's faith alive, he gathered money from his staff and friends. He failed to collect hundred pesos and collected only seventy pesos. He,then, put the money in an envelope and signed it as 'God'.

Next Sunday, Lencho received the money but was disappointed to find only seventy pesos. He did not believe that God made a mistake. So, he wrote another letter to God asking for the rest of the money. In this letter, he asked God not to send the money through the mail because he believed that the post office employes might have stolen his money.

यह अध्याय एक किसान, लेन्चो की ईश्वर में दृढ़ आस्था के बारे में है। लेन्चो अपने परिवार के साथ एक निचली पहाड़ी की चोटी पर रहता था। वह उत्सुकता से अच्छी वर्षा की प्रतीक्षा कर रहा था, जिससे उसकी फसल अच्छी हो सके तथा वह अपने परिवार के लिए धन अर्जित कर सके। जैसा कि लेन्चो ने अपेक्षा की थी, रात के खाने के समय बारिश शुरू हो गई। वह बहुत खुश था, लेकिन अचानक बारिश ओलावृष्टि में बदल गई, जिससे लेन्चो का मक्का का खेत पूर्ण रूप से नष्ट हो गया। लेन्चो जानता था कि उसके परिवार को कष्ट सहना पड़ेगा, क्योंकि उनके पास खाने के लिए पर्याप्त भोजन नहीं होगा।

अपनी कठिन परिस्थिति के भी बावजूद लेन्चो और उसका परिवार मदद के लिए ईश्वर पर विश्वास करता रहा। अपने दृढ़ विश्वास के साथ, लेन्चो ने भगवान को एक पत्र लिखा। उसने फसल उगाने और अपने परिवार का भरण-पोषण करने के लिए 100 पीसोज की माँग की। वह उस पत्र को डाकघर ले गया, जिसमें उसने पते के रूप में 'भगवान' लिखा। उस पत्र को पढ़ने के बाद पोस्टमास्टर हँस पड़ा। लेकिन पोस्टमास्टर एक दयालु व्यक्ति था और वह लेन्चो के दृढ़ विश्वास से प्रभावित हुआ। लेन्चो के विश्वास को जीवित रखने के लिए, उसने अपने कर्मचारियों और अपने दोस्तों से धन एकत्रित किया। लेकिन 100 पीसोज एकत्रित करने में असफल रहा और केवल 70 पीसोज ही एकत्र कर सका। फिर, उसने उन पैसों को एक लिफाफे में रखा और उस पर 'भगवान' के नाम से हस्ताक्षर कर दिए।

अगले रविवार, को लेन्चो को पैसे मिले, लेकिन केवल 70 पीसोज पाकर वह निराश हो गया। उसे विश्वास नहीं हुआ कि 'भगवान' ने गलती की है। इसलिए उसने बाकी पैसे माँगते हुए भगवान को पुनः पत्र लिखा। इस पत्र में, उसने ईश्वर से यह अनुरोध भी किया कि वे डाक से पैसे ने भेजें, क्योंकि लेन्चो को विश्वास था कि डाकघर के कर्मचारियों ने उसके पैसे चुरा लिए होंगे।

Objective Questions

Extract Based Questions

Read the following extracts carefully and answer the questions that follow.

1 But suddenly a strong wind began to blow and along with the rain very large hailstones began to fall. These truly did resemble new silver coins. The boys, exposing themselves to the rain, ran out to collect the frozen pearls.

(i) How did Lencho feel when he saw his fields covered with the curtain of rain?
लेन्चो ने कैसा महसूस किया, जब उसने अपने खेतों को बारिश के पर्दे से ढका हुआ देखा?
(a) Satisfied
(b) Unsatisfied
(c) Well-pleased
(d) None of the above

(ii) What happened to the rain suddenly?
अचानक बारिश को क्या हुआ?
(a) It changed into hailstorm.
(b) It changed into storm.
(c) It changed into gale.
(d) None of the above

(iii) Along with the rain .... began to fall.
बारिश के साथ .... गिरना शुरू हो गए।
(a) stones
(b) hailstones
(c) silver coins
(d) pearls

2 It was during the meal that, just as Lencho had predicted, big drops of rain began to fall. In the North-East huge mountains of clouds could be seen approaching. The air was fresh and sweet. The man went out for no other reason than to have the pleasure of feeling the rain on his body, and when he returned he exclaimed, "These aren't raindrops falling from the sky, they are new coins. The big drops are ten cent pieces and the little ones are fives."

(i) When did the rain begin to fall?
बारिश कब शुरू हुई?
(a) During the meal (b) In the morning
(c) After lunch (d) During brunch

(ii) Who predicted about the rain?
बारिश के बारे में भविष्यवाणी किसने की थी?
(a) A wise man in the village
(b) His wife
(c) Lencho
(d) An old monk

(iii) What could be seen approaching in the North-East?
उत्तर-पूर्व दिशा से आता हुआ क्या देखा जा सकता था?
(a) Dark clouds (b) Thunderstorm
(c) Rainbow (d) None of these

3 So, in order not to shake the writer's faith in God, the postmaster came up with an idea to answer the letter. But when he opened it, it was evident that to answer it, he needed something more than goodwill, ink and paper. But he stuck to his resolution : he asked for money from his employees, he himself gave part of his salary, and several friends of his were obliged to give something 'for act of charity'.

(i) The postmaster answered the letter
पोस्टमास्टर ने पत्र का उत्तर दिया
(a) as he was a good friend of the writer
(b) as he was dutiful
(c) as he did not want to help the writer
(d) in order not to shake the writer's faith in God

(ii) Who is the 'writer' described in the paragraph?
लेखक ने अनुच्छेद में किसका वर्णन किया है?
(a) G.L. Fuentes
(b) The Postmaster
(c) Lencho
(d) Postman

4 Immediately, Lencho went up to the window to ask for paper and ink. On the public writing-table, he started to write, with much wrinkling of his brow, caused by the effort he had to make to express his ideas. When he finished, he went to the window to buy a stamp which he licked and then affixed to the envelope with a blow of his fist. The moment the letter fell into the mailbox the postmaster went to open it. It said: "God: Of the money that I asked for, only seventy pesos reached me. Send me the rest, since I need it very much."

(i) The moment the letter fell into the mailbox, who went to open it?
जिस क्षण पत्र मेलबॉक्स में आया, उसे खोलने कौन गया?
(a) The postman (b) The postmaster
(c) The clerk (d) None of these

(ii) How much money did Lencho get?
लेन्चो को कितने पैसे प्राप्त हुए?
(a) Forty pesos (b) Fifty pesos
(c) Seventy pesos (d) Eighty pesos

(iii) What did Lencho ask for in his second letter?
लेन्चो ने दूसरे पत्र में क्या माँगा था?
(a) More money
(b) Remaining amount and the request to not send it by mail
(c) Remaining amount and send it by mail only
(d) He didn't ask for anything

5 It was nothing less than a letter to God.
'God,' he wrote, " If you don't help me, my family and I will go hungry this year. I need a hundred pesos in order to sow my field again and to live until the crop comes, because the hailstorm ...."

(i) .... wrote a letter a God.
भगवान को पत्र .... ने लिखा था।
(a) The postmaster (b) A postman
(c) A child (d) Lencho

Ans. (d) Lencho

(ii) He needed a hundred pesos in order to ....
उसे .... के लिए 100 पीसोज की आवश्यकता थी।
(a) purchase a new field (b) water his field
(c) sow his field again and to live until the crop comes
(d) do some business instead of farming

Ans. (c) sow his field again and to live until the crop comes

6 One of the employees, who was a postman and also helped at the post office, went to his boss laughing heartily and showed him the letter to God. Never in his career as a postman had he known that address. The postmaster–a fat, amiable fellow– also broke out laughing, but almost immediately he turned serious and, tapping the letter on his desk, commented, 'What faith!
I wish I had the faith of the man who wrote 'this letter. Starting up a correspondence with God !"

(i) The postman showed .... to his boss.
डाकिए ने अपने बॉस को .... दिखाया।
(a) a pen (b) a stamp paper
(c) an inkpot (d) a letter

(ii) The postmaster was
पोस्टमास्टर .... था।
(a) a fraud
(b) an amiable fellow
(c) an intelligent employee
(d) a dishonest person

Multiple Choice Questions (MCQs)

1. Where was Lencho's house situated?
(a) At the bottom of the hill
(b) At the top of a low hill
(c) At the top of a plateau
(d) In a city

2. Whose house was the only house in the entire valley?
(a) Postmaster's house
(b) Lencho's house
(c) Farmer's house
(d) None of the above

3. Lencho's field was full of ....
(a) riped maize (b) riped corn
(c) riped potato (d) riped rice

4. What happened during supper (dinner) time?
(a) It started raining
(b) Strong winds began
(c) Storm
(d) Snowfall began

5. Lecho wrote to God, "If you don't help me, my family and I will go .... this year."
(a) to the dogs (b) dry
(c) mad (d) hungry

6. What did Lencho compare the large raindrops with?
(a) Silver coins (b) Pearls
(c) Diamond (d) New coins

7. The postmaster was a .... amiable man.
(a) rude (b) friendly
(c) lazy (d) fat

8. Why did Lencho become angry when he counted the money?
(a) It was less than he expected.
(b) God made a mistake in sending money.
(c) He thought that post office employees had stolen some money.
(d) Both (a) and (c)

9. What did Lencho think of the post office employees?
(a) Bunch of crooks (b) Rude
(c) Unhelpful (d) Proud

10. Lencho wrote a letter to God asking for a .... pesos.
(a) thousand (b) hundred
(c) fifty (d) sixty

11. What did Lencho hope for?
(a) A good shower of rain
(b) Bright sunshine
(c) A good crop
(d) Cloudy weather

12. What quality of Lencho impressed the postmaster most?
(a) His foolishness
(b) His great faith in God
(c) His simplicity
(d) None of the above

Answers

Extract Based Questions

1. (i) (a), (ii) (a), (iii) (b), 2. (i) (a), (ii) (c), (iii) (a) 3. (i) (d), (ii) (c) 4. (i) (b), (ii) (c), (iii) (b) 5. (i) (d), (ii) (c) 6. (i) (d), (ii) (b)

Multiple Choice Questions

1. (b) 2. (b) 3. (b) 4. (a) 5. (d) 6. (a) 7. (b) 8. (d) 9. (a) 10. (b) 11. (a) 12. (b)

02 Nelson Mandela : Long Walk to Freedom

Summary of the Lesson पाठ का सार

This chapter is an extract from the autobiography of Nelson Mandela, the first black President of South Africa. It starts with the description of the ceremonial installation of the first democratic government of South Africa which took place on 10th May, 1994. Dignitaries and world leaders had gathered to pay their respects, making it the largest gathering of international leaders ever in South Africa.

The inauguration occurred at the Union Building in Pretoria. Mandela was accompanied by his daughter Zenani. Mr. De Klark was sworn as second Deputy President and then Thabo Mbeki as first deputy president. Mandela took his oath of office, promising to uphold the Constitution and serve the Republic and its people.

In his speech, Mandela reflected on South Africa's transition from apartheid to democracy. He thanked international guests for their support and recognised the sacrifices made for political freedom. Mandela pledged to fight poverty, deprivation, and discrimination for all citizens, as he believed that the greatest wealth of a nation are its people, not gems.

South African jets displayed the military power. Highest military generals of South African defence force and police saluted him and pledged their loyalty. Both the old 'Nkosi Sikelel' and new 'Die Stem' national anthems were sung.

Nelson Mandela remembers the days when the whites had formed a system of racial dominance against the blacks. He says that the policy of apartheid (policy of racial segregation) created a deep and lasting wound on his country and its people. He also praised the bravery of his people. He recalled great freedom fighters like Oliver Tambos, Walter Sisulus, Chief Luthulis, Yusuf Dadoos, etc.

Mandela believed that every man has two obligations-one to his family and the other to his nation. A black man born in South Africa, just like him, cannot fulfill both. In order to do something for his nation, Mandela was taken away from his family.

Mandela remembered that as a child, freedom for him meant being able to do what he wanted. As a student, he wanted freedom just for himself. Then as a young man in Johannesburg, he wanted freedom to achieve his dreams, start a family, earn for himself, etc. As he grew up, he started realising that the freedom that he enjoyed as a child was just an illusion.

Mandela joined the African National Congress with a desire to gain freedom, respect and dignity for his community. Mandela realised that he could not enjoy his freedom when his community was not free. As a result, he was imprisoned. He also realised that just like the oppressed (tortured), the oppressor (torturer) is also not free.

यह अध्याय अफ्रीका के प्रथम अश्वेत राष्ट्रपति नेल्सन मण्डेला की आत्मकथा से लिया गया उद्धरण है। इसका प्रारम्भ दक्षिण अफ्रीका की प्रथम लोकतान्त्रिक सरकार की औपचारिक स्थापना के वर्णन से होता है, जो 10 मई, 1994 को हुई थी। गणमान्य व्यक्ति और विश्व के नेता अपना सम्मान प्रकट करने के लिए यहाँ एकत्र हुए थे, जिससे यह दक्षिण अफ्रीका में अन्तर्राष्ट्रीय नेताओं की अब तक की सबसे बड़ी सभा बन गई।

उद्घाटन प्रिटोरिया की यूनियन बिल्डिंग में हुआ था। मण्डेला के साथ उनकी बेटी जेनानी थी। श्रीमान डी क्लार्क ने द्वितीय उपराष्ट्रपति के रूप में शपथ ली और फिर श्रीमान थाबो मबेकी ने प्रथम उपराष्ट्रपति के रूप में शपथ ली। मण्डेला ने संविधान को बनाए रखने और गणतन्त्र तथा उसके लोगों की सेवा करने का वादा करते हुए अपने पद की शपथ ली।

अपने भाषण में, मण्डेला ने दक्षिण अफ्रीका के रंगभेद से लोकतन्त्र में बदलाव को प्रतिबिम्बित किया। उन्होंने अन्तर्राष्ट्रीय मेहमानों को उनके समर्थन के लिए धन्यवाद दिया और राजनीतिक स्वतन्त्रता के लिए किए गए बलिदानों का सम्मान किया। मण्डेला ने सभी नागरिकों के लिए गरीबी, अभावों और भेदभाव से लड़ने की प्रतिज्ञा की, क्योंकि उनका मानना था कि किसी राष्ट्र की सबसे बड़ी सम्पत्ति उसके लोग होते हैं, न की रत्न।

दक्षिण अफ्रीका के जेट विमानों ने अपनी सैन्य शक्ति का प्रदर्शन किया। दक्षिण अफ्रीका के रक्षा एवं पुलिस के सर्वोच्च सैन्य अधिकारियों ने मण्डेला को सलाम किया एवं उनके एवं राष्ट्र के प्रति निष्ठा की प्रतिज्ञा ली। पुराने 'नकोसी सिकेलल' और नए 'डाइ स्टेम' दोनों राष्ट्रगान गाए गए।

नेल्सन मण्डेला उन दिनों को याद करते हैं, जब श्वेत लोगों के द्वारा अश्वेत लोगों के विरुद्ध नस्लीय प्रभुत्व की प्रणाली बनाई गई थी। वह कहते हैं कि रंगभेद की नीति (नस्लीय अलगाव की नीति) ने उनके देश व इसके लोगों को गहरा और कभी न भरने वाला घाव दिया है। उन्होनें अपने लोगों की बहादुरी की प्रशंसा की। उन्होंने ओलिवर टैम्बोस, वाल्टर सिसुलस, चीफ लुथुलिस, यूसुफ दादूस आदि जैसे महान स्वतन्त्रता सेनानियों को याद किया।

मण्डेला का मानना था कि प्रत्येक व्यक्ति के दो दायित्व होते हैं- एक अपने परिवार के प्रति तथा दूसरा अपने राष्ट्र के प्रति। उनकी तरह दक्षिण अफ्रीका में जन्म लेने वाला अश्वेत व्यक्ति दोनों को पूरा नहीं कर पाता। अपने देश के हित में कुछ करने के लिए मण्डेला को अपने परिवार से दूर किया गया था।

मण्डेला ने याद किया कि एक बच्चे के रूप में, उनके लिए स्वतन्त्रता का अर्थ—वह करने में सक्षम होना था, जो वे करना चाहते थे। विद्यार्थी के रूप में वह केवल स्वयं के लिए स्वतन्त्रता चाहते थे। फिर जोहानसबर्ग में एक युवा व्यक्ति के रूप में वह अपने सपनों को हासिल करने, परिवार प्रारम्भ करने, स्वयं के लिए कमाने की स्वतन्त्रता चाहते थे। जैसे-जैसे वे बड़े हुए, उन्हें यह अहसास होने लगा कि एक बच्चे के रूप में उन्होंनें जो स्वतन्त्रता का आनन्द लिया था, वह केवल एक भ्रम था।

मण्डेला अपने समुदाय के लिए स्वतन्त्रता सम्मान और आत्म-सम्मान प्राप्त करने की इच्छा के साथ अफ्रीकन राष्ट्रीय कांग्रेस में शामिल हो गए। मण्डेला ने अनुभव किया कि जब तक उनका समुदाय स्वतन्त्र नहीं होगा, तब तक वे स्वतन्त्रता का आनन्द नहीं उठा सकते। फलस्वरूप, उन्हें बन्दी बना लिया गया। उन्होंने यह भी अनुभव किया कि उत्पीड़ित (यातना पाने वाले) के समान उत्पीड़क (यातना देने वाला) भी स्वतन्त्र नहीं होता है।

Objective Questions

Extract Based Questions

Read the following extracts carefully and answer the questions that follow.

1 We, who were outlaws not so long ago, have today been given the rare privilege to be host to the nations of the world on our own soil. We thank all of our distinguished international guests for having come to take possession with the people of our country of what is, after all, a common victory for justice, for peace, for human dignity.

We have, at last, achieved our political emancipation. We pledge ourselves to liberate all our people from the continuing bondage of poverty, deprivation, suffering, gender and other discrimination.

Never, never, and never again shall it be that this beautiful land will again experience the oppression of one by another.

(i) What privilege did they (people of South Africa) get?
उन्हें (दक्षिणी-अफ्रीका के लोगों को) क्या विशेषाधिकार प्राप्त हुआ था?
(a) To host the nations of the world on their own soil
(b) To led the first non-racial government
(c) To achieved a victory
(d) Appointed as a first Deputy President of South Africa

(ii) 'We have achieved our political emancipation'. What is the meaning of word 'emancipation'?
'We have achieved our political emancipation'.
में 'Emancipation' शब्द का क्या अर्थ है?
(a) Freedom from restrictions (b) Enslavement
(c) Slavery (d) Both (b) and (c)

(iii) What did they (people of South Africa) achieve at last?
आखिरकार उन्होंने (दक्षिणी-अफ्रीका के लोगों ने) क्या हासिल कर लिया?
(a) Their moral values (b) Their dignity
(c) Their political emancipation (d) Their victory

2 But then I slowly saw that not only was I not free, but my brothers and sisters were not free. I saw that it was not just my freedom that was curtailed, but the freedom of everyone who looked like I did. That is when I joined the African National Congress, and that is when the hunger for my own freedom became the greater hunger for the freedom of my people. It was this desire for the freedom of my people to live their lives with dignity and self-respect that animated my life, that transformed a frightened young man into a bold one.

(i) The freedom of the black people of his country was ....
उनके देश के अश्वेत लोगों की स्वतन्त्रता .... थी।
(a) sanctioned (b) supported
(c) curtailed (d) opposed

(ii) The author felt the greater hunger for ....
लेखक ने .... के लिए और अधिक लालसा महसूस की
(a) the freedom of his parents
(b) the freedom of his people
(c) the freedom of his friends
(d) the freedom of his neighbours

(iii) Mr. Mandela was not free but his brothers and sisters were ....
श्रीमान मण्डेला स्वतन्त्र नहीं थे, परन्तु उनके भाई और बहन .... थे।
(a) free (b) praying (c) apologising (d) also not free

(iv) Mr. Mandela joined the African National Congress when ....
श्रीमान मण्डेला अफ्रीकन राष्ट्रीय कांग्रेस में शामिल हुए जब ....
(a) he found he was free
(b) he found himself in jail
(c) he found that he was unsuccessful
(d) he found that his freedom and the freedom of everyone who looked like him, was curtailed

3 I knew that the oppressor must be liberated just as surely as the oppressed. A man who takes away another man's freedom is a prisoner of hatred, he is locked behind the bars of prejudice and narrow mindedness.

(i) Who, according to Mandela, is not free?
मण्डेला के अनुसार, कौन स्वतन्त्र नहीं है?
(a) Oppressor (b) Oppressed
(c) Both (a) and (b) (d) None of these

(ii) Who are robbed of their humanity?
किनसे उनकी मानवता छीन ली गई है?
(a) People of other country
(b) Corrupt political leaders
(c) Both the oppressor and the oppressed
(d) All of the above

(iii) A man who takes away another man's freedom is ....
एक आदमी, जो दूसरे आदमी की स्वतन्त्रता छीन लेता है वह ....
(a) white (b) criminal
(c) a prisoner of hatred (d) rude

Multiple Choice Questions (MCQs)

1. Nelson Mandela became the first black .... of South Africa.
(a) Prime Minister (b) Vice-President
(c) President (d) Defence Minister

2. Democracy elections were held in South Africa in .... and Mandela became the first black President of a new nation.
(a) 1990 (b) 1950 (c) 1994 (d) 1984

3. "The brave man is not he who does not feel afraid but he who conquers that fear." Who said the given statement?
(a) Nelson Mandela (b) Thabo Mbeki
(c) Zenani (d) Walter Sisulu

4. What change brought international leaders to South Africa?
(a) End of Apartheid (b) Humanity
(c) Peace (d) Trade negotiations

5. Whom did Mandela thank for attending the ceremony that represented a common victory of justice, peace and human dignity?
(a) The International Leaders
(b) The National Leader
(c) The Military
(d) Deputy President

6. On the podium, ... was first sworn in as second Deputy President.
(a) Thabo Mbeki (b) Nelson Mandela
(c) Zenani (d) Mr. De Klerk

7. Who sang 'Nkosi Sikelel' the old song?
(a) The blacks (b) The whites
(c) Both (a) and (b) (d) None of these

8. Which National Anthem was sung by the Blacks?
(a) Nkosi Sikelel (b) Die Stem
(c) Both (a) and (b) (d) None of these

9. The .... took place in the lovely sandstone amphitheater formed by the Union Building in Pretoria.
(a) wedding (b) festival
(c) ceremonies (d) party

10. According to Mandela, what is the greatest wealth of a nation?
(a) Minerals (b) Gems
(c) Diamonds (d) People

11. Nelson Mandela had to spend .... years in prison.
(a) thirty-three (b) twenty
(c) thirty (d) twenty-nine

Answers

Extract Based Questions

1. (i) (a), (ii) (a), (iii) (c), **2.** (i) (c), (ii) (b), (iii) (d), (iv) (d) **3.** (i) (c), (ii) (c), (iii) (c)

Multiple Choice Questions

1. (c) 2. (c) 3. (a) 4. (a) 5. (a) 6. (d) 7. (b) 8. (b) 9. (c) 10. (d) 11. (c)

03 From the Diary of Anne Frank

Summary of the Lesson पाठ का सार

This chapter is an extract from the diary of Anne Frank, a 13-year old Jewish girl. She had written her dairy while hiding with her family and friends in Amsterdam during the German occupation of the Netherlands in Second World War. On 20th June, 1942, Anne Frank started writing her diary, just eight days after her birthday. At first, she wasn't sure if anyone would care about her thoughts. But she needed to let out her feelings, so she kept writing. Even though, she seemed to have everything-a loving family and some friends, she felt lonely and wanted a true friend. So, she started writing the diary and named it 'Kitty'.

Anne provides a brief description of her early childhood. Her father and mother moved to Holland from Frankfurt in 1933. Margot, her elder sister, and Anne were sent to Aachen to live with their grandmother for a little while. She tells us that in 1941, her grandma fell ill and died. Anne says that she still misses her grandma.

She also talks about Mrs. Kuperus, her headmistress in the sixth form, and how both of them cried when Anne had to bid farewell to the school.

यह अध्याय एक 13 वर्षीय यहूदी लड़की, ऐनी फ्रेंक की डायरी का अवतरण है। उसने अपनी डायरी तब लिखी थी, जब वह अपने परिवार और मित्रों के साथ, द्वितीय विश्व युद्ध के दौरान जर्मनी के द्वारा नीदरलैण्ड पर आधिपत्य कर लेने के कारण एम्सटरडम में छिपी हुई थी। ऐनी फ्रेंक ने अपने जन्मदिन के मात्र आठ दिनों बाद 20 जून, 1942 को अपनी डायरी लिखना प्रारम्भ किया था। प्रारम्भ में, वह निश्चित नहीं थी कि किसी को उसके विचारों की कोई परवाह होगी, लेकिन उसे अपनी भावनाओं को व्यक्त करने की आवश्यकता थी, इसलिए वह लिखती रही। हालाँकि, ऐसा लगता है कि उसके पास सब कुछ था – एक प्यारा परिवार और कुछ मित्र, वह अकेलापन महसूस करती थी और एक सच्चा मित्र चाहती थी। इसलिए, उसने डायरी लिखना प्रारम्भ किया और उसे 'किट्टी' नाम दिया।

ऐनी ने अपने पूर्व बाल्यकाल का संक्षिप्त वर्णन प्रस्तुत किया है। उसके पिताजी और माताजी वर्ष 1933 में फ्रेंकफर्ट से हॉलैण्ड चले गए थे। ऐनी की बड़ी बहन, मार्गोट और ऐनी को कुछ समय के लिए आचेन उनकी दादी के साथ रहने के लिए भेजा गया था। वह हमें बताती है कि वर्ष 1941 में, उसकी दादी बीमार हुई और उनकी मृत्यु हो गई। ऐनी कहती है कि वह अभी भी अपनी दादी को याद करती है।

वह अपनी छठी कक्षा की प्रधानाध्यापिका, श्रीमती कूपरस के बारे में भी बात करती है कि कैसे वह दोनों रोए थे, जब ऐनी को विद्यालय छोड़ना पड़ा था।

After setting her background for the readers, she narrates what is currently happening with her. She tells us that all the students at her school are worried about who would be moving to the next level. She tells us that she and her friends are going to pass, but she is unsure about Maths. She also tells us that her Maths teacher Mr. Keesing was annoyed with her because she talked too much. So, he gave her a punishment to write an essay on the subject 'A Chatterbox'. Anne wrote about the benefits of talking and even Mr. Keesing laughed at it. However, when she kept talking all through the next class too, she was punished again. She had to write an essay on 'An Incorrigible Chatterbox'. Later, she was punished again for talking. This time he assigned her another essay titled 'Quack, Quack, Quack, Said Mistress Chatterbox'. This time Anne wrote a poem on the topic about a mother duck and a father swan with three baby ducklings who were bitten to death by the father because they quacked too much. This time, her teacher took it lightly and recited it in the class and in other classes as well. He even allowed Anne to talk without assigning any extra homework.

पाठकों के लिए अपनी पृष्ठभूमि स्थापित करने के उपरान्त, वर्तमान में जो उसके साथ हो रहा था, वह उसका वर्णन करती है। वह हमें बताती है कि उसके विद्यालय के सभी विद्यार्थी इस बारे में चिन्तित थे कि अगली कक्षा में कौन पहुँचेगा? वह हमें बताती है कि वह और उसके मित्र उत्तीर्ण हो जाएंगे, परन्तु वह गणित के बारे में निश्चित नहीं थी। वह हमें यह भी बताती है कि उसके गणित के अध्यापक, श्रीमान कीसिंग उससे नाराज थे, क्योंकि वह बहुत अधिक बातें करती थी इसलिए, उन्होंने उसे सजा के रूप में एक 'A Chatterbox' विषय पर निबन्ध लिखने के लिए दिया था। ऐनी ने बातें करने के लाभों के बारे में लिखा और श्रीमान कीसिंग को इस पर हँसी भी आई थी। हालाँकि, वह अगली कक्षा में भी लगातार बातें करती रही थी, उसे पुनः सजा मिली। उसे 'An Incorrigible Chatterbox' विषय पर निबन्ध लिखना पड़ा। बाद में, उसे पुनः बात करने पर सजा मिली।

इस बार उन्होंने उसे 'Quack, Quack, Quack Said Mistress Chatterbox' नामक शीर्षक पर निबन्ध लेखन का कार्य दिया। इस बार ऐनी ने एक माँ बत्तख और एक हंस पिता तथा उनके तीन बत्तख बच्चों के विषय पर कविता लिखी, जिन्हें उनके पिता ने पीट-पीट कर मार दिया था, क्योंकि वह बहुत ज्यादा बोलते थे। इस बार उसके अध्यापक ने इसे सहजता से समझा और कक्षा में पढ़कर सुनाया, साथ ही उन्होंने इस कविता को अन्य कक्षाओं में भी इस बार पढ़कर सुनाया। उन्होंने ऐनी को अतिरिक्त गृहकार्य का भार ना प्रदान करते हुए बात करने की अनुमति भी प्रदान कर दी।

Objective Questions

Extract Based Questions

Read the following extracts carefully and answer the questions that follow.

1 Let me put it more clearly, since no one will believe that a thirteen-year-old girl is completely alone in the world. And I'm not. I have loving parents and a sixteen-year-old sister, and there are about thirty people I can call friends. I have a family, loving aunts and a good home.

No, on the surface I seem to have everything, except my one true friend. All I think about when I'm with friends is having a good time. I can't bring myself to talk about anything but ordinary everyday things. We don't seem to be able to get any closer, and that's the problem. Maybe it's my fault that we don't confide in each other. In any case, that's just how things are and unfortunately they're not liable to change. This is why I've started the diary.

(i) Who is the thirteen-year-old-girl in the passage?
गद्यांश में तेरह वर्षीय लड़की कौन है?
(a) Hollander Frank (b) Otto Frank
(c) Margot Frank (d) Anne Frank

(ii) How old is Anne's elder sister?
ऐनी की बड़ी बहन की आयु कितनी है?
(a) Thirteen-year-old (b) Seventeen-year-old
(c) Sixteen-year-old (d) Ten-year-old

(iii) Why did Anne decide to write a diary?
ऐनी ने डायरी लिखने का निर्णय क्यों लिया?
(a) Because she felt lonely (b) For her friend
(c) For time pass (d) None of these

2 My father, the most adorable father I've ever seen, didn't marry my mother until he was 36 and she was 25. My sister Margot was born in Frankfurt in Germany in 1926. I was born on 12th June, 1929. I lived in Frankfurt until I was four. My father emigrated to Holland in 1933.

(i) When was Anne Frank born?
ऐनी फ्रैंक का जन्म कब हुआ था?
(a) 13th June, 1929 (b) 22nd June, 1929
(c) 17th June, 1929 (d) 12th June, 1929

(ii) The author's father did not marry until he was
लेखिका के पिता ने तब तक विवाह नहीं किया, जब तक कि वे
(a) twenty-five (b) twenty-seven
(c) thirty-four (d) thirty-six

(iii) Find out the opposite of 'immigrated' used in the passage.
गद्यांश में प्रयुक्त आव्रजन का विलोम शब्द खोजिए।
(a) Apigrated (b) Emigrated
(c) Exigrated (d) Semigrated

3 Our entire class is quaking in its boots. The reason, of course, is the forthcoming meeting in which the teachers decide who'll move up to the next form and who'll be kept back. Half the class is making bets. G.N. and I laugh ourselves silly at the two boys behind us, C.N. and Jacques, who have staked their entire holiday savings on their bet. From morning to night, it's "You're going to pass", "No, I'm not", "Yes, you are", "No, I'm not".

Even G's pleading glances and my angry outbursts can't calm them down. If you ask me, there are so many dummies that about a quarter of the class should be kept back, but teachers are the most unpredictable creatures on Earth.

I'm not so worried about my girlfriends and myself. We'll make it. The only subject I'm not sure about is Maths. Anyway, all we can do is wait. Until then, we keep telling each other not to lose heart.

(i) Why is the entire class is quaking?
पूरी कक्षा डर से क्यों काँप रही है?
(a) Because there is no teacher
(b) Because the exams have been delayed
(c) Because the exams result are to be declared soon
(d) All of the above

(ii) What does the idiom 'quaking in its boots' mean?
'Quaking in its boots' मुहावरे का क्या अर्थ है?
(a) To be scared
(b) To be relaxed
(c) To be calm
(d) To be settled

(iii) What did Anne expect about her result?
ऐनी को अपने परिणाम के बारे में क्या उम्मीद थी?
(a) She would expect to pass the exams.
(b) She would expect to fail in the exams.
(c) She would expect not to promote in the next class.
(d) All of the above

Multiple Choice Questions (MCQs)

1. Who was Anne Frank?
(a) A thirteen-year-old Jewish girl
(b) A ninteen-year-old Jewish girl
(c) A seventeen-year-old Jewish girl
(d) A nineteen-year-old Jewish girl

2. Who was Margot Frank?
(a) Anne's friend (b) Anne's mother
(c) Anne's sister (d) Anne's father

3. Who gifted a diary to Anne?
(a) Her mother (b) Her sister
(c) Her brother (d) Her father

4. Who felt that paper had more patience than people?
(a) Anne (b) Otto Frank
(c) Hollander Frank (d) Mr. Keesing

5. Anne considered the diary to be ....
(a) a real friend (b) a great time pass
(c) a real hero (d) a great thing

6. Anne Frank wants to keep a diary because
(a) she is fond of keeping a diary.
(b) she has no friend to talk and share her feelings.
(c) she wants to keep a record in it.
(d) Mr. Keesing, her teacher, had asked her to do so.

7. Why does Anne want to keep a diary?
(a) She has no close friends.
(b) She loves to write.
(c) She wants people to read about her later.
(d) She likes the idea of it.

8. What was the name of Anne's diary?
(a) Kitty (b) Otto
(c) Margot (d) Keesing

9. Who gave Anne a heart-breaking farewell?
(a) Mrs. Kuperus
(b) Otto Frank
(c) Mr. Keesing
(d) Margot Frank

10. The poem was about a mother duck and .... swan.
(a) a sister (b) a brother
(c) a father (d) a grandfather

Answers

Extract Based Questions

1. (i) (d), (ii) (c), (iii) (a), 2. (i) (d), (ii) (d), (iii) (b) 3. (i) (c), (ii) (a), (iii) (a)

Multiple Choice Questions

1. (a) 2. (c) 3. (d) 4. (a) 5. (a) 6. (b) 7. (a) 8. (a) 9. (a) 10. (c)

04 Mijbil the Otter

Summary of the Lesson पाठ का सार

The story 'Mijbil the Otter' by Gavin Maxwell is about the author's pet Mijbil who was an otter. The narrator remembers his journey to Southern Iraq in 1956. He had gone with the intention of getting an otter as a pet. He had learnt that otters are common in the Tigris marshes and can be tamed by the locals. One day he received an otter.

Mijbil looked like a muddy dragon at first. But when the narrator cleaned him up, he discovered that Mijbil was a species unknown to science. The zoologists named him 'Lutrogale perspicillata maxwelli' or Maxwell's Otter. Initially Mijbil ignores the narrator. However, the otter quickly forms a bond with the narrator. The otter exhibits playful behaviour, particularly enjoying water activities like swimming and splashing.

As the narrator prepares to take Mijbil back to England, he faces challenges due to airline regulations. He knew that the British Airline would not allow him to carry an animal to London. So, he booked another flight to Paris and then, Paris to London. For the journey, he constructs a small box for Mijbil to travel in but the otter tries to escape from the box and gets injured. After finding Mijbil injured and covered in blood, the narrator removes the box's lining to ensure that the box could not harm Mijbil further. With little time left before their flight, the narrator quickly put Mijbil into the box, and held the lid with his hand to prevent any further escapes.

Inside the aircraft, the narrator informs the air hostess about Mijbil's presence and gives her a parcel of fish for him. However, soon after takeoff, Mijbil manages to escape from the box and runs down the aisle of the plane. As a result, there is chaos among the passengers. There are squawks and screams, with one passenger mistaking Mijbil for a rat. Eventually, Mijbil finds his way back to the narrator and settles on his knee. The narrator spends the remainder of the journey comforting Mijbil and ensuring his safety.

Maxwell and Mijbil stayed in London for a month. There, Mijbil would spend his time playing with his toys, ping-pong balls, marbles, rubber fruits and a terrapin shell that Maxwell had bought from the marshes. Maxwell would also take Mijbil for exercise and walks. Just like the school children, he would run, play and walk in the streets. In London, many people had not seen an otter. When they saw Mijbil, they made guesses about it. They guessed that it could be a baby seal, a walrus, a hippo, a beaver, a bear cub, a leopard, etc. All of these guesses made the narrator laugh.

गेविन मैक्सवेल द्वारा लिखित कहानी 'Mijbil the Otter' लेखक के पालतू जानवर के बारे में है, जो एक ऊदबिलाव था। कथावाचक वर्ष 1956 की अपनी दक्षिणी इराक की यात्रा को स्मरण करता है। वह पालतु जानवर के रूप में एक ऊदबिलाव लाने के इरादे से गया था। उसे ज्ञात हुआ था कि टिगरिस के दलदली क्षेत्रों मे ऊदबिलाव बहुत सामान्य है और उन्हें स्थानीय निवासियों द्वारा प्रशिक्षित किया जा सकता है। एक दिन उसे ऊदबिलाव प्राप्त हुआ।

प्रारम्भ में, मिजबिल कीचड़ से सने हुए ड्रेगन जैसा दिख रहा था। लेकिन जब कथावाचक ने उसे साफ किया, तो उसे पता चला कि मिजबिल की प्रजाति से विज्ञान भी अनजान था। जीव वैज्ञानिकों ने उस ल्यूट्रोगेल पर्सपिसिल़टा या मैक्सवेल का ऊदबिलाव नाम दिया था। प्रारम्भ में, मिजबिल कथावाचक को अनदेखा करता है। हालाँकि, ऊदबिलाव बहुत शीघ्र कथावाचक के साथ गहरा सम्बन्ध स्थापित कर लेता है। ऊदबिलाव चंचल स्वभाव को प्रदर्शित करता है, विशेषतया पानी के क्रियाकलापों में, जैसे—तैरना और पानी को इधर-उधर उछालना।

जैसे ही कथावाचक मिजबिल को इंग्लैण्ड ले जाने की तैयारी करता है, हवाईयात्रा के नियमों के कारण उसे चुनौतियों का सामना करना पड़ता है। वह जानता था कि ब्रिटिश सरकार हवाईयात्रा से उसे एक जानवर को लन्दन ले जाने की अनुमति नहीं देगी, इसलिए उसने पेरिस तक की हवाईयात्रा निर्धारित की और फिर पेरिस से लन्दन की। यात्रा के लिए, उसने मिजबिल के सफर हेतु एक छोटा बक्सा बनाया, लेकिन ऊदबिलाव उस बक्से से भागने का प्रयास करता है और घायल हो जाता है। मिजबिल को घायल और खून में लथपथ देखने के बाद, कथावाचक बक्से की परत को निकाल देता है, जिससे आगे से बक्सा मिजबिल को नुकसान ना पहुँचा सके। हवाईयात्रा से थोड़े समय पहले, कथावाचक जल्दी से मिजबिल को बक्से में रख देता है और ऊपरी भाग को अपने हाथ से ढक लेता है, जिससे वह फिर से ना निकल पाए।

हवाईजहाज में, कथावाचक वायुयान परिचारिका को मिजबिल की उपस्थिति की सूचना देता है और उसके लिए उसे एक मछलियों का डिब्बा देता है। यद्यपि, हवाई जहाज के उड़ान भरने के कुछ समय पश्चात् ही, मिजबिल बक्से में से बचकर निकलने में कामयाब हो जाता है और हवाईजहाज के गलियारे में दौड़ता है। फलस्वरूप, यात्रियों के बीच उथल-पुथल मच जाती है। एक यात्री मिजबिल को चूहा समझने की भूल करता है और वहाँ चीख-पुकार मच जाती है। अन्ततः मिजबिल कथावाचक तक पहुँचने का अपना मार्ग खोज लेता है और अपने घुटने पर बैठ जाता है। कथावाचक अपनी बची हुई यात्रा मिजबिल को आराम देने में और उसकी सुरक्षा को सुनिश्चित करने में बिताता है।

एक महीने तक मैक्सवेल और मिजबिल लन्दन में रहते है। वहाँ, मिजबिल अपना समय अपने खिलौनों पिंग-पोंग वाली गेंदो, कंचों, रबर के फलों और कछुए के कवच से खेलने में बिताता है, जिन्हें मैक्सवेल ने दलदली क्षेत्र से खरीदा था। मैक्सवेल मिजबिल को व्यायाम कराने व टहलाने के लिए भी ले जाता था। विद्यालय के बच्चों की भाँति, वह गलियों में दौड़ता, खेलता और टहलता था। लन्दन में, अधिकांश लोगों ने ऊदबिलाव नहीं देखा था। जब वे मिजबिल को देखते तो इसके बारे में अनुमान लगाते थे। वे अनुमान लगाते थे कि यह एक शील का बच्चा वॉलरस, दरियाई घोड़ा, ऊदबिलाव, भालू का बच्चा, तेन्दुआ आदि हो सकता है। इन सभी अनुमानों से कथावाचक को हँसी आती थी।

Objective Questions

Extract Based Questions

Read the following extracts carefully and answer the questions that follow.

1 Two days later, Mijbil escaped from my bedroom as I entered it and I turned to see his tail is appearing round the bend of the corridor that led to the bathroom. By the time I got there he was up on the end of the bathtub and fumbling at the chromium taps with his paws. I watched, amazed; in less than a minute he had turned the tap far enough to produce a trickle of water and after a moment or two achieved the full flow.

(i) Mijbil was a/an ....
मिजबिल एक .... था।
(a) cat (b) otter (c) dog (d) seal

(ii) By nature, Mijbil was ....
स्वभाव से, मिजबिल .... था।
(a) friendly (b) indifferent
(c) anti-social animal (d) not liked by the author

(iii) Where did Mijbil go?
मिजबिल कहाँ गया था?
(a) Bathroom (b) Pool (c) Garden (d) Veranda

2 The days passed peacefully at Basra, but I dreaded the prospect of transporting Mijbil to England and to Camusfearna. The British airline to London would not fly animals, so I booked a flight to Paris on another airline and from there to London. The airline insisted that Mijbil should be packed into a box not more than eighteen inches square, to be carried on the floor at my feet. I had a box made and an hour before we started, I put Mijbil into the box so that he would become accustomed to it and left for a hurried meal.

(i) The author ....
लेखक ....
(a) was fearful of carrying Mijbil to England.
(b) did not want to take Mijbil with him.
(c) wanted to carry Mijbil without box in the plane.
(d) did not want to board the flight.

(ii) How did Mijbil feel in the box?
मिजबिल को डब्बे में कैसा लगा था?
(a) Uncomfortable (b) Angry
(c) Sad (d) Shocked

(iii) What was the size of the box?
डब्बे का माप क्या था?
(a) Less than seventeen inches
(b) Eighteen to twenty inches
(c) Not more than eighteen inches
(d) None of the above

3 When I returned, there was an appalling spectacle. There was complete silence from the box, but from its airholes and chinks around the lid, blood had trickled and dried. I whipped off the lock and tore open the lid, and Mijbil, exhausted and blood-spattered, whimpered and caught at my leg. He had torn the lining of the box to shreds; when I removed the last of it so that there were no cutting edges left, it was just ten minutes until the time of the flight, and the airport was five miles distant. I put the miserable Mijbil back into the box, holding down the lid with my hand. I sat in the back of the car with the box beside me as the driver tore through the streets of Basra like a ricocheting bullet.

(i) Choose the word which means the same as 'whimpered'.
वह शब्द चुनिये, जिसका अर्थ 'whimpered' के समान हो।
(a) Moaned (b) Shouted
(c) Bit (d) Loud

(ii) How was Mijbil feeling when he was put in the box again?
मिज को दोबारा डब्बे में डाले जाने पर कैसा महसूस हुआ था?
(a) Flustered (b) Angry
(c) Miserable (d) Sad

(iii) Which of the following options correctly states Maxwell's likely feelings, in the situation below?
"... I put the miserable Mij back into the box, holding down the lid with my hand."
निम्न में से कौन-सा विकल्प नीचे दी गई स्थिति में मैक्सवेल की सम्भावित भावनाओं को सही ढंग से बताता है?
"...... मैने अपने हाथ से ढक्कन को पकड़कर, दुखी मिज को वापस बाक्स में डाल दिया।"
(a) Anxious (b) Terrified
(c) Guilty (d) Both (a) and (c)

Multiple Choice Questions (MCQs)

1. What was the name of the author's pet dog in the chapter 'Mijbil the Otter'?
(a) Jennie (b) Jonnie
(c) Jammie (d) Jinnie

2. Early in the new year of 1956, Maxwell travelled to ....
(a) London (b) Southern Iraq
(c) India (d) Arabia

3. What did the otter look like?
(a) Small dog (b) Small cat
(c) Small dragon (d) Small rabbit

4. How many days later did the author's mail arrive?
(a) 2 (b) 4 (c) 5 (d) 7

5. The otter was brought to the author by ....
(a) his friend (b) two Arabs
(c) hotel staff (d) None of these

6. Who sent the following note to the author: "Here's your otter..."?
(a) Consulate General (b) Two Arabs
(c) Air hostess (d) His friend

7. Choose the correct scientific name given to otters by zoologist.
(a) Lutrogale Maxwelli
(b) Lutrogale Perspicillata
(c) Lutrogale Perspicillata Maxwelli
(d) Maxwelli Perspicillata Lutrogale

8. In the beginning, the otter was ....
(a) friendly (b) hostile
(c) aloof and indifferent (d) sad

9. Why did the driver drive through the streets of Basra like a ricochetting bullet?
(a) Author was late for his flight
(b) Mijbil had hurt himself
(c) Someone was after the driver
(d) All of the above

10. How did the airline wanted him to carry Mijbil?
(a) In a separate compartment
(b) In a box
(c) In his bag
(d) None of the above

11. For the first twenty-four hours Mijbil was neither hostile nor ....
(a) helpful
(b) friendly
(c) opposed
(d) supportive

Answers

Extract Based Questions

1. (i) (b), (ii) (a), (iii) (a), 2. (i) (a), (ii) (a), (iii) (c) 3. (i) (a), (ii) (c), (iii) (d)

Multiple Choice Questions

1. (b) 2. (b) 3. (c) 4. (c) 5. (b) 6. (d) 7. (c) 8. (c) 9. (a) 10. (b) 11. (b)

05 Madam Rides the Bus

Summary of the Lesson पाठ का सार

This story is about an eight-year-old girl named Valliammai (Valli). She lives in a village from where a bus passes. She is fascinated by the bus that travels between her village and the nearest town. She wants to experience a bus ride by herself. Valli gathered information about the bus timings by listening to the conversations of her neighbours who used the bus regularly. She saves money for the fare by cutting down her spending on candies, peppermints etc., and she plans to go on the bus when her mother is asleep in the afternoon. She gets on the bus. The conductor is amused by her and calls her 'madam'. He gives her a ticket and shows her a seat.

Valli enjoys the bus ride and observes the scenery outside. She sees mountains, fields, palm trees, and grasslands. She also sees a cow running across the road. She is thrilled by everything she sees and feels like she is in a dream. An elderly passenger in the bus calls Valli a child and he asks her not to stand. At the stand, an elderly woman came and sat beside Valli. Valli found the lady ugly. She had big holes in her ears and was wearing ugly earrings. She was chewing betel nuts.

यह कहानी वल्लियमाई (वल्ली) नाम की एक आठ वर्षीय लडकी की है। वह एक गाँव में रहती है, जहाँ से बस गुजरती है। वह उस बस के प्रति बहुत आकर्षित थी, जो उसके गाँव और कस्बे के बीच चलती थी। वह स्वयं बस की यात्रा का अनुभव करना चाहती है। वल्ली ने अपने उन पड़ोसियों की बातचीत को सुनकर बस की समय सारिणी की जानकारी प्राप्त की, जो नियमित रूप से बस का प्रयोग करते थे। उसने अपने मिठाईयों और पेपरमिण्ट, टोफी आदि पर होने वाले खर्च को कम करके किराए के लिए धनराशि बचाई और उसने दोपहर में बस यात्रा करने की योजना बनाई जब उसकी माँ सोती है। वह बस में चढ़ती है। बस कण्डक्टर उससे बहुत प्रसन्न होता है और उसे मैडम कहता है। वह उसे टिकट देता है और उसे उसकी सीट दिखाता है।

वल्ली बस की सवारी का आनन्द उठाती है और बाहर के दृश्य का अवलोकन करती है। वह पर्वत, खेत, खजूर के पेड़ और घास के मैदान देखती है। वह एक गाय को सड़क पर दौडते हुए भी देखती है। वह अपने देखे हुए प्रत्येक दृश्य से रोमांचित होती है और उसे ऐसा महसूस होता है, जैसे वह सपने में हो। बस में एक वृद्ध यात्री वल्ली को बच्ची बोलता है और वह उसे खड़े रहने से मना करता है। बस के स्टैण्ड पर, एक बुजुर्ग महिला आकर वल्ली के पास बैठ जाती है। वल्ली को महिला अच्छी नहीं लगती है। उसके कानों में बड़े-बड़े छेद थे और उसने बदसूरत झुमके पहने हुए थे। वह सुपारी चबा रही थी।

Valli does not talk to anyone on the bus and gets annoyed because she does not like being treated like a child and considers herself an adult. She does not get off the bus when bus reaches the town. She tells the conductor that she is there only for the ride. She buys a return ticket and stays on the bus.

On the way back, she sees the same cow lying dead on the roadside. She is shocked and saddened by the sight. She sat on the bus silently for the rest of the journey. She does not tell anyone about what she saw, and she keeps it to herself. She gets off the bus and goes back to her house. She pretends that nothing happened, and does not tell her mother about her adventure. She thinks that she will go on another bus ride someday, but she also feels that she has grown up a little.

वल्ली बस में किसी से बात नहीं करती और क्रोधित हो जाती है, क्योंकि उससे बच्चों की तरह व्यवहार किया जाता है। वल्ली को यह व्यवहार पसन्द नहीं आता क्योंकि वह स्वयं को व्यस्क समझती है। जब बस शहर में पहुँच जाती है, वह बस से नहीं उतरती। वह कण्डक्टर को बताती है कि वह वहाँ केवल सवारी करने के लिए है। वह लौटने का टिकट खरीदती है और बस में ही रुकी रहती है।

लौटते समय, वह उसी गाय को सड़क के किनारे मरा हुआ पड़ा देखती है। वह यह दृश्य देखकर हैरान और दुःखी हो जाती है। बाकी की यात्रा में वह चुपचाप बस में बैठी रहती है। वह किसी को नहीं बताती कि उसने क्या देखा, और इसे स्वयं तक ही रखती है। वह बस से उतरकर अपने घर वापस चली जाती है। वह ऐसा व्यवहार प्रदर्शित करती है जैसे कुछ भी न हुआ हो और अपने रोमांच के बारे में अपनी माँ को नहीं बताती है। वह सोचती है कि किसी अन्य दिन वह दूसरी बस यात्रा पर जाएगी, लेकिन उसे ऐसा भी अनुभव होता है कि वह थोड़ी बड़ी हो गई है।

Objective Questions

Extract Based Questions

Read the following extracts carefully and answer the questions that follow.

1 There was a girl named Valliammai who was called Valli for short. She was eight years old and very curious about things. Her favourite pastime was standing in the front doorway of her house, watching what was happening in the street outside. There were no playmates of her own age on her street, and this was about all she had to do. But for Valli, standing at the front door was every bit as enjoyable as any of the elaborate games other children played. Watching the street gave her many new unusual experiences.

(i) What was the full name of Valli?
वल्ली का पूरा नाम क्या था?
(a) Narrator (b) Harshita (c) Valliammai (d) Anne

(ii) How old was Valli?
वल्ली की आयु कितनी थी?
(a) 9 years old (b) 10 years old
(c) 6 years old (d) 8 years old

(iii) Why did she spend her time by standing in the front doorway of her house?
वह अपने घर के मुख्य द्वार पर खड़े रहकर अपना समय क्यों व्यतीत करती थी?
(a) Because the bus filled with new passengers everyday and wished to ride in the bus.
(b) Because no one of her age plays with her.
(c) Because she want to watch the vehicles on the road.
(d) Because her father went to city she used to wait for him.

2 The most fascinating thing of all was the bus that travelled between her village and the nearest town. It passed through her street each hour, once going to the town and once coming back. The sight of the bus, filled each time with a new set of passengers, was a source of unending joy for Valli.

Day after day she watched the bus, and gradually a tiny wish crept into her head and grew there: she wanted to ride on that bus, even if just once. This wish became stronger and stronger, until it was an overwhelming desire. Valli would stare wistfully at the people who got on or off the bus when it stopped at the street corner.

(i) What was the most fascinating scene for Valli in the street?
सड़क पर वल्ली के लिए सबसे आकर्षक दृश्य कौन-सा था?
(a) The bus with new set of curtains every time.
(b) The bus with new set of passengers every time.
(c) The bus with new drivers every time.
(d) The bus with new conductor every time.

(ii) 'Valli would be jealous to listen ....'. This indicates Valli's
'Valli would be jealous to listen ....' यह वल्ली के बारे में क्या संकेत देता है?
(a) longing to ride the bus
(b) nature as an envious person
(c) denial to accept her situation
(d) inclination to trouble travellers

(iii) What does the line 'gradually, a tiny wish crept into her head and grew there' mean?
"Gradually, a tiny wish crept into her head and grew there" पंक्ति का क्या अर्थ है?
(a) The wish developed in her head over a period of time.
(b) The wish was a feeling of wanting to prove her strength.
(c) The wish was planted in her head by someone's suggestion.
(d) The wish was small and was overpowered by a sense of doubt.

3 Over many days and months Valli listened carefully to conversations between her neighbours and people who regularly used the bus, and she also asked a few discreet questions here and there. This way she picked up various small details about the bus journey. The town was six miles from her village. The fare was thirty paise one way—"which is almost nothing at all," she heard one well-dressed man say, but to Valli, who scarcely saw that much money from one month to the next, it seemed a fortune.

(i) Complete the sentence by choosing the most suitable option.
सबसे उपयुक्त विकल्प चुनकर वाक्य को पूर्ण कीजिए।
The town was .... from Valli's village.
शहर वल्ली के गाँव से .... दूर था।
(a) ten miles
(b) five miles
(c) six miles
(d) very near

(ii) Why did Valli listen to the conversations?
वल्ली बातचीत क्यों सुनती थी?
(a) Because she was curious.
(b) Because she wanted to travel in the bus.
(c) Becase it was hed hobby.
(d) Because she had nothing else to do.

(iii) Complete the sentence by choosing the most suitable option.
सबसे उपयुक्त विकल्प चुनकर वाक्य को पूर्ण कीजिए।
The fare of the bus was .... one way.
बस का एक तरफ का किराया .... था।
(a) thirty paise (b) fifty paise
(c) twenty paise (d) forty paise

Multiple Choice Questions (MCQs)

1. Valli was a .... year old girl.
(a) ten (b) seven
(c) eight (d) twenty

2. What would make Valli jealous?
(a) Strangers travelling by bus
(b) Hearing the story of her friend's bus journey
(c) Both (a) and (b)
(d) None of the above

3. The girl Valliammi was called .... for short.
(a) Usha (b) Valli
(c) Amma (d) Kutti

4. The bus fare from Valli's village to the town was .... paise one way.
(a) thirty (b) forty
(c) fifty (d) twenty

5. Valli (Madam Rides the Bus) decided to board the bus at one o'clock so that she could be back by two forty-five because ....
(a) it was lunchtime
(b) it was her mother's nap time
(c) it was the scheduled time of the bus
(d) All of the above

6. How many passengers were in the bus when Valli was riding in the bus?
(a) 6-7 passengers (b) 8-9 passengers
(c) 9-10 passengers (d) 10-11 passengers

7. Who offered Valli to sit at the front seat of the bus?
(a) One passenger in the bus
(b) Lady in the bus
(c) The bus driver
(d) The bus conductor

8. What was the source of unending joy for Valli in the chapter 'Madam Rides the Bus'?
(a) The sight of the bus (b) New set of passengers
(c) The sight of people (d) Both (a) and (b)

9. 'Valli was excited to see the view outside', but what obstructed her view?
(a) Other passenger (b) Window cover
(c) Canvas blind (d) The curtain

10. What was on the other side of the road?
(a) Deep ditch (b) Acres of green fields
(c) Mountain (d) Both (a) and (b)

Answers

Extract Based Questions

1. (i) (c), (ii) (d), (iii) (b), 2. (i) (b), (ii) (a), (iii) (a) 3. (i) (c), (ii) (b), (iii) (a)

Multiple Choice Questions

1. (c) 2. (b) 3. (b) 4. (a) 5. (b) 6. (a) 7. (d) 8. (d) 9. (c) 10. (d)

06 The Proposal

Summary of the Lesson पाठ का सार

The Proposal is a one-act comedy that makes fun of the greed and hypocrisy of the upper-class society.

The story is about three people :

- **Ivan Lomov,** a rich man who wants to marry Natalya Stepanovna, the daughter of his neighbour Stepan Chubukov
- **Natalya,** a young woman who wants to get married
- **Stepan Chubukov** a proud and greedy father who wants his daughter to marry a rich man.

The story begins with Lomov visiting Chubukov's house, dressed in a formal suit. He tells Chubukov that he has a proposal to make, but Chubukov misunderstands him and thinks that he wants to borrow money. Lomov says that he wants to marry Natalya, after which Chubukov became very happy. He calls Natalya and leaves them alone to talk.

Lomov starts by saying nice things about Natalya, but soon they start to argue over a piece of land called Oxen Meadows. Both Lomov and Natalya say that the meadow is theirs. They say mean things to each other and start a fight. Chubukov joins the fight and Lomov leaves in anger. He does not ask Natalya to marry him. Chubukov yells at Natalya for making Lomov go away. He tells her that Lomov came to propose to her, and Natalya feels sorry for what she did. She asks her father to bring him back, and he agrees.

Lomov comes back and Natalya tries to be nice and friendly. She says that he can have Oxen Meadows, and he is happy but then they start to fight again over their dogs, Squeezer and Guess. They continue arguing suddenly, Lomov falls down from a heart problem. Chubukov comes in and thinks that Lomov is dead. He tries to wake him up with water, after a while Lomov moves a bit and opens his eyes. Chubukov quickly gives Natalya's hand to Lomov and blesses them, but they continue to argue over their dogs. The play ends with Chubukov shouting at them to stop.

'The Proposal' एक हास्यप्रधान एकांकी नाटक है, जो उच्च-वर्गीय समाज के लालच व पाखण्ड का मजाक बनाता है।

यह कहानी तीन व्यक्तियों के बारे में है

- **इवान लोमोव**, एक अमीर व्यक्ति, जो अपने पड़ोसी स्टीफन चुबुकोव की बेटी नताल्या स्टीपनोवना से विवाह करना चाहता है।
- **नताल्या**, एक युवा महिला, जो विवाह करना चाहती है।
- **स्टीफन चुबुकोव**, एक घमण्डी और लालची पिता, जो अपनी बेटी का विवाह एक अमीर व्यक्ति से करवाना चाहता है।

कहानी की शुरूआत लोमोव औपचारिक सूट पहनकर चुबुकोव के घर जाने से होती है। वह चुबुकोव को बताता है कि वह एक प्रस्ताव लेकर आया है, परन्तु चुबुकोव उसे गलत समझ लेता है और सोचता है कि वह पैसे उधार लेना चाहता है। लोमोव कहता है कि वह नताल्या से विवाह करना चाहता है यह सुनकर चुबुकोव बहुत खुश होता है। वह नताल्या को बुलाता है और उन्हें बात करने के लिए अकेला छोड़ देता है।

लोमोव नताल्या के बारे में अच्छी बाते बोलने से शुरू करता है, लेकिन शीघ्र ही वे एक जमीन के टुकड़े को लेकर बहस करने लगते हैं, जिसे ऑक्सन मेडोज कहते थे। लोमोव और नताल्या दोनों कहते हैं कि मैदान उनके हैं। वे एक-दूसरे को तुच्छ बातें बोलते हैं और लड़ना शुरू कर देते है। चुबुकोव भी लड़ाई में शामिल होता है और लोमोव गुस्से में वहाँ से चला जाता है। वह नताल्या से शादी करने के लिए नहीं पूछता है। चुबुकोव लोमोव को भगा देने के लिए नताल्या पर चिल्लाता है। वह उसे बताता है कि लोमोव उसे विवाह का प्रस्ताव लेकर आया था और नताल्या ने जो किया, उसे उसके लिए दु:ख होता है। वह अपने पिता से उसे वापस लाने के लिए कहती है और वह मान जाता है।

लोमोव वापस आता है और नताल्या उसके साथ अच्छा एवं मित्रवत् रहने का प्रयास करती है। वह कहती है कि वह ऑक्सन मेडोज रख सकता है और वह प्रसन्न हो जाता है, लेकिन वे पुन: अपने कुत्तों, स्कवीजर और गैस के बारे में लड़ने लगते हैं। वे एक-दूसरे को भला-बुरा कहते रहते हैं और अचानक से लोमोव दिल की बीमारी के कारण नीचे गिर जाता है। चुबुकोव अन्दर आता है और सोचता है कि लोमोव मर चुका है। वह पानी से उसे होश में लाने की कोशिश करता है, कुछ समय बाद लोमोव अपनी आँखे खोलता है। चुबुकोव शीघ्रता से नताल्या का हाथ लोमोव को देता है और उन्हें आशीर्वाद देता है, लेकिन वे अपने कुत्तों के बारे में लगातार बहस करते रहते हैं चुबुकोव के उन्हें चुप करने के लिए चिल्लाने के साथ नाटक समाप्त हो जाता है।

Objective Questions

Extract Based Questions

Read the following extracts carefully and answer the questions that follow.

1 "Natalya Stephenova is an excellent housekeeper, not bad looking, well-educated. What more do I want? But I'm getting noise in my ears from excitement. (Drinks) And it's impossible for me not to marry. In the first place, I'm already 35-a critical age so to speak. In the second place, I ought to lead a quiet and regular life."

(i) When the speaker says, "What more do I want?", he means that
जब वक्ता कहता है, "मुझे इससे ज्यादा क्या चाहिए?" उसका अर्थ है कि
(a) he wants to get married soon.
(b) Natalya is a good match for him.
(c) he and Natalya are both quarrelsome.
(d) Natalya would add to his glory.

(ii) The statement that is true about the speaker, according to the passage is
गद्यांश के अनुसार, वक्ता के बारे में सत्य कथन है कि
(a) he is an old man.
(b) he suffers from attacks of excitements.
(c) he wants to make Natalya his business partner.
(d) he wants to travel to the world.

(iii) Who is the speaker of the given lines?
दी गई पंक्तियों का वक्ता कौन है?
(a) Lomov
(b) Chubukov
(c) Natalya's housekeeper
(d) Chubukov's wife

2 Lomov Hear me out, I implore you! The peasants of your father's grandfather, as I have already had the honour of explaining to you, used to bake bricks for my aunt's grandmother. Now my aunt's grandmother, wishing to make them a present.

Natalya I can't make head or tail of all this about aunts and grandfathers and grandmothers. The Meadows are ours, that's all.

Lomov Mine.

Natalya Ours! You can go on proving it for two days on end, you can go and put on fifteen dress jackets, but I tell you they're ours, ours, ours! I don't want anything of yours and I don't want to give anything of mine. So there!

(i) Natalya and Lomov were ....
नताल्या और लोमोव .... रहे थे।
(a) talking to each other (b) abusing each other
(c) arguing with each other (d) in love with each other

(ii) What did Lomov forget in the midst of the argument?
लोमोव बहस के बीच में क्या भूल गया था?
(a) Marriage proposal for Natalya
(b) Ownership documents of Oxen Meadows
(c) His dog
(d) None of the above

(iii) Which of the following correctly point out Natalya's tone in the given lines?
निम्नलिखित में से कौन-सा विकल्प दी गई पंक्तियों में नताल्या के स्वर की ओर संकेत करता है?
(a) Shocked (b) Calm
(c) Angry (d) Irritated

Ans. (c) Angry

3 "But, please, Stephen Stepanovitch, how can they be yours? Do be a reasonable man !My aunt's grandmother gave the Meadows for the temporary and free use of your grandfather's peasants. The peasants mused the land for forty years and got accustomed to it as if it was their own, when it happened that ....

(i) Why did the peasants treat the land as their own?
कृषक जमीन को अपनी जमीन के समान क्यों मानते थे?
(a) They used the land for forty years
(b) They got accustomed to using the land
(c) Both (a) and (b)
(d) None of the above

(ii) What light do these lines throw on the speaker's character?
ये पंक्तियाँ वक्ता के चरित्र पर क्या प्रकाश डालती हैं?
(a) Logical (b) Rational
(c) Polite (d) All of these

(iii) How does the listener react to the speaker?
श्रोता वक्ता के प्रति कैसी प्रतिक्रिया करता है?
(a) The listener aggressively refuses the speaker, Lomov's claims.
(b) The listener politely refutes the speaker, Lomov's assertions.
(c) The listener abused the speaker, Lomov.
(d) None of the above

Multiple Choice Questions (MCQs)

1. What is the play about?
   (a) Tendency of wealthy families to seek ties with other wealthy families
   (b) Tendency of wealthy families to increase their estates
   (c) Encouragement of marriages that make good economic sense
   (d) All of the above
2. What was Lomov wearing when he entered the scene?
   (a) Dress jacket and white gloves
   (b) Evening coat with hat
   (c) Waistcoat and trousers
   (d) Shirt and trousers
3. What request did Chubukov think Lomov would make?
   (a) Ask for her daughter's hand in marriage
   (b) Borrow money
   (c) Borrow land
   (d) All of the above
4. Chubukov was blessing Lomov because he ....
   (a) gave Oxen Meadows to Chubukov
   (b) gave his pet dog guess to Natalya
   (c) asked Chubukov's daughter's hand in marriage
   (d) None of the above
5. What was the first point of disagreement between Natalya and Lomov?
   (a) Pet dog (b) Oxen Meadows
   (c) House (d) None of these
6. What happens to Lomov when he gets in an excited state?
   (a) He starts running
   (b) His heart beat increases
   (c) His brain started working
   (d) His starts coughing
7. Who gave the Meadows to Natalya's father?
   (a) Lomov's Aunt's grandmother
   (b) Lomov's Aunt
   (c) Lomov's grandmother
   (d) Lomov's mother
8. What had Natalya been doing when Lomov called for her?
   (a) Cleaning the house (b) Washing clothes
   (c) Shelling peas (d) Cooking food
9. How much are the meadows worth?
   (a) 100 roubles (b) 200 roubles
   (c) 300 roubles (d) 400 roubles
10. Who does Chubukov call a 'lovesick cat'?
   (a) Lomov (b) himself
   (c) his maid (d) Natalya

Answers

Extract Based Questions

1. (i) (b), (ii) (b), (iii) (a), **2.** (i) (c), (ii) (a), (iii) (c) **3.** (i) (c), (ii) (d), (iii) (b)

Multiple Choice Questions

1. (d) 2. (a) 3. (b) 4. (c) 5. (b) 6. (b) 7. (a) 8. (c) 9. (c) 10. (d)

07 Glimpses of India

Part–I A Baker from Goa

Summary of the Lesson पाठ का सार

This part of the chapter is a pen-portrait of a traditional Goan village baker or 'Pader' who still has an important place in Goan culture.

The narrator recalls his childhood in Goa. In the old Portuguese days of Goa, the Portuguese were famous for their loaves of bread. The Portuguese left Goa a long time ago but the mixers, moulders, traditional bakers and furnaces (a machine for baking) still exist in Goa. Bakers are known as Pader and they still carry on the traditional baking practices.

The baker used to arrive with a jingling sound of the bamboo stick that woke up everyone. The children ran to meet the baker when they heard the sound. They ran to get the bread-bangles specially made of sweet bread. The baker supported the bread basket on his head. His one hand supported the basket and other hand banged the bamboo stick on the ground. The children would be pushed aside and the loaves would be delivered to the maid-servant.

Bakers were important in Goa. Marriages or any festival were incomplete without the sweet bread known as Bol. Sandwiches were prepared by the lady of the house for her daughter's engagement. Cakes and bolinhas were essential for Christmas and other festivals.

The baker in Goa wore a special dress known as Kabai. During the narrator's childhood, bakers wore shirt trousers which were shorter than full-length and longer than half pants. The baker usually collected his bills at the end of the month.

In old days, baking was a profitable profession. A baker's family and servants were always happy and prosperous.

पाठ का यह भाग गोवा के गाँव के पारम्परिक बेकर या पैडर का एक लिखित चित्रण है, जिसका गोवा की संस्कृति में अभी भी एक महत्त्वपूर्ण स्थान है।

कथावाचक गोवा में अपने बचपन के समय को याद करता है। गोवा के पुरातन पुर्तगाली शासनकाल के दिनों में, पुर्तगाली अपने ब्रेड की पाव-रोटियों के लिए प्रसिद्ध थे। पुर्तगालियों ने बहुत समय पहले ही गोवा छोड़ दिया था, किन्तु मिश्रण बनाने की मशीन, साँचे, परम्परागत बेकर और भट्टियाँ (ब्रेड सेकने की मशीन) अभी भी गोवा में है। बेकर को पैडर कहते हैं और वे अभी भी ब्रेड की सिकाई के लिए परम्परागत तरीके का प्रयोग करते हैं।

बेकर बाँस की छड़ियों की टनटनाहट की आवाज के साथ आया करते थे, जो प्रत्येक व्यक्ति को नींद से जगा देती थी। बच्चे जब आवाज को सुनते, तो वे बेकर से मिलने के लिए दौड़ पड़ते थे। वे ब्रेड के गोल छल्ले लेने के लिए दौड़ते, जो विशेषत: मीठी ब्रेड से बनते थे। बेकर अपने सिर पर रखी ब्रेड की टोकरी को सँभालता। उसका एक हाथ टोकरी को सँभालता था और दूसरे हाथ से वह बाँस की छड़ी को जमीन पर ठोकता रहता था। बच्चों को एक तरफ धकेलकर पाव नौकरानी को दे दिए जाते थे।

बेकर्स गोवा में महत्त्वपूर्ण थे। विवाह या अन्य कोई त्योहार मीठी ब्रेड के बिना अधूरा था, जिसे बोल कहा जाता था। घर की महिला के द्वारा अपनी बेटी की सगाई के लिए सेण्डविच बनाए जाते थे। क्रिसमस और अन्य त्योहारों के समय केक और बोलिन्हास बहुत आवश्यक होते थे।

गोवा के बेकर एक विशेष परिधान पहनते थे, जिसे कबाई कहा जाता था। कथावाचक के बचपन में, बेकर्स कमीज और पतलून पहनते थे, जो पतलून की नाप से छोटी और हॉफ पैण्ट से थोड़ी बड़ी होती थी। सामान्यतया बेकर महीने के अन्त में अपने बिल एकत्रित करता था।

पुराने दिनों में, बेकिंग एक लाभदायक पेशा था। एक बेकर का परिवार और नौकर हमेशा प्रसन्न और समृद्ध रहते थे।

Objective Questions

Extract Based Questions

Read the following extracts carefully and answer the questions that follow.

1 Our elders are often heard reminiscing nostalgically about those good old Portuguese days, the Portuguese and their famous loaves of bread. Those eaters of loaves might have vanished but the makers are still there. We still have amongst us the mixers, the moulders and those who bake the loaves. Those age-old, time-tested furnaces still exist. The fire in the furnaces has not yet been extinguished. The thud and jingle of the traditional baker's bamboo, heralding his arrival in the morning, can still be heard in some places. Maybe the father is not alive but the son still carries on the family profession. These bakers are, even today, known as pader in Goa.

(i) What were the Portuguese famous for?
पुर्तगाली किस लिए प्रसिद्ध थे?
(a) Their traditional dresses (b) Their loaves of bread
(c) Their ceremonies (d) The moulders

(ii) The narrator says that the furnaces were 'time-tested' because
कथावाचक कहता है कि भट्टियों का लम्बे समय से परीक्षण किया गया था, क्योंकि
(a) they had been thoroughly tested each time before being used
(b) they had proved the test of time and were working well
(c) they had been tested by modern day experts
(d) they had the power to withstand inexperienced usage

(iii) Who carries on the family profession?
पारिवारिक पेशे को आगे कौन बढ़ाता है?
(a) Son (b) Daughter (c) Baker (d) Elders

2 During our childhood in Goa, the baker used to be our friend, companion and guide. He used to come at least twice a day. Once, when he set out in the morning on his selling round, and then again, when he returned after emptying his huge basket. The jingling thud of his bamboo woke us up from sleep and we ran to meet and greet him. Why was it so? Was it for the love of the loaf? Not at all. The loaves were bought by some Paskine or Bastine, the maid-servant of the house! What we longed for were those bread-bangles which we chose carefully. Sometimes it was sweet bread of special make.

(i) What role did the baker play during author's childhood?
लेखक के बचपन के दौरान बेकर ने क्या भूमिका निभाई?
(a) Friend (b) Companion (c) Guide (d) All of these

(ii) How many times did the baker come in a day?
बेकर एक दिन में कितनी बार आता था?
(a) Only one time (b) Three times
(c) Twice a day (d) Seven times

(iii) The loaves of bread were bought by whom?
ब्रेड की पाव-रोटी किसके द्वारा खरीदी गई?
(a) The daughter of the house
(b) The son of the house
(c) The maid-servant of the house
(d) All of the above

Multiple Choice Questions (MCQs)

1. Who left Goa a long time ago?
(a) Portuguese (b) Author
(c) Sandwich maker (d) Bakers

2. What still exists in Goa?
(a) Old Portuguese
(b) The traditional bakers and their furnaces
(c) Pader
(d) The Goan baker

3. What sound can still be heard in some places in Goa?
(a) The sound of the baker's bamboo
(b) The sound of Portuguese
(c) The sound of birds
(d) The sound of bakers

4. Bakers are also known as ....
(a) bol
(b) traditional bakers
(c) pader
(d) bread-bangles

5. Which one of the following task is done by bakers?
(a) Bake the loaves (b) Bake the dough
(c) Bake the mould (d) None of these

6. During our childhood in Goa, the baker used to be our friend, companion and ....
(a) teacher (b) guide (c) helper (d) friend

7. How is the traditional baker recognised?
(a) With the thud and jingle of the bamboo
(b) With his baking style
(c) With his clothing style
(d) All of the above

8. The author is .... when he says 'Loaves for the elders and the bangles for the children'.
(a) despairing (b) proud
(c) nostalgic (d) regretful

9. What did the children eat with tea?
(a) Cakes
(b) Sandwiches
(c) Biscuit
(d) Bread-bangles made of sweet bread

10. Marriages or any festival were incomplete without ....
(a) sandwiches (b) sweet bread
(c) bakers (d) pizza

11. The bakers of Goa used to wear
(a) Kabai (b) Bol
(c) Long Frock (d) All of these

12. Baking was indeed a profitable .... in the old days.
(a) service (b) job
(c) business (d) profession

Answers

Extract Based Questions

1. (i) (b), (ii) (b), (iii) (a), **2.** (i) (d), (ii) (c), (iii) (c)

Multiple Choice Questions

1. (a) 2. (b) 3. (a) 4. (c) 5. (a) 6. (b) 7. (a) 8. (c) 9. (d) 10. (b) 11. (a) 12. (c)

Part–II Coorg – *Lokesh Abrol*

Summary of the Lesson पाठ का सार

This part describes Coorg which is situated between Mysore and the coastal town of Mangalore.

Coorg or Kodavu is the smallest district of Karnataka. It is like a heaven on Earth with evergreen forests, coffee and spice plantation. During monsoon, it receives a lot of rain. So, the best season to visit Coorg starts in September and ends in March. The weather is pleasant during these months and the smell of coffee is all around.

The people of Coorg are possibly descendents of Greeks and Arabs. It is believed that Alexander's army moved South along the coast and settled there. These people married among the locals and their culture can be witnessed by their martial traditions, marriages and religious rites. The Kodavus (residents of Coorg) wear a long black coat with an embroidered waist belt known as Kuppia. It resembles Kuffia worn by the Arabs and the Kurds.

Kodavus or Coorgi are known for their hospitality. There are many tales of bravery related to the people of Coorg. The Coorg Regiment is one of the most decorated regiments of the Indian Army. The First Chief of the Indian-Army, General Cariappa was a Coorgi. Kodavus are the only people in India permitted to carry firearms without a licence.

The river Kaveri originates in the hills of Coorg. In the waters of the river, a large freshwater fish, Mahseer, kingfishers and other animals such as squirrels, langurs can be seen. Coorg offers many adventurous activities such as river rafting, canoeing, rappelling, rock climbing, mountain biking and trekking.

One can have a panoramic view of the entire Coorg by climbing the Brahmagiri hills. Other interesting places are the Nisargadhama and the largest Tibetan settlement of Buddhist monks at Bylakuppe.

Coorg can be reached by road and by rail. If one prefers to go by air, then the nearest airports are Bangalore and Mangalore. By road, it is around 250-260 km from Bangalore.

यह भाग कुर्ग का वर्णन करता है, जो मैसूर और मैंगलोर के तटीय कस्बे के बीच में स्थित है।

कुर्ग या कोडावु कर्नाटक का सबसे छोटा जिला है। यह स्थान सदाबहार वनों, कॉफी और मसालों के बागानों के कारण धरती पर स्वर्ग के समान है। मानसून के दौरान, यहाँ बहुत अधिक वर्षा होती है। इसलिए, कुर्ग भ्रमण का सर्वश्रेष्ठ समय सितम्बर से प्रारम्भ होता है और मार्च में समाप्त होता है। इन महीनों के दौरान मौसम बहुत ही खुशनुमा होता है और चारों और कॉफी की सुगन्ध रहती है।

कुर्ग के लोग (निवासी) सम्भवतया ग्रीक और अरब के लोगों के वंशज हैं। यह माना जाता है कि सिकन्दर की सेना समुद्र किनारे से होकर दक्षिण गई और वहाँ बस गई। उन लोगों ने स्थानीय निवासियों से विवाह किया और उनकी संस्कृति को उनकी सामरिक परम्पराओं, विवाह एवं धार्मिक संस्कारों में देखा जा सकता है। कोडावु (कुर्ग के निवासी) कशीदाकारी वाले कमरबन्द के साथ एक लम्बा काला कोट पहनते हैं, जिसे कुप्पियाँ कहते हैं। यह अरब और कुर्ग द्वारा पहने जाने वाले कुफियाँ से मिलता-जुलता है।

कोडावस और कुर्गी अपनी मेहमान नवाजी के लिए जाने जाते हैं। कुर्ग के लोगों की वीरता के सम्बन्ध में अनेक कथाएँ है। कुर्ग सैन्य दल भारतीय सेना का सबसे अधिक सज्जित सैन्य दल है। भारतीय सेना के प्रथम मुख्य जनरल (सेनाध्यक्ष) जनरल करियप्पा कुर्गी थे। कोडावु भारत के एकमात्र निवासी (लोग)हैं, जिन्हें बिना अनुज्ञा-पत्र के हथियार रखने की अनुमति है।

कुर्ग की पहाड़ियों से कावेरी नदी का उद्‌गम होता है। नदी के पानी में, एक मीठे पानी की बड़ी मछली, महासीर, नीलकण्ठ और अन्य जानवर; जैसे– गिलहरियाँ और लंगूर देखे जा सकते हैं। कुर्ग में कई प्रकार के साहसिक कार्य भी किए जा सकते हैं; जैसे– रीवर राफ्टिंग, डोंगी चलाना, चट्टानों से रस्सी द्वारा उतरना, पहाड़ियाँ चढ़ना, पर्वतों पर मोटरबाइक चलाना व ट्रेकिंग।

कोई व्यक्ति सम्पूर्ण कुर्ग का सुन्दर दृश्य ब्रह्मगिरि पहाड़ियों पर चढ़कर देख सकता है। अन्य रुचिकर स्थानों में निसर्गधाम और तिब्बत के बौद्ध भिक्षुओं का सबसे बड़ा निवास बाइलाकुप्पे है।

कुर्ग तक सड़कमार्ग और ट्रेन द्वारा पहुँचा जा सकता है। यदि कोई हवाई जहाज से जाना चाहे, तो सबसे नजदीकी एयरपोर्ट बैंगलोर और मैंगलोर है। सड़कमार्ग द्वारा, बैंगलोर से इसकी दूरी लगभग 250-260 किलोमीटर है।

Objective Questions

Extract Based Questions

Read the following extracts carefully and answer the questions that follow.

1 Coorg, or Kodavu, the smallest district of Karnataka, is home to evergreen rainforests, spices and coffee plantations. Evergreen rainforests cover thirty per cent of this district. During the monsoons, it pours enough to keep many visitors away. The season of joy commences from September and continues till March. The weather is perfect, with some showers thrown in for good measure. The air breathes of invigorating coffee. Coffee estates and colonial bungalows stand tucked under tree canopies in prime corners.

(i) Which is the smallest district of Karnataka?
कर्नाटक का सबसे छोटा जिला कौन-सा है?

(a) Coorg (b) Mysore
(c) Mangalore (d) Raichur

(ii) What type of plantations are found in Coorg?
कुर्ग में किस प्रकार के बागान पाए जाते हैं?
(a) Coffee
(b) Spice plantations
(c) Kuppia
(d) Both (a) and (b)

(iii) Coorg or Kodavu, the smallest district of Karnataka, is home to
कुर्ग या कोडावु, कर्नाटक का सबसे छोटा जिला का .... घर है।
(a) evergreen rainforests and spices
(b) evergreen rainforests, spices and coffee plantations
(c) spices and coffee plantations
(d) evergreen rainforests and coffee plantations

(iv) In which state of India is Coorg situated?
भारत के किस राज्य में कुर्ग स्थित है?
(a) Karnataka (b) Goa
(c) Kerala (d) Rajasthan

(v) The best season to visit Coorg is ....
कुर्ग जाने का सबसे अच्छा मौसम .... है।
(a) April to June (b) July to August
(c) September to March (d) None of these

2 The fiercely independent people of Coorg are possibly of Greek or Arabic descent. As one story goes, a part of Alexander's army moved South along the coast and settled here when return became impractical. These people married amongst the locals and their culture is apparent in the martial traditions, marriage and religious rites, which are distinct from the Hindu mainstream. The theory of Arab origin draws support from the long, black coat with an embroidered waist-belt worn by the Kodavus, known as Kuppia, it resembles the Kuffia worn by the Arabs and the Kurds.

(i) The people of Coorg are of which origin?
कुर्ग के लोग किस मूल के हैं?
(a) Greek or Arabic descent
(b) Nisargadhama
(c) Mangalore
(d) Mysore

(ii) Where did a part of Alexander's army move?
अलेक्जेण्डर की सेना की एक टुकड़ी किस दिशा में चली गई थी?
(a) East (b) North-West
(c) South (d) West

(iii) With whom did the people of Alexander's army marry?
अलेक्जेण्डर की सेना के लोगों ने किनसे विवाह किया था?
(a) Nisargadhama (b) The locals
(c) Greek (d) Arabic desert

Multiple Choice Questions (MCQs)

1. Which is a piece of heaven situated in the midway between Mysore and the coastal town of Mangalore?
(a) Coorg (b) Karnataka
(c) Madikeri (d) Uduki

2. The season of joy commences from September and continues till March. The given line suggests that
(a) September to March is the best time to visit Coorg
(b) September to March are the month of rainfall
(c) Coorg becomes even more beautiful between September and March
(d) Both (a) and (c)

3. In which months is the weather pleasant in Coorg and smell of coffee is all around?
(a) September to March (b) March to October
(c) January to March (d) March to September

4. Which traditions show that Coorgi culture is distinct from Hindu mainstream?
(a) Martial traditions (b) Marriage
(c) Religious (d) All of these

5. Who was Kodavus?
(a) Residents of Mysore (b) Residents of Coorg
(c) Residents of Karnataka (d) Residents of Jammu

6. The Kodavus wear a long black coat with an embroidered waist belt known as ....
(a) Kuppia (b) Kurta (c) Kupper (d) Kullia

7. The main crop of Coorg is
(a) rice (b) coffee (c) tea (d) spices

8. Which kind of tales related to the people of Coorg?
(a) The Tales of Love (b) The Tales of Spark
(c) The Tales of Magic (d) The Tales of Bravery

9. Mahseer is a large fish found in the freshwater of ....
(a) Krishna (b) Godavari (c) Kaveri (d) Ganga

10. The land between Mysore and Mangalore is .... by proud race of martial men and beautiful women.
(a) left (b) inhabited
(c) filled (d) surrounded

Answers

Extract Based Questions

1. (i) (a), (ii) (d), (iii) (b), (iv) (a), (v) (c) **2.** (i) (a), (ii) (c), (iii) (b)

Multiple Choice Questions

1. (a) 2. (d) 3. (a) 4. (d) 5. (b) 6. (a) 7. (b) 8. (d) 9. (c) 10. (b)

Part–III Tea from Assam

– Arup Kumar Datta

Summary of the Lesson पाठ का सार

This part describes Assam which has the largest concentration of tea plantation in the world. The narrator tried to explain the importance of tea in the country through a dialogue between two school students Rajvir and Pranjal.

Pranjal and Rajvir were classmates studying in the same school in Delhi. Pranjal belonged to Assam and his father was the manager of a tea garden in Assam. He had invited Rajvir to visit his home during the summer vacation. So, both of them were travelling to Assam by a train. In the train they bought tea from a vendor.

While sipping tea, Rajvir told Pranjal that over 80 crore cups of tea are drunk everyday around the world. It is thus, a very popular drink. As the train started moving, Rajvir looked out of the window. He was amazed to see the beautiful scenery of greenery outside. On the other hand, Pranjal was reading his detective book. Pranjal was born and bought up in a tea plantation and thus was not as excited.

Rajvir told Pranjal that Assam has the largest concentration of tea plantations in the world. He told Pranjal that there are many legends or stories about the discovery of tea. According to a legend, a Chinese emperor discovered tea when he was boiling water for drinking. When the water was put to boil, a few leaves of the twigs (stems) fell into the water giving it a delicious flavour. The twigs are believed to be tea leaves.

Another legend from India said the Bodhidharma, an ancient Buddhist monk, cut off his eyelids because he felt sleepy during meditation. Ten tea plantations grew out of his eyelids. It is believed that the leaves of these plants when put in hot water and drunk, banished sleep.

Rajvir further told Pranjal that tea was first drunk in China in 2700 BC and the words like 'tea', 'chai' and 'chini' are also Chinese. He also mentioned that tea first came to Europe in the sixteenth century and it was drunk more as medicine than as a beverage.

Rajvir and Pranjal reached the Mariani Junction where Pranjal's parents received them. In car, they went to Dhekiabari, the tea estate managed by Pranjal's father. On both the sides of the road, there were huge acres of tea bushes. Looking at the tea, Rajvir told Pranjal's father that it was the second flush or sprouting season. He also told him that this season lasts from May to July and yields the best tea.

यह भाग असम का वर्णन करता है, जहाँ दुनिया में सबसे ज्यादा चाय बागानों का संकेन्द्रण है। वर्णनकर्ता विद्यालय के दो विद्यार्थियों राजवीर और प्रांजल के बीच हुए संवाद के माध्यम से देश में चाय के महत्त्व की व्याख्या करने का प्रयास कर रहा है।

प्रांजल और राजवीर दिल्ली के एक ही विद्यालय में अध्ययनरत् सहपाठी थे। प्रांजल असम से सम्बद्ध था और उसके पिताजी असम के एक चाय बागान में मैनेजर थे। उसने ग्रीष्मकालीन अवकाश के दौरान राजवीर को अपने घर आने का निमन्त्रण दिया। इसलिए वे दोनों ट्रेन से असम की यात्रा कर रहे थे। ट्रेन में उन्होंने एक विक्रेता से चाय खरीदी।

चाय की चुसकी लेते हुए, राजवीर ने प्रांजल को बताया कि दुनिया में प्रतिदिन लगभग 80 करोड़ कप चाय के पिए जाते हैं। इसीलिए यह एक प्रसिद्ध पेय पदार्थ है। जैसे ही ट्रेन ने रफ्तार पकड़ना प्रारम्भ किया, राजवीर खिड़की से बाहर देखने लगा। वह बाहर के सुन्दर हरियाली भरे दृश्य को देखकर बहुत अचम्भित था। दूसरी तरफ, प्रांजल अपनी जासूसी की पुस्तक पढ़ रहा था। प्रांजल का जन्म और पालन-पोषण चाय के बागानों में हुआ था और इसलिए वह उत्सुक नहीं था।

राजवीर ने प्रांजल को असम के बारे में बताया की असम दुनिया के सबसे बड़े चाय बागानों का संक्रेद्रण है। उसने प्रांजल को बताया कि चाय की खोज के बारे में अनेक पौराणिक कथाएँ और कहानियाँ हैं। एक पौराणिक कथा के अनुसार, एक चीनी शासक ने चाय की खोज की थी, जब वह पीने के लिए पानी उबाल रहा था। जब पानी को उबालने के लिए रखा गया, तो टहनियों से कुछ पत्तियाँ पानी में गिर गई, जिससे उसमें स्वाद आ गया। इन छोटी टहनियों को चाय की पत्तियाँ माना गया।

भारत की एक अन्य पौराणिक कथा के अनुसार, एक प्राचीन बौद्ध साधु, बोधिधर्मा ने अपनी आँखो की पलकों को काट दिया था, क्योंकि ध्यान के समय उन्हें नींद आती थी। उनकी पलको से दस चाय के बागान उग गए। यह विश्वास किया जाता है कि जब इन पौधों की पत्तियों को गर्म पानी में डाल कर पिया जाता है, तो नींद खत्म हो जाती है।

इसके अतिरिक्त राजवीर ने प्रांजल को बताया कि पहली चाय चीन में 2700 ईसा पूर्व पी गई थी और 'टी', 'चाय' और 'चीनी' जैसे शब्द चीनी शब्द हैं। उसने यह भी बताया कि यूरोप में चाय प्रथम बार सोलहवीं शताब्दी में आई थी और इसे एक पेय पदार्थ के स्थान पर एक औषधि के रूप में अधिक पिया जाता था।

राजवीर और प्रांजल मारियानी जंक्शन पहुँचे, जहाँ प्रांजल के माता-पिता उन्हें लेने आए थे। कार से, वे चाय के बागान ढेकियबारी पहुँचे जिसे प्रांजल के पिताजी सम्भालते थे। सड़क के दोनों ओर, कई एकड़ में फैली हुई चाय की झाड़ियाँ थीं। चाय को देखकर राजवीर ने प्रांजल के पिताजी से कहा कि यह द्वितीय प्रफुल्लता या अंकुरण का मौसम था। उसने उन्हें यह भी बताया कि यह मौसम मई से लेकर जुलाई तक रहेगा और चाय की सबसे उत्तम पैदावार प्रदान करेगा।

Objective Questions

Extract Based Questions

Read the following extracts carefully and answer the questions that follow.

1 "CHAI-GARAM... garam-chai," a vendor called out in a high-pitched voice.
He came up to their window and asked,"Chai, sa'ab?"
"Give us two cups," Pranjal said.
They sipped the steaming hot liquid. Almost everyone in their compartment was drinking tea too.
"Do you know that over eighty crore cups of tea are drunk everyday throughout the world?" Rajvir said.
"Whew!" exclaimed Pranjal. "Tea really is very popular."

(i) Who was selling the tea?
चाय कौन बेच रहा था?
(a) A tea vendor (b) Pranjal
(c) Rajvir (d) None of these

(ii) As per the given extract how many cups of tea are drunk everyday throughout the world?
दिए गए गद्यांश के अनुसार सम्पूर्ण विश्व में पूरे दिन में कितने कप चाय पी जाती है?
(a) Over eighty crore (b) Over eighty
(c) Over seventy crore (d) Almost eighty crore

2 The train pulled out of the station. Pranjal buried his nose in his detective book again. Rajvir too was an ardent fan of detective stories, but at the moment he was keener on looking at the beautiful scenery.

It was green, green everywhere. Rajvir had never seen so much greenery before. Then the soft green paddy fields gave way to tea bushes.

It was a magnificent view. Against the backdrop of densely wooded hills a sea of tea bushes stretched as far as the eye could see. Dwarfing the tiny tea plants were tall sturdy shade-trees and amidst the orderly rows of bushes busily moved doll-like figures.

(i) What was Pranjal doing after train left the station?
रेलगाड़ी के स्टेशन से निकलने के बाद प्रांजल क्या कर रहा था?
(a) Reading detective book (b) Seeing the greenery outside
(c) Watching movie (d) None of these

(ii) What was Rajvir keen on?
राजवीर को किस चीज का शौक था?
(a) Looking at the garden
(b) Looking at the beautiful scenery
(c) Looking at the bus
(d) Looking at the tea-pluckers

(iii) What gave way to the tea bushes?
चाय की झाड़ियों को किसने रास्ता दिया?
(a) Maize fields (b) Cows
(c) Tea-pluckers (d) Paddy fields

Multiple Choice Questions (MCQs)

1. Who has invited his friend Rajvir to visit his home in Assam?
(a) Pranjal (b) Mr. Barua
(c) Pranjal's aunt (d) None of these

2. Who was excited to see the tea plantation of Assam?
(a) Pranjal (b) Rajvir
(c) Mr. Barua (d) Rajvir's father

3. Who was the manager of a tea garden in upper Assam?
(a) Rajvir (b) Pranjal
(c) Mr. Barua (d) Rajvir's father

4. Who were Pranjal and Rajvir?
(a) Brothers (b) Cousins
(c) Classmates (d) Roommates

5. Pranjal and Rajvir were travelling to Assam by ..... .
(a) a bus (b) an airplane
(c) a car (d) a train

6. In ancient Europe, tea was drunk as more of a .... than ....
(a) medicine, beverage (b) beverage, medicine
(c) sleep waver, medicine (d) sleep banishes, medicine

7. Who told Pranjal that over eighty crore cups of tea are drunk everyday around the world?
(a) Mr. Barua (b) Rajvir
(c) Pranjal's aunt (d) None of these

8. According to Rajvir, which is a very popular drink?
(a) Coffee (b) Cocktail
(c) Tea (d) Coconut water

9. Who was fascinated by the vast stretch of the tea bushes?
(a) Rajvir (b) Pranjal
(c) Mr. Barua (d) Rajvir's aunt

Answers

Extract Based Questions

1. (i) (a), (ii) (a), 2. (i) (a), (ii) (b), (iii) (d)

Multiple Choice Questions

1. (a) 2. (b) 3. (c) 4. (c) 5. (d) 6. (a) 7. (b) 8. (c) 9. (a)

Unit-11

01 The Lost Child

In the story 'The Lost Child', the author highlights a child's love for his parents. It is a story about a young child who gets attracted by things around him, on the way to the fair. In the fair, he wants many things. He knows that his parents would refuse to buy them and so he moves ahead. When he gets separated from his parents, all those things do not tempt him.

Important Characters

The Lost Child	The main character of the story who gets fascinated with the items at the village fair and gets separated from his parents.
खोया हुआ बच्चा	कहानी का मुख्य पात्र जो गाँव के मेले के सामानों से आकर्षित होता है, और अपने माता-पिता से बिछड़ जाता है।
The Parents माता-पिता	They are in hurry and keep on asking the child to remain with them. But they are careless enough that they lose him (the child) at the fair. वे जल्दी में हैं, और बच्चे को अपने साथ रहने के लिए कहते रहते हैं। लेकिन इतने लापरवाह हैं, कि बच्चे को मेले में खो देते हैं।

Summary of the Lesson पाठ का सार

Child Goes to Spring Fair with His Parents

It was the festival of spring. Everyone was going to the spring fair. The child was going to the fair with his parents. The child was very happy and excited. He was attracted by many things around him especially, the toys. The child was also attracted by the purple dragon-flies, a black bee and butterfly fluttering over the mustard flowers. He wanted to catch one of them but his mother called him. He was also attracted by small insects and worms along the footpath. He also collected the petals in the grove. He also heard the cooing of doves and ran round the banyan tree.

Entry into the Fair

The parents and the child entered the fair passing through the mustard fields. In the fair, the child heard the sweetmeatseller selling sweets like gulab jamuns, rasgulla, burfi, jalebi, etc.

The child was attracted towards *burfi* that was his favourite sweet and wanted it. But he knew that if he asked for it, his parents would call him greedy. So without waiting for their answer, he moved on. Then, the child was attracted towards the garlands of gulmohur and he also wanted a garland. But, this time also, he knew that his parents would call it cheap and would refuse to buy so he moved on. Further, the child saw a balloon seller and desired to buy all the colourful balloons. But, he knew that his parents would call him too old to play with them. So, he walked away.

बच्चे का अपने माता-पिता के साथ बसंत के मेले में जाना

यह बसंत ऋतु का त्योहार था। सभी लोग बसंत के मेले में जा रहे थे। बच्चा अपने माता-पिता के साथ मेले में जा रहा था। बच्चा बहुत प्रसन्न और उत्सुक था। वह अपने आस-पास की प्रत्येक वस्तु से, विशेष रूप से खिलौनों से आकर्षित था। बच्चा सरसों के फूलों पर मंडराती बैंगनी पंखों वाले पतंगों, काली मधुमक्खी और तितलियों से भी आकर्षित था। वह उनमें से किसी एक को पकड़ना चाहता था, लेकिन उसकी माँ ने उसे बुला लिया। फुटपाथ पर वह छोटे-छोटे कीटों और कीड़ों से भी आकर्षित था। उसने वाटिका से फूलों की पंखुडियाँ भी एकत्रित की। उसने कपोत पक्षी की आवाज भी सुनी और बरगद के पेड़ के चारों ओर दौड़ लगाई।

मेले में प्रवेश

सरसों के खेतों से होते हुए माता-पिता और बच्चे ने मेले में प्रवेश किया। मेले में बच्चे ने मिठाई बेचने वाले की आवाज सुनी जो गुलाब जामुन, रसगुल्ला, बर्फी, जलेबी आदि मिठाइयाँ बेच रहा था।

बच्चा बर्फी की ओर आकर्षित हो गया जो उसकी सबसे पसन्दीदा मिठाई थी और वह उसे खाना चाहता था। लेकिन वह जानता था कि यदि वह इसे (बर्फी) माँगता तो उसके माता-पिता उसे लालची कहेंगे। इसलिए जवाब का इन्तजार किए बिना वह आगे बढ़ गया। फिर बच्चा गुलमोहर की मालाओं से आकर्षित हो गया और उसे भी प्राप्त करना चाहता था। लेकिन इस बार भी वह जानता था कि उसके माता-पिता इसे बेकार का सामान बताएँगे और खरीदने से मना कर देंगे इसलिए वह आगे बढ़ गया। आगे बच्चे ने गुब्बारे बेचने वाले को देखा और सभी रंगीन गुब्बारे खरीदना चाहता था। लेकिन वह जानता था कि उसके माता-पिता उसे गुब्बारों से खेलने की उम्र के लिए अधिक बड़ा बताएँगे, इसलिए वह वहाँ से चला गया।

The Child is Lost

As the child walked, he saw a snake charmer. He was playing a flute to the snake. He went towards it but then remembered that his parents had told him not to hear such music. So, he moved away. Then he saw a roundabout. He requested his parents to ride the roundabout. However, there was no reply. The child looked back around to look for his parents, but couldn't find them. He, then realised that he was separated from his parents and was lost.

The Child was in Trouble

As the child realised that he was lost, he started crying. He was filled with panic and called out for his parents. He looked around in all directions with the hope of finding them. However, he could not see them. His clothes were now muddy and his yellow turban was untied. He ran quickly to a shrine which was crowded by the people.

The Kind Man helps the Child

There was a huge rush of people near the temple. The child struggled to search his parents in the crowd but he was pushed back by the crowd. A man picked up the child in his arms when he heard his cry in the crowd. He asked the child about his parents and how he reached there. But the child only said that he wanted his mother and father. The man took the child to the roundabout. He asked him to have a ride but the child continued crying for his parents. The man offered many things to the child to divert his attention. The man took him to the place where a snake-charmer was playing the flute and asked the child to listen to the music. The man also took him near the balloons and offered him a balloon.

He also took him to the flower seller and offered the child a garland to put round his neck. He further took the child to the sweet shop and offered him sweets. But the child had no fascination for all these things now. He only wanted his parents and cried for them.

बच्चे का खो जाना

जैसे ही बच्चा आगे चलता है, उसे एक सपेरा दिखता है। वह साँप के लिए बीन बजा रहा था। वह उसकी ओर जा ही रहा था कि उसे याद आया कि उसके माता-पिता ने उसे इस प्रकार का संगीत सुनने के लिए मना किया था। इसलिए, वह आगे बढ़ गया। फिर उसने चक्करदार झूला देखा। उसने अपने माता-पिता से चक्करदार झूले पर झूलने की विनती की। हालाँकि, कोई जवाब नहीं आया। बच्चा अपने माता-पिता को देखने के लिए पीछे पलटा, लेकिन वह उन्हें नहीं खोज सका। तब उसे अनुभव हुआ कि वह अपने माता-पिता से बिछड़ गया था और खो गया था।

बच्चे का मुसीबत में होना

जैसे ही बच्चे को अनुभव हुआ कि वह खो गया था वह रोने लगा। वह घबरा गया और अपने माता-पिता को पुकारने लगा। उसने उन्हें खोजने की उम्मीद में चारों दिशाओं में उन्हें देखा। हालाँकि वह उन्हें देख न सका। उसके कपड़े अब तक धूल से भर गए थे और उसकी पीली पगड़ी खुल गई थी। वह जल्दी से मन्दिर की ओर दौड़ा जहाँ लोगों की भीड़ थी।

एक दयालु व्यक्ति द्वारा बच्चे की सहायता करना

मन्दिर के पास लोगों की भारी भीड़ थी। बच्चे ने भीड़ में अपने माता-पिता को खोजने के लिए संघर्ष किया, लेकिन भीड़ ने उसे पीछे धकेल दिया। एक व्यक्ति ने उसके रोने की आवाज सुनकर उसे अपनी बाहों में उठा लिया। उसने बच्चे से उसके माता-पिता और वह वहाँ कैसे पहुँचा के विषय में पूछा। लेकिन बच्चे ने केवल यही कहा कि उसे उसके माता-पिता चाहिए। व्यक्ति उसे झूले के पास ले गया। उसने उससे झूले की सवारी करने के लिए पूछा, लेकिन वह अपने माता-पिता के लिए लगातार रोता रहा। उस व्यक्ति ने बच्चे का ध्यान भटकाने के लिए उसके सामने बहुत-सी वस्तुओं की पेशकश की। वह व्यक्ति उसे वहाँ ले गया जहाँ सपेरा बीन बजा रहा था और उससे संगीत सुनने के लिए कहा। वह व्यक्ति उसे गुब्बारों के पास ले गया और उसे गुब्बारे देने की पेशकश की।

वह उसे फूल बेचने वाले के पास भी लेकर गया और बच्चे से गले में फूलों की माला पहनने के लिए पूछा। उसके बाद वह बच्चे को मिठाई की दुकान पर लेकर गया और उसके सामने मिठाइयाँ प्रस्तुत की। लेकिन अब बच्चे को इन सभी वस्तुओं के प्रति कोई आकर्षण नहीं था। वह केवल अपने माता-पिता चाहता था और उनके लिए रोता रहा।

Objective Questions

1. Which festival is mentioned in 'The Lost Child'?
(a) Festival of Summer (b) Festival of Winter
(c) Festival of Monsoon (d) Festival of Spring

2. How does the child feel when he goes to the fair?
(a) Happy and excited (b) Happy but nervous
(c) Sad
(d) Resentful

3. How was everyone travelling to the fair?
(a) Some people were walking.
(b) Some people were riding on the horses.
(c) Some people were travelling through the bamboo and bullock carts.
(d) All of the above

4. The child's father looked at him like a ...... when he asked for the toy.
(a) goon (b) fool
(c) wolf (d) tyrant

5. What did his mother point him towards?
(a) A rainbow coloured balloon
(b) A flowering mustard-field
(c) A gulmohur garland
(d) A snake charmer playing the flute

6. The group of dragon flies were bustling about on their ....
(a) big beautiful wings (b) green sparkling wings
(c) gaudy purple wings (d) blue pale wings

7. What did the child want to do when he saw the dragon-flies?
(a) He wanted to keep seeing them.
(b) He wanted to fly like them.
(c) He wanted to catch them.
(d) He wanted to catch the black bee.

8. 'Come child come'. Who said this to whom?
(a) Child's parents to child
(b) Snake charmer to child
(c) The man to the child
(d) Child's uncle to the child

9. The flowering mustard field looked ....
(a) like a group of dragon flies
(b) pale like melting gold
(c) like Sun rise
(d) like liquid gold

10. 'Come child, come, come on to the footpath' Who said this ?
(a) His father (b) His mother
(c) Snake charmer (d) The man

11. Which bird did the child hear cooing?
(a) The cuckoo (b) The dove
(c) The peacock (d) The sparrow

12. What was the child's favourite sweet?
(a) Gulab Jamun (b) Rasgulla
(c) Burfi (d) Jalebi

13. What was the colour of the child's turban?
(a) Red (b) Blue
(c) Yellow (d) Green

14. The man tried to soothe the child by taking him to ....
(a) the nake charmer (b) the sweet shop
(c) roundabout (d) the horse

15. "Will you have a ride on the horse?" Who said this to the child?
(a) The man (b) Snake charmer
(c) His father (d) His mother

Answers

1. (d) 2. (a) 3. (d) 4. (d) 5. (b) 6. (c) 7. (c) 8. (a) 9. (b) 10. (b) 11. (b)
12. (c) 13. (c) 14. (c) 15. (a)

02 Iswaran the Storyteller

The story revolves around a junior construction supervisor, Mahendra and his cook Iswaran. Iswaran was fond of telling stories to Mahendra so he would narrate a story every evening.

His stories were influenced by the popular Tamil thrillers that he read everyday. He got inspired by reading these stories. His one such story of a female ghost, disturbed Mahendra so much that he decided to leave the place the very next day.

Important Characters

Mahendra महेन्द्र	He is a junior construction supervisor who loves to hear Iswaran's stories but gets scared by his ghost story. वह एक कनिष्ठ निर्माण निरीक्षक है, जो ईश्वरन की कहानियाँ सुनना पसन्द करता है, लेकिन उसकी भूत वाली कहानी से डर जाता है।
Iswaran ईश्वरन	He is a wonderful cook, domestic helper and fascinating storyteller. who scares Mahendra with his ghost story. वह एक अद्‌भुत रसोइया, घरेलू सहायक और शानदार कहानीकार है, जो महेन्द्र को अपनी भूत की कहानी से डरा देता है।

Summary of the Lesson पाठ का सार

Mahendra : A Junior Supervisor

Mahendra was a junior supervisor in a firm. The firm offered various construction sites including factories, bridges, dams, etc. to supervisors on hire. Mahendra's job was to keep an eye on the activities at the work site. Due to his job, he had to move from one place to another. Mahendra was a bachelor who led a simple life. His requirements were less, so he could adjust to all conditions.

महेन्द्र : एक कनिष्ठ सुपरवाइजर (निरीक्षक)

महेन्द्र एक संस्थान में कनिष्ठ सुपरवाइजर था। संस्थान विभिन्न निर्माण स्थानों; जैसे—कारखानों, पुलों, बाँधों पर निरीक्षक नियुक्त करती थी। उसका (महेन्द्र) का कार्य कार्य-स्थल की गतिविधियों पर नजर रखना था। अपनी नौकरी के कारण उसे एक स्थान से दूसरे स्थान पर जाना पड़ता था। महेन्द्र कुँवारा था जो एक साधारण जीवन व्यतीत करता था। उसकी जरूरतें कम थीं, इसलिए वह सभी परिस्थितियों से समायोजन कर लेता था।

Iswaran, Mahendra's Cook

Mahendra had a cook named Iswaran. Iswaran did all household works of Mahendra. He would cook, wash his clothes and entertain him with his stories. Iswaran also had an amazing capacity to produce vegetables and cooking ingredients which were not found anywhere.

Iswaran's Daily Routine

Mahendra would leave for work early in the morning with some food. After Mahendra left for work, Iswaran would clean the shed, wash the clothes and would take a bath while praying. After eating his lunch, he used to read popular Tamil thrillers and then would go off to sleep.

Iswaran : A Great Storyteller

Iswaran was greatly influenced by the Tamil thrillers that he had read. This influence was visible in his methods of story telling. He would narrate even the smallest incidents with suspense and surprise. For example, he described an uprooted tree as a bushy beast (wild animal) in a dramatic gesture.

Iswaran's Story of a Tusker

Iswaran narrates an incident about a mad tusker (elephant) to Mahendra. He narrated that one day a mad elephant escaped from the timber yard in his hometown and destroyed everything that came in his way. It tore up the creepers and broke the branches.

After sometime, the elephant reached Iswaran's town. It came to the main road and smashed the stalls selling fruits, mud pots and clothes. Then, the elephant entered the school ground and destroyed everything in it.

Suddenly, Iswaran, a young boy of school, took a cane (stick) from one of his teachers. He ran to the ground and hit the third toenail of the elephant and the elephant fell down. At this point, Iswaran would leave the story unfinished.

Iswaran's Concludes the Tusker Story

After sometime, Iswaran concluded the story and told Mahendra that an animal doctor was called to examine the elephant. After two days, the elephant was taken to the jungle by his mahout. When Mahendra asked Iswaran, how he had controlled the elephant, then Iswaran told that it was related to Japanese martial art Ju-jitsu or karate which paralysed his nervous system.

Story of a Female Ghost

One day, Iswaran prepared a delicious dinner because it was the auspicious day of feeding the spirits of the ancestors. While Mahendra had his dinner, Iswaran told Mahendra about the factory where they were staying.

He informed Mahendra that this factory area was initially a burial ground. He himself had come across skulls and bones on the path and saw ghosts at night. He further told Mahendra about an horrible female ghost who would roam around at midnight during full moon. She would appear to be a skeleton carrying a foetus in her arms.

महेन्द्र का रसोइया ईश्वरन

महेन्द्र के पास ईश्वरन नाम का रसोइया था। ईश्वरन महेन्द्र के घर का सारा काम करता था। वह खाना पकाता, कपड़े धोता और अपनी कहानियों से महेन्द्र का मनोरंजन करता था। ईश्वरन में सब्जियाँ और खाना पकाने की सामग्री उत्पन्न करने की अद्भुत क्षमता थी जो कहीं नहीं मिलती थी।

ईश्वरन की दिनचर्या

महेन्द्र सबुह जल्दी खाना लेकर काम पर चला जाता था। महेन्द्र के काम पर जाने के बाद ईश्वरन घर को साफ करता, कपड़े धोता और प्रार्थना करते हुए नहाता था। दोपहर का भोजन करने के उपरान्त वह प्रसिद्ध तमिल पुस्तकें पढ़ता और फिर सो जाता था।

ईश्वरन : एक महान कहानी वक्ता

ईश्वरन रोमांचक तमिल कहानियाँ, जो उसने पढ़ी थी से अत्यधिक प्रभावित था। यह प्रभाव उसके कहानी सुनाने के तरीके में दिखता था। वह छोटी-सी घटना का भी रोमांच और आश्चर्य के साथ वर्णन करता था। उदाहरण के लिए, वह जड़ सहित उखड़े हुए पेड़ को नाटकीय अन्दाज में झाड़ीदार जानवर (जंगली जानवर) के रूप में वर्णन करेगा।

ईश्वरन की एक हाथी की कहानी

ईश्वरन ने महेन्द्र को एक पागल हाथी की एक घटना सुनाई। उसने बताया की एक दिन उसके गृहनगर में एक पागल हाथी लकड़ियों के कारखाने से भाग निकला और उसने अपने रास्ते में आने वाली प्रत्येक वस्तु को बर्बाद कर दिया। उसने लताएँ और डालियाँ तोड़ दीं।

कुछ देर बाद, वह ईश्वरन के कस्बे तक पहुँच गया। वह मुख्य सड़क पर आया और फलों, मिट्टी के बर्तनों और कपड़ों की दुकानों को तोड़ दिया। फिर हाथी स्कूल के मैदान में घुस गया और वहाँ उसने सब कुछ बर्बाद कर दिया।

अचानक, ईश्वरन जो की स्कूल का एक छात्र था, ने अध्यापक से एक छड़ी ली। वह मैदान की ओर दौड़ा और हाथी के पैर के तीसरी उँगली के नाखून पर मारा और हाथी नीचे गिर गया। इस बिन्दु पर ईश्वरन ने कहानी को अधूरा छोड़ दिया।

ईश्वरन की हाथी की कहानी का निष्कर्ष

कुछ समय बाद ईश्वरन ने कहानी को पूरा किया और महेन्द्र को बताया कि एक पशु चिकित्सक को हाथी की जाँच के लिए बुलाया गया। दो दिन बाद हाथी का महावत उसे जंगल में ले गया। जब महेन्द्र ने ईश्वरन से पूछा कि उसने हाथी को कैसे नियन्त्रित किया, तब ईश्वरन ने बताया कि इसका सम्बन्ध जापानी कला जू-जित्सू या कराटे से है जिसने उसकी (हाथी की) तन्त्रिका तन्त्र को कमजोर कर दिया था।

एक महिला के भूत की कहानी

एक दिन, ईश्वरन ने स्वादिष्ट खाना बनाया, क्योकि यह पूर्वजों की आत्माओं को भोजन करवाने का पवित्र दिन था। जब महेन्द्र डिनर कर रहा था तो ईश्वरन ने उसे फैक्ट्री के विषय में बताया जहाँ वे रह रहे थे।

उसने महेन्द्र को बताया कि फैक्ट्री की जगह पहले कब्रिस्तान था। उसने स्वयं रास्ते में खोपड़ी, हड्डियाँ, और रात में भूत देखे थे। उसने आगे महेन्द्र को एक भयानक पिशाच स्त्री के बारे में बताया जो पूर्णिमा की आधी रात में घूमती रहती है। वह अपनी बाहों में भ्रूण को लिए कंकाल जैसी दिखती है।

Hearing this, Mahendra was scared and shivered at the description of the ghost. He scolded Iswaran stating that ghosts don't exist. Soon, he retired to bed but could not sleep as the discussion about the ghost woman was going on in his mind.

यह सुनने के बाद, महेन्द्र डर गया ओर भूत के वर्णन पर काँपने लगा। उसने यह कर ईश्वरन को डाँटा की भूत नहीं होते। जल्द ही, वह अपने बिस्तर पर चला गया परन्तु वह सो नही पाया क्योंकि पिशाच स्त्री की चर्चा उसके दिमाग में चल रही थी।

Mahendra's Decision to Leave the Place

From that day onwards, Mahendra would go tot sleep feeling uneasy thinking about the female ghost. One night as Mahendra was sleeping, he suddenly woke up from his sleep by a low moaning sound coming from his window. Out of curiosity, he looked out of the the window and saw the night sky was filled with moonlight outside and noticed a dark cloud-shaped structure that was clutching a bundle. Seeing this, Mahendra stated sweating profusely and fell on his pillow. The next morning, Iswaran enquired his master about the female ghost and the moaning sound that was coming from his room. Mahendra was so terrified that he decided to leave the place immediately and forever.

महेन्द्र का स्थान छोड़ने का निर्णय

उस दिन के बाद से, महेन्द्र जब सोने के लिए जाता उसे महिला के भूत बारे में सोच कर बैचेनी होती। एक रात जब महेन्द्र सो रहा था, वह अचानक खिड़की से आ रही धीमी करहाने की आवाज सुनकर नींद से उठा। उत्सुकता वंश, उसने खिडकी के बाहर देखा और उसने देखा रात का आसमान चाँद की रोश्नी से भरा हुआ था और उसने ध्यान से देखा एक गहरे रंग की बादल की आकृति का ढाँचा जिसने गठरी पकड़ी हुई थी। यह देखकर महेन्द्र को बूरी तरह पसीने आने लगे और वह अपने तकिए पर गिर गया। अगली सुबह, ईश्वरन ने अपने मलिक से महिला के भूत ओर उसके कमरे से आ रही करहाने की आवाज के बारे में पूछा। महेन्द्र इतना डर गया था कि उसने उस जगह को तुरन्त और हमेशा के लिए छोड़ने का निश्चय किया।

Objective Questions

1. What was the occupation of Mahendra ?
(a) Teacher
(b) Engineer
(c) Junior Supervisor
(d) Cook

2. From which place to which other did Mahendra have to move when orders came from his head office?
(a) From a coal mining area to a railway bridge construction site
(b) From Iswaran's home in the village to the jungle nearby
(c) From a railway bridge construction site to a chemical plant
(d) Both (a) and (c)

3. Which of the following statements is false?
(a) Mahendra was married.
(b) Mahendra was able to adjust himself to all conditions.
(c) Iswaran chatted with Mahendra at night.
(d) Iswaran was attached to Mahendra.

4. Which of the following tasks was not done by Iswaran?
(a) He washed Mahendra's clothes.
(b) He told stories to Mahendra.
(c) He evoked Mahendra's food.
(d) He ironed Mahendra's clothes.

5. What was Iswaran fond of reading?
(a) Book
(b) Comics
(c) Drama
(d) Popular Tamil thrillers

6. Mahendra claimed himself to be a .... person.
(a) well-read (b) intelligent
(c) curious (d) brave and rational

7. The place 'I' comes from is famous for
(a) tusker (b) timber
(c) ghost (d) mad elephant

8. What did the elephant do when it came into the main road?
(a) It smashed all the stalls
(b) It danced around to present a show
(c) It poured water everywhere from his trunk
(d) It stamped its feet and showed anger

9. Which class was Iswaran in when the elephant entered the school ground?
(a) Primary class (b) Junior class
(c) Senior class (d) Middle class

10. What did Iswaran do to the elephant after it lifted its trunk and trumpeted loudly?
(a) He whacked the elephant's first toenail
(b) He whacked the elephant's second toenail
(c) He whacked the elephant's third toenail
(d) He whacked the elephants' trunk

11. From where was Iswaran watching the elephant Incident?
(a) From a room (b) From a bridge
(c) From the rooftop (d) From a tree

12. Iswaran made up for the absence of a .... in Mahendra's quarters?
(a) VCR (b) TV
(c) radio (d) jukebox

13. According to Iswaran, what was the entire factory area before?
(a) A burial ground
(b) A battlefield
(c) Another family's home
(d) Property of the ghost woman

14. Who narrated the story?
(a) Ganesh (b) Mahendra
(c) Ghost (d) None of these

15. Whose story did Iswaran tell Mahendra?
(a) Leopard's (b) Tiger's
(c) Mad Elephant's (d) None of these

16. The Elephant is also known as
(a) moti (b) tusker
(c) timber (d) None of these

17. Where did the elephant enter?
(a) House (b) Room
(c) School ground (d) Hall

18. Who always admired the beauty of full moon night in the story 'Iswaran the Story Teller'?
(a) Mahendra
(b) Ganesh
(c) Author
(d) Iswaran

19. After hearing Iswaran's stand of female ghost, Mahendra
(a) kept looking out of his window
(b) closed his window
(c) avoided looking out of his window on full moon nights
(d) avoided looking out of his window on-moon nights

Answers

1. (c)	2. (d)	3. (a)	4. (d)	5. (d)	6. (d)	7. (b)	8. (a)	9. (b)	10. (c)	11. (c)
12. (b)	13. (a)	14. (b)	15. (b)	16. (b)	17. (c)	18. (a)	19. (c)			

03 The Happy Prince

The story 'The Happy Prince' is a story of a Prince and a little swallow. It highlights that love and sacrifice are important aspects in human life. Hence, disparity and sorrow in society can be overcome by compassion, generosity and sharing. The generous Prince and the gentle swallow sacrificed themselves to bring happiness to the poor and needy people.

Important Characters

The Happy Prince प्रसन्नचित्त राजकुमार	He is a beautiful statue which parts with all its wealth to help the poor and needy. वह एक सुन्दर प्रतिमा है, जो गरीबों और जरूरतमन्दों की मदद करने के लिए अपना सारा धन खर्च करती है।
The Swallow अबाबील पक्षी	He is a migrant bird who sacrifices his life to help the prince in distributing his valuables among the poor. वह एक प्रवासी पक्षी है, जो गरीबों के बीच कीमती सामान को वितरित करने में राजकुमार की मदद करने के लिए अपने जीवन का बलिदान करता है।

Summary of the Lesson पाठ का सार

The Statue of Happy Prince

A beautiful statue was installed on a tall column (Pillar) high above the city. It was the statue of Happy Prince. The statue was covered with thin layers of gold. It had two bright sapphires fixed in the eyes. A bright ruby stone was placed in the hilt (handle) of his sword.

The Swallow Arrives

One night, a little swallow who was going to Egypt, arrived in the city. He was tired, so he decided to spend the night at the feet of the statue. He was going to sleep but was disturbed by a large drop of water that fell on his head. The swallow was amazed as the sky was clear. When the second drop fell, he decided to fly away. But, when the third drop fell, he looked at the statue. He found that the statue was crying.

प्रसन्नचित्त राजकुमार की प्रतिमा

शहर में सबसे ऊँचे, लम्बे स्तम्भ पर एक खूबसूरत प्रतिमा लगाई गई थी। यह प्रतिमा प्रसन्नचित्त राजकुमार की थी। प्रतिमा सोने की पतली-सी परत से ढकी हुई थी। उसकी आँखों में दो चमकीले नीलम जड़े हुए थे। एक चमकीला मणिक उसकी तलवार के हत्थे पर लगाया गया था।

अबाबील पक्षी का आगमन

एक रात, एक छोटा-सा अबाबील पक्षी, जो मिस्र जा रहा था शहर में आया। वह थका हुआ था, इसलिए उसने रात प्रतिमा के पैरों में बिताने का निश्चय किया। वह सोने ही जा रहा था लेकिन तभी पानी की एक बड़ी-सी बूँद उसके सिर पर गिरी जिससे वह विचलित हो उठा। अबाबील पक्षी हैरान था, क्योंकि आसमान बिल्कुल साफ था। जब दूसरी बूँद गिरी, तो उसने उड़ जाने का निश्चय किया। लेकिन, तीसरी बूँद गिरने पर उसने प्रतिमा की ओर देखा। उसने देखा कि प्रतिमा रो रही थी।

The Happy Life of Prince

The Swallow asked the statue, the reason behind his tears. The statue of Happy Prince told the Swallow that when he was alive, he did not know about miseries and sorrows.

He lived a happy life. So, his courtiers called him the Happy Prince. However, now after his death, his statue was set up very high and he could see the misery, poverty and all the sadness that people face.

The Prince wants to help the Poor People

The Prince told the Swallow that he wanted to help the poor people but he couldn't move. So, he requested the Swallow to stay with him and help him to do so. The Swallow agreed to help the Prince.

Helping the Seamstress and her ill Child

The Prince told the Swallow that a poor seamstress lived in the city. She was embroidering flowers on a gown for the Queen's loveliest maid of honour. By her side her little boy was lying ill and asking for oranges. But the poor woman did not have money.

So, the Prince requested the Swallow to pick out the ruby from his sword and give it to the seamstress. The Swallow agreed and put the ruby beside the poor seamstress. He also fanned the sick boy's forehead with its wings and left.

Helping the Playwright

The Swallow wanted to go Egypt but the Prince requested him to stay for another night. The Prince requested the Swallow to help the playwright.

The young playwright was trying to finish his play for the Director of the theatre but he couldn't do so. It was very cold to write anything and he was hungry which had made him faint.

The Prince asked the Swallow to pluck a sapphire and give it to the playwright who became happy after receiving it.

Helping the Poor Matchstick Girl

Next day, the Swallow came to the Prince to tell him good bye but the Prince again requested him to stay. The Prince told the Swallow that a little matchstick girl was standing and crying in the square. Her matchsticks had fallen in the drain and were all spoiled. Her father would beat her if she failed to take home some money.

The Happy Prince commanded the Swallow to take another sapphire from his eye and give it to the poor girl. The Swallow was not ready to do so because that would make the Prince completely blind, but the Prince forced him. The Swallow put the sapphire into the little girl's hand. The little girl felt very happy after getting the sapphire. The Prince became blind now. So, the Swallow decided to stay with the Prince always.

राजकुमार का खुशहाल जीवन

अबाबील पक्षी ने प्रतिमा से उसके रोने का कारण। पूछा प्रसन्नचित्त राजकुमार की प्रतिमा ने अबाबील पक्षी को बताया कि जब वह जीवित था, तब वह तकलीफों और दु:खों के बारे में नहीं जानता था।

उसने एक खुशहाल जीवन व्यतीत किया। इसलिए उसके दरबारी उसे प्रसन्नचित्त राजकुमार कहते थे। हालाँकि अब उसकी मृत्यु के बाद, उसकी प्रतिमा को ऊँचे स्थान पर स्थापित किया गया और अब वह लोगों की तकलीफों, गरीबी और सारे दु:खों को देख सकता था।

राजकुमार की गरीब लोगों की सहायता करने की इच्छा

राजकुमार ने अबाबील पक्षी को बताया, कि वह गरीब लोगों की मदद करना चाहता था, लेकिन वह हिल नहीं सकता। इसलिए उसने अबाबील पक्षी से उसके साथ रहने और लोगों की मदद करने में उसकी सहायता करने की विनती की। अबाबील पक्षी राजकुमार की सहायता करने के लिए तैयार हो गया।

दर्जिन और उसके बीमार बच्चे की सहायता

राजकुमार ने अबाबील पक्षी को बताया कि एक गरीब दर्जिन शहर में रहती थी। वह रानी की सबसे प्यारी दासी के गाउन पर कशीदेकारी से फूल बना रही थी। उसके समीप ही उसका छोटा बेटा बीमार लेटा हुआ था, जो अपनी माँ से सन्तरे माँग रहा था। लेकिन बेचारी औरत के पास पैसे नहीं थे।

इसलिए, राजकुमार ने अबाबील पक्षी से निवेदन किया, कि वह उसकी तलवार में से मणिक निकालकर उसे दर्जिन को दे दे। अबाबील पक्षी मान गया और मणिक को दर्जिन के पास रख दिया। उसने बीमार बच्चे के सिर पर अपने पंखों से हवा की और चला गया।

नाटककार की सहायता

अबाबील पक्षी मिस्र जाना चाहता था, लेकिन राजकुमार ने उससे एक रात और रुकने का निवेदन किया। राजकुमार ने अबाबील पक्षी से नाटककार की सहायता करने की विनती की।

युवा नाटककार रंगमंच के निर्देशक के लिए अपने नाटक को पूरा करने का प्रयास कर रहा था, लेकिन वह ऐसा नहीं कर पा रहा था। कुछ भी लिखने के लिए सर्दी बहुत अधिक थी और वह भूखा था जिसके कारण उसे बेहोशी आ रही थी।

राजकुमार ने अबाबील पक्षी से नीलम निकालकर उसे नाटककार को देने के लिए कहा जो उसे प्राप्त करके बहुत प्रसन्न हुआ।

गरीब माचिस बनाने वाली लड़की की सहायता

अगले दिन, अबाबील पक्षी राजकुमार को अलविदा कहने के लिए आया, लेकिन राजकुमार ने उससे पुन: रुकने की विनती की। राजकुमार ने अबाबील पक्षी को बताया कि छोटी-सी माचिस बनाने वाली लड़की चौराहे पर खड़ी होकर रो रही थी। उसकी सारी माचिस नाले में गिरकर नष्ट हो गई थी। यदि वह घर पर कुछ रुपये नहीं लेकर गई तो उसके पिता उसकी पिटाई करेंगे।

प्रसन्नचित्त राजकुमार ने अबाबील पक्षी को उसकी आँख से दूसरा नीलम भी निकालकर गरीब लड़की को देने की हिदायत दी। अबाबील पक्षी यह करने के लिए तैयार नहीं था, क्योंकि इससे राजकुमार पूरी तरह से अंधा हो जाता, लेकिन राजकुमार ने ऐसा करने के लिए उसे (अबाबील पक्षी) मजबूर किया। अबाबील पक्षी ने नीलम छोटी लड़की के हाथ में रख दिया। छोटी लड़की नीलम पाकर बहुत प्रसन्न हुई। अब राजकुमार अंधा हो गया था, इसलिए अबाबील पक्षी ने हमेशा राजकुमार के साथ रहने का निश्चय किया।

Swallow Reports the Matter

The Prince asked the Swallow to fly over his city and tell him what he saw there. The Swallow informed the Prince that the poor were leading a miserable life. The Prince requested the Swallow to take the gold leaf by leaf from his statue and give it to the poor. The Swallow did the same as per the request and made poor people happy.

Swallow Died

Now, the weather had become extremely cold. The Swallow could not tolerate the extremely cold weather. But the Swallow didn't leave the Prince. He tried to keep himself warm but was not able to do so. He soon realised that he was going to die. He requested the Prince to kiss on his hand, but the Prince told the Swallow to kiss on his lips. After kissing the Prince's lips, the Swallow fell down and died. When the Swallow died, the statue's leaden heart broke into two pieces.

The Statue is Removed

The Mayor of the city along with the town councillors visited the place. They found the statue to be ugly and useless as it was no longer beautiful. Hence, it was removed and sent to be melted. But the broken lead heart couldn't be melted so it was thrown away.

God Sends the Angel

God sent one of his angels to bring him the two most precious things from the city. The Angel brought the leaden heart of the Happy Prince along with the dead bird. The God praised the angel. He also stated that the Swallow would sing forever in his garden of paradise and the Happy Prince would praise him forever in his City of Gold.

अबाबील पक्षी द्वारा सारे मामले का विवरण

राजकुमार ने अबाबील पक्षी से शहर के ऊपर उड़कर उसे यह बताने के लिए कहा कि उसे वहाँ क्या दिखाई दिया। अबाबील ने उसे सूचना दी कि गरीब लोग दुःख से भरा जीवन जी रहे थे। राजकुमार ने अबाबील पक्षी से उसकी प्रतिमा से एक-एक सोने की पत्ती निकालकर गरीबों को देने के लिए कहा। अबाबील पक्षी ने राजकुमार की विनती के अनुसार वैसा ही किया और गरीब लोगों को खुशी प्रदान की।

अबाबील पक्षी की मृत्यु

अब, मौसम बहुत ठण्डा हो गया था। अबाबील पक्षी इतना ठण्डा मौसम सहन नहीं कर सकता था। लेकिन अबाबील पक्षी ने राजकुमार का साथ नहीं छोड़ा। उसने स्वयं को गर्म रखने का प्रयास किया, लेकिन वह ऐसा नहीं कर सका। जल्द ही उसे अनुमान हो गया कि वह मरने जा रहा था। उसने राजकुमार से उसके हाथ पर चुम्बन करने की विनती की, लेकिन राजकुमार ने अबाबील पक्षी से उसके होठों पर चुम्बन करने के लिए कहा। राजकुमार के होठों पर चुम्बन करने के बाद अबाबील पक्षी गिरकर मर गया। जब अबाबील पक्षी मर गया तो प्रतिमा का सीसे का दिल दो टुकड़ों में टूट गया।

प्रतिमा का हटना

शहर के मेयर और कस्बे के पार्षदों ने उस स्थान का दौरा किया। उन्हें वह प्रतिमा भद्दी और बेकार लगी, क्योंकि वह अब सुन्दर नहीं थी। इसलिए उसे हटा कर पिघलाने के लिए भेज दिया गया। लेकिन टूटा हुआ सीसे का दिल पिघल नहीं सका इसलिए उसे फेंक दिया गया।

ईश्वर द्वारा देवदूत को भेजना

ईश्वर ने शहर से दो सबसे कीमती वस्तुओं को लाने के लिए अपने एक देवदूत को भेजा। देवदूत प्रसन्नचित्त राजकुमार के सीसे के दिल और मृत पक्षी को उठा लाया। ईश्वर ने देवदूत की प्रशंसा की। उन्होंने घोषणा की कि अबाबील पक्षी उनके स्वर्ग के बाग में हमेशा गाता रहेगा और सोने के शहर में प्रसन्नचित्त राजकुमार हमेशा उसकी प्रशंसा करता रहेगा।

Objective Questions

1. .... glowed on the hilt of the sword of the Happy Prince.
(a) A large red sapphire (b) A large red ruby
(c) Two larged sapphires (d) Two longe red rubies

2. The swallow decided to put up at the statue on the tall column as
(a) it was a fine position
(b) there was plenty of fresh air
(c) Both (a) and (b)
(d) his friends were also staying there

3. Where had the swallow's friends gone?
(a) To an island near Egypt (b) To their homes
(c) To the swallow's home (d) To Egypt

4. How many drops of water had fallen on the swallow before he looked up?
(a) Three (b) Two (c) Five (d) Four

5. Who said the following line?
"I don't think I like boys"
(a) The Happy Prince (b) The seamstress
(c) The playwright (d) The swallow

6. What did the swallow think when the prince told him that his heart was made of lead ?
(a) Is the Prince not solid ruby?
(b) Is the Prince not solid gold?
(c) Is the Prince not solid sapphire?
(d) Is the Prince not solid lead?

7. What did the Happy Prince say about the sapphires in his eyes?
(a) They were rare sapphires.
(b) They were bought from India a thousand years ago.
(c) They were bought from Chan.
(d) Both (a) and (b)

8. What were the swallow's friends doing in Egypt?
(a) Flying up and down the Nile
(b) Talking to the large lotus flowers
(c) Probably sleeping
(d) Both (a) and (b)

9. Which place did the swallow not pass on his way to the seamstress's house?
(a) The river (b) The cathedral tower
(c) The palace (d) The valley

10. Why did the boy feel cold?
(a) The swallow had poured cold water on his head.
(b) The swallow was fanning his forehead with his wings.
(c) His mother had poured cold water on his head.
(d) His mother was fanning his forehead with his wings.

11. The statue of the Happy Prince was covered with the layer of
(a) gold (b) silver
(c) diamond (d) brass

12. The little swallow was going to
(a) France (b) Africa
(c) India (d) Egypt

13. The hands of the poor woman were red as she got hurt by
(a) sword (b) blade
(c) needle (d) scissor

14. The poor woman was making a gown for
(a) Queen's maid (b) herself
(c) daughter (d) Queen

15. The colour of the hair of the poor writer was
(a) black
(b) white
(c) brown
(d) grey

16. "He is no longer beautiful, he is no longer useful" said the
(a) Town Clerk (b) Mayor
(c) Art Professor (d) Town Councilor

17. The swallow decided to spend the night
(a) on a tree near the statue of the happy Prince
(b) on the shoulder of the Happy Prince
(c) under the tall column where the statue stood
(d) between the feet of the Happy Prince

18. "My feet are fastened to this pedestal and I cannot move." Who said this?
(a) The poor woman (b) The little swallow
(c) The little boy (d) The Happy Prince

19. The Prince was called happy because
(a) he never cried
(b) he had everything
(c) he was very lucky
(d) he always smiled and was living in palace of happiness

20. Who said the following line?
"This broken heart will not melt in the furnace. We must throw it away."
(a) The overseer at the foundry (b) The Art Professor
(c) The Mayor
(d) The Town Councillor

Answers

1. (b) 2. (c) 3. (d) 4. (a) 5. (d) 6. (b) 7. (d) 8. (d) 9. (d) 10. (b)
11. (a) 12. (d) 13. (c) 14. (a) 15. (c) 16. (c) 17. (d) 18. (d) 19. (d) 20. (a)

04 The Last Leaf

This chapter is a short story written by O.Henry. This story focuses on the friendship of two artist friends Sue and Johnsy, who live together. In this chapter, the author tells about the power of hope and how it helps in facing various obstacles in life, and also shows the effects of depression that can lead to disaster. The chapter also depicts the value of art and sacrifice. Thus, the story underlines the fact that even a poor, neglected person is capable of doing a noble act.

Important Characters

Sue	She is an artist, who shares a small flat with her friend Johnsy. She helps Johnsy in getting well.
स्यू	वह एक कलाकार है, जो अपनी दोस्त जौन्सी के साथ एक छोटा सा फ्लैट साझा करती है।
Johnsy	She is the friend of Sue and lives with her. She is suffering from pneumonia. She is also an artist.
जौन्सी	वह स्यू की दोस्त है और उसके साथ रहती है। वह निमोनिया से पीड़ित है। वह भी एक कलाकार है।
Behrman	Behrman is a sixty year old painter and neighbour of Sue and Johnsy. He saves the life of Johnsy.
बहरमन	बहरमन साठ वर्षीय चित्रकार है तथा स्यू और जौन्सी का पड़ोसी हैं। वह जौन्सी का जीवन बचाता है।

Summary of the Lesson पाठ का सार

Sue and Johnsy

Sue and Johnsy were two young artists who lived together in a small flat. It was located on the third storey of an old house.

Once Johnsy fell ill in November due to pneumonia. In her illness Johnsy would lie on the bed without moving and kept looking out of the window. Johnsy's behaviour worried Sue, so she called the doctor.

The Doctor's Visit

The doctor came everyday but there was no improvement in Johnsy's health. One day, the doctor informed Sue that Johnsy had lost her willingness to live. Therefore, without hope and willingness, no medicine would cure her.

Since then, Sue tried to make Johnsy take an interest in things. She would talk about clothes and fashion, but nothing interested Johnsy. Sue even brought her drawing board into Johnsy's room to complete her work.

Johnsy's Strange Belief

One day, Sue noticed that Johnsy was looking out of the window and counting backwards.

Sue found out that Johnsy was looking at an old ivy creeper that was climbing the brick wall opposite to their window. The creeper was shedding its leaves due to the strong winds. Sue was shocked when she came to know that Johnsy believed that she would die when the last leaf of the creeper would fall.

Sue disregarded Johnsy's belief. She told Johnsy to think positively and also requested her to not look at the ivy creeper.

The Old Behrman

Sue had to paint an old miner, so she called Behrman to be her model. Behrman was a sixty-year old painter who lived on the ground floor of the same house.

Behrman was not a successful artist. He always had a dream of painting a masterpiece but was not successful in doing so.

Sue told Behrman about Johnsy's condition and her belief.

Later, Sue and Behrman went to Johnsy's room and saw that only one last leaf remained on the ivy creeper.

The Leaf does not Fall

Next morning, Johnsy saw that the last leaf was still hanging on the ivy creeper. She was surprised to see that even after the strong winds and storm, the leaf had not fallen. In fact, it looked green and healthy. Looking at the leaf, Johnsy realised her mistake. She called Sue and apologised to her for losing hope.

Even the doctor now told Sue that Johnsy would get cured soon. He also informed Sue that Behrman was suffering from pneumonia and would die soon.

स्यू और जौन्सी

स्यू और जौन्सी दो युवा कलाकार थी जो एक साथ एक छोटे से फ्लैट में रहती थी। यह एक पूराने घर की तीसरी मंजिल पर स्थित था।

एक बार जौन्सी निमोनिया के कारण नवम्बर में बीमार पड़ गई। अपनी बीमारी में जौन्सी अपने बिस्तर में बिना हिले डुले लेटी रहा करती थी और खिड़की के बाहर देखा करती थी। जौन्सी के व्यवहार ने स्यू को चिन्तित कर दिया, इस कारण उसने डाक्टर को बुलाया।

डाक्टर का आगमन

डाक्टर रोजाना आता था, परन्तु जौन्सी के स्वास्थ में कोई सुधार नहीं था। एक दिन, डाक्टर ने स्यू को बताया कि जौन्सी अपनी जीने की इच्छा खो चुकी थी। इस कारण बिना आशा और इच्छा के, कोई दवा उसे ठीक नहीं कर सकती।

उसके बाद, स्यू ने जौन्सी को चीजों में रूचि उत्पन्न करवाने का प्रयास किया। वह कपड़ों और फैशन के बारे में बात किया करती परन्तु जौन्सी को कुछ भी प्रभावित नहीं करता था। यहाँ तक की स्यू अपना ड्राईंग बोर्ड अपना कार्य पूरा करने जौन्सी के कमरे में ले आयी थी।

जौन्सी का आसामान्य विचार

एक दिन, स्यू ने ध्यान दिया कि जौन्सी खिड़की के बाहर देख रही थी और उल्टी गिनती कर रही थी।

स्यू ने पाया कि जौन्सी पुरानी आइवी लता जो उनकी खिड़की के सामने ईंट की दीवार पर चढ़ रही थी उसे देख रही थी। तेज हवा के कारण लता अपनी पत्तियाँ गिरा रही थी। स्यू को जब पता चला कि जौन्सी यह मानती कि जब लता की अन्तिम पत्ती गिर जाएगी तो उसकी मृत्यु हो जाएगी।

स्यू ने जौन्सी के विचार पर ध्यान नहीं दिया। उसने जौन्सी को सकारात्मक सोच रखने को कहा और उससे आइवी लता को ना देखने का अनुरोध किया।

बुजुर्ग बहरमन

स्यू को बूढे खनिक का चित्र बनाना था, इसलिए उसने अपने मॉडल के लिए बहरमन को बुलाया बहरमन साठ वर्षीय बूढ़ा चित्रकार जो उसी इमारत में निचली मंजिल पर रहता था।

बहरमन सफल चित्रकार नहीं था। उसका हमेशा से सपना था कि वह उत्कृष्ट कृति बनाए परन्तु वह उसमें सफल नहीं हुआ था।

स्यू ने बहरमन को जौन्सी की स्थिति और उसके विचार के बारे में बताया।

बाद में, जौन्सी और बहरमन जौन्सी के कमरे में गए और उन्होने देखा कि आइवी लता पर केवल एक पत्ती शेष थी।

पत्ती गिरी नहीं

अगली सुबह, जौन्सी ने देखा कि अन्तिम पत्ती आइवी लता पर अभी लगी हुई थी। उसे यह देख कर आश्चर्य हुआ कि इतनी तेज हवा और तुफान के बाद भी, पत्ती नहीं गिरी। बल्कि, वह हरी और स्वस्थ दिख रही थी। पत्ती को देखकर, जौन्सी को अपनी गलती का अहसास हुआ। उसने स्यू को बुलाया और निराश हाने के लिए माफी माँगी।

यहाँ तक कि डाक्टर ने स्यू को बताया कि जौन्सी जल्दी ही ठीक हो जाएगी। उसने स्यू को यह भी बताया कि बहरमन को निमोनिया हो गया और उसकी शीघ्र ही मृत्यु हो जाएगी।

Behrman's Masterpiece and Sacrifice

Next morning, Sue informed Johnsy that Behrman had died of pneumonia and he had been ill only for two days.

The Janitor found Behrman on his bed and his clothes and shoes were wet. When Sue and Johnsy went to see Behrman, they found a ladder and a lantern near his bed.

Sue had realised what happened to Behrman and told Johnsy that the last leaf was infact a painted leaf. It was painted by Behrman in the stormy night when the real leaf had fell. He had painted his masterpiece and had sacrificed his own life to save Johnsy.

बहरमन की उत्कृष्ट कृति और बलिदान

अगली सुबह, स्यू ने जौन्सी को बताया की बहरमन की निमोनिया के कारण मृत्यु हो गई और वह केवल दो दिन से ही बीमार था।

चौकीदार ने बहरमन को उसके बिस्तर पर पाया और उसके कपड़े और जूते गीले थे। जब स्यू और जौन्सी बहरमन को देखने गए, उन्हे उसके पंलग के पास एक सीढ़ी और लालटेन मिली।

स्यू को पता चल गया कि बहरमन को क्या हुआ और उसने जौन्सी को बताया कि अन्तिम पत्ती वास्तव में चित्रित पत्ती थी। वह बहरमन द्वारा तूफानी रात में बनाई गई थी। जब वास्तविक पत्ती गिर गई थी। उसने अपनी उत्कृष्ट कृति बनाई थी और उसने जौन्सी को बचाने के लिए अपने जीवन का बलिदान कर दिया।

Objective Questions

1. The flat in which Sue and Johnsy stayed was on the .... storey of on old house.
(a) second (b) fourth
(c) first (d) third

2. Sue ...... while painting to get Johnsy's attention.
(a) clapped (b) whistled
(c) shouted (d) whispered

3. Which of the following statements is false?
(a) Sue and Johnsy were artists.
(b) The ivy creeper was shedding its leaves.
(c) The doctor was confident that Johnsy would get better.
(d) Medicines did not help Johnsy.

4. Sue refused to draw the curtain as she needed .... to paint.
(a) light (b) pen
(c) someone (d) darkness

5. Which floor did Behrman lived on?
(a) Second (b) Tenth
(c) Ground (d) Basement

6. According to the doctor, what was the cure for Johnsy's illness?
(a) Medicines
(b) Therapy
(c) Love and care
(d) Her own desire to live

7. Who said the following line? "How can she be so foolish?"
(a) Sue (b) Johnsy
(c) The Janitor (d) Behrman

8. How old was Behrman?
(a) Sixty years old (b) Sixty one years old
(c) Sixty two years old (d) Fifty eight years old

9. .... looked after Johnsy.
(a) Behrman (b) Doctor
(c) Sue (d) None of these

10. .... was brought by Sue into Johnsy's room.
(a) Blackboard (b) Masterpiece
(c) Painting (d) Drawing board

11. Johnsy was looking the ...... out of the window.
(a) flowers (b) leaves (c) birds (d) sky

12. .... had developed a strange superstition.
(a) Sue (b) Behrman (c) Doctor (d) Johnsy

13. .... refused to eat or drink in the story.
(a) Sue (b) Johnsy
(c) Behrman (d) None of them

14. .... Johnsy asked Sue to draw the curtains.
(a) In a feeble voice (b) In an exclaimed voice
(c) In a sad voice (d) Both (a) and (b)

15. .... was the masterpiece of Behrman.
(a) The ivy leaf (b) The temple
(c) The painting of god (d) All of these

Answers

1. (d) 2. (b) 3. (c) 4. (a) 5. (c) 6. (d) 7. (d) 8. (a) 9. (c) 10. (d)
11. (b) 12. (d) 13. (b) 14. (a) 15. (a)

05 The Accidental Tourist

The story 'The Happy Prince' is a story of a Prince and a little swallow. It highlights that love and sacrifice are important aspects in human life. Hence, disparity and sorrow in society can be overcome by compassion, generosity and sharing. The generous Prince and the gentle swallow sacrificed themselves to bring happiness to the poor and needy people.

Important Characters

The Happy Prince प्रसन्नचित्त राजकुमार	He is a beautiful statue which parts with all its wealth to help the poor and needy. वह एक सुन्दर प्रतिमा है, जो गरीबों और जरूरतमन्दों की मदद करने के लिए अपना सारा धन खर्च करती है।
The Swallow अबाबील पक्षी	He is a migrant bird who sacrifices his life to help the prince in distributing his valuables among the poor. वह एक प्रवासी पक्षी है, जो गरीबों के बीच कीमती सामान को वितरित करने में राजकुमार की मदद करने के लिए अपने जीवन का बलिदान करता है।

Summary of the Lesson पाठ का सार

The Accidental Tourist by Anne Tyler follows Macon Leary, a man whose life is turned upside down after the sudden death of his young son, Daniel. Macon is a travel writer who specializes in guidebooks for people who prefer to travel without straying too far from their comfort zones. His personal life, however, is far from comfortable. He struggles with depression, alienation, and a strained marriage with his wife, Sarah.

When Sarah leaves him, Macon moves back in with his eccentric siblings in Baltimore. He begins to rebuild his life with the help of a quirky dog trainer named Muriel. Over time, Macon starts to open up emotionally and confront his past, learning to navigate relationships and heal from his grief.

The novel explores themes of loss, family, and emotional healing, with Tyler's signature blend of humor, empathy, and depth. Macon's journey is one of personal growth, as he learns to accept the messiness of life and the possibility of happiness.

In "The Accidental Tourist" the writer narrates the incidences where he acts strangely. On various air trips, he spills drinks on co – passengers.

Its as if his arms work on their own, move towards the tray and knock – off the glass without his directions.

He would be unable to get the air miles because either he could not present his card or the clerk refused to give him the points. Once while opening his bag to get the card, he threw all the articles on the floor.

Things flew here and there and there was complete chaos. Also, on another trip, the ink from his pen smeared his mouth, teeth, gums and chin. His face turned blue and would remain like that for a couple of days.

Once he bend forward to tie his shoelace when the front seat went into a recline position and his head got stuck there.

Whenever he ate a meal, the dining table was a complete mess and it appeared as if an earthquake had struck the place.

His family was accustomed to it and when they got their meal, they would get alert to prevent being victims of the spillovers.

While travelling alone, he would not eat, drink or bend forward. He would even keep his hands under him to avoid mishaps.

He never managed to get the airmiles and would not travel free of cost to Bali but that was good in a way. He could not remain without food on such a long flight.

Objective Questions

1. Who is the protagonist of The Accidental Tourist?
(a) Sarah Leary (b) Macon Leary
(c) Muriel Pritchett (d) Daniel Leary

2. What is Macon Leary's profession?
(a) Travel agent (b) Author of travel books
(c) Pilot (d) Tour guide

3. What tragic event affects Macon and his family at the beginning of the novel?
(a) The death of his wife
(b) The loss of his job
(c) The death of his son
(d) A financial crisis

4. How does Macon cope with his grief after Daniel's death?
(a) He isolates himself
(b) He goes on a world tour
(c) He moves to a new city
(d) He starts a new relationship

5. What is the main source of conflict between Macon and his wife, Sarah?
(a) Financial troubles
(b) Sarah's affair
(c) Their differing attitudes toward grief and healing
(d) Sarah's desire for children

6. Where does Macon move to after his wife Sarah leaves him?
(a) A small apartment
(b) His family home in Baltimore
(c) A hotel
(d) His childhood house

7. Who helps Macon with his dog training in the novel?
(a) Sarah
(b) Muriel Pritchett
(c) His brother Charles
(d) His father

8. How would you describe Muriel Pritchett's character?
(a) Reserved and shy
(b) Quirky, unconventional and caring
(c) Strict and judgmental
(d) Wealthy and sophisticated

9. What does Macon learn from his relationship with Muriel?
(a) That he should return to his wife
(b) To open up emotionally and allow himself to heal
(c) That he should never trust anyone again
(d) To travel more frequently

10. What role do Macon's siblings play in the story?
(a) They are a source of conflict
(b) They help him regain his emotional strength
(c) They encourage him to travel more
(d) They criticize his work

11. What is the name of Macon's wife?
(a) Muriel (b) Sarah (c) Ruth (d) Lillian

12. What kind of dog does Macon have?
(a) Poodle (b) Labrador Retriever
(c) Weimaraner (d) Beagle

13. What is one of the quirks of Macon's family?
(a) They are all involved in politics
(b) They run a bakery together
(c) They are very close-knit and eccentric
(d) They are all doctors

14. How does Macon feel about the idea of traveling after Daniel's death?
(a) He is excited to visit new places
(b) He becomes indifferent and prefers staying home
(c) He is fearful of traveling alone
(d) He continues to write travel books but dislikes it

15. What does Sarah suggest to Macon during their separation?
(a) That they should start fresh together
(b) That they should continue living in the same house
(c) That Macon should go on a long vacation
(d) That they should get a divorce

16. What is Macon's attitude toward change throughout most of the novel?
(a) He embraces it eagerly
(b) He resists it and prefers stability
(c) He is indifferent to change
(d) He constantly seeks new experiences

17. What role does the character of Charles, Macon's brother, play in the story?
(a) He provides financial support to Macon
(b) He tries to fix Macon's relationship with Sarah
(c) He provides emotional support, despite his own issues
(d) He convinces Macon to travel for work

18. According to the writer, How does Macon's relationship with his dog, Edward, change over the course of the novel?
(a) The dog becomes a source of constant frustration
(b) Macon becomes more attached to Edward and learns to care for him
(c) Macon gives away the dog to Muriel
(d) Edward becomes ill and Macon grows distant from him

19. What is Muriel's main reason for becoming involved with Macon?
(a) She wants to help him with his writing
(b) She feels a deep sympathy for him and is drawn to his vulnerability
(c) She is in need of financial support
(d) She is looking for adventure in her life

20. According at the end of the novel, what is Macon's outlook on life?
(a) He decides to travel the world
(b) He remains emotionally closed off
(c) He opens himself to love and is willing to take risks
(d) He moves back to his childhood home permanently

21. What is Macon's main occupation as a writer?
(a) Writing novels
(b) Writing travel books for the fearful traveler
(c) Writing for magazines
(d) Writing about history and culture

22. According to the writer, what is Macon's approach to life before the tragic death of his son?
(a) He is carefree and adventurous
(b) He is emotionally distant and controlled
(c) He is impulsive and spontaneous
(d) He is constantly seeking new experiences

23. Who is the first to suggest that Macon seek help for his grief?
(a) Muriel (b) His therapist
(c) Sarah (d) His brother, Charles

24. What does Macon do after Sarah leaves him?
(a) He goes on a long vacation
(b) He moves in with his parents
(c) He stays at his family's home in Baltimore
(d) He relocates to another city

25. How does Macon feel about Muriel when they first meet?
(a) He is immediately attracted to her
(b) He feels uncomfortable and critical of her
(c) He sees her as a potential business partner
(d) He does not trust her

26. What event causes Macon to reconsider his rigid, controlled lifestyle?
(a) His dog's behavior improves
(b) He begins to care more about his relationship with Muriel
(c) His sister suggests he take a vacation
(d) A tragic accident happens in his family

27. How does Macon's family react to his relationship with Muriel?
(a) They strongly disapprove of her
(b) They are indifferent to it
(c) They warmly accept her
(d) They try to break them up

28. What is the most significant turning point in Macon's emotional journey?
(a) His decision to travel for work
(b) His interaction with his ex-wife Sarah
(c) His realisation that he can love again, especially with Muriel
(d) His relationship with his siblings

29. How does Macon's relationship with his brother Charles affect him?
(a) It helps Macon open up emotionally
(b) It causes Macon to question his life choices
(c) It deepens his sense of loneliness
(d) It encourages Macon to go on a trip

30. What is Macon's main struggle throughout the novel?
(a) Overcoming his fear of travel
(b) Coping with the death of his son and the end of his marriage
(c) Finding a new career path
(d) Reconnecting with his childhood friends

31. What was the reason for Sarah and Macon's separation?
(a) Macon's emotional distance
(b) Sarah's affair with another man
(c) Financial problems
(d) Macon's desire to live overseas

32. What is the symbolic significance of the title The Accidental Tourist?
(a) It refers to the idea that Macon is forced into new experiences rather than seeking them
(b) It symbolises Macon's love for travel
(c) It suggests a journey of self-discovery
(d) It alludes to the character of Muriel, who is an accidental traveler

33. According to the writer, how does Macon view relationships at the beginning of the novel?
(a) As a source of joy and fulfillment
(b) As a necessary but burdensome part of life
(c) As something that should be avoided
(d) As a deep emotional connection

34. What is Macon's biggest fear regarding his relationship with Muriel?
(a) That she will hurt him
(b) That he will lose his independence
(c) That she is not truly interested in him
(d) That she will want him to change

35. How does Macon's perspective on love change by the end of the novel?
(a) He decides love is a weakness
(b) He learns to accept love and embrace vulnerability
(c) He rejects the idea of love forever
(d) He believes love should be based on practicality

36. How does Macon feel about the idea of traveling after his son's death?
   (a) He becomes obsessed with traveling
   (b) He completely abandons the idea of travel
   (c) He continues to write his travel books but feels detached
   (d) He finds solace in exploring new places

37. What is the nature of Macon's relationship with his dog, Edward?
   (a) The dog is an obstacle to Macon's emotional growth
   (b) The dog is a constant source of comfort and companionship
   (c) The dog is a symbol of Macon's lost childhood
   (d) Macon is indifferent to the dog

38. According to the writer, what does Muriel do to help Macon in his healing process?
   (a) She listens to him without judgment
   (b) She encourages him to leave his family
   (c) She helps him write a book about his grief
   (d) She pressures him to make quick decisions about his life

39. How does Macon's family react when he begins a relationship with Muriel?
   (a) They encourage the relationship
   (b) They actively discourage it
   (c) They are indifferent
   (d) They are supportive, but concerned about his emotional state

40. What lesson does Macon learn by the end of the novel?
   (a) That he should always prioritise work over relationships
   (b) That healing is a gradual process and requires vulnerability
   (c) That travel is the key to overcoming grief
   (d) That he should never let anyone get close to him again

Answers

Multiple Choice Questions

1. (b)	2. (b)	3. (c)	4. (a)	5. (c)	6. (b)	7. (b)	8. (b)	9. (b)	10. (b)
11. (b)	12. (c)	13. (c)	14. (b)	15. (d)	16. (b)	17. (c)	18. (b)	19. (b)	20. (c)
21. (b)	22. (b)	23. (d)	24. (c)	25. (b)	26. (b)	27. (a)	28. (c)	29. (a)	30. (b)
31. (a)	32. (a)	33. (b)	34. (b)	35. (b)	36. (c)	37. (b)	38. (a)	39. (b)	40. (b)

Unit-12

01 A Triumph of Surgery

Summary of the Lesson पाठ का सार

The story narrates the episode where the narrator (Dr. James Herriot), a veterinary surgeon, saves the life of a dull dog, Tricki. The story starts when Dr. James was driving, he saw Mrs. Pumphrey and Tricki walking down the street. He was shocked to see that Tricki had become very fat and was ill. So, he enquired about Tricki's health from Mrs. Pumphrey.

Mrs. Pumphrey explained to Dr. James that she felt that Tricki was suffering from malnutrition. So, she had been giving him some extra food. Furthermore, she added that Tricki only walked with her and did not play games.

After learning about Tricki's condition and his routine, Dr. James informed Mrs. Pumphrey that if she did not reduce his food and increase his exercise, her dog would fall ill. After a few days, Mrs. Pumphrey called and informed Dr. James that Tricki was not eating anything and had been vomiting.

Dr. James suggested Mrs. Pumphrey to hospitalise him for a fortnight for observation, so that proper treatment could follow. Mrs. Pumphrey was sad but she allowed him to take Tricki. Dr. James carried Tricki wrapped in a blanket to his car while the maids started keeping the things that Tricki would need during hospitalisation in Dr. James' car.

In the hospital, Tricki was put on a water diet for first two days. At the end of the second day, Tricki started to show some interest in his surroundings. On the third day, he walked slowly and joined the greyhound (hunting dog) in the garden. Later, he ran with enthusiasm when the food was served. He also ate the food kept for him.

While Tricki was recovering, Mrs. Pumphrey used to phone Dr. James' clinic several times a day to know about Tricky's recovery. Dr. James assured her that Tricki was out of danger. Hearing this, Mrs. Pumphrey started sending eggs and wine for Tricki. The food sent for Tricki was eaten by Dr. James and his team.

After a fortnight, Dr. James called and informed Mrs. Pumphrey that Tricki was fit and could go home. Mrs. Pumphrey reached the surgery within half an hour. As soon as the dog saw his owner, he jumped into her lap and started licking her face. Mrs. Pumphrey was very happy at finding Tricki as excited as he used to be. She thanked Dr. James Herriot and called the treatment 'A triumph of surgery'.

यह कहानी उस प्रसंग का वर्णन करती है, जहाँ वर्णनकर्ता (डॉ. जेम्स हेरियट) एक पशुचिकित्सक, एक सुस्त कुत्ते, ट्रिकी की जान बचाते हैं। कहानी तब शुरू होती है, जब डॉ. जेम्स गाड़ी चला रहे थे और उन्होंने श्रीमती पम्फ्रे व ट्रिकी को सड़क पर जाते हुए देखा। वह यह देखकर हैरान रह गए कि ट्रिकी बहुत मोटा हो गया और बीमार, इसलिए उन्होंने श्रीमती पम्फ्रे से ट्रिकी के स्वास्थ्य के बारे में पूछा।

श्रीमती पम्फ्रे ने डॉ. जेम्स को बताया कि उन्हें लगता है कि ट्रिकी कुपोषण से पीड़ित था, इसलिए, वह उसे मुख्य भोजन के बीच कुछ अतिरिक्त भोजन दे रही थी। इसके अतिरिक्त, उन्होंने कहा कि ट्रिकी केवल उनके साथ ही टहलता था और कोई खेल भी नहीं खेलता था।

ट्रिकी की स्थिति और दिनचर्या के बारे में जानने के बाद, डॉ. जेम्स ने श्रीमती पम्फ्रे को बताया कि यदि उन्होंने उसका खाना कम नहीं किया और व्यायाम नहीं बढ़ाया, तो उनका कुत्ता बीमार पड़ जाएगा। कुछ दिनों के बाद श्रीमती पम्फ्रे ने डा. जेम्स को फोन किया और उन्हें सूचित किया कि ट्रिकी कुछ भी नहीं खा रहा था और उसे उल्टियाँ हो रही थी।

डॉ. जेम्स ने श्रीमती पम्फ्रे को दो सप्ताह के लिए निगरानी रखने के लिए उसे अस्पताल में भर्ती करने का सुझाव दिया, जिससे उसका उचित उपचार किया जा सके। श्रीमती पम्फ्रे दु:खी थीं, लेकिन उन्होंने ट्रिकी को ले जाने की अनुमति दे दी। डॉ. जेम्स ट्रिकी को कम्बल में लपेटकर अपनी कार तक ले गए, जब तक नौकरानियों ने डॉ. जेम्स की कार में वे वस्तुएँ रखना शुरू कर दिया, जिनकी ट्रिकी को अस्पताल में भर्ती होने के दौरान आवश्यकता होगी।

अस्पताल में, शुरू के दो दिनों तक ट्रिकी को पानी ही आहार के रूप में दिया गया। दूसरे दिन के अन्त में, ट्रिकी ने अपने आस-पास कुछ रुचि दिखानी शुरू कर दी। तीसरे दिन, वह धीरे-धीरे चलने लगा और बगीचे में ग्रेहाउण्ड (शिकारी कुत्ते) के साथ शामिल हो गया। बाद में, जब भोजन परोसा गया, तो वह उत्साह से दौड़ पड़ा। उसने अपने लिए रखा खाना भी खा लिया।

जब ट्रिकी ठीक हो रहा था, तब श्रीमती पम्फ्रे ट्रिकी की सेहत के बारे में जानने के लिए दिन में कई बार डॉ. जेम्स के क्लीनिक में फोन करती थी। डॉ. जेम्स ने उन्हें आश्वासन दिया कि ट्रिकी अब खतरे से बाहर है। यह सुनकर श्रीमती पम्फ्रे ने ट्रिकी के लिए अण्डे और वाइन भेजना शुरू कर दिया। ट्रिकी के लिए भेजा गया खाना डॉ. जेम्स और उनके समूह के लोगो ने खाया।

दो सप्ताह के बाद, डॉ. जेम्स ने फोन करके श्रीमती पम्फ्रे को सूचित किया कि ट्रिकी बिल्कुल स्वस्थ है और घर जा सकता था। श्रीमती पम्फ्रे आधे घण्टे के अन्दर ही चिकित्सालय पहुँच गईं। जैसे ही कुत्ते ने अपनी मालकिन को देखा, वह उसकी गोद में कूद गया और उसका चेहरा चाटने लगा। ट्रिकी को पहले के जैसा उत्साहित पाकर श्रीमती पम्फ्रे बहुत खुश हुईं। उन्होनें डॉ. जेम्स हेरियट को धन्यवाद दिया और इलाज को 'चिकित्सा की सफलता' कहा।

Objective Questions

1. Mrs. Pumphrey was a ....
   (a) poor lady (b) selfish lady
   (c) rich lady (d) gentle lady

2. Mrs. Pumphrey was a ....
   (a) maid (b) caretaker
   (c) nurse (d) mistress

3. Who was Tricki?
   (a) A cat (b) A monkey
   (c) A dog (d) A rabbit

4. Tricki's actual problem was
   (a) malaria
   (b) malnutrition
   (c) fever
   (d) vomiting because of excess of food

5. Tricki would tackle a meal at any hour because his only fault was
   (a) attraction (b) hunger
   (c) willingness (d) greed

6. During treatment of the dog, doctor
   (a) operated the dog
   (b) gave the dog many things to eat
   (c) kept an eye on the dog, giving him no food, but plenty of water
   (d) gave the dog a lot of food, but no water

7. In how many hours did Mrs. Pumphrey reached the surgery of Tricki?
   (a) Two an hour
   (b) One an hour
   (c) Half an hour
   (d) Three an hour

8. In two weeks, Tricki had been transformed into a lithe, hard-muscled
   (a) human being (b) bird
   (c) animal (d) insect

9. When Mrs. Pumphrey came to pick up Tricki, ... opened the door of her car.
   (a) Mr. Herriot (b) The cook
   (c) The chauffeur (d) The maid servant

10. What type of questions did Dr. Herriot avoid when Tricki was hospitalised?
    (a) Whether Tricki was out of hunger
    (b) Whether Tricki's cushions were being formed regularly
    (c) Whether Tricki had worn the correct coat according to the weather
    (d) Both (b) and (c)

11. At the clinic, the doctor gave Tricki
    (a) fruits and vegetables (b) injections and medicines
    (c) no food for two days (d) chocolates

12. For how many days was Tricki given no food?
    (a) One day (b) Four days
    (c) Two days (d) Six days

13. Who was Mr. Herriot?
    (a) A compounder
    (b) A doctor
    (c) A neighbour of Mrs. Pumphrey
    (d) A trainer of dogs

14. What was Tricki's only fault?
    (a) Barking (b) Attacking
    (c) Biting (d) Greed

Answers

1. (c) 2. (d) 3. (c) 4. (d) 5. (d) 6. (c) 7. (c) 8. (c) 9. (c) 10. (d) 11. (c) 12. (c)
13. (b) 14. (d)

02 The Thief's Story

In this story, a young thief named Hari Singh encounters a trusting and kind man named Anil. Hari met Anil when he was 15 years old while he was watching a wrestling match. Hari thought that he could easily steal from Anil. So, he goes to Anil and asks to work for him, even though Anil can't pay him. Anil agrees and Hari begins living with him on the condition that Hari has to cook.

On the first day, Anil finds that Hari has lied to him. However, he still keeps Hari and tells him that he would teach him how to cook. Apart from cooking, Anil also taught Hari to write his name and promised to teach him how to write whole sentences and to add numbers.

One evening, Anil returns home with money from selling a book to a publisher, which he keeps under the mattress. Hari feels tempted to steal it. He remembers that he has been working for Anil for almost a month and had gained Anil's trust. Anil had given the key of the room to Hari. For Hari, this was the opportunity to rob Anil. However, due to Anil's trust, it was a difficult task for Hari. But he put away these thoughts and decided to rob Anil that night. Hari goes into Anil's room while he's asleep, takes the money from under the mattress and plans to catch a train to Lucknow. When he counted the money, he was happy to find ₹ 600.

Hari arrives at the train station but does not catch the train. Hari realised that he had no friends except for Anil, the man he robbed. Hari decided to leave the station and thought about how Anil would feel when he would come to know about the theft. Soon, he reached the maidan. It was november and it had started raining.

In the excitement of theft, Hari forgot that apart from giving him some money, Anil also educated him. He understood that it was easy to steal but it was difficult to be respected like Anil. Finally, Hari decided to go back to Anil. He went back into the room and put back the wet currency notes under the mattress and went to sleep.

Hari woke up late in the morning. He found that Anil had already prepared tea. Anil gave a fifty rupee note to Hari which was still wet. He told Hari that he had earned some money by selling a book to a publisher and now would be able to pay him regularly. He also told Hari that they would start writing sentences from that day. Hari felt that Anil knew about the theft but he didn't say anything to him about it.

इस कहानी में, एक हरी सिंह नामक युवा चोर एक विश्वास करने वाले और दयालु व्यक्ति अनिल से मिलता है। हरी अनिल से 15 वर्ष की आयु में मिला था, जब वह कुश्ती का मुकाबला देख रहा था। हरी ने सोचा कि वह आसानी से अनिल के यहाँ चोरी कर सकता था। इसलिए, वह अनिल के पास जाता है और उससे अपने लिए काम माँगता है, यद्यपि अनिल उसे वेतन नहीं दे सकता था। अनिल सहमत हो जाता है और हरी उसके साथ इस शर्त पर रहना प्रारम्भ कर देता है कि हरी को खाना पकाना पड़ेगा।

पहले दिन ही, अनिल जान जाता है कि हरी ने उससे झूठ बोला था। हालाँकि, वह फिर भी हरी को रखता है और उससे कहता है कि वह उसे सिखा देगा कि खाना कैसे बनाया जाता है। खाना पकाने के अतिरिक्त, अनिल ने हरी को उसका नाम लिखना सिखाया और उसे पूरा वाक्य लिखना और अंकों को जोड़ना सिखाने का वायदा किया।

एक शाम, अनिल एक पुस्तक प्रकाशक को पुस्तक बेचने पर मिली धनराशि के साथ घर वापस लौटता है, जिसे वह गद्दे के नीचे रख देता है। हरी उसे चुराने के लिए ललचाता है। उसे याद आता है कि वह लगभग एक महीने से अनिल के लिए कार्य कर रहा है और अनिल का विश्वास प्राप्त कर चुका था। अनिल ने कमरे की चाबी हरी को दी थी। हरी के लिए, यह अनिल को लूटने का अवसर था। हालाँकि, अनिल के भरोसे के कारण, हरी के लिए एक मुश्किल कार्य था। लेकिन उसने इन विचारों को दूर किया और उस रात अनिल को लूटने का निश्चय किया। जब अनिल सो रहा होता है, तो हरी उसके कमरे में जाता है, गद्दे के नीचे से धनराशि निकाल लेता है और लखनऊ की ट्रेन पकड़ने की योजना बनाता है। जब उसने धनराशि गिनी, तो उसे ₹ 600 प्राप्त करके प्रसन्नता हुई।

हरी स्टेशन पर पहुँचता है, लेकिन ट्रेन नहीं पकड़ता। हरी को महसूस होता है कि अनिल जिसे उसने लूट लिया था उसके अतिरिक्त उसका अन्य कोई मित्र नहीं है, हरी स्टेशन से निकलने का निश्चय करता है और सोचता है कि चोरी के बारे में पता चलने पर अनिल को कैसा महसूस होगा। जल्दी ही, वह मैदान में पहुँच जाता है। वह नवम्बर का महीना था और बारिश होने लगी थी।

चोरी की उत्तेजना में हरी भूल गया था कि थोड़ी धनराशि देने के अतिरिक्त अनिल ने उसे शिक्षित भी किया था। वह समझ जाता है कि चोरी करना आसान है, लेकिन अनिल के समान सम्मान प्राप्त करना मुश्किल है। अन्ततः हरी अनिल के पास वापस जाने का निश्चय करता है। वह कमरे में वापस गया और गीली धनराशि को वापस गद्दे के नीचे रखकर सोने चला गया।

हरी सुबह देर से जागा। उसने देखा कि अनिल ने पहले ही चाय बना ली थी। अनिल ने हरी को पचास रुपये का नोट दिया, जो अभी भी गीला था। उसने हरी को बताया कि उसने प्रकाशक की एक पुस्तक बेचकर कुछ धनराशि अर्जित की थी और अब नियमित रूप से उसे वेतन देगा। उसने हरी को यह भी बताया कि वे उसी दिन से वाक्य लिखना प्रारम्भ करेंगे। हरी को महसूस हुआ कि अनिल चोरी के बारे में जानता था, लेकिन उसने उससे चोरी के बारे में कुछ भी नहीं कहा।

Objective Questions

1. Who is the narrator of the story 'The Thief's Story'?
(a) Ruskin Bond (b) Anil
(c) Hari Singh (d) Anil's friend

2. What did Anil do to the food cooked by the boy on the first day?
(a) Ate it happily
(b) Kept it in the refrigerator
(c) Threw it to a stray dog
(d) Asked the boy to eat it all

3. What made Anil give up on his decision to throw Hari Singh out?
(a) His happy face (b) His honesty
(c) His appealing smile (d) His hard work

4. Who was watching a wrestling match?
(a) The Narrator (b) Hari Singh
(c) Anil (d) None of these

5. Who was the thief in the story 'The Thief's Story'?
(a) Hari Singh (b) Anil
(c) Mangal Pandey (d) Suresh

6. What was the name of the shop above which Anil lived?
(a) Laddu Sweet Shop
(b) Ganga Sweet Shop
(c) Jumna Sweet Shop
(d) Jogi Sweet Shop

7. What did Hari Singh want from Anil?
(a) Work (b) Money
(c) Home (d) Eatables

8. Hari Singh did not to cook, but told that he could cook, because ....
(a) he wanted work and food
(b) he wanted some place to sleep for a night
(c) he wanted to train Anil as a cook
(d) he wanted to learn cooking

9. What kind of jobs did Hari Singh do for Anil?
(a) Making tea
(b) Bringing day's supplies
(c) Doing odd jobs
(d) All of the above

10. When the train had gone, the thief found himself
(a) out of the station
(b) away from home
(c) at the ticket office
(d) on the deserted platform

11. How old was Hari Singh when he met Anil?
(a) 15 years (b) 17 years
(c) 20 years (d) 21 years

12. Anil taught Hari Singh to ....
(a) write only his name
(b) cook and add numbers
(c) cook, write and add numbers
(d) cook and write

13. Who does 'I' refer to in the story, 'The Thief's Story'?
(a) Hari Singh
(b) Anil
(c) The writer of the story
(d) The previous employer of the thief

14. Who came with a small bundle of notes one evening?
(a) The thief
(b) A publisher
(c) Anil
(d) A master

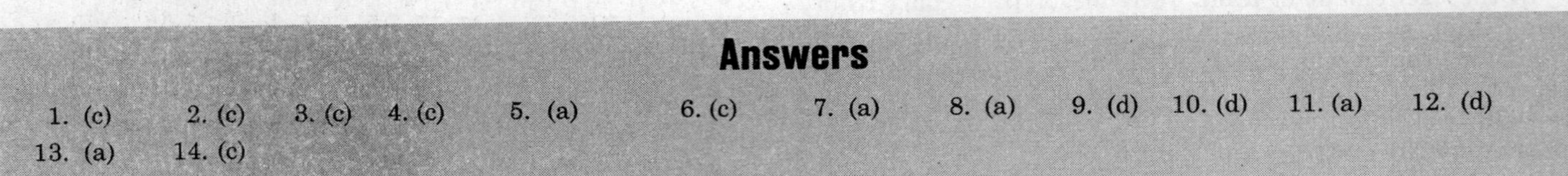

Answers

1. (c) 2. (c) 3. (c) 4. (c) 5. (a) 6. (c) 7. (a) 8. (a) 9. (d) 10. (d) 11. (a) 12. (d) 13. (a) 14. (c)

03 The Necklace

Summary of the Lesson पाठ का सार

This story revolves around Matilda Loisel, a beautiful young woman born into a family of clerks. Matilda desires a life of luxury and elegance. Despite her beauty and charm, Matilda marries a clerk who worked in the office of Education. Therefore, she leads a life of dissatisfaction and desires for wealth and social status.

One evening, M. Loisel returned from his office with a large envelope. The envelope consisted of an invitation to a ball (party) at the Minister's residence. M. Loisel thought that his wife would be happy to read the invitation but she was not happy to see the invitation. She denied the invite as she does not have a suitable attire and accessories. Her husband, eager to please her, offered money for a new dress. After Matilda got her new dress, she wanted new jewellery to complete her look. So, her husband advised her that she should go to Madam. Forestier, her friend and borrow her jewellery. Next day, Matilda went to her friend's house. She told Mme. Forestier her problem and borrowed a diamond necklace. The night of the ball arrived and Matilda was happy at the occasion. She looked very beautiful. She danced with great enthusiasm and happiness and went home at 4 am. When Matilda returned home and was changing her dress, she noticed that the necklace was not around her neck. She cried and informed her husband that she had lost the necklace. So, they searched everywhere but the necklace was not found.

Now, Matilda and Loisel urgently needed a replacement of the necklace. They found a similar one at a shop at Palais Royal, priced at forty thousand francs. They bought the necklace for thirty-six thousand, but that was still too much. Loisel had only eighteen thousand francs from his father, so he borrowed the rest from various lenders. This put them in a tough financial situation, and they spent years struggling to pay off their debts.

After replacing the necklace, Liosels changed their lifestyle. They moved to a smaller house and even dismissed their maid. Matilda did household chores. Matilda's appearance also changed. They repaid the debts after 10 years.

One Sunday, while walking in the Champs-Elysees, Matilda encountered Mme. Forestier. Matilda approached her and revealed the truth about the necklace. Madam. Forestier was touched by Matilda's honesty. However, she revealed that the original necklace had been fake and worth only five hundred francs.

यह कहानी मटिल्डा लोइसेल के इर्द-गिर्द घूमती है, जो लिपिकों के परिवार में पैदा हुई एक खूबसूरत युवा महिला है। मटिल्डा समृद्धि और उत्तम जीवन चाहती है। अपनी सुन्दरता और आकर्षण के बावजूद मटिल्डा ने एक लिपिक से शादी की, जो शिक्षा के कार्यालय में कार्य करता था। इसलिए वह असन्तोषपूर्ण जीवन गुजारती है एवं धन तथा सामाजिक प्रतिष्ठा की प्राप्ति की इच्छा रखती है।

एक शाम एम. लोइसेल एक बड़ा लिफाफा लेकर अपने कार्यालय से लौटे। लिफाफे में मन्त्री के आवास पर एक नृत्य (समारोह) का निमन्त्रण था। एम. लोइसेल ने सोचा कि उसकी पत्नी निमन्त्रण पढ़कर खुश होगी, लेकिन वह निमन्त्रण देखकर प्रसन्न नहीं हुई। उसने निमन्त्रण अस्वीकार कर दिया, क्योंकि उसके पास उपयुक्त पोशाक एवं जेवरात नहीं थे। उत्सुकतावश उसके पति ने उसे खुश करने के लिए नई पोशाक के लिए पैसे दे दिए। अपनी नई पोशाक प्राप्त करने के पश्चात् मटिल्डा सम्पूर्ण वेशभूषा को पूर्ण करने के लिए नए आभूषण चाहती थी, तो उसके पति ने उसे सुझाव दिया कि उसे अपनी मित्र मैडम फॉरेस्टर के पास जाना चाहिए। अगले दिन मटिल्डा अपनी मित्र के घर गई। उसने मैडम फॉरेस्टर को अपनी समस्या बताई और एक हीरों का हार उधार ले लिया। बॉल पार्टी की रात आ गई और इस अवसर पर मटिल्डा प्रसन्न थी। वह बहुत सुन्दर लग रही थी। वह बहुत ही उत्साह और खुशी से नाच रही थी और सुबह चार बजे पार्टी से घर चली गई। जब मटिल्डा घर लौटी और अपनी पोशाक बदल रही थी, तब उसने देखा कि हार उसके गले में नहीं था। उसने रोते हुए अपने पति को बताया कि उसने हार खो दिया है, इसलिए उन्होंने प्रत्येक जगह हार को खोजा, लेकिन वह नहीं मिला।

अब, मटिल्डा और लोइसेल को तत्काल उस हार को बदलकर दूसरा हार लेने की आवश्यकता थी। उन्हें पैलेस रॉयल की दुकान में उस हार के जैसा समान हार मिला, जिसकी कीमत चालीस हजार फ्रेंक थी। उन्होंने हार छत्तीस हजार में खरीदा, लेकिन अभी भी बहुत महँगा था। लोइसेल के पास अपने पिता से प्राप्त हुए केवल अट्ठारह हजार फ्रेंक थे, इसलिए उसने बाकी राशि विभिन्न उधारदाताओं से उधार ली। इसके कारण वे कठिन वित्तीय स्थिति में आ गए थे और उन्होंने अपना कर्ज चुकाने के लिए संघर्ष करते हुए कई वर्ष बिताए।

हार बदलने के बाद, लोइसेल ने अपनी जीवन-शैली बदल दी। वे एक छोटे से घर में रहने लगे और यहाँ तक की उन्होंने अपनी नौकरानी को भी हटा दिया। मटिल्डा घर का कार्य किया करती थी। मटिल्डा का रूप-रंग भी बदल गया था। उन्होंने दस वर्ष बाद धीरे-धीरे अपना कर्ज चुकाया।

एक रविवार को चैप्स-एलिसीज में घूमते समय मटिल्डा का सामना मैडम फॉरेस्टयर से हुआ। मटिल्डा ने उससे सम्पर्क किया और हार के बारे में सच्चाई बताई। मैडम फॉरेस्टियर मटिल्डा की ईमानदारी देखकर प्रभावित हो गई। हालाँकि उसने खुलासा किया कि असली हार नकली था और उसकी कीमत केवल पाँच सो फ्रेंक थी।

Objective Questions

1. Name a pretty young women who married to a clerk.
   (a) Madam Forestier (b) Narrator
   (c) Matilda Loisel (d) None of these

2. Matilda's husband was
   (a) a minister (b) a businessman
   (c) an officer (d) a petty clerk

3. Who was Madam Forestier and what did she give to Matilda?
   (a) Good friend of Matilda
   (b) Husband of Matilda
   (c) Necklace
   (d) Both (a) and (c)

4. In which family was Matilda born?
   (a) Rich family (b) Small family
   (c) Family of clerks (d) None of these

5. Where did M. Loisel use to work?
   (a) Board of Education
   (b) Board of Public Education
   (c) Ministry of Education
   (d) Ministry of Public Instruction

6. For what had Loisel saved four hundred francs?
   (a) To buy a bicycle (b) To buy a music player
   (c) To buy a shirt (d) To buy a gun

7. Where did Matilda's husband receive the invitation from?
   (a) Ministry of Health and Family Welfare
   (b) Ministry of Public Instruction
   (c) Ministry of External Affairs
   (d) None of the above

8. What did her husband (M. Loisel) tell her after realising Matilda's distress?
   (a) Buy a new car
   (b) Buy a new dress
   (c) Buy a sandal
   (d) None of the above

9. Madam Loisel suffered from
   (a) the poverty of her apartment
   (b) the shabby walls
   (c) the worm chairs
   (d) All (a), (b) and (c) are correct

10. Matilda always remained
    (a) unhappy
    (b) happy
    (c) delighted
    (d) contended

11. Who had invited Matida's husband for the ball (Party)?
    (a) The Prime Minister
    (b) The President
    (c) The Minister of Public Instruction
    (d) The Governor

12. Which of the following statments is correct?
    (a) Matilda borrowed a necklace of real diamonds and returned a necklace of real diamonds.
    (b) Matilda borrowed a necklace of real diamonds but returned a necklace of artificial diamonds.
    (c) Matilda borrowed a necklace of artificial diamonds but returned a necklace of real diamonds.
    (d) Matilda borrowed a necklace of artificial diamonds and returned a necklace of artificial diamonds.

Answers

1. (c) 2. (d) 3. (d) 4. (c) 5. (a) 6. (d) 7. (b) 8. (b) 9. (d) 10. (a) 11. (c) 12. (c)

04 The Midnight Visitor

Summary of the Lesson पाठ का सार

This is a story about two smart secret agents who try to trick each other. Ausable, a secret agent is expecting to receive a very important report about some new missiles. Another secret agent, Max also wants to get the report and so, threatens Ausable.

The story begins with Fowler, a young writer, meeting Ausable, a supposed secret agent, at a French hotel. Ausable, did not fit the typical image of a spy. Fowler was disappointed to see Ausable as he could not find any characteristics of a secret agent in Ausable as he had read. Ausable told Fowler that soon he would receive a very important report that could change the course of history.

As they enter Ausable's room, they were surprised to find a man named Max standing inside with a pistol. Max demands the paper Ausable was expecting, claiming it will be safer with him. Ausable calmly sat down and complained about the balcony that is attached to his room. He told Fowler that this was the second time that someone used the balcony to secretly enter his room.

Ausable explained to Fowler that it was actually not his balcony, but the balcony of the next apartment. He further told him that his room and the next apartment were earlier a larger unit. Now, the unit had been divided, but the balcony still existed. The management had done nothing to block the balcony.

Max, then, told Ausable that the report would arrive in half an hour. Ausable wanted to know how Max came to know about the report, but Max asked Ausable how his people had got that report. Just then, someone knocked on the door. Ausable calmly explained that he had asked the police to check on him for safety. This made Max nervous. He insisted they send the police away and escaped from the balcony with a loud scream.

When the door opened, it was not the police, but a waiter with a drink for Ausable. Ausable clarified that there were no police, just the waiter he was expecting. Fowler asked about the balcony and was shocked when Ausable revealed the truth that there was no balcony. This surprising twist left both Fowler and the reader amazed at Ausable's clever plan to outsmart Max and protect the important report.

यह कहानी दो चतुर गुप्तचरों के विषय में है, जो एक-दूसरे को धोखा देने का प्रयास करते हैं। आजेबल, एक गुप्तचर कुछ नई मिसाइलों के बारे में एक बहुत ही महत्त्वपूर्ण रिपोर्ट (खबर) प्राप्त करने की आशा कर रहा है। एक अन्य गुप्तचर, मैक्स भी रिपोर्ट प्राप्त करना चाहता है और इसलिए आजेबल को धमकी देता है।

कहानी की शुरुआत एक युवा लेखक, फाउलर के एक तथा कथित गुप्तचर, आजेबल से एक फ्रांसीसी होटल में मुलाकात से होती है। आजेबल एक जासूस की विशिष्ट छवि में उपयुक्त नहीं बैठता। फाउलर आजेबल को देखकर निराश हो जाता है, क्योंकि उसने जैसा पढ़ा था, वैसी गुप्तचर जैसी कोई विशेषता उसे आजेबल में नजर नहीं आई थी। आजेबल फाउलर को बताता है कि जल्द ही उसे एक बहुत ही महत्त्वपूर्ण रिपोर्ट मिलेगी, जो देश के इतिहास की दिशा बदल सकती है।

जैसे ही वे आजेबल के कक्ष में प्रवेश करते हैं, वे मैक्स नाम के एक व्यक्ति को पिस्तौल के साथ अन्दर खड़ा हुआ देखकर आश्चर्यचकित हो जाते हैं। मैक्स उस दस्तावेज की माँग करता है, जिसकी प्रतीक्षा आजेबल कर रहा था और यह दावा करता है कि यह उसके पास अधिक सुरक्षित रहेगा। आजेबल शान्तिपूर्वक बैठ जाता है और अपने कमरे से जुड़ी हुई बालकनी के बारे में शिकायत करता है। वह फाउलर को बताता है कि यह दूसरी बार था, जब किसी ने बालकनी का प्रयोग करके चोरी-छिपे उसके कमरे में प्रवेश किया था।

आजेबल ने फाउलर को समझाया कि वह वास्तव में उसकी बालकनी नहीं है, बल्कि अगले मकान की बालकनी है। उसने आगे बताया कि उसका कमरा और अगला मकान पहले एक ही थे, अब यह विभाजित हो चुके थे, लेकिन बालकनी अभी भी थी। प्रबन्धन (मैनेजमैंट) ने बालकनी को बन्द करने के सम्बन्ध में कुछ नहीं किया था।

इसके बाद, मैक्स ने आजेबल को बताया कि रिपोर्ट आधे घण्टे में आ जाएगी। आजेबल जानना चाहता था कि मैक्स को सूचना-पत्र के बारे में कैसे पता चला, लेकिन मैक्स ने आजेबल से पूछा कि उसके लोगों को यह रिपोर्ट कैसे प्राप्त हुई? तभी किसी ने दरवाजा खटखटाया। आजेबल ने शान्ति से बताया कि उसने पुलिस से उसकी सुरक्षा का ध्यान रखने के लिए कहा था। इससे मैक्स घबरा गया। उसने जोर देकर कहा कि वे पुलिस को वापस भेज दें और एक तेज चीख के साथ बालकनी से बच निकला।

जब दरवाजा खुला, तो वहाँ पुलिस नहीं थी, बल्कि एक वेटर आजेबल के लिए पेय (ड्रिंक) के साथ खड़ा था। आजेबल ने स्पष्ट किया कि वहाँ कोई पुलिस नहीं थी, केवल वेटर था, जिसकी उसे प्रतिक्षा थी। फाउलर ने बालकनी के बारे में पूछा और उसे आश्चर्य हुआ, जब आजेबल ने सच्चाई बताई कि वह कोई बालकनी नहीं थी। इस आश्चर्यजनक मोड़ ने फाउलर और पाठक दोनों को आजेबल की फाउलर को चकमा देने और महत्त्वपूर्ण रिपोर्ट को सुरक्षित रखने की चतुर योजना ने हैरान कर दिया।

Objective Questions

1. Who came to meet Ausable in the story 'The Midnight Visitor'?
(a) Fowler (b) A policeman
(c) Ausable's father (d) Max

2. Ausable did not fit any description of a ....
(a) secret agent (b) teacher
(c) stuntman (d) policeman

3. Ausable had never lost the American accent he had brought to Paris from ....
(a) London (b) Japan
(c) Boston (d) Russia

4. Some day soon, that paper may well affect the course of ....
(a) History (b) Math
(c) Geography (d) Economy

5. As the light came on, Fowler has his first .... of the day.
(a) surprise (b) authentic thrill
(c) gift (d) project

6. Ausable moved to an .... and sat down heavily.
(a) armchair (b) cupboard (c) door (d) desk

7. Max said that he did not know about the ....
(a) room (b) secret report
(c) Ausable (d) balcony

8. Fowler was standing stiffly not far from ....
(a) Max (b) Henry
(c) Ausable (d) Balcony

9. Ausable said that the police will not hesitate to ....
(a) arrest (b) beat (c) shoot (d) torture

10. Max's face was black with ....
(a) joy (b) sorrow
(c) disappointment (d) anger

11. Max grasped the frame with his free hand to .... himself.
(a) support (b) jump (c) climbed (d) stood

Answers

1. (a) 2. (a) 3. (c) 4. (a) 5. (b) 6. (a) 7. (d) 8. (c) 9. (c) 10. (d) 11. (a)

05 Bholi

Summary of the Lesson पाठ का सार

The story 'Bholi' by K.A. Abbas follows the life of a young girl named Sulekha who is called Bholi due to her simplicity. Bholi is the fourth daughter of Ramlal, a rich and successful farmer. From a young age, Bholi faces several challenges. At ten months old, she has fallen off the cot which had damaged some part of her brain. Since then she remained a backward child. When she was two years old, she suffered from smallpox which left her disfigured with deep black marks. Bholi also struggled to speak and stammered. So, other children often made fun of Bholi.

When a girls' primary school opens in their village, the Tehsildar encourages Ramlal to send his daughters to school as an example. So, Ramlal and his wife decide to send Bholi to school. Bholi was initially scared to go to school as she feels that she is going to be sold. On the day of the school, she is bathed, her hair is oiled and she is given new clothes to wear. When Bholi reaches the school, Bholi was happy to see other girls of her same age. In school, Bholi finds comfort and encouragement from her kind teacher. She begins to learn and gains confidence

के. एस. अब्बास द्वारा लिखित कहानी 'भोली' सुलेखा नाम की एक युवा लड़की के जीवन का अनुकरण करती है, जिसे उसकी सादगी के कारण भोली कहा जाता है। भोली एक अमीर और सफल किसान रामलाल की चौथी बेटी है। बहुत छोटी आयु से ही भोली को अनेक चुनौतियों का सामना करना पड़ा है। दस महीने की आयु में वह चारपाई से गिर गई थी, जिसके कारण उसके मस्तिष्क का कुछ हिस्सा क्षतिग्रस्त हो गया। तभी से वह एक पिछड़ी हुई बच्ची बनकर रह गई, जब वह दो वर्ष की थी, तब उसे चेचक हो गया, जिससे उसका चेहरा काले गहरे निशानों के कारण विकृत हो गया। भोली को बोलने में भी कठिनाई होती थी और वह हकलाती थी। इसलिए अन्य बच्चे अक्सर भोली का मजाक उड़ाते थे।

जब उनके गाँव में लड़कियों के लिए प्राथमिक विद्यालय खुलता है, तो तहसीलदार, अन्य लोगों के लिए मिसाल बनने हेतु रामलाल को अपनी बेटियों को विद्यालय भेजने के लिए प्रोत्साहित करता है। इसलिए रामलाल और उसकी पत्नी भोली को विद्यालय भेजने का फैसला करते हैं। प्रारम्भ में भोली विद्यालय जाने से डर रही थी, क्योंकि उसे लगता था कि उसे बेच दिया जाएगा। विद्यालय जाने के दिन उसे नहलाया जाता है, उसके बालों में तेल लगाया जाता है और पहनने के लिए नए कपड़े दिए जाते हैं, जब भोली विद्यालय पहुँचती है, तो अपनी आयु की अन्य लड़कियों को देखकर प्रसन्न होती है। विद्यालय में भोली को अपने दयालु शिक्षक से सांत्वना और प्रोत्साहन मिलता है। वह सीखना शुरू करती है और आत्मविश्वास अर्जित करती है।

Years later, Bholi's family receives a marriage proposal from Bishamber Nath, an old but rich grocer. Bholi initially agreeed due to her sense of duty towards her family's honor. The wedding preparations begin. However, when Bishamber saw Bholi's disfigured face, he demanded a large sum of money as dowry. Ramlal, to save his family's honour, agrees to pay. But when Bholi learns of Bishamber's greed, she refuses to marry him in front of everyone.

Bholi's refusal shocks her family and guests. When Bishamber and everyone went away, Bholi informed her family that she would not marry and take care of her parents in their old age. She also told them that she would teach at the school just like her teacher. Sulekha's teacher who was watching all this drama approved Bholi's decision. She smiled at her with satisfaction just like an artist who is satisfied after completing her masterpiece.

वर्षों बाद, भोली के परिवार को एक बूढ़े, लेकिन अमीर किराना व्यापारी बिशम्भर नाथ से शादी का प्रस्ताव मिलता है। शुरू में भोली अपने परिवार के सम्मान के प्रति अपने कर्त्तव्य की भावना के कारण सहमत हो जाती है। शादी की तैयारियाँ शुरू हो जाती हैं, हालाँकि जब बिशम्भर ने भोली का विकृत चेहरा देखा, तो उसने दहेज के रूप में एक बड़ी धनराशि की माँग की। अपने परिवार के सम्मान को बचाने के लिए रामलाल धनराशि देने के लिए मान जाता है, लेकिन जब भोली को बिशम्भर के लालच के बारे में पता चलता है, तो वह सबके सामने उससे शादी करने से इंकार कर देती है।

भोली के इंकार से उसके परिवार और मेहमानों को सदमा लगता है, जब बिशम्भर और अन्य लोग चले जाते हैं, तो भोली अपने परिवार को बताती है कि वह शादी नहीं करेगी और वृद्धावस्था में अपने माता-पिता की देखभाल करेगी। वह उन्हें यह भी बताती है कि अपनी टीचर की तरह वह भी विद्यालय में पढ़ाएगी। सुलेखा की टीचर, जो यह सम्पूर्ण नाटक देख रही थी, भोली के निर्णय का समर्थन करती है। वह सन्तोष के साथ उनकी ओर देखकर मुस्कुराई, बिल्कुल उस कलाकार की तरह, जो अपनी उत्कृष्ट कृति को पूर्ण करने के बाद सन्तुष्ट हो जाता है।

Objective Questions

1. Ramlal's eldest daughter was
(a) Radha (b) Rekha (c) Sulekha (d) Kamala

Or Who was Ramlal's eldest daughter?
(a) Mangla (b) Champa
(c) Radha (d) Sulekha

2. What was Bholi's real name?
(a) Priya (b) Geeta
(c) Sulekha (d) Sita

3. Why did Tehsildar come to Ramlal's village?
(a) To meet the villagers people
(b) To attend Radha's wedding
(c) To perform the opening ceremony of the girl's school
(d) All of the above

4. Numberdar Ramlal had seven children ....

Or Bholi's father Ramlal had
(a) two sons and five daughters
(b) five sons and two daughters
(c) three sons and four daughters
(d) four sons and three daughters

5. Bholi was the daughter of
(a) Collector Ramlal (b) Tehsildar Ramlal
(c) Inspector Ramlal (d) Numberdar Ramlal

6. In which age, Bholi's suffered from an attack of small pox and her entire body was disfigured by deep black pock-marks?
(a) 3 years (b) 2 years
(c) 4 years (d) 5 years

7. How was Bholi treated in his family?
(a) She was not given new clothes
(b) No one cared to wash her clothes
(c) No one cared to comb her hair
(d) All of the above

8. What did Bishamber demand as dowry?
(a) Two thousand rupees
(b) Five thousand rupees
(c) Three thousand rupees
(d) Twenty thousand rupees

9. Why did Bholi talk very little?
(a) She stammered
(b) Other kids mimicked and made fun of her
(c) She was an introvert
(d) None of the above

10. Who used to wear old clothes by her sisters?
(a) Mangla (b) Champa
(c) Radha (d) Bholi

11. Who comforted Bholi in the classroom?
(a) Her friend
(b) Her teacher
(c) Her principal
(d) The monitor of the class

12. I will not have such a mean, greedy and contemptible coward as my ....
(a) husband (b) companion
(c) friend (d) classmate

Answers

1. (a) 2. (c) 3. (c) 4. (c) 5. (d) 6. (d) 7. (d) 8. (d) 9. (d) 10. (d) 11. (b) 12. (a)

Unit-13

01 Rain on the Roof

Stanza-Wise Explanation of the Poem

Stanza-wise Explanation परीक्षा में नहीं पूछा जाता है, यह केवल विद्यार्थियों को Poem का अर्थ समझाने के लिए दिया गया है।

1

When the humid shadows hover
Over all the starry spheres
And the melancholy darkness
Gently weeps in rainy tears,
What a bliss to press the pillow
Of a cottage-chamber bed
And lie listening to the patter
Of the soft rain overhead!

Word-Meaning

Word	Pronunciation	English Meaning	Hindi Meaning
Humid shadows	हुमिड शेडोज	clouds	बादल
Hover	होवर	hang	मँडराना
Starry spheres	स्टेरी स्फेर्अस	stars	तारों का समूह
Melancholy	मेलनचोली	sad	उदास
Bliss	ब्लिस	utmost joy	परमानन्द, हर्ष
Cottage chamber	कोटेज चेम्बर	room in a cottage	झोंपड़ी में कमरा
Patter	पैटर	sound of rain falling on the roof	बारिश की पटपटाहट की आवाज
Over head	ओवर हैड	above the head	सिर के ऊपर

Explanation In these lines, the poet describes a rainy night. The poet says that the stars in the sky are not visible as they are covered by the dark rainy clouds. The sky looks sad and the rain looks as if tears are falling from human eyes. This weather represents the poet's sorrowful mood. In such a mood, the only thing that can bring joy in the poet's heart is to lay down on the pillow of his bed in his cottage and listen to the soft sound of the rain falling on the roof.

2

Every tinkle on the shingles
Has an echo in the heart;
And a thousand dreamy fancies
Into busy being start,
And a thousand recollections
Weave their air-threads into woof,
As I listen to the patter
Of the rain upon the roof.

Word-Meaning

Word	Pronunciation	English Meaning	Hindi Meaning
Tinkle	टिन्कल	ringing sound	झंकार, टनटनाहट
Shingles	शिंगल्ज	rectangular tiles used on sloping roof	तख्ता
Echo	इको	resounding	गूँजना
Dreamy fancies into busy being	ड्रीमी फेन्सीज इनटु बिजी बींग	imaginary stories in my mind	काल्पनिक सपनों में व्यस्त व्यक्ति
Recollections	रिक्लेक्शन	memories / remembrances	स्मृतियाँ, यादें
Air threads	ऐअर-थ्रेड्स	dreamy memories	स्वप्नमय यादें
Woof	वूफ	the yarn women across the warp yarn in meaning. (also called pick, weft)	बुनना

Explanation In these lines, the poet now describes how the raindrops make a tinkling sound as they fall on the tiled rooftop of his cottage. According to the poet, each sound made by the rain is echoed by the beatings of his heart (heart beat). In other words, the sound of the rain affects the poet deeply. As he is listening to the sound, many images (dreamy fancies) come into his mind. He starts recollecting many memories of his childhood. These memories appear to be interwoven together to form a beautiful picture.

3

Now in memory comes my mother,
As she used in years agone,
To regard the darling dreamers
Ere she left them till the dawn:
O! I feel her fond look on me
As I list to this refrain
Which is played upon the shingles
By the patter of the rain.

Word-Meaning

Word	Pronunciation	English Meaning	Hindi Meaning
In memory comes	इन मेमोरी कम्स	remember	यादों में आती है
Agone	अगॉन	past time	बीता हुआ समय
Regard	रिगार्ड	observe	देखना, निहारना
The darling dreamers	द डार्लिंग ड्रीमर्स	one who dreams	प्यारे सपने देखने वाले
Ere	एरे	before	पहले
Dawn	डॉन	morning	भोर, सुबह
Fond look	फोंड लुक	a look of affection	प्यार भरी नजर
Refrain	रिफ्रेन	part of song that is repeated	गीत का दोहराया हुआ अंश
Played upon	प्लेइड अपॉन	the sound coming due to rain falling on	बारिश के गिरने की ध्वनि

Explanation In these lines, the poet says that out of the many memories the poet recollects, he identifies one fond memory of his mother. He remembers how many years ago, his mother used to look at him and his siblings lovingly while they slept and used to dream. She would look at her sleeping children every night because she knew she won't see them till the next morning. The poet can still feel the look of his mother while he lays on his bed and listens to the soft musical sound of the rain falling on the roof.

Central Idea of the Poem कविता का सार

परीक्षा में Poetry भाग की किन्हीं भी तीन Poems के नाम दिए जाते हैं, जिनमें से किसी एक Poem का Central Idea लिखना होता है। इसके लिए 3 अंक निर्धारित हैं।

The poem describes the poet's thoughts when he hears the sound of rain falling on the tiled roof of his cottage. The sound produced by the rain reminds the poet of a memory of his mother. This memory stays in his mind and calms him. Through rain, the poet highlights the healing power of nature.

According to him, the music produced by the simple act of falling of rain holds the power to bring back some of our fondest memories. These memories, then, provides us with comfort and calm us.

कविता कवि के उन विचारों का वर्णन करती है, जब वह अपनी झोंपड़ी की टाइल वाली छत पर गिरती हुई बारिश की आवाज सुनता है। बारिश से उत्पन्न आवाज कवि को उसकी माँ की याद दिलाती है। यह याद उसके मस्तिष्क में रहती है और उसे शान्त रखती है। बारिश के द्वारा, कवि प्रकृति की उपचारात्मक शक्ति को उजागर करता है।

उसके अनुसार, बारिश के गिरने के साधारण से कार्य से उत्पन्न संगीत में हमारी कुछ सबसे पसन्दीदा यादों को पुन: जीवित करने की शक्ति है। तब, ये यादें, हमें आराम और शान्ति प्रदान करती हैं।

Objective Questions

Read the stanzas given below and answer the questions that follow.

1 When the humid shadows hover
Over all the starry spheres,
And the melancholy darkness
Gently weeps in rainy tears,

(i) What time of the day is discussed in the given extract?
(a) Early morning (b) Afternoon
(c) Night (d) None of these

(ii) Why does the poet call the melancholy darkness 'weeping'?
(a) Because he is in a sad mood.
(b) Because it is dark all around.
(c) Because it is raining.
(d) Both (b) and (c)

(iii) Where is the poet when it is raining?
(a) In his cottage (b) In his school
(c) In his office (d) In his hostel

(iv) Which word in the stanza means 'humid'?
(a) Moist (b) dry (c) wet (d) chill

(v) What does the poet like to do when it rains?
(a) Eating snacks
(b) Listening to the music
(c) Roaming on the roof
(d) Lie on the bed and listen to the pitter- patter sound of the rain

2 Every tinkle on the shingles
Has an echo in the heart;
And a thousand dreamy fancies
Into busy being start,
And a thousand recollections weave their
air-threads into woof,

(i) What is the meaning of 'woof'?
(a) Noise (b) Weft
(c) Disgust (d) Peace

(ii) How does the heart echo?
(a) With sound sleep
(b) With the falling of the rain on the shingles
(c) With peace and happiness
(d) With the falling of the rain on the ground

(iii) How does the poet's mind get busy?
(a) With memories (b) With dreams
(c) With music (d) With peace

(iv) Which word in the extract means "rectangular wooden tiles used on roofs"?
(a) Shingles (b) Tinkle
(c) Echo (d) Fancies

(v) Which dreamy fancy is most dear to the poet?
(a) Of playing in the rain
(b) Of childhood bonding with siblings
(c) Of travel
(d) Of his mother

3 As she used in years agone,
To regard the darling dreamers,
Ere she left them till the dawn :
O! I feel her fond look on me
As I list to this refrain

(i) The poet of the poem from which these lines have been taken is
(a) Adrienne Rich
(b) Subramania Bharati
(c) Coates Kinney
(d) Robert Frost

(ii) Which sound is the poet listening to?
(a) The sound of the wind (b) The sound of the lightening
(c) The sound of the rain (d) The sound of the train

(iii) In the given lines, the poet is feeling
(a) sorrowful (b) relaxed
(c) nostalgic (d) regretful

(iv) The sound reminds the poet of
(a) his happy relaxed days
(b) his childhood
(c) the natural marvellous beauty of past
(d) his siblings

(v) 'Darling dreamers' in the extract refers to
(a) the poet and his siblings
(b) the poet and his friends
(c) the poet and his classmates
(d) the poet and his neighbours

Answers

1. (i) (c), (ii) (d), (iii) (a), (iv) (a), (v) (d) **2.** (i) (b), (ii) (b), (iii) (a), (iv) (a), (v) (d) **3.** (i) (c), (ii) (c), (iii) (c), (iv) (b), (v) (a)

02 The Lake Isle of Innisfree

Stanza-Wise Explanation of the Poem

Stanza-wise Explanation परीक्षा में नहीं पूछा जाता है, यह केवल विद्यार्थियों को Poem का अर्थ समझाने के लिए दिया गया है।

1 I will arise and go now, and go to Innisfree,
And a small cabin build there, of clay and wattles made:
Nine bean-rows will I have there, a hive for the honeybee,
And live alone in the bee-loud glade.

Word Meanings

Word	Pronunciation	English Meaning	Hindi Meaning
Arise	अराइज	stand up	उठना
Innisfree	इनिस्फ्री	an island in a lake	झील में एक द्वीप
Cabin	केबिन	a small wooden shelter	कुटिया, झोंपड़ी
Clay	क्ले	mud	मिट्टी
Wattles	वेट्ल्स	fences	बाड़े
Bean rows	बीन-रॉज	rows of bean plants	फली के पौधों की पंक्तियाँ
Hive	हाइव	structure made by bees, honeycomb	छत्ता
Bee-loud	बी-लाउड	the loud sound of bees buzzing	मधुमक्खियों की भिनभिनाहट
Glade	ग्लेड	path in a forest	जंगल का मार्ग

Explanation In the first line, the poet repeats the word 'go' to express his determination of going to the lake Isle of Innisfree. The poet says that he will wake up and go to an island of Innisfree. On the island, he would build a small house from clay and wattles (fences). He would grow nine rows of bean and would also have a hive for honey. The honeybees residing (living in the hive) will fill the place with a buzzing sound. The poet here intends to live alone on the island full of natural beauty.

2 And I shall have some peace there, for peace comes dropping slow Dropping from the veils of the morning to where the cricket sings
There midnight's all a glimmer, and noon a purple glow,
And evenings full of the linnet's wings.

Word Meaning

Word	Pronunciation	English Meaning	Hindi Meaning
Peace	पीस	calm	शान्ति
Veils	वेल्स	misty atmosphere in morning or a piece of cloth used to cover face of a woman	घूँघट, परदा
Cricket	क्रिकेट	an insect	झिंगुर
All a glimmer	आल अ ग्लीमर	shining	चमकना
Purple glow	पर्पल ग्लो	the light of afternoon	दोपहर की रोशनी/चमक
Linnet	लिनेट	a small bird of brown and grey colour	भूरे व गेहुँए रंग का पक्षी

Explanation In the first line, the poet repeats the word 'peace' to reveal the real reason for moving away from his current lifestyle.

The poet states that in the countryside, peace can be found at every location. It comes as naturally as the morning sun comes in the sky. It comes slowly just like the morning drops the veil of darkness.

In the morning the poet would hear the crickets singing. At noon, he would see the purple sky and at midnight he would look at the shining sky. In the evenings, poet would hear the sound of linnet flapping its wings.

3 I will arise and go now, for always night and day
I hear the lake water lapping with low sounds by the shore;
While I stand on the roadway or on the pavements grey,
I hear it in the deep heart's core

Word Meanings

Word	Pronunciation	English Meaning	Hindi Meaning
Lapping	लेपिंग	hit gently	टकराना
Low	लो	soft	कोमल, धीमा
Shore	शोर	bank of a river	किनारा
Roadway	रोडवे	road in the town	कस्बे की सड़क
Pavements grey	पेवमेन्ट्स ग्रे	dull and drab paths	फीका और नीरस रास्ता/ पगडण्डियाँ
Deep heart's core	डीप हर्टस् कोर	deep in my heart	दिल की गहराई में

Explanation In these lines, the poet takes a resolution to wake up and to go to Innisfree right now. He decides so because, in his mind, he hears for all day and night, the low and soft sound of the water reaching the shore of the island. He hears this sound even when he is standing on a road or a pavement in the city. The poet can hear the sound of the lake which makes a deep effect on his heart.

Central Idea of the Poem कविता का सार

परीक्षा में Poetry भाग की किन्हीं भी तीन Poems के नाम दिए जाते हैं, जिनमें से किसी एक Poem का Central Idea लिखना होता है। इसके लिए 3 अंक निर्धारित हैं।

The Poem 'The Lake Isle of Innisfree' is about the beauty and charm associated with the countryside as compared to the dull, grey and boring life of the city. This poem reveals the poets desire to escape from the noisy hustle and bustle of the city life and lead a simple life in the natural landscape of Innisfree, a lake island. For the poet, a simple and peaceful life with only a few simple needs is more delightful than the restless life of the city.

'The Lake Isle of Innisfree' कविता ग्रामीण क्षेत्र की सुन्दरता और आकर्षण के विषय में है, जिसकी तुलना शहर के नीरस, उदास और उबाऊ जीवन से की गई है। यह कविता, कवि की शहर के व्यस्त जीवन से बचकर इनिस्फ्री के टापू पर प्राकृतिक परिदृश्य में साधारण जीवन जीने की चाहत को दर्शाती है। कवि के लिए, केवल सामान्य जरूरतों के साथ साधारण और शान्तिपूर्ण जीवन, शहर के व्यस्त जीवन से अधिक आनन्दमय है।

Objective Questions

Read the stanzas given below and answer the questions that follows.

I will arise and go now and go to Innisfree,
And a small cabin build there, of clay and wattles made:
Nine bean-rows will I have there, a hive for the honeybee,
And live alone in the bee-loud glade.

(i) The fact that the poet of the given lines wants to go to Innisfree shows that
- (a) his childhood is spent in Innisfree
- (b) he wants peace and quiet
- (c) he loves nature
- (d) he is an old man

(ii) What is the rhyme scheme of the given stanza?
(a) abcb (b) abca
(c) abcd (d) abab

(iii) The kind of a house that the poet wants to live in reflects
(a) luxury (b) ancient times
(c) simplicity (d) All of these

(iv) What does the poet want to build?
(a) A big cabin (b) A small cabin
(c) A house (d) A room

(v) Which word in the stanza rhymes with 'made'?
(a) wattles (b) glade (c) honey bee (d) these

2 And I shall have some peace there, for peace comes dropping slow
Dropping from the veils of the morning to where the
cricket sings;
There midnight's all a glimmer, and noon a purple glow,
And evenings full of the linnet's wings.

(i) Who is the poet of this poem?
- (a) William Wordsworth
- (b) W.B Yeats
- (c) James Williams
- (d) P.B. Shelley

(ii) In the given lines, 'there' refers to
(a) a town (b) a village
(c) on mountains (d) Innisfree Island

(iii) How will you most probably describe the night 'there'?
(a) Dark and gloomy
(b) Charming and glimmering
(c) Peaceful and satisfactory
(d) Dark and glimmering

(iv) Find the opposite of the word 'fast'.
(a) good (b) slow
(c) dim (d) dark

(v) What does the poet hope to get there?
(a) Wealth (b) Money
(c) Peace (d) Parents

3 I will arise and go now, for always night and day
I hear the lake water lapping with low sounds by the shore;
While I stand on the roadway, or on the pavements grey,
I hear it in the deep heart's core.

(i) What will the poet hear?
(a) The lapping sound of water (b) The roaring of lion
(c) The singing sound (d) The laughing sound

(ii) Who is the poet of the poem?
(a) William Wordsworth
(b) William Shakespeare
(c) William Butler Yeats
(d) William Heats

(iii) 'Lake water lapping with low sounds' what image do these words draw in the mind?
(a) Flowing stream
(b) Sound of flowing stream
(c) Low soft sound of lake's water washing the shore
(d) None of the above

(iv) In the given lines, the poet shows
(a) a desire for peace
(b) a desire to go back to Innisfree
(c) a love for natural beauties
(d) a need to go away from the city

(v) The lines in the extract have been taken from
(a) Isle of Innisfree
(b) The Lake Isle of Innisfree
(c) The Road Not Taken
(d) No Men are Foreign

Answers

1. (i) (b), (ii) (d), (iii) (c), (iv) (b), (v) (b) **2.** (i) (b), (ii) (d), (iii) (b), (iv) (b), (v) (c) **3.** (i) (a), (ii) (c), (iii) (c), (iv) (b), (v) (b)

03 Wind

Stanza-Wise Explanation of the Poem

Stanza-wise Explanation परीक्षा में नहीं पूछा जाता है, यह केवल विद्यार्थियों को Poem का अर्थ समझाने के लिए दिया गया है।

1 Wind, come softly.
Don't break the shutters of the windows.
Don't scatter the papers.
Don't throw down the books on the shelf.

Word-Meaning

Word	Pronunciation	English Meaning	Hindi Meaning
Softly	सॉफ्टली	slowly	धीरे से
Shutters	शटर्स	hinged panel used to close and open windows	खिड़की का लोहे/लकड़ी का फ्रेम
Scatter	स्कैटर	throw in different directions	बिखेरना, फैला देना

Explanation In these lines, the poet requests the wind to blow gently and not destroy anything with its force. He asks the wind not to break the shutters of the windows and scatter the papers here and there. He also asks the wind not to throw down the books from the shelf. The repetition of the word 'don't' in these lines highlight the requests of poet for mercy.

2 There, look what you did –
You threw them all down.
You tore the pages of the books.
You brought rain again.

Word-Meaning

Word	Pronunciation	English Meaning	Hindi Meaning
Tore	टोर	separate by pulling	फाड़ना
Brought	ब्रोट	fetch, bring in	लाना

Explanation In these lines, as the wind had not paid any attention to the poet's request of not blowing strongly. The poet says that the wind has thrown down the books from the shelf and it torn the pages of the books. The poet also accuses that the wind has also bring rain with it.

3 You're very clever at poking fun at weaklings.
Frail crumbling houses, crumbling doors, crumbling rafters, crumbling wood, crumbling bodies, crumbling lives, crumbling hearts–the wind God winnows and crushes them all.

Word-Meaning

Word	Pronunciation	English Meaning	Hindi Meaning
Poking fun	पोकिंग फन	making fun of	मजाक उड़ाना
Weaklings	वीकलिंग्स	weak	कमजोर
Frail	फ्रेल	weak	दुर्बल
Crumbling	क्रम्बलिंग	breaking up	टुकड़े-टुकड़े करना
Rafters	राफ्टर्स	sloping beams supporting a roof	कड़ी
Winnows	विन्नोज	separate by throwing	छाँटना
Crushes	क्रशीस	destroy	कुचलना

Explanation In these lines, the poet seems to be little sad as well as accusatory (critical tone). The poet calls the wind clever as it makes fun of all weak things. The strong wind represents all the difficulties and struggles that an individual faces in life. The poet says that the wind destroys all weak things such as houses, doors, rafters and wood. It even destroys people, their lives and their hearts with its mighty power. The wind God continues destroying or separating weak people until, only the strong people (who can go through hardships and face challenges) remain.

4 He won't do what you tell him.
So, come, let's build strong homes,
Let's joint the doors firmly.
Practise to firm the body.
Make the heart steadfast.
Do this, and the wind will be friends with us.

Word-Meaning

Word	Pronunciation	English Meaning	Hindi Meaning
Firmly	फर्मलि	strongly	मजबूती से/दृढ़ता से
Firm	फर्म	make strong	मजबूत बनाना
Steadfast	स्टैडफास्ट	unmoved	अटल

Explanation In these lines, the poet addresses the readers and asks them to make themselves strong as the wind will not listen to them. The poet asks the readers to build strong houses and to close/fix the doors tightly so that wind cannot harm them.

He encourages his readers to become bold and strong so as to face all the troubles in life. The poet asks the readers to practice hard to get a firm mind as well as a strong body so that they can face the wind and any challenge of life. If they are able to do so, the wind will become their friend and will not harm them.

5 The wind blows out weak fires.
He makes strong fires roar and flourish.
His friendship is good.
We praise him everyday.

Word-Meaning

Word	Pronunciation	English Meaning	Hindi Meaning
Blow out	ब्लो आउट	extinguish	बुझाना
Roar	रोर	loud sound	गड़गड़ाहट
Flourish	फ्लरिश	*to develop*	बढ़ाना
Praise	प्रेज	admire	तारीफ/प्रशंसा करना

Explanation In these lines, the poet describes wind as both a destroyer and a creator.

As a destroyer, the wind blows out the weak fires. As a creator, it encourages and nurture strong fires. In other words, wind can destroy all weak things and can also flourish a thing which is already strong. The poet states that if we are strong, then the wind is a good friend to us and nothing can harm us. We will praise the wind God everyday for building our strength. Thus, we should make ourselves physically and mentally ready to accept all challenges. Once we are strong, we will easily overcome the challenges and live our lives comfortably.

Central Idea of the Poem कविता का सार

परीक्षा में Poetry भाग की किन्हीं भी तीन Poems के नाम दिए जाते हैं, जिनमें से किसी एक Poem का Central Idea लिखना होता है। इसके लिए 3 अंक निर्धारित हैं।

This poem depicts the power of wind and how it is destructive. The wind, as described in the poem, blows violently and breaks everything around. The poet has linked this powerful wind with the difficulties, obstacles and struggles of life. Just like the wind that destroys everything that is weak, these difficulties also easily break down weak people. Only strong people can withstand them. So, the poem, encourages us to have courage and firm determination. It gives a message that we must have strong hearts as well as will power to face any trouble or hardship of life.

यह कविता हवा की शक्ति और यह किस प्रकार विनाशकारी हो सकती है, इसका वर्णन करती है। कविता के वर्णन के अनुसार, हवा बहुत तीव्र गति से बहती है और अपने चारों ओर सब कुछ तोड़ देती है। कवि ने इस शक्तिशाली हवा को जीवन की कठिनाइयों, बाधाओं और संघर्ष से जोड़ा है। जिस प्रकार हवा प्रत्येक उस वस्तु को तोड़ देती है जो कमजोर है, जीवन की कठिनाइयाँ भी कमजोर लोगों को आसानी से तोड़ देती हैं। केवल शक्तिशाली लोग ही इसका सामना कर सकते हैं। इसलिए कविता हमें साहस और दृढ़ निश्चय के लिए प्रोत्साहित करती हैं। यह कविता सन्देश देती है कि हमें मजबूत दिल के साथ-साथ जीवन की कठिनाइयों या मुश्किलों का सामना करने की इच्छा शक्ति रखनी चाहिए।

Objective Questions

Read the stanzas given below and answer the questions that follow.

1 Wind, come softly.
Don't break the shutters of the windows,
Don't scatter the papers.
Don't throw down the books on the shelf.

(i) Who is the poet?
(a) William Wordsworth (b) Robert Frost
(c) Subramania Bharati (d) James Kirkup

(ii) From the given lines, the tone of the poet can be said to be
(a) friendly (b) order
(c) angry (d) requesting

(iii) The given lines tell us that the wind is blowing
(a) gently (b) forcefully
(c) continuously (d) slowly

(iv) In the poem, wind is symbolic of
(a) difficult times (b) trials and tribulations
(c) emotional outbursts (d) stress and suffering

(v) Find a word for 'thrown in different directions'.
(a) throw (b) blow
(c) scatter (d) None of these

2 There, look what you did –
You threw them all down.
You tore the pages of the books.
You brought rain again.
You're very clever at poking fun at weaklings.

(i) Name the poem from which this extract has been taken.
(a) Rain On The Roof
(b) On Killing a Tree
(c) A Legend of The Northland
(d) Wind

(ii) Whom does the poet address as 'you'?
(a) The hailstorm (b) The bird
(c) The wind (d) The squirrel

(iii) The given lines indicate that the poet is
(a) trying to give readers a moral lesson
(b) angry at the wind
(c) trying to stop the damage
(d) trying people to be strong

(iv) How does it deal with the 'weaklings'?
(a) It treats them kindly.
(b) It terrifies them with its fierce power.
(c) It ignores them.
(d) It does not harm them.

(v) What did the wind bring again?
(a) Fog (b) Storm
(c) Rain (d) Cloud

3 Frail crumbling houses,
crumbling doors,crumbling rafters,
crumbling wood, crumbling bodies,
crumbling lives crumbling hearts–
The wind god winnows and crushes them all.

(i) Why does wind first winnow and then crush?
(a) To separate weak from strong
(b) To show its power
(c) To play before killing
(d) All of the above

(ii) How does the poet describe the wind?
(a) Good (b) Forgiving
(c) Hasty (d) Cruel

(iii) Why is the word 'crumbling' repeated in the extract?
(a) For no obvious reason
(b) To improve the rhyming of the poem
(c) To emphasise the destruction caused by the wind
(d) To ignore the destruction caused by the wind

(iv) "The wind god winnows and crushes them all" indicates that
(a) the weak always lose
(b) only the strong remain in the world
(c) the wind god is always powerful
(d) the wind tests the courage of the people

(v) The word in the extract that does not indicate destruction is
(a) crumbling (b) crushes (c) frail (d) winnows

4 He won't do what you tell him.
So, come, let's build strong homes,
Let's joint the doors firmly.
Practise to firm the body.
Make the heart steadfast.

(i) What sort of houses does the poet ask us to build?
(a) Huts (b) Luxury houses
(c) Strong homes (d) Weak houses

(ii) Why will 'he' not listen?
(a) As he is deaf.
(b) As it is his nature to exploit the weak.
(c) As it is his nature to exploit the strong.
(d) As he is in a hurry.

(iii) 'You' in the first line refers to
(a) the poet (b) the strong people
(c) the poet's friend (d) the listener

(iv) "He won't do what you tell him". Who is 'He' in this line?
(a) Wind (b) God (c) Sun (d) All of these

(v) Which word is opposite of 'firmly' as used in the extract?
(a) Tightly (b) Highly (c) Loosely (d) Securely

Answers

1. (i) (c), (ii) (d), (iii) (b), (iv) (b), (v) (c) 2. (i) (d), (ii) (c), (iii) (b), (iv) (b), (v) (c) 3. (i) (a), (ii) (d), (iii) (c), (iv) (b), (v) (c)
4. (i) (c), (ii) (b), (iii) (d), (iv) (a), (v) (c)

04 A Slumber Did My Spirit Seal

Stanza-Wise Explanation of the Poem

Stanza-wise Explanation परीक्षा में नहीं पूछा जाता है, यह केवल विद्यार्थियों को Poem का अर्थ समझाने के लिए दिया गया है।

A slumber did my spirit seal-
I had no human fears.
She seemed a thing that could not feel
The touch of earthly years.

Word Meaning

Word	Pronunciation	English Meaning	Hindi Meaning
Slumber	स्लम्बर	sleep	निद्रा
Spirit	स्पिरिट	soul	आत्मा
Seemed	सीम्ड	appeared .	प्रतीत होना
Earthly	अर्थलि	related or pretaining to earth	सांसारिक

Explanation In this stanza, the poet has expressed his grief over the death of his loved one. He says that she had no usual human fears now as death is the ultimate fear for human beings.

When a person is alive, then he has many apprehensions and many fears like disease, famine etc. But death makes the end of all these fears because earthly years or usual fears seem to have no effect on his beloved now. She has passed away peacefully leaving everything behind.

No motion has she now, no force-
She neither hears nor sees,
Rolled round in Earth's diurnal course
With rocks and stones and trees.

Word Meaning

Word	Pronunciation	English Meaning	Hindi Meaning
Motion	मोशन	movement	हलचल
Force	फोर्स	strength	ताकत/शक्ति
Rolled	रोल्ड	moved	घूमना
Diurnal	ड्यूरनल	daily "earth's diurnal course" is earth's daily rotation on its axis.	दैनिक

Explanation In this stanza, the poet mentions that there is no motion in the body of his beloved as death has overcome her. Also, death has deprived her of her strength. She is unable to see and unable to hear. All her senses are dead now. She has adjusted herself with the routine activity of earth now. As the earth completes its routine of day and night with the rocks, stones and trees; so does the beloved of the poet now. She has become a part of the nature.

Central Idea of the Poem कविता का सार

परीक्षा में Poetry भाग की किन्हीं भी तीन Poems के नाम दिए जाते हैं, जिनमें से किसी एक Poem का Central Idea लिखना होता है। इसके लिए 3 अंक निर्धारित हैं।

In this poem the poet has expressed his grief over the death of his loved one. The poet is deeply grieved and troubled over this. He says that the death has affected his soul deeply. His beloved who is dead now has become a part of nature. She can not sense anything and has no fears. She is now above the worldly affairs and is now resting peacefully within the Earth.

इस कविता में कवि ने अपने किसी प्रियजन की मृत्यु पर अपना दुख व्यक्त किया है। कवि इस बात से अत्यधिक दुखी और परेशान है। वह कहता है कि इसकी मृत्यु ने उसकी आत्मा को गहराई से प्रभावित किया है। उसकी प्रेमिका जो अब मर चुकी है, प्रकृति का हिस्सा बन चुकी है। अब वह कुछ भी महसूस नहीं कर सकती और उसे कोई डर नहीं है। अब वह सांसारिक मामलों से ऊपर है और पृथ्वी के अन्दर शन्ति से आराम कर रही है।

Objective Questions

Read the stanzas given below and answer the questions that follow.

A slumber did my spirit seal—
I had no human fears.
She seemed a thing that could not feel
The touch of earthy years.

(i) By the use of the word 'slumber', the author is referring to ....

(a) sleep
(b) death
(c) unconsciousness
(d) None of these

(ii) Who is 'she' in the above extract?
(a) A loved one of the poet
(b) A mortal enemy of the poet
(c) An unknown person
(d) An immortal person

(iii) What does death do to human fears?
(a) Starts them (b) Ends them
(c) Increases them (d) Decreases them

(iv) 'She' in the above extract cannot feel the touch of earthy years. Why?
(a) She is lost (b) She has died
(c) She has left Earth (d) She is immortal

(v) What is the tone of the above extract?
(a) Sorrowful (b) Happy
(c) Nostalgic (d) Suspicious

2 No motion has she now, no force—
She neither hears nor sees,
Rolled round in Earth's diurnal course
With rocks and stones and trees.

(i) Identify the poem from which the above lines have been taken.
(a) The Road Not Taken
(b) A Slumber did My Spirit Seal
(c) A Legend of the Northland
(d) No Men are Foreign

(ii) What has death deprived her of?
(a) Strength (b) Sight
(c) Hearing (d) All of these

(iii) Following her death, what has she become?
(a) A ghost (b) A form of energy
(c) A part of nature (d) An angel

(iv) What does the author mean by 'Earth's diurnal course'?
(a) Earth's rotation on its axis
(b) Earth's revolution
(c) Earth's rotation on sun's axis
(d) All of the above

(v) Who does she roll around with now?
(a) Rocks (b) Stones
(c) Trees (d) All of these

3 A slumber did my spirit seal-
I had no human fears.
She seemed a thing that could not feel
The touch of earthly years.

(i) What actually is a 'slumber' here?
(a) Denote death (b) End of era
(c) Birth of new child (d) None of these

(ii) Who has sealed spirit of the poet?
(a) Death of his grand parents
(b) Death of his beloved
(c) Loss of child
(d) None of the above

(iii) Who is 'she' here in the third line?
(a) His mother (b) His beloved
(c) His daughter (d) None of these

(iv) Why did she can't feel the touch of Earthly years?
(a) Because she is senseless
(b) Because she is ill
(c) Because she has died
(d) Becasue she is lost

(v) The phrase 'the touch of Earthly years' means
(a) active and living
(b) life on Earth
(c) The touch of beauty of the Earth
(d) None of the above

4 No motion has she now, no force-
She neither hears nor sees,
Rolled round in earth's diurnal course
With rocks and stones and trees.

(i) What does the poet think of death?
(a) As a relief (b) As a peaceful sleep
(c) As a fear (d) None of these

(ii) Why has she no motion?
(a) Because she is sleeping
(b) Because she can't move
(c) Because she is dead
(d) None of the above

(iii) What does the Earth's 'diurnal course' imply?
(a) Rising of Sun
(b) Coming of night
(c) Daily rotation on it's axis
(d) Day and night

(iv) She has been mingled with what?
(a) In soil (b) In water
(c) With nature (d) In ocean

(v) What does she do now?
(a) She moves all around (b) Buried
(c) Lying in caffin (d) Under water

Answers

1. (i) (b), (ii) (a), (iii) (b), (iv) (b), (v) (a) **2.** (i) (b), (ii) (a), (iii) (c), (iv) (a), (v) (d) **3.** (i) (a), (ii) (b), (iii) (b), (iv) (c), (v) (a)
4. (i) (b), (ii) (c), (iii) (c), (iv) (c), (v) (a)

05 A Legend of the Northland

Stanza-Wise Explanation of the Poem

Stanza-wise Explanation परीक्षा में नहीं पूछा जाता है, यह केवल विद्यार्थियों को Poem का अर्थ समझाने के लिए दिया गया है।

1-2
Away, away in the Northland,
Where the hours of the day are few,
And the nights are so long in winter
That they cannot sleep them through;
Where they harness the swift reindeer
To the sledges, when it snows;
And the children look like bear's cubs
In their funny, furry clothes:

Word-Meaning

Word	Pronunciation	English Meaning	Hindi Meaning
Away, away	अवे, अवे	very far away (away is repeated for emphasis)	बहुत दूर
Northland	नॉर्थलैण्ड	a place located in the far North of Europe	उत्तरी यूरोप में स्थित दूरस्थ प्रदेश
Hours of the day	आवर्स ऑफ द डे	daylight hours	दिन का समय
Cannot sleep them through	केननॉट स्लीप देम थ्रो	cannot sleep through the entire night	पूरी रात नहीं सो सके
Harness	हारनेस	tie	बाँधना
Reindeer	रेन्डियर	animal residing in the far North	उत्तरी दूरस्थ स्थानों पर पाया जाने वाला जानवर
Sledges	स्लेज्स	animal drawn carriage used for transportation over snow	बर्फ में चलने वाली जानवरों द्वारा खींची जाने वाली गाड़ी
Furry	फरी	made of fur	फर से बना हुआ

Explanation In the first two stanzas, the poet describes the place from where the story had originated. The story originated in the cold region of Northland where the days are short and nights are very long in winter. The people of the Northland can't sleep due to extreme cold conditions in the night at this place.

When the snow falls in Northland, the people living there tie their reindeers to sledges to travel (reindeer pull the sledges). The children wear warm furry clothes that make them look like bear cubs.

3-4
They tell them a curious story,
I don't believe 'tis true;
And yet you may learn a lesson
If I tell the tale to you.
Once, when the good Saint Peter
Lived in the world below,
And walked about it, preaching,
Just as he did, you know,

Word-Meaning

Word	Pronunciation	English Meaning	Hindi Meaning
Curious	क्यूरियस	(here) strange	अजीब, विचित्र
Tis	टिस	short form of it is	*'it is'* का छोटा रूप
Lesson	लेसन	teaching	शिक्षा
Tale	टेल	story	कहानी
Saint Peter	सेंट पीटर	an apostle of christ	ईसा मसीह से प्रेरित शिष्य
Preaching	प्रीचिंग	giving sermons	उपदेश देना

Explanation In Northland, parents tell their children a story. The poet does not think that the story is true but still tells the tale. The poet believes that it contains an important lesson which we all must learn.

The poet, then, begins the tale. Once, Saint Peter lived on Earth as a human. He travelled the world teaching about God.

5-6
He came to the door of a cottage,
In travelling round the Earth,
Where a little woman was making cakes,
And baking them on the hearth;
And being faint with fasting,
For the day was almost done,
He asked her, from her store of cakes,
To give him a single one.

Word-Meaning

Word	Pronunciation	English Meaning	Hindi Meaning
Cottage	कॉटेज	small house	कुटिया
Travelling	ट्रैवलिंग	wandering place to place	यात्रा करना
Baking	बेकिंग	cooking	पकाना
Hearth	हर्थ	fireplace	भट्ठी
Being faint	बींग फेन्ट	feeling like fainting	बेहोशी जैसा महसूस होना
Fasting	फास्टिंग	abstinence from all food	उपवास रखना
Store	स्टोर	place for stocking	भण्डार
Single one	सिंगल वन	'one' is emphasised for showing that it is a small amount	'एक' को थोड़ी मात्रा पर जोर देने के लिए प्रयुक्त किया गया है

Explanation While travelling round the Earth, Saint Peter came to a cottage door. In the cottage, a little woman was baking cakes in the fireplace.

Saint Peter had been fasting for the whole day and he was hungry and weak. The day was now almost over. So, Saint Peter asked the woman to give him a cake from her store of cakes.

7-8 So she made a very little cake,
But as it baking lay,
She looked at it, and thought it seemed
Too large to give away.
Therefore she kneaded another,
And still a smaller one;
But it looked, when she turned it over,
As large as the first had done.

Word-Meaning

Word	Pronunciation	English Meaning	Hindi Meaning
Baking lay	बेकिंग ले	was being baked	पकाया, बनाया
Seemed	सीम्ड	appeared	प्रतीत होना
Give away	गिव अवे	donate free	मुफ्त में दान करना
Kneaded	नीडेड	moulded the dough	आटा गूँथा
Turned it over	टर्नड् इट ओवर	reversed while baking	पकाते समय घुमाना या पलटना

Explanation So, the woman started baking a small cake for Saint Peter. But, she felt that it was too big to give away. So, the woman went to make another small cake, but when she turned it over, the cake looked as big as the first one.

9-10 Then she took a tiny scrap of dough,
And rolled and rolled it flat;
And baked it thin as a wafer —
But she couldn't part with that.
For she said, "My cakes that seem too small
When I eat of them myself
Are yet too large to give away."
So she put them on the shelf.

Word-Meaning

Word	Pronunciation	English Meaning	Hindi Meaning
Tiny scrap	टाइनी स्क्रेप	very small piece	बहुत छोटा टुकड़ा
Dough	डो	kneaded flour	गुँथा हुआ आटा
Wafer	वेफर	thin slice like a leaf	पतला पापड़ जैसा टुकड़ा
Part with	पार्ट विद	give away	देना
Shelf	शेल्फ	place of storage	दराज/सामान रखने की जगह

Explanation Then the woman took a small piece of dough and rolled it as thin as she could. The cake baked from it was as thin as wafer but the woman could not also give it to Saint Peter. She felt that her cakes seemed too small when she would eat them.

However, those cakes became too large to give away for free. Consequently, she put all the cakes on the shelf and did not give any cake to Saint Peter.

11-12 Then good Saint Peter grew angry,
For he was hungry and faint;
And surely such a woman
Was enough to provoke a saint.
And he said, "You are far too selfish
To dwell in a human form,
To have both food and shelter,
And fire to keep you warm.

Word-Meaning

Word	Pronunciation	English Meaning	Hindi Meaning
For	फॉर	because	क्योंकि
Surely	श्योरली	definitely	अवश्य ही
Provoke	प्रोवोक	to make angry	क्रोध दिलाना
Selfish	सेल्फिश	greedy or not considerate	स्वार्थी
Dwell	ड्वेल	live	जीवन जीना

Explanation The selfish behaviour of the woman made Saint Peter angry. He was very weak and hungry. It is not easy for a compassionate and kind saint like Saint Peter to become angry but the actions of the woman had been able to do so.

Hence, Saint Peter told her that she was very selfish. She did not deserve to be a human being and live a comfortable life with good food to eat, a house to live in with fire to keep her warm.

13-14 Now, you shall build as the birds do,
And shall get your scanty food
By boring, and boring, and boring,
All day in the hard, dry wood."
Then up she went through the chimney,
Never speaking a word,
And out of the top flew a woodpecker,
For she was changed to a bird.

Word-Meaning

Word	Pronunciation	English Meaning	Hindi Meaning
Build	बिल्ड	make your nest	घोंसला बनाना
Scanty	स्कैनटि	too small in amount	बहुत कम मात्रा में
Boring	बोरिंग	making holes in the tree trunks with the beak to find food	चोंच से पेड़ के तने में भोजन खोजने के लिए छेद बनाना
Woodpecker	वुडपेकर	a kind of bird	कठफोड़वा पक्षी

Explanation Saint Peter cursed the woman and transformed her into a bird. As a bird, the woman would now have to build her own nest and get her own food. To get food, she must dig holes into the hard dry wood. As a result, the women went out through the chimney of her house without speaking a word. She had now changed into a woodpecker.

15-16 She had a scarlet cap on her head,
And that was left the same;
But all the rest of her clothes were burned
Black as a coal in the flame.
And every country schoolboy
Has seen her in the wood,
Where she lives in the trees till this very day,
Boring and boring for food.

Word-Meaning

Word	Pronunciation	English Meaning	Hindi Meaning
Scarlet	स्कारलेट	bright red	गहरा लाल रंग
Flame	फ्लेम	flame of fire	आग की लपटें
Wood	वुड	forest	जंगल
This very day	दिस वेरी डे	today	आज

Explanation As a human, the little woman wore a red cap. When she was converted into a woodpecker, only her red cap remained and all her clothes had burned. In other words, the woodpecker had a red head but the rest of its body was black.

The poet then says that since then every school boy has seen the woodpecker (the little woman) in the forest. She still lives there digging into the dry and hard wood (bark of tress) to look for her food.

Central Idea of the Poem कविता का सार

परीक्षा में Poetry भाग की किन्हीं भी तीन Poems के नाम दिए जाते हैं, जिनमें से किसी एक Poem का Central Idea लिखना होता है। इसके लिए 3 अंक निर्धारित हैं।

The poem 'A legend of the Northland' is a folktale (ballad) that is passed from one generation to another in Northland. In the tale, Saint Peter, once reached the place after travelling the wholeday. He was hungry and asked a woman who was baking cakes to give him a single piece. However, the woman did not give him even the smallest and thinnest cake. Thus, the angry saint cursed her and changed her into a woodpecker, a bird who would have to work hard to get food.

Throughout the story, the woman was punished for her greed and selfishness. The legend teaches us not to be greedy and that we should acquire the qualities of kindness and empathy.

'A Legend of the Northland' कविता एक लोककथा है, जिसे नॉर्थलैण्ड में एक पीढ़ी से दूसरी पीढ़ी को हस्तान्तरित किया जाता है। कहानी में, एक बार संत पीटर पूरे दिन की यात्रा के बाद एक स्थान पर पहुँचे। वह भूखे थे और उन्होंने एक महिला जो केक बना रही थी, से केक के एक टुकड़े की माँग की। हालाँकि, महिला ने उन्हें सबसे छोटा और पतला केक का टुकड़ा भी नहीं दिया। इसलिए, क्रोधित संत ने उसे श्राप दिया और उसे कठफोड़वा पक्षी में बदल दिया, जो एक ऐसा पक्षी है, जिसे भोजन प्राप्ति के लिए कठोर मेहनत करनी पड़ती है। पूरी कहानी में, महिला को अपने लालच और स्वार्थ के लिए सजा मिली।

यह कथा हमें लालच नहीं करने की सीख देती है, और सिखाती है कि हमें दया और सहानुभूति के गुणों को अपनाना चाहिए।

Objective Questions

Read the stanzas given below and answer the questions that follow.

1 Where they harness the swift reindeer
To the sledges, when it snows;
And the children look like bear's cubs
In their funny, furry clothes:
They tell them a curious story
I don't believe 'tis true;
And yet you may learn a lesson
If I tell the tale to you.

(i) Who is the poet of the poem?
(a) WB Yeats
(b) Robert Frost
(c) Phoebe Cary
(d) William Shakespeare

(ii) How do the children look like wearing furry clothes?
(a) They look like a fawn.
(b) They look like bear's cubs.
(c) They look like little pups.
(d) They look like deer.

(iii) The tale referred to, in the extract is related to
(a) how the woodpecker came into being
(b) how Saint Peter got angry once
(c) how greed results in doom
(d) how a bird is often seen by people

(iv) The poet calls the tale curious because
(a) it is imaginative
(b) he does not believe in it
(c) it is just to teach the students against greed
(d) it is very interesting

(v) 'They' in the extract refers to
(a) the people of Northland
(b) the poet and his relatives
(c) the people of the poet's country
(d) the children of Northland

2 So she made a very little cake,
But as it baking lay,
She looked at it, and thought it seemed
Too large to give away.
Therefore she kneaded another,
And still a smaller one;
But it looked, when she turned it over,
As large as the first had done.

(i) For whom the cake was baked by the woman?
(a) Family
(b) Friends
(c) The Saint
(d) Herself

(ii) What did she think about it as she saw it being baked?
(a) That the cake was too small for the charity.
(b) That the cake was too big to be given away in charity.
(c) That the cake didn't look attractive.
(d) That the cake will not be sufficient for one person.

(iii) What aspect of her character is highlighted in the above stanza?
(a) Smart
(b) Overthinker
(c) Greed
(d) Innocence

(iv) The poetic device used in the sixth line of the extract is
(a) Metaphor (b) Simile
(c) Anaphora (d) Alliteration

(v) 'Kneaded' in the extract means
(a) to press (b) to charge
(c) to divide (d) to boil

3 Then good Saint Peter grew angry,
For he was hungry and faint;
And surely such a woman
Was enough to provoke a saint!

(i) Who was angry?
(a) Poet (b) Woman
(c) Saint Peter (d) The child

(ii) Saint Peter was about to faint because
(a) he had not taken his medicines
(b) he had taken the wrong medicine
(c) he had preached and fasted the whole day
(d) he fell from the stairs

(iii) The word 'provoke' in the extract means
(a) to make someone angry
(b) to make someone comfortable
(c) to make someone happy
(d) to make someone hungry

(iv) Which word rhymes with 'faint'?
(a) Surely (b) Enough
(c) Saint (d) Grew

(v) How is Saint Peter described in the extract?
(a) Hungry (b) Good
(c) Faint (d) All of these

4 And he said, "You are far too selfish
To dwell in a human form,
To have both food and shelter,
And fire to keep you warm.
Now, you shall build as the birds do,
And shall get your scanty food
By boring, and boring, and boring,
All day in the hard, dry wood."

(i) Who is 'he' in the given extract?
(a) St. Francis (b) St. Peter
(c) St. John (d) St. Vincent

(ii) Why does he call the listener selfish?
(a) Because she did not give him water.
(b) Because she did not give him time to rest.
(c) Because she did not give him even the smallest of cakes.
(d) Because she had asked him to go away from her house.

(iii) The given lines are taken from a ballad whose purpose seems to
(a) teach children how to be kind and not selfish
(b) entertain the children
(c) to tell the story of the bird they had seen
(d) to teach them about the story regarding their town

(iv) Which figure of speech is used in the second-last sentence of the extract?
(a) Personification (b) Simile
(c) Metaphor (d) Repetition

(v) 'dwell' in the extract means
(a) to live (b) to die
(c) to enjoy (d) to argue

Answers

1. (i) (c), (ii) (d), (iii) (a), (iv) (b), (v) (a) 2. (i) (c), (ii) (b), (iii) (c), (iv) (d), (v) (a) 3. (i) (c), (ii) (c), (iii) (a), (iv) (c), (v) (d)
4. (i) (b), (ii) (c), (iii) (a), (iv) (d), (v) (a)

Unit-14

01 Dust of Snow

Stanza-Wise Explanation of the Poem

1
The way a crow
Shook down on me
The dust of snow
From a hemlock tree.

Explanation In this stanza, the poet remembers a small incident that changed his mood. Once, the poet was in a depressed mood and was hopeless. He was standing (It is not clear in the poem whether the poet was standing under or passing by a hemlock tree). Suddenly, a crow sitting on the tree shook it and some powdery snow from the tree fell on the poet.

व्याख्या इस पद्य में, कवि एक छोटी घटना को याद करता है जिसने उसकी मनोदशा को बदल दिया था। एक बार, कवि का मन बहुत उदास था और आशाहीन था। वह एक धतूरे के वृक्ष के नीचे खड़ा था (कविता में यह स्पष्ट नहीं है कि कवि वृक्ष के नीचे खड़ा था या उसके पास से गुजर रहा था)। अचानक, वृक्ष पर बैठे एक कौए ने, उसे (वृक्ष को) हिलाया और वृक्ष से बर्फ के अत्यन्त छोटे कण कवि पर गिर गए।

2
Has given my heart
A change of mood
And saved some part
Of a day I had rued

Explanation The powdery snow which fell on the poet changed his mood to happiness. Earlier, he was depressed and sad but now, he started feeling refreshed. This incident saved some part of the poet's day which he would have spent in regret.

व्याख्या बर्फ के वे कण जो कवि पर गिरते हैं वे उसके उदास मन को प्रसन्नता में परिवर्तित कर देते हैं। पहले वह उदास एवं दुखी था। लेकिन अब वह तरोताजा महसूस करना शुरु करने लगा। इस घटना ने कवि के दिन का कुछ भाग बचा लिया जो वह पछतावे में गुजार देता।

Central Idea of the Poem

परीक्षा में Poetry भाग की किन्हीं भी तीन Poems के नाम दिए जाते हैं, जिनमें से किसी एक Poem का Central Idea लिखना होता है।

'Dust of snow' is a beautiful short poem written by Robert Frost. This poem expresses the significance of small things that can change one's mood. The poet has mentioned crow and hemlock tree in this poem that are believed to be symbols of bad omen. The poet describes the dark, depressive and bitter side of nature to present his similar mood but when the crow shook the hemlock tree and snow particles fell on the poet, his mood changed suddenly. Through this poem, we get a message that we should hope for the best even in the worst of situations. We must also remember that nature and its objects have the ability to make one happy and come out of hopelessness.

'Dust of Snow' रॉबर्ट फ्रॉस्ट द्वारा लिखी गई एक सुन्दर छोटी कविता है। यह कविता किसी की मनोदशा को बदलने में छोटी चीजों के महत्त्व को दर्शाती है। कवि ने इस कविता में कौए एवं धतूरे (हेमलॉक) के वृक्ष का उल्लेख किया है, जो बुरे शगुन का प्रतीक माना जाता है। कवि स्वयं की मनोदशा को दर्शाने हेतु प्रकृति के अन्धकारमय, उदास एवं कटु पक्ष का वर्णन करता है, किन्तु जब कौआ धतूरे के वृक्ष को हिलाता है और बर्फ के छोटे कण कवि पर गिरते हैं, तो उसकी मनोदशा सहसा बदल जाती है। इस कविता के माध्यम से, हमें यह सन्देश प्राप्त होता है कि हमें अत्यन्त बुरी परिस्थितियों में भी सर्वश्रेष्ठ की आशा रखनी चाहिए। हमें यह भी स्मरण रखना चाहिए कि प्रकृति एवं उसकी वस्तुएँ किसी को खुश करने एवं निराशा से बाहर निकालने की क्षमता रखती हैं।

Objective Questions

Read the following extracts carefully and answer the questions that follow.

1
The way a crow
Shook down on me
The dust of snow
From a hemlock tree

(i) Name the poet of the above lines.
उपरोक्त पंक्तियों के कवि का नाम बताइए।

(a) Robert Frost (b) Wordsworth
(c) Shelley (d) WB Yeats

(ii) What is a 'Dust of Snow'?
'Dust of Snow' क्या है?

(a) Particles of clay (b) Particles of sand
(c) Particles of plants (d) Particles of snow

(iii) Who was sitting on the tree?
पेड़ पर कौन बैठा था?
(a) A cuckoo (b) A sparrow
(c) A pigeon (d) A crow

(iv) Where was the poet standing?
कवि कहाँ खड़ा था?
(a) Under a hemlock tree (b) Under a banyan tree
(c) Under a peepal tree (d) Under a neem tree

(v) Choose the correct statement.
सही कथन का चुनाव करें।
(a) Hemlock is a tree with sweet healthy fruits
(b) Hemlock is a tree known for furniture making
(c) Hemlock is a tree bearing fragrant flower
(d) Hemlock is a poisonous tree

2 Has given my heart
A change of mood
And saved some part
Of a day I had rued.

(i). What was the poet's mood in the above lines?
उपरोक्त पंक्तियों में कवि की मनोदशा कैसी थी?
(a) Happy
(b) Sorrowful
(c) Anguish
(d) Nostalgic

(ii) What was the effect of the fall of the Dust of Snow on the poet?
बर्फ के कणों के गिरने का कवि पर क्या प्रभाव पड़ा था?
(a) It changed his mood
(b) It changed his luck
(c) It changed his car
(d) It changed his job

(iii) How did the poet feel for the rest of the day?
कवि बचे हुए दिन में कैसा महसूस करता है?
(a) He felt gloomy
(b) He felt positive and happy
(c) He felt hopeless
(d) Both (a) and (c)

Answers

1. (i) (a), (ii) (b), (iii) (d), (iv) (a), (v) (d) **2.** (i) (a), (ii) (a), (iii) (b)

02 A Tiger in the Zoo

Stanza-Wise Explanation of the Poem

1 He stalks in his vivid stripes
The few steps of his cage,
On pads of velvet quiet,
In his quiet rage.

Explanation In these lines, the poet is describing a tiger in a cage. The tiger with bright and clear stripes moves inside the cage. The cage is very small so the tiger can hardly take a few steps along its length. His pads are soft like velvet so no one can hear the sound of his footsteps. In spite of being the most powerful creature, he is imprisoned inside a cage. This situation has made the tiger angry but he is keeping quiet as he knows that he is helpless in this situation.

व्याख्या इन पंक्तियों में, कवि पिंजरे में कैद एक बाघ का विवरण कर रहा है। साफ चमकदार धारियों वाला बाघ पिंजरे के अन्दर घूमता है। पिंजरा बहुत छोटा है, इसलिए बाघ उसकी लम्बाई के साथ कठिनता से मात्र कुछ ही कदम चल पाता है। उसके पंजों का निचला भाग मखमल की भाँति नर्म है, इसलिए कोई भी उसके कदमों की आवाज नहीं सुन सकता है। सर्वशक्तिशाली प्राणी होने के बावजूद, वह एक पिंजरे में कैद है। इस परिस्थिति ने बाघ को क्रोधित कर दिया है। किन्तु वह चुप है, क्योंकि वह जानता है कि वह इस परिस्थिति में असहाय है।

2 He should be lurking in shadow,
Sliding through long grass
Near the water hole
Where plump deer pass.

Explanation In these lines, the poet is filled with sorrow for the caged tiger. He feels that a tiger should be free in his natural habitat.

He should be hiding in the shadows and quietly moving through the long grass near the water hole. He should be waiting for a fat and healthy deer to pass, in the hopes of getting a heavy meal. The poet wants to convey that the actual life of a tiger is in a jungle and not in a cage.

व्याख्या इन पंक्तियों में कवि पिंजरे में कैद बाघ के प्रति शोक से भर गया है। उसे महसूस होता है कि बाघ को अपने प्राकृतिक परिवेश में मुक्त होना चाहिए।

उसे परछाई में छिपना चाहिए एवं पानी के गड्ढे के पास वाली लम्बी घास में चुपचाप घूमना चाहिए। उसे भारी भोजन मिलने की आशा से, एक मोटे एवं स्वस्थ हिरण के गुजरने की प्रतीक्षा करनी चाहिए। कवि यह कहना चाहता है कि बाघ का वास्तविक जीवन जंगल में है न कि पिंजरे में।

3 He should be snarling around houses
At the jungle's edge,
Baring his white fangs, his claws,
Terrorising the village!

Explanation In these lines, the poet explains what a tiger in his natural habitat should be doing.

According to him, a free tiger should be roaring around the houses located at the jungle's edge. He should be showing his sharp white teeth and his claws to terrorise the villagers.

व्याख्या इन पंक्तियों में, कवि समझाता है कि बाघ को उसके प्राकृतिक परिवेश में क्या करना चाहिए।

उसके अनुसार, एक मुक्त बाघ को जंगल के किनारे पाए जाने वाले घरों के इर्द-गिर्द दहाड़ना चाहिए। उसे गाँव वालों को भयभीत करने के लिए अपने नुकीले सफेद दाँत और पंजे दिखाने चाहिए।

4 But he's locked in a concrete cell,
His strength behind bars,
Stalking the length of his cage,
Ignoring visitors.

Explanation In these lines, the poet's focus returns to the angry tiger in the cage. The poet explains that unlike the tiger in the jungle, this tiger is not free. He is locked in the concrete cell. His strength and power is of no use, behind the bars of the cage. He is moving in his cage ignoring the visitors who are continuously visiting to have a look at him.

व्याख्या इन पंक्तियों में, कवि का ध्यान पिंजरे में बन्द क्रोधित बाघ पर वापस लौटता है। कवि समझाता है कि जंगल के बाघ के विपरीत यह बाघ आजाद नहीं है। वह सीमेन्ट से बने पिंजरे में बन्द है। उसकी शक्ति एवं ताकत, पिंजरे की सलाखों के पीछे व्यर्थ है। वह उसकी एक झलक पाने के लिए लगातार आने वाले आगन्तुकों को अनदेखा करते हुए अपने पिंजरे में टहल रहा है।

5 He hears the last voice at night,
The patrolling cars,
And stares with his brilliant eyes
At the brilliant stars.

Explanation In these lines, the poet says that even at night the tiger is disturbed. He hears the last sound of the patrolling cars of the zoo officials. The tiger stares at the brilliant stars shining brightly in the sky with his brilliant eyes which hope for freedom.

व्याख्या इन पंक्तियों में, कवि कहता है कि रात में भी बाघ परेशान रहता है। वह चिड़ियाघर के अधिकारियों की गश्त लगाती गाड़ियों की आखिरी आवाज़ सुनता है। बाघ अपनी चमकदार आँखों से, जो मुक्त होने की आशा रखती हैं, आसमान में चमकते सितारों को देखता है।

Central Idea of the Poem

परीक्षा में Poetry भाग की किन्हीं भी तीन Poems के नाम दिए जाते हैं, जिनमें से किसी एक Poem का Central Idea लिखना होता है।

In this poem 'A Tiger in the Zoo', the poet tries to depict the poor conditions of a caged tiger. He contrasts and compares the life of a caged tiger with a tiger living in natural habitat, i.e. a jungle. Through the poem, the poet tries to convey that wild animals should be allowed to live freely in their natural habitat. Freedom is loved by all living beings and not just by human beings. The life of captivity breeds rage, intolerance and stress.

इस कविता, *'A Tiger in the Zoo'* में कवि ने एक पिंजरे में बन्द बाघ की दरिद्र स्थिति का चित्रण करने का प्रयास किया है। वह पिंजरे में बन्द बाघ के जीवन की तुलना प्राकृतिक परिवेश अर्थात् जंगल में रहने वाले बाघ से करता है। कविता के माध्यम से, कवि यह बताने का प्रयास करता है कि जंगली जानवरों को उनके प्राकृतिक परिवेश में स्वतन्त्र रूप से रहने की अनुमति देनी चाहिए। आजादी सभी जीवित प्राणियों को प्रिय है न कि केवल मनुष्यों को। अधीनता का जीवन क्रोध, असहिष्णुता तथा तनाव को जन्म देता है।

Objective Questions

Read the following extracts carefully and answer the questions that follow.

1 He stalks in his vivid stripes,
The few steps of his cage,
On pads of velvet quiet,
In his quiet rage.

(i) Who is the poet of the poem from which the above stanza has been extracted?
उस कविता का कवि कौन है, जिससे उपरोक्त पद्यांश जिस कविता से लिया गया है?
(a) Walt Whitman (b) Leslie Norris
(c) Robert Frost (d) Robin Klein

(ii) Which of the following is in a cage?
निम्न में से कौन पिंजरे में है?
(a) Tiger (b) Dog (c) Bear (d) Horse

(iii) How are the pads of a tiger?
बाघ के पंजे कैसे हैं?
(a) Hard (b) Velvet (soft)
(c) Vigorous (d) None of these

(iv) What is the title of the poem?
कविता का शीर्षक क्या है?
(a) Animals
(b) Fire and Ice
(c) A Tiger in the Zoo
(d) The Trees

2 He should be lurking in shadow,
Sliding through long grass,
Near the water hole,
Where plump deer pass.

(i) Where should the tiger be lurking?
बाघ कहाँ छिपा हुआ है?
(a) Behind the tree
(b) In the shadow
(c) In the house
(d) None of the above

(ii) Where did the tiger wait for his prey?
बाघ अपने शिकार की प्रतीक्षा कहाँ कर रहा था?
(a) He was hiding in the shadow of trees
(b) He was hiding in the long grasses
(c) Both (a) and (b)
(d) Near the river

(iii) Point out the rhyming words in the stanza.
पद्यांश में तुकान्त वाले शब्द निकालिए।
(a) Grass and pass
(b) Lurking and sliding
(c) Long and near
(d) None of the above

3 But he's locked in a concrete cell,
His strength behind bars,
Stalking the length of his cage,
Ignoring visitors.

(i) Where has the tiger been locked?
बाघ को कहाँ बन्द किया गया है?
(a) In a concrete cell
(b) In a safari
(c) In a zoo
(d) None of the above

(ii) What is the reaction of the tiger towards the visitors?
आंगतुक के प्रति बाघ का क्या रवैया है?
(a) Attacking them
(b) Ignoring them
(c) Growling them
(d) None of the above

(iii) Is the tiger's strength useful?
क्या बाघ की शक्ति उपयोगी है?
(a) It is useful to show it of in circus
(b) It is useful to attack on his prey
(c) It is of no use in the cage
(d) None of the above

4 He hears the last voice at night,
The patrolling cars,
And stares with his brilliant eyes,
At the brilliant stars.

(i) What is the tiger's attitude towards visitors?
आंगतुको के प्रति बाघ का व्यवहार कैसा है?
(a) Loving
(b) Hating
(c) Ignoring
(d) Threatening

(ii) What is patrolling at night?
रात्रि में गश्त कौन लगाता है?
(a) Cars (b) Tigers
(c) Deer (d) All of these

Answers

1. (i) (b), (ii) (a), (iii) (b), (iv) (c) **2.** (i) (b), (ii) (c), (iii) (a) **3.** (i) (a), (ii) (b), (iii) (c) **4.** (i) (c), (ii) (a)

03 The Ball Poem

Stanza-Wise Explanation of the Poem

1 What is the boy now, who has lost his ball,
What, what is he to do? I saw it go
Merrily bouncing, down the street, and then
Merrily over - there it is in the water!
No use to say 'O there are other balls':

Explanation The poem starts with the poet looking at the boy who has lost his ball. The poet wants to know about him and his reaction after losing his ball. The poet himself saw the ball bouncing happily down the street and then falling into the water. The poet says that there is no use to tell the boy that there are other balls because he would get many other balls, but he would never be able to get the lost ball and the memories associated with it.

व्याख्या कविता की शुरूआत कवि द्वारा उस लड़के को देखने से होती है जिसने अपनी गेंद खो दी है। कवि लड़के की गेंद के खो जाने के पश्चात् उसके और उसकी प्रतिक्रिया के बारे में जानना चाहता है। कवि ने स्वयं गेंद को सड़क पर खुशी से उछलते हुए एवं पानी में गिरते हुए देखा था। कवि कहता है कि लड़के को यह बताने का कोई फायदा नहीं था कि अन्य गेंदें भी हैं, क्योंकि, वह बहुत सारी अन्य गेंदें प्राप्त कर सकता था, किन्तु वह कभी भी खोई हुई गेंद एवं उससे जुड़ी स्मृतियाँ वापस नहीं पा सकता था।

2 An ultimate shaking grief fixes the boy
As he stands rigid, trembling, staring down
All his young days into the harbour where
His ball went. I would not intrude on him;
A dime, another ball, is worthless.

Explanation In these lines, the poet describes the condition of the boy after losing his ball. The boy feels very sad by the loss of his ball. He is standing like a statue at one place, shivering and staring down the ball which symbolises the memories of his young days. He is filled with sorrow and just keeps standing and looking in the direction where his ball is going. The poet says that he would not interfere with the boy's thoughts as he feels that through this experience, the boy will learn the meaning of loss. The poet says that it is not worth to tell the boy that another ball can be bought for only a dime (ten cents). Because, he was very attached to his lost ball which was with him from his very childhood.

व्याख्या इन पंक्तियों में, कवि गेंद खोने के पश्चात् लड़के की स्थिति का वर्णन करता है। लड़के को अपनी गेंद खोने का बहुत दुःख होता है। वह एक मूर्ति की तरह एक ही जगह खड़ा है, काँप रहा है और गेंद की ओर घूर रहा है जो उसके बचपन के दिनों की स्मृतियों का प्रतीक है। वह शोकपूर्ण है एवं केवल उसी दिशा में खड़ा रहता है जिस दिशा में उसकी गेंद जा रही है। कवि कहता है कि वह लड़के के विचारों में हस्तक्षेप नहीं करेगा क्योंकि उसे यह महसूस होता है कि इस अनुभव के माध्यम से लड़का खोने का अर्थ सीख लेगा। कवि कहता है कि लड़के को यह बताना व्यर्थ है कि केवल एक पैसे (दस सेंट) में दूसरी गेंद खरीदी जा सकती है, क्योंकि वह उस खोई हुई गेंद से बहुत जुड़ा हुआ था जो बचपन से ही उसके साथ थी।

3 .... Now
He senses first responsibility
In a world of possessions. People will take
Balls, balls will be lost always, little boy.
And no one buys a ball back. Money is
external.

Explanation In these lines, the poet says that the boy is learning his first responsibility of taking care of his things and how to bear the loss of something in a world of possessions. The poet makes a broad statement that people will take balls and these balls will be lost. In other words, the boy will keep losing things and would buy another one to replace the lost thing. But he would never be able to buy back that lost thing and the memories associated with it. Money is external as it cannot buy memories nor can it replace the lost things.

व्याख्या इन पंक्तियों में, कवि कहता है कि लड़का स्वयं की वस्तुओं का ध्यान रखने की एवं भौतिकवादी संसार में किसी वस्तु की हानि को सहन करने की अपनी पहली जिम्मेदारी सीख रहा है। कवि एक प्रभावशाली कथन देता है कि लोग गेंद लेंगे और ये गेंद खो जाँएगी। दूसरे शब्दों में, लड़का वस्तुओं को खोता रहेगा और खोई हुई वस्तुओं के स्थान पर नई खरीदता रहेगा। किन्तु वह कभी भी खोई हुई वस्तु एवं उससे जुड़ी स्मृतियों को वापस खरीद नहीं पाएगा। पैसा बाहरी है क्योंकि वह स्मृतियाँ नहीं खरीद सकता और न ही वह खोई हुई वस्तुओं का स्थान ले सकता है।

4 He is learning, well behind his desperate eyes,
This epistemology of loss, how to stand up
Knowing what every man must one day know
And most know many days, how to stand up.

Explanation In these lines, the poet suggests that from the loss of the ball, the boy is learning the meaning of loss. He is also learning how to stand up from the loss. The poet says that knowing that every man has to stand up after such losses, the boy too will learn how to stand up and leave the losses behind. He would have understood the true meaning and nature of loss.

व्याख्या इन पंक्तियों में, कवि सुझाव देता है कि गेंद को खोने से, लड़का क्षति का अर्थ समझ रहा है। वह नुकसान का सामना करना भी सीख रहा है। कवि कहता है कि यह जानते हुए कि हर व्यक्ति को ऐसे नुकसान का सामना करना पड़ता है, लड़का भी सीख जाएगा कि किस प्रकार जिम्मेदारी समझे और नुकसानों को पीछे छोड़ें। वह हानि का वास्तविक अर्थ तथा हानि की प्रकृति समझ चुका होगा।

Central Idea of the Poem

परीक्षा में Poetry भाग की किन्हीं भी तीन Poems के नाम दिए जाते हैं, जिनमें से किसी एक Poem का Central Idea लिखना होता है।

The poet John Berryman in this poem describes the grief of a boy over the loss of his ball. With that loss, he senses his first responsibility in a materialistic world. The poet suggests that the people whom we love and our material possessions will not be with us forever. One has to understand the nature of loss and learn to cope up with the loss. The child has to learn that loss is a part of everyday life and still life goes on.

इस कविता में कवि जॉन बैरीमैन ने एक लड़के की गेंद खोने पर उसे होने वाले दु:ख का वर्णन किया है। इस हानि के साथ वह (लड़का) इस भौतिकतावादी संसार में अपनी पहली जिम्मेदारी समझता है। कवि सुझाव देता है कि जिन लोगों को हम प्रेम करते हैं तथा हमारी भौतिक वस्तुएँ, सदा के लिए हमारे साथ नहीं रहेंगी। प्रत्येक व्यक्ति को क्षति की प्रकृति समझनी होगी एवं इस हानि का सामना करना सीखना होगा। बच्चे को यह समझना पड़ेगा कि हानि रोजमर्रा के जीवन का एक हिस्सा है एवं जीवन फिर भी चलता रहेगा।

Objective Questions

Read the following extracts carefully and answer the questions that follow.

1 What is the boy now, who has lost his ball,
What, what is he to do? I saw it go
Merrily bouncing, down the street, and then
Merrily over- there it is in the water!
An ultimate shaking grief fixes the boy
As he stands rigid, trembling, staring down
All his young days into the harbour where
His ball went. I would not intrude on him;

(i) The poem begins with a question. Based on your reading of the poem, the speaker
कविता प्रश्न के साथ प्रारम्भ होती है। अपने कविता के अध्ययन के आधार पर वक्ता
(a) wants the boy to answer the question.
(b) expects the passers-by to respond.
(c) is looking for answers in a self-help book.
(d) is thinking to himself.

(ii) The poet seems to have indicated the 'merry bouncing of the ball' to
ऐसा प्रतीत होता है कि कवि ने गेंद के 'अनंदमय उछाल' की ओर संकेत किया है।
(a) create a sense of rhythm in these lines.
(b) support the happiness of the experience of playing.
(c) contrast with the dejected feeling of the boy.
(d) indicate the cheerful mood of the boy.

(iii) The extract suggests that the poet is
पद्यांश यह बताता है कि कवि
(a) an onlooker observing
(b) a parent recounting the incident
(c) the boy talking about himself
(d) imagining the incident

2 Now he senses first responsibility
In a world of possessions. People will take
Balls, balls will be lost always, little boy.
And no one buys a ball back.
Money is external.

(i) What does the poet mean by 'money is external'?
'Money is external' से कवि का क्या तात्पर्य है?
(a) Money has to be earned
(b) Money is meant to be spent
(c) Money is not fixed
(d) Money can be earned with hard work

(ii) Who is 'He' in the given extract?
दिए गए पद्यांश में 'He' कौन है?
(a) The poet (b) The young boy
(c) The poet's son (d) A teen boy

(iii) What does the poet mean by 'In a world of possessions'?
'In a world of possessions' से कवि का क्या तात्पर्य है?
(a) Sense of loss
(b) Material things
(c) Every one loves to possess things
(d) World of wealth and prosperity

(iv) Who is the poet of the poem, 'The Ball Poem'?
कविता 'The Ball Poem' का कवि कौन है?
(a) Robert Frost (b) WB Yeats
(c) Sylvia Plath (d) John Berryman

3 Money is external.
He is learning, well behind his desperate eyes,
The epistemology of loss, how to stand up
Knowing what every man must one day know
And most know many days, how to stand up

(i) The boy is learning ......
लड़का ...... सीख रहा है।
(a) the meaning of life (b) meaning of responsibility
(c) to cope with loss (d) meaning of happiness

(ii) The word 'epistemology' in the above extract means
उपरोक्त पद्यांश में 'Epistemology' शब्द का अर्थ है
(a) imitation (b) methodology
(c) philosophy (d) assertion

(iii) What is the rhyming scheme of the stanza?
पद्यांश की तुकबन्दी योजना क्या है?
(a) abcbc (b) ababab
(c) abcba (d) No rhyming scheme

Answers

1. (i) (d), (ii) (c), (iii) (a) **2.** (i) (b), (ii) (b), (iii) (d), (iv) (d) **3.** (i) (c), (ii) (d), (iii) (d)

04 Amanda

Stanza-Wise Explanation of the Poem

1 Don't bite your nails, Amanda!
Don't hunch your shoulders, Amanda!
Stop that slouching and sit up straight,
Amanda!

Explanation In these lines, Amanda, a little girl, is being scolded and instructed by her mother for her actions. Amanda is advised to stop biting her nails, which is a bad habit. She is told to sit up straight without bending her shoulders because her mother wants her to sit in the right posture.

The last word 'Amanda!' is used with an exclamation mark, which shows the irritation and frustration of Amanda's mother.

व्याख्या इन पंक्तियों में, अमाण्डा, एक छोटी बच्ची अपने कार्यों के लिए अपनी माँ से डाँट खा रही है तथा हिदायत (सीख) ले रही है। अमाण्डा को अपने नाखून नहीं कुतरने की सलाह दी जाती है, क्योंकि यह एक बुरी आदत है। उसे बिना कंधे झुकाए सीधे बैठने को भी कहा जाता है, क्योंकि उसकी माँ उसे सही मुद्रा में बिठाना चाहती है।

अन्त में 'अमाण्डा !' शब्द को एक विस्मयादिबोधक चिह्न के साथ उपयोग किया गया है, जो अमाण्डा की माँ की चिड़चिड़ाहट एवं निराशा को दर्शाता है।

2 There is a languid, emerald sea,
where the sole inhabitant is me—
a mermaid, drifting blissfully.

Explanation Amanda is lost in her world of imagination while her mother is instructing her. In her world, she imagines that she is a mermaid that lives alone in the beautiful green sea. She imagines an imaginary sea creature having a woman's head and body with a fish's tail instead of legs that as a mermaid she would move in the soft waves of the sea. She believes that as a mermaid, her life would be peaceful and relaxing.

व्याख्या अमाण्डा अपनी काल्पनिक दुनिया में खोई है, जबकि उसकी माँ उसे हिदायत दे रही हैं। अपनी दुनिया में, वह कल्पना करती है कि वह एक जलपरी है, जो सुन्दर हरे समुद्र में अकेली रहती है। वह कल्पना करती है कि एक जलपरी की भाँति वह समुद्र की मंद लहरों में तेरेगी। उसका विश्वास है कि एक जलपरी के रूप में उसका जीवन शान्तिपूर्ण एवं आरामदायक होगा।

3 Did you finish your homework, Amanda?
Did you tidy your room, Amanda?
I thought I told you to clean your shoes,
Amanda!

Explanation In these lines, Amanda is being inquired about her work. Amanda's mother is asking whether she has finished her homework and whether she has cleaned her room. Amanda is also reminded that she was told to clean her shoes.

व्याख्या इन पंक्तियों में, अमाण्डा से उसके कार्य के विषय में पूछा जा रहा है। अमाण्डा की माँ पूछ रही है कि उसने अपना गृहकार्य पूर्ण किया अथवा नहीं तथा अपना कमरा व्यवस्थित किया अथवा नहीं। अमाण्डा को उसके जूते साफ करने के बारे में भी याद दिलाया जाता है।

4 I am an orphan, roaming the street.
I pattern soft dust with my hushed, bare feet.
The silence is golden, the freedom is sweet.

Explanation Again, Amanda is not paying any attention to her mother. Amanda is in her world of imagination. She imagines that she is an orphan child who is freely roaming around the street. She has no shoes on her feet and is making patterns on the soft dust with her quiet and bare feet. She is loving the silence and freedom to do anything in her world of imagination.

व्याख्या एक बार फिर, अमाण्डा अपनी माँ की ओर ध्यान नहीं दे रही है। अमाण्डा स्वयं की काल्पनिक दुनिया में है। वह कल्पना करती है कि वह एक अनाथ बालिका है, जो आजादी से गलियों में भटक रही है। उसके पैरों में जूते नहीं हैं और वह अपने नंगे पैरों से शान्ति से नर्म धूल पर चित्र बना रही है। वह काल्पनिक दुनिया में मिलने वाली शान्ति एवं कुछ भी करने की आजादी से प्रेम कर रही होती है।

5 Don't eat that chocolate, Amanda!
Remember your acne, Amanda!
Will you please look at me when I'm speaking
to you, Amanda!

Explanation In these lines, Amanda is instructed by her mother not to eat chocolates. She is reminded that eating chocolates had previously caused her acne (pimples). However, as Amanda is lost in her own thoughts, she is not paying attention to her mother. So, her mother strictly asks her to listen to what is being told to her.

व्याख्या इन पंक्तियों में, अमाण्डा को उसकी माँ द्वारा चॉकलेट न खाने की हिदायत दी जा रही है। उसको यह याद दिलाया जाता है कि चॉकलेट खाने की वजह से अतीत में उसे मुहांसे हो गए थे। हालाँकि, अमाण्डा अपने ही विचारों में खोई हुई है, वह अपनी माँ पर ध्यान नहीं दे रही है। इसलिए उसकी माँ उसे सख्ती से, जो कहा जा रहा है, उसे सुनने को कहती है।

6 I am Rapunzel, I have not a care;
life in a tower is tranquil and rare;
I'll certainly never let down my bright hair!

Explanation Amanda is still in her world of imagination. Now, she dreams of herself as Rapunzel (character of a

German fairy tale) who lived alone in a tower. As Rapunzel, she will not have to worry about anything and her life would be calm and peaceful in the tower. She emphasises that unlike Rapunzel, she would never let her hair down or permit anyone to come inside the tower.

व्याख्या अमाण्डा अब भी अपनी काल्पनिक दुनिया में है। अब, वह स्वयं की रेप्यूनजल के रूप में कल्पना कर रही है (परियों की एक जर्मन कहानी का किरदार) जो एक मीनार में अकेली रहती थी। रेप्यूनजल के रूप में, उसको किसी चीज की चिन्ता नहीं करनी पड़ेगी एवं मीनार में उसका जीवन शान्तिपूर्ण रहेगा। वह इस बात पर बल देती है कि रेप्यूनजल के विपरीत, वह कभी अपने लम्बे बाल नहीं खोलेगी और किसी को भी मीनार में स्वयं के पास आने की अनुमति नहीं देगी।

7 Stop that sulking at once, Amanda!
You're always so moody, Amanda!
Anyone would think that I nagged at
you, Amanda!

Explanation In these lines, Amanda seems annoyed due to constant instructions.

Amanda's mother is asking her to stop being upset and moody. She said that her (Amanda) upset behaviour will show to anyone that she is disturbed due to her mother's constant instructions.

व्याख्या इन पंक्तियों में, अमाण्डा अपनी माँ की हिदायतों पर कोई प्रतिक्रिया नहीं दे रही है। ऐसा प्रतीत होता है कि वह लगातार दी जाने वाली हिदायतों से परेशान है।

अमाण्डा की माँ उसे निराश एवं उदासीन रहना बन्द करने के लिए कह रही है। वह कहती है कि अमाण्डा का निराशापूर्ण व्यवहार किसी को भी यह दर्शाएगा कि वह अपनी माँ द्वारा निरन्तर दी जाने वाली हिदायतों से परेशान है।

Central Idea of the Poem

परीक्षा में Poetry भाग की किन्हीं भी दो Poems के नाम दिए जाते हैं, जिनमें से किसी एक Poem का Central Idea लिखना होता है।

'Amanda' is a poem about child psychology. The poem tells us about a little girl, Amanda. She is constantly and continuously being scolded most probably by her mother. But she is lost in her own world. The frequent interferences make her very unhappy. She wants freedom from all restrictions and dreams of leading the life of a mermaid in the emerald sea where she is the only inhabitant. She feels that an orphan has more freedom than her. The little girl does not pay attention to what her mother is saying. The poem thus, asserts that parents must give some freedom to growing children. Constant scolding may adversely affect a child's development.

कविता 'अमाण्डा' बच्चे की मनोवृत्ति के विषय में है। यह कविता हमें एक छोटी बच्ची 'अमाण्डा' के बारे में बताती है। वह हमेशा एवं निरन्तर रूप से सम्भवत: उसकी माँ से डाँट खाती रहती है, किन्तु वह स्वयं की दुनिया में खोई रहती है। बार-बार होने वाली टोका-टाकी उसे बहुत अप्रसन्न कर देती है। वह सभी पाबन्दियों से मुक्ति चाहती है तथा एक जलपरी के समान जीवन जीने का स्वप्न देखती है, जहाँ चमकीले हरे समुद्र की वह एकमात्र निवासी हो। वह यह महसूस करती है कि एक अनाथ बच्चे के पास उससे ज्यादा आजादी है। यह छोटी बच्ची अपनी माँ द्वारा कही गई बातों पर ध्यान नहीं देती है। कविता फिर यह दावा करती है कि अभिभावकों को बड़े होते बच्चों को निश्चित रूप से थोड़ी आजादी देनी ही चाहिए। लगातार डाँट लगाना सम्भवत: बच्चे के विकास पर प्रतिकूल प्रभाव डालता है।

Objective Questions

Read the following extracts carefully and answer the questions that follow.

1 Don't bite your nails, Amanda!
Don't hunch your shoulders, Amanda!
Stop that slouching and sit up straight,
Amanda!

(i) Who is getting all the instructions?
सभी निर्देश किसे दिए जा रहे हैं?
(a) Amanda (b) Wanda
(c) Peggy (d) Maddie

(ii) What is Amanda doing to her nails?
अमाण्डा अपने नाखूनों के साथ क्या कर रही है?
(a) Painting (b) Cutting
(c) Biting (d) None of these

(iii) What is the meaning of 'slouching' in the extract?
पद्यांश में 'Slouching' का क्या अर्थ है?
(a) Bend
(b) Sit in a lazy way
(c) Lie down
(d) Bend backwards

2 There is a languid, emerald sea,
where the sole inhabitant is me—
a mermaid, drifting blissfully.

(i) Who is the sole inhabitant of the sea?
समुद्र का एकमात्र निवासी कौन है?
(a) Wanda (b) Peggy (c) Maddie (d) Amanda

(ii) What has Amanda become in her imagination?
अमाण्डा अपनी कल्पना में क्या बन जाती है?
(a) Mermaid (b) Scientist
(c) School teacher (d) None of these

(iii) How is the sea?
समुद्र कैसा है?
(a) Emerald green in colour (b) Peaceful
(c) Solitary (d) Both (a) and (b)

3 Did you finish your homework, Amanda?
Did you tidy your room, Amanda?
I thought I told you to clean your shoes,
Amanda!

(i) What was Amanda supposed to finish?
अमाण्डा को क्या खत्म करना था?
(a) Cooking (b) Homework
(c) Milk (d) None of these

(ii) What was Amanda told to clean?
अमाण्डा को क्या साफ करने के लिए कहा गया था?
(a) Her table
(b) Her uniform
(c) Her room
(d) Her book shelf

(iii) 'I thought I told you to clean your shoes'. Who is 'I' here?
'I thought I told you to clean your shoes'. यहाँ 'I' कौन है?
(a) Amanda (b) Amanda's mother
(c) The poet (d) Amanda's friend

4 I am an orphan, roaming the street.
I pattern soft dust with my hushed, bare feet.
The silence is golden, the freedom is sweet.

(i) What has Amanda imagined herself to be in this stanza?
अमाण्डा ने इस छन्द में स्वयं के क्या बनने की कल्पना की है?
(a) Orphan
(b) Mermaid
(c) Rapunzel
(d) None of the above

(ii) Where does the orphan roam?
अनाथ कहाँ भटकता है?
(a) Village
(b) City
(c) Streets
(d) None of these

(iii) What does she want to do as an orphan?
एक अनाथ के रूप में वह क्या करना चाहती है?
(a) Walk freely in the streets
(b) Play in dust with bare feet
(c) Both (a) and (b)
(d) None of the above

Answers

1. (i) (a), (ii) (c), (iii) (b) **2.** (i) (d), (ii) (a), (iii) (d) **3.** (i) (b), (ii) (c), (iii) (b) **4.** (i) (a), (ii) (c), (iii) (c)

05 On Killing a Tree

Stanza-Wise Explanation of the Poem

1 It takes much time to kill a tree,
Not a simple jab of the knife
Will do it. It has grown
Slowly consuming the earth,
Rising out of it, feeding
Upon its crust, absorbing
Years of sunlight, air, water,
And out of its leprous hide
Sprouting leaves.

Explanation In this stanza, the poet comments on the way a person cuts down a tree in order to serve his purpose. The poet says that it is not easy to cut down a tree because a simple jab of the knife is never enough to wipe out its existence. The reason behind its strength is its consuming the resources which it has got from the earth's crust so powerfully. Years of absorption of sunlight, air and water from which the earth has made its growth so perfect that a jab of knife won't do much. It will come out with leaves again and will grow as ever.

2 So hack and chop
But this alone wont do it.
Not so much pain will do it.
The bleeding bark will heal
And from close to the ground
Will rise curled green twigs,
Miniature boughs
Which if unchecked will expand again
To former size.

Explanation In this stanza, the poet further states the ways of cutting a tree. As the jab of the knife was not sufficient, the poet advises us to hit the tree severely in the form of hacking and chopping. But, the poet contrasts that even that won't be enough to kill the tree. This hacking and chopping would raise a pain to the tree but not good enough to kill it. The bark will ooze (leak) out with the liquid secretion, but over a period of time, it gets healed. Then, the fighting spirit of the tree will make it alive again. From close to the ground, it will start a new life again by giving rise to new leaves and small boughs. These will make the tree so glorious again that it will acquire its former size. Therefore, it is not easy to cut or kill a tree.

3 No,
The root is to be pulled out—
Out of the anchoring earth;
It is to be roped, tied,
And pulled out—snapped out
Or pulled out entirely,
Out from the earth-cave,
And the strength of the tree exposed
The source, white and wet,
The most sensitive, hidden
For years inside the Earth.

Explanation In the previous stanzas, the poet has discussed the various ways of killing the tree, but still the tree has managed to survive. So, the poet came up with another idea. He says that the root needs to be pulled out of the earth where it has stocked its strength. To do this, one needs to rope the roots, then pull out the whole mass outside.

When the roots are out of the Earth cave, then the actual strength of the tree i.e. the roots are exposed to the sun or environment. The source of life of the tree, which is roots, is now exposed and out and its root matter is white and wet with absorption of water. It is now subjected to the outside world. This is the actual start of the death of the tree as the life-source of tree, it roots, are exposed.

—— Then the matter
Of scorching and choking
In Sun and air,
Browning, hardening,
Twisting, withering,
And then it is done.

Explanation In the previous stanza, the poet discussed the way a tree is uprooted and exposed to the surrounding. When the tree is uprooted and left open in the surrounding, then the sun starts drying it up with the burning heat. This intense heat makes the root of the tree getting choked in the air and sunlight. Heat makes the root brown which was white earlier and hardens it by soaking all the moisture content. Then, the root starts twisting from its original shape and finally gets withered from its parts. This brings the actual end to the life of the tree and that is how it is done in the end. The poet takes us into a detailed account of how we kill a tree, what suffering it has to face and how harsh our attitude is for the one which is the breath of our lives.

Central Idea of the Poem कविता का सार

परीक्षा में Poetry भाग की किन्हीं भी तीन Poems के नाम दिए जाते हैं, जिनमें से किसी एक Poem का Central Idea लिखना होता है। इसके लिए 3 अंक निर्धारित हैं।

The poem 'On Killing a Tree' is like an instruction manual of killing a tree. It tells its reader that trees are like living beings. They are not cut but killed properly by uprooting the roots that are stuck deeply in the soil. Through the poem, the poet teaches us many lesson. Firstly, it depicts the courage and strength of trees, through which it teaches us to be strong and determined. Then, it points out that evils are just like roots. They exist deep within us and even we feel we had gotten rid of it, it suddenly appears. Therefore, to kill evils we must put on best efforts to uproot it from deep. Thirdly, it teaches us that we must bring all our work to a proper end. Lastly, it appeals (requests) not to cut trees as they sustain our lives.

'On Killing a Tree' कविता एक पेड़ की हत्या के लिए एक निर्देश नियमावली है। यह अपने पाठक को बताती है, कि पेड़ जीवित प्राणियों के समान हैं। उन्हें काटा नहीं जाता बल्कि उन्हें जड़ों से जो मिट्टी में गहरी जमी हुई हैं उखाड़कर समुचित तरीके से उनकी हत्या की जाती है। कविता के द्वारा कवि हमें बहुत सी शिक्षाएँ देता है। सर्वप्रथम, वह पेड़ के साहस और शक्ति का चित्रण करता है, जिसके द्वारा वह हमें शाक्तिशाली और दृढ़ निश्चयी बनने की शिक्षा देता है। उसके बाद, वह बताता है कि बुराईयाँ पेड़ की जड़ो के समान होती हैं वह हमारे अन्दर गहराई तक समाई हुई हैं और यदि हम यह महसूस करते हैं कि हमने उनसे छुटकारा प्राप्त कर लिया है, वे अचानक वापस उभरकर सामने आ जाती हैं। अत: बुराइयों को समाप्त करने के लिए हमें सर्वोत्तम प्रयासों के द्वारा इन्हें जड़ों से उखाड़ना होगा। तीसरा, यह हमें सिखाती है कि हमें हमारे प्रत्येक कार्य का उचित अन्त करना चाहिए। अन्त में यह कविता निवेदन करती है, कि हमें पेड़ों को नहीं काटना चाहिए, क्योंकि वे हमारे जीवन के स्रोत हैं।

Objective Questions

Read the stanzas given below and answer the questions that follow.

1 It takes much time to kill a tree,
Not a simple jab of the knife
Will do it. It has grown
Slowly consuming the Earth,
Rising out of it, feeding
Upon its crust, absorbing
Years of sunlight, air, water,
And out of its leprous hide
Sprouting leaves.
So hack and chop
But this alone wont do it.
Not so much pain will do it.
The bleeding bark will heal

(i) From which poem the above lines have been taken?
(a) On killing a tree
(b) A slumber did my spirit seal
(c) The road not taken
(d) The lake isle of Innisfree

(ii) What slowly consumes the Earth?
(a) People (b) Tress
(c) Animals (d) Knife

(iii) What does a tree absorb for years?
(a) Sunlight (b) Air
(c) Water (d) All of these

(iv) What does a tree feed on?
(a) The Earth's soil (b) The Earth's air
(c) The Earth's crust (d) The Earth's soil

(v) Which part of a tree bleeds, as per the poem?
(a) Stem (b) Leaves
(c) Bark (d) Roots

2 And from close to the ground
Will rise curled green twigs,
Miniature boughs
Which if unchecked will expand again
To former size. No,
The root is to be pulled out —
Out of the anchoring Earth
It is to be roped, tied,
And pulled out — snapped out
Or pulled out entirely,
Out from the earth-cave

(i) Identify the poet who wrote above lines.
(a) Gieve Patel (b) William Wordsworth
(c) Robert Frost (d) WB Yeats

(ii) According to the extract, ... rises from close to the ground.
(a) Green twigs (b) Miniature trees
(c) New roots (d) Fresh fruits

(iii) Which characteristic of the trees is mentioned in the given lines?
(a) Resilience (b) Strength
(c) Rejuvenation (d) Immortal

(iv) How should the root be pulled out?
(a) Not at all (b) Not completely
(c) Entirely (d) None of these

(v) If 'hack and chop' won't do it, what would be able to do it?
(a) Burning it (b) Relocating it
(c) Killing it roots (d) Re-growing it

3 It takes much time to kill a tree,
Not a simple jab of the knife
Will do it. It has grown
Slowly consuming the Earth,
Rising out of it, feeding
Upon its crust, absorbing
Years of sunlight, air, water,
And out of its leprous hide
Sprouting leaves.

(i) Write the name of the poem and its writer.
(a) Robert Frost (b) Gieve Patel
(c) William Wordsworth (d) Coates Kinney

(ii) Why is it not easy to cut down a tree?
(a) Single knife is not enough to jab it
(b) It has grown to it full length
(c) Both (a) and (b)
(d) None of the above

(iii) How does a tree get its strength?
(a) From water
(b) From Nutrients
(c) From Earth which nourishes and feed it
(d) None of the above

(iv) What does a tree absorb from the Earth?
(a) Sunlight (b) Air
(c) water (d) All of these

(v) How does a tree grow?
(a) By the timepasses (b) Feeding upon Earth's crust
(c) Both (a) and (b) (d) None of these

4 So hack and chop
But this alone wont do it.
Not so much pain will do it.
The bleeding bark will heal
And from close to the ground
Will rise curled green twigs,
Miniature boughs
Which if unchecked will expand again
To former size.

(i) What alone is not sufficient to kill a tree?
(a) Hacking (b) Chopping
(c) Both (a) and (b) (d) None of these

(ii) What start rising from close to the ground?
(a) Grass (b) Green twigs
(c) Small branches (d) Both (b) and (c)

(iii) How does a chopped tree start a new life again?
(a) By giving rise to new leaves
(b) Rising small boughs
(c) Both (a) and (b)
(d) None of the above

(iv) How can a tree gets its former size?
(a) When unchecked after cutting
(b) Watering
(c) By providing fertilisers
(d) All of the above

Answers

1. (i) (a), (ii) (b), (iii) (d), (iv) (c), (v) (c) **2.** (i) (a), (ii) (a), (iii) (c), (iv) (c), (v) (c) **3.** (i) (b), (ii) (c), (iii) (c), (iv) (d), (v) (b)
4. (i) (a), (ii) (d), (iii) (b), (iv) (d)

Unit-15

01 A Prayer for My Daughter

Summary of the Lesson

- "A prayer of my daughter" is one of the most significant poems of William Butler Yeats. This poem was composed by the poet soon after the birth of his first daughter on 26 February, 1919. This poem was composed by Yeats soon after the composition of another significant poem 'The second coming'.
- In that poem the poet said that the "ceremony of innocence is drowned". But in this poem he speaks about innocence as the chief laurel of his daughter.
- Yeats begin the poem with the image of his newly -beauty daughter sleeping calmly and peacefully in her cradle while a fierce storm rages outside. The intensity of the storm brings into the mind the idea that the world is about to come to an end.
- A Prayer for my Daughter" has ten stanzas, with each stanza eight lines long. The lines are written in iambic pentameter and iambic tetrameter. The first person speaker of the poem is a new father, Yeats, writing about his daughter, Anne, in 1919.
- The poem opens with a storm raging while the speaker's child sleeps, protected by her cradle. The next lines contain a description of the land surrounding the child's home: Only a neighbor's wood and a small hill (with a haystack on it) buffer the home during strong winds from the Atlantic Ocean. The speaker explains he has been walking and praying because of his gloomy thoughts for the past hour.
- While walking and praying, the speaker has been listening to the wind hitting the tower where he lives, a bridge, and trees above a stream.
- The speaker imagines the future and compares it to a dancer coming out of the sea like the wind. In the next stanza, the speaker prays his daughter be given beauty-but not too much, as excessive beauty would cause unwanted attention from strangers; cause his daughter to believe beauty is more important than other qualities, like kindness and rightness; and leave her friendless. The speaker uses Helen of Troy for an example of excessive beauty.
- The Judgement of Paris-a Greek myth-is discussed: Helen's beauty is the reason Paris chose Aphrodite for the winner of his judgement. Aphrodite, in turn, chose Hephaestus.
- The decisions surrounding these beautiful women are examples of how a symbol of bountiful beauty-the Horn of Plenty-is ruined.
- In the next stanza, the speaker returns to praying for qualities he wants his daughter to learn, focusing on manners. He believes a kind demeanor will make a woman who is not excessively beautiful still somewhat attractive to the right suitor. Foolish men often value beauty, but most men will stick beside the woman who values kindness.
- The speaker compares his daughter to a tree. He hopes her thoughts will resemble a bird or, in other words, that she will be entertaining. Also, the speaker prays she will be rooted: have a long-term home.
- Next, the speaker reflects on how loving excessively beautiful women has stagnated his mind. He is only certain that hate will ruin the chances a woman has and reverts to the bird metaphor: The absence of hate will allow the bird to stay on its leaf in the tree or, in other words, have a home.
- The speaker's condemnation of hate is narrowed to intellectual hatred in the following stanza. He believes a woman's hateful opinions can ruin even a bounty of beauty; he repeats the symbol of a corrupted Horn of Plenty to describe this. Returning to the storm imagery, he compares hateful speech to the wind.
- In the next stanza, the poem changes direction and looks at what an absence of hate brings: a deep-rooted innocence of the soul. The soul can amuse itself and enact the will of Heaven. Once she has rediscovered the soul's innocence, his daughter must remain happy, despite any metaphoric (or literal) storm.
- The speaker prays his daughter will find a husband who will provide her with a proper home. To the speaker, ceremony and custom are the only places where one can find beauty and innocence, respectively. He defines ceremony/beauty as the Horn of Plenty and custom/innocence as a victorious laurel tree, harkening back to the stable home of the linnet bird.
- The poem concludes with a prayer for the daughter's happiness, regardless of the external circumstances. The speaker wishes that her husband will take her to a home filled with tradition and ceremony, where purity and beauty are fostered. He emphasises the importance of upholding customs and respecting order as a means of preserving these qualities.
- "A Prayer for My Daughter" is a reflective and emotional poem in which the speaker prays for his daughter's well-being and happiness. The poem investigates themes of beauty, kindness, education, and the power of the mind.
- It offers a glimpse into a father's hopes and concerns for his child's future, set against the backdrop of a stormy and uncertain world.

Objective Questions

1. William Butler Yeats was the son of a well-known-------, John Butler Yeats.
(a) Irish painter (b) Irish carpenterc.
(c) Irish mechanicd. (d) Irish businessman

2. Where was WB Yeats born?
(a) Edinburgh (b) London
(c) Dublin (d) Glasgow

3. WB Yeats was deeply involved in ---------in Ireland.
(a) The moment of liberty
(b) Politics
(c) Studies
(d) Fighting with his enemies

4. The poetry of WB Yeats reflected a pessimism about the .... situation in his country and the rest of Europe.
(a) Political (b) Economical
(c) Social (d) Cultural

5. W. B. Yeats was awarded the Nobel Prize in ....
(a) 1920 (b) 1921 (c) 1923 (d) 1924

6. WB Yeats was one of the founders of the famous Abbey Theatre in ....
(a) Dublin (b) Edinburgh
(c) London (d) Glasgow

7. WB Yeats is .... poet.
(a) An Indian (b) A British
(c) An Irish (d) An American

8. Who has composed the poem, 'A Prayer for My Daughter'?
(a) W. H. Davies (b) T. S. Eliot
(c) W. B. Yeats (d) W. H. Auden

9. WB Yeats had involved ...., a movement against the cultural influences of English rule in Ireland during the Victorian period, which sought to promote the spirit of Ireland's native heritage.
(a) French revolution
(b) Celtic revival
(c) Romantic revival
(d) Pre-Raphaelite movement

10. What was the Celtic Revival?
(a) It was a movement against the cultural influences of English rule in Ireland .
(b) It was a movement against the economical influences of English rule in Ireland .
(c) It was a movement against the cultural influences of English rule in England .
(d) It was a movement against the economical influences of English rule in England .

11. Which movement promoted the spirit of Ireland's native heritage?
(a) French revolution
(b) Celtic revival movement
(c) Romantic revival movement
(d) Pre-Raphaelite movement

12. WB Yeats verse reflected .... about the political situation in his country and the rest of Europe
(a) An optimism (b) A pessimism
(c) Anti-romanticism (d) Idealism

13. WB Yeats was one of the founders of the famous .... in Dublin.
(a) Capel Street Theatre (b) Focus Theatre
(c) Abbey Theatre (d) Irish Literary Theatre

14. W. B. Yeats was awarded the .... in 1923.
(a) Pulitzer Prize (b) Poet Laureate
(c) Nobel Prize (d) Booker award

15. The poem, 'A Prayer for My Daughter' by Yeats is addressed to-------, his daughter.
(a) Anne (b) Jenney (c) Laura (d) Amanda

16. The poem, 'A Prayer for My Daughter' begins by describing " -------------".
(a) The first birth day of poet's daughter
(b) Storm
(c) Flood
(d) Draught

17. What does the 'Storm' symbolize in the poem, 'A Prayer for My Daughter' by Yeats?
(a) The Irish War of Independence
(b) The African War of Independence
(c) The Indian War of Independence
(d) The American War of Independence

18. What were the common subjects of WB Yeats' poetry?
(a) Conflict between Science and Religion
(b) Conflict between Ireland and the United Kingdom
(c) Conflict between Reality and Illusion
(d) Conflict between Good and Worst

19. How many stanzas are there in the poem, 'A Prayer for My Daughter' by Yeats?
(a) Seven (b) Eight
(c) Nine (d) Ten

20. Which is not the following poem written by WB Yeats?
(a) Among School Children
(b) A Prayer for My Daughter
(c) Journey of Magi
(d) Sailing to Byzantium

21. 'A Prayer for My Daughter' by W. B. Yeats opens with an image of the newborn child .... in a cradle.
(a) Crying
(b) Playing
(c) Sleeping
(d) Laughing

22. W. B. Yeats is in a state of .... in the poem, 'A Prayer for My Daughter' .
(a) Happiness (b) Reverie
(c) Nightmare (d) Dream

23. W. B. Yeats feels a kind of gloom and worry about the .... of his daughter in the poem, 'A Prayer for My Daughter'?
(a) Present
(b) Past
(c) Future
(d) All of the above

24. What does Yeats want that her daughter possess in future?
(a) Some qualities to face independently with confidence
(b) A nice bungalow with all amenities
(c) Some weapons to fight with enemies
(d) Gold and land in big amount

25. What is the last wish of WB Yeatsin the poem, 'A Prayer for My Daughter'?
(a) His daughter should become a poet
(b) His daughter should have weapons to fight with enemies
(c) His daughter should marry a person of aristocratic family
(d) His daughter should lead the country

26. 'A Prayer for My Daughter' is a prayer for .... in a damaged civilization.
(a) Order and grace
(b) Harshness and crudeness
(c) Clumsiness and ugliness
(d) Deformity and unkindness

27. 'A Prayer for My Daughter' is a reflection of the poet's --------for his daughter.
(a) Hate (b) Love
(c) Sorrow (d) None of these

28. Who is the speaker in the poem, 'A Prayer for My Daughter'?
(a) The mother of the daughter
(b) The sister of the daughter
(c) The poet himself
(d) The God.

Answers

1. (a)	2. (c)	3. (b)	4. (a)	5. (c)	6. (a)	7. (c)	8. (c)	9. (b)	10. (a)
11. (b)	12. (b)	13. (c)	14. (c)	15. (a)	16. (b)	17. (a)	18. (c)	19. (b)	20. (a)
21. (c)	22. (c)	23. (c)	24. (a)	25. (c)	26. (a)	27. (b)	28. (c)		

02 Indian Weavers

Summary of the Lesson

- Indian Weavers is a poem by Sarojini Naidu is a short poem consisting of three stanzas having four lines each. The poetess talk about three types of dresses that the Indian Weavers weave at three particular times of the day.
- Metaphorically each time and the dress weaved in the different time of the day symbolises a particular stage of life.
- The poem has a rhyme scheme AABB. The poet uses a number of literary devices to express her ideas like similie, imagery, metaphor etc. the poem consists of a discussion between the poetess and the weavers; the poet asks the weavers and the latter reply.
- In the first stanza, the poetess asks the weavers why they are weaving cloths early in the morning which seem to be quite beautiful and charming (gay).
- The clothes are blue as the wing of a halcyon wild (the bird Kingfisher).
- The wings of the kingfisher are bright blue in colour. In addition blue colour also symbolises loyalty. The blue colour thus symbolises something beautiful and precious. Hence, in this stanza, the clothes weaved by the weavers are quite special and this is why the poetess is curious to know about them.
- The Indian weavers reply, We weave the robes of a new-born child i.e. they are weaving the beautiful dress for a young one who has just came to the world.
- In this stanza, a number of images are used to describe the first stage of human life like break of day, garments so gay, and blue as the wing of halcyon wild. This stage is full of happiness, freshness, hope and beauty etc. there is no sorrow at this stage.
- In the second stanza, the poetess again meets the Indian weavers, this time during the fall of night. It probably refers to the evening or dusk when the sun sets and darkness paves the way. Moreover it is also the time during which most of the Indian marriages take place.

- The poetess questions the weavers why they weave the garments so bright like the plumes of the peacock, purple andgreen.
- The garment at this time is bright and full of colours like feathers of peacock unlike the one colour-blue (during the morning time).
- The weavers reply that they weave the marriage-veils of a queen, thus referring to the second or in other words adult stage of life. During this stage, humans are quite active. They love each other, get married and quest for a better prosperous life.
- The colour purple and green symbolise sorrow and happiness or struggle and ease in one's adult stage and these all colours or ups and downs of life make the adulthood bright.
- In the last stanza, the poet finds the weavers solemn and still i.e. they are quite sorrowful, grieved and silent. They are weaving something weird in the moonlight chill i.e. in the dead of the night which is white as a feather and white as a cloud, i.e. colourless, lifeless.
- As the poetess fails to figure out what it is (clothes) and why they are sorrowful and silent, she asks them what are they weaving rather than why are weaving. They reply that they are weaving shroud (cloth put on the dead body) for a dead person.
- Thus the third and the final is death which is emotionless and lifeless like a white colour or feather. In this way, the life which begins with life, joy, hope etc. ends with sorrow and grief.

Objective Questions

1. Who composed the poem' Indian Weavers'?
(a) Rabindranath Tagore (b) Sarojini Naidu
(c) William Wordsworth (d) John Keats

2. In Indian Weavers, what do the weavers weave in the morning?
(a) Gold threads (b) Garlands
(c) Purple robes for a queen
(d) Soft and silken threads for the night

3. What do the weavers weave in the evening according to the poem' The Indian weavers'?
(a) Scarlet threads for a bride's wedding
(b) White cloth for a funeral
(c) Silk garments for a king
(d) Blue and green scarves for festivals

4. What do the weavers weave in the night in the poem Indian Weavers?
(a) Garlands of flowers
(b) Soft and silken threads for the night
(c) Coffins for the dead
(d) Bright and shiny ribbons

5. What is the central theme of the poem 'Indian Weavers'?
(a) The beauty of nature
(b) The cycle of life and death
(c) The simplicity of rural life
(d) The role of women in society

6. In The poem 'Indian Weavers', what does the poet praise about the weavers?
(a) Their creativity
(b) Their craftsmanship
(c) Their ability to create clothes
(d) Their role in the wedding ceremonies

7. How does the poet describe the work of the weavers in the morning?
(a) Weaving bright yellow and red threads
(b) Weaving dark, heavy cloth
(c) Weaving purple robes for a queen
(d) Weaving light and airy garments

8. According to poem 'Indian weavers ',What emotion does the poem Indian Weavers evoke about life?
(a) Joy and celebration (b) Sadness and melancholy
(c) Anger and frustration (d) Confusion and mystery

9. The poem Indian Weavers uses which of the following literary devices?
(a) Metaphor (b) Simile
(c) Personification (d) Imagery

10. From the given options,What does the poet imply through the weavers' work in the night?
(a) They are preparing for a grand feast.
(b) They are part of the natural cycle of life and death.
(c) They are creating luxurious clothes for the rich.
(d) They are preparing for the upcoming festival.

11. In poem Indian Weavers, the weavers weave "purple robes for a queen" in the morning. What does this symbolize?
(a) Youth and vitality
(b) Joy and celebration
(c) Royalty and power
(d) Simplicity and peace

12. According to the poem,The weavers in the poem Indian Weavers represent a metaphor for which aspect of human life?
(a) The unpredictability of life
(b) The continuity of work
(c) The cycle of life, death, and rebirth
(d) The struggle for wealth and power

13. According to the poem"Indian Weavers', what do the weavers weave at night?
(a) Clothes for kings (b) Garlands for festivals
(c) A coffin for the dead (d) Blankets for warmth

14. The phrase "Soft as the blossoms of the night" in Indian Weavers refers to the weaving of what?
(a) Morning robes for the queen
(b) Evening bridal garments
(c) Funeral garments for the dead
(d) Wedding garlands for the bride

15. What emotion does the poet convey in the third stanza of The poem Indian Weavers?
(a) Hope (b) Joy (c) Sorrow (d) Anger

16. The imagery in Indian Weavers is mostly associated with which of the following elements?
(a) Fire
(b) Seasons of the year
(c) Elements of nature and life
(d) Sounds of the city

17. What does the "scarlet threads" woven by the weavers in the evening symbolise in Indian Weavers?
(a) The joy of the festival
(b) Wedding garments and the beginning of life
(c) The colors of the sunset
(d) The royal robes for the king

18. The use of purple in the first stanza of the poem symbolizes which of the following?
(a) Death (b) Luxury and royalty
(c) Fertility and growth (d) Peace and harmony

19. Which of the following best describes the tone of the poem Indian Weavers?
(a) Cheerful and lively
(b) Reflective and melancholic
(c) Excited and joyful
(d) Angry and rebellious

20. The line "Weavers, weaving at night" in Indian Weavers suggests the weavers are engaged in which activity?
(a) Preparing for a celebration
(b) Engaged in their daily work
(c) Reflecting on the passage of time
(d) Grieving over loss

21. What does the color "scarlet" represent in the second stanza of Indian Weavers?
(a) Youth and vitality (b) Love and marriage
(c) Mourning and death (d) Wealth and prosperity

22. In the poem Indian Weavers, which of the following seasons is NOT mentioned as the time of the weavers' work?
(a) Morning (b) Evening(c) Night (d) Winter

23. In Indian Weavers, the weavers' craft is depicted as symbolic of:
(a) The passage of time and life's transitions
(b) Wealth and luxury
(c) The struggle for social equality
(d) The eternal pursuit of happiness

24. What is the mood of the poem Indian Weavers?
(a) Festive and celebratory
(b) Hopeful and optimistic
(c) Melancholic and reflective
(d) Angry and rebellious

25. In Indian Weavers, the weavers work during the night to weave ....
(a) The future of India
(b) Coffins for the dead
(c) Garments for a royal wedding
(d) Gifts for the queen

26. What does the line "Soft as the blossoms of the night" in the poem Indian Weavers refer to?
(a) The silk garments woven in the morning
(b) The wedding robes woven in the evening
(c) The funeral shroud woven in the night
(d) The colors of the sunrise

27. Which of the following best describes the structure of Indian Weavers?
(a) The poem follows a free verse form without a regular meter.
(b) The poem has a consistent rhyme scheme and meter.
(c) The poem is written as a dialogue between two characters.
(d) The poem is written in long prose paragraphs.

28. In Indian Weavers, the poet speaks about the weavers' work as a ....
(a) Celebration of life's achievements
(b) Metaphor for life, death, and rebirth
(c) Challenge and struggle for survival
(d) Representation of eternal joy

29. What does the poem Indian Weavers primarily explore?
(a) The importance of artisans in society
(b) The relationship between the weavers and the royal family
(c) The cycle of life, from birth to death
(d) The future of the Indian textile industry

30. The weavers in 'Indian Weavers' are engaged in their craft at different times of the day. What does this convey about their work?
(a) They work according to a strict schedule
(b) Their work is based on the natural cycle of life
(c) Their work is purely artistic with no practical purpose
(d) Their work is associated only with wealth and luxury

Answers

1. (b)	2. (c)	3. (a)	4. (c)	5. (b)	6. (b)	7. (c)	8. (b)	9. (d)	10. (b)
11. (c)	12. (c)	13. (c)	14. (c)	15. (c)	16. (c)	17. (b)	18. (b)	19. (b)	20. (b)
21. (b)	22. (d)	23. (a)	24. (c)	25. (b)	26. (c)	27. (b)	28. (b)	29. (c)	30. (b)

03 Ode to Autumn (John Keats)

Summary of the Lesson

- The poem 'Ode to Autumn' is a remarkable poem which has been composed by the great Romantic poet 'John Keats'.
- It was composed in 1819 and published in the next year 1820.
- In this poem poet describes the beauty and characteristic spirit of autumn in a series of memorable pictures, exhibiting the principle of beauty in nature.
- The poem is divided into three stanzas, each highlighting a different feature of fall and a concluding stanza considering life's revolving-door nature and the certainty of death.
- The apples were bending the branches of the trees they were growing on and were covered with moss, the thick green stuff that can grow on almost anything. The fruit was filled with ripeness to the core by which the poet meant that the fruit had grown to its fullest size and needed to be harvested.
- The gourd became big and full and hazel shells grew fat with a sweet nut inside. The flowers were growing new buds and kept growing more, and when these buds bloomed, bees gathered around the flowers' pollen.
- Those bees thought that the warmth would last forever, because summer brought so many flowers and so much pollen that the beehives were now overflowing with honey.
- In the first stanza of the poem the poet talked about autumn, the season associated with mists and a general sense of calm abundance.
- Autumn was scheming with the sun to put on and bless with fruit, the vines that were running around the roof. Thatch was reeds or some other plant that was used as roof covering. The apples
- In the second stanza of the poem, the poet asked a question to the Autumn season that who had not noticed it.
- Further he explained that any person who found themselves wandering about how to find the Autumn season, was likely to find it sitting lazily on the floor of a building where grains were stored.
- The poet talked about the season's hair being lifted by a light wind that separated the strands of the hair by which he meant how a harvester might separate the components of a grain of wheat.
- Autumn was asleep with the toxic smell of poppies in her nose. Therefore the next section of a long strip of land on which crops had been cut and the twisted flowers would be saved from being cut.
- According to the poet Sometimes, Autumn was like the agricultural laborer who picked up loose cuttings from the fields after the harvest. Autumn had gleaned lots of leftovers and put them on her head.
- So the poet had described the Autumn season as a laborer, who had to be observant, who watched the stream with a full, heavy head of fruit and leaves. Other times Autumn would watch the cyder-press noting how the juice and pulp slowly oozed out of the machine over the course of many hours.
- In the last stanza of the poem, the poet expressed sadness that spring was not here. He asked where the music that characterises spring and he repeated himself where it was by asking a question.
- The poet suggested not to think about the spring and its typical music as autumn had its own music. The poet described the background for the music as a scene in which beautiful, shadowed clouds expanded in the evening sky and filtered the sunlight such that it casted pink upon the fields, which had been harvested.
- The music included gnats, which hummed mournfully in a chorus among the willows that grew along the riverbanks, and which rose and fell according to the strength of the wind.
- They were mourning because of the dying day and also as the end of the summer was approaching.
- The poet also described that there were mature, fully grown lambs who were making loud sounds from the fence of their hilly enclosure. It included crickets singing in the bushes and a red-breasted bird that softly whistled from a small garden.
- And lastly, it included the growing flock of swallows, which rose and sang together against the darkening sky.

Objective Questions

1. **From the given options,Who has composed the poem, 'Ode to Autumn' ?**
(a) Keats (b) Wordsworth
(c) Coleridge (d) Shelley

2. **Ode To Autumn' is written in-**
(a) October 1819 (b) September 1819
(c) November 1819 (d) December 1819

3. **The Poem 'Ode To Autumn' is-**
(a) an epic (b) an elegy
(c) an ode (d) a ballad

4. **In 'Ode to Autumn' poet deals with .... in detail.**
(a) Spring (b) Winter
(c) Summer (d) Autumn

5. **How many stanzas The Poem 'Ode To Autumn' consists of -**
(a) four stanzas (b) three stanzas
(c) five stanzas (d) six stanzas

6. **The theme of Autumn is --**
(a) scarcity (b) abundance
(c) fulfilment/maturity (d) None of these

7. **Who called 'Ode to Autumn'Keats' most satisfying of all the odes ?**
(a) Dryden (b) Coleridge
(c) Wordsworth (d) Arthur Compton-Rickett.

8. **Each stanza of The Poem'Ode To Autumn' consists-**
(a) 11 lines (b) 12 lines (c) 13 lines (d) 14 lines

9. **Who has been personified in 'Ode To Autumn' ?**
(a) Spring (b) Autumn
(c) Winter (d) Summer

10. **John Keats has written the poem-**
(a) An Epitaph (b) Ode To Autumn
(c) The Soldier (d) Fire-Hymn

11. **According to the poet,Autumn is a season of mellow-**
(a) no wind (b) fruitlessness
(c) fruitfulness (d) None of these

12. **In which season Autumn starts with the departure.**
(a) winter (b) spring
(c) rainy (d) summer

13. **Who scene was a great lover of nature.**
(a) John Keats (b) John Donne
(c) W.H. Auden (d) Walt Whitman

14. **In .... new leaves and fruits come out on trees.**
(a) spring (b) autumn
(c) summer (d) winter

15. **And gathering swallows twitter in the skies' is taken from -**
(a) snake
(b) The soldier
(c) ode to Autumn
(d) An Epitaph

16. **Season of mists and inellow fruitfulness' is written by-**
(a) John Donne (b) Walt Whitman
(c) W.H. Auden (d) John Keats

17. **Which of the following best describes the tone of the poem 'ode to Autumn"?**
(a) Reflective and celebratory
(b) Melancholic and despairing
(c) Joyful and energetic
(d) Angry and critical

18. **In the poem 'ode to Autumn' what is Autumn described as being a close friend of?**
(a) The sun (b) The moon
(c) The stars (d) The wind

19. **Which literary device is used in the line "Close bosom-friend of the maturing sun"?**
(a) Metaphor (b) Simile
(c) Personification (d) Alliteration

20. **Which natural activity is mentioned in the first stanza?**
(a) Bees collecting honey (b) Leaves falling from trees
(c) Rivers freezing over (d) Birds building nests

21. **Which of the following Natural activity is mentioned in the first stanza?**
(a) Bees collecting honey
(b) Leaves falling from trees
(c) Rivers freezing over
(d) Birds building nests

22. **In the poem 'ode to Autumn' what is a theme of To Autumn?**
(a) The inevitability of death
(b) The beauty of change and transition
(c) The power of human creativity
(d) The destruction caused by nature

23. **Which type of the music of Autumn described in the poem?**
(a) As loud and celebratory
(b) As soft and harmonious
(c) As harsh and foreboding
(d) As silent and still

24. **Which phrase from the poem 'ode to Autumn 'suggests the passage of time?**
(a) "Where are the songs of Spring?"
(b) "Season of mists and mellow fruitfulness"
(c) "Thy hair soft-lifted by the winnowing wind"
(d) "The red-breast whistles from a garden-croft"

25. **In the poem 'ode to Autumn', what is the purpose of the line "Thou hast thy music too"?**
(a) To emphasize that Autumn has its own unique beauty
(b) To dismiss the importance of Spring's music
(c) To compare Autumn's song to a lullaby
(d) To criticize those who dislike Autumn

26. What type of imagery is predominantly used in the poem'ode to Autumn'?
(a) Visual and tactile (b) Auditory and gustatory
(c) Visual and auditory (d) Olfactory and tactile

27. What does the poet mean by "barred clouds bloom the soft-dying day"?
(a) The clouds are tinged with the colors of sunset.
(b) The clouds signify the coming of rain.
(c) The clouds symbolize the end of harvest.
(d) The clouds are a metaphor for Autumn's melancholy.

28. What does the poet mean by "thou watchest the last oozings hours by hours"?
(a) Autumn is leisurely observing the process of making cider.
(b) Autumn is busy completing its duties.
(c) Autumn is mourning the end of harvest.
(d) Autumn is impatient for winter to arrive.

29. What emotion dominates the final stanza of the poem'ode to Autumn'?
(a) Nostalgia for spring and summer
(b) Celebration of nature's bounty
(c) Sadness for the coming winter
(d) Acceptance of life's cycles

30. What time of day is described in the final stanza of the poem?
(a) Morning (b) Noon
(c) Evening (d) Midnight

Answers

1. (a)	2. (b)	3. (c)	4. (d)	5. (b)	6. (c)	7. (d)	8. (a)	9. (b)	10. (b)
11. (c)	12. (d)	13. (a)	14. (b)	15. (c)	16. (d)	17. (a)	18. (a)	19. (c)	20. (a)
21. (a)	22. (b)	23. (b)	24. (a)	25. (a)	26. (c)	27. (a)	28. (a)	29. (d)	30. (c)

04 Our Casuarina Tree (Toru Dutt)

Summary of the Lesson

- Our casuarina Tree is one of the notable poem of Toru Dutt.
- It was published in her childhood collection of the poems Ancient ballads and Leagends of Hindustan in 1882.
- The poem "Our Casuarina Tree" is a beautiful symbolic poem harmonising both matt er and manner in accurate proportion.
- The tree stands for a symbolic representation of Toru's past memory. Apparently it symbolises the rich tradition of Indian culture and philosophy which played an important role in shaping the poetic and aesthetic sensibility of the poets. In Keats' "Ode to a Nightingale", the bird symbolizes the world of art and beauty. In Shelley's "To a Skylark", the bird is the symbol of freedom and liberty.
- Similarly, in Toru Dutt's "Our Casuarina Tree", the tree connotes the nostalgic feelings and memor y of Toru Dutt. This is the tree under which she played with his brother and sister- Abju and Aru. So the very thought of the tree transported her to her golden past days.
- The poem opens with the use of the simile- "L ike a huge python..." and the poet says that a huge creeper like plant has wound around the trun k of the Casuarina tree and has crept upto the mast of the tree. Immediately later she says tha t any other tree would have found it difficult to live under that stifling throttle. But the Casuarina wears it like a scarf on its head.
- At once a magnanimous appearance of the tree is env isioned. This giant tree is an abode of peace for all the birds, the flowers that blossom o n the tree attract the bees. At night a sweet song of a bird would reverberate all around the garden. Thus in the first stanza, the poet establishes how beautiful and heavenly the place wo uld seem like. The action described took place in the past.
- In the second stanza too, the description of n ature comes again. In the morning when the poet would look at the tree, she would see a gray b aboon sitting on the top of the tree and experiencing the sunrise. His little baby would pla y in the branches. The scenic beauty is far beyond words to describe. In another part of the ga rden, the water lilies would bloom together underneath the shadow of the tree.
- In the third stanza, the poet becomes personal and declares that not because of its beauty is the tree dear to her, "But not because of its magnificence / Dear is the Casuarina to my soul:" Rather she has spent a great number of her childhood years underneath this tree with her sweet siblings, those kindred souls whom death has untimely taken away. The beaut y of the tree is no more

than an added gift. Its actual importance lies in the fact that i t is a part of the Dutts' existence, a reminder of family ties, of the warmth shared by three siblings . The Abju-Aru-Toru bonding was indeed strong and in Sita Toru mentions, "Three happy children..." sitting in a dark room listening to a story and then sighs because she knows that they will never again "by their mother's side/Gather". Like Keats, she had to suffer a lot. She had seen bitter struggle for life and death, untold miseries after the death of her belov ed brother and sister.

- The fourth stanza is highly philosophical. The poet observes "Unknown yet well-known to the eyes of faith" . Here the term 'unknown' denotes not simply the na tive home of the poet but also the world of the departed soul. A man who has the eye of faith can see the unknown as well-known. This is what exactly Toru Dutt feels here. Interestingly Toru's mystical and spiritual approach to poetry is center ed to her profound knowledge of great Sanskrit epics and scriptures.
- The music which Toru refers here is not an ordinary music which we hear in our day to day life; it is music of the soul, which once it is attained, never dies and continues to vibrate with the highest perc ipience in the mind of the seeker.
- Toru Dutt is not like the "Skylark" of Shelley, "the scorner of the ground" but she is the "Skylark" of Wordsworth "a pilgrim of the sky" and does not despise the earth where cares abound.At the end of the poem she absolutely transcends th e mortal, materialistic and mundane frame of mind and attains the power of love to over come the negative forces of life like death and darkness, terror and fear. In this stanza, the w ords and the phrases like 'trembling hope', 'love', 'death', 'the skeleton', 'and oblivion' are very suggestive. She means to say that a man of unflinching love and devotion never fears th e blows of death. Toru does not express any desire to fade "far away" and "dissolve".
- Their Casuarina tree does not make her long for "easeful" death. Instead, even though its "timelessness" mocks the transience of the human world, the tree is to her a support, a remind er of the joy she once experienced with Abju and Aru. So, in the final stanza, Toru Dutt, aware both of Druidism and the customary tree-worship in India, wishes to "consecrate a lay" in the Casuarina Tree's honour. To sum up, the poem "Our Casuarina Tree" shows a pe rfect blending of feelings and forms, matter and manner. It contains what Eliot means by his phrase "unified sensibility".
- o It is a combination of both the East and the West. In form, it is very near to the Romantic and the Victorian poems. In theme it dives deep into the` un fathomable ocean of the Vedanta and the Upanishad of body and soul, life and death.

Objective Questions

1. Who composed the poem 'Our Casuarina Tree'?
(a) Sarojini Naidu (b) Toru Dutt
(c) Rabindranath Tagore (d) Kamala Das

2. According to the poet,What does the casuarina tree symbolize in the poem '?
(a) Strength and permanence
(b) Love and nostalgia
(c) Both A and B
(d) The beauty of nature

3. What is the tone of the toru dart's Poem Our Casuarina Tree?
(a) Light and humorous
(b) Nostalgic and melancholic
(c) Angry and defiant (d) Romantic and passionate

4. What kind of imagery is prominently used in the poem?
(a) Urban imagery
(b) Pastoral and natural imagery
(c) Futuristic imagery
(d) Industrial imagery

5. Which of the following creature is described as climbing the casuarina tree?
(a) A monkey (b) A python
(c) A squirrel (d) A bird

6. The poet associate the tree with?
(a) Childhood memories and lost loved ones
(b) The struggles of life
(c) The beauty of urbanization
(d) The horrors of colonial rule

7. Which season is vividly described in the poem 'our casuarina Tree'?
(a) Summer
(b) Autumn
(c) Winter
(d) Spring

8. The poet wish to immortalize the casuarina tree,why?
(a) To preserve its beauty for future generations
(b) To honor its connection to her childhood and loved ones
(c) To celebrate nature's role in human life
(d) To express her desire to protect the environment

9. Which literary devices are prominently used in the poem 'Our Casuarina Tree'?
(a) Metaphor and personification
(b) Hyperbole and satire
(c) Allegory and irony
(d) Euphemism and understatement

10. What does the poet Toru Dutt mean by "a presence that disturbs me with the joy of elevated thoughts"?
(a) The tree inspires her with deep, reflective thoughts.
(b) The tree makes her feel uneasy and anxious.
(c) The tree reminds her of her responsibilities.
(d) The tree disturbs her with its towering height.

11. What is the primary theme of The poem "Our Casuarina Tree"?
(a) The beauty of nature
(b) The passage of time and nostalgia
(c) The importance of preserving trees
(d) The joy of childhood play

12. What does the poet wish to achieve by writing the poem ' our casuarina Tree'?
(a) To protect the casuarina tree
(b) To immortalize her memories and loved ones
(c) To promote the conservation of forests
(d) To criticize modern lifestyles

13. What is the poetic form of The poem 'Our Casuarina Tree'?
(a) A sonnet
(b) A free verse poem
(c) A lyric poem
(d) An epic poem

14. Form the given options,Which classical allusion does Toru Dutt use in the poem?
(a) Greek gods and myths
(b) Italian landscapes
(c) The immortal yew trees of literature
(d) Biblical references

15. Which of the following role does the python play in the poem?
(a) It adds an element of danger.
(b) It highlights the tree's grandeur and timelessness.
(c) It symbolizes the struggle of life.
(d) It represents death and decay.

16. According to the poem 'The casuarina Tree',What kind of relationship does the poet have with the tree?
(a) A spiritual and emotional connection
(b) A fear and respect for its power
(c) An indifferent relationship
(d) A purely aesthetic appreciation

17. What is the significance of the tree in the poet's childhood?
(a) It was a source of shade during hot days.
(b) It was a silent witness to her childhood joys and losses.
(c) It was a barrier against storms.
(d) It provided fruits and resources.

18. The poet refer to the tree as "giant" because..
(a) To emphasize its physical size and grandeur
(b) To symbolize its strength and timelessness
(c) To portray it as a protector of memories
(d) All of the above

19. According to you,What does the casuarina tree remind the poet of?
(a) Her lost siblings and their shared childhood
(b) The hardships of life
(c) The beauty of Indian flora
(d) The cultural importance of nature

20. What mood is evoked at the end of the poem 'The casuarina Tree'?
(a) A sense of sorrow and finality
(b) A hopeful and eternal connection to memories
(c) A feeling of detachment from nature
(d) A longing to return to the past of the tree.

21. How does the poet describe the casuarina tree's flowers?
(a) They are small and red.
(b) They are large and fragrant.
(c) They are tiny and clustered.
(d) They are golden and glowing.

22. From the given options,Which literary device is used in the line "like a huge Python, winding round and round"?
(a) Simile
(b) Metaphor
(c) Alliteration
(d) Personification

23. The casuarina tree stands as a symbol of what in the Toru Dutt's life?
(a) Change and uncertainty
(b) Stability, love, and memories
(c) Growth and success
(d) Nature's mysteries

24. What significance does the casuarina tree hold for the poet's siblings?
(a) They used to play around it during their childhood.
(b) It provided them with shade while they studied.
(c) They carved their initials on it.
(d) They never interacted with it.

25. How does the poet immortalize the casuarina tree?
(a) By planting more trees
(b) By dedicating her poem to it
(c) By preserving it in a photograph
(d) By writing about its fruit-bearing qualities

26. What is the significance of the phrase "a grey baboon sits statue-like alone"?
(a) It reflects the stillness of the morning.
(b) It symbolizes the tree's role as a shelter for wildlife.
(c) It highlights the mysterious atmosphere of the tree.
(d) Both A and B.

27. The poet reference yew trees in the poem.why?
(a) To draw a parallel between yew trees and the casuarina tree as symbols of immortality.
(b) To emphasize the casuarina tree's historical significance.
(c) To show her interest in European landscapes.
(d) To compare different types of trees.

28. What emotion does Toru Dutt associate with the chirping of birds around the tree?
(a) Joy and contentment (b) Nostalgia and longing
(c) Sadness and regret (d) Anxiety and fear

29. From the given options What poetic technique is used in the phrase "Time the shadow, and light the intervening"?
(a) Personification (b) Oxymoron
(c) Metaphor (d) Symbolism

30. How does the poet describe the morning scene around the tree?
(a) As noisy and crowded
(b) As serene and filled with natural activity
(c) As dark and gloomy
(d) As chaotic and wild

31. What does Toru Dutt hope to achieve by writing about the casuarina tree?
(a) Immortalize the tree and her cherished memories
(b) Advocate for environmental conservation
(c) Criticize industrialization
(d) Provide a botanical description

32. What does the casuarina tree represent for Toru Dutt in terms of time?
(a) The fleeting nature of life
(b) The permanence amidst the transience of life
(c) The inevitability of death
(d) The gradual passage of years

33. From the given options,What is the poet's connection to the casuarina tree in adulthood?
(a) It serves as a reminder of her happy childhood.
(b) It is no longer significant to her.
(c) It becomes a symbol of her spiritual beliefs.
(d) It provides her with shade while she writes.

34. What does the poet describe as "a blessing on the landscape"?
(a) The sunlight falling on the fields
(b) The casuarina tree
(c) The chirping birds
(d) The baboon and its young

35. From the given options,What aspect of the tree reflects its grandeur and age?
(a) The giant trunk and winding branches
(b) The sound of its leaves in the wind
(c) The animals and birds it shelters
(d) Its ability to produce fruit

36. How does Toru Dutt view nature in the poem?
(a) As indifferent to human emotions
(b) As a source of inspiration, solace, and nostalgia
(c) As something to be controlled and tamed
(d) As an object of scientific study

37. What does the poet associate the casuarina tree with in terms of loss?
(a) The death of her parents
(b) The untimely loss of her siblings
(c) The destruction caused by industrialization
(d) The fading of her youthful innocence

38. How does the poet use the imagery of the python in the poem 'The casuarina Tree'?
(a) To show the tree's danger
(b) To symbolize the strength and majesty of the tree
(c) To depict a scene of battle
(d) To introduce an element of fear

39. From the given options,What does the poet's longing for the casuarina tree signify?
(a) Her regret for moving away
(b) Her deep emotional bond with the past
(c) Her fear of losing memories
(d) Her desire to return to her childhood home

40. How does 'Our Casuarina Tree' reflect toru Dutt's personal life?
(a) It echoes her grief for her siblings and childhood memories.
(b) It portrays her connection with Indian mythology.
(c) It represents her love for traveling.
(d) It mirrors her spiritual struggles.

41. What does the poet compare the casuarina tree to in the poem?
(a) A watchtower (b) A giant sentinel
(c) A wise old sage (d) A sheltering roof

42. What does the line "Its rugged trunk indented deep with scars" signify?
(a) The tree's long history and endurance
(b) The tree's suffering and pain
(c) The tree's struggle against storms
(d) The tree's loss of beauty

43. What makes The poem 'Our Casuarina Tree' a blend of personal and universal themes?
(a) The combination of childhood memories and reflections on immortality
(b) Its focus on environmental preservation
(c) Its celebration of nature's beauty
(d) Its critique of modern life

44. Why is 'The casuarina tree' described as a "blessing on the landscape"?
(a) It protects the surrounding land from storms.
(b) It stands as a symbol of comfort and continuity.
(c) It provides economic resources to the villagers.
(d) It offers fruit to animals and humans alike.

45. What does the poet hope will preserve the memory of the poem 'The casuarina tree'?
(a) The poem itself
(b) The stories told by her family
(c) The tree's ability to grow forever
(d) Its fame in the local community

46. How does the poet create a sense of harmony in the poem 'The casuarina Tree'?
(a) By describing the relationship between humans, animals, and nature
(b) By focusing solely on the tree
(c) By emphasizing human struggles
(d) By ignoring the negative aspects of life

47. Why does the poet mention the "unknown land" in the poem?
(a) To reflect her belief in an afterlife
(b) To symbolize the spiritual connection between the tree and her siblings
(c) To highlight the tree's ability to transcend time and space
(d) All of the above

48. How does the poet use the casuarina tree to explore the theme of loss?
(a) By portraying the tree as a witness to her siblings' absence
(b) By associating the tree with fading childhood memories
(c) By showing the tree as a link to her lost loved ones
(d) All of the above

49. What does Toru Dutt mean by the phrase "my own loved dead"?
(a) Her ancestors who planted the tree
(b) Her siblings who passed away
(c) The local villagers who admired the tree
(d) The animals who lived near the tree

50. Which poetic device is used in the line "Thy form, O Tree, as in my happy prime"?
(a) Apostrophe (b) Simile
(c) Alliteration (d) Hyperbole

51. How does the poet view the casuarina tree's relationship with the surrounding landscape?
(a) As a dominating force that overshadows everything
(b) As a harmonious and integral part of the natural world
(c) As a lonely figure disconnected from its surroundings
(d) As a symbol of urbanization

Answers

1. (b)	2. (c)	3. (b)	4. (b)	5. (b)	6. (a)	7. (c)	8. (b)	9. (a)	10. (a)
11. (b)	12. (b)	13. (c)	14. (c)	15. (b)	16. (a)	17. (b)	18. (d)	19. (a)	20. (b)
21. (c)	22. (a)	23. (b)	24. (a)	25. (b)	26. (d)	27. (a)	28. (b)	29. (d)	30. (b)
31. (a)	32. (b)	33. (a)	34. (b)	35. (a)	36. (b)	37. (b)	38. (b)	39. (b)	40. (a)
41. (b)	42. (a)	43. (a)	44. (b)	45. (a)	46. (a)	47. (d)	48. (d)	49. (b)	50. (a)
51. (b)									

05 The Sky is Your Platter

Summary of the Lesson

- In the poem The Sky is Your Platter, Guru Nanak Dev conveys a powerful message of the interconnectedness between humans and the universe.
- The sky is depicted as a vast and infinite platter, symbolizing the boundless opportunities and resources available to all. Guru Nanak encourages people to recognize that everything in the world, including the natural elements, is provided by the divine.
- The poem emphasizes the idea of unity and equality, urging people to understand that the earth and sky, which provide sustenance, are available to everyone, regardless of their background. Guru Nanak's teachings in this poem stress living in harmony with nature, being humble, and recognizing the divine presence in all aspects of life.
- The "platter" of the sky represents the vastness of God's gifts to humanity, and it serves as a reminder that the world is a shared gift, not meant for individual possession or greed.
- The poem "The Sky is Your Platter" by Guru Nanak Dev consists of four stanzas. Each stanza presents an important message, focusing on the interconnectedness of all beings with nature and the divine, while encouraging humility, equality, and respect for the world around us.
- In "The Sky is Your Platter", Guru Nanak Dev uses the imagery of the sky as a vast, boundless platter to convey profound spiritual lessons. The poem emphasizes that the universe is a creation of the divine, and everything within it, including nature, is a gift to humanity. The "sky" symbolizes infinite opportunities, abundance, and the interconnectedness of all living beings.
- The poem calls on people to understand that the resources of the world are meant to be shared and are available to all equally. It reminds us to be humble and to recognize that we are all part of a greater cosmic order. The natural world and the sky do not belong to any one individual but are gifts from the Creator for everyone.

- Through this poem, Guru Nanak Dev encourages us to live selflessly, live in harmony with nature, and understand the unity that connects all life forms. It is a call to respect the divine in all aspects of the world and to treat others with kindness, equality, and compassion.
- Overall, the poem promotes the values of selflessness, sharing, and respect for all living beings, encouraging a life that acknowledges the divine in everything around us.

Objective Questions

1. Who composed the poem The Sky is Your Platter?
(a) Rabindranath Tagore (b) Guru Nanak Dev
(c) Sarojini Naidu (d) Swami Vivekananda

2. In the poem, what is the sky referred to as?
(a) A vast ocean (b) A vast platter
(c) A golden crown (d) A great mountain

3. What is the main message of the poem The Sky is Your Platter?
(a) The importance of wealth
(b) The need for personal growth
(c) Unity and equality of all beings
(d) The pursuit of knowledge

4. In the poem, what does the "platter" symbolize?
(a) Divine gifts and opportunities
(b) Earthly possessions
(c) Personal achievements
(d) Power and wealth

5. What does Guru Nanak Dev urge people to recognize in the poem?
(a) The superiority of human beings
(b) The connection between humans and nature
(c) The importance of material success
(d) The need to conquer the world

6. How does the poem portray the natural world?
(a) As a place of suffering
(b) As a gift from the divine
(c) As something to be conquered
(d) As irrelevant to human life

7. What is the tone of the poem The Sky is Your Platter?
(a) Angry
(b) Hopeful
(c) Humble and reflective
(d) Sad

8. What does the poet encourage people to do in relation to the gifts of the sky?
(a) Take them for granted
(b) Use them for personal gain
(c) Share them equally with others
(d) Hoard them

9. What is the central theme of The Sky is Your Platter?
(a) The pursuit of individual wealth
(b) Equality, humility, and spiritual connection
(c) The importance of political power
(d) The significance of personal identity

10. The poem teaches that the resources of the world are meant to be:
(a) Hoarded (b) Exploited (c) Shared (d) Wasted

11. The "sky" in the poem can be interpreted as a metaphor for:
(a) Human suffering
(b) Endless possibilities and opportunities
(c) War and conflict
(d) A place of chaos

12. What does the poet's use of the term "platter" suggest about the sky?
(a) The sky is full of obstacles
(b) The sky is abundant and generous
(c) The sky is empty and unyielding
(d) The sky is dangerous and difficult to reach

13. According to the poem, the sky is a gift from whom?
(a) The kings and rulers (b) The divine or God
(c) Nature alone (d) Human beings

14. Which of the following values does the poem The Sky is Your Platter emphasize?
(a) Greed (b) Equality and humility
(c) Competition (d) Power and control

15. The poem conveys that the earth and sky are meant to be:
(a) Controlled and dominated
(b) Shared and respected
(c) Exploited for personal gain
(d) Ignored

16. What is the poet's perspective on material wealth in The Sky is Your Platter?
(a) It should be prioritized over spiritual values
(b) It is a divine gift for only a few
(c) It is less important than spiritual and moral values
(d) It is the ultimate goal of human life

17. How does the poem relate to the concept of selflessness?
(a) Encourages people to focus only on themselves
(b) Emphasizes the need to share the gifts of life
(c) Suggests that one should seek personal power
(d) Calls for domination over others

18. From the given options,The poet uses the metaphor of the sky being a platter to convey the idea of:
(a) An endless source of material wealth.
(b) Spiritual generosity and abundance
(c) A place to store personal belongings
(d) A hard, unyielding surface

19. What does Guru Nanak Dev imply about human beings' relationship to the divine gifts in the poem ' The sky is your platter'?
(a) They should claim ownership over them
(b) They are entitled to them without responsibility
(c) They should humbly accept and share them
(d) They should reject them as unimportant

20. From the given options,What is the ultimate lesson of The Sky is Your Platter?
(a) Life is about accumulating wealth
(b) Everyone should act in their own self-interest
(c) Humans should live in harmony with nature and each other
(d) Only the elite are worthy of divine gifts

21. In The Sky is Your Platter, Guru Nanak Dev encourages people to:
(a) Hoard wealth and resources for future generations
(b) Live in competition with each other
(c) Accept the gifts of nature with humility and share them
(d) Seek power and control over nature

22. According to the poem, who is the "platter" of the sky meant for?
(a) Only the rich (b) Only the rulers
(c) All of humanity (d) Only the wise

23. The poet uses the metaphor of the "sky" to convey the idea that:
(a) Nature is infinite and offers endless possibilities to all
(b) The sky is a place for the elite to claim
(c) Humans are separate from nature
(d) Only the mighty can reach the sky

24. What does the phrase "The sky is your platter" symbolize in the poem?
(a) The sky is a place of danger
(b) The sky is a place for seeking personal success
(c) The sky represents unlimited opportunities given by the divine
(d) The sky is meant for the rich and powerful only

25. What does the poet suggest people should do with the gifts of the sky?
(a) Use them to dominate others
(b) Use them to build their empires
(c) Share them with all, without greed
(d) Hoard them for their own benefit

26. What does Guru Nanak Dev's poem The Sky is Your Platter emphasize about material possessions?
(a) They are essential for happiness
(b) They should be valued above spiritual wealth
(c) They are temporary and should not be hoarded
(d) They are the only means of achieving success

27. According to the poem, the sky is not meant for:
(a) The rich and powerful alone
(b) The poor and needy
(c) Nature and animal
(d) Only those who work hard

28. Which of the following best describes the poet's message regarding the gifts of nature in the poem?
(a) They should be hoarded for future use
(b) They are meant to be enjoyed alone
(c) They are meant to be shared equally among all
(d) They should be used for personal gain

29. How does Guru Nanak Dev view the relationship between humans and nature in the poem?
(a) Humans should dominate nature
(b) Humans should live in harmony with nature and use its gifts responsibly
(c) Nature should be exploited for personal gain
(d) Humans should reject nature

30. The poet's tone in The Sky is Your Platter can be described as:
(a) Angry and forceful
(b) Inspirational and reflective
(c) Satirical and mocking
(d) Frustrated and hopeless

31. According to Guru Nanak Dev, the sky and its resources are:
(a) A reward for the hardworking
(b) A divine gift meant for everyone
(c) Only for the spiritually advanced
(d) Only for those who are wealthy

32. What does the poem The Sky is Your Platter suggest about the role of individuals in society?
(a) Individuals should prioritize their own happiness
(b) Individuals should exploit the resources of nature
(c) Individuals should live in harmony with others and share nature's gifts
(d) Individuals should focus solely on personal success

33. In the poem, Guru Nanak Dev urges people to:
(a) Be selfish and protect their resources
(b) Acknowledge the unity of all life and the gifts from the divine
(c) Pursue material wealth above all else
(d) Ignore the gifts of nature

34. What is the primary focus of The Sky is Your Platter?
(a) The beauty of the natural world
(b) The importance of spiritual knowledge
(c) The idea that resources and opportunities are meant for all, not just the few
(d) The celebration of individual success

35. What message does Guru Nanak Dev convey about personal possessions in the poem?
(a) They are a sign of spiritual success
(b) They should be used selfishly for personal benefit
(c) They should be used to serve others and promote equality
(d) They are a burden to carry

36. What does the sky symbolize in The Sky is Your Platter?
(a) Heaven and spiritual enlightenment
(b) The harshness of life
(c) The divine abundance and opportunities available to all
(d) A place to store material wealth

37. What does the poet suggest about equality in The Sky is Your Platter?
(a) Only the strong deserve the gifts of nature
(b) All people, regardless of status, should have equal access to the gifts of the world
(c) The wealthy should control the resources of nature
(d) The poor are not entitled to the gifts of nature

38. According to the poem, the sky's platter is a symbol of:
(a) The rewards of hard work
(b) The divine presence in all aspects of life
(c) The journey to spiritual enlightenment
(d) Materialistic desires

39. Guru Nanak Dev's poem is an expression of which of the following?
(a) The importance of individual struggle
(b) The need for collective harmony and shared responsibility
(c) The pursuit of worldly success
(d) The dominance of human beings over nature

40. What does the poet imply by saying "the sky is your platter"?
(a) Humans should take control of nature
(b) The sky offers only limited resources
(c) The sky provides an abundance of opportunities for all to share
(d) Only the strongest can claim the sky's gifts

Answers

1. (b)	2. (b)	3. (c)	4. (a)	5. (b)	6. (b)	7. (c)	8. (c)	9. (b)	10. (c)
11. (b)	12. (b)	13. (b)	14. (b)	15. (b)	16. (c)	17. (b)	18. (b)	19. (c)	20. (c)
21. (c)	22. (c)	23. (a)	24. (c)	25. (c)	26. (c)	27. (a)	28. (c)	29. (b)	30. (b)
31. (b)	32. (c)	33. (b)	34. (c)	35. (c)	36. (c)	37. (b)	38. (b)	39. (b)	40. (c)

Unit-16

01 On Going a Journey

Summary of the Lesson

- The essay, "On Going a Journey", contains Hazlitt's ideas and thoughts about making a journey. A journey in his essay means a short or a long waking trip undertaken voluntarily as a change from daily routine of one's own life. He talks about a journey which is a kind of diversion from one's practical ongoing affairs.
- It's a process of leaving and arriving, of losing yourself and finding it again with some more freshness and inner strength. And if these are our only criteria, anything can be a journey, as long as you are intentional.
- Journeys define us. They are the important markers of our lives. And they remind us that we are all travelers of some sort. Also, reveal our shortcomings. They show us we are not alone in this world and there are other wanderers out there, in searching of truth and meaning in this great big, confusing universe. Journeys teach us about life and this is what William Hazlitt tries to explain through his essay "On Going a Journey". However Hazlitt's journey has different meaning and interpretations.
- One of the most pleasant things in the world, says Hazlitt, is going on a journey all by himself. He would not like to have a companion with him when he goes on a journey. He can enjoycompany in a room; but out of the doors, he finds Nature as a complete companion, with nature, he is never less alone when alone.
- If he would take a companion with him, the two would naturally enter into a conversation; but Hazlitt does not find any point in walking and talking at the same point. A conversation would disturb the mood of relaxation and idleness. He wants some time to meditate upon all kinds of unimportant matters. He wants to lose himself in contemplation.
- If one has a companion during a journey, one can sometimes talk to him, can sometimes become silent and thus lose oneself in one's own thoughts. But Hazlitt does not want any half-hearted companionship. Also Hazlitt seems to have company of other literary works of eminent writers during the journey of his life.
- Hazlitt favors the synthetical method on a journey, in preference to the analytical. On a journey he wants to have all things all his own way, and this can be had only if he is alone. He would have no objection to arguing point with anyone for twenty miles of the road, but then he would not regard such a discussion as a part of pleasure of the journey.
- Hazlitt thinks, it is a mark of extravagance or affectation to express his feelings in the presence of a companion; and he thinks, it is an arduous task to have explained to a companion, the mystery of human existence and human experience in the world. There are certain things which need only to be understood and not to be stated or described to a companion. Though. Charles Lamb could do both the things, namely understand things and describe them also.
- Lamb could deliver a regular discourse to explain the beauties of hills and dales; he could indeed convert a landscape into a poem with a moral. But Hazlitt does not have that talent, and he cannot clothe his ideas in high-sounding and flowering words. Hazlitt does not claim to possess the poetic powers of Wordsworth and Coleridge. Hazlitt, however, is of the view that there is one subject on whom it is pleasant to talk in the course of a journey, and that subject is what one would have for supper at the inn where he would be spending the night.
- Journey, however, shows most effectively, the short-sightedness or arbitrariness of the human imagination. With every change of the place, we change our ideas, and we change even our opinions and feelings. Hazlitt says that, in travelling through a wild, barren country, he can form no idea of a woody and cultivated one. While travelling through a barren country, he feels that the entire world must be barren. In the country, one forgets the town; and in town one begins to despise the country. All the part of the world which one does not see before one's eyes is blank. A man tends to measure the universe by the dimension of his own understanding.
- This essay can be read from another angle i.e. a literary journey. Hazlitt uses lines, references and phrases from other famous writers like Milton, Shakespeare, Coleridge, Charles Lamb, Neither Stowcy, Michael Drayton, John Fletcher, William Cowper, Sancho Panza, Wordsworth ete. These quotes and phrases from the eminent works of other authors make this essay more illustrative and embellished from literary angle and the readers too feel a panoramic view through the journey of this essay having a vast experience in minimum bare words. There is no denying the fact that this essay is not less than a filigree work from Hazlitt.

Objective Questions

1. Who is the author of "On Going Journey"?
(a) George Orwell (b) J.B. Priestley
(c) Virginia Woolf (d) William Shakespeare

2. In "On Going Journey," what is the primary theme?
(a) The importance of nature
(b) The journey of life
(c) Political power
(d) War and its effects

3. What does Priestley compare life to in the essay?
(a) A river (b) A journey
(c) A storm (d) A mountain

4. What metaphor does Priestley use to describe life's path?
(a) A straight line (b) A circular path
(c) A winding road (d) A broken bridge

5. According to Priestley, what should one do during their journey?
(a) Avoid distractions (b) Rush to the destination
(c) Embrace the unknown (d) Look for shortcuts

6. In the essay, Priestley reflects on the importance of what in life?
(a) Knowledge (b) Material wealth
(c) Understanding time (d) Relationships

7. What does Priestley say about the destination of life's journey?
(a) It is always clear (b) It is irrelevant
(c) It should be the focus (d) It is unpredictable

8. Which of the following best describes Priestley's tone in the essay?
(a) Cynical (b) Humorous
(c) Reflective (d) Angry

9. In "On Going Journey," how does Priestley describe time?
(a) A continuous process
(b) A finite resource
(c) A challenge to overcome
(d) An illusion

10. What does Priestley believe is a critical aspect of traveling through life?
(a) Financial stability (b) Keeping a fast pace
(c) Curiosity and learning (d) Avoiding risks

11. Which of the following best describes the structure of the essay?
(a) A series of personal anecdotes
(b) A fictional narrative
(c) A chronological account of events
(d) A philosophical reflection

12. What role do reflections play in the essay?
(a) They distract from the journey
(b) They highlight the significance of experience
(c) They focus on the past
(d) They describe material successes

13. From the given options,How does Priestley view the concept of arrival at the end of the journey?
(a) It is a comforting thought
(b) It is irrelevant
(c) It is a moment of peace
(d) It is the ultimate goal of life

14. According to Priestley, life's journey should be about:
(a) Achievement of goals
(b) Constant movement
(c) Reaching the end
(d) Avoiding mistakes

15. Priestley suggests that the journey of life can be:
(a) Planned in advance
(b) Measured by success
(c) Enjoyed at a slow pace
(d) Free from all challenges

16. What does Priestley think about the idea of a final destination in life?
(a) It is essential to keep in mind
(b) It is a comforting idea
(c) It is a myth
(d) It is the only goal

17. From the given options,How does Priestley suggest one should handle obstacles in life?
(a) By avoiding them
(b) By learning from them
(c) By giving up
(d) By complaining about them

18. From the given options,Priestley emphasizes the importance of what aspect of life in the essay?
(a) Material possessions
(b) Emotional connections
(c) Financial success
(d) Accomplishments

19. What does Priestley say about the unpredictable nature of the journey?
(a) It is a cause for concern
(b) It should be embraced
(c) It can be avoided
(d) It is unpleasant

20. According to Priestley, life's journey requires one to be:
(a) Prepared for every outcome
(b) Completely in control
(c) Open to new experiences
(d) Always on the right track

21. What aspect of human nature does Priestley explore in the essay?
(a) Greed
(b) Fear of change
(c) The desire for control
(d) The need for understanding

22. Which element of nature does Priestley associate with life's journey?
(a) Mountains
(b) Rivers
(c) Forests
(d) Clouds

23. In the essay, Priestley discusses the importance of:
(a) Traveling alone
(b) Rushing through life
(c) Making the most of the present
(d) Settling down

24. Priestley believes the journey of life should be treated as:
(a) A race
(b) A series of obstacles to overcome
(c) A constant adventure
(d) A task to be completed

25. What does Priestley say about the role of time in the journey of life?
(a) Time is the enemy of the journey
(b) Time should be strictly controlled
(c) Time should be embraced as part of the journey
(d) Time is irrelevant to the journey

26. How does Priestley suggest people view challenges in life?
(a) As punishments
(b) As learning opportunities
(c) As avoidable experiences
(d) As signs of failure

27. What does Priestley think of the concept of "destination" in life?
(a) It is important to have a final destination
(b) It should be a focus of all actions
(c) It is an illusion that distracts from the journey
(d) It is the only way to find peace

28. Priestley argues that the journey of life:
(a) Ends too soon
(b) Is filled with constant clarity
(c) Requires constant reassessment
(d) Is predictable and easy

29. What role does experience play in the essay?
(a) It is something to be avoided
(b) It is central to understanding the journey
(c) It is a barrier to progress
(d) It has little relevance

30. Priestley say about the pace of life's journey?
(a) It should be fast and hurried
(b) It should be measured and steady
(c) It should be slow and contemplative
(d) It should be rushed to reach the end

31. Priestley believes that people should focus on:
(a) Reaching the end of the journey
(b) Success and achievements
(c) The journey itself, not the destination
(d) Avoiding hardships

32. Which of the following does Priestley discuss in relation to life's journey?
(a) Material success (b) Emotional growth
(c) Political power (d) Financial independence

33. What is one of the key takeaways from the essay?
(a) To always look ahead
(b) To stay in the same place
(c) To focus on the present and learn from it
(d) To avoid challenges at all costs

34. How does Priestley suggest we face uncertainty in life?
(a) By avoiding it
(b) By embracing it with confidence
(c) By ignoring it
(d) By resisting change

35. What does Priestley say about the journey's ultimate purpose?
(a) To accumulate wealth
(b) To reach a fixed destination
(c) To experience and learn
(d) To meet the right people

36. How does Priestley view the concept of "arrival"?
(a) As a necessary part of life
(b) As an unnecessary goal
(c) As a final point of peace
(d) As something to be avoided

37. According to the writer, Priestley encourages readers to
(a) Plan every step of the journey
(b) Embrace spontaneity and adventure
(c) Avoid life's obstacles
(d) Rush to the destination

38. What does Priestley suggest about learning during life's journey?
(a) It is irrelevant
(b) It is essential for growth
(c) It should be avoided
(d) It is a secondary concern

39. In "On Going a Journey," Priestley emphasizes:
(a) The pursuit of perfection
(b) The importance of the destination
(c) The beauty of the journey itself
(d) The need for wealth

40. What does Priestley think about the future in the essay?
(a) It should be controlled at all costs
(b) It is unpredictable and should be embraced
(c) It is something to fear
(d) It should be ignored

41. What is the overall message of "On Going a Journey"?
(a) Life is a fixed path
(b) Life's journey should be embraced with an open mind
(c) Success is the only goal of the journey
(d) The destination is all that matters

42. According to the writer, how does Priestley feel about life's challenges?
(a) They should be avoided
(b) They are obstacles that must be overcome at all costs
(c) They are opportunities for learning and growth
(d) They are irrelevant

43. What does Priestley imply about the speed of life's journey?
(a) Life should be rushed to reach the end
(b) Life's speed is irrelevant as long as one learns from it
(c) Life should be lived slowly without change
(d) Life should be hurried to avoid boredom

Answers

1. (b)	2. (b)	3. (b)	4. (c)	5. (c)	6. (d)	7. (d)	8. (c)	9. (a)	10. (c)
11. (d)	12. (b)	13. (b)	14. (b)	15. (c)	16. (c)	17. (b)	18. (b)	19. (b)	20. (c)
21. (d)	22. (b)	23. (c)	24. (c)	25. (c)	26. (b)	27. (c)	28. (c)	29. (b)	30. (b)
31. (c)	32. (b)	33. (c)	34. (b)	35. (c)	36. (b)	37. (b)	38. (b)	39. (c)	40. (b)
41. (b)	42. (c)	43. (b)							

02 On Umbrella Morals

Summary of the Lesson

- This essay is a satire on the people's habit of picking up others' things and then at the same moment losing them by the others. The narrator once loses his silk umbrella and gets a cotton umbrella in exchange. He thinks that the man who would have picked up his silk umbrella might be feeling smart. For such people the narrator has not at all a good opinion. He thinks that these people have umbrella conscience.
- In On Umbrella Morals by A.G. Gardiner we have the theme of honesty, morality, guilt, appearance, acceptance and social opinion. Taken from his Pebbles on the Shore collection the reader realises after reading the essay that Gardiner may be exploring the theme of honesty. For Gardiner there are two types of honesty.
- One in whereby a genuine mistake is made and one where an individual knows he is being dishonest. For the case of the essay Gardiner is discussing the former.
- An honest mistake can be made where a man takes another man's umbrella. However this does not mean that the same man is pleased at what has happened to his umbrella. If anything he takes exception to the fact. Even though he himself (Gardiner) may not necessarily own the umbrella he is carrying. Gardiner also uses other incidents in the essay to highlight the morality of an honest mistake.
- Some people, may travel on a train without the proper ticket. These people are not to be scorned at as they are only doing what others might do. However it is unlikely that the rail company would see things in the same light.

Objective Questions

1. What does the term "umbrella morals" most likely refer to?
(a) A specific set of rules for one culture
(b) Overarching ethical principles that guide behavior in various situations
(c) A collection of religious teachings
(d) A political philosophy on justice

2. Which of the following is an example of a universal moral value?
(a) The right to bear arms
(b) The importance of honesty
(c) The concept of monarchy
(d) The idea of free-market capitalism

3. According to the essay, what is a common characteristic of umbrella moral values?
(a) They apply only in certain contexts
(b) They are specific to each culture
(c) They serve as general principles for decision-making
(d) They are based solely on religion

4. Which of the following is considered a "moral absolute"?
(a) Lying is always wrong
(b) It is acceptable to lie in some situations
(c) The morality of lying depends on the outcome
(d) Lying is an individual choice

5. What is moral relativism?
(a) The belief that moral principles are fixed
(b) The idea that moral judgments are determined by personal feelings and cultural context
(c) The belief in universal moral truths
(d) The idea that laws should reflect moral principles

6. What is the role of ethical theories under the umbrella of morality?
(a) To provide a rigid set of rules for all scenarios
(b) To offer frameworks for understanding and solving moral dilemmas
(c) To encourage adherence to political ideologies
(d) To focus solely on religious teachings

7. Which moral theory focuses on the consequences of actions to determine their morality?
(a) Deontological ethics (b) Virtue ethics
(c) Utilitarianism (d) Contractarianism

8. Who is the philosopher most commonly associated with utilitarianism?
(a) Immanuel Kant (b) Aristotle
(c) John Stuart Mill (d) Confucius

9. What is the central idea behind Kantian ethics?
(a) The greatest good for the greatest number
(b) Actions are morally right if they align with universal moral laws
(c) The outcome of actions is the most important factor
(d) Character traits define the morality of actions

10. What does "moral autonomy" mean?
(a) The freedom to follow personal desires
(b) The ability to make moral decisions independently based on reason
(c) The belief that morality is relative
(d) The obligation to follow social norms

11. Which principle is at the core of deontological ethics?
(a) Consequences are irrelevant to morality
(b) The action itself must align with moral laws or duties
(c) Happiness is the ultimate goal
(d) It is morally acceptable to break rules for greater good

12. What is a criticism of moral absolutism?
(a) It can be too flexible in situations
(b) It overlooks the importance of consequences
(c) It does not account for context and can lead to harsh judgments
(d) It is too reliant on personal choice

13. What is the "Golden Rule" in moral philosophy?
(a) Do what makes you happy
(b) Treat others as you would like to be treated
(c) Always seek revenge for wrongdoings
(d) Follow the laws of your government

14. Which of the following is a common critique of utilitarianism?
(a) It ignores the importance of emotions
(b) It can justify harmful actions if they benefit the majority
(c) It fails to consider the moral quality of the person making the decision
(d) It focuses too much on individual rights

15. What does virtue ethics emphasize?
(a) The greatest good for the greatest number
(b) Following moral laws regardless of consequences
(c) Developing good character traits such as honesty and courage
(d) The importance of rational decision-making

16. What is an ethical dilemma?
(a) A situation where there are clear right and wrong choices
(b) A situation where multiple moral principles conflict
(c) A situation where the law determines the correct action
(d) A situation where no action is needed

17. What is the "veil of ignorance" as proposed by philosopher John Rawls?
(a) A tool for making decisions while considering personal biases
(b) The concept of acting in complete ignorance of one's personal interests to ensure fairness
(c) The idea that individuals should ignore cultural norms when making decisions
(d) A method to remove all emotions from decision-making

18. Which ethical approach would argue that breaking a promise could be acceptable if it leads to greater happiness?
(a) Virtue ethics (b) Kantian ethics
(c) Utilitarianism (d) Social contract theory

19. Who is most associated with the concept of the "categorical imperative"?
(a) Aristotle (b) Immanuel Kant
(c) John Stuart Mill (d) Friedrich Nietzsche

20. Which ethical theory believes in prioritizing the well-being of the majority over the minority?
(a) Virtue ethics
(b) Social contract theory
(c) Utilitarianism
(d) Deontological ethics

21. What is moral relativism?
(a) The belief that morals are determined by society and culture
(b) The idea that moral laws are fixed and universal
(c) The notion that actions are always judged by their consequences
(d) The belief that morality can only be understood in religious terms

22. Which ethical theory focuses on following moral duties and rules regardless of consequences?
(a) Consequentialism (b) Deontology
(c) Utilitarianism (d) Hedonism

23. A major advantage of the umbrella moral approach is
(a) It offers specific rules for all scenarios
(b) It provides flexibility and considers multiple moral perspectives
(c) It encourages ignoring the consequences of actions
(d) It leads to a one-size-fits-all moral solution

24. What does "moral realism" suggest?
(a) Morality is subjective and varies by individual
(b) Morality is defined by the state
(c) There are objective moral facts that exist independently of human opinions
(d) Morality is purely based on religious teachings

25. Which of the following is a moral duty in Kantian ethics?
(a) Seek the greatest happiness for the most people
(b) Always treat others as ends in themselves, not as means to an end
(c) Pursue personal pleasure above all
(d) Break promises when it benefits others

26. What does "moral universalism" assert?
(a) Moral principles are subjective
(b) There are universal moral truths that apply to all people at all times
(c) Moral values differ from culture to culture
(d) There is no such thing as morality

27. Which moral theory is most concerned with individual rights and freedoms?
(a) Utilitarianism
(b) Virtue ethics
(c) Libertarianism
(d) Communitarianism

28. What is the "social contract" in moral philosophy?
(a) An agreement among individuals to prioritize personal happiness
(b) A theoretical agreement to abide by common moral principles for societal benefit
(c) A legal contract to follow state laws
(d) A form of economic exchange

29. What does "moral subjectivism" suggest about morality?
(a) Morality is based on objective truths
(b) Individuals create their own moral truths
(c) There are universal moral principles
(d) The state determines morality

30. Who introduced the idea of the "social contract"?
(a) Immanuel Kant
(b) Jean-Jacques Rousseau
(c) John Stuart Mill
(d) Karl Marx

31. What is an example of a moral rule under the umbrella of ethics?
(a) Always act to promote the greatest happiness
(b) Always seek personal pleasure
(c) Always follow your cultural norms without question
(d) Always disregard others' well-being for personal gain

32. Which of the following is an example of a deontological moral rule?
(a) Always tell the truth, even if it may cause harm
(b) Maximize happiness for the most people
(c) Prioritize your personal happiness over others
(d) Break promises if the outcome is beneficial

33. The concept of "moral courage" refers to:
(a) Following the law regardless of moral considerations
(b) Acting in accordance with moral beliefs even in the face of adversity
(c) Following the crowd in moral decisions
(d) Disregarding personal safety for moral beliefs

34. What role does empathy play in moral decision-making?
(a) It helps individuals identify what will benefit them personally
(b) It allows people to ignore societal norms and make their own rules
(c) It helps individuals understand and consider the feelings of others
(d) It encourages individuals to act in their own self-interest

35. What is the central ethical question in moral philosophy?
(a) How can I achieve personal success?
(b) What is the right thing to do?
(c) What makes a good leader?
(d) What is the best form of government?

36. What is the relationship between ethics and law?
(a) Ethics and law are always identical
(b) Ethics provides guidance beyond what the law covers
(c) Laws are purely based on moral principles
(d) Ethics is irrelevant to the law

37. Who is associated with the concept of "virtue ethics"?
(a) John Stuart Mill (b) Aristotle
(c) Immanuel Kant (d) Jean-Paul Sartre

38. In moral decision-making, which of the following is often emphasized in umbrella ethics?
(a) Strict obedience to rules
(b) Consideration of all possible consequences
(c) Freedom from moral responsibility
(d) Avoiding all ethical dilemmas

39. How does the "slippery slope" argument relate to moral discussions?
(a) It argues that small ethical violations can lead to larger, more harmful actions
(b) It encourages people to avoid ethics in favor of practical decision-making

(c) It suggests that all moral decisions are subjective
(d) It advocates for ignoring consequences in favor of moral purity

40. According to the essay, which ethical theory focuses on the character of the person making the decision?
(a) Deontology
(b) Virtue ethics
(c) Utilitarianism
(d) Pragmatism

41. From the given options,What is a key feature of ethical pluralism?
(a) There is one correct moral code for all situations
(b) It embraces different moral perspectives and acknowledges their value
(c) Ethics is a purely individual experience
(d) It rejects all forms of universal ethics

42. Which concept is emphasized in moral consequentialism?
(a) Actions are evaluated based on their inherent nature
(b) Moral duties must be followed regardless of outcomes
(c) The consequences of actions are the most important aspect
(d) Actions are morally neutral

43. What does "moral empathy" mean?
(a) Ignoring others' feelings to avoid personal discomfort
(b) Understanding and sharing in the emotional experiences of others
(c) Prioritizing one's own interests over others' well-being
(d) Rejecting moral obligations based on self-interest

44. Which of the following is an example of a virtue?
(a) Lying to protect someone's feelings
(b) Always seeking happiness at the expense of others
(c) Compassion for others' suffering
(d) Following social norms without question

45. Which is a criticism of utilitarianism in moral decision-making?
(a) It does not consider the character of the decision-maker
(b) It fails to maximize overall happiness
(c) It overlooks the importance of intentions and duties
(d) It applies universal moral principles in every situation

46. What does "moral duty" mean?
(a) Acting in accordance with personal desires
(b) Acting in a way that adheres to universal principles of right and wrong
(c) Acting based on the immediate outcome of an action
(d) Acting in a way that avoids any inconvenience

47. According to the essay, what does the ethical principle of "justice" focus on?
(a) Ensuring fairness and equality in how people are treated
(b) Ensuring that personal desires are met above all else
(c) Ensuring that all laws are followed strictly
(d) Ensuring that individual pleasure is maximized

48. What role does reason play in moral decision-making?
(a) It is irrelevant to ethical choices
(b) It helps people apply universal principles logically
(c) It encourages people to act on emotional impulses
(d) It promotes conformity over individual moral choices

49. What is "ethical integrity"?
(a) The ability to ignore ethical dilemmas
(b) The consistency of one's moral beliefs and actions
(c) The ability to maximize personal gain through ethics
(d) The rejection of all external moral influences

50. What is the goal of moral education?
(a) To enforce specific cultural values
(b) To encourage individual freedom above all
(c) To teach individuals how to make ethical decisions
(d) To help people follow religious commands

Answers

1. (b)	2. (b)	3. (c)	4. (a)	5. (b)	6. (b)	7. (c)	8. (c)	9. (b)	10. (b)
11. (b)	12. (c)	13. (b)	14. (b)	15. (c)	16. (b)	17. (b)	18. (c)	19. (b)	20. (c)
21. (a)	22. (b)	23. (b)	24. (c)	25. (b)	26. (b)	27. (c)	28. (b)	29. (b)	30. (b)
31. (a)	32. (a)	33. (b)	34. (c)	35. (b)	36. (b)	37. (b)	38. (b)	39. (a)	40. (b)
41. (b)	42. (c)	43. (b)	44. (c)	45. (a)	46. (b)	47. (a)	48. (b)	49. (b)	50. (c)

03 Of Studies

Summary of the Lesson पाठ का सार

About the Author

Francis Bacon was an English Renaissance statesman and Philosopher, best known for his promotion of the scientific method. Bacon was born on 22nd January, 1561 in London England. He is known as 'the father of English Essay'. It was by his essays that Bacon proved himself a great writer of his own language Bacon served as attorney general and Lord Chancellor of England, resigning amid changes of corruption. His more valuable work was philosophical. Bacon took up Aristotelian ideas, arguing for an empirical inductive approach, known as 'the scientific method' which is the foundation of modern scientific inquiry.

So, Alexander Pope, the 18th century satirist, sums up the character of the great Lord Bacon, to a large extent, but not the more important-part is written in Latin, Bacon's style of writing is aphoristic and compact. His works are full of practical wisdom.

लेखक का परिचय

फ्रेन्सिस बैकन एक ब्रिटिश पुनार्जागरण राजनेता और दार्शनिक थे। वे अपने वैज्ञानिक तरीकों को बढ़ावा देने के लिए विख्यात थे।

बैकन का जन्म 22 जनवरी, 1561 में लन्दन, इंग्लैण्ड में हुआ था। वे 'अंग्रेजी निबन्ध के जनक' के नाम से जाने जाते हैं। अपनी निबन्ध कृतियों के कारण ही वे अपनी भाषा के महान् लेखक के रूप में प्रसिद्ध हुए। इंग्लैण्ड के अटॉर्नी जनरल और लार्ड चांसलर और के रूप में बैकन ने अपनी सेवा प्रदान की, परन्तु भ्रष्टाचार के कारण अपनी सेवा से त्याग-पत्र दे दिया। उनकी मुख्य कृतियाँ दर्शन से सम्बन्धित हैं। उन्होंने अरस्तु के विचारों का चयन करके उनका समर्थन किया। उन्होंने प्रयोगसिद्धि और अधिष्ठापन दृष्टिकोण के लिए तर्क-वितर्क किया, जोकि वैज्ञानिक पद्धति के नाम से जाने जाते थे और आधुनिक विज्ञान की नींव थे।'

इसलिए एलैक्जेन्डर पोप, जो 18वीं सदी के प्रसिद्ध व्यंग्यकार थे, ने लॉर्ड बैकन के चरित्र को पर्याप्त सीमा तक विस्तार से लिखने की पूर्ण कोशिश की; परन्तु बैकन की जिन्दगी का विशेष भाग लैटिन में लिखा गया है जो कि सघन और सूत्रपात व्यवस्थित है। उनके कार्य प्रयोगात्मक बुद्धिमत्ता से भरे होते हैं।

Bacon's Literary Career

During his career as counsel and statesman, Bacon often wrote for the court. In 1584, he wrote his first political memorandum, ' A Letter of Advice to Queen Elizabeth'. In 1592, to celebrate the anniversary of the queen's coronation, he wrote an entertaining speech in praise of knowledge. The year 1597 marked Bacon's first publication, a collection of essays about politics. The collection was later expanded and published in 1612 and 1625.

Bacon's, even today, is widely regarded as a major figure in scientific methodology and natural philosophy during the English renaissance. In his essays, he takes up the role of a practical moralist and presents a philosophy of his own. As a moralist, Bacon makes no pretence to system. Having advocated an organised system of obtaining knowledge with a humanitarian goal in mind, he is largely credited with ushering in the new early modern era of human understanding.

Bacon died of pneumonia on 9th April, 1926.

बैकन की साहित्यिक यात्रा

अपनी यात्रा में, एक सलाहकार और राजनेता के रूप में बैकन ने कोर्ट के बारे में लिखा। सन् 1584 में उन्होंने अपना पहला राजनैतिक ज्ञापन 'ए लैटर ऑफ़ एडवाइस टु क्वीन एलिजाबेथ (रानी एलिजाबेथ को एक सुझाव पत्र)' लिखा। सन् 1592 में उन्होंने रानी के राज्याभिषेक की वर्षगांठ के उत्सव में ज्ञान की प्रशंसा में रूचिकर भाषण लिखा। सन् 1597 बैकन के 'राजनैतिक निबन्धों के संग्रह' के प्रकाशन के लिए प्रसिद्ध है। यह संग्रह आगे विस्तारित रूप में सन् 1612 और सन् 1625 में पुन: प्रकाशित हुआ।

आज भी बैकन, वैज्ञानिक प्रणाली और अंग्रेजी पुनर्जागरण के समय के प्राकृतिक दर्शन में विशेष चरित्र के रूप में जाने जाते हैं। अपने निबन्धों में उन्होंने प्रयोगात्मक नीतिज्ञ का चरित्र निभाकर स्वयं की विचारधारा का प्रदर्शन किया, नीतिज्ञ होने के कारण बैकन ने कभी कोई दिखावा नहीं किया। मानवीय लक्ष्य को ध्यान में रखकर, व्यवस्थित प्रणाली में प्राप्त होने वाले ज्ञान को बैकन बढ़ावा देते हैं। उन्हें 'मानवीय समझ या ज्ञान' के आधुनिक युग को अक्षुण्ण रखने का श्रेय दिया जाता है।

न्यूमोनिया के कारण 9 अप्रैल, 1926 को बैकन का निधन हो गया।

Important Works By Bacon

Essays (1st Edition 10 essays, 1597)

Essays (2nd Edition, 38 essays , 1612)

Essays, or Counsels Civil and Moral (3rd final edition, 58 essays. 1625).

बैकन के द्वारा रचित मुख्य पुस्तकें

1. निबन्ध (प्रथम संस्करण, 10 निबन्ध, 1597)
2. निबन्ध (द्वितीय संस्करण, 38 निबन्ध 1612)
3. निबन्ध, 'तीसरा अन्तिम संस्करण, 58 निबन्ध, 1625)

Introduction to the Essay

Francis Bacon is a very important figure in the history of knowledge, and we can learn a lot from his essay, 'Of Studies'. Bacon points that it is study that depicts over the enjoyed moment, attraction and capabilities. 'Of Studies' was published in 1597.

Bacon, here, first tells us the three chief uses of studies, he then speaks of those who spend too much time in studies those who use studies too much for ornament and those who form judgements wholly by the rules emerging from their studies. The writer then goes on the speak of the value of practical experience but even more abruptly, goes on to say that craft men condemn studies, simple men admire them and wise men use them.

Bacon tells us why we should study and then abruptly classifies books into three or four categories-those that are to be tasted, those that are to be swallowed, those that are to be chewed and digested and finally those that may be read 'By Deputy'. In the paragraph that follows, he speaks of the contribution that reading, conference and writing make towards the development of a man.

'Of Studies' explains how we can read and study and get the most benefit out of it. It connects learning and self-improvement in very practical way.

Bacon opens up by asserting three purpose for reading: delight-reading for the fun of it, ornament-being able to show off that we known stuff and ability. The essay focuses on study to increase out ability to succeed in life.

He makes an important point in saying that we do not need to read every book all the way, though, we can skim or select passages.

The central theme of the essay is that specific fields of study sharpen the mind in specific ways. Study, Bacon asserts, is for the mind what exercise is for the body. We would exercise one way to be able to run faster and another way to be able to dance. And, we would choose the type of exercise depending on what we wanted to achieve and also on an honest assessment of our weakness.

निबन्ध का परिचय

फ्रेन्सिस बैकन ज्ञान के इतिहास में महत्त्वपूर्ण चरित्र हैं। हमें उनके निबन्ध 'ऑफ़ स्टड़ीज़' से बहुत कुछ सीखने को मिलता है। बैकन बताते हैं कि यह आनन्दित पल, आकर्षण और सक्षमता का अध्ययन है। 'ऑफ़ स्टडीज़' का प्रकाशन 1597 ई० में हुआ था।

बैकन सर्वप्रथम हमें अध्ययन के तीन मुख्य प्रयोग बताते हैं। उसके बाद वे उन लोगों के बारे में बताते हैं, जो अध्ययन में बहुत समय व्यतीत करते हैं। वे उन लोगों के बारे में भी बताते हैं, जो अध्ययन को आभूषण मानते हैं और उनके बारे में वर्णित किया है जो अपने निर्णय अध्ययन पर आधारित नियमों से लेते हैं।

इसके बाद लेखक प्रायोगिक अनुभव की महत्ता के बारे में विस्तार से बताते हैं। साधारण व्यक्ति अध्ययन की प्रशंसा करते हैं और समझदार लोग अध्ययन को जिन्दगी में प्रयोग करते हैं।

बैकन हमें बताते हैं कि हमें अध्ययन क्यों करना चाहिए और वे पुस्तकों को तीन या चार श्रेणियों में विभाजित करते हैं— (1) वे जिन्हें सिर्फ़ चखा जा सकता है अर्थात् सरसरी निगाहों से पढ़ा जा सके (2) वे जिन्हें (उसकी अध्ययन सामग्री) निगला जा सके (3) तीसरी जिन्हें चबाया और पचाया जा सकता है अर्थात् पढ़कर कुछ पलों के लिए याद रखा जा सके और आखिर में वे जिन्हें डिप्टी (मनुष्य) द्वारा कण्ठस्थ किया जा सके और उसमें निहित ज्ञान को व्यावहारिक जीवन में प्रयोग में लाया जा सके। अग्रिम अनुच्छेद में लेखक ने पढ़ाई, सम्मेलन और लिखावट में 'मनुष्य के विकास' में योगदान को वर्णित किया है।

'ऑफ़ स्टडीज़' में वर्णित है कि हम किस प्रकार पढ़ सकते हैं और किस प्रकार उसका अधिकतम प्रयोग कर सकते हैं। यह सीखने और आत्म-सुधार को प्रयोगात्मक तरीके से जोड़ता है अर्थात् शिक्षा के द्वारा हम सीखकर स्वयं में सुधार कर सकते हैं।

बैकन पढ़ने के तीन मुख्य उद्देश्यों पर जोर देते हैं, आनन्दित पठन, जो सिर्फ़ आनन्द के लिए पढ़ा जाता है। दूसरे वे लोग जो आभूषण की तरह शिक्षा का सिर्फ़ दिखावा करते हैं, उन्हें अत्यधिक ज्ञान है और वे सक्षम हैं। बैकन का यह निबन्ध हमारी जिन्दगी में सफलता के लिए हमारी सक्षमता और योग्यता को बढ़ाने पर ज़ोर देता है।

निबन्ध का केन्द्र बिन्दु है कि अध्ययन के विशिष्ट अंग: अध्ययन मस्तिष्क का विभिन्न तरीकों से विकास कर सकते हैं। बैकन कहते हैं जिस प्रकार स्वस्थ शरीर के लिए व्यायाम महत्त्वपूर्ण है, उसी प्रकार स्वस्थ मस्तिष्क के लिए अध्ययन ज़रूरी है। हम व्यायाम का चयन अपनी ज़रूरत के अनुसार करते हैं; जैसे- हमें तेज भागने के लिए व्यायाम करना है या नृत्य के लिए करना है। हमारे व्यायाम का चयन हमारे लक्ष्य और हमारी कमज़ोरी पर निर्भर करता है।

Explanation of the Prose

Explanation The essay opens up with Bacon's view on study. Study as an activity in whatever form, brings us joy and enhances our thinking, speaking and writing ability adding charm to our personality.

According to Bacon, study is always a private or individual activity which people engage in when they are alone or in the privacy of their homes. In this way studies become a means of relaxation or passing time fruitfully.

If one studies for ornamentation or show off, such person will show off knowledge in general takes. The aim of show studies is to earn praise for one's knowledge. Studies also sharpen our intellect helping us to judge things soundly. It helps us to go about our life's business in a more capable-way.

The third use of studies is to apply the learning in living life. If one's learning is put into practice, while making judgements or carrying out plans, this is studies for abilities.

There are experts who have studied extensively to critically examine issues and arrive at the right conclusions. They can garner data, facts and agreements or against a particular view rationally. Such intelligent analysis of fact improves the soundness and quality of their judgement.

Though it is good to devote time in studies, but is not wise to overdo it. Over indulgence in studies leads to undesirable consequences, setting aside long hour in a day to study will make a man indolent. Overuse of the wisdom to analyse ordinary commonplace issues may make the man appear pretentious and vainglorious. Sticking too

Studies add finesses and perfection to human nature. A person's abilities inherited by birth are raw, only when they are carefully worked upon and honed, the in-born abilities yield the best benefits to us. Studying is the whetstone that we use to sharpen our abilities. But inferences from study may lead to misleading conclusions. In such situations one's experience in life comes in handy to arrive at the right conclusion. Experience helps in perfecting studies, so it is a valuable asset.

Cunning people who try to deceit others have no appreciation for studies as they accomplish their objectives through many crafty ways. They in fact misguide others by taking them away from the path of studies. Simple folks, however, greatly value the role of studies in human life.

Wise people inherently draw upon their knowledge to solve any problem in life. Knowledge by itself is of no use if not put to use for the betterment of others. One should realise that use of knowledge lies outside it. It is a pearl of wisdom one can earn by experience.

The aim of reading and acquiring knowledge must not be to aggressively refute other's views or accept the writer's views as gospel truth. It should not be used to engage in useless or pointless discussion and arguementation. Perfect use of knowledge lies in to weigh facts and analyze then rationally.

There are different books and uses of them are also different. Books of varying content and genre are to be made use of differently. Some books require only cursory reading, some others can be quickly sifted through. But other important looks are to be read slowly and minutely so as to understand the meaning and underlying idea in it. Such books cannot be and should not be read in extracts or in parts or by some assistant. They require first hand studies.

Reading makes a man perfect and practical. Discussing with others about the contents of a book imparts social practical skills to the reader. Writing removes all the residual weaknesses and ignorance from the person and enables him to remember the contents of a book. By reading one can keep oneself updated in life. And it is by discussing his reading with others, that a person will be able to improve his wit. If he does not read, he will remain a somewhat ignorant person. When one puts his thoughts on the paper that one realises what one actually known or thinks on a certain matter. So those who do not write much must have a good memory. And those who do not read much must have cunning manner to make it look as if they know what they actually do not.

Studying History makes men wise while that of poetry witty. Study of mathematics makes them subtle and analytical and study of science gives sound logical sense and study of morality and philosophy imparts valuable lesson and people are able to argue persuasively. In fact there is no ailment of life that cannot be cured by doing proper studies.

Wit is a God given gift but it can be sharpened by selective studying. This is akin to the way certain weaknesses of the human body are cured by appropriate physical exercises. Just as bowling is good for the store and reins, shooting for the lungs and breast, gentle walking for the stomach, in the same way if a person is unable to concentrate he must study Mathematics. Studying Mathematics restrains the mind from darting off elsewhere. If a person does not have the ability to discern, he will be benefitted by studying philosophy. If a person is unable to garner facts and manipulate them to put across his views convincingly, studying law will certainly help him. Thus every deficiency of mind can be addressed by appropriate reading.

व्याख्या बैकन के 'अध्ययन' से सम्बन्धित विचारों से निबन्ध की शुरुआत होती है। अध्ययन एक ऐसी प्रक्रिया है जो किसी भी तरह से की जाए, बदले में हमें आनन्द ही मिलता है। अध्ययन हमारी सोचने, बोलने और लिखने की क्षमता को बढ़ाकर हमारे व्यक्तित्व में चार चाँद लगाता है।

बैकन के अनुसार अध्ययन व्यक्तिगत प्रक्रिया है, जो लोग अकेले में ही करते हैं। इसलिए अध्ययन विश्राम का साधन है और समय के सदुपयोग का तरीका है। यदि कोई सिर्फ दिखावे के लिए अध्ययन करता है, तो वह सामान्य बातों और मामलों में भी दिखावा ही करेगा। दिखावा करने का उद्देश्य झूठे ज्ञान के लिए दूसरों से झूठी प्रशंसा को पाना है।

अध्ययन हमारे सोचने-समझने की शक्ति का विकास करने में सहायता करता है, जिससे हम सही-गलत की पहचान कर सकते हैं। हमारी जिन्दगी के सही निर्णय लेने में भी अध्ययन हमारी सहायता करता है।

अध्ययन का तीसरा प्रयोग यह है कि हम जो भी सीखते हैं, उसे अपनी जिन्दगी में व्यावहारिक तरीके से प्रयोग भी करें। यदि कोई अपनी सीखी हुई बात का प्रयोग ज़िन्दगी के निर्णय लेने में करता है, तो यह अध्ययन की क्षमता एवं योग्यता है। बहुत-से कुशल लोग हैं जो अध्ययन को विस्तारित रूप से ग्रहण कर, जाँच-परख करते हुए जिन्दगी में काम में लेते हैं और सही निष्कर्ष निकालते हैं। वे किसी भी विशिष्ट विचार के लिए तथ्य-आँकड़ों को संचित कर सकते हैं। इसलिए तथ्यों का विश्लेषण उनकी गुणवत्ता में वृद्धि करता है।

हालाँकि अध्ययन में समय व्यतीत करना अच्छा है, लेकिन अति प्रत्येक वस्तु की बुरी होती है अर्थात् सीमित अध्ययन ही सफलता दिला सकता है। अत्यधिक अध्ययन नकारात्मक और अनचाहे परिणामों का जनक है। दिनभर एक अकेले कोने में अध्ययन करके व्यक्ति एकान्तवासी हो जाता है। सामान्य विषयों के लिए बुद्धि का अधिक प्रयोग मनुष्य को अभिमानी और अंहकारी बना देता है। सामान्य पारिस्थितियों को सुलझाने के लिए यदि कोई व्यक्ति अधिक नियम-कानून को मानता है अर्थात् क्या करना चाहिए और क्या नहीं। इसके लिए बहुत विचार करता है, तो वह दूसरों के लिए उपहास का विषय बन जाता है।

अध्ययन, व्यक्ति के व्यवहार में चालाकी और उत्तमता को बढ़ाता है। ज़िन्दगी के अनुभव व्यक्ति के लिए कच्चे माल की तरह होते हैं, जब व्यक्ति उन गुणों में अपनी कोशिशों से सुधार करता है, तभी सही अर्थ में वे गुण उसके लिए लाभकारी होते हैं। अध्ययन हमारी योग्यताओं को तीक्ष्ण बनाने में सहायक होता है।

चालाक लोग, दूसरों को छलने की कोशिश करते हैं, उनके अध्ययन की कभी प्रशंसा नहीं होती, क्योंकि वे कुटिल/कपटी तरीकों से अपने लक्ष्य को पूरा करते हैं। यहाँ तक कि वे दूसरों को भी भ्रमित कर के अध्ययन से पथभ्रष्ट देते हैं। सामान्य कथाओं का अध्ययन भी मानव जीवन में महत्ता रखता है।

समझदार लोग बचपन से ही अपनी समस्याओं के समाधान के लिए अध्ययन द्वारा प्राप्त ज्ञान को काम में लेते हैं। ज्ञान जब तक दूसरों की भलाई के लिए काम में न लिया जाए, तब तक वह किसी काम का नहीं रहता। सभी को यह विश्वास होना चाहिए कि ज्ञान, बुद्धिमत्ता का वह मोती है जिसे अनुभव से ही प्राप्त किया जा सकता है।

पठन और ज्ञान प्राप्त करने का उद्देश्य दूसरों के विचारों का खण्डन या लेखक की बात को सच मानकर स्वीकार कर लेना नहीं है। अध्ययन को निरर्थक तर्क-वितर्क या वाद-विवाद के लिए प्रयोग में नहीं लेना चाहिए। तथ्यों की समझ और संश्लेषण करना ही ज्ञान का सही प्रयोग है।

विभिन्न प्रकार की पुस्तकों का अलग-अलग प्रयोग होता है। विभिन्न प्रकार की पुस्तकों की सामग्री और शैली अलग-अलग होती है। कुछ पुस्तकों को सिर्फ सतही/सरसरी निगाहों से पढ़ने की आवश्यकता होती है, कुछ ज़ल्दी से परख ली जाती हैं, लेकिन महत्त्वपूर्ण पुस्तकों को आराम और बारीकी से पढ़ा जाता है, ताकि उनमें निहित अर्थ और विचारों को समझा जा सके। ऐसी महत्त्वपूर्ण पुस्तकों को किसी की सहायता से या टुकड़ों में नहीं पढ़ना चाहिए, बल्कि पूर्ण लगन के साथ स्वयं की मेहनत से पढ़ना चाहिए।

पठन व्यक्ति को उपयुक्त बनाता है और उस पठन की दूसरों से चर्चा करने पर पाठक को सामाजिक-व्यावहारिक कौशल प्रदान करता है। लेखन से पाठक की बची हुई कमज़ोरियाँ दूर हो जाती हैं और पुस्तक में दी गई सामग्री/ज्ञान उसे याद रहता है।

पठन व्यक्ति को ज़िन्दगी में नए ज्ञान से अवगत कराकर उसे आधुनिक बनाता है। दूसरों से ज्ञान की चर्चा करने से मानसिक विकास होता है और ज्ञान की वृद्धि होती है। जब कोई व्यक्ति अपने विचारों को कागज़ पर उतारता है, तो इससे पता चलता है कि वह उस मुद्दे के बारे में क्या सोचता है अर्थात् उसके विचार क्या हैं, जो लोग लिखते नहीं हैं, उनकी स्मृति तीक्ष्ण होती है और जो अधिक नहीं पढ़ते, वे लोगों को चालाकी से यह दिखाते हैं कि उन्हें बहुत कुछ आता है, परन्तु वास्तविकता और होती है।

इतिहास का अध्ययन मनुष्य को समझदार बनाता है, जबकि कविताएँ कुशाग्र बुद्धि बनाती हैं। गणित का अध्ययन व्यक्ति को तीक्ष्ण और विश्लेषणात्मक बनाता है। विज्ञान का अध्ययन तर्कों की समझ को सिखाता है। नैतिकता और दर्शन का अध्ययन मूल्यात्मक ज्ञान में वृद्धि करता है और व्यक्ति को प्रेरक रूप से तर्क-वितर्क करने में सक्षम बनाता है। ज़िन्दगी का ऐसा कोई भी कार्य नहीं है, जो अध्ययन के द्वारा पूर्ण नहीं किया जा सकता।

बुद्धि हमारे लिए प्रकृति/भगवान का उपहार है, परन्तु इसे तीक्ष्ण बनाने के लिए अध्ययन आवश्यक है; जैसे- मानव शरीर की कमज़ोरी दूर करने के लिए व्यायाम आवश्यक है। जैसे-गेंदबाजी नसों के लिए, निशानेबाज़ी फेफड़ों के लिए, सामान्य घूमना पेट के लिए आवश्यक है, उसी प्रकार यदि कोई व्यक्ति ध्यान केन्द्रित करने में सक्षम नहीं है, तो उसे गणित का अध्ययन करना चाहिए। गणित के अध्ययन से एकाग्रता का विकास होता है और मन तथा मस्तिष्क इधर-उधर नहीं भटकते। यदि किसी व्यक्ति में पहचानने या परखने की योग्यता की कमी है, तो दर्शन का अध्ययन उसके लिए लाभकारी है, यदि कोई व्यक्ति तथ्यों को स्वीकार नहीं करता और सन्तोषजनक तरीके से अपने विचारों को दूसरों के सामने रखने की योग्यता रखता है तो 'कानून पढ़ाई' उसकी सहायता करेगी। अतः किसी भी प्रकार की मानसिक कमी को अध्ययन के द्वारा ठीक किया जा सकता है।

Word Meanings (शब्द-अर्थ)

Word (शब्द)	Meaning (अर्थ)
Delight	Here it means intellectual pleasure derived from reading (यहाँ 'डिलाइट' से अभिप्राय 'पठन/अध्ययन से प्राप्त होने वाले मानसिक आनन्द से है।')
For Ornament	Use of highly difficult-words to show off during conversation with others (दूसरों से वार्तालाप करते समय दिखावा करने के लिए कठिन शब्दों का प्रयोग करना।)
Privateness	When one is alone or in solitude (जब कोई अकेला और एकान्त में हो।)
Discourse	Conversation, written or spoken communication or debate (वार्तालाप, लिखित या मौखिक विवाद।)
Disposition	A person's inherent-qualities of mind and character ("एक मनुष्य को मस्तिष्क और चरित्र के विरासत (उत्तराधिकार) में मिले गुण।")
General Counsels	Piece of advice on general matters (सामान्य मामलों पर दी गई सलाह।)
Marshalling	Set out in an orderly manner (पुराने तरीके से व्यवस्थित।)
Sloth	Idleness or laziness (आलस्य)
Pruning	To cut or chop superfluous or undesired twigs, branches or roots (सीमाओं से बँधा हुआ।)
Bounded	Having limits (आवश्यकता से अधिक को काटना (अनचाही टहनियाँ या जड़ें)
Condemn	To indicate strong disapproval of, censure (कठोर निन्दा या नामंजूरी को इंगित करना।)
Observation	Register on record (नामांकन करना/ अवलोकन करना)
Swallowed	To gulp down (निगलना)
Dilligence	Constant and earnest effort to accomplish what is undertaken (किसी कार्य को पूरा करने के लिए निरन्तर और जोशीली कोशिश।)
Concert	To dismiss an arguement. Take for granted. (तर्क को ख़ारिज कर देना/ झूठा ठहराना)
Present wit	Ability to answer quickly (हाज़िर-जवाब / जल्दी से उत्तर देने में सक्षम)
Subtle	Requiring mental acuteness, penetration or discernment (मानसिक तीक्ष्णता, सूझ-बूझ)

Objective Questions

1. Bacon belonged to the
(a) 15th century (b) 16th century
(c) 17th century (d) 18th century

2. Bacon was essentially known as a
(a) poet (b) prose writer
(c) novelist (d) critic

3. Who was the father of Francis Bacon?
(a) Sir Nicholas Bacon (b) Sir Charles Bacon
(c) Sir John Bacon (d) None of these

4. Who was the mother of Francis Bacon?
(a) Anne Bacon (b) Anne James
(c) Marry Bacon (d) Julie Bacon

5. In which year was 'Of Studies' published'
(a) 1610 (b) 1601
(c) 1620 (d) 1602

6. Where was Francis Bacon born?
(a) Liverpool (b) London
(c) Cambridge (d) Paris

7. Where did Francis Bacon complete his Law study?
(a) Inner temple (b) Middle temple
(c) Lincoln's inn (d) Gray's inn

8. When did Francis Bacon publish "Advancement of Learning"?
(a) 1605 (b) 1600
(c) 1598 (d) 1596

9. Where did Francis bacon die?
(a) England (b) Marlborough
(c) Shrewsbury (d) Netherwood

10. The Renaissance term means
(a) Rebirth (b) evidence
(c) period (d) None of these

11. Bacon's first collection of essays was published in
(a) 1597 (b) 1605
(c) 1616 (d) 1625

12. The epithet 'Augustan' was first applied by Dryden to
(a) Bacon (b) Addison
(c) Dr Johnson (d) Steele

13. "Studies serve for delight, for ornament and for ability". Who wrote these lines?
(a) Lamb (b) Bacon
(c) DH Lawrence (d) Swift

14. The concern of the Neo Classical writers was
(a) nature (b) love
(c) revenge (d) human nature

15. Bacon's essays are ....in style.
(a) aphoristic (b) compact
(c) condensed (d) All of these

16. Bacon's essays are known as
(a) Dispersed Meditations (b) Handbook
(c) Essays of Elia (d) None of these

17. "Some books are to be tasted, others to be swallowed, and some few to be chewed and digested". The above line appears in the essay.
(a) On Spelling (b) Recollections of Childhood
(c) Of Studies (d) An Apology for Idlers

18. Which of the following is incorrect about Bacon's essays?
(a) They belonged to the reign of James I
(b) He was not clogged with long sentences like the writers of his age
(c) He was inclined to American authors who studied brevity
(d) He was imprisoned for bribery

19. Bacon's major contribution is
(a) His practical wisdom has universal appeal
(b) His wisdom is devoid of moral pretensions
(c) His wisdom is for the man of the world
(d) All of these

20. Bacon's style
(a) terse and pithy
(b) Packed with thought
(c) reflects the intellectual power in the great mind
(d) All of the above

21. A pioneer in the field of philosophical prose was
(a) Bacon (b) Lamb
(c) Steele (d) Addison

22. Bacon belonged to the ....faith.
(a) Indian (b) Anglican
(c) Puritan (d) Elizabethan

23. Bacon was the translator of ....essays.
(a) Ciero (b) Plato
(c) Montaigne (d) Pope

24. "Of Marriage and Single Life" is written by
(a) Joseph Addison (b) Richard Steele
(c) Charles Lamb (d) Francis Bacon

25. What does 'Of Studies' display?
(a) Wide learning (b) Deep scholarship
(c) Sound Wisdom (d) All of these

26. Bacon explains the multifarious aspect of studies in
(a) Human affairs (b) Love affairs
(c) Nature is environment (d) None of these

27. What is the chief use of studies for delight?
(a) One's private life (b) One's public life
(c) For adventure (d) None of these

28. What is the dominant spirit of the essay?
(a) Didactism (b) Patribtism
(c) Secularism (d) Democracy

29. Which of the following is the professional work of Bacon?
(a) Maxims of the Law (b) The De Augment
(c) The New Atlantis (d) The Novum organum

30. Which of the following is the literary work of Bacon?
(a) A Popthegms New and Old
(b) Reading on the Statute of Uses
(c) The Advancement of Learning
(d) The De Augments

31. Bacon's Famous essay 'Of Studies' is full of
(a) aphorisms (b) criticisms
(c) admiration23 (d) excitement

32. Truth may perhaps come to the price of a
(a) diamond (b) gold
(c) pearl (d) None of these

33. Through an exquisite metaphor drawn from Botany, Bacon compares human mind to a
(a) growing child
(b) growing plant
(c) developing humanity
(d) growing environment

34. What purpose do studies serve?
(a) Creation (b) Ornaments
(c) Innovation (d) Invention

35. What kind of view simple do men have about studies?
(a) Admiring (b) Criticism
(c) Support (d) Pull over

36. Francis Bacon's "The Advancement of Learning" is related to
(a) Philosophy (b) Literary
(c) Profession (d) None of these

37. What did bacon advise in all the cases of excessiveness in studies?
(a) Avoid (b) Reject (c) Accept (d) Admir

38. "Reading maketh a full man ". Who gave this statement?
(a) Francis Bacon (b) Richard Steele
(c) Charles Lamb (d) Oliver Goldsmith

39. How many of Bacon's essay's are the subjects of human interest?
(a) 52 essays (b) 37 essays
(c) 58 essays (d) 30 essays

40. Bacon was an
(a) essayist (b) historian
(c) thinker (d) All of these

41. "The English reader will find difficulties in Bacon's language of style," Who said this for Bacon?
(a) Mr. Wright (b) Mr. Machiavelli
(c) Mr. Humes (d) Mr. Hudson

42. Who calls the essays of bacon "Good Advice for Satan's Kingdom"?
(a) Henry Hudson (b) William Blake
(c) Joseph Addison (d) Charles Lamb

43. Who influenced Bacon's political morality?
(a) Plato (b) Socrates
(c) Aristotle (d) Machiavelli

44. Bacon's essays were written in
(a) French and English (b) Latin and French
(c) Latin and English (d) Greek and Latin

45. "Proper Study of mankind is man", a dictum of the Augustan age means that
(a) they emphasised on the importance of only men and not women
(b) they believed in the study of physical nature
(c) they believed in the study of human nature
(d) None fo these

46. The Royal Society of science is the result of .... emphasis on the collection of facts.
(a) Bacon's (b) Byron's
(c) Yeats (d) None of these

47. Name the writer who called an essay "Dispersed Meditations"?
(a) Addison (b) Johnson
(c) Lamb (d) Bacon

48. The author of the novel 'The New Atlantis' is
(a) Sir Thomas Moore (b) Dean Church
(c) Goethe (d) Francis Bacon

49. Which constituency did Francis Bacon represent in the Parliament in 1586-1588?
(a) Middlesex (b) Ipswich
(c) Tounton (d) Kent

50. Bacon believes that the human mind easily misuses its......... in many ways.
(a) reason (b) intellect
(c) gray matter (d) purpose

51. Bacon says that .... is more precious than anything on Earth.
(a) intellect
(b) philosophy
(c) true understanding
(d) a meeting of the minds

52. Bacon believes that the meeting between the two entities must return to its
(a) womb (b) previous incarnation
(c) original condition (d) self

53. Many things may be improved by using instruments of
(a) God (b) fellowship
(c) logic (d) intuition

54. Bacon states that people tend to lean towards false and hasty
(a) conclusion (b) allise
(c) decision (d) beliefs

55. Bacon suggests that man should try to focus on their .... power.
(a) true (b) limited
(c) God given (d) inevitable

56. When was Francis Bacon born?
(a) 22nd January, 1561 (b) 4th May, 1549
(c) 16th July, 1548 (d) 11th November, 1564

57. "Distilled books are like common distilled water, flashy things". This statement was used by
(a) Addison (b) Bacon
(c) Steele (d) Goldsmith

58. What makes people witty?
(a) Prose (b) Maths
(c) Poetry (d) Philosophy

59. How studies are used by the wise men ?
(a) Intellectual way
(b) Mathematical way
(c) Advantageous way
(d) All of the above

60. Bacon is remembered only for his
(a) drama (b) prose
(c) essays (d) fiction

61. What qualities does the essay "Of studies" bear for human beings? It is
(a) significant (b) helpful
(c) entertaining (d) All of these

62. The mode of the study is
(a) reading (b) writing
(c) confidence (d) All of these

63. 'The New Atlantis' is a work done by
(a) Steele (b) Smith (c) Bacon (d) Burton

64. Which of the following is incorrect about Bacon's essays?
(a) Of Marriage and Single Life
(b) Poor Relations
(c) Of Studies
(d) Of Simulation and Dissimulation

65. Bacon's style of writing is
(a) Sorrowful
(b) terse and pity
(c) the usage of intellectual power of mind
(d) All of these

66. The essay " Of Truth" belongs to
(a) Charles Lamb (b) Francis Bacon
(c) William Hazlitt (d) None of these

67. Crafty people think that their cleverness can better serve their ends than
(a) student's knowledge (b) bookish knowledge
(c) teacher's knowledge (d) None of these

68. Bacon's famous essay "Of studies" serves purpose that includes
(a) pleasure (b) ornament
(c) ability (d) All of these

69. In Bacon's essay, cunning person don't like
(a) studies (b) games
(c) play (d) None of these

70. Studies become a source of pleasure when a man is
(a) in natural environment (b) all alone
(c) in social life (d) None of these

71. According to Bacon virtues are like
(a) precious (b) odours
(c) most fragrant (d) All of these

72. "Crafty men condemn studies, simple men admire them and wise men use them." The above line appears in the essay.
(a) Of Adversity
(b) Of Studies
(c) Of Marriage and Single Life
(d) Of Friendship

73. "The disease of the body may have appropriate exercise". The above line belongs to
(a) Francis Bacon's essay (b) Charles Camb
(c) Richard Steele (d) Joseph Addison

74. Bacon's books recommend studies as to be of
(a) three types (b) four types
(c) six types (d) None of these

75. Which of the following pairs is incorrect?
(a) Charles Lamb "The Convalescent
(b) Francis Bacon 'Of Studies'
(c) Richard Steele 'On Shaking Hands'
(d) Joseph Addison 'Sir Roger at Church'

76. Bacon's literary works are full of
(a) system (b) practical wisdom
(c) adversity (d) None of these

77. What kind of view do simple men have about studies, according to Bacon?
(a) Supportive (b) Entertaining
(c) Admiring (d) Helpful

78. Bacon's moral consideration gives to
(a) entertaining (b) morality
(c) aloofness (d) creativity

Answers

1. (b)	2. (b)	3. (a)	4. (c)	5. (b)	6. (b)	7. (d)	8. (a)	9. (a)	10. (b)
11. (d)	12. (a)	13. (a)	14. (a)	15. (b)	16. (d)	17. (c)	18. (a)	19. (c)	20. (c)
21. (a)	22. (c)	23. (a)	24. (b)	25. (c)	26. (d)	27. (d)	28. (a)	29. (a)	30. (a)
31. (a)	32. (a)	33. (a)	34. (c)	35. (b)	36. (b)	37. (a)	38. (a)	39. (a)	40. (a)
41. (c)	42. (a)	43. (a)	44. (b)	45. (d)	46. (c)	47. (c)	48. (a)	49. (d)	50. (b)
51. (c)	52. (a)	53. (c)	54. (c)	55. (c)	56. (a)	57. (a)	58. (a)	59. (b)	60. (c)
61. (c)	62. (c)	63. (d)	64. (d)	65. (c)	66. (a)	67. (c)	68. (b)	69. (b)	70. (b)
71. (a)	72. (b)	73. (d)	74. (b)	75. (a)	76. (b)	77. (c)	78. (b)		

01 David Copperfield

Summary of the Lesson

- David copperfield relates the story of a young boy's growth and development into maturity. It is written from the point of view of the mature adult who recounts his own obstacles and the obstacles of those around him and how it all shaped his life and his beliefs.
- David Copperfield is deeply attached to his mother, who waswidowed six months before his birth. His early childhood is a very happy one, and once, he goes with his nurse Peggotty, for a holiday to Yarmouth. They stay with her brother Mr. Peggotty and other relatives in a boat-house.
- On his return, David finds that his mother has remarried. He is ill-treated by his stepfather, Mr. Murdstone, and sentaway to Salem House, a school run by a cruel man named Creakle. After his mother's death, David is sent to work for a few shillings aweek at Murdstone and Grinby's warehouse in London.
- He lodges with Mr. Micawber and his family and becomes very attached to them. But they leave London and David decides to go and find his great aunt, Miss Betsy Trotwood, who lives at Dover. But he is robbed of his money and has to walk the whole way to her house. Miss Betsy is very kind to him and sends him to an excellent school in Canterbury, wherhe boards with Mr. Wickfield and his daughter Agnes. Mr. Wickfield has a weakness for drink and his cunning clerk, Uriah Heep, takes advantage of this. After leaving school, David is articled to the firm of Spenlow and Jorkins in London.
- He meets Mr. Spenlow's daughter, Dora and falls madly in love with her, but Mr. Spenlow refuses to consider him as a son-in-law. Miss Trotwood loses her money andcomes to live in London. David works extremely hard and becomes a successful reporter and writer. After Mr. Spenlow's death, David and Dora are married. Dora ispretty but silly and immature, and wishes to be regarded as a "childwife".
- She loses a child, is very ill, and weakens slowly and dies. To forget his grief, David goes abroad and is away for three years. During this time, he realizes that he loves Agnes, but is sure that sheregards him as a brother.
- He returns to England and realizes that she has always loved him. They are married. Miss Trotwood's fortune isrestored, and Uriah Heep is imprisoned for fraud. Mr. Peggotty's family, as well as Mr. Micawber's family emigrate to Australia and live happily there.

Objective Questions

Here are 50 multiple-choice questions (MCQs) and answers based on David Copperfield, a novel by Charles Dickens:

1. Who is the narrator of David Copperfield?
(a) David Copperfield (b) Charles Dickens
(c) Mr. Micawber (d) Agnes Wickfield

2. What is the name of David Copperfield's mother?
(a) Clara Copperfield (b) Peggotty
(c) Miss Betsey Trotwood (d) Dora Spenlow

3. Who is David Copperfield's stepfather?
(a) Mr. Murdstone (b) Mr. Wickfield
(c) Mr. Micawber (d) Mr. Peggotty

4. What is the name of David Copperfield's first wife?
(a) Dora Spenlow (b) Agnes Wickfield
(c) Emily (d) Clara Copperfield

5. Who is David's aunt who cares for him after his mother's death?
(a) Miss Betsey Trotwood (b) Mrs. Gummidge
(c) Mrs. Micawber (d) Peggotty

6. Where is David born?
(a) London (b) Dover
(c) Blunderstone (d) Canterbury

7. Who is David's closest friend throughout the novel?
(a) Steerforth (b) Tom Traddles
(c) James Steerforth (d) Mr. Micawber

8. What is the occupation of Mr. Micawber?
(a) Lawyer (b) Shopkeeper
(c) Clerk (d) Magistrate

9. Who is the villain of the novel?
(a) Mr. Murdstone
(b) James Steerforth
(c) Uriah Heep
(d) David Copperfield

10. Who is the first person to tell David about his inheritance?
(a) Miss Betsey Trotwood (b) Mr. Wickfield
(c) Mr. Micawber (d) Dora Spenlow

11. What is Uriah Heep's most notable characteristic?
(a) Arrogance (b) Humility
(c) Wealth (d) Beauty

12. Who does David marry after Dora's death?
(a) Agnes Wickfield (b) Emily
(c) Miss Betsey (d) Peggotty

13. What profession does David take up after his education?
(a) Teacher (b) Lawyer
(c) Doctor (d) Merchant

14. Who does David meet in the debtors' prison?
(a) Mr. Micawber (b) Steerforth
(c) Mr. Wickfield (d) Peggotty

15. What is the relationship between Miss Betsey Trotwood and David?
(a) Mother (b) Aunt
(c) Sister (d) Grandmother

16. Who is Steerforth's mother?
(a) Miss Betsey (b) Mrs. Gummidge
(c) Mrs. Steerforth (d) Clara Copperfield

17. What happens to Steerforth at the end of the novel?
(a) He becomes rich (b) He dies in a shipwreck
(c) He marries Agnes (d) He goes to prison

18. Who is the first person to express concern for David's future?
(a) Miss Betsey Trotwood (b) Clara Copperfield
(c) Mr. Wickfield (d) Dora Spenlow

19. What is the name of Mr. Wickfield's daughter?
(a) Dora (b) Agnes
(c) Emily (d) Peggotty

20. How does David's mother, Clara Copperfield, die?
(a) Illness (b) Childbirth
(c) Drowning (d) Old age

21. Who is Mr. Peggotty?
(a) A lawyer (b) A servant
(c) A sailor (d) A doctor

22. What type of character is Uriah Heep?
(a) Arrogant (b) Charitable
(c) Scheming (d) Honest

23. Who is the first to recognize the wickedness of Uriah Heep?
(a) Agnes (b) Miss Betsey
(c) David (d) Mr. Wickfield

24. What is the name of the school where David attends as a child?
(a) Salem House
(b) Dr. Blimber's Academy
(c) Mr. Creakle's School
(d) Miss Pinkerton's Academy

25. Who is the headmaster of Salem House?
(a) Dr. Blimber (b) Mr. Creakle
(c) Mr. Spenlow (d) Mr. Wickfield

26. Who is the character that David takes pity on because of her mistreatment?
(a) Agnes (b) Dora
(c) Emily (d) Peggotty

27. What is Steerforth's relationship to David Copperfield?
(a) Uncle (b) Father (c) Friend (d) Rival

28. What is the name of the servant who is very loyal to David's family?
(a) Peggotty (b) Miss Betsey
(c) Dora (d) Mrs. Gummidge

29. What does David initially plan to do after leaving school?
(a) Become a lawyer (b) Become a merchant
(c) Travel the world (d) Become a clerk

30. How does David feel about his stepfather, Mr. Murdstone?
(a) He loves him (b) He respects him
(c) He hates him (d) He is indifferent to him

31. Who rescues David from being beaten by Mr. Murdstone?
(a) Miss Betsey (b) Peggotty
(c) Tom Traddles (d) Mr. Wickfield

32. What happens to Mr. Micawber's financial situation at the end of the novel?
(a) He goes to prison
(b) He becomes wealthy
(c) He becomes a successful lawyer
(d) He remains poor

33. Who does David first meet in London?
(a) Steerforth (b) Mr. Micawber
(c) Miss Betsey (d) Tom Traddles

34. What is the relationship between David and Dora Spenlow?
(a) Cousins (b) Friends
(c) Husband and wife (d) Siblings

35. Where does David eventually move after his marriage to Agnes?
(a) Australia (b) London
(c) Blunderstone (d) Dover

36. Who reveals Uriah Heep's true nature?
(a) Miss Betsey (b) David
(c) Agnes (d) Mr. Wickfield

37. How does Uriah Heep end up at the end of the novel?
(a) He is forgiven (b) He is arrested for his crimes
(c) He dies in prison (d) He escapes

38. Who does David Copperfield eventually inherit his wealth from?
(a) Miss Betsey (b) Mr. Wickfield
(c) Mr. Spenlow (d) His father

39. How does Steerforth treat Emily?
(a) He marries her (b) He abandons her
(c) He mistreats her (d) He helps her

40. Who does Tom Traddles marry?
(a) Emily (b) Agnes (c) Dora (d) Sophy

41. The major theme of David Copperfield is..
(a) The importance of education
(b) The dangers of greed
(c) The quest for personal happiness
(d) The power of family

42. What type of character is David Copperfield?
(a) Static (b) Dynamic (c) Antagonist (d) Villain

43. Who is David's first true friend at school?
(a) Steerforth (b) Tom Traddles
(c) Mr. Wickfield (d) Mr. Micawber

44. Which character has an obsession with the idea of humility?
(a) Mr. Wickfield (b) Uriah Heep
(c) David Copperfield (d) Peggotty

45. Where does Miss Betsey Trotwood live?
(a) London (b) Blunderstone
(c) Dover (d) Canterbury

46. According to the novel,What is David Copperfield's main internal conflict throughout the novel?
(a) His desire to be rich
(b) His struggle to forgive Steerforth
(c) His search for a career
(d) His struggle to find true love

47. How does Dora Spenlow die?
(a) In childbirth (b) From a fever
(c) In an accident (d) Of a broken heart

48. What was David's reaction when he first saw Miss Betsey Trotwood?
(a) He was afraid of her
(b) He was confused by her
(c) He was immediately fond of her
(d) He didn't like her

49. The relationship between David and his father is..?
(a) They are very close
(b) They rarely interact
(c) David's father is dead before the story starts
(d) David resents his father

50. How does the novel David Copperfield end?
(a) With David in prison
(b) With David inheriting a fortune and marrying Agnes
(c) With Steerforth escaping
(d) With David leaving London

Answers

1. (a)	2. (a)	3. (a)	4. (a)	5. (a)	6. (c)	7. (b)	8. (c)	9. (c)	10. (a)
11. (b)	12. (a)	13. (b)	14. (a)	15. (b)	16. (c)	17. (b)	18. (a)	19. (b)	20. (b)
21. (b)	22. (c)	23. (b)	24. (a)	25. (b)	26. (c)	27. (c)	28. (a)	29. (a)	30. (c)
31. (a)	32. (b)	33. (a)	34. (c)	35. (b)	36. (b)	37. (b)	38. (a)	39. (b)	40. (d)
41. (c)	42. (b)	43. (b)	44. (b)	45. (b)	46. (b)	47. (a)	48. (c)	49. (c)	50. (b)

02 Mrs. Dalloway

Summary of the Lesson

Clarissa Dalloway, an upper-class, fifty-two-year-old woman married to a politician, decides to buy flowers herself for the party she is hosting that evening instead of sending a servant to buy them. London is bustling and full of noise this Wednesday, almost five years after Armistice Day. Big Ben strikes. The king and queen are at the palace. It is a fresh mid-June morning, and Clarissa recalls one girlhood summer on her father's estate, Bourton. She sees herself at eighteen, standing at the window, feeling as if something awful might happen. Despite the dangers, and despite having only a few twigs of knowledge passed on to her by her childhood governess, Clarissa loves life. Her one gift, she feels, is an ability to know people by instinct.

Clarissa next runs into her old friend Hugh Whitbread. Hugh and Clarissa exchange a few words about Hugh's wife, Evelyn, who suffers from an unspecified internal ailment. Beside the proper and admirable Hugh, Clarissa feels self-conscious about her hat.

Past and present continue to intermingle as she walks to the flower shop. She remembers how her old friend Peter Walsh disapproved of Hugh. She thinks affectionately of Peter, who once asked her to marry him. She refused. He made her cry when he said she would marry a prime minister and throw parties. Clarissa continues to feel the sting of his criticisms but now also feels anger that Peter did not accomplish any of his dreams.

- She continues to walk and considers the idea of death. She believes she will survive in the perpetual motion of the modern London streets, in the lives of her friends and even strangers, in the trees, in her home. She reads lines about death from a book in a shop window. Clarissa reflects that she does not do things for themselves, but in order to affect other people's opinions of her. She imagines having her life to live over again. She regrets her face, beaked like a bird's, and her thin body. She stops to look at a Dutch picture, and feels invisible. She is conscious that the world sees her as her husband's wife, as Mrs. Richard Dalloway.

- Clarissa looks in the window of a glove shop and contemplates her daughter, Elizabeth, who cares little for fashion and prefers to spend time with her dog or her history teacher, Miss Kilman, with whom she reads prayer books and attends communion. Clarissa wonders if Elizabeth is falling in love with Miss Kilman, but Richard believes it is just a phase. Clarissa thinks of her hatred for Miss Kilman, which she is aware is irrational, as a monster.
- A car backfires while Clarissa is in the flower shop, and she and several others turn to observe the illustrious person passing in a grand car. They wonder if it is the queen or the prime minister behind the blinds. The car inspires feelings of patriotism in many onlookers.
- Septimus Warren Smith, a veteran of World War I who is about thirty years old, also hears the car backfire. He suffers from shell shock, a mental illness brought on by the horrors of war, and believes he is responsible for the traffic congestion the passing car causes. Lucrezia, or Rezia, his young Italian wife, is embarrassed by his odd manner and also frightened, since Septimus recently threatened to kill himself. She leads him to Regent's Park, where they sit together. Septimus's thoughts are incomprehensible to his wife. He believes he is connected to trees and that trees must not be cut down. He believes that if he looks beyond the park railings he will see his dead friend, Evans, and fears the world might burst into flames.
- Septimus, Rezia, and many minor characters observe a plane overhead writing letters in the sky. The letters eventually seem to read "TOFFEE." Septimus believes someone is trying to communicate with him in a code language.
- Rezia cannot stand to see him so broken, staring and talking out loud, and she walks to the fountain. She sees a statue of an Indian holding a cross. She feels alone and for a moment is angry with Septimus-after all, Dr. Holmes has said that Septimus has nothing at all the matter with him. Suddenly, Rezia feels her devotion to her husband clearly and returns to where he sits. A young woman, Maisie Johnson, asks them directions, and as she walks away she thinks about how strange the couple is. An older woman, Carrie Dempster, observes Maisie and feels regret about her own life.

Objective Questions

1. Who is the protagonist of Mrs. Dalloway?
(a) Septimus Warren Smith
(b) Clarissa Dalloway
(c) Sally Seton
(d) Richard Dalloway

2. Where does Mrs. Dalloway take place?
(a) Paris (b) London
(c) New York (d) Edinburgh

3. What is Clarissa Dalloway's primary concern at the beginning of the novel?
(a) Her mental health
(b) Her preparations for a party
(c) Her marriage to Richard
(d) Her relationship with Sally Seton

4. Who is Septimus Warren Smith?
(a) Clarissa's ex-lover
(b) A war veteran suffering from PTSD
(c) Clarissa's husband
(d) Clarissa's best friend

5. What is the significance of the bell in the novel?
(a) It marks the time for Clarissa's party
(b) It signals the death of Septimus
(c) It signals Clarissa's marriage to Richard
(d) It symbolizes the passage of time

6. What theme is most prominent in Mrs. Dalloway?
(a) Social class (b) Time and memory
(c) Love and marriage (d) Political revolution

7. How does Clarissa feel about her past choices?
(a) She is content with them
(b) She is regretful and nostalgic
(c) She is indifferent
(d) She is angry with herself

8. Who does Clarissa encounter while preparing for her party?
(a) Sally Seton (b) Richard Dalloway
(c) Peter Walsh (d) Septimus Warren Smith

9. How does Clarissa view Peter Walsh?
(a) As a symbol of lost love (b) As a friend
(c) As a rival (d) As a political ally

10. What is the relationship between Sally Seton and Clarissa?
(a) They are childhood friends
(b) They are romantic partners
(c) They are sisters
(d) They are cousins

11. What event causes Septimus's mental deterioration
(a) The death of his wife
(b) The trauma from the war
(c) His relationship with Clarissa
(d) His loneliness

12. What is the central setting of the novel?
(a) Clarissa's house and garden
(b) London streets
(c) Septimus's home
(d) A psychiatric hospital

13. What is Clarissa's primary source of inner conflict
(a) Her ambition to become a writer
(b) Her dissatisfaction with her marriage
(c) Her relationship with Sally
(d) Her struggle with her identity and choices

14. What does the novel suggest about the roles of women?
(a) Women are empowered and independent
(b) Women are trapped by societal expectations
(c) Women are given total freedom in their choices
(d) Women are presented as passive characters

15. What is the role of Clarissa's party in the novel?
(a) A symbol of social status
(b) A chance to escape her past
(c) A plot device to bring characters together
(d) A place of rebellion

16. Who is Richard Dalloway?
(a) Clarissa's lover (b) Clarissa's husband
(c) Clarissa's father (d) Septimus's doctor

17. How does Septimus die?
(a) He is murdered (b) He dies from a war injury
(c) He commits suicide (d) He is killed by the doctors

18. What role does the theme of mental illness play in the novel?
(a) It is irrelevant to the plot
(b) It is only seen in Septimus's character
(c) It highlights the differences between men and women
(d) It reflects societal neglect and misunderstanding of mental health

19. Who is Sally Seton married to in the novel?
(a) Richard Dalloway
(b) Septimus Warren Smith
(c) Peter Walsh
(d) A wealthy man from India

20. How does Clarissa react to her reunion with Sally Seton?
(a) She feels uncomfortable
(b) She is overjoyed and nostalgic
(c) She is indifferent
(d) She is angry

21. What is the significance of the London setting in the novel?
(a) It represents Clarissa's independence
(b) It symbolizes the passage of time and social change
(c) It represents Clarissa's isolation
(d) It is irrelevant to the themes

22. How is time portrayed in Mrs. Dalloway?
(a) As linear and straightforward
(b) As fragmented and subjective
(c) As static and unchanging
(d) As predictable and ordinary

23. How does Peter Walsh react to his reunion with Clarissa?
(a) He is angry at her
(b) He is deeply moved and nostalgic
(c) He is indifferent to her
(d) He criticizes her choices

24. What does Clarissa think of death?
(a) She fears it (b) She is obsessed with it
(c) She is indifferent to it (d) She sees it as a release

25. Which of the following does the character of Septimus symbolize?
(a) The failure of modern medicine
(b) The trauma of war and the alienation of veterans
(c) The consequences of neglecting family duties
(d) The fear of death

26. Which of the following does Clarissa's relationship with Richard Dalloway represent?
(a) A passionate and romantic love
(b) A comfortable and stable marriage
(c) A source of deep dissatisfaction and alienation
(d) A political partnership

27. What is Peter Walsh's reaction to Clarissa's marriage to Richard?
(a) He is relieved (b) He is angry and resentful
(c) He is happy for her (d) He is indifferent

28. How does Clarissa view her own identity?
(a) As a mother and wife
(b) As an individual struggling for independence
(c) As someone defined by social norms
(d) As a successful career woman

29. Who is the character who represents the conventional British society?
(a) Sally Seton (b) Richard Dalloway
(c) Clarissa Dalloway (d) Septimus Warren Smith

30. How does the novel handle the concept of the "stream of consciousness"?
(a) It does not use this technique
(b) It uses it to explore the inner thoughts and emotions of characters
(c) It uses it to present a disjointed narrative
(d) It uses it exclusively for Clarissa's character

31. What role does Sally Seton play in Clarissa's life?
(a) She is Clarissa's rival
(b) She is a figure from Clarissa's past that represents freedom
(c) She is a political ally
(d) She is Clarissa's business partner

32. How does the novel depict the relationship between men and women?
(a) As equal and supportive
(b) As a source of tension and misunderstanding
(c) As free from societal constraints
(d) As romantic and idealized

33. What is the significance of the character of Richard Dalloway in the novel?
(a) He represents wealth and success
(b) He represents societal stability and normalcy
(c) He represents the failure of traditional masculinity
(d) He represents an ideal romantic partner

34. What is the impact of the First World War on the characters in Mrs. Dalloway?
(a) It unites the characters in a common cause
(b) It affects Septimus, leading to his mental breakdown
(c) It causes financial hardship for the Dalloways
(d) It is mentioned but has no significant impact

35. What does the novel suggest about the role of memory?
(a) Memory is unreliable and fades over time
(b) Memory is an essential part of one's identity
(c) Memory is a distraction from the present
(d) Memory is irrelevant in shaping one's life

36. How does the novel portray the impact of societal expectations on individuals?
(a) It shows the freedom of individuals from societal norms
(b) It highlights the burden of societal expectations and their impact on personal identity
(c) It suggests that societal expectations are irrelevant
(d) It celebrates societal norms

37. What does Clarissa think about her past relationship with Peter Walsh?
(a) She regrets it deeply
(b) She sees it as a source of deep happiness
(c) She feels it was an important part of her life
(d) She is indifferent to it

38. How is the theme of death explored in the novel?
(a) Death is seen as an escape from societal pressure
(b) Death is ignored by the characters
(c) Death is portrayed as inevitable and oppressive
(d) Death is only explored through Septimus's death

39. What is the primary narrative structure of Mrs. Dalloway?
(a) Linear and chronological
(b) Nonlinear, using flashbacks and shifts in perspective
(c) Told entirely from one character's perspective
(d) Told in the form of letters

40. What is Clarissa's relationship with Sally Seton?
(a) They have a romantic relationship
(b) They were once close friends and share a deep emotional bond
(c) They are business partners
(d) They are rivals

41. Who is the character that represents modernity in Mrs. Dalloway?
(a) Sally Seton
(b) Clarissa Dalloway
(c) Richard Dalloway
(d) Septimus Warren Smith

42. What is the significance of the title Mrs. Dalloway?
(a) It reflects Clarissa's role as a mother
(b) It focuses on the social expectations placed on women in society
(c) It is simply the name of the main character
(d) It refers to Clarissa's relationship with her husband

43. From the given options What is the impact of Clarissa's party on her life?
(a) It brings her closer to her past and brings resolution to her internal conflict
(b) It allows her to forget her past
(c) It causes a breakdown in her marriage
(d) It has no significant impact

44. What is Peter Walsh's role in the novel?
(a) He is Clarissa's love interest
(b) He is an outsider who contrasts Clarissa's world
(c) He is a representation of societal norms
(d) He is a symbol of freedom and modernity

45. Which of the following does the character of Septimus represent in Mrs. Dalloway?
(a) The trauma and alienation of war veterans
(b) A symbol of mental illness
(c) A reflection of Clarissa's own struggles
(d) All of the above

46. According to the Author,What does the stream-of-consciousness narrative technique allow readers to do?
(a) See the events from an objective point of view
(b) Experience the characters' internal thoughts and emotions directly
(c) Follow the plot chronologically
(d) Understand the motives of secondary characters

47. How does the novel portray relationships between men and women?
(a) As equal partnerships
(b) As unequal, with power struggles and expectations
(c) As purely transactional
(d) As deeply romantic and idealistic

48. What does Clarissa fear the most?
(a) Losing her social status
(b) Losing her identity and individuality
(c) Losing Peter's love
(d) The death of her daughter

Answers

1. (b)	2. (b)	3. (b)	4. (b)	5. (d)	6. (b)	7. (b)	8. (c)	9. (a)	10. (a)
11. (b)	12. (b)	13. (d)	14. (b)	15. (c)	16. (b)	17. (c)	18. (d)	19. (d)	20. (b)
21. (b)	22. (b)	23. (b)	24. (b)	25. (b)	26. (c)	27. (b)	28. (b)	29. (b)	30. (b)
31. (b)	32. (b)	33. (b)	34. (b)	35. (b)	36. (b)	37. (c)	38. (c)	39. (b)	40. (b)
41. (a)	42. (b)	43. (a)	44. (b)	45. (d)	46. (b)	47. (b)	48. (b)		

01 The Merchant of Venice

Summary of the Lesson

- The Merchant of Venice, comedy in five acts by William Shakespeare, written about 1596-97 and printed in a quarto edition in 1600 from an authorial manuscript or copy of one.
- The play centers around the themes of mercy, justice, and revenge. The story follows Antonio, a merchant in Venice, who borrows money from the Jewish moneylender Shylock to help his friend Bassanio court the wealthy heiress Portia. Shylock agrees to lend the money without interest, but in exchange, he demands a pound of Antonio's flesh if the loan is not repaid on time.
- When Antonio's ships are delayed and he cannot repay the debt, Shylock demands the pound of flesh as agreed. The case goes to court, where Portia, disguised as a male lawyer, defends Antonio. She cleverly argues that while Shylock is entitled to a pound of flesh, he is not allowed to spill any of Antonio's blood, as the contract does not mention blood. Shylock loses the case and is forced to convert to Christianity and give up his wealth.
- Meanwhile, Bassanio and his friend Gratiano both find happiness. Bassanio marries Portia, and Gratiano marries Nerissa, Portia's maid. The play concludes with a mix of resolutions to the main conflicts, though it leaves some questions about mercy and justice unanswered.
- The play opens with Antonio, a wealthy merchant in Venice, who is sad but unsure why. His best friend, Bassanio, wants to court the wealthy heiress Portia but has no money. Antonio agrees to lend Bassanio the money for the journey to win Portia's hand in marriage, but since Antonio's wealth is tied up in his ships, he borrows the money from the Jewish moneylender Shylock. Shylock agrees to lend the money on the condition that if Antonio cannot repay it within three months, he will owe Shylock a pound of his own flesh. Antonio agrees to the terms, confident his ships will return in time.
- Meanwhile, Portia is bound by her father's will, which stipulates that suitors must choose between three caskets (gold, silver, or lead) to win her hand. The suitor who chooses correctly will marry her, while the others must leave. Bassanio chooses the right casket, and Portia agrees to marry him.
- Back in Venice, Antonio's ships are delayed, and he cannot repay the loan to Shylock. Shylock, enraged by Antonio's past insults and treatment of him, insists on the pound of flesh. The case goes to court, and Portia, disguised as a lawyer named Balthazar, defends Antonio. She argues that while Shylock is entitled to the flesh, the contract does not allow him to spill any of Antonio's blood. Shylock is defeated, as he cannot take the flesh without causing Antonio's death, and he is ordered to give up his wealth and convert to Christianity.
- Portia and Nerissa (Portia's maid) return home, where Bassanio and Gratiano (Bassanio's friend) await. As a token of gratitude for saving Antonio, Bassanio gives Portia the ring he promised never to part with. Gratiano also gives Nerissa a ring, though they both end up giving the rings to the disguised Portia and Nerissa, leading to a humorous conclusion.
- The play ends with a sense of justice, but also leaves open questions about mercy, revenge, and the power dynamics between the characters. It highlights both the positive and negative aspects of human nature, with moments of generosity and forgiveness contrasting with cruelty and greed.

About the Author

William Shakespeare was born in a small English town called Stratford -upon- Avon in Warwickshire, England on 23rd April, 1564. He studied at a local school in Stratford. When he was 14 years old, his father lost his property and the boy had to leave school to support his family. In 1582, he got married to Anne Hathaway, who was 8 years older to him.

The author left Stratford in 1585 and reached London in 1586. It is believed that he started his career doing modest jobs in the theaters of London. By 1592, Shakespeare found himself earning his living as an actor and playwright. Documents have shown that by early 1590s, Shakespeare was a partner in an acting company in London called Lord Chamberlain's Men. He remained in London till 1610 and left for Stratford. He died on 23rd April, 1616 at his Stratford home.

Shakespeare's most flourishing period is claimed to be between 1590 and 1610. He has been credited with 37 plays which are divided into three main categories–tragedies, comedies and tragicomedies. His works also comprise 154 sonnets, 2 long narrative poems and few other verses. As one of the greatest dramatists of all times, Shakespeare's genius lies in his characterisation. His characters are not mechanical puppets but true to life human beings. They are not totally blameless or error free but realistic characters with human flaws.

About the Play

'The Merchant of Venice' is a play of revenge and exhibition of cruelty, mercy and encouragement. Antonio, a leading merchant of Venice is a wealthy, respected, rich and popular trader. He tries to help his dear friend Bassanio by lending money from Shylock (a Jew moneylender). Antonio never wanted to take money from Shylock, but has to due to shortage of money as his ships have not arrived as yet. The money was given by signing a bond which stated that if money is not paid in time, Shylock will take a pound of flesh from Antonio's body.

Bassanio wanted this money to go to Belmont and to fulfill the terms of Portia's father's will to marry her. Bassanio and Portia marry but the news arrives that Antonio's ships have been lost at sea. Antonio cannot repay his debt and Shylock gets his chance for revenge. Shylock insists that he should be paid in accordance with his contract, i.e. he wants his pound of flesh.

At the point, Portia disguised as a lawyer and Nerissa dressed as her law clerk enter the courtroom. Portia begins her case with a plea for mercy. She begs Shylock to forfeit the bond and accept three times the money that Bassanio had offered. Upon refusal by Shylock, Portia makes another claim. She informs Shylock that he can take exact one pound of flesh from Antonio's body but he has to do so without spilling a single drop of blood. If he fails, all his lands and goods will be confiscated. Knowing that the act is impossible, Shylock agrees to take the triple amount or the return of original amount but Portia refuses.

The Duke of Venice decides to spare Shylock's life and gives half of Shylock's money to Antonio and half to the state. As a reward, the young lawyer asks for Bassanio's ring which his wife has given to him. The play starts reaching its end on a humorous and happy tone when Antonio, Bassanio and Gratiano return to Belmont. After much comical agonising moments, Portia and Nerissa confess everything and Jessica inherits the money from Shylock to settle down. The play ends as Antonio is informed about three of his ships have arrived safely in port.

Characters in the Play (Brief Intro)

- **Antonio** A wealthy Venetian Merchant who occasionally lends money
- **Bassanio** Antonio's dear friend
- **Portia** An intelligent, witty and wealthy lady who marries Bassanio
- **Shylock** A strict Jew Moneylender
- **Gratiano** A friend of Bassanio who accompanies him to Belmont and marries Nerissa
- **Lorenzo** Friend of Antonio and Bassanio who loves Jessica
- **Jessica** Shylock's daughter
- **Nerissa** Portia's confidant and lady in waiting
- **Salarino** Antonio's friend
- **Salanio** Antonio's friend
- **Launcelot Gobbo** Shylock's servant
- **Tubal** Shylock's friend
- **Balthazar** Portia dressed as a lawyer
- **Salerio** Messenger
- **The Duke of Venice** The judge of the court
- **The Prince of Morocco** Portia's suitor
- **The Prince of Arragon** Portia's suitor
- **Leonardo** Bassanio's servant
- **Dr. Bellario** A lawyer from Padua
- **Stephano** Portia's servant

ACT-I (Scene I, II & III)

Summary of Act I Scene I

Antonio, a Venetian merchant, complains to his friends, Salarino and Salanio, that a sadness has overtaken him and dulled his faculties. He cannot explain why he is sad. Salarino and Salanio suggest that his sadness must be due to his commercial investments as Antonio has dispatched several trade ships to various ports. Salarino says it is impossible for Antonio not to feel sad at the thought of the sinking of his entire investment in the ocean, but Antonio assures his friends that his business ventures do not depend on the safe passage of any one ship. Salanio then declares that Antonio must be in love, but Antonio dismisses the suggestion too. Then, Salarino suggests Antonio feels sad because of his melancholic disposition.

The three men encounter Bassanio, Antonio's dear friend, walking with two friends named Lorenzo and Gratiano. Salarino and Salanio bid Antonio farewell and depart. When Gratiano notices Antonio's unhappiness and suggests that the merchant worries too much about business, Antonio responds that he is a player on a stage destined to play a sad part. Gratiano warns Antonio against becoming the type of man who remains serious in order to gain a wise reputation and then, takes his leave with Lorenzo.

As soon as Gratiano and Lorenzo leave, Bassanio assures Antonio and asks him not to worry about Gratiano's remarks. Changing the subject, Antonio asks Bassanio to tell him about the love that Bassanio is harboring for someone. In reply, Bassanio admits that although he already owes Antonio a substantial sum of money from his earlier days, he has fallen in love with Portia, a rich heiress from Belmont. He hopes to win her heart by contending against her other wealthy and powerful suitors. He adds that in order to woo Portia, he needs to borrow more money from Antonio. Antonio replies that he cannot give Bassanio another loan as all his money is tied up in his present business ventures, but offers to help him. He tells Bassanio to take up loan on his name and guarantee.

Analysis of Act I Scene I

The introduction or the exposition of the play is crucial as it introduces the central characters of the play to us. Through this scene we are introduced to the world of wealthy, upper-class Christian men living in Venice. Their conversation reveals that they are men of business who take great risks with money and are careful to avoid seeming overly concerned about their investments. From the conversation we come to know about Antonio being a rich merchant, his melancholic disposition and his deep friendship with Bassanio. We are also introduced with other important details which are crucial to the play. These include-the risks involved in the merchant ships and the love story of Bassanio and Portia. The act also points out the significance of money not just for Antonio but also for Bassanio. All of these together act as a forewarning of something bad which may happen in the play.

Summary of Act I Scene II

The scene shifts to Belmont wherein Portia complains to her lady-in-waiting, Nerissa, that she is tired of the world because of her dead father's will. According to her father's will, Portia cannot marry the man of her choice. Instead, Portia has to conduct a casket test in which her suitors must choose between three chests in the hopes of selecting the one that contains her portrait. The man who guesses correctly will win Portia's hand in marriage, but those who guess incorrectly must swear never to marry anyone. Nerissa assures Portia and tells her that her father would only choose or do well for her. But Portia is not certain as she does not like any man who had come as her suitors.

When Nerissa lists the suitors who have come to guess–a Neapolitan prince, a Palatine count, a French nobleman, an English baron, a Scottish lord and the nephew of the Duke of Saxony–Portia criticises their many hilarious faults. She describes the Neapolitan prince as being too fond of his horse, the Palatine count as being too serious, Monsieur Le Bon for lacking personality, the Englishman as lacking any knowledge of Italian or any of the other languages Portia speaks, the Scottish lord for cowardice and the German suitor of drunkenness.

Each of these suitors has left without even attempting a guess for fear of the penalty for guessing wrong. This fact relieves Portia and both she and Nerissa remember Bassanio, who has visited once before, as the suitor most deserving and worthy of praise. A servant enters to tell Portia that the Prince of Morocco will arrive soon. It is a news that Portia is not at all happy to hear.

Analysis of Act I Scene II

Much like the first introductory scene, Scene II of this act introduces the female protagonist of the play-Portia. From the characterisation, we come to understand her not just as a beautiful and wealthy girl but also as an intelligent and witty lady who does not approve of her father's will. She, from her introduction, comes out as a powerful character who can hold her own stance. Apart from coming to meet Portia, we are also introduced with the Casket Test plot of the play as well as Portia's interest in Bassanio.

Summary of Act I Scene III

The scene shifts back to Venice where Bassaino seeks out Shylock, a Jewish moneylender for the loan. Shylock agrees to loan Bassanio three thousand ducats for a term of three months. Bassanio assures Shylock that Antonio will guarantee the loan, but the moneylender is doubtful. Shylock knows Antonio's wealth is currently invested in business ventures that may fail. In the end, however, Shylock decides that Antonio's guarantee of the loan will be sufficient assurance and asks to speak with him. Bassanio agrees and invites him to dinner which Shylock refuses. Shylock states that while he can do business with Christians, he cannot eat or pray with them.

Just then Antonio arrives and Shylock, in an aside, confesses his hatred for the man. Shylock's hatred is based on the fact that Antonio is a Christian who lends money without interest, which makes the practice of usury or money lending at exorbitant interest rates difficult. Shylock is also incensed by Antonio's frequent public denunciations of Shylock. Antonio makes it clear to Shylock that he is not in the habit of borrowing or lending money, but has decided to make an exception on behalf of his friend Bassanio. Their conversation leads Antonio to chastise the business of usury which Shylock defends as a way to thrive.

As he calculates the interest on Bassanio's loan, Shylock remembers the many times that Antonio has cursed him, insulted him, spit on him and called him a 'dog'. Antonio responds that he is likely to do so again and insists that Shylock lend him the money as an enemy. Such an arrangement, Antonio claims, will make it easier for Shylock to exact a harsh penalty if the loan is not repaid. Assuring Antonio that he means to be friends, Shylock offers to make the loan without interest. Instead, he suggests that Antonio forfeit a pound of his own flesh should the loan not be repaid in due time. Bassanio warns Antonio against entering such an agreement, but Antonio assures him that he will have no trouble repaying the debt as his ships will soon bring him wealth that far exceeds the value of the loan. Shylock attempts to dismiss Bassanio's suspicions, asking what profit he stands to make by procuring a pound of Antonio's flesh.

As Shylock heads off to the notary's office to sign the bond, Antonio remarks on Shylock's newfound generosity. Bassanio remains suspicious of the arrangement, but Antonio reminds him that his ships will arrive within the next two months.

Analysis of Act I Scene III

The third scene of Act I has two main purpose-to introduce Shylock and to set the base for the Bond. Shylock, from the very beginning, has an arresting presence and although Antonio may be the character for whom the play is named, it is Shylock's character that depicts the playwright's powerful dramatisation. Shylock's physical presence shows the business acumen that Antonio may perhaps be lacking. In his presence in the scene, Bassanio and Antonio seem to be naïve. Shylock knows what he is doing and makes it clear to the audience watching the play.

The aside section is crucial as we come to know about Shylock's intentions through them. An aside is a device used by playwrights in which a character addresses the audience giving them information not known to other characters of the play. Due to the aside mentioned in the this scene, we may easily pin Shylock to be a thorough villain. However, this soon changes to sympathy as we realise that Antonio's treatment of Shylock is unexpectedly harsh and brutal.

Even though Bassanio and Antonio require a favour from Shylock, Antonio's tone of imperious command and his past, present and future attitude toward Shylock is one of exceptional contempt. Shylock, as a Jew, is an outcast who is vilified and spat upon by the Christian characters. Shylock, thus, is a victim in spite of being cunning, cautious and crafty.

In his presence, Shylock also exposes the Christians present in the play. He understands the Christians and their culture much better than they understand him. The Christian characters only interact with Shylock within a framework of finance and law—he is not part of the friendship network portrayed in Act I, Scene I. However, Shylock is able to cite the New Testament as readily as Jewish scripture. As we see more of Shylock, he does not become a hero or a fully sympathetic character, but he is an unsettling figure insofar as he exposes the inconsistencies and hypocrisies of the Christian characters. Shylock never quite fits their descriptions or expectations of him. Most significantly, they think he is motivated solely by money, when in fact his resentment against Antonio and the other Christians outweighs his desire for monetary gain.

Word Meanings (Act I)

Ado–difficulty; **Argosies**–large merchant ships; **Portly**–stout, plump, fat; **Venture forth**–business ventures; **Burghers**–a citizen of a town or city typically a member of a wealthy bourgeoise; **Ague**–a fever or shivering fit; **Fie**–used to express disgust or outrage; **Mirth**–amusement; **Mortifying**– suppressing, restraining; **Visages**–facial expression; **Gudgeon**–easily fooled person; **Exhortation**–insistence, persuasion; **Bushels**–heap; **Ere**–before; **Prodigal**–extravagant, spendthrift; **Presages**–warming of an event typically an unwelcome one; **Chaff**–husk of corn of other seed; **Edofice**–building; **Dock'd**–run as horse; **Enrobe**–cover; **Leap**–frisk, jump; **Aught**–anything at all; **Curbed**–restrain or keep in check; **Colt**–a young uncastrated male horse; **Requite**–respond to love or affection; **Doublet**–a pair of similar things; **Sibylla**–prophetess; **Chaste**–virgin; **Wooers**–suitor; **Sirrah**–used as a term of address for a man or boy; **Surfeit**–satiate; **Superfluity**–something unnecessary; **Throstle**–a machine for continuously spinning wool or cotton; **Vilely**–revoltingly, disgustingly; **Capering**–jumping; **Shrive**–give spiritual consolation;

Ducats–a gold coin, formerly currency in most European countries; **Imputation**–charge, accusation; **Squandered**–spent money like water; **Peril**–serious and immediate danger; **Gratis**–without charge or fee; **Congregate**–assemble; **Albeit**–though; **Wrought**–made or fashioned in the specified way; **Compromise**–settle a dispute by mutual concession; **Streaked**–striped; **Ewe**–a female sheep; **Borne**–tolerated; **Badge**–characteristic; **Gabardine**–a long, loose upper garment; **Rheum**–a watery fluid that collects in nose or eyes; **Spurn**–reject with disdain or contempt; **Cur**–a contemptible man; **Bated**–anxious; **Exaction**–the action of demanding and obtaining something from someone; **Estimable**–worthy of great respect; **Adieu**–goodbye; **Forthwith**–immediately, without delay; **Unthrifty**–wasteful, not using money and other resources carefully; **Knave**–a dishonest or unscrupulous man; **Dismay**–concern and distress caused by something unexpected; **Argosy**–merchant ship.

ACT-II (Scene I to IX)

Summary of Act II Scene I

Act II shifts to Belmont where the Prince of Morocco arrives to attempt to win Portia's hand in marriage. The Prince asks Portia not to judge him by his dark complexion, assuring her that he is as valorous as any European man who has come to court the lady. Portia reminds the Prince that her own tastes do not matter since the process of picking chests, stated in her father's will, makes the Prince as worthy as any other suitor. The Prince of Morocco tells Portia that he had killed three Persian princes. Further, he has the capability of snatehing aways a bear's babies and of teasing a hungry lion. He, then, compares himself to Hercules, a hero, who was beaten in a game of chess by his servant Lichas even if he was the strongest man in Greece. With a lengthy proclamation of his own bravery and heroism, the Prince asks Portia to lead him to the caskets, where he may make his guess.

She reminds him that the penalty for guessing incorrectly is that he must remain unmarried forever. The Prince accepts this stipulation and Portia leads him off to dinner after which they will go for the casket test.

Anaylsis of Act II Scene I

The first scene of Act II stands in stark contrast to the business like atmosphere of Act I. The scene begins with much pomp and show with the entrance of the Prince of Morocco and Portia. The elaborate excuse the Prince of Morocco makes for his dark colouring serves to call attention to it and to his cultural difference from Portia and from Shakespeare's audience. His extravagant praise of his own valor also makes him seem both less well-mannered and less attractive. Moreover, his assertion that the best ladies of his community have loved him makes him less attractive to Portia. He is simply a self- assured warrior with an imposing presence. Special focus is given to his character so as to differentiate between the three suitors of Portia one of whom is Bassanio.

Portia response to the Prince's claims is polite showing her good breeding and her virtuous acquiescence to her dead father's wishes. But her words also clearly convey that she does not want to marry him.

Summary of Act II Scene II

The act shifts back to Venice where Launcelot Gobbo, a servant of Shylock's, struggles to decide whether or not he should run away from his master. Part of him wants to leave, while his conscience reminds him of his honest nature and urges him to stay. Although Launcelot has no specific complaints, he seems troubled by the fact that his master is Jewish. Just when Launcelot determines to run away, his father, Old Gobbo, enters.

The old man is blind and asks how to get to Shylock's house where he hopes to find young Launcelot. Because his father does not recognise him, Launcelot decides to play a prank on him—he gives the old man confusing directions and reports that Launcelot is dead. When Launcelot reveals the deception, Old Gobbo doubts that the man before him is his son, but Launcelot soon convinces his father of his identity. Launcelot confesses to his father that he is leaving Shylock's employment in the hopes of serving Bassanio.

Just then, Bassanio enters and old Gobbo pleads with him to accept Launcelot as his servant. However, Bassanio cannot understand anything as both the old Gobbo and young Launcelot Gobbo start speaking together. Finally, when Bassanio understands their bumbling proposition, he accepts the offer. Bassanio then, warns Launcelot regarding his change of employment. He tells Launcelot that it is not advisable to leave work/service of a wealthy merchant and work for a poor master like Bassanio. But Launcelot is determined to work for Bassanio and goes on to flatter him. Bassanio then meets Gratiano, who asks to accompany him to Belmont. Bassanio agrees on the condition that Gratiano tame his characteristically wild behaviour. Gratiano promises to be on his best behaviour and the two men plan a night of merriment to celebrate their departure.

Analysis of Act II Scene II

The scene between the young and the old Gobbo is typical of Shakespeare who frequently employs servants and members of the working class to provide comic interludes in his plays.

Gobbos in the scene are what we call clowns or jests who entertained the audience with their physical comedy and in their dialogues presented important themes. The humor presented in this scene is created by confusions created by Launcelot.

The comic element is so simple that it is hard to overlook and mistake. Seen in this light, we forgive things that might otherwise seem cruel to us, like Launcelot's shabby treatment of his blind and doting father.

This humor is comedy at its simplest, where laughs are derived not from quick wit but from confusion and foolery. At the same time, we see a thematic concern in his rejection of Shylock's employment as an implication of Shylcok being Jew. His rejection paves the way for Bassanio's journey to Belmont and the love story between Lorenzo and Jessica.

Summary of Act II Scene III

This scene belongs to Shylock's house where his daughter Jessica bids good-bye to Launcelot. She tells him that his presence made life with her father more bearable. Jessica gives Launcelot a letter to carry to Bassanio's friend Lorenzo.

As Launcelot leave, Jessica confesses that although she feels guilty for being ashamed of her father, she is only his daughter by blood and not by actions. Still, she hopes to escape her damning relationship to Shylock by marrying Lorenzo and converting to Christianity.

Analysis of Act II Scene III

This scene completes the exposition of the play. By now we are introduced to everyone crucial to the plot. First and foremost, we are introduced to Jessica whose character makes us understand the character of Shylock in a much better manner. Although Shylock does not appear in many scenes of act II like this scene, our view of him is further shaped by the opinions of those closest to him. Even though his servant and daughter do not like him, their descriptions of him inadvertently make him a more sympathetic figure in our eyes.

Much like Launcelot, Jessica, too voices no real complaint about her father but seems eager to escape her Jewish heritage which she sees as a stain on her honor.

The negative impression that Shylock has given us with his first appearance is somewhat counteracted by the words of those closest to him who feel guilty even as they speak ill of him.

Summary of Act II Scene IV

On a street in Venice, Gratiano, Lorenzo, Salarino and Salanio discuss the plan for Bassanio's dinner party and masque that night. Gratiano worries that they are not well prepared, but Lorenzo assures the men that they have enough time to gather the necessary disguises and torchbearers. As they talk, Launcelot enters bearing Jessica's letter. Lorenzo recognises the writing and asks Launcelot, who is going to Shylock's house to invite Shylock to the dinner, to assure Jessica secretly that Lorenzo will not let her down. Launcelot departs and Lorenzo orders his friends to prepare for the night's festivities. Salarino and Salanio leave and Lorenzo relates to Gratiano that Jessica will escape from Shylock's house by disguising herself as Lorenzo's torchbearer. He also tells Gratiano that she will escape with enough gold and jewellery for a proper dowry. Lorenzo gives Gratiano the letter and asks him to read it, then leaves excited for the evening's outcome.

Analysis Act II Scene IV

The scene does not hold any special significance in the play apart from telling us more about Jessica's elopement.

Summary of Act II Scene V

After having accepted Bassanio's invite for the dinner, Shylock warns Launcelot regarding his employment. He tells his previous servant that Bassanio will not be as lenient a master as Shylock himself has been and that Launcelot will no longer be at liberty to overeat and oversleep. Shylock calls for Jessica and tells her that he has been summoned for dinner.

Worried by a premonition that trouble is brewing, Shylock gives Jessica the keys and asks her to keep the doors and windows locked. When Launcelot informs him about the masque, Shylock is filled with hatred for now he has to see a Christian Masque and asks Jessica to not look out at the masque taking place in the streets.

Launcelot whispers to Jessica that she must disobey her father and look out the window for the Christian who is actually Lorenzo. Shylock asks Jessica about her conversation with Launcelot and says that though Launcelot is kind, he eats and sleeps too much to be an efficient servant. After Shylock has left to see Bassanio, Jessica bids him farewell, thinking that if nothing goes wrong, Shylock will soon have lost a daughter and she, a father.

Analysis Act II Scene V

The scene tells us about the material obsession of Shylock. The villain is too concerned with his possession and continuously makes sure that Jessica locks every door and window. He states that he would return soon for his miserliness does not allow him any confidence in the safety of his material possession. It is ironical since we as audience know that Shylock loses not only some material belongings but also his daughter.

Summary of Act II Scene VI

As planned, Gratiano and Salarino meet masked and costumed in front of Shylock's house. They are especially anxious because Lorenzo is late and they think that lovers tend always to be early. Then, Gratiano explains Salarino's theory that love is at its best when the lover chases the object of his affection and that once the lover captures his lady and consummates the relationship, he tends to tire and lose interest.

Soon, Lorenzo joins them, apologises for being late and calls up to Jessica. Jessica appears on the balcony dressed as a torch bearer and tosses him a casket of gold and jewels. Before coming down Jessica states her anxiety at playing her role of the torchbearer. She is also ashamed that she is eloping with Lorenzo while being dressed as a boy. She tells Lorenzo that she might be exposed but Lorenzo reassures her. Jessica finally comes down after locking everything and taking some more money. All of them exit the scene as Gratiano praises her as wise, fair and true. Just then, Antonio enters to report that the masquerade is cancelled and that Bassianio must sail for Belmont immediately as the wind is moving in the favourable direction. Gratiano is obliged to leave the festivities and join Bassanio at once.

Analysis Act II Scene VI

In continuation with the previous scene, this scene only sets up the romantic mood for Jessica and Lorenzo's love. It does not serve any other purpose.

Summary of Act II Scene VII

Back in Belmont, Portia takes the Prince of Morocco to the caskets where he will attempt to win her hand by guessing which chest contains her portrait. The first casket, made of gold, is inscribed with the words, "Who chooseth me shall gain what many men desire". The second, made of silver, reads, "Who chooseth me shall get as much as he deserves". The third, a heavy leaden casket, declares, "Who chooseth me must give and hazard all he hath". Portia tells the Prince that the correct casket contains her picture.

The Prince thinks that no other suitor deserves portia more than him because of his high rank, noble birth and great wealth and power. He reviews the inscriptions and rejects the lead and silver caskets for not being worthy.After much pondering, he chooses the gold casket reasoning that only the most precious metal could house the picture of such a beautiful woman. He opens the chest to reveal a skull with a scroll in its eye socket. The scroll states that a person who is guarded by the glitter of things is generally deceived.

After reading a short poem chastising him for the folly of his choice, the Prince makes a hasty departure. Portia is glad to see him go.

Analysis Act II Scene VII

The scene holds importance because of the presence of the inscriptions and the folly of the Prince of Morocco. The inscriptions are important as they influence the choice of caskets by the suitors. They are ambiguous in nature pointing out that they can be interpreted in many ways. Further, we see the Prince's folly in believing in outer appearance. He is superficial man who makes the most obvious choice of the caskets.

Summary of Act II Scene VIII

Salanio had witnessed Shylock's rage upon learning of Jessica's elopement and so describes the scene to Salarino. He tells that Shylock railed against the loss of his daughter and his ducats and shouted a loud, urgent appeal for justice and law to prevail. Shylock demanded the Duke to check Bassanio's ship as he believed that Lorenzo and Jessica were on it. Antonio, however, assured the Duke that it was not the case.

Salanio shows his worry for Antonio. He knows that with Jessica's elopement and Antonio claiming that Bassanio was not a part of the escape, Shylock will become revengeful against Antonio. He hopes that Antonio is able to pay his debt, but Salarino reminds him of rumors that the long-awaited ships have capsized in the English Channel. The two men warmly remember Bassanio's departure from Antonio wherein the merchant insisted that his young friend not allow thoughts of debt or danger to interfere with his courtship of Portia. They leave to visit Antonio and break the news to him. They also realise that Antonio may need some cheering up after hearing the news.

Analysis of Act II Scene VIII

The dialogue between Salarino and Salanio are crucial as they serve primarily to fill us in on events that take place offstage—in this case, Shylock's reaction to his daughter's flight and the parting of Antonio and Bassanio. Shylock's cries of "My daughter! O, my ducats! O, my daughter!" are meant to be comic. He bemoans the loss of his money as much as his loss of Jessica, suggesting that greed is as important to him as familial love. At one point we may feel that Shylock's desire for revenge against Antonio may be justified as he has lost his only child to a Christian. However, the cry for the daughter comes with the cry for money which indicates that for Shylock, his daughter is just another one of his possessions.

Summary of Act II Scene IX

At Belmont, another suitor arrives for Portia. The Prince of Arragon comes to try his luck at winning Portia's hand in marriage. When Portia informs him of the conditions of the test, he also puts forward his conditions. First, if he fails to choose the correct casket he would not reveal his choice second, he would never court another woman and third he would leave Belmont immediately. When brought to the caskets, he rejects the lead casket for not being worthy of the risk of losing everything. He also rejects the gold casket for it will be desired by many. This Prince does not want to possess things that are desired by common people. Finally, he selects the silver one, confident that he deserves Portia's hand. Inside, he finds a portrait of a blinking idiot and a poem that condemns him as a fool. Keeping his oath, the Prince of Arragon leaves Belmont. After he departs, Portia claims that fools who do excessive deliberation also lose.

Soon a messenger arrives to tell Portia that a promising young Venetian, who seems like the perfect suitor, has come to Belmont to try his luck at the casket game. Hoping that it is Bassanio, Portia and Nerissa go out to greet the new suitor.

Analysis Act II Scene IX

The purpose of this scene is to present the character of another suitor in the casket test. This suitor is a proud and arrogant Spanish noble man. He feels that Portia is 'deserved'. There is no semblance of love or affection in this suitor.

Word Meanings (Act II)

Cornets–a brass instrument resembling a trumpet but shorter and wider; **Livery**–a special uniform worn by a servant, an official, or a member of a city company; **Burnish'd**–polish (something, especially metal) by rubbing; **Thaws**–melts; **Icicles**–a hanging, tapering piece of ice formed by the freezing of dripping water; **Clime**–a region considered with reference to its climate; **Hue**–a colour or shade; **Scanted**–provide grudgingly; **Hedged**–limit or qualify (something) by conditions or exceptions; **Scimitar**–a short sword with a curved blade that broadens towards the point, used originally in Eastern countries; **Slew**–killed; **Alcides**–another name for Hercules; **Blest**–blessed; **Fiend**–an evil spirit or demon; **Scorn**–feel or express contempt; **Budge**–change an opinion; **Reverence**–deep respect for someone; **Incarnation**–a living being embodying a deity or spirit; **Begotten**–bring (a child) into existence by the process of reproduction; **Sand-blind**–half-blind; **High gravel blind**–more than half blind; **Ergo**–therefore; **Beseech**–ask someone urgently; **Cudgel**–a short, thick stick used as a weapon; **Hovel post**–simply constructed dwelling; **Alack**–used to express, regret or dismay; **Famished**–extremely hungry; **Anon**–soon; **Gramercy**–used to express gratitude; **Cater-cousins**–on friendly terms; **Trifle**–a thing of little value or importance; **Bestow'd**–confer or present; **Endeavours**–try hard to do or achieve something; **Yonder**–at some distance in the direction indicated; over there; **Allay**–diminish or put at rest; **Misconstrued**–interpret; **Demurely**–quiet and modest; **Ostent**–a significant sign; **Grandam**–grandmother; **Gauge**–estimate or determine the amount; **Mirth**–amusement, especially as expressed in laughter; **Adieu**–goodbye; **Pagan**–non-believer; **Heinous**–deadly; **Strife**–conflict. **Slink**–sneak away, slip; **Torch-bearers**–a person who inspires others in walking towards a valued goal; **Quaintly**–strangely, unusual; **Page's**–young attendant at formal function; **Peruse**–examine carefully; **Gormandise**–eat good food in excess; **Rend**–tear into pieces; **Bid forth**–invited; **Prodigal**–reckless; **Loth**–reluctant, unwilling; **A-brewing**–mischief in the air; **Beseech**–ask someone urgently to do; **Conspired**–plot; **Black-Monday**–easter Monday; **Ash-Wednesday**–a day of fasting before easter; **Vile squealing**–shrill-notes; **Wry-neck'd**–asymmetrical position of neck; **Fife**–flute; **Casements**–a window; **Foppery**–foolish action; **Hagars off-spring**–hagar's child; **Patch**–fellow; **Drones**–murmur, whisper; **Hives**–lives; **Not Crost**–cross (Here, if nothing goes wrong with the plans). **Pent-house**–a flat on the top floor of a tall building; **Out-dwells**–late past the appointment; **Unabated**–without any reduction in intensity or strength; **Yonker**–smart boy; **Cupid**–God of love; **Beshrew**–curse; **Gentile**–a person who is not Jewish. **Withal**–with that; **Stoops**–bends; **Dross**–worthless things; **Virgin hue**–white colour; **Shrine**–temple; **Brook**–a small stream; **Cerecloth**–waxed cloth used for wraping a corpse; **Obscure**–unclear, hidden; **Immured**–confined, jailed; **Thrive**–prosper, flourish; **Carrion**–decaying flesh or dead animal; **Gilded**–cover thinly with gold; **Inscroll'd**–to write on a scroll; **Frost**–cold, disappointment; **Riddance**–relief; **Gondola**–a light flat-bottomed boat used on Ventian canals; **Amorous**–loving; **Narrow seas**–english channel; **Fraught**–loaded; **Treads**–walk in a specified ways; **Slubber**–spoil; **Chiefest**–first or foremost; **Wrung**–shook; **Quicken**–cheer up; **Heaviness**–having relatively high density; **Ostents**–displays, **Outcries**–complaints; **Solemnised**–performed; **To woo**–try to gain the love of a woman; **Injunctions**–conditions; **Enjoin'd**–bound; **Mastlet**–a bird; **Barbarous**–extremely brutal; **Cozen**–trick or deceive; **Peasantry**–a member of a class of low social status; **Glean'd**–obtain information from various sources; **Chaff**–rubbish; **Linger**–stay in place longer than necessary; **Wroth**–anger; **Heresy**–rumour; **Bringeth**–bring; **Regreets**–greetings, cleverness; **Commends**–praise formally; **Fore-spurres**–one who rides before.

ACT-III (Scene I to IV)

Summary of Act III Scene I

In Venice, Salarino and Salanio discuss the rumors that yet another of Antonio's ships has been wrecked off the southeast coast of England. They are joined by Shylock, who accuses them of having helped Jessica escape. The two Venetians proudly take credit for their role in Jessica's elopement. Shylock curses his daughter's rebellion, to which Salarino responds by telling him that she and Shylock are very different from each other. Salarino then, asks Shylock whether he can confirm the rumors of Antonio's lost vessels. Shylock replies that Antonio will soon be bankrupt and swears to collect his bond.

Salarino doubts Shylock's resolve, wondering what the old man will do with a pound of flesh, to which Shylock chillingly replies that Antonio's flesh will feed his revenge for the many insults. In a short monologue, Shylock says Antonio has mistreated him solely because Shylock is a Jew, but now Shylock is determined to apply the lessons of hatred and revenge that Christian intolerance has taught him so well.

Salarino and Salanio go to meet with Antonio, just as Tubal, a friend of Shylock's and a Jew, enters. Tubal announces that he has heard about Jessica being in Genoa but he cannot find her. Shylock rants against his daughter and he wishes her dead as he cries for his losses. He is especially embittered when Tubal reports that Jessica has taken a ring—given to Shylock in his bachelor days by a woman named Leah, presumably Jessica's mother—and has traded that ring for a monkey. Shylock's spirits brighten, however, when Tubal reports that Antonio's ships have run into trouble and that Antonio's creditors are certain that Antonio is ruined. The scene ends with Shylock instructing Tubal to pay a police sergeant in advance to arrest Antonio if he forfeits the bond.

Analysis of Act III Scene I

The scene breaks the unity of time and moves to three months later when the news of Antonio's losses have come. As Antonio's losses increase, Shylock's villainous plan becomes apparent. His villainy has intensified not just by the fact that Antonio had time and again insulted him publicly but also by the fact that he had lost his daughter and some money to Lorenzo- a Christian. Anger and revenge is burning in Shylock and this persuades him to give his one of the most powerful speeches on human tolerance. Despite his mounting obsession with the pound of Antonio's flesh, however, he maintains his dramatic dignity. Even as we recognise that Shylock's plans are terribly wrong, we can appreciate the logic of his speech. By asserting his own humanity, he points to the pretensions of the Christian characters to value mercy, charity and love above self-interest. Shylock's speech is so powerful that no one else can speak. His hatred reaches an all time high as he does not want to relent from getting his revenge. Shylock's dignity lapses in his scene with Tubal, who keeps his supposed friend in agony by alternating between good and bad news. Shylock lurches from glee to despair and back.

But even here he rouses our sympathy, because we hear that Jessica stole a ring given to him by his late wife and traded it for a monkey.

Villain though he may be, we can still feel sorrow that Jessica—who is suddenly a much less sympathetic character—would be heartless enough to steal and sell a ring that her dead mother gave her father.

Summary of Act III Scene II

In Belmont, Portia begs Bassanio to delay choosing between the caskets for a day or two. If Bassanio chooses incorrectly, Portia reasons, she will lose him forever. Bassanio insists that he make his choice now to avoid prolonging the torment of living without Portia as his wife. Portia orders that music be played while her love makes his choice and compares Bassanio to the Greek hero and demigod Hercules.

Like the suitors who have come before him, Bassanio carefully examines the three caskets and puzzles over their inscriptions. He rejects the gold casket, saying that he will not be fooled by appearences, while the silver he deems to be a common metal. After much debate, Bassanio picks the lead casket, which he opens to reveal Portia's portrait, along with a poem congratulating him on his choice and confirming that he has won Portia's hand. The happy couple promises one another love and devotion and Portia gives Bassanio a ring that he must never part with, as his removal of it will signify the end of his love for her.

Nerissa and Gratiano congratulate them and confess that they too have fallen in love with one another. They ask to be married and suggest a double wedding. Portia agrees to the suggestion. Lorenzo and Jessica arrive in the midst of this rejoicing, along with Salerio, who gives a letter to Bassanio. As Bassanio reads the letter, Portia welcomes her husband's old friends. Bassanio reads the letter and grows pale. In the letter, Antonio writes that all of his ships are lost and that Shylock plans to collect his pound of flesh. Looking at her husband, Portia asks Bassanio about the letter. Bassanio informs Portia of the deal. The news provokes a fit of guilt in Bassanio, which in turn prompts Portia to offer to pay twenty times the sum. Jessica, however, worries that her father is more interested in revenge than in money.

Understanding the friendship between Bassanio and Antonio, Portia tells Bassanio that he should leave for Venice as soon as they are married. She adds that while their husbands are gone, she and Nerissa will live as maids and widows. Soon after, the couples are married. Then, Bassanio reads out loud the letter from Antonio, who asks only for a brief reunion before he dies. Portia urges her husband to rush to his friend's aid and Bassanio leaves for Venice.

Analysis Act III Scene II

The scene presents the conclusion to the casket story with Bassanio choosing the correct casket and getting married to Portia. The whole deliberation he does and the song are of special importance because they take Bassanio away from the world of outer appearances. The choice made of Bassanio- Lead casket stands in strong opposition to the money centric mind of Shylock. For Shylock, possession is important but for Bassanio, love has no value in front of wealth.

Further, the scene presents an idyllic setup for romance. Love is triumphing as two couples have formed and married but the shadow of evil wealth and Shylock looms over it. The letter from Antonio disrupts the happy serenity enjoyed by the couples. Herein, the strong minded character of Portia comes to play as she immediately reacts to a crisis. She quickly makes a decision and asks Bassanio to leave for Venice to save his dear friend. Such a character development makes it easy for us to see Portia as a Lawyer in the future scenes.

Summary of Act III Scene III

Antonio has been arrested for the forfeiture of the Bond. Shylock escorts the bankrupt Antonio to prison. Antonio pleads with Shylock to listen, but Shylock refuses. Remembering the many times Antonio condemned him as a dog, Shylock advises the merchant to beware of his bite. Assured that the Duke will grant him justice, Shylock insists that he will have his bond and tells the jailer not to bother speaking to him of mercy.

Salanio declares that Shylock is the worst of men while Antonio reasons that the Jew hates him for bailing out many debtors. He had paid the debts of many of Shylock's debtors. Salanio attempts to comfort Antonio by suggesting that the Duke will never allow such a ridiculous contract to stand, but Antonio is not convinced. Venice, Antonio claims, is a wealthy trading city with a great reputation for upholding the law and if the Duke breaks that law, Venice's economy may suffer. As Salanio departs, Antonio prays desperately that Bassanio will arrive to "see me pay his debt and then I care not".

Analysis Act III Scene III

The Plot of the Bond has now quickened its pace. Antonio has been arrested and Shylock is consumed by his need for revenge. Now, it is difficult to sympathise with Shylock for his need to get the Bond- the pound of flesh is an act of cruelty. When Antonio tells Salanio that Shylock is getting revenge for his practice of lending money without interest, he seems to miss the bigger picture. Shylock's mind has been warped into obsession not by Antonio alone, but by the persecutions visited on him by all of Christian Venice. He has taken Antonio as the embodiment of all his persecutors so that, in his pound of flesh, he can avenge himself against everyone.

The institution of law comes to the forefront of the play in these scenes and we may be tempted to view the law as a sort of necessary evil, a dogmatic set of rules that can be forced to serve the most absurd requests. Law is cast as the very backbone of the Venetian economy, as Antonio expresses. Trade is the city's lifeblood and an integral part of trade is ensuring that merchants of all religions and nationalities are extended the same protections as full-blooded Venetian citizens.

In principle, the Duke's inability to bend the law is sound, as the law upholds the economy that has allowed Antonio and his friends to thrive. However, Shylock's furious rants about justice and his bond make it seem as if his very law-abiding nature has perverted a bastion of Christian uprightness.

Summary of Act III Scene IV

At Belmont after Bassanio's departure, Lorenzo assures Portia that Antonio is worthy of all the help she is sending him and that if Portia only knew the depths of Antonio's love and goodness, she would be proud of her efforts to save him. Portia replies that she has never regretted doing a good deed and goes on to say that she could never deny help to anyone so close to her dear Bassanio. Indeed, Antonio and Bassanio are so inseparable that Portia believes saving her husband's friend is no different than saving her own husband. She has sworn to live in prayer and contemplation until Bassanio returns to her and announces that she and Nerissa will retire to a nearby monastery. She further declares that Lorenzo and Jessica will rule the estate in her absence.

Portia then sends her servant-Balthazar-to Padua, where he is to meet her cousin, Doctor Bellario, who will provide Balthazar with certain documents and clothing. From there, Balthazar will take the ferry to Venice, where Portia will await him. After Balthazar departs, Portia informs Nerissa that the two of them, dressed as young men, are going to pay an incognito visit to their new husbands. When Nerissa asks why but Portia dismisses the question and promises to disclose the whole of her purpose on the coach ride to Venice.

Analysis of Act III Scene IV

This scene presents many more qualities of Portia. She is a noble woman very similar to Antonio. Earlier Antonio took the role of a selfless giver for Bassanio and now it is Portia who is doing the same. The generosity shown by Portia and Antonio stand in stark contrast to Shylock who is obsessed with his own possessions.

An interesting feature of this scene is cross dressing or dressing up as a member of the opposite gender. Portia's cross-dressing is a device typical of women in Shakespeare's comedies. Indeed, the play has already shown Jessica dressed as a boy in her escape from Shylock's house. However, it is Portia's cross dressing that takes significance. Dressing as a man is necessary since Portia is about to play a man's part, appearing as member of a male profession. The demands placed upon her by her father's will are gone and she feels free to act and to prove herself more intelligent and capable than the men around her. Portia, thus, comes out to be a woman of the world.

Summary of Act III Scene V

The scene comes back to a garden in Belmont where Launcelot is teasing Jessica. Quoting the adage that the sins of the father shall be delivered upon the children, Launcelot says he fears for Jessica's soul. When Jessica claims that she will be saved because she has become a Christian due to her marriage to Lorenzo, Launcelot complains that the conversion of the Jews, who do not eat pork, will have disastrous consequences on the price of bacon.

Lorenzo enters and chastises Launcelot. He appears jealous and asks Launcelot to go inside to get dinner prepared. Launcelot delivers a dazzling series of puns in reply and departs to prepare for dinner. When Lorenzo asks Jessica what she thinks of Portia, she responds that the woman is without match, nearly perfect in all respects. Lorenzo jokes that he is as good a spouse as Portia and leads them off to dinner.

Analysis of Act III Scene V

The scene functions to provide a light comic relief before the heavy drama of the court begins. The presence of Jessica is important to understand the change that she undergoes in Belmont. She is not of nobility and is an outsider who is born and brought up by a miser Jew. The time she spends in Belmond changes her immensely.

Word Meanings (Act III)

Rialto–stock exchange at Venice; **Carcasses**–dead bodies of animals; **Prolixity**–long windedness; **Fledged**–having wings that are large enough for flight; **Smug**–self-satisfied; **Hindered**–hampered, delayed; **Thwarted**–obstructed, blocked; **Humility**–forbearance; **Hearsed**–put in coffin; **Fourscore**–eighty; **Plague**–persecute; **Synagogue**–a Jewish temple. **Tarry**–wait; **Forsworn**–swear falsely; **Beshrew**–curse; **Peize**–retard; increase the action of bet saying someone of something; **Amity**–friendly agreement; **Torment**–severe physical or mental suffering; **Aloof**–conspicuously uninvolved; **Dulcet**–sweet and soothing; **Howling**–producing a long wailing sound; **Dardan**–a native or inhabitant of tray; **Bleared**–make dim/Blur; **Visages**–faces; **Begot**–cause, bring about; **Knell**–sound of a bell rung solemnly for a death or funeral; ; **Excrement**–appearance; **Wanton**–unprovoked, deliberate; **Sepulchre**–a small room or a movement in which, a dead person is buried or laid; **Drudge**–slave; **Grossness**–disgusting; **Shuddering**–tremble as a result of fear; **Surfeit**–desire to do no more of somethings as a result of having done it in excess; **Counterfeit**–forged fake; **Gnats**–small insects; **Oration**–a formal speech; **Solemnise**–celebrate; **Pertains**–concern; **Infidel**–the Jewess; **Hither**–to or towards this place; **Ere**–before; **Fleece**–golden fleece; **Blotted paper**–stained paper; **Braggart**–someone who boasts about their achievements or possessions; **Gaping wound**–deep and wide open wound; **Marring**–spoil; **Plies**–pursue; **Interposer**–separate; **Twixt us twain**–between two extremes. **Gratis**–without charge, free;

Gaoler–jailor; **Impenetrable**–which cannot be satisfied; **Cur**–a contemptible man; **Bootless**–useless; **Bated**–in great suspence; **Forfeitures**–penalties; **Intercessors**–pleaders; **Impeach**–to bring an scusation against; **Conceit**–idea; **Lineaments**–features; **Bestow'd**– give granted; **Semblance**–likeness; **Husbandry**–control; **Contemplation**–consideration; **Monastery**–religious house of monks; **Padua**–a city in North-East Italy; **Tranect**–a Ferry to the lending place; **Wager**–bet; **Accountred**–equipped; **Reed**–shrill; **Mincing**–short, quick; **Frays**–heated dispute; **Bragging**–boasting; **Quaint**–charming; **Withal**–in addition, consideration; **Repent**–feel or express since regret; **Puny**–small and weak, little; **Haste away**–rapidly; **Jacks**–fellows.

ACT-IV (Scene I & II)

Summary of Act IV Scene I

Act IV Scene I is the largest and the most important scenes of the play. For better understanding, we have divided it into parts.

Shylock Wants the Pounds of Flesh

In Venice, the court convenes for Antonio's trial. The Duke of Venice greets Antonio and expresses pity for him, calling Shylock an inhuman monster who can summon neither pity nor mercy. Antonio says he knows the Duke has done all that he can to lawfully counter Shylock's malicious intentions and that since nothing else can be done, Antonio will accept Shylock's rage.

The Duke summons Shylock into the courtroom and addresses him, saying that he believes that Shylock only means to frighten Antonio by extending this drama. According to the Duke, no one believes that Shylock actually means to inflict such a horrible penalty on Antonio who has already suffered the loss of his ships.

Shylock reiterates his intentions and says that should the court deny him his right, the city's very laws and freedoms will be forfeit. Shylock offers no explanation for his insistence other than to say that certain hatreds, like certain passions, are lodged deep within a person's heart. Shylock hates Antonio and for him that is reason enough.

Bassanio, who has arrived from Belmont, attempts to argue with Shylock, but Antonio tells him that his efforts are vain. Antonio suggests that hatred comes naturally to some men. Bassanio offers Shylock six thousand ducats, twice the amount of the original loan, but Shylock turns down the offer saying he would not forfeit his bond.

When the Duke asks Shylock how he expects to receive mercy when he offers none, Shylock replies that he has no need for mercy as he has done nothing wrong. Just as the slave-owning Christians of Venice would refuse to set their human property free, Shylock will not relinquish the pound of flesh that belongs to him. Shylock then call for an immediate judgement.

The Coming of a Learnew Lawyers-Balthazar

The Duke postpones the judgement stating that he has sent messages to the learned lawyer, Doctor Bellario, as he believes that the case is serious and needs another mind. News comes that a messenger has arrived from Bellario and Salarino runs off to fetch him. Meanwhile, Bassanio tries, without much success, to cheer up the despairing Antonio. Nerissa enters, disguised as a lawyer's clerk and gives the Duke a letter from Bellario. Shylock takes out his knife anticipating a judgment in his favour much to the horror of Antonio's friends. The Duke then tells the court that Bellario's letter mentions that he is ill and cannot come to court, but that he has sent the learned young Balthazar to judge in his stead. The Duke orders the disguised Nerissa to admit the young man to the court.

Portia enters, disguised as Balthazar. The Duke greets her and asks whether she is familiar with the circumstances of the case. Portia answers that she knows the case well and, then, proceeds with the case. Portia asks Antonio if he admits to owing Shylock money. When Antonio answers yes, Portia concludes that the Jew must be merciful. Shylock asks why he must show mercy and, in one of the play's most famous speeches, Portia responds that mercy is a blessing to both those who provide and those who receive it. Portia reasons that because mercy is an attribute of God, humans approach the divine when they exercise it. Shylock brushes aside her pretty speech by reiterating his demands for justice and revenge.

Portia as Balthazar Saves Antonio

The trail moves and Portia asks whether Antonio is able to pay the money and Bassanio offers Shylock twice the sum owed. Bassanio says that he is willing to pay the bond ten times over and even with his own life.

Bassanio begs the court to bend the law slightly in order to exonerate Antonio. Portia replies that the law shall not be broken and Shylock joyfully extols Portia's wisdom giving her the bond for inspection. She looks it over, declares it legal and binding and again asks Shylock to be merciful.

Shylock remains deaf to reason and Portia tells Antonio to prepare himself for the knife. She orders Shylock to have a surgeon on hand to prevent the merchant from bleeding to death, but Shylock refuses because the bond stipulates no such safeguard.

Antonio bids Bassanio farewell. He asks his friend not to grieve for him and tells Bassanio that he is happy to sacrifice his life for his friend. Both Bassanio and Gratiano say that, though they love their wives, they would give them up in order to save Antonio. In a pair of sarcastic asides, Portia and Nerissa mutter that Bassanio's and Gratiano's wives are unlikely to appreciate such sentiments.

Shylock is on the verge of cutting into Antonio when Portia suddenly reminds him that the bond stipulates a pound of flesh only and makes no allowances for blood. She urges Shylock to continue collecting his pound of flesh, but reminds him that if a drop of blood is spilled, then he will be guilty of conspiring against the life of a Venetian citizen and all his lands and goods will be confiscated by the state. Stunned, Shylock agrees to accept three times the sum, but Portia is insistent, saying that Shylock must have the pound of flesh or nothing.

Shylock's Punishment

When Shylock finds out that he cannot even take the original three thousand ducats in place of the pound of flesh, he drops the case, but Portia stops him reminding him of the penalty that non-citizens face when they threaten the life of a Venetian. In such a case, Portia states, half of Shylock's property would go to the state, while the other half would go to the offended party—namely Antonio. Portia orders Shylock to beg for the Duke's mercy.

The Duke declares that he will show mercy and spare Shylock's life. But Shylock claims that they may as well take his life as it is worthless without his estate. Antonio offers to return his share of Shylock's estate, on the condition that Shylock convert to Christianity and bequeath all his goods to Jessica and Lorenzo upon his death. Shylock consents and departs.

The Lawyer's Reward

After Shylock leaves, the Duke invites Portia, still in the disguise of a young lawyer, to dinner. Portia declines, saying that she must leave immediately for Padua. As she leaves, the Duke tells Antonio to reward the young law clerk since it was he who saved Antonio's life. Bassanio thanks Portia, though he does not see through her disguise and offers her the money he brought with him in order to pay off Shylock. Portia declines the gift and says that having delivered Antonio from Shylock's clutches is payment enough. Bassanio insists that she take some token from him and she eventually agrees. Portia asks Antonio for his gloves and Bassanio for his ring, which she herself gave Bassanio on the condition that he never part with it. Bassanio pulls his hand away calling the ring a trifle and claiming that he will not dishonor the judge by giving him such a lowly gift.

Instead, Bassanio offers to find the most valuable ring in Venice, but Portia remains firm and demands the trifle or nothing. When Bassanio admits that the ring was a gift from his wife, who made him promise never to part with it, Portia claims that the excuse is convenient and used by many men to hold onto possessions they would rather not lose. With that, she takes her leave. Antonio urges Bassanio to let the law clerk have the ring, saying that he should value Antonio's love and the gentleman's worth more than his wife's orders. Bassanio gives in and sends Gratiano to run after Portia and present her with the ring. Antonio and Bassanio then leave for Antonio's house to plan their trip to Belmont.

Analysis Act IV Scene I

The trial scene is the longest in the play and stands as one of the most dramatic scenes in all of Shakespeare. Almost every plot reaches its climax- Shylock is defeated, Antonio is saved and the lovers are free to return to Belmont.

The beginning of the scene sees us sympathising with only Antonio. Shylock is the Villain. Almost all authorities- The Duke and Portia as Balthazar give Shylock a chance to give away the idea of revenge. But he does not relent. The portion of the scene that passes before Portia's entrance shows a triumphant and merciless Shylock. When asked to explain his reasons for wanting Antonio's flesh, he says, "I am not bound to please thee with my answers". The only answer that the court gets, ultimately, is that Shylock merely emulates Christian behavior. Just as some Christians hate cats, pigs and rats, Shylock hates Antonio. Just as some Christians own slaves, Shylock owns a pound of Antonio's flesh. Shylock has the law on his side and his chief emotion seems to be outrage that Christian Venice would deny him what is rightfully his. Shylock is not so much attacking the Venetian worldview as demanding that he be allowed to share in it. His speech about slavery is emphatically not an antislavery: he is in favor of owning people, as long as he can own Antonio. In spite of itself, Venetian society is made an accomplice to Shylock's murderous demands and while this complicity certainly does not exonerate Shylock, it has the almost equally desirable effect of bringing everyone else down with him. Shylock's intention is not to condemn the institution of slavery and certainly not to urge its eradication—it is to express that his urges simply mirror those already found among wealthy Venetians and to demand that his desires be greeted with the same respect.

Even though we see Shylock as just, we cannot ignore his villainy. He does not want to do away with his bond and that is what leads to his downfall. In the end, he cannot get the flesh, the money and is stripped of his identity. His profession, his money and even his religion is taken away from him. He is defeated so badly that he wants to die. He will forfeit his estate to the man responsible for stealing his daughter and he will abandon his religion for one that forbids him from practicing the trade by which he earns his livelihood. The whole downfall of Shylock seems to be too harsh making him the tragic figure of the story. However, this downfall is essential for comedies always end in the punishment of hate and evil which Shylock had come to embody.

An important aspect of this scene is the institution of law. The presiding Duke-the authority representing the law is far from impartial; Portia appears as an unbiased legal authority, when in fact she is married to the defendant's best friend and appears in disguise, under a false name. While Portia bends the rules of the court, the actual decision taken by her is nonetheless legally accurate. This absolute power is appropriate for her character because she alone has the strength to wield it. None of the men seem a match for Shylock: Gratiano shouts and curses with anti-semitic energy, Bassanio pleads uselessly and Antonio seems resigned to his fate.

Coming back to Shylock's punishment we may feel that the punishment Portia exacts is too heavy. Perhaps the court's verdict fits Shylock's crimes but the court indulges in an equally literal and severe reading of the law in order to effect the same vicious end that Shylock has demanded. Before doling out Shylock's punishment, the Duke assures him that he will "see the difference of our spirit," but the spirit of the Venetians proves to be as vindictive as the Jew's. Thus, our views regarding the Jew's destruction remain ambivalent- we cannot completely hate him or love him.

The last part of the scene is the ring game. Once Shylock makes his way offstage, the mood of the play is decidedly light. In devising the game in which Bassanio sacrifices his wedding ring, Portia once again proves herself cleverer and more competent than any of the men with whom she shares the stage.

Summary of Act IV Scene II

Still in Venice, Portia sends Nerissa to Shylock's house to ensure that Shylock signs the deed that will leave his fortune to Lorenzo and Jessica. Portia observes that Lorenzo will be happy to have this document. Once they complete this task, the disguised women plan to leave for Belmont, which will ensure their arrival a full day before their husbands'.

Gratiano enters, offers Bassanio's ring to Portia and invites her to dinner. Portia accepts the ring, but declines the invitation. Portia asks Gratiano to show Nerissa to Shylock's house and Nerissa, before leaving, tells Portia that she will likewise try to convince Gratiano to part with his ring. The plan satisfies Portia, who imagines how Gratiano and Bassanio will swear up and down that they gave their rings to men and she looks forward to embarrassing them. Nerissa turns to Gratiano and asks him to lead her to Shylock's house.

Analysis of Act IV Scene II

This scene holds no significance except taking the ring game forward.

Word Meanings (Act IV)

Stony–cruel; **Adversary**–opponent; **Dram**–a small drink of whisky; **Void**–bereft of; **Obdurate**–obstinate; **Remorse**–compassion; **Huddled**–crowded; **Enow**–enough; **Commiseration**–pity; **Flint**–a hard fine grained quartz; **Sabbath**–seventh day of the week observed as rest; **Carrion**–pity; **Gaping**–with open mouth; **Inevitable**–impossible; **Serpent**–snake; **Fretten**–blown; **Beseech**–to beg; **Abject**–degrading; **Palates**–appetite; **Viands**–rich food; **Tainted**–sick; **Wether**–sheep; **Epitaph**–an inscription on grave; **Whet**–rub; **Inexecrable**–deserving of being cursed; **Currish**–vile, wicked; **Gallows**–wooden framework, where persons are put to death; **Dam**–mother; **Ravenous**–starving; **Importunity**–request; **Impediment**–hindrance; **Scruple**–very small unit of cut; **Infidel**–dishonest; **Contrive**–conspire; **Predicament**–situation; **Christening**–baptism; **Mercenary**–greedy; **Outswear**–swear loudly; **Tarry**–wait.

ACT-V

Summary of Act V Scene I

In moonlit Belmont, Jessica and Lorenzo are on the avenue leading to Portia's house. They compare themselves to famous lovers from classical literature, like Troilus and Cressida, Pyramus and This be and Dido and Aeneas. The couple goes back and forth with endless declarations of love, when a messenger named Stephano suddenly interrupts them. The messenger informs them that Portia and Nerissa will soon return from the monastery and Lorenzo and Jessica need to prepare to greet the mistress of the house. Launcelot enters and announces that Bassanio will return to Belmont the next day.

Lorenzo calls for music and he and Jessica sit on a grassy bank beneath the stars. The musicians arrive and begin to play and Lorenzo decides that anyone who is not moved by music deserves the worst cruelties and betrayals. Portia and Nerissa enter and hear the music before they reach the estate. Portia believes that the music is made more beautiful by the night and the flickering candles lighting up her estate enchant her. She states that the worth of things is determined largely by the context in which they are experienced. Lorenzo recognises Portia's voice and greets Portia who requests that he not mention her absence to her husband.

Trumpets sound as Bassanio, Antonio and Gratiano arrive. Portia greets Bassanio, who introduces her to Antonio. Antonio tells Portia that he has been acquitted in the courts of Venice. Gratiano and Nerissa begin to argue over the ring with which he promised never to part. Nerissa chastises her husband not for hurting her feelings, but for breaking his own promise. Gratiano insists that he gave the ring to a lawyer's clerk as a fee and Portia criticizes him for parting with so precious a gift, saying that her own husband would never have parted with his ring. Gratiano corrects her and reveals that Bassanio has, in fact, given his ring to the lawyer who saved Antonio. Portia declares that her husband's heart is as empty as his finger and she promises never to visit his bed until he produces the ring.

Bassanio pleads with Portia to understand that he gave the ring to a worthy man to whom he was indebted, but Portia dismisses his reasoning saying it is more likely that Bassanio gave the ring to another woman. Portia vows to be equally unfaithful, threatening to offer the same worthy man anything she owns including her body or her husband's bed. Antonio intercedes on behalf of Bassanio and Gratiano asking the women to accept his soul should either Bassanio or Gratiano prove unfaithful again. Portia and Nerissa relent giving each of their husbands a ring and suggesting that they exercise more care in keeping these rings.

Bassanio and Gratiano recognise these as the same rings they gave to the lawyer and his clerk and Portia and Nerissa claim that they lay with the gentlemen in order to get back the rings. Before either Bassanio or Gratiano can become too upset at being cheated, Portia reveals that she was the lawyer in Venice and Nerissa her clerk. Antonio receives news that some of his ships have miraculously arrived in port and Lorenzo is told that he will inherit Shylock's fortune. The company rejoices in its collective good fortune.

Analysis of Act V Scene I

The act, decidedly lighter in tone, delivers the happy ending required of a comedy: the lovers are restored to their loving relationships, Antonio's supposedly lost ships arrive miraculously in port and no threatening presence looms in the distance to suggest that this happiness is only temporary.

The act begins with the romantic setup wherein Lorenzo and Jessica are expressing their love and consequently the harmony. Jessica and Lorenzo keep comparing themselves to a catalogue of famous lovers. They mean to place themselves in a league of romantic figures whose love was so great that it inspired praise from generations of poets, but all of the lovers named—Troilus and Cressida, Pyramus and Thisbe, Dido and Aeneas, Medea and Jason—end tragically. Newly weds should not necessarily hope to take their place in this lineup, as it promises misunderstanding, betrayal and death. However, we do not really focus on this.

The ring episode in this act ends with a comic tone. The comedy comes with an ironic note regarding the knowledge that Portia, Nerissa and the audience has which the husbands do not have. The ring sequence, then, ties all the open ends of the play. Everyone knows that true saviors of Antonio and shows the happy ending of all couples.

Word Meanings (Act V)

Avenue–a broad road in a town, typically having trees at regular intervals; **Willow**–a symbol of unhappy love; **Unthrift**–ceaseless; **Shrew**–scolding woman; **Slander**–malicious statement; **Out-night you**–beat you in the game of making speeches about nights; **Hark**–listen; **Wedlockhour**–married life; **Patines**–plates; **Orb**–spherical body; **Cherubins**–angels; **Muddy vesture**–body of perishable flesh; **Wanton herd**–mischievous group; **Bellowing**–deep roar of large animal; **Perchance**–by any chance; **Feign**–imagine; **Treasons**–betrayal, treachery; **Stratagems**–deception; **Antipodes**–people living in the other part of the globe; **Scant**–cease to express; **Vehement**–strong; **Besmear**–disgrace; **Come to Manna**–divine drink; **Inter' gatories**–questions.

Characters Descriptions

While there are many characters, there are some central characters that become a part of the various plots present in the play. These characters are discussed below

Antonio

Antonio is the Merchant referred to in the title of the play 'The Merchant of Venice'. However, as a central figure he is a rather lackluster character. He emerges in Act I, Scene I as a hopeless depressive, someone who cannot name the source of his melancholy. He is a rich, comfortable and a popular man who throughout the course of the play, reduces into a self-pitying figure, unable to muster the energy required to defend himself against execution. As a reader of play that is to be performed on stage, we understand that this melancholy is a deliberate act by Shakespeare's part. The playwright cannot give Antonio much to say except for stating his deep friendship with Bassanio and pointing out his melancholy simpley because he has to make space for more complex characters.

An important characteristic shown by Antonio is his generosity. He had been generous to Bassanio on multiple previous occasions but it reaches its pinnacle when he offers his pound of flesh. Antonio had also helped many debtors of a fellow businessman Shylock and provided debts without any interest rate. Antonio, as such, is an honorable man who is ready to fulfill his end of the bond. He, even resigns to his fate after Shylock is not ready to have mercy and fulfill the bond.

The positive characteristics of Antonio make us sympathetic of him. However, all sympathy is lost when we realise that Antonio had insulted Shylock because he was Jew. He had called him a 'dog' along with many other names and had even spit on him publicly.

Bassanio

Bassanio is Antonio's dear friend who serves as a kind of catalyst throughout 'The Merchant of Venice', provoking much of the play's action. At the beginning, Bassanio is a good-natured but irresponsible young man who has gotten himself into debt by living beyond his means. He is rash, selfish and extravagant. To put in other words, he is financially careless and it is perfectly natural for him to ask Antonio for more money. He hopes to get out of debt by marrying a wealthy heiress, but he first needs to court Portia. While men like Antonio attempt to profit by making investments in commerce and trade, Bassanio takes his risks in the realm of love and desire. His confidence is ultimately rewarded since Portia falls in love with him.

As a character, Bassanio is shown to be a soldier but he does not act on it. Rather, he comes out to be romantic hero-noble and kind but vain. His sound judgement and emotion comes only when Bassanio is faced with the riddle of the caskets. He is not fooled by the superficial beauty of the gold and silver caskets, noting that his success in solving the riddle indicates his worthiness as a suitor for Portia. His honesty, truthfulness and his romantic nature comes out whenever he is with Portia.

Even though Bassanio exploits his friendship with Antonio by constantly borrowing his money, Bassanio's reaction to Antonio's misfortune reveals the love he has for his companion. His immediate uncalculated concern for his friend shows that Bassanio is not an opportunist who uses Antonio for money. Bassanio has just achieved his heart's desire by winning Portia's hand in marriage, but when he learns that Antonio defaulted on his loan and owes Shylock a pound of his flesh, Bassanio's focus immediately shifts to how to help Antonio and he hurries back to Venice. Bassanio remains steadfastly supportive of Antonio throughout the trial. He also shows his newfound sense of caution by initially being unwilling to give his ring to Portia while she is disguised as Balthazar. However, Bassanio proves that he is still somewhat susceptible to social pressure by ultimately giving in to Antonio's urging and handing over the ring.

Portia

Quick-witted, wealthy and beautiful, Portia is the female lead of the play who embodies the virtues that are typical of Shakespeare's heroines. She is essentially an ideal woman who possesses elegance, grace, charm, wit, humour, sensitivity, kindness and modesty. From her very first presence, we see Portia as a quick, determined and vocal woman who does not shy away from speaking what is in her mind. She dislikes her father controlling her choice of husband and expresses it clearly. Portia, we know is formed of the rarest of combinations—a free spirit who abides rigidly by rules. Rather than ignoring the stipulations of her father's will, she watches a stream of suitors pass her by, happy to see these particular suitors go, but sad that she has no choice in the matter.

It is interesting to note that Portia could have easily married the man of choice and constantly keeps reminding the audience of this. But, she does not do so for the love and respect for her dead father.

While we see her as a bold woman, Portia's true potential for initiative and resourcefulness comes out when Bassanio arrives. She begs the man she loves to stay a while before picking a chest and starts finding loopholes in the will's provision that we never thought possible. In her doing so, she shows a feminine weakness of love but that is what makes her human.

Portia, as a character, reaches her pinnacle after Bassanio receives the news of Antonio's trial. Without wasting time, she makes arrangements and takes decisions. She comes up with a strategy and meticulously implements it. It comes as no surprise that such a strong female emerges as the antidote to Shylock's malice. Portia's intelligence reaches a new standard when she quickly turns the tables on Shylock. In her courtroom appearance, she vigorously applies the law, but still rejects convention by appearing disguised as a man. Her presence is so strong that no one can speak when she is speaking and in the end her decision becomes absolute. Her mercy speech is commendable on her part.

Portia, thus, displays not just courage and resourcefulness but also confidence and strength which appeals to the audience. However, in the end she emerges as a good natured, faithful and a gentle wife who knows how to poke fun at her husband. After depriving Bassanio of his ring, she teases him but stops the prank before it goes too far.

Shylock

Shylock, the play's antagonist, is a Jew who poses a serious danger to the happiness of Venice's businessmen and young lovers alike. One of the most prominent characters of the play, Shylock's role as an antagonist has often come to question. We, as, audience sympathise with him for he has suffered a lot just for being a Jew amidst Christians. As a character we are introduced to him as a moneylender approached by Bassanio for loan.

Shylock is a moneylender who gives loans on high interest rates. He is an adamant and unyielding materialist who is obsessed with his possessions and money. He is so obsessed with money that his love for money overpowers his love for his daughter. He does not reduce interests or help his debtors. He is intolerant against Christianity and is a miser. As a father, he is a strict and controlling man disliked by his daughter. In other words, he is a man disliked by almost everyone except Tubal.

Our knowledge of him being an antagonist comes to question when we realise that his negativity against Antonio springs from the treatment given to him. Antonio has time and again insulted Shylock, called him names and even spit on him publicly. Antonio claims that he would keep on doing so for Shylock is a greedy Jew. Hence, Shylock's hate for Antonio is quite natural. In this light, his hatred for Christianity can also be quite understood.

As a result, we start sympathising with him. Shylock comes out to be a creation of circumstance; even in his single-minded pursuit of a pound of flesh, his frequent mentions of the cruelty he has endured at Christian hands make it hard for us to label him a natural born monster. But Shylock's coldly calculated attempt to revenge the wrongs done to him by murdering his persecutor, Antonio, prevents us from viewing him in a primarily positive light. Our pity for the villain reduces when we realise that he is a cruel and a cunning man who is going to get the pound of flesh from Antonio and perhaps kill him.

Shylock shrewdly creates a bond as a agent and revenge and uses it as a weapon. Unmoved by appeals by anyone in the court, Shylock almost seems obsessed with getting his revenge. He appears to be bloodthirsty and this leads to his downfall. In the end, he is stripped of his profession, religion and his property. He is thoroughly defeated.

It is interesting to note that while we should feel happy for the punishment received by him, we do not do so. We feel sorry for the man.

We question the Christians who have not themselves upheld the idea of mercy they were preaching to him. In fact, Shylock himself ascertains that Christians do not follow their own rules and morals while preaching others to do so. We also think about whether Shylock's fault was so great to have received such a punishment.

Jessica

Daughter of the antagonist Jew- Shylock, Jessica is an attractive, good-looking, sweet, polite, wise, faithful, witty and a generous lady who abandons her father and her Jewish identity in order to marry Lorenzo and convert to Christianity. Her presence in the story is to form the romantic atmosphere of the play with Lorenzo and present her father's character in more detail. She, from the very start, makes it clear that she is unhappy living with Shylock who is strict and a miser. She reveals her intelligence and independence when she escapes her father's house by disguising herself in male clothing and taking money and other valuables with her.

Jessica is aware that she is violating traditional expectations of showing loyalty to her father, but she ultimately chooses Lorenzo in hopes of becoming a loving wife. This shows that unlike her father, she had no scrupulous about Christianity and falling in love with Lorenzo.

As a young woman with a particular suitor in mind, Jessica faces a similar challenge to Portia because both women are controlled by their fathers (dead or alive) and unable to freely choose whom they want to marry. In contrast with Portia, who honors her father's wishes and takes a gamble in hoping that Bassanio will make the right choice, Jessica is more proactive and takes control of her own destiny. At the end, the play suggests that Jessica makes the right decision, as she enjoys a happy marriage and is rewarded with an income and inheritance that Antonio secured for her after Shylock lost the court case.

Gratiano

Gratiano is a friend of Bassanio's who accompanies him to Belmont. As a minor character, he is a joyful and a friendly person who functions to relieve the gloom and gravity of the situation. Gratiano is a faithful friend to both Antonio and Bassanio. Not only does he follow Bassanio but he even rebukes the Jew for Antonio. He is essentially Shylock's most vocal and insulting critic during the trial. While Bassanio courts Portia, Gratiano falls in love with and eventually weds Portia's lady-in-waiting, Nerissa.

Lorenzo

A friend of Bassanio and Antonio, Lorenzo is another minor character in the play. He is in love with Shylock's daughter, Jessica and this is his only role in the play. He schemes to help Jessica escape from her father's house and he eventually elopes with her to Belmont.

Nerissa

Portia's lady-in-waiting and confidante, Nerissa is not just a mere servant in the play. As a lady without any noble background, she had retained some of Portia's wisdom, nobility and elegance. She is a witty and cheerful girl who marries Gratiano and even goes to the court as Portia's clerk.

Launcelot Gobbo

Launcelont Gobbo is a servant throughout the play. First he is a servant of Shylock and later of Bassanio. A comical, clownish figure, Gobbo make up one of the most critically studied characters of the jester present in Shakespearean plays. As a Jester, Gobbo's main role is to bring comedy in the drama. However, unlike the jesters present in other plays, he does not come out as a clever or an intellectual person.

His role in the play is limited to physical comedy that he does with his old and blind father and to be a messenger between Lorenzo and Jessica.

The Prince of Morocco

A Moorish prince who seeks Portia's hand in marriage, the Prince of Morocco asks Portia to ignore his dark countenance and seeks to win her by picking one of the three caskets. He is a proud and self-respecting person who does not forget his worth in the face of his dark complexion. Conscious of his own as well as Portia's worth, the Prince chooses the gold casket which is the wrong casket.

The Prince of Arragon

Another suitor of Portia is an arrogant Spanish nobleman named the Prince of Arragon. Like the Prince of Morocco, however, the Prince of Arragon also has a flaw. He is extremely arrogant, proud and over confident. He hates to be a part of the multitude and feels that he deserves Portia because of his merits. He picks the silver casket which is incorrect. However, this does not deter him as he starts to argue his case till Portia reminds him of the rules of the game.

Major Themes of the Play

The play deals with many themes which are discussed below.

Self-Interest Versus Love

One of the themes of the play is the value one places on human relationships. On the surface, we understand that the main difference between the Christian characters and Shylock appears to be that the Christian characters value human relationships over business ones, whereas Shylock is only interested in money. Merchants like Antonio lend money free of interest and put themselves at risk for those they love, whereas Shylock agonizes over the loss of his money and is reported to run through the streets crying, "O, my ducats! O, my daughter!" With these words, he apparently values his money at least as much as his daughter, suggesting that his greed outweighs his love. However, upon closer inspection, this supposed difference between Christian and Jew breaks down. When we see Shylock in Act III, scene 1, he seems more hurt by the fact that his daughter sold a ring, that was given to him by his dead wife before they were married, than he is by the loss of money. Some human relationships do indeed matter to Shylock more than money. Moreover, his insistence that he have a pound of flesh rather than any amount of money shows that his resentment is much stronger than his greed.

Just as Shylock's character seems hard fit into a single category, the Christian characters also present an inconsistent picture. Though Portia and Bassanio come to love one another, Bassanio seeks her hand in the first place because he is monstrously in debt and needs her money. Bassanio's friendship with Antonio is also more based on selfish reasons than love. Finally, Shylock eloquently argues that Jews are human beings just as Christians are, but Christians such as Antonio hate Jews simply because they are Jews. Thus, while the Christian characters may talk more about mercy, love and charity, they are not always consistent in how they display these qualities.

The Divine Quality of Mercy

The mercy speech by Portia lends another important theme to the story- the idea of Mercy. The conflict between Shylock and the Christian characters comes to a head over the issue of mercy and justice. The other characters acknowledge that the law is on Shylock's side, but they all expect him to show mercy, which he refuses to do. When, during the trial, Shylock asks Portia what could possibly compel him to be merciful, Portia's long reply states its divine quality. Human beings should be merciful because God is merciful: mercy is an attribute of God himself and therefore greater than power, majesty or law.

However, while Portia preaches mercy, she and other Venetians do not themselves give mercy. Once she has turned Shylock's greatest weapon—the law—against him, Portia has the opportunity to give freely the mercy which she so beautifully advocates. Instead, she backs Shylock into a corner, where she strips him of his bond, his estate and his dignity, forcing him to kneel and beg for mercy. Given that Antonio decides not to seize Shylock's goods as punishment for conspiring against him, we might consider Antonio to be merciful. But we may also question whether it is merciful to return to Shylock half of his goods, only to take away his religion and his profession. By forcing Shylock to convert, Antonio disables him from practicing usury, which, according to Shylock's reports, was Antonio's primary reason for berating and spitting on him in public. Antonio's compassion, then, seems to stem as much from self-interest as from concern for his fellow man. Mercy, as delivered in 'The Merchant of Venice', never manages to be as sweet, selfless or full of grace as Portia presents it.

Friendship, Love and Loyalty

Being a comedy in nature, the play is expected to focus on the themes of friendship and love. It is the theme of friendship that drives most of the action in the play. Bassanio needs money and turns to Antonio, who has already offered him substantial financial support in the past. Antonio immediately and unquestioningly agrees to do whatever he can to help his friend, including offering a pound of his own flesh to Shylock if he defaults on the loan. Antonio never rebukes Bassanio for leading him into the situation that later threatens his life. Instead, Antonio repeatedly says that he is happy to die for the sake of his friend. Thus, the play depicts friendship as one of the most intense and important emotional bonds humans can experience and suggests that the bond of friendship between Antonio and Bassanio may even run deeper than romantic love. The importance of friendship is also displayed between Bassanio and Gratiano and between Portia and Nerissa. Gratiano and Nerissa show great loyalty to and trust in their friends and they even fall in love with each other after being brought together by their friends. The final double marriage means that the four friends will never have to be separated from one another, which further supports the importance placed on friendship.

Love accounts for the movement of action in the play. There are three couples in the story which point to the poetic quality of romance. The three couples: Bassanio- Portia, Nerissa- Gratiano and Lorenzo- Jessica, are sincerely in love with each other. They are faithful, dedicated and would do anything for each other. The presence of love as a theme is central to end the play on a happy note.

Loyalty is a part of each and every character in the story. Portia is loyal to her father, Antonio and his friends are loyal to each other, Jessica while disloyal to her father is loyal to her husband and Shylcok is loyal to his religion.

Wealth

'The Merchant of Venice' highlights the complexities of wealth and treats this theme with ambivalence. Several wealthy characters are depicted as unhappy despite their vast fortunes. At the beginning of the play, Antonio is a prosperous merchant on the verge of more financial success, but he still suffers from a sense of melancholy. He cannot figure out why he is so miserable. Likewise, Portia is a wealthy heiress but complains of sadness. The uneven distribution of wealth causes problems for several characters. Bassanio seems to be a noble person, but he suffers from a lack of money, forcing him to selfishly borrow from Antonio, while the vengeful Shylock makes substantial profits by exploiting others. Moreover, wealth is presented as fickle and liable to disappear at any moment. For example, Antonio is confident that he will have more than enough money to repay his loan, but he ends up losing his fortune.

While money is depicted as a source of greed and dissatisfaction, the play also asserts that wealth gives individuals freedom and power. For instance, Bassanio is only able to court Portia because he gains access to money.

Then, when Bassanio and Portia find out that Antonio is unable to pay back his loan, Portia suggests a solution in the form of money. Portia's wealth allows her to help resolve a dangerous situation. At the end of the play, the redistribution of wealth functions as both a punishment and reward. Shylock is punished for his viciousness by losing half of his income and Antonio is rewarded with the surprising news that not all of his ships were lost after all and Jessica and Lorenzo secure an income from the money extracted from Shylock.

The theme of money or wealth is important to understand Shylock's character who is greedy and a miser. The idea of money obsesses him and he cannot part with it. Thus, when he cries for the loss his daughter, it comes after the cries for the loss of the money she has taken. This obsession with money stays with Shylock till he loses his daughter. As he realises that Antonio cannot pay back his debt, his obsession with money changes to obsession with revenge.

Prejudice

Prejudice is a force that creates barriers and divisions between the people of Venice. As a Jewish man, Shylock deeply disdains Christians. When he first appears in the play, Shylock describes his feelings about Antonio, saying, "I hate him for he is a Christian" (I.iii.34). Shylock continuously refers to his animosity toward Christians, such as when he warns Jessica to shut up the house because he does not trust "the Christian fools with varnished faces" (II.v.32). Shylock's strong prejudice against Christians is one reason Jessica runs away to be with Lorenzo, which permanently destroys the relationship between father and daughter. For his part, Shylock sees his daughter's choice to marry a Christian as the ultimate betrayal.

The Christian characters also show deep prejudice toward Shylock because of his Jewish identity. Antonio not only insults him and spits on him publicly but also makes it clear that borrowing money from Shylock does not change his opinion of him. After Antonio's failure to repay his loan, many characters prejudicially link Shylock's Jewish identity to his refusal to compromise or show mercy and Antonio's insistence that Shylock convert to Christianity indicates a desire to undermine Shylock's identity.

While anti-Jew is the most apparent type of prejudice in the play, many characters are also prejudiced against outsiders and anyone who is different than them. After the dark-skinned Moroccan prince fails to solve the casket riddle, Portia responds with relief by saying, "Let all of his complexion choose me so" (II.vii.83). She does not want anyone who looks like him to correctly solve the riddle and win her hand in marriage, indicating her deep-seated prejudice against people who look different from herself.

Revenge

Revenge is a powerful, corrupting and destructive force in the play. Shylock wants to hurt Antonio because of Shylock's desire for revenge against the entire Christian community, which he blames for persecuting and degrading him and also for stealing his daughter and the money she took when she ran away. Shylock feels he has been wronged by Christians and is entitled to seek revenge in response to their dehumanisation.

He views this revenge as a natural human response to mistreatment. Because of his desire for revenge, Shylock will not consider altering the conditions of Antonio's bond in any way. Ironically, his insistence on the exact nature of the law being enacted is what leads to his downfall when Portia finds a legal loophole and then uses the same law to condemn him. Shylock's desire for revenge makes him behave in an emotional rather than a logical way and he ends up losing everything as a result.

Appearance and Reality

The play is partly constructed on the theme of appearance and reality. From the moment we are introduced to Shylock's character, we know that appearances can be deceptive. Shylock's decision to give loan to Bassanio on the bond may seem a simple business deal for he makes it seems like a joke. But we, as audience, know the real intentions of Shylock. We know that he is a cruel and a manipulative man who is agreeing to the bond to get revenge.

The theme becomes even more apparent with the casket test. The three caskets and its inscriptions along with the failures of the Prince of Morocco and the Prince of Arragon show how people make decisions on the basis of appearances.

Another instance of the theme is the character of Jessica who at first seems to be a obedient and a good daughter to Shylcok but is actually rebellious.

Motifs of the Play The Law

The Merchant of Venice depends heavily upon laws and rules—the laws of the state of Venice and the rules stipulated in contracts and wills. Laws and rules can be manipulated for cruel purposes, but they are also capable of producing good when executed by the right people. Portia's virtual imprisonment by the game of caskets seems, at first, like a questionable rule. The game keeps a host of suitors at bay and of the three who try to choose the correct casket to win Portia's hand, only the man of Portia's desires succeeds. By the time Bassanio picks the correct chest, the choice seems like a more efficient indicator of human nature than any person could ever provide.

A similar phenomenon occurs with Venetian law. Until Portia's arrival, Shylock is the law's strictest adherent and it seems as if the city's adherence to contracts will result in tragedy. However, when Portia arrives and manipulates the law most skillfully of all, the outcome is the happiest ending of all, at least to the audience of the time when the play was written: Antonio is rescued and Shylock forced to abandon his religion. The fact that the trial is such a close call does, however, raise the fearful specter of how the law can be misused. Without the proper guidance, the law can be wielded to do horrible things.

Cross-dressing

Daring escapes are executed with the help of cross-dressing. Jessica escapes Shylock's house by dressing as a page, while Portia and Nerissa rescue Antonio by posing as officers of the Venetian court. This device was not only familiar to drama of the time Shakespeare wrote, but essential to its performance: women were banned from the stage and their parts were performed by young boys. Shakespeare was a great fan of the potentials of cross-dressing and used the device often, especially in his comedies. But Portia reveals that the donning of men's clothes is more than mere comedy. She 'in her statements' implies that male authority is a kind of performance that can be imitated successfully. She feels confident that she can outwit any male competitor. In short, by assuming the clothes of the opposite sex, Portia enables herself to assume the power and position denied to her as a woman.

The Play as a Romantic Comedy

The Merchant of Venice is a typical example of a Shakespearean comedy in that its central conflict finds resolution before real harm comes to anyone. As in many comedies, the conflict at the heart of the play has the potential to end tragically. After Antonio forfeits his deadly bond, Shylock demands the pound of flesh he's been promised and he almost succeeds in claiming it after making his argument in court. However, Shylock's plan falls apart when Portia shows up in court disguised as a young male 'doctor of the law'. Not only does Portia twist Shylock's argument against him, but she also cites a law declaring that Shylock must suffer punishment for threatening the life of a Venetian citizen. Despite an initial suggestion that he should be hanged for his attempt to forfeit Antonio's life, Shylock ends up with a less serious sentence: he loses half of his fortune and has to convert to Christianity. This resolution is certainly devastating for Shylock, but nevertheless, the lack of fatalities marks the play's ending as an appropriately 'comic'.

Although *Merchant* shares the basic structure of Shakespeare's other comedies, the play also makes subtle deviations from typical comedic form. Take, for instance, the play's treatment of lovers. Like other comedies, *Merchant* features lovers who are initially kept apart by circumstance and family interference, but who all unite in marriage before the play ends. What is unusual, however, is the fact that the lovers overcome their obstacles and marry each other midway through the play, before the main conflict has been resolved in Act IV. In other words, the lovers occupy a much less significant position in the play's plot. Furthermore, only two pairs of lovers—Portia and Bassanio as well as Jessica and Lorenzo—have any meaningful obstacles to overcome. The third pair—Nerissa and Gratiano—get married at the spur of the moment, inspired by Portia and Bassiano's successful union. This third marriage only has significance insofar as it makes it possible for Portia and Nerissa to play a parallel trick on their new husbands in the final act.

Another twist on the typical comedy has to do with Shakespeare's complex and ambiguous treatment of Shylock. Shylock is clearly the play's villain, as indicated by his unrelenting insistence on taking his pound of flesh. And yet, despite the dehumanising way other characters treat him, Shakespeare portrays Shylock as a complex and sympathetic figure. We often sympathise with Shylock, who ends up alone, destitute, alienated from his daughter and forced to abandon the faith of his 'tribe.' Such a miscarriage of justice is no small problem, particularly given the play's emphasis on the sanctity of Venetian law. On this reading, Shylock's sad end makes the play's final act and the lovers' quarrel at its center seem frivolous.

It is important to note here that the plot of 'The Merchant of Venice' can be divided into various sub-plots

- The Bond Story
- The Trial Scene
- The Casket Test
- The Ring Test
- Lorenzo and Jessica's Story

Further, it is important to point out that Antonio is the Merchant of Venice referred to in the title because he is the only character who can be directly or indirectly associated with all the sub plots of the play. The Bond Story and the Trial Scene finds Antonio as the central character. The Casket Test succeeds because Antonio could arrange loan for Bassanio. The ring test happens because Antonio succeeds in convincing Bassanio to give away the ring his wife has given him to the lawyer and lastly, Antonio is taken to task for Jessica's elopement and her marriage to a Christian.

Objective Questions

1. Who is the title character of The Merchant of Venice?
(a) Shylock (b) Bassanio
(c) Antonio (d) Gratiano

2. What does Shylock demand as collateral for the loan?
(a) A pound of flesh
(b) A pound of gold
(c) A pound of silver
(d) A pound of diamonds

3. What is the name of the heiress whom Bassanio wishes to marry?
(a) Nerissa (b) Jessica (c) Portia (d) Belaria

4. Form the given options, How many caskets does Portia's suitor have to choose from?
(a) Two (b) Three (c) Four (d) Five

5. Which casket does Bassanio choose to win Portia's hand?
(a) Gold (b) Silver (c) Lead (d) Bronze

6. What condition does Shylock set for the loan to Antonio?
(a) Antonio must repay the loan within one month
(b) Antonio must give a pound of his flesh if the loan is not repaid
(c) Antonio must agree to a 10% interest rate
(d) Antonio must convert to Judaism

7. According to the play,Who is the first suitor to choose the caskets in the play?
(a) Bassanio (b) Prince of Morocco
(c) Prince of Arragon (d) Gratiano

8. What is Antonio's mood at the beginning of the play?
(a) Angry (b) Happy
(c) Sad (d) Nervous

9. Who convinces Shylock to lend the money to Antonio?
(a) Jessica (b) Lancelot
(c) Bassanio (d) Gratiano

10. Who is Jessica's father?
(a) Gratiano (b) Antonio
(c) Shylock (d) Lancelot

11. Where is Bassanio from?
(a) Venice (b) Belmont
(c) Verona (d) Milan

12. Who disguises herself as a lawyer in the play?
(a) Nerissa (b) Portia
(c) Jessica (d) Gratiano

13. Which of the following is Shylock's profession?
(a) Merchant (b) Moneylender
(c) Lawyer (d) Soldier

14. What does Shylock want to do to Antonio after the loan is not repaid?
(a) Take Antonio's wealth
(b) Convert Antonio to Judaism
(c) Demand the pound of flesh
(d) Kill Antonio

15. How does Portia save Antonio from Shylock's bond?
(a) She convinces Shylock to forgive the debt
(b) She argues that Shylock can take the flesh, but not spill any blood
(c) She offers to pay the debt
(d) She gets the Duke to rule in Antonio's favor

16. Who is the Duke of Venice?
(a) Antonio
(b) Shylock
(c) Gratiano
(d) The ruler who presides over the trial

17. Who does Bassanio give the ring to?
(a) The Duke (b) Portia
(c) The disguised lawyer (d) Shylock

18. According to the play, who gives away his/her ring in exchange for the lawyer's help?
(a) Bassanio (b) Gratiano
(c) Antonio (d) Nerissa

19. What happens to Shylock at the end of the trial?
(a) He is executed
(b) He wins the case
(c) He is forced to convert to Christianity
(d) He is forgiven

20. How does Bassanio react when he finds out Portia was the lawyer?
(a) He is angry (b) He is relieved
(c) He is grateful (d) He is confused

21. Who is Gratiano's love interest in the play?
(a) Jessica (b) Nerissa
(c) Portia (d) Shylock's daughter

22. What does Shylock demand in return for his loan to Antonio?
(a) A ring (b) A pound of flesh
(c) A piece of land (d) A house

23. Where does the final trial take place?
(a) Portia's house
(b) Antonio's mansion
(c) The Duke's court in Venice
(d) The marketplace

24. How does Jessica escape from Shylock's house?
(a) She bribes the guards
(b) She disguises herself as a boy
(c) She steals money and jewels
(d) She runs away with Lorenzo

25. What does Bassanio choose to do before marrying Portia?
(a) Go to Venice (b) Give away his ring
(c) Repay his debts (d) Take a trip to Egypt

26. What does the inscription on the gold casket say?
(a) "Who chooseth me shall gain what many men desire."
(b) "Who chooseth me shall get the prize."
(c) "Who chooseth me shall find the greatest joy."
(d) "Who chooseth me shall win the fairest maiden."

27. How does Shylock feel about his daughter's marriage?
(a) He is supportive
(b) He is angry and disapproving
(c) He is indifferent
(d) He is happy

28. Who does Gratiano marry at the end of the play?
(a) Nerissa (b) Jessica
(c) Portia (d) Belaria

29. What is the relationship between Antonio and Bassanio?
(a) Brothers (b) Best friends
(c) Father and son (d) Rivals

30. Who tries to persuade the Duke to show mercy to Shylock?
(a) Gratiano (b) Antonio
(c) Bassanio (d) Portia

31. What happens to Shylock's wealth after the trial?
(a) He loses everything (b) He gets a large fine
(c) He is allowed to keep it (d) He donates it to charity

32. How does Antonio react to the loss of his wealth?
(a) He is unconcerned
(b) He is devastated but accepts it
(c) He asks the Duke for mercy
(d) He curses Shylock

33. What does the silver casket say on the inscription?
(a) "Who chooseth me shall get the lady."
(b) "Who chooseth me shall get all that he deserves."
(c) "Who chooseth me shall find his fate."
(d) "Who chooseth me shall have his heart's desire."

34. What does Bassanio do to help Antonio?
(a) He pays off the loan
(b) He offers to give up his life for Antonio
(c) He defends Antonio in court
(d) He brings Portia's lawyer to the trial

35. Accroding to the play, what role does Gratiano play in the final scene of the trial?
(a) He defends Shylock
(b) He assists in the trick to save Antonio
(c) He brings Bassanio's ring to Portia
(d) He negotiates with Shylock

36. What is Shylock's attitude toward Christians?
(a) He dislikes them but is tolerant
(b) He is indifferent to them
(c) He hates them
(d) He converts to Christianity

37. What is the ultimate fate of Jessica in the play?
(a) She becomes a Christian and lives happily
(b) She is disowned by her father
(c) She returns to Shylock
(d) She marries Antonio

38. Who provides the legal defense for Antonio in court?
(a) Nerissa (b) Bassanio
(c) Gratiano
(d) Portia (disguised as Balthazar)

39. According to the play,What does Portia do to test Bassanio's love for her?
(a) She asks him to choose between her and money
(b) She asks him to give her a ring
(c) She makes him solve a riddle
(d) She asks him to give up his wealth

40. Why does Shylock want to take a pound of flesh from Antonio?
(a) To settle a grudge
(b) To satisfy his anger
(c) To get revenge for the loss of his money
(d) To prove his superiority

41. What does the lead casket say on its inscription?
(a) "Who chooseth me must give and risk all."
(b) "Who chooseth me shall find true love."
(c) "Who chooseth me must hazard all."
(d) "Who chooseth me shall gain all things."

42. Who is Shylock's daughter?
(a) Jessica (b) Nerissa (c) Portia (d) Belaria

43. What is the name of Shylock's servant?
(a) Lancelot (b) Gratiano (c) Nerissa (d) Lorenzo

44. What is the central theme of the play "The marchent of Venice"?
(a) Love and loyalty (b) Mercy and justice
(c) Wealth and poverty (d) Revenge and betrayal

45. Who marries Jessica?
(a) Gratiano (b) Antonio (c) Bassanio (d) Lorenzo

46. According to the play,Who is the Prince of Morocco?
(a) A suitor of Portia (b) The Duke of Venice
(c) Antonio's rival (d) A friend of Bassanio

47. Who is the Prince of Arragon?
(a) A suitor of Portia (b) Bassanio's rival
(c) Gratiano's brother (d) Shylock's enemy

48. What is the condition of the bond between Antonio and Shylock?
(a) A loan of 3,000 ducats
(b) A loan of 6,000 ducats
(c) A pound of flesh if the loan is not repaid
(d) A penalty of 2,000 ducats

49. According to the play,What is the name of the court in which the trial takes place?
(a) Court of Venice (b) Court of Belmont
(c) Court of Milan (d) Court of the Duke

50. What does the ring symbolize in the play?
(a) Wealth (b) Loyalty (c) Love (d) Power

Act- I (Scene I, II & III)

1. As the play opens, with whom does Antonio discuss his troubles?
(a) Bassanio and Gratiano (b) Bassanio and Lorenzo
(c) Salerio and Bassanio (d) Salarino and Salanio

2. What appears to be the "problem" as the play opens?
(a) Bassanio owes a lot of money to Antonio
(b) Antonio's ships are all at sea
(c) Bassanio is in love
(d) Antonio is sad

3. Which character speaks the following lines?
"Believe me, sir, had I such venture forth, The better part of my affections would Be with my hopes abroad."
(a) Bassanio (b) Antonio (c) Gratiano (d) Solanio

4. What aspect of Gratiano does Bassanio joke about after Gratiano has left?
(a) His small stature (b) His empty speech
(c) His social status (d) His physical appearance

5. In Act I scene 2, which character says, "my little body is aweary of this great world"?
(a) Solarino (b) Nerissa (c) Portia (d) Jessica

6. Which of the suitors that have arrived in Belmont does Portia say she could tolerate marrying?
(a) None of them
(b) Baron Falconbridge
(c) County Palatine
(d) The Duke of Saxony's nephew

7. At Belmont, what reason does Portia give Nerissa for being weary of the world?
(a) Her inheritance is gone
(b) Her father has died
(c) Can't choose her husband
(d) Has to get married

8. What word best describes how Portia feels about her fate as it relates to a getting a husband?
(a) Excited (b) Frustrated (c) Calm (d) Sad

9. Portia can be described as ....
(a) quick-witted (b) daring
(c) loyal (d) All of these

10. According to Portia, what is a character fault of the English suitor who came to guess the correct casket?
(a) Poor language skills
(b) Drunkenness
(c) An obsession with horses
(d) Overly serious

11. How do Nerissa and Portia know Bassanio?
(a) He has arrived with the other suitors in Act I.
(b) He visited them once and presented himself as a scholar and a soldier.
(c) They met him once on the rialto.
(d) They don't know him at all.

12. How much money does Bassanio ask to borrow from Shylock?
(a) 6,000 ducats (b) 3,000 ducats
(c) 2,000 ducats (d) 1,000 ducats

13. In the aside, what does Shylock confess?
(a) He hates Antonio
(b) He hates Bassanio
(c) He hates his daughter
(d) He hates Venice

14. What does Antonio tell Shylock that he never does?
(a) He never worries about his ships.
(b) He never speaks to a Jew.
(c) He never eats pork.
(d) He neither lends nor borrows with interest

15. What are the two primary reasons Shylock says he hates Antonio?
(a) Antonio has spit on him and ruined his business
(b) Antonio plans to run off with his daughter and he is a Christian.
(c) Antonio is a Christian and his Christian business practices hurt Shylock's business.
(d) Antonio has spit on him and he has kicked him.

16. What is it that Antonio criticises and that Shylock does as a regular business practice?
(a) Loans (b) Usury
(c) Advertise his services (d) Bribery

17. What does Shylock say that Antonio has done to him in the past?
(a) Failed to repay money (b) Been a good friend
(c) Spat on him (d) Told him jokes

18. In what capacity does Antonio insist Shylock lend him the money?
(a) As a friend (b) As a business partner
(c) As a shareholder (d) As an enemy

19. What is Antonio required to forfeit if he fails to repay the amount he borrowed from Shylock within the time specified in the bond?
(a) A pound of his flesh
(b) Three times the sum he had borrowed
(c) His friendship with Bassanio
(d) All his wealth and property

20. What does Shylock say he will not do with a Christian?
(a) Walk, talk or stay with
(b) Sell, buy or deal with
(c) Lend, borrow or buy with
(d) Eat, drink or pray with

21. What does Shylock reference many times during his conversation with Antonio and Bassanio?
(a) The old testament
(b) His hatred of Christians
(c) His love of the Jewish people
(d) The present rates of interest

Act-II (Scene I, II & III)

1. Who is the first suitor that actually chooses a casket?
(a) Bassanio (b) Antonio
(c) The Prince of Morocco (d) The Duke of Burgundy

2. Who wants to "prove whose blood is reddest"?
(a) Antonio (b) Morocco
(c) Lancelot (d) Shylock

3. What does Portia tell Morocco he must do before selecting a casket?
(a) Go to the temple
(b) Put down his sword
(c) Seal his fate with a kiss
(d) Go wash his hands

4. To what is Portia referring when she speaks of 'the lottery of my destiny'?
(a) Her dead father (b) The three caskets
(c) Her great fortune (d) Bassanio

5. As Act II Scene II opens, who/what is telling Launcelot to flee the Jew?
(a) Jessica (b) Lorenzo
(c) Bassanio (d) His conscience

6. Why does Launcelot want to leave his master Shylock?
(a) Because Shylock pays badly
(b) Because Shylock has abused him
(c) Because Shylock is Jewish
(d) Because Shylock is annoying

7. Who does Launcelot want to work for instead of Shylock?
(a) Bassanio (b) Antonio (c) Gratiano (d) Portia

8. Why is Old Gobbo looking for Shylock's house?
(a) To find Launcelot (b) To give him a present
(c) To ask for money (d) We never find out

9. Who does Launcelot tell Old Gobbo to go see?
(a) Jessica (b) Antonio
(c) Lorenzo (d) Bassanio

10. Bassanio is hesitant to let Gratiano go with him to Belmont because
(a) he is too loud and rude (b) he is uneducated
(c) he is poorly dressed (d) he is unattractive

11. In Act II Scene III, Jessica believes that this will solve the misery of life with Shylock.
(a) Becoming a more devout Jew
(b) Locking herself in her room
(c) Marrying Lorenzo, a Christian
(d) Ensuring Shylock loses his bond to Antonio

12. What is true and perhaps unusual about Jessica's character in this play?
(a) She speaks in blank verse
(b) She seems to be a strong female character
(c) She speaks in prose
(d) Her character doesn't seem to fit into the action of the play

13. When Shylock talks to Jessica about Launcelot, how does he describe Launcelot?
(a) A terrible person (b) A fine servant
(c) Untrustworthy (d) Kind but lazy

14. Who brings Lorenzo a letter?
(a) Old Gobbo (b) Bassanio
(c) Launcelot (d) Gratiano

15. What does the letter say?
(a) That Jessica has decided to stay with Shylock
(b) That Shylock is staying home and Lorenzo should wait until morning
(c) Antonio has lost a ship bound for Tripolis
(d) That Shylock will be out of the house and Lorenzo should go tonight to get Jessica

16. In Act II, Scene (VI), who meets in front of Shylock's house?
(a) Bassanio and Antonio
(b) Gratiano, Salarino and Lorenzo
(c) Gratiano, Salanio and Lorenzo
(d) Gratiano, Salarino and Launcelot

17. Who is the last one to arrive outside Shylock's house?
(a) Solario (b) Bassanio
(c) Gratiano (d) Lorenzo

18. Why does Jessica say she is ashamed?
(a) She doesn't want to be seen with Christians
(b) She is dressed like a boy
(c) She is a girl going out at night
(d) She is running away from her father

19. What does Jessica tell Lorenzo is "worth the pains"?
(a) Leaving Shylock
(b) Catching the casket of ducats and jewels she throws out the window
(c) Marriage
(d) Becoming a Christian

20. Which of Portia's caskets bears the inscription "Who chooseth me must give and hazard all he hath"?
(a) The gold casket (b) The silver casket
(c) The lead casket (d) All three caskets

21. Over in Belmont in Scene (VII), Morocco chooses the casket that says
(a) "Who chooseth me shall gain what many men desire."
(b) "Who chooseth me shall get as much as he deserves."
(c) "Who chooseth me must give and hazard all he hath."
(d) "Pick me! Pick me!"

22. In Scene (IX), The Prince of Aragon explains that the conditions of the oath he must take require all EXCEPT the following
(a) Never woo another maid in way of marriage.
(b) Never tell anyone which casket he chose.
(c) He must swear to remain true to Portia should he choose correctly.
(d) He must leave immediately if he chooses incorrectly.

23. How will Morocco know if he chooses the correct casket?
(a) It will simply have a note in it that says, "You won."
(b) It will contain the deed to Portia's castle.
(c) It will have a picture of Portia in it.
(d) It will be filled with gold and jewels.

24. As Scene VIII opens, who do Salerio and Solanio say was not on Bassanio's ship?
(a) Gratiano (b) Lorenzo
(c) Bassanio (d) Launcelot

25. Solanio heard Shylock crying in the streets. About what does Solanio imply Shylock was most upset?
(a) Getting locked out of his house
(b) That a Christian tricked him
(c) Losing his daughter
(d) Losing his ducats and jewels

26. What did a Frenchman tell Salerio?
(a) Bassanio has set sail for Belmont.
(b) Antonio is still sad.
(c) A ship has sunk in the English Channel.
(d) Lorenzo and Jessica have eloped.

27. As scene XIII closes, who does Salerio see shake hands "with affection wondrous sensible"?
(a) Bassanio and Gratiano (b) Antonio and Shylock
(c) Lorenzo and Gratiano (d) Antonio and Bassanio

28. What is contained in the casket Aragon chooses?
(a) Nothing
(b) A skull
(c) A portrait of Portia
(d) The portrait of a blinking idiot

29. What news does a messenger bring Portia once Aragon has departed?
(a) All the suitors have left Belmont
(b) A young Venetian has arrived to see her
(c) He would like to try a casket
(d) Nerissa has run away

Act-III

1. What does Shylock lament in the Scene 1 of the Act?
(a) His wife's death
(b) His daughter's death
(c) The loss of an expensive diamond
(d) His daughter eloping with a Christian

2. When Shylock speaks of Jessica's elopement he exclaims, 'My own flesh and blood to rebel!' What feeling do his words convey?
(a) Pride (b) Envy
(c) Betrayal (d) Remorse

3. Tubal returns from Genoa with news both good and bad, for Shylock. Which of the following did he not say to Shylock?
(a) That he met Jessica, Shylock's daughter in Genoa.
(b) That, in Genoa, he had heard of Antonio's misfortunes.
(c) That Jessica had spent eighty ducats in one night in Genoa.
(d) That he had been shown Shylock's ring that Jessica has traded in Genoa for a monkey.

4. Tubal reports Jessica has stolen a ring of Shylock's. What does she trade the ring for?
(a) A monkey (b) Fine clothes
(c) Portia's ring (d) Thousands of ducats

5. What cheers up Shylock after hearing of his daughter's theft?
(a) Bassanio's financial ruin
(b) News of Jessica's marriage
(c) Tubal tells a joke
(d) Antonio's financial ruin

6. Shylock in his speech compares Christians with Jews. Which of the following comparisons does he not make?
(a) Both Jews and Christians bleed when cut
(b) Both Jews and Christians die if poisoned
(c) Both Jews and Christians treat each other with humility
(d) Both Jews and Christians seek revenge when wronged

7. Which of the following words would you use to describe Shylock's state of mind after this impassioned speech?
1. Hurt 2. Angry 3. Vindictive 4. Resourceful
(a) 1, 2 and 3 (b) 2, 3 and 4
(c) 3, 4 and 1 (d) 4, 1 and 2

8. As Scene (II) opens, what does Portia ask of Bassanio?
(a) Don't hazard a guess at the caskets
(b) Not to select either the gold or silver casket
(c) To wait a few days before he chooses a casket
(d) Just to leave Belmont

9. Portia says, "I am locked in one of them." The word 'one' refers to ....
(a) silver casket (b) golden casket
(c) bronze casket (d) lead casket

10. To whom does portia compare Bassanio as he steps forward to take the casket test?
(a) Midas (b) Mercury
(c) Hesione (d) Hercules

11. Portia compares Nerissa and the rest to ....
(a) Alcides and the sea-monster
(b) Alcides and the Dardanian wives
(c) Alcides and Hesione
(d) The Dardanian wives with tearstained faces

12. Bassanio rejected the golden casket because....... ..
(a) he knew that Midas has found gold hard to digest
(b) he knew that outward appearance are often deceptive
(c) he found gold too shiny for his taste
(d) he had been told which casket contains Portia's portrait

13. Who/what is Bassanio referring to in the following lines?
"thou pale and common drudge/'tween man and man"
(a) Shylock (b) The gold casket
(c) The lead casket (d) Portia

14. What rare quality of Bassanio helps him choose the right casket?
(a) This honesty and integrity
(b) This desperate need for money
(c) This dislike for gold and silver
(d) This ability to look beyond outword appearances

15. Soon after Portia and Bassanio declare their love for each other, another pair also declare their love and ask to be married at the same time as Portia and Bassanio. They are............ .
(a) Gratiano and Nerissa
(b) Gratiano and Jessica
(c) Lorenzo and Nerissa
(d) Lorenzo and Jessica

16. Who arrives from Venice towards the end of the scene bringing news of Antonio's misfortunes?
(a) Salerio, Lorenzo and Jessica
(b) Salerio, Gratiano and Nerissa
(c) Salerio, Lorenzo and Nerissa
(d) Salerio, Gratiano and Jessica

17. What piece of bad news interrupts the celebrations at Belmont?
(a) The outbreak of war
(b) Shylock's arrival
(c) Gratiano and Nerissa's engagement
(d) Antonio's bankruptcy

18. How much money does Portia tell Bassanio to pay to 'deface the bond'?
(a) 6,000 ducats
(b) 12,000 ducats
(c) 36,000 ducats
(d) 72,000 ducats

19. What animal does Shylock remember Antonio comparing him to?
(a) A hind (b) A wolf
(c) A dog (d) A sheep

20. Lorenzo and Portia discuss helping Antonio. Why does Portia agree to help?
(a) She hates Shylock
(b) Antonio is kind
(c) Antonio is Bassanio's friend
(d) For the challenge

21. .... was Portia's faithful servant.
(a) Bellario (b) Balthazar
(c) Launcelot (d) Stephano

22. When Portia left for Venice she put .... in charge of her house.
(a) Lorenzo (b) Gratiano
(c) Jessica (d) Launcelot

23. Which of the following statements in NOT true?
(a) At the beginning of the scene Portia urges Bassanio to wait a while before taking the casket test.
(b) At the begining of the esene Bassanio is eager to take the test as he finds waiting a form of torture.
(c) At the beginning of the scene Bassanio wants to wait and take the test later as he wants to spend some time with Portia.
(d) At the beginning of the scene portia is afraid that Bassanio might choose the wrong casket and be lost to her forever.

Act-IV (Scene I & II)

1. "My deeds upon my head! I crave the law. The penalty and forfeit of my bond."
Who says these words and to whom?
(a) Portia to Antonio (b) Shylock to Portia
(c) Bassanio to Portia (d) Antonio to Shylock

2. Which of the following words best describes Antonio's attitude during the trial?
(a) Jealous (b) Angry
(c) Generous (d) Resigned

3. "Go, one and call the Jew into the court."
Who said these words and to whom?
(a) Antonio to Salerio (b) Antonio to Salarino
(c) Duke to Salarino (d) Duke to Salerio

4. What explanation does Shylock give for continuing to pursue his bond?
(a) To scare people (b) It amuses him
(c) He hates Antonio (d) For the attention

5. Antonio says that trying to reason with Shylock was like ....
(a) standing on the beach and ordering the waves to wash away the sands.
(b) reasoning with a ewe which was crying out in distress at the loss of her lamb.
(c) trying to soften a rock.
(d) commanding the pine trees on the mountain side to remain quiet and motionless when battered by strong winds.

6. As Act IV opens, the Duke speaks to Antonio. How does the Duke feel about Antonio's predicament?
(a) He doesn't seem to care one way or the other
(b) He is angry with Antonio
(c) He hopes Antonio has to pay the forfeiture of the bond
(d) He feels sorry for him

7. When Shylock enters the courtroom what does the Duke suggest has been Shylock's plan all along?
(a) To exact the forfeiture of the bond
(b) Not to arrive at court
(c) To accept payment late from Antonio
(d) In the end, to show great mercy toward Antonio

8. What does Bassanio offer Shylock to persuade him to forfeit his bond?
(a) Six thousand ducats (b) Three thousand ducats
(c) Nothing (d) Portia's ring

9. When she is disguised as Balthazar, what argument does Portia make for Shylock showing mercy?
(a) Mercy is a blessing (b) Shylock will be respected
(c) It is the law (d) Shylock will feel good

10. What does Bassanio beg the court to do for Antonio's sake?
(a) Kill Shylock (b) Give Shylock money
(c) Take Shylock's knife (d) Bend the rules

11. Who does the Duke call into the courtroom?
(a) Bassanio
(b) Bellario - a learned doctor (lawyer)
(c) Balthazar - a learned doctor (lawyer)
(d) Antonio

12. "A Daniel come to judgement! Yea a Daniel" Who is being described in these words? By whom?
(a) Shylock, by Portia (b) Bassanio, by Gratiano
(c) Antonio, by Portia (d) Portia, by shylock

13. As Antonio prepares his bosom for cutting what does he hold on to?
(a) A Bible (b) Shylock's bond
(c) Bassanio's hand (d) A crucifix

14. What does Antonio ask of Bassanio?
(a) Give Shylock the money after I am gone
(b) Give me a Christian burial
(c) Take over my merchant fleet
(d) Tell your wife how much I loved you

15. Why did Portia ask Shylock if he had arranged for a surgeon to be present at Antonio's trial?
(a) She wanted to make sure that Antonio would not bleed to death.
(b) It was mentioned in the bond.
(c) She wanted to stop Bassanio from harming Shylock.
(d) She was afraid she would faint at the sight of blood.

16. Portia says that Shylock can take his pound of flesh from Antonio but he must not ....
(a) be too slow (b) laugh about it
(c) spill any blood (d) be boastful

17. What will the state seize if Shylock spills a drop of blood while extracting the pound of flesh?
(a) His entire estate
(b) His knife
(c) His daughter
(d) His Venetian citizenship

18. To what is Shylock referring when he calls Portia a 'Daniel'?
(a) The New Testament (b) The Old Testament
(c) A Christian judge (d) His lost son

19. What is the Duke's final decision?
(a) Antonio gets half of Shylock's possessions.
(b) Shylock is free to tear up the bond and leave.
(c) Both Shylock and Antonio will be put in jail together.
(d) Antonio and Shylock must not do business again.

20. Antonio offers to return half of Shylock's estate on the condition Shylock ....
(a) apologises (b) duels with him
(c) gives him a loan (d) converts to Christianity

21. What reason does portia give for refusing the Duke's invitation to dinner?
(a) She had to hurry back to Belmont before Bassanio's return.
(b) She already felt rewarded and satisfied at having saved Antonio.
(c) She was afraid of being found out.
(d) She had to return to Padua that night.

22. What does Bassanio do when faced with Portia, still in her disguise as Balthazar?
(a) Offers her money
(b) Gets angry with her
(c) Sees through her disguise
(d) Ignores her

23. Why doesn't Bassanio want to give the ring as payment to Balthazar?
(a) It was a very expensive ring that Portia gave to him.
(b) He had bought the ring as a gift to Portia.
(c) Portia gave it to him with a promise to never lose it.
(d) His father gave him that ring before his death.

24. What tokens does Portia ask from Antonio and Bassanio?
(a) Gloves and a ring (b) Boots and a ring
(c) Diamonds and rubies (d) A letter of thanks

25. Antonio tells Bassanio to give Balthazar the ring, reasoning that Antonio's love and Balthazar's worth are more valuable than______.
(a) Bassanio's pride (b) mercy
(c) his wife's orders (d) Antonio's gloves

26. Who gives Bassanio's ring to Portia?
(a) Antonio (b) Shylock (c) Nerissa (d) Gratiano

27. What does Nerissa, still in disguise, promise Portia that she will get from Gratiano?
(a) His boots (b) His ring (c) His gloves (d) His jerkin

28. As Act IV ends, where does Portia send Nerissa?
(a) To Shylock's house (b) Back to Belmont
(c) To find Bassanio (d) To find Antonio

Act-V

1. "Did This be fearfully o'ertrip the dew
And saw the lion's shadow ere himself"
Who said these words and to whom?
(a) Thisbe to Pyramus (b) Lorenzo to Jessica
(c) Pyramus to Thisbe (d) Jessica to Lorenzo

2. Which of the young lovers died tragically because of a misunderstanding caused by the appearance of a lion?
(a) Troilus and Cressida (b) Pyramus and Thisbe
(c) Dido and Aeneas (d) Medea and Aeson

3. What does Lorenzo ask Stephano to do when he arrives with news of Portia's arrival in Act V Scene I?
   (a) To tell him where she went
   (b) To have the musicians come outdoors and play
   (c) To inform Bassanio of her arrival
   (d) To help him plot for her and Bassanio's death
4. What does Lorenzo think of people who don't like music?
   (a) He has no opinion (b) They deserve cruelties
   (c) They are clever (d) They amuse him
5. According to Lorenzo, a man who is unmoved by music is ....
   (a) tone-deaf (b) not to be trusted
   (c) self-absorbed (d) not fit to live
6. What does Portia believe makes the music she and Nerissa hear more beautiful?
   (a) The lonely setting (b) Her victories
   (c) Her intellect (d) The night
7. How does Lorenzo recognise Portia even before he sees her when the two young women return from Venice?
   (a) By the clothes she wears
   (b) By the sound of her voice
   (c) By the perfume she uses
   (d) By her touch
8. Why does Nerissa chastise her husband Gratiano, who has given away her ring?
   (a) For hurting her feelings
   (b) For breaking his promise
   (c) For being so careless
   (d) For not selling it
9. What special 'deed of gift' does Jessica give to Lorenzo at the end of the play?
   (a) The news that Shylock has forgiven them for eloping.
   (b) The bond signed by Shylock making Lorenzo heir to all his wealth.
   (c) The three thousand ducats that Antonio owed to Shylock.
   (d) The news that Shylock has agreed to become Christain.
10. Why does a quarrel breaks out between Nerissa and Gratiano in the final Act?
   (a) Gratiano admits that he had given away the ring which Nerissa had given to him.
   (b) Nerissa admits that she had accompanied Portia to Venice disguised as a lawyer's clerk.
   (c) Gratiano is annoyed with Nerissa for giving away his ring to a stranger in Venice.
   (d) Nerissa is angry with Gratiano for leaving for Venice on the very day they were married.

Answers

1. (b) 2. (b) 3. (a) 4. (b) 5. (b) 6. (b) 7. (c) 8. (c) 9. (b) 10. (c)
11. (b) 12. (c) 13. (a) 14. (a) 15. (d) 16. (b) 17. (b) 18. (a) 19. (d) 20. (a)
21. (a) 22. (b) 23. (d) 24. (a) 25. (c) 26. (a) 27. (b) 28. (a) 29. (b) 30. (a)
31. (c) 32. (c) 33. (a) 34. (b) 35. (b) 36. (c) 37. (d) 38. (d) 39. (b) 40. (c)
41. (c) 42. (b) 43. (b) 44. (b) 45. (c) 46. (d) 47. (a) 48. (b) 49. (b) 50. (c)

Act-I

1. (d) 2. (d) 3. (d) 4. (b) 5. (c) 6. (a) 7. (c) 8. (d) 9. (d) 10. (a)
11. (b) 12. (b) 13. (a) 14. (d) 15. (a) 16. (b) 17. (c) 18. (d) 19. (a) 20. (d)
21. (a)

Act-II

1. (c) 2. (b) 3. (a) 4. (b) 5. (d) 6. (c) 7. (a) 8. (a) 9. (d) 10. (a)
11. (c) 12. (a) 13. (d) 14. (c) 15. (d) 16. (b) 17. (d) 18. (b) 19. (b) 20. (c)
21. (a) 22. (c) 23. (c) 24. (b) 25. (d) 26. (c) 27. (d) 28. (d) 29. (b)

Act-III

1. (d) 2. (c) 3. (a) 4. (a) 5. (d) 6. (c) 7. (a) 8. (c) 9. (d) 10. (d)
11. (d) 12. (b) 13. (c) 14. (d) 15. (a) 16. (a) 17. (d) 18. (c) 19. (c) 20. (c)
21. (b) 22. (a) 23. (c)

Act-IV

1. (b) 2. (d) 3. (c) 4. (c) 5. (b) 6. (d) 7. (d) 8. (a) 9. (b) 10. (d)
11. (b) 12. (d) 13. (c) 14. (d) 15. (a) 16. (c) 17. (a) 18. (b) 19. (a) 20. (d)
21. (d) 22. (a) 23. (c) 24. (a)

Act-V

1. (d) 2. (b) 3. (b) 4. (b) 5. (b) 6. (d) 7. (b) 8. (b) 9. (b) 10. (a)

02 The Silver Box

Summary of the Lesson

- The Silver Box" is Galsworthy's most discussed and controversial problem play which unveils disparity, discrimination, snobbery and hypocrisy in the society.
- Mr. John Barthwick is an M.P. belonging to the Liberal Party, very jealous of his position and unwilling that it should be compromised in any way. His wife does not endorse his political views and is a typical lady of the upper class. They have a son, Jack. This young man is the Pampered child of well-to-do parents. He is given to drinking, is extravagant in his expenses and has all the vices of his class. The establishment of the Barthwicks consists of Marlow, their man-servant; Wheeler, their maidservant and Mrs. Jones, their charwoman, besides others.
- Now, past midnight of Easter Monday, Jack Barthwick comes home heavily drunk. He has his latchkey with him, for, it appears he is usually in the habit of returning home late unknown to his father or mother. He is so stupefied with drink that he cannot find out the keyhole. As he is thus engaged, a man named Jones happening to pass by that place, helps Jack to open the door and get into the house. Jack goes in, but returns almost immediately inviting Jones into the house to have a drink as he had no money with him to give for the help Jones had rendered. Jones is an unfortunate man without work, habituated to drink because of long unemployment, and happens to be the husband of the Barthwicks' charwoman.
- Jack goes straight to the dining-room followed by Jones. They drink whisky there and after some time Jack falls asleep on sofa in the dining-room. Jones has more whisky from the decanter on the table. While so occupied, he finds on the floor a lady's purse. This purse has fallen out of the bag that Jack had been carrying and which he had shown to Jones and also given a hint as to how it had come into his possession. Jones suddenly realises, though he had lost his sobriety, the world of difference between himself, the starved and hungry man, and Jack, the prosperous and well-fed one. He is filled with bitterness and out of spite he takes away the silver cigarette-box he finds on the whisky tray and also the purse and leaves the house.
- That morning the silver box is missing. When it cannot be found anywhere in the house, suspicion falls on Mrs. Jones as she was alone for a while in the dining-room where the silver box was and as it transpires that her husband is a drunkard without employment and there is perpetual want in their household. Mr. John Barthwick thereupon engages a detective to trace the missing box and find out the thief. Previous to this a young lady had arrived and had called to see Jack Barthwick. The father had seen her instead and learnt from her that his son had picked up her acquaintance on Good Friday, was at her house the previous night and being rather the worse for liquor, had a quarrel with her and later at supper outside,he had snatched from her the reticule containing her purse in which was all the money she had. Jack being unable to produce the purse or to return the money that was in it, Mr. Barthwick, afraid of scandal and fearing that the matter might get publicity in the papers, pays the lady her money and gets rid of her.
- In the Jones' lodgings at half-past two in the afternoon that day, when their landlady demands rent, Jones surprises his wife and the landlady by producing a sovereign towards payment of the arrear rent. On the landlady's departure, he tells his wife that he had picked up a purse containing a good sum of money.
- Mrs. Jones does not support the idea of the money so found to himself. Then, as she shakes out her husband's coat, the silver box, which had been missing from the Barthwicks and for which suspicion had fallen upon her, drops from the pocket. Mrs. Jones is shocked at this and while her husband assures her that he did not steal it, the detective enters the room. Seeing the silver box and being definite that it was the one he had been engaged to trace, he places Mrs. Jones under arrest, though she says that she is innocent. As he prepares to leave, Jones says that it was he who had taken the box and wants the detective to release his wife. Finding the detective unwilling to let his wife off, he gives the former a blow upon which he is also arrested for assault.
- He had snatched from her the reticule containing her purse in which was all the money she had. Jack being unable to produce the purse or to return the money that was in it, Mr. Barthwick, afraid of scandal and fearing that the matter might get publicity in the papers, pays the lady her money and gets rid of her.
- In the Jones' lodgings at half-past two in the afternoon that day, when their landlady demands rent, Jones surprises his wife and the landlady by producing a sovereign towards payment of the arrear rent. On the landlady's departure, he tells his wife that he had picked up a purse containing a good sum of money.

- Mrs. Jones does not support the idea of the money so found to himself. Then, as she shakes out her husband's coat, the silver box, which had been missing from the Barthwicks and for which suspicion had fallen upon her, drops from the pocket. Mrs. Jones is shocked at this and while her husband assures her that he did not steal it, the detective enters the room. Seeing the silver box and being definite that it was the one he had been engaged to trace, he places Mrs. Jones under arrest, though she says that she is innocent. As he prepares to leave, Jones says that it was he who had taken the box and wants the detective to release his wife. Finding the detective unwilling to let his wife off, he gives the former a blow upon which he is also arrested for assault.
- The Magistrate then sums up the charges against Jones and gives him one month's hard labour. Jones makes an unavailing protest against the injustice meted out to him, for the M. P.'s son, though guilty of the same offence as he, gets off scot-free by force of money, and ridicules Justice.

Objective Questions

1. Who wrote The Silver Box?
(a) George Bernard Shaw (b) John Galsworthy
(c) Oscar Wilde (d) Henrik Ibsen

2. When was The Silver Box first performed?
(a) 1906 (b) 1907
(c) 1909 (d) 1912

3. What is the central theme of The Silver Box?
(a) Class conflict
(b) Love and sacrifice
(c) The struggle for power
(d) Revenge and betrayal

4. Which character is the first to be introduced in the play?
(a) John (b) Mrs. Jones
(c) The magistrate (d) Mr. Barrow

5. What does the silver box symbolize in the play?
(a) Greed (b) Innocence
(c) Wealth (d) Justice

6. What is the crime that takes place in The Silver Box?
(a) Murder (b) Theft (c) Forgery (d) Arson

7. Who is the character accused of stealing the silver box?
(a) Mrs. Jones (b) John
(c) Jones (d) Mr. Barrow

8. According to the play,Who is John in the play?
(a) A magistrate (b) A businessman
(c) A working-class man (d) A lawyer

9. Which character represents the law and justice in the play?
(a) John (b) The magistrate
(c) Mrs. Jones (d) Mr. Barrow

10. Who is the victim of the theft in the play?
(a) Mrs. Jones (b) John
(c) Mr. Barrow (d) The police

11. What happens to Jones at the end of the play?
(a) He is found innocent
(b) He is punished for his crime
(c) He is given a reward
(d) He escapes punishment

12. Form the given options,What social class is John part of?
(a) Upper class (b) Middle class
(c) Working class (d) Lower class

13. What is the attitude of the magistrate towards John?
(a) Sympathetic (b) Harsh
(c) Indifferent (d) Paternalistic

14. What is Mr. Barrow's occupation?
(a) A businessman (b) A judge
(c) A policeman (d) A shopkeeper

15. Who is the character who brings the silver box to court?
(a) Jones (b) Mrs. Jones
(c) The magistrate (d) Mr. Barrow

16. According to the play, Who helps to reveal the truth in the play?
(a) Mrs. Jones (b) The magistrate
(c) John (d) The police officer

17. How does the play address the issue of social class?
(a) It criticizes the lower class
(b) It shows the inequality between the upper and lower classes
(c) It celebrates the success of the working class
(d) It ignores social class issues

18. What is the relationship between Jones and Mrs. Jones?
(a) Husband and wife (b) Employer and employee
(c) Friends (d) Father and daughter

19. According to the play,What was the silver box used for?
(a) A gift for Mrs. Jones (b) A bribe
(c) A piece of jewelry (d) It contained money

20. Which character represents the working-class perspective in the play?
(a) John (b) Mr. Barrow
(c) The magistrate (d) Mrs. Jones

21. How does the play portray the legal system?
(a) As fair and just (b) As corrupt
(c) As impartial (d) As biased

22. What does the magistrate's decision symbolize at the end of the play?
(a) Mercy (b) Equality before the law
(c) Class bias (d) Vengeance

23. Which character is in favor of a strict punishment for Jones?
(a) John (b) Mrs. Jones
(c) The magistrate (d) Mr. Barrow

24. According to playwright,What was the reason behind the theft?
(a) Desperation for money (b) Revenge
(c) Greed (d) Accident

25. How does Mrs. Jones react when the silver box is found?
(a) She is indifferent (b) She is angry
(c) She is relieved (d) She is remorseful

26. Who is the first to defend Jones in the courtroom?
(a) Mrs. Jones (b) John
(c) The magistrate (d) Mr. Barrow

27. What does John try to do in order to help Jones?
(a) Bribe the magistrate (b) Speak on his behalf
(c) Pay for the silver box (d) Hide the evidence

28. What is the primary conflict in The Silver Box?
(a) Man versus man (b) Man versus society
(c) Man versus himself (d) Man versus nature

29. Who is the character who feels guilty about the theft?
(a) Mrs. Jones (b) John
(c) Mr. Barrow (d) The magistrate

30. What is the main setting of The Silver Box?
(a) A courtroom (b) A police station
(c) A hotel (d) A wealthy mansion

31. What is John's relationship with Mr. Barrow?
(a) Business partners
(b) Employer and employee
(c) Acquaintances
(d) Strangers

32. What aspect of society does the play critique the most?
(a) Family dynamics
(b) Education system
(c) Social and class divisions
(d) Government policies

33. What decision does the magistrate make regarding Jones' punishment?
(a) Imprisonment
(b) Fine
(c) Probation
(d) Release without punishment

34. Who is the character that represents the rich, upper class in the play?
(a) John (b) Mr. Barrow
(c) The magistrate (d) Mrs. Jones

35. According to the play, how does the play address issues of justice?
(a) By showing bias in the legal system
(b) By showing that all people, regardless of class, deserve justice
(c) By suggesting that the legal system is corrupt
(d) By demonstrating that the rich can manipulate justice

36. What motivates Jones to steal the silver box?
(a) Desire for power
(b) Revenge against Mr. Barrow
(c) Financial desperation
(d) Greed for wealth

37. According to the playwright, what is the silver box used for in the play?
(a) A valuable family heirloom
(b) A gift from Mr. Barrow
(c) A means to bribe someone
(d) A container for stolen money

38. Which of the following character represents the lower class perspective in the play?
(a) The magistrate (b) Mrs. Jones
(c) Mr. Barrow (d) John

39. How is the theme of mercy explored in The Silver Box?
(a) Through the harsh punishment of Jones
(b) Through the judge's decision to show mercy to Jones
(c) Through John's attempt to cover up the crime
(d) Through Mr. Barrow's charitable actions

40. What is the outcome for John at the end of the play?
(a) He is found guilty
(b) He is rewarded for his honesty
(c) He is let off with a warning
(d) He is pardoned by the magistrate

41. What motivates Mr. Barrow's actions in the play?
(a) Revenge against Jones (b) Desire to make money
(c) Commitment to justice (d) Fear of being caught

42. What is the significance of the silver box to the plo of the play?
(a) It represents the innocence of the accused
(b) It serves as evidence in the crime
(c) It symbolizes the wealth of the characters
(d) It is a gift to Mrs. Jones

43. How does The Silver Box reflect Galsworthy's views on social inequality?
(a) By showing that the rich always win in court
(b) By focusing on the relationship between the working and upper classes
(c) By portraying the poor as corrupt and dishonest
(d) By celebrating the achievements of the wealthy

44. What is the character of the magistrate's attitud towards Jones?
(a) Indifferent (b) Sympathetic but firm
(c) Harsh and unforgiving (d) Apathetic

45. What is Mrs. Jones' role in the play?
    (a) To serve as a moral guide
    (b) To act as a barrier to justice
    (c) To show support for her husband, John
    (d) To show the impact of the theft on the family

46. According to the play ,What is John's main concern throughout the play?
    (a) His own reputation (b) The fate of Jones
    (c) His wife's happiness (d) The future of his family

47. What is the role of the court in the play?
    (a) To deliver justice
    (b) To create conflict between the characters
    (c) To support the working class
    (d) To manipulate the outcome of the case

48. What is the main message of the play 'The Silver Box'?
    (a) The rich should be punished for their crimes
    (b) All people, regardless of social class, deserve justice
    (c) Social class determines guilt and innocence
    (d) People cannot escape their social status

49. According to the play,How does the play explore the theme of morality?
    (a) By showing the importance of following the law
    (b) By depicting characters who struggle with ethical decisions
    (c) By focusing on the hypocrisy of the upper class
    (d) By showing that morality is irrelevant in the legal system

50. What does the ending of The Silver Box suggest about justice?
    (a) Justice is unattainable for the poor
    (b) Justice is reserved for the wealthy
    (c) Justice is fair and impartial
    (d) Justice is ineffective in a corrupt system

Answers

1. (c)	2. (a)	3. (c)	4. (b)	5. (a)	6. (b)	7. (b)	8. (c)	9. (c)	10. (c)
11. (b)	12. (b)	13. (b)	14. (c)	15. (b)	16. (d)	17. (c)	18. (a)	19. (c)	20. (c)
21. (b)	22. (b)	23. (c)	24. (d)	25. (b)	26. (a)	27. (b)	28. (a)	29. (b)	30. (d)
31. (a)	32. (b)	33. (b)	34. (b)	35. (c)	36. (c)	37. (a)	38. (d)	39. (b)	40. (c)
41. (a)	42. (a)	43. (a)	44. (b)	45. (d)	46. (a)	47. (a)	48. (c)	49. (d)	50. (b)

01 The English Teacher

Summary of the Lesson

The English Teacher (1945) is a semi-autobiographical novel by R.K. Narayan. It is the third book in his Malgudi series, following 'Swami and Friends' and 'The Bachelor of Arts'. The novel explores themes of love, loss, spirituality, and self-discovery.

The story follows Krishna, an English teacher at Albert Mission College in the fictional town of Malgudi. Though he has a stable job, he feels disconnected from his work and yearns for a more meaningful existence.

Krishna's life takes a joyful turn when his wife, Susila, and their young daughter, Leela, move in with him. He deeply loves Susila, and their relationship brings him happiness. However, their joy is short-lived when Susila falls ill with typhoid and tragically passes away. Krishna is devastated and struggles to cope with her loss.

As he grieves, Krishna begins experiencing supernatural occurrences-he receives messages from Susila's spirit.

With the help of a medium, he establishes a spiritua connection with her, which brings him peace an understanding. This journey transforms his perspective o life, love, and death.

At the same time, Krishna undergoes another change i his professional life. He realises that teaching at the rigid colonial-style college does not fulfill him. Instead, he find purpose in a new role at a local kindergarten, where h embraces a more compassionate and child-center approach to education.

By the end of the novel, Krishna attains inner peace as h accepts both his personal loss and his new sense of purpos in life.

The English Teacher is a poignant story about love, grie and self-discovery. Through Krishna's journey, R.K Narayan reflects on his own life experiences, making th novel deeply personal and touching.

Objective Questions

1. What in the name of the protagonist in the novel 'The English Teacher'?
(a) Kumar (b) Krishna
(c) Kishan (d) Krishn

2. In which college does, krishna teach?
(a) Stain Mission College
(b) Albert Mission Collage
(c) Albert Einstein Collage
(d) None of these

3. In this novel Albert Mission college is located at ....
(a) America (b) Singapore
(c) Malgudi (d) London

4. Krishna receives a letter from .... informing that he should start living with his wife and daughter in his own house.
(a) his father (b) his uncle
(c) his daughter (d) his wife

5. Krishna find house on rent of .... per month
(a) twenty rupees (b) twenty five rupees
(c) thirty rupees (d) thirty five rupees

6. Who helped Krishna in starting his own household?
(a) His father (b) His mother in law
(c) His wife (d) His mother

7. Who trained susila to be a responsible housewife ?
(a) Her mother (b) Her mother in law
(c) Her husband (d) Her aunt

8. Krishna mother sends .... to help Susila hi own kitchen .
(a) Her sister (b) an old lady
(c) young women (d) none of the above

9. .... is very sharp in keeping nack of all th expenses .
(a) Leela (b) krishna
(c) susila (d) Krishna mother's

10. Who encourager krishna to write poem?
(a) Susila (b) Leela
(c) His mother (d) His father

11. who accuses krishna of copying and urges to b original ?
(a) Susila (b) Leela
(c) His father (d) Mr. Brown

12. What caused first serious quarrel between Krishn and Susila.
(a) Susila's cooking
(b) Susila's accusation
(c) Krishna's irresponsible behaviour
(d) Susila's selling of Krishna's old clock and papers

13. Where Krishna takes Susila for breakfast after their first quarrel ?
(a) Bombay Ananda Bhawan
(b) salary street
(c) street market
(d) none of the Above

14. On the .... birthday of Krishna daughter ,he received after of money from hisfather to buy his own houses in malgudi.
(a) fifth (b) sixth
(c) ninth (d) third

15. Susila and Krishna search various houses in Lawley Extension with the help of Krishna collage ....
(a) Sashi (b) Dr. Menon
(c) Gopal (d) Kumar

16. Who said," I would love to call this house the Jasmine house, it's perfume greets us ever as well as ?
(a) Krishna (b) susila
(c) shastri (d) none of the above

17. Krishna goes to call .... for susila's treatment.
(a) Dr. Raman (b) Dr. shivam
(c) Dr. Shankar (d) Dr.Sharma

18. What is the name of Dr. Shankar's clinic?
(a) krishna Medical Center
(b) krishns Medical Home
((c) Krishna medical hub
(d) krishna Medical Hall

19. Who called Dr. Shankar's "the greatest physician on the earth ?
(a) Krishna (b) Gopal
(c) Rangappa (d) Shastri

20. Initially, Susila is diagnosed with ....
(a) Malaria (b) Normal Fever
(c) cancer (d) typhoid

21. Later, Doctor confirms that susila is suffering from ....
(a) cancer (b) back pain
(c) typhoid (d) Mental illness

22. In this novel susila dies in the......... chapter .
(a) Third (b) fifth
(c) sixth (d) seventh

23. Krishna decides not to............. again
(a) teach (b) write
(c) Marry (d) speak

24. In which chapter krishna receives letter which contains message from his dead wife?
(a) Fourth (b) Fifth
(c) Sixth (d) Seventh

25. Who wants to communicate with Krishna?
(a) His father (b) His mother
(c) Spirit of his dead wife (d) None of the above

26. Who became medium of communication between krishna and dead spirit of his wife ?
(a) His father
(b) Her daughter
(c) His mother
(d) Cheerful peasant

27. The medium asek krishna to come every........... .
(a) Wednesday (b) Thursday
(c) Saturday (d) Friday

28. How many letters susila had wrote for Krishna ?
(a) Ten (b) Twelve
(c) Thirteen (d) Fourteen

29. At the end of The story (told by her school's head master) Leela demand a ....
(a) story book (b) cat
(c) dog (d) none of these

30. Who considers children as good on the Earth?
(a) Dr.Shankar (b) krishna
(c) Shastri (d) Head master

31. Who tries to bring a new system in education?
(a) Shastri (b) Gopal
(c) Dr. Menon (d) Head master

32. Whose death time is predicted by an astrology ?
(a) Krishna (b) Headmaster
(c) Dr. Shankar (d) subsbalen

33. In which chapter krishna succeeds in directly communicating with susila?
(a) fifth (b) sixth
(c) seventh (d) Eighth

34. Who wants krishna to take charge of the school?
(a) Headmaster (b) susila
(c) krishna himself (d) leela

35. In which chapter krishna resigns from his job in Albert Mission college?
(a) Sixth (b) Seventh
(c) Eighth (d) none of these

36. Who is called "an uncompromising idealist?
(a) Ms. Brown C (b) Headmaster
(c) Dr. shankar (d) Krishna

37. After quitting his job at Albert Mission College, Krishna joins ....
(a) Farming (b) Headmaster's school
(c) Another college (d) None of the above

38. How much krishna is paid at Headmaster's School ?
(a) Twenty five rupees (b) Twenty rupees
(c) Fifty rupees (d) Fifty four rupees

39. How much krishna was paid at Albert Mission college?
(a) fifty rupees (b) sixty rupees
(c) Hundred rupees (d) Eighty rupees

40. Who was the head of department of English at albert Mission college ?
(a) Krishna (b) Shastri
(c) Dr. Menon (d) Gajapthy

41. What inspired headmaster to start school for children ?
(a) School of cities
(b) Memory of his own early days
(c) His wife's nature
(d) None of the above

42. Which system headmaster wants to bring in School education ?
(a) Leave alone system (b) Bring together System
(c) Divide System (d) None of the above

43. Who arranged for an exorcist to visit krishna's house?
(a) His wife (b) His mother
(c) His mother in law (d) His father

44. Who says there is no escape from loneliness and separation ?
(a) Krishna (b) Susila
(c) The headmaster (d) Krishna's Father

45. Who says school is house hereafter?
(a) Leela (b) The Head master
(c) Krishna (d) Susila

46. What bored the Headmaster?
(a) School (b) Children
(c) Holidays (d) Susila

47. What did krishna call his wife?
(a) Susila (b) Jasmine (c) Dalling (d) Madan

48. what price susila got for the old clock?
(a) Ten annas (b) Twenty aanas
(c) Twelve Aaanas (d) Fifty aanas

49. Who was a "Phantom Delight for Krishna
(a) Leela (b) His mother
(c) Susila (d) His father

50. Who is leela in the novel ?
(a) His wife (b) His mother
(c) His mother in law (d) His daughter

Answers

1. (b)	2. (b)	3. (c)	4. (d)	5. (b)	6. (d)	7. (b)	8. (b)	9. (c)	10. (a
11. (a)	12. (d)	13. (a)	14. (d)	15. (a)	16. (a)	17. (c)	18. (d)	19. (c)	20. (a
21. (c)	22. (a)	23. (c)	24. (b)	25. (c)	26. (d)	27. (a)	28. (d)	29. (b)	30. (d
31. (d)	32. (b)	33. (c)	34. (a)	35. (?)	36. (d)	37. (?)	38. (a)	39. (c)	40. (d
41. (b)	42. (a)	43. (c)	44. (a)	45. (b)	46. (c)	47. (b)	48. (c)	49. (d)	50. (d

02 The Room on the Roof

Summary of the Lesson

- "The Room on the roof" is a first novel of famous Indian author Ruskin Bond and he wrote it when he was just 17 years old. The novel was originally published in 1956 and it has won John Llewellyn Rhys Prize in 1957. The story of novel center around Rusty, a 17 years old Anglo Indian orphaned boy who lives with his guardian named Mr. John Harrison and Mrs. Harrison.
- The Second important character of novel is Mr. John Harrison, very strict English man who don't like Indian at all and want Rusty to stay away from Indian because he want him to be a complete Englishman. The third important character of novel is Kishan, a neighbour of Rusty who learned daily English from him.
- The Story of novel starts with Rusty, a 17 years old boy with no parents who lives in Dehradun, Uttarakhand with his guardian named Mr. John Harrison. His guardians are very strict who don't like Indian at all and they does not allow Rusty to live or play with Indian because they wa him to be a complete Englishman.
- Rusty do not like living with his guardian because of th strict behavior towards him for Indian and he longs liberation.
- One day in morning during light rain when Rusty w returning home he meets a boy named Somi and Ran who helps him by giving him lift through bicycle and th go on to become Rusty's best friends.
- When Mr. and Mrs. Harrison were not in home Ru decides to go in market with his best friends Somi a Ranbir and after enjoying with his best friends wh Rusty return back to home he find out that his guardi has came back early and he gets punishment for going market.
- The next day he goes to play Holi with his best frie Somi and Ranbir and one more time when he came back get punishment for playing with his friends but this ti

Rusty gets angry and in anger he starts fighting with Mr. John Harrison, and when Mr. Harrison wife comes he runs away from their home.

- Rusty spend first time in his life whole night outside the home crying and waiting for his best friend Somi who will come in morning to take him in his home because he don't want to go back at his guardian home. In morning Somi comes and takes him in his home and help Rusty in getting a job as English teacher in Mr. and Mrs. Kapoor home.
- Mr. and Mrs. Meena Kapoor hired him as English teacher for their son named Kishan and they gave him room on the roof in their home to live freely. Mr. Kapoor is a alcoholic man who is 20 years older than his wife, Meena and don't care for her at all.
- Rusty starts attracting towards Mrs. Kapoor because of her beauty and on the other hand Mrs. Meena Kapoor also seem attracted towards him as she feel uncared by her spouse. One day Mr. and Mrs. Meena Kapoor goes in Delhi for their personal work and after few days Rusty gets a horrific news that Mr. & Mrs. Meena Kapoor had an car accident in which Mrs. Meena died.
- Kishan and Rusty were shocked after hearing the news of Meena's death and they feel very sad and heart broken for their lost. Mrs. Meena Kapoor's death make Rusty orphaned again and now he live alone in his room on the roof. Rusty decides to go England by taking help from British Embassy and before going England he goes to meet his friend Kishan who is living in Haridwar with his aunt.
- When he went to Haridwar to meet Kishan he learns that Mr. Kapoor has married another woman and Kishan don't live with them anymore. When Rusty meet Kishan he learns that he has chosen a life of crime and became a thief. Rusty advises him to quit a life of crime and thief because he don't want to see him in prison, he told him to start a new life in Dehradun. The next morning Rusty and Kishan leaves for Dehradun to start a new life together.

Objective Questions

Here are 50 multiple-choice questions (MCQs) based on the book The Room on the Roof by Ruskin Bond. These questions cover key events, characters, and themes from the story.

1. Who is the protagonist of The Room on the Roof?
(a) Mr. John (b) Suraj
(c) Rusty (d) Som

2. What is Rusty's full name in the novel?
(a) Rustam (b) Rusty Roberts
(c) Rustom Singh (d) Rustom Mehta

3. Where does Rusty live at the beginning of the novel?
(a) Dehradun (b) Delhi
(c) Shimla (d) Mussoorie

4. Who are Rusty's guardians?
(a) His aunt and uncle (b) His parents
(c) His grandparents (d) His teacher

5. What is the main reason Rusty leaves his guardians' house?
(a) He wants to study abroad.
(b) He does not like the strictness of his aunt and uncle.
(c) He wants to escape his mundane life.
(d) He wants to find a new place to live.

6. Who helps Rusty when he first leaves his guardian's house?
(a) Somi (b) Mrs. Singh
(c) Narayan (d) Mr. Kapoor

7. Where does Rusty stay after leaving his guardians' house?
(a) In a hotel
(b) In a room on the roof
(c) With a friend
(d) At a hostel

8. Who owns the house where Rusty finds a room?
(a) Mr. Kapoor (b) Mrs. Singh
(c) Mr. Bhatia (d) Som's family

9. What is Rusty's relationship with Somi in the novel?
(a) They are cousins
(b) They are strangers
(c) They are best friends
(d) They are neighbours

10. What type of relationship does Rusty have with his aunt and uncle?
(a) Loving and caring
(b) Strict and oppressive
(c) Distant and indifferent
(d) Supportive and nurturing

11. Which city does Rusty initially want to escape to?
(a) Delhi (b) Mussoorie
(c) London (d) Dehradun

12. How does Rusty feel when he is living alone for the first time?
(a) Lonely and scared (b) Excited and free
(c) Sad and homesick (d) Confused and lost

13. What is the primary theme of The Room on the Roof?
(a) Friendship and loyalty
(b) The journey to self-discovery
(c) Family and relationships
(d) Adventure and exploration

14. Which of the following is a key event in the story?
(a) Rusty goes on a road trip to Delhi.
(b) Rusty learns to ride a bike.
(c) Rusty's friendship with Somi grows.
(d) Rusty discovers his passion for painting.

15. What does Rusty learn from his experience in the novel?
(a) The importance of material wealth
(b) The value of independence and friendship
(c) The need to stay within family boundaries
(d) The necessity of following social norms

16. What does Rusty do to earn money after leaving his guardians?
(a) He starts tutoring children
(b) He gets a job in a bookstore
(c) He writes articles for magasines
(d) He works in a restaurant

17. Which of the following characters plays a major role in helping Rusty?
(a) Mr. Kapoor
(b) Somi
(c) Mrs. Singh
(d) Mr. Bhatia

18. How does the novel The Room on the Roof end?
(a) Rusty returns home to his guardians.
(b) Rusty moves to a new city to study.
(c) Rusty decides to stay in Dehradun and continue his life there.
(d) Rusty goes on an adventure to the mountains.

19. What is the relationship between Rusty and Somi?
(a) They are childhood friends.
(b) They are distant cousins.
(c) They are roommates.
(d) They are mentor and mentee.

20. How does Rusty describe his aunt and uncle in the book?
(a) Loving and supportive
(b) Strict and controlling
(c) Caring but distant
(d) Warm and understanding

21. Who is the character that Rusty initially feels a strong connection with in the novel?
(a) Somi (b) Mr. Kapoor
(c) Mrs. Singh (d) His uncle

22. Which city does Rusty find himself in after running away?
(a) Delhi (b) Dehradun
(c) Mussoorie (d) Shimla

23. What role does Mrs. Singh play in Rusty's life?
(a) She is his aunt
(b) She is a friend and guide
(c) She is his tutor
(d) She is his landlord

24. How does Rusty feel about his life in the city after leaving home?
(a) He feels free and happy.
(b) He feels lonely and abandoned.
(c) He feels trapped and scared.
(d) He feels excited and determined.

25. What is Rusty's primary internal conflict?
(a) Deciding between staying with his guardians or being independent.
(b) Deciding whether to move to another country.
(c) Deciding whether to follow his passion for art.
(d) Deciding how to deal with his fear of the unknown.

26. Which of these themes is most explored in The Room on the Roof?
(a) The power of love (b) The struggle for identity
(c) The importance of family bonds
(d) The pursuit of career success

27. According to the Author,What is Rusty's greatest fear?
(a) Losing his friends (b) His uncle's anger
(c) The unknown future (d) Being alone forever

28. Who is the first person to encourage Rusty to stay independent?
(a) Mr. Kapoor (b) Somi
(c) Mrs. Singh (d) His uncle

29. What does Rusty like to do in his free time?
(a) Go hiking in the mountains
(b) Write stories and poems
(c) Paint and draw (d) Play the guitar

30. What does Rusty learn about friendship from his experiences?
(a) Friendship can only survive in perfect conditions.
(b) Real friends are always there, even in difficult times.
(c) Friendships are not important in life.
(d) Friendship requires constant effort and sacrifice.

31. What does Rusty miss the most after leaving his home?
(a) His art supplies
(b) His aunt and uncle's attention
(c) The mountains and nature
(d) His old life of comfort

32. What happens when Rusty's uncle finds out he's left home?
(a) He forbids Rusty from returning home.
(b) He is angry but eventually understands Rusty's need for independence.
(c) He sends the police after him.
(d) He ignores Rusty completely.

33. What does the "room on the roof" symbolise in the novel?
(a) A place of freedom and independence for Rusty
(b) A symbol of Rusty's escape from family pressure
(c) A physical space where Rusty finds solace
(d) All of the above

34. How does Rusty's relationship with Somi change over time?
(a) They grow closer and become best friends.
(b) They drift apart due to misunderstandings.
(c) They compete for the same job.
(d) They become rivals.

35. What is the main reason Rusty feels alienated at the beginning of the novel?
(a) He is living in a foreign city.
(b) He doesn't get along with his guardians.
(c) He has no friends in the city.
(d) He is struggling with financial problems.

36. Who is the first person to notice Rusty's art talent?
(a) Mr. Kapoor (b) Somi
(c) Mrs. Singh (d) His uncle

37. What does Rusty begin to realise about himself by the end of the novel?
(a) That he wants to return to his old life.
(b) That he is capable of standing on his own.
(c) That he wants to become a teacher.
(d) That he dislikes the city life.

38. How does Somi help Rusty?
(a) He gives him a place to stay.
(b) He helps Rusty find a job.
(c) He teaches Rusty how to live independently.
(d) All of the above

39. What does the room on the roof represent for Rusty?
(a) A place of refuge from the world.
(b) A symbol of self-reliance and growth.
(c) A temporary place to stay.
(d) A place to escape from his feelings.

40. Which emotion best describes Rusty's feeling towards his life in Dehradun by the end of the book?
(a) Resentment (b) Relief
(c) Satisfaction (d) Indifference

41. Who gives Rusty emotional support throughout his journey?
(a) Mrs. Singh (b) Somi
(c) His aunt (d) Mr. Kapoor

42. What lesson does Rusty learn about independence?
(a) Independence is easy and without challenges.
(b) Independence requires courage and responsibility.
(c) Independence means being completely isolated.
(d) Independence is irrelevant to happiness.

43. How does Rusty's attitude toward his family evolve by the end of the novel?
(a) He becomes completely resentful of them.
(b) He recognizes their importance but chooses his own path.
(c) He wishes to reunite with them.
(d) He feels the need to please them at all costs.

44. According to the Author,What motivates Rusty to leave his home and seek a new life?
(a) A desire for adventure and freedom
(b) A sudden realisation about his future
(c) A conflict with his uncle and aunt
(d) Pressure to follow a career path

45. What role does Somi's family play in Rusty's life?
(a) They provide him with shelter and warmth.
(b) They discourage his journey for independence.
(c) They act as obstacles in Rusty's decisions.
(d) They have no role in his life.

46. How does the novel portray the theme of friendship?
(a) It shows friendship as an obstacle to independence.
(b) It emphasizes the importance of genuine connections.
(c) It suggests that friends are unreliable.
(d) It dismisses friendship as unimportant.

47. Which of the following setting is crucial to the development of Rusty's character?
(a) The mountains (b) The city streets
(c) The room on the roof (d) The family home

48. What does Rusty learn about people in Dehradun?
(a) They are unfriendly and cold.
(b) They are kind and welcoming.
(c) They are only interested in material wealth.
(d) They are too busy to care about others.

49. What is one of the first signs of Rusty's growth in the story?
(a) He starts painting more seriously.
(b) He becomes financially independent.
(c) He helps Somi with his personal issues.
(d) He starts a new relationship.

50. According to the Author,What is Rusty's ultimate goal by the end of the novel?
(a) To return to his guardians' house
(b) To go to college abroad
(c) To become a successful artist
(d) To live a self-sufficient life on his own terms

Answers

1. (c)	2. (b)	3. (a)	4. (a)	5. (b)	6. (a)	7. (b)	8. (a)	9. (c)	10. (b)
11. (c)	12. (b)	13. (b)	14. (c)	15. (b)	16. (a)	17. (b)	18. (c)	19. (a)	20. (b)
21. (a)	22. (b)	23. (b)	24. (a)	25. (a)	26. (b)	27. (c)	28. (b)	29. (c)	30. (b)
31. (c)	32. (b)	33. (d)	34. (a)	35. (b)	36. (c)	37. (b)	38. (d)	39. (b)	40. (c)
41. (b)	42. (b)	43. (b)	44. (c)	45. (a)	46. (b)	47. (c)	48. (b)	49. (b)	50. (d)

03 Kabuliwala

Summary of the Lesson

- The short story "Kabuliwala" is composed by Rabindranath Tagore and set in Kolkata, India. It a famous short story. It revolves around the relationship between a young girl named Mini and a Kabuliwala, a fruit-seller from Afghanistan.
- The story begins with Mini's father, a writer, noticing the Kabuliwala on the street and inviting him into their home. The Kabuliwala, named Rahamat, is a tall and bearded man who wears a long robe and a turban. He carries a bag of dry fruits and sells them to earn a living.
- Mini is initially afraid of Rahamat due to his appearance, but she gradually warms up to him and becomes curious about his life and homeland. Rahamat, too, is fond of Mini and treats her like his own daughter. He brings her gifts from his homeland, including almonds and raisins.
- As time passes, Rahamat's visits become less frequent, and Mini grows up and gets married. Years later, when Mini returns to Kolkata after a long absence, she sees Rahamat on the street. However, she fails to recognize him, as he has aged and his appearance has changed.
- Rahamat is overjoyed to see Mini and tries to remind her of their past relationship. He shows her the gifts he had given her as a child, hoping that she will remember. But Mini, now a grown woman with different priorities, fails to recall their bond.
- The story ends on a poignant note, highlighting the passage of time and the changes that occur in relationships. It explores themes of friendship, innocence, and the impact of time on human connections.
- Overall, "Kabuliwala" is a touching tale that explores the bond between a young girl and an immigrant fruit-seller, highlighting the power of human connection and the lasting impact of childhood memories.

Objective Questions

1. Who is the author of "Kabuliwala"?
(a) Leo Tolstoy (b) Rabindranath Tagore
(c) Charles Dickens (d) William Wordsworth

2. The name of the little girl in the story?
(a) Mini (b) Rina
(c) Aarti (d) Kamala

3. Where does the Kabuliwala come from?
(a) Bengal (b) Kabul
(c) Dhaka (d) Lahore

4. What is the Kabuliwala's profession?
(a) Farmer (b) Merchant
(c) Street vendor (d) Soldier

5. How does Mini react when she first meets the Kabuliwala?
(a) She gets scared
(b) She laughs and talks to him
(c) She runs away
(d) She cries

6. Why does the Kabuliwala come to Kolkata?
(a) For trade (b) To find his daughter
(c) To meet his friend (d) To seek work

7. What does the Kabuliwala carry in his bag?
(a) Sweets (b) Fruits
(c) Spices (d) Cloth

8. What does the Kabuliwala promise Mini?
(a) To bring her a gift
(b) To return with his daughter
(c) To play with her every day
(d) To give her his bag

9. What happens to the Kabuliwala after he is arrested?
(a) He is sent to prison
(b) He is deported to Afghanistan
(c) He is fined
(d) He is set free

10. How long does the Kabuliwala stay in prison?
(a) 5 years (b) 7 years
(c) 10 years (d) 12 years

11. What is the Kabuliwala's emotional attachment to Mini?
(a) She reminds him of his own daughter
(b) He loves her like his own daughter
(c) He is afraid of her
(d) He feels pity for her

12. What is Mini's father's profession?
(a) Teacher
(b) Writer
(c) Doctor
(d) Shopkeeper

13. What does Mini's father think of the Kabuliwala initially?
(a) He trusts him completely
(b) He thinks he is a criminal
(c) He is suspicious of him
(d) He considers him a friend

14. What does the Kabuliwala give Mini as a gift?
(a) A ring (b) A doll
(c) A dry fruit (d) A toy

15. Why does the Kabuliwala become emotional in the story?
(a) He misses his homeland
(b) He misses his daughter
(c) He wants to go back to Kabul
(d) He feels rejected by society

16. What is the reason for Mini's father's change of heart towards the Kabuliwala?
(a) He sees the Kabuliwala as a friend
(b) He understands the Kabuliwala's love for his daughter
(c) He feels sorry for the Kabuliwala
(d) He realizes the Kabuliwala is a victim of circumstance

17. How does the Kabuliwala react when he is reunited with Mini?
(a) He weeps
(b) He feels angry
(c) He hugs her tightly
(d) He asks her to return home

18. What is the central theme of "Kabuliwala"?
(a) Friendship
(b) Sacrifice
(c) Separation and longing
(d) Betrayal

19. What emotion does Mini's father experience at the end of the story?
(a) Guilt (b) Happiness
(c) Compassion (d) Anger

20. What type of character is the Kabuliwala depicted as?
(a) A villain (b) A tragic hero
(c) A kind-hearted man (d) A mysterious figure

21. What does the Kabuliwala's love for Mini symbolize?
(a) The love of a father for his daughte
(b) The friendship between strangers
(c) The hardship of immigrants
(d) The poverty of the poor

22. How does Mini's father view the Kabuliwala after the latter's imprisonment?
(a) He is indifferent to him
(b) He is disappointed in him
(c) He sees him as a victim of fate
(d) He is angry at him

23. According to the Author, what does the Kabuliwala's interaction with Mini demonstrate about human nature?
(a) That people are inherently selfish
(b) That people are capable of deep emotional connections
(c) That people are afraid of strangers
(d) That people cannot change their fate

24. What does the Kabuliwala do for a living?
(a) Selling clothes
(b) Selling fruits and dry fruits
(c) Selling books
(d) Selling carpets

25. How does Mini change throughout the story?
(a) She becomes more independent
(b) She becomes more selfish
(c) She matures and understands the world better
(d) She loses interest in the Kabuliwala

26. What kind of the role of the Kabuliwala's daughter in the story?
(a) She is a distant memory that drives the Kabuliwala's emotions
(b) She is a character who appears frequently in the story
(c) She represents happiness for the Kabuliwala
(d) She is never mentioned in the story

27. How does the Kabuliwala's daughter affect the plot of the story?
(a) She is the source of the Kabuliwala's longing and sadness
(b) She changes Mini's behavior
(c) She makes Mini's father angry
(d) She causes the conflict between the Kabuliwala and Mini's family

28. What emotion does Mini's father feel when he sees the Kabuliwala's situation?
(a) Sympathy (b) Indifference
(c) Happiness (d) Anger

29. Why is the Kabuliwala arrested?
(a) For stealing
(b) For causing trouble
(c) For a violent crime
(d) For an altercation with a man

30. How does Mini change in her attitude towards the Kabuliwala?
(a) She becomes more indifferent to him
(b) She begins to see him as a fatherly figure
(c) She fears him
(d) She becomes angry with him

31. What cultural significance does "Kabuliwala" hold?
(a) It shows the struggles of immigrants
(b) It represents the importance of family bonds
(c) It illustrates the effects of colonialism
(d) It criticizes the caste system

32. Which of the following is the climax of the story?
(a) The Kabuliwala is released from prison
(b) Mini grows up and forgets him
(c) The Kabuliwala and Mini are reunited
(d) Mini's father helps the Kabuliwala

33. What does the Kabuliwala carry in his bag that Mini finds interesting?
(a) Clothes (b) Dry fruits
(c) Books (d) Toys

34. How does the Kabuliwala's emotional journey reflect the immigrant experience?
(a) It highlights the emotional toll of being away from family
(b) It emphasizes the need for revenge
(c) It focuses on the economic struggles
(d) It shows the violence faced by immigrants

35. How does the Kabuliwala's connection with Mini evolve by the end?
(a) He no longer cares about her
(b) He views her as his own daughter
(c) He becomes resentful of her
(d) He forgets about her entirely

36. What role does time play in the story of the Kabuliwala?
(a) It causes conflict between characters
(b) It symbolizes the separation of loved ones
(c) It has no significant role
(d) It only represents physical aging

37. How does Mini's growth in the story reflect a shift in perspective on human relationships?
(a) She learns to value money
(b) She starts to understand the complexities of love and separation
(c) She becomes more selfish
(d) She becomes more materialistic

38. "Kabuliwala" considered a poignant story, why?
(a) Because of its moral lesson
(b) Due to its depiction of love and longing
(c) Because of its complex characters
(d) Because of the tragic ending

39. How does the story illustrate the universal nature of father-daughter relationships?
(a) Through Mini's father's behavior
(b) Through the Kabuliwala's deep love for his daughter
(c) Through Mini's growth
(d) Through the change in cultural settings

40. According to you, What lesson can we learn from the story of the Kabuliwala?
(a) The importance of material wealth
(b) The strength of familial love and sacrifice
(c) The dangers of separation
(d) The unimportance of cultural differences

41. What does the Kabuliwala's relationship with Mini signify in a broader social context?
(a) Friendship across cultural boundaries
(b) The clash of different cultures
(c) The importance of economic success
(d) The need for societal control

42. What transformation does the Kabuliwala undergo in the story?
(a) He becomes more bitter and distant
(b) He becomes a symbol of love and fatherly sacrifice
(c) He becomes disillusioned with society
(d) He gives up his profession entirely

43. What does the Kabuliwala's yearning for his daughter tell us about human emotion?
(a) It reflects the universal longing for home and family
(b) It emphasizes the importance of wealth
(c) It highlights the insignificance of family
(d) It suggests that distance leads to forgetfulness

44. How does Mini's perspective of the Kabuliwala evolve?
(a) She begins to see him as a source of amusement
(b) She learns to understand his pain
(c) She becomes afraid of him
(d) She forgets him completely

45. How is the theme of separation depicted in the story?
(a) Through the Kabuliwala's absence from his daughter
(b) Through Mini's growing independence
(c) Through the conflict between cultures
(d) Through the relationship between the Kabuliwala and Mini

46. What does the story of the Kabuliwala convey about the nature of time?
(a) Time heals all wounds
(b) Time can make people forget
(c) Time causes both separation and reunion
(d) Time is irrelevant

Answers

1. (b)	2. (a)	3. (b)	4. (b)	5. (b)	6. (a)	7. (c)	8. (b)	9. (a)	10. (b)
11. (a)	12. (b)	13. (c)	14. (c)	15. (b)	16. (b)	17. (a)	18. (c)	19. (c)	20. (c)
21. (a)	22. (c)	23. (b)	24. (b)	25. (c)	26. (a)	27. (a)	28. (a)	29. (d)	30. (b)
31. (b)	32. (c)	33. (b)	34. (a)	35. (b)	36. (b)	37. (b)	38. (b)	39. (b)	40. (b)
41. (a)	42. (b)	43. (a)	44. (b)	45. (a)	46. (c)				

Unit-20

01 Indian Writing in English

Inspired by Western Modals

Indian writing in English has a vibrant history with gigantic expansion globally. In the beginning, the Indian writers were inspired by Western models towards prose, translation, biographies and political essays.

The first book in English by an Indian was written in 1793 by Sake Dean Mahomed titled 'The Travels of Dean Mahomed'. The emergence of the Indian English novel underwent assorted phases from imitation, assimilation and finally to genuine self expression.

However, most early Indian writing in English was non-fictional work, such as biographies and political essays.

Bankim Chandra Chatterjee as Father of Indian Novel

The first Indian English novel, titled 'Rajmohan's Wife' was published in the year 1864 by Bankim Chandra Chatterjee, and it marked a significant epoch in the history of Indian writing in English. He is considered to be the father of the novel in Indian literature.

The 'Poison Tree' (1873) and 'Krishna kanta's Will' (1878) were other two popular novels of Chatterjee that prompted Krishna Kripalani to compare him with international novelists. Other contributions in this period were Raj Lakshi Devi's 'The Hindu Wife' (1876), 'H. Dutt's Bijoychand' (1888), 'Roshinara' by Kali Krishna Lahiri's (1881) and 'Khetrapal Chakravarti's Sarata and Hingana (1895).

Rabindranath Tagore entered into Indian English Writing

This began to change in the late 1800s, when famous Indian authors who wrote mostly in their mother tongue, began to try their hand at writing in English.

In the early 1900s, Rabindranath Tagore began translating his works from Bengali to English with the release of his first substantial poems by 1877 and was acclaimed for his best-known works novels, stories, songs, dance-dramas and essays.

Beginning of Children Stories

Starting in 1917, Dhan Gopal Mukerji wrote many children's stories that were set in India. He was awarded the Newbery medal in 1928 for 'Gay-Neck, the Story of a Pigeon'.

Era of R.K. Narayanan and Mulk Raj Anand

Soon after, a new generation of Indian authors, who wrote almost exclusively in English, hit the bookshelves, beginning in 1935, 'Swami and Friends' by R.K. Narayan and 'Untouchable by' Mulk Raj Anand's. Raja Rao's 'Kanthapura' followed in 1938. What made Narayan's, Anand's and Rao's writing different from the Indian authors before them was that their stories were about the contemporary man on the street. There was also Indianness to their work, in terms of the words they used and their style of writing. This resonated with the new, but growing ranks of Indians reading English literature. Their works were the forerunners to the magnificent diversity of Indian writing in English that we see today.

Crusaders of Contemporary and Modern Era

The crusaders of the contemporary and modern era include Salman Rushdie, Amitav Ghosh, Vikram Seth and many more. They elucidate and substantiate strength of the emerging modern voice of India, which has the vibrancy and energy of a gushing artesian along with an unmatched resolve to experiment and explore new avenues of writing novels. A host of contemporary post – colonial writers like Rushdie, Arundhati Roy, Meena Alexander, Anita Nair and Jhumpa Lahiri have initiated the process of decolonising the 'Colonial English' and using it as a medium to express Indian thoughts and sensibilities with a distinctive Indian style.

National Freedom Movement Inspired Literature in India

The freedom movement spearheaded by Gandhi inspired a flurry of activity in the literary world. There was a flourish of novels in both regional and as well as in the national stream.

This burst of energy in regional literature, laid the ground work of fine–tuning and enhancing the vibrancy and the scope of the Indian English Fiction. The dual combination of independent movement and nationalist consciousness gave much impetus and spur to the outflow of novels in which affection for motherland was the crux and this served to invoke the patriotic sentiments of the masses. Post - independent India also produced number of novels involving the causes and aftermaths of the freedom movement. The novels that belong to this category include 'A Time to be Happy' by Nayantara Sahgal (1952), 'Inquilab by Khwaja Ahmad Abbas (1955), 'Waiting for the Mahatma' by R.K. Narayan (1955) etc.

Role of Women Novelists

Women novelists have played a crucial and momentous role in enhancing the quality and quantity of the Indian English Fiction. They have further added the woman's perspective and feministic dimensions to the novels. These rich contributions have widened the spectrum of issues deliberated in the novel.

In the 19th century, more and more women actively participated in India's reformist movement against the British rule. It again led to the women's literature.

At that time, their write ups mainly concentrated on the country's freedom struggle. Over the years, the world of feminist ideologies began to influence the English literature of India. Among the women writers Sarojini Naidu, the great poetess charmed the readers with her writings. Feminism themes have also been used by authors like Nayantara Sahgal and Rama Mehta. Regional fiction theme has been aptly used by Kamala Das, Anita Nair and Susan Viswanathan. Novelists, like Kamala Markandaya and Anita Desai captured the spirit of Indian cultures and its traditional values. During 1990's India became a popular literary nation as a number of women authors made their debut in this era. Chitra Banerjee Divakaruni, Suniti Namjoshi and Anuradha Marwah Roy used realism as main theme of their novels. The novels of authors like Namita Gokhale or Shobha De are really out - spoken.

Most of these female novelists are known for their bold views that are reflected in their novels. Basically, these are the novels of protest and an outburst of reservations and contaminations.

Indian Literature on the Verge of being the Best Seller

These authors make use of Indian phrases alongside English words and have tried to reproduce a blend of the Indian and the Western cultures.

While Indian poets, novelists, essayists, dramatists have been making momentous and considerable contributions to world literature since the pre-independence era, the past few years have witnessed a thriving of Indian English writing in the global market. The works of Indian authors writing in English are often to be found on the best seller list. They are also incurring and earning an immense amount of critical fame.

Exercise

1. The Jataka stories are related to the previous lives of whom?
(a) Krishna (b) Mahabir
(c) Budha (d) Guru Nanak

2. In which year Salman Rushdie cancelled his visit of Jaipur Literature Festival for threats to his life?
(a) 2008 (b) 2010
(c) 2011 (d) 2012

3. Wings of Fire is an autobiography of
(a) Indira Gandhi
(b) A. P. J. Abdul Kalam
(c) Subhash Chandra Bose
(d) Pranab Mukherjee

4. The fictional South Indian city 'Malgudi' is a creation of
(a) Ruskin Bond
(b) Mulk Raj Anand
(c) Rabindranath Tagore
(d) RK Narayan

5. Who has received the Sahitya Akademi Award for his short story collection, 'Our Trees Still Grow in Dehra?
(a) RK Narayan
(b) Chetan Bhagat
(c) Ruskin Bond
(d) Anita Desai

6. For which book Salman Rushdie won the Booker Prize?
(a) The Satanic Verses
(b) Midnight's Children
(c) Fury
(d) Shalimar the Clown

7. In which year Salman Rushdie won the Booker Prize?
(a) 1981 (b) 1984
(c) 1987 (d) 1990

8. Which Indian writer is also a member of the US President's Committee on the Arts and Humanities, appointed by US President Barack Obama?
(a) Arundhati Roy
(b) VS Naipaul
(c) Jhumpa Lahiri
(d) Salman Rushdie

9. Where the Head Office of the Sahitya Akademi is located?
(a) Kolkata (b) New Delhi
(c) Lucknow (d) Pune

10. In which year National Book Trust was founded?
(a) 1947 (b) 1949
(c) 1952 (d) 1957

11. In 2011, who won the Pulitzer Prize for the book 'The Emperor of All Maladies: A Biography of Cancer'?
(a) Siddhartha Mukherjee
(b) Geeta Anand
(c) Jhumpa Lahiri
(d) Gobind Behari Lal

12. Jhumpa Lahiri won the Pulitzer Prize in the section of
(a) Public Service
(b) Fiction
(c) Poetry
(d) Drama

13. Who is the author of the book 'Hajar Churashir Maa'?
(a) Aparna Sen
(b) Taslima Nasrin
(c) Ashapoorna Devi
(d) Mahasweta Devi

14. Who was the first elected fellow of Sahitya Akademi Fellowship?
(a) C Rajagopalachari
(b) DR Bendre
(c) Dr S Radhakrishnan
(d) Gopinath Kaviraj

15. Which foundation instituted Saraswati Samman annual award?
(a) KK Birla Foundation
(b) TATA Foundation
(c) Smile Foundation
(d) M Gandhi Foundation

16. Who translated the book 'The Story of My Experiments with Truth' written by MK Gandhi from Gujrati to English?
(a) Mahadev Desai
(b) JB Kripalani
(c) Mohanlal Pandya
(d) Vinoba Bhave

17. 'The Autobiography of an Unknown Indian' is an autobiography of
(a) Inder Kumar Gujral
(b) Nirad C. Chaudhuri
(c) Mahatma Gandhi
(d) Jawaharlal Nehru

18. Who wrote the famous novel 'Anandamath'?
(a) Sarat Chandra Chattopadhyay
(b) Bankim Chandra Chatterjee
(c) Rabindranath Tagore
(d) Michael Madhusudan Dutt

19. The first English translation of the Bhagavad Gita was done by
(a) Charles Wilkins
(b) William Jones
(c) Warren Hastings
(d) Henry Thomas Colebrooke

20. Who is the first woman to receive Sahitya Akademi Award?
(a) Mahasweta Devi
(b) Bani Basu
(c) Ashapoorna Devi
(d) Amrita Pritam

21. Who is the first winner of Sahitya Akademi Award for Hindi?
(a) Acharya Narendra Dev
(b) Nagendra
(c) Makhanlal Chaturvedi
(d) Amritlal Nagar

22. Indian origin writer VS Naipaul won the Nobel Prize in Literature in the year?
(a) 1998 (b) 2001
(c) 2003 (d) 2008

23. Who wrote the the National Anthem of Bangladesh's 'Amar Shonar Bangla'?
(a) Kazi Nazrul Islam
(b) Michael Madhusudan Dutt
(c) Faraaz Kazi
(d) Rabindranath Tagore

24. Which Bengali poet is also known as 'Bidrohi Kobi (Rebel Poet)' during independence movement?
(a) Jibanananda Das
(b) Rabindranath Tagore
(c) Kazi Nazrul Islam
(d) Daulat Qazi

25. When the famous novel 'Godaan' of Munshi Premchand was first published?
(a) 1930 (b) 1936
(c) 1940 (d) 1942

26. What is the other pen name of Munshi Premchand?
(a) Nawab Rai
(b) Dhanpat Das
(c) Gopal Sharma
(d) Prem Das

27. In which novel, the fictitious town 'Malgudi' was first mentioned?
(a) The Bachelor of Arts
(b) The English Teacher
(c) Under the Banyan Tree
(d) Swami and Friends

28. From which year Sahitya Akademi Award was started?
(a) 1949
(b) 1951
(c) 1954
(d) 1962

29. Satyajit Ray's famous film 'shatranj ke Khilari' is based on a novel written by
(a) Prem Chand
(b) RK Narayan
(c) Girish Karnad
(d) Anita Desai

30. The fictional character 'Mowgli' is the creation of
(a) Ruskin Bond
(b) RK Narayan
(c) Mulk Raj Anand
(d) Rudyard Kipling

31. Which one is the first novel of Chetan Bhagat?
(a) One Night at the Call Center
(b) 2 States
(c) Five Point Someone
(d) The 3 Mistakes of My Life

32. The story in the book 'God of Small Things' is based on which state
(a) Goa
(b) Kerala
(c) Andhra Pradesh
(d) Tamil Nadu

33. Who is the writer of of the book 'Train to Pakistan'?
(a) Amrita Pritam
(b) Khushwant Singh
(c) Anita Desai
(d) Subodh Javadekar

34. Which one is the longest Indian novel ever published in a single volume in the English language?
(a) Revolution 2020
(b) The God of Small Things
(c) A Suitable Boy
(d) Train to Pakistan

35. Who is the first women to received Jnanpith Award?
(a) Amrita Pritam
(b) Ashapoorna Devi
(c) Mahadevi Verma
(d) Mahasweta Devi

36. Who is the first winner of Jnanpith Award?
(a) G Sankara Kurup
(b) Ashapoorna Devi
(c) Umashankar Joshi
(d) Amrita Pritam

37. For which book Kiran Desai won the Man Booker Prize?
(a) Life of Pi
(b) The White Tiger
(c) Last Orders
(d) The Inheritance of Loss

38. Beside Arundhati Roy and Kiran Desai, who is the other one to win Man Booker Prize from India?
(a) Aravind Adiga
(b) Amitav Ghosh
(c) Rohinton Mistry
(d) Anita Desai

39. Who is the writer of the book 'Devdas'?
(a) Satyajit Ray
(b) Bankim Chandra Chattopadhyay
(c) Mahasweta Devi
(d) Sarat Chandra Chattopadhyay

40. Who is the writer of the book 'A Suitable Boy'?
(a) Vikram Seth
(b) Arundhati Roy
(c) Salman Rushdie
(d) Kiran Desai

41. Famous Indian writer Dhanpat Rai Srivastav is also known as
(a) Lakshminath Bezbaroa
(b) Rabindranath Tagore
(c) Premchand
(d) Sumitranandan Pant

Answers

1. (a)	2. (d)	3. (b)	4. (d)	5. (c)	6. (b)	7. (a)	8. (c)	9. (b)	10. (d)
11. (a)	12. (b)	13. (d)	14. (c)	15. (a)	16. (a)	17. (b)	18. (b)	19. (a)	20. (d)
21. (c)	22. (b)	23. (d)	24. (c)	25. (b)	26. (a)	27. (d)	28. (c)	29. (a)	30. (d)
31. (c)	32. (b)	33. (b)	34. (c)	35. (b)	36. (a)	37. (d)	38. (a)	39. (d)	40. (a)
41. (c)									